CONSTITUTIONAL AND ADMINISTRATIVE LAW

Text with Materials

FOURTH EDITION

David Pollard
Officier des Palmes Académiques,
Formerly of the Faculty of Law,
The University of Leicester
Sometime Professeur invité at the Université Jean Moulin, Lyon

Neil Parpworth
De Montfort University, Leicester

David Hughes FRSA, ILTM
Professor of Housing and Planning Law,
De Montfort University, Leicester

OXFORD
UNIVERSITY PRESS

OXFORD
UNIVERSITY PRESS

Great Clarendon Street, Oxford OX2 6DP

Oxford University Press is a department of the University of Oxford.
It furthers the University's objective of excellence in research, scholarship,
and education by publishing worldwide in

Oxford New York

Auckland Cape Town Dar es Salaam Hong Kong Karachi
Kuala Lumpur Madrid Melbourne Mexico City Nairobi
New Delhi Shanghai Taipei Toronto

With offices in

Argentina Austria Brazil Chile Czech Republic France Greece
Guatemala Hungary Italy Japan Poland Portugal Singapore
South Korea Switzerland Thailand Turkey Ukraine Vietnam

Oxford is a registered trade mark of Oxford University Press
in the UK and in certain other countries

Published in the United States
by Oxford University Press Inc., New York

© Oxford University Press, 2007

British Library Cataloguing in Publication Data

Data available

Library of Congress Cataloging in Publication Data

Data available

Typeset by Newgen Imaging Systems (P) Ltd., Chennai, India
Printed in Great Britain
on acid-free paper by
Ashford Colour Press, Gosport, Hants

ISBN 978–0–19–928637–9

10 9 8 7 6 5 4 3 2 1

PREFACE

The three authors continue to have several reasons for producing the fourth edition of this work and in doing so we have been guided by the many kind and thoughtful comments by both colleagues and students which were made with regard to the previous editions. Of course, one significant factor is that so much has happened and changed as a result of political developments and well over a decade of active judicial interventionism. Another factor, although not good, is the continuing immense pressure on resources continually felt by all law schools. The underfunding of law teaching—a cause for sorrow which looks likely to continue (we said this in 1990)—means that even if the libraries provided for law schools were large enough to accommodate the ever-growing numbers of law students, there could not be a sufficiency of monographs, statutes, law reports and other essential source materials to meet the legitimate requirements of such students. Furthermore, as the authors believe they will demonstrate in the following pages, the student of constitutional and administrative law must seek as his or her sources not merely the traditional food of statutes and judicial decisions of the United Kingdom. The student must become aware of and use legal materials from the Commonwealth and other jurisdictions, especially materials emanating from the institutions of the European Community and Union and the European Court of Human Rights, and must become aware of and use non-legal materials, especially official publications, such as House of Commons Papers, Command Papers and statements in Parliament. Many of these materials may simply not exist in some law school libraries. The law student of today, accordingly, must look to source books which can be used in the lecture room and in places of study and residence. A further reason for the creation of this particular work emerges from an educational need of so many of today's law students. Constitutional and administrative law is a 'core' subject and can be a popular one. However, many students are often denied the satisfaction of a thorough understanding of the subject because of a lack of knowledge of the constitutional history of the United Kingdom and its current and political life, especially if they come from countries where such subjects do not form part of the school curriculum. Sadly that is now often true of 'home based' students whose 'A' level studies may have included no history at all.

We have, therefore, continued to produce a work of particular (perhaps peculiar) nature, designed to fulfil certain fundamental views which we each have on the nature and teaching of constitutional and administrative law. First, the work reflects our belief that constitutional and administrative law can only be studied and understood within the context of its historical development and its current political environment. Much of that recent development and environment has emanated from the increasing movement for European integration and this continues to be reflected in this edition. Second, the content has been largely determined by what we consider to be the 'common core' or the highest common denominator of constitutional and administrative law in our law schools. There is not, however, as yet, a national curriculum and arrangements for teaching the subject still vary from law school to law school. However, there is a recognisable irreducible basic course content. Third, because of our view that this work should be a portable library, we decided for the first edition that it is preferable, on the whole, to reproduce generous extracts of material from a reasonable number and a wide variety of sources. That continues to be our view as we place before the world our fourth edition. We were enjoined by commentators on the first edition to 'let the materials speak for themselves' and we have continued to do this, though as a radical departure for this edition we have integrated text and materials for the first time. Even so we remain true to the hope that guided previous editions, namely that our work will enable students to understand principles rather than mere series of facts, while we trust we still do justice to the arguments of those from whose work we have selected. Fourth, we have compiled the text and selected the source materials with the needs of the first year law student in mind. This means that there must be adequate explanatory background to the academic rigour which we wish to encourage, and that both text and the source materials must be presented, if we may descend to modern language, in a 'user-friendly manner'.

In the first edition, prefatory statements at the start of each chapter were written as introductory essays highlighting central issues and problems, guiding students through the pages which followed, and arousing a spirit of inquiry. However, we were enjoined thereafter to expand those essays in order to provide a self-standing work on the subject which would enable ever poorer students to discover sufficient in the way of essential text within one set of covers. This we did and now, as already stated, we have taken the step of integrating the entire content of the book. We still, however, believe that the essence, nay more than the essence, of what the first year law student both will need and may comprehend is to be found in this volume. We hope that this work will create an enthusiasm to delve deeper into the subject and for this reason, the chapters include a selection of further reading. We also include a selection of websites wherefrom students may obtain information that is both relevant and free.

The production of this edition has also involved the substantial rewriting of many of the chapters, especially those on the developing and devolved United Kingdom constitution, the European Community and Union, judicial review, where there continue to be so many developments in the law, and those on human rights following the enactment of the Human Rights Act 1998. The significance of this legislation continues to grow and to affect the perceptions of the constitutional roles of both legislators and judges.

David Pollard, Neil Parpworth, and David Hughes
September 2006

ACKNOWLEDGMENTS

Grateful acknowledgement is made to all the authors and publishers of copyright material which appears in this book, and in particular to the following for permission to reprint material from the sources indicated:

The Court of Justice of the European Communities

W Green, the Scottish Law Publisher, for *Gibson v Lord Advocate* (1975) SLT 134; *Sillars v Smith* (1982) SLT 539

The Incorporated Council for Law Reporting for England and Wales

House of Commons for *Annual Report of the Commissioner for 2005–06: Making a Difference (HC 1363 of 2005–2006), Minutes of Evidence taken before the Public Administration Select Committee (HC 1081–I of 2005–2006)*

International Thompson Publishing Services Ltd for extracts from *Handyside v United Kingdom, The Sunday Times v United Kingdom* ([1976] 1 EHRR 757, [1979] 2 EHRR 245)

Justice (the British section of the International Commission of Jurists)

Thompson Legal and Regulatory Group Aisa and Pacific Ltd for *New South Wales v Bardolph* (1934) 52 CLR 455

Oxford University Press for Marshall *Constitutional Conventions: The Rules and Forms of Political Accountability* (1984), pp. 216–17

The Scottish Council for Law Reporting, for *McCormick v Lord Advocate* [1953] SC 396

The Stationery Office

Sweet & Maxwell Ltd/Stevens, for extracts from *Bentley v Brudzinski* (1982) 74 Cr App Rep 217, *Hirst & Agu v Chief Constable of West Yorkshire* (1987) 85 Cr App Rep143, *Atkin v DPP* (1989) 89 Cr App Rep 199, *DPP v Clarke* (1992) 94 Cr App Rep 359, *The Republic of Ireland v United Kingdom* (1978) 2 EHRR 25, *Branningan & McBride v United Kingdom* (1993) 17 EHRR 539, *Welch v United Kingdom* (1995) 20 EHRR 247, *SW v United Kingdom; CR v United Kingdom* (1996) 21 EHRR 363; Denning, Lord *A Freedom under the Law* (1949); Ganz, Professor G *Quasi Legislation* (1987), p 1; Wass, Sir D., 'Checks and Balances in Public Policy Making' [1987] Public Law 181 at 182

Every effort has been made to trace and contact copyright holders prior to publication but this has not been possible in every case. If notified, the publisher will undertake to rectify any errors or omissions at the earliest opportunity.

A SELECTION OF WEBSITES OF CONSTITUTIONAL SIGNIFICANCE

Government Information	http://www.open.gov.uk/
Cabinet Office	http://www.cabinet-office.gov.uk
Department for Constitutional Affairs	http://www.dca.gov.uk
ECJ	http://www.curia.eu.int/
Home Office	http://www.homeoffice.gov.uk
HMSO	http://www.tsonline.co.uk
HMSO	http://www.official-documents.co.uk/menu/ukpinf.htm
HMSO	http://www.hmso.gov.uk
ECHR	http://www.echr.coe.int/
Central Office of Information	http://www.nds.coi.gov.uk/coi/coipress.nsf
UK Parliament	http://www.parliament.uk
The Monarchy	http://www.royal.gov.uk
The Parliamentary and Health Service Ombudsman	http://www.ombudsman.org.uk
Legislation	http://www.hmso.gov.uk/acts.htm
SIs	http://www.hmso.gov.uk/stat.htm

CONTENTS—SUMMARY

8 The Parliamentary Commissioner for Administration

9 The Availability of Judicial Review

10 Grounds for Judicial Review

11 Public Order

12 Police Powers

13 European Convention on Human Rights and Fundamental Freedoms and the Human Rights Act 1998

DETAILED CONTENTS

5 Parliament: Composition and Privileges

6 Parliament: Procedures and Functions

7 The United Kingdom and the European Community and Union

10 Grounds for Judicial Review

TABLE OF STATUTES

TABLE OF STATUTORY INSTRUMENTS

TABLE OF CASES

1 CONSTITUTIONAL AND ADMINISTRATIVE LAW: NATURE, SOURCES AND HISTORY

1. The Nature of Constitutional and Administrative Law

Constitutional law is the fountain head from which other laws flow and derive validity. It describes how a state is constituted and functions. Furthermore, the enormous importance of state action cannot be overstressed. There are few spheres of human activity in modern Britain in which government agencies are not to some extent active. Government influences, so far as it is able, the economy; through subsidiary agencies it provides, for example, welfare services, housing, education, roads, transport and employment; it is responsible for law and order, defence and foreign relations; it draws up new laws and replaces old ones; it regulates trade, and keeps something of a watchful eye on the arts, cultural and leisure activities. Laying down general principles to guide the exercise of these functions is one task for administrative law, especially as regards that part emanating from the courts, though it is not always easy to draw a clear distinction between constitutional law on the one hand and administrative on the other. But, clearly, the law no longer exists solely to provide a framework within which individuals may deal fairly with one another: it is concerned with the allocation of resources between geographical areas and sections of society; relationships of groups within society; and the relationship of the citizen to the state.

Law is not a value-free system of rules, nor the equivalent of justice or morality. Law is a phenomenon within society, acting upon, and being acted upon, by society. Law may arguably be an expression of the desire of humankind to live in a civilised and ordered way, but individual laws and legal systems are the result of political processes within society whereby values and interests are promoted and given protection. The Human Rights Act 1998,[1] for example, enshrines *certain* rights and liberties, but is by no means a comprehensive catalogue of what some might consider basic human rights, for example it contains no 'right of life'

---

[1] See chapter 13 below.

provisions for the unborn. Controversy and disagreement surround such issues. Individual laws may promote the interests of particular sections within society, or seek to redress imbalances, or advance the claims of those who have suffered historic disadvantages. Law may enshrine economic and social ideologies within a state, or be used to promote and protect values, sometimes because there is a broad, general, national agreement on particular issues, or because a dominant group controls the law-making process and can use law to promote its interests. This phenomenon cannot be fully understood without a knowledge of constitutional and administrative law because, inter alia, they provide the legal framework for the law-making process—a process over which political and social forces compete to secure dominance.

Constitutional law lies somewhere between constitutional history and constitutional politics. Lawyers often make statements about the constitution that may, historically, have been true, but which are now less than accurate. However, the tasks of lawyers and historians are different. The latter seek to establish an impeccable factual record and then to interpret it: the former are concerned with creating principles and rules to ensure that like situations are treated alike. That pursuit *may* involve departure from *strict* respect for the historical record. Equally, lawyers cannot delve too deeply into day-to-day reportage of politics: the task is, normally, to stand back and see the broad developing pattern of constitutional practice. The lawyer's prime task is not the study of politics, or how political parties work, or the rights and wrongs of particular ideologies, though students of law cannot understand how constitutional systems are used unless they bear in mind the historical, political and social context. And, of course, they will bring to the subject their own moral and political persuasions which they will utilise in any given situation to evaluate the law and its operation.

II. The Sources of Constitutional and Administrative Law

While the United Kingdom of Great Britain and Northern Ireland has no one single document called *The Constitution*, it is not true to say that the constitution is unwritten. The constitution is *not codified:* part is to be found in *decisions of the courts*, either as statements of principle, or as interpretations of statute; part is found in the *Royal Prerogative*; part must be taken to emanate from Brussels, Luxembourg and Strasbourg as we fulfil our *obligations to our European partners*[2] and also under the European Convention on Human Rights.[3] Yet another part is found in those, strictly, *extra-legal* historic constitutional arrangements and practices known as *conventions*, part is the *law and custom of Parliament*, and part is to be found in the *opinions of learned authors* such as Coke, Hale and Blackstone. The issue of conventions will be returned to in chapters 3 and 4 below. Here it is sufficient to note that these constitutional practices though not 'law' as such are a crucial feature of our constitution without which it could not work. They are that part of our constitutional system which must merit the epithet 'unwritten' for so much with them depends on historic practice and political reality. However, the majority of the legal rules are found written down in the form of *statutes*. In the United

---

[2] See further chapter 7 below.   [3] See further chapter 13 below.

Kingdom enactments will be found corresponding to many, if not indeed most, provisions normally found in written constitutions.

Not all would agree. Dicey in *Law of the Constitution* said: 'the general principles of the constitution are with us as the result of judicial decisions determining the rights of private persons in particular cases brought before the Courts'.[4] However, Jennings in *The Law and the Constitution* points out that legislation is the most potent force nowadays for constitutional change and that: 'the truth is that Dicey . . . was concerned mainly with the principles which are inserted in many constitutions for the protection of private rights'.[5] No doubt judicial decisions as to the rights of citizens are of great importance; however, not only is statute law of equal importance here, but it also governs many other basic liberties such as the right to vote, the right to belong to a trades union, and to be free from racial or sexual discrimination. Legislation, in one form or another, is today the principal means whereby government policies are implemented.

However, British constitutional law has *no special pre-eminence* over other bodies of law. The sources of constitutional law are as for other laws. Constitutional statutes have no status of unrepealability. Our constitution is *descriptive* not *prescriptive*; ie no document lays down general, overarching, paramount rules and principles, as in, eg, the United States.

Administrative law (in the sense of the body of legal administrative powers and duties) is particularly statute based, though the judicial contribution to its application, especially over the last 60 years, has been considerable. In addition, because so many statutes devolving functions to administrative bodies grant powers in broad, general discretionary terms, much of the actual substance of the law can only be discovered by a study of how administrators use their powers; how they are guided by central and local government policies, departmental practices and professional standards of conduct and ethics.

III. The History and Nature of British Constitutional and Administrative Law

Politically what makes a constitution operable is acceptance, however obtained, of the established order. If the people as a whole, or a sufficiently powerful group (eg the army), refuse to accept and overthrow that order, there is a revolution and a new legal order has to be created. In the non-revolutionary situation which pertains for most of the time, some theory other than social acceptance must, from a legal standpoint, be found for why a constitution is valid. Nations feel the need to appeal to some higher form of authority as a validation for their constitutions. In the USA the Preamble to the Constitution states that: 'We the people . . . do ordain and establish this Constitution.' There is not just an agreement by the people to a common contract binding themselves together—the constitution is 'ordained'. It takes on a formal life of its own apart from individual persons and generations. In the former USSR the constitution derived its validity from the collectivist principles of Marxism; the political foundation of the USSR was the Soviets of Working People's Deputies and the dictatorship of the proletariat.[6]

---

[4] 9th edn, (Macmillan, London).   [5] 5th edn, (University of London Press, London), pp. 39–41.
[6] Article 2 of the 1936 Soviet Constitution.

The United Kingdom has never experienced any sufficiently traumatic national event to force a thinking-out of basic constitutional principles. The constitution has evolved: 'evolution not revolution' and 'the inevitability of gradualism' spring to mind as descriptive of the process. We must search through history for the principles of our constitution.

(a) The medieval origins

A most important date is the Norman conquest of 1066. Then constitutional principles were inextricably intertwined with those applicable to landholding, for those who owned land enjoyed *power* and *jurisdiction* over the vast majority who were landless. By the time of the Domesday survey (1086) there were some 1500 'tenants-in-chief' as the principal landholders, though they had subordinates who 'held' land by the performance of, for example, services for superiors. The result was noted by Stubbs in his *Constitutional History of England*:[7] 'the creation of several intermediate links between the body of the nation and the king'. Nevertheless, the notion that all land was ultimately held 'of the king' became, over time, the basis of a general body of law applying *throughout the nation*, in itself a unifying force. Additionally, William the Conqueror exacted in 1086 an oath of allegiance from *all* who possessed land. As Stubbs points out[8] the oath provided: 'a direct tie between the sovereign and all freeholders which no inferior relation existing between them and the mesne [intermediate] lords would justify them in breaking'. The oath of allegiance to the King subsequently became an indispensable feature of the system of holding land.

Since the Conquest the Crown, as an institution, has remained central to the life of the nation and the constitution. The Crown remains responsible for defence, administration of justice, and the control of public affairs generally; so much so that the United Kingdom is best described as a limited monarchy rather than a democracy.

That is not to say the monarch rules in person: 'Crown' and 'monarch' have become somewhat separate constitutional ideas. The powers of the Crown are today exercised by ministers who hold office, in *political* terms, because they are the leaders of the majority party in the House of Commons. The development of this constitutional pattern demonstrates the flexibility, adaptability and pragmatism of British constitutional thinking and practice, particularly with regard to the adaptation of old institutions to serve new ends. A conspectus of constitutional development is necessary if the current position is to be understood.

Under William the Conqueror England became a feudal state, but one in which all landholders owed allegiance to the King who, of course, ruled in person. Law-making was an act of the King, who received advice from his principal tenants in chief and bishops on a conciliar basis. Writing of the reign of Henry II (1154–89), Stubbs[9] argued for the existence of a 'national council . . . a complete council of feudal tenants in chief'. This was not, of course, a 'Parliament'; conciliar arrangements were fluid with sometimes only the greater landholders in attendance.

Magna Carta (1215) in the reign of King John (1199–1216) has been argued for as the origin of English statute law, but the Charter was re-issued in differing forms in 1216, 1217 and 1225. The Charter was finally confirmed in 1297, and Chapter 29 is one of the foundation stones of our constitution.

---

[7] 4th edn, vol I, p. 283.   [8] Op cit at p. 290.   [9] Op cit at p. 604.

Magna Carta (1297) (25 Edw 1)

'the great charter of the liberties of england, and of the liberties of the forest; confirmed by King Edward, in the Twenty-fifth Year of his Reign. Edward by the grace of God King of England, Lord of Ireland, and Duke of Guyan, to all archbishops, bishops &c. . . .

Chapter 1. Confirmation of Liberties

First, we have granted to God, and by this our present charter have confirmed, for us and our heirs for ever, that the church of England shall be free, and shall have all her whole rights and liberties inviolable. We have granted also, and given to all the freemen of our realm, for us and our heirs for ever, these liberties underwritten, to have and to hold to them and their heirs, of us and our heirs for ever . . .

Chapter 29. Imprisonment, etc contrary to law

No freeman shall be taken or imprisoned, or be disseised of his freehold, or liberties, or free customs, or be outlawed, or exiled, or any other wise destroyed; nor will we not pass upon him, nor condemn him, but by lawful judgment of his peers, or by the law of the land. We will sell to no man, we will not deny or defer to any man either justice or right.'

About this time distinctions began to emerge between the 'National' or 'Great' Council, and the small body of personal advisers to the King on the daily work of government. The matter is neatly summed up in Mackenzie's *The English Parliament*.[10]

'Parliament is the child of the occasional national assembly and retains today its essential character as an advisory—critical if you like—assembly representative of the nation. In the course of time it has found the means to enforce its advice and to make its criticisms effective but it does not itself govern. The King and his private council have developed into the whole complex machine which we call "the government", ie the ministry and the civil service.'

In 1236 'Parliamentum' was used to describe a great council of bishops and peers; the word had acquired a certain official currency by 1258. In 1265 representatives of the shires and the towns were summoned; the 'communes' thus entered Parliament though there was no guarantee of their being summoned to every Parliament thereafter; they were on occasions omitted.

Edward I (1272–1307) called a 'Parliament' of bishops, peers, knights, citizens and burgesses, and the Statute of Westminster the First 1275 declared it had received the assent of the Lords Spiritual and Temporal and the 'Community' of the land. In 1295 the foundations of what was to become Parliament were laid. The writ of summons stated: 'that which touches all should be approved by all'. In 1297 Edward I issued The Confirmation of the Charters and undertook, inter alia, not to levy new taxes without the consent of the realm, and in this connection the 'Revocation of the New Ordinances of 1322' should also be noted.

'And that for ever hereafter, all manner of ordinances or provisions, made by the subjects of our lord the King or of his heirs, by any power or authority whatsoever, concerning the royal power of our lord the King or of his heirs, or against the estate of our said lord the King or of his heirs, or against the estate of the Crown, shall be void and of no avail or force whatever; but the matters which are to be established for the estate of our lord the King and of his heirs, and for the estate of the realm and of the people, shall be treated, accorded, and established in Parliaments, by our lord the King, and by the assent of the prelates, earls, and barons, and the commonalty of the realm; according as it hath been heretofore accustomed.'

[10] At pp. 11–12.

At these early Parliaments judicial business was also transacted. The notion of Parliament as a 'High Court' led to the institution being more than a place for giving advice to the King; legal decisions could be made; Parliament was a law-making body.

These early, infrequent, Parliaments, however, were far from the modern institution in that they transacted *both* legislative and judicial business. They were a 'fleshing out' of the King's Council which would often meet without the Commons being present. However, by 1322, as we have seen, the principle had been recorded that a statute required the assent of the Lords *and* the Commons and, by 1327, the understanding was that statute was *perpetual* law, not simply limited to the reign of a particular monarch.

The method of making law was, however, very different from that of modern Parliaments. Edward I asserted a wide power to redress grievances not otherwise remediable at law, particularly in response to individual or collective petitions presented at a Parliament: the system was well established by 1280. By the early fourteenth century attempts were being made to put petitions into a collected form for the King to remedy by permanent legislation. These collected petitions—precursors of the Bills nowadays presented to Parliament to be enacted—were presented by the Commons, the first recorded instance being in 1327. Parliament became a place where law was made by the Crown in response to the petitions of the people.

The reign of Edward III (1327–77) witnessed great developments in constitutional matters. Stubbs claimed: 'The definite and final arrangement of Parliament in two houses must be referred to this period.'[11] The Knights of the Shires and the Burgesses of the Boroughs began to deliberate together regularly after 1340. Subsequently they were given places in which to meet, though they had no permanent home until after 1547. Regular presentation of collective grievances to the King for grants of redress emerged after 1340, and the Commons started to make the vote of taxes to the King ('supply') conditional upon grants of redress: in 1348 they stipulated redress should come *before* supply.

In 1330 and 1362 statutes required the holding of Parliament every year, though these were disregarded from time to time. Edward III held 48 Parliaments during his reign, largely because regular wars required the voting of taxes. Too much should not be read into this, nor into the apparent increase in influence of the Commons. They were still not a regular corporate body, and were certainly not representative of all the people, being frequently nominees of great landholders: 'House of Commons' has never meant 'House of the Common People'. Furthermore, the Commons would merely be called into the presence of King and Council where they would stand to hear his proposals and show their assent by silence. This is echoed today in the State Opening of Parliament: the Queen takes the throne in the House of Lords surrounded by peers, bishops and judges; the Commons are summoned to the bar of the House where they hear in silence the proposals the Queen's Government will introduce, and then depart. Moreover, the influence of Parliament depended on the King's need of taxation. A monarch able to 'live of his own' from feudal revenues, or who received a life grant of customs duties, as happened for example in 1397, 1415 and 1453, could well manage without summoning Parliament. Henry VII, who left a vast fortune for his time of £1,800,000, held Parliaments only seven times in a reign of 24 years. Monarchs frequently also amended the petitions received from the Commons, a practice that continued down to the reign of Queen Elizabeth I.

The fifteenth century saw the continued slow evolution of Parliament. In 1418 the 'Modus Tenendi Parliamentum' (the Method of Holding Parliaments) was issued to the Lord Lieutenant of Ireland. Though earlier versions of this exist, its special issue to Ireland points

---

[11] Op cit vol II, p. 393.

to the existence of practices having a degree of authority. In 1430 electoral qualifications to vote for shire representatives were laid down: voters had to be freeholders of land worth '40 shillings' (£2), a high figure for the time. In the boroughs there was more flexibility about the franchise, but effectively only *men* of substance enjoyed the vote; much also depended on which boroughs the King chose to be represented. Edward I chose 166 boroughs: they had declined to 99 by the fifteenth century. Henry VI added 8 boroughs after 1445 and Edward IV a further 5. Despite legal requirements for annual Parliaments, they were summoned only sporadically with new elections each time. The monarch further determined the form of Parliament, finding it convenient that the bishops, abbots and peers, the greatest landowners, should meet as one while the knights and burgesses should also consult together.

Parliament became accepted as the place where taxes were imposed by law, and without whose consent the King could not impose new taxes. Moreover, grants of taxation were accepted as having to be initiated in the Commons. In 1433 the words 'by the authority of the same Parliament' appear in the enacting preamble of a statute for the first time. By the end of the century the *active* assent of the Commons was accepted as essential to the validity of a statute. However, though Fortescue CJ asserted that the King could only rule his people: 'bi . . . lawes . . . such as thai assenten unto',[12] the constitutional balance was utterly different from today's. The King possessed enormous personal powers: he summoned Parliament, determining its form by his summons; he prorogued, suspended, and dissolved it *as of right*. The King retained vague powers to 'ordain' law in his council, and to suspend a statute, though having no power to repeal a statute by his own act. Moreover the King was commander-in-chief in time of war; the wealth of the nation was his personally; he was the keeper of the peace, and the appointer of public officials. What had in essence emerged, however, was the two streams of government existing today ie under prerogative powers and under laws made in Parliament.

By the end of the fifteenth century the old 'great' or 'national' council had been replaced by Parliament; a Parliament, however, very different from today's. The sixteenth century saw the institutional development of Parliament, principally because Tudor monarchs found it a compliant forum in which to fashion legislative powers needed to implement their policies. Both Houses of Parliament experienced great changes. Amongst lay peers, the right to a hereditary place in the upper house having been established, their numbers grew from 43 in 1509 to 53 in 1563. In 1531 statutes gave the King power to appoint bishops and in 1540 (following the final abolition of the monasteries in 1539) abbots disappeared from Parliament. The Church was brought under the control of the King, effectively completing the process whereby the whole realm was made subject to one system of law and government. This was also hastened by the Laws in Wales Act 1535 incorporating Wales with England. The House of Commons also increased in size: Edward VI added 48 members, Mary I, 21, Elizabeth I added 60 and James I, 27. The Commons grew from under 300 members in 1485 to 450 in 1603. Henry VIII also began the practice of continuing the life of Parliament over a number of sessions, though sessions were not continuous and were of unequal length. Members began to be regularly re-elected and the phrase 'Member of Parliament' achieved some vogue. The corporate identity of the Commons was enhanced by their being granted the former Chapel of St Stephen at Westminster as a permanent home.

As Parliament's status increased so did that of statute as an increasingly important type of law. In 1589 Sir Thomas Smith, a Secretary of State, wrote: 'the Parliament of England . . . representeth and hath the power of the whole realm, both the head and the body'.[13] Too much

---

[12] *De Laudibus Legum Angliae*, 1469.
[13] *De Republica Anglorum (The Commonwealth of England and the Manner of Government thereof)*.

should not be read into that statement, nevertheless Parliament asserted throughout the sixteenth century certain rights and privileges as against the monarch.

Though claims for freedom of speech for the Commons can be found before the sixteenth century, eg Yonge's petition of 1455, it was not until 1512 that there was any form of statutory recognition of this. Legislation was passed following the imprisonment of a member, Strode, by the Stannary Court for having proposed tin mine regulation Bills in Parliament. This Act declared the proceedings against Strode void, and though there was to be future doubt whether the Act was of general application, the legislation marks some increase in importance for the Commons. In 1523 Sir Thomas More, as Speaker, petitioned the King for indulgence towards what was said in debate. By 1541 the Speaker claimed freedom of speech as one of the ancient and undoubted rights and privileges of the Commons: the practice was well established by 1565. Other privileges began to emerge contemporaneously: freedom from arrest (1543); power to punish for contempt (1548). The existence of these powers was not always acceptable to the Crown. Elizabeth I attempted to restrict freedom of speech in 1566, 1571 and in 1592–93: James I actually did so in 1614 and 1621. Nevertheless the Commons' estimation of its own importance grew. In 1586 it insisted it alone had the right to determine disputed elections, and in 1593 the Commons resented a 'reminder' from the Lords to vote taxes to the queen.

By the beginning of the seventeenth century many elements of the current constitution existed—the monarchy, peerage, House of Commons, a service of permanent officials (though not a modern 'civil service'), courts, and an 'inner council' of advisers to the monarch, some bearing titles continuing today: Lord Chancellor, Lord President of the Council, Lord Privy Seal and Secretary of State. What differed from today was the relationship between those elements.

(b) The crisis of the seventeenth century

The seventeenth century, in particular the years 1642–49, transformed the medieval constitution. One major *legal* feature of interest was the merging of interests of the common lawyers with those of Parliament. There was then no unified system of courts—there were many courts whose jurisdictions dated from different times, with largely separate personnel. The lawyers of the common law courts, the ancestors of the modern Queen's Bench Division of the High Court, feared alternative systems of redress of grievance developed under the Tudors. Particularly, they distrusted the Court of Star Chamber, whose existence could be traced back to a Statute of 1487 enabling a body of stated persons to punish various offences. By 1562 Star Chamber was a recognised court. The Council of The North, created by Royal Command in 1536, had a criminal jurisdiction in the North of England, and the existence of the Court of the Council of Wales was acknowledged by legislation in 1542. In 1558 the Act of Supremacy gave the monarch power to set up a Court of High Commission in ecclesiastical matters. By the end of the sixteenth century this had a wide jurisdiction to fine and imprison in relation to religious matters, at a time when adherence to forms of worship provided by law was regarded as a test of loyalty. From time to time the Crown also resorted to what was called 'martial law', a system of setting up Commissions to try a variety of persons in response to perceived emergencies, such as in 1569, 1595, 1617, 1620 and 1624.

The ingredients were present for a conflict, not just political but also legal. The conflict of various sources of law—Parliament, the common law and the jurisdictions of the other bodies mentioned above—reinforced political, religious and economic uncertainties and controversies. The legal issues were summarised by Maitland.

'The system by which England has of late been governed is a questionable system, it is being questioned in parliament, it is being questioned in the law courts. The more men look at history (and history is now being minutely examined for controversial purposes) the more they see that the constitution is not what it was under the Lancastrian Kings—that the mode of government conflicts with unrepealed statutes, that there is at least plausible excuse for pronouncing a great deal of it illegal.'[14]

The common law courts did not resist the claims of the Crown on all occasions. The judges were willing to hold isolated acts of royal authority illegal, but not to face the issue that the whole business of government might be corrupted by illegality. In the *Case of Monopolies*[15] Popham CJ held the King could not dispense, for a private gain, with an Act passed for the general public good. In 1605–06, as a result of controversy over whether common law courts could forbid ecclesiastical courts from trying cases the common lawyers maintained should lie in lay courts, the King (James I) maintained it was for him to decide to which court cases should go. Coke CJ responded with the medieval dictum that the King is under God and under the law. However, in *Bates' Case*[16] the court accepted the prerogative power of the King to tax, without parliamentary consent, merchandise entering the country, on the tenuous basis that the tax was not imposed to raise revenue, but rather was an act of foreign policy which, it was admitted, lay within the King's prerogative. In the case of *Prohibitions del Roy*,[17] however, it was stated that the King personally could not adjudicate in cases, though it is doubtful whether that was accepted by the King. Again, in the *Case of Proclamations*,[18] the judges held the King could not create new offences solely by proclamation, and further that the prerogative was only what the law allowed. Despite this the monarch in Council continued to issue proclamations, and have them enforced in the Star Chamber. In 1611 Coke CJ held that the Court of High Commission had no power to fine or imprison, and in 1616 in the *Case of Commemdams* Coke entertained an action in which the legality of the royal prerogative to grant a bishop two other church offices, and their income, together ('in Commemdam') with his bishopric was questioned. The King ordered the judges not to try the case. Coke refused to obey and the King dismissed him, which was legal, for the judges were but the King's servants. In the *Five Knights' Case*[19] the judges accepted the King had power to imprison without showing cause, even when the issue arose out of a refusal to pay a forced loan.

The Petition of Right 1627 asserted taxation was not to be levied without the consent of Parliament.

'To the Kings most excellent Majestie.
   Humbly shew unto our soveraigne lord the King the lords spirituall and temporall and commons in Parliament assembled that

1 Reciting that by (25) 34 Edw 1 st 4 c 1 by authority of Parliament holden 25 Edw 3, and by other laws of this realm, the King's subjects should not be taxed but by consent in Parliament

whereas it is declared and enacted by a Statute made in the tyme of the raigne of King Edward the First comonly called Statutum de Tallagio non concedendo, that no tallage or ayde should be layd or levyed by the King or his heires in this realme without the good will and assent of the archbishopps bishopps

[14] *Constitutional History of England*, p. 275.
[15] (1602) 11 Co Rep 84b.
[16] *A-G v Bates* (1610) 2 State Trials 371.
[17] (1607) 12 Co Rep 63.
[18] (1611) 12 Co Rep 74, 2 State Trials 723.
[19] *Darnel's Case* (1627) 3 State Trials 1.

earles barons knights burgesses and other freemen of the comonaltie of this realme, and by authoritie of Parliament holden in the five and twentieth yeare of the raigne of King Edward the Third, it is declared and enacted, that from thenceforth no person should be compelled to make any loanes to the King against his will because such loanes were against reason and the franchise of the land, and by other lawes of this realme it is provided that none should be charged by any charge or imposicion called a benevolence nor by such like charge by which the statutes before mencioned and other the good lawes and statutes of this realme your subjects have inherited this freedome that they should not be compelled to contribute to any taxe tallage ayde or other like charge not sett by comon consent in Parliament.

2 And that commissions have of late issued on which proceedings have been had contrary to law

Yet nevertheless of late divers comissions directed to sundry comissioners in severall counties with instructions have issued, by meanes whereof your people have been in divers places assembled and required to lend certaine somes of mony unto your Majestie, and many of them upon their refusall soe to doe have had an oath administred unto them not warrantable by the lawes or statutes of this realme and have been constrayned to become bound to make apparance and give attendance before your privie councell and in other places; and others of them have been therefore imprisioned confined and sondry other waies molested and disquieted and divers other charges have been laid and levied upon your people in severall counties by lord lieutenants deputie lieutenants comissioners for musters justices of peace and others by comaund or direccion from your Majestie or your privie councell against the lawes and free customes of the realme.

7 Reciting 25 Edw 3, and that commissions have issued under the great seal for proceedings according to martial law

And wheras alsoe by authoritie of Parliament in the five and twentieth yeare of the raigne of King Edward the Third it is declared and enacted that no man should be forejudged of life or limbe against the forme of the Great Charter and the lawe of the land, and by the said Great Charter, and other the lawes and statutes of this your realme no man ought to be adjudged to death but by the lawes established in this your realme, either by the customes of the same realme or by Acts of Parliament. And whereas no offendor of what kinde soever is exempted from the proceedings to be used and punishments to be inflicted by the lawes and statutes of this your realme, neverthelesse of late tyme divers comissions under your Majesties great seale have issued forth, by which certaine persons have been assigned and appointed comissioners with power and authoritie to proceed within the land according to the justice of martiall lawe against such souldiers or marriners or other dissolute persons joyning with them as should comitt any murther robbery felony mutiny or other outrage or misde-meanor whatsoever, and by such sumary course and order as is agreeable to martiall lawe and as is used in armies in tyme of warr to proceed to the tryall and condemnacion of such offenders, and them to cause to be executed and putt to death according to the lawe martiall.

8 The Petition

They doe therefore humblie pray your most excellent Majestie, that no man hereafter be compelled to make or yield any guilt loane benevolence taxe or such like charge without common consent by Acte of Parliament, and that none be called to make aunswere or take such oath or to give attendance or be confined or otherwise molested or disquieted concerning the same or for refusall thereof. . . . And that the afforesaid comissions for proceeding by martiall lawe may be revoked and annulled. And that hereafter no comissions of like nature may issue forth to any person or persons whatsoever to be executed as aforesaid, lest by colour of them any of your Majesties subjects be destroyed or put to death contrary to the lawes and franchise of the land.

All which they most humblie pray of your most excellent Majestie as their rights and liberties according to the lawes and statutes of this realme, and that your Majestie would alsoe vouchsafe to declare that the awards doings and proceedings to the prejudice of your people in any of the premises shall not be drawn hereafter into consequence or example. And that your Majestie would be alsoe graciouslie pleased for the future comfort and safetie of your people to declare your royall will and pleasure, that in the things aforesaid all your officers and ministers shall serve you according to the lawes and statutes of this realme as they tender the honor of your Majestie and the prosperitie of this kingdome.'

The King replied that right would be done as desired: shortly thereafter Parliament was dissolved and the King (Charles I) attempted to rule alone. To manage without grants of taxation, the King had to exploit other sources of revenue. In 1635 and 1636 he attempted to collect 'ship money', ie grants of funds to pay for ships to defend the realm, not just from coastal areas but the whole nation. He relied on previous authority that he could raise such funds to meet an emergency. At this time, however, no emergency existed, to which the King's response was that he was sole judge, under prerogative, of whether an emergency existed, and that his power to act for the public good in time of crisis could not be taken away even by statute. The legality of this action was challenged in the *Case of Ship Money (R v Hampden)*[20] but the judges upheld the legality of the King's action 7 to 5.

Lack of finance to fund military action against Scotland forced the King to summon a Parliament which met in 1640. The King had to make substantial concessions: triennial Parliaments, no dissolution of Parliament without its consent, no taxation without consent and abolition of the Courts of Star Chamber and High Commission. The English Civil War (1642–49) which followed saw the defeat and execution of the King, and a brief flirtation with a non-monarchical form of government, with Cromwell as Lord Protector operating under 'The Instrument of Government' of 1653.

On Cromwell's death the remnants of the Parliament summoned originally in 1640, and which had been dismissed in 1653, formally dissolved themselves. A 'Convention Parliament' of Lords and Commons invited the son of the executed monarch to resume the throne. The new King's first regular Parliament of 1661 retrospectively validated all that had been done by the Convention Parliament, an indication that supreme legal authority lay with the King *in* Parliament.

From 1660 to his death in 1685 Charles II managed to co-exist with Parliament (despite being dependent on it for finance following the abolition of feudal revenues in 1660) by, inter alia, the use of patronage as a way of securing votes in Parliament, by living within his means (the customs and excise revenues settled on him in 1660 in return for the feudal dues) and by playing off factions within Parliament against one another. These various factions began in the period 1673–81 to be known as 'Whigs' (effectively those who distrusted royal power, wished to limit it, and who favoured what to them was 'liberty', ie freedom of trade, property and enterprise) and 'Tories' (who tended to value the monarch as the guarantor of order and stability and who supported royal power). From this period dates a predominantly 'two party' form of government that has developed down to the present, though we should not think of 'Whigs' and 'Tories' as political parties. Indeed, the various factions were to coalesce, break up, reform and regroup many times until the start of the twentieth century—even today, of course, it is not unknown for politicians 'to change their colour'.

---

[20] (1637) 3 State Trials 826.

Royal influence received a number of checks in court and in Parliament, however. The first parliamentary commission of public accounts was created in 1667 to ensure that taxation was spent for the purpose for which it had been voted. In *Thomas v Sorrell*[21] the court held that the King could not dispense with a general penal law made 'pro bono publico' or for the good of a third party.

James II (1685–88) proved, for a variety of reasons, unable to operate the constitution. From a legal point of view the chief features of interest of his short reign are the decisions in *Godden v Hales*[22] where the judges held the King could dispense with a penal law upon particular occasions for particular reasons, of which the King himself was the only judge, and the *Seven Bishops' Case*[23] in which *Thomas v Sorrell* was cited with approval for the proposition that the King had no general power to suspend an Act of Parliament.

In 1688, following intense religious controversy, consequent on the King's overt adherence to Roman Catholicism, a revolution occurred. As Maitland states 'Passing to the events of 1688 we see it was extremely difficult for any lawyer to make out that what had been done was lawful.'[24] William of Orange, the King's son-in-law, was 'invited' by a group of peers (Whig *and* Tory) to 'deliver the nation' on 30 June, shortly after the birth of a son to the King which raised the spectre of a Roman Catholic succession, a horrendous prospect to many. In July the King dissolved Parliament, and on 5 November William landed. James departed the realm on 22 December. There being no Parliament, William summoned an *assembly* of peers and members of the Commons who had sat under Charles II, and the Aldermen of the City of London. They advised the calling of a *Convention* of peers and representatives of the shires and boroughs. This met and resolved that James II had subverted the constitution and had abdicated by his flight. The Crown was 'offered' to William and his wife Mary, though there was little choice about this as William's Dutch army had effectively occupied the nation! The Convention also passed an Act declaring itself to be Parliament and furthermore passed The Bill of Rights 1688 which abolished the 'dispensing and suspending' power, secured freedom of speech in Parliament (which can be argued to be the basis on which our courts have bowed to the will of Parliament and recognised its supremacy), and declared the levying of money for the use of the Crown without parliamentary consent to be illegal. In 1680–90 a new Parliament summoned by William and Mary passed statutes declaring all the actions of 1688–89 lawful.[25] This gave a cloak of legality and continuity to the previous events, for there can be little doubt that the flight and deposition of James II was a result of revolution, albeit comparatively quiet and reasonably bloodless. The part played by the courts in this bloodless revolution will be considered below in the context of the sovereignty of Parliament debate.

The Bill of Rights (1688) (1 Will & Mar sess 2 c 2)

'An Act declaring the Rights and Liberties of the Subject and Setleing the Succession of the Crowne . . .

The heads of declaration of lords and commons, recited—Whereas the late King James the Second by the assistance of diverse evill councillors judges and ministers imployed by him did endeavour to subvert and extirpate the Protestant religion and the lawes and liberties of this kingdome.

Dispensing and suspending power—**By assumeing and exerciseing a power of dispensing with and suspending of lawes and the execution of lawes without consent to Parlyament**.

---

[21] (1673) Vaugh 330.   [22] (1686) 11 State Trials 1166.   [23] (1688) 12 State Trials 183.
[24] *Constitutional History of England*, p. 283.   [25] The Crown and Parliament Recognition Act 1689.

Committing prelates—*By committing and prosecuting diverse worthy prelates for humbly petitioning to be excused from concurring to the said assumed power.*

Ecclesiastical commission—*By issueing and causeing to be executed a commission under the great seale for erecting a court called the court of commissioners for ecclesiasticall causes.*

Levying money—*By levying money for and to the use of the Crowne by [pretence] of prerogative for other time and in other manner then the same was granted by Parlyament.*

Standing army—*By raising and keeping a standing army within this kingdome in time of peace without consent of Parlyament and quartering soldiers contrary to law.*

Disarming Protestants, etc—*By causing severall good subjects being protestants to be disarmed at the same time when papists were both armed and imployed contrary to law.*

Violating elections—*By violating the freedome of election of members to serve in Parlyament.*

Illegal prosecutions—*By prosecutions in the Court of King's Bench for matters and causes cognizable onely in Parlyament and by diverse other arbitrary and illegall courses.*

Juries—*And whereas of late yeares partiall corrupt and unqualifyed persons have been returned and served on juryes in tryalls and particularly diverse jurors in tryalls for high treason which were not freeholders.*

Excessive bail—*And excessive baile hath beene required of persons committed in criminall cases to elude the benefitt of the lawes made for the liberty of the subjects.*

Fines—*And excessive fines have beene imposed.*

Punishments—*And illegall and cruell punishments inflicted.*

Grants of fines, etc before conviction, etc—*And severall grants and promises made of fines and forfeitures before any conviction or judgement against the persons upon whome the same were to be levyed.*

All which are utterly and directly contrary to the knowne lawes and statutes and freedome of this realme.

And whereas the said late King James the Second haveing abdicated the government and the throne being thereby vacant his Highnesse the Prince of Orange (whome it hath pleased Almighty God to make the glorious instrument of delivering this kingdome from popery and arbitrary power) did (by the advice of the lords spirituall and temporall and diverse principall persons of the commons) cause letters to be written to the lords spirituall and temporall being protestants and other letters to the severall countyes cityes universities boroughs and cinque ports for the choosing of such persons to represent them as were of right to be sent to Parlyament to meete and sitt at Westminster upon the two and twentyeth day of January in this yeare one thousand six hundred eighty and eight in order to such an establishment as that their religion lawes and liberties might not againe be in danger of being subverted, upon which letters elections haveing beene accordingly made.

The subject's rights—***And thereupon the said lords spirituall and temporall and commons pursuant to their respective letters and elections being now assembled in a full and free representative of this nation takeing into their most serious consideration the best meanes for attaining the ends aforesaid doe in the first place (as their auncestors in like case have usually done) for the vindicating and asserting their auntient rights and liberties, declare***.

Suspending power—*That the pretended power of suspending or laws or the execution of laws by regall authority without consent of Parlyament is illegall.*

Late dispensing power—*That the pretended power of dispensing with laws or the execution of laws by regall authoritie as it hath beene assumed and exercised of late is illegal.*

Ecclesiastical courts illegal—*That the commission for erecting the late court of commissioners for ecclesiastical causes and all other commissions and courts of like nature are illegal and pernicious.*

Levying money—*That levying money for or to the use of the Crowne by pretence of prerogative without grant of Parlyament for longer time or in other manner than the same is or shall be granted is illegal.*

Rights to petition—*That it is the right of the subjects to petition the King and all commitments and prosecutions for such petitioning are illegal.*

Standing army—*That the raising or keeping a standing army within the kingdome in time of peace unlesse it be with consent of Parlyament is against the law.*

Subject's arms—*That the subjects which are protestants may have arms for their defence suitable to their conditions and as allowed by law.*

Freedom of election—*That election of members of Parlyament ought to be free.*

Freedom of speech—*That the freedome of speech and debates or proceedings in Parlyament ought not to be impeached or questioned in any court or place out of Parlyament.*

Excessive baile—*That excessive baile ought not to be required nor excessive fines imposed nor cruell and unusuall punishments inflicted.*

Juries—*That jurors ought to be duly impannelled and returned . . .*

Frequent Parliaments—*And that for redresse of all grievances and for the amending strengthening and preserving of the lawes Parlyaments ought to be held frequently . . .*

The said lords spirituall and temporall and commons assembled at Westminster doe resolve that William and Mary Prince and Princesse of Orange be and be declared King and Queene of England France and Ireland and the dominions thereunto belonging to hold the crowne and royall dignity of the said kingdomes and dominions to them the said prince and princesse dureing their lives and the life of the dominions to them the said prince and princesse dureing their lives and the life of the survivour of them. And that the sole and full exercise of the regall power be onely in and executed by the said Prince of Orange in the names of the said prince and princesse dureing their joynt lives and after their deceases the said crowne and royall dignitie of the said kingdoms and dominions to be to the heires of the body of the said princesse and for default of such issue to the Princesse Anne of Denmarke and the heires of her body to be to the heires of the body of the said princesse and heires of her body and for default of such issue to the heires of the body of the said Prince of Orange. And the lords spirituall and temporall and commons doe pray the said prince and princesse to accept the same accordingly . . .

Upon which their said Majestyes did accept the crowne and royall dignitie of the kingdoms of England France and Ireland and the dominions thereunto belonging according to the resolution and desire of the said lords and commons contained in the said declaration. And thereupon their Majestyes were pleased that the said lords spirituall and temporall and commons being the two Houses of Parlyament should continue to sitt and with their Majesties royall concurrence make effectuall provision for the settlement of the religion lawes and liberties of this kingdome soe that the same for the future might not be in danger againe of being subverted, to which the said lords spirituall and temporall and commons did agree and proceede to act accordingly. Now in pursuance of the premises the said lords spirituall and temporall and commons in Parlyament assembled for the ratifying confirming and establishing the said declaration and the articles clauses matters and things therein contained by the force of a law made in due forme by authority of Parlyament doe pray that it may be declared and enacted that all and singular the rights and liberties asserted and claimed in the said declaration are the true auntient and indubitable rights and liberties of the people of this kingdome and soe shall be esteemed allowed adjudged deemed and taken to be and that all and every the particulars aforesaid shall be firmly and strictly holden and observed as they are expressed in the said declaration. And all officers and ministers whatsoever shall serve their Majestyes and their successors according to the same in all times to come. And the said lords spirituall and temporall and commons seriously considering how it hath pleased Almighty God in his marvellous providence and mercifull goodness to this nation to provide and preserve their said Majestyes royall persons most happily to raigne over us upon the throne of their auncestors . . . doe hereby recognize acknowledge and declare that King James the Second haveing abdicated the government and their Majestyes having accepted the crowne and royall dignity as aforesaid their said Majestyes did become were are and of right ought to be by the lawes of this realme our soveraigne liege lord and lady King and Queene of England . . . And for preventing all questions and divisions in this realme by reason of any pretended titles to the crowne and for preserveing a certainty in the succession thereof in and upon which the unity peace tranquillity and safety of this nation doth under God wholly consist and depend the said lords spirituall and temporall and commons doe beseech their Majestyes that it may be enacted established and declared that the crowne and regall government of the said kingdoms and dominions with all and singular the premises thereunto belonging and appertaining shall bee and continue to their said Majestyes and the survivour of them dureing their lives and the life of the survivour of them and that the entire perfect and full exercise of the regall power and government be onely in and executed by his Majestie in the names of both their Majestyes dureing their joynt lives and after their deceases and said crowne and premises shall be and remaine to the heires of the body of her Majestie and for default of such issue to her royall Highnesse the Princess Anne of Denmarke and the heires of her body and for default of such issue to the heires of the body of his said Majestie ... And whereas it hath beene found by experience that it is inconsistent with the safety and welfare of this protestant kingdome to be governed by a popish prince or by any King or Queene marrying a papist the said lords spirituall and temporall and commons doe further pray that it may be enacted that all and every person and persons that is are or shall be reconciled to or shall hold communion with the see or church of Rome or shall professe the popish religion or shall marry a papist shall be excluded and be for ever uncapeable to inherit possesse or enjoy the crowne and government of this realme and Ireland and the dominions thereunto belonging or any part of the same or to have use or exercise any regall power authoritie or jurisdiction within the same.'

From this point on the Crown was in the gift of Parliament. Under the Coronation Oath Act, passed immediately after the revolution, the monarch's coronation oath contained a pledge to govern 'according to the statutes in Parliament agreed on'.[26] In 1694 the Meeting of Parliament Act established that Parliament should meet at least once every three years, though Parliament effectively secured at least one yearly meeting by providing that the army should be controlled by a Mutiny Act which had to be annually renewed. In 1700 the Act of Settlement conferred the Crown on the House of Hanover, from whom the present Royal House of Mountbatten-Windsor are descended. Section 2 of this Act excluded Roman Catholics, or those married to Roman Catholics, from the Royal Succession as follows:

'Provided always and it is hereby enacted that all and every person and persons who shall or may take or inherit the said crown by vertue of the limitation of this present Act and is are or shall be reconciled to or shall hold communion with the see or church of Rome or shall profess the popish religion or shall marry a papist shall be subject to such incapacities as in such case or cases are by the said recited Act provided enacted and established.'

By this time it must be accepted the supreme legal power was *The King in Parliament*. Parliament further regulated the succession to the Crown by the Royal Marriages Act 1772, the Accession Declaration Act 1910, the Regency Act 1937 and the Royal Titles Act 1953. It also became an established practice that bills granting taxation revenue to the Crown could only be initiated in the Commons and could not be amended by the Lords.

The reign of the final Stuart monarch, Queen Anne, saw the Union with Scotland Act 1706 and the last exercise of the royal refusal of assent to legislation, since when it has become the conventional rule that the monarch always assents to legislation passing the Commons and the Lords.

[26] The Coronation Oath Act 1688, section 3.

(c) The slow decline of the personal power of the monarch

It would be wrong, however, to think that the eighteenth century had a system of government much like that of the present. *Elements* of the current system were present, and royal absolutism was a spent force, but otherwise matters differed. Parliament was not representative of the whole people—few had the right to vote. Elections were local personal contests (only in 1701 and 1789 were they fought as issues of choice and policy). Moreover, the Septennial Act of 1715 provided only for a minimum of an election every seven years. What did occur, however, was the emergence of important current constitutional institutions: the growth of the Cabinet is an excellent example of this.

In the early middle ages the King ruled in person, advised by his Great Council. As the centuries passed this was replaced, for day-to-day administration, by the King's 'Privy Council' consisting of his principal advisers. This was the body most used by the Tudors. By the end of the seventeenth century meetings of the principal members of this council were known as Cabinet Councils, from which the modern Cabinet is descended. At first the King was present at these meetings, but George I ceased to attend and consulted with ministers privately—thus separating monarch and Cabinet by a rule of practice which has now become the convention whereby the Prime Minister and the monarch have Tuesday afternoon meetings, usually weekly, at which the monarch is informed of developments, and *may* exercise the right to warn and/or encourage.

It also became established that the King's principal advisers or ministers who formed the Cabinet must be members of one or other of the Houses of Parliament. Though the King still ruled and made policy in consultation with ministers, they had to secure majority support in the House of Commons, if votes of finance were to be assured. Thus they had to advise pursuit of policies likely to attract support in the Commons. Support could be obtained, however, in a number of ways, for example by the use of corruption, though there were never enough 'spoils' of office to satisfy all those who might have wished for them, and much support came about through ties of personal loyalty to the King, or via friendships, family, or common interest. But it must be remembered that over half the members of the Commons were what would nowadays be called 'independents', and astute and persuasive political management was needed in order to ensure their support. Even so the *personal* influence of the monarch declined throughout the eighteenth century. In 1779 Lord Shelburne stated in the House of Lords the monarch: 'cannot act but through the medium of his ministers in their several departments'. By 1807 Lord Erskine could be even more direct: 'The King can perform no act of government himself . . . he cannot act but by advice; and he who holds office sanctions what is done, from whatever source it may proceed.'

The status of 'Prime Minister' emerged also at this time, though in *legal* terms the post of premier was recognised only in 1905 when a royal warrant placed the officeholder behind the Archbishop of Canterbury in terms of precedence for state occasions.

(d) Reform and the emergence of the modern constitution

Following the union of Great Britain and Ireland to form the United Kingdom[27] the constitutional history of the nineteenth century is primarily concerned with the gradual emergence of the constitution in recognisably modern form. In 1832 the Great Reform Bill abolished the old electoral qualifications in the counties, and extended the franchise to a wider range of property holders in both urban and rural areas. Though the increase in the numbers of the electorate was not great, from some 500,000 to 813,000 (with only one adult male in seven having the vote), the *proportional* increase was larger. Nevertheless, the percentage of adult males entitled to vote rose only slowly thereafter, increasing from 5 per cent in 1831 to 7 per cent in 1832, 16 per cent in 1867 and 23.5 per cent in 1884. Seats in the Commons were redistributed to ensure some representation for new industrial areas. There were other imbalances to correct: Yorkshire with 17,000 voters and Rutland with 600 each returned two members; England had 489 MPs, 25 per cent of whom came from the five South Western counties, of which Cornwall returned 44 members. The 1832 Act established 20 new boroughs with two MPs and 20 with one, principally in the Midlands and North. Royal influence over Parliament declined and effective power passed to ministers who, though many were great aristocrats, began to have to rely increasingly on political organisation to ensure their policies and proposals would be acceptable to Parliament. Political parties emerged from registration societies created to ensure that all those entitled to vote and known to support a particular policy were registered to vote, and from the growth of political clubs in London such as the Carlton and Reform.

The Second Reform Act of 1867 gave the franchise to virtually all male town householders, and country householders were similarly enfranchised by the Third Reform Act of 1880. Parliament became the principal legislative body concerned to lay down general rules while leaving to ministers and civil servants day-to-day administration of the increasing range of government activities.

(e) New roles for government

Basic government functions had been for long concerned with protecting the state from external aggression, maintaining law and order within the realm, raising taxation to pay for such activities, together with regulating the nation at the local level. For hundreds of years, defence had been, as it still is, a government function of the highest order; therefore national resources (eg land, wood, coal, and men) and major 'government departments' (such as the Admiralty and the War Office) were devoted to the prosecution of defence policies. As well as defending the nation, monarchs maintained their power and status within the country: rebellions were crushed, official religion maintained, the monarch's lands protected, the laws of the realm enforced. In order to carry out these functions means of ensuring that the royal will was carried out in the provinces was needed. Monarchs could not rely on officials in London to do this in an era of poor communication and slow travel: someone was needed at

[27] The Union with Ireland Act 1800. We shall return to the problems raised by the Acts of Union with Scotland and Ireland in chapter 2.

grass-roots level and already in a position of authority in the regions. The chosen local representatives from medieval times were the justices of the peace. More functions were given to them over the centuries. These were not simply criminal concerns but administrative matters such as: ensuring disabled soldiers received pensions; checking attendance at church; controlling local fairs and supervising local public works, such as the upkeep of the roads and keeping rivers and harbours clear. All the foregoing were historic functions of government, but with the coming of the industrial and agrarian revolutions of the mid to late eighteenth century changes in society led to changes in the tasks of government.

It is impossible to point to a single date and to claim that then the 'limited' state whose functions are outlined above gave way to an 'interventionist' state with many functions, at which point government assumed full responsibility for the welfare of the nation. Some governmental functions, as we have seen, had existed for many centuries, together with a rudimentary and charitable system of welfare for the poor, the disabled, orphans and the mentally ill. However, it is usual to point to the nineteenth century, especially its second half, as the period of economic, social and legal history which gave birth to the framework of the modern interventionist administrative state. At this time certain matters, traditionally considered not within the role of the state and left to be carried on, if at all, by private individuals, landowners, merchants and factory owners, came into the realm of government responsibility. It was at this time that the ill effects of the Industrial Revolution came increasingly to public notice.

That change in society was founded on individualism, a phenomenon often given the name 'laissez faire'. This was a doctrine that demanded the minimum interference by government in economic and political affairs. Economists preached freedom: the removal of customs barriers would lead to the sale of more and more goods; this would create a strong economy. Additionally individuals, if left to their own devices, would achieve more social good than state monopolies. Competition to increase profit would lead to improved techniques and lower prices. Individualism also meant the survival of those fitted to survive. (It may be noted that these arguments are still attractive to many at the current time.)

Individualism was aided by the common law and its strong principles of freedom of the person, freedom of property and freedom of contract. As Lord Denning commented in *Freedom Under the Law*:

'But just as the property owners were entitled to prefer their own interest to public good, so also anyone who had a bargaining lever was able to exploit it for his own benefit. It was all done under the name of freedom of contract. It mattered not to the judges of the day that one party had the power to dictate the terms of the contract and the other had no alternative but to submit. So in the days of housing shortage, when men with families were looking in vain for a furnished room in which to live, the law, as laid down by the judges of the nineteenth century, would have us believe that there was freedom of contract between the landlord and tenant. [In] 1863 it was held "There is no law against letting a tumble down house" [*Robbins v Jones* (1863) 33 LJCP 1]. This meant that a landowner could put up ramshackle back to back houses with no sanitation and let them for whatever rent he could get; and no matter that the roof leaked, and the damp rose up the walls so that the tenant and his family fell sick, or the stairs gave way so that he broke his leg, nevertheless the law gave no remedy. The judges who laid down this law were only conforming to the political thought of their time.'[28]

However, 'the very success of laissez faire was its undoing'.[29] The industrial revolution which brought fortune to some also brought intolerable working conditions, overcrowding in manufacturing towns, disease caused by insanitary housing, uncontrolled industrial pollution, epidemics of cholera and typhoid, and widespread poverty. 'The Administration had to

---

[28] At p. 67.   [29] Griffith and Street, *Principles of Administrative Law*, p. 1.

intervene in the interests of public safety and health.'[30] Victorian liberalism and humanitari-
anism demanded that something be done: the authority to do it was the Crown; the responsibilities of government had to be expanded enormously. If humanitarian principles were to
prevail, freedom of property and freedom of contract had to be abated, while freedom from
want and disease became important issues, especially after the extension of the franchise
referred to above. Political power changed—political masters began to rely on the support of
the electorate, pursuing policies which commanded their agreement. From the nineteenth
century through to the present day the role of government has thus expanded enormously.

An early target for Victorian reformist zeal was the alleviation of working conditions in
cotton and wool mills in the north of England, metal industries in the Midlands and coal
mines throughout the nation. The hours for which children could be employed were progressively reduced, as were those for adult male workers, while women were excluded altogether
from underground work in coal mines. The power of legislation here superseded the common
law of contract which had hitherto governed employment. Public health protection also
received the attention of Parliament after a series of cholera, typhoid fever and influenza
epidemics in the 1830s and 1840s. Various local boards—the ancestors of our modern local
authorities—were given powers to secure the removal of 'nuisances', such as piles of festering
manure, and the creation of a system of sanitation by means of the creation of public sewers
and the provision of wholesome water. By the latter half of the nineteenth century attention
was also being given to the demolition of insanitary dwellings, and the first faltering steps were
taken towards the provision of better quality housing by the state itself, again via the medium
of local authorities. In the early years of the twentieth century these initiatives led to the
beginnings of a statutory system of town planning (from 1909) and the mass provision of
council housing (from 1923). The nineteenth century witnessed only rudimentary provision
of income support for those unable to maintain themselves and their families by virtue of
unemployment, illness, accidents, disabilities or old age. However, the Asquith government,
elected in 1906, undertook the introduction of both state pensions for the elderly and 'labour
exchanges' where the unemployed could seek work. In 1911 the National Insurance Act
created a scheme of compulsory sickness insurance for manual workers.

The themes outlined above continued to develop throughout the twentieth century and
remain central to the role of government in the life of the nation at the beginning of the
twenty-first century. As the successor to the Victorian Factories Acts we have modern Health
and Safety laws; the protection of public health has broadened out to become general
environmental protection; the provision of which is variously called 'social' or 'affordable'
housing has continued, albeit with less of a role for local authorities and more emphasis on the
work of voluntary organisations such as Housing Associations; benefits for those in need of
state assistance have vastly increased so that the government's social security spending is one of
the greatest items of national expenditure, way exceeding, for example, spending on defence.

It must not be supposed, however, that the increasing managerial role of the state has led to
governments being as powerful as they might seem—or wish—to be. By the latter years of the
twentieth century it was clear that the notion of 'command and control', ie the concept of
governments being able to deal with issues and problems by the passage of legislation and the
creation of regulation, was less and less capable of being easily and universally applied. The
reasons for this are many, but to a large measure depend on the globalisation of financial and
labour markets. It is hard nowadays to think of any industrialised state that is truly self
contained and self sufficient—the essential prerequisites for 'command and control' to work.

[30] Loc cit.

Nations are dependent on one another for the supply of raw materials and for markets in their goods and services. Multinational companies with vast budgets can transfer their resources and operations with a degree of ease from one part of the world to another. International organisations such as the United Nations and, in the economic sphere particularly, the World Trade Organisation and World Bank, act as major constraints on the freedom of governments to do as they wish. At the same time it is clear even within nations that the ability of governments to achieve their objectives depends at least as much upon the willing cooperation of organisations and individuals as it does on the coercive power of the law. Many commentators on government and policy would nowadays argue that the chief role of government is akin to that of a choreographer who has to persuade national and international bodies and companies and individuals to dance in time to the 'tune' of policy.

At the same time, however, the vast growth in the communications industry via radio, television, newspapers and the internet, means that politicians have ever more opportunities for putting forward their views and policies. Individuals and organisations also have become much more sophisticated in using the media to press their own individual cases. One result of this is that governments can be far too ready to promise action and to give the impression that by the passage of legislation they can meet the claims—which may often be incompatible—of the various sections of society. 'Soundbite' policy making is a feature of twenty-first century Britain, and it has severe drawbacks in that it can so often lead to the raising of aspirations which cannot then easily be satisfied. The consequence of that is that the political process becomes discredited and politicians and policy makers are increasingly seen as untrustworthy.

The student of the modern constitution must bear all this in mind and must adopt a somewhat sceptical approach to the making of policy and the passage of legislation. The former is not contingent solely upon the actions of government but rather is subject to a whole range of external constraints, the latter is not a simple and easy way to 'magic away' a problem.

(f) Some features of the modern constitution

(i) The position of the monarch

By the early years of the twentieth century both the current constitution, and the basic framework of what is called 'the Welfare State', were essentially present. Certain events of importance, however, were still to come. The Parliament Act 1911 laid down that the House of Lords may only delay legislation passed by the Commons, they may not veto it. The personal influence of the monarch over the formulation of policy also declined. Queen Victoria exercised a degree of influence over ministers; her son, Edward VII, influenced foreign policy, while in 2004 it became clear that George V had personally intervened to try to prevent the outbreak of the First World War by pleading with his cousin the Czar of Russia for the demobilisation of the Russian army.[31] However, in the twentieth century the role of the monarch was not that of policy formulation—that became exclusively a task for ministers. A series of popular monarchs—King George V (1910–36), King George VI (1937–52) and Queen Elizabeth II (1952 to date)—made the monarchy instead a focus of unity for the whole nation. Governments are Her Majesty's Government and the opposition is Her Majesty's 'Loyal' Opposition, but the monarch herself is above politics, and separate from politicians

---

[31] *Sunday Times*, 18 July 2004.

who are collectively less than popular and generally distrusted. The monarch, on the other hand, is a national symbol to whom all can give loyalty and allegiance, even though of diverse political persuasions. Another role often argued for as especially appropriate to modern monarchs is that of *guarantor of the constitution*. Ministers come and go, the monarch goes on. Ministers are associated with the policies they pursue and the laws made in Parliament during their period of office—the monarch is above party politics.

While the powers, theoretical or otherwise, of the monarch will be discussed in chapter 3, it is appropriate to pause and consider the current position of the monarchy in the United Kingdom. While the personal popularity of Queen Elizabeth II is not in serious doubt, the institution of monarchy has been increasingly called in question by a number of people. There are a number of reasons for this.

Many argue that it is inappropriate for Britons to be subjects rather than citizens, and that the monarch is an outmoded symbol of a heritage of deference to authority and a hierarchical ordering of society which no longer survives.[32] However, it may well be that many who espouse this view confuse the existence of monarchy with another issue to be returned to below, namely the overwhelming power of government—which is carried on in the Queen's name—and the so-called 'democratic deficit'. It is essential to disaggregate these issues.

Rather more important may be the question of the overall 'style' of the Royal Family from whose behaviour and conduct it is hard to disengage the monarch herself and the institution of monarchy. In previous centuries the conduct of a reigning monarch's children has brought the institution into question. This happened in the reigns of George III in the eighteenth century and of Queen Victoria in the nineteenth, in both instances largely being fuelled by questions over the conduct of the heir to the throne. While Sir Ivor Jennings was right to assert 'the influence of the Crown depends on him who wears it', it is now the case that the public's esteem of the monarchy has also become tied into the perception of the character and worth of the monarch's family, together with matters such as the cost of the institution to the nation. This has been accompanied by over intrusiveness by the media who have glamorised the Royal Family (and even its very distant relatives) to an unsustainable degree, while the Royal Family have not always resisted this tendency as they might have been better advised to do.

There can be little doubt that unfortunate events in the private lives of some of the Queen's children have had an effect on the public standing of the monarchy. The death in a car crash of Diana, Princess of Wales on 31 August 1997 was to cause a degree of perturbation amongst students of the constitution.

The marriage of the Prince and Princess of Wales in 1981 was portrayed as a fairytale event. The subsequent story of an unhappy marriage leading to a highly public divorce was exploited by authors, journalists and broadcasters and did little to enhance the position of the monarchy. The death of Diana, Princess of Wales, led to a massive public outpouring of grief, though this was probably over-estimated at the time; for instance only a minority of the population signed one of the special books of condolence that were opened nationwide. Even so that grief, coupled with the Prime Minister's televised characterisation of her as 'the people's princess' (a phrase initially applied by the journalist Julie Burchill) caused a surge of emotion to the effect that the Royal Family was aloof and distant from a nation (as described by the Press) in the throes of virtually irreconcilable grief. Why, for example, the Press cried, did the Queen stay in Scotland when the nation needed her? It was almost heresy to argue that the Queen was performing the entirely proper task of comforting and protecting two young princes who had suffered a greater loss than anyone else in the country.[33]

[32] See Ben Summerskill, 'The Future of the Monarchy' 3/4, 2001, RSA Journal p. 12.
[33] Ben Pimlott, 'The People v Regina', *Sunday Times*, 21 October 2001.

In the event a live broadcast by the Queen to the nation, the alteration of protocol so that on the day of Diana's funeral the Union flag flew at half mast over Buckingham Palace, and the entire Royal Family's publicly dignified acceptance of the criticism that was, to a considerable extent, unjustly heaped on them, did much to take the heat out of the situation. Within a year a public opinion poll in the *Sunday Times* (25 August 1998) revealed, inter alia, that 63 per cent of Britons considered the nation would be worse off without the monarchy, while only 19 per cent considered it would be better off. 62 per cent of those polled believed the Queen should never abdicate, while 58 per cent of them believed that the Prince of Wales was fit to become King. Yet other polls (*The Times*, 27 August 1998) indicated that the personal popularity of the Prince of Wales had increased markedly. Figures reported in *The Times*, 19 June 2000, indicated that three quarters of people surveyed in a poll believed the monarchy would survive. However, over half of those surveyed still considered the institution to be out of touch with the views and hopes of the nation and the real danger to the monarchy may not be active republicanism, but rather a slow erosion of its perceived relevance to people. Too much cannot be read into such polls as they only give a 'snapshot' at any given moment. Many commentators have, however, argued that within the year from August 1997 to August 1998 the Royal Family had largely transformed its public image. The Queen appointed a 'communications director' (portrayed by the Press as a royal 'spin doctor') to ensure the best construction of events is publicly received; Union flags now fly over royal residences when the Queen is absent—an indication they are national as well as royal homes; royal diaries are less rigidly organised so that time can be made available to respond to emergencies; the royal website has been promoted; protocol has been relaxed on royal visits and it has been re-stated that bowing and curtseying are optional. There was in addition a considerable upsurge of sympathy for the Royal Family following the death of the Queen Mother in 2002, and that was consolidated only a little later in that year by the celebrations for the Queen's Golden Jubilee. During her joint address to both Houses of Parliament on that occasion the Queen emphasised for herself and the nation: 'the tradition of service. The willingness to "honour one another and seek the common good" transcends social change.'

A degree of republicanism remains intellectually active in the United Kingdom, both on the left and the right of politics. Left wing thinkers view the institution of monarchy as encapsulating class division, private privilege and the dominance of birth and inherited wealth: those on the right see it as a barrier to casting out old ways of thinking and the emergence of a radical entrepreneurial capitalist society along American lines where virtually all positions are open to popular election. These views sit oddly together: excessively entrepreneurial societies tend to be those most obviously divided by wealth. Even so the rejection of moves to republican status in Australia in November 1999—albeit because the particular form of republican proposal was repugnant to many Australians, was no encouragement to republicanism here. There are also those who while not advocating abolition of the monarchy argue for a complete ending of all the monarch's personal political powers such as the appointment of the Prime Minister and the granting of the Royal Assent, and the total separation of church and state. These were proposals put forward variously by the Demos 'think tank' in 1998 and the Fabian Society in 2003, adopting a Scandinavian model where, for example, in Sweden, the King lost his powers in 1975. But if the monarch does not appoint the Prime Minister, for example, who does? The Speaker of the House of Commons has been suggested, but the Speaker is a political, not an impartial, figure. It is wise to remember these words of Professor Vernon Bogdanor: 'In the modern world, constitutional monarchy and democracy are complementary rather than conflicting notions.'[34]

---

[34] Vernon Bogdanor, 'Let's be really radical and not change the monarchy', *The Times*, 16 July 2003.

It remains clear that the monarchy retains its place only with the consent of the people. While without a great deal of actual political power the monarch retains considerable influence, and while not the effective head of national government, the monarch remains head of state, and that is a source of strength to the institution as an apolitical focus of national unity. The way forward for the monarchy may well be to weld together its unifying rôle with broad general support from the people. This should not be impossible; throughout the twentieth century the House of Windsor displayed considerable skill in adapting to changes in society, but it may need all of that skill in the twenty-first century.

(ii) What then would the role of the monarchy be?

The people of the United Kingdom are no longer as politically culturally or racially homogeneous as they used to believe themselves to be. They are also less deferential to old ideas and institutions. Many commentators argue that the very concept of 'Britishness' only dates from the eighteenth century following union with Scotland, and certainly the devolution of powers to the Scottish Parliament and the Welsh Assembly (see further below) has done much to stimulate a degree of separate identity in those parts of the United Kingdom. However, opinion polls carried out in Scotland have indicated a majority of Scottish voters (61%) wish to retain the British monarch as head of state.[35] Furthermore, the forces that unite are more important and should be more powerful than those which divide. There are qualities which, while not uniquely found in the United Kingdom, are often thought of as 'British'—belief in toleration and liberty, love of fair play, and an embracing of pluralism which allows people to have a number of allegiances which are seen as complementary not competing. These aspects of our society need to be developed so that it is not anachronistic to be Scottish *and* British, or English *and* British, irrespective of ethnicity, but also embracing the cultural strength such diversity brings. An obvious task for the monarchy is thus to be a major proactive force for *unity in diversity*.

No one should suppose that task is easy and it cannot be undertaken in a mechanistic way as one would create an artefact. The old forces of imperial patriotism, religion and hierarchical class structures are no longer of much account, so the early twentieth century model of the monarchy as an above-the-political fray arbiter, the social pinnacle of society, the source of imperial, legal and moral authority is no longer apt. In a society where the overwhelming majority of people are, in financial terms at least, middle class, the task is one of reaching out to as many sections of the community as possible. The monarchy will have to earn respect and to learn the hard lesson that authority nowadays is personal and not dependent upon status.

A further task is to promote *unity by inclusion*. While the enormously increased rôle of government in the provision of services has been outlined above, it now seems clear that state action alone can neither meet all the needs of society, nor even identify them. Indeed it is desirable that it should not, for a society where the welfare of its members depended entirely on state action would be excessively bureaucratic, with individuals becoming increasingly apathetic as to the needs and interests of their fellows. Individual involvement in the civic, voluntary, religious and charitable workings of the nation is essential to the health of society.

[35] *Sunday Times*, 6 September 1998.

Traditionally the monarchy has been associated with voluntary and charitable activity, but a much greater emphasis now needs to be placed on that rôle.

Mention has been made of the largely middle class nature of our society, but that should not blind us to the existence of large numbers of people who are excluded from general affluence and who are alienated from, and largely ignored by, the rest of society. Politicians to a considerable extent are in thrall to the electorate and cannot ignore the wishes of voters who, on the whole, do not want to see any redistribution of wealth from the middle to the working classes by any major increase in taxes: the monarchy does not have to worry about votes in this sense. The monarchy as a force to counteract social disintegration would draw the attention of society to the existence of the needs of outsiders.

To a considerable extent this new role for monarchy has already been prefigured in the work undertaken by the Prince of Wales through the Prince's Trust, and by the late Diana, Princess of Wales, so that Professor Pimlott could justly argue that: 'both Charles and Diana in their contrasting ways deserve credit for a significant change of emphasis—towards using the royal status to help groups the public prefers to forget. Traditionally royals bestowed their favour on the long established mainstream charities. The Waleses shifted it (sometimes controversially) onto the margins . . . While Diana assisted desperate people by investing them with a kind of underclass chic merely by being photographed in their company, Charles has sought to help the disadvantaged by helping them to help themselves. . . . [By] pinpointing problems and seeking solutions of a kind vote-seekers often shy away from, the . . . work [of the Prince's Trust] has begun to open up a new opportunity for modern monarchy in the era of the often-excluding consensus.'[36]

In the early 1990s particular criticism arose over the Queen's exemption from the payment of tax on her private income and on the other payments made to her and members of her family via the annual 'civil list'. This latter institution dates back to 1760 when George III surrendered the income from the Crown Estate to the Treasury in return for what was effectively an annual salary. Since then at the beginning of each reign the Crown Estate is given over to the Treasury. In 1992–93 the Civil List for the Queen and other members of her family came to £10,457,000 (the Queen received £7,900,000 of this) with a separate budget of £24m in respect of the royal palaces—£636,000 of the Civil List was, however, refunded by the Queen. The Treasury was not thereby out of pocket, for the income from the Crown Estate came to £70m.

The Royal exemption from tax was not historically well founded. Queen Victoria was persuaded to pay income tax on all her income from 1842, and this continued under Edward VII (1901–10). From the time of George V, however, secret agreements between monarch and government reduced the burden of taxation on royal finances, and in 1937 George VI struck a deal with the Prime Minister, Stanley Baldwin, which exempted the monarch from income tax—largely because the King undertook to fund his brother, the former Edward VIII, in exile following his abdication. The royal exemption from tax did not, however, come to light until 1971.

Criticism of royal tax exemption combined with concern at the total running cost of the monarchy, which was some £57m by 1992. It was argued that the Queen should meet more of these costs from her own private resources. Here, however, there arose a problem because of the entangled nature of what the monarch owns personally and what are, in effect, inalienable state-controlled assets, such as the Crown Jewels, royal palaces and their contents, which it is inconceivable the monarch would sell. In 2002 the Queen's personal fortune was estimated to

---

[36] *Sunday Times*, 30 August 1998.

he some £275m, though the total wealth of the Royal Family in 2001 was estimated to be over £2bn—rather less than the wealth of the Duke of Westminster at £3.9bn and Sir Richard Branson at £2.3bn. Broadly, however, the Queen's personal wealth derives from investments and property, certain works of art which could conceivably be sold, and £7.3m per annum (2002) from the Duchy of Lancaster estates which funds expenditure not covered by the Civil List.

The fire at Windsor Castle in November 1992, followed by the government's announcement that the state would pay restoration costs brought criticism to a head—with many people believing that the Queen should either pay for the work herself or pay tax. In fact in the spring of 1992 the Queen had told the Prime Minister she wished to pay income tax, though the Queen remains exempt from inheritance tax. There then followed six months of secret negotiations between the Queen's staff, the Treasury and the Inland Revenue Service. The Prime Minister appears to have been much involved in these negotiations, and deflected parliamentary involvement on 26 November 1992 by turning down a suggestion that the issue of royal finances should be examined by a Commons Select Committee. A measure of bilateral political party support was obtained for the proposal that the Queen should pay tax by the Leader of the Opposition being informed, confidentially, of the matter a few days before the proposal was made in public in Parliament. The Queen also opened Buckingham Palace to the public to raise funds for the restoration of Windsor Castle.

On 26 November 1992 the Prime Minister announced that the Queen had voluntarily agreed to pay income tax at the rate of 40 per cent on her private income, and to pay council tax on Balmoral and Sandringham, opening her accounts to the Treasury and Inland Revenue Services, and making her £3m annual income from the Duchy of Lancaster estates and investments, which is used to pay for her public duties, subject to their scrutiny. It appeared the Queen would have to pay between £1.2 and £2m per annum in tax. In addition the Queen undertook to meet the Civil List costs of the Princess Royal, the Duke of York, Prince Edward, Princess Margaret and Princess Alice, Duchess of Gloucester; some £870,000 per annum, thus leaving only herself, the Duke of Edinburgh and the Queen Mother as charges on tax revenue. However, it has subsequently appeared that this sum of £870,000 would be paid out of the revenues of the Duchy of Lancaster and set against tax liability otherwise payable on that income.

Further amendments to royal finances have occurred since 1992. The settlement of the Civil List made in 1991 assumed an annual inflation rate of 7.5%, while in fact it averaged 3.25%, leading to a notional 'overpayment' of £34m. In 1998, to correct the anomaly, payment was suspended for four years from 2001, and when payment recommenced in 2005–2006 it was apparently limited to an annual increase of 2.5%, the official annual inflation target. Indeed in June 2000 it was stated that the Civil List would be capped at £7.9m per annum until 2011, with any shortfall being met from the £35m reserve that had built up in the 1990s. Even so there remains a degree of official secrecy surrounding royal finance and the Civil List in particular. This leads many to believe, incorrectly, that the public 'bank rolls' the entire extended Royal Family: in fact payment is made only to the Queen and the Duke of Edinburgh. It has to be remembered that the annual cost of the monarchy at some £36.2m (2003 figures), a reduction since 1998, was then only 58p a year for each person in the nation. That was almost the cost of a loaf of bread, and since 1992 the annual cost of the monarchy has been reduced by 50% or more. Inflation raised the annual cost of the monarchy to the tax payer in 2004 to £36.8m, but the *real* cost reduced by 1%, and the annual cost is hardly more than one-fifth of the £170m which the Treasury receives from the Crown Estate. It is true that in 2005 the cost per head of the monarchy rose to 62p, but that is still a fraction of the cost of the monarchy in the early 1990s before stringent financial reforms were undertaken. It should also be remembered that the above figures do not include the costs of security services for members of the Royal Family. These are not disclosed and are borne by the taxpayer via funding for the police. That cost is believed to be considerable.

Furthermore as part of the restructuring of the Civil List and to introduce transparency into royal finances an annual statement of the cost of the monarchy to taxpayers will be produced. Furthermore the Queen has undertaken to pay pension contributions for the 300 staff of the royal household. At the same time the National Audit Office now investigates the costs of maintaining Buckingham Palace, St James' Palace, Windsor Castle, Kensington Palace, Clarence and Marlborough Houses, etc which are separately funded by a grant-in-aid from the Department for Culture, Media and Sport. In 2002 the Queen undertook to publish her Civil List accounts as a move towards greater public accountability in her finances, though in 2005 the House of Commons Public Accounts Committee argued it should be able to investigate the accounts of the Duchies of Lancaster and Cornwall. This was resisted on the basis that both Duchies are not public bodies but are simply well-run private estates which provide finance helping to underpin the independence of the monarchy and its political neutrality.

In the less deferential society in which we now live, however, where the role of the monarch may be moving in the direction of being 'first citizen' it is, however, legitimate to argue for disclosure of how and where public finance is being applied by the monarch, and that the monarch should as a matter of obligation pay tax like everyone else, and not as a matter of voluntary agreement.

The Prince of Wales is generally separately funded from the Duchy of Cornwall. The Prince of Wales receives income from the Duchy, but cannot spend its capital. Some tax is paid on the income, but there is no liability for capital gains tax on the capital which has led the Duchy to be worth an estimated £463m.[37] The Duchy had an annual income of some £12m in 2004/2005 of which £5.9m went to meet the Prince of Wales's official and charitable activities, while £4.4m was devoted to the (voluntary) payment of tax and other personal expenditure. It remains questionable whether payment of tax on a voluntary basis is easily defensible. In 2005 the Prince of Wales's income from the Duchy rose by £800,000, but there was only a £33,000 increase in tax paid. The explanation for this was increased costs incurred in discharging royal duties which could be set against tax. While the income from the Duchy ensures the Prince of Wales is not a burden on the taxpayer, his London house, Clarence House, is funded and costs £1.9m per annum, an annual charge of 3.5p per head of the population.

In August and September 1996 it appeared that senior members of the Royal Family were discussing proposals apparently initiated by the Queen herself to (i) modify the relationship of the Crown with the Church of England by abolishing the title 'Defender of the Faith' (which appears on the coinage under its Latin abbreviation 'Fid Def'), (ii) end the ban on marriage by members of the Royal Family to members of the Roman Catholic Church, (iii) end the rule that the Crown descends to the monarch's eldest son so as to enable the eldest child to succeed irrespective of sex, (iv) 'downsize' the Royal Family by taking royal status away from the monarch's cousins, uncles and aunts, and (v), and, most controversially, give up the civil list and resume the revenues from the Crown Estates in order to finance the Royal Family's operations. Most of these changes would require legislation, and there was some disquiet on the basis that (a) the very considerable revenue from the Crown Estate (which includes high

[37] *The Times,* 9 April 2005.

rental properties such as Regent Street and Trafalgar Square in London) might make the monarch less accountable to Parliament, while (b) the proposals did not make it clear who would pay for the upkeep of royal palaces, the security of the Royal Family, and their travel and clothing costs. These changes would require primary legislation, for which no parliamentary time has been found. In July 2001, however, the Queen approved a set of guidelines in connection with the pursuit of commercial activities by members of the Royal Family. These are designed to ensure that members of the Royal Family do not make a profit solely out of their status, and should consult the Lord Chamberlain before accepting official engagements or participating in commercial ventures that could lead to a conflict of interest. These guidelines are designed to prevent 'trading on the royal connection'.

(iii) A democratic deficit

The twentieth century has seen the adoption of *'residence'* as a qualification to vote, as opposed to property holding. This was accepted in the Representation of the People Act 1918, which also gave women over 30 the vote, a right extended to women over 21 by the Representation of the People (Equal Franchise) Act 1928. The principle of 'one person, one vote' was enshrined in the Representation of the People Act 1948, and the age at which a person may vote is currently 18. These changes have served to confirm the need for organised party politics: only well disciplined parties with adequate fund raising (such as from wealthy private donors or from groups such as trade unions), and well articulated and clearly presented policies, can survive in a nation where the overwhelming majority can vote and are used to reading, hearing and seeing regular political debate in the media. This has had consequences for Parliament. In the eighteenth century it could exercise a real degree of control not just over legislation but also over the administrative implementation of law and policy. In the nineteenth century its role became largely confined to making legislation in response to government proposals. In the twentieth century Parliament has found it impossible to pass all the legislation needed and has conferred subordinate law-making powers on ministers. Furthermore, the increasingly strict nature of party discipline within the House of Commons has made it ever more unlikely for a government having a working majority there to have its legislative proposals rejected or modified to any real extent (see chapter 6).

In more recent years, however, a focus of *some* opposition to government emerged in the House of Lords. At the start of the twentieth century when it was comprised, effectively, of hereditary peers with an inbuilt conservative bias, the upper house could well be described by Lloyd-George as 'Mr Balfour's Poodle'. After 1958, however, with the ability granted to the Crown to create life peers, and the withdrawal from active political life of many hereditary peers, the nature of the House has changed greatly. Its working strength came to consist of experienced politicians, quite reasonably balanced between the main political parties, and was also marked by the presence of independent 'cross bench' peers owing allegiance to no party. This, combined with weaker party discipline than is found in the Commons, meant that the Lords were certainly not anyone's poodle. The reform of the composition of the House of Lords, albeit on an apparently interim basis, in 1999, and the exclusion from membership of all but a minority of hereditary peers has, if anything, increased the apparent willingness of the Upper House to resist proposals from the government. Thus in the early days of the new century government legislative proposals were defeated in the House of Lords. These matters will be returned to in chapter 6.

However, it is still the case that many commentators point to a 'democratic deficit' in the United Kingdom. These ideas particularly drove the thinking of many who became associated with the 'Charter 88' movement, which, inter alia, called for major constitutional overhaul and, in particular, for a written constitution. It is not hard to appreciate why such ideas became popular. From a purely descriptive point of view the United Kingdom scores highly as a democracy. We have universal suffrage, free, multi-party elections, there is freedom of speech and of association and a general subscription to the idea of the rule of law: see further below. However, what is the *quality* of our democracy? Many argue that while it is clearly impossible in a modern complex state for everyone to play a full participatory role in every decision, our system does not provide for effective control over those who are the decision takers.

The United Kingdom is still best described as a 'limited monarchy': the ultimate responsibility for governing still lies with the Crown. Parliament is simply the place where that power to govern can be expressed in the most solemn and potent way, ie the passage of legislation. Ministers' presence in, and answerability to, Parliament have, historically, been argued for as the means of legitimating the exercise of the power to govern, ie of making it politically acceptable. This legitimacy has been enhanced as Parliament has become increasingly democratically elected. However, the essential point remains true that the central power to govern lies with the Crown, and that is a major feature of our constitution. As LS Amery said in *Thoughts on the Constitution*: 'Our constitution . . . has never been one in which the active and originating element has been the voter . . . the starting point and mainspring of action has always been the government.'[38] And again: 'The function of legislation . . . has always been predominantly exercised by Government.'[39] And again: 'Our system is one of democracy, but of democracy by consent not by delegation, of government of the people, for the people *with but not by* the people.'[40] It is in our system for the Crown, not the people, to make policy. That policy can only be made into law via the active participation and assent of the elected representatives of the people, but, given the nature of modern party politics, that assent is usually forthcoming. Every four or five years, in normal circumstances, the electorate of the United Kingdom has the right to elect its legislature. Out of that election will, normally, emerge a victorious party and its leader who, by constitutional convention, have the right to become (or to continue to be) the group from whom the monarch will choose her ministers. Provided, however, those ministers can retain the confidence of the majority in Parliament— which is likely for they are leaders of that majority—their power is what Lord Hailsham, a former Lord Chancellor, described as an 'elective autocracy'.

It should not be assumed, however, that our system is not without its own *internal* checks and balances. Much depends upon the size of a government's majority and the cohesiveness of that majority. Political parties are often described as 'broad churches', ie they contain members of widely differing points of view who, nevertheless, being agreed on a number of points of principle will agree to sink their differences in a common cause. When in power ministers sometimes have to tread warily to ensure that they do not stretch party loyalty beyond its limits. The point is well illustrated by comparing the Thatcher governments of 1979 to 1991 with those of her successor John Major (1991–97). Mrs Thatcher enjoyed large majorities and a high degree of party loyalty. Mr Major, however, had following 1992 a small and constantly declining majority with open conflict in his party between 'Euro sceptics' and 'Euro enthusiasts'. This conflict was at one point sufficiently acute for some Conservative MPs in 1995 to resign the party whip (ie to give up membership of the party) to indicate their

---

[38] At p. 15.   [39] At p. 12.   [40] At p. 20.

opposition to particular policies. Even so, and even when down to a majority of one, Mr Major was able to secure parliamentary approval for most of his policies. The reason for that has much to do with the realisation among members of the party whose leaders form the government that should they refuse their support, so that the government is defeated on an issue of confidence, the result will be a general election which, if they are shown to be weak and divided, they are likely to lose.

The question now, however, is whether such an 'elective autocracy' is acceptable. Leading thinkers in the Charter 88 movement argued that we need to move away from our present system towards a more democratic one.

In order to understand what has driven the development of such thinking it is necessary to consider certain features of the British constitution as it had developed in the second half of the twentieth century and then to turn our attention to arguments that the nation suffers from a 'democratic deficit': that in turn will lead to a consideration of what is meant by 'democracy'.

(iv) Conclusions of the Royal Commission

The Royal Commission on the Constitution 1969–73,[41] identified certain principal features of the constitution as they then appeared. These were as follows.

- Common loyalty owed to the monarch and a common citizenship enjoyed by the people of the United Kingdom.
- A single supreme law making body in the form of the Westminster Parliament.
- The United Kingdom is a unitary state in both economic and political terms, with a single currency, and a single central bank. All citizens are entitled to move, settle and to trade anywhere within its boundaries.
- The role of government grew markedly throughout the twentieth century, so that very few areas of public, economic and even personal, life are nowadays untouched by government activity at either, or both, central and local levels. This increased role for government was accompanied by an increase in its size. Thus up to the end of the nineteenth century the non-industrial civil service numbered no more than 50,000, by the end of the 1960s there had been a tenfold increase to around 500,000. At the same time the total population had risen by only 50 per cent. There has been a dramatic increase in government spending. In 1870 government spent about £3 per annum per head of the population, one hundred years later the figure was £400, and as a proportion of national income expenditure had risen in that period from 9 per cent to 43 per cent. 'Transfer payments', ie money redistributed *from* taxation of one section of society *to* benefits paid to other sections also rose in this period from 0.2 per cent of national income to 12.5 per cent. By 1970 government claimed over 23 per cent of the annual national output of resources for its own use.
- The balance between central and local government had changed dramatically, with the latter losing many of its functions to the former.
- Ministers were no longer able to maintain a close watch on all the work of their departments and to take all major policy decisions personally. Much of the business of government had become the preserve of the Civil Service. Yet the pressure for government to intervene more and more in every aspect of the nation's life had grown. People expect not just defence, law and order and protection from disease, but also protection from poverty, provision of equal opportunities, more and constantly improving services, and, indeed, constantly enhanced

[41] Cmnd 5460.

standards of living.
- While all this has occurred the institutional life of the nation had changed hardly at all. Parliament went about its business at the end of the twentieth century largely as it did at the beginning.
- By the end of the twentieth century the United Kingdom had become the largest unitary state in Europe, and one of the most centralised industrial nations in the world. This led to a feeling that, as the Royal Commission put it: 'only those at the centre can know all that goes on, and that only they are properly qualified to assess all the possible repercussions of taking any particular action. They must therefore have the last word. The contrary argument is that while the growth in the volume of government has increased the power of those at the centre, it has resulted in ever greater demands upon them and made it quite impossible for them to have a full grasp of all that is going on . . . The recipients of their edicts out in the regions have become uneasy about the quality of the decisions being taken, and have come to question the need for centralisation of so much power in London . . . '42

By the end of the 1980s these concerns had coalesced to produce the argument that the United Kingdom had a 'democratic deficit'. To understand this it is necessary to put forward a model of what democracy is. The arguments on this issue were well summarised by Professor David Beetham in 'Democratic Audit' published by the Charter 88 Trust in 1993 to which indebtedness is acknowledged.

(v) Addressing the deficit

The basic principles of democracy are *popular control* and *political equality*. The former in modern societies, where it is impossible for people to exercise direct control over events personally and to take part in deciding every rule and policy which is to apply, results in a *representatives system*.

'Democracy' nowadays describes a procedure for securing control over decision making and taking. Such control needs to be effective, in other words there must first be institutional arrangements to ensure control, ie a guaranteed electoral system, limits to the powers of judges, ministers and legislators, a real degree of openness and accountability on the part of those in power, effective systems to ensure redress for citizens against illegal state action or maladministration. Then there has to be a set of guaranteed civil liberties such as freedom of speech so that the people have the opportunity to express their views and to influence government in policy making. Political equality on the other hand is a moral principle which states that all people should be equal in the exercise of popular control. This is underpinned by the argument that people are self determining agents who have a right to express views on what may affect their lives, and that they have an equal capacity for self determination. This means that in democratic states citizens have equal rights at law and equal citizenship rights and obligations, the votes of all voters have equal weight and all have the opportunity to seek public office, or to influence those who are elected and to seek a remedy where governments commit illegal acts.

To determine whether a nation satisfies the criteria outlined above it is necessary first to examine whether it has effective institutional arrangements to ensure a distribution of power between people and government and between different arms and levels of government—and to define the procedures by which alone power can be exercised. 'Effective' in this context

---

[42] Cmnd 5460 para 270.

means more than just the existence of formal institutional arrangements which could, for example, be apparently clear under a written constitution, but which in practice may be inadequate because, inter alia, parliamentary control over executive power is weakened by governmental control of the parliamentary majority—a problem which does affect the United Kingdom. On the other hand token participation in decision taking by large numbers of individuals is equally a false image of democracy unless that participation results in a real exercise of power by the people rather than the government. In a mature, well culturally developed democracy large numbers of people will participate in a variety of ways, for example by voting, by being members of political parties, by lobbying members of the legislature and local authorities and by being prepared generally to exercise legally established rights. Even so within such a society participation may not be evenly distributed between all sections of society—those with more leisure, resources and a feeling of commitment will participate more—those with less may conversely feel alienated and excluded. Even so formal legal structures remain important, for before civil rights can be exercised they must be clearly defined and publicised. In this latter respect the United Kingdom would qualify as a well established democratic state.

However, institutional systems alone are not enough to ensure true democracy. Not only does a government need to gain its legitimacy from having an electoral mandate, it also needs to have effective power to govern if it is to retain the confidence of the electorate. Indeed erosion of confidence in a government which is ineffective may lead to disaffection with the entire machinery of democracy. A democratic system of government requires politicians to have sufficient power to bring about the programmes on whose basis they have been elected, coupled with well functioning institutional and political arrangements to ensure that in the exercise of that power they are always responsive to the views of the electorate. Furthermore to be effective in government politicians need policies which are carefully thought through, but equally effective policy implementation requires the co-operation of those who are subject to government, both as to the goal to be achieved and the means of achieving it.

In this respect there is an arguable democratic deficit within the United Kingdom for central government has gained effectively total dominance over local government, so that the latter has become simply the means whereby central policy is executed at a local level. This has been brought about largely as a result of central government assuming since 1945 responsibility for the provision and management of large numbers of services and utilities, for example the provision of health care, the imposition of national standards of delivery on those services which remain local, for example education, and the denial of budgetary freedom to local authorities. Local government thus lacks the power to deliver its agenda in an effective way, and this results in frequently poor turnouts in local elections. On the other hand the central government at Westminster has seen power over many issues pass to the European Community where the issue of democratic accountability remains open to debate. It remains unclear whether the EC is an international organisation where accountability is achieved via domestic legislative oversight of the ministers who make up its Council, or a quasi-national body where accountability is achieved via the elected European Parliament which has certain scrutiny and legislative powers. Where the EC does make legislation it is far from certain that there is effective national oversight over this activity, while the European Parliament lacks power to hold EC institutions accountable on a regular basis.

It is arguable that for the democratic deficit to be addressed that there needs to be a clear division of power between the various levels at which government can operate—local, regional, national and, in the case of the EC, supra national. Furthermore it needs to be established that policy should be determined at that level of government most able to implement it—and that should be the lowest level practicable. Beetham further argues that this 'lowest level practicable' should often be identified as that of local government for that is the level where elected representatives are most accessible, and where direct personal involvement by individuals, for example by membership of residents' and tenants' associations, is likely to be most effective. Truly effective local government is, on this view, essential to the overall democratic vitality of society. There is also an argument—an argument which has only recently begun to be addressed in the United Kingdom in the devolution of power to Scotland, Wales and Northern Ireland (see below)—that regional government should be a feature of a truly democratic system to reflect the legitimate aspirations of people in particular areas of the nation. At the national level also the democratic deficit is reflected in, and reinforced by, the British attachment to simple majoritarian, or 'first past the post', systems of electing the legislature. The result is that the winner takes all under such a system, and this ignores the fact that a nation comprises a considerable diversity and plurality of social and political forces. To put all power in the hands of one group who come first in an election has the consequence of excluding all others and the interests they represent. At the moment the British people at the time of a general election are forced to make simplistic choices between one party or another, with no real chance of influencing the style and content of government by being able to express preferences for particular policies from the range of choice offered by a variety of parties. A majority of the people may thus be frustrated in their electoral wishes and choices, and that may have the long term effect of weakening respect for democracy as a form of government.

For many years the British, and in particular the English, people have clung to a notion well expressed by the couplet:

'For forms of Government let fools contest,
Whate'er is best administered is best.'

On the whole we have been well administered, and we have come to regard effective and strong government as good government. But we should not confuse the two notions. To be 'good' government also needs to be answerable to the people, and nowadays that has the added element of recognising that 'the people' are culturally and socially diverse and wish to express that diversity. The form and structure of government is therefore an issue, for a proper sharing of power between different levels of government not only prevents concentrations of power in too few hands, but also allows a wider range or people to share in government. This enhances people's sense of inclusion and the self-respect that flows from self determination. On that basis popular control and political equality are two sides of one coin.

Debate about more accountable government at Westminster, however, is unlikely to come to anything without tackling the major problem of the electoral system which remains wedded to the concepts of 'first-past-the-post/winner-takes-all'.

(vi) Ever more opportunities for conflict between individuals and the state

The twentieth century has also witnessed great growth in the development of administrative law—that body of law evolved to respond to the growth of state intervention described above. Modern government affects us all, not only with respect to foreign policy, defence, the criminal law and taxation, but also with regard to, for example, prices and incomes, parking regulations, and the provision of various grants, and benefits. The individual comes into contact with government functions from before birth (ante-natal care in National Health Service hospitals) to after death (death certificates and burial plots).

The increase in government functions has brought with it increased administrative machinery to plan, execute and supervise. Today there are many government departments, ranging from Customs and Excise, Defence, the Environment and Agriculture, Transport, Health, the Home Office, Social Security, Trade and Industry to the Treasury. All these have civil servants in London, in regional and local offices in many towns and cities. In addition many functions are discharged for central government by 'next steps' or executive agencies whose staff are not civil servants, but whose activities impinge directly on the public, eg the Child Support and Environment Agencies, and who are subject to ministerial powers of direction. In the nineteenth century many functions were given to counties and large boroughs, in place of small parishes. Today there is a mix of unitary, metropolitan, district and county councils and London borough councils, each having a range of activities, depending on the status of the local authority. Many are employed by such authorities as, for example, town planners, dustmen and teachers. In addition it has been found necessary for special Quasi-Autonomous-Non-Governmental-Organisations (Quangos) to be created to administer or advise on a particular function, for example, the Equal Opportunities Commission. The distinction between quangos and executive agencies is not easily drawn. The latter are 'hived off' parts of the civil service, while the former are a diffuse set of bodies many of which function at a local level, eg National Health Service Trusts. Perhaps the best distinction is that the latter are particularly 'directable' by ministers.

The individual is thus much regulated and needs expert advice to allow the achieving of the maximum amount of happiness with the minimum amount of friction. If there should be a conflict between the individual and the state, the former needs adequate opportunity for resolving that conflict. The purpose of administrative law is to provide legal rules, institutions and machinery which try to guarantee that governmental functions are exercised efficiently to produce beneficial effects for the individual; that government policies are operated in such a way that, so far as possible, they will not produce conflict; that such policies should be exercised openly, fairly and impartially, and that individuals aggrieved by governmental action should, so far as is possible, have recourse to independent dispute settlement machinery and expert advice. Greater government responsibility, functions and regulation provide opportunities for conflicts to increase. Granted that private rights are to be subordinate to the public interest, the public interest must not smother all private rights. The state may cause harm to the individual. The creation, for example, of public works, such as airports, reservoirs and motorways may result in the loss of land and the creation of hazards and nuisance.

Most administrative decisions are as near correct as may be. For example, it is, despite the plethora of case law, comparatively rare to get wrong decisions about housing or planning applications. However, administrators may make wrong decisions, and there must be opportunity to obtain redress against these. Almost more important is the situation where the individual thinks that an administrator has 'got it wrong' and wants an opportunity of questioning the decision and having it explained openly and without official jargon. For example, there may be complaints about the standard and service of education, or a claim to have a child educated at a particular school or to have a child educated in a particular religion or language; there may be complaints that a local authority has not carried out such duties as refuse disposal or has not enforced a prohibition on ice-cream vans disturbing the peace. For accounts of 'political' and 'legal' redress of grievances see chapters 8–10 below.

Some words of warning must, however, be given: legal rules, institutions and machinery cannot by themselves create Utopia. A lawyer cannot solve every problem put forward by a client. Many disputes between individuals and the state fall beyond the range of law. There are inevitable and intractable conflicts of interest involved in every compulsory transfer of property from the individual to the state, be it in the form of taxation or the compulsory purchase of land. Complaints about the personal style of administrators and the ways in which they behave towards those whose lives they affect, and the manifold range of conflicts that arise merely from the fact of being governed, are also unlikely to receive adequate redress in court.

If it is decided to impose certain taxes or not to compensate persons whose property is adversely affected by a new airport, such controversy cannot be made to vanish by a legal magic wand. If, for example, it is desired to reduce levels of poverty, increased benefits for the less well off must be paid for. Decisions on such matters belong to Parliament and particularly to Her Majesty's Government.

(g) The constitution under New Labour and the institution of devolution

When Tony Blair swept into power in May 1997 with a parliamentary majority many of his predecessors would have envied, he did so as a self-proclaimed 'moderniser'. The first fruits of this policy included a constitutional reform programme whose implications still remain to be entirely worked out. Some of the reforms were included in Labour's election manifesto—for example reform of the House of Lords, and devolution of power to Scotland. In addition while 'New' Labour proclaimed 'we have no plans to replace the monarchy' considerable changes have, as has been seen, taken place, and that process continues. Interim reform of the House of Lords has occurred which will be returned to in chapter 5, and devolution to Wales and Scotland has taken place (see below). Reform of the system of electing MPs to replace 'first-past-the-post' has yet to bear fruit.

With devolution, however, rather more has been achieved—with some surprising political consequences.

What is devolution? It is an attempt to address some of the issues highlighted by the debate on the democratic deficit. It is designed to give to the people of Wales, Scotland and Northern Ireland a real measure of independent, decentralised control over the development of their societies.

What forms does devolution take? These have been diverse.

(i) Scotland

Devolution to Scotland was originally more extensive than that to Wales. Following the issue of 'Scotland's Parliament'[43] in July 1997 a referendum on the devolution proposals was held under the Referendums (Scotland and Wales) Act 1997. A large majority in Scotland voted for a Parliament with tax-varying powers. The government further proposed that in relation to any matter not specifically reserved to Westminster the Scottish Parliament should have full legislative power, and this has been enshrined in section 29 of the Scotland Act 1998.

---

[43] Cm 3658.

In addition sections 44 to 63 of that Act created the Scottish Administration which is the effective government of Scotland in relation to devolved issues and which assumed the functions of the Scottish Office. The head of that Administration is the First Minister. Sections 73 to 80 of the Act provide the Parliament with its taxation powers including power to vary the basic rate of income tax in Scotland by up to 3 pence.

(ii) Elections to the Scottish Parliament

The government's White Paper proposed a Parliament built on fairness based on a new form of electoral system combining traditional constituency links with a proportional element to ensure the fair reflection of party preferences in the Parliament. The principal features of these arrangements, under sections 1–18 of the 1998 Act, are:

- a general election to the Parliament takes place every four years, while extraordinary general elections may happen in certain circumstances;
- the Executive has no power to determine the dates of general elections;
- electors are able to vote twice in each election—for a constituency member *and* for a regional member;
- regional members may be either representatives of registered political parties or individuals standing in their own right;
- regional members are returned to the Parliament on a basis taking account of seats already won on a constituency basis.

Members of the Parliament are known as MSPs.

(iii) Administration and working of the Parliament

Section 19 requires the election, by MSPs, of a Presiding Officer who has a role similar to that of the Speaker at Westminster. This section also provides for the appointment of appropriate Clerks and other staff, and for a management body for the Parliament—the Scottish Parliamentary Corporate Body (SPCB).

Section 22 of the 1998 Act together with Schedule 3 give the Parliament powers to determine its own detailed procedures and committee structure. Standing orders deal with certain matters in a limited number of cases such as the preservation of good order in parliamentary proceedings and the declaration of members' interests.

Sections 23–26 give the Parliament extensive powers to call for witnesses to give evidence and documents to assist in investigating matters. These provisions are intended to ensure that the Parliament is able to hold the Scottish Administration to account.

Sections 28–36 and Schedule 5 lie at the heart of the Act and establish the Parliament's powers to make laws, and set out the basis for determining distinctions between devolved and 'reserved' matters. Schedule 5 of the Act actually lists matters that are 'reserved' to the UK Parliament at Westminster: any matter not 'reserved', or otherwise defined in section 29 as outwith the Parliament's competence, falls within the Parliament's powers.

The devolved matters generally are: Health (including the NHS in Scotland); Education and Training (including schools, further and higher education, training and life long learning, careers advice and guidance); Local Government and Housing (including local government finance, social work, area regeneration, planning, building control, economic development, promoting trade and exports, tourism, passenger and road transport, ports and harbours, inland waterways); Law and Home Affairs (including criminal law, civil law, electoral law, judicial appointments—save for the posts of Lord President and Lord Justice Clerk—criminal justice, courts, tribunals, legal aid, prisons, police and fire services, civil defence, liquor licensing); Environment (including the functions of the Scottish Environmental Protection Agency, natural and built heritage, flood control, agriculture, food standards, forestry and fishers); Sport and the Arts.

Schedule 5 of the Act sets out the reserved matters in two parts. The Parliament, however, has powers to *debate* both devolved *and* reserved matters. Section 30 makes provision for amending the list of reserved matters. Orders under this provision have to be approved by both Houses of the UK Parliament *and* by the Scottish Parliament. It is beyond the Parliament's powers to legislate in ways which are incompatible with EC law or the European Convention on Human Rights. Section 33 enables Law Officers of the UK government or the Scottish Executive to refer to the Judicial Committee of the Privy Council questions whether any Bill of the Scottish Parliament, or any provision in such a Bill, is within the bounds of legislative competence.

The reserved matters generally are: The UK constitution (including the Crown, the Westminster Parliament, electoral law, the Civil Service, titles); UK foreign policy; UK defence and national security; Protection of borders (including immigration, extradition and regulation of drugs); the stability of the UK fiscal, economic and monetary system and currency; common markets for UK goods and services (including company law, insurance, insolvency, intellectual property, regulation of financial services, competition, consumer protection, regulation of energy supply, international trade policy, telecommunications, postal services, weights and measures, time zones); Employment legislation (including industrial relations and equal opportunities); Social Security (including benefits and contributions, child support, occupational and personal pension regulation); Regulation of certain professions (including the medical, dental, nursing, veterinary, architects, auditors, estate agents, and insolvency professions). In addition certain matters of transport safety and regulations are reserved to Westminster, including rail, marine and aviation safety, as are nuclear safety, and the control and safety of medicines, together with Ordnance Survey matters, oversight of broadcasting, theatre and cinema licensing, gambling and the National Lottery, data protection, abortion and human fertilisation and equality legislation.

While the Scottish Parliament and Executive have a considerable degree of autonomy, Scotland remains an integral part of the United Kingdom. Relations between the UK government and the Scottish Executive are conducted on the basis of formal, non-statutory understandings between Departments. Within the Department for Constitutional affairs in Whitehall there is the Scotland Office headed by the Secretary of State for Scotland who represents Scotland's interests at Westminster and is the guardian for the constitutional settlement contained in the devolution legislation.

Sections 35 and 58 of the Act grant certain intervention powers to the UK government. Primarily designed to enable the UK to be compliant with international obligations and to protect the interests of defence or national security, section 35 additionally enables the Secretary of State to prohibit a Bill from being submitted for Royal Assent if (a) it contains provisions which make modifications of the law applying to reserved matters and (b) which the Secretary of State has reasonable grounds to believe would adversely affect the operation of that law.

(iv) The constitution of the Scottish Executive and Administration

The Scottish Executive is accountable to the Scottish Parliament. Section 44 of the 1998 Act establishes the Scottish Executive as the First Minister, other ministers appointed by him and the Lord Advocate and the Solicitor General. They are known collectively and for legal purposes as 'the Scottish ministers'. Section 52 provides for their collective responsibility and liability of members of the Scottish Executive.

Sections 45 and 46 lay down the procedure for choosing and appointing the First Minister. Sections 47, 48 and 49 provide for the appointment of other ministers, the Scottish Law Officers and junior Scottish ministers. Section 48, and section 29(2)(e), guarantee continued independence for the Lord Advocate as head of the systems of criminal prosecution and investigation of deaths in Scotland.

The Scottish Administration consists of the Executive, junior ministers, the Keeper of the Registers of Scotland, the Registrar General of Births, Deaths and Marriages for Scotland, the Keeper of the Records, other non-ministerial office holders appointed by the Executive and their staff. Section 51, however, empowers Scottish ministers to appoint staff who remain members of the Home Civil Service.

(v) Miscellaneous matters

Members of the Westminster Parliament representing Scottish constituencies continue to play their traditional roles in proceedings at Westminster. Section 86 of the Act, however, fulfils the White Paper commitment to end the legal requirement which stipulated a minimum number of Scottish seats.

Since the inception of the Scottish Parliament these matters do not appear to have given rise to controversy. One argument against the introduction of devolution was the so called 'West Lothian question', ie if Scotland has a Parliament of its own able to deal with a whole range of issues to the exclusion of English and Welsh MPs at Westminster, why should a Scottish MP at Westminster, such as the MP for 'West Lothian', have the right to legislate on those same issues south of the border? To date this matter has not, however, resulted in any controversy, for while Scottish MPs remain able to vote on English domestic matters, their numbers were reduced for the 2005 general election from 72 to 59, thus ending the previous over-representation of Scotland at Westminster and largely defusing the 'West Lothian' issue. Furthermore even amongst voters who vote for the Scottish National Party (SNP) there appears to be no real demand for independence from the rest of the UK—rather more a desire for an alternative Scottish Executive not dominated by the Labour Party.

The Scottish Parliament is required under section 91 of the 1998 Act to have arrangements for handling complaints about maladministration concerning administrative acts by or on behalf of members of the Scottish Executive or other office holders in the Scottish Administration. The Parliament has power to make arrangements for investigating complaints concerning Scottish public authorities.

Sections 98 to 103 and Schedule 6 of the Act make provision for legal challenges over whether an Act of the Scottish Parliament, or subordinate legislation made by the Scottish Executive, or action by a member of the Executive, is within relevant powers. They specify the circumstances in which challenges are to be made in the ordinary courts, or when reference is to be made to the Judicial Committee of the Privy Council.

Even in areas which are reserved legislatively to Westminster, 'executive devolution' can occur, so that the Scottish Executive is responsible for carrying out UK legislation. In general the functions concerned relate to Betting, Gaming and Lotteries (including gaming hours and certification issues); the Police (including firearm licensing and payment of grants to police authorities); certain Home Affairs issues (including extradition to/from Scotland); Cultural Affairs (including powers to fund Gaelic television and radio); Tribunals; Employment; Energy (including permitting generating stations, powers over civil nuclear installations, construction of pipelines in Scotland); Transport (including certain powers concerning noise at airports, designation restricted roads, etc); Public sector pensions; Health (including approval of abortion facilities and the enforcement of medicines legislation).

Furthermore Scottish ministers are consulted by UK ministers before specified functions are exercised, including licensing areas of the seas around Scotland for oil or gas exploration, granting licences to generate, transmit or supply electricity, appointing members to bodies such as the Independent Television Commission and the Broadcasting Standards Commission, the Equal Opportunities Commission, Commission for Racial Equality and National Disability Council.

(vi) Wales

Under the Government of Wales Act 1998 the National Assembly for Wales was established. This had no legislative powers comparable to those of the Scottish Parliament, but it had transferred to it the powers and responsibilities of the Secretary of State for Wales, and power to allocate funds made available to Wales from the Treasury. However, Wales remains part of the United Kingdom, and the Secretary of State for Wales and members representing Welsh constituencies in the UK Parliament still play a full part in the life of Westminster and laws passed at Westminster still apply in Wales.

Considerable changes to the government of Wales are introduced by the Government of Wales Act 2006. This provides for, inter alia:

- an assembly elected on a constituency basis;
- general elections to the assembly;
- the creation of an executive governing body—the Welsh Assembly Government—with its own First Minister (nominated by the Assembly but appointed by the Queen) which is no longer a mere committee of the Assembly but is a legally separate organisation;
- the creation of a consolidated fund for Wales;
- enhanced legislative powers to pass 'measures' for the Assembly in relation to matters approved and delegated by Parliament;
- a referendum to be held in Wales on the future acquisition of even more extensive legislative powers to pass 'Acts of the Assembly'.

It will be seen that while the new situation in Wales is not a replication of that for Scotland, there are considerable parallels between the devolved systems. This legislation continues the propulsion of the United Kingdom along the path to a form of federalism, with the Westminster Parliament losing control over domestic issues concerning Scotland and Wales and the consequent question of why Scottish and Welsh MPs should have the right to debate and vote on English domestic matters.

(vii) Northern Ireland

Following a generation of direct rule by Westminster, as part of the initiative to bring civil peace back to Northern Ireland, under the Northern Ireland (Elections) Act 1998 a Northern Ireland Assembly was established with powers over Agriculture, Economic Development, Education, Environment, Finance, Health and Social Services. The executive of the Assembly took office on a power sharing basis to reflect the various sectors of the community in Northern Ireland and the Assembly's 108 members were elected on a proportional representation basis. The application of these arrangements has been bedevilled by continuing civil unrest in Northern Ireland, and devolved government was suspended in February 2000, restored in May 2000, and suspended again in 2002. While elections to the Assembly were held in November 2003 it remains suspended, and the Secretary of State for Northern Ireland directs government activities in the province.

(viii) Devolution in practice

Devolution may be seen as a partial answer to the problem of the 'democratic deficit' alluded to above, partly because powers have been devolved to new elected bodies, and partly because each of those bodies has found it necessary to operate on some sort of a power sharing basis. It has also become clear that the devolved bodies are sturdily independent and unwilling to act simply at the behest of the central government.

It remains unclear how far the development of the devolved assemblies will go. Scotland has already seen the creation of a new system of funding university entrants with the scrapping of tuition fees, and banned fox hunting with hounds before that happened in England. It is clear that there is more enthusiasm for devolution in Scotland, with its historic memories of independent nationhood, than in Wales. The Labour Party in Scotland was keen on devolution, while that in Wales was not and would only agree to a small Assembly with no legislative power, while only one adult in four voted in the referendum on devolution in Wales. However, the new institutions exist and in political terms cannot be easily controlled from Westminster. Devolution has led to a dispersal of power and a diversity of forms of government. It also leads to rising expectations and aspirations amongst those who live in Scotland and Wales. In other nations, eg France and Spain, granting limited devolution to certain areas led to demands for wholesale regional restructuring of government. The English regions as yet have no formal structure or powers. They appear unlikely to get them, for while the Blair government has favoured elected regional administrations, a pilot programme for North East England was defeated in a referendum on 4 November 2004. The weakness of the proposal was that the region would be no more than a rearrangement of existing local government, lacking even the limited powers of the Welsh Assembly. 'Democratic deficit' thus continues in England.

In concluding this historical survey of our constitution we may ask whether we are currently moving from the traditional uncodified constitution towards both codification and a more federally structured nation. There is evidence for the latter in the existence of the Scottish Parliament, the Welsh Assembly and the Northern Ireland Assembly which are effectively in control of the development of domestic affairs within their respective areas of the United Kingdom. Indeed the Standing Orders of the House of Commons now provide that members may not table questions to ministers on devolved issues. This development has certain 'untidy' consequences:

• the 'United' Kingdom in legislative terms consists of four parts with regard to domestic policy issues;

• the Westminster Parliament retains responsibility for domestic law making in England, but in respect of the rest of the nation its responsibilities are limited;

• Members of Parliament sitting for Scottish and Welsh constituencies cannot raise issues relating to domestic policies within those constituencies at Westminister, and that inevitably reduces their role as members of the legislature.

So far as codification is concerned, it is arguable that the European Communities Act 1972 (see further chapter 7 below) was the first step in altering the constitutional relationship between Parliament and the courts. This process has been continued under the Blair government's 'modernisation agenda' since 1997 by the enactment of the devolution legislation referred to above, the Human Rights Act 1998 (see further chapters 2 and 13), the House of Lords Act 1999 (see chapter 5) and the Constitutional Reform Act 2005 (see chapter 2) all of which have given the constitution a much more 'statute based' appearance.

It is certainly true, as will be examined at length in the following chapter, that the judiciary has of late asserted a degree of independent thought and action that might have seemed impossible half a century ago. In addition, as will also be argued at greater length in the following chapter, the constitutional balance between the three historic principles of our constitution, namely the Rule of Law, the Separation of Powers and the Supremacy of Parliament can be seen to have shifted in favour of the first two at the expense of the third consequent on the enactment of the Human Rights Act 1998 and the Constitutional Reform Act 2005.

However, we should still remember that our constitution is still largely the product of history and practice. Much still depends on the Royal Prerogative and constitutional conventions (see chapters 2, 3 and 4), while the willingness of the judiciary to 'strike out' independently is limited. Recent case law suggests that the courts are much less likely to utilise their powers to make declarations of incompatibility in respect of UK statutes and the provisions of the European Convention on Human Rights under the 1998 Act in relation to what may be called social and economic issues, for example, matters of housing and planning law, than they are in relation to more traditional civil rights and constitutional issues such as deprivation of liberty and the right to a fair trial.[44] Similarly while the judges have been able to review the legality of the exercise of certain prerogative powers for over twenty years, as will be examined in greater detail in the following chapter, there is still a degree of judicial self restraint which inhibits the judiciary from inquiring into the exercise of certain prerogative powers which relate to matters of state policy such as the conduct of foreign relations and decisions to go to war. Thus where certain protesters alleged that they were entitled to disrupt activities at certain UK military bases on the basis that they were preventing a 'crime of agression' by the British government against the people of Iraq and that their actions were

---

[44] Contrast *Kay and others and another (Appellants) v London Borough of Lambeth and others (Respondents), Leeds City Council (Respondents) v Price and others and others (Appellants)* [2006] UKHL 10 with *Secretary of State for the Home Department v MB, The Times*, 17 April 2006.

therefore lawful under section 3 of the Criminal Law Act 1967, their case failed. This was partly because the House of Lords would not accept that the 'crime of agression' was a crime under UK domestic law and so did not fall within the terms of the 1967 Act, but also because the decision of the UK government to go to war with Iraq was a matter falling within the royal prerogative which courts should be slow to review as it concerned the conduct of foreign relations and the deployment of the armed forces.[45]

Our constitution thus continues to be a mixture of the old and the new, the established and the innovative, the cautious and the exploratory. That makes it hard to understand, but fascinating to study.

FURTHER READING

Amery LS *Thoughts on the Constitution* (OUP, London, 1964).

Bagehot W *The English Constitution* (Collins/Fontana, London, 1963).

Bogdanor V *The Monarchy and the Constitution* (Clarendon Press, Oxford, 1995).

Bogdanor V 'Our New Constitution' (2004) 120 LQR 242.

Bogdanor V 'Tomorrow's Government' (2006) Royal Society of Arts Journal, April, 34–37.

Burgess G *Absolute Monarchy and the Stuart Constitution* (Yale University Press, New Haven and London, 1996).

Burrows N *Devolution* (Sweet & Maxwell, London, 2000).

Denning AT *Freedom Under the Law* (Stevens, London, 1949).

Lyon A *A Constitutional History of the United Kingdom* (Cavendish, London, 2003).

Maitland FW *The Constitutional History of England* (CUP, Cambridge, 1950).

---

[45] *R v Jones (and others), Aycliffe and others v DPP, Swain v DPP* [2006] UKHL 16; *The Times*, 30 March 2006.

2 CONSTITUTIONAL LAW AND CONSTITUTIONAL PRINCIPLES

Individual rules of law are predicated on a basic understanding that like situations should be treated alike and this represents a legal application of generally accepted moral notions of the desirability of fair, equal and consistent dealing between persons. Of course in practice there is much room for argument as to whether situations are indeed 'alike', and as to the precise meaning and ambit of any given rule in any particular situation; but the core notion remains valid; a legal rule is a mechanism for identifying which situations are alike and for ensuring that these situations, and the persons who find themselves in them, are treated alike. Principles on the other hand are not so fixed. They guide the application and formulation of rules, and they may be used to criticise situations in which rules have not been applied or have been mis-applied. Principles can also exist in a large number of guises from inspirational statements of 'high morality' through to more concrete expressions which may appear to be much more akin to rules in their form and content. However, a principle which cannot be accorded some generally accepted core meaning is hardly worth the name and is probably no more than a somewhat pious aspiration.

Our constitutional law demonstrates such a distinction between rules and principles. In particular three principles may be identified as underlying our body of constitutional rules.

---

1. The Rule of Law

Particularly associated with the name of AV Dicey who made an influential statement of what he considered to be the rule of law in his *Introduction to the Law of the Constitution*, the concept of a principle identifiable as the rule of law is of much greater antiquity than this. It is traceable back to ancient Greece, and can be found in Plato's works, and in those of Aristotle in the third century BC. Taken up by the Romans and then considerably developed by Christian thinking, particularly in the works of St Thomas Aquinas in the thirteenth century, the principle of the rule of law has since become a central feature of western liberal democratic governments. However, its exact content, application, and indeed desirability, remain a subject of intense controversy and debate. The basic core notion is clear: all persons must be subject to law, and government must take place according to law. That said, it must be admitted that there is much less agreement as to the elaboration or worth of the principle. Much here depends on the philosophical, moral and political viewpoints of individual theorists. How one defines and views the rule of law will depend on a mix of factors such as: subscription to beliefs in a highly individualist, libertarian view of society, or a more collectivist position in which individual rights are given less prominence in relation to common rights and obligations; adherence to natural law traditions which assert that law's authority derives from, and is subject to, some higher authority—such as a religious or moral system, or to a 'positivist' position which makes a strict separation between what *is* and what *ought* to be (so that a law may be criticised for its moral content, or lack of it, but nevertheless remains a law until legally altered). According to the multiplicity of combinations in which such fundamental philosophical, moral and political beliefs can be held so will one's view of the content and usefulness of the rule of law vary. However, beginning with the core notion, a 'family' of elaborations can be identified—not all of which achieve general acceptability. Most commentators agree:

- no person or institution is above the law, and the state itself is subject to legal regulation;
- rules of law must be clearly defined and precisely stated;
- rules of law should be adjudicated upon and applied by independent judges—and thus the rule of law implies the existence of some concept of the separation of powers (see below).

There is general agreement that the UK constitution today demonstrates these features. Rather more controversially some argue:

- the rule of law implies a notion of equality before the law, which, so far as the United Kingdom is concerned, means at least that there should be equal access for all to law, vindication of their rights and protection of their interests;
- the rule of law guarantees liberty, and accepts the notion of natural justice (see chapters 9 and 10 below).

Thereafter theorists begin to part company somewhat alarmingly. Thus some would argue:

- the rule of law implies that a system of laws has a basis in morality, and a system of laws which does not comply with such a moral requirement is not truly a 'legal' system;
- the law should promote and serve the interests of all those subject to it.

However, others would argue the law is the law while it is clear to those subject to it what they must do to stay within its limits, and thus a legal system must be recognised as such, provided its laws are publicised so all may know what the law is. This is the position in the United Kingdom.

The vast majority of commentators agree that law must possess a degree of stability in order for those subject to it to know in advance the likely consequences of their acts according to law. It is also generally agreed that the rule of law requires that the law should, in general, not be retrospective in effect, ie conduct innocent at a past point of time should not be made criminal by a later change in the law. Similarly legal rules should be coherent and not contradictory.

It is, however, easy to confuse the concept of the rule of law with calls for the maintenance of 'law and order'. No doubt one mark of a society which subscribes to the notion of the rule of law is that those who commit crime should be apprehended by the police, and punished for breach of established laws following a fair trial before an independent judge. However, in pursuit of 'law and order', in the sense of a quiet and compliant populace, it may well be that those who legitimately dissent from, or sincerely criticise, the views of the state are labelled as criminals simply because of their dissentient views, and may have their arguments silenced by imprisonment. That is hardly the rule of law. But sadly this noble principle can become so bound up with the concept of 'law and order' that some may be led to argue (as has been the fashion amongst Marxist and other critical legal scholars) that the rule of law is, at best, a highly conservative way of justifying as little change as possible in the law, or, at worst, a cloak for injustice, whereby those subject to the law are led (by the argument that laws properly made should be obeyed until they are lawfully changed) to accept structured inequalities which are imposed by the powerful in society via law.

However, within the United Kingdom, the rule of law is accepted as underlying the basic requirement that government should operate according to laws made by a democratically elected Parliament and applied and interpreted by an independent judiciary. As such it clearly has links with both the doctrine of the separation of powers and that of the sovereignty of Parliament, for it relies on the former to limit the latter.

II. The Separation of Powers

It is sometimes said that the 'separation of powers' applies within the United Kingdom.[1] But if it does so it is as a principle guiding the formulation of rules for particular situations rather than as a highly formal rule in its own right. Indeed if one reads the views of the members of the House of Lords, they appear to be as much concerned with upholding the rule of law and the supremacy of Parliament as the separation of powers.

Lord Diplock:

'at a time when more and more cases involving the application of legislation which gives effect to policies that are the subject of bitter public and parliamentary controversy, it cannot be too strongly emphasised that the British Constitution, though largely unwritten, is firmly based on the separation of powers; Parliament makes the laws, the judiciary interpret them. When Parliament legislates to remedy what the majority of its members at the time perceive to be a defect or a lacuna in the existing law (whether it be the written law enacted by existing statutes or the unwritten common law as it has been expounded by the judges in deciding cases), the role of the judiciary is confined to ascertaining from the words that Parliament has proved as expressing its intention what that intention was, and to giving effect to it. Where the meaning of the statutory words is plain and unambiguous it is not for the judges to invent fancied ambiguities as an excuse for failing to give effect to its plain meaning because they themselves consider that the consequences of doing so would be inexpedient, or even unjust or immoral. In controversial matters such as are involved in industrial relations there is room for differences of opinion as to what is expedient, what is just and what is morally justifiable. Under our Constitution it is Parliament's opinion on these matters that is paramount . . .

It endangers continued public confidence in the political impartiality of the judiciary, which is essential to the continuance of the rule of law, if judges, under the guise of interpretation, provide their own preferred amendments to statutes which experience of their operation has shown to have had consequences that members of the court before whom the matter comes consider to be injurious to the public interest . . .

The legitimate questions for a judge in his role as interpreter of the enacted law are, "How has Parliament, by the words that it has used in the statute to express its intentions, defined the category

---

[1] *Duport Steels Ltd v Sirs* [1980] 1WLR 142.

of acts that are entitled to the immunity? Do the acts done in this particular case fall within that description?" . . .'

Lord Edmund Davies:

'a judge's sworn duty to "do right by all manner of people after the laws and usages of this realm" sometimes puts him in difficulty, for certain of those laws and usages may be repugnant to him. When that situation arises, he may meet it in one of two ways. First, where the law appears clear, he can shrug his shoulders, bow to what he regards as the inevitable, and apply it. If he has moral, intellectual, social or other twinges in doing so, he can always invoke Viscount Simonds LC who once said (in *Scruttons Ltd v Midland Silicones Ltd* [1962] AC 446 at 467):

> "For to me heterodoxy or, as some might say, heresy, is not the more attractive because it is dignified by the name of reform. Nor will I easily be led by an undiscerning zeal for some abstract kind of justice to ignore our first duty, which is to administer justice according to law, the law which is established for us by Act of Parliament or the binding authority of precedent."

Alternatively, a judge may be bold and deliberately set out to make new law if he thinks the existing legal situation unsatisfactory. But he risks trouble if he goes about it too blatantly, and if the law has been declared in statutory form it may prove too much for him, dislike it though he may. . . .'

Lord Scarman:

'When one is considering law in the hands of the judges, law means the body of rules and guidelines within which society requires its judges to administer justice. Legal systems differ in the width of the discretionary power granted to judges: but in developed societies limits are invariably set, beyond which the judges may not go. Justice in such societies is not left to the unguided, even if experienced, sage sitting under the spreading oak tree.'

The concept of the separation of powers goes back along with the rule of law to ancient Greece, but it was elevated to the rank of a grand constitutional principle by the French theorist Montesquieu in his great work *De L'Esprit des Lois* (1748) which argued for a strict separation of the legislature (which makes the law), the executive or administration (which governs the state), and the judiciary (who apply the law) in order to protect the liberty of the individual. It should not be supposed that Montesquieu's views were based on a literal understanding of British constitutional arrangements during his own time. His arguments represent an idealised system in which the separation of powers guarantees individual liberty. His desire for that cannot be separated from the background of continental despotisms, particularly his own France, where the King could easily state 'L'Etat c'est moi' for the entire power of the state resided in him.

In the United Kingdom there is no *absolute* formal separation of the principal constitutional organs—Parliament, Crown and Cabinet and the judiciary—so that the personnel of each are kept rigidly distinct with no overlap. As Bagehot wrote in *The English Constitution* (1867): 'the efficient secret of the English Constitution may be described as the close union, the nearly complete fusion of the executive and legislative powers'.[2] Indeed Bagehot went to considerable lengths to denigrate arguments that there was a complete separation of the legislative, executive and judicial powers, pointing instead to the balance that was achieved by the close association of legislative and executive power in the Cabinet system of government. In this context Bagehot was speaking of checks and balances historically existing between the personal power of the monarch, the power deriving from possession of land and inherited

---

[2] Bagehot, W, op cit, Fontana Library Edition, p. 65.

titles then enjoyed by the House of Lords and the democratic power enjoyed by an elected House of Commons. Nevertheless Bagehot's arguments point to a fundamental truth, in the United Kingdom powers may be *distributed* between various organs, agencies and levels of government, but ultimately legislative and executive powers are closely approximated in Parliament by value of the existence of Cabinet government. Thus, though government and Parliament are legally separate institutions, the leaders of the former gain the *legitimacy* they need to exercise their powers through being also the leaders of the majority in the latter. Even so the influence of the doctrine of the separation of powers as a formulative principle for other laws is visible in our constitution. Thus there are many persons who are excluded from membership of Parliament by virtue of the offices they hold.[3] It is also true that the independence of the judiciary, and their unwillingness to step outside what they regard as their proper sphere, so that for instance they claim no power to review the constitutionality of legislation, is also attributable in part to a notion that each of the major constitutional bodies has a proper sphere outside which it should not venture.

On the other hand there are also instances where it is clear that the doctrine is of little applicability. There is no absolute formal separation of powers which forbids *all* members of the executive from being members of the legislature; while one member of the judiciary, the Lord Chancellor, historically has been a member of the Cabinet, the presiding officer of the House of Lords, and the nation's most senior and powerful judge. This anomalous situation has been amended recently, see p 47 below. Similarly at a functional level it is not possible to find a strict allocation of tasks so that law-making functions are carried out only by legislative bodies, judicial functions are carried out only by full-time members of the judiciary, and executive tasks are undertaken only by those who are appointed to office in central and local government. Thus ministers of the Crown frequently have law-making functions delegated to them by Parliament, and many adjudications on legal entitlements are made by specialist tribunals which are not part of the ordinary structure of the courts. However, even in such cases the influence of the doctrine can be seen. No one should suppose because an individual's entitlement to a particular state benefit is subject to adjudication by an administrative tribunal that that tribunal operates at the behest of, and is subject to the ruling of, the central government. Indeed it is in relation to the preservation of the independence of the judicial function that the influence of the doctrine as a constitutional principle is most clearly seen in the United Kingdom, and where the doctrine is seen as being very closely allied to the principle of the rule of law.

(a) The Constitutional Reform Act 2005— reinforcing the separation of powers?

The background to this legislation was the desire of the government to reform national institutions by, according to official statements, strengthening democracy and public engagement with decision-taking, enhancing the trust in and accountability of public bodies together with enhancing their credibility and effectiveness. This is the so called 'modernising' agenda which has the aims of discarding confusing traditions and introducing transparent

---

[3] See further The House of Commons Disqualification Act 1975.

government systems which, it is claimed, will better reflect societal values. The ancient office of Lord Chancellor, and the dual role of the House of Lords as both a chamber of Parliament and the highest court in the land thus came under scrutiny, especially after questions had arisen following the enactment of the Human Rights Act 1998 as to whether a 'fair' system of justice could exist where the head of the judiciary was also a Cabinet minister and Speaker of the House of Lords.

As the first step to reform the Lord Chancellor's Department was retitled the Department for Constitutional Affairs (DCA) in 2003, a change which did not need legislation as the names and the function of government departments can be altered under the Ministers of the Crown Act 1975. Controversial proposals were put before Parliament in 2004, namely the abolition of the post of Lord Chancellor and the creation of a new Supreme Court. The former proposal attracted considerable opposition in the House of Lords, some of whose members argued that they desired strongly to retain the ancient title for their Speaker, and by mid-June 2003 there was evidence that the government might be prepared to compromise its proposals in relation to this issue. The proposals were also attacked by senior judges who feared a disguised attempt to interfere with judicial independence unless new safeguards were built into the legislation. The fears of the judiciary were that the abolition of the office of Lord Chancellor and its replacement by a Secretary of State for Constitutional Affairs would result in the creation of just another minister who would very likely sit in the House of Commons and be a political appointee who might not act as a voice for the judiciary, thus removing one of the 'checks and balances' of the constitution. That led to further promises from the government in December 2003 that judicial independence would be protected, and by January 2004 a 'concordat' had been reached between the Lord Chancellor and the Lord Chief Justice confirming the latter as head of the judiciary and protecting the budget of the judiciary and the courts from political interference by the Treasury. It was also agreed that the new legislation would impose on ministers a duty to uphold judicial independence, while the responsibility for appointing judges would be entrusted to an independent Judicial Appointments Commission (JAC) chaired by someone who is not a judge nor a lawyer. The Lord Chancellor would thus lose this task, and there would be in addition a 'judicial ombudsman' charged with oversight of the judicial recruitment process to ensure its fairness and to arbitrate in disputes. The government, however, determined to press ahead with plans to exclude senior judges from membership of the House of Lords, and for membership of the newly proposed Supreme Court to be subject to ministerial veto in respect of names put forward by the JAC. The proposals remained, however, politically controversial and were resisted in the House of Lords, particularly on the basis that the proposed reforms had been precipitately introduced without due consultation. This led to the government making further compromises in December 2004, such as the retention of the title 'Lord Chancellor' in order to secure the passage of other parts of the legislation, while the House of Lords also attempted to retain the Lord Chancellor as a member of their house. Throughout 2004 there was also further controversy over where the new Supreme Court should sit once it became separated from the House of Lords, and by May 2004 it appeared that there would be a period of considerable delay in implementing that change, even assuming it became enshrined in law.

The outcome of this controversial proposal is the Constitutional Reform Act 2005. This begins (section 1) by declaring that it does not adversely affect the principle of the Rule of Law, and proceeds to lay down 'requirements' in section 2 for the holder of the office of Lord Chancellor, but effectively leaves the choice open to the discretion of the Prime Minister provided the appointee has experience of legal or ministerial life considered to be 'relevant'. Section 3 contains the guarantee of judicial independence and in particular lays down a requirement that ministers must not seek to influence individual judicial decisions 'through any special access to the judiciary'. This would not seem to preclude the making of speeches on legal topics. The Lord Chief Justice, as Head of the Judiciary and President of the Courts of England and Wales, is empowered by section 5 to represent the views of the judiciary to Parliament, the Lord Chancellor and other ministers. The Lord Chief Justice will be supported by a new 'Judicial Office', which is an Associated Office of the Department for Constitutional Affairs and which will be based in the Royal Courts of Justice in London.

Part 3 of the 2005 Act provides for the new Supreme Court which will consist of a President, Deputy President and ten other Justices of the Supreme Court, and the first holders of these positions will be the current Lords of Appeal in Ordinary. Provision is made by Schedule 8 for Supreme Court Selection Commissioners to exist in relation to future appointments. It appears that, following internal modification, the new court will commence sitting in the Middlesex Guildhall, currently a Crown Court, sometime in 2008. The name 'Supreme Court' formerly applied to the Court of Appeal and High Court of Justice is replaced by the title 'Senior Courts of England and Wales'. To further ensure the independence of the judiciary and to provide for transparency in judicial appointments Part 4 of the 2005 Act creates the new Judicial Appointments Commission which has fifteen members, a Chairman and fourteen other members, to include five lay persons, five judges, one barrister, one solicitor, one tribunal member and one magistrate. Three of the fourteen are appointed by the Judges' Council under the terms of the 2005 Act, while the remaining eleven are appointed by means of an open competition. In addition section 62 of the Act provides for the Office of Judicial Appointments and Conduct Ombudsman. The sole criterion for appointment to judicial office will be merit.

The Lord Chancellor is likely also to hold the office of Secretary of State for Constitutional Affairs under the regime created by the 2005 Act and will continue as 'Lord Keeper' to be the custodian of the Great Seal of England. However, it is not necessary for the Lord Chancellor any longer to be a member of the House of Lords and provision is made under section 18 for there to be a Speaker of the House of Lords to whom the Lord Chancellor's functions in this regard will be transferred, see section 19. The first election to this post was held at the end of June 2006 when the Lords elected Baroness Hayman as their Lord Speaker. On 23 January 2006 it was announced that the Judicial Appointments Commission would be brought into force on 3 April 2006, at the same time the Lord Chancellor's position as a judge would terminate. The fifteen members of the Commission, who will serve for up to five years each, are drawn from the judiciary, the legal professions, listed tribunals, lay magistrates and the lay public, and, as from April 2007 will assume responsibility for making recommendations for appointment to judicial office, see Schedule 12 to the 2005 Act.

The 2005 Act may be considered to strengthen the application of the principle of the separation of powers within the United Kingdom in that it enhances the formal independence of the judiciary and vastly reduces the role of the office of Lord Chancellor in respect of the appointment and functioning of judges. Whether, however, it will led to a reduction in conflicts between ministers and judges—a conflict that has become particularly acute following the enactment of the Human Rights Act 1998 and the pursuit of a 'tough on crime, tough on the causes of crime' policy by the Blair government—can only remain to be seen.

What may be predicted, however, is that in a constitutional system such as ours with no written constitution and no 'supreme' court in the American sense, and where the role and character of state activity has changed so radically and grown so much, there will continue to be a degree of instability in the relationship between the courts and ministers, and maybe between the courts and Parliament. The boundaries between the powers of these three institutions are no more than conventional, and are in some cases most indistinct. We may expect judges to cross at times from the realm of 'lawyers' law' into areas of much greater political controversy, and this is an issue to be returned to later in the context of the Human Rights Act 1998.

III. Sovereignty or Supremacy— Principle or Rule?

Though it has undergone subsequent change and development, the UK constitution was principally forged during the conflicts of the seventeenth century between 1642 and 1689. In those struggles there were a number of participants; the monarch and his supporters, Parliament (which then represented certain landholding and major trading interests) and the courts being the most prominent. Though force of arms finally determined many of the issues, from a legal standpoint the greatest changes were brought about by the alliance of the courts (by which is meant the common law courts served by the members of the historic Inns of Court) and Parliament. The so-called doctrine of the Sovereignty of Parliament was one of the matters which emerged over a long period of time, finally reaching full maturity in the writings of Dicey at the end of the nineteenth and beginning of the twentieth centuries. Nevertheless it represents new ideas forged during the working out of that alliance, and the question, to which there is probably no answer satisfactory to all, is whether what emerged was a rule of law of some sort, or a *principle* to guide the relationship of courts and Parliament, to enable individual answers to be reached in individual and highly varied circumstances.

Modern Britain is a unitary and highly centralised nation. Parliament is the forum within which legislation is given its formal shape and legal force, but there can be no doubt that the principal power responsible for making and executing policy, and for ensuring that policy is enshrined in statute where necessary, is the Crown in the form of the Queen's ministers. But what is the role of the courts in relation to this matter?

Some talk of 'the sovereignty of Parliament' but this confuses legal and political issues, for sovereignty is primarily a concept of political thought related to the notion of the independence of states. In legal terms we need to concentrate on issues such as *who* is the supreme law-making body, and *how* are its wishes recognised by courts? It is thus preferable to speak of the *supremacy* of Parliament. Secondly, confusion also stems from fundamental divergences of view already alluded to as to whether parliamentary supremacy is 'the' basic rule of the British constitution, or rather a way of describing the relationship between Parliament and the courts. Let us proceed by considering first the argument that what we are considering is a rule of law. We need then to ask 'what sort of rule is it?'

The legal philosopher Hans Kelsen argued that every legal system must have some basic rule or 'grundnorm' upon which the whole body of laws depends. Following a revolution in which the political structure of a nation is changed, there must be a complete rethinking of the basic rule. If, for example a totalitarian monarchy becomes a republic, the continuance of the monarch was the grundnorm for the former constitutional system; his/her removal will ultimately involve a complete reordering of the legal system to take account of the changed political situation. It is open to question whether such an analysis is appropriate to an ancient constitution such as that of the United Kingdom where it may be impossible to find a 'basic rule.' However, there have been those, before and after Kelsen, who have attempted to find such a rule.

What then is or could be the British grundnorm? Many argue that Parliament (ie Crown, Lords and Commons) is legally competent to do anything it likes. We live under a legal system historically largely formed by judges; yet, since the seventeenth century, the judges have bowed to the will of Parliament as the supreme source of law. It is therefore natural to assume that an argument that Parliament is the supreme law-making source and the body whose legal will must be obeyed should be the legal bedrock of the constitution. There are some who find this unsatisfactory. They point out that while Parliament may be democratically elected, the majority of adult citizens having the right to vote, the United Kingdom is far from being a democracy with the electorate able to participate in public policy choices. Political power also does not simply inhere in the electorate. It is to be found in self-interest groups having economic and social power, for example, a trades union: those groups will be broadly represented by the major political parties. The choice the electorate has is choosing which of the parties shall be in the majority in the House of Commons and so in control of the most powerful law-making organ. Such commentators are unhappy that lawyers divorce legal theory from political fact by distinguishing 'legal sovereignty', ie power to make law unrestricted by any legal limit, from 'political sovereignty' which is concerned with where power lies in a state. They are keen that lawyers should consider how power is to be controlled and distributed. Some would have lawyers develop ideas of how those who wield power can be made more accountable, calling for the development of new controls over power.[4] However, students *may* consider it safer to stay with the conventional stance of English lawyers and reiterate a primary concern with legal rules not power politics, and with the concept that Parliament is the supreme law-making source—the body whose will must be obeyed.

There are a number of 'groups' of legal opinion on the sovereignty/supremacy issue.

The 'traditional' view, associated with Dicey (1835–1922), asserts that Parliament's power is unlimited, subject to no procedural bounds, and 'continuing' in that Parliament cannot bind itself in any way.

The 'new' view asserts that there are no limits of substance to Parliament's power, but *procedural* limitations can be imposed.

A third group consider that Parliament can limit itself and some matters are beyond its competence. This is a view among some Scots lawyers.

More recently, many have begun to argue that sovereignty is better thought of not as a rule of law at all but rather as a guiding principle or set of relationships between Parliament and the courts: others argue that sovereignty does not consist of one 'rule', but is a 'family' of propositions each of whose validity is separately debatable.

(a) The traditional view's historical development

Sir Edward Coke in the early part of the 17th century considered, at least from time to time, there were rules of law superior to statute. As witness his comments below:

'If an Act of Parliament be penned by assent of the King, and of the Lords Spiritual and Temporal, and of the Commons, or, it is enacted by authority of Parliament, it is a good Act; but the most usual way is,

[4] See further McAuslan, P. and McEldowney, J. (eds), *Law, Legitimacy and the Constitution* (Sweet & Maxwell, London, 1985), chapter 3.

that it is enacted by the King by the assent of the Lords, Spiritual and Temporal and of the Commons . . . but if an Act be penned, that the King, with the assent of the Lords, or with the assent of the Commons, it is no Act of Parliament, for three ought to assent to it, *scil.* the King, the Lords, and the Commons or otherwise, it is not an Act of Parliament; . . .'[5]

'And it appears in our books, that in many cases, the common law will control Acts of Parliament, and sometimes adjudge them to be utterly void: for when an Act of Parliament is against common right and reason, or repugnant, or impossible to be performed, the common law will control it, and adjudge such an Act to be void; and, therefore, in 8 E 3 39 a.b. *Thomas Tregor's* case on the statute of W2 c 38 et Artic Super Chartas, c 9. Herle saith, some statutes are made against law and right, which those who made them perceiving, would not put them in execution.'[6]

For his alternative view see his 4 Inst 36 where he considered Parliament's power transcendent and absolute! Coke could, however, claim the authority of medieval precedent for the view that statute is not the 'supreme' law. Fortescue argued in *De Natura Legis Naturae* and *De Laudibus Legum Angliae* that a statute was void if contrary to the Law of God. Other lawyers held not dissimilar views. Bacon (James I's Lord Chancellor) argued for the right of the Crown to dispense with statutes, thus exalting prerogative above statute. Such views held currency for a while. However, following the general alliance between the courts and Parliament in the struggle with the King from 1642 onwards, and certainly after 1688, the common lawyers submitted to the supremacy of Parliament, though even then one or two still argued that Parliament was bound by reason. See on this point the somewhat contradictory arguments of Holt CJ:

'[A] by-law is liable to have its validity brought into question, but an Act of Parliament is not; . . .

And what my Lord Coke says in *Dr Bonham's case* in his 8 Co is far from any extravagancy, for it is a very reasonable and true saying, that if an Act of Parliament should ordain that the same person should be party and Judge, or, which is the same thing, Judge in his own cause, it would be a void Act of Parliament; for it is impossible that one should be Judge and Party, for the Judge is to determine between party and party, or between the Government and the party; and an Act of Parliament can do no wrong, though it may do several things that look pretty odd . . . but it cannot make one that lives under a Government judge and party. An Act of Parliament may not make adultery lawful, that is, it cannot make it lawful for A to lie with the wife of B but it may make the wife of A to be the wife of B and dissolve her marriage with A.'[7]

Parliament was the chief law-making organ, but with uncertainty as to the extent of its powers; the judges seemingly abdicated responsibility for determining that extent. Older arguments were abandoned by English lawyers. Blackstone said of Parliament: 'It can, in short, do everything that is not naturally impossible; and therefore some have not scrupled to call its power, by a figure rather too bold, the omnicompetence of Parliament. True it is, that what the parliament doth, no authority upon earth can undo.'[8] In addition the Bill of Rights 1688 had also declared that freedom of speech and debate in Parliament should not be questioned in any court, a vague declaration but one giving a degree of supremacy to Parliament.

The doctrine of parliamentary sovereignty, which has come to be associated with the name of AV Dicey[9] asserts there are no legal limits to what Parliament can do. This grew out of the

---

[5] *The Prince's Case* (1606) 8 Co Rep 1a at 206. [6] *Dr Bonham's Case* (1610) 8 Co Rep 114a at 118a.

[7] *City of London v Wood* (1701) 12 Mod Rep 669 at 678 and 687–699.

[8] *Commentaries on the Law of England,* Book 1, 4th edn, p. 161.

[9] See particularly *An Introduction to the Study of the Law of the Constitution* (10th edn, Macmillan, London, 1967), Part I.

emergence of Parliament as the major law creating institution. The notion derived from a desire, however, to *limit* arbitrary personal monarchical power. Because the Crown could only make new laws via the agency of Parliament, the two Houses would be able to act as a check upon the King's ambition. *Political* control over executive power was at the heart of this notion, hence there was no perceived need to formulate doctrines of fundamental *legal* limits to the power of the executive, nor for the judges to assert a power to control legislation. Today it is patently clear that governments are well able, through party discipline, to ensure they can generally get their way in terms of finance, legislation and the approval of policy in Parliament. What began as a fetter on executive power has become its most potent weapon. Governments can see their wishes reflected in the statute book, and claim, with constitutional and legal propriety, those laws are *the will of Parliament*—the product of a democratic process, having been assented to by a majority of the elected representatives of the people.

(b) A 'new' view of sovereignty

One of Dicey's contemporaries, Sir Frederick Pollock formulated a notion which has become an alternative theory to the traditional view. This was developed considerably by RTE Latham in *The Law and the Commonwealth*[10] and is tersely described by Marshall in *Constitutional Theory*.[11] 'Supreme legal power is . . . limited by the rules which prescribe how it shall be exercised. Even if no constitutional rule places a limit or boundary to what can be done by sovereign legal authority, the organs which are to exercise it must be delimited and defined by rules.' Proponents of the 'new view' further argue 'that to achieve its purposes Parliament must be properly constituted', and 'the constitution and procedure of Parliament may be altered in such a way as to prevent certain objects from being attained by any except by a specified procedure'.[12]

There has been considerable judicial support in the Commonwealth for the 'new' view.[13] There are disagreements as to whether such limits could apply in this country. Commonwealth authorities are not strictly relevant to the position here for the relevant legislatures operated under the terms of prior written constitutions which limited their freedom, and there is no doubt that a written constitution, as in the USA, can impose limitations on the law-making power.

In *The Law and the Constitution*[14] Sir Ivor Jennings pointed out difficulties for a court attempting to investigate whether procedural requirements had been satisfied with regard to legislation. A court cannot look behind the 'Parliamentary Roll' (ie the official vellum copies of legislation as passed) to seek for irregularities. However Professor Heuston in his *Essays on Constitutional Law*[15] argued powerfully that a court could look behind the Roll, and could intervene to strike down a purported Act not enacted by the component parts of Parliament acting together in the manner and form required by law. On the other hand, we have the

---

[10] (OUP, Oxford, 1949).   [11] (OUP, Oxford, Clarendon Law Series, 1971), pp. 40–41.

[12] Op cit p. 52.

[13] *R (O'Brien) v Military Governor North Dublin Union Internment Camp* [1924] 1 IR 32; *A-G for New South Wales v Trethowan* (1931) 44 CLR 394; *Harris v Minister of the Interior* 1952 (2) SA 428(A); *Bribery Commissioner v Ranasinghe* [1965] AC 172.

[14] (5th edn, 6th impression, University of London Press, London, 1967), chapter 4.

[15] (2nd edn, Stevens and Sons, London, 1964), chapter 1.

reassertion in *British Railways Board v Pickin*[16] that the courts do not sit as courts of appeal from Parliament.

In that case in the Court of Appeal Lord Denning suggested that where Parliament had been misled into passing legislation (in this case because the existence of certain old legislation guaranteeing rights to Mr Pickin had not been brought to Parliament's attention before it enacted legislation taking those rights away), the courts had power to review the legality of the legislation. The House of Lords completely rejected this argument.

Nevertheless, it is still a *common academic* view that the United Kingdom Parliament could impose limits on itself as to the manner and form of legislation, probably only by an entrenched provision, ie one protected against any repeal save in a specified manner (eg both houses sitting as one chamber) and with, probably, the entrenching provision itself being made subject to repeal only in the specified manner (double entrenchment). Certainly some clear indication that a fundamental constitutional change has been made would be needed for such an argument to succeed.

Professor Heuston in *Essays on Constitutional Law* considered there might be such provisions already. He argued that Parliament was bound by section 1(2) of the Ireland Act 1949: 'It is hereby declared that Northern Ireland remains part of His Majesty's dominions and of the United Kingdom and it is hereby affirmed that in no event will Northern Ireland or any part thereof cease to be part of His Majesty's dominions and of the United Kingdom *without the consent of the Parliament of Northern Ireland.*' This *may*, argued Professor Heuston, have amounted to a redefinition of Parliament. The 1949 Act was, however, repealed and replaced by the Northern Ireland Constitution Act 1973, stating that Northern Ireland shall not cease to be part of the United Kingdom without the consent of the people of Northern Ireland which is to be expressed in a poll. The better view of the law is that, European obligations and the requirements of the Human Rights Act 1998 apart, even if the UK Parliament could impose a procedural limitation on itself, there are currently no such requirements in existence.

(c) Substantive limits to Parliament's power

With regard to what may be the subject matter of legislation it is generally agreed in England and Wales there is no limit. Certain Scots lawyers, however, argue there may be limits to the area of sovereignty. In 'The Sovereignty of Parliament: Yet Again',[17] Professor JDB Mitchell put forward a suggestion that there are provisions of the 1707 Union between England and Scotland intended to be fundamental and binding upon the legislature of the unified realm. In *Minister of Prestonkirk v The Heritors*[18] Lord Justice Clerk Hope said: 'Our ancestors at the Union, provided that the regulations applicable to our national church should be irrevocable, and that the Parliament of Great Britain should have no power to alter or repeal those provisions.'

---

[16] [1974] AC 765.   [17] (1963) 79 LQR 196.
[18] (3 February 1808, Session Papers in Connell, *Tithes* vol 3 p. 321).

In this connection we should note certain terms from the preamble to the Union with Scotland Act 1706 and Article XIX:

'Whereas articles of union were agreed on the twenty second day of July in the fifth year of your Majesties reign by the commissioners nominated on behalf of the kingdom of England under your Majesties great seal of England bearing date at Westminster the tenth day of April then past in pursuance of an Act of Parliament made in England in the third year of your Majesties reign and the commissioners nominated on the behalf of the kingdom of Scotland under your Majesties great seal of Scotland bearing date the twenty-seventh day of February in the fourth year of your Majesties reign in pursuance of the fourth Act of the third session of the present Parliament of Scotland to treat of and concerning an union of the said kingdoms. And whereas an Act hath passed in the Parliament of Scotland at Edinburgh the sixteenth day of January in the fifth year of your Majesties reign wherein 'tis mentioned that the estates of Parliament considering the said articles of union of the two kingdoms had agreed to and approved of the said articles of union with some additions and explanations and that your Majesty with advice and consent of the estates of Parliament for establishing the Protestant religion and Presbyterian Church government within the kingdom of Scotland had passed in the same session of Parliament an Act intituled Act for securing of the Protestant religion and Presbyterian Church government which by the tenor thereof was appointed to be inserted in any Act ratifying the treaty and expressly declared to be a fundamental and essential condition of the said treaty or union in all times coming the tenor of which articles as ratified and approved of with additions and explanations by the said Act of Parliament of Scotland follows. . . .

Article XIX

1 That the Court of Session or colledge of justice do after the union and notwithstanding thereof remain in all time coming within Scotland as it is now constituted by the laws of that kingdom and with the same authority and privileges as before the union subject nevertheless to such regulations for the better administration of justice as shall be made by the Parliament of Great Britain . . . And that all other courts now being within the kingdom of Scotland do remain but subject to alterations by the Parliament of Great Britain and that all inferiour courts within the said limits do remain subordinate as they are now to the supreme courts of justice within the same in all time coming And that no causes in Scotland be cognoscible by the courts of Chancery Queen's Bench Common Pleas or any other court in Westminster Hall and that the said courts or any other of the like nature after the union shall have no power to . . . review or alter the acts or sentences of the judicatures within Scotland or stop the execution of the same . . . '

Note must also be taken of Scottish judicial pronouncements on the issue.

'The principle of the unlimited sovereignty of Parliament is a distinctively English principle which has no counterpart in Scottish constitutional law . . . Considering that the Union legislation extinguished the Parliaments of Scotland and England and replaced them by a new Parliament, I have difficulty in seeing why it should have been supposed that the new Parliament of Great Britain must inherit all the peculiar characteristics of the English Parliament but none of the Scottish Parliament, as if all that happened in 1707 was that Scottish representatives were admitted to the Parliament of England. That is not what was done. Further, the Treaty and the associated legislation, by which the Parliament of Great Britain was brought into being as the successor of the separate Parliaments of Scotland and England, contain some clauses which expressly reserve to the Parliament of Great Britain powers of subsequent modification, and other clauses which either contain no such power or emphatically exclude subsequent alteration by declarations that the provision shall be fundamental and unalterable in all time coming, or declarations of a like effect. I have never been able to understand how it is possible to reconcile with elementary canons of construction the adoption by the English constitutional theorists of the same attitude to these markedly different types of provisions.

The Lord Advocate conceded this point by admitting that the Parliament of Great Britain could not repeal or alter such fundamental and essential conditions . . . I have not found in the Union legislation any provision that the Parliament of Great Britain should be "absolutely sovereign" in the sense that that Parliament should be free to alter the Treaty at will . . .

But the petitioners have still a grave difficulty to overcome on this branch of their argument. Accepting it that there are provisions in the Treaty of Union and associated legislation which are "fundamental law", and assuming for the moment that something is alleged to have been done—it matters not whether with legislative authority or not—in breach of that fundamental law, the question remains whether such a question is determinable as a justiciable issue in the courts of either Scotland or England, in the same fashion as an issue of constitutional vires would be cognisable by the Supreme Courts of the United States, or of South Africa or Australia. I reserve my opinion with regard to the provisions relating expressly to this court and to the laws "which concern private right" which are administered here. This is not such a question, but a matter of "public right" (articles 18 and 19). To put the matter in another way, it is of little avail to ask whether the Parliament of Great Britain "can" do this thing or that, without going on to inquire who can stop them if they do . . . This at least is plain, that there is neither precedent nor authority of any kind for the view that the domestic Courts of either Scotland or England have jurisdiction to determine whether a governmental act of the type here in controversy is or is not conformable to the provisions of a Treaty, least of all when that Treaty is one under which both Scotland and England ceased to be independent states and merged their identity in an incorporating union. From the standpoint both of constitutional law and of international law the position appears to me to be unique, and I am constrained to hold that the action as laid is incompetent in respect that it has not been shown that the Court of Session had authority to entertain the issue sought to be raised.'[19]

'The submission of the appellants to the sheriff was in effect that Parliament acted unlawfully in resolving that the Scotland Act 1978 (which made provision for the setting up of a Scottish Assembly with certain legislative powers) should be repealed. The Scotland Act 1978 accordingly stood with legislative effect, and the provisions thereof in relation to the legislative powers of the Assembly precluded the passing by Parliament of the Criminal Justice (Scotland) Act 1980. The purported passing of that Act therefore constituted an illegality which rendered that Act, and consequently section 78 thereof, invalid. The supremacy of Parliament was not unchallengeable in the Scottish courts, and accordingly it was competent for a Scottish court to determine that illegality and give effect to the consequents thereof by holding that a charge based on the illegal section of that illegal Act was itself fundamentally illegal . . . We go straight to the fundamental question whether the vires of an Act of Parliament which has gone through the whole parliamentary process, has received the Royal Assent and been brought into operation can be competently challenged in a Scottish court. That question has been definitely answered by two Scottish cases which span over a century in time. In *Edinburgh and Dalkeith Rly Co v Wauchope* (1842) 1 Bell's App Cas 252 in the House of Lords Lord Campbell said at p 279: "All that a court of justice can look to is the parliamentary roll"; . . . In *McCormick v Lord Advocate* 1953 SLT 255, 1953 SC 396 Lord President Cooper said: "This at least is plain that there is neither precedent nor authority of any kind for the view that the domestic Courts of either Scotland or England have jurisdiction to determine whether a governmental act of the type here in controversy is or is not conform to the provisions of a Treaty" . . . '[20]

The view of the English judiciary has, historically, seemed clear.

'Can you seriously (he said) contend that an act of parliament can be brought before this court, like an order at sessions, to be quashed as invalid? . . . there is no judicial body in the country by which the validity of an act of parliament could be questioned. An act of the legislature is superior in authority to

[19] *McCormick v Lord Advocate* (1953) SC 396: The Lord President at 411–413.
[20] *Sillars v Smith* (1982) SLT 539n at 541: The Lord Justice-Clerk.

any court of law. We have only to administer the law as we find it, and no court could pronounce a judgment as to the validity of an act of parliament.'[21]

It may, however, be argued that some of the statements from the Scottish courts reinforce the argument that the sovereignty doctrine is truly a principle governing relationships between the judiciary and the legislature. Scottish judges may believe there are fundamental limits to Parliament's power, but consider themselves unable to do anything about a situation where those limits are transgressed.

If Parliament surrenders an area of sovereign power to another legislature, is it then incapable of getting that power back? This argument may not be fruitful in that the doctrine of sovereignty is a purely *legal* matter. The United Kingdom Parliament can, in pure law, revoke independence, and *United Kingdom* courts would be bound to recognise the validity of the repeal. However, in 'The Government of Ireland Bill and the Sovereignty of Parliament',[22] Anson argued: 'the statement that Parliament cannot bind its successors may be taken to be true subject to two exceptions. The first of these is where Parliament surrenders its sovereign powers over a certain area to another person or body.' It may be asked whether this statement confuses political and legal concepts of sovereignty. Parliament may give away *political* sovereignty over an area by, for example, granting it independence from British rule; *legally* Parliament remains able to repeal the legislation granting independence. *British* courts would have to accept the repeal as good law.

In 1931, by virtue of section 4 of the Statute of Westminster, Parliament declared that British legislation should not extend to Commonwealth countries without a declaration of their consent and request. However, in *British Coal Corpn v R*[23] Viscount Sankey LC alleged that Parliament 'could, as a matter of abstract law, disregard section 4 of the Statute'. For alternative views see Marshall *Constitutional Theory*,[24] and Lord Denning's obiter dictum in *Blackburn v A-G*: 'take the acts that have granted independence to the Dominions and territories overseas. Can anyone imagine that Parliament could or would reverse those laws and take away their independence? Most clearly not. Freedom once given cannot be taken away. Legal theory must give way to practical politics.'[25]

The traditional view was reasserted by Lord Reid, however, in *Madzimbamuto v Lardner-Burke and George*[26] and from a purely *legal* point of view it is preferable not to confuse law with politics.

(d) A principle governing relationships

In relation to this question some of the most recent thinking on the sovereignty issue is most relevant. Turning to Professor Hart's *The Concept of Law*[27] we find he pointed out that the 'Sovereignty of Parliament' was a rule of recognition whereby courts could recognise the validity of a rule of law. Statute law is the most potent 'type' of law because Parliament is recognised as the ultimate law-making body. However, Hart points out, this is only an arrangement we have come to accept. Arguably the doctrine of sovereignty is simply a label for the way in which courts conduct themselves relative to Parliament. The relationship is

[21] *Ex p Canon Selwyn* (1872) 36 JP Jo 54: Cockburn CJ at 55.   [22] (1886) 2 LQR 427 at 440.
[23] [1935] AC 500 at 520.   [24] Marshall, op cit Chapter III.   [25] [1971] 1 WLR 1037 at 1040.
[26] [1969] 1 AC 645.   [27] (OUP, Oxford, Clarendon Law Series, 1961).

essentially one of subservience by the courts; need this necessarily continue? The courts may come to recognise the organs of the European Communities as legitimate alternative law-making bodies with a status equivalent to that of Parliament, and whose legal will is to be taken as paramount. This is, of course, the theory of Community law, which is conceived of as a supra-national body of law binding both the member states of the Community and their nationals. This was recognised by Lord Denning MR in *Blackburn v A-G* where he said: 'It does appear that if this country should go into the Common Market and sign the Treaty of Rome, it means that we will have taken a step which is irreversible. The sovereignty of these islands will thence forward be limited. It will not be ours alone but will be shared with others.'[28]

Recent thinking thus stresses that the heart of the sovereignty debate is the relationship between courts and Parliament. This is dynamic. It makes little sense to speak of a single 'rule' of sovereignty: 'rules' are only needed where there are a succession of instances all needing similar treatment. Issues in sovereignty are not matters of that sort: they are individual problems requiring individual answers. Statements on sovereignty thus form a 'family' of propositions. This is an idea developed by Munro in *Studies in Constitutional Law*:[29] see also Allan 'Parliamentary Sovereignty: Lord Denning's Dextrous Revolution',[30] and Bradley 'The Sovereignty of Parliament—in Perpetuity?'[31] In the past the courts have accepted that an Act of Parliament cannot be held invalid by reference to some principle of overriding inalienable liberty[32] or of international law,[33] but the question remains whether they *must* necessarily do so in the future. Thus in *R v Secretary of State for Transport, ex p Factortame (No 2)*,[34] following a decision by the European Court of Justice (ECJ)[35] that provisions of the Merchant Shipping Act 1988 were in contravention of the Treaty of Rome, the House of Lords responded ingeniously to the situation. The ECJ had stated that national courts were under a duty to give effect to Community rights and should set aside rules of national law which could be an impediment to effective implementation of such rights. The House of Lords 'disapplied' the UK statute. In other words they declined to give effect to the offending provisions without declaring the legislation void or ultra vires. Arguably in doing this they were actually obeying the will of Parliament in the European Communities Act 1972 where the primacy of European Community law was declared. This had been recognised by Lord Denning MR in *McCarthys Ltd v Smith* '. . . priority is given by our own law. It is given by the European Communities Act 1972 itself.'[36] However, the same judge in earlier litigation between the same parties stated: 'If the time should come when our Parliament *deliberately* passes an Act with the *intention* of repudiating the Treaty or any provisions in it or *intentionally* of acting inconsistently with it and says so in *express terms*, then I should have thought it would be the duty of our Courts to follow the statute of Parliament.'[37] Emphasis has been added to what are clearly the key words in that passage, which shows also that Lord Denning's thought had developed since his earlier remarks in *Blackburn's* case.

The position thus appears to be that the legislative competence of the European Community within the areas where it may act has been recognised by our courts. While the United Kingdom remains part of the Community our courts will give primacy to EC law by disapplying UK laws that are in inescapable conflict with it. But should there be UK legislation

---

[28] [1971] 1 WLR 1037 at 1039.   [29] (Butterworths, London, 1987), chapter 5.

[30] (1983) 3 Oxford Journal of Legal Studies, p. 22.

[31] In Jowell, J. and Oliver, D. (eds), *The Changing Constitution* (3rd edn, OUP, Oxford, 1994), and see Professor Bradley's current thinking in the 5th edition of this title (2004), at chapter 2.

[32] *R v Jordan* [1967] Crim LR 483.   [33] *Cheney v Conn* [1968] 1 All ER 779.

[34] [1991] 1 AC 603.   [35] Case C-213/89 [1990] ECR 1–2433.   [36] [1981] QB 180 at 200.

[37] [1979] 3 All ER 325 at 329.

that is deliberately and expressly made in contravention of EC law then the old relationship of subservience between the courts and Parliament would reassert itself.

It is at this point that the weakness of regarding the doctrine of supremacy as a single entity becomes clearly apparent. It is, even if we accept it as a 'rule' as opposed to a 'principle', a series of connected propositions each of which may be individually debated as to its truth and applicability. It has been the practice of courts to accept the latest expression of Parliament's will in the form of a statute as binding upon them. Thus if Parliament passes a later statute that is expressly or clearly impliedly inconsistent with an earlier one, the courts have considered the earlier to be repealed, no matter how mandatory its language with respect to its subject matter and its continued place on the statute book. Thus the Union with Ireland Act 1800 which united the Kingdoms of Great Britain and Ireland, declared that the Union should last 'for ever after' and furthermore that the Church of England and the Church of Ireland should be united as one, and that 'shall remain in full force for ever'. Even so the Church of Ireland was separated from the Church of England in 1869, and, as we have already seen, in 1872 in *Ex p Canon Selwyn* the English courts refused to declare the Irish Church Disestablishment Act invalid. Furthermore Ireland itself was divided into two portions by the Government of Ireland Act 1920, and the southern portion granted full independence by the Ireland Act 1949.

Our membership of the European Communities would appear, however, to have changed the thinking of at least some judges on this issue. In *Thoburn v Sunderland City Council*[38] certain traders had been prosecuted for offences related to continuing to sell goods measured and prices set in terms of Imperial measures as opposed to metric measures. The change from Imperial to metric was required by the Units of Measurement Regulations SI 1994/2867 which had been made to fulfil EC obligations under section 2(2) and (4) of the European Communities Act. Their defence was that the Weights and Measures Act 1985 had permitted the continued use of Imperial measures and, as it was subsequent to the European Communities Act 1972 it had impliedly repealed the power under the 1972 Act to make regulations requiring the use of metric measures. They relied on *Vauxhall Estates Ltd v Liverpool Corporation*[39] where Avory J said: 'if [two statutes] are inconsistent . . . then the earlier Act is impliedly repealed by the latter . . .', and *Ellen Street Estates Ltd v Minister of Health*,[40] where Maugham LJ said: 'The legislature cannot, according to our constitution, bind itself as to the form of subsequent legislation, and it is impossible for Parliament to enact that in a subsequent statute dealing with the same subject matter there can be no implied repeal.'

The Divisional Court rejected the defence on the narrow ground that there was no inconsistency between the 1972 and 1985 Acts on the basis that the former contained a general and wide-ranging power to change the law while the latter dealt only with the 'for the time being' use of Imperial measures. Laws LJ went on to make comments of wider application. While denying that Parliament could by statute stipulate that the European Communities Act 1972 cannot be wholly or partly repealed and asserting that neither the European Court of Justice nor any other EC institution has power to 'touch or qualify' the supremacy of Parliament within the UK, because the UK Parliament cannot abandon its sovereignty, Laws LJ continued by adding that the traditional doctrine of supremacy had been modified. He argued that the doctrine of implied repeal is a creation of the common law, and the common law recognises the existence of a class of statutes which are 'constitutional' or 'fundamental', which are not capable of implied repeal. Constitutional statutes are those, Laws LJ argued,

---

[38] [2003] QB 151, [2002] EWHC 195.   [39] [1932] 1 KB 733 at 734.   [40] [1934] 1 KB 590 at 597.

which condition legal relationships between the citizen and the state in a general or overarching way, or which enlarge or diminish the scope of fundamental constitutional rights. As examples of these he cited Magna Carta, 1297, the Bill of Rights, 1689, the Union with Scotland Act, 1706, the Representation of the People Acts of 1832 to 1884, the Scotland Act 1998, the Government of Wales Act 1998, the Human Rights Act 1998 *and* the European Communities Act 1972. Such statutes, he argued, may only be expressly repealed or affected by words in a later statute so specific that there is an irresistible argument that Parliament has intended to change the law. To alter a constitutional statute requires unambiguous words. This, Laws LJ further argued, gives us most of the benefits which a written constitution confers while preserving the flexibility of an unwritten constitution and the supremacy of Parliament.

This new strand of judicial thinking represents a trend towards what has been termed the 'juridification' of the constitution whereby the traditional system of 'checks and balances' which has operated primarily via the political system, argument in Parliament and in the media and the force of public opinion, is being replaced by a more legalised and judicialised framework.[41] In this new era judges are less willing to accept 'the latest word from Parliament' as something to which they must unhesitatingly bow.

This is a change which is in part due to the actions of Parliament itself in passing the European Communities Act 1972 which transformed the previous bi-partite relationship of the courts and Parliament—a relationship in which Parliament was clearly the senior partner—into a tri-partite relationship between the UK courts, the UK Parliament and the EC. In this new relationship our judges have a degree of freedom to decide to whose will they should submit.

The change is also due to judicial realisation that the doctrine of supremacy may no longer always serve democracy well. It has already been argued that given a working majority in Parliament, modern governments are normally assured of seeing their policies enshrined in law, and thus the doctrine of supremacy becomes a dangerous tool in the hands of an over-mighty executive. It is against that background that we must now consider the impact of the Human Rights Act 1998.

(e) The impact of the Human Rights Act 1998

The 1998 Act is best thought of as a radical but not a revolutionary measure. It is radical in that it gives certain 'convention rights' (ie those derived from the European Convention on Human Rights—see further chapter 13) a primary constitutive significance. It is radical in that it injects a value base into our public law. Thus into our highly procedural constitution which says much about how laws are made and how they are recognised and received by the courts, but which has been rather silent on the values underpinning these laws or the morality they could or should reflect, new values are injected. These will serve to underpin respect for the autonomy, dignity, status and security of individuals, but they will also advance collective values such as the accountability of governments, the freedom of press and political expression, the rule of law, transparency and consistency in decision-making and, to a degree, freedom of information. But it is not revolutionary in that it is not entrenched and does not

---

[41] See generally Jowell, J. and Oliver, D. *The Changing Constitution* (5th edn, OUP, Oxford, 2004), pp. XV–XVI.

abrogate the principle of parliamentary supremacy. Rather it is arguable it will lead to a development and enhancement of existing principles.

Indeed Professor David Feldman, to whose work indebtedness is acknowledged, has argued in 'The Human Rights Act 1998 and constitutional principles':[42] 'The Act's ability to inject values which could fill the ethical vacuum at the heart of public life depends on the perceived legitimacy of the Convention rights, which in turn depends on their capacity to accommodate the most important elements of the United Kingdom's constitutional heritage.' That heritage is not founded on unlimited individualism, rather it has proceeded on the basis of striking balances between individual and collective 'goods'. The Convention rights follow that pattern. There are statements of rights, but these are generally subject to exceptions allowing interference in the public interest—however, only those grounds for interference set out in the Act can be relied on by public authorities. To that extent limits are set to their powers, and standards created for assessing their use of those powers.

The 1998 Act will certainly establish practical limits to the power of Parliament in that, though not entrenched, *politically* it will be hard to amend it. Furthermore under section 3(1) of the Act all legislation, whether passed before or after 1998, is to be interpreted, wherever possible, in such a way as to achieve compatibility with Convention rights. Indeed section 3(2)(c) appears to require incompatible subordinate legislation, in general, to be treated as invalid or ineffective. In this the judges build on similar approaches to EC and international legal obligations to ensure wherever possible that a harmonious interpretation is given to UK law, see *Raymond v Honey*[43] and *R v Lord Chancellor, ex p Witham*.[44] Indeed speaking on 5 February 1998 in the House of Lords on the third reading of the Bill leading to the 1998 Act the Lord Chancellor considered that in 99% of cases our courts will be able to interpret and apply UK legislation in a fashion compatible with Convention Rights.

However, the supremacy of Parliament is maintained, for the 1998 Act provides in section 6(2) that Parliament is not a 'public body' required to act in conformity with the legislation. The 1998 Act also accepts that there may be cases where it is not possible to achieve an interpretation of UK law consistent with the Convention under section 3, and there all the judges can do is to give effect to the inconsistent legislation and make a declaration of incompatibility (under section 4)—which may lead to amending legislation being made (under section 10), though not necessarily. The *legal* principle of supremacy thus remains intact.

However, there is an alteration in the balance of power between courts and Parliament. The judges now have power to declare that Parliament has acted incompatibly with Convention rights. Such a declaration amounts to a statement that Parliament has acted wrongly—which runs counter to formulations of supremacy stating that nothing Parliament does can be legally wrong, or that no Act of Parliament can be legally wrong. However, the 'wrong' that Parliament has done in such a case is a non-legal one, for the courts can only declare it, they can give no remedy. Nevertheless as Feldman concludes: 'making a declaration about a non-legal wrong takes the judges into a new field'.

It is furthermore at least arguable that a 'manner and form' limitation may have crept into our law by virtue of section 19 of the 1998 Act. This requires ministers to state whether Bills before Parliament are compatible with Convention rights, or that such a statement cannot be made but nevertheless Parliament is to proceed with the Bill. Is the making of such a statement a condition precedent to the ability of Parliament to proceed with the Bill? Could a failure to provide a statement allow the judges to declare the subsequent legislation ultra vires in that a

[42] (1999) 19 Legal Studies (No 2) 165.   [43] [1983] 1 AC 1.   [44] [1997] 2 All ER 779.

procedural requirement had been ignored? Traditionally our courts will not look behind the words of legislation to inquire into how it was passed—the 'enrolled-Bill rule'—and also have been unwilling to interfere with Parliament's exclusive right to regulate its own procedures, see *British Railways Board v Pickin*.[45] But could these matters be regarded as altered by section 19? Time may tell.

It is, however, the principle of the Rule of Law which is most affected by the 1998 Act. There are situations where there is an interference with a Convention right by a public authority where the courts demand much more by way of legal justification—and the adequacy of the arguments supporting it—than historically was the case. It is unlawful either by subordinate legislation or by an administrative action to violate a Convention right. Furthermore the rights themselves contain various procedural guarantees, which are more clearly articulated than notions of 'fairness' under the General Principles of Administrative Law. Where a violation is found, the 1998 Act, section 8, empowers courts to grant 'such relief or remedy, or to make such order within its powers as it considers just and appropriate'.

(i) The 1998 Act in practice

The 1998 Act has given rise to some controversy and has become less than popular amongst many politicians, including some of those who supported its initial enactment. In general terms it can be argued that the Act has strengthened the influence of the Rule of Law, particularly in its insistence on the need for correct and lawful authority for executive action to be demonstrable, and, to an extent, weakened the powers of both Parliament and the executive. This is the consequence of a small number of cases that have achieved considerable media exposure in which declarations of incompatibility have been made. Before, however, considering them it is pertinent to ask whether section 3 of the Act is not more influential, albeit in a less patent way, to exalt the powers of judges and to reduce those of Parliament. It will be remembered that section 3 requires primary and subordinate legislation to be read 'so far as it is possible to do so' in a way which is compatible with the Convention Rights. This must be read in conjunction with section 2 of the 1998 Act which requires our courts to take into account judgments, decisions, declarations and advisory opinions of the European Court of Human Rights, what is known as 'the Strasbourg Jurisprudence'. The question has therefore arisen how far can a UK court go in altering the wording and application of an Act of Parliament in order to achieve compatibility?

R v A (No 2)[46] concerned the interpretation of the Youth Justice and Criminal Evidence Act 1999 which had, inter alia, been passed to prevent questions being put to rape victims about their sexual history so as to give the impression to a jury that the victim was of 'easy virtue' and had consensually indulged in sexual activities. A, who had been charged with rape, wished to argue that the intercourse had been consensual, or that he believed consent had been given, and sought at a preliminary stage in the proceedings to have the complainant cross-examined about the previous sexual activities that had previously occurred between her and A. In those proceedings it was ruled that the complainant could be cross-examined about her relationship with a friend of A's, but not about what had occurred between her and A. This, however, gave rise to a prima facie breach of A's right to a fair trial under Article 6 of the European Convention on Human Rights. In the outcome the House of Lords found a means of

---

[45] [1974] AC 765.   [46] [2001] UKHL 25, [2002] 1 AC 45.

interpreting the provisions of the 1999 Act in such a way as to avoid incompatibility with Convention Rights, however Lord Steyn made general observations on the powers of the courts:

'. . . the interpretative obligation under section 3 of the 1998 Act is a strong one. It applies even if there is no ambiguity in the language in the sense of the language being capable of two different meanings . . . the obligation goes far beyond the rule which enabled the courts to take the convention into account in resolving any ambiguity in a legislative provision . . . Section 3 of the 1998 Act places a duty on the court to strive to find a possible interpretation compatible with convention rights. Under ordinary methods of interpretation a court may depart from the language of the statute to avoid absurd consequences: section 3 is more radical in its effect. . . . [It] will sometimes be necessary to adopt an interpretation which linguistically may appear strained. The techniques to be used will not only involve the reading down of express language in a statute but also the implication of provisions. A declaration of incompatibility is a measure of last resort. It must be avoided unless it is plainly impossible to do so.'[47]

Subsequent judicial pronouncements have gone even further in the direction initially pointed out in *R v A*. In *Ghaidan v Godin Mendoza*[48] the defendant had shared a flat with his same-sex partner from 1972 until that partner's death. That partner had been a Rent Act protected tenant of the flat in which he lived in a stable relationship with the defendant. On the death of the tenant a question arose as to the succession rights of the defendant. Under the decision in *Fitzpatrick v Sterling Housing Association*[49] he was entitled to succeed to an assured tenancy under paragraph 3(1) of Schedule 1 to the Rent Act 1977 (as amended) because he was considered to be a member of the original tenant's 'family'. The rights of *assured tenants* are, however, less than those of *protected tenants*, and the defendant wished to achieve protected status. The issue was whether the status of assured tenant was compatible with the defendant's Convention Rights under the Human Rights Act 1998. A number of questions had to be addressed:

• Was the previous interpretation of the law, that persons in same-sex relationships could not succeed to a statutory tenancy as surviving spouses, incompatible with Convention Rights under Articles 8 and 14 of the European Convention on Human Rights?

• If so, was it possible to interpret the 1977 Act in such a way as to render the relevant provision compatible?

• The Court of Appeal answered 'yes' to both these questions. The House of Lords, despite a strong dissent from Lord Millett who considered that the exercise undertaken by the House transgressed the boundary between interpretation and creativity, affirmed the Court of Appeal's decision.

We are concerned here with the issue of the interpretation of the 1977 Act to render it compatible with the defendant's Convention Rights once they were found to be infringed, that infringement being based on an unjustifiable difference in the treatment of the defendant as a homosexual man compared with the rights enjoyed by cohabiting heterosexual couples.

Having determined that the defendant had been subjected to unjustifiable discrimination, Lord Nicholls proceeded to the issue of whether it was possible to interpret the legislation in such a way as to make it compatible with Convention Rights. He pointed out that under section 3 of the Human Rights Act 1998 it is the intention of Parliament that all legislation is to be read and given effect so as to be compatible with Convention Rights 'so far as it is

[47] [2001] UKHL 25 para [44].   [48] [2004] UKHL 30.   [49] [1999] 4 All ER 705.

possible to do so'. However, he asked, what does 'possible' mean here? It certainly includes resolving ambiguities, so that if a phrase can have two meanings the compatible one is to be chosen, but does the process go further than that? He argued: 'Section 3 [of the Human Rights Act 1998] may require the court to depart from . . . the intention of Parliament . . . The question of difficulty is how far, and in what circumstances, Section 3 requires a court to depart from the intention of the enacting Parliament.'[50]

He proceeded to argue that section 3 enables language to be interpreted restrictively or expansively: 'But Section 3 goes further than this. It is also apt to require a court to read in words which change the meaning of enacted legislation so as to make it Convention-compliant.'[51]

The limit to this power is that section 3 does not allow a meaning inconsistent with the fundamental features of the legislation in question, in other words 'the meaning imported by application of section 3 must be compatible with the underlying thrust of the legislation construed'. In the instant case Lord Nicholls concluded, the legislation could be effectively reworded to make it compatible but not in a way which conflicted with the underlying purpose of Parliament which was to confer security of tenure on certain people.

Lord Steyn, agreeing with Lord Nicholls, argued:

'If the core remedial purpose of section 3(1) [of the 1998 Act] is not to be undermined a broader approach [than the purely literal and technical] is required. That is, of course, not to gainsay the obvious proposition that inherent in the use of the word "possible" . . . is the idea that there is a Rubicon which courts may not cross. If it is not possible within the meaning Section 3, to reach or give effect to legislation in a way which is compatible with Convention rights, the only alternative is to exercise, where appropriate, the power to make a declaration of incompatibility. Usually, such cases should not be too difficult to identify.'[52]

Lord Rodger was also concerned to explore the limit of the courts' interpretative powers. He pointed out that the obligation on the court is twofold, it is 'to read' and 'to give effect to'. These are complementary but distinct obligations. In other words, interpretation is only part of the task of the court which, as a public authority, must ensure that legislation is given effect in those ways which are compatible with Convention Rights. There are, as Lord Rodger conceded, limits to this obligation, such as where the clear and unavoidable words of Parliament impose a duty to act in a particular way. However, the key to understanding that limit is to realise that they are cases where the entire substance of the provision is incompatible with the Conventions, in which case only Parliament can amend the law, though the court will make a declaration of incompatibility. Thus section 3 of the 1998 Act does not allow a court to change the substance of a legislative provision completely, eg so as to say something must happen when Parliament has said it must not. The courts are also not to turn legislative schemes inside out, they must not by interpretation create something entirely different from what Parliament has provided. Neither can they negative explicit powers given to ministers by Parliament. In addition courts must be wary not to cross the boundary line between interpretation and amendment where the result may have important practical repercussions a court may not be equipped to evaluate. In short it is not possible for the process of interpretation to allow a court to do anything inconsistent with the cardinal principles of legislation, for example by introducing something into an Act which was not there in some way before.

---

[50] [2004] UKHL 30 para 30.   [51] [2004] UKHL 30 para 32.   [52] [2004] UKHL 30 para 49.

However, Lord Rodger then went on to say:

'this is not to say that, where a provision can be read compatibly with the Convention without contradicting any principle that it enshrines or the principles of the legislation as a whole, such an interpretation is not possible simply because it may involve reading into the provision words which go further than the specific words used by [Parliament]. . . . the key to what is possible for the courts to imply into legislation without crossing the border from interpretation to amendment does not lie in the number of words that have to be read in. The key lies in a careful consideration of the essential principles and scope of the legislation being interpreted. If the insertion of one word contradicts those principles or goes beyond the scope of the legislation it amounts to impermissible amendment. On the other hand, if the implication of a dozen words leaves the essential principles and scope of the legislation intact but allows it to be read in a way which is compatible with Convention rights, the implication is a legitimate exercise of the powers conferred [by the 1998 Act].'[53]

For those familiar with Gilbert and Sullivan's *Iolanthe*, Lord Roger's allusion is clear. In that Savoy opera the Fairy Law provides that it is death for a fairy to marry a mortal. By the end of the opera *all* the fairies have married members of the House of Lords, so all have incurred death. The Lord Chancellor neatly solves the problem by inserting a single word: it is death for a fairy *not* to marry a mortal. Such a stroke of Gilbertian logic is not possible under section 3 of the Human Rights Act 1998.

Declarations of incompatibility under section 4 of the 1998 act have been uncommon, but those that have occurred have tended to be controversial, particularly where issues of criminal justice or national security have been involved. While such a declaration does not force a change in the law to take place, the practice has been for amendments to follow declarations, albeit at some distance of time and sometimes with ill grace.

R (on the application of Anderson) v Secretary of State for the Home Department[54] concerned a prisoner who was serving a life sentence for murder. This crime carries a mandatory life penalty, but 'life' can mean less than 'lifetime'. A's trial judge and the Lord Chief Justice had recommended a sentence of 15 years' imprisonment but the Home Secretary fixed the period at 20 years—before which A could not be considered for release by the Parole Board under section 29 of the Crime (Sentences) Act 1997. A challenged the Home Secretary's decision arguing his powers were incompatible with the European Convention on Human Rights, in particular alleging that these powers were incompatible with Article 6(1) of the Convention, which requires that matters of sentencing should be carried out by an independent and impartial tribunal, which the Home Secretary, as a member of the executive, was not.

In the House of Lords, Lord Bingham reviewed the development of the case and statute law on the issue and referred to the progress of case law from the European Court of Human Rights (the 'Strasbourg Jurisprudence') in particular the decision in *Stafford v United Kingdom*[55] in which the Court had expressed growing unease about the Home Secretary's powers and the apparent clash with the principle of the separation of powers. Lord Bingham stated:

'While the duty of the House under section 2(1)(a) of the Human Rights Act 1998 is to take into account any judgment of the European Court, whose judgments are not strictly binding, the House will not without good reason depart from the principles laid down in a carefully considered judgment of the court sitting as a Grand Chamber . . . Here, there is strong reason to support the decision . . . I am satisfied that the House should, in accordance with the will of Parliament expressed in the Human Rights Act 1998, seek to give effect to the decision of the European Court in *Stafford*.'[56]

---

[53] [2004] UKHL 30 paras 117 and 122. [54] [2002] UKHL 46.
[55] Application No 46295/99, 28 May 2002. [56] [2002] UKHL 46 para 18.

Lord Bingham further referred to the decision of the court in *Benjamin and Wilson v United Kingdom*[57] in which the court further condemned the role of the Home Secretary in fixing sentences because the post is an executive one which contradicts the fundamental principles of the separation of powers by detracting from the concept of impartiality in sentence fixing, and thus also undermines the concept of the rule of law. Lord Bingham concluded that the Home Secretary should no longer play a part in fixing the sentence tariff for a convicted murderer and that his power to do so under section 29 of the Crime (Sentences) Act 1997 was incompatible with the Convention.

Lord Steyn pointed out that while the UK constitution has never embraced a rigid doctrine of the separation of powers, there is clearly a considerable degree of separation between the judiciary on the one hand and the legislative and executive arms of government on the other. However, the principle of the supremacy of Parliament is paramount in the UK constitution and on that basis the Home Secretary had, at law, a role in the sentencing of convicted murderers. However, what was the effect on that of the 1998 Act and the Convention? Lord Steyne was clear: 'Article 6(1) requires effective separation between the courts and the executive, and further requires that what can in shorthand be called judicial functions may only be discharged by the courts.'[58] He too relied on the decisions in *Stafford* and *Benjamin and Wilson* to argue that members of the executive may not play any part in what is essentially a judicial function. He went on to expand on this. 'One can readily accept that it is sometimes difficult to categorise a function as judicial or non-judicial. . . . It is recognised that there are functions which, by their very nature, may only be exercised by courts and, on the other hand, there are functions which by their very nature are inappropriate for such exercise. Between these functions there lies a "borderland" in which functions may be exercised either by the executive or the courts.'[59] Lord Steyn argued that the only way forward in such situations is to ask what the predominant characteristic feature of a function is, and whether it is comparable with those functions and processes historically performed by courts. On that basis Lord Steyn considered the powers of the Home Secretary to be anomalous, and that the power to punish by imprisonment both historically and as a matter of principle is a judicial function performable only by a court. Lord Steyn concluded that this anomaly could not be dealt with simply by using the interpretative powers of section 3 of the 1998 Act: 'It would not be interpretation but interpolation inconsistent with the plain legislative intent to entrust the decision to the Home Secretary who was intended to be free to follow or reject judicial advice.'[60] He too concluded that a declaration of incompatibility was the only remedy.

This decision *in effect* stripped the Home Secretary of the power to fix sentences for murder and there followed a period of some acrimony between certain politicians and some senior judges in which there was a tussle over the future direction of the law. Parliament subsequently passed the Criminal Justice Act 2003, Part 12 of which creates an independent Sentencing Guidelines Council which will issue guidance on the length, etc. of sentences which must be taken into account by the courts in fixing penalties, and which further impose on courts an obligation to give reasons for and explain the effect of sentences imposed, in particular such reasons must be given where sentencing guidelines are departed from. In effect this legislation may be seen as a concession by the executive to the judiciary acknowledging the former's primacy with regard to sentencing, though the Act was not simply the outcome

---

[57] Application No 28212/95, 26 September 2002.   [58] [2002] UKHL 46 para 40.
[59] [2002] UKHL 46 para 50.   [60] [2002] UKHL 46 para 59.

of the decision in *Anderson* but was also the product of a number of searching research reports into the functioning of sentencing.

A cause of even greater controversy was the decision in *A and others v Secretary of State for the Home Department*.[61] This concerned certain persons detained under certificates from the Home Secretary issued under sections 21 and 23 of the Anti-terrorism, Crime and Security Act 2001. All of the detainees were foreign nationals who had not been charged with a criminal offence. Their detention took place under the 2001 Act and the Human Rights Act 1998 (Designated Derogation) Order SI 2001/3644 which achieved legal force very swiftly after the terrorist attacks on the United States of America on 11 September 2001. The provisions enable the Home Secretary to detain non-British nationals and were designed to circumvent the provisions of the Human Rights Act 1998, the European Convention on Human Rights and decisions of the European Court of Human Rights and of UK courts whereunder detention of a foreign national deemed a danger to the UK is permissible only for such a period of time as is necessary for the process of deportation to be carried out, while such a deportation cannot take place where the deportee would face a real risk of death or torture if deported to the country from whence he came. Each of the detainees was considered by the Home Secretary to be dangerous to the UK by virtue of involvement in terrorism, but equally each claimed he would face death or torture if deported.

The action taken by the UK government included making a derogation order under Article 5 of the Convention, claiming to rely on the ability enjoyed by member states to derogate from their obligations under the Convention in times of war or other public emergency, and arguing that there was a terrorist threat to the UK from suspected foreign nationals who were present in the country. The Anti-terrorism, Crime and Security Act 2001 then conferred extensive powers on the Home Secretary to certify suspected terrorists as a risk to national security and to order their deportation and/or indefinite detention where deportation would not otherwise be lawful or practicable. It was the detention of the suspects that was challenged as contrary to the Convention.

Lord Bingham reviewed the history of the legislation and in particular pointed to the report of a Committee of Privy Councillors on the operation of the 2001 Act which pointed out that, despite threats by terrorists to other European nationals, only the UK had found it necessary to make a derogation from the Convention.[62] He went on to point out that Article 15 of the Convention requires that any steps taken by way of derogation must not go beyond what is strictly required in the particular situation, ie they must be no more than what is proportionally necessary. Having considered the case law from Strasbourg on the issue, and the stress laid thereon on granting to national governments some freedom of decision making in determining what is needful and necessary for their nations, Lord Bingham nevertheless pointed out the fundamental principle that the Convention Rights set limits to executive and legislative decision taking, and adjudicating on those limits is a responsibility the courts cannot abdicate. He said:

'It is . . . of course true that the judges in this country are not elected and we are not answerable to Parliament. It is also true . . . that Parliament, the executive and the courts have different functions. But the function of independent judges charged to interpret and apply the law is universally recognised as a cardinal feature of the modern democratic state, a cornerstone of the rule of law itself. The Attorney-General is fully entitled to insist on the proper limits of judicial authority, but he is wrong to stigmatise judicial decision making as in some way undemocratic.'[63]

---

[61] [2004] UKHL 56.   [62] Anti-terrorism, Crime and Security Act 2001 Review: Report HC 100.
[63] [2004] UKHL 56 at para 42.

He added that in pursuing this function judges are performing a duty laid on them by Parliament itself in the 1998 Act, and that the supreme will of Parliament has to be obeyed even if a declaration of incompatibility is made as under section 4(6) of the 1998 Act as that does not affect the validity of the legislation, provided it is an Act of Parliament.

On the facts of the case Lord Bingham concluded that the action taken in respect of the detainees was disproportionate and was further discriminatory in that it was action that could not have been taken against a British subject. He found, as did the rest of the House, against the government. A declaration of incompatibility was made in respect of section 23 of the 2001 Act.

Baroness Hale's succinct but tersely analytical speech sets out the issues in the case well:

'Before us is a challenge to the validity of the law under which the detainees are detained. That law is contained in an Act of Parliament, the Anti-terrorism, Crime and Security Act 2001. The Human Rights Act 1998 is careful to preserve the sovereignty of Parliament. The courts cannot strike down the laws which the Queen in Parliament has passed. However, if the court is satisfied that a provision in an Act of Parliament is incompatible with a Convention right, it may make a declaration of that incompatibility (under section 4 of the 1998 Act). This does not invalidate the provision or anything done under it. But Government and Parliament then have to decide what action to take to remedy the matter.

The Convention right in question here is the right under article 5(1):

"Everyone has the right to liberty and security of person. No one shall be deprived of his liberty save in the following cases. . . .".

There are then listed six possible reasons for depriving a person of his liberty, none of which applies here. These people are not detained under articled 5(1)(f) "with a view to deportation or extradition" because they cannot be deported and no other country has asked for their extradition. They are being detained on suspicion of being international terrorists, a reason which does not feature in article 5. It does not feature because neither the common law, from which so much of the European Convention is derived, nor international human rights law allows indefinite detention at the behest of the executive, however well-intentioned. It is not for the executive to decide who should be locked up for any length of time, let alone indefinitely. Only the courts can do that and, except as a preliminary step before trial, only after the grounds for detaining someone have been proved. Executive detention is the antithesis of the right to liberty and security of person.

Yet that is what the 2001 Act allows. The Home Secretary may issue a certificate (under section 21) if he reasonably (a) believes that a person's presence here is a risk to national security, and (b) suspects that he is a terrorist. A terrorist is someone who takes part in acts of international terrorism, belongs to an international terrorist group, or merely supports or assists such a group. These are all likely to be criminal offences under the Terrorism Act 2000 or other legislation. But a person so certified can be detained indefinitely (under section 23) without being charged with or tried for any criminal offence. . . .

Article 5 applies to 'everyone'. States who are parties to the European Convention are required by article 1 to secure the rights and freedoms defined in the Convention to 'everyone within their jurisdiction'. This includes everyone physically present within their territory. So it was necessary for the United Kingdom to depart from its normal obligations under the Convention in order to enact this legislation. Departure is permitted under article 1:

"In time of war or other public emergency threatening the life of the nation any High Contracting Party may take measures derogating from its obligations under the Convention to the extent strictly required by the exigencies of the situation, provided that such measures are not inconsistent with its other obligations under international law."

The rights defined in the Convention have become rights in United Kingdom law by virtue of the Human Rights Act: but section 1(2) provides that the rights defined in the Convention articles shall have effect subject to any 'designated derogation'. This means a derogation designated in an order made by the Secretary of State under section 14, in this case the Human Rights Act 1998 (Designated Derogation) Order 2001. Such an order would not be within his powers if it provided for a derogation which was not allowed by the Convention. Section 30(2) and (5) of the 2001 Act allow the detainees to challenge this derogation from their article 5(1) rights in proceedings before SIAC and in an appeal from SIAC's decision. Thus it is that we have power to consider the validity of the Derogation Order made by the Secretary of State and to quash it if it is invalid. If the Derogation Order is invalid, it follows that detention powers under the 2001 Act are incompatible with the Convention rights as defined in the Human Rights Act and that we have power to declare it so. It will then be for Parliament to decide what to do about it.

The courts' power to rule on the validity of the derogation is another of the safeguards enacted by Parliament in this carefully constructed package. It would be meaningless if we could only rubber-stamp what the Home Secretary and Parliament have done. But any sensible court, like any sensible person, recognises the limits of its expertise. Assessing the strength of a general threat to the life of the nation is, or should be, within the expertise of the Government and its advisers. They may, as recent events have shown, not always get it right. But courts too do not always get things right. It would be very surprising if the courts were better able to make that sort of judgment than the Government. Protecting the life of the nation is one of the first tasks of a Government in a world of nation states. That does not mean that the courts could never intervene. Unwarranted declarations of emergency are a familiar tool of tyranny. If a Government were to declare a public emergency where patently there was no such thing, it would be the duty of the court to say so. But we are here considering the immediate aftermath of the unforgettable events of 11 September 2001. The attacks launched on the United States on that date were clearly intended to threaten the life of that nation. SIAC were satisfied that the open and closed material before them justified the conclusion that there was also a public emergency threatening the life of this nation. I, for one, would not feel qualified or even inclined to disagree.

But what is then done to meet the emergency must be no more than "is strictly required by the exigencies of the situation". The Government wished to solve a problem which had three components: (1) it suspected certain people living here of being international terrorists—in the very broad definition given to that term by the Act; but (2) either it could not or it did not wish to prove this beyond reason-able doubt by evidence admissible in a court of law; and (3) it could not solve the problem by deporting them, either for practical or for legal reasons.

The Government knew about certain foreign nationals presenting this problem, because they were identified during the usual immigration appeals process. But there is absolutely no reason to think that the problem applies only to foreigners. Quite the reverse. There is every reason to think that there are British nationals living here who are international terrorists within the meaning of the Act; who cannot be shown to be such in a court of law; and who cannot be deported to another country because they have every right to be here. Yet the Government does not think that it is necessary to lock them up. Indeed, it has publicly stated that locking up nationals is a Draconian step which could not at present by justified. But it has provided us with no real explanation of why it is necessary to lock up one group of people sharing exactly the same characteristics as another group which it does not think necessary to lock up. . . .

The conclusion has to be that it is not necessary to lock up the nationals. Other ways must have been found to contain the threat which they present. And if it is not necessary to lock up the nationals it cannot be necessary to lock up the foreigners. It is not strictly required by the exigencies of the situation.

It is also inconsistent with our other obligations under international law from which there has been no derogation, principally article 14 of the European Convention. This states:

"The enjoyment of the rights and freedoms set forth in this Convention shall be secured without discrimination on any ground such as sex, race, colour, language, religion, political or other opinion, national or social origin, association with a national minority, property, birth or other status."

This has five components, some of which overlap: (i) people belonging to a particular group or status (ii) must not be singled out for less favourable treatment (iii) from that given to other people who are in the same situation (iv) in relation to the enjoyment of their Convention rights (v) unless there is an objective justification for the difference in treatment.

Article 14 would make it unlawful to single out foreign nationals for less favourable treatment in respect of their article 5 rights whether or not the derogation from those rights was "strictly required by the exigencies of the situation". It is wrong to single them out for detention without trial if detention without trial is *not* strictly required to meet the exigencies of the situation. It is also wrong to single them out for detention without trial if detention without trial *is* strictly required, if there are other people who are in the same situation and there is no objective justification for the difference in treatment. Like cases must be treated alike. . . .

Even [if a] difference in treatment might have an objective justification . . . it must [still] serve a legitimate aim and be proportionate to that aim. Once again, the fact that it is sometimes permissible to treat foreigners differently does not mean that every difference in treatment serves a legitimate aim. If the situation really is so serious, and the threat so severe, that people may be detained indefinitely without trial, what possible legitimate aim could be served by only having power to lock up some of the people who present that threat? This is even more so, of course, if the necessity to lock people up in this way has not been shown.

Democracy values each person equally. In most respects, this means that the will of the majority must prevail. But valuing each person equally also means that the will of the majority cannot prevail if it is inconsistent with the equal rights of minorities. As Thomas Jefferson said in his inaugural address:

"Though the will of the majority is in all cases to prevail, that will to be rightful must be reasonable . . . The minority possess their equal rights, which equal law must protect, and to violate would be oppression."

No one has the right to be an international terrorist. But substitute "black", "disabled", "female", "gay", or any other similar adjective for "foreign" before "suspected international terrorist" and ask whether it would be justifiable to take power to lock up that group but not the "white", "able-bodied", "male", or "straight" suspected international terrorists. The answer is clear.

I would therefore allow the appeals, quash the derogation order, and declare section 23 of the 2001 Act incompatible with the right to liberty in article 5(1) of the European Convention.'[64]

These decisions achieved a high degree of media publicity, and were also politically controversial, provoking adverse criticism of the judiciary by ministers, and some judicial ripostes thereto! It is necessary therefore to set this controversy in context. Let us begin by defining in very basic terms what in the present context is meant by the words 'legal right'. A legal right is a mechanism for achieving some desirable objective, or for preventing some undesirable consequence of action or inaction, such mechanism being clearly defined—as is what it seeks to achieve—and enforceable at the suit of an individual. These mechanisms may regulate the relationships of individuals between themselves or between the individual and

---

[64] [2004] UKHL 56 at paras 221–223, 227–228, 231–234, 236–239.

the state. Judges are very familiar with such rights—they are the traditional realm of the law. Nearly all such rights will be individual in nature, for while they may be given to all, they will be pursued and enforced by individuals on individual occasions. Collective rights are, in comparison, generally poorly developed in our law. They are rights whose impact is only determined by the collective exercise of the mechanism of those entitled to utilise it. Perhaps the best example of such a right is the franchise at election time—it is the collective exercise of that right to vote by the electorate that has an effect on the persons subject to the duty to comply with the right, namely those seeking election.

The Convention Rights in the above sense of mechanisms are largely individual in nature, even though available generally to people, and are well understood and well applied by judges who traditionally are concerned to protect the individual against the encroaching power of the state.

Ministers on the other hand are much concerned—and rightly so—with the collective *interests* of citizens—these being much less defined than rights and largely social or political in nature. However, it is not logically acceptable for criticism of judges by ministers to be based on an argument that the former are too concerned with individual rights at the expense of the collective interest of the population to live in peace and tranquility—a claim made in relation to these cases where the judges made declarations of incompatibility in relation to situations concerning the powers of ministers to fix sentences for offences, or to detain those they deem to be a public danger. The characterisation of the public interest as a 'right' by ministers is the problem. While we all have an interest in pursuing our lives in peace, free of the threat of crime and violence, this can hardly be conceived of as a 'right' in the sense of the foregoing definition—it is simply too general and too ill-defined to be pursued and enforced on either a collective or individual basis. The issue between judges and ministers is thus to some extent linguistic—they are not talking about the same thing! Unfortunately for ministers, and in a sense for Parliament also, the 1998 Act has been passed, and lies on the statute book, and until repealed it creates new opportunities for the judges to pursue their role as the protectors of the individual—especially against the state. As with the European Communities Act 1972, we must assume that ministers and Parliament knew what they were doing when the legislation was enacted, and what the consequences could be—if they did, then they should not subsequently complain, while if they did not, very serious questions as to the competence and collective understanding of both the executive and the legislature must arise.

(f) Whither, or wither, supremacy?

The cases we have been considering indicate a degree of judicial unease with the traditional doctrine of supremacy. The judges have come to appreciate that it could be a dangerous implement in the hands of a government able to secure a compliant majority in the House of Commons—as indeed has been the case with most British governments for most of their periods of office during the last half century or so. While it may be that political forces such as the force of public or international opinion, or the wise counsel of the civil service, or 'elder statesmen' may serve to restrain the wilder excesses of a government flushed with the power of a large majority, it is not hard to find examples of legislation that has been passed by Parliament that has proved to be deeply socially divisive—the example of the Community Charge or 'Poll Tax' under the Thatcher government springs particularly to mind. This tax was initially proposed in 1985 as a flat rate contribution to be paid by effectively all adult citizens in order to finance local government. It formed part of the Conservative Party's 1987 election manifesto and was passed into law in 1988. The tax was generally regarded as unfair because it took no account of ability to pay, and riots broke out, including one attended by 200,000 protesters on 31 March 1990. In due course this unfortunate tax was replaced in the 1993/94 financial year, but its unpopularity contributed to the fall from power of Mrs Thatcher, who had vigorously promoted it, in 1990.

In such circumstances it is not surprising that the judges seem to be casting about for some means of restricting the doctrine of supremacy. Notions such as that of 'Constitutional statutes' which can only be repealed by the clearest of words, or the ability of UK courts to 'disapply' provisions of UK law that conflict with EC law, and the ability of the courts to make declarations of incompatibility in respect of statutes which inescapably conflict with Convention Rights, are examples of this search. Certainly it would appear that the judiciary is no longer prepared to treat supremacy as a single monolithic notion, but rather to see it as a family of propositions which may be individually debatable. However, we must ask how far along this path of searching our judges might be prepared to go. Many of the recent developments have built on the quite radically new notion in the *Thoburn* case that all statutes cannot any longer be treated as equal, and that it is the will of Parliament that some should be treated as having some sort of special significance. In this context the Acts of 1972 and 1998 come most quickly to mind. In pursuing this argument the judges claim to be doing the will of Parliament, and so avoid any clash with supremacy. But we must ask whether they would be prepared to go further and challenge the clear words of Parliament in a statute that purported for example to legislate in a manner clearly contrary to EC law. Past experience suggests not, and that the doctrine of supremacy would be reasserted, but might the past be an uncertain guide to the future?

This brings us to the most recent case on supremacy. *Jackson v Her Majesty's Attorney General*[65] concerned the validity of the ban on hunting with dogs contained in the Hunting Act 2004 which was passed under the terms of the Parliament Acts 1911 and 1949 in order to bypass opposition to the legislation in the House of Lords. The 1911 Act was passed following a series of constitutional crises between the Liberal Party, who formed the government, in the House of Commons and the Conservative Party who had a majority in the House of Lords. The Act finally established the predominance of the Lower, democratically elected, House of Parliament by taking away the power of veto of the Upper House and replacing it with a limited power of delay, initially of two years which was reduced to one year in 1949. Little use of the Parliament Act procedure was made for many years, the only legislation being passed in that way being the Welsh Church Act 1914, the Home Rule Act 1914 (which was never in fact brought into force) and the Parliament Act of 1949. More recently, however, the procedure has been relied on to pass the War Crimes Act 1991, the European Parliamentary Elections Act 1999, the Sexual Offences (Amendment) Act 2000 and the Hunting Act 2004, and its use was threatened in the case of the Trade Union and Labour Relations Act 1976 and the Aircraft and Shipbuilding Industries Act 1977.

The principal provisions of the 1911 Act (as amended) are as follows:

'1.–(1)If a Money Bill, having been passed by the House of Commons, and sent up to the House of Lords at least one month before the end of the session, is not passed by the House of Lords without amendment within one month after it is so sent up to that House, the Bill shall, unless the House of Commons direct to the contrary, be presented to His Majesty and become an Act of Parliament on the Royal Assent being signified, notwithstanding that the House of Lords have not consented to the Bill.

---

[65] [2005] UKHL 56.

(2)A Money Bill means a Public Bill which in the opinion of the Speaker of the House of Commons contains only provisions dealing with all or any of the following subjects, namely, the imposition, repeal, remission, alteration, or regulation of taxation; the imposition for the payment of debt or other financial purposes of charges on the Consolidated Fund [the National Loans Fund] or on money provided by Parliament, or the variation or repeal of any such charges; supply; the appropriation, receipt, custody, issue or audit of accounts of public money; the raising or guarantee of any loan or the repayment thereof; or subordinate matters incidental to those subjects or any of them. In this subsection the expressions "taxation", "public money", and "loan" respectively do not include any taxation, money, or loan raised by local authorities or bodies for local purposes.

(3)There shall be endorsed on every Money Bill when it is sent up to the House of Lords and when it is presented to His Majesty for assent the certificate of the Speaker of the House of Commons signed by him that it is a Money Bill. Before giving his certificate, the Speaker shall consult, if practicable, two members to be appointed from the Chairmen's Panel at the beginning of each Session by the Committee of Selection.

2.–(1)If any Public Bill (other than a Money Bill or a Bill containing any provision to extend the maximum duration of Parliament beyond five years) is passed by the House of Commons [in two successive sessions] (whether of the same Parliament or not), and, having been up to the House of Lords at least one month before the end of the session, is rejected by the House of Lords in each of those sessions, that Bill shall, on its rejection [for the second time] by the House of Lords, unless the House of Commons direct to the contrary, be presented His Majesty and become an Act of Parliament on the Royal Assent being signified thereto, notwithstanding that the House of Lords have not consented to the Bill: Provided that this provision shall not take effect unless [one year has elapsed] between the date of the second reading in the first of those sessions of the Bill in the House of Commons and the date on which it passes the House of Commons [in the second of those sessions].

(2)When a Bill is presented to His Majesty for assent in pursuance of the provisions of this section, there shall be endorsed on the Bill the certificate of the Speaker of the House of Commons signed by him that the provisions of this section have been duly complied with.

(3)A Bill shall be deemed to be rejected by the House of Lords if it is not passed by the House of Lords either without amendment or with such amendments only as may be agreed to by both Houses.

(4)A Bill shall be deemed to be the same Bill as a former Bill sent up to the House of Lords in the preceding session if, when it is sent up to the House of Lords, it is identical with the former Bill or contains only such alterations as are certified by the Speaker of the House of Commons to be necessary owing to the time which has elapsed since the date of the former Bill, or to represent any amendments which have been made by the House of Lords in the former Bill in the preceding session, and any amendments which are certified by the Speaker to have been made by the House of Lords [in the second session] and agreed to by the House of Commons shall be inserted in the Bill as presented for Royal Assent in pursuance of this section:

Provided that the House of Commons may, if they think fit, on the passage of such a Bill through the House [in the second session], suggest any further amendments without inserting the amendments in the Bill, and any such suggested amendments shall be considered by the House of Lords, and, if agreed to by that House, shall be treated as amendments made by the House of Lords and agreed to by the House of Commons; but the exercise of this power by the House of Commons shall not affect the operation of this section in the event of the Bill being rejected by the House of Lords.

3. Any certificate of the Speaker of the House of Commons given under this Act shall be conclusive for all purposes, and shall not be questioned in any court of law.

4.–(1) In every Bill presented to His Majesty under the preceding provisions of this Act, the words of enactment shall be as follows, that is to say:

"Be it enacted by the King's most Excellent Majesty, by and with the advice and consent of the Commons in this present Parliament assembled, in accordance with the provisions of the Parliament Acts, 1911 and 1949, and by authority of the same, as follows."

(2)Any alteration of a Bill necessary to give effect to this section shall not be deemed to be an amendment of the Bill. . . .'

Over the years a number of questions concerning the validity of the Parliament Act procedure had been raised by academics. In particular there were two arguments.

• Could the Act of 1949 be regarded as secondary as opposed to primary legislation as it depended for its validity on the 1911 Act, and, if so, would courts be prepared to inquire into that validity?

• Under the Act of 1911 could the Crown, the Lords and the Commons be considered to have delegated legislative power to the Crown and the Commons in certain situations, thus creating a subordinate legislative body which would be unable to extend its powers (as it purported to do in 1949) without the further express authority of the 'whole' Parliament?

These questions were relied on by those who opposed the Hunting Act 2004 on the basis that it was invalid having been passed under the terms of the Parliament Act 1949, which was itself invalid as it went beyond what was allowed by the Parliament Act 1911 in reducing the Lords' delaying powers from two years to one without the specific consent of the House of Lords.

The House of Lords encountered little difficulty in rejecting these arguments. Lord Bingham stated:

' . . . sections 1(1) and 2(1) of the 1911 Act provide that legislation made in accordance with those provisions shall "become an Act of Parliament on the Royal Assent being signified". The meaning of the expression "Act of Parliament" is not doubtful, ambiguous or obscure . . . It is used, and used only, to denote primary legislation . . . The 1911 Act did, of course, effect an important constitutional change, but the change lay not in authorising a new form of sub-primary parliamentary legislation but in creating a new way of enacting primary legislation. I cannot, secondly, accept that the 1911 Act can be understood as a delegation of legislative power or authority by the House of Lords, or by Parliament, to the House of Commons . . . Section 1 of the 1911 Act involved no delegation of legislative power and authority to the Commons . . . the overall object of the Act was not to enlarge the powers of the Commons but to restrict those of the Lords.'[66]

Lord Bingham took his stance on the clear lines of authority stretching from *Edinburgh and Dalkeith Railway Co. v Wauchope*[67] to *Pickin v British Railways Board*[68] that no court in this country can declare a duly enacted law invalid. He furthermore specifically rejected the argument that the procedure laid down by the 1911 Act could not be used to amend that Act, as in fact happened in 1949. '[The] 1911 Act did not involve any delegation of power and the Commons, when invoking the 1911 Act, cannot be regarded as a subordinate body . . . There was nothing in the 1911 Act to preclude use of the procedure laid down by the Act to amend the Act.'[69]

The conclusions of the other members of the House of Lords on the substantive issues in this case were similar to those of Lord Bingham. The problems in the case arise from speculation amongst their Lordships about whether there are matters that could not be passed by means of the Parliament Act procedure. Lord Nichols considered that, on the basis of the clear wording of the 1911 Act, the procedure could *not* be used by the Commons to pass a Bill extending the life of Parliament, and he found, by implication, that the procedure could not

---

[66] [2005] UKHL 56 at paras 24–25.   [67] (1842) 8 CL & F 710.   [68] [1974] AC 765.
[69] [2005] UKHL 56 at para 36.

be used on a 'two steps' basis, ie by first utilising the Parliament Act procedure to repeal the express prohibition on the use of that procedure to put through an extension Bill and then utilising the procedure to secure enactment of an extension of Parliament's life. Apart from that, however, he thought there is no restriction as to the subject matter of what may be enacted using the Parliament Act procedure.

Lord Steyn, considering this point, stated: 'There are two possible views about the limitation on the duration of Parliament. First, it may be a strict condition which must be complied with at all times. Secondly, it may be possible by means of the 1911 Act to eliminate this limitation albeit in two stages. It is a point of construction. In the context of a parliamentary democracy the language of section 2(1) and section 7 supports the former interpretation.'[70] Thus far Lord Steyn is agreeing with Lord Nichols, but then he adds: 'Parliament acting as ordinarily constituted may functionally redistribute legislative power in different ways. For example, Parliament could for specific purposes provide for a two-thirds majority in the House of Commons and the House of Lords. This would involve a redefinition of Parliament for a specific purpose. Such a redefinition could not be disregarded.'[71] This seems to suggest that the UK Parliament could limit its supremacy by procedural requirements. He then added:

'The Attorney General said at the hearing that the government might wish to bring about constitutional changes such as altering the composition of the House of Lords. The logic of this proposition is that the procedure of the 1949 Act could be used by the government to abolish the House of Lords. Strict legalism suggests that the Attorney General may be right. But I am deeply troubled about assenting to the validity of such an exorbitant assertion of government power in our bi-cameral system . . . If the Attorney General is right the 1949 Act could also be used to introduce oppressive and wholly undemocratic legislation. For example, it could theoretically be used to abolish judicial review of flagrant abuse of power by a government . . .'[72]

Lord Steyn argued that it is implausible now to assert that the UK has such an uncontrolled constitution and pointed out that Dicey's argument that the doctrine of supremacy is pure and absolute is out of place in a nation that is a member of the EC and has incorporated the European Convention on Human Rights into its law. He added further that supremacy as a notion was created by the judges, and thus other judges might amend or modify it, and might conclude that there are certain constitutional fundamentals, such as the power of Judicial Review and the existence of the courts which even a sovereign Parliament cannot abolish. At this point Lord Steyn goes far beyond the opinion of Lord Nicholls.

Lord Craig of Hopehead, a Law Lord appointed from Scotland, pointed out that the notion of a supreme Parliament nowadays has to be set in the context of restrictions that some courts, such as those of the EC, might impose, while also referring to the impact of the European Convention on Human Rights and the view, already encountered from Scotland, that some provisions of the Act of Union of 1707 are beyond Parliament's legislative powers. He furthermore identified the Rule of Law as 'the ultimate controlling factor on which our constitution is based'.[73] He was also certain that the Parliament Act procedure would not be utilised to force through a bill to extend the life of Parliament, but beyond that he was uncertain about where any legal limits to the powers of Parliament might lie, adding that a principle which states the absolute ability of a legislature to pass any legislation it likes is somewhat empty of meaning if the consequence is the passage of legislation that is absurd or which the population at large refuses to recognise as law.

---

[70] [2005] UKHL 56 at para 79.   [71] [2005] UKHL 56 at para 81.
[72] [2005] UKHL 56 at paras 101–102.   [73] [2005] UKHL 56 at para 109.

Baroness Hale considered that the 1911 Act's procedure can be used to pass legislation other than Bills to extend the duration of Parliament. In her view the courts would treat any attempt by Parliament to interfere with fundamental rights with considerable care and would not accept any such interference unless it was phrased in unmistakable language. In addition she considered that for the time being the Acts of 1972 and 1998 limit Parliament's powers, but impliedly accepted that, again by clear words, Parliament could dispose of those restrictions and concluded the constraints on Parliament's powers are primarily political and diplomatic rather than constitutional. She did, however, argue that Parliament might redesign itself for general or particular purposes and that such a redesign might be binding on future Parliaments.

It can be seen that there is only a very limited consensus amongst their Lordships on the issues considered. There appears to be a degree of agreement that the procedure created by the 1911 Act could not be used to push through legislation extending the duration of Parliament. Apart from that there is no clear view on whether any permanent limits to the powers of Parliament could exist and, if they do, what they might be. The European Communities Act 1972 and the Human Rights Act 1998 appear, however, for the time being, to impose limitations. It is, however, equally obvious that the old Diceyan certainties can no longer be relied on. Judicial deference to the notion of an omnipotent legislature cannot be guaranteed.

In part the issue is linguistic. In legal terms it makes more sense to speak of the 'supremacy' of Parliament in order to identify the supreme law making body, rather than to use the word 'sovereignty' which has overtones of international legal relations between states and concepts of state independence and autonomy, as well as the more political question of where the actual power to govern resides and originates. This was recognised by Professor JAG Griffith when he wrote:

'We speak of the sovereignty of Parliament but less confusion would be caused if we spoke of the sovereignty of the Government . . . The executive force of Governments derives from the power of the Queen to govern through her ministers and that power is ultimate . . . Sovereignty . . . in this wider sense is an attribute of the Government. That is its origin and its only resting place . . . The process of legislating is . . . a Governmental process but the assent of the Houses of Parliament must be obtained. But the strength of the Government's position lies in its power to command that assent.'[74]

It may be that what is required is a clear separation of thinking between questions of supremacy and those of sovereignty. The latter is truly a political concept, and its intrusion into constitutional law is to be regretted. Our judiciary must be criticised for using the words 'supremacy' and 'sovereignty' on occasion as if they are interchangeable, when conceptually they are quite separate. Sovereignty may exist in a state where the legislature is subject to the 'higher law' of a written constitution—as witness the USA. Dicey wrote at a time when it was fatally easy to confuse the concepts—at the height of empire, when the British parliamentary system was, confusingly, apparently intertwined with the exercise of sovereign imperial power. Ministers appeared to rule, in the name of the Crown, an Empire on which—quite truthfully in geographical terms—the sun never set, and they did so equally apparently while being answerable for their actions to a Parliament which passed laws for that Empire. It is easy to see how the concept of imperial might, which was essentially political in nature, became confused with that of the role and function of Parliament which is a legal issue. The power of

---

[74] 'Legislation' in Hanson, AH and Crick, B, *The Commons in Transition* (Fontana/Collins, London, 1970) pp. 18–19.

Empire became confused with the power of Parliament, and too much authority was accordingly ascribed to the latter.

Today the power of Empire has departed, but the confusion over the power of Parliament remains. The UK would still be a sovereign power even if its legislature did not have supreme power to pass any legislation it likes—the two concepts are not mutually interdependent. Supremacy, as already stated, is, however, simply a judicial construct designed to ensure a recognisable hierarchy of laws and law making powers. What the judiciary has constructed they may dismantle: or may they?

FURTHER READING

Allan TRS 'Parliamentary Sovereignty: Lord Denning's Dextrous Revolution' (1983) 3 Oxford Journal of Legal Studies 22.

Bogdanor V *The Monarch and the Constitution* (Clarendon Press, Oxford, 1995).

Dike C 'The Case against Parliamentary Sovereignty' [1976] Public Law 283.

Edwards RA 'Reading down Legislation under the Human Rights Act' (2000) 20 Legal Studies (No 3) 353.

Feldman D 'The Human Rights Act 1998 and Constitutional Principles' (1999) 19 Legal Studies (No 2) 165.

Feldman D 'None, One or Several? Perspectives on the UK's Constitution(s)' [2005] CLJ 329.

Hailsham (Lord) *The Dilemma of Democracy* (Collins, London, 1978).

Heuston RFV *Essays in Constitutional Law* (2nd edn, Stevens, London, 1964).

Jennings Sir Ivor *The Law and the Constitution* (5th edn, University of London Press, London, 1959).

Jowell J and Oliver D (eds) *The Changing Constitution* (4th edn, Clarendon Press, Oxford, 2004).

Marshall G *Constitutional Theory* (Clarendon Press, Oxford, 1971) Chapter III.

McAuslan P and McEldowney JF (eds) *Law, Legitimacy and the Constitution* (Sweet & Maxwell, London, 1985) ch 3.

Mitchell JDB 'The Sovereignty of Parliament: Yet Again' (1963) 79 LQR 196.

Munro C *Studies in Constitutional Law* (2nd edn, Butterworths, London, 1999) chs 1, 2, 5, 6, 9 and 10.

Nicol D 'The Human Rights Act and the Politicians' (2004) 24 Legal Studies (No 3), 451.

Upton M 'Marriage Vows of the Elephant: The Contribution of 1707' (1989) 105 LQR 79.

Wade HWR 'The Basis of Legal Sovereignty' [1955] CLJ 155.

Winterton G 'The British Grundnorm: Parliamentary Supremacy Re-examined' (1976) 92 LQR 591.

Woodhouse D 'The Constitutional and Political Implications of a United Kingdom Supreme Court' (2004) 24 Legal Studies (Nos 1 & 2), 134.

3 THE ROYAL PREROGATIVE

The prerogative is an ancient source of power. Understanding of what it comprises has changed over time. 'Prerogative' can be used to mean (a) those powers peculiar to the Crown, for example, granting titles; (b) powers and rights not derived from statute but from (or recognised by) common law; (c) personal rights enjoyed by the monarch. We are principally concerned with 'prerogative' in the sense of that body of powers, rights, immunities and duties belonging to the Crown and not statute based. Primarily this means, as Blackstone states: 'that special pre-eminence which the King hath over and above all persons, and out of the ordinary course of the common law . . . And . . . only applied to those rights and capacities which the King enjoys in contradistinction to others'.[1] Long usage also includes what Dicey called: 'every act which the executive government can do without the authority of an Act of Parliament'.[2] However, there are particular features of the prerogative which must be noted.

---

1. The Origins of the Prerogative and its Subdivisions

It is customary and ultimately derived from the ruler–subject relationship, one which demands from the ruler protection, both at home and overseas, and from the subject faithful allegiance. This was explained by Nourse LJ in *R v Secretary of State for the Home Department, ex p Northumbria Police Authority:*[3]

'It has not at any stage in our history been practicable to identify all the prerogative powers of the Crown. It is only by a process of piecemeal decision over a period of centuries that particular powers are seen to exist or not to exist, as the case may be. From time to time a need for more exact definition arises. The present need arises from a difference of view between the Secretary of State and a police authority over what is necessary to maintain public order, a phenomenon which has been observed only in recent times. There has probably never been a comparable occasion for investigating a prerogative of keeping the peace within the realm.

The Crown's prerogative of making war and peace, the war prerogative, has never been doubted. Its origins may not have been fully explored. Here it is important to remember that the Royal prerogative was never regarded as a collection of mere powers, to be exercised or not at the will of the sovereign.

---

[1] *Commentaries* vol 1, p. 239.   [2] *The Law of the Constitution* (10th edn, Macmillan, London), p. 425.
[3] [1988] 2 WLR 590 between 611 and 614.

The King owed certain duties to his subjects, albeit duties of imperfect obligation whose performance could not be enforced by legal process . . . They included a duty to protect the lives and property of the King's subjects.' . . .

A duty of protection seems to have been recognised from earliest times. In *Calvin's Case* (1608) 7 Co Rep 1a,4b we find this statement based on some observations of Glanville on the connection which there ought to be between a lord and his tenant by homage:

> "But between the Sovereign and the subject there is without comparison a higher and greater connexion; for as the subject oweth to the King his true and faithful ligeance and obedience, so the Sovereign is to govern and protect his subjects . . ." . . .

Reverting to the war prerogative, it is natural to suppose that it was founded, at least in part, on the wider prerogative of protection. That seems to have been the view of Lord Erskine, speaking in the House of Lords in 1808 [8 March 1808, 10 Cobbett *Parliamentary Debates* 961] and cited in *Chitty's Prerogatives of the Crown* p. 50:

> "What is termed the war prerogative of the King is created by the perils and exigencies of war for the public safety, and by its perils and exigencies it is therefore limited."

The wider prerogative must have extended as much to unlawful acts within the realm as to the menaces of a foreign power. There is no historical or other basis for denying to the war prerogative a sister prerogative of keeping the peace within the realm . . .

[The] scarcity of references in the books to the prerogative of keeping the peace within the realm does not disprove that it exists. Rather it may point to an unspoken assumption that it does.'

The prerogative is divided into that which is exercised by ministers, the 'political' prerogative, see further below, and that which is 'personal' to the monarch, though even here constitutional conventions, see also below, indicate that these powers are exercised on ministerial advice—effectively today *prime* ministerial advice. It is, however, also common nowadays to speak of a 'reserve' prerogative which could be exercised personally by the monarch in extraordinary situations.

The prerogative coalesces with the general power of government to govern, a power both *political* in that ministers are drawn from those forming the *elected* majority in Parliament, and *legal* in that *ministers* are the Crown's principal *servants* and are entrusted with the Crown's powers. This legal power, it should be remembered, is original, not electorally derived. Government needs no mandate from Parliament to decide how, when and where to exercise existing powers and policy-making functions.

(a) The residuary character of the prerogative

The prerogative is residuary, but the question whether statute supplants prerogative in any given area is an issue of statutory interpretation, and whether the prerogative has/has not been supplanted may give rise to acute conflicts of opinion.

The leading authority is *A-G v De Keyser's Royal Hotel Ltd.*[4] In May 1916, the Crown, purporting to act under the Defence of the Realm Regulations, took possession of a hotel for the purpose of housing the headquarters personnel of the Royal Flying Corps, and denied the legal right of the owners to compensation. The owners yielded up possession

---

[4] [1920] AC 508.

under protest and without prejudice to their rights, and by a Petition of Right they asked for a declaration that they were entitled to a rent for the use and occupation of the premises, or, in the alternative, that they were entitled to compensation under the Defence Act 1842.

Lord Dunedin, having reviewed the previous authorities, concluded:

'The most that could be taken from them is that the King, as *suprema potestas* endowed with the right and duty of protecting the Realm, is for the purpose of the defence of the realm in times of danger entitled to take any man's property, and that the texts give no certain sound as to whether this right to take is accompanied by an obligation to make compensation to him whose property is taken . . . As to the necessity for the taking over of the particular subject, the Crown authorities must be the judge of that . . .

None the less, it is equally certain that if the whole ground of something which could be done by the prerogative is covered by the statute, it is the statute that rules. On this point I think the observation of the learned Master of the Rolls [in the court of Appeal when considering the action] is unanswerable. He says: "What use would there be in imposing limitations, if the Crown could at its pleasure disregard them and fall back on prerogative?"

The prerogative is defined by a learned constitutional writer as "The residue of discretionary or arbitrary authority which at any given time is legally left in the hands of the Crown." Inasmuch as the Crown is a party to every Act of Parliament it is logical enough to consider that when the Act deals with something which before the Act could be effected by the prerogative, and specially empowers the Crown to do the same thing, but subject to conditions, the Crown assents to that, and by that Act, to the prerogative being curtailed.'

Lord Atkinson concurred:

'The conclusion, as I understand it, is this: that it does not appear that the Crown has ever taken for these purposes the land of the subject without paying for it, and there is no trace of the Crown having, even in the times of the Stuarts, exercised or asserted the power or right to do so by virtue of the Royal Prerogative . . .

It is quite obvious that it would be useless and meaningless for the Legislature to impose restrictions and limitations upon, and to attach conditions to, the exercise by the Crown of the powers conferred by a statute, if the Crown were free at its pleasure to disregard these provisions, and by virtue of its prerogative do the very thing the statutes empowered it to do . . . It was suggested that when a statute is passed empowering the Crown to do a certain thing which it might theretofore have done by virtue of its prerogative, the prerogative is merged in the statute. I confess I do not think the word "merged" is happily chosen. I should prefer to say that when such a statute, expressing the will and intention of the King and of the three estates of the realm, is passed, it abridges the Royal Prerogative while it is in force to this extent: that the Crown can only do the particular thing under and in accordance with the statutory provisions, and that its prerogative power to do that thing is in abeyance . . . [After] the statute has been passed, and while it is in force, the thing it empowers the Crown to do can thenceforth only be done by and under the statute, and subject to all the limitations, restrictions and conditions by it imposed, howsoever unrestricted the Royal Prerogative may therefore have been.'

Lord Parmoor reached a similar conclusion:

'The Royal Prerogative connotes a discretionary authority or privilege, exercisable by the Crown, or the Executive, which is not derived from Parliament, and is not subject to statutory control. This authority or privilege is in itself a part of the common law, not to be exercised arbitrarily, but "per legem" and "sub modo legis" . . .

The growth of constitutional liberties has largely consisted in the reduction of the discretionary power of the executive, and in the extension of Parliamentary protection in favour of the subject, under a series of statutory enactments. The result is that, whereas at one time the Royal Prerogative gave legal sanction to a large majority of the executive functions of the Government, it is now restricted within comparatively narrow limits. The Royal Prerogative has of necessity been gradually curtailed, as a settled rule of law has taken the place of an uncertain and arbitrary administrative discretion . . .

The constitutional principle is that when the power of the Executive to interfere with the property or liberty of subjects has been placed under Parliamentary control, and directly regulated by statute, the Executive no longer derives its authority from the Royal Prerogative of the Crown but from Parliament, and that in exercising such authority the Executive is bound to observe the restrictions which Parliament has imposed in favour of the subject . . .

It would be an untenable proposition to suggest that Courts of law could disregard the protective restrictions imposed by statute law where they are applicable. In this respect the sovereignty of Parliament is supreme. The principles of construction to be applied in deciding whether the Royal Prerogative has been taken away or abridged are well ascertained. It may be taken away or abridged by express words, by necessary implication, or, as stated in Bacon's Abridgement, where an Act of Parliament is made for the public good, the advancement of religion and justice, and to prevent injury and wrong. Statutes which provide rent or compensation as a condition to the right of the Executive to take over the temporary possession of lands or buildings on the occasion of public exigency come, in my opinion, within the category of statutes made for the advancement of justice and to prevent injury and wrong . . . I am further of opinion that where a matter has been directly regulated by statute there is a necessary implication that the statutory regulation must be obeyed, and that as far as such regulation is inconsistent with the claim of a Royal Prerogative right, such right can no longer be enforced.'

Note, however, the decision in *R v Secretary of State for the Home Department, ex p Northumbria Police Authority.*[5] The Secretary of State for the Home Department issued a circular to all chief officers of police and clerks to police authorities in England and Wales, informing them that police requirements for plastic baton rounds and CS gas for use in the event of serious public disorder would be met from a central store to be maintained by the Secretary of State. A chief officer wishing to obtain such equipment would be able to purchase it, with the financial approval of his police authority. Where, however, a chief officer anticipated refusal to approve his request for such equipment, the circular set out a procedure for obtaining the equipment directly from the central store. A police authority sought to challenge the issue of the circular on the grounds that the Secretary of State had no power either by virtue of the Police Act 1964 or otherwise to maintain a central supply of such equipment, or to supply the equipment without the approval of the relevant police authority save in a situation of grave emergency. It applied for an order to quash the decision of the Secretary of State to issue and apply the circular.

Clearly in this case one issue turned on whether the prerogative power had survived the passing of the Police Act 1964. Purchas LJ on the question whether the prerogative had survived the passing of the Police Act 1964:

'[The] Act is mainly a consolidating Act and does not, in my judgment, affect any prerogative power otherwise enjoyed by the Crown . . . The continued existence of prerogative has never been questioned. Indeed the police authority conceded that it still exists in the case of national emergency—although as a concept this was difficult to define beyond the obvious extremes of war or threat of war, civil or otherwise. So far as I know, it has never been suggested that in assenting to any of the enactments referred to in this judgment the Monarch has in any way derogated from the Royal

---

[5] [1988] 2 WLR 590.

prerogative to maintain the peace of the realm . . . [In] considering the powers of ministers exercising as a Secretary of State the Royal prerogative, one must distinguish between the existence of the prerogative and the machinery set up to enable the expeditious and efficient use of that prerogative . . .

In the present case the Secretary of State contended that if he does not have the power to make equipment available to police forces under the Act, he must have this power under the Royal Prerogative for the purpose of promoting the efficiency of the police. In order to dispute this the police authority had to contend that the combined effect of sections 4(1), (4) and 41 is to prevent the Secretary of State from supplying equipment unless it is requested by the police authority . . . Even if I am not justified in holding that these sections afford positive statutory authority for the supply of equipment, they must fall short of an express and unequivocal inhibition sufficient to abridge the prerogative powers, otherwise available to the Secretary of State, to do all that is reasonably necessary to preserve the peace of the realm.

Mr Keene referred us to *Chitty's Prerogatives of the Crown* (1820) for the purposes of demonstrating that there was then no recognisable "prerogative to provide or equip a police force". With respect to Mr Keene, in my judgment this argument begs the question. One is not seeking a prerogative right to do this. The prerogative power is to do all that is reasonably necessary to keep the Queen's peace. This involves the commissioning of justices of the peace, constables and the like. The author clearly identifies the prerogative powers inherent in the Crown in relation to the duty placed on the Sovereign to protect his dominions and subjects. At p. 4 the author adopts the definition of prerogative by Sir William Blackstone:

> "By the word 'prerogative' we usually understand", observes Sir William Blackstone, "that special pre-eminence which the King hath over and above all other persons, and out of the ordinary course of the common law, in right of his royal dignity. It signifies, in its etymology (from prae and rogo), something that is required or demanded before, or in preference to, all others. And hence it follows, that it must be in its nature singular and eccentrical; that it can only be applied to those rights and capacities which the King enjoys alone, in contradistinction to others; and not to those which he enjoys in common with any of his subjects; for if once any one prerogative of the Crown could be held in common with the subject, it would cease to be prerogative any longer. And therefore Finch [*Law, or, a discourse thereof* (1759, at page 5)] lays it down as a maxim, 'that the prerogative is that law in case of the King, which is law and no case of the subject.' The splendour, rights, and powers of the Crown were attached to it for the benefit of the people, and not for the private gratification of the sovereign; they form part of, and are, generally speaking, as antient as the law itself." . . . '

Purchas LJ further cited Chitty (at 71) on the issue:

'The *duties* arising from the relation of sovereign and subject are reciprocal. Protection, that is, the security and governance of his dominions according to law, is the duty of the sovereign; and allegiance and subjection, with reference to the same criterion, the constitution and laws of the country, form, in return, the duty of the governed, as will be more fully noticed hereafter. We have already partially mentioned this duty of the sovereign, and have observed that the prerogatives are vested in him for the benefit of his subjects, and that His Majesty is under, and not above, the laws.' . . .

Purchas LJ concluded:

'In my judgment, the prerogative powers to take all reasonable steps to preserve the Queen's peace remain unaffected by the Act and these including the supply of equipment to police forces which is reasonably required for the more efficient discharge of their duties.'[6]

---

[6] [1988] 2 WLR 590 between 603 (Letter G) and 610 (Letter G).

(b) The prerogative is subject to the law

'The rule of law' requires government to operate through and according to law. The Crown has no reserve of discretion to operate outside the limits of legality.

This was made clear in *The Zamora* by Lord Parker:[7]

'The idea that the King in Council, or indeed any branch of the Executive, has power to prescribe or alter the law to be administered by Courts of law in this country is out of harmony with the principles of our Constitution. It is true that, under a number of modern statutes, various branches of the Executive have power to make rules having the force of statutes, but all such rules derive their validity from the statute which creates the power, and not from the executive body by which they are made. No one would contend that the prerogative involves any power to prescribe or alter the law administered in Courts of Common Law or Equity . . .'

The limits of prerogative power are declared by the courts; no new powers may be created but the limits of existing prerogatives are unknown. These propositions have been the subject of a number of judicial pronouncements over the centuries. In *The Case of Proclamations* it was stated:

' . . . Note, the King by his proclamation or other ways cannot change any part of the common law, or statute law, or the customs of the realm, 11 Hen 4.37. Fortescue De Laudibus Angliae Legum, cap 9 18 Edw 5 35, 36, &c 31 Hen 8 cap 8 *hic infra*: also the King cannot create any offence by his prohibition or proclamation, which was not an offence before, for that was to change the law, and to make an offence which was not; for *ubi non est lex, ibi non est transgressio: ergo*, that which cannot be punished without proclamation, cannot be punished with it. *Vide* le stat. 31 Hen 8 cap 8 which Act gives more power to the King than he had before, and yet there it is declared that proclamations shall not alter the law, statutes, or customs of the realm, or impeach any in his inheritance, goods, body, life, &c. But if a man shall be indicted for a contempt against a proclamation, he shall be fined and imprisoned; and so impeached in his body and goods. *Vide* Fortescue, cap 9 18.34 36, 37, &c.

But a thing which is punishable by the law, by fine, and imprisonment, if the King prohibit it by his proclamation, before that he will punish it, and so warn his subjects of the peril of it, there if he permit it after, this as a circumstance aggravates the offence; but he by proclamation cannot make a thing unlawful, which was permitted by the law before: and this was well proved by the ancient and continual forms of indictments; for all indictments conclude *contra legem et consuetudinem Angliae*, or *contra leges et statuta*, &c. But never was seen any indictment to conclude *contra regiam proclamationem* . . .

In the same term it was resolved by the two Chief Justices, Chief Baron, and Baron Altham, upon conference betwixt the Lords of the Privy Council and them, that the King by his proclamation cannot create any offence which was not an offence before, for then he may alter the law of the land by his proclamation in a high point; for if he may create an offence where none is, upon that ensues fine and imprisonment: also the law of England is divided into three parts, common law, statute law, and custom; but the King's proclamation is none of them: also *malum aut est malum in se aut prohibitum*, that which is against common law is *malum in se, malum prohibitum* is such an offence as is prohibited by Act of Parliament, and not by proclamation.

Also it was resolved, that the King hath no prerogative, but that which the law of the land allows him.'[8]

These strictures were repeated in *A-G v Brown*.[9] By a Proclamation known as the Prohibition of Imports (No 32) Proclamation 1919, and dated June 25 last, His Majesty,

[7] [1916] 2 AC 77, (PC) at 90.   [8] (1611) 12 Co Rep 74.   [9] [1920] 1KB 773 at 792–793.

purporting to act under section 43 of the Customs Consolidation Act 1876, prohibited the importation into the United Kingdom of chemicals of all descriptions, unless under licence. Section 43 provides as follows: 'The importation of arms, ammunition, gunpowder, or any other goods may be prohibited by Proclamation or Order in Council.' On or about 17 August 1919, the defendant, John Brown, trading as Brown and Forth, chemical manufacturers of Manchester and London, imported into the United Kingdom at Manchester six casks of pyrogallic acid on the steamship *Bovic* from New York. On 29 August 1919, at Manchester, an officer of Customs and Excise seized the goods as forfeited to the Crown, and duly notified the defendant of the seizure. The defendant's firm claimed the goods as not so forfeited. The defendant took the position that the Proclamation under which the King purported to act was of no legal force and effect and that he had no power to make it.

Sankey J:

'Considerable argument was addressed to me as to the state of the King's prerogative at [the time when the statute under which the purported proclamation was made] in respect of trade and commerce. Reference was made to Lord Chief Justice Hale's opinion as set out in Hargrave's *Law Tracts*, Article "De Portibus Maris", chap 9, ed 1787, p 97, concerning the *jus regium* in ports of the sea in relation to commerce and trade, where the learned author in the last paragraph says: "And thus I have passed through the consideration of the King's prerogative in ports, for their opening and shutting in relation to trade and commerce. And upon the whole matter, it will appear from the several Acts of parliament that have been made for the support and increase of trade, and for the keeping of the sea open to foreign and English merchants and merchandize, that there is now no other means for the restraint of exportation or importation of goods and merchandizes in times of peace, but only when and where an Act of parliament puts any restraint. Several Acts of parliament having provided *que la mere soit overt*, it may not be regularly shut against the merchandize of English, or foreigners in amity with this Crown, unless an Act of parliament shut it, as it hath been done in some particular cases, and may be done in others." . . .'

In 1776 an embargo was placed by proclamation on the export of wheat because of a scarcity of flour. Parliament was not sitting at the time; the King acted solely on the advice of ministers. Parliament passed an Act of Indemnity to regularise the position.

Similar limits on the power to govern by prerogative proclamation were imposed in *A-G v Wilts United Dairies*.[10] As part of a scheme to encourage milk production and equalise production prices and rates in various parts of the country under section 3 of the New Ministries and Secretaries Act 1916, the Food Controller required persons living outside the south west of England to obtain licences if they wished to buy milk within that area. A condition of the licence then imposed a 2d per gallon fee on such milk if taken outside the area.

Lord Buckmaster:

'The question before this House is . . . whether there was any power conferred upon the Food Controller to do what he did. The Attorney-General has urged your Lordships to consider the extreme difficulty of the situation in which this country found itself owing to the war . . . but it cannot possibly give to any official a right to act outside the law; nor can the law be unreasonably strained in order to legalise that which it might be perfectly reasonable should be done if in fact it was unauthorised.

---

[10] [1922] 91 LJKB 897 at 899.

The real answer to such an argument is to be found in this, that in times of great national crisis Parliament should be, and generally is, in continuous session, and the powers which are required for the purpose of maintaining the integrity of the country, both economic and military, ought always to be obtained readily from loyal Houses of Parliament. The only question here is, Were such powers granted?

There are only two sources from which those powers can possibly be derived. One is the Act creating the Ministry, and the other the Regulations under the Defence of the Realm Act. Neither of these either directly or, in my opinion, by inference, enabled the Food Controller to levy the payment of any sums of money from any of His Majesty's subjects. The statute of 1916 confines his duties to regulating the supply and consumption of food and taking the necessary steps for maintaining a proper supply of food. The powers so given are no doubt very extensive and very drastic but they do not include the power of levying upon any man payment of money which the Food Controller must receive as part of a national fund and can only apply under proper sanction for national purposes. However the character of this payment may be clothed by asking your Lordships to consider the necessity for its imposition. In the end it must remain a payment which certain classes of people were called upon to make for the purpose of exercising certain privileges, and the result is that the money so raised can only be described as a tax the levying of which can never be imposed upon subjects of this country by anything except plain and direct statutory means.'

Issues become more problematic, however, when the limits of *existing* prerogatives are in question. This became apparent in the *Northumbria Police Authority* litigation already considered above. It will be remembered that this involved a claim by the Home Secretary to issue baton rounds and CS gas to police forces. The question arose whether these modern articles could be issued under the terms of a vague, old prerogative power.

Croom Johnson LJ:

'Although there has always been what is called the war prerogative, which is the Crown's right to make war and peace, Mr Keene submitted that there is no corresponding prerogative to enforce the keeping of what is popularly called the "Queen's peace within the realm". Mr Keene based his submission by reference to *Chitty's Prerogatives of the Crown* (1820) and pointed out that there is no power referred to in it for keeping the peace. It does, however, contain an extensive section on "The King as the Fountain of Justice" and courts and gaols. The argument is that if there was no prerogative power to keep the peace in 1820, at which date no organised police force existed, then all police forces exist and are controlled only by the later statutes by which they were created, and there is no residual prerogative power to draw on in cases of necessity . . . There were constables long before the establishment of Peel's Metropolitan Police in 1829. At all events, the assumption was early made that keeping the peace was part of the prerogative. The position of the Secretary of State is that he is one of a number of secretaries of state through whom the prerogative power is exercised. In *Harrison v Bush* (1856) 5 E & B 344 at 353, Lord Campbell CJ stated:

"In practice, to the Secretary of State for the Home Department . . . belongs peculiarly the maintenance of the peace within the Kingdom, with the superintendence of the administration of justice as far as the Royal prerogative is involved in it." . . .

In *Coomber v Berkshire Justices* (1883) 9 App Cas 61 the question for decision was whether a block of buildings comprising county assize courts and a police station were liable to income tax under Schedule A. If they were erected as part of the function of government in the administration of justice, then notwithstanding the fact that they were built by the county and paid for out of the county rates, the Crown's exemption from payment of taxes would apply. The House of Lords held that they both were exempt, the police being ultimately a Crown responsibility. Lord Blackburn, at p. 67:

"I do not think it can be disputed that the administration of justice, both criminal and civil, and the preservation of order and prevention of crime by means of what is now called police, are among the most important functions of Government, nor that by the constitution of this country, these functions do, of common right, belong to the Crown." . . .

By its very nature the subject of maintaining the Queen's peace and keeping law and order has over the years inevitably been dealt with by statute much more than the war prerogative has been . . . but I have no doubt that the Crown does have a prerogative power to keep the peace, which is bound up with its undoubted right to see that crime is prevented and justice administered. This is subject to Mr Keene's next submission, which was that any prerogative power may be lost by being overtaken by statute law . . .

It is clear that the Crown cannot act under the prerogative if to do so would be incompatible with statute. What was said here is that the Secretary of State's proposal under the circular would be inconsistent with the powers expressly or impliedly conferred on the police authority by section 4 of the Police Act 1964. The Divisional court rejected that submission for reasons with which I wholly agree; namely that section 4 does not expressly grant a monopoly, and that granted the possibility of an authority which declines to provide equipment required by the chief constable there is every reason not to imply a Parliamentary intent to create one.

Mr Keene's last submission was that if there is a prerogative power it can only be used in emergency and that this does not allow its use beforehand in circumstances of peace and quiet. One need only quote and adapt . . . passages from the speeches in *Burmah Oil Co Ltd v Lord Advocate* [1965] AC 75. That was a case concerning the war prerogative, but the same point was taken. Lord Reid said, at p. 100:

"it would be very strange if the law prevented or discouraged necessary preparations until a time when it would probably be too late for them to be effective." . . .

The same reasoning must apply to the provision of equipment to the police, and to their being trained in its use, in times when there is reason to apprehend outbreaks of riot and serious civil disturbance.'[11]

Purchas LJ:

'[It] is convenient to notice the distinction between the underlying prerogative power which undisputably resides in the Crown to "protec:t the realm", "keep the Queen's peace", "make treaties", etc, and the various ways in which that power is exercised and has been exercised over many centuries. Whether the prerogative powers variously described are merely different aspects of the same fundamental power to protect the realm, or are separate individual prerogative powers, may be more important academically than in the resolution of the issues raised in this appeal. The exercise of the prerogative of keeping the peace and the enforcement of law and order was effected by proclamation and statute from earliest times . . . The constable's powers and duties have been described . . . by Lord Denning in *R v Metropolitan Police Comr, ex p Blackburn* [1968] 2 QB 118 at 135:

"The office of Commissioner of Police within the Metropolis dates back to 1829 when Sir Robert Peel introduced his disciplined force. The commissioner was a justice of the peace specially appointed to administer the police force in the metropolis. His constitutional status has never been defined either by statute or by the courts. It was considered by the Royal Commission on the Police in their Report in 1962 (Cmnd 1728). But I have no hesitation in holding that, like every constable in the land, he should be, and is, independent of the executive. He is not subject to the orders of the Secretary of State, save that under the Police Act 1964, the Secretary of State can call upon him to give a report, or to retire in the interests of efficiency. I hold it to be the duty of the Commissioner of Police of the Metropolis, as it is of every chief constable, to enforce the law of the land. He must take steps so to post his men that crimes may be detected; and that honest citizens may go about their affairs in peace. He must decide whether or not suspected persons are to be prosecuted; and, if need be, bring the prosecution or see that it is brought. But in all these things he is not the servant of anyone,

---

[11] [1988] 2 WLR 590 between 598 (post letter H) to 601 (post letter F).

save of the law itself. No Minister of the Crown can tell him that he must, or must not, keep observation on this place or that; or that he must, or must not, prosecute this man or that one. Nor can any police authority tell him so. The responsibility for law enforcement lies on him. He is answerable to the law and to the law alone." . . .

In carrying out these duties, the powers of the chief constables must stem from delegated power to exercise the prerogative power to keep the peace . . . From early times the courts have not been averse to considering whether a power does or does not exist within the prerogative—see *Laker Airways Ltd v Department of Trade* [1977] QB 643 at 705, per Lord Denning MR:

"The prerogative is a discretionary power exercisable by the executive government for the public good, in certain spheres of governmental activity for which the law has made no provision, such as the war prerogative (of requisitioning property for the defence of the realm), or the treaty prerogative (of making treaties with foreign powers). The law does not interfere with the proper exercise of the discretion by the executive in those situations: but it can set limits by defining the bounds of the activity: and it can intervene if the discretion is exercised improperly or mistakenly. That is the fundamental principle of our constitution." . . . '[12]

Prerogative power is generally subject to judicial review. In *Council of Civil Service Unions v Minister for the Civil Service*[13] ('*GCHQ*') the House of Lords made it clear that there are a number of qualifications to be satisfied before judicial review of a decision taken under prerogative powers can be obtained. In particular Lord Diplock argued that the decision in question must have consequences for a person either by altering his/her rights or obligations or by depriving him/her of some benefit or advantage previously enjoyed. In addition the decision must be taken by a person empowered to take it by public law and not by way of mere agreement between parties, and the decision must be tainted with illegality, irrationality or procedural unpropriety. Lords Diplock, Scarman and Roskill further stated that in addition to the foregoing requirements the prerogative power in question must be justiciable, ie of such a character that the courts will review, for it is clear that there are some matters which the courts may be unwilling to review. These excluded matters Lord Roskill considered would include the making of treaties, the defence of the realm, the prerogative of mercy, the granting of honours, the dissolution of Parliament and the appointment of ministers.

Lord Fraser of Tullybelton recited the facts in *GCHQ* and continued:[14]

'My Lords, Government Communications Headquarters ("GCHQ") is a branch of the public service under the Foreign and Commonwealth Office, the main functions of which are to ensure the security of the United Kingdom military and official communications and to provide signals intelligence for the Government. These functions are of great importance and they involve handling secret information which is vital to the national security. The main establishment of GCHQ is at Cheltenham where over 4,000 are employed. There are also a number of smaller out-stations one of which is at Bude in Cornwall.

Since 1947, when GCHQ was established in its present form, all the staff employed there have been permitted, and indeed encouraged, to belong to national trade unions, and most of them did so. Six unions were represented at GCHQ. They were all members, though not the only members, of the Council of Civil Service Unions ("CCSU"), the first appellant. The second appellant is the secretary of CCSU. The other appellants are individuals who are employed at GCHQ and who were members of one or other of the unions represented there. A departmental Whitley Council was set up in 1947 and, until

---

[12] [1988] 2 WLR 590 between 602 (post letter A) to 603 (post letter C).   [13] [1985] 1 AC 374.
[14] [1985] 1 AC 374 between 394 (post letter A) and 403 (post letter D).

the events with which this appeal is concerned, there was a well-established practice of consultation between the official side and the trade union side about all important alterations in the terms and conditions of employment of the staff.

On 25 January 1984 all that was abruptly changed. The Secretary of State for Foreign and Commonwealth Affairs announced in the House of Commons that the Government had decided to introduce with immediate effect new conditions of service for staff at GCHQ, the effect of which was that they would no longer be permitted to belong to national trade unions but would be permitted to belong only to a departmental staff association approved by the director of GCHQ. The announcement came as a complete surprise to the trade unions and to the employees at GCHQ, as there had been no prior consultation with them. The principal question raised in this appeal is whether the instruction by which the decision received effect, and which was issued orally on 22 December 1983 by the respondent (who is also the Prime Minister), is valid and effective in accordance with article 4 of the Civil Service Order in Council 1982. The respondent maintains that it is. The appellants maintain that it is invalid because there was a procedural obligation on the respondent to act fairly by consulting the persons concerned before exercising her power under article 4 of the Order in Council, and she failed to do so. Underlying that question, and logically preceding it, is the question whether the courts, and your Lordships' House in its judicial capacity, have power to review the instruction on the ground of a procedural irregularity, having regard particularly to the facts (a) that it was made in the exercise of a power conferred under the royal prerogative and not by statute, and (b) that it concerned national security . . .

The mechanism on which the Minister for the Civil Service relied to alter the terms and conditions of service at GCHQ was an "instruction" issued by her under the Order in Council of 1982, article 4. That article so far as relevant provides as follows:

> "As regards Her Majesty's Home Civil Service—(a) the Minister for the Civil Service may from time to time make regulations or give instructions—. . . (ii) for controlling the conduct of the service, and providing for the classification of all persons employed therein and . . . the conditions of service of all such persons; . . ."

The Order in Council was not issued under powers conferred by any Act of Parliament. Like the previous Orders in Council on the same subject it was issued by the sovereign by virtue of her prerogative, but of course on the advice of the government of the day. In these circumstances Mr Alexander submitted that the instruction was not open to review by the courts because it was an emanation of the prerogative. This submission involves two propositions: (1) that prerogative powers are discretionary, that is to say they may be exercised at the discretion of the sovereign (acting on advice in accordance with modern constitutional practice) and the way in which they are exercised is not open to review by the courts; (2) that an instruction given in the exercise of a delegated power conferred by the sovereign under the prerogative enjoys the same immunity from review as if it were itself a direct exercise of prerogative power . . .

As *De Keyser* shows, the courts will inquire into whether a particular prerogative power exists or not, and, if it does exist, into its extent. But once the existence and the extent of a power are established to the satisfaction of the court, the court cannot inquire into the propriety of its exercise. That is undoubtedly the position as laid down in the authorities to which I have briefly referred and it is plainly reasonable in relation to many of the most important prerogative powers which are concerned with control of the armed forces and with foreign policy and with other matters which are unsuitable for discussion or review in the law courts. In the present case the prerogative power involved is power to regulate the Home Civil Service, and I recognise there is no obvious reason why the mode of exercise of that power should be immune from review by the courts. Nevertheless to permit such review would run counter to the great weight of authority to which I have briefly referred. Having regard to the opinion I have reached on Mr Alexander's second proposition, it is unnecessary to decide whether his first proposition is sound or not and I prefer to leave that question open until it arises in a case where a decision upon it is necessary. I therefore assume, without deciding, that his first proposition is correct and that all powers exercised directly under the prerogative are immune from challenge in the courts. I pass to consider his second proposition.

The second proposition depends for its soundness upon whether the power conferred by article 4 of the Order in Council of 1982 on the Minister for the Civil Service of "providing for . . . the conditions of service" of the Civil Service is subject to an implied obligation to act fairly. (Such an obligation is sometimes referred to as an obligation to obey the rules of natural justice, but that is a less appropriate description, at least when applied, as in the present case, to a power which is executive and not judicial.) There is no doubt that, if the Order in Council of 1982 had been made under the authority of a statute, the power delegated to the minister by article 4 would have been construed as being subject to an obligation to act fairly. I am unable to see why the words conferring the same powers should be construed differently merely because their source was an Order in Council made under the prerogative. It is all the more difficult in the face of article 6(4) of the Order in Council of 1982 which provides that the Interpretation Act 1978 shall apply to the Order; it would of course apply to a statutory order. There seems no sensible reason why the words should not bear the same meaning whatever the source of authority for the legislation in which they are contained. The Order in Council of 1982 was described by Sir Robert Armstrong in his first affidavit as primary legislation; that is, in my opinion, a correct description, subject to the qualification that the Order in Council, being made under the prerogative, derives its authority from the sovereign alone and not, as is more commonly the case with legislation, from the sovereign in Parliament. Legislation frequently delegates power from the legislating authority—the sovereign alone in one case, the sovereign in Parliament in the other—to some other person or body and, when that is done, the delegated powers are defined more or less closely by the legislation, in this case by article 4. But whatever their source, powers which are defined, either by reference to their object or by reference to procedure for their exercise, or in some other way, and whether the definition is expressed or implied, are in my opinion normally subject to judicial control to ensure that they are not exceeded. By "normally" I mean provided that considerations of national security do not require otherwise . . .

Mr Blom-Cooper submitted that the minister had a duty to consult the CCSU, on behalf of employees at GCHQ, before giving instruction on 22 December 1983 for making an important change in their conditions of service. His main reason for so submitting was that the employees had a legitimate, or reasonable, expectation that there would be such prior consultation before any important change was made in their conditions.

It is clear that the employees did not have a legal right to prior consultation. The Order in Council confers no such right, and article 4 makes no reference at all to consultation. The Civil Service handbook makes no reference at all to consultation. The Civil Service handbook (Handbook for the New Civil Servant, 1973 edn as amended 1983) which explains the normal method of consultation through the departmental Whitley Council, does not suggest that there is any legal right to consultation; indeed it is careful to recognise that, in the operational field consideration of urgency may make prior consultation impracticable. The Civil Service Pay and Conditions of Service Code expressly states:

"The following terms and conditions also apply to your appointment in the Civil Service. It should be understood, however, that in consequence of the constitutional position of the Crown, the Crown has the right to change its employees' conditions of service at any time, and that they hold their appointments at the pleasure of the Crown."

But even where a person claiming some benefit or privilege has no legal right to it, as a matter of private law, he may have a legitimate expectation of receiving the benefit or privilege, and, if so, the courts will protect his expectation by judicial review as a matter of public law.

. . . Legitimate, or reasonable, expectation may arise either from an express promise given on behalf of a public authority or from the existence of a regular practice which the claimant can reasonably expect to continue . . .

The submission on behalf of the appellants is that the present case is of the latter type. The test of that is whether the practice of prior consultation of the staff on significant changes in their conditions of service was so well established by 1983 that it would be unfair or inconsistent with good administration for the Government to depart from the practice in this case. Legitimate expectations such as are now under consideration will always relate to a benefit or privilege to which the claimant has no right in private law, and it may even be to one which conflicts with his private law rights. In the present case the evidence shows that, ever since GCHQ began in 1947, prior consultation has been the invariable rule when conditions of service were to be significantly altered. Accordingly in my opinion if there had been no question of national security involved, the appellants would have had a legitimate expectation that the minister would consult them before issuing the instruction of 22 December 1983. The next question, therefore, is whether it has been shown that consideration of national security supersedes the expectation.

The issue here is not whether the minister's instruction was proper or fair or justifiable on its merits. These matters are not for the courts to determine. The sole issue is whether the decision on which the instruction was based was reached by a process that was fair to the staff at GCHQ. As my noble and learned friend Lord Brightman said in *Chief Constable of the North Wales Police v Evans* [1982] 1 WLR 1155, 1173: "Judicial review is concerned, not with the decision, but with the decision-making process."

I have already explained my reason for holding that, if no question of national security arose, the decision-making process in this case would have been unfair. The respondent's case is that she deliberately made the decision without prior consultation because prior consultation "would involve a real risk that it would occasion the very kind of disruption [at GCHQ] which was a threat to national security and which it was intended to avoid" . . .

The question is one of evidence. The decision on whether the requirements of national security outweigh the duty of fairness in any particular case is for the Government and not for the courts; the Government alone has access to the necessary information, and in any event the judicial process is unsuitable for reaching decisions on national security. But if the decision is successfully challenged, on the ground that it has been reached by a process which is unfair, then the Government is under an obligation to produce evidence that the decision was in fact based on grounds of national security. Authority for both these points is found in *The Zamora*. The former point is dealt with in the well-known passage from the advice of the Judicial Committee delivered by Lord Parker of Waddington, at p. 107:

"Those who are responsible for the national security must be the sole judges of what the national security requires. It would be obviously undesirable that such matters should be made the subject of evidence in a court of law or otherwise discussed in public."

The second point, less often referred to, appears at p. 106 and more particularly at p. 108 where this passage occurs:

"In their Lordships' opinion the order appealed from was wrong, not because, as contended by the appellants, there is by international law no right at all to requisition ships or goods in the custody of the court, but because the judge had before him *no satisfactory evidence* that such a right was exercisable . . ." (Emphasis added.)

In *Chandler v DPP* [1964] AC 763, which was an appeal by persons who had been convicted of a breach of the peace under section 1 of the Official Secrets Act 1911 by arranging a demonstration by the Campaign for Nuclear Disarmament on an operational airfield at Wethersfield, Lord Reid said, at p. 790:

"The question more frequently arises as to what is or is not in the public interest. I do not subscribe to the view that the Government or a minister must always or even as a general rule have the last word about that. But here we are dealing with a very special matter—interfering with a prohibited place which Wethersfield was."

But the court had had before it evidence from an Air Commodore that the airfield was of importance for national security. Both Lord Reid and Viscount Radcliffe, at p. 796, referred to the evidence as being relevant to their refusal of the appeal.

The evidence in support of this part of the respondent's case came from Sir Robert Armstrong in his first affidavit . . . it does set out the respondent's view that to have entered into prior consultation would have served to bring out the vulnerability of areas of operation to those who had shown themselves ready to organise disruption. That must be read along with the earlier parts of the affidavit in which Sir Robert had dealt in some detail with the attitude of the trade unions which I have referred to earlier in this speech. The affidavit, read as a whole, does in my opinion undoubtedly constitute evidence that the Minister did indeed consider that prior consultation would have involved a risk of precipitating disruption at GCHQ. I am accordingly of the opinion that the respondent has shown that her decision was one which not only could reasonably have been based, but was in fact based, on considerations of national security, which outweighed what would otherwise have been the reasonable expectation on the part of the appellants for prior consultation . . . '

Lord Scarman ([1985] 1 AC 374, 404 letter C to 407 letter A):

'My Lords, I would dismiss this appeal for one reason only. I am satisfied that the respondent has made out a case on the ground of national security. Notwithstanding the criticisms which can be made of the evidence and despite the fact that the point was not raised, or, if it was, was not clearly made before the case reached the Court of Appeal, I have no doubt that the respondent refused to consult the unions before issuing her instruction of the 22 December 1983 because she feared that, if she did, union-organised disruption of the monitoring services of GCHQ could well result. I am further satisfied that the fear was one which a reasonable minister in the circumstances in which she found herself could reasonably entertain. I am also satisfied that a reasonable minister could reasonably consider such disruption to constitute a threat to national security. I would, therefore, deny relief to the appellants upon their application for judicial review of the instruction, the effect of which was that staff at GCHQ would no longer be permitted to belong to a national trade union . . .

My Lords, I conclude, therefore, that where a question as to the interest of national security arises in judicial proceedings the court has to act on evidence. In some cases a judge or jury is required by law to be satisfied that the interest is proved to exist: in others, the interest is a factor to be considered in the review of the exercise of an executive discretionary power. Once the factual basis is established by evidence so that the court is satisfied that the interest of national security is a relevant factor to be considered in the determination of the case, the court will accept the opinion of the Crown or its responsible officer as to what is required to meet it, unless it is possible to show that the opinion was one which no reasonable minister advising the Crown could in the circumstances reasonably have held. There is no abdication of the judicial function, but there is a common sense limitation recognised by the judges as to what is justiciable: and the limitation is entirely consistent with the general development of the modern case law of judicial review.'

Lord Diplock ([1985] 1 AC 374, 408 post letter E to 413 post letter B):

'Judicial review, now regulated by RSC, Ord 53, provides the means by which judicial control of administrative action is exercised. The subject matter of every judicial review is a decision made by some person (or body of persons) whom I will call the "decision-maker" or else a refusal by him to make a decision.

To qualify as a subject for judicial review the decision must have consequences which affect some person (or body of persons) other than the decision-maker, although it may affect him too. It must affect such other person either:

(a) by altering rights or obligations of that person which are enforceable by or against him in private law; or

(b) by depriving him of some benefit or advantage which either (i) he had in the past been permitted by the decision-maker to enjoy and which he can legitimately expect to be permitted to continue to do until there has been communicated to him some rational grounds for withdrawing it on which he has been given an opportunity to comment; or (ii) he has received assurance from the decision-maker will not be withdrawn without giving him first an opportunity of advancing reasons for contending that they should not be withdrawn. (I prefer to continue to call the kind of expectation that qualifies a decision for inclusion in class (b) a "legitimate expectation" rather than a "reasonable expectation", in order thereby to indicate that it has consequences to which effect will be given in public law, whereas an expectation or hope that some benefit or advantage would continue to be enjoyed, although it might well be entertained by a "reasonable" man, would not necessarily have such conse-quences. . . . "Reasonable" furthermore bears different meanings according to whether the context in which it is being used is that of private law or of public law. To eliminate confusion it is best avoided in the latter.)

For a decision to be susceptible to judicial review the decision-maker must be empowered by public law (and not merely, as in arbitration, by agreement between private parties) to make decisions that, if validly made, will lead to administrative action or abstention from action by an authority endowed by law with executive powers, which have one or other of the consequences mentioned in the preceding paragraph. The ultimate source of the decision-making power is nearly always nowadays a statute or subordinate legislation made under the statute; but in the absence of any statute regulating the subject matter of the decision the source of the decision-making power may still be the common law itself, ie, that part of the common law that is given by lawyers the label of "the prerogative". Where this is the source of decision-making power, the power is confined to executive officers of central as distinct from local government and in constitutional practice is generally exercised by those holding ministerial rank.

It was the prerogative that was relied on as the source of the power of the Minister for the Civil Service in reaching her decision of 22 December 1983 that membership of national trade unions should in future be barred to all members of the home civil service employed at GCHQ . . .

My Lords, I see no reason why simply because a decision-making power is derived from a common law and not a statutory source, it should *for that reason only* be immune from judicial review. Judicial review has I think developed to a stage today when without reiterating any analysis of the steps by which the development has come about, one can conveniently classify under three heads the grounds upon which administrative action is subject to control by judicial review. The first ground I would call "illegality", the second "irrationality" and the third "procedural impropriety". That is not to say that further development on a case by case basis may not in course of time add further grounds. I have in mind particularly the possible adoption in the future of the principle of "proportionality" which is recognised in the administrative law of several of our fellow members of the European Economic Community; but to dispose of the instant case the three already well-established heads that I have mentioned will suffice.

By "illegality" as a ground for judicial review I mean that the decision-maker must understand correctly the law that regulates his decision-making power and must give effect to it. Whether he had or not is par excellence a justiciable question to be decided, in the event of dispute, by those persons, the judges, by whom the judicial power of the state is exercisable.

By "irrationality" I mean what can by now be succinctly referred to as *"Wednesbury* unreasonable-ness". It applies to a decision which is so outrageous in its defiance of logic or of accepted moral standards that no sensible person who had applied his mind to the question to be decided could have arrived at it. Whether a decision falls within this category is a question that judges by their training and experience should be well equipped to answer, or else there would be something badly wrong with our judicial system . . .

I have described the third head as "procedural impropriety" rather than failure to observe basic rules of natural justice or failure to act with procedural fairness towards the person who will be affected by the decision. This is because susceptibility to judicial review under this head covers also failure by an administrative tribunal to observe procedural rules that are expressly laid down in the legislative instrument by which its jurisdiction is conferred, even where such failure does not involve any denial of natural justice . . .

As respects "procedural propriety" I see no reason why it should not be a ground for judicial review of a decision made under powers of which the ultimate source is the prerogative. Such indeed was one of the grounds that formed the subject matter of judicial review in *R v Criminal Injuries Compensation Board, ex p Lain* [1967] 2 QB 864. Indeed, where the decision is one which does not alter rights or obligations enforceable in private law but only deprives a person of legitimate expectations, "procedural impropriety" will normally provide the only ground on which the decision is open to judicial review. But in any event what procedure will satisfy the public law requirement of procedural propriety depends upon the subject matter of the decision, the executive functions of the decision-maker (if the decision is not that of an administrative tribunal) and the particular circumstances in which the decision came to be made.

My Lords, in the instant case the immediate subject matter of the decision was a change in one of the terms of employment of civil servants employed at GCHQ. That the executive functions of the Minister for the Civil Service, in her capacity as such, included making a decision to change any of those terms, except in so far as they related to remuneration, expenses and allowances, is not disputed. It does not seem to me to be of any practical significance whether or not as a matter of strict legal analysis this power is based upon the rule of constitutional law to which I have already alluded that the employment of any civil servant may be terminated at any time without notice and that upon such termination the same civil servant may be re-engaged on different terms. The rule of terminability of employment in the civil service without notice, of which the existence is beyond doubt, must in any event have the consequence that the continued enjoyment by a civil servant in the *future* of a right under a particular term of his employment cannot be the subject of any right enforceable by him in private law; at most it can only be a legitimate expectation.

Prima facie, therefore, civil servants employed at GCHQ who were members of national trade unions had, at best, in December 1983, a legitimate expectation that they would continue to enjoy the benefits of such membership and of representation by those trade unions in any consultations and negotiations with representatives of the management of that government department as to changes in any term of their employment. So, but again prima facie only, they were entitled, as a matter of public law under the head of "procedural propriety", before administrative action was taken on a decision to withdraw that benefit, to have communicated to the national trade unions by which they had theretofore been represented the reason for such withdrawal, and for such unions to be given an opportunity to comment on it.

The reason why the Minister for the Civil Service decided on 22 December 1983 to withdraw this benefit was in the interests of national security. National security is the responsibility of the executive government; what action is needed to protect its interests is, as the cases cited by my learned friend, Lord Roskill, establish and common sense itself dictates, a matter upon which those upon whom the responsibility rests, and not the courts of justice, must have the last word. It is par excellence a non-justiciable question. The judicial process is totally inept to deal with the sort of problems which it involves.

The executive government likewise decided, and this would appear to be a collective decision of cabinet ministers involved, that the interests of national security required that no notice should be given of the decision before administrative action had been taken to give effect to it. The reason for this was the risk that advance notice to the national unions of the executive government's intention would attract the very disruptive action prejudicial to the national security the recurrence of which the decision barring membership of national trade unions to civil servants employed at GCHQ was designed to prevent.

There was ample evidence to which reference is made by others of your Lordships that this was indeed a real risk; so the crucial point of law in this case is whether procedural propriety must give way to national security when there is conflict between (1) on the one hand, the prima facie rule of "procedural propriety" in public law, applicable to a case of legitimate expectations that a benefit ought not to be withdrawn until the reason for its proposed withdrawal has been communicated to the person who has theretofore enjoyed that benefit and that person has been given an opportunity to comment on the reason, and (2) on the other hand, action that is needed to be taken in the interests of national security, for which the executive government bears the responsibility and alone has access to sources of information that qualify it to judge what the necessary action is. To that there can, in my opinion, be only one sensible answer. That answer is "Yes".'

Subsequent case law has indicated that the power to issue passports is susceptible of review. The decision in *R v Secretary of State for Foreign and Commonwealth Affairs, ex p Everett* illustrates the approach of the courts to issues of justiciability.[15]

O'Connor LJ:

'The facts giving rise to this case can be simply stated. The applicant has been living in Marbella in the south of Spain since June 1984. He was the holder of a British passport which was due to expire on 20 May 1986. In April of that year he filled in the necessary form to apply for a new passport with the supporting documents. That can be issued by a consul in Malaga via the consular department of the British Embassy in Madrid. The matter went to Madrid, but no passport was forthcoming. On 12 May the applicant sent a lawyer to the British Embassy to find out why he had not received a new passport and according to the affidavit of the notary he was told that a passport was not going to be issued but that a travel document, which was effectively a one-way ticket to England, could be issued. The report of this interview does not record whether the Spanish lawyer asked why his client was not getting a passport, nor does it record being told why he was not given one. In the result solicitors in London on behalf of the applicant wrote to the Passport Office. It turns out that, when passports are issued abroad, it is handled by the Foreign Office, as one might expect, from the embassy or consulate as the case may be. Thus it was that a reply came back on 24 July asking why no passport had been issued. That letter reads:

> "I refer to your letter of 2 June addressed to the Passport Office.
> . . . However, British passports are issued overseas at the discretion of the Secretary of State for Foreign and Commonwealth Affairs and it is a fundamental principle that they should not be issued to persons for whose arrest a warrant has been issued in the United Kingdom. Such a warrant has been issued in respect of [the applicant] and it would clearly not be in the interests of justice if, in these circumstances, a passport were to be issued to him. We therefore consider that the British Embassy in Madrid were justified in refusing to issue a standard passport to [the applicant], who has however been offered an emergency passport to enable him to travel to the United Kingdom only. I regret that we are not in a position to give you details of the warrant for arrest and can only advise that you contact the UK police authorities if you wish to have these."

As a result of that letter these proceedings were launched in October 1986. The relief sought by way of judicial review was certiorari to quash both the oral decision on 12 May in Madrid and that contained in the letter on 24 July, together with an order for mandamus requiring the passport application to be considered in a proper and lawful manner.

The grounds which were given for the relief were that no particulars of the warrant had been made available to the applicant, that he was afforded no opportunity for a hearing before the decision was made in Spain and that therefore the decision was made in a manner which failed to comply with natural justice. So, too, was the attack in the letter of 24 July . . . the Secretary of State objected that

---

[15] [1989] QB 811, between 814 (post letter H) to 819 (post letter C), and 820 (post letter B to post letter F).

judicial review did not lie against the refusal of a passport. That forms the first ground of appeal, because the judge rejected the submission. Once again it can be simply stated. Until the decision of the House of Lords in *Council of Civil Service Unions v Minister for the Civil Service* [1985] AC 374 it was generally assumed that the law was that decisions of the administration taken under the prerogative were not amenable to judicial review, and so one finds a whole series of matters which were not amenable to review. In that case it will be remembered that the order that employees of GCHQ were not to be union members was taken under an Order in Council issued under the prerogative by the Minister for the Civil Service. The first question which had to be decided was whether judicial review of the decision lay at all.

Three of their Lordships, Lord Diplock, Lord Scarman and Lord Roskill, unequivocally held that judicial review of decisions taken under the prerogative did lie. Lord Scarman in his speech stated that it was not the origin of the administrative power, but was the actual factual application which had to be considered. It is quite clear since that decision that there are areas of the exercise of the prerogative which the courts can and will review. There are other areas, some of which were identified in that case, which they will not. Obvious examples are the making of treaties, which the court would not entertain by way of judicial review: so, too, policy decisions on foreign affairs and other matters which are to be found in Lord Roskill's speech. I need not refer to them in this judgment.

The judge held that the issue of a passport fell into an entirely different category. That seems common sense. It is a familiar document to all citizens who travel in the world and it would seem obvious to me that the exercise of the prerogative in the discretion of the Secretary of State is an area where common sense tells one that, if for some reason a passport is wrongly refused for a bad reason, the court should be able to inquire into it. I would reject the submission made on behalf of the Secretary of State that the judge was wrong to review the case.

. . . It seems to me that the Secretary of State, in the fair exercise of his discretion, was entitled to refuse the passport but to give his reason for so doing; and the fair giving of the reason, if the reason be that there is a warrant for the applicant's arrest outstanding, was to tell him when the warrant was issued and what offence was charged. Once he has done that he has all but discharged his duty, but he should, when notifying the applicant that that was the reason for refusing the passport, tell him that if there were any exceptional grounds which might call for the issue of a passport he would consider them. We have been told very properly by counsel for the Secretary of State that it is possible that exceptions may arise on compassionate grounds, eg if such a person were desperately ill in hospital in a foreign country it might be that a passport would be issued or an exception made. Had that been done, no one could challenge the proper exercise of the discretion.

In the present case it has been submitted that the letter of 24 July gives all the information, coupled with the visit of a lawyer on behalf of the applicant in Madrid, and one could assume that the lawyer must have asked why the passport was refused.

Unfortunately I do not think one can assume if he did ask such a question that he necessarily got the answer which would be required and it seems to me that the decision letter of 24 July was not sufficient to give the information which ought to have been given.

That is not an end of the matter, because judicial review is a discretionary remedy and one must look at the position at the time when the application came before the judge. At that stage the applicant knew everything. He was fully armed with lawyers in this country, solicitors and counsel, and there is not a word from him of any sort. There is no suggestion that there are any exceptional circumstances in this case. There is no suggestion from him that there is anything wrong with the warrant, or that he was not wanted on a warrant for an offence of obtaining a false passport or obtaining a passport in the name of Ronald Page by deception: he knew everything which he ought to have been told. He certainly knew when he made representations in the launching of the proceedings.

In those circumstances I cannot see that there are any grounds for thinking that, had the decision letter contained the information which he got later and contained the offer to consider any representations as to exceptional circumstances, any different result would have come about. When the court finds itself in that position, namely that the applicant has suffered no injustice and that to grant the remedy would produce a barren result there are no grounds for granting relief . . .'

Taylor LJ:

'I am in no doubt that the court has power to review the withdrawal or refusal to grant or renew a passport. The House of Lords in *Council of Civil Service Unions v Minister for the Civil Service* [1984] 3 All ER 935, [1985] AC 374 made it clear that the powers of the court cannot be ousted merely by invoking the word "prerogative". The majority of their Lordships indicated that whether judicial review of the exercise of prerogative power is open depends on the subject matter and in particular on whether it is justiciable. At the top of the scale of executive functions under the prerogative are matters of high policy, of which examples were given by their Lordships: making treaties, making law, dissolving Parliament, mobilising the armed forces. Clearly those matters, and no doubt a number of others, are not justiciable. But the grant or refusal of a passport is in a quite different category. It is a matter of administrative decision, affecting the rights of individuals and their freedom of travel. It raises issues which are just as justiciable as, for example, the issues arising in immigration cases. Counsel for the Secretary of State sought to put the grant of passports under the umbrella of foreign affairs and thereby elevate it to that level of high policy which would preclude the intervention of the courts. He says that the grant of a passport involves a request in the name of the Queen to a foreign power to afford the holder free passage and protection. It also extends the protection and assistance of the Crown to the holder whilst he is abroad.

However, those considerations do not, to my mind, render issues arising on the refusal of a passport non-justiciable. The ready issue of a passport is a normal expectation of every citizen, unless there is good reason for making him an exception. The issues arising are no more likely to have foreign policy repercussions than those arising, to take the same analogy as before, in immigration cases . . .'[16]

Clearly much depends in these cases on the issue of the 'legitimate expectation' of the applicant for review. The approach of the Courts to this issue is illustrated by *R v Secretary of State for the Home Department, ex p Ruddock*.[17] The case concerned the 'tapping' of telephones, and an initial issue was whether a simple plea of 'this was done in the interests of national security' would be enough to prevent further consideration of the matter by the courts.

Taylor J referred to the *GCHQ Case* and continued:

'Mr Laws [Counsel for the Secretary of State] does not challenge here the jurisdiction of the court to decide the issues raised. He bases his submission on a plea to the court's discretion. In effect the plea amounts to this: the Secretary of State invariably maintains silence in the interests of national security on issues such as are raised here. The court in its discretion should do likewise, and since making findings to decide the case may break that silence, the court should, in Lord Scarman's phrase, abdicate its judicial function. I cannot agree with that, either as a general proposition or in this particular case. I do not accept that the court should never inquire into a complaint against a minister if he says his policy is to maintain silence in the interests of national security. To take an extreme and one hopes unlikely example, suppose an application were put before the court alleging a warrant was improperly issued by a Secretary of State against a political opponent, and suppose the application to be supported by the production of a note in the minister's own hand acknowledging the criteria did not apply but giving instructions that the phone be tapped nevertheless to see if anything discreditable could be learnt. It could not be sensibly argued that the department's invariable policy of silence

---

[16] [1989] 1 QB 811, 820 post letter A to letter F.

[17] [1987] 1 WLR 1482, between 1491 (post letter E) to 1492 (post letter F), and 1497 (post letter A to post letter G).

should require the court meekly to follow suit and decline to decide such a case. At the other extreme, I recognise there could occur a case where the issue raised was so sensitive and the revelations necessarily following its decision so damaging to national security that the court might have to take special measures (for example sitting in camera or prohibiting the mention of names). Conceivably (although I would reserve the point) in an extreme case the court might have to decline to try the issues. But in all such cases, cogent evidence of potential damage to national security flowing from the trial of the issues would have to be adduced, whether in open court or in camera, to justify any modification of the court's normal procedure. Totally to oust the court's supervisory jurisdiction in a field where ex hypothesi the citizen can have no right to be consulted is a draconian and dangerous step indeed. Evidence to justify the court's declining to decide a case (if such a course is ever justified) would need to be very strong and specific.

What is the evidence here? Sir Brian Cubbon explains why it is the invariable policy of the Secretary of State neither to confirm nor deny the existence of a warrant in any case so that no inferences can be drawn in regard to that case or any other from what is or is not said by the Secretary of State or his department. But that policy is not vitiated if in a case where evidence is before the court concerning an alleged warrant the court proceeds to consider it. The respondent's policy remains intact. He and his department maintain their silence. No inferences can be drawn about the given case or any later case from anything which they either say or do not say. Moreover, Sir Brian Cubbon does not say in his affidavit that it would be prejudicial to national security if the court were to make findings in this case. Counsel for the Secretary of State has argued the court should not do so, but without any evidence to that specific effect. Apart from the plea to the court to follow the department's policy of non-disclosure, no other argument based on national security or the wider public interest was advanced. It was not, for example, suggested here, as elsewhere, that the need for MI5 to appear leakproof should inhibit the court. No application was made that Miss Massiter's affidavit should not be read aloud, or that it should be heard in camera. Its main contents had already been relayed to the nation on television over a year ago. In these circumstances I see no grounds for refusing, as a matter of discretion, to deal with this application which I undoubtedly have jurisdiction to hear. I bear in mind that every citizen has a right to come to the courts for relief, and it is well established that even where statute is relied on, only the most clear and unequivocal words would entitle the courts to deny him access.'

Taylor J referred to the discussion of 'legitimate expectation' in the *GCHQ* case and other authorities and continued:

'On those authorities I conclude that the doctrine of legitimate expectation in essence imposes a duty to act fairly. Whilst most of the cases are concerned, as Lord Roskill said, with a right to be heard, I do not think the doctrine is so confined. Indeed, in a case where ex hypothesi there is no right to be heard, it may be thought the more important to fair dealing that a promise or undertaking given by a minister as to how he will proceed should be kept. Of course such promise or undertaking must not conflict with his statutory duty or his duty, as here, in the exercise of a prerogative power. I accept the submission of counsel for the Secretary of State that the respondent cannot fetter his discretion. By declaring a policy he does not preclude any possible need to change it. But then if the practice has been to publish the current policy, it would be incumbent on him in dealing fairly to publish the new policy, unless again that would conflict with his duties. Had the criteria here needed changing for national security reasons, no doubt the respondent could have changed them. Had those reasons prevented him also from publishing the new criteria, no doubt he could have refrained from doing so. Had he even decided to keep the criteria but depart from them in this single case for national security reasons, no doubt those reasons would have afforded him a defence to judicial review as in the *GCHQ* case. It is no part of the Secretary of State's evidence or argument here, however, that the published criteria were inapplicable, either because they had been changed or abandoned or because for good reason (eg national security) it was justifiable to depart from them. Sir Brian Cubbon's evidence amounts to an acceptance that the criteria were throughout regarded as binding and an assertion that all decisions under his purview have been made in accordance with them. So the argument of counsel for the Secretary of State that provided he acts in good faith for a proper purpose the respondent could grant a warrant outside the criteria and not be subject to judicial review is irrelevant on the evidence he had adduced.

As to the strength of the legitimate expectation here, not only were the criteria repeated publicly in similar terms some six times between 1952 and 1982, the Home Secretary in office at the relevant time adopted them in the most trenchant terms which Sir Brian quotes in his affidavit as follows: "I would authorise interception only in those cases where the criteria set out in the White Paper were clearly met." It would be hard to imagine a stronger case of an expectation arising in Lord Fraser's words "either from an express promise given on behalf of a public authority or from the existence of a regular practice which the claimant can reasonably expect to continue". Here it was both.'

However, the general power to conduct foreign relations and to make treaties appears non-justiciable. This seems to follow from *R v Secretary of State for Foreign and Commonwealth Affairs, ex p Rees Mogg*.[18] To enable understanding of this case a few definitions must initially be given (for the development of the European Community see chapter 7):

(a) a treaty—an international agreement between states intended to have legal consequences for their relationships (sometimes known as a 'convention'—this use of the word should *not* be confused with constitutional conventions);

(b) a protocol—a subsidiary or ancillary agreement to a main treaty;

(c) dualism—in international law a dualist state is one where any changes required in national law as a result of making a treaty have to be brought about by national legislation, and do not automatically occur—the United Kingdom is a dualist state.

In December 1991 the leaders of the governments of the EC member states agreed the Maastricht Treaty—The Treaty on European Union. This contained seven main sections (or 'titles') and was followed by a number of protocols. In international law the fact that a state signs a treaty does not commit it to sign any subsidiary protocols, and in the case of Maastricht the United Kingdom did not sign the protocol on social policy—thus John Major performed the so-called 'opt out'. For the treaty as agreed to come into force it had to be ratified formally by all the member states according to their own constitutional arrangements (eg referendums in Denmark and France). In the United Kingdom this involved (because the United Kingdom is 'dualist') the passage of legislation because some changes in the European Communities Act 1972 were needed. The European Communities (Amendment) Act 1993 was passed, after the government survived a vote of confidence on the issue, in July 1993, and the United Kingdom government then had to face a challenge to the legality of its action from Lord Rees-Mogg, the former editor of *The Times* and a campaigner for a UK referendum on the Maastricht Treaty.

There was one major issue concerning the prerogative.

Under the prerogative the Crown is free to make such treaties as it desires; the approval of Parliament is, in general, only required if a treaty will lead to a change in UK law. So far as the Maastricht Treaty was concerned certain parts—Titles II, III and IV—did require Parliamentary approval because they required changes in the European Communities Act 1972, and the 1993 Act made consequential provision for their approval. Title V, however, which created a 'common foreign and security policy' for the EC, including 'all questions related to the security of the Union, including the eventual framing of a common defence policy, which might in time lead to a common defence', was not specifically dealt with by the

[18] [1994] 1 All ER 457.

1993 Act because it related solely to matters within the royal prerogative, ie the conduct of foreign relations and the disposition of forces, and was an intergovernmental agreement which could have no impact on UK domestic law. Counsel for Lord Rees-Mogg argued this amounted to the abandonment or transfer of prerogative power by the Crown, and that was something the Crown could not do without statutory authority. He submitted that the effect of Title V of the Maastricht Treaty would be that the Crown had transferred its prerogative power in relation to foreign policy, security and ultimately defence to the European Council without statutory authority.

How could the court deal with the claim? There were two avenues open:

(1) to accept the argument of counsel for the Secretary of State, Mr Kentridge QC, that such a matter is not one for judges to deal with, ie it is one of the prerogative actions which simply cannot be dealt with in court: see *Blackburn v A-G*[19] and *J H Rayner (Mincing Lane) Ltd v Department of Trade and Industry*;[20]

(2) to accept that the court had jurisdiction to decide the matter. The court followed the latter course because it appears open for the courts to *examine* the text of an international agreement to determine whether any rule of the common law or statute, or any constitutional convention, has been contravened: see *ex p Molyneaux*.[21] Thus, in the instant case the court proceeded on the *assumption* that it was entitled to consider the issue, and appeared to accept that the principle of the non justiciability of treaties is not absolute, though the *negotiation and signing* of treaties is non justiciable.

The court examined Title V and concluded that in fact it did not amount to a transfer of prerogative power. The United Kingdom is a party to a number of international security and defence treaties, eg the UN Treaty and the NATO Treaty, and no one has ever suggested that they are illegal transfers of prerogative power. Title V should be read in the same way. Lloyd LJ stated: 'In the last resort, as had been pointed out in argument, it could presumably be open to the government to denounce the treaty or at least to fail to comply with its international obligations under Title V.' The court therefore rejected the argument on the prerogative.

Turning to another of Lord Roskill's excluded matters, the prerogative of mercy, further development has also occurred. To set *R v Secretary of State for the Home Department, ex p Bentley*[22] in context it is necessary to rehearse the background facts of what has become one of the most controversial British murder trials of the last half century—the subject of numerous books, documentaries and even a film.

In December 1952 Derek Bentley (B) and Christopher Craig (C) were convicted of the murder of PC George Miles. B and C had been involved in an attempted burglary; both were armed, B with a knife and knuckle-duster, C with a gun. They were interrupted by the police; B was captured. C held the police at bay with his gun, and B who broke free was then alleged to say: 'Let him have it, Chris.' C then shot and *wounded* a policeman. B was then recaptured, *after which* C shot and killed PC Miles. Though C did the shooting both he and B were engaged in an alleged 'joint venture' and so, in law, both were equally guilty of the killing of PC Miles. Both were charged with murder, found guilty, and sentenced—C to be detained 'during Her Majesty's pleasure' for he was only 16 and too young to hang. B, however, was sentenced to death. He was 19—but illiterate, with a mental age of 11 and an IQ of 66. B was hanged, despite recommendations for mercy from his trial jury. B's family thereafter fought to establish that B should not have been executed. It is, for instance, arguable that at the time

---

[19] [1971] 1 WLR 1037.   [20] [1990] 2 AC 418.   [21] [1986] 1 WLR 331.   [22] [1994] QB 349.

PC Miles was shot any joint venture between B and C was over for B was in custody. It is also most certain that when B said: 'Let him have it, Chris' he was actually pleading with C to surrender his gun; he was not urging armed resistance. After the death of B's parents his sister, Iris, continued the struggle to establish his innocence.

In October 1992 the then Home Secretary, Mr Kenneth Clarke, refused to exercise the prerogative of mercy, and declined to grant a pardon. He stated that a free pardon could 'by long-established policy' only be granted to a person whose 'moral as well as technical innocence . . . can be established. I do not believe that this is the case on either point in relation to Derek Bentley.' Iris Bentley sought judicial review of *that* decision.

Watkins LJ in the Divisional Court began by rehearsing the history of the case and then stated the law relating to judicial review of the royal prerogative. He reiterated that powers are not beyond judicial review simply because they are part of the prerogative, and that it established that 'some aspects of the exercise of the royal prerogative were reviewable'. But for a review to take place there must be illegality, irrationality or procedural impropriety. What was the legal basis of Iris Bentley's claim? Watkins LJ stated: 'the substance of the applicant's case was that the Home Secretary had failed to recognise the fact that the prerogative of mercy was capable of being exercised in many different circumstances and over a wide range and therefore failed to meet the facts of the present case'.

In particular the Home Secretary could have considered granting a pardon less than a free pardon: a pardon may be conditional. It may substitute a lesser sentence for the original penalty. There is no objection in principle to the grant of a posthumous conditional pardon. The prerogative of mercy is a flexible power which nowadays is a constitutional safeguard against mistakes. The grant of a conditional pardon could thus be a recognition that a mistake had been made.

Watkins LJ declared he was not satisfied that Mr Clarke had given sufficient consideration to this power to grant some other form of pardon which would be suitable to the circumstances of the present case. In the circumstances the court, while not considering it appropriate to make a specific order, 'invited' the Home Secretary to look at the matter again 'and to examine whether it could be just to exercise the prerogative of mercy in such a way as to give full recognition to the now generally accepted view that Bentley should have been reprieved'.

The interest of the case from a constitutional point of view is that it indicates that the Home Secretary made a mistake of law in declining to grant a full pardon. He should have realised the prerogative is a broad, flexible power capable of adaptation to many circumstances. Though it is not for a court to direct *how* the prerogative of mercy should be used in any given case, the court may intervene in any case where the prerogative is misapplied in contravention of the law. The court may not say to the Home Secretary, 'you shall pardon Derek Bentley', but it may say: 'you were legally wrong not to consider the width and flexibility of your prerogative powers, for then you might have found a way of putting right something that is now generally considered to have been an injustice'.

On 30 July 1993 the Home Secretary granted a unique 'partial' pardon to Derek Bentley, while in *R v Bentley*[23] the Court of Appeal stated that Derek Bentley had not been fairly tried. It still appears, however, that the court would not enquire into an exercise of the prerogative of mercy where there was no issue of law as there was in the Bentley case: see *Hanratty v Lord Butler*.[24] In other parts of the British Commonwealth, however, it appears the prerogative of mercy remains unreviewable, see *Reckley v Minister of Public Services (No 2)*.[25]

---

[23] [1999] Crim LR 330.   [24] [1971] 115 Sol Jo 386.   [25] [1996] AC 527.

In the United Kingdom it has been further accepted, in principle, that prerogative decisions on the composition of the armed forces, for example a ban on homosexuals, are justiciable, though hard to impugn on grounds of irrationality, see *R v Ministry of Defence, ex p Smith*.[26]

In the context of justiciability, regard must also be had to *Burmah Oil Co Ltd v Lord Advocate*.[27] The issue in this case, whether the Crown was bound to pay compensation for damage done in the Second World War, has been dealt with by the War Damage Act 1965 which abolished any right at common law to receive compensation for any damage to, or destruction of, property, within or outside the United Kingdom, as a consequence of acts lawfully done by, or under the authority of, the Crown during, or in contemplation of the outbreak of, a war. The speeches in the House of Lords, however, cast light on problems inherent in determining the extent of prerogative powers.

Lord Reid:

'It is not easy to discover and decide the law regarding the royal prerogative and the consequences of its exercise . . .

The definition of Dicey (*Law of the Constitution*, 10th edn, p 424), always quoted with approval: "The residue of discretionary or arbitrary authority, which at any given time is legally left in the hands of the Crown", does not take us very far. It is extremely difficult to be precise because in former times there was seldom a clear-cut view of the constitutional position . . . I am no historian but I would suppose that Maitland is as good a guide as any. In his *Constitutional History* he says: "I do not wish you to think that a definite theory to the effect that while legislative power resides in king and parliament, the so-called executive power is in the king alone, was a guiding theory of mediaeval politics. On the contrary, the line between what the king could do without a parliament, and what he could only do with the aid of parliament, was only drawn very gradually, and it fluctuated from time to time." (p 196) . . . So it appears to me that we must try to see what the position was after it had become clear that sovereignty resided in the King in Parliament. Any rights thereafter exercised by the King (or the executive) alone must be regarded as a part of sovereignty which Parliament chose to leave in his hands. There is no doubt that control of the armed forces has been left to the prerogative . . . subject to the power of Parliament to withhold supply and to refuse to continue legislation essential for the maintenance of a standing army: and so also has the waging of war . . . [The] prerogative certainly covers doing all those things in an emergency which are necessary for the conduct of war . . . '

Viscount Radcliffe:

'What, then, do we mean by the prerogative in this connection? I say "this connection" because in our history the prerogatives of the Crown have been many and various, and it would not be possible to embrace them under a single description. Some of them were or came to be beneficial or sources of profit to the Crown—these, I suppose, had their origin in the military tenures and the status of the feudal superior, and examples of them would be wardship . . . and the right to the royal minerals. Others were as much duties as rights and were vested in the Sovereign as the leader of the people and the chief executive instrument for protecting the public safety. No one seems to doubt that a prerogative of this latter kind was exercisable by the Crown in circumstances of sudden and extreme emergency which put that safety in peril . . . I do not think that for present purposes we need say more than that the outbreak or imminence of war, provided that it carried with it the threat of imminent invasion or attack, did arm the Crown with what may be called the war prerogative.

---

[26] [1996] QB 517.

[27] [1965] AC 75 at 99 (post letter D) to 100 (post letter D), 114 (post letter F) to 116 (post letter B), and 147 (post letter G) to 156 (post letter E).

It is of some importance to speak of this as the war, not as the defence, prerogative. Whatever else may be deduced from the lengthy historical researches made for the purposes of the *De Keyser Hotel* case, it does seem clear that the Crown never claimed or sought to exercise in time of peace a right to take land, however much required for the defence of the realm, except by agreement or under statutory powers . . .

I do not know who is in a position to say on what occasions and for what purposes this war preroga-tive was exercised in our history. Nevertheless, it has remained a matter of general acceptance that there was such a power and, since it was a power that came into existence on the occurrence of a sudden emergency, no one could well be in a position to categorise the acts that it authorised, since, depending on the necessity of the occasion, their nature would be determined by the nature of that occasion. To put the matter quite generally, the Crown was supposed to have the right in such an emergency to command and direct the services of its subjects and to take their land and property for the purpose of protecting the realm from its enemies . . .

An instance of an undoubted exercise of the war prerogative in recent time is the proclamation issued by the Crown on 3 August, 1914 (one day before the war began), authorising the Admiralty to requisition British ships for war purposes. No statute authorised the making of this Proclamation, and in both *The Broadmayne* [1916] P 64 and *The Crown of Leon* [1921] 1 KB 595 it was accepted as an act of prerogative power . . .'

Lord Pearce pointed out that the Crown enjoys a much wider power in emergencies than ordinary citizens, encompassing not only *what* may be done, but *when* and *where* and *how* it may be done. He continued, however:

'Bracton's theory that the Crown was subject to the rule of law has, after some vicissitudes in Stuart times, prevailed . . . And even in Stuart times, Crooke J in his dissenting judgment in *Hampden's case* in 1637 [3 State Tr 826 at 1130], after referring to Magna Carta said: "Fortescue Chief Justice setteth down what the law of England is in that kind, as instructions for the young prince. Saith he, 'The king governeth his people by power, not only royal but also politic.' If this power over them were royal only, then he might change the laws of his realm, and charge his subjects with taillage, and other burdens, without their consent. Thus the king can change no laws, nor yet charge them with strange impositions against their wills. He setteth down, as the head is the chief of the body, so the King is the head of his people: He cannot take any thing from them, without their ordinary consent; the common consent it is in parliament . . ." . . .

The prerogative is the residue of the power of sovereignty that has not been superseded or abridged or supplanted temporarily by the power of the King in Parliament . . . There is and there should be a wide residue of power to govern in the crisis of war if, for any reason, Parliament were unable to pass the necessary legislation in time. It is right that in time of war the Government or the armed forces should have the power to take or destroy the property of the subject so far as they deem necessary for the safety of the realm.'

The issues of the justiciability of the Royal Prerogative, and of the willingness of the judiciary to become involved in that process were further highlighted in *R v Secretary of State for the Home Department, ex p Fire Brigades Union*,[28] a case involving some quite acute divisions of judicial opinion.

In 1964 a Criminal Injuries Compensation Scheme was created using prerogative powers to pay compensation to victims of crimes of violence, with payments being made, using the principles of common law damages, and assessed by the Criminal Injuries Compensation Board. The existence of this scheme was put onto a statutory basis by the Criminal Justice Act 1988, which also provided that the relevant provisions were to come into effect on a day or

[28] [1995] 2 AC 513.

days to be appointed by the Secretary of State, until when the prerogative scheme remained in force. These orders were not made, so the old prerogative was never supplanted by statute—a point of distinction between the present case and earlier authorities such as the *De Keyser* case considered above. Then, in 1993, a further government White Paper proposed the introduction of a new non-statutory scheme of compensation in which the tortious basis of compensation previously used was to be replaced by flat-rate tariffs. This would considerably reduce the cost of the scheme. The White Paper also announced that the relevant provisions of the 1988 Act would not be brought into effect, while in 1994 the government announced that the new non-statutory scheme would come into effect on 1 April of that year. This would effectively render the commencement of the statutory scheme impossible. The decision of the government to proceed in this way was challenged as illegal by trades unions representing workers who were likely to suffer from criminal injuries in the course of their employment. The case turned on whether the decision not to commence the 1988 Act scheme was illegal, in view of the introduction of the 1994 new non-statutory scheme, and, if so, whether that decision was open to judicial review, or whether, irrespective of its alleged illegality, such a matter was solely one for Parliament who might hold the Secretary of State to account for failure to commence the 1988 Act.

The House of Lords divided on these issues, the majority opinion being that of Lord Browne Wilkinson,[29] while Lord Mustill[30] gave a solitary but powerfully argued dissenting opinion.

Lord Browne Wilkinson:

'Although the application for judicial review identifies for attack two decisions by the Secretary of State, in reality the Secretary of State made either a number of interlocking decisions or one composite decision having a number of strands. In order to reach a position in which the new prerogative tariff scheme should come into operation on a permanent basis without Parliament repealing the statutory scheme contained in the 1988 Act, the Secretary of State had to take all the following steps: (1) to resolve not to exercise either immediately or in the future the power or duty conferred on him by section 171(1) to bring the statutory scheme into effect; (2) to discontinue under prerogative power the old, non-statutory, scheme which was in operation down to 1 April 1994; and (3) to introduce under prerogative powers the new tariff scheme. The second of those steps is not directly attacked by the application for judicial review. But, in my judgment, that is not material since all three steps are inextricably interlinked and the legality of the decision to introduce the new tariff scheme must depend, at least in part, on the legality of steps (1) and (2). . . .

It is of central importance in this case that section 171(1) of the 1988 Act (providing that, inter alia, the statutory scheme "shall come into force on such day as the Secretary of State may . . . appoint") is itself in force. It is the applicants' case that, although the section confers a discretion as to the date on which the statutory scheme is to be brought into force, it in addition imposes on him a statutory duty to bring the sections into force at some time . . . if the argument of the applicants is right, there must come a time when the Secretary of State comes under a duty to bring the statutory provisions into force and accordingly the court could grant mandamus against the Secretary of State requiring him to do so. Indeed, the applicants originally sought such an order in the present case. In my judgment it would be most undesirable that, in such circumstances, the court should intervene in the legislative process by requiring an Act of Parliament to be brought into effect. That would be for the courts to tread dangerously close to the area over which Parliament enjoys exclusive jurisdiction, namely the making of legislation. In the absence of clear statutory words imposing a clear statutory duty, in my

---

[29] [1995] 2 AC 513, 549 (post letter D) to 554 (post letter G).
[30] [1995] 2 AC 513, 560 (post letter C) to 568 (post letter C).

judgment, the court should hesitate long before holding that such a provision as section 171(1) imposes a legally enforceable statutory duty on the Secretary of State.

Power

It does not follow that, because the Secretary of State is not under any duty to bring the section into effect, he has an absolute and unfettered discretion whether or not to do so. So to hold would lead to the conclusion that both Houses of Parliament had passed the Bill through all its stages and the Act received the royal assent merely to confer an enabling power on the executive to decide at will whether or not to make the parliamentary provisions a part of the law. Such a conclusion, drawn from a section to which the sidenote is "commencement", is not only constitutionally dangerous but flies in the face of common sense. The provisions for bringing sections into force under section 171(1) apply not only to the statutory scheme but to many other provisions. For example, the provisions of Pts I, II and III relating to extradition, documentary evidence in criminal proceedings and other evidence in criminal proceedings are made subject to the same provisions. Surely, it cannot have been the intention of Parliament to leave it in the entire discretion of the Secretary of State whether or not to effect such important changes to the criminal law. In the absence of express provisions to the contrary in the Act, the plain intention of Parliament in conferring on the Secretary of State the power to bring certain sections into force is that such power is to be exercised so as to bring those sections into force when it is appropriate and unless there is a subsequent change of circumstances which would render it inappropriate to do so.

If, as I think, that is the clear purpose for which the power in section 171(1) was conferred on the Secretary of State, two things follow. First, the Secretary of State comes under a clear duty to keep under consideration from time to time the question whether or not to bring the section (and therefore the statutory scheme) into force. In my judgment he cannot lawfully surrender or release the power contained in section 171(1) so as to purport to exclude its future exercise either by himself or by his successors. In the course of argument, the Lord Advocate accepted that this was the correct view of the legal position. It follows that the decision of the Secretary of State to give effect to the statement in para 38 of the 1993 White Paper (Cm 2434) that "the provisions in the 1988 Act will not now be implemented" was unlawful. The Lord Advocate contended, correctly, that the attempt by the Secretary of State to abandon or release the power conferred on him by section 171(1), being unlawful, did not bind either the present Secretary of State or any successor in that office. It was a nullity. But, in my judgment, that does not alter the fact that the Secretary of State made the attempt to bind himself not to exercise the power conferred by section 171(1) and such attempt was an unlawful act.

There is a second consequence of the power in section 171(1) being conferred for the purpose of bringing the sections into force. As I have said, in my view, the Secretary of State is entitled to decide not to bring the sections into force if events subsequently occur which render it undesirable to do so. But if the power is conferred on the Secretary of State with a view to bringing the sections into force, in my judgment, the Secretary of State cannot himself procure events to take place and rely on the occurrence of those events as the ground for not bringing the statutory scheme into force. In claiming that the introduction of the new tariff scheme renders it undesirable now to bring the statutory scheme into force, the Secretary of State is, in effect, claiming that the purpose of the statutory power has been frustrated by his own act in choosing to introduce a scheme inconsistent with the statutory scheme approved by Parliament.

The lawfulness of the decision to introduce the tariff scheme

The tariff scheme, if validly introduced under the royal prerogative, is both inconsistent with the statutory scheme contained in sections 108 to 117 of the 1988 Act and intended to be permanent. In practice, the tariff scheme renders it now either impossible or at least more expensive to reintroduce the old scheme or the statutory enactments of it contained in the 1988 Act. The tariff scheme involves the winding up of the old Criminal Injuries Compensation Board together with its team of those skilled in assessing compensation on the common law basis and the creation of a new body, the Criminal

Injuries Compensation Authority, set up to assess compensation on the tariff basis at figures which, in some cases, will be very substantially less than under the old scheme. All this at a time when Parliament has expressed its will that there should be a scheme based on the tortious measure of damages, such will being expressed in a statute which Parliament has neither repealed nor (for reasons which have not been disclosed) been invited to repeal.

My Lords, it would be most surprising if, at the present day, prerogative powers could be validly exercised by the executive so as to frustrate the will of Parliament expressed in a statute and, to an extent, to pre-empt the decision of Parliament whether or not to continue with the statutory scheme even though the old scheme has been abandoned. It is not for the executive, as the Lord Advocate accepted, to state as it did in the White Paper (para 38) that the provisions in the 1988 Act "will accordingly be repealed when a suitable legislative opportunity occurs". It is for Parliament, not the executive, to repeal legislation. The constitutional history of this country is the history of the prerogative powers of the Crown being made subject to the overriding powers of the democratically elected legislature as the sovereign body. The prerogative powers of the Crown remain in existence to the extent that Parliament has not expressly or by implication extinguished them. But under the principle in *A-G v De Keyser's Royal Hotel Ltd* [1920] AC 508, if Parliament has conferred on the executive statutory powers to do a particular act, that act can only thereafter be done under the statutory powers so conferred: any pre-existing prerogative power to do the same act is pro tanto excluded.

How then is it suggested that the executive has power in the present case to introduce under the prerogative power a scheme inconsistent with the statutory scheme? First, it is said that since sections 108 to 117 of the Act are not in force, they confer no legal rights on the victims of crime and impose no duties on the Secretary of State. The *De Keyser* principle does not apply since it only operates to the extent that Parliament has conferred statutory powers which in fact replace pre-existing powers: unless and until the statutory provisions are brought into force, no statutory powers have been conferred and therefore the prerogative powers remain. Moreover, the abandonment of the old scheme and the introduction of the new tariff scheme does not involve any interference by the executive with private rights. The old scheme, being a scheme for ex gratia payments, conferred no legal rights on the victims of crime. The new tariff scheme, being also an ex gratia scheme, confers benefits not detriments on the victims of crime. How can it be unlawful to confer benefits on the citizen, provided that Parliament has voted the necessary funds for that purpose?

In my judgment, these arguments overlook the fact that this case is concerned with public, not private, law. If this were an action in which some victim of crime were suing for the benefits to which he was entitled under the old scheme, the arguments which I have recited would have been fatal to his claim: such a victim has no legal right to any benefits. But these are proceedings for judicial review of the decisions of the Secretary of State in the discharge of his public functions. The well-known passage in the speech of Lord Diplock in *Council of Civil Service Unions v Minister for the Civil Service* [1985] AC 374 at 408–410 demonstrates two points relevant to the present case. First, an executive decision which affects the legitimate expectations of the applicant (even though it does not infringe his legal rights) is subject to judicial review. Second, judicial review is as applicable to decisions taken under prerogative powers as to decisions taken under statutory powers save to the extent that the legality of the exercise of certain prerogative powers (eg treaty making) may not be justiciable.

The *GCHQ* case demonstrates that the argument based on the ex gratia and voluntary nature of the old scheme and the tariff scheme is erroneous. Although the victim of a crime committed immediately before the White Paper was published had no legal right to receive compensation in accordance with the old scheme, he certainly had a legitimate expectation that he would do so. Moreover, he had a legitimate expectation that, unless there were no proper reasons for further delay in bringing sections 108 to 117 of the Act into force, his expectations would be converted into a statutory right. If those legitimate expectations were defeated by the composite decision of the Secretary of State to discontinue the old scheme and not to bring the statutory scheme into force and those decisions were unlawfully taken, he has locus standi in proceedings for judicial review to complain of such illegality.

Similar considerations apply when considering the legality of the minister's decisions. In his powerful dissenting judgment in the Court of Appeal, Hobhouse LJ . . . decided that, since the statutory provisions had not been brought into force, they had no legal significance of any kind. He held, in my judgment correctly, that the *De Keyser* principle did not apply to the present case: since the statutory provisions were not in force they could not have excluded the pre-existing prerogative powers. Therefore the prerogative powers remained. He then turned to consider whether it could be said that the Secretary of State had abused those prerogative powers and again approached the matter on the basis that since the sections were not in force they had no significance in deciding whether or not the Secretary of State had acted lawfully. I cannot agree with this last step. In public law the fact that a scheme approved by Parliament was on the statute book and would come into force as law if and when the Secretary of State so determined is in my judgment directly relevant to the question whether the Secretary of State could in the lawful exercise of prerogative powers both decide to bring in the tariff scheme and refuse properly to exercise his discretion under section 171(1) to bring the statutory provisions into force.

I turn then to consider whether the Secretary of State's decisions were unlawful as being an abuse of power. In this case there are two powers under consideration: first, the statutory power conferred by section 171(1); second, the prerogative power. In order first to test the validity of the exercise of the prerogative power, I will assume that the 1988 Act, instead of conferring a discretion on the Secretary of State to bring the statutory scheme into effect, had specified that it was to come into force one year after the date of the royal assent. As Hobhouse LJ held, during that year the *De Keyser* principle would not apply and the prerogative powers would remain exercisable. But in my judgment it would plainly have been an improper use of the prerogative powers if, during that year, the Secretary of State had discontinued the old scheme and introduced the tariff scheme. It would have been improper because in exercising the prerogative power the Secretary of State would have had to have regard to the fact that the statutory scheme was about to come into force: to dismantle the machinery of the old scheme in the meantime would have given rise to further disruption and expense when, on the first anniversary, the statutory scheme had to be put into operation. This hypothetical case shows that, although during the suspension of the coming into force of the statutory provisions the old prerogative powers continue to exist, the existence of such legislation basically affects the mode in which such prerogative powers can be lawfully exercised.

Does it make any difference that the statutory provisions are to come into effect, not automatically at the end of the year as in the hypothetical case I have put, but on such day as the Secretary of State specifies under a power conferred on him by Parliament for the purpose of bringing the statutory provisions into force? In my judgment it does not. The Secretary of State could only validly exercise the prerogative power to abandon the old scheme and introduce the tariff scheme if, at the same time, he could validly resolve never to bring the statutory provisions and the inconsistent statutory scheme into effect. For the reasons I have already given, he could not validly so resolve to give up his statutory duty to consider from time to time whether to bring the statutory scheme into force. His attempt to do so, being a necessary part of the composite decision which he took, was itself unlawful. By introducing the tariff scheme he debars himself from exercising the statutory power for the purposes and on the basis which Parliament intended. For these reasons, in my judgment the decision to introduce the tariff scheme at a time when the statutory provisions and his power under section 171(1) were on the statute book was unlawful and an abuse of the prerogative power. . . . '

It will be seen that the core of Lord Browne Wilkinson's argument is that by using the prerogative power to bring forward a new non-statutory scheme of compensation, the Secretary of State in effect debarred himself from considering whether and at what point he should commence the statutory scheme under the 1988 Act. Parliament had granted the Secretary of State a discretion as to when any such decision should be taken, and it would not be for any court to say to a Minister of the Crown, 'You must at this point of time take the decision.'

However, a court may intervene under the principles of judicial review where an administrative authority—and that includes a Minister—acts illegally by placing a fetter on its discretion, in other words where it does something or decides something that prevents it from exercising its discretion. The introduction of the 1994 non-statutory scheme was such a fetter as it precluded the Secretary of State from considering whether and at what point he should exercise his discretion, and thus the Court could say, 'You must not do anything which stops you from taking the decision.' This is a clearly very narrow and technical point of law.

Lord Mustill:

'It will be seen that two, and only two, aspects of the controversy are before the court. The proceedings call in question first the announcement that Pt VII of the 1988 Act will not be brought into force (at any rate during the lifetime of the present government), and secondly, the plan to pre-empt the unimplemented statutory scheme by installing a wholly different regime. It is with these challenges, and with these alone, that the Appellate Committee, reporting to your Lordships' House in its judicial capacity, can be concerned.

My Lords, I put the matter in this way to emphasise that although the issues arising on the appeal are of great constitutional importance they are limited in range. The present appeal is directly concerned only with the relationship between the executive and the public. Save to the extent necessary for a ruling upon the lawfulness of what the Secretary of State has said and done the Appellate Committee has no competence to express any opinion on the relationship between the executive and parliament. By way of example, stress was laid by the applicants on the statement in the White Paper (para 38) that the provisions of the 1988 Act relating to compensation for criminal injuries "will accordingly be repealed when a suitable legislative opportunity occurs" as demonstrating at the best a forgetfulness that it is Parliament, not the Secretary of State or a government, which decides whether an existing enactment shall be repealed. This may be so, or it may not, but it is of no consequence here. If the attitude of the Secretary of State is out of tune with the proper respect due to parliamentary processes this is a matter to which Parliament must attend. It is true that in some cases the frame of mind in which a minister approaches the exercise of a statutory or common law discretion may be relevant to the lawfulness of his decision. But this is not such an occasion. It is not suggested that the Secretary of State has acted in bad faith, simply that when his duties under statute and at common law are properly understood it can be seen that what he has done, omitted to do and proposed to do are contrary to law. Criticisms of the manner, rather than the matter, of his actions are for political debate, not legal argument.

Equally, your Lordships are not concerned in your appellate capacity to inquire whether the Secretary of State's decisions were sound. The task of the courts is to ensure that powers are lawfully exercised by those to whom they are entrusted, not to take those powers into their own hands and exercise them afresh. A claim that a decision under challenge was wrong leads nowhere, except in the rare case where it can be characterised as so obviously and grossly wrong as to be irrational, in the lawyers' sense of the word, and hence a symptom that there must have been some failure in the decision-making process. No such proposition is advanced here, nor could it have been; for, whatever their rights and wrongs, if the decisions manifested by the Secretary of State's words and actions are otherwise lawful it is impossible to say that no decision maker acting rationally could have arrived at them. Once again, it is for Parliament to intervene if it finds the new policies unacceptable.

My Lords, I have begun in this way because the narrow focus of the inquiry is blurred if factors, highly relevant in a wider perspective but not germane to the questions of law for decisions, are allowed to intrude. In broad terms, these questions are as follows. First, does section 171(1) impose on the Secretary of State a legally enforceable duty to bring into force all the provisions of the Act to which it applies, including Pt VII? If so, what considerations are relevant in determining when the duty must be performed? Was the announcement that Pt VII would not be implemented a separate breach of duty? Second, was either the winding up of the existing scheme or the inauguration of the new scheme, or both, (a) a breach of a duty created by section 171(1), or (b) an abuse of the prerogative power? . . .

I will begin with the first question, since in my opinion the answer to it is an essential starting point for consideration of the second. It is common ground that this part of the dispute turns on the interpretation of section 171(1). There are I believe three possible meanings. The first is that the Secretary of State has no obligations at all as regards the implementation of the sections to which it applies; his discretion is entirely free from control. This need not be considered at length, for the Lord Advocate does not propose it, and indeed it must be unsound. Parliament cannot have intended that the minister could simply ignore the power, or exercise it for his own personal advantage. He must give consideration to the exercise of the power, and do so in good faith.

At the other extreme is the interpretation for which the applicants contend, that the Secretary of State is under a legally enforceable obligation to bring the relevant sections into force, not immediately for that would be absurd but as soon as it is administratively practicable to do so. For this purpose, so they maintain, questions such as financial and political feasibility must be left entirely out of account. I am quite unable to accept that Parliament can have intended to hamstring the discretion in such a mechanical and unrealistic way. Parliamentary government is a matter of practical politics. Parliament cannot be taken to have legislated on the assumption that the general state of affairs in which it was thought desirable and feasible to create the power to bring a new regime into effect will necessarily persist in the future. Further study may disclose that the scheme has unexpected administrative flaws which would make it positively undesirable to implement it as enacted, or (for example) it might happen that a ruling of the European Court of Human Rights would disclose that persistence with the scheme would contravene the international obligations of the United Kingdom. Financial circumstances may also change, just as the Secretary of State maintains that they have changed in the present case; the scheme may prove unexpectedly expensive, or a newly existing or perceived need for financial stringency may leave insufficient resources to fund public expenditures which might otherwise be desirable. I cannot attribute to Parliament an intention that all the provisions of this Act falling within section 171(1), not limited as we have seen to the criminal injuries scheme, and all the relevant provisions of the numerous other statutes in which a similar formula is used, will be brought inexorably into effect as soon as it is physically possible to do so, even if the country can no longer afford them.

A less extreme version of this submission, albeit one which would not yield success for the applicants in the present dispute, is that the Secretary of State is entitled and bound to take into account all relevant considerations, including financial practicability, but that as soon as it becomes feasible in the more general sense to do so he is compelled to appoint a day. My Lords, I am constrained to hold that this alternative must also be rejected, for more than one reason. In the first place, it postulates that instead of reserving to itself the power, through the use of its own methods, to ensure that ministers do not delay unduly in the appointment of a day, Parliament has chosen to create and through the medium of section 117(1) has expressed in the Act, a duty owed to the public at large and capable of enforcement in the courts.

If this is right, it must follow inevitably that though there is implicit in section 171(1) a surrender by Parliament to the courts of a power not only to investigate whether the Secretary of State in failing to appoint a day and hence to bring primary legislation into force has acted in a way which is, in a legal sense, irrational but also, if all else fails, and if the Secretary of State is obdurate in the face of a declaration as to the true legal position, to make an order of mandamus against him, backed by the threat of imprisonment. That this is indeed the consequence of the applicants' submission is shown by the fact that just such an order forms part of the relief claimed in these proceedings. For the courts to grant relief of this kind would involve a penetration into Parliament's exclusive field of legislative activity far greater than any that has been contemplated even during the rapid expansion of judicial intervention during the past 20 years. Recalling that your Lordships, in your appellate capacity, are concerned when dealing with the first question brought before them solely with a question of statutory interpretation it must be asked whether Parliament, jealous as it is of its prerogatives and possessed as it is of its own special means to scrutinise and control the actions of ministers, can have intended to create, through the medium of section 171(1), any such rights and remedies. I do not believe that it can.

The second reason is that a legal regime of this kind would be so lacking in precision that it can scarcely have been the intention of Parliament to create it. Where the exercise of power is challenged it is possible for the court to assess the question of irrationality in the light of the relevant factors as they stood at the relevant time. Once taken, the decision can once and for all be put in question. But if the applicants are right and the non-exercise of the power was intended by Parliament to be controllable by the courts, a continuing omission to appoint a day, under any one of the innumerable statutory provisions subject to the same regime as is created for the 1988 Act by section 171(1), would be continuously open to challenge in the light of the changing interplay of practicality and policy in the light of which decisions of this kind must be made. It seems to me highly improbable that Parliament would have wished to make justiciable in court what are essentially political and administrative judgments, rather than retain them for its own scrutiny and enforcement.

The third and simplest reason is that the words of section 171(1) do not mean what the applicants wish them to say. It is true that "may" is capable of denoting "shall" if the context so demands, but this is not the customary usage. If one looks to the Act at large, taking Pt VII as an example, the words appear more than 30 times, omitting compound expressions such as "shall only" and "shall not". It is to my mind beyond doubt that in every one of these instances "may" invokes a choice and "shall" an order. Looking next at the immediate context of the word "may" in section 171(1), we find that, only a few words before, "shall" is used in its natural sense, which makes it unlikely that the draftsman immediately afterwards chose "may" to convey the same meaning; and if one seeks guidance elsewhere in the section there is no need to go further than sub-section (3), where it is quite clear that "may" does not denote an unqualified obligation. If Parliament had intended to compel the Secretary of State to bring Pt VII and all the other provisions governed by section 171(1) into force just as soon as practicable, it could easily have said so. In my opinion it has not. . . .

For these reasons I would reject the argument that the continuing omission to implement the statutory scheme was a breach of any duty arising from section 171(1). There remains the question whether the positive act of the Secretary of State in announcing that he would not implement the scheme in the interval which remained before the statutory underpinnings were removed was in itself an unlawful act. At first acquaintance an alternative answer can be made to seem quite plausible. The tone of the White Paper and of the utterances in Parliament can be presented as a defiance of the will of Parliament, embodied in Pt VII of the Act. There may be substance in this complaint, which has already been voiced in Parliament, and which may be voiced again if the Houses ever have occasion to discuss the obligations owed by a minister to Parliament in respect of powers entrusted to him under provisions such as section 171(1). But the substance, if there is any, is one of Parliamentary practice, expectation and courtesy, not of public law. If there is no duty to bring the relevant provisions into force, there can be no breach of duty simply by announcing in advance that the non-existent duty will not be performed. I must emphasise the words "simply by", for it is possible that such an announcement could be evidence of a lack of the good faith which, as the Lord Advocate freely acknowledged, is an indispensable element of the lawful exercise of the discretion conferred by section 171(1), as much as of any other statutory discretion. But this is out of context here. Although the applicants, and no doubt others, object to the substance of the change as well as to the way in which it has been done, it has not been suggested, and on the facts could not properly have been suggested, that the Secretary of State has acted in bad faith, in any sense relevant to such control of his discretion as the courts can properly exercise through the medium of judicial review. . . .

I turn to the second area of complaint, which relates to the implementation of the new scheme in a form which differs radically from that contained in Pt VII of the Act. This complaint is advanced in two ways. First, that the actions and statements of the Secretary of State were an abuse of the powers conferred by section 171(1). Secondly, that the powers exercisable under the royal prerogative were limited by the presence in the background of the statutory scheme.

At first sight a negative answer to each of these averments seems inevitable, once given the premise that section 171(1) creates no duty to appoint a day. As regards the Act, in a perspective which may never yield a statutory scheme, the possibility of substituting one non-statutory scheme for another must have been just as much envisaged and tolerated as was the continuation of the existing non-statutory scheme, or indeed the termination of any scheme at all. The interval between the passing of the Act and the bringing into force of Pt VII, if it ever happened, was simply a statutory blank.

So too, it would appear, as regards the argument based on the royal prerogative. The case does not fall within the principle of *A-G v De Keyser's Royal Hotel Ltd* [1920] AC 508. There, in the words of Lord Dunedin, it was established that "if the whole ground of something which is covered by the prerogative could be done by the statute, it is the statute that rules". Thus, if in the present case Pt VII had been brought into force there was no room left for the exercise of that aspect of the prerogative which had enabled the Secretary of State to establish and maintain the scheme. Once the superior power of Parliament has occupied the territory, the prerogative must quit the field. In the present case, however, the territory is quite untouched. There is no Parliamentary dominion over compensation for criminal injuries, since Parliament has chosen to allow its control to be exercised today, or some day, or never, at the choice of the Secretary of State. Until he chooses to call the Parliamentary scheme into existence there is a legislative void and the prerogative subsists untouched. The position is just the same as if Pt VII had never been enacted, or had been repealed soon afterwards.

This is not to say that the decisions of the Secretary of State in the exercise of the prerogative power to continue, modify or abolish the scheme which his predecessor in the exercise of the same power had called into existence are immune from process. They can be called into question on the familiar grounds: *R v Criminal Injuries Compensation Board, ex p Lain* [1967] 2 QB 864. But no question of irrationality arises here, and the decision to inaugurate a new scheme cannot be rendered unlawful simply because of its conflict on paper with a statutory scheme which is not part of the law. . . .

My Lords, I introduced the preceding discussion with the words "At first sight" because the applicants have a further (and to my mind altogether more formidable) argument which challenges the implicit assumption that in the absence of a duty to appoint a day the Secretary of State's dealings with the compensation scheme are entirely free from statutory restraint. Contrary to this assumption, it is said, there is no statutory void; for although Pt VII is not itself in force, section 171(1) is in force and must not be ignored. The continued existence of section 171(1) means that, even if there is no present duty to appoint a day, there is a continuing duty, which will subsist until either a day is appointed or the relevant provisions are repealed, to address in a rational manner the question whether the power created by section 171(1) should be exercised. This continuing duty overshadows the exercise by the Secretary of State of his powers under the royal prerogative.

To some degree this argument is uncontroversial. I accept, and indeed the Lord Advocate does not dispute, that the Secretary of State cannot simply put out of his mind the subsisting discretion under section 171(1). But I part company with the argument at the next stage. One must look at the practicalities, which Parliament must be taken to have envisaged. Pending the appointment of a day it is impossible for the Secretary of State to remain completely inactive. He has no choice but to do something about compensation for criminal injuries: whether wind up the existing scheme and put nothing in its place; or keep the existing scheme in force; or modify it; or copy the statutory scheme. It seems to me inevitable, once it is acknowledged that it may be proper at any given time for the Secretary of State to say, "It is inappropriate at present to put the statutory scheme into force", that it can be proper for him to install something different from the statutory scheme. Otherwise there would be the absurdity that the Secretary of State is obliged to do something under the royal prerogative which he is not obliged to do under the statute. Thus, merely to introduce a cheaper scheme cannot in itself be an abuse of the prerogative powers which subsist in the interim. If the Secretary of State had made an announcement as follows:

"I have come to the conclusion after careful study that for the reasons which I have explained the Parliamentary scheme must now be seen as too expensive, slow and top-heavy; that its priority is not sufficiently high to justify the great expense when there are other calls on the country's resources; that the scheme which I propose will do substantial justice in a more efficient way; and that accordingly I shall run the scheme for a while to see how it works and if, as I confidently expect, it is a success I will ask Parliament to agree with me and repeal the statutory scheme",

it is hard to see what objection could have been taken. Does not the minister's actual stance, although perhaps more likely to provoke hostility, really come to the same thing?

The applicants reply that it does not, essentially for two reasons. First, they contend that the Secretary of State has renounced the statutory duty which still dominates the prerogative in this field: not the duty, as under the argument already discussed and rejected, to bring Pt VII into force, but the duty to keep under review the powers conferred by section 171(1). I would reject this argument. Perhaps the Secretary of State has laid himself open to attack more than he need have done by the tone of his announcement, but I cannot read him as having said that however much circumstances may change he will never think again; and even if he had said this his statement would have been meaning-less since, leaving aside questions arising from the doctrine of "legitimate expectation" which do not arise here, nothing that he says on one day could bind him in law, or bind his successor, not to say and do the opposite the next day.

Furthermore, even if the argument were sound it would not yield any useful relief. The most that the court could do would be to grant a declaration that the Secretary of State is now and in the future obliged to keep the power under review in a spirit of good faith: something which the Lord Advocate on his behalf has not denied. To this declaration he could respond: "As for the present, you can see that I have not only kept the appointment of a day under review but have examined it in depth, and have come to a conclusion which, even if you do not care for it, is undeniably rational. As for the future, I will continue to keep the power under review, although I cannot at present foresee circum-stances which will impel me or my successors to a different view." Such a reply would in practice be impregnable, and for my part I would not be prepared as a matter of discretion to grant relief so empty of content.

The applicants' second contention is that the Secretary of State has frustrated the intentions of Parliament by bringing in his own inconsistent scheme and hence nullifying any realistic possibility that he will perform his continuing duty to keep the implementation of the statutory scheme under review. I do not accept this. No doubt if Pt VII had been the subject of section 171(6) and hence due to come into force inevitably on a fixed day the creation of any different scheme otherwise than purely as an interim measure would have been a breach of duty. It is also possible to imagine cases where the pro-visions to be brought into force on an appointed day are such as to become incapable of execution if irreversible changes have been made in the meantime, and it may be that to make such changes would be an abuse of the prerogative. But this is not so here. The new scheme is not in tablets of stone. Certainly, it would be an inconvenient, time-consuming and expensive business to dismantle the scheme and return to something on the former lines. But it would be feasible to do so, just as it proved feasible to pull down the original scheme which has been firmly established over many years. Nothing is certain in politics. Who is to say that a successor in office, under the present or some future adminis-tration, with wholly different ideas on social policy and financial means and priorities, might not decide that the present Secretary of State has taken a completely wrong turning and that after all the Parliamentary scheme is best? If he did so, and made an order under section 171(1), accompanied by the necessary regulations and by executive action to wind up the new scheme, there is nothing in what the present Secretary of State has done that could stand in his way. His words have no lasting effect, he has not put an end to the statutory scheme; only Parliament can do that. So long as he and his succes-sors in office perform in good faith the duty to keep the implementation of Pt VII under review there is in my opinion no ground for the court to interfere.

In reaching these conclusions I have left out of account the evidence as to subsequent debates and votes in Parliament upon which the Secretary of State has sought to rely, for these cannot be permis-sible guides to the meaning of the 1988 legislation and its relationship to the minister's powers.

In particular I have attached no direct significance to the fact that Parliament has recently thought fit, through the medium of the Appropriation Act 1994, to make public money available for the conduct of the scheme which is now under attack. Nevertheless, it is I believe legitimate to observe, in company with Hobhouse LJ . . . , that there is something strange about the proposition that it is an abuse for the minister to apply moneys voted by Parliament for a stated purpose to that purpose, and I believe that, all other considerations apart, the court should hesitate long before employing its discretionary remedies in such a case.

This prompts one final observation. It is a feature of the peculiarly British conception of the separation of powers that Parliament, the executive and the courts have each their distinct and largely exclusive domain. Parliament has a legally unchallengeable right to make whatever laws it thinks right. The executive carries on the administration of the country in accordance with the powers conferred on it by law. The courts interpret the laws, and see that they are obeyed. This requires the courts on occasion to step into the territory which belongs to the executive, not only to verify that the powers asserted accord with the substantive law created by Parliament, but also, that the manner in which they are exercised conforms with the standards of fairness which Parliament must have intended. Concurrently with this judicial function Parliament has its own special means of ensuring that the executive, in the exercise of delegated functions, performs in a way which Parliament finds appropriate. Ideally, it is these latter methods which should be used to check executive errors and excesses; for it is the task of Parliament and the executive in tandem, not of the courts, to govern the country. In recent years, however, the employment in practice of these specifically Parliamentary remedies has on occasion been perceived as falling short, and sometimes well short, of what was needed to bring the performance of the executive into line with the law and with the minimum standards of fairness implicit in every Parliamentary delegation of a decision-making function. To avoid a vacuum in which the citizen would be left without protection against a misuse of executive powers the courts have had no option but to occupy the dead ground in a manner, and in areas of public life, which could not have been foreseen 30 years ago. For myself, I am quite satisfied that this unprecedented judicial role has been greatly to the public benefit. Nevertheless, it has its risks, of which the courts are well aware. As the judges themselves constantly remark, it is not they who are appointed to administer the country. Absent a written constitution much sensitivity is required of the parliamentarian, administrator and judge if the delicate balance of the unwritten rules evolved (I believe successfully) in recent years is not to be disturbed, and all the recent advances undone. I do not for a moment suggest that the judges of the Court of Appeal in the present case overlooked this need. The judgments show clearly that they did not. Nevertheless some of the arguments addressed would have the court push to the very boundaries of the distinction between court and Parliament established in, and recognised ever since, the Bill of Rights 1688. Three hundred years have passed since then, and the political and social landscape has changed beyond recognition. But the boundaries remain; they are of crucial significance to our private and public lives; and the courts should, I believe, make sure that they are not overstepped. . . .

For these reasons I would allow the appeal and dismiss the cross-appeal.'

The prerogative is diverse. Adopting the usual sub-classification of the 'everyday' or 'political prerogatives', we find executive, judicial and legislative prerogatives. The first relate to national and international affairs, covering matters such as: hiring and firing military and civil servants; disposition of forces (including the use of the armed forces within the UK to assist the police and other emergency services and to maintain peace); granting of honours; powers to give information to subjects; conduct of the realm in time of war and emergency (which includes the power to govern British overseas territories, the organisation of the civil service, and the power to appoint ministers); declaring war and peace; issuing passports; making treaties and the general conduct of external relations, including recognising foreign states and the consequential diplomatic privileges and immunities flowing therefrom. The Crown exercises these powers without needing *prior* authorisation by Parliament; the powers being exercised by ministers who are generally responsible to Parliament making the position constitutional. Where treaties are made, parliamentary confirmation is required where a treaty will affect private rights of British subjects, where an alteration of British law will be produced, or where the treaty was made conditional on parliamentary confirmation (see the European Assembly Elections Act 1978, section 6(1)). Judicial prerogatives include that of mercy (power to issue pardons for offences). Legislative prerogatives include declaring existing law by proclamations and the principle that statute is presumed not to bind the Crown unless that is expressly stated or it is the statute's necessary implication.

In *Bombay Province v Bombay Municipal Corpn*[31] the question arose whether the Crown was bound by statutory provisions enabling laying of water mains. The City of Bombay wished to lay a main across Crown land. The Crown was only willing to allow this subject to conditions, some of which the city found unacceptable. The city gave notice that it intended to rely on statutory powers of compulsion enabling it to proceed without having to agree to any conditions.

Lord Du Parcq:

'The general principle to be applied in considering whether or not the Crown is bound by general words in a statute is not in doubt. The maxim of the law in early times was that no statute bound the Crown unless the Crown was expressly named therein, "Roy n'est lie par ascun statute si il ne soit expressement nosme." But the rule so laid down is subject to at least one exception. The Crown may be bound, as has often been said, "by necessary implication". If, that is to say, it is manifest from the very terms of the statute, that it was the intention of the legislature that the Crown should be bound, then the result is the same as if the Crown had been expressly named. It must then be inferred that the Crown, by assenting to the law, agreed to be bound by its provisions . . .

It was contended on behalf of the respondents that whenever a statute is enacted "for the public good" the Crown, though not expressly named, must be held to be bound by its provisions and that, as the Act in question was manifestly intended to secure the public welfare, it must bind the Crown. This contention, which did not meet with success in the High Court, was again raised before their Lordships. The proposition which the respondents thus sought to maintain is supported by early authority, and is to be found in Bacon's Abridgement and other text-books, but in their Lordships' opinion it cannot now be regarded as sound except in a strictly limited sense. Every statute must be supposed to be "for the public good", at least in intention, and even when, as in the present case, it is apparent that one object of the legislature is to promote the welfare and convenience of a large body of the King's subjects by giving extensive powers to a local authority, it cannot be said consistently with the decided cases, that the Crown is necessarily bound by the enactment . . .

Their Lordships prefer to say that the apparent purpose of the statute is one element, and may be an important element, to be considered when an intention to bind the Crown is alleged. If it can be affirmed that, at the time when the statute was passed and received the royal sanction, it was apparent from its terms that its beneficent purpose must be wholly frustrated unless the Crown were bound, then it may be inferred that the Crown has agreed to be bound. Their Lordships will add that when the court is asked to draw this inference, it must always be remembered that, if it be the intention of the legislature that the Crown shall be bound, nothing is easier than to say so in plain words.'

Note also the conclusion of Lord Keith in *Lord Advocate v Dumbarton District Council*:[32]

'Accordingly, it is preferable, in my view, to stick to the simple rule that the Crown is not bound by any statutory provision unless there can somehow be gathered from the terms of the relevant Act an

---

[31] [1947] AC 58, 61–63. [32] [1990] 2 AC 580, 604 (post letter C to post letter D).

intention to that effect. The Crown can be bound only by express words or necessary implication. The modern authorities do not, in my opinion, require that any gloss should be placed on that formulation of the principle. However, as the very nature of these appeals demonstrates, it is most desirable that Acts of Parliament should always state explicitly whether or not the Crown is intended to be bound by any, and if so which, of their provisions.'

(c) The prerogative and Parliament

This issue was examined by the House of Commons Public Administration Committee in its Fourth Report for the session 2003–04[33] which pointed out that the considerable executive prerogative powers of the Crown have in effect been transferred to ministers leading the Committee to argue that these powers should be renamed 'ministerial executive' rather than 'royal prerogative'. While some limits have been placed in recent years on these powers by replacing them with statutory powers, such as the Interception of Communications Act 1985, the Security Service Act 1989 and the Intelligence Services Act 1994, and while the exercise of many prerogative powers is subject to judicial review, and while certain conventional understandings have been reached, for example the so called 'Ponsonby rule' under which any international treaty which requires ratification must be laid before Parliament twenty days before it is ratified, the Committee still concluded that the restrictions on executive powers were still too limited. In general the Committee was concerned by the lack of any obligation on ministers to report to Parliament about the use of prerogative powers on particular occasions, by the argument that ministers may do anything not prohibited by statute or the common law, and by the fact that ministerial accountability to Parliament for the exercise of prerogative powers arises only retrospectively.

In particular terms the Committee was exercised by the powers ministers hold to go to war without having explicit parliamentary approval, by their ability to negotiate treaties without parliamentary involvement, though, of course, once a treaty which would lead to changes in UK law is made parliamentary approval is required, by their control over the management and organisation of the Civil Service which is not subject to parliamentary approval, in which connection the Committee pointed to Canada where parliamentary approval is required for governmental reorganisations. The Committee also argued that parliamentary oversight of public appointments should be enhanced and that successful candidates for major posts should be questioned by parliamentary Committees about their fitness for appointment. Furthermore the Committee was concerned that such a fundamental right as freedom of movement should be subject to unregulated prerogative control via the powers that exist to grant and revoke passports.

The Committee concluded that there was an 'unanswerable' case for reform if ministerial accountability to Parliament is to be enhanced. This could take place either on a piecemeal pragmatic basis whereby individual prerogative powers are made subject to parliamentary control, or via the means of new comprehensive legislation. The latter was the preferred option for most of those giving evidence to the Committee as it would reinforce the notions of parliamentary supremacy, executive accountability and the overall rule of law. Such legislation, following suggestions placed before the Committee by Professor Rodney Brazier,

---

[33] *Taming the Prerogative: Strengthening Ministerial Accountability to Parliament*, HC 422.

could require the listing of 'ministerial executive' powers within six months of the passing of the Act to be followed by other legislation considered by a joint committee of both Houses of Parliament, to put in place such statutory safeguards as might be considered necessary. Particular requirements could be laid down in respect of prerogative decisions on military conflicts, the making of treaties and the issue of passports to ensure that early information about the exercise of such powers is given to Parliament. In addition the Committee strongly urged that decisions to engage in armed conflict should be subject to parliamentary approval, either prior to such an event or as soon thereafter as is possible.

In July 2004 the Department for Constitutional Affairs issued the government's response to the Committee. This seized on the point that no recommendation had been made for abolition of prerogative powers and emphasised their importance for flexible and responsive governmental action, particularly in complex and dangerous circumstances. The government, however, conceded that in some respects the prerogative is an historical anachronism, but argued that the enactment of the Human Rights Act 1998 places extended judicial constraints on the powers ministers hold. Even so the particular concerns of the Committee were largely rejected. Thus, while acknowledging a need for Parliament to be kept informed of developments during an armed conflict, and reinforcing assurances that Parliament will be given opportunities to debate and scrutinise decisions on the deployment of British forces in overseas conflicts, the government declined to extend Parliament's powers to require prior approval of entry into conflict. Similarly there was a rejection of the arguments for enhanced parliamentary scrutiny of treaties at the pre-ratification stage, for further statutory regulation of the powers to grant or revoke passports, and for parliamentary scrutiny of the most important public appointments.

In general terms there was a complete rejection of the notion of increased statutory regulation of the prerogative. It was argued that ministers are already accountable to Parliament in political terms for their prerogative powers, for example via the work of Departmental Select Committees.[34] This *political* accountability was considered to be sufficient without any further form of *legal* control. The most the government would concede was that a case-by-case argument may be put forward for the selective transfer of prerogative powers to statutory systems or for further non-statutory parliamentary scrutiny.

It is strange to note such conclusions emerging from a Labour government when in 1994 the current Leader of the House of Commons, Mr Straw, wrote '[t]he royal prerogative has no place in a modern western democracy . . . [The prerogative] has been used as a smoke screen by Ministers to obfuscate the use of power for which they are insufficiently accountable'[35] while the 'official' party line on the issue in 1989 was that there should be enhanced political and statutory control over the prerogative.[36] It would appear, however, that for the present enhanced parliamentary control over prerogative powers is unlikely to occur.

However, since 6 February 2006 it has been the policy of the Conservative Opposition that the decision to go to war should be entrusted to Parliament and not the Prime Minister. While in 2003 before the invasion of Iraq MPs were allowed to vote on the issue, this had no binding significance, and decisions to deploy troops may often be known to the press (via ministerial releases) before Parliament hears of them. However, on 27 July 2006 the House of Lords Select Committee on the Constitution called for the establishment of a convention that future military action should be justified by ministers in Parliament, together with details of any legal

---

[34] See below pp. 282–287.
[35] *Taming the Prerogative: Strengthening Ministerial Accountability to Parliament*, para 10.
[36] Op cit para 14.

advice received in relation to taking such action. By the same convention, Parliament's consent for the deployment of troops would be needed. Both Houses of Parliament would be free to vote on the action, but in the event of disagreement between them the view of the House of Commons should prevail. Once approved operational control of military action would be left to military commanders, but Parliament would be kept informed of developments and would have the right to hold a new vote should circumstances alter.

The Committee argued that proceeding down the convention route would be in keeping with the unwritten nature of our constitution, would avoid the risk of judicial review which could arise if a statutory regime were put in place, and would allow for flexibility in time of emergencies.

(d) The prerogative and convention

The exercise of prerogative powers is largely governed by 'conventions'. Thus even in relation to the daily exercise of 'political' prerogative powers, say, to determine the disposition of troops, it is convention that determines that it is ministers who actually wield the power and not the monarch in person. But what is a convention?

All systems of government, even those operating under highly-detailed written constitutions, develop 'ways of going about things', in other words general practices and understandings as to how particular powers will be exercised. In the United Kingdom because of the lack of a written constitution such practices assume a major importance. Indeed someone who simply read the various rules of law which pertain to our constitution would have a rather imperfect and partial view of what that constitution is and how it works.

However, there is a fundamental distinction between a convention and a rule of law, and that relates to the consequence of a breach. If a rule of law is broken then there is, in theory at least, a legal consequence, for example the imposition of a penalty or the issue of some order from the court. Of course, in everyday life many breaches of rules of law go unsanctioned either because they are not detected or because they are so minor as not to warrant attention, but that should not deflect us from understanding that rules of law are best thought of as essentially being particularly formalised requirements to impose order on events and to ensure that like situations are treated alike. The breach of such a requirement, if detected, must *at very least* merit a decision by the person responsible for enforcing and applying the rules as to whether formal steps should be taken to secure compliance with the law by some appropriate means. The breach of a convention, however, gives rise only to political consequences—even though these may be more dire and immediate than a legal sanction.

Thus, for example, if a minister does something for which he/she has no legal power the *legal* consequence may be that the action is subject to judicial review with the minister's decision being quashed: see chapters 9 and 10 below. The minister is, however, not made to suffer a personal legal punishment such as a fine or term of imprisonment. However, where ministers broke a conventional requirement, say the understanding that a government defeated on a vote of 'no confidence' in the House of Commons should resign, the political consequences for their party at the next election, and for their own political careers, would be dire for they would almost certainly be voted out of office. And yet there would be no immediate legal sanction in respect of those ministers' actions: it would only be at a point where they would need to have the approval of Parliament for an action, say the raising of finance by taxation, that they would find themselves *legally* unable to govern because they could not then command the support of the Commons whose clearly expressed 'no confidence' vote they had ignored.

Conventions are thus essentially political in nature, though Dicey preferred to use the somewhat dangerous expression 'the morality of the Constitution'. They are 'practices' which have emerged from the repeated habitual acts of the principal constitutional actors, so that it may be said they are principles of constitutional behaviour whose breach is unthinkable. Thus while a particular action in our constitution, say the refusal of the Royal Assent to legislation by the monarch, could be perfectly *lawful*, it would also be conventionally unconstitutional, for it is nowadays unthinkable that the monarch should refuse assent.

The matter of what a convention is has been examined by Jaconelli in 'The Nature of Constitutional Convention'[37] to which indebtedness is acknowledged. Arguably a constitutional convention in the strictest sense of the expression is more than just a custom, practice or usage; it is something that inhibits or constrains the actions of a constitutional actor, such as the monarch, so that a particular course of action has to be adopted even though there are very strong arguments for pursuing some other course of action. Sir Ivor Jennings argued[38] that a constitutional convention would in general possess the characteristics of being based on precedent, on the belief of constitutional actors that they are bound to act in a particular way, and by there being a good reason for the convention. He added: 'A single precedent with a good reason may be enough to establish the rule. A whole string of precedents without such a reason will be of no avail . . . ' Jaconelli points out that Jennings does not elaborate on what a 'good reason' is in the above context, but nevertheless accepts: 'it is the habitual practice which is observed *for the time being*—provided it has "some reason to it"—which has some claim to the title, "convention"'. On this basis Jaconelli concludes constitutional conventions are 'social rules' and argues: 'A constitutional convention is no mere habit that certain governmental situations are dealt with in a particular way. It is a rule, characterised by a "critical reflective attitude", which looks on the outward pattern of behaviour as a standard to be followed. Any deviation from the practice attracts—and is rightly regarded as attracting—criticism and pressure to conform.'

On this basis Jaconelli argues for a very narrow definition of 'constitutional convention', and even while acknowledging that they can be characterised by 'various possible degrees of "bindingness" . . . ' goes on to assert that: 'The more narrowly are drawn the confines of an alleged convention, the higher the degree of conformity that is likely to be found with its requirements.' He then goes on to argue that a truly constitutional convention is one which imposes a 'framework of rules the observance of which transcends the sectional interests of political party. . . . Matters constitutional are those which regulate the *manner* in which the business of government is to be conducted in such areas as . . . relations between the government as a whole and Parliament; relations between the two Houses of Parliament; relations between the United Kingdom and member countries of the Commonwealth.' This leads him to exclude from the definition of 'convention' any 'rules which do not regulate the mode of conduct of government', eg 'rules and practices, etc that govern purely intra political party conduct'.

Jaconelli's arguments are powerful and attractive, but they leave us with a problem: if we restrict the term 'constitutional convention' to a narrow set of circumstances, how do we characterise all the other usages, practices and habits of the constitution? Even Jaconelli accepts that conventions may emerge from 'understandings', 'habits' and 'practices', and there

---

[37] (1999) 19 Legal Studies (No 1) 24.
[38] Jennings, Sir I, *The Law and the Constitution*, (5th edn, University of London Press, 1967), p. 136.

can be considerable doubt as to whether something is merely a convenient practice, and also when such a practice turns into a binding convention. For the purposes, therefore, of this work just as the term 'prerogative' is given a wide meaning, so the notion of convention itself, it is argued, is best thought of as a continuum which ranges from those 'social rules' which clearly are 'constitutional conventions' on the basis of Jaconelli's definition, and whose content is well known, though to much vaguer 'conventional requirements and practices'. At one end of this continuum we encounter rules hardly distinguishable from rules of law, certainly in relation to their importance for the regular functioning of the constitution. At the other end there are 'requirements' which are ill established, whose observation depends on political circumstances, whose breach, no matter what the antiquity of the practice, may give rise to lesser or greater political consequences of a more (or less) immediate and severe nature, depending on the political context of the events in question. 'True' constitutional conventions are undoubtedly absolutely obeyed and the only question that arises is what are the circumstances in which constitutional actors may be freed from the duty of observance. But it seems over restrictive to exclude from the general notion of 'convention' those instances where there is a general degree of latitude as to observance.

In this chapter we shall be primarily concerned with those conventions of a clearly fixed and absolute nature; those which relate to the personal prerogatives of the monarch, and which centre on the general principle that the monarch in person must not be drawn into political conflict. The following chapter will deal further with the conventional position of the Cabinet and ministers where requirements may be found to be a little freer, and where the topic of conventions will be further examined.

Before dealing with the personal prerogative there are certain remaining issues concerning the exercise of political prerogative powers which must be addressed.

---

ii. The Crown and the Giving and Withholding of Evidence

In litigation discovery of documents is a pre-trial process whereby parties list and make available to each other (if necessary under a court order) documents material to their dispute. It is not an independent course of action, and cannot be pursued merely speculatively. Is the Crown able to refuse to discover documents, or even deny their existence on the pretext this is desirable 'in the public interest'? For many years the answer was 'yes' following *Duncan v Cammell Laird & Co Ltd*[39] where the House of Lords held the Crown could claim, by ministerial affidavit, that a document should not be produced either on grounds of its contents, or in that it belonged to a class of documents which should not be withheld in order to protect the functioning of the public service. Such a claim of 'Crown privilege' could not be resisted by the court.

In *Conway v Rimmer*[40] the House of Lords departed from its previous decision and denied that a minister's affidavit should any longer be conclusive. The plaintiff, a former probationary

---

[39] [1942] AC 624.   [40] [1968] AC 910 per Lord Reid at 937 to 954.

police constable, began an action for malicious prosecution against his former superintendent. In the course of discovery, the defendant disclosed a list of documents in his possession
or power, relevant to the plaintiff's action, including four reports made by him about the
plaintiff during his period of probation, and a report by him to his chief constable for transmission to the Director of Public Prosecutions in connection with the prosecution of the
plaintiff on the criminal charge, on which he was acquitted. The Secretary of State for Home
Affairs objected in proper form to the production of all five documents on the ground that
each fell within a class of documents the production of which would be injurious to the
public interest.

Lord Reid:

'The question whether such a statement by a Minister of the Crown should be accepted as conclusively
preventing any court from ordering production of any of the documents to which it applies is one of
very great importance in the administration of justice. If the commonly accepted interpretation of the
decision of this House in *Duncan v Cammell Laird & Co Ltd* [1942] AC 624 is to remain authoritative the
question admits of only one answer—the Minister's statement is final and conclusive . . . I have no
doubt that the case of *Duncan v Cammell Laird & Co Ltd* was rightly decided. The plaintiff sought
discovery of documents relating to the submarine *Thetis* including a contract for the hull and
machinery and plans and specifications. The First Lord of the Admiralty had stated that "it would be
injurious to the public interest that any of the said documents should be disclosed to any person." . . . It is universally recognised that here there are two kinds of public interest which may clash.
There is the public interest that harm shall not be done to the nation or the public service by disclosure
of certain documents, and there is the public interest that the administration of justice shall not be
frustrated by the withholding of documents which must be produced if justice is to be done. There are
many cases where the nature of the injury which would or might be done to the nation or the public
service is of so grave a character that no other interest, public or private, can be allowed to prevail
over it. With regard to such cases it would be proper to say, as Lord Simon did [in *Duncan*], that to order
production of the document in question would put the interest of the state in jeopardy. But there are
many other cases where the possible injury to the public service is much less and there one would think
that it would be proper to balance the public interests involved . . .

There are now many large public bodies, such as British Railways and the National Coal Board, the
proper and efficient functioning of which is very necessary for many reasons including the safety of
the public . . . I find it difficult to see why it should be *necessary* to withhold whole classes of routine
"communications with or within a public department" but quite unnecessary to withhold similar
communications with or within a public corporation. There the safety of the public may well depend on
the candour and completeness of reports made by subordinates whose duty it is to draw attention to
defects. But, so far as I know, no one has ever suggested that public safety has been endangered by the
candour or completeness of such reports having been inhibited by the fact that they may have to be
produced if the interests of the due administration of justice should ever require production at any
time . . . I cannot think that it is satisfactory that there should be no means at all of weighing, in any civil
case, the public interest involved in withholding the document against the public interest that it should
be produced . . . Two questions will arise: first, whether the court is to have any right to question the
finality of a Minister's certificate and, secondly, if it has such a right, how and in what circumstances that
right is to be exercised and made effective.

A Minister's certificate may be given on one or other of two grounds: either because it would be
against the public interest to disclose the contents of the particular document or documents in
question, or because the document belongs to a class of documents which ought to be withheld,
whether or not there is anything in the particular document in question disclosure of which would be
against the public interest. It does not appear that any serious difficulties have arisen or are likely to
arise with regard to the first class. However wide the power of the court may be held to be, cases would

be very rare in which it could be proper to question the view of the responsible Minister that it would be contrary to the public interest to make public the contents of a particular document . . .

But in this field it is more than ever necessary that in a doubtful case the alleged public interest in concealment should be balanced against the public interest that the administration of justice should not be frustrated. If the Minister, who has no duty to balance these conflicting public interests, says no more than that in his opinion the public interest requires concealment, and if that is to be accepted as conclusive in this field as well as with regard to documents in his possession, it seems to me not only that very serious injustice may be done to the parties, but also that the due administration of justice may be gravely impaired for quite inadequate reasons.

It cannot be said that there would be any constitutional impropriety in enabling the court to overrule a Minister's objection. That is already the law in Scotland . . .

I would therefore propose that the House ought now to decide that courts have and are entitled to exercise a power and duty to hold a balance between the public interest, as expressed by a Minister, to withhold certain documents or other evidence, and the public interest in ensuring the proper adminis-tration of justice. That does not mean that a court would reject a Minister's view: full weight must be given to it in every case, and if the Minister's reasons are of a character which judicial experience is not competent to weigh, then the Minister's view must prevail. But experience has shown that reasons given for withholding whole classes of documents are often not of that character . . .

I do not doubt that there are certain classes of documents which ought not to be disclosed whatever their content may be. Virtually everyone agrees that Cabinet minutes and the like ought not to be disclosed until such time as they are only of historical interest . . . And that must, in my view, also apply to all documents concerned with policy making within departments including, it may be, minutes and the like by quite junior officials and correspondence with outside bodies. Further it may be that deliberations about a particular case require protection as much as deliberations about policy. I do not think that it is possible to limit such documents by any definition . . . [It] is important that the Minister should have a right to appeal before [a] document is produced. This matter was not fully investigated in the argument before your Lordships. But it does appear that in one way or another there can be an appeal if the document is in the custody of a servant of the Crown or of a person who is willing to co-operate with the Minister. There may be difficulty if it is in the hands of a person who wishes to produce it.'

Subsequent cases indicate the courts do not grant the Crown a privileged position. The law considers there is some evidence which, *no matter who the parties are*, should be given 'public interest immunity' ('PII'). This was further developed in *Burmah Oil Co Ltd v Bank of England*[41] and *Air Canada v Secretary of State for Trade (No 2)*.[42]

In *Burmah Oil Co Ltd v Bank of England*, in January 1975, an agreement was made between the plaintiffs, an oil company, and the Bank of England acting in close contact with and under the direction of the government, with the object of rescuing the company from grave financial difficulties arising out of the international oil crisis on terms consistent with the government's national economic policy. A term of the agreement involved the sale and transfer to the Bank of nearly 78 million ordinary stock units in British Petroleum held by the company at £2.30 per unit, the price required by the government.

In October 1976 the oil company began an action against the Bank claiming a declaration that the sale was unconscionable and inequitable and an order that the Bank should transfer the stock units back to the company at the price paid in 1975, about £179 million. In March 1977 the company sought an order for discovery of all documents held by the Bank relevant

---

[41] [1980] AC 1090 per Lord Keith at 1130–1134 and Lord Scarman at 1141–1145.

[42] [1983] 2 AC 394 per Lord Fruser at 432–435, Lord Wilberforce at 438–440 and Lord Scarman at 444–446.

to the issues pleaded. The Bank disclosed quantities of material relevant to the issues, but on government instructions resisted production of 62 documents in its possession and control. On the hearing of the summons the Crown intervened by the Attorney-General, the Bank taking no part in the proceedings. Objection to production was taken by the Chief Secretary to the Treasury in a certificate stating that he had personally read and considered each of the 62 documents listed in a schedule and had formed the opinion that their production would be injurious to the public interest. He particularised the documents in three categories: categories A and B consisted of classes of documents relating to the formulation of government policy. Category C documents concerned commercial or financial information communicated in confidence to the government or the Bank by major business companies and other businessmen.

On the plaintiff's appeal to the House of Lords the list of 62 documents, discovery of which the company originally sought, was reduced to 10 (2 in category A and 8 in category B).

Lord Keith:

'My Lords, this appeal is concerned with the legal topic known formerly as Crown privilege and now as public interest immunity . . .

It is convenient to start with the points of distinction between what are commonly called "class" and "contents" claims to immunity. In *Conway v Rimmer* [1968] AC 910 . . . Lord Hodson . . . at p 979 said that he did not regard the classification which places all documents under the heading either of contents or class as being wholly satisfactory. I agree with him. What really matters is the specific ground of public interest upon which the ministerial objection is based, and it scarcely needs to be said that the more clearly this ground is stated the easier will be the task of the court in weighing it against the public interest in the administration of justice. The weight of a contents claim is capable of being very readily measured. Obvious instances are documents relating to defence of the realm or relations with other states. It might be said that such documents constitute a class defined by reference to the nature of their contents. But I would prefer to regard the claim in regard to such a document as being in substance a contents claim . . . Claims to immunity on class grounds stand in a different category because the reasons of public interest upon which they are based may appear to some minds debatable or even nebulous . . . Over a considerable period it was maintained, not without success, that the prospect of the disclosure in litigation of correspondence or other communications within government departments would inhibit a desirable degree of candour in the making of such documents, with results detrimental to the proper functioning of the public service . . . This contention must now be treated as having little weight, if any . . . Nowadays the state in multifarious manifestations impinges closely upon the lives and activities of individual citizens. Where this has involved a citizen in litigation with the state or one of its agencies, the candour argument is an utterly insubstantial ground for denying him access to relevant documents. I would add that the candour doctrine stands in a different category from that aspect of public interest which in appropriate circumstances may require that the sources and nature of information confidentially tendered should be withheld from disclosure . . .

In my opinion, it would be going too far to lay down that no document in any particular one of the categories mentioned should never in any circumstances be ordered to be produced . . . Something must turn upon the nature of the subject matter, the persons who dealt with it, and the manner in which they did so. In so far as a matter of government policy is concerned, it may be relevant to know the extent to which the policy remains unfulfilled, so that its success might be prejudiced by disclosure of the considerations which led to it . . .

The ministerial certificate should offer all practicable assistance on these aspects. But the nature of the litigation and the apparent importance to it of the documents in question may in extreme cases demand production even of the most sensitive communications at the highest level.'

Lord Scarman:

'Discovery of documents remains, ultimately, a matter for the discretion of the court. It is a discretion governed by two general rules of law. The first is that discovery is not to be ordered unless necessary for fairly disposing of the case or for saving costs . . . The second is that only documents in a party's possession and control which relate to the matters in issue are required to be disclosed, but all such documents, subject to certain exceptions, are to be disclosed, whether or not admissible in evidence. Public interest immunity is, of course, an exception . . .

In *Conway v Rimmer* [1968] AC 910 this House had to consider two questions. They were formulated by Lord Reid in these terms, at p 943:

> " . . . first, whether the court is to have any right to question the finality of a minister's certificate and, secondly, if it has such a right, how and in what circumstances that right is to be exercised and made effective."

The House answered the first question, but did not, in my judgment, provide, nor was it required to provide, a complete answer to the second . . .

Having established the principle of . . . review, the House had in *Conway v Rimmer* [1968] AC 910 a simple case on the facts to decide . . .

In reaching its decision the House did indicate what it considered to be the correct approach to the clash of interests which arises whenever there is a question of public interest immunity . . .

The essence of the matter is a weighing, on balance, of the two public interests, that of the nation or the public service in non-disclosure and that of justice in the production of the documents. A good working, but not logically perfect, distinction is recognised between the contents and the classes of documents. If a minister of the Crown asserts that to disclose the contents of a document would, or might, do the nation or the public service a grave injury, the court will be slow to question his opinion or to allow any interest, even that of justice, to prevail over it. Unless there can be shown to exist some factor suggesting either a lack of good faith (which is not likely) or an error of judgment or an error of law on the minister's part, the court should not (the House held) even go so far as itself to inspect the document. In this sense, the minister's assertion may be said to be conclusive. It is, however, for the judge to determine whether the minister's opinion is to be treated as conclusive . . .

In "class" cases the House clearly considered the minister's certificate to be more likely to be open to challenge. Undoubtedly, however, the House thought that there were certain classes of documents, which ought not to be disclosed however harmless the disclosure of their contents might be, and however important their disclosure might be in the interest of justice. Cabinet minutes were cited as an example. But the point did not arise for decision . . .

The point does arise in the present case. The documents are "high level". They are concerned with the formulation of policy . . . In such circumstances the minister may well be right in his view that the public service would be injured by disclosure. But is the court bound by his view that it is *necessary* for the proper functioning of the public service that they be withheld from production? And, if non-disclosure is necessary for that purpose, is the court bound to hold that the interest in the proper functioning of the public service is to prevail over the requirements of justice? . . . [Is] the secrecy of the "inner workings of the government machine" so vital a public interest that it must prevail over even the most imperative demands of justice? If the contents of a document concern the national safety, affect diplomatic relations or relate to some state secret of high importance, I can understand an affirmative answer. But if they do not (and it is not claimed in this case that they do), what is so important about secret government that it must be protected even at the price of injustice in our courts? . . .

Sometimes the public service reasons will be decisive of the issue: but they should never prevent the court from weighing them against the injury which would be suffered in the administration of justice if the document was not to be disclosed. And the likely injury to the cause of justice must also be assessed and weighed. Its weight will vary according to the nature of the proceedings in which disclosure is sought, the relevance of the documents, and the degree of likelihood that the document will be of importance in the litigation. In striking the balance, the court may always, if it thinks it necessary, itself inspect the documents.'

In *Air Canada v Secretary of State for Trade* the British Airports Authority ('BAA'), a statutory body which owned and managed several airports including Heathrow airport, fixed the charges which airlines had to pay for using the airport. The BAA embarked on a programme of major improvements originally to be financed in part from reserve funds and in part from borrowing. However, the Secretary of State for Trade (under the Airports Authority Act 1975) required the BAA to finance the improvements from internal revenues. The BAA imposed a 35 per cent increase in charges at Heathrow airport. The plaintiffs brought an action against the Secretary of State and the BAA claiming, inter alia, declarations that the former had acted unlawfully and that the increase in charges imposed by the latter was excessive and illegal. They alleged that the Secretary of State's power to give financial directions to the BAA was confined to the purposes of the Act of 1975 and since his dominant motive in giving the instructions to the BAA was to reduce the public sector borrowing requirement, the directions were ultra vires and unlawful.

In order to investigate the Secretary of State's dominant purpose, the plaintiffs sought the production of certain documents for which the Secretary of State claimed public interest immunity and certificates to that effect were signed by the permanent secretaries of the government department concerned. The documents in category A consisted of high level ministerial papers relating to the formulation of government policy and those in category B consisted of inter-departmental communications between senior civil servants.

Lord Fraser:

'In considering the present law of England on what has come to be called public interest immunity, in relation to the production of documents, it is not necessary to go further back than *Conway v Rimmer* [1968] AC 910 where this House decided that a certificate by a minister stating that production of documents of a certain class would be contrary to the public interest, was not conclusive . . . I do not think that even Cabinet minutes are completely immune from disclosure in a case where, for example, the issue in a litigation involves serious misconduct by a Cabinet Minister . . . But while Cabinet documents do not have complete immunity, they are entitled to a high degree of protection against disclosure. In the present case the documents in category A do not enjoy quite the status of Cabinet minutes, but they approach that level in that they may disclose the reasons for Cabinet decisions and the process by which the decisions were reached. The reasons why such documents should not normally be disclosed until they have become of purely historical interest were considered in *Burmah Oil Co Ltd v Bank of England* [1980] AC 1090, where Lord Wilberforce said this, at p. 1112:

"One such ground is the need for candour in communication between those concerned with policy making. It seems now rather fashionable to decry this, but if as a ground it may at one time have been exaggerated, it has now, in my opinion, received an excessive dose of cold water. I am certainly not prepared—against the view of the minister—to discount the need, in the formation of such very controversial policy as that with which we are here involved, for frank and uninhibited advice from the bank to the government, from and between civil servants and between ministers . . . Another such ground is to protect from inspection by possible critics the inner working of government while forming important governmental policy. I do not believe that scepticism has invaded this, or that it is for the courts to assume the role of advocates for open government. If, as I believe, this is a valid ground for protection, it must continue to operate beyond the time span of a particular episode. Concretely, to reveal what advice was *then* sought and given and the mechanism for seeking and considering such advice might well make the process of government more difficult *now*. On this point too I am certainly not prepared to be wiser than the minister." . . .

But it has been claimed, and the onus therefore is on the plaintiffs, as the parties seeking disclosure, to show why the documents ought to be produced for inspection by the court privately. The question of whether the court, having inspected them privately, should order them to be produced publicly is a separate question which does not arise at this stage, although as I shall seek to show in a moment it is in my opinion relevant . . .

[A] party who seeks to compel his opponent, or an independent person, to disclose information must show that the information is likely to help his own case. It would be illogical to apply a different rule at the stage of inspection from that which applies at the stage of production. After all, the purpose of inspection by the court in many cases, including the present, would be to let the court see whether there is material in favour of disclosure which should be put in the scales to weigh against the material in favour of immunity. Inspection is with a view to the possibility of ordering production, and in my opinion inspection ought not to be ordered unless the court is persuaded that inspection is likely to satisfy it that it ought to take the further step of ordering production . . .

In *Burmah Oil Co Ltd v Bank of England* [1980] AC 1090 at 1117, Lord Wilberforce said that it was not desirable for the court to assume the task of inspection

> "except in rare instances where a strong positive case is made out, certainly not upon a bare unsupported assertion by the party seeking production that something to help him may be found, or upon some unsupported—viz, speculative—hunch of its own."

Of all the formulations I have seen, that is, I think, the one least favourable to inspection. Lord Edmund-Davies in the *Burmah Oil* case, at p. 1129 . . . expressed the view that a judge should not hesitate to call for production of documents for his private inspection if they are " 'likely' to contain material substantially useful to the party seeking discovery". At p. 1135 Lord Keith of Kinkel referred to

> "situations where grave doubt arises, and the court feels that it cannot properly decide upon which side the balance falls without privately inspecting the documents."

And Lord Scarman said, at p. 1145:

> "Inspection by the court is, I accept, a power to be exercised only if the court is in doubt, after considering the certificate, the issues in the case and the relevance of the documents whose disclosure is sought."

My Lords, I do not think it would be possible to state a test in a form which could be applied in all cases. Circumstances vary greatly. The weight of the public interest against disclosure will vary according to the nature of the particular documents in question; for example, it will in general be stronger where the documents are Cabinet papers than when they are at a lower level. The weight of the public interest in favour of disclosure will vary even more widely, because it depends upon the probable evidential value to the party seeking disclosure of the particular documents, in almost infinitely variable circumstances of individual cases. The most that can usefully be said is that, in order to persuade the court even to inspect documents for which public interest immunity is claimed, the party seeking disclosure ought at least to satisfy the court that the documents are very likely to contain material which would give substantial support to his contention on an issue which arises in the case, and that without them he might be "deprived of the means of . . . proper presentation" of his case: see *Glasgow Corpn v Central Land Board* 1956 SC (HL) 1 at 18, per Lord Radcliffe.'

Lord Wilberforce:

'What then are the criteria upon which a decision should be made to inspect, or not to do so? . . . [There] are three questions which have now to be answered. (1) What is it that the documents must be likely (in whatever degree) to support? (2) What is the degree of likelihood that must be shown? (3) Is that degree of likelihood attained? (1) . . . [There] must be a likelihood that the documents would support the case of the party seeking discovery . . . In a contest purely between one litigant and another, such as the present, the task of the court is to do, and be seen to be doing, justice between the parties—a duty reflected by the word "fairly" in the rule. There is no higher or additional duty to ascertain some independent truth . . . (2) The degree of likelihood (or providing support for the plaintiff's case) may be variously expressed: "likely" was the word used by Lord Edmund-Davies in *Burmah Oil:* a "reasonable probability" by Lord Keith of Kinkel. Both expressions must mean something beyond speculation, some concrete ground for belief which takes the case beyond a mere "fishing" expedition. One cannot attain greater precision in stating what must be a matter of estimation. I would accept either formula . . .

As [to (3)] the judgment of Bingham J [at first instance] contains this important passage:

"If it were necessary for the plaintiffs . . . to show a likelihood that the documents, if produced, would help them I could not on the material put before me conclude that they had done so. There are indications both ways. It would be wrong to guess."

I respectfully agree.'

Lord Scarman:

'The Crown having made its objection to production in proper form, in what circumstances should the court inspect privately the documents before determining whether they, or any of them, should be produced? . . .

If it is a "class" objection and the documents (as in *Conway v Rimmer* [1968] AC 910) are routine in character, the court may inspect so as to ascertain the strength of the public interest in immunity and the needs of justice before deciding whether to order production. If it is a "contents" claim, eg, a specific national security matter, the court will ordinarily accept the judgment of the minister. But if it is a class claim in which the objection on the face of the certificate is a strong one—as in this case where the documents are minutes and memoranda passing at a high level between ministers and their advisers and concerned with the formulation of policy—the court will pay great regard to the minister's view (or that of the senior official who has signed the certificate). It will not inspect unless there is a likelihood that the documents will be necessary for disposing fairly of the case or saving costs. Certainly, if, like Bingham J in this case, the court should think that the documents might be "determinative" of the issues in the action to which they relate, the court should inspect: for in such a case there may be grave doubt as to which way the balance of public interest falls . . . But, unless the court is satisfied on the material presented to it that the documents are likely to be necessary for fairly disposing of the case, it will not inspect for the simple reason that unless the likelihood exists there is nothing to set against the public interest in immunity from production . . .

The learned judge rejected, in my view rightly, the view which has commended itself to the Court of Appeal and to some of your Lordships that the criterion for determining whether to inspect or not is whether the party seeking production can establish the likelihood that the documents will assist his case or damage that of his opponent . . .

I would think it better in principle to retain the formulation of the interests to be balanced which Lord Reid gave us in *Conway v Rimmer* [1968] AC 910 at 940:

"It is universally recognised that here there are two kinds of public interest which may clash. There is the public interest that harm shall not be done to the nation or the public service by disclosure of certain documents, and there is the public interest that the administration of justice shall not be frustrated by the withholding of documents which must be produced if justice is to be done." . . .

Basically, the reason for selecting the criterion of justice, irrespective of whether it assists the party seeking production, is that the Crown may not have regard to party advantage in deciding whether or not to object to production on the ground of public interest immunity. It is its duty to bring the objection, if it believes it to be sound, to the attention of the court. It is for the court, not the Crown, to balance the two public interests.'

Discovery is always at the court's discretion; there is no rule that a class of documents is automatically immune from discovery merely because they are of a high level of public importance. (For the 'discovery' powers of the Parliamentary Commissioner for Administration see chapter 8.)

The law relating to PII continued to develop thereafter. In *Re HIV Haemophiliac Litigation*,[43] 962 haemophiliacs, their wives and children who had developed, or who would develop, AIDs claimed their condition arose from being treated for haemophilia with the preparation known as Factor VIII concentrate. This had been imported from the USA by the National Health Service. They made various claims in tort, including allegations of negligence, against the authorities who had treated them and the Department of Health (DoH). In one instance they alleged, for example, that the DoH had been negligent in failing to ensure that the United Kingdom was self-sufficient in blood supplies and blood-based products so that infected material from the USA had to be imported. To help prove their case the plaintiffs sought production of various documents, production of which was resisted by the DoH on the basis that they related to ministerial briefings on blood products etc, and the allocation of resources. The DoH argued that disclosure should not be made because the plaintiff's claims did not add up to good causes of action in law. At first instance Rougier J ordered discovery of some documents only. The plaintiffs appealed against his partial order, and the defendants against any order at all. In the Court of Appeal Ralph Gibson LJ adopted a two-stage approach ie:

(a) to consider, first, whether the claim of public interest immunity was made out generally;

(b) then ask whether, nevertheless, that claim could be overridden by a greater public interest in securing justice.

Ralph Gibson LJ accepted that (a) had been made out, as did the plaintiffs; the documents in question were extremely sensitive. As to (b), however, he applied the *Air Canada* test that those seeking discovery had to show that: 'the documents are very likely to contain material which would give substantial support to [their] contention on an issue which arises in the case and that without them [they] might be deprived of the means of . . . proper presentation of [their] case'. Ralph Gibson LJ, however, added: 'The test must, of course, be understood and applied with regard to the fact that the party seeking disclosure, and the court, know only the class of documents as described and do not know what is in them.' This 'gloss' on the *Air Canada* test lightens the burden on those seeking discovery just a little for clearly less can be demanded by them by way of proof if they have no absolutely certain knowledge of the content of the documents of which they seek discovery.

Ralph Gibson LJ went on to argue, on the basis of the evidence so far, there was a *prima facie* case (ie a good, 'first sight' case) of negligence on the part of the DoH. That negligence he ascribed to 'the result of failure at some level within the department to pass [the] available information [about American Factor VIII] to those [within the department] who were required to make the decisions [on its use]'. He concluded that the material in issue in the case 'would give substantial support to the plaintiffs' contentions and that without [it] the plaintiffs might be deprived of the means of proper presentation of their case'. The material would show whether or not there was a failure to give due regard to known risks of using US Factor VIII, and why such a failure of judgement occurred. Disclosure was needed in order to ensure the 'fair and proper disposal of the case'.

---

[43] [1990] NLJR 1349.

The law was further developed in *Balfour v Foreign and Commonwealth Office*.[44] Balfour alleged he had been unfairly dismissed by his employers, the FCO, and he took a case before an industrial tribunal under the employment protection legislation. During the course of this he sought discovery of certain documents in the possession of the Crown, in respect of which PII was claimed. Before the industrial tribunal Balfour failed because the tribunal chairman made an error of law and considered he was absolutely bound by the ministerial affidavits claiming PII. There was an appeal to the Employment Appeal Tribunal.

Knox J made a number of specific points:

- not all cases of PII claims are the same, even where the state is involved;
- in some cases a minister's reasons for claiming PII are capable of being evaluated according to the experience and knowledge of judges, in which case the decision to disclose is the product of a simple balancing exercise between the two cases for/against disclosure—ie has a claim to immunity been made out, but nevertheless has the applicant made out a claim that there should be disclosure;
- in other cases, eg where non-disclosure is claimed on grounds of national security, it is harder for judges to decide the issue. On the basis of *Thorburn v Herman*[45] the court will pay great respect to a claim of non-disclosure on grounds of national security. The court will accept that a ministerial affidavit claiming PII on grounds of national security means what it says and will not dispute that security issues are involved. That does *not* mean, however, that the Crown's claim is absolutely predeterminative of the issue. It is, rather, that the scale against which the applicant has to establish his/her need for disclosure is more demanding. Thus where a PII claim involves allegations that national security is involved it is not, *in general*, appropriate for a subordinate court to allow a claim for disclosure in the face of 'a ministerial certificate as regards national security considerations including, in particular, the assessment of dangers involved in the disclosure of classes of document'.

The general position would thus seem to be:

(1) *no* document is absolutely immune from an order for disclosure;

(2) the court makes the decision on disclosure, no one else;

(3) the court in making its decision has a discretion whether or not to inspect the documents before ordering disclosure;

(4) where PII is claimed by *anyone* the first question is whether it has been established in general that the document(s) in question are entitled to PII, and then, if the answer is affirmative, to ask whether nevertheless there is a greater public interest in the proper administration of justice to be served by overriding the PII claim. In this context the PII claim must be supported by evidence linking the document(s) to the claim for non-disclosure;

(5) in answering the *second* question it is for the *person seeking disclosure* to show that the document(s) is/are very likely to contain material giving substantial support to his/her contentions, and without which he/she will be deprived of a proper means of arguing the case;

(6) in cases where PII is claimed on grounds of national security by way of a ministerial affidavit, inferior or subordinate courts such as industrial tribunals should *generally* accept the ministerial claim;

---

[44] [1993] ICR 663, affirmed [1994] 2 All ER 588 (CA).   [45] *The Times*, 14 May 1992.

(7) in *any* case where PII is claimed on national security grounds a court has to go through a balancing exercise of weighing the interests of the proper administration of justice against those of preserving national security, with the scales initially weighted in favour of preserving security, though here much depends on the reason why disclosure is sought.

(a) Are ministers bound to claim PII?

This issue arose in the context of the 'arms to Iraq' or 'Matrix-Churchill' scandal, the unfolding of which has considerable implications for ministerial responsibility to Parliament: see further chapter 4 below.

In 1984 the UN, as a matter of international law which bound the United Kingdom, placed an embargo on the sale of weapons and similar goods to Iraq. Subsequently Messrs Henderson, Allen & Abraham (executives of the Matrix-Churchill Co) were accused of and prosecuted for illegally exporting arms-making equipment to Iraq. They were further accused of misleading government officials by claiming the machinery they were exporting to Iraq was for peaceful purposes only. In fact 17 British firms were encouraged to exhibit at the 1989 Baghdad arms fair and Mr Henderson claimed that he had in fact been an agent of the British government discovering details of Iraqi arms procurement for Whitehall, and that the government, or at least a number of its members, knew what he was about in doing business with President Saddam Hussein. Into that matter a separate judicial inquiry under Scott LJ was appointed. What is of interest for this chapter was the attempt by the Crown to prevent certain evidence being given in court during the trial on grounds of PII. A number of ministers, including Mr Heseltine, Mr Clarke, Mr Rifkind and Mr Garel-Jones, signed affidavits claiming PII for information in the possession of their departments—some 500 pages of confidential and classified ministerial communications in all.

The ministers, it was subsequently claimed, believed they *had* to claim immunity because of the highly sensitive nature of the information in question, though they also knew the trial judge could override their affidavits. The legal basis for this contention was a statement by Lord Scarman in the *Air Canada* case that when claiming PII ministers were 'discharging a duty'. Quite what Lord Scarman meant by that was not clear.

At the trial of Mr Henderson, Mr Allen and Mr Abraham, the trial judge, Smedley J, ordered that the secret ministerial papers should not be granted PII but should be disclosed to the defence, in the interests of a fair trial; the prosecution subsequently collapsed. Other exporters who had been similarly charged, and convicted, of illegally exporting arms to Iraq, and whose claims for discovery of documents had been resisted by the Crown on the basis that there were *no* documents showing the turning of an official 'blind eye' to arms exports, subsequently successfully appealed against conviction.[46] It is clear that PII can be claimed in criminal as well as civil proceedings, but in the former case the claim has to be weighed against the weighty interests of justice and the need to secure a fair trial for the defendant.[47]

Before the Scott inquiry into the affair the Attorney General, Sir Nicholas Lyell, appeared to admit that the argument that ministers have an absolute 'duty' to claim PII was untenable, and that rather the decision was one for ministers acting on legal advice. By mid 1995 new

---

[46] *R v Blackledge* [1996] 1 Cr App Rep 326.
[47] *R v Governor of Brixton Prison, ex p Osman* [1991] 1 WLR 281, and see further the Crown Prosecution Service Legal Guidance on such cases (*http://www.eps.gov.uk/legal/section20/chapter_i.html*).

guidance on the use of PII claims had been drafted and these were promulgated in December 1996. Documents *must* be disclosed unless disclosure would cause real harm or damage to the public interest, *and this must be specified*, for example harm to an informant, or to international relations, or to the national economic interest. 'Class claims' in respect of documents will not be made. The new principle is maximum disclosure consistent with protecting essential public interests. This is also consistent with the decision of the House of Lords in *R v Chief Constable of West Midland Police, ex p Wiley*[48] where it was stated that as a general principle documents relevant and material to litigation should be disclosed unless that would result in substantial harm. Ministers should exercise discretion as to where the balance of the public interest lies, and this, it appears, has led to a reduction in the number of PII claims.

(b) Do Crown servants enjoy special privileges with regard to contempt of court?

This issue arose in *M v Home Office*.[49] M, a 28 year old teacher and citizen of Zaire, came to the UK on a false passport in September 1990 seeking political refuge after having been beaten and imprisoned for anti-government strike activities. His claim was processed by the Home Office who concluded he was not a bona fide political refugee, and in April 1991 they indicated M should be returned to Zaire by May 1991. M had already made an application for judicial review of the deportation decision in March 1991 and that had been rejected. On the afternoon of the proposed date of deportation M appealed against the refusal of leave for judicial review but was unsuccessful. *A few hours later a fresh application on new grounds was made to Garland J.* This occurred after M changed his solicitors. That application was technically incorrectly made. The new application should have been made to the Court of Appeal who had taken jurisdiction in the matter by hearing the appeal against the earlier refusal, Garland J received the application at 5.30 pm, while M was due to be deported at 6.00 pm. Realising the complexities of the legal issues involved Garland J had indicated he needed time to consider the matter and asked for M's deportation to be postponed. Garland J received at 5.50 pm from counsel for the Home Office what appeared to be an undertaking to that effect. However, neither counsel nor the solicitors for the Home Office had instructions to give such an undertaking.

What followed was an embarrassing blunder. Garland J proceeded on the basis that undertaking had been given, the Home Office then had to try to fulfil the undertaking they had never contemplated being made. Officials tried to prevent M's deportation, but it was too late and his flight took off at 6.47 pm. It was even too late to intercept his flight in Paris, despite an order from Garland J, made when he learned that M had left the UK, that he should be returned so that the matter could be calmly considered the next morning. There were clear administrative failings in the Home Office in that those responsible for executing M's deportation were not kept fully informed as to the progress of court proceedings concerning the deportation. Similarly, when on the following day it was clear that M had been sent beyond Paris, Garland J made a further order at 2.15 pm that M should be brought back to the United Kingdom. The Home Secretary was not personally informed of the situation until 4.00 pm when it was clearly probably too late to do anything. However, the Home Secretary, being

48 [1995] 1 AC 274.   49 [1992] QB 270 (CA); affirmed [1994] 1 AC 377.

advised that there was no illegality in ignoring Garland J's order, *chose personally* not to comply with the order. That then became a legal issue: in choosing not to comply with Garland J's order once he had learned of all the facts had the Home Secretary committed contempt of court? Garland J formally set aside in his order the next day but the damage was done by then.

The matter came at first instance before Simon Brown J[50] who concluded the Home Secretary could not be liable for contempt of court, because he believed that orders of the court made against ministers were not enforceable by compulsion against ministers, and the same applied to undertakings given on a minister's behalf. 'Orders' in such cases become really no more than 'requests'. The matter was appealed. The Master of the Rolls in the Court of Appeal giving the principal judgment argued that, irrespective of any mistake Garland J had made about the order he had made (because of the complex legalities already referred to above) there was no doubt he had jurisdiction in the issue. The MR stated: 'The High Court was a court of unlimited jurisdiction, and its judges could make any order which was not illegal . . . The present order was irregular, and should not have been made, but it was not made without jurisdiction.'[51]

Given that Garland J had acted within jurisdiction, what effect did his having made an inappropriate order have? The MR argued that the effect was that the order was binding until set aside, and thus the Home Secretary and his officials should have complied with it until released by a finding on appeal against the order: they certainly should not simply have done nothing. The MR then turned to the most contentious issue; could the Home Secretary be guilty of contempt for his failure to obey Garland J's order? The MR argued that contempt proceedings could not lie against the disembodied entities of the Crown and the Home Office: only a natural person or body with a legal personality (eg a company) can commit contempt of court, and the Home Secretary had committed a serious contempt by withholding action on M's return to Zaire. There was a further appeal to the House of Lords, where the Court of Appeal's decision was confirmed. The House of Lords added, however, that a finding of contempt of court against a minister in his/her official capacity may be made, as it also may against a department of state. In such circumstances the contempt proceedings may not be personal or punitive, but the finding of contempt indicates the subordination of ministers to the law, (and see above chapter 2 on the rule of law) and an order for costs may be made to reinforce the significance of the finding. The *political* consequences of such a finding for ministers are, however, for Parliament to determine.

That decision was historic. No minister of the Crown had ever been made liable for contempt in the execution of his functions before. Counsel for the Home Secretary had argued that ministers were above the contempt jurisdiction because the courts are the Crown's courts and ministers are the Crown's servants and the Crown cannot be seen to be punishing itself. This echoed arguments (from the seventeenth century) that the executive is above the law, and the courts' rejection of the argument is a reassertion of the principle of the rule of law 'The King is under no man, but under God and under the law'.

The constitutional importance of the decision is great. Ministers as individuals cannot shelter behind the shield of Crown immunity, but are responsible if what they do results in an order of the court being flouted.

In the House of Lords, Lord Templeman stated: 'the argument that there was no power to enforce the law by injunction or contempt proceedings against a minister in his official

---

[50] [1992] 4 All ER 97.   [51] [1992] QB 270 at 299 (post letter A).

capacity would, if upheld, establish the proposition that the executive obeyed the law as a matter of grace, not of necessity, a proposition that would reverse the result of the Civil War'.[52] Note also *R v IRC, ex p Kingston Smith*[53] where the Inland Revenue Service had to apologise for the failure of its officials to act in accordance with an injunction. The problem nevertheless remains that the Crown itself remains immune from judicial process, and it is not always easy to determine where 'the Crown' begins and 'the Crown's servants' end. There is an argument for a statutory rule to impose corporate liability on the government when it acts in the name of the Crown.

III. The Personal Prerogatives

The television documentary 'Elizabeth R' (6 February 1992) gave a glimpse of the monarch's otherwise highly confidential relationships with ministers. The Queen made *general* remarks about how she had 'got on' with her nine prime ministers from 1952 to 1992. She claimed to be a 'sounding board'; 'they unburden themselves or they tell me what's going on'. The Queen continued 'If they've got any problems . . . sometimes one can help in that way too.' She added: 'It's rather nice to feel that one's a sort of sponge and everybody can come and tell one things. Some things stay there and some things go out the other ear and some things never come out at all. Occasionally you can put one's point of view when perhaps they hadn't seen it from that angle.' This was hardly an earth-shattering revelation but was perhaps a little more than was known before. Rather more is known from Ben Pimlott's biography *The Queen*[54] which resulted from interviews with a range of persons including other members of the Royal Family, courtiers and close friends of the Queen, together with access to royal archives allowed by Buckingham Palace. Though more exposed to media coverage than any previous monarch, the Queen, however, remains in public formal and unemotional.

The personal prerogatives of the monarch remain a subject shrouded in history and mystery. From a strictly legal point of view there are enormous personal powers to change governments, alter the course of legislation and to intervene in the political life of the nation. In practice none of these things happens because of the growth of constitutional conventions which have largely served to distance the monarch from the day-to-day business of government and from political controversy, so that it is the monarch's ministers chosen, by convention, from the elected majority in Parliament, who take responsibility for the Crown's actions, and on whose advice the monarch is conventionally required to act.

It may thus be stated that convention demands that:

- the monarch will give the Royal Assent to legislation unless advised to refuse it by ministers;
- the Prime Minister will be the leader of the party with a majority of seats in the House of Commons and will be a member of that House;
- Parliament will be dissolved only on the advice of ministers.

In normal circumstances these requirements operate without being questioned and the monarch's influence is limited to what Rodney Brazier terms the 'usual powers' ie the right to

---

[52] [1994] 1 AC 377 (post letter G).   [53] [1996] STC 1210.   [54] (HarperCollins, London, 1996).

be informed, the right to warn, the right to encourage.[55] No doubt these 'rights' are exercised by the monarch during her regular totally private *and* unrecorded Tuesday afternoon audiences with the Prime Minister of the day. It is, however, possible for subtle monarchical encouragement to take place in relation to *other* ministers. In his memoirs *Time and Chance* Lord Callaghan recalled being seated next to the Queen at a supper hosted by the Italian embassy during the time of the Rhodesian independence crisis in the late 1960s. The then Mr Callaghan was Foreign and Commonwealth Secretary in the 1964–70 Wilson government with responsibility for dealing with the situation and he outlined to the Queen various initiatives which had been taken and which had led to a number of choices opening up for further action, including the option of doing nothing for a while. The following day Lord Callaghan records receiving a letter written by the Queen's private secretary which stated: 'she recognises that any initiative you take may prove ineffective but none the less believes it would be worthwhile to make the effort'. Lord Callaghan added that the Queen's opinion was 'enough to tip the scales' in favour of action.[56]

Brazier[57] records a number of historic 'warnings' from monarch to Prime Minister, such as George V's worries that combining the tasks of Prime Minister and Foreign Secretary might be too much for Ramsay MacDonald, the urging of Baldwin in 1924 to take 'powerful' action on housing, unemployment, the cost of food and education, and George VI's strong admonition to Churchill that he should not place himself in danger by being personally present to watch the D-Day landings in 1944. Also worth remembrance was the veiled warning given by the Queen in her silver jubilee response to a loyal address from both Houses of Parliament in 1977. This was at a time of strong separatist tensions in Scotland and Wales. The Queen stated she would not forget she had been crowned monarch of the *United Kingdom*. Pimlott in his biography further records expressions of disquiet by the Queen when the UK government acquiesced in the invasion of Grenada, a Commonwealth country, by the USA in 1983, and over Baroness Thatcher's opposition to sanctions against South Africa in respect of the apartheid regime.

However, matters rarely come to the point where any kind of warning has to be given, and tactful advice will normally be the pattern of the monarch's relationship with the Prime Minister, both being aware of the fundamental constitutional needs for neither to embarrass the other politically, for there to be complete confidentiality in the relationships between the monarch and her ministers, and for the monarch not to be associated with particular political policies. The monarch may drop hints, may refer to letters she has received from her subjects—a considerable number of people write to the Queen on all sorts of issues—and may rely on 'behind the scenes' communications between her private secretary and the Prime Minister's private secretary. She may also rely on the weight that inevitably attaches to her considerable experience of public affairs. Even before she assumed the throne in 1952 the then Princess Elizabeth was involved as much as was constitutionally proper in matters of state by her father King George VI (the Prince of Wales sees a variety of state papers today, and also receives both individual ministers and opposition leaders privately), and just as Queen Victoria was able to tell Gladstone what Wellington had told her about Pitt, so Queen Elizabeth II may be able to relate what Churchill told her about the conduct of government during and before the First World War. Pimlott argues that the Queen never directly criticises

---

[55] *Constitutional Practice* (3rd edn, OUP, Oxford, 1999), p. 184 et seq.
[56] *Time and Chance* (William Collins Sons & Co, London, 1987), pp. 380–381.
[57] Op cit pp. 186–187.

government policies, but she expresses her views by hints, or by asking leading questions, or by referring to other persons known to hold alternative views. If the Queen approves of policy she says so openly: a failure to comment indicates disapproval.

Of course there will be considerable differences of outlook, emphasis, and values between the Queen and any given Prime Minister, as Hugo Young described in his study of Baroness Thatcher's years in government, *One of Us*. Young describes the entire Royal Family as 'worried paternalists' concerned about issues of care and compassion, and standing for certain societal values which came under intense pressure during the years of the Thatcher governments.[58] Even so Young exploded one of the prevalent political myths of the time that the Queen had been 'worried to the point of outrage' over certain government policies and had taken steps to 'leak' her views via Palace officials to the press. Young found not a shred of evidence to support such arguments.[59] The Queen's respect for 'punctilious' constitutionalism would never allow her to ventilate her opinions so openly, and certainly not through the press. It is generally understood that the Queen extends to her ministers what the then Mr Macmillan called in 1972 an invariable graciousness and 'understanding'.[60] Pimlott nevertheless argues that the Queen indicated subtle disapproval of the general trend of some 'Thatcherite' policies, particularly with regard to the treatment of the less well-off in society, the abandonment of a general consensus on social policies, and the confrontation with striking miners in 1984.

Though it rarely happens, the monarch may see individual ministers to discuss issues affecting their departments, however, it is more usual for the Queen's private secretary to pass to a minister correspondence received from a subject, the implication being that the Queen feels the matter raised is of some importance, and this is enough to secure action of some sort. The Chancellor of the Exchequer also has an annual audience to brief the monarch on budget proposals. Occasionally the monarch may grant an audience to the Leader of the Opposition, who in any case as a member of the Privy Council has the right to speak to the Queen confidentially. Of course no formal advice can be given by the Leader of the Opposition, nor may the Queen act on his advice. Nevertheless there is clear evidence in Pimlott's work that the Queen has her own views on policy issues, and that she expresses these as part of the system of checks and balances within the constitution to bring alternative views and warnings to the notice of those who have executive power and who are able to control the legislature also—ie the Queen's ministers.

(a) Other members of the Royal Family

The strict conventions separating the monarch from involvement in political controversy are somewhat less well defined with regard to other members of the Royal Family. It would be, for example, unthinkable for a 'Royal' to espouse in any way open to public knowledge the cause of one political party against the others. Too much of that occurred under the Hanoverians in the eighteenth century when the heir to the throne could be a focus for politicians seeking office. However, if one defines politics quite properly and more widely than merely 'party politics' to include any question on the organisation of society, then it is hard for members of the Royal Family, given their close involvement with social and philanthropic causes, not to be

---

[58] *One of Us* (Macmillan, London, 1989), pp. 488–489.   [59] See also Brazier, op cit pp. 188–189.
[60] *Pointing the Way* (Macmillan, London, 1972), p. 39.

at least touched by some controversy. The Prince of Wales's comment criticising the proposed redevelopment of the Mappin and Webb site near the Mansion House in London was certainly controversial and undoubtedly played its part in the decision that the initial proposal should not proceed. Similarly on Friday 8 December 1995 *The Independent* reported anger amongst Conservative MPs that the Princess of Wales had appeared to support critics of government policy on homelessness by sharing a platform on the issue with a Labour MP, Mr Jack Straw. On the other hand Prince Charles was reported as having annoyed *Labour* ministers by not attending an official banquet for the President of China—which some newspaper commentators tried to portray also as a rift between the Queen and the Prince of Wales.[61] Similarly the Prince was stated to have annoyed ministers by joining the Beaufort Hunt and eating beef on the bone while it was banned by law for health reasons.[62]

In March 2001 it was reported that the Prince of Wales had agreed to undergo self-imposed silence on the issue of the government's handling of the foot and mouth disease outbreak, lest his open support for farmers whose livelihoods were at risk during that event might be seen to be 'stepping over the line' into political issues. This was a sensitive issue as a general election was due.[63] However, by September 2002 concern in the Labour Party and the Fabian Society was reported over the number of letters and phone calls received by ministers from the Prince of Wales on issues as wide-ranging as law and order, 'red tape' and genetically modified foods. In response to this, sources at St James's Palace—the Prince's then London base—stated that there was a need to represent views that might otherwise go unheard.[64] This led *The Times* to comment on 25 September 2002 that while the Prince's well-known ability to speak his mind was an example of his sincerity, he should be wary of becoming involved in 'hot' political issues. It was then reported that every government from the late 1960s onwards had been subject to a degree of lobbying from the Prince of Wales, and it appears he has been the most outspoken holder of that position since George IV, who before his appointment as Prince Regent actively courted political opposition to his father, George III.[65] On the other hand, some of Prince Charles's causes, such as environmental concern, have ceased to be fringe matters and are now at the centre of national and international politics. To ensure that there should be a more discreet and formalised link between the Prince and ministers, it was stated that a minister would take responsibility for acting as a conduit between Whitehall and St James's Palace.[66]

Even so, allegations have continued to be made about strained relationships between the Prince of Wales and the government. It is argued that these date back to 1999, when the Prince declined to attend a state banquet in honour of the President of China as an expression of concern over China's action in Tibet. In May 2004 the Prince then hosted a reception for the exiled Dalai Lama of Tibet which the Prime Minister declined to attend, citing 'diary pressures' as the reason. The Prince of Wales further indicated his dislike of China's record in regard to human rights by being absent from a Chinese banquet in honour of the Queen and refused to accompany President Jiang Zemin on official functions during a visit to this country. This caused embarrassment to the Foreign and Commonwealth Office.[67] Further evidence of tension emerged in November 2004 when Prince Charles allegedly made critical comments on certain aspects of education policy.[68] A 'cooling off' period was arranged by the

[61] *The Sunday Times*, 24 October 1999.   [62] *The Times*, 1 November 1999.
[63] *The Times*, 22 March 2001.   [64] *The Times*, 24 September 2002.
[65] *The Times*, 26 September 2002.   [66] *The Sunday Times*, 29 September 2002.
[67] *The Times*, 26 May 2004, and *The Times*, 21 January 2006.
[68] *The Times*, 18 November, 19 November, 22 November 2004, *The Sunday Times*, 21 November 2004.

Prince's principal private secretary and the Prime Minister's principal private secretary who act as the channel of communication between Clarence House—the Prince's current London home—and 10 Downing Street.[69] The Prince of Wales has, however, continued to make his views known on issues which may be the subject of government policy, for example the proposal to bulldoze whole areas of Victorian terraced housing in the North and Midlands of England; a policy, it should be added that, at the time, appeared to be less than unanimously supported by all government departments, so a 'head-to-head' clash did not occur.[70]

The matter assumed a greater public significance in 2006 when the Prince of Wales took court action against certain newspapers alleging breach of confidentiality and copyright when extracts from his private journals concerning his views on the 1997 handover of Hong Kong to China were published. A former royal servant made allegations in his witness statement in the case to the effect that the Prince of Wales had a view of himself as a 'dissident' able to take on a campaigning role with regard to controversial issues. Ministers who had received arguments from the Prince of Wales on, inter alia, farming, rural pursuits, architecture, heritage, education, human rights and foreign affairs, had also adopted a tactic of receiving these statements, but not acting on them, while attempting to ensure that the Prince does not become a focus of political opposition to the government. It is one thing to pester ministers with letters and phone calls, but quite another to adopt a seriously partial position on controversial issues which are matters of policy for ministers to determine and Parliament to debate.

The constitutional position of those 'in line' to succeed to the throne is unenviable as our constitution assigns no formal role to them. Each person who steps into the positions of heir apparent and heir presumptive (currently the Prince of Wales and Prince William) has to create that role for themselves. It must be borne in mind, however, that he or she who would be a constitutional monarch must learn to behave in a constitutional fashion and avoid becoming involved in political issues, especially those of a party nature, but that does not mean a life of enforced idleness. The current Prince of Wales has been heir apparent for over fifty years and has consistently and conscientiously sought to avoid the mistakes of his two predecessors George IV and Edward VII who found themselves similarly placed. He has devoted much of his life to the charitable and voluntary sector and has inevitably encountered the problems and points of view of particular, and arguably vulnerable, sections of society. Is he to ignore what he sees and hears? If so, he runs the risk of appearing cold and aloof. If, however, he expresses a point of view, particularly in an age where his public—and private—appearances are recorded and broadcast, his statements may well be misinterpreted. Furthermore any action he takes to improve his public standing may bring him into conflict with a government which is also sensitive about its 'image'. It appears to be unacceptable to the Prince of Wales for him not to speak on issues of which he believes he has knowledge and experience. Constitutional propriety, however, demands that he must only do so in a way that does not embarrass the elected government of the day by appearing to undermine what is clear policy. In theory the gentle assertion of a point of view by the Prince of Wales in a private capacity on an issue where government policy is as yet unformed or unclear might appear to be acceptable. However, it is hard to see how such an expression could ever be considered as 'just another' point of view from a private citizen by ministers. Furthermore there is the problem of embarrassing 'leaks' of the Prince's views by, for example, his former employees.

One possible way forward was reported in *The Times* on 16 January 2006. As Her Majesty the Queen reduces some of her public engagements on account of her age, the Prince of Wales

---

[69] *The Times*, 23 November 2004.   [70] *The Times*, 25 May 2005.

may take some of them over, for example by being granted greater access to state papers, presiding at investitures and meeting foreign dignitaries. The Prince of Wales had two private audiences with the Prime Minister in 2005 and more may take place on a regular basis. These would enable the Prince to express his views in the security of privacy. Such meetings would not, of course, replace the Queen's weekly audience with the Prime Minister, even though this has, it appears, *once* been 'modernised' to take place over the telephone!

(b) The 'reserve powers' of the monarch

The monarch is often said to have two ultimate duties: the first to avoid constitutional conflict, maintain stability and to ensure that government is carried on normally; the second is to be a 'constitutional referee' in extraordinary situations. In support of this it is contended that the monarch's religious authority as Supreme Governor of the Church of England (not 'Head' as is frequently and doctrinally incorrectly stated) and as 'Defender of the Faith' coupled with her unique social position reinforce the performance of these duties. However, in our secularised and less deferential modern society it may be countered that no monarch would lightly involve him or herself in political controversy without having the overwhelming force of united public opinion on his/her side—and that is not likely to exist given the diversity and plurality of modern British society. On the other hand it may also be supposed that no Prime Minister would propose legislation that would upset the fundamental balance of the constitution, and its democratic working, without also having such overwhelming united public opinion on his/her side.

What then would be the situations in which the 'reserve powers' (a term utilised by Professor Brazier in his study *Constitutional Practice*[71] to which indebtedness is acknowledged) could be used, and what are they?

(c) Refusal of the Royal Assent to legislation

It is well known that the formula 'La reine s'avisera' ('the Queen will think about it') was last used in 1707, since when the Royal Assent has always been given to legislation passing both Houses of Parliament. The Royal Assent could, however, be constitutionally refused to such legislation if this was advised by ministers, for example if there was a change of government without a dissolution of Parliament, and the incoming ministers had 'second thoughts' about the proposals. Could it be otherwise withheld? Professor Brazier puts forward a number of instances including Bills to prolong the life of Parliament for no proper reason, or to subvert the democratic basis of the constitution, eg by gerrymandering constituency boundaries so as to favour the government party and prevent the exercise of democratic choice by the electorate. However, he concludes that in the exceptionally unlikely event of such a situation occurring the monarch would constitutionally be limited to 'vigorous private protest . . . or to insisting on a dissolution (but assenting to the Bill if passed again in the new Parliament)'.[72] Professor Brazier thus seems to agree with the strong tide of modern thinking that the

---

[71] (3rd edn, OUP, Oxford, 1999).   [72] Brazier, op cit p. 196.

monarch is bound to act on ministerial advice, even if that advice itself is unconstitutional. His conclusion is that: 'the Queen would, therefore, be justified today in using her legislative veto only over a Bill designed to postpone, without all-party agreement, a dissolution in peacetime'.[73] Indeed it may be supposed that a government bent on such unconstitutional action would not be averse to sweeping away the monarchy altogether, provided it had the support of public opinion. But then it should not be forgotten that Hitler came to power in Germany democratically via the ballot box.

(i) Dismissing ministers

Refusal of the Royal Assent would certainly lead to the resignation of the monarch's ministers and hence their 'indirect dismissal', but what of direct dismissal? Professor Brazier suggests that the one situation in which the Queen could dismiss ministers is where they had lost a vote of confidence in the House of Commons, but had refused to resign and had also not requested a dissolution of Parliament. However, even in such a circumstance the wiser course of action would be for the monarch to dissolve Parliament, for any other course of action directly involves the Crown in party politics.

(ii) Dissolving Parliament

If the monarch may insist on a dissolution of Parliament where ministers have lost its confidence but have not themselves requested a dissolution (for only the monarch can dissolve Parliament) are there other cases where a dissolution could be justified against ministerial advice? The only circumstances in which this might be constitutionally proper is where there is a government proposal to 'swamp' the House of Lords with newly created peers in order to ensure the passage of legislation which has the support of the House of Commons. This was the situation which arose in 1909–1911 when the Conservative-dominated House of Lords, acting in defiance of a long-standing convention, refused its assent to Lloyd George's 'people's budget' of 1909 which had the overwhelming support of the Liberal-dominated House of Commons. This led to proposals to introduce a Bill to reduce the powers of the Upper House; the Bill was, however, not likely to be enacted in the face of the Conservative dominance of the House of Lords. Ministers argued that the monarch might have to use the prerogative power to create new peers to cancel the Conservative majority in the Upper House. Winston Churchill, a Liberal at that time, delivered a speech in which he hinted that such a creation of peers *would* take place *on the decision of the cabinet*—a claim which certainly involved the monarch in politics to the angered embarrassment of King Edward VII. However, that monarch, and his son George V who succeeded to the throne in 1910, were both insistent that before the prerogative was used to create new peers, ministers should test their support by 'going to the country' in a general election, and this in fact occurred in December 1910. Thereafter the Conservative majority in the Lords gave way once the King's conditional guarantee to create peers was made public.

What of the converse situation of *refusing* a dissolution requested by ministers? If the monarch is to discharge the duty of seeing that government is carried on, is it constitutionally

---

[73] Brazier, op cit pp. 195–196.

proper to refuse a dissolution on a Prime Ministerial request for one where it is clear that such a dissolution has nothing to do with the national interest and is only designed to impose order on the majority party in Parliament? It was rumoured, for example, in November 1992 that Mr Major might seek a dissolution in order to fight a general election should he fail to gain support for his measures to ensure parliamentary ratification of the Maastricht Treaty, yet he had only recently been returned to power in such an election. Could the Queen have refused his request? It would certainly appear constitutionally proper for the monarch to seek advice, for example from her private secretary and senior privy councillors such as former ministers, before responding to a request for what may be termed an 'irregular' dissolution where there is no clear need for one. Likewise in private the monarch could urge the Prime Minister to continue in office, or to test the confidence of the House of Commons in the government by seeking a vote of confidence. However, any refusal to refuse a dissolution request would inevitably involve the monarch in political controversy, and the position must be, as Sir Alan Lascelles, George VI's private secretary, wrote (under a pseudonym) in a letter to *The Times* in 1950, that a dissolution is not to be refused unless the monarch is convinced that '(1) the existing Parliament was still vital, viable and capable of doing its job; (2) a general election would be detrimental to the national economy; (3) he could rely on finding another Prime Minister who could carry on his government for a reasonable period, with a working majority in the House of Commons'.

Since the end of the Second World War most Parliaments have lasted for about four years of their statutory five. Only occasionally have Prime Ministers with unworkable majorities sought an election with a view to seeking return to office with a working majority—though Harold Wilson did so in both his periods of government from 1964 to 1970 and from 1974 to 1976. On the other hand once a Parliament has run for four years or so there is nothing unconstitutional in the Prime Minister seeking a dissolution at the time which seems most suited to him/her to favour his/her reelection. It is to cancel out that 'built-in' advantage for the party in power that calls have been made for fixed-term Parliaments.

(d) The appointment of ministers

It is for the Prime Minister to appoint other ministers and it would be 'unthinkable' today for the Queen to either dismiss a minister over the head of the Prime Minister or to refuse to accept the appointment of the Prime Minister's nominees for office. This is a far cry from the last century when Queen Victoria's request went to Gladstone not to include Sir Charles Dilke among his ministers on the basis of moral turpitude as Dilke had been involved in a divorce case, or when the same monarch considered dismissing Palmerston for approving the seizure of power in France by Louis-Napoleon without first consulting her, despite an earlier undertaking from Palmerston that he would always first inform the Queen before executing foreign policy in her name. To save royal embarrassment and to avoid dragging the Crown into politics the Prime Minister, Russell, himself removed Palmerston from office.

However, who appoints the Prime Minister? Now that all the major political parties have mechanisms for electing a leader there is no problem in giving the 'normal' answer. The monarch must send for the Leader of the majority party in Parliament to be Prime Minister and 'to form a government'. But what if something then happens to that leader; for example what if Mrs Thatcher had been killed in the IRA bomb attack on the Conservative Party Conference in Brighton in 1984? Where a party's constitution provides for a deputy leader—as the Labour Party's does—that person will assume the leadership, at least temporarily, and so presumably would have to be sent for as Prime Minister. The interesting situation then could arise that that person might be defeated in the subsequent leadership election, and yet might refuse to resign the office of Prime Minister. Would the monarch be constitutionally justified in dismissing that Prime Minister so that the duly elected leader could take over? The situation is even more complex where a party's constitution does not provide for a deputy, as is the case with the Conservative Party. In such cases the death in office of the leader might lead to the monarch having to take advice from senior politicians on a suitable 'stand in' Prime Minister until the election for the new leader has taken place. It has been suggested[74] that in such a situation it might even be constitutional for the monarch to select a member of the House of Lords to be the 'temporary' Prime Minister. Professor Brazier[75] outlines a number of other, highly particular but nevertheless possible, situations in which the monarch might be forced to exercise creative choices with regard to appointing a Prime Minister, these include: where a coalition government is needed during a parliamentary dissolution; where the Labour Party electoral college system produces a new leader for the party while it is in power but that person is rejected by the Parliamentary Labour Party; where the electoral college ousts an incumbent Labour Prime Minister from the Party leadership; and where an incumbent Labour Prime Minister fails to retain his seat as a result of the mandatory reselection process to which all Labour MPs must submit themselves and no other seat can be found for him.

What of the situation where there is no majority party in the House of Commons, either because the party in power's majority is whittled away by death, defections, or by election defeats, or because following an election no party has a clear majority? It is clear that an incumbent Prime Minister who loses his/her majority, or who finds, after an election, that his/her party no longer has the largest number of seats in a Parliament where there is no majority party, is not automatically required to resign office, but is entitled to try to see whether he/she can gain the confidence of the House of Commons, for example by reaching a pact with another party. Mr Edward Heath did not thus immediately resign in March 1974 when, after the general election his party held 297 seats to Mr Harold Wilson's 301. Where the Prime Minister in such a circumstance finds it impossible to proceed, or fails to gain the confidence of the Commons on a vote, constitutionally he/she must resign. There is no obligation at that point on the monarch to seek advice from the outgoing Prime Minister, nor to act on it if it is asked, though in 1974 the Queen did seek Mr Heath's advice and, acting on it, sent for Mr Wilson, who was able to gain the confidence of the Commons with support from the minor parties. Had he been unable, however, to gain that confidence then he too would have been constitutionally required to resign. What would then have been the position?

According to Lord Armstrong of Illminster (formerly Cabinet Secretary) speaking on Radio 4 and quoted by Peter Hennessy[76] the first concern of the monarch in such a situation would be to keep the Crown away from political controversy, but that it would be entirely proper for the monarch to find that course of action 'most likely to command the widest possible degree of political and public acceptance'. The Queen might be justified in resisting requests for a further dissolution of Parliament if that was not considered to be in the national interest and to seek some course of action such as the formation of an all party government. King George V took that step in 1931 when no one party leader could command the confidence of the Commons and asked Ramsay Macdonald to form a 'national government'. However, that possibility had already been agreed on as acceptable by all the established

---

[74] Simon Heffer, *The Times*, 6 January 1994.   [75] Brazier, op cit pp. 20–29.
[76] *The Independent*, 3 July 1991.

political parties so arguably the King merely facilitated the solution to a problem and did not act on his own initiative.

Truly uncharted waters would, however, be encountered if after one inconclusive election a dissolution of Parliament was followed by a further inconclusive general election. In such circumstances the monarch, advised initially by her private secretary, the Secretary of the Cabinet and the Prime Minister's private secretary would have to seek further advice from a range of notable persons including past Prime Ministers and Lord Chancellors, past Cabinet Secretaries, other long-serving statesmen and eminent academics. But whatever is done it would be essential for the monarch to bear in mind the force of public opinion. If the monarch is to continue to be the national focus of affection and respect and to be identified as the guarantor of the continuation of democratic government then nothing can be done that would identify the monarch with one party as against all others.[77]

FURTHER READING

Barendt E 'Constitutional Law and the Criminal Injuries Compensation Scheme' (1995) Public Law 357.

Daintith T *The Executive in the Constitution: Structure, Autonomy and Internal Control* (Oxford University Press, Oxford, 1999).

Forsyth C 'Public Interest Immunity—Recent and Future Developments' [1997] CLJ 51.

Ganz G 'Criminal Injuries Compensation: The Constitutional Issue' (1996) 59 MCR 95.

Jennings Sir Ivor *Cabinet Government* (3rd edn, Cambridge University Press, Cambridge, 1969) chs XII and XIII.

Marshall G *Constitutional Conventions* (Clarendon Press, Oxford, 1984) ch II.

Marshall G and Moodie GC *Some Problems of the Constitution* (4th edn, Hutchinson and Co (Publishers) Ltd, London, 1967) ch 3.

Munro CR *Studies in Constitutional Law* (2nd edn, Butterworths, London, 1999) ch 8.

Pimlott B *The Queen* (Harper Collins, London, 1996).

Sedley S 'The Sound of Silence: Constitutional Law Without a Constitution' (1994) 110 LQR 270.

Sunkin M and Payne S (eds) *The Nature of the Crown: A Legal and Political Analysis* (Clarendon Press, Oxford, 1999).

Turpin C *British Government and the Constitution* (4th edn, Butterworths, London, 1999) ch 3.

---

[77] See further Brazier, op cit, chapter 3.

4 THE CABINET: MINISTERS AND THEIR RESPONSIBILITIES

Historically a central connecting feature of the constitution has been the Cabinet—Her Majesty's senior ministers collected together. Lord Haldane writing in 1917, considered the Cabinet to be the 'mainspring of all the mechanism of Government',[1] the place where policy is finally determined before being laid before Parliament, the supreme controller of the execution of policy approved by Parliament, and the coordinator of the work of the various departments of state. To this end Haldane considered the Cabinet should have no more than 12 members who met frequently, it should possess all the information needed in order to enable it to make decisions, after due consultation with affected ministers, and it should have the means to ensure that its decisions are effectually carried out. Though the Cabinet is still a most important institution, since 1945, at least, power increasingly has, in politically real terms, passed to the Prime Minister who, legally, as 'First Lord of the Treasury' is the monarch's principal servant, but is, politically, the national leader, as leader of the elected majority in Parliament. In 1969 DJ Heasman identified 'the need to project the image of the leader to a mass democracy'[2] as the prime cause of this development. It is clear that the old notion of the Prime Minister being 'first among equals' is no longer applicable. Certainly ministers are not all equal, most are not in the Cabinet, holding assistant rank within particular departments. Even within the Cabinet some ministers, no matter how ancient their title, will be subordinate to others, for example Sir Edward Heath when Lord Privy Seal (1960–1963) assisted the Foreign Secretary.

1. Cabinets and Prime Ministers: Changing Roles

It is the Prime Minister who to a considerable degree 'sets the pace' of Cabinet activity. The Prime Minister is part of the Cabinet, but can also stand back from it, and he/she will also have a very considerable body of central staff to assist in the task of leadership. Lord Callaghan, Prime Minister from 1976 to 1979, listed in this connection: the Central Policy Review

---

[1] Quoted in Hennessy, P, *Whitehall* (Secker & Warburg, London, 1989), p. 296.
[2] 'The Prime Minister and the Cabinet', in King, A, *The British Prime Minister: A Reader* (MacMillan, London, 1955), p. 55.

Staff; the Policy Unit; Private Office; Political Office; the Press Office; and the Cabinet Office.[3] Baroness Thatcher, Prime Minister from 1979 to 1990, disbanded the Central Policy Review Staff, however, she strengthened her own 'in house' Policy Unit which worked closely only with her—the Policy Unit was also retained and relied on by John Major, Prime Minister from 1990 to 1997. She retained the Private Office which kept No 10 Downing Street operating 'round the clock', and, of course, a considerable staff of private secretaries, headed by a principal private secretary. These private secretaries, in Lord Callaghan's description, were selected personally by the Prime Minister from a list of 'high fliers' in the departments of state. One of their principal tasks was to sort out those matters that it is important for the Prime Minister to see and consider—and Baroness Thatcher recorded that some four to seven thousand letters were received by the Private Office every week. Baroness Thatcher also retained the Political Office, which, as under Lord Callaghan, was made up of non-Civil Service staff *not* funded by the taxpayer, and paid for by money the Prime Minister had to raise, and this continues to be the case under Mr Blair. The Cabinet Office *is* a publicly funded body which serves all members of the Cabinet but which, as Lord Callaghan records, tends to be more at the service of the Prime Minister than other ministers, should there be, as is usual, a close working relationship between the Prime Minister and the Cabinet Secretary.

Baroness Thatcher also made considerable use of her Press Office to control the flow of information to the media.

(a) Prime Ministerial control over policy making

Under Tony Blair, Prime Minister since 1997, the premiership has assumed an even more overtly presidential role. Indeed it is arguable that the period 1970—2000 saw more change in this respect than the century before 1970. Mr Blair created another central unit in July 1998—the Performance and Innovation Unit—consisting of civil servants and other experts to give advice to the Prime Minister on specific issues, and forming part of the Cabinet Office. By 2001 the Cabinet Office had 1,200 staff, with some permanent staff, some on secondment from departments of state, others on shorter term appointments from the public and private sectors; its tasks included reporting to and advising the Prime Minister.

By the summer of 2006 the Cabinet Office had the following tasks:

- supporting the Prime Minister in defining and delivering the government's objectives;
- supporting the Cabinet in driving forward the coherence, quality, and delivery of policy on a cross departmental basis;
- strengthening the Civil Service in ensuring that it is organised effectively and has appropriate skills, values and leadership to deliver the objectives of government.

To this end the Cabinet Office had both a 'support and development' function, with 'divisions' devoted to Financial Management, Infrastructure, the Private Office Group, and a number of 'cross government units' including the Better Regulation Executive and the Parliamentary Counsel Office. There were various other 'units', 'secretariats' and 'groups' including 'Strategy', 'Delivery', 'E Government', 'Economic and Domestic Affairs', 'Overseas and Defence', 'Intelligence, Security and Resilience', 'European', 'Ceremonial', 'Corporate Development', 'Government Communication' and 'Property and Ethics'.

---

[3] See generally Callaghan, J, *Time and Chance* (Collins, London, 1987).

The Cabinet Office may be seen as an 'inner' Civil Service whose members mirror the work of colleagues in the actual departments of state. This is *not* a phenomenon that began under Tony Blair: it has been developing since the creation of the Cabinet Office in 1916. In the early years of the twentieth century the Treasury was the main coordinating actor with regard to the policies of departments and ministries, but towards the end of the century it is the Cabinet Office which has assumed the function of support for government, policy coordination, policy advice and formulation. Under Tony Blair the Cabinet Office has become much more of a 'Prime Minister's Department' than before, and it is understandable how the apparently ever closer links between the Cabinet Office and the Prime Minister should lead to suspicions of politicisation of what is supposedly neutral service. The information which the Cabinet Office and his own private staff and advisers supply to him enables the Prime Minister to voice an opinion and make a statement on virtually any issue. That gives him an advantage over the opposition in Parliament and over his own colleagues in government.

Alongside the Cabinet Office the Prime Minister can also draw on other sources of information and advice. Tony Blair merged the Policy Unit and the Private Office at No 10 Downing Street into the Policy Directorate in 2001. He has also relied on the services of 'special advisers'—as indeed have other ministers—some salaried, some unpaid, and the public profile of such advisers has been much greater under Blair than under previous Prime Ministers. The term 'special adviser' is not easily defined, but it can refer to an aide who is an expert in relation to a particular policy, or who may have expertise in more than one area. This has led to allegations of 'cronyism' and 'spin doctoring', ie the manipulation of news media to put the best possible construction on events for the benefit of the government. This is not easily reconciled with the notion that those who are employed as civil servants are politically neutral. It is somewhat unfair to attribute all this to Tony Blair. Previous Prime Ministers used the services of advisers, some coming from outside the traditional ranks of the civil service, and they too could be the subject of criticism if it was considered they were becoming 'over mighty subjects', eg in the last forty years, Marcia Williams, who served Harold Wilson, Bernard Ingham and Alan Walters who served Margaret Thatcher, and Sarah Hogg who served John Major. Once again, however, we may see an intensification of pre-existing trends under Tony Blair with regard to the role and functioning of special advisers. John Major's government employed 38 special advisers in 1997, but under Tony Blair the number grew rapidly to 70 or so and by July 2000 it was 78, falling to 75 in July 2002. Of these the Prime Minister had 19 in 1998 and 27 in 2002. This was in conflict with the Code of Conduct for ministers which allowed Cabinet ministers to appoint only two advisers and in 2001 the Code was revised to allow the appointment of excess numbers in special circumstances. The number of special advisers has increased from 39, immediately before Mr Blair's election, to 84 in 2006. The cost of those advisers, who are employed under the terms of the Ministerial Code of Conduct, to the public purse was £5.9 million. Twenty five such advisers are employed by No 10 Downing Street: there are only 23 cabinet members.

Once again the existence of the network of special advisers spread throughout Whitehall, but centred on 'No 10' has tended to favour the pre-eminence of the Prime Minister by enabling him to know what is happening in departments so that he can deal with contentious issues before they reach cabinet level. However, this also raises the difficult question of the extent to which the Prime Minister, and his aides, can give instructions to civil servants generally. The power exists under the Royal Prerogative and was formalised by Civil Service Order in Council of 1995 as amended, but its extent is unclear as is the question of who, other than the Prime Minister, can exercise it. This order allows appointments to be made by ministers to the Civil Service outside the normal requirements of fair and open competition for the purpose of providing assistance to a minister, though for only so long as a government is in power. It also permits the minister (ie the Prime Minister) to control the conduct of the Civil Service—a vague power indeed.

The vagueness of prerogative powers in this area was highlighted by the issue of a revised Code of Conduct for Special Advisers in July 2005 which took place without parliamentary or public debate simply by the device of altering the Civil Service Order in Council by the Privy Council. This was criticised by the Committee on Standards on Public Life which continues to press for a Civil Service Act which enshrines standards for both permanent civil servants and special advisers in a legislative form. The Committee did, however, welcome it being made clear that special advisers report to ministers, not the permanent secretaries of the departments to which they are attached and that they are not allowed to convey ministerial instructions to civil servants. On the other hand the Committee expressed concern that the revised Code for Special Advisers does not make it clear that they are clearly outside normal departmental hierarchies, and that their appointments may be made without due regard to the normal criterion of appointment on the basis of merit. The Committee also expressed concern over the revised wording of the code which enables advisers to provide assistance, as opposed to advice, to ministers, and their ability to 'request' work from civil servants.

(b) A presidential Prime Minister?

Perhaps even more of a sign that we have moved towards a more overtly presidential style of government comes from arguments that Mr Blair has lessened emphasis on a number of basic constitutional fundamentals—the apolitical Civil Service, the supremacy of Parliament in law making, parliamentary control over the executive, the centrality of the Cabinet in decision making and the value of the monarchy as a kind of 'national cement'. The apolitical Civil Service has been undermined by the appointment of 'special advisers' alluded to above. The supremacy of Parliament in law making and control over the executive has been, some would argue, weakened by ever more power passing to the unelected bodies of the European Community, while the removal of the hereditary peers from the House of Lords has not resulted in any marked democratisation of that body—see further chapter 5 below. In addition the government has, despite lip service to the ideals of modernisation, failed to reform the system for elections to the House of Commons and has largely resisted calls to improve parliamentary powers to scrutinise government and to hold it to account, again see chapter 5 below. The Prime Minister has also been accused of spending little time in the House of Commons, being rarely present for debates and generally present only for Prime Minister's question time. Mr Blair's voting record is the worst of any Prime Minister in the last thirty years, and he was present for only 6 per cent of votes during the session 2003–04, slightly better than his 'record' for 1997–98 which was 5 per cent. Could this account for a general decline in attendance by MPs?[4] The centrality of the Cabinet has been undermined by an apparent curtailing of debate within that body, while many Cabinet meetings now last for only about forty to sixty minutes.

Writing in *The Times* on 25 September 2000 in advance of the publication of his work *The Prime Minister: The Office and its Holders since 1945*,[5] Professor Peter Hennessy argued

---

[4] *The Times*, 24 December 2004.   [5] (Palgrave, London, 2001).

that under Mr Blair the premiership has become particularly personalised and 'Napoleonic', with important decisions, such as that to place responsibility for fixing interest rates with the Bank of England Monetary Policy Committee, being taken without full Cabinet consultation. The Cabinet's meetings now have no proper agenda, simply headings of 'regular business' eg 'domestic and economic affairs'. However, there are statements of the timing and presentation of ministerial and departmental statements—evidence of the government's preoccupation with publicity perhaps? The move away from the older model of Cabinet government has been accompanied by the transformation of the functioning of the Cabinet Office and the other agencies answerable to the Prime Minister considered above.

Dennis Kavanagh and Anthony Seldon, in their study, *The Powers Behind the Prime Minister: The Hidden Influence of Number 10*,[6] argue that the role of the British Prime Minister has not altered in *content* for well over a century: it is to be the national leader, to be the chief formulator of policy, the leader of the majority party in Parliament and the chief appointer to offices within the nation. However, they point to an increase in the complexity of the tasks and a change of balance between the roles. Certainly under Tony Blair the job has had a particularly 'international statesman' aspect to it, and there is an increased demand for answers to difficult questions on policy from the media. A modern British Prime Minister is far from *primus inter pares* amongst his Cabinet colleagues, but is much less powerful vis-à-vis other world leaders, and, indeed, even the heads of power of multinational corporations whose financial decisions can have profound effects on national economies.

By way of contrast the Cabinet as a collective body does not enjoy the levers of power available to the Prime Minister. Cabinets have grown in size. Haldane in the early years of the century contemplated Cabinets of no more than 12 members, but by the 1980s the Cabinet usually consisted of 20 or more members. Baroness Thatcher's first Cabinet of May 1979 consisted of 23 members, while her last, of November 1990, had 24. Secondly membership of the Cabinet can change quite often. Under Baroness Thatcher the Cabinet was reconstituted after an election, or 'shuffled' during the course of a Parliament, 21 times, and nearly always some ministers left office while others moved to new posts: all the time the Prime Minister remained unchanged. Mr Blair has generally resisted massive Cabinet reshuffles; even so four Cabinet ministers lost their posts in July 1998, while there were other changes in October 1999 when one minister lost his post, two others resigned to take on other commitments and one moved to new responsibilities within the government, and further changes in 2001 and even more following the general election of 2005 and the English local elections of 2006 when, inter alia, the Home Secretary lost his position, the Foreign Secretary was effectively demoted and the Secretary of State for Education was 'moved sideways'. Thirdly it is clear that Prime Ministers can easily determine the character of the Cabinet by the appointments they are prepared to make. Though even here, let it be noted, that a Prime Minister will need to ensure that the Cabinet reflects the broad spectrum of opinion within his or her party—something that was more of a problem for Mr Major than it was for Baroness Thatcher. Indeed, the larger a Prime Minister's majority, and the more unified his/her party, the less he/she will have to worry about unifying all shades of party opinion within the Cabinet. Such a situation inevitably strengthens the 'presidential' position of the Prime Minister, as witness 'Napoleonic' premiers such as Baroness Thatcher and Mr Blair, as contrasted with 'chairmen of the board' figures such as Lord Callaghan and Mr Major.

---

[6] (HarperCollins, London, 1999).

II. The Cabinet in Decline?

Further reasons for the decline in the importance of the Cabinet relative to that of the Prime Minister lie in the number of meetings of the Cabinet held, the amount of paper work seen by the Cabinet and the number of other committees through which business is channelled. Clement Atlee, Sir Winston Churchill and Harold Macmillan usually held two Cabinet meetings per week, Baroness Thatcher usually held only one. Similarly the number of Cabinet papers in the 1980s fell to some 60–70 per annum, a sixth of the level of 30 to 40 years previously. Furthermore while Baroness Thatcher had fewer committees of Cabinet ministers than some of her predecessors, it is clear that a great deal of important policy formulation was carried out via ad hoc groups such as on the 'Economic Seminar' whose membership was varied according to the issues in hand. It appears now to be an inescapable fact of public life that the amount of public business that has to be carried on makes it inevitable that modern Prime Ministers have increasingly to work through smaller groups rather than the full Cabinet. This tendency has, as has been argued above, continued apace under Mr Blair.

Anthony Seldon in his chapter 'The Cabinet System' in *The British Constitution in the Twentieth Century*[7] identifies the current Cabinet as no more than a forum within which political friends may discuss policy, air disagreements and foster a sense of teamwork and common ownership of policy, though the number of Cabinet meetings has declined from a high of 72 in 1970 to only 36 in 2000. The structure and functioning of the Cabinet has become looser and much less formal, and it has ceased to be the only or principal decision taking body, as it was from 1900 to 1939. Indeed it is no longer even the principal decision ratifying body, nor even the most important discussion and information giving body. What the modern Cabinet has become is a fluid informal gathering where views are exchanged, and highly dependent on the personally relaxed style of the Prime Minister.

Seldon, to whose work indebtedness is acknowledged, identifies certain reasons for this change in the status of the Cabinet. These include:

- the need to bring in expert opinion from outside the body of the Cabinet;
- the pressure of business which has made it impossible for the cabinet to discuss all issues and has forced delegation to committees and sub-committees;
- demands from the media for comment on political events meaning that issues could not be left until after the next Cabinet meeting;
- the shift of focus away from Westminster as the seat of government consequent on the UK's membership of the EU and the taking of many of the most important decisions in Brussels and Strasbourg;
- the personality of powerful Prime Ministers such as Baroness Thatcher and Tony Blair who have sought to bypass the traditional Cabinet system.

One major issue, however, links both Prime Minister and Cabinet: that is that their existence is a matter of convention not law. *Legally* the Prime Minister is the First Lord of the Treasury, and the appellation 'Prime Minister' appears only sporadically in statute, eg the Chequers Estate Act 1917. The post dates from the time of Sir Robert Walpole who held office from 1721

[7] Bogdanor, V (ed) (OUP, Oxford, 2003).

to 1742, yet even for a while after his time the technical leader of the group possessing the confidence of the House of Commons might not, historically, be recognised as the most important statesman of the day. The notion of a first or 'prime' minister was, however, well established by the end of the eighteenth century, though throughout the nineteenth century some of those who held that office did so only for a short while, and the post changed hands frequently within the life of given Parliaments and not just on an electoral defeat as has become the predominant position in the twentieth century. Likewise convention has increasingly made it requisite that the Prime Minister should be a member of the House of Commons, a matter effectively settled by the appointment of Mr Baldwin as Prime Minister in 1923 when many thought Lord Curzon was the obvious 'leader' of the Conservative party. The matter was surely put beyond doubt in 1963 when the Earl of Home gave up his title and became Sir Alec Douglas-Home in order to hold office as Prime Minister.

Similarly the Cabinet is a conventional institution. *Legally* the monarch's private advisers are the Privy Council, a body now having important legal and ceremonial functions. It is the development of the political life of the nation that has led to the emergence of a much smaller group of members of the Privy Council, all of whom share a common political allegiance and who command the support of the majority in Parliament, as the Cabinet, the body charged with responsibility for developing policy and guiding the course of the nation.

The student of the constitution is thus here within yet another area where rules of law, ie rules designed to identify like situations as such and then to ensure they are always treated alike, play, at most, only a supplementary role. Throughout much of the area of Cabinet and ministerial responsibilities 'procedures', 'practices', 'arrangements' rather than 'rules' largely apply. These 'procedures' etc are characterised as 'conventions', a notion already encountered in connection with the royal prerogative in chapter 3, though as was said then not all commentators are agreed as to what constitutes a convention, preferring to reserve the use of that term for the most solemn and historically well established practices.

In *Constitutional Conventions: The Rules and Forms of Political Accountability*[8] Geoffrey Marshall identified the historic conventions centred on the notion that the monarch always acts on ministerial advice, and designed to ensure royal prerogative powers are effectively exercised by ministers answerable to Parliament (see chapter 3). He adds other situations governed by convention, such as relationships between the Prime Minister and the Cabinet, between ministers collectively and Parliament and between ministers and civil servants. Conventions, as defined by Dicey are: 'understandings, habits or practices which, though they may regulate the conduct of . . . the Ministry . . . are not in reality laws . . . since they are not enforced by the courts'.[9] As such 'we find [conventions] of every degree of stringency and definiteness'.[10] Indeed, the preferable modern approach is to admit of conventions that 'their precision and obligatoriness are variable'.[11] 'The non-legal rules . . . may be viewed as on a continuum. Some few may be stated with precision, others are harder to formulate. Some are more or less invariably obeyed, while there are others to which, by degrees, a lesser sense of obligation adheres'.[12] Geoffrey Marshall reached very similar conclusions stating that: 'Conventions are rules that define major non-legal rights, powers and obligations of office-holders in the three branches of government, or the relations between governments or organs of government . . . Conventions have as their main general aim the effective working of the

---

[8] (Clarendon Press, Oxford, 1984).   [9] (Macmillan, London, 1885), p. 24.
[10] Maitland, *Constitutional History of England* (CUP, Cambridge, 1950), p. 398.
[11] Munro, *Studies in Constitutional Law* (2nd edn, Butterworths, London, 1999), p. 81.
[12] Munro, op cit p. 86.

machinery of political accountability. Conventions can in most cases be stated only in general terms, their applicability in some circumstances being clear but in other circumstances uncertain and debatable.'[13]

The 'continuum' view of conventions conflicts, of course, with that of Jaconelli already examined in chapter 3: 'A constitutional convention is no mere habit that certain governmental situations are dealt with in a particular way. It is a rule characterised by a "critical reflective attitude" which looks on the outward pattern of behaviour as a standard to be followed. Any deviation from the practice attracts—and is rightly regarded as attracting criticism and pressure to conform.' Many of the procedures we shall encounter in this chapter would not meet that strict definition because, for example, their confines are broadly drawn and hence it may be easier in particular circumstances to escape pressure to conform. Jaconelli would, for example, exclude from the definition of convention 'rules which do not regulate the mode of conduct of government', and would certainly exclude arguments that there is a 'convention that a minister must always resign in the wake of a sexual scandal, *not* because such a resignation does not always occur, but rather 'because it fails to meet the threshold requirement of governmental consequence'.[14]

However, if Jaconelli is right, how is one to classify practices and understandings which do play an enormous part in the functioning of our unwritten constitution such as the resignation of ministers following proof of individual misconduct—albeit not on every occasion? While admitting the intellectual force of Jaconelli's arguments, this work nevertheless continues to incline towards a rather more pragmatic view of the matter.

Professor Munro's argument that conventions can be viewed as a continuum helps us understand why some conventions can be quite precise and invested with a character that approaches that of a rule of law: they impose more than a simple moral obligation, rather one that is effectively imperative. This is particularly true of conventions relating to the exercise of the monarch's personal prerogative powers, for example the requirement that royal assent is 'always' given to legislation that has passed both Houses of Parliament. (See chapter 3.) These conventions have been formulated since the constitutional settlement of the seventeenth century in which government under laws made by the Crown in Parliament acquired supremacy over government under prerogative powers. The desire to ensure that royal power is exercised in accordance with ministerial advice is in a real sense a natural concomitant of the fact that statutes made by the Crown in Parliament are the most potent form of law. As statute is so potent it is desirable that statutes should only be made after advice has been given by ministers who command the confidence of Parliament. This group of conventions may be characterised as 'strong'. Today, however, it might be objected that what is necessary is not a conventional limit on the monarch's personal powers but rather limits to the powers of the leaders of the majority in Parliament. Other conventions approach the status solely of moral requirements, and may be very broadly characterised as of 'middling strength' or 'weak.' As moral principles can conflict with one another, it is possible for conventional requirements to be set aside if a greater moral purpose may be served, for example, the Labour Party's 1975 decision not to require unanimity amongst cabinet ministers during the campaign preceding the referendum on membership of the European Communities. In other cases conventions may be fluid and subject to change or to little degree of consensus as to what their requirements are, or not so clearly formulated by practice or understanding as to be capable of easy

[13] Marshall, op cit p. 210.
[14] 'The Nature of Constitutional Conventions' (1999) 19 Legal Studies (No 1) 24.

application to novel situations. This is acknowledged by Geoffrey Marshall:

'The practice of revising or changing conventions suggests that conventions are in a number of ways unlike both legal rules and ordinary moral rules. They are unlike legal rules because they are not the product of a legislative or of a judicial process. They differ from ordinary moral rules because their content is determined partly by special agreement, and many of them govern matters that apart from such agreed arrangements would be morally neutral . . . One form of conventional change is then the deliberate abrogation of an old convention or creation of a new one by agreement, if the old rule is felt to be outdated or inconvenient. In this sense, of course, conventions are not rules that have to be followed unconditionally or permanently. It will always be possible for governments or politicians to propose a change of convention. They must be followed only in the sense that they cannot be changed unilaterally and must be complied with if in force until changed by agreement. But conventions can also develop or extend in new directions by being applied to fresh political circumstances . . . [It] will be the case that the rules ultimately reflect what people do. In that sense conventions will become in the end whatever politicians think it right to do. But at any one time what politicians in fact do may conflict with and infringe a rule based on existing precedents or agreements.'[15]

The continuum notion is particularly applicable to those conventions relating to the Cabinet, intra-Cabinet relationships, ministers and their responsibilities (especially those relating to collective and individual ministerial responsibility), the retention of the Commons' confidence and relationships between civil servants and ministers. These illustrate how the understanding and application of convention alters over time.

III.   Relationships within the Cabinet

It has already been argued that the nature of any given Cabinet is determined by a variety of forces including the personality of the Prime Minister, the degree of control he/she enjoys over the parliamentary majority, and the degree of freedom he/she has in choosing ministers to serve in the Cabinet and to preserve a balance between the various points of view in his/her party. Once a Cabinet has been formed, however, its working depends primarily on conventional procedures—procedures initially collected together in 1945 in *Questions of Procedure for Ministers* which was a kind of code of etiquette in Cabinet affairs, and which grew considerably over the years, even though its issue to ministers was not public knowledge: the 1976 edition's existence, for example, was only publicly declared in *The New Statesman* for 14 February 1986. The weakness of that document was demonstrated by the Westland affair of 1986.

(a) Westland—a most illustrative and cautionary tale

The Westland affair grew out of a difference of opinion between Cabinet ministers. The Prime Minister and Secretary of State for Trade and Industry (Mr Leon Brittan), favoured the purchase of the Westland helicopter company by the American Sikorsky company, while the

---

[15] Marshall, op cit pp. 216–217.

Secretary of State for Defence, Mr Heseltine, favoured a rescue bid mounted by a European consortium. The normal conventional understanding is, as will be examined further below, that once a Cabinet decision is taken it is binding on *all* members of the government. However, it had been the understanding before 1986 that the legitimacy of this convention depended on full and frank prior discussion of the issues involved by ministers before a decision was taken, and that that discussion should be private. To facilitate this it was further understood that any member could ask for an item to be discussed in Cabinet and that this would be agreed by the Prime Minister, unless there were to be an unacceptably long or unmanageable agenda, though not even that reason could suffice to justify excluding a matter on which a Cabinet minister felt strongly that an issue should be examined and arguments heard.

That the favoured bid for Westland should come from Sikorsky had apparently been agreed in December 1985 in ad hoc committees of the Cabinet, and the fact that this important issue had not been formally decided and recorded in Cabinet minutes was to have many later repercussions. Mr Heseltine believed that he had requested a further ad hoc meeting of relevant ministers before whom he could argue his case: Baroness Thatcher believed there had been no decision to hold such a meeting, only an agreement to have a meeting if events warranted it; but there was no formal record of what had been agreed.

Mr Heseltine continued to advance his cause by writing various letters to people involved in the European consortium rescue package, and these were published: indeed a major feature of the whole episode became the use of 'non-attributable' press briefings by career civil servants acting on behalf of ministers. The opinion of the Solicitor-General was at that point sought by the Prime Minister as to whether some of Mr Heseltine's statements made in his letters went beyond what the facts could warrant. The Solicitor-General reviewed the information and wrote to Mr Heseltine cautiously suggesting there were 'material inaccuracies' to correct. Copies of this letter were also sent to the Prime Minister and Mr Brittan, and within a few hours a civil servant at the Department of Trade and Industry (Colette Bowe) had released the text of the letter to Press Association news agency.

Ms Bowe stated she had obtained 'cover' for her action from Bernard Ingham, the Chief Press Secretary, and Charles Powell, a private secretary, both from No 10 Downing Street. However, the entire affair is shrouded in obscurity. Mr Brittan himself apparently considered the letter should be in the public domain, but only subject to the approval of 'No 10'. The Prime Minister's staff were not prepared to 'leak' the letter themselves, but did not sufficiently strongly advise the unfortunate Ms Bowe not to have anything to do with the matter. In the event the leak of a letter from one of the law officers, apparently by a fellow minister to discredit yet another minister, led to two Cabinet resignations and major repercussions which will be further examined below in the context of collective and individual ministerial responsibility and the relationship between ministers, civil and other public servants. What is important at this point is for students to appreciate the light that the events cast on our constitutional arrangements which in many ways are excessively fluid and ad hoc. To use a cosmetic term we may call them 'incremental', to be more brutally frank we can say 'we make them up as we go along'. The British are generally a pragmatic not a dogmatic people, but sometimes we take this too far and it is hard to disagree with the comment of Professor JAG Griffith, the eminent constitutional lawyer, made in conversation with Peter Hennessy and quoted in *Whitehall*: 'The Constitution is what happens.'[16]

---

[16] (Secker & Warburg, London, 1989), p. 307.

iv. Subsequent Developments

Questions of Procedure for Ministers, the guidance to ministers, was (officially) made public for the first time on 19 May 1992. Following further comment on *Questions* by the Nolan Report (Standards in Public Life Cm 2850) in 1995, an entirely new documentation was drawn up for the incoming Labour government in 1997.

The Code in its 1997 version was a much more detailed document than its predecessors. It stressed the primacy of the Prime Minister over other ministers in a number of ways. Similarly restrictions were applied to journalistic activities by ministers, and they were forbidden while in office to publish books on their ministerial experiences.

The current code of *Ethics and Procedural Guidance for Ministers* was issued by the Cabinet Office in July 2005 and selected extracts follow:

'1. Ministers of the Crown

1.1 Ministers of the Crown are expected to behave according to the highest standards of constitutional and personal conduct in the performance of their duties.

1.2 This Code provides guidance to Ministers on how they should act and arrange their affairs in order to uphold these standards. It lists the principles which may apply in particular situations drawing on past precedent. It applies to all members of the Government (and covers Parliamentary Private Secretaries in section 2).

1.3 Ministers are personally responsible for deciding how to act and conduct themselves in the light of the Code and for justifying their actions and conduct in Parliament. The Code is not a rulebook, and it is not the role of the Secretary of the Cabinet or other officials to enforce it or to investigate Ministers although they may provide Ministers with private advice on matters which it covers.

1.4 Ministers only remain in office for so long as they retain the confidence of the Prime Minister. He is the ultimate judge of the standards of behaviour expected of a Minister and the appropriate consequences of a breach of those standards, although he will not expect to comment on every allegation that is brought to his attention.

1.5 The Code should be read against the background of the overarching duty on Ministers to comply with the law, including international law and treaty obligations, to uphold the administration of justice and to protect the integrity of public law. They are expected to observe the Seven Principles of Public Life set out in the first report of the Committee on Standards in Public Life, repeated in annex A, and the following principles of Ministerial conduct:

a. Ministers must uphold the principle of collective responsibility;

b. Ministers have a duty to Parliament to account, and be held to account, for the policies, decisions and actions of their departments and agencies;

c. it is of paramount importance that Ministers give accurate and truthful information to Parliament, correcting any inadvertent error at the earliest opportunity. Ministers who knowingly mislead Parliament will be expected to offer their resignation to the Prime Minister;

d. Ministers should be as open as possible with Parliament and the public, refusing to provide information only when disclosure would not be in the public interest which should be decided in accordance with the relevant statutes and the Freedom of Information Act 2000;

e. Ministers should similarly require civil servants who give evidence before Parliamentary Committees on their behalf and under their direction to be as helpful as possible in providing accurate, truthful and full information in accordance with the duties and responsibilities of civil servants as set out in the Civil Service Code;

f. Ministers must ensure that no conflict arises, or appears to arise, between their public duties and their private interests;

g. Ministers should avoid accepting any gift or hospitality which might, or might reasonably appear to, compromise their judgement or place them under an improper obligation;

h. Ministers in the House of Commons must keep separate their roles as Minister and constituency Member;

i. Ministers must not use government resources for Party political purposes. They must uphold the political impartiality of the Civil Service and not ask civil servants to act in any way which would conflict with the Civil Service Code.

1.6 Ministers must also comply at all times with the requirements which Parliament itself has laid down, including in particular the Codes of Conduct for their respective Houses. For Ministers in the Commons, these are set by the Resolution carried on 19 March 1997 (Official Report columns 1046–47), and for Ministers in the Lords the Resolution can be found in the Official Report of 20 March 1997 column 1057.

. . .

Parliamentary Private Secretaries

2.7 Parliamentary Private Secretaries are not members of the Government and should be careful to avoid being spoken of as such. They are Private Members, and should therefore be afforded as great a liberty of action as possible; but their close and confidential association with Ministers imposes certain obligations on them. Official information given to them should generally be limited to what is necessary for the discharge of their Parliamentary and political duties. This need not preclude them from being brought into Departmental discussions or conferences where appropriate, but they should not have access to secret establishments, or information graded secret or above, except on the personal authority of the Prime Minister. While, as Private Members, they need not adhere to the rules on private interests which apply to Ministers, they should, as a general rule, seek to avoid a real or perceived conflict of interest between their role as a Parliamentary Private Secretary and their private interests.

2.8 Ministers choose and appoint their own Parliamentary Private Secretaries with the written approval of the Prime Minister. The Chief Whip should, however be consulted about the choice of a Parliamentary Private Secretary; and in view of the special position which Parliamentary Private Secretaries occupy in relation to the Government, the Prime Minister's approval must also be sought before any such appointment is offered and announced.

2.9 Ministers should ensure that their Parliamentary Private Secretaries are aware of certain principles which should govern the behaviour of Parliamentary Private Secretaries in the House of Commons. Like other Private Members, Parliamentary Private Secretaries are expected to support the Government in all important divisions. However, their special position in relation to the Government imposes an additional obligation which means that no Parliamentary Private Secretary who votes against the Government may retain his or her position. Parliamentary Private Secretaries should not make statements in the House or put Questions on matters affecting the Department with which they are connected. Parliamentary Private Secretaries are not precluded from serving on Select Committees but they should not do so in the case of inquiries into their own Minister's Departments and they should avoid associating themselves with recommendations critical of or embarrassing to the Government. They should also exercise discretion in any speeches or broadcasts which they may make outside the House, taking care not to make statements which appear to be made in an official or semi-official capacity, and bearing in mind at the same time that, however careful they may be to make it clear that they are speaking only as Private Members, they are nevertheless liable to be regarded as speaking with some of the authority which is attached to a member of the Government. Generally they must act with a sense of responsibility and with discretion; and they must not associate themselves with particular groups advocating special policies.

2.10 Parliamentary Private Secretaries making official visits in the United Kingdom may receive the normal Civil Service travelling and subsistence allowances in respect of absences on official (or Departmental) business, as would other MPs undertaking work for Government Departments. It is for the Minister concerned to decide whether or not the Parliamentary Private Secretary, when accompanying the Minister, is engaged on Departmental business. It may occasionally be useful for a Parliamentary Private Secretary to accompany the Minister on an official visit abroad but no such arrangements should be made without the prior written approval of the Prime Minister. Where a Minister has to pull out of an event (United Kingdom or overseas) at the last minute and no other Minister is available to represent the Government, a Parliamentary Private Secretary may stand in for the Minister. However, such attendance should be exceptional and very much a last resort. It is for the Minister in charge of the relevant Department to justify the use of a Parliamentary Private Secretary in individual cases. The Prime Minister's approval will be required where this involves attendance at an overseas event.

Special Advisers

2.11 The employment of Special Advisers on the one hand adds a political dimension to the advice available to Ministers, and on the other provides Ministers with the direct advice of distinguished "experts" in their professional field, while reinforcing the political impartiality of the permanent Civil Service by distinguishing the source of political advice and support. With the exception of the Prime Minister, Cabinet Ministers may each appoint up to two Special Advisers. The Prime Minister may also authorise the appointment of one or two Special Advisers by Ministers who regularly attend Cabinet. The Government expects the appointment of experts normally to be made to permanent or temporary Civil Service posts in accordance with the rules of the Civil Service Commissioners. Where, however, an individual has outstanding skills or experience of a non-political kind which a Minister wishes to have available while in a particular post, the Prime Minister may exceptionally permit their appointment as an expert adviser within the usual limit of two advisers per Cabinet Minister. All appointments require the prior written approval of the Prime Minister, and no commitments to make such appointments should be entered into in the absence of such approval. Any departures from the rule of two Special Advisers per Cabinet Minister will need to be explained publicly. All such appointments should be made, and all Special Advisers should operate, in accordance with the terms and conditions of the Model Contract for Special Advisers and the Code of Conduct for Special Advisers will also apply to expert advisers except for those aspects which relate to political commitment.

2.12 The responsibility for the management and conduct of Special Advisers, including discipline, rests with the Minister who made the appointment. Individual Ministers will be accountable to the Prime Minister, Parliament and the public for their actions and decisions in respect of their Special Advisers. It is, of course, also open to the Prime Minister to terminate employment by withdrawing his consent to an individual appointment.

2.13 The Government is committed to making an annual statement to Parliament setting out the numbers, names and paybands of Special Advisers, the appointing Minister and the overall salary cost. This statement will also include similar details in respect of expert and Unpaid Advisers. Where an adviser has a particular expertise or works mainly in a particular area of the department's work, this will also be indicated.

Unpaid Advisers

2.14 The appointment of an Unpaid Adviser is to provide advice to a Minister in their ministerial capacity. Such appointments are exceptional, and the prior written approval of the Prime Minister should be sought for any such appointment before a commitment is entered into. These appointments carry no remuneration or reimbursement from public funds. The appointment of an Unpaid Adviser is a personal appointment by the Minister concerned and there is no contractual relationship between such an adviser and the Department. In making an appointment Ministers must ensure that there is no conflict of interest between the matters on which the Unpaid Adviser will be advising and their private concerns. A letter of appointment must be issued by the employing Minister making this clear. Where an adviser is acting on similar terms to a Special Adviser but on an unpaid basis then they should conduct themselves as if they were a Special Adviser. As with Special Advisers, Unpaid Advisers are required to uphold the political impartiality of the Civil Service. The letter should indicate the subjects with which an Unpaid Adviser may (or may not) deal and their access to papers. The normal rules of confidentiality also apply. Unpaid Advisers are subject to the Official Secrets Act and Business Appointment Rules. Aside from the provision of a furnished office, use of a telephone, and access to typing facilities, a personal computer and internal departmental messenger system, an Unpaid Adviser should constitute no cost to the public purse. Ministers are responsible for the management and conduct of Unpaid Advisers.

3 Ministers and civil servants

3.1 Ministers have a duty to give fair consideration and due weight to informed and impartial advice from civil servants, as well as to other considerations and advice, in reaching policy decisions; a duty to uphold the political impartiality of the Civil Service, and not to ask civil servants to act in any way which would conflict with the Civil Service Code; [see further below at pages 179–181] a duty to ensure that influence over appointments is not abused for partisan purposes; and a duty to observe the obligations of a good employer with regard to terms and conditions of those who serve them. Civil servants should not be asked to engage in activities likely to call in question their political impartiality, or to give rise to the criticism that people paid from public funds are being used for Party political purposes.

The role of the Accounting Officer

3.2 Heads of Departments and the chief executives of executive agencies are appointed as Accounting Officers. The essence of the role is a *personal* responsibility for the propriety and regularity of the public finances for which he or she is responsible; for keeping proper accounts; for the avoidance of waste and extravagance; and for the efficient and effective use of resources. Accounting Officers answer personally to the Committee of Public Accounts on these matters, within the framework of Ministerial accountability to Parliament for the policies, actions and conducts of their Departments.

3.3 Accounting Officers have a particular responsibility to see that appropriate advice is tendered to Ministers on all matters of financial propriety and regularity and more broadly as to all considerations of prudent and economical administration, efficiency and effectiveness and value for money. If a Minister in charge of a Department is contemplating a course of action which would involve a transaction which the Accounting Officer considers would breach the requirements of propriety or regularity, the Accounting Officer will set out in writing his or her objection to the proposal, the reasons for the objection and the duty to inform the Comptroller and Auditor General should the advice be overruled. If the Minister decides nonetheless to proceed, the Accounting Officer will seek a written instruction to take the action in question. The Accounting Officer is obliged to comply with the instructions, send relevant papers to the Comptroller and Auditor General, and inform the Treasury of what has occurred. A similar procedure applies where the Accounting Officer has concerns as regards the value for money of a proposed course of action. The procedure enables the Committee of Public Accounts to see that the Accounting Officer does not bear personal responsibility for the actions concerned.

The role of Accounting Officers is described in detail in the Treasury memorandum, *The Responsibilities of an Accounting Officer*. There is also a Treasury handbook, *Regularity, Propriety and Value for Money*.

Civil servants and Party Conferences

3.5 Ministers should not ask civil servants to attend, or take part in, Party Conferences or meetings of policy or subject groups of any of the Parliamentary parties. In their official capacity, civil servants should not accept invitations to conferences convened by party political organisations except when their presence is required for carrying through essential Departmental business unconnected with the conference. An exception to this rule is made for Special advisers who, under the terms of their contracts, may attend Party functions, including the annual Party conference (but they may not speak publicly at the conference) and maintain contact with Party members. Further guidance is available in the *Directory of Civil Service Guidance, Volume* 2 (*www.cabinet-office.gov.uk/guidance*). If a Minister wishes to have a factual brief for a party political occasion to explain Departmental policies or actions, there is no reason why this should not be provided.

. . .

5. Ministers' private interests

General principle

5.1 Ministers must ensure that no conflict arises, or appears to arise, between their public duties and their private interests, financial or otherwise.

Responsibility for avoiding a conflict

5.2 It is the personal responsibility of each Minister to decide whether and what action is needed to avoid a conflict or the perception of a conflict, and to defend that decision, if necessary by accounting for it in Parliament. The role of the Permanent Secretary is to ensure that advice is available when it is sought by the Minister, either by providing it personally, drawing on precedent and if need be other parts of government including the Secretary of the Cabinet, or to arrange for expert or professional advice from inside or outside Government. In cases of serious difficulty or doubt the matter may be referred to the Prime Minister for a view. But ultimately it is the responsibility of Ministers individually to order their own private lives in such a way as to avoid criticism, and the final decision about what action to take to achieve that is theirs.

Procedure

5.3 On appointment to each new office, Ministers are advised to provide their Permanent Secretary with a full list in writing of all interests which might be thought to give rise to a conflict. The list should cover not only the Minister's personal interests but those of a spouse or partner, of children who are minors, of trusts of which the Minister or a spouse or partner is a trustee or beneficiary, or of closely associated persons. The list should cover all kinds of interest including financial instruments and partnerships, financial interests such as unincorporated businesses and real estate, as well as relevant non-financial private interests such as links with outside organisations, and previous relevant employment.

5.4 On receipt of the written list the Permanent Secretary will arrange a meeting with the Minister to discuss it and to consider what advice is necessary and from what source, and what further written information is needed. The Permanent Secretary will stand ready either to give a considered view on the issues which the Minister raises, drawing on precedent and the help of the Cabinet Office as necessary, or to arrange for expert or professional advice also to be made available to the Minister from inside or outside government. At the end of the exercise Ministers are advised to record in writing what action has been considered and taken, and to provide the Permanent Secretary with a copy of that record.

5.5 Where it is proper for a Minister to retain a private interest it is the rule that he or she should declare that interest to Ministerial colleagues if they have to discuss public business which in any way affects it and that the Minister should remain entirely detached from the consideration of that business. Similar steps may be necessary if a matter under consideration in the Department relates in some way to a Minister's previous or existing private interests such that there is or may be thought to be a conflict of interest. Particular care needs to be taken where financial interests are involved: see paragraphs 5.11 to .18 below.

5.6 The personal information which Ministers disclose to those who advise them is treated in confidence. Should the Department receive a request for this information it will take account of a range of factors including the confidentiality of the information. The relevant Minister will also be consulted and his or her views taken into account before a decision would be made on disclosure. If an allegation is made that a particular Minister has a conflict of interest it must be for that Minister to explain their position and justify what has been done. In doing so, they may wish to make public the list of their private interests (required under paragraph 5.3) and the steps taken to avoid an actual or perceived conflict. It is open to them if they wish to confirm (if it is the case) that they have consulted their Permanent Secretary in accordance with the Code. The Minister should however consult the Permanent Secretary about the content of any such statement before making it to ensure that there is agreement about the content, and any disagreement should be referred to the Prime Minister.

5.7 The intention of these procedures is not to inhibit the holding of Ministerial office by individuals with wide experience, whether of industry, a profession or some other walk of life, but to ensure that systemic steps are taken to avoid the danger of an actual or perceived conflict of interests. The following paragraphs set out in more detail particular measures which should be taken based on experience over successive governments.

Public appointments

5.8 When they take up office Ministers should give up any other public appointment they may hold. Where it is proposed that such an appointment should be retained, the Prime Minister must be consulted.

Non-public bodies

5.9 Ministers should take care to ensure that they do not become associated with non-public organisations whose objectives may in any degree conflict with Government policy and thus give rise to a conflict of interest. Hence Ministers should not normally accept invitations to act as patrons of or otherwise offer support to pressure groups, or organisations dependent in whole or in part on Government funding. There is normally less objection to a Minister associating him or herself with a charity (subject to the points above) but Ministers should take care to ensure that in participating in any fund-raising activity, they do not place or appear to place, themselves under an obligation as Ministers to those to whom appeals are directed (and for this reason they should not normally approach individuals or companies personally for this purpose). In any case of doubt, the Prime Minister should be consulted before a Minister accepts an association with such bodies. Ministers should also exercise care in giving public support for petitions, open letters etc.

Trade unions

5.10 There is, of course, no objection to a Minister holding trade union membership but care must be taken to avoid any actual or perceived conflict of interest. Accordingly, Ministers should arrange their affairs so as to avoid any suggestion that a union of which they are a member has any undue influence; they should take no active part in the conduct of union affairs, should give up any office they may hold in a union and should receive no remuneration from a union (a nominal payment purely for the purpose of protecting a Minister's future pension rights is acceptable).

Financial interests

5.11 Ministers must scrupulously avoid any danger of an actual or apparent conflict of interest between their Ministerial position and their private financial interests. In order to avoid such a danger, they should be guided by the general principle that they should either dispose of any financial interest giving rise to the actual or apparent conflict or take alternative steps to prevent it. It is particularly important that the procedure described in paragraphs 5.3 and 5.4 is followed in the case of financial interests. The Permanent Secretary as Accounting Officer has a personal responsibility for financial propriety and regularity across the Department's business, and his or her advice must be given particular weight where such issues arise.

5.12 Two particular ways in which a conflict of financial interest, or the perception of it, can arise are as follows:

a. from the exercise of powers or other influence in a way that does or could be considered to affect the value of interests held; or

b. from using special knowledge acquired in the course of their Ministerial activities in ways which bring benefit or avoid loss (or could arouse reasonable suspicion of this) in relation to their private financial interests.

Apart from the risk to the Minister's reputation, two legal obligations must be born in mind:

a. any exercise or non-exercise by a Minister (including a Law Officer) of a legal power or discretion or other influence on a matter in which the Minister has a pecuniary interest could be challenged in the courts and, if the challenge is upheld, could be declared invalid. The courts interpret conflict of interest increasingly tightly;

b. Ministers are bound by the provisions of Part V of the Criminal Justice Act 1993 in relation to the use or transmission of unpublished price-sensitive information obtained by virtue of their Ministerial office.

Financial interests: alternatives to disposal

5.14 If for any reason the Minister is unable or unwilling to dispose of a relevant interest, he or she should consider, with the advice of the Permanent Secretary of the Department and, where necessary, an external adviser what alternative measures would sufficiently remove the risk of conflict. These fall into two types: those relating to the interests of themselves, and those relating to the handling of the decisions to be taken or influenced by the Minister.

Steps to be taken where financial interests are retained

5.15 As regards steps other than disposal which might be taken in relation to interests, the Minister might consider placing all investments (including derivatives) into a 'blind' trust, i.e one in which the Minister is not informed of changes in investments or of the state of the portfolio, but is still fully entitled to receive regular reports on the performance of the trust, and to receive both the capital and income generated. A blind trust is only blind in the case of a widely-spread portfolio of interests, managed by external advisers. Once a blind trust has been established the Minister should not be involved or advised of decisions on acquisition or disposal relating to the portfolio, although he can advise on the overall structure of the portfolio to be acquired. Ministers should remember that Part VI of the Companies Act 1985 allows companies to require information as to the true owners of its shares, which could result in the fact of a Minister's interest becoming public knowledge despite the existence of a trust. It should also be remembered that even with a trust the Minister could be assumed to know the contents of the portfolio for at least a period after its creation, so the protection a trust offers against conflict of interest is not complete. Alternatively a power of attorney may be suitable. However, this is a complex area and the Minister should seek professional advice because, among other things there may be tax consequences in establishing this kind of arrangement.

5.16 Another step which (perhaps in conjunction with other steps) might provide a degree of protection would be for the Minister to accept an obligation to refrain from dealing in the relevant shareholdings etc. for a period.

5.17 Unless adequate steps can be taken in relation to the financial interests themselves, the Minister and the Department must put processes in place to prohibit access to certain papers and ensure that the Minister is not involved in certain decisions and discussions. The extent to which this can be done depends on the specific powers under which the Minister would be required to take decisions. For example:

a. in the case of a junior Minister, it should be possible for the Ministerial head of the Department to take the decision or for the case to be handled by another junior Minister in the Department;

b. in the case of the Ministerial head of Department or the holder of a specific office in whom powers are vested, it will normally be possible without risk of legal challenge to pass the handling of the matter to a junior Minister or appropriate official in the Department, or, exceptionally, to another Secretary of State. In such cases, legal advice should always be sought to ensure that the relevant powers can be exercised in this way.

5.18 In some cases, it may not be possible to devise such a mechanism to avoid actual or perceived conflict of interest, for example because of the nature or size of the investment or the nature of the Department's work. In such a case, or in any case where, after taking legal advice of the Permanent Secretary, the Minister is in doubt whether adequate steps have been or can be taken, he or she should consult the Prime Minister. In such a case it may be necessary for the Minister to cease to hold the office in question.

Partnerships

5.19 Ministers who are partners, whether in professional firms, for example solicitors, accountants etc., or in other businesses should, on taking up office, cease to practise or to play any part in the day-to-day management of the firm's affairs. They are not necessarily required, however, to dissolve their partnership or to allow, for example, their annual practising certificate to lapse. Beyond this it is not possible to lay down precise rules applicable to every case; but any continuing financial interest in the firm would make it necessary for the Minister to take steps to avoid involvement in relevant decisions, as described in paragraph 5.17 above. Ministers in doubt about their personal position should consult the Prime Minister.

Directorships

5.20 Ministers must resign any directorships they hold when they take up office. This applies whether the directorship is in a public or private company and whether it carries remuneration or is honorary. The only exception to this rule is that directorships in private companies established in connection with private family estates or in a company formed for the management of flats of which the Minister is a tenant may be retained subject to the condition that if at any time the Minister feels that conflict is likely to arise between this private interest and public duty, the Minister should even in those cases resign the directorship. Directorships or offices held in connection with charitable undertakings should also be resigned if there is any risk of conflict arising between the interests of the undertakings and the Government.

Membership of Lloyd's

5.21 A Minister holding office as Prime Minister, Chancellor of the Exchequer or Secretary of State for Trade and Industry, or a Minister holding office as a Minister in the Treasury who is responsible under the Chancellor of the Exchequer for taxation matters relating specifically to Lloyd's, or as a Minister in the Department of Trade and Industry responsible under the Secretary of State for Trade and Industry for insurance matters relating specifically to Lloyd's, should not become an underwriting member of Lloyd's. Such a Minister, if already a member of Lloyd's on appointment, should cease underwriting during tenure of office.

5.22 Other Ministers who are underwriting members of Lloyd's should not take an active part in the management of the affairs of syndicates of which he/she is a member, and should on appointment as a Minister withdraw from any such active participation in its management. Ministers with underwriting connections to Lloyd's (whether past or present) should seek the advice of their Permanent Secretary as there can be implications for handling Departmental or collective discussions or decisions which are not always obvious.

Nomination for prizes and awards

5.23 From time to time, the personal support of Ministers is requested for nominations being made for international prizes and awards, e.g the annual Nobel prizes. Ministers should not sponsor individual nominations for any awards, since it would be inevitable that some people would assume that the Government was itself thereby giving its sponsorship.

Acceptance of gifts and hospitality

5.24 It is a well established and recognised rule that no Minister or public servant should accept gifts, hospitality or services from anyone which would, or might appear to, place him or her under an obligation. The same principle applies if gifts etc. are offered to a member of their family.

5.25 This is primarily a matter which must be left to the good sense of Ministers. But any Minister in doubt or difficulty over this should seek the Prime Minister's guidance. The same rules apply to the acceptance of gifts from donors with whom a Minister has official dealings in this country as to those from overseas . . ., that is:

a. Receipt of gifts should be reported to the Permanent Secretary;

b. Gifts of small value (currently this is set at up to £140) may be retained by the recipient;

c. Gifts of a higher value should be handed over to the Department for disposal, except that:
   i. the recipient may purchase the gift at its cash value (abated by £140);
   ii. if the Department judges that it would be of interest, the gift may be displayed or used in the Department;
   iii. if the disposal of the gift would cause offence or if it might be appropriate for the recipient to use or display the gift on some future occasion as a mark of politeness, then the gift should be retained in the Department for this purpose for a period of up to five years;

d. Gifts received overseas worth more than the normal travellers' allowances should be declared at importation to Customs and Excise who will advise on any duty and tax liability. In general, if a Minister wishes to retain a gift he or she will be liable for any tax or duty it may attract.

5.26 Gifts given to Ministers in their Ministerial capacity become the property of the Government and do not need to be declared in the Register of Members' or Peers' Interests. Gifts given to Ministers as constituency MPs or members of a political Party fall within the rules relating to the Registers of Members' and Peers' Interests.

Annual list of gifts

5.27 The Government publishes an annual list of gifts received by Ministers valued at more than £140. The list provides details of the value of the gifts and whether they were retained by the department or purchased by the Minister. Departments must ensure that they maintain records of gifts received in such a way as to be able to provide this information on an annual basis to the Cabinet Office.

5.28 In the event of a Minister accepting hospitality on a scale or from a source which might reasonably be thought likely to influence Ministerial action, it should be declared in Register of Members' or Peers' Interests. Registration of hospitality would normally be required for hospitality over £550 in value for the Commons and £1000 for the Lords.

Acceptance of appointments after leaving ministerial office

5.29 On leaving office, Ministers should seek advice from the independent Advisory Committee on Business Appointments about any appointments they wish to take up within two years of leaving office. This is not necessary for unpaid appointments in non-commercial organisations or appointments in the gift of the Government, such as Prime Ministerial appointments to international organisations. Although it is in the public interest that former Ministers should be able to move into business or other areas of public life, it is equally important that there should be no cause for any suspicion of impropriety about a particular appointment. The Advisory Committee may recommend a delay of up to two years before the appointment is taken up if:

a. an appointment could lead to public concern that the statements and decisions of the Minister, when in Government, have been influenced by the hope or expectation of future employment with the firm or organisation concerned;

b. an employer could make improper use of official information to which a former Minister has had access.

....

Annex A

The seven principles of public life

Selflessness

Holders of public office should act solely in terms of the public interest. They should not do so in order to gain financial or other material benefits for themselves, their family, or their friends.

Integrity

Holders of public office should not place themselves under any financial or other obligation to outside individuals or organisations that might seek to influence them in the performance of their official duties.

Objectivity

In carrying out public business, including making public appointments, awarding contracts, or recommending individuals for rewards and benefits, holders of public office should make choices on merit.

Accountability

Holders of public office are accountable for their decisions and actions to the public and must submit themselves to whatever scrutiny is appropriate to their office.

Openness

Holders of public office should be as open as possible about all the decisions and actions that they take. They should give reasons for their decisions and restrict information only when the wider public interest clearly demands.

Honesty

Holders of public office have a duty to declare any private interests relating to their public duties and to take steps to resolve any conflicts arising in a way that protects the public interest.

Leadership

Holders of public office should promote and support these principles by leadership and example.

. . .

PART II—Procedural guidance for Ministers

6 Ministers and the Government

. . .

Cabinet and Ministerial Committee business

6.2 The business of the Cabinet and Ministerial Committees consists in the main of:

a. questions which significantly engage the collective responsibility of the Government because they raise major issues of policy or because they are of crucial importance to the public;

b. questions on which there is an unresolved argument between Departments.

6.3 Matters wholly within the responsibility of a single Minister and which do not significantly engage collective responsibility as defined above need not be brought to the Cabinet or to a Ministerial Committee unless the Minister wishes to inform his colleagues or to have their advice. A precise definition of such matters cannot be given: in borderline cases a Minister is advised to seek collective consideration. Questions involving more than one Department should be examined interdepartmentally, before submission to a Ministerial Committee, so that the decisions required may be clearly defined.

Collective responsibility

6.16 The internal process through which a decision has been made, or the level of Committee by which it was taken, should not be disclosed. Decisions reached by the Cabinet or Ministerial Committees are binding on all members of the Government. They are, however, normally announced and explained as the decision of the Minister concerned. On occasions it may be desirable to emphasise the importance of a decision by stating specially that it is the decision of Her Majesty's Government. This, however, is the exception rather than the rule.

6.17 Collective responsibility requires that Ministers should be able to express their views frankly in the expectation that they can argue freely in private while maintaining a united front when decisions have been reached. This in turn requires that the privacy of opinions expressed in Cabinet and Ministerial Committees should be maintained. Moreover Cabinet and Committee documents will often contain information which needs to be protected in the public interest. It is therefore essential that, subject to the requirements on the disclosure of information set out in the Freedom of Information Act 2000, Ministers take the necessary steps to ensure that they and their staff preserve the privacy of Cabinet business and protect the security of Government documents.

6.18 The principle of collective responsibility and the need to safeguard national security, relations with other countries and the confidential nature of discussions between Ministers and their civil servants impose certain obligations on former Ministers who are contemplating the publication of material based upon their recollection of the conduct of Government business in which they took part. They are required to submit their draft manuscript to the Secretary of the Cabinet for comment and approval and to conform to the principles set out in the Radcliffe Report of 1976 (Cmnd 6386).

. . .

Cabinet documents

6.19 Ministers relinquishing office without a change of Government should hand over to their successors those Cabinet documents required for current administration and should ensure that all others have been destroyed. Former Ministers may at any time, and subject to undertakings to observe the conventions governing Ministerial memoirs, have access in the Cabinet Office to copies of Cabinet or Ministerial Committee papers issued to them while in office.

6.20 On a change of Government, the outgoing Prime Minister issues special instructions about the disposal of the Cabinet papers of the outgoing Administration.

Some Ministers have thought it wise to make provision in their wills against the improper disposal of any oficial or Government documents which they might have retained in their possession by oversight.

. . .

9 Ministers and the presentation of policy

Coordination of Government policy

9.1 Official facilities financed out of public funds can be used for Government publicity and advertising, but may not be used for the dissemination of material which is essentially party political. The conventions governing the work of the Government Communication Network are set out in *Guidance on Government Communications*.

9.2 In order to ensure the effective presentation of government policy, all major interviews and media appearances, both print and broadcast, should be agreed with the No 10 Press Office before any commitments are entered into. The policy content of all major speeches, press releases and new policy initiatives should be cleared in good time with the No 10 Private Office. The timing and form of announcements should be cleared with the No 10 Strategic Communications Unit.

Press conferences

9.3 In order to explain policies or to announce new policies a Minister may decide to hold a press conference. This will be convened by the Department's Communications Directorate. All press conferences are on the record and open to any representative of the home and overseas media. It is often the practice of Ministers to give separate radio and TV interviews afterwards in order to secure the most effective presentation of their views or announcement. Where a Minister wishes to address the Lobby the No 10 Press Office should be consulted both about the desirability of such a briefing and the method of organising it. This paragraph applies to overseas as well as to the home media.

Publication of White and Consultation Papers

9.4 Before publishing a White or a Consultation Paper, Departments should consider whether it raises issues which require full collective Ministerial consideration, and, after consulting the Cabinet Office as necessary, seek clearance through the appropriate Cabinet Committee. Any Command Paper containing a major statement of Government policy should be circulated to the Cabinet before publication. This is usually done at the Confidential Final Revise (CFR) stage and should be done under cover of a letter from the Minister's Private Secretary. This rule applies to Papers containing major statements even when no issue requiring collective consideration is required.

. . .

Speeches

9.7 Ministers cannot speak on public affairs for themselves alone. In all cases other than those described in paragraph 4.6 they speak as Ministers; and the principle of collective responsibility applies. They should ensure that their statements are consistent with collective Government policy and should not anticipate decisions not yet made public. Ministers should exercise special care in referring to subjects which are the responsibility of other Ministers. Any Minister who intends to make a speech which deals with, or makes observations which bear upon, matters which fall within another Minister's responsibilities should consult that Minister.

9.8 The Prime Minister should always be consulted before any mention is made of matters which either affect the conduct of the Government as a whole or are of a constitutional character. The Foreign and Commonwealth Secretary should always be consulted before any mention is made of matters affecting foreign and Commonwealth affairs, relations with foreign and Commonwealth countries and the political aspects of the affairs of dependent territories. Ministers wishing to refer in a speech or any other public statement to economic policy or to proposals involving additional public expenditure or revenue costs should in all cases consult the Chancellor of the Exchequer or the Chief Secretary. Ministers wishing to refer to defence policy should in all cases first consult the Secretary of State for Defence. Ministers wishing to discuss or refer to Northern Ireland should in all cases first consult the Secretary of State for Northern Ireland.

9.9 Ministers should use official machinery for distributing texts of Ministerial speeches only when such speeches are made on official occasions and deal with Government as distinct from Party policy. Speeches made in a party political context should be distributed through the Party machinery.

9.10 Ministers should not accept payment for speeches of an official nature or which directly draw on their responsibilities or experience . . .

Broadcasts

9.11 The provisions of paragraphs 9.1–9.3 apply to Ministerial broadcasts as well.
. . .

Press articles

9.15 Ministers may contribute occasionally to a book, journal or newspaper (including a local news-paper in their constituency) for the purpose of supplementing other means of informing the public about the work of their Department provided that publication will not be at variance with their obligations to Parliament and their duty to observe the principle of collective Ministerial responsibility. Any Minister wishing to practice regular journalism, including the contribution of weekly or fortnightly articles to local newspapers in their constituencies, must have the prior approval of the Prime Minister. In cases of doubt, and in all cases where a Minister is contemplating the contribution of an article going beyond the strict confines of his or her Departmental responsibility, the Prime Minister should be consulted, before work has begun and in any case before any commitment to publish is entered into. In all cases where an article contains material which falls within the Departmental responsibility of another Minister, that Minister must be consulted. Ministers should not accept payment for writings, either on their own or on their Department's account, or with a view to donating the fee to charity. If the organisation receiving the Minister's written contribution insists on making a donation to a charity then it should be a charity of the organisation's choice. This is to avoid any criticism that a Minister is using his or her official position position to influence or take the credit for donations to charity.

9.16 Ministers are advised not to engage in controversy in the correspondence columns of either the home or the overseas press. Ministers may however see advantage in correcting serious errors or misstatements of fact which led to false conclusions. Such letters should be brief and confined to the exposition of facts.

Books

9.17 Ministers may not, while in office, write and publish a book on their Ministerial experience. Nor, while serving as a Minister, may they enter into any agreement to publish their memoirs on leaving their Ministerial position, without the agreement of the Prime Minister. Former Ministers are required to submit their manuscript to the Secretary of the Cabinet and to conform to the principles set out in the Radcliffe Report of 1976 (Cmnd 6386) . . . Ministers may not receive payment for a book written before becoming a Minister if the decision to publish was taken afterwards.'

At this point it should be pointed out that the provisions of the code relating to books written by ministers and ex-ministers refer back to an incident in the 1970s known as the 'Crossman Diaries Affair'. This led to the case of *A-G v Jonathan Cape Ltd*,[17] which casts light on the nature of conventions and the attitude of the courts towards them.

Between 1964 and 1970 a Cabinet minister, with the knowledge of his Cabinet colleagues, kept a diary recording Cabinet discussions and political events with a view to their publication as a book. Following his death in April 1974, volume one of the book, *Diaries of a Cabinet Minister*, which covered the years 1964–66, was sent to the Secretary of the Cabinet for his approval, but was rejected on the ground that publication was against the public interest in that the doctrine of collective responsibility would be harmed by the disclosure of details of Cabinet discussions, the revelation of differences between members of the Cabinet and the disclosure of advice given by, and discussions regarding the appointment of, civil servants. In July 1974 the literary executors gave an undertaking not to publish the book without giving prior notice to the Treasury Solicitor but, in January 1975, the first extracts from the book were published in the *Sunday Times* without the consent of the Secretary of the Cabinet.

Lord Widgery CJ:[18]

'It has always been assumed by lawyers . . . that Cabinet proceedings and Cabinet papers are secret, and cannot be publicly disclosed until they have passed into history . . . [The] Attorney-General contends . . . the court . . . will . . . positively forbid the disclosure of such papers and proceedings if publication will be contrary to the public interest.

The basis of this contention is the confidential character of these papers and proceedings, derived from the convention of joint Cabinet responsibility whereby any policy decision reached by the Cabinet has to be supported thereafter by all members of the Cabinet . . . It is contended that Cabinet decisions and papers are confidential for a period to the extent . . . that they must not be referred to . . . in such a way as to disclose the attitude of individual Ministers in the argument which preceded the decision. Thus, there may be no objection to a Minister disclosing (or leaking, as it was called) the fact that a Cabinet meeting has taken place, or, indeed, the decision taken, so long as the individual views of Ministers are not identified. . . .

The defendants' main contention is that whatever the limits of the convention of joint Cabinet responsibility may be, there is no obligation enforceable at law to prevent the publication of Cabinet papers and proceedings, except in extreme cases where national security is involved. In other words, the defendants submit that the confidential character of Cabinet papers and discussions is based on a true convention as defined in the evidence of Professor Henry Wade, namely, an obligation founded in conscience only. Accordingly, the defendants contend that publication of these Diaries is not capable of control by any order of this court. . . .

[17] [1976] QB 752.   [18] [1976] QB 752 at 764 (post letter D) to 771 (post letter F).

It seems to me, therefore, that the Attorney-General must first show that whatever obligation of secrecy or discretion attaches to former Cabinet Ministers, that obligation is binding in law and not merely in morals. . . .

The general understanding of Ministers while in office was that information obtained from Cabinet source was secret and not to be disclosed to outsiders.

There is not much evidence of the understanding of Ministers as to the protection of such information after the Minister retires. It seems probable to me that those not desirous of publishing memoirs assumed that the protection went on until the incident was 30 years old, whereas those interested in memoirs would discover on inquiry at the Cabinet Office that draft memoirs were normally submitted to the Secretary of the Cabinet for his advice on their contents before publication . . .

However, the Attorney-General has a powerful reinforcement for his argument in the developing equitable doctrine that a man shall not profit from the wrongful publication of information received by him in confidence. This doctrine, said to have its origin in *Prince Albert v Strange* (1849) 1 H & TW 1, has been frequently recognised as a ground for restraining the unfair use of commercial secrets transmitted in confidence. Sometimes in these cases there is a contract which may be said to have been breached by the breach of confidence, but it is clear that the doctrine applies independently of contract: see *Saltman Engineering Co. Ltd v Campbell Engineering Co. Ltd* (1948) 6 RPC 203 . . .

This extension of the doctrine of confidence beyond commercial secrets has never been directly challenged, and was noted without criticism by Lord Denning MR in *Fraser v Evans* [1969] 1 QB 349 at 361 . . . I cannot see why the courts should be powerless to restrain the publication of public secrets, while enjoying . . . powers in regard to domestic secrets . . . I conclude, therefore, that when a Cabinet Minister receives information in confidence the improper publication of such information can be restrained by the court, and his obligation is not merely to observe a gentleman's agreement to refrain from publication . . .

I find overwhelming evidence that the doctrine of joint responsibility is generally understood and practised and equally strong evidence that it is on occasion ignored. The general effect of the evidence is that the doctrine is an established feature of the English form of government, and it follows that some matters leading up to a Cabinet decision may be regarded as confidential. Furthermore, I am persuaded that the nature of the confidence is that spoken for by the Attorney-General, namely that since that confidence is imposed to enable the efficient conduct of the Queen's business, the confidence is owed to the Queen and cannot be released by the members of the Cabinet themselves. I have been told that a resigning Minister who wishes to make a personal statement in the House, and to disclose matters which are confidential under the doctrine obtains the consent of the Queen for this purpose. Such consent is obtained through the Prime Minister . . .

The Attorney-General must show (a) that . . . publication would be a breach of confidence; (b) that the public interest requires that the publication be restrained, and (c) that there are no other facts of the public interest contradictory of and more compelling than that relied upon. Moreover, the court, when asked to restrain such a publication, must closely examine the extent to which relief is necessary to ensure that restrictions are not imposed beyond the strict requirement of public need . . .

There must, however, be a limit in time after which the confidential character of the information, and the duty of the court to restrain publication, will lapse. Since the conclusion of the hearing in this case I have had the opportunity to read the whole of volume one of the Diaries, and my considered view is that I cannot believe that the publication at this interval of anything in volume one would inhibit free discussion in the Cabinet of today . . .

It may, of course, be intensely difficult in a particular case, to say at what point the material loses its confidential character, on the ground that publication will no longer undermine the doctrine of joint Cabinet responsibility . . . The court should intervene only in the clearest of cases where the continuing confidentiality of the material can be demonstrated. In less clear cases—and this, in my view, is certainly one—reliance must be placed on the good sense and good taste of the Minister or ex-Minister concerned.'

Following this decision the issue was referred to a Committee of Privy Councillors, whose report, Cmnd 6386, 1976, is referred to in the current Ministerial Code. After considering the foregoing case the report made certain recommendations:

'**64** There are three considerations arising from this Judgment's exposition of the law which we will set out briefly below, because they seem to us to be critical for the purposes of our own inquiry.

(a) The common law does extend so far as to be capable of prohibiting an ex-Minister or his inheritors from publishing in his memoirs information which he has received in confidence by virtue of his office . . .

(b) The impropriety of disclosure which the Court needs to find in order to justify its intervention must be proved before it by evidence in each case . . .

(c) The categories of information described as (1) advice given by senior Civil Servants to their Ministers and (2) observations made by Ministers on the capacity of individual senior Civil Servants and their suitability for specific appointments do not, it seems, qualify for legal protection from disclosure on the ground of any intrinsic confidentiality . . .

71 . . . [Every] Minister on taking office should have his attention drawn explicitly to the obligations with regard to the future that he is assuming by virtue of that office . . . [It] has been the practice of successive Prime Ministers in the past to circulate to each incoming colleague a confidential document drawing his attention to the general principles of Ministerial conduct and some other matters of Ministerial procedure. A Minister on first appointment is required also to sign a declaration that his attention has been drawn to the provisions of the Official Secrets Act . . .

73 We recommend that . . . every ex-Minister who wishes to make public an account bearing on his Ministerial life should make it his business to let the Secretary of the Cabinet see in advance the full text of what he proposes to say . . .

75 The comments that he offers and the advice that he tenders are not those of a censor . . . Those representations are advisory and must be understood as such. If his advice is not accepted in any matter whether supported by reference to the opinion of the Prime Minister or not, the consequences of publication must in the last resort lie with the author himself . . . The Prime Minister should not be required to direct his attention to every one of the . . . detailed questions that may arise from the scrutiny of a projected memoir. It is enough that it should be realised that his position and responsibilities involve him in a continuing concern for the maintenance of the conventions that we have reviewed and that he is at all times available for reference to give a ruling or an opinion on disputed points . . .

78 . . . [The] Cabinet Secretary will have several duties to perform when he receives the text of a proposed publication . . .

79 On the one hand there is the need for clearance in respect of national security and the preservation of international relations. For this he will submit the text to the Government Department or, very possibly, Departments concerned for scrutiny and advice. If objections are raised under either head he will transmit them to the author . . . [If] in the end the objection stands, it is in our opinion the positive duty of the author to give way to it . . . These are not matters upon which in the last resort he is at liberty to set his judgment against the official view. It may be that an unabated sense of dissatisfaction will lead him to ask for the issue to be referred to the decision of the Prime Minister himself. If so, he should, we think, have this right of reference, and he should be heard. But that should be the end. The Prime Minister's decision should be accepted as final.

80 On the other hand lie those various considerations that we have discussed and formulated under the category of 'Confidential Relationships' in Part II . . . [This] is not a range of subject upon which we feel justified in recommending that it should be the duty of the author in the last resort to give way to the view of the Cabinet Secretary or of the Prime Minister, if the issue reaches the latter . . . On all these questions we think that the author must take upon his own shoulders the responsibility for deciding what he is going to say and how he is going to express himself. What he must do is to pay careful attention to the advice that he receives from the Cabinet Secretary and give fair weight to the reflection that he is one of a somewhat special class of privileged writers for whose situation a special set of conventions has been gradually evolved . . . At some point of time the secrets of one period must become the common learning of another. How then to find any working rule for the ex-Minister author which will do justice to the proper claims of governmental and administrative life on the one side and to the demand of genuine historical inquiry on the other?

. . .

83 Reviewing the various categories of restriction that we have recommended, we see that the time factor has not the same significance for all of them. In this respect questions of national security and international relations impose their own time limits simply by virtue of their own special circumstances . . . The only thing that matters for this purpose is that the intending author should always clear his material through the Cabinet Secretary before he offers it to the public.

84 But the problem is fundamentally different for those issues which we have classed as Confidential Relationships . . . [We] are led to the conclusion that a fixed time limit, at the expiry of which the restrictions proposed under this heading of Confidential Relationships will be lifted, is the only satisfactory way of reconciling the interests of the State, the needs of the author, and the demands of the interested public.

85 Any such time limit must necessarily be arbitrary and general. It does not admit of any reasoned process of measurement . . . What we propose for the time limit is a period of 15 years . . . What we mean to secure by it is that, while in dealing with incidents or affairs or matters which are less than 15 years ago at the date of intended publication an author should regard himself as bound by the approved rules and procedures governing Confidential Relationships, he can, if he so wishes, take his own unrestricted line in dealing with any subject of an earlier date . . .

86 We must note however that there is one principle which we have outlined earlier which cannot be adequately covered by the observance of a simple time limit. That is the rule that an ex-Minister should not reveal the advice given to him in confidence by those in the Service whose duty it has been to advise him. If he gives the weight of it, it must be given without attributing it to any identifiable persons . . . It is a rule that, according to our recommendation, should be adhered to during the whole period of the adviser's Service life, not just for the sake of his own protection but also because successive Governments have accepted a convention that neither the views of predecessors in office nor the advice tendered to them by their departmental officers should be made available to their successors.'

The problem with these various guidelines set out above is that they are not binding rules and apply only to ministers. In July 2006 the House of Commons Public Administration Committee called for one set of rules that should apply to ministers, special advisers, diplomats, and public officials requiring them to have a contractual obligation to submit for scrutiny any proposed memoirs of their periods in office before publication. Such a requirement could be made a contractual term in the contracts of employment of the home civil and diplomatic services, though it might be harder to impose it on the much more nebulous appointment of being a minister of the Crown. Even so it is very arguable that those who are privy to confidential information should not be too easily able to reveal details of splits, leaks and disagreements at Cabinet level if trust between ministerial colleagues and harmonious relationships between ministers and officials is to be preserved. On the other hand it would not be in the public interest to attempt to ban such memoirs entirely.

(a) Enforcement of the Ministerial Code

In 2001 the Code was examined by the House of Commons Public Administration Select Committee who argued that it was a document of constitutional significance which should be treated as 'law' rather than 'lore', with the Prime Minister being given a specific enforcement role under the Code.[19] The Committee on Standards in Public Life also addressed the issue in 2003, calling in March 2006 for more effective means of investigating alleged infringements of the Code,[20] and repeated its call for an independent body with powers to investigate alleged infringements. A few days later the government responded by agreeing to:

- the appointment of an independent Adviser on Ministerial Interests to advise incoming ministers on arrangements necessary to prevent actual or perceived conflicts between public duties and private interests, and to maintain records of any interests a minister is required to disclose;
- the nomination by the Prime Minister, in consultation with the leaders of other parties, at the beginning of each Parliament, of a panel from whom individuals may be selected to investigate alleged infringements of the Code.

These developments were welcomed by the Committee on Standards in Public Life which also, however, reserved judgment on their operation in practice arguing that much will depend on the independence, clarity, openness and publication of investigations. In September 2006 the Committee on Standards in Public Life further welcomed the most recent call from the Public Administration Select Committee that alleged breaches of the Ministerial Code should be subject to an independent investigative mechanism while leaving the final decision on any action to be taken to the Prime Minister.

It cannot be sufficiently stressed that the enforcement of the Ministerial Code is a crucial issue. However, it has to be admitted that the attitude of the Prime Minister is the key issue here. Public confidence in the Code is eroded and the suspicion of 'sleaze' in the conduct of government business increases unless the Prime Minister is seen to be both conscious of the need for clearly defined ethical standards for ministers and vigilant to enforce those standards.

---

v. Defeat and Resignation, the Conventional Understanding

It might be supposed that the argument that a government defeated on a policy issue is conventionally bound to resign is unassailable. It seems close to the argument that only those statutes should be passed in relation to which ministers can command confidence in the Commons. Such an argument was generally academically accepted into the late 1960s: but over recent years the convention has become that governments should resign if defeated on a vote specifically declared one of confidence. Indeed, Harold Wilson as Prime Minister made a statement to that effect in 1974.[21] It is therefore for a government, more probably the Prime Minister, to decide whether to declare that a matter is one of confidence. Even the loss of a Bill will now not necessarily bring about a confidence vote. Even though Mr Major's increasingly frail majority from 1992 onwards led to a number of reverses for his government, the last Prime Minister to be forced from office on a vote of 'no confidence' was Lord Callaghan in 1979. This was the first time since 1924 that a vote of no confidence had been carried against

---

[19] See further Peter Riddell, *The Times*, 14 February 2001.
[20] Ninth Report of the Committee on Standards in Public Life, Cm 5775 (HMSO, London, 2003).
[21] 870 HC Official Report (5th Series) cols 71–72, 12 March 1974.

a government, forcing it to resign. In July 1993 Mr Major, however, survived a confidence vote after he had been defeated on a vote in the Commons where he sought authority to ratify the 1992 Maastricht Treaty.

Of course, a government having a comfortable majority in the Commons is unlikely to be defeated there, particularly on a confidence vote. But defeats can happen, for example that of the government's Shops Bill, to liberalise Sunday trading laws, in 1986, when there was a refusal by 68 Conservative members to obey a three-line whip. However, for most of the time 'retaining the confidence of the House of Commons' means not so much a need to survive votes in the House but rather an obligation to explain policy and defend decisions, both to the Opposition and to the government's own back bench supporters.

(a) The requirement for collective responsibility

Collective responsibility involves collective resignation if there is a 'no confidence' vote in the Commons, but what of the argument that it also involves unanimity amongst ministers? In the early 1930s the National Government 'agreed to differ' on certain issues; Harold Wilson in 1974 relaxed requirements in relation to the European Communities membership referendum; James Callaghan allowed dissent in relation to the European Assembly Elections Bill in 1977. These 'agreements to differ' allowed by Prime Ministers, are, however, very different from out and out public disagreements between ministers, such as occurred in the Westland affair of 1985–86, see above. The Ministerial Code, also see above, once again stresses the collective responsibility of ministers.

While the conventional understanding assists in promoting the clear articulation of policy, it is clear that is subject to stresses. One of these is the less than honourable device of the 'unattributable leak' which is characterised by Rodney Brazier[22] as 'the life saver' of the convention. Indeed, Brazier is reasonably relaxed in his description of the practice: 'A day rarely passes without some item in the newspapers giving details of Cabinet or Cabinet Committee business which could only have been obtained by a leak. Leaking is periodically and hypocritically condemned by Prime Ministers and Ministers; sometimes leak inquiries [are] set up under the Cabinet Secretary; civil servants and Ministers are questioned; usually nothing comes of them.'[23] In the Westland affair such leaking achieved a totally unacceptable significance, however. On other, rare, occasions the convention has been relaxed by a Prime Minister who has allowed open dissent and debate on policy issues, such as occurred in 1932 on trade and tariff matters, and in 1975 and 1977 over the question of membership of the European Community, the national referendum on that matter and the subsequent introduction of direct elections from the UK to the European Assembly. A number of commentators (Geoffrey Marshall and Rodney Brazier among them) also argue that 'open disagreements openly arrived at' may be desirable if government and policy formation are to become more transparent, for the 'downside' of the convention is the prevention of open debate and the promotion of secrecy in government.[24]

Normally, however, a public façade of unanimity is maintained by ministers even in respect of Cabinet decisions with which they privately disagree. Internal dissent can, however, be

---

[22] *Constitutional Practice* (3rd edn, OUP, Oxford, 1999), p. 145.   [23] Brazier, op cit p. 129.
[24] Brazier, op cit p. 149.

made patent by 'non-attributable leaks', or by the delivery of public speeches in which a 'coded message' is given which expresses a minister's individual view on an issue. Rodney Brazier again neatly sums up the issue: 'near or actual breaches of collective responsibility provoke no automatic penalty; much will depend on the particular minister's political strength, his ability to brazen out any demands for his resignation, and the attitude of the Prime Minister'.[25] Clearly there is no effective conventional requirement for unanimity amongst ministers in the sense of *total* solidarity in all things at all times and in all places. This indicates that this particular convention is less 'strong' than those relating to the powers of the monarch. Equally there are times when ministers must resign or must be required to resign because of their dissent. Again as Rodney Brazier points out Cabinets must hang together on essential policies and too much departure from the conventional understanding could be politically dangerous for the government—and confusing for the nation it may be added. The *normal* understanding is that ministers who cannot accept a Cabinet decision should resign, or keep their dissent private, and those who do not resign accept responsibility for decisions taken and should speak, and vote, for such policies as the occasion demands.

Two comparatively recent resignations illustrate the working of the convention. On 18 March 2003 Mr Robin Cook resigned from the government because he considered that the decision to invade Iraq was lacking in international agreement and domestic support. He announced his intention then to vote against going to war in the vote the government had agreed to hold in the House of Commons on the issue, even though there was no legal requirement for such a vote. Such an action by Mr Cook would have been incompatible with membership of the government and he therefore had to resign. After the invasion had begun Ms Clare Short also resigned on 12 May 2003. She too had been troubled by the decision to go to war, considering it a mistake, but though she tendered her resignation the Prime Minister and others had persuaded her to stay in office, which she did so as not to weaken the government at a particularly delicate time. Her resignation when it came was triggered by mistakes made by the UK/US coalition *after* the invasion had occurred. Ms Short felt she had to resign, but it is interesting to note that for a while at least her legitimate desire not to weaken the government overcame her misgivings about the action the government was taking.

(b) The 'creative leak'

Leaking may occur for purposes other than indicating a degree of disagreement between ministers. Documents may for example be leaked by a variety of persons—perhaps in order to allow a government department to 'get its blow in first' before criticism of a particular policy is made in Parliament. One apparent instance of this arose in 1998 consequent on allegations of British involvement in the internal affairs of Sierra Leone, and an investigation into this by a Commons Select Committee. The Foreign Secretary, Mr Robin Cook, allegedly attempted to limit the investigation, but then further allegations were made of British involvement in illegal arms shipments to Sierra Leone. An *official* inquiry into the allegations was also proceeding and the report of this on 27 July 1998 was critical of certain actions by British officials and companies. This, however, did not prevent continuing criticism by some members of the Commons Select Committee, and there was open tension between Mr Cook and the Committee over his attempts to deny access to relevant Foreign Office communications.

---

[25] Brazier, op cit p. 146.

When the Select Committee finally reported they too were critical of particular officials, though ministers were cleared of conniving in plots to supply arms illegally to factions in Sierra Leone, and of any attempt to mislead Parliament. However, in the present context the most serious issue would appear to be reports carried in *The Times* of 5 March 1999 alleging that Mr Cook had received a leaked version of the Committee's Report. Mr Cook admitted receiving leaked information—which, of course, enabled him and his department to prepare arguments in their own defence.

Leaks may also take place, for even more questionable reasons, to advance the political careers of ministers by besmirching their colleagues. From the early days of the Blair government there have been press allegations of rivalry between Mr Blair and his supporters and the Chancellor of the Exchequer, Gordon Brown, and his supporters. By Christmas 1998 the allegations of feuding were allegedly being fuelled by 'unauthorised press briefings' given by the press officers of the various parties. This led on 4 January 1999 to the departure from office of Mr Charlie Whelan, the Chancellor's press secretary who had been, it was alleged by some, implicated in leaking. It was also argued by some commentators that Dr Mo Mowlam's decision to resign from ministerial office on the calling of the next general election (announced on 4 September 2000) was partly motivated by leaks and 'whispering campaigns' against her in government circles. Even so allegations continue to be circulated—as witness *The Independent* for 4 July 2000—that ministers are undermined by the associates and allies of other ministers—including the Prime Minister.

Leaking, by, for or against ministers, goes on, despite official condemnation and claims that either it does not exist, or has ceased. The real questions (leaving aside the probably inevitably dirty business of day to day politics) are for what reasons does it occur, and could there be less leaking if there was more open policy making?

Anthony Seldon has argued that collective responsibility now only applies to public disagreements between ministers, and not to leaks or private disagreements. Ministers, he claims, however, will avoid public disagreements not only because of the notion of collective responsibility but because 'they know insufficient detail to dispute the decision'. He nevertheless points to the criticisms made by a number of ministers about the Millennium Dome because they felt 'they had been overruled' by Blair in the summer of 1997 (when the decision to proceed with the Dome had been taken).[26]

VI. The Individual Responsibility of Ministers

The individual responsibility of ministers illustrates further Professor Munro's continuum theory. Ministers are individually accountable for their own private conduct, the general running of their departments and acts done, or omitted to be done, by their civil servants; responsibility in the first two cases is clearer than in others. A minister involved in sexual or financial scandals, particularly those having implications for national security, may have to

---

[26] Seldon, A, 'The Cabinet System,' chapter 4 in Bogdanor, V, (ed) *The British Constitution in the 20th Century* (OUP, Oxford, 2004), p. 133.

resign because his activities will so attract the attention of the press that he will no longer be able to carry out departmental duties.

The provisions in the 1997 Code of Conduct for Ministers on their private interests related primarily to financial affairs. The current Code does require ministers to observe the 'highest standards of . . . personal conduct' but even so the position here is governed by conventional principles whose content appears to be fluid, capable of changing with public perceptions of morality, and the seriousness of the issues involved. Thus in 1963 the Secretary of State for War, Mr John Profumo, was forced to resign following discoveries that he had lied to the House of Commons over his alleged involvement with Christine Keeler who was also allegedly involved with the naval attaché at the Russian Embassy, so that there could have been a security risk. The real 'offence' on Profumo's part was, however, the lie to the Commons.

In 1973 Lord Lambton resigned from office following disclosure that he had been allegedly photographed in bed with two call girls, and Earl Jellicoe resigned a few days later after alleged involvement in a vice ring scandal. In these cases it was clear the notoriety of the issue would have adversely prevented these ministers from doing their jobs. When, however, in 1983 it emerged that, the then Mr, Cecil Parkinson had had an affair with Sarah Keays, his Secretary, Baroness Thatcher did not immediately accept his offer to resign from office—nor did the issue subsequently prevent Mr Parkinson from returning to office and then proceeding to the House of Lords as an 'elder statesman'.

It is certainly the case that the fact of divorce is no longer enough to prevent a person from holding ministerial office, nor will a person's sexual orientation bar him/her from office provided he/she behaves discreetly *so that no hint of scandal arises*. But once a scandal of either a financial or sexual nature arises the position may alter dramatically.

In January 1994 allegations were made about Mr Tim Yeo, a minister in the Department of the Environment, that he had had an extra-marital affair with a local councillor and had fathered an illegitimate child. On 6 January 1994 Mr Yeo resigned apparently because he had lost the support of his local constituency party whose officers voiced deep concern over widespread criticism of his conduct. It appears that it was this loss of Mr Yeo's constituency support which persuaded the Prime Minister's close advisers that the hapless minister could no longer continue in office and, following a meeting with the Chief Whip, Mr Yeo finally laid down his office.

A further scandal afflicted Mr Major's government on 19 October 1994 when Mr Tim Smith, a minister in the Northern Ireland Department resigned on admitting that he had taken a fee from a wealthy businessman in return for asking questions on that person's behalf in Parliament. Allegations were also made against Mr Neil Hamilton, a Trade and Industry minister, in respect of the same issue. Mr Hamilton at first refused to resign, denied he had been involved and commenced a defamation action in respect of the allegations. However, on 26 October 1994 Mr Hamilton resigned—or, it appears, was forced to resign in respect of further allegations made against him which, according to the Prime Minister, disabled Mr Hamilton from carrying out his ministerial duties. Subsequent resignations included Mr Jonathan Aitken, the Chief Secretary to the Treasury, who resigned in 1995 following allegations of financial scandal, Mr Rod Richards, a Welsh Office minister, in June 1996 following allegations of marital infidelity and Mr David Willetts in December 1996 following criticism from an all-party Commons committee.

Between 1945 and 1997 a total of 65 ministers resigned for causes including sexual scandals, financial misdealings, failure in office, political principles and general public criticism. Under Baroness Thatcher's long tenure of office (1979–1991) 14 ministers resigned, while 12 resigned under Mr Major. Sex scandals are not the most common cause of resignation; they account for only 11 cases, while financial scandals account for only six. Resignation on a point of principle, ie when a minister cannot accept the collective 'line' of the government, is the most common situation, as, for example, the case of Mr Heseltine following the Westland affair, and, more recently, the resignations of Mr Robin Cook and Ms Clare Short examined above. Public criticism accounted for only a few resignations, as did failures in office, such as when Hugh Dalton, the Chancellor of the Exchequer, resigned in 1947 after inadvertently revealing details of the budget to a journalist before informing the House of Commons. Ministers do not have to resign, however, simply because their policies either do not work or fail to reach the statute book. Thus, in early 1994, Mr Michael Howard, the Home Secretary, did not resign following a series of defeats in the House of Lords on the Police and Magistrates' Courts Bill, many of these defeats leading to substantial departures from what had been the policy of the government. Similarly at the end of 1994 Mr Heseltine, then President of the Board of Trade, did not resign after there was considerable backbench resistance by Conservative MPs in the House of Commons to his proposals to privatise the Post Office and he was forced to withdraw them.

However, incautious remarks by a minister can lead to his/her being in an impossible position and having to resign, such as Mrs Currie's remarks about salmonella in British eggs in 1989, and Mr Ridley's intemperate comments on German influence in the EC in 1990. Likewise apparent incompetence in handling a delicate issue can lead to such serious backbench criticism of a minister that there may be calls from leaders of backbench opinion among the government's political supporters for the minister to 'fall on his sword' to save further embarrassment for the government and, in particular, the Prime Minister. This was the fate of the then Mr Leon Brittan following the disclosure of the Solicitor-General's letter to Mr Heseltine during the Westland Crisis by Colette Bowe who was, of course, one of Mr Brittan's officials.

Under Mr Blair, who, of course, during his early years in office enjoyed a much larger parliamentary majority than his immediate predecessor, there were fewer resignations. In July 1998 Mr Frank Field resigned ministerial office apparently after failing to obtain the post of Secretary of State for Social Security. On 27 October 1998 Mr Ron Davies, the Secretary of State for Wales, resigned after 'a serious lapse of judgement' had led to his being robbed of his wallet, mobile telephone and car by a group of strangers, one of whom he had met on Clapham Common while walking there alone. Mr Davies accepted that the incident would cause embarrassment to the government. On 23 December 1998 both Mr Peter Mandelson, Secretary of State for Trade and Industry, and Mr Geoffrey Robinson, the Paymaster-General, both resigned. The ostensible reason was a possible allegation of 'sleaze' in that Mr Robinson had loaned Mr Mandelson a very considerable sum of money to purchase a dwelling. Mr Robinson had been under previous investigation into his business dealings, and these had concerned Mr Mandelson's department. There was also a question as to whether Mr Mandelson had broken the rules of the House of Commons by failing to declare the loan in the Register of Members' Interests (see chapter 5). In this instance there were also press allegations that Mr Mandelson had been 'undermined' by leaks from ministerial opponents. Nevertheless Mr Mandelson accepted that what had happened had become an embarrassment to the government. However, these events did not prevent Mr Mandelson returning to the Cabinet as Secretary of State for Northern Ireland on 11 October 1999. Mr Mandelson left office once more in January 2001 following allegations he had misled the House of Commons about his involvement in a passport application by a person who had helped to sponsor the Millennium Dome, a project for which he had had ministerial responsibility. It appears the Prime Minister had little option but to point his colleague in the direction of resignation, as Mr Mandelson's statements on the matter had also misled the Prime Minister's own press officer—clearly a situation of great embarrassment.

More recent ministerial resignations under Mr Blair have included those of: Stephen Byers who resigned in May 2002 following allegations of deception of Parliament, particularly in connection with the departure from their posts of two of his press advisers; Estelle Morris in October 2002, and Beverley Hughes in April 2004, the latter following a series of sustained allegations about failures of immigration policy. Estelle Morris cited as her reason for resignation her feeling that she was not effective in her job as Secretary of State for Education, and while a minister is not personally responsible for every failure of administration within his/her department, Estelle Morris had identified herself with certain policies which were not being effectively implemented. In the cases of Mr Byers and Ms Hughes it became clear that their continued presence in power was an embarrassment to the government, and, in particular, the Prime Minister. Even so the influence of political events in each of these instances points to the continuing lack of clarity about the convention of individual ministerial responsibility and mark it as one that is 'weak' and uncertain in its operation.

In this context 'official utterances' such as the 1954 statement by Sir David Maxwell Fyfe following the 'Crichel Down' affair are only partially helpful.

This scandal arose following the requisitioning of three farms during the Second World War. After the war the Ministry of Agriculture wished to keep the land as one unit and declined to sell one farm back to its original owners. Public disquiet over what was seen as bureaucratic intransigence ultimately led to the resignation of the minister concerned.

'There has been considerable anxiety . . . as to how far the principle of Ministerial responsibility goes. We all recognise that we must have that principle in existence and that Ministers must be responsible for the acts of civil servants. Without it, it would be impossible to have a Civil Service which would be able to serve Ministries and Governments of different political faiths and persuasions with the same zeal and honesty which we have always found . . .

There has been criticism that the principle operates so as to oblige Ministers to extend total protection to their officials and to endorse their acts, and to cause the position that civil servants cannot be called to account and are effectively responsible to no one. That is a position which I believe is quite wrong, and I think it is the cardinal error that has crept into the appreciation of this situation. It is quite untrue that well-justified public criticism of the actions of civil servants cannot be made on a suitable occasion. The position of the civil servant is that he is wholly and directly responsible to his Minister. It is worth stating again that he holds his office "at pleasure" and can be dismissed at any time by the Minister, and that power is none the less real because it is seldom used. The only exception relates to a number of senior posts, like permanent secretary, deputy secretary, and principal financial officer, where, since 1920, it has been necessary for the Minister to consult the Prime Minister, as he does on appointment.

I would like to put the different categories where different considerations apply . . . [In] the case where there is an explicit order by a Minister, the Minister must protect the civil servant who had carried out his order. Equally, where the civil servant acts properly in accordance with the policy laid down by the Minister, the Minister must protect and defend him.

I come to the third category, which is different . . . Where an official makes a mistake or causes some delay, but not on an important issue of policy and not where a claim to individual rights is seriously involved, the Minister acknowledges the mistake and he accepts the responsibility, although he is not personally involved. He states that he will take corrective action in the Department . . . [He] would not, in those circumstances, expose the official to public criticism . . .

But when one comes to the fourth category, where action has been taken by a civil servant of which the Minister disapproves and has no prior knowledge, and the conduct of the official is reprehensible, then there is no obligation on the part of the Minister to endorse what he believes to be wrong, or to defend what are clearly shown to be errors of his officers. The Minister is not bound to defend action of which he did not know, or of which he disapproves. But, of course, he remains constitutionally responsible to Parliament for the fact that something has gone wrong, and he alone can tell Parliament what has occurred and render an account of his stewardship.

The fact that a Minister has to do that does not affect his power to control and discipline his staff. One could sum it up by saying that it is part of a Minister's responsibility to Parliament to take necessary action to ensure efficiency and the proper discharge of the duties of his Department. On that, only the Minister can decide what is right and just to do, and he alone can hear all sides, including the defence.'[27]

What do these various events therefore tell us about the conventional rules relating to ministerial resignation?

(1) The press can be very influential in undermining a minister's position. Indeed the power of the press to harry a minister who has made political blunders is very great—great enough in some cases to make it impossible for him/her to carry on functioning efficiently as a minister and thus ensuring either dismissal or resignation.

(2) The Prime Minister's support for a minister can be a most powerful force to keep that minister in office.

(3) Even Prime Ministerial support and friendship, however, are of little avail where there is a strong tide of backbench, press or public opinion (or possibly 'undermining' by colleagues) to the effect that a minister has become an embarrassment to the government.

(4) A sexual or financial scandal *alone* is not inevitably going to lead to resignation, but such a scandal can leave a minister vulnerable to other attacks.

Ministers may feel it incumbent on them to resign following major misjudgements or mal-administration within their departments, as witness Lord Carrington, Mr Atkins and Mr Luce in 1982 following the misjudgement of Argentinian intentions towards the Falklands Islands. However, with regard to acts or omissions of individual civil servants it is impossible to argue that a minister is completely responsible, in the sense of culpability, for everything done by *every* official within his department. As Brazier puts it, and this illustrates the continuum notion well, 'the further the minister was, geographically or hierarchically, from the people or events complained of, the less he will generally be expected to take the blame for mistakes and resign'.[28] Once again, much will depend on the politics and circumstances of any given issue, as was recognised by S E Finer: 'If the minister is yielding, his Prime Minister unbending, and his party out for blood—no matter how serious or trivial the reason—the Minister will find himself without Parliamentary support.'[29]

VII. Ministers and Civil Servants

Moving further into the day-to-day discharge of ministerial responsibilities we continue to find much depending upon practice and procedure. True, in many cases, statute declares 'the minister' or 'the Secretary of State' shall make a particular decision. Yet as Peter Hennessy points out: 'For the Civil Service the buck-stopping question is of crucial importance. Under the doctrine of ministerial responsibility, ministers are the ultimate can-carriers for

---

[27] 530 HC Official Report (5th Series) cols 1285–1287. [28] Brazier, op cit p. 154.
[29] 'The Individual Responsibility of Ministers' (1956) 34 Public Administration 377 at 394.

everything done by the civil service in their name.'[30] Thus a minister heads his/her department, is technically responsible for all decisions taken and must be prepared to answer for them to the House of Commons. In practice it is impossible for a minister to know of all the decisions taken in his/her name. Routine decisions of comparatively minor civil servants cannot be known to the minister, and even some greater decisions taken by senior civil servants can hardly be known in detail. The need for, and the legitimacy of, delegation of powers to civil servants has been judicially recognised. However, that was on the basis that civil servants were anonymous instruments of ministers who would be fully answerable to Parliament.[31] The size of the Civil Service and the number and complexity of the issues it has to decide weaken ministerial control over permanent officials. Even where a decision is of such importance that it has to be made by a minister, he/she will have to listen most carefully to the advice of his/her permanent staff before making it. The reasons for this are not hard to understand. Rapid rates of change in ministerial appointments, even within the lifetime of a ministry, mean that individuals may frequently change jobs or achieve new office, while civil servants are permanent officials able to take a long-term view of individual issues. In addition ministerial time is limited and subject to the demands of the department, Parliament, the Cabinet, colleagues, the party, the media, and a constituency, while ministerial knowledge in general and particular terms may also be limited. Ministers are thus forced to depend to a degree at least upon senior officials. Those officials traditionally have tended to be conservative with a small 'c', fond of continuity and consensus in policy and administration, averse to rapid reversals of policy, and imbued with considerable knowledge of, and experience in, their areas of responsibility. This might lead to a particular 'line' of departmental advice being given which ministers could find uncongenial. Furthermore, once a policy is implemented, resources committed to it, contracts made under it and public expectations raised by it, it is very difficult to alter course. An incoming ministry may find it virtually impossible to depart radically, for some years at least, from the policies of their predecessors, even though they have denounced them in Parliament and campaigned against them in an election.

Since 1990, however, there have been major changes in the organisation of the Civil Service and its relationships with ministers. Under Mrs Thatcher the idea of 'Next Steps' agencies was floated, and between February 1988 and October 1990 some 80,000 civil servants were transferred to such agencies, and there were 96 agencies by 1994. By May 1999 three quarters of civil servants worked in such agencies. Even so, the agencies are a management innovation, not a constitutional one. They are now responsible for services as diverse as Customs and Excise, Inland Revenue, Highways and Social Security Benefits. The basic idea for such an agency is to reduce the number of decision-making tiers between central policy advisers and those who actually carry out the work of the service, in the interests of improving public service, and enhancing efficiency and economy. Thus where a function of government is *effectively* discharged by people who are well removed from the centre, that function may be removed from other departmental responsibilities and will become a 'Next Steps' or, more correctly, an 'Executive Agency' headed by a chief executive, who may be appointed from outside the Civil Service and who will administer the agency according to objectives set by ministers. The line of accountability with regard to such executive agencies is clearly more attenuated than was previously the case, and within the Civil Service it has become the practice to modify the traditional formulae of ministerial responsibility by talking about 'ultimate accountability' which lies to Parliament via ministers.

30 *Whitehall* (Secker & Warburg, London, 1989), p. 502.
31 *Carltona v Commissioners of Works* [1943] 2 All ER 560.

However, problems of accountability and ministerial responsibility were nevertheless highlighted by events in 1994 and 1995 concerning the prison service. In late 1994 a report into lax discipline at Whitemoor Prison raised public fears that prisoners were living a 'pampered' existence with officers apparently being sent on extensive shopping trips for inmates. The lax discipline had also led to escapes from the prison by armed IRA members imprisoned there. It also appeared that the Home Secretary, Mr Michael Howard, had been warned two months before that escape about lax security at Whitemoor. Though there was early parliamentary criticism of Mr Howard, there was also speculation about the future of Mr Derek Lewis, the Director General of the Prison Service. The Prison Service became an executive agency in March 1994, and under ministerial objectives day-to-day operational decisions were entrusted to the Director General and a board of 10 directors. It was laid down that the Home Secretary was 'accountable to Parliament for the prison service' but was not to be 'involved' in day-to-day management, though he would be 'consulted . . . on the handling of operational matters which could give rise to grave public or parliamentary concern'. The Home Secretary was also informed about any incident or issue likely to arouse parliamentary or public concern. Under this system there would be fortnightly contact between the Home Secretary and the Director General who has day-to-day managerial responsibilities and the ability to *recommend* policy changes. That distinction between operational issues (the responsibility of the Director General), and policy matters (the responsibility of the Home Secretary) which is by no means clearly or sharply definable was to give rise to further problems.

The escape of three 'extremely dangerous' inmates from Parkhurst Prison and riots at Everthorpe Prison in January 1995 once again brought into question the issue of who should bear responsibility. By October 1995 it was alleged that Mr Howard had intervened in managerial affairs in the Prison Service by seeking the suspension of the Governor of Parkhurst Prison following the escape of inmates. By way of counter allegation the Home Office stated the decision to suspend the Governor had been taken by the Director General, and that the Home Secretary had not intervened. Mr Lewis was then dismissed by the Home Secretary, for which he was subsequently paid £200,000 by way of compensation, and the matter became one of acute political controversy, which, however, Mr Howard survived. There can be little doubt that Mr Howard's considerable political astuteness was responsible for his survival in office. Furthermore, previous prison incidents did *not* lead to the resignation of the incumbent Home Secretaries, eg in 1966 when, the then, Roy Jenkins did not resign over the escape of the spy George Blake, or in 1983 when Lord Prior did not resign over the escape of 38 prisoners from the Maze Prison, or in 1991–1992 when Kenneth Baker did not resign over the escape of prisoners from Brixton Prison.

Nevertheless, there is a degree of consensus that the emergence of the executive agencies has weakened ministerial responsibility. It is clear that the distinction between 'policy' and 'operations' though neat is unconvincing, and the two matters cannot always be separated, particularly where an operational failure leads to public outcry. Indeed the then Chief Inspector of Prisons, Judge Stephen Tumin, was reported as saying the distinction was 'bogus' in that 'Nothing is created by policy. What has created trouble is created by operational failure. That means the Home Secretary takes credit but is free of responsibility.'[32] In effect this can amount to ministerial *irresponsibility*. Procedural rules which have a flexible content on accountability enable ministers to be the judges of when they have broken those rules. This will be returned to further below.

---

[32] *The Independent*, 18 October 1995.

All this may appear to be a very far cry from the Crichel Down Affair considered earlier where Sir Thomas Dugdale, the Minister of Agriculture, resigned over a bungled land transaction by his officials. This is often cited as a vindication of the principle of ministerial responsibility where a minister sacrificed his job (and in Sir Thomas's case his entire political future) because of actions by junior civil servants of which he did not even know. Indeed Sir Winston Churchill as Prime Minister in accepting Dugdale's resignation saluted his sense of honour and called the resignation 'chivalrous in a high degree'. However, as has subsequently become clear, Dugdale resigned not because of the blunder but because of backbench criticism of his conduct. There is no absolute rule that ministers should resign because something within their portfolio has gone awry: what is, apparently, more important is that they should be able to retain the confidence of their own backbenchers.

(a) The anonymity of civil servants

An understanding correlative to that of ministerial responsibility was that individual civil servants should not be named, and that they should not therefore have to bear in public the responsibility, and odium, of any failures of policy, nor are they to be identified with any particular procedure or policy. A further corollary is that the Civil Service is politically neutral. However, the principle of anonymity has been eroded over the last 20 years or so. Problems within the Child Support Agency (CSA) in the early 1990s showed how far former understanding of the role of an anonymous public service had altered.

The CSA is an executive agency charged with administering a statutory policy whereby absent fathers are required to pay towards the support of their children. From its inception the CSA was the subject of controversy, not only over the policy issue, but also over its mode of operation. Demands for maintenance were made to deceased persons, to men who had never met the mothers of their alleged children, and for sums of money which actually exceeded their recipients' gross income. The style of operation of the CSA was considered by many to be punitive: it alienated many men, and there were claims that its activities had resulted in a number of suicides. On top of this the CSA did not work. Its first annual report of July 1994 indicated that of the £530m it was set to save by recouping, from absent fathers, state benefits paid to mothers, it had actually only recovered £418m. Much of the opprobrium which was directed against the CSA was in particular concentrated on its director, Ros Hebblethwaite. The combination of public dislike, plus the failure of the CSA to meet targets, forced Mrs Hebblethwaite to resign on 2 September 1994.

The accountability of public officials was also raised by the resignation of Mr Chris Woodhead on 3 November 2000. Mr Woodhead was Chief Inspector of Schools at OFSTED, the government agency charged with the oversight and improvement of educational standards. He became no stranger to controversy during his period of office and often took a line arguably independent of, and certainly somewhat at variance with, central government policy, though for most of his period in office ministers supported him in public. Disagreements seem to have led to his resignation following his criticism of proposals to expand Higher Education and to modify the law relating to consideration of homosexuality by schools. He was also greatly critical of A level standards only shortly after ministers had introduced new syllabuses. Matters came to a head in early November 2000 when Mr Woodhead was engaged in heated exchanges with the Commission for Racial Equality and a number of MPs. He offered his resignation on being offered a post as a newspaper columnist and leader writer. Mr Woodhead's controversial period of office raises questions such as:

- whether the traditional convention of anonymity for public servants means very much any more when particular functions of government are entrusted to executive agencies whose heads become media personalities in their own right;
- how far such a public servant is entitled to go in developing and then pursuing the agenda of his/her office;
- who is in day to day control of the formulation and implementation of policy—elected, and in theory, accountable, ministers, or appointed and unaccountable public officials?

The anonymity issue was further tragically highlighted by the death of Dr David Kelly in 2003. Dr Kelly was a civil servant who worked for the Ministry of Defence (MoD) with expertise in biological warfare, though he also acted as a media liaison officer, but not as an 'official spokesman'. In the events leading to the invasion of Iraq in 2003 the government commissioned via its Joint Intelligence Committee a dossier on 'Weapons of Mass Destruction' (WMD) allegedly possessed by the Iraqi regime. Dr Kelly had access to this dossier and was concerned over some of the claims made in connection with Iraq's WMD capacity. Dr Kelly subsequently met with a BBC journalist on the basis of an 'unattributable' conversation, a problem of British government to which allusion has already been made. In due course allegations were made that Mr Alistair Campbell, the Prime Minister's Director of Communications, had included information in the dossier on WMD to bolster the case for the invasion. This led to a political furore between the government and the BBC with the former seeking to discover the identity of the BBC's source of information.

Dr Kelly informed his superiors at the MoD that he *might* have been the BBC's source, and in due course other journalists guessed at Dr Kelly's involvement in the matter and that, somewhat unusually, was confirmed, though Dr Kelly was not told at the time that his name had become known to the press. Dr Kelly was subsequently interviewed by the House of Commons Foreign Affairs Sub-Committee and the Intelligence and Security Committee. One meeting was held in public, further exposing Dr Kelly as the possible source of the BBC's information. Dr Kelly was found dead in July 2003 and his death was officially confirmed as being due to suicide. The matter was subsequently investigated by Lord Hutton's *Report of the Inquiry into the Circumstances Surrounding the Death of David Kelly CMG*[33] and Lord Butler's *Review of Intelligence on Weapons of Mass Destruction. Report of a Committee of Privy Counsellors.*[34] These we shall return to below in the context of considering how government policy is formulated. For the moment we should note that two matters are highlighted by this tragic sequence of events. The anonymity of civil servants can no longer be taken for granted: their involvement in policy issues may be discovered by the media or disclosed by their employers. Secondly the affair was a distressing illustration of the capacity of our governmental system to leak, and for those within it to go to the media if they are unhappy with policy developments. This may, however, be an inescapable feature of a system within which the government controls the 'levers' of information and uses them to its own advantage while the democratically elected representatives of the people in Parliament have less ability to discover what is happening until after the event. This is a matter to which we shall return in chapter 6.

[33] HC 247 (HMSO, London, 2004).   [34] HC 898 (HMSO, London, 2004).

However, despite these high profile and unfortunate incidents attempts have been made over a number of years to set proper limits to the functioning of the civil service and the use ministers can make of it. A Civil Service Code was implemented over ten years ago, and was further revised in 1999. A new Code was promulgated on 6 June 2006. The new Code is the result of work between the government and the Civil Service Commissioners, and a detailed consultation that elicited over 2000 responses from civil servants across a broad range of grades, departments, disciplines and regions.

Particular revisions of note to the Code include:

• For the first time the Code provides for the independent Civil Service Commissioners to consider a complaint direct from a civil servant.

• The Code forms part of the terms and conditions for civil servants. For the first time, the Code makes clear that it forms part of the contractual relationship between a civil servant and their employer.

Speaking at the launch Sir Gus O'Donnell, the Head of the Civil Service stated:

'Our traditional values of integrity, objectivity, impartiality and honesty are our bedrock. They are just as important today as when they were first developed and are essential to everything we do, whether its policy, delivery or corporate services. They need to be expressed clearly in a way which is relevant to all our staff.

We need to ensure we live up to these values. And I want all civil servants to reflect some additional qualities in everything we do. These bring the dynamism needed to deliver 21st century public services. So as well as these traditional values, we need pace, pride, passion and professionalism.'

The terms of the Code are as follows:

'Civil Service values

1. The Civil Service is an integral and key part of the government of the United Kingdom. It supports the Government of the day in developing and implementing its policies, and in delivering public services. Civil servants are accountable to Parliament.

2. As a civil servant, you are appointed on merit and on the basis of fair and open competition and are expected to carry out your role with dedication and a commitment to the Civil Service and its core values: integrity, honesty, objectivity and impartiality. In this Code:

• 'integrity' is putting the obligations of public service above your own personal interests;

• 'honesty' is being truthful and open;

• 'objectivity' is basing your advice and decisions on rigorous analysis of the evidence; and

• 'impartiality' is acting solely according to the merits of the case and serving equally well Governments of different political persuasions.

3. These core values support good government and ensure the achievement of the highest possible standards in all that the Civil Service does. This in turn helps the Civil Service to gain and retain the respect of Ministers, Parliament, the public and its customers.

4. This Code sets out the standards of behaviour expected of you and all other civil servants. These are based on the core values. Individual departments may also have their own separate mission and values statements based on the core values, including the standards of behaviour expected of you when you deal with your colleagues.

Standards of behaviour

Integrity

5. You must:

- fulfil your duties and obligations responsibly;

- always act in a way that is professional and that deserves and retains the confidence of all those with whom you have dealings;

- make sure public money and other resources are used properly and efficiently;

- deal with the public and their affairs fairly, efficiently, promptly, effectively and sensitively, to the best of your ability;

- handle information as openly as possible within the legal framework; and

- comply with the law and uphold the administration of justice.

6. You must not:

- misuse your official position, for example by using information acquired in the course of your official duties to further your private interests or those of others;

- accept gifts or hospitality or receive other benefits from anyone which might reasonably be seen to compromise your personal judgement or integrity; or

- disclose official information without authority. This duty continues to apply after you leave the Civil Service.

Honesty

7. You must:

- set out the facts and relevant issues truthfully, and correct any errors as soon as possible; and

- use resources only for the authorised public purposes for which they are provided.

8. You must not:

- deceive or knowingly mislead Ministers, Parliament or others; or

- be influenced by improper pressures from others or the prospects of personal gain.

Objectivity

9. You must:

- provide information and advice, including advice to Ministers, on the basis of the evidence, and accurately present the options and facts;

- take decisions on the merits of the case; and

- take due account of expert and professional advice.

10. You must not:

- ignore inconvenient facts or relevant considerations when providing advice or making decisions; or

- frustrate the implementation of policies once decisions are taken by declining to take, or abstaining from, action which flows from those decisions.

Impartiality

11. You must:

- carry out your responsibilities in a way that is fair, just and equitable and reflects the Civil Service commitment to equality and diversity.

12. You must not:

• act in a way that unjustifiably favours or discriminates against particular individuals or interests.

Political impartiality

13. You must:

• serve the Government, whatever its political persuasion, to the best of your ability in a way which maintains political impartiality and is in line with the requirements of this Code, no matter what your own political beliefs are;

• act in a way which deserves and retains the confidence of Ministers, while at the same time ensuring that you will be able to establish the same relationship with those whom you may be required to serve in some future Government; and

• comply with any restrictions that have been laid down on your political activities.

14. You must not:

• act in a way that is determined by party political considerations, or use official resources for party political purposes; or

• allow your personal political views to determine any advice you give or your actions.

Rights and responsibilities

15. Your department or agency has a duty to make you aware of this Code and its values. If you believe that you are being required to act in a way which conflicts with this Code, your department or agency must consider your concern, and make sure that you are not penalised for raising it.

16. If you have a concern, you should start by talking to your line manager or someone else in your line management chain. If for any reason you would find this difficult, you should raise the matter with your department's nominated officers who have been appointed to advise staff on the Code.

17. If you become aware of actions by others which you believe conflict with this Code you should report this to your line manager or someone else in your line management chain; alternatively you may wish to seek advice from your nominated officer. You should report evidence of criminal or unlawful activity to the police or other appropriate authorities.

18. If you have raised a matter covered in paragraphs 15 to 17, in accordance with the relevant procedures, and do not receive what you consider to be a reasonable response, you may report the matter to the Civil Service Commissioners. The Commissioners will also consider taking a complaint direct. Their address is:

3rd Floor, 35 Great Smith Street, London SW1P 3BQ.
Tel: 020 7276 2613
email: *ocsc@civilservicecommissioners.gov.uk*

If the matter cannot be resolved using the procedures set out above, and you feel you cannot carry out the instructions you have been given, you will have to resign from the Civil Service.

19. This Code is part of the contractual relationship between you and your employer. It sets out the high standards of behaviour expected of you which follow from your position in public and national life as a civil servant. You can take pride in living up to these values.'

It will be noted that the Code has legal force by virtue of being part of a civil servant's contract of employment. It may, however, be asked whether a statutory provision binding not just civil servants but also ministers, the media, pressure groups, etc might not at some point be desirable. There can be no doubt that despite the changes and stresses that the Civil Service had undergone in the last quarter century, in particular the erosion of the principle of anonymity and the introduction into its ranks of temporary senior staff brought in from industry, commerce and the media as ministerial aides and advisers which have led to a limited degree of politicisation of the Civil Service, the core values of political neutrality, admission to the service by open competition, promotion by merit and the general accountability of ministers to Parliament remain basically intact.[35] What should not be forgotten, however, is that while the 'core' permanent Civil Service retains its values, the advice given by senior civil servants may be weakened by contrary advice given by those brought into government by ministers and who may well have been appointed on a political basis. Such advisers may well have an interest in telling ministers what they want to hear, not what they ought to.[36]

It is therefore further appropriate that we should remind ourselves of how far the organisational and structural changes have gone in altering the Civil Service, even if we acknowledge the continuing force of its institutional values.

Over the last 25 years the Civil Service has undergone radical changes—not least because of the introduction of Next Steps Agencies referred to above. It also shrank in size from 750,000 in the 1970s to 460,000 in 1999, however, total public sector employment increased by 530,000 between 1997 and 2004, while in 2003 central government employment increased by 14,800. At the same time much more emphasis began to be placed on civil servants being more effective *managers* of policy implementation, and moves were also made to introduce resource accounting and budgeting which make individual civil servants more obviously responsible for the ways in which resources are deployed by them to bring about given objectives of policy.

After the 1997 Election the Civil Service had to work with a government committed to modernisation, on the delivery of specific outcomes untrammelled by older views of individual departmental responsibilities—Mr Blair's famous commitment to 'joined-up government'. Thus on 30 March 1999 the government issued 'Modernising Government' Cm 4310, which emphasised better policy making, better responsiveness to public needs and more effective public services. As part of this barriers to the delivery of effective and convenient services based simply on the way in which government is organised were identified as a major target for reform. This demanded a considerable amount of rethinking and further managerial reorganisation within the Civil Service—eg the delivery of public services 24 hours a day, seven days a week and the creation of 'one stop shops' for service where demand justifies this. All of that, however, is once again a matter of management as opposed to constitutional change. Similarly so was the acceptance that the Civil Service must become more diverse in its structures and recruiting policies.

It is at this point that questions have arisen as to whether the changes to the Civil Service are moving from the purely managerial to having a constitutional significance. Proposals to induce more recruits from the private sector to join the Civil Service—so that by 2005 some 65 per cent of civil servants should have had experience in the private or voluntary sectors—coupled with others for enhanced pay bonuses for 'high performers', and rewards for those prepared to move between departments and/or who gain outside experience, led to fears of politicisation on the part of Civil Service unions who considered ministers could utilise the system to ensure that their supporters obtain key jobs in departments. Certainly the secondment of private sector managers into the Civil Service has led to some radical questions about the current shape of departments and whether some of them are needed at all in their present

---

[35] See further Bogdanor, V, 'The Civil Service' in *The British Constitution in the 20th Century*, Bogdanor, V, (ed) (OUP, Oxford, 2004), chapter 7.

[36] 'How not to run a country' Lord Butler of Brockwell interviewed by Boris Johnson (2004) *The Spectator*, 11 December, p. 12.

form. On the other hand it is arguable that the proposals merely reflect a recognition by the Civil Service that, as with the wider world of commerce and industry, it needs better quality leadership, improved business planning, better incentives to reward better performance, greater sexual and ethnic diversity, and proper management training skills. In other words it must be part of the world we all inhabit.

VIII. The Formulation of Policy

The formulation of policy, its translation, where necessary, into law, and subsequent implementation by administrative bodies and measures also reflect the lack of formal structured rules already encountered above. In 'Checks and Balances in Public Policy Making',[37] Sir Douglass Wass (former Permanent Secretary to the Treasury and Joint Head of the Home Civil Service) pointed out that policy making, ie the act of reviewing policies to see whether they are achieving their desired objectives, together with examining alternative policy strategies and taking decisions on existing policies, 'is largely a closed business in our society'. Wass pointed out:

'Whatever the impetus may be . . . the process of policy review, analysis and decision usually takes place within the government machine and without the systematic participation of outsiders. The last stage—that of decision—must always be that of the government, subject of course to its being able to carry parliament with it; and the process of taking that decision—the business of taking the essentially political choice from the available options—has to take place within the privacy of government committee rooms. But the first two stages are by no means so obviously the sole prerogative of government. And yet in our system they do not often involve anyone else.'[38]

Of course governments do expose their policy formulation to public consultation on occasions, but there is no *legal* requirement that they should do so. Wass pointed out that policy review has, historically, been unsystematic; appraisal has not been regular. Nor has it conformed to any ideal of participatory democracy; the public have no real opportunity to pass judgement on proposals.

'What the public has not enjoyed has been access to the detailed work, the detailed information, the thorough analysis . . . which has come before ministers . . . No doubt not all of this material has been supportive of the policy line that ministers have selected, and this above may be cause enough for not exposing it to critical inspection. But the fact that policy may not be as perfect as ministerial statements would imply is itself an argument that the public, which has to live with the policy, should be aware of its limitations. Nor is the public made aware of all the options which may have been displayed to ministers before the final decisions have been made . . . '.[39]

The issue of secrecy surrounding the formulation of policy was raised by the Scott Inquiry into the 'Arms to Iraq' affair (see above chapter 3). Briefly, it will be remembered that certain businessmen had been prosecuted for illegally selling to Iraq material capable of being used in weapons manufacturing. Their defence was that they were only acting in accordance with government policy. That the government appeared to have one policy on arms sales to Iraq

---

[37] [1987] PL 181. [38] [1987] PL 181 at 182. [39] [1987] PL 181 at 186–187.

while it was secretly operating a very different one caused a political uproar which led to the appointment of a Committee of Inquiry, led by, the then, Scott LJ. Some years later, and after the Scott Inquiry's voluminous but not particularly illuminating findings, the sad tale of who was responsible for what during the period in question remains unclear. No minister resigned as a result of the inquiry and the sheer size, expense, and complexity of the Report prevented it from having a great public impact.

The *basic* findings of the inquiry were that in December 1988 Mr William Waldegrave, then a minister at the Foreign Office, assisted by Mr Alan Clark and Lord Trefgarne, who also held middle rank ministerial posts, relaxed the guidelines under which the supply of defence-related equipment to Iraq was regulated. Mr Waldegrave claimed in his defence there had been no actual change in the guidelines which were flexible to begin with. This led the Report to condemn 'the duplicitous nature of the flexibility claimed for the guidelines'. What is, how-ever, more certain is that such changes as did occur were kept secret and MPs, indeed Parliament as a whole, were misled by being told there had been no change of policy. At one point during the running of the inquiry Mr Waldegrave appeared to indicate that ministers do not have to tell 'the truth, the whole truth and nothing but the truth'. This was when he said to a Commons select committee on 8 March 1994 that 'in exceptional cases it is necessary to say something that is untrue in the House of Commons . . . Much of government activity is much more like playing poker than playing chess. You don't put all your cards up at one time.' He then went on to add that such situations would be 'exceptional', though there would be other situations where a minister while taking care not to mislead the Commons would not 'display everything he knows about [the] subject . . .'. Subsequently Mr Waldegrave attempted to extricate himself from the criticism engendered by his remarks by saying that the basic rule is always that ministers must not mislead Parliament, and that the only exception to this is where the Chancellor of the Exchequer has to give an inaccurate statement in order to protect sterling pending a devaluation decision.

An argument to reconcile the issue was put forward to the Scott Inquiry in February 1994 by Sir Robin Butler, the Cabinet Secretary—the guardian of the constitution in many eyes—which was that it is possible for a minister to give 'an accurate but incomplete answer'. Sir Robin defended this later by arguing that an incomplete statement is not the same as a misleading one, and that there is a duty to avoid misleading statements wherever possible. However, he added: 'In the real world it is frequently the case that one cannot say all one knows.' But, as the Scott Report made clear, the problem of such a 'half the picture' approach is that those who receive the statement may be unaware that other material is, for good reason perhaps, being withheld, and they are therefore almost certain to be misled in effect, if not consciously. Scott's conclusion was that though it may be impossible to give every fact to Parliament there should be a fair summation of the 'full picture' given in response to requests about policy. To this general principle Scott indicated there could be, however, exceptions, such as matters relating to security and the intelligence services, and imminent changes in interest or exchange rates. But such exceptions can only be made where there are cogent reasons for so acting, and the general principle has to remain that ministerial accountability requires that where a minister speaks in Parliament, or to a select committee, or answers a parliamentary question, he/she is under an obligation to give full information, for without that the legislature cannot hold the executive fully to public account. This has been accepted and reinforced by the Code of Conduct for Ministers, see above, in a clear and determined attempt to root out, and make unacceptable, any continuing culture of secrecy within government. It is certainly unacceptable for a partial answer to be given for reasons of conve-nience or to avoid political embarrassment. Denial of information to the public also takes away their ability to come to an informed decision on the record in office of ministers.

IX. Accountability and Responsibility

The Scott Inquiry also examined a claim made by Sir Robin Butler (now Lord Butler of Brockwell, to whom allusion has been made above) that a distinction has to be made between 'ministerial accountability' and 'ministerial responsibility'. The former is the general constitutional burden which is an inescapable fact of ministerial life. Ministerial accountability covers that sphere of 'operational' departmental business for which a minister *must* answer to Parliament but which does not involve the acceptance of personal blame by a minister if some error or failure occurs within his/her department. The justification for this 'line of argument' is that modern government is now such a complex business that ministers must delegate some responsibilities to their officials and so should not be held to blame if something goes wrong. Ministerial responsibility arises where a minister has personal involvement in what has gone wrong. On the Butler formulation, however, surely a minister could be 'responsible' if he/she had become personally involved in an 'operational' issue. Sir Richard Scott, however, while pointing out that the Butler formulation does not enjoy universal support (and has important constitutional implications), also stated he found it hard to disagree with the process of thinking behind it. Even so Scott concluded that where a minister is ignorant of acts or omissions within his/her department, there is still an obligation to be honest with Parliament and people and there is an obligation to be forthcoming with information about the incident once it comes to light if there is to be a fair and informed judgement as to whether blame should lie. Scott further concluded that any re-examination by the government of its practices in answering parliamentary questions should take account of the claimed distinction between 'accountability' and 'responsibility'.

In an attempt to introduce some order into these issues in July 1996 the House of Commons Public Service Committe called for a resolution in the House of Commons laying down the obligations of ministers to be open and honest about their conduct and requiring resignation in cases where rules of conduct are broken. In addition all MPs, ministers and witnesses called before any Commons' committees would be required to assist the committee and not to obstruct or impede it. Civil servants and staff from executive agencies would be under a duty to give frank and clear answers to committee questions, rather than 'toeing the departmental line'. Ministers would be required: to provide full and accurate information to Parliament; to behave themselves with frankness and candour; not to mislead Parliament knowingly; and to correct inadvertent errors at the earliest opportunity. Furthermore, the report recommended that the Prime Minister should assume responsibility for ensuring ministers reach the standards required of them, though in reaching a judgement on an individual he would also have to take into account how far that minister retained the confidence of the House of Commons.

This report marked a major attempt to create a Parliamentary Code of Ministerial Responsibility and for the first time saw Parliament itself laying down what it expects of ministers by way of accountability. Most of the recommendations are reflected in the Code of Conduct for Ministers, and the Civil Service Code, see above.

The Public Service Committee report should also be seen in the light of other developments. Following allegations in 1994 that certain MPs had accepted money for asking questions in Parliament, a Committee on Standards in Public Life was created. This body conducted its first deliberations at the same time as the Scott Inquiry into 'Arms to Iraq'. There thus was a very considerable examination of how those who are elected to office should behave—and in the absence of a written constitution good behaviour as opposed to legal conduct is the best that can be hoped for in many situations. The Nolan Committee produced its first report in July 1995 and the government accepted its recommendations that ministers should observe the highest standards of constitutional and personal conduct.

The present government in its Response to the Sixth Report from the Committee on Standards in Public Life[40] agreed that there should be changes with regard to ministerial responsibility, for which see above. In addition while reiterating the basic duty of ministers to uphold the highest standards of conduct, the government's response added significantly: 'Ministers can only remain in office for so long as they retain the confidence of the Prime Minister. There is no gap in the lines of accountability.' This again reinforces the Prime Minister's position as the person to whom all other ministers are accountable. In accordance with the Committee's proposals the government appeared happy to accept that no new office for investigating allegations of ministerial misconduct should be established.

---

x. The Formulation of Legislative Proposals: Turning Policy into Law

Remembering that the initiation of legislative proposals is primarily a government function, the comments of Sir Douglass Wass considered earlier are particularly relevant to the legislative process. This begins for government proposals long before Bills are introduced to Parliament. Desire to have legislation on a particular issue may arise out of a commitment in an election manifesto, though there is *no* doctrine of the mandate in the British constitution requiring a government to honour its election promises. Equally it may arise from some problem or difficulty encountered as the years progress. Proposals may result from Royal Commissions, the Law Commission or a committee of inquiry; governments may decide to pass legislation to give effect to them. In each session, of the Bills introduced by the government, most will *not* be part of the government's political programme: some amend earlier statutes; some deal with specific problems encountered by central and local government, some consolidate earlier statutes. Though most Bills are not of first-rank political importance, they do take time, and a government can only expect to get a limited number of proposals enacted because of the constraints imposed by the parliamentary timetable. Ministers have to decide what measures need the most urgent action and which may be left, perhaps until after a further election which they, naturally, hope to win.

Bills begin their progress to 'legal life' in many ways. There are, however, a number of traditional phases through which proposals go: (1) identifying the issue involved, ie 'perception of circumstances which appear to necessitate a response the form of which may require the enactment of legislation'—during this phase the issue is placed on 'the political agenda'; (2) evaluation and investigation, which will involve the examination and evaluation of alternative strategies; (3) consultation. Historically this would take place within the department concerned, thereafter other relevant departments are involved, and also the Treasury. Such internal consultation is effectively mandatory if collective responsibility is to apply, and if government is to be coherent. This historic pattern has been somewhat upset since 1997 by Tony Blair's insistence on 'joined up government', to which are shall return below.

---

[40] Cm 4817, (HMSO, London, 2000).

Whether and how the public is involved is a matter for the discretion of government. Green Papers setting out proposals *may* be printed and published generally, and the views of the public sought. Thereafter, *or independently*, White Papers *may* be issued containing firm legislative proposals. More commonly private consultation may take place with those likely to be affected by legislative proposals, and consultation papers may be issued to identified groups or individuals. Sometimes, as in the case of the Housing Act 1988, consultation papers on detailed issues may be issued *after* the White Paper has set out the main proposals. The important point is that there is no set, formal general order requiring consultation or specifying its manner and form. Governments may choose not to consult those known to be likely to oppose particular proposals, but the common practice is now to consult those likely to be affected either because their economic interest will be affected by legislation, or because they form a particular pressure group. The consultation of the general public is rarer.

The usually cited reasons for consultation are: (1) it helps to ensure that legislation once finally made is workable; (2) it is something of an exercise in democratic government for it ensures that the views of consultees are taken into account and their expertise and knowledge can be relied on. However, the involvement of pressure groups can carry with it the risk that the views of other persons are ignored.

It is further important to note that, historically, the House of Commons has been almost totally excluded from 'the processes whereby legislative initiatives are decided upon and formulated'. And while individual MPs may put pressure on government through all party alliances on particular issues, or via debates, etc, *formally* they are effectively excluded from the stage of formulation of legislative proposals. We shall return to this issue in chapter 6.

(a) 'Joined-up government'

The Blair government came to power in 1997 committed to a programme of national renewal and reform—one aspect of which was to modernise government to make it work better for individuals and for companies. This involves a need for 'joined-up government', an idea with wide reaching implications—for example enabling citizens to inform all government departments with which they have dealings of a change of address by one single electronic transaction. However, the concept has implications for policy making also. It involves arguments that departmental boundaries are not sacrosanct, that 'pooled' cross departmental budgets can be created to ensure that policy issues are dealt with 'in toto' and not piecemeal, that policies themselves should not be seen in isolation, or simply as issues of political expedience. Effective solutions to problems must thus be found across departments—for example, to tackle the worst conditions on council housing estates, problems with rough sleepers and issues concerning teenage parenthood the matters must be treated together as issues of social exclusion rather than as isolated phenomena. This, of course, has led to greater prominence being given to the work of the specialist units alluded to above, and to the need to bring into the civil service people from outside.

The government has also welcomed the notion of the pre legislative scrutiny of draft Bills— which enhances both the role of Parliament with regard to the formulation of the law as well as enabling greater public involvement in the process. However, not all Bills are dealt with in this way, see further chapter 6. It has also been accepted that where issues cut across the boundaries between departments that it should be possible for ministers to be asked to answer questions from all relevant Departmental Select Committees in the House of Commons, not just that Committee normally shadowing the work of 'their' department.

XI. The Cabinet, Policy Formulation and the Conduct of Government: Some Pointers from the Blair Administration

Many of the changes considered above in relation to the position of the Cabinet, the collective and individual responsibility of ministers and the role and function of the Civil Service have their roots in a time long before Tony Blair came to power in 1997. However, there have been significant intensifications of those changes during Mr Blair's time as Prime Minister. Broadly these are:

- the increasing influence of politically appointed 'advisers' to government which may have the effect of reducing the influence of the traditional Civil Service leading to the pursuit of policies which suit individual ministers' political desires and agendas but which might otherwise be discouraged;

- a considerable emphasis on the presentation and 'selling' of policy to the electorate, as opposed to prior deliberation and rigorous analysis;

- the replacement of collective Cabinet decision taking by policy making centred on small groups who may not be representative of all shades of opinion within government;

- an intensification of an historic tendency within British government to respond to perceived problems—especially those 'pushed' by vociferous pressure groups—by an almost relentless resort to fresh legislation and new policy initiatives, rather than an inquiry into whether existing provisions are adequate to achieve goals—as witness the twelve legislative interventions made with regard to the criminal justice system between 1998 and 2005;[41]

- the promotion of the Prime Minister as 'national leader' with a 'finger in every policy pie', (something that has also happened to an extent with regard to domestic policy in respect of Mr Blair's likely acknowledged successor, Gordon Brown, the Chancellor of the Exchequer) with an inevitable demotion of the status of other Cabinet ministers.

These issues were highlighted by the two official reports into the death of Dr David Kelly to which earlier allusion has been made, ie the Hutton and Butler Reports. The findings of those reports are extensively reviewed in: *Hutton and Butler: Lifting the Lid on the Workings of Power*.[42] While this work concentrates on particular policy issues and practices relating to the decision to invade Iraq, and most especially the gathering and evaluation of the intelligence reports used to justify that invasion by the Prime Minister, it nevertheless casts light on the general style of government under Mr Blair. Thus we are told that during the period while an invasion was under discussion there was a considerable reliance on unscripted oral presentations and arguments and a failure to consider papers presented by permanent officials in either the full Cabinet or in relevant Cabinet committees, and likewise a reliance on informal

---

[41] The Crime and Disorder Act 1998, the Access to Justice Act 1999, the Youth Justice and Criminal Evidence Act 1999, the Criminal Justice and Courts Services Act 2000, the Powers of Criminal Courts (Sentencing) Act 2000, the Proceeds of Crime Act 2002, the Courts Act 2003, the Criminal Justice Act 2003, the Sexual Offences Act 2003, the Domestic Violence, Crime and Victims Act 2004, the Serious Organised Crime and Police Act 2005, the Constitutional Reform Act 2005.   [42] Runciman, WG (ed) (OUP, Oxford, 2004).

gatherings of indeterminate status. Particular criticisms were voiced in the Butler Report about the informality of decision taking processes which undermine the ability for the Cabinet to reach collective political judgements. Discussing this issue, Lord Wilson of Dinton (formerly Sir Richard Wilson, the Cabinet Secretary between 1998 and 2002) made the following points:

'I believe there is a connection between proper processes and good government.

Different Prime Ministers have different ways of doing business and there is no 'right' way of running a government. It is quite possible to reconcile due process with informal style. But the risk is that informality can slide into something more fluid and unstructured, where advice and dissent may either not always be offered or else may not be heard.'[43]

In the wake of the Hutton and Butler Reports there appears to have been something of a return to more correct, ie properly minuted, meetings at No 10 Downing Street, and an acknowledgement that informal ad hoc policy groups should be more formally recognised as Cabinet Committees. Nevertheless the following comments from Sir Michael Quinlan, Permanent Under-Secretary of State at the Ministry of Defence, 1988 to 1992 are worthy of note:

'It is . . . open to question, as we survey the scene disclosed by Hutton and Butler whether the changes—often, it seemed, reflecting a marked impatience with collective process—always rested upon sufficient understanding that existing patterns had not been developed without practical reason, . . . Where . . . there is no written constitution and governmental practice rests largely upon convention rather than entrenched rule or statute, changes may be more easily made than in a more formalized setting; but that does not render thorough, timely and transparent evaluation any the less important.'[44]

It is important to remember, however, that modern government functions in a world where the economy and political movements are globalised. The ability of any government to control events within national boundaries are severely constrained by the economic power of multinational corporations and their ability to move their investment and operations from one part of the world to another. There are, moreover, other powerful political actors in the form of trade unions and well organised, well informed and vociferous pressure groups, often functioning on an international basis. Furthermore the outplacing of executive decision taking to next steps agencies within the state creates alternative focuses of power and responsibility who may well develop their own agendas and practices of which governments have little day to day knowledge. This has resulted in governments losing much of the ability simply to 'command and control'. The task of a modern administration is to organise and to 'choreograph' the various players within a state referred to above. Modern government must therefore to some extent move away from the older structures of decision taking, policy formulation and implementation within which the historic conventions of collective and individual ministerial responsibility developed. There is today much less ability to command and much more need to achieve consensus.

Tony Blair's style of government has reflected the developments outlined above, and during his premiership new styles of regulating economic and social relationships have been introduced using contract as a model, and taking the form of Public Service Agreements and Framework Documents under which 'targets' may be set which allow ministers to exercise a degree of control over those with whom the 'agreement' has been made, and to be able to point to particular achievements as government successes where targets are met. These have been a feature of an attempt to find a 'third way' between the market forces of the private sector and

[43] Runciman, op cit p. 85.   [44] Runciman, op cit p. 127.

dirigiste, highly centralised, highly planned traditions of state provided schemes. These new forms, which are often considered as 'governance' rather than 'government' because of their consensual and contractual basis have been utilised to change the delivery of health and social service provision, often by the introduction of an element of competition for the provision of a service by the disaggregated elements of the monolithic organisation, such as the National Health Service, which previously undertook the task. A further example of this development has been the use of 'Private Finance Initiatives' (pfi) whereby the private sector has undertaken to develop public facilities such as hospitals which are then rented and paid for over a number of years by service providers. At the personal level the same use of new forms of governance can be seen in the development of Youth Offender Contracts, Acceptable Behaviour Contracts, Parenting Contracts and Jobseeker's Agreements as alternatives to more traditional forms of regulatory activity involving various forms of punishment and sanctions.[45]

This move from government to governance, however, can result in an over-concentration on delivery, ie the achievement of practical results, and an over concern with outcomes and targets with a consequent disregard for appropriate and reflective prior policy formulations. Indeed in the modern world, *governance* demands due process of consultation, involvement and ownership by all affected parties if the activities of *government* are to be accepted as legitimate. To that end outcome must be rooted in properly recorded policy discussions whose development can be audited and in respect of which there must be a clear system of accountability. Sir Michael Quinlan's comments on this issue should be heeded: 'Cabinet Government of the traditional model has manifestly atrophied over the past seven years, and moreover by deliberate neglect, not accident. . . . If a collective Cabinet system no longer functions well, and Parliament is in practice docile or impotent, we may be nearer to "elective dictatorship" than when Lord Hailsham's coining of that phrase a quarter of a century ago was widely dismissed as hyperbole.'[46]

XII. Quasi Legislation

Another area of government activity very relevant to the implementation of policy yet subject to little formal regulation is the issue of what was first identified as 'administrative quasi legislation' in 1944.[47] This was subsequently examined in detail in Professor Ganz's book *Quasi-Legislation: Recent Developments in Secondary Legislation*.[48] She wrote: 'quasi legislation is problematical because it is not a term of art. It is used here to cover a wide spectrum of rules whose only common factor is that they are not directly enforceable through criminal or civil proceedings . . . [but] there are degrees of legal force and many of the rules . . . do have some legal effect. It is also not possible to draw a clear distinction between law and quasi-legislation on purely formal lines, ie the mechanism by which it is made. A legally binding provision may be contained in a circular whilst a code of practice may be embodied in a statutory instrument.'[49] Much will depend on the wording of any relevant legislation, for example, with regard to the form of documents, their degree of force, and whether and to what extent Parliament has

---

[45] See generally Vincent Jones, P, *The New Public Contracting: Regulation Responsiveness, Relationality* (OUP, Oxford, 2006).   [46] Runciman, op cit p. 129.

[47] Megarry, RE, 'Administrative Quasi-Legislation' (1944) 40 LQR 125.

[48] (Sweet & Maxwell, London, 1987).   [49] Ganz, op cit p. 1.

any supervision of them. Thus where a statute states a local authority are 'to have regard to' ministerial guidance any such guidance has to be taken into account in local decision-making, though a degree of local discretion will be retained. Where, on the other hand, authorities are directed to 'act in accordance with' ministerial guidance there is no local discretion. However, much policy guidance is not issued under the direct authority of a statutory provision and may be only 'a factor to be taken into account' by the receiving authority in the exercise of its statutory functions (see further chapter 10). Such quasi legislation is, nevertheless, a potent force in transmitting central government's views on how law and policy should be implemented and applied by local and other subordinate authorities.

The forms of 'quasi legislation' are many and varied.

Circulars are essentially letters from government to subordinate authorities containing guidance on the exercise of statutory functions, such as planning, housing, education, social services, finance and local government superannuation. They may be printed and made available for sale to the public in a numbered series, though a more usual source of dissemination nowadays is via the website of the issuing department.

Codes of Guidance may be issued. A good example is the Code of Guidance in relation to responsibilities of local authorities for homeless persons and with regard to allocating tenancies. The basic rules are statutory—being initially found in Part III of the Housing Act 1985, but now replaced by the Housing Act 1996—the Code advises authorities on discharging functions. The Code is not 'law': the advice it contains does not have to be accepted. If, however, an authority can be shown to have failed to consider the Code when deciding how to act, its actions can be challenged by a person affected thereby.[50]

Codes of Practice are many and various: examples are those under sections 60, 66 and 67 of the Police and Criminal Evidence Act 1984.

Guidance Notes can also take many forms. An example is the Guidance Notes issued under the Pollution Prevention and Control Act to supplement the statutory rules on regulating polluting processes. Such Notes can, if not applied with care, supplant other statutory requirements in the minds of regulators.[51]

Guidelines are informal and persuasive and do not have a legal force, and can consist of no more than a letter from a central to a local authority.

Other relevant forms of quasi legislation include National Health Service Notices and Family Practitioner Notices. It was the issue of a memorandum of guidance by the Department of Health and Social Security on family planning which contained material on contraceptive advice for those aged under 16 which led to *Gillick v West Norfolk and Wisbech Area Health Authority*[52] in which Lord Bridge stated:

'If a government department, in a field of administration in which it exercises responsibility, promulgates in a public document, albeit non-statutory in form, advice which is erroneous in law, then the court, in proceedings in appropriate form commenced by an applicant or plaintiff who possesses the necessary locus standi, has jurisdiction to correct the error of law by an appropriate declaration . . . But the occasions of a departmental non-statutory publication raising . . . a clearly defined issue of law . . . will be rare. In cases where any proposition of law implicit in a departmental advisory document is interwoven with questions of social and ethical controversy, the court should . . . exercise its jurisdiction with the utmost restraint, [and] confine itself to deciding whether the proposition of law is erroneous.'

[50] *R v Newham London Borough Council ex p Ojuri (No 3)* (1998) 31 HLR 631.
[51] *Thornby Farms v Daventry District Council* [2002] Env LR 28.
[52] [1986] AC 112 at 193 (post letter G) to 194 (post letter A).

It is interesting to note that while the Department of Health ceased to issue Family Practitioner Notices in 1998, it still issues a considerable array of other quasi-legislative documents such as: Advance Letters—which detail agreements on conditions of working for health service staff; CMO updates—bi-annual newsletters from the Chief Medical Officer to doctors in England; Dear Colleague Letters—conveying general information, policy updates or requests for action and addressed to various Health Service and Social Care bodies; Estates Alerts—which deal with risk management etc in Health Service premises; Fire codes—including Health Technical Memoranda and Fire Practice Notes on fire precautions for the Health Service; Health Service Circulars—formal communications addressed to Health Service Chief Executives, and requiring significant or specific action; Local Authority Circulars—similar to the foregoing but addressed to local authorities; Local Authority Social Services Letters—conveying information or requesting short term action; Professional Letters—these are addressed to relevant Health Service personnel from the heads of relevant professions such as the Chief Medical and Chief Nursing Officers. Interestingly, only the Circulars are stated to have a possible quasi-legislative effect, but clearly anything affecting the care of patients, the availability of drugs and services etc is capable of affecting patients' interests and may become a relevant consideration in any litigation that might arise.

Professor Ganz identified the following as features of quasi legislation:

(a) use of non-technical language easily understood by lay persons;

(b) flexibility in that the documents in question are quite easily drawn up and replaced;

(c) the documents are often designed to secure uniformity of action amongst those to whom they are addressed, particularly where the legal rules under which those persons operate give them a great measure of discretion as to *how* they will exercise their functions;

(d) the documents are a product of a belief, current in both central and local government, that persuasion is often better than compulsion: it is preferable to achieve an object by voluntary means than by the force of law, with the language used being that of exhortation rather than command;

(e) the documents can be a halfway house between doing nothing in relation to an issue and introducing legislation to control the matter: this may serve to satisfy pressure groups otherwise demanding legislation;

(f) there is considerable diversity in the amount of parliamentary involvement in the promotion of quasi legislation;

(g) there is similar diversity as to the publication of quasi legislation, and public involvement in, and consultation over, the drawing up of documents. For example circulars and Guidance Notes may be sent out in draft for comment by local authorities and local government representative organisations, but there is no general legal requirement that this should happen.

However, the formlessness and lack of legal structures surrounding quasi legislation bring with them their own problems.

(a) There is no clear rule as to which quasi-legislative form should be used for which purpose. For example consider the diversity of documentation issued by the Department of Health and outlined above.

(b) Despite the clear legal understanding that quasi legislation does not normally make law it nevertheless can have a legal significance as a factor to be taken into account in decision-taking. From this flow a number of problems. There is the increasingly specific nature of some guidance—coupled in some cases with a considerable increase in its bulk. A particularly good example of this was Department of the Environment Circular 11/94 *Environmental Protection Act 1990: Part II Waste Management Licensing, the Framework Directive on Waste* which ran to 199 pages with 11 annexes. Not only did this give guidance on the detailed application of ministerial regulations made in pursuance of EC obligations relating to the contentious environmental issue of waste management, it also contained a very detailed exposition of what was centrally believed to be the meaning of relevant pieces of EC legislation. The problem with such a level of detail, however, is that when those bodies and agencies who have responsibility for regulatory activity have to apply the law, there is a temptation not to look to the words of the primary EC and UK legislation but to the words and definitions of the guidance, as occurred in the *Thornby Farms* case.[53] Despite departmental disclaimers that circulars and other forms of guidance cannot be taken as absolutely authoritative statements of law there is an increasing tendency for the bulk, complexity and degree of specificity of some of them to erode the distinction between law and guidance.

(c) A further contentious issue is the ability of quasi legislation to drastically alter *the effect in practice* of the words of Parliament as contained in statute. When, for example, Parliament created the Environment Agency under the Environment Act 1995 it gave the Agency wide powers to regulate the environment, to control the activities of those whose legitimate industrial and commercial activities can have undesirable environmental consequences, and to prosecute and punish those who pollute air, land and water or who overstep the limits which have been set to their otherwise allowed activities. Offences against the environment in the United Kingdom are generally of strict liability, ie it is not necessary to prove a specific mental element such as an intention to damage the environment. Certain activities are simply prohibited and those who commit them, even unintentionally, are technically open to prosecution. That is, the law on the face of the statute: the reality of law enforcement is very different. That was clear from the publication on 14 May 1996 of the Agency's initial Enforcement Code of Practice which stated that the Agency would use discretion in deciding whether or not to mount a prosecution, and in the exercise of that discretion one factor which it was clear would be taken into account is the view taken by the Agency of the moral quality of the offender's action. Thus while the law itself did not require there to be a culpable mental element as part of an environmental offence, *in practice where a comparatively minor infraction had occurred* and it was considered that no moral blame attached to it, a prosecution was unlikely. The 1996 Code was replaced by the Agency's Enforcement and Prosecution Policy, 1998 which retained, inter alia, a reference to the intent of the offender as a factor in considering mounting a prosecution. These policy statements modify the effect of the relevant statutes in practice. But where was Parliament's voice in all of this? It is quite clear that Parliament can lay down broad general rules in legislation, but quasi legislation drawn up by ministers, civil and other public servants can subtly alter the practical effect of Parliament's words, and over the quasi-legislative process there is no democratic control.

(d) Finally it should be noted that courts may experience problems with quasi legislation. It has already been noted that where there is a clash between quasi legislation and the law it is the latter which must prevail. However, it is rare for quasi-legislative documents to contain erroneous statements of the law. The problem usually arises because, as factors administrative bodies such as local authorities are bound to take into account, statements in quasi legislation have to be capable of being given a clear meaning. However, where a document is designed to give broad general guidance on a particular policy it is unlikely to be couched in the precise terms used in the formulation of statutes and statutory instruments. There have been complaints by judges about the vagueness of guidance issued with regard to planning controls

---

[53] See n 51 above.

in relation to sensitive issues such as controlling development in greenbelt areas, ie areas of land around major urban centres which it is desired to keep open.[54]

Despite such strictures quasi legislation is alluring to central government because it is an alternative way of achieving the implementation of policy, particularly where legislative action might result in political controversy. Furthermore, central guidance given repeatedly on a particular issue tends to harden into something akin to a rule of law.[55] However, it appears that where a minister issues non-statutory guidance to a subordinate authority that guidance is only subject to review in court where it actually states the law incorrectly.[56]

Quasi legislation in all its multiplicity of forms is nevertheless an excellent example of how much the governance of the United Kingdom depends upon practice and procedure as opposed to formal rules of law.

FURTHER READING

Blick A *People who Live in the Dark: The History of the Special Adviser in British Politics* (Politico's, London, 2004).

Bogdanor V (ed) *The British Constitution in the Twentieth Century* (OUP, Oxford, 2004), chs 4, 7 and 8.

Brazier R *Constitutional Practice* (Clarendon Press, Oxford, 2nd edn, 1994) chs 5, 6 and 7.

Charter 88 *Unlocking Democracy* (Charter 88, London, 2000).

Ganz G *Quasi-Legislation: Recent Developments in Secondary Legislation* (Sweet & Maxwell, London, 1987).

Ingham B *The Wages of Spin* (John Murray, London, 2003).

Jennings (Sir Ivor) *Cabinet Government* (3rd edn, Cambridge University Press, Cambridge, 1969) chs I, V, VIII and IX.

Jowell J and Oliver D (eds) *The Changing Constitution* (5th edn, Clarendon Press, Oxford, 2004) chs 11 and 17.

Kavanagh D and Seldon A *The Powers Behind the Prime Minister, the Hidden Influence of Number 10* (HarperCollins, London, 1999), chs 9 and 10.

King A (ed) *The British Prime Minister* (Macmillan and Co Ltd, London, 1969) Pts I and IV.

Marshall G *Constitutional Conventions* (Clarendon Press, Oxford, 1984) chs I, IV, VI and XIII.

Marshall G and Moodie GC *Some Problems of the Constitution* (4th edn, Hutchinson and Co (Publishers) Ltd, London, 1967) chs 2 and 4.

Munro C *Studies in Constitutional Law* (2nd edn, Butterworths, London, 1999) ch 3.

Runciman WG (ed) *Hutton and Butler: Lifting the Veil on The Workings of Power* (OUP, Oxford, 2004).

Wass D 'Checks and Balances in Public Policy Making' [1987] Public Law 181.

Weir S and Beetham D *Political Power and Democratic Control in Britain* (Routledge, London, 1999).

---

[54] *Barnet Meeting Room Trust v Secretary of State for the Environment* [1993] JPL 739.
[55] See per Lord Wilberforce in *Coleshill and District Investment Co Ltd v Minister of Housing and Local Government* [1969] 1 WLR 746 at 765.
[56] *R v Secretary of State for the Home Department, ex p Westminster Press Ltd*, The Times, 18 December 1991.

5 PARLIAMENT: COMPOSITION AND PRIVILEGES

The Queen's ministers must, by convention, be members of one or other Houses of Parliament, while The House of Commons Disqualification Act 1975 (as amended) excludes from membership of the House of Commons effectively all of the Queen's judicial, military and civil servants. Convention further demands that the Prime Minister must be a member of the House of Commons, and when a member of the House of Lords holds high ministerial rank, for example Secretary of State, he/she should have a suitably high ranking colleague to speak on his/her departmental responsibilities in the House of Commons. (The converse is not true.) Furthermore, Parliament is the place where the most important type of law—statute—is created, with all its three component elements, the Crown, Lords and Commons assenting. The Queen does not *have* to signal her assent *within* the Palace of Westminster. The Royal Assent Act 1967 provides that she may notify her assent via the speaker of each House of Parliament and this is the method nowadays adopted. However, it must be appreciated that *Government and Parliament are separate institutions*. This chapter is, accordingly, concerned with the two Houses of Parliament.

Since Henry VIII left the Palace of Westminster for Whitehall in 1512 the former has become the 'home' of the two Houses, with the Lords and Commons, who certainly met separately from 1377 onwards, having their own chambers.

---

1. The House of Lords

The 'upper house' met from 1377 in the White Chamber at Westminster, moving to the Court of Requests in 1801. A new chamber was provided following the fire of 1834. This contains cross benches for politically non-aligned peers in addition to those for supporters of the government and the opposition. This is a special feature of what is a very British institution.

In the middle ages the King was principally advised by those who held great estates of land. These principal landholders sat with the King in his Council or 'Curia Regis'. Some were lay men, others clerics representing that great landholder, the Church. Arguably, the House of Lords is the descendant, by a tortuous route admittedly, of the King's Council (which is why it is both a legislative chamber and a court), for an assembly of bishops, earls and barons called in 1081 to give advice on a dispute *subsequently* had the name 'Parliament' ascribed to it, though resembling only the House of Lords.

The House consisted, historically, of noblemen representing the continuing importance of inherited land and wealth plus twenty-six bishops representing 'The Church by Law Established'. In practice, however, after the introduction of life peerages under the Life Peerages Act 1958 for distinguished men and women in science, industry, the arts, commerce, voluntary activities, charities, education and, *particularly*, political life, hereditary peers have played a diminishing role in the House. The Conservative Party was not *guaranteed* a majority in the Upper House, but it was the *ability* of the hereditary 'backwoods men' to come up to Parliament in answer to the Conservative Party's call to vote down proposals by other parties which particularly angered the Labour Party and which led that body to propose abolition entirely of the rights of hereditary peers.

The House's chief task is to act as a revising and scrutinising chamber. The atmosphere of the House has lacked the political 'cut and thrust' of the Commons and numbers of ambitious members attempting to attract the favourable gaze of their leaders. The considered elucidation of the meaning of proposed statutory provisions is a task well befitting the House. It matters little that the House cannot (under the Parliament Acts 1911 and 1949) veto legislation and can only delay it, see further chapter 2, or that it has no real power over public finance. Indeed in its last 'unreformed' year (1998/99) the House worked extremely hard and economically, sitting for almost eight hours a day, considering 7,762 proposed amendments to Bills, and agreeing 2,972 of them, asking 4,149 written questions, and with an average daily attendance of 458 the annual running cost was £43.3m, compared with £260m for the Commons. It could well be said the 'old' House of Lords represented at least good value for money.

The Labour Party was, however, committed to reform on its return to power in 1997, and by 1998 appeared to have public opinion on its side, though this was mostly in the form of opposition to the status quo with no real consensus as to what composition a reformed upper house should have. Stung by criticism that simply excluding hereditary peers altogether would create a 'super quango' of appointed life peers who would be the Prime Minister's 'poodle', the government accepted the long term need for an elected upper house, and there was much talk of an independent commission being set up to oversee appointments to the interim reformed house. The initial reform proposals were introduced to Parliament in 1998, and the Reform Bill to exclude hereditary peers was introduced into the House of Commons in January 1999. It was then envisaged that a Royal Commission report on the next stage of reform would be considered by a joint committee of both houses in 2000 with further reform legislation coming about in 2000 or 2001 to turn the House of Lords into a partly elected, partly nominated chamber.

The outcome has been somewhat different. The initial reform legislation, the House of Lords Act 1999, came into effect, but not all the hereditary peers were excluded. A 'behind-the-scenes' accommodation reached between the Prime Minister and Viscount Cranbourne, leader of the Conservative peers, led to amendments to the initial Bill under which a number of peers were elected by their fellows to the upper house. In addition a number of peers were automatically returned as office holders. There were also a number of hereditary peers who had life peerages conferred upon them. Thus as from November 1999 102 'elected or appointed' hereditary peers survived, 42 Conservatives, 3 Liberal Democrats, 2 Labour, 28 'Crossbenchers' (peers who do not take a party whip), 15 Deputy Speakers, 6 hereditary peers of 'first creation' returned as life peers, six hereditary former leaders of the upper house returned as life peers and two holders of great Offices of State—the Duke of Norfolk as Earl Marshall and the Marquis of Cholmondely as Lord Great Chamberlain. The overall political composition of the House of Lords *then* became about 220 Conservatives, 166 Labour, 160 Crossbenchers, and 54 Liberal Democrats.

The initial 'tranche' of House of Lords reform under the Blair government thus followed the historic British pattern of incrementalism, with the remaining hereditary peers preserving the continuity of the new House with the old in the persons of 2 Dukes, 1 Marquis, 24 Earls, 1 Countess, 15 Viscounts, 55 Barons and 4 Baronesses.

(a) But what of the future?

In the short term attention clearly focused on the appointed life peers. By 31 March 2000 Mr Blair had appointed 209 new life peers since his coming to power in 1997—this compared with 203 for Mrs Thatcher's 13 years in office—and led to early fears about the amount of Prime Ministerial political patronage being exercised. A further cause for concern was the poor record of attendance in the House of some life peers, and this, particularly though *not* exclusively amongst Labour peers, led to embarrassing reverses in the upper house for the government—by March 2000 Labour's 182 peers could still be defeated by 232 Conservatives, 54 Liberal Democrats and 161 Crossbenchers. Labour's 20 'working' life peers appointed in March 2000 had it impressed upon them they were indeed expected 'to work' and spend at least three evenings a week in the House for late night, three line whip votes.

Proposals for further reform were put forward by the Wakeham Commission (Royal Commission on the Reform of the House of Lords)—'A House for the Future' Cm 3534, January 2000. These proposals were as follows:

- An Upper House of some 550 members, mainly nominated but partly elected:
  - the elected minority would represent the regions while the appointed majority would be emplaced by an Independent Appointments Commission whose duties would include ensuring that the Upper House would reflect proportionately the balance of political opinion within the nation according to votes cast at the previous general election, but with no single party having an overall majority, and with about 20 per cent cross bench representation;
  - three models for election of regional members were included, A (65 members reflecting votes cast in the previous general election), B (81 members directly elected at the time of European Parliament Elections, on a regional list basis), C (195 members elected by proportional representation at the time of European Parliament Elections);
  - regional members should serve for three electoral cycles, and appointed members should have a fixed term of fifteen years, though both would have a right of reappointment for a period of up to fifteen years;
  - election/appointment to the Upper House should bar membership of the Commons until a period of ten years has elapsed following the end of membership of the Upper House.
- The Appointments Commission should ensure that at least 30 per cent of members of the Upper House are female with the objective of securing gender balance over a period of time, with ethnic minorities being represented at least in proportion to their levels in the overall population.
- Existing life peers should be able to be members of the reformed upper house.
- There should be an end to party political patronage over appointments, with the Prime Minister having no control over the size, balance and membership of the Upper House.

- Members of the House should receive a daily attendance payment rather than merely the reimbursement of expenses as at present.
- The Upper House should retain its existing supervisory powers only over legislation, and should respect the election manifesto of the governing party, and its clearly expressed views on policy:
  - There should be, however, enhanced powers to delay, and voice concerns over, delegated legislation.
  - There should be a Constitutional Committee to scrutinise the implications of all legislation, and a further Human Rights Committee to scrutinise all Bills for their implications in this area.
  - Senior ministers in the Commons should make occasional statements in and answer questions in an appropriate Committee of the Upper House.
  - The Law Lords should continue to sit in the Upper House.
- Sixteen Bishops of the Church of England should be members, with five places for representatives of other denominations of the Christian Church, and at least five members should be specifically selected to represent non-Christian faith communities.
- No name was suggested for the new Upper House, and while existing life peers would remain as members for life, following the passage of the necessary legislation possession of a life peerage granted as an honour should no longer qualify for membership, while the newly appointed/elected members should not be offered peerages, and, of course, possession of an hereditary peerage would be no qualification for membership.
- The role of the Upper House should be to bring various perspectives to bear on the development of policies, to give the various sections of British society a voice in Parliament, to continue the current role of the House of Lords as part of the constitutional system of checks and balances, and to enable the nations and regions of the UK to have their voices heard at Westminster, while deferring to the House of Commons as the principal political forum.

On publication the Wakeham Commission report was variously attacked:

- By Charter 88 who wanted a fully elected Upper House and who portrayed the proposals as leading to a house full of 'Tony's Clones';
- By some Labour politicians who distrusted the electoral elements in the proposals as giving a degree of elected legitimacy to the Upper House;
- By commentators who argued that the report had not been bold enough, particularly with regard to the lack of formal powers to control legislation on constitutional or human rights grounds, by, for example the use of special delaying powers, or the power to require a referendum to be held;
- It was also possible to characterise the reform proposals as being no more than a rehash of the current revising chamber nature of the Lords, to which would be added some vague additional scrutiny functions;
- The balance between appointed and elected elements was also seen as unacceptable by some—far too many seats would go to the appointed 'great and good'—even though the Appointments Commission would be made up of eight persons, three nominated by the major political parties, one 'crossbencher' and four independents;
- Guaranteed representation for women, religious groups and ethnic minorities drew the criticism why was there no such representation for rural areas or for the professions;

- Many people found the whole notion of a predominantly appointed house fundamentally unacceptable in a democratic society, while there were also fears that only bland and 'non-awkward' appointments would be made.

(b) After the Wakeham Commission

The history of House of Lords reform in the early years of the twenty-first century has been both tangled and inconclusive—the former in that, as we shall see, it has become enmeshed in the issues of the financing of political parties and the alleged 'purchase' of honours and influence by wealthy business people, the latter in that it appears we are hardly nearer to consensus on *how* the Upper House of Parliament should be composed and, more importantly, what its powers should be.

The sad story can be begun in the summer of 2001 when, following a government statement committing it to a fully appointed House, there was disagreement over the issue of consultation between the government and the Conservatives and Liberals in the House of Lords regarding its future reform. Reform proposals were drafted by October 2001 but early reservations were raised about the power of the Prime Minister to appoint peers, which raised the issue of political patronage. The proposals were launched in the form of a White Paper in November 2001 and included the removal of the remaining hereditary peers, the election of 120 members by the public, the appointment of 120 non-party political peers by an Appointments Commission, the nomination of 332 political peers by party leaders, with the majority of these being nominated by the Prime Minister, the abolition of the titles 'Lord' and 'Baroness', a possible retirement age of 75, the guarantee of more women and members of ethnic minorities in the Upper House, and the reduction of the numbers of Bishops from 26 to 16. The Appointments Commission would itself be appointed on a cross-party basis. The scheme was complex, with different lengths of service for different types of member, while there was to be no change in the powers of the Upper House. These proposals proved to be unpopular with both the members of the House of Lords and the government's own supporters in the House of Commons who had been in favour of a much greater number of elected members in the Upper House.

By 2002 it appeared there could be a compromise reached with the number of elected members being increased to 40 per cent of the total and by October 2002 it was reported that the Prime Minister might be prepared to accept proposals which would allow the election of over 50 per cent of the members. A joint committee of both Houses of Parliament had been tasked in May 2002 with taking the proposal forward and to find a scheme acceptable to both Houses. This had the effect of shielding the government from the task of having to come up with its own proposals after considerable opposition to the notion of a largely appointed second chamber. However, by January 2003 it appeared the Prime Minister had reversed his position and was opposed to the notion of a 'hybrid' Upper House consisting of both elected and appointed elements. This, apparently, was on the basis that a partially elected Upper House might be tempted to assert its authority against the House of Commons and because having two classes of members would be an inherently unstable position to adopt. However, in December the Joint Committee on Lords Reform called for detailed costings of how much a reformed Upper House might cost when it appeared that could be up to three times the current cost of some £200m p.a. That would be a consequence of paying salaries to the members of the reformed House and giving them enhanced working conditions. In February 2003 all the proposed reform options were rejected by the House of Commons, including the Prime Minister's preferred option of a fully appointed Upper House. This occurred after the House of Commons rejected the 'all nominated' option, and government whips then so organised the voting of their party members that all other options were also rejected. At this point the Joint Committee on Lords Reform voted to wind itself up.

In September 2003 it appeared the government was proposing to remove the only elected element in the Upper House, namely the 92 'elected' hereditary peers, and to set up a statutory Appointments Commission itself appointed on a cross-party basis, to make appointments to the Upper House on the basis of some nominations by political parties and some selected independent persons. These proposals were included in the 2003 Queen's Speech as a Lords Reform Bill. However, by March 2004 it appeared the Cabinet had decided to wait until after the next general election before proceeding with further reforms.

Following the May 2005 general election the number of new life peers appointed to the Upper House gave the Labour Party parity for the first time with the Conservatives, with both parties having 208 members. At the same time the Department for Constitutional Affairs committed itself to a reform proposal concerning the *powers* of the Upper House, not its composition, by putting forward the notion that there should be a time limit on the period a Bill may spend in the Upper House, though it was stressed this was simply a matter of clarifying the timescale of legislation and was not an attempt to further reduce the legislative powers of the Lords.

The reform issue came back on the political agenda in March 2006 when it appeared the Prime Minister might be prepared to abandon his attachment to a nominated Upper House and agree to a majority of the House being elected, though perhaps with a statutory limit on the powers of the House to block any policy that has been the subject of the government's election manifesto. That last issue raises, of course, the crucial issue of the powers and purposes of the Upper House. If one attempts to make the Upper House a less aristocratic and more democratic, and therefore more legitimate, body, one begins to compromise the position of the House of Commons. A largely elected Upper House could claim it had a mandate to resist proposals that have been passed by the Lower House. Furthermore there is no national consensus either inside or outside Parliament as to the path of reform. Many appear to want a strengthened Upper House to act as a check on the powers of government, but equally there is apparent majority support for the argument that the will of the Commons must ultimately prevail. There is no agreement either on the election/nomination issue, with many people believing that nomination secures a degree of independence from the political process for the Upper House, while yet others believe election is essential for the legitimacy of the institution. Some argue that if the Upper House became a 'senate' with a majority of elected members it would be unthinkable for it not to have extensive powers; others respond that such a development could turn the Upper House into a mere mirror image of the Commons in which case why, they ask, is it needed? To this one answer is that the Upper House should not be elected at the same time as the Lower House or should be elected on a different basis. That, however, could lead to a Parliament with a divided authority and to confusion in the mind of the electorate about who is responsible for what in policy terms.

The lastest proposals for reform contained in a White Paper of 8 February 2007, Cm 7027, suggest a hybrid House, 50 per cent appointed and 50 per cent elected. This would not challenge, it is claimed, the primacy of the House of Commons, and would neither be a replica of nor a rival to the Commons.

(c) Relationships between the Houses

Even in its interim reformed state, the government cannot take the House of Lords for granted. Between 1979 and 1986 the House inflicted 10 defeats on the government, particularly where crossbench peers voted with the opposition and the support of Conservative peers wavered. By 1992 the number of defeats had risen to 155, with further defeats in 1993 on the Railways Bill, in 1994 on the Police and Magistrates' Courts Bill, and in 1995 on the Pensions Bill. Many of these defeats were not reversed, and in 1985–86 of the 19 amendments resulting from government defeats in the Lords, 12 effectively survived in the final form of the legislation and in 4 other cases a compromise was effected.

There have been a number of 'causes célèbrès' down the years. In the early summer of 1990 the Lords rejected the government's War Crimes Bill which would have allowed proceedings to be taken in this country, in respect of alleged Nazi atrocities committed *overseas* during the Second World War, against their perpetrators who subsequently managed to disappear as immigrants into the fabric of British society. The Bill was opposed on the grounds that it was retrospective legislation—a favourite device of tyrannical governments the world over to criminalise for their own purposes past behaviour which was then innocent or legal. When the Lords defeated the principle of the Bill (as opposed to its mere detail) the question arose whether they had acted unconstitutionally. It had long been accepted they should not challenge the principle of Government Bills which have featured in an election manifesto—the so-called 'Salisbury Convention' (named after Lord Salisbury, Conservative leader in the Lords 1942–1957). However, in this case the convention was not broken:

1) the Bill was not part of an election manifesto;
2) it was not truly a Government Bill, being essentially derived from a motion tabled by a Conservative backbencher in December 1989;
3) the government had allowed a free vote on the Bill at all stages in the Commons and 3 Cabinet ministers had actually voted against.

The 'Salisbury Convention' is supplemented by the 'Carrington Convention'—derived from a declaration made by Lord Carrington, the Conservative Leader in the Upper House in 1967, namely that the Lords should not normally dissent from the views of the Commons, not even by resort to the power to delay legislation under the Parliament Act 1911. However, this is subject to the vague condition that, exceptionally, and as a matter of last resort on a matter of great constitutional importance which is either known to be dividing the nation deeply, or on which public opinion is, as yet, unknown, the Upper House may use the power of delay to give time for reflection.

Before the 1999 reforms the Labour government faced revolts in the House of Lords—usually as a result of alliances by Conservative, Liberal Democrat and crossbench peers. Writing in *The Times* on 30 November 2000, Professor Bogdanor pointed out that:

• In the first three months of 2000 the government suffered ten defeats in the Lords—and though able to reverse most of these in the Commons, particularly with the threat of resort to the Parliament Acts, there were situations where subordinate legislation (which is not subject to the Parliament Acts) was lost;
• Removal of most of the hereditary element, enables the Upper House to point to a legitimacy based on selection or election (albeit by a small constituency), and the decidedly expert nature of the House's composition;

- The Upper House thus began to change from a revising to an opposing chamber, with even the Salisbury Convention being questioned as no longer appropriate to an age where *no* party has a guaranteed majority in the Upper House.

Since 1999 the conventional understanding that the Upper House should concentrate on the task of detailed revision of legislation and rarely, if ever, challenge the will of the House of Commons has been eroded. The Upper House has a greater degree of self confidence, and figures indicate that since 1997 the present government has been defeated on nearly 400 occasions. Most of these defeats have then been reversed in the House of Commons and the House of Lords has then given way, but on nearly four out of ten occasions the defeat has not been reversed, and this has resulted in some changes to government policy. A particular recent example of some notoriety relates to the Racial and Religious Hatred Act 2006. The Blair government tried on a number of occasions to create an offence of inciting hatred against a person on grounds of religion. The measure was originally included in the Anti-Terrorism, Crime and Security Bill in 2001 but was withdrawn following opposition in the House of Lords. It was included once more in the Serious Organised Crime and Police Bill of 2004 but was again withdrawn, largely because of the need to get the majority of that Bill's provisions through Parliament before its dissolution in respect of the 2005 General Election. The government brought the proposals once more before Parliament in July 2005. The House of Lords made amendments to the Bill restricting the ambit of the offence of stirring up religious hatred to situations where the accused had the *specific intent* of stirring up hatred. In a somewhat controversial vote on 31 January 2006 the House of Commons voted, very narrowly, to accept the Lords' amendments.

It may also be asked why governments only rarely resort to the Parliament Act 1911 in respect of those matters which do fall within its terms. The answer appears to be that such resort takes time, and may be seen nationally as a heavy-handed response to a defeat. Furthermore some defeats in the Upper House will be accepted by governments as a compromise. Some reverses are accepted as the price for getting the majority of legislative proposals on the statute book expeditiously.

II. The House of Commons

The Commons acquired a permanent home in St Stephen's Chapel at Westminster in 1547. Its shape has had an enduring influence on subsequent political development. As a 'Chapel Royal' St Stephen's followed the pattern of 'Oxbridge' college chapels so the seating did not run across the building but rather was in long rows from West to East. The Speaker's chair, and the Clerks' table before it where ministers and Opposition leaders stand and where the results of votes are received, took the place of the altar. The opposing rows of seating running the length of the old building helped to foster the predominantly two party, and overtly confrontational, nature of British politics. They were reproduced in the rebuilding of Westminster following the Palace's destruction by fire in 1834. In the past a distinction in the House was between members who were the King's ministers and those who were not (see chapter 1). Today the distinction is between ministers (though their numbers are limited by the House of Commons Disqualification Act 1975, as amended), sitting on the front or 'Treasury' bench on the left of the House, looking towards the Speaker, together with their 'backbench' support, and the opposition parties sitting on the right. These latter have their own leaders who 'shadow' the work of ministers. The Conservative Party, as the largest in opposition, has a 'shadow cabinet' (a body with no legal or conventional existence) whose members occupy the bench opposite to ministers with the table of the House between them: even they are technically ordinary members. Only the leader of the Opposition and his three senior whips receive a degree of official recognition by receiving a special salary. The rows behind the shadow cabinet are occupied by backbench opposition supporters.

The House is open to both men and women, under the Parliament (Qualification of Women) Act 1918, and all races and religions, though few members of the ethnic minorities are members. 128 women were elected to the House of Commons in the 2005 General Election, the highest number ever, while there was a small increase in the number of black and ethnic minority MPs from 13 to 15. In terms of the racial and sexual composition of the nation, some would argue that these figures constitute a gross under-representation of women and ethnic minorities. Others might respond that a person is elected to serve all the members of a constituency, and that sex and race are not the only determinants of a constituent's interests and concerns.

Members are not 'delegates' but 'representatives', ie they do not have to comply with their constituents' instructions, nor do they have to reside in their constituencies. The right to vote is *generally* held by all those aged over 18. It is a right to cast a single vote in a constituency, and depends upon residence there according to sections 1 and 2 of the Representation of the People Act 1983, as amended in 2000. The nation is divided into constituencies which are kept under regular review by Boundary Commissions created under the Parliamentary Constituencies Act 1986. The party which at a general election wins the majority of constituencies in the nation is victorious: there is no requirement that they should secure a majority of the popular vote as a whole. Proposals to reform the voting system emerge from time to time. In 1997 the Labour Party's election manifesto pledged a referendum on reform but in office the Labour government has been less enthusiastic. A Commission on reform headed by Lord Jenkins made recommendations in 1998 and recommended an 'alternative vote plus, or Additional Member' system for electing MPs whereby some 15 per cent to 20 per cent of members would be elected on a 'top-up' basis to ensure that the House of Commons more accurately reflects the number of votes cast. An alternative method of securing a modified system of representation would be the 'alternative vote' system under which voters list the candidates in order of preference, and those with fewer votes are progressively eliminated, with their votes being redistributed according to the listed preference until one candidate emerges with more than 50 per cent of the votes cast. For a strictly proportional representation system a Single Transferable Vote with large multi-member constituencies would be required. This has the merit of ensuring parliamentary composition in line with overall voter-preferences, but breaks the traditional link between member and quite small geographical constituencies.

The Labour Party initiated an internal consultation exercise on the Jenkins proposals, but the majority of Labour MPs indicated their opposition to any change in the 'first past the post' system, despite the fact that the 'Additional Member' is already in use for the Scottish Parliament and Welsh Assembly where it has led to coalition administrations and the possibility of permanent multi-party governments. By the summer of 2000 it appeared the government's promised referendum would not take place during the lifetime of that Parliament and for the moment there seems to be little chance of further reform of the 'first past the post' system.

Members are elected to represent their constituents' interests, irrespective of party, and to scrutinise, debate and criticise government policy—they are not elected to make policy. For years there has been debate as to the degree of influence members have, individually and collectively, over government, and as to whether party discipline in the House is too strong. The arguments were summarised by the Royal Commission on the Constitution (Cmnd 5460) as long ago as 1969–73:

• There is a public impression that the task of MPs is simply to vote for their party.

• Members are unable to influence policy making and so may find a destructive role in simply criticising government, rather than advising the formulation of policy (see also chapter 6).

• Members lack the power and status of Congressmen in the United States, and are lacking access to information available to government via civil servants or businesses via their research departments.

• Because the party in power will seek to preserve its parliamentary majority, at times a minority of members on one wing of that party can demand disproportionate attention is given to their views as the 'price' of their support.

There are, however, counter arguments:

• While members are reluctant to question 'the party line' in public, they nevertheless have considerable behind the scenes influence in committee and in party meetings;

• The content of legislation is decided very much in the light of what the government's supporters are thought likely to accept;

• The views of members as a matter of fact are sought before legislation is drafted and policies formulated;

• When an important vote is to take place there is much canvassing and seeking of the support of individual members.

The 'whips' (a name derived from whipping in a pack of hunting dogs) of the parties certainly do their best to mobilise support in the House, indicating to 'their' members the importance of an issue by the number of underlinings it receives (hence 'one', 'two' and 'three line whips') on communications sent. Whips are, however, primarily parliamentary business managers, rather than disciplinarians. Most members support their particular party not out of fear but because of general agreement with its policies and opposition to those of other parties, though when a government's majority is small the need for the whips to manage it assiduously is even more necessary. See further on this issue chapter 6 below. Members may also wish to advance their political careers with their leaders, though whips nowadays do not distribute honours, and the government chief whip lost his 'secret service' fund to spend as he pleased in 1886. Members can vote against their party's proposals, or in favour of a private member's proposal opposed by the government of the day. This happened, for example, in January 1988. A Conservative private member introduced a proposal to reform official secrets law which received support from both the opposition and some Conservatives, in the latter case in the form of votes for and abstentions. The proposal was defeated by only 271 votes to 234. Nevertheless, though backbenchers exercised more freedom of action during the 1980s than in the 1950s and 60s, party discipline and identity is still strong, much aided by the confrontational nature of the shape of the House alluded to already, and members normally 'toe the party line', particularly when in receipt of three line whips, though this cannot always be guaranteed.

The measures used by the whips in 'managing' the Commons include not only 'whipping' their supporters but also, wherever possible, close and effective liaison with the major opposition parties so as to ensure agreed timetables for the consideration of legislation (see further chapter 6 below). Inevitably, however, much depends on the size of the government's majority. Where there is a large and cohesive majority it is clearly easier for the government to achieve its legislative wishes, particularly where these are controversial.

This has been particularly clear since the 2005 General Election when the Blair government's majority was substantially reduced and elements within the Parliamentary Labour Party disaffected with the Prime Minister have asserted themselves by 'rebelling' against the government on a number of occasions, leading at times, to retreats on policy issues and at other times to only very narrow victories for the government, or even defeat. An example of a policy retreat was the decision on 11 January 2006 to allow MPs a free vote on whether smoking should be banned in all public houses, when it became clear that there would be strong opposition to the government's initial proposal to exempt licensed premises not serving food. An example of a narrow victory was the vote on 15 February 2006 on legislation outlawing the glorification of terrorism which saw the government's majority reduced to only 38, while the restriction of the ambit of the offence of stirring up religious hatred discussed earlier is an example, admittedly rare, of a government defeat.

III. The Law and Custom of Parliament

Though part of the law of the land, and an important source of constitutional law, this is a body of law subject to the jurisdiction of, and enforcement by, the 'High Court of Parliament'. Parliamentary privilege is the major part of this *lex et consuetudo parliamento*, and the privileges of the Commons are that area of law capable of giving rise to most controversy. Some of this body of law is now supplemented by statute, for example the settling of disputed elections, but much remains subject to the jurisdiction of the House, subject in some cases to the claimed jurisdiction of the courts. In those areas where overlaps of jurisdictions occur there is no legal machinery to decide between the institutions should they come to opposing decisions in any given circumstance.

The early history of privilege has been touched on in chapter 1. Privileges were claimed in 1404 and the various privileges—freedom of speech, from arrest, of access to the monarch, and of having the most favourable construction placed on the Commons' proceedings—were to a degree established by the end of the sixteenth century, with the Committee of Privileges (which considers alleged breaches of privilege) itself dating from 1630. The Commons may also take action against 'contempts', that is, actions likely to interfere with the work of the House and its officers or to bring it into disrepute, or disobedience to its orders. Breaches of privilege are contempts, but the notion of contempt extends beyond that of breach. Though no new privileges can be created save by statute, it is far from clear what the exact scope of existing privileges is. The Bill of Rights 1688, while securing freedom of speech in Parliament, by declaring 'the freedome of speech and debates or proceedings Parlyament ought not to be impeached or questioned in any court or place out of Parlyament', adds to the confusion by failing to define what constitutes proceedings in Parliament. The House gave a wide meaning to the term in the *Duncan Sandys* case, but decided not to accept such a wide definition in the subsequent *Strauss* case.

Fifth Report from the Committee of Privileges, Session 1956–57
(HC 305, the *Strauss* case)

'On the 8th April 1957, Mr G R Strauss, the Member for Vauxhall, drew the attention of the House to communications between himself and the Paymaster General, . . . the London Electricity Board, and the Solicitors for that Board. Mr Strauss stated that the Board . . . threatened to institute against him proceedings for libel in respect of statements made by him in a letter written . . . on the 8th February 1957, to the Paymaster General . . .

The answer to the questions whether these threats constitute in themselves a breach of privilege depends, in the main, upon the meaning of article 9 of the Bill of Rights of 1689, which declared and enacted that "The freedom of speech and debates or proceedings in Parliament ought not to be impeached or questioned in any Court or Place out of Parliament".

Three questions arise, namely:

(a) Was the letter written on the 8th February 1957 . . . part of "a proceeding in Parliament"?

(b) Is the threat to institute proceedings for libel in respect of a speech, debate or proceeding in Parliament an interference with the freedom of Members of Parliament so as to amount to an impeachment or questioning of that freedom in a Court or Place out of Parliament and is thus a breach of privilege?

(c) If the answers to (a) and (b) are in the affirmative, would the House be acting contrary to the Parliamentary Privilege Act 1770, if it treated the issue of a writ against a Member of Parliament in respect of a speech or proceeding by him in Parliament as a breach of its privileges? . . .

In considering the meaning borne by the words of the Bill of Rights it is proper to have in mind the conditions prevailing at the time the Act was passed. Debates took place and speeches were made in Parliament but questions to Ministers were unknown; the system of questions as it is now practised was developed in the nineteenth century. A recognised practice has grown which is now in regular and frequent use and that is that a Member of Parliament, instead of putting down a question for answer in Parliament by a Minister, or bringing the matter to the attention of the Minister and the House in debate, writes to the Minister. Mr Strauss did so in this case . . .

No one today would question the claim that the system of questions by Members to Ministers and the answers given by Ministers are "proceedings in Parliament", even though the question be written down outside Parliament and sent by post to the House of Commons.

The question of the extent of the privilege claimed in respect of "proceedings in Parliament" was considered by the Select Committee on the Official Secrets Acts which reported to the House in the Session 1938–39 (House of Commons Paper No 101). [The *Duncan Sandys* case.]

The report of the Select Committee is so relevant to the matter here in issue that it is proper to set out the paragraphs in full—for the House of Commons resolved on the 21st November 1939, "That it agreed with the Committee in their conclusions". The paragraphs are:

"**2** The privilege to which your Committee were directed by the order of reference to have due regard is that usually referred to as the privilege of freedom of speech. This privilege is declared by the Bill of Rights . . .

3 The . . . Bill of Rights is not necessarily an exhaustive definition of the cognate privileges. But even assuming that it is, the privilege is not confined to words spoken in debate or to spoken words, but extends to all proceedings in parliament. While the term 'proceedings in parliament' has never been construed by the courts, it covers both the asking of a question and the giving written notice of such question, and includes everything said or done by a member in the exercise of his functions as a member in a committee of either House, as well as everything said or done in either House in the transaction of parliamentary business.

4 The privilege of freedom of speech being confined to words spoken or things done in the course of parliamentary proceedings, words spoken or things done by a member beyond the walls of parliament will generally not be protected. Cases may, however, easily be imagined of communications between one member and another, or between a member and a minister, so closely related to some matter pending in, or expected to be brought before, the House, that though they do not take place in the chamber or a committee room they form part of the business of the House, as, for example, where a member sends to a minister the draft of a question he is thinking of putting down or shows it to another member with a view to obtaining advice as to the propriety of putting it down or as to the manner in which it should be framed.

5 There is authority for saying that an act not done in the immediate presence of the House may yet be held to be done constructively in parliament and therefore protected. Sir Robert Atkyns, sometime Lord Chief Baron of the Exchequer, in his Argument upon the case of Sir William Williams, says that the Common's 'rights and privilege so far extends, that not only what is done in the very House sitting the parliament, but whatever is done relating to them . . . during the parliament and sitting the parliament, is nowhere else to be punished but by themselves or a succeeding parliament, although done out of the House . . . In a just sense, any offence committed by a member relating to the parliament, though done out of the House, is termed an offence in parliament.' [13 State Trials 1434 at 1435.]

6 Sir Gilbert Campion expressed the opinion that 'the immunity of members from the criminal law in respect of acts done by them in the exercise of the functions of their office' could 'not be confined to acts done within the four walls of the House'. This conclusion was, he considered, involved in Mr Justice O'Connor's dictum in *R v Bunting* (1885) 7 OR 524 at 563 that a member of parliament 'is privileged and protected by *lex et consuetudo parliament*' in respect of 'anything he may say or do within the scope of his duties in the course of parliamentary business' . . .

Mr Justice O'Connor's dictum must, your Committee think, command general assent; and it would, in their view, be unreasonable to conclude that no act is within the scope of a member's duties in the course of parliamentary business unless it is done in the House or a committee thereof and while the House or committee is sitting.

The courts and parliamentary privilege

8 The House of Commons has long claimed, as stated in the resolutions of the House of the 20th May 1837, 'That by the law and privilege of parliament, the House has the sole and exclusive jurisdiction to determine upon the existence and extent of its privileges', and 'that for any court or tribunal to assume to decide upon matters of privilege inconsistent with the determination of either House of Parliament thereon is contrary to the law of parliament, and is a breach and contempt of the privileges of parliament'. The courts, however, claim the right, where privilege of parliament is pleaded by way of defence, to determine whether the alleged privilege exists and whether the case falls within it, and in determining these questions the judges would not regard as conclusive a resolution of the House declaring any particular matter to be within its privileges. There is, therefore, a possibility of the courts taking a different view from that taken by the House. It is true that the prosecution of a member for an act which the House adjudged to be within his privileges as a member would itself be a breach of privilege, and that all parties concerned in the prosecution would subject themselves to the penalties incurred by those guilty of a contempt of the House, but this would not solve the difficulty. Your Committee do not think that any conflict between the two jurisdictions is likely to arise in practice." . . .

Where a Member of Parliament writes to a Minister concerning a Nationalised Industry and criticises the administration of that industry or the conduct of the Minister, the Statutory Authority or its Subordinate Board and is not satisfied with the reply he has from the Minister, the Authority or the Board, it is a reasonable possibility that he will seek an opportunity to debate the matter in the House. That debate would certainly be a debate or proceeding in Parliament.

We adopt and follow the arguments and reasoning of the Select Committee of November 1939, and we are of the opinion that Mr Strauss in writing to the Paymaster General on 8 February 1957, directing his attention to matters of administration in the London area of the Nationalised industry of Electricity and criticising the London Electricity Board, was conducting or engaged in a "proceeding in Parliament" and that in so doing he is protected by the privilege declared to belong to Parliament by the Bill of Rights 1688.

If that conclusion is right, then Mr Strauss has been threatened with the issue of a writ for libel to be brought before a Court of Law, that is: "out of Parliament in respect of a 'proceeding in Parliament' " taken by him . . .

The issue and service of a writ from the High Court of Justice against a Member of Parliament in respect of a "proceeding by him in Parliament" is an impeachment or questioning of his freedom to pursue the "proceeding in Parliament" and an impeachment or questioning of his freedom in a "Court or Place out of Parliament". A threat to issue such a writ falls into the same category as the actual issue and service of the writ.

It appears, therefore, clear that the letters of the Board and their Solicitors of 8th March, 27th March, and 4th April 1947 were in direct conflict with the declared privilege of Parliament and a distinct breach of such privilege.

The attention of the Committee was drawn, however, to an Act of 1770, entitled the Parliamentary Privilege Act 1770, and it is contended that the effect of that Act, reading it with the Bill of Rights of 1688, is that institution (or the threat of the institution), of legal proceedings against a Member of Parliament, even in respect of his speech, part in debate, or proceeding in Parliament, cannot be treated as a breach of privilege, that the Member must enter an appearance within the proper time to the writ and state that he intends to defend the action, and that when the matter comes before the Court, he can then claim that the Court has no jurisdiction to entertain the proceedings as he is entitled to the protection of the Bill of Rights of 1688.

As the question of the effect of this Act of 1770 upon the privileges of the House as declared in the Bill of Rights of 1688 is a legal one involving the correct interpretation of these Acts of Parliament we recommend that the opinion of the Judicial Committee of the Privy Council should be sought on the question whether the House would be acting contrary to the Parliamentary Privilege Act 1770, if it treated the issue of a writ against a Member of Parliament in respect of a speech or proceeding by him in Parliament as a breach of its privileges.'

The matter was referred to the Judicial Committee of the Privy Council: *Re Parliamentary Privilege Act 1770* [1958] AC 331. Viscount Simonds gave the opinion that the Act of 1770 applied 'only to proceedings against Members of Parliament in respect of their debts and actions as individuals and not in respect of their conduct in Parliament as Members of Parliament, and does not abridge or affect the ancient and essential privilege of freedom of speech in Parliament'. He then went on to state:

'Their Lordships repeat that they answer this and no other question. It was referred to them and it became their duty to answer it. But they do not intend expressly or by implication to pronounce upon any other question of law. In particular they express no opinion whether . . . the mere issue of a writ would in any circumstances be a breach of privilege. In taking this course they have been mindful of the inalienable right of Her Majesty's subjects to have recourse to her courts of law for the remedy of their wrongs and would not prejudice the hearing of any cause in which a plaintiff sought relief.'

The House of Commons did not, however, in the *Strauss* case accept its Committee's recommendation, thus leaving open the meaning of 'proceeding in Parliament'. The issue is complicated by the claim of the judiciary to interpret the meaning of the law and its application.

In *Stockdale v Hansard*[1] Lord Denman CJ stated:

'The inspectors of prisons made a report to the Secretary of State, in which improper books were said to be permitted in the prison, of Newgate; . . . adding that the improper books were published by the plaintiff . . . These documents were printed by . . . order from the House of Commons, who had come to a resolution to publish and sell all the papers they should print for the use of the members, and who also resolved . . . that the power of publishing such . . . reports . . . as they thought conducive to the public interest, [was] an essential incident . . . of the functions of Parliament . . . The . . . defence involved in this plea is, that the defendant committed the grievance by order of the House of Commons in a case of privilege, and that each House of Parliament is the sole judge of its own privileges . . . But it by no means follows that the opinion that either House may entertain of the extent of its own privileges is correct, or its declaration of them binding . . .

I will dispose of the notion that the House of Commons is a separate Court, having exclusive jurisdiction over the subject matter, on which, for that reason, its adjudication must be final. The argument placed the House herein on a level with the Spiritual Court and the Court of Admiralty. Adopting this analogy, it appears to me to destroy the defence attempted to the present action. Where the subject matter falls within their jurisdiction, no doubt we cannot question their judgment; but we are now enquiring whether the subject matter does fall within the jurisdiction of the House of Commons. It is contended that they can bring it within their jurisdiction by declaring it so. To this claim, as arising from their privileges, I have already stated my answer: it is perfectly clear that none of these Courts could give themselves jurisdiction by adjudging that they enjoy it.'[2]

Littledale J continued:

'It is said that the House of Commons is the sole judge of its own privileges: and so I admit as far as the proceedings in the House and some other things are concerned; but I do not think it follows that they have a power to declare what their privileges are, so as to preclude enquiry whether what they declare are part of their privileges.

The Attorney-General admits that they are not entitled to create new privileges; but they declare this to be their privilege. But how are we to know that this is part of their privileges, without enquiring into it, when no such privilege was ever declared before? . . .

The decision and dicta of the Judges, who have said that the House of Commons are the only judges of their own privileges, and that the Courts of Common law cannot be judges of the privileges of the House of Commons, are chiefly where the question has arisen on commitments for contempt, upon which no doubt could ever be entertained but that the House are the only judges of what is a contempt to their House generally, or to some individual member of it: but no cause has occurred where the Courts or Judges have used any expressions to shew that they are concluded by the resolution of the House of Commons in a case like the present. I think, therefore, that the Courts of Westminster Hall are not precluded from going into the enquiry from the decisions and dicta of Judges . . .

There is no doubt about the rights as exercised by the two Houses of Parliament with regard to contempts or insults offered to the House, either within or without their walls; there is no doubt either as to the freedom of their members from arrest, or of their right to summon witnesses, to require the production of papers and records, and the right of printing documents for the use of the members of the constituent body; and as to any other thing which may appear to be necessary to carry on and conduct the great and important functions of their charge.

In the case of commitments for contempts, there is no doubt but the House is the sole judge whether it is a contempt or not; and the Courts of Common Law will not enquire into it . . .'

---

[1] (1839) 9 Ad & EL 1.   [2] (1839) 9 Ad & EL 1 at 113–148.

Littledale J then proceeded to consider the effect of the Bill of Rights on the issue:

'I think this is not such a proceeding in Parliament as the Bill of Rights refers to; it is something out of Parliament. The privileges of Parliament appear to me to be confined to the walls of Parliament, for what is necessary for the transaction of the business there, to protect individual members so that they may always be able to attend their duties, and to punish persons who are guilty of contempts to the House, or against the orders and proceedings of other matters relating to the House, or to individual members in discharge of their duties to the House, and to such other matters and things as are necessary to carry on their Parliamentary functions; and to print documents for the use of the members.'[3]

Patterson J added:

'It is clear that no action can be maintained for anything said or done by a member of either House in the House: and the individual members composing the House of Commons, whether it be a Court of Record or not, may, like other members of a Court of Record, be free from personal liability on account of the orders issued by them as such members. Yet, if the orders themselves be illegal, and not merely erroneous, upon no principle known to the laws of this country can those who carry them into effect justify under them. The mere circumstance, therefore, that the act complained of was done under the order and authority of the House of Commons, cannot of itself excuse that act, if it be in its nature illegal: . . . Now, if the House of Commons, by declaring that it has power to publish all the defamatory matter which it may have ordered to be printed in the course of its proceedings with impunity to its publisher, can prevent all enquiry into the existence of that power, I see not why it may not, by declaring itself to have any other power in any other matter, equally preclude all enquiry in Courts of Law or elsewhere, as to the existence of such power. And what is this but absolute arbitrary dominion over all persons, liable to [no] question or control? It is useless to say that the House cannot by any declaratory resolution give itself new powers and privileges; it certainly can, if it can preclude all persons from enquiring whether the powers and privileges, which it declares it possesses, exist or not: for then how is it to be ascertained whether those powers and privileges be new or not? If the doctrine be true that the House, or rather the members constituting the House, are the sole judges of the existence and extent of their powers and privileges, I cannot see what check or impediment exists to their assuming any new powers and privileges which they may think fit to declare . . .'[4]

In *the Case of the Sheriff of Middlesex*[5] Stockdale, having successfully sued *Hansard*, was entitled to damages. To the Sheriff of Middlesex fell the task of executing judgment. The House of Commons resolved such execution was a contempt of its privileges, authorising its sergeant-at-arms to take the Sheriff into custody. The legality of this action was challenged by way of habeas corpus proceedings. The sergeant-at-arms produced in court a certificate from Mr Speaker simply stating the Sheriff was 'guilty of a contempt and a breach of the privileges of this House'.

Lord Denman CJ:

'The only question upon the present return is, whether the commitment is sustained by a legal warrant . . . The great objection remains behind, that the facts which constitute the alleged contempt are not shewn by the warrant. It may be admitted that words containing this kind of statement have appeared in most of the former cases; indeed there are few in which they have not . . . In *Earl of Shaftesbury's case* (1677) 6 State Tr 1270, 1 Mod 144, the form was general; and it was held unnecessary to set out the facts on which the contempt arose. That case is open to observation on other grounds; but I think it has not been questioned on this. In *R v Paty* ((1705)2 Ld Raym 1105), three of the Judges adopted the doctrine of that case to the extent of holding that the Court could not inquire into the ground of commitment even when expressed in the warrant.

---

[3] (1839) 9 Ad & EL 1 at 162–185.   [4] (1839) 9 Ad & EL 1 at 189–215.
[5] (1840) 11 Ad & EL 273.

[In *Burdett v Abbot* (1811) 14 East 1 Lord Ellenborough said]:

"If a commitment appeared to be for a contempt of the House of Commons generally, I would neither in the case of that Court, or of any other of the Superior Courts, inquire further: but if it did not profess to commit for a contempt, but for some matter appearing on the return, which could by no reasonable intendment be considered as a contempt of the Court committing, but a ground of commitment palpably and evidently arbitrary, unjust; I say, that in the case of such a commitment, (if it ever should occur, but which I cannot possibly anticipate as ever likely to occur), we must look at it and act upon it as justice may require from whatever Court it may profess to have proceeded . . . In the present case, I am obliged to say that I find no authority under which we are entitled to discharge these gentlemen from their imprisonment." ' [6]

Littledale J added:

'If the warrant returned be good on the face of it, we can inquire no further. The principal objection is, that it does not sufficiently express the cause of commitment; and instances have been cited in which the nature of the contempt was specified. But the doctrine laid down in *Burdett v Abbot* (14 East 1) in this Court and before the House of Lords, sufficiently authorises the present form. If the warrant declares the grounds of adjudication, this Court, in many cases, will examine into their validity; but, if it does not, we cannot get into such an inquiry.' [7]

The instant cause of contention was removed by the Parliamentary Papers Act 1840, granting rights to summary stays of any proceedings brought against those publishing under the direct authority of either House of Parliament. The issue of who is to judge the extent of parliamentary privilege remains unsettled; the Commons remain able to circumvent the courts by committing those they judge to be in breach simply for contempt without giving reasons.

Thus in *Rivlin v Bilainkin*[8] the plaintiff, in an action for libel, was granted an interim injunction to restrain the defendant from repeating the alleged libels. The defendant took to the House of Commons communications which repeated the alleged libels. He delivered one by hand to the messenger of the House of Commons for delivery to a Member of Parliament. On application by the plaintiff for an order committing the defendant to prison for breach of the injunction:

McNair J stated:

'It is argued on behalf of the defendant that this court has no jurisdiction to make an order for committal, since the matter complained of . . . occurred in the precincts of the House of Commons and was connected with an attempt to obtain parliamentary redress for an alleged grievance.

Having examined the authorities, I am satisfied that no question of privilege arises, for a variety of reasons, and particularly I rely on the fact that the publication was not connected in any way with any proceedings in that House.' [9]

In *Church of Scientology of California v Johnson-Smith*[10] the plaintiffs brought an action for libel against the defendant, a Member of Parliament, for defamatory remarks made during a television interview. The defendant pleaded fair comment and privilege. In order to defeat those pleas the plaintiffs by their reply alleged malice and in order to establish that the defendant had acted with malice they sought to adduce evidence, including extracts from *Hansard*, of what the defendant had done and said in Parliament.

---

[6] (1840) 11 Ad & EL 273 at 287–290.   [7] (1840) 11 Ad & EL 273 at 293.   [8] [1953] 1 QB 485.
[9] [1953] 1 QB 485 at 488.   [10] [1972] 1 QB 522.

Browne J stated:

'It is quite plain of course, that the privilege of Parliament is the privilege of Parliament as a whole and not the privilege in any individual member . . . The principle as to the privilege of Parliament is, of course, entirely clear. It comes for modern purposes from article 9 of the Bill of Rights (1688) . . . It is quite clear, therefore, that no action for defamation could be brought in respect of anything said in the House of Commons itself. The Attorney-General says that the privilege goes further and that what is said or done in the House in the course of any proceedings there cannot be examined outside Parliament for the purpose of supporting a cause of action, even though the cause of action itself arises out of something done outside the House . . . I accept the Attorney-General's argument that the scope of Parliamentary privilege extends beyond excluding any cause of action in respect of what is said or done in the House itself. And I accept his proposition which I have already tried to quote, that is, that what is said or done in the House in the course of proceedings there cannot be examined outside Parliament for the purpose of supporting a cause of action even though the cause of action itself arises out of something done outside the House. In my view this conclusion is supported both by principle and authority.'[11]

The issue of 'proceeding in Parliament' has been considered by a number of parliamentary committees. In 1976–77 the third Report from the Committee of Privileges HC 417 set the matter in the wider context of privileges and contempts generally, recommending a statutory definition of 'proceeding in Parliament' and replacement of the Commons' power to imprison for contempt with a power to fine.

The courts have been further called upon to adjudicate on the meaning of 'proceedings in Parliament', with somewhat inconclusive results. In *Rost v Edwards*,[12] a case involving an alleged libel by a newspaper on an MP in which some of the evidence consisted of correspondence between the MP and the Clerk of the House of Commons together with the Register of Members' Interests (see further below), Popplewell J ruled that the correspondence could not be produced in evidence as it fell within the definition of 'proceedings in Parliament' while the Register of Interests did not as it was a public document. However, in *Prebble v Television New Zealand Ltd*[13] the Privy Council effectively gave a very wide meaning to the phrase by agreeing that without a waiver of privilege by the New Zealand House of Representatives a number of Parliamentary papers could not be adduced in evidence. On the other hand in *Pepper v Hart*[14] despite arguments from the Attorney-General that to allow courts to refer to *Hansard* in deciding how to interpret a statute would contravene the Bill of Rights as amounting to inquiring with or questioning 'proceedings in Parliament', the House of Lords nevertheless determined that *Hansard* may be used in certain circumstances as an aid to statutory interpretation, particularly where legislation is unclear or ambiguous.

To a certain extent the problems in the *Rost* and *Prebble* cases have now been alleviated by section 13 of the Defamation Act 1996. This provides that where the conduct of a person (effectively an MP) in or in relation to proceedings in Parliament is in issue in defamation proceedings that person may waive so far as he/she is concerned (for the purposes of the proceedings) the protection of 'any rule of law' which prevents proceedings in Parliament being impeached or questioned in any court or place outside Parliament. The provision makes it clear that the concession made does not take away from MPs, or indeed any person, their protection from legal liability for words spoken or things done in the course of, or for the purposes of or incidental to, any proceedings in Parliament.

[11] [1972] 1 QB 522 at 528 (post letter B) to 530 (letter A).   [12] [1990] 2 QB 460.
[13] [1995] 1 AC 321.   [14] [1993] AC 593.

The 1996 Act does not, however, define 'proceedings in Parliament', though section 13(4) and (5) interestingly state that in particular nothing in the 1996 legislation takes away protection from 'a person' from legal liabilities in respect of 'words spoken or things done' with regard to giving evidence before either House or a committee, the presentation or submission of documents to either House or a committee, the *preparation* of a document for purposes of or incidental to the transacting of any such business, or the formulation, making or publication of a document or report by, or pursuant to, an order of either House or a committee. It may be by implication that this particularised list gives *some* indication of modern parliamentary thinking on the extent of the phrase 'proceedings in Parliament' but we are no nearer to a comprehensive definition acceptable to both courts and Parliament. In *Hamilton v Al Fayed*[15] the Court of Appeal argued that the Bill of Rights only prohibits the attachment by a court of any form of legal penalty to an MP for anything said in Parliament, or the direct criticism by a court of anything said or done in the course of a parliamentary proceeding, for the vice the Bill of Rights is directed against was inhibition of parliamentary speech and debate which might follow from condemnation by the courts which in this context are an arm of government. The court also accepted that an inquiry and report by the Parliamentary Commissioner for Standards, and a resolution of the House of Commons, all fell within the definition of a 'proceeding in Parliament'.

No court would presume to claim jurisdiction over the power of the Commons to regulate its own internal proceedings. In *Bradlaugh v Gossett*[16] the plaintiff, returned as member for the borough of Northampton, required the Speaker to call him to the table for the purpose of taking the oath required by 29 Vict c 19. In consequence of something which had transpired on a former occasion the Speaker declined to do so: and the House, upon motion, resolved 'that the Sergeant-at-Arms do exclude Mr B (the plaintiff) from the House until he shall engage not further to disturb the proceedings of the House'.

In an action against the sergeant-at-arms praying for an injunction to restrain him from carrying out this resolution. Stephen J stated:

'Taken by itself, the order of the 9th of July stated nothing except that the House had by resolution excluded a member, who in the judgment of the House had disturbed its proceedings, till he undertook not further to disturb it. It is obvious that we could not interfere with what might be a mere measure of internal discipline . . .

Suppose that the House of Commons forbids one of its members to do that which an Act of Parliament requires him to do, and, in order to enforce its prohibition, directs its executive officer to exclude him from the House by force if necessary, is such an order one which we can declare to be void and restrain the executive officer of the House from carrying out? In my opinion, we have no such power. I think that the House of Commons is not subject to the control of Her Majesty's Courts in its administration of that part of the statute law which has relation to its own internal proceedings, and that the use of such actual force as may be necessary to carry into effect such a resolution as the one before us is justifiable . . .

Blackstone says [1 Com 163]: "The whole of the law and custom of Parliament has its original from this one maxim, 'that whatever matter arises concerning either House of Parliament ought to be examined, discussed, and adjudged in that House to which it relates, and not elsewhere'."

---

[15] [1999] 3 All ER 317, affirmed by the House of Lords, [2001] 1 AC 395.   [16] (1884) 12 QBD 271.

Apply the principle thus stated to the present case. We are asked to declare an order of the House of Commons to be void, and to prevent its execution in the only way in which it can be executed, on the ground that it constitutes an infringement of the Parliamentary Oaths Act. This Act requires the plaintiff to take a certain oath. The House of Commons have resolved that he shall not be permitted to take it. Grant, for the purposes of argument, that the resolution of the House and the Parliamentary Oaths Act contradict each other; how can we interfere without violating the principle just referred to? Surely the right of the plaintiff to take the oath in question is "a matter arising concerning the House of Commons", to use the words of Blackstone . . . Whatever may be the reasons of the House of Commons for the conduct, it would be impossible for us to do justice without hearing and considering those reasons; but it would be equally impossible for the House, with any regard for its own dignity and independence, to suffer its reasons to be laid before us for that purpose, or to accept our interpretation of the law in preference to its own. It seems to follow that the House of Commons has the exclusive power of interpreting the statute, so far as the regulation of its own proceedings within its own walls is concerned; and that, even if that interpretation should be erroneous, this Court has no power to interfere with it directly or indirectly.'

Stephen J went on to state, however, that he knew of no authority for arguments that the courts have no jurisdiction over an 'ordinary crime' committed in the House of Commons. The principle is otherwise where the House is dealing with its own privileges and procedures.

'The House of Commons is not a Court of Justice: but the effect of its privilege to regulate its own internal concerns practically invests it with a judicial character when it has to apply to particular cases the provisions of an Act of Parliament. We must presume that it discharges this function properly and with due regard to the laws, in the making of which it has so great a share. If its determination is not in accordance with law, this resembles the case of an error by a judge whose decision is not subject to appeal . . . The assertion that the resolution of the House goes beyond matter of procedure, and that it does in effect deprive both Mr Bradlaugh himself and his constituents of legal rights of great value, is undoubtedly true if the word "procedure" is construed in the sense in which we speak of civil procedure and criminal procedure, by way of opposition to the substantive law which systems of procedure apply to particular cases. No doubt, the right of the burgesses of Northampton to be represented in Parliament, and the right of their duly-elected representative to sit and vote in Parliament and to enjoy the other rights incidental to his position upon the terms provided by law are in the most emphatic sense legal rights, legal rights of the highest importance, and in the strictest sense of the words. Some of these rights are to be exercised out of Parliament, others within the walls of the House of Commons. Those which are to be exercised out of Parliament are under the protection of this Court, which, as has been shewn in many cases will apply proper remedies if they are in any way invaded, and will in so doing be bound, not by resolutions of either House of Parliament, but by its own judgment as to the law of the land, of which the privileges of Parliament form a part. Others must be exercised, if at all, within the walls of the House of Commons; and it seems to me that, from the nature of the case, such rights must be dependent upon the resolutions of the House . . . If they misunderstand [the law], or (I apologize for the supposition) wilfully disregard it, they resemble mistaken or unjust judges; but in either case, there is in my judgment no appeal from their decision. The law of the land gives no such appeal; no precedent has been or can be produced in which any Court has ever interfered with the internal affairs of either House of Parliament, though the cases are no doubt numerous in which the Courts have declared the limits of their powers outside of their respective Houses. This is enough to justify the conclusion at which I arrive.'

However, where the House 'reaches out', as it were, from its own walls to affect the rights and entitlements of parties existing under the general law, then a conflict with the courts may arise. In such a conflict the Commons have the advantage, at least during parliamentary sessions, of being able to commit parties for contempt without stating reasons—a matter into which the courts cannot inquire. Conflicts are rare, though there have been periods when the House has seemed to be more than jealous of its privileges. In 1978 the House approved the Committee of Privileges' recommendation that the House's penal jurisdiction over contempt should be used sparingly and only in cases where there is actual or threatened improper obstruction likely to interfere substantially with the functions of the House, its members or officers. Since then the House seems to have taken a generally robust attitude to what is said by the media, and to have become rather more conscious of the need to maintain decorum and moral standing.

First Report from the Select Committee on Procedure, Session 1988–89, Conduct of Members in the Chamber and the Alleged Abuse of Parliamentary Privilege (HC 290)

'[A] certain level of noise and disturbance is inevitable in a gathering whose main characteristic is that it represents the clash of opinion in the country as a whole and whose Members, by their very nature, hold their views more passionately than the population at large. This is reflected in the confrontational arrangement of the Chamber, which differs so markedly from the Continental tradition of a semi-circular lay-out with Members seated at individual desks. We echo the view of the Clerk of the House that . . . conduct of a public meeting at large bears no relation to what is going on in the House of Commons, where the conflicts within politics and public life are ranged against each other deliberately in a confrontational way, which calls for response and reaction, not only of incredulity and dissent from the Members sitting opposite one, but support from colleagues sitting around one. There are also all kinds of reactions which, although they reduce sometimes to the sort of noises which upset the public, are read in quite a sophisticated way by other parliamentarians, who are realizing that a colleague is not holding the House, and so forth . . . All this said, it is clear that, in any legislative body, a point is reached from time to time at which the conduct of a Member, or group of Members, or even of the House as a whole, has gone beyond the acceptable, and has become such a hindrance to the efficient despatch of business that the Chair is obliged to invoke its powers of discipline laid down in Standing Orders . . .

The disciplinary powers of the Chair and the House are explained by the Clerk of the House in his memorandum submitted for our . . . enquiry, the relevant section of which is as follows:

"There are several gradations in the powers available to the Chair in relation to disorderly conduct. They are confined to offences committed in the Chamber during a sitting and dealt with by means of an *ad hoc* Motion . . . in which cases the House may impose any penalty it considers appropriate.

The Chair does not normally invoke its disciplinary powers without careful warning to the Member involved of what is likely to happen. If the Member persists in his conduct, the Chair may consider the situation adequately dealt with by requesting the Member to leave the Chamber. This is an informal procedure not governed by any Standing Order, and if the Member complies with the request he is not prevented from taking part in Divisions of the House or staying in the precincts: he simply absents himself from the chamber itself for the remainder of the day.

If a Member declines to withdraw voluntarily, or if the Chair considers that lesser sanction to be adequate, he may direct him to withdraw immediately from the House for the remainder of the day's sitting. . . . Its consequence is that the Member must leave the precincts of the House . . . for the rest of the day . . .

If a Member refuses to comply with the Speaker's direction just referred to, it is possible (though rarely done) for the Speaker to direct the Serjeant at Arms to ensure that the Member does so. The more normal course (after a solemn warning) is for the Chair to proceed to a formal 'naming'—which, if he judges the offence to warrant it, he can do in any case, without either of the preliminary steps so far described. . . ."

[The report continues:]

The most striking feature of the period since 1945 is the sharp increase since 1980–1981 in the use of the Chair's formal disciplinary powers and, in particular, in the incidence of namings. Even more noticeable is the further steep rise which occurred in the session 1987–1988 . . . [The] 1979–83 Parliament saw 12 cases, of which five involved naming, while in the 1983–87 Parliament the relevant Standing Orders were invoked nine times, including five namings. In the first Session of the current Parliament alone no fewer than nine cases occurred, of which eight led to naming and suspension . . . and the other consisted of an *ad hoc* Motion for suspension . . . [We] are conscious of a recent decline—not, of course, recorded in any figures—in what might be termed parliamentary manners. As the Clerk of the House put it: "Exchanges are sharper, I think, and formal courtesies are fewer and there are fewer expected." This has been accompanied by an increase in what the Clerk described in another context as "low grade abuse" in Members' dealings with one another. This may be unedifying but it hardly qualifies as disorderly behaviour. It rests very much in the hands of individual Members to avoid such discourtesies and not least for more senior Members to set a proper example.

Taking all the relevant factors into account—statistics for namings and suspensions of the House in grave disorder, varying degrees of strictness of different Speakers, and anecdotal evidence, we find it difficult to conclude that the last decade as a whole has witnessed a decline of standards of behaviour which could reasonably be described as unprecedented in recent history, particularly having regard to the example of the 1920s, when political tempers were high. Whilst the figures for 1987–88 are certainly without parallel over this period, we hesitate to form a firm judgement on the basis of a single abnormally long Session during which special factors may have applied, such as the number of newly elected, inexperienced Members.

[The Committee nevertheless considered whether it was desirable to reduce the "namings" by stressing the need for high standards of Parliamentary behaviour. One method of proceeding, previously considered in 1983, would be for a period of suspension to be accompanied by loss of salary as a disincentive to misbehaviour. However, there are arguments against such action, as the Clerk of the House explained:]

". . . one would be inflicting, in addition to the indignity of suspension, the loss of facilities, the possibility of speaking, voting and asking questions, and the carrying out of one's duties generally, a substantial fine which, I think, would make the introduction of such a penalty controversial. If it is controversial, it might increase the number of Members who voted against the suspension of a Member . . . that, I think would not be a development welcome to the Chair . . . I also think that . . . it might affect the willingness of the Chair to invoke its powers. I am not saying it would be decisive, but I would just advance those as considerations to be borne in mind . . ."

[The Committee endorsed the Clerk's view, but, however, also urged the general observance of good behaviour.]

We wish . . . to make some more general observations about Members' conduct in the Chamber. The first is that we see little point in addressing the particular issue of the naming of individual Members in isolation from the wider question of overall standards of parliamentary behaviour. We [refer to] the insidious practice, which appears to have grown in recent years, of concerted disruption of another Member's speech, either by continuous barracking or by the deliberate holding of conversations at a noise level just enough to render the Member who has the floor almost inaudible without shouting. Background noise is not, of course, a new phenomenon and Members cannot expect always to be heard in awed silence . . .

However, the methods sometimes employed today go well beyond the legitimate cut and thrust of debate and spontaneous reactions to opposing viewpoints, without which the Chamber would be a mere sounding-board. They are intended, by means which render it virtually impossible for the Chair to identify individual culprits, to deny a fair hearing to a fellow Member. As such they are, in our view, every bit as subversive of the parliamentary ethos as the more overt disruptions—which they can themselves provoke—which lead to the naming and suspension of individual Members. Whilst we have no evidence that such behaviour is organised or co-ordinated by the Whips, we find it difficult to believe that they could not, if they wished, take action to stop or at least curb it. Accordingly, we urge those responsible for the management of business in the House, in the strongest possible terms, to do all within their power to ensure that collective discipline is as strict as that applying to individuals . . .

The alleged abuse of parliamentary privilege

Background

The practice of making defamatory statements about named individuals under the cover of parliamentary privilege was a question touched on in our Third Report of 1986–87 . . . At that time we . . . echoed the view expressed by Mr Speaker on 19 February 1987: "We should use our freedom of speech and the freedom of the Notice Paper with the greatest care, particularly if we impute any motives or dishonourable conduct to those outside the House who have no right of reply". [110 HC Official Report (6th series) col 1084.]

Historical origins and definition of privilege

Before considering the alleged abuse of parliamentary privilege, it is necessary to examine the definition of the concept and the purposes for which it exists. The Clerk of the House began his memorandum on the subject thus: "The word 'privilege' literally means 'private law'—the right (in this case) of an institution to regulate its own affairs without control or interference from outside, together with the power to deal with those who seek to 'breach' its privileges, either by direct acts or by conduct that tends to undermine its authority." The Clerk described the purpose of privilege as being "to protect the institution, and not to set individual Members of Parliament outside the law . . . It was not until the Bill of Rights gave statutory confirmation to freedom of speech in 1689, as part of the Revolution Settlement, that the Commons' position was safeguarded beyond dispute." The key section of the Bill of Rights is article 9, which states. "That the freedom of speech, and debates or proceedings in Parliament, ought not to be impeached or questioned in any court or place out of Parliament."

The term "proceedings"—which sets the boundaries of parliamentary privilege—has been defined neither in statute nor by Resolution of the House . . . It is usually assumed, for everyday practical purposes, that proceedings in this context applies to the formal transaction of business by the House and its Committees. To this, Erskine May adds the following rider: " . . . it does not follow that everything that is said or done within the Chamber during the transaction of business forms part of proceedings in Parliament. Particular words or acts may be entirely unrelated to any business which is in course of transaction, or is in a more general sense before the House as having been ordered to come before it in due course. This is a test which may be useful in deciding how far crimes committed during a sitting may be entitled to privilege. But it may be used to dispose immediately of the most obvious case, that of a casual conversation between two Members which takes place during the progress of a debate." [20th edn, p. 94.] However, only a few of the many grey areas at the margins of this working definition have ever been clarified in the form of rulings in specific cases . . .

As the Clerk of the House underlined, the privilege enjoyed by Members is not unfettered and must be exercised within the rules laid down by the House itself for the regulation of its business and the preservation of order in debate. A Member may not, for instance, attack the motives or conduct of certain holders of public office (including judges) except on a substantive Motion; he must use language which is temperate, and which is not unbecoming or in any other way unparliamentary; he may not in any circumstances accuse a fellow Member of dishonesty; and he may not infringe the House's *sub-judice* rule by seeking to canvass issues which are currently awaiting adjudication in a court of law . . . The privilege of freedom of speech is an important and necessary element in the work of Parliament. However, because of the immunity it confers, its misuse can have serious effects . . . Your Committee consider it right to emphasise the obligation upon all Members to have regard, in any decision to make statements in the House which, if made outside the House, would be defamatory or even criminal, to the widespread effect of such statements when reported through newspaper reports and broadcasts of proceedings, and to the prejudice and possibly underservedly injury which may result to individual citizens who have neither remedy nor right of reply . . . There can, it is true, be no clear dividing line between statements which represent a legitimate exercise of freedom of speech, on the one hand, and those which constitute an abuse, on the other. Nevertheless, it is possible to imagine at one end of the spectrum the example of a Member who, for some political purpose, wilfully makes highly damaging accusations against a named individual for which he has no basis whatever in evidence. Equally, a Member might knowingly and mischievously divulge, during the course of proceedings, highly classified information, the publication of which carried a threat to national security or, more particularly, to the lives of individuals. We find it hard to believe that the House would regard these two, admittedly extreme, cases as anything other than a misuse of parliamentary privilege . . .

In considering these matters we have been conscious that there already exists a wide range of venues which can be pursued by an aggrieved person who wishes to correct or rebut remarks made about him in the House. He can approach his Member of Parliament . . . there may be cases which can be raised through Questions if some ministerial responsibility can be established; he can petition the House, through a Member; and he can approach directly the Member who made the allegations in the hope of persuading him that they are unfounded and that a retraction would be justified . . . We believe that there would be great advantage in securing wider publicity for the remedies outlined above. These parliamentary channels, whilst not perfect, also have to be set alongside the normal access to the media open to any citizen who wishes to advance a particular cause . . . The strongest safeguard against so-called abuses is the self-discipline of individual Members. This means, for instance, that a Member should take steps, before making a potentially damaging accusation against a named individual, to ensure not only that evidence exists but that it comes from a normally reliable source. This does not imply that a Member needs to have evidence that would satisfy a court, but that he should act on the basis of something firmer than mere rumour or supposition . . .

Appendix 7

Definition of proceedings in Parliament

[A *proposed* definition dating from the 1970 Joint Committee on the Publication of Proceedings in Parliament:]

(1) For the purpose of the defence of absolute privilege in an action or prosecution for defamation the expression "proceedings in Parliament" shall without prejudice to the generality thereof include

   (a) all things said done or written by a Member or by any Officer of either House of Parliament or by any person ordered or authorised to attend before such House, in or in the presence of such House and in the course of a sitting of such House, and for the purpose of the business being or about to be transacted, wherever such sitting may be held and whether or not it be held in the presence of strangers to such House: provided that for the purpose aforesaid the expression 'House' shall be deemed to include any Committee sub-Committee or other group or body of Members or Members and Officers of either House of Parliament appointed by or with the authority of such House for the purpose of carrying out any of the functions of or of representing such House; and

   (b) all things said done or written between Members or between Members and Officers of either House of Parliament or between Members and Ministers of the Crown for the purpose of enabling any Member or any such officer to carry out his functions as such provided that publication thereof be no wider than is reasonably necessary for that purpose.

(2) In this section "Member" means a Member of either House of Parliament; and "Officer of either House of Parliament" means any person not being a Member whose duties require him from time to time to participate in proceedings in Parliament as herein defined . . .

The recommended statutory definition of proceedings in Parliament arose from consideration of the Strauss case, which involved threatened libel proceedings, and it was subsequently commended by the Faulks Committee on Defamation. It is no doubt for these reasons that the definition is specifically limited to actions or prosecutions for defamation. The issues before the present Committee of

Privileges however have suggested that there might be other types of legal action where a definition of proceedings in Parliament would be helpful to a court, in the areas of the enforcement of injunctions and contempt of court. The Committee may wish to consider whether the proposed statutory definition might not with advantage be made general, by stating that it is for the purpose of defining the expression "proceedings in Parliament" contained in the 9th Article of the Bill of Rights, rather than for the purpose of the defence in a particular type of action. Such a definition might also be helpful to Members in providing a broad description, easily accessible in the Act of Parliament, of those parts of their functions as Members which are protected by absolute privilege . . .

[The definition in (1) (b) supra qualifies] closely the extent to which communications between Members should attract absolute privilege: first "all things said done or written between Members" must be "for the purpose of enabling any Member . . . to carry out his functions as such"; and secondly that "publication (of such communications) be no wider than is reasonably necessary for that purpose", so that the reasonableness would have to be decided in each case.'

See now, however, the very limited changes made by section 13 of the Defamation Act 1996 discussed above in the text.

(a) Members: their business interests and their independence

Most MPs do not live solely on their parliamentary salaries and other expense allowances—the cost of maintaining more than one house (London and the constituency) and of paying for research and other secretarial staff over and above that covered by allowances means that other income has to be found, either from employment, professional earnings or sponsorship. It is known that a certain few members do live very frugally in bed and breakfast accommodation and exist only on their parliamentary salaries, but this does not appeal to many. The fact that our MPs are not full-time legislators explains some of the oddities of parliamentary procedure—why, for example, the real business of Parliament does not get under way until the afternoon when it may be assumed lawyer members will have finished the day in court. The outside pay of MPs, however, raises another issue: can their independence be compromised by the sources of their outside earnings?

The House of Commons itself has taken the view since 1695 that it is illegal to offer money to a member for the purpose of promoting any issue in Parliament, a view repeated in 1858. Since 1945 the offer of money etc to members to induce them to ask parliamentary questions has been a breach of privilege. Since 1975 the House of Commons has required that a member should disclose any relevant pecuniary interest or benefit (direct or indirect) he/she may have, or may have had or may be expecting to have when taking part in debates or proceedings of the House or any of its committees' deliberations. However, the issue remains uncertain as to how far there may be overlapping jurisdictions between Parliament and the courts on this matter. While it is clear that the acceptance of a bribe by a member is a contempt punishable by the House of Commons, the Nolan Committee (see further below) has also argued that the *acceptance* of bribes could also constitute a common law offence.

It has only been since 1975 that there has been any obligation, however, on members to declare income additional to parliamentary salaries (and that only by resolution of the House of Commons). The change was made following an example of what has now come to be called 'sleaze'—a word connoting the financial misdoings of parliamentary figures. The questionable dealings under consideration can be traced back to 1963 when T Dan Smith, a leading local government politician on Tyneside, allegedly gave £250 to the then Leader of the House of Commons. There would have been nothing necessarily wrong with that, but Mr Smith was subsequently convicted of corruption offences and it transpired the 'gift' had been deliberately kept quiet. Following press criticism of such activities the Commons adopted the resolution referred to above that members must disclose relevant pecuniary etc interests in debate, etc. In due course there was also created a Register of Members' Interests 'to provide information of any pecuniary interest or other material benefit which a member . . . may receive which might be thought to affect his conduct as a member . . . or influence his actions, speeches or votes in Parliament'.

Over the years the requirements of registration have been tightened up so that members must now register: remuneration from company directorships; remuneration from employment, trading, professional and vocational activities; the names and other details of clients of lobbying companies for whom members have a parliamentary role; any gifts, benefits or hospitality received above specified levels; financial sponsorships; overseas visits consequential on membership of the Commons where the costs have not been borne by the individual member(s) involved or by public funds; payments, benefits or advantages received from foreign governments, organisations or persons; land or property producing a substantial income; names of companies in which members have share holdings above a specified level. So far as ministers are concerned the rules are even more strict, as they may not act as company directors and may not hold investments which could give rise to conflicts of interest with their responsibilities.

In 1994 the *Sunday Times* alleged that two Conservative MPs had accepted money in return for tabling questions of ministers in the House of Commons. The issue was referred to the Committee of Privileges which found the allegations substantiated and imposed penalties of 10 and 20 days' suspension respectively on the MPs in question.

The allegations made against Mr Tim Smith and Mr Neil Hamilton that they had accepted money in return for asking questions on a wealthy businessman's behalf which led to their resignation as ministers also had further consequences in the so-called 'cash for questions' affair.

In response to the public disquiet aroused by this affair the government created the Nolan Inquiry—The Committee on Standards in Public Life. The affair highlighted a number of issues. These were that there was no comprehensive statement of the standards expected of MPs in relation to external payments received, and indeed it was unclear whether there was a criminal offence of attempting to bribe a member, or of a member accepting a bribe. Furthermore, a feeling had grown up in Parliament that simply to register and declare interests was an adequate discharge of the obligations members have in respect of outside private interests—and that was open to question.[17]

The Nolan Committee was created as a standing body with a membership appointed for a three-year period. The Committee undertook a programme of inquiry into the general issue of standards of conduct in public life, and produced its first report in May 1995, *First Report on Standards in Public Life*.[18] In essence, with regard to Parliament, the Committee proposed that there should be a prohibition on agreements or other forms of connection between MPs and multi-client lobbying firms. It was also proposed that there should be a new Parliamentary Commissioner for Standards, together with a tightening up of the rules on the disclosure of interests and the avoidance of conflicts of interest, as well as a new Code of Conduct to be drawn up by the House of Commons for itself.

---

[17] See further Oliver, D, 'Standards of Conduct in Public Life—What Standards?' [1995] Public Law 497.
[18] Cm 2850.

A Commons Select Committee on Standards in Public Life reported in July 1995 and recommended acceptance in principle, though with some minor modifications, of all the Nolan proposals. The Commons itself accepted their Committee's report on 19 July 1995. In due course on 6 November 1995 the Commons further resolved that paid advocacy by members in respect of any speech, question, motion, introduction of legislation, or amendments to motions or to legislation should be forbidden. There is thus now a parliamentary rule against paid advocacy. It was, secondly, resolved that any member entering into an agreement for the provision of services in his/her capacity as a member should deposit the terms of that agreement with the Parliamentary Commissioner for Standards contemporaneously with entering these details in the Register of Members' Interests. The terms to be deposited include the amount of remuneration to be received by the member, within bands. The Commons further resolved to create a new Committee on Standards and Privileges which subsumed the roles of the former Privileges and Members' Interests Committees.

The Office of Parliamentary Commissioner for Standards has had a somewhat chequered existence, despite the existence of the Code of Conduct for Members of the House of Commons, dating from 1995, and the extensive guidance which has been issued on it, see further below. Controversy surfaced at the end of 2001 when it emerged some MPs were unhappy at the way in which the then Commissioner was going about her work, alleging over-zealous inquiries into complaints of failures to observe the Code, while others defended her as an independent public servant who was not given sufficient backing by the Standards and Privileges Committee, while moves were also in train to reduce the status of the office by reducing its hours from four to three days a week. The issue became politically even more controversial when the Commissioner sent a letter to the Speaker of the House alleging that her investigations on occasions had been obstructed by ministers, MPs and civil servants. This letter was 'leaked' to the media, and the Commissioner, who was about to leave her post, also argued that there had been a 'whispering campaign' about her suitability for the post since her appointment in 1999. The *Sunday Times* of 9 December 2001 illustrated how relations between the Commissioner and the House of Commons had deteriorated, with an erosion of trust and confidence on both sides, with a distinct impression on the part of the Commons that the Commissioner had investigated too many minor issues to the exclusion of, arguably, more important matters, while in defence of the Commissioner it was pointed out that she had insufficient staff and resources to undertake her tasks. On 20 December 2001 the Speaker stated that the Commissioner had failed to substantiate claims of the alleged 'whispering campaign'. The issued was referred to the Committee on Standards in Public Life (the Wicks Committee), while in February 2002 a new Commissioner was appointed. The Wicks Committee made its report in November 2002 and argued that the Commissioner should be seen as someone who holds an office paid for by the House of Commons, and who is appointed by that House, but is not an employee of the House so as to preserve the integrity and independence of the post. Legislation enshrining this principle has not been made, but the Standing orders of the House of Commons were amended in 2003 to provide that:

• the Commissioner will be appointed for a non-renewable term of five years;

• the Commissioner may only be dismissed as a result of a motion approved by the House following a reasoned report from the Committee on Standard and Privileges that the Commissioner is unable to function or is unfit for office;

• the Standards and Privileges Committee will consist of equal numbers of government and opposition members chaired by a member of the Opposition.

This goes some way to meeting the recommendation of the Wicks Committee, but does not provide the Commissioner with independent status and the power to call for witnesses and papers.

Since these alterations the current Commissioner has stressed his role as being one of education and the prevention of abuse. The guidance issued to MPs has been augmented and clarified, and minor infringements are unlikely to result in major formal investigations. It has been stressed, however, that MPs should not indulge in 'tit-for-tat' allegations against one another.

The Guide to the Rules Relating to the Conduct of Members
(HC papers 2005 351, 13 July 2005)

'Introduction

1. The purpose of this Guide is to assist Members in discharging the duties placed upon them by the Code of Conduct agreed by the House. It replaces the Guide approved by the House on 24 July 1996 (HC 688 (1995–96)).

2. No written guidance can provide for all circumstances; when in doubt Members should seek the advice of the Parliamentary Commissioner for Standards who, if necessary, will seek adjudication from the Committee on Standards and Privileges.

3. The Guide is divided into four Sections dealing with (1) Registration of Interests (paras 8–54); (2) Declaration of Interests (paras 55–70); (3) Lobbying for Reward or Consideration (paras 71–82); and (4) Procedure for Complaints (paras 83–93).

4. The Code of Conduct provides a framework within which acceptable conduct should be judged. The purpose of the Resolution of 6 November 1995 relating to "Conduct of Members" is to remove a major area of potential conflict of interest by prohibiting lobbying for reward or consideration. This Guide contains guidelines (para 75) to assist Members in applying the new rule. A further rule (para 82) deals with the conflict of interest that may arise when a Member holding a relevant financial interest takes part in a delegation involving the source of that interest.

5. Other Resolutions of the House, agreed on 19 July and 6 November 1995, supplement and strengthen the long established rules on disclosure of financial interest. The House has two distinct but related methods for the disclosure of the personal financial interests of its Members: registration of interests in a Register which is open for public inspection; and declaration of interest in the course of debate in the House and in other contexts. The main purpose of the Register is to give public notification on a continuous basis of those pecuniary interests held by Members which might be thought to influence their parliamentary conduct or actions. The main purpose of declaration of interest is to ensure that fellow Members of the House and the public are made aware, at the appropriate time when a Member is making a speech in the House or in Committee or participating in any other proceedings of the House, of any past, present or expected future pecuniary interest which might reasonably be thought to be relevant to those proceedings. The Resolution of 19 July 1995 provides for declaration of interest in respect of all written notices (para 60). The Resolution of 6 November 1995 relating to certain employment agreements requires the deposit of such agreements with the Commissioner for Standards (paras 49–54).

6. The rules described in this Guide derive their authority from Resolutions of the House, rather than from statute or common law, and are therefore enforceable by the House of Commons.

7. Ministers of the Crown who are Members of the House of Commons are subject to the rules of registration, declaration and advocacy in the same way as all other Members (although Ministerial office is not registrable and the restrictions imposed by the ban on lobbying for reward or consideration do not apply to Ministers when acting in the House as Ministers). In addition, Ministers are subject to further guidelines and requirements laid down by successive Prime Ministers in order to ensure that no conflict arises, nor appears to arise, between their private interests and their public duties

('The Ministerial Code'). These requirements are not enforced by the House of Commons and so are beyond the scope of this Guide.

Registration of Members' interests

Rules of the House

"Every Member of the House of Commons shall furnish to a Registrar of Members' Interests such particulars of his registrable interests as shall be required, and shall notify to the Registrar any alterations which may occur therein, and the Registrar shall cause these particulars to be entered in a Register of Members' Interests which shall be available for inspection by the public."

(Resolution of the House of 22 May 1974)

"For the purposes of the Resolution of the House of 22 May 1974 in relation of disclosure of interests in any proceeding of the House or its Committees, any interest declared in a copy of the Register of Members' Interests shall be regarded as sufficient disclosure for the purpose of taking part in any division of the House or in any of its Committees."

(Part of the Resolution of the House of 12 June 1975)

8. Under the Resolution agreed by the House on 22 May 1974, and under the Code of Conduct, Members are required to register their pecuniary interests in a Register of Members' Interests. The duty of compiling the Register rests with the Parliamentary Commissioner for Standards whose functions, set out in a Standing Order of the House, include those formerly exercised by the Registrar of Members' Interests.

Definition of the Register's purpose

9. The main purpose of the Register of Members' interests is "to provide information of any pecuniary interest or other material benefit which a Member receives which might reasonably be thought by others to influence his or her actions, speeches or votes in Parliament, or actions taken in his or her capacity as a Member of Parliament." [Select Committee on Members' Interests, First Report, Session 1991–92, "Registration and Declaration of Financial Interests", HC 326, paragraph 27.] The registration form specifies ten Categories of registrable interests which are described below. Apart from the specific rules, there is a more general obligation upon Members to keep the overall definition of the Register's purpose in mind when registering their interests.

10. The purpose of registration is openness. Registration of an interest does not imply any wrongdoing.

Duties of Members in respect of registration

11. Members of Parliament are required to complete a registration form and submit it to the Commissioner for Standards within three months of their election to the House (whether at a general election or a by-election). After the initial publication of the Register (or, in the case of Members returned at by-elections, after their initial registration) it is the responsibility of Members to notify changes in their registrable interests within four weeks of each change occurring.

12. Any Member having a registrable interest which has not at the time been registered, shall not undertake any action, speech or proceeding of the House (save voting) to which the registration would be relevant until notification has been given to the Commissioner for Standards of that interest.

13. Members are responsible for making a full disclosure of their interests, and if they have relevant interests which do not fall clearly into one or other of the specified categories, they are nonetheless expected to register them.

14. A reference in any Category to a spouse includes a Member's partner.

15. Interests the value of which does not exceed 1 per cent of the current parliamentary salary do not have to be registered. All single benefits of whatever kind which exceed that threshold should be

registered in the appropriate Category (unless a higher threshold is specified in the relevant Category). All benefits received from the same source in the course of a calendar year, which cumulatively amount to more than 1 per cent of the current parliamentary salary, should also be registered. In addition, if a Member considers that any benefit he or she has received falls within the definition of the main purpose of the Register set out in paragraph 9, even though it does not exceed the 1 per cent threshold, the Member should register it in the appropriate Category or under Category 10 (Miscellaneous).

Publication and public inspection

16. The Register is published soon after the beginning of a new Parliament, under the authority of the Committee on Standards and Privileges, and annually thereafter. Between publications the Register is regularly updated in a loose leaf form and, in that form, is available for public inspection in the Committee Office of the House of Commons. At the discretion of the Commissioner copies of individual entries in the Register may be supplied on request. However, the employment agreements deposited with the Commissioner which relate to registered interests (para 35) are available for personal inspection only.

The Categories of registrable interest

[Note: Each of the [categories] in this section contains a description of one of the Categories of interest which the House has agreed should be registered and which appear in the registration form]

Category 1

Directorships: Remunerated directorships in public and private companies including directorships which are individually unremunerated, but where remuneration is paid through another company in the same group.

17. In this Category, and in others, "remuneration" includes not only salaries and fees, but also the receipt of any taxable expenses, allowances, or benefits, such as the provision of a company car. Remuneration which in the course of a calendar year does not exceed 1 per cent of the current parliamentary salary may be disregarded. It is necessary to register the name of the company in which the directorship is held and to give a broad indication of the company's business, where that is not self-evident from its name. In addition to any remunerated directorships, a Member is also required to register any directorships he or she holds which are themselves unremunerated but where the companies in question are associated with, or subsidiaries of, a company in which he or she holds a remunerated directorship. Otherwise, Members are not required to register unremunerated directorships (see Category 10).

18. Companies which have not begun to trade or which have ceased trading need not be registered, either under this Category or under Category 9 (shareholdings). "Not trading" should, however, be interpreted in a strict sense; if a company is engaged in any transaction in addition to those required by law to keep it in being, then a remunerated directorship in that company should be registered. If a Member wishes to register a directorship in a company which is not trading the Minister should make the position clear by adding the words "not trading" after the name of the company.

Category 2

Remunerated employment, office, profession, etc: Employment, office trade, profession or vocation (apart from membership of the House or ministerial office) which is remunerated or in which the Member has any pecuniary interest. Membership of Lloyd's should be registered under this Category.

19. All employment outside the House and any sources of remuneration which do not fall clearly within any other Category should be registered here if the value of the remuneration exceeds 1 per cent of the current parliamentary salary. When registering employment, Members should not simply state the employer company and the nature of its business, but should also indicate the nature of the

post which they hold in the company or the services for which the company remunerates them. Members who have paid posts as consultants or advisers should indicate the nature of the consultancy, for example "management consultant", "legal adviser", "parliamentary and public affairs consultant".

20. Members who have resigned from Lloyd's should continue to register their interest as long as syndicates in which they participated continue to have years of account which are open or in run-off. The date of resignation should be registered in such circumstances. Members of Lloyd's are also required to disclose the categories of insurance business which they are underwriting. Any member of Lloyd's receiving financial assistance (including relief from indebtedness or other loan concessions but excluding any general settlement available to all Lloyd's members) from a company, organisation or person within or outside the United Kingdom should register that interest under Categories 5 or 7, as appropriate.

21. Members who have previously practised a profession may wish to register that profession under this Category with a bracketed remark such as "[non practising]" after the entry. This is particularly desirable in cases of sleeping partnerships and where it is likely that the Member will resume the profession at a later stage.

22. Further guidance about media work is given in paragraph 54.

Category 3

Clients: In respect of any paid employment registered in Category 1 (Directorships) and Category 2 (Remunerated employment, office, profession, etc.), any provision to clients of services which depend essentially upon, or arise out of, the Member's position as a Member of Parliament should be registered under this Category. All clients to which personal services are provided should be listed together with the nature of the client's business in each case. Where a Member receives remuneration from a company or partnership engaged in consultancy business which itself has clients, the Member should list any of those clients to whom personal services or advice is provided, either directly or indirectly.

23. The types of services which are intended to be covered here include those connected with any parliamentary proceedings, or other services relating to membership. A Member who has clients in a non-parliamentary professional capacity (for example as a doctor, solicitor or accountant) is not required to register those clients, provided it is clear beyond doubt that the services which are being provided do not arise out of or relate in any manner to membership of the House.

24. Under this Category, if a Member is employed as a parliamentary adviser by a firm which is itself a consultancy and therefore is providing such advice and services to its clients, the Member should disclose those of the consultancy's clients with whom he or she has a personal connection or who benefit from the Member's advice and services. The same requirement applies where a Member, on his or her own account, accepts payment or material benefit for providing such services, but not on such a regular basis as to warrant registration as employment under Category 2. Where a company is named as a client, the nature of the company's business should be indicated.

Category 4

Sponsorships:

(a) Any donation received by a Member's constituency association which is linked either to candidacy at an election or to membership of the House; and

(b) any other form of financial or material support as a Member of Parliament,

amounting to more than £1,000 from a single source, whether as a single donation or as multiple donations of more than £200 during the course of a calendar year.

25. This Category deals with sponsorship or other forms of support by companies, trade unions, professional bodies, trade associations, other organisations and individuals. Political donations which

Members are required to report to the Electoral Commission should be entered under this Category unless —

a) it would be more appropriate to enter them under another Category, such as Category 5 (Gifts, benefits and hospitality (UK)) or Category 6 (Overseas visits); or

b) they are exempt from registration.

26. Category 4(a) deals with financial contributions to *constituency associations*. Support should be regarded as "linked" directly to a Member's candidacy or membership of the House if it is expressly tied to the Member by name, e.g. if it is a contribution to the Member's fighting fund or a donation which has been solicited or encouraged by the Member. Financial contributions to constituency associations which are not linked to a Member's candidacy or membership of the House do not have to be registered.

27. Category 4(b) covers support from which the Member receives any financial or material benefit in support of his or her role as a Member of Parliament. (Any contribution for the *personal benefit* of a Member should be entered under Category 5 (Gifts, benefits and hospitality (UK)).) The types of support which should be registered under this Category include the services of a research assistant or secretary whose salary, in whole or in part, is met by an outside organisation or individual; the provision of free or subsidised accommodation for the Member's use, other than accommodation provided by a local authority to a Member for the sole purpose of holding constituency surgeries or accommodation provided solely by the constituency party; and financial contributions towards such services or accommodation.

Category 5

Gifts, benefits and hospitality (UK): Any gift to the Member or the Member's spouse or partner, of any material benefit, of a value greater than 1 per cent of the current parliamentary salary from any company, organisation or person within the UK which in any way relates to membership of the House.

28. The specified financial value above which tangible gifts (such as money, jewellery, glassware etc.), or other benefits (such as hospitality, tickets to sporting and cultural events, relief from indebtedness, loan concessions, provision of services etc.) must be registered is 1 per cent of a Member's annual parliamentary salary.

29. The rule means that any gift, or other benefit, which in any way relates to membership of the House and which is given gratis, or at a cost below that generally available to members of the public, should be registered whenever the value of the gift or benefit is greater than the amounts specified . . . above. Any similar gift or benefit which is received by any company or organisation in which the Member, or the Member and the Member's spouse jointly, have a controlling interest should also be registered.

30. Gifts and other benefits from the same source in the course of a calendar year which *cumulatively* are of a value greater than 1 per cent of the current parliamentary salary should be registered, even if each single gift or benefit is of lesser value.

31. Benefits, such as tickets to sporting or cultural events, received by another person together with or on behalf of a Member should be registered as if they had been received by the Member.

32. Gifts, or other benefits, from another Member of Parliament are registrable in the same way as those from anyone else.

33. There are three important exceptions to this rule:

a) gifts and benefits known to be available to all Members of Parliament need not be registered;

b) a Member need not register attendance at a conference or a site visit within the United Kingdom where the organiser meets reasonable travel costs and subsistance only; and

c) hospitality provided by Her Majesty's Government, any of the devolved institutions in Scotland, Wales or Northern Ireland, or non-departmental public bodies, including a Member's local authorities or health authorities, is exempt from registration.

34. Gifts and material benefits in this Category (and other Categories) are exempt from registration if they do not relate in any way to membership of the House. The extent to which this exemption applies in any particular case is necessarily a matter of judgement. Both the possible motive of the giver and the use to which the gift is put have to be considered: if it is clear on both counts that the gift or benefit is entirely unrelated to membership of the House, or would not reasonably be thought by others to be so related, it need not be registered. If there is any doubt it should be registered.

Category 6

Overseas visits: With certain specified exceptions, overseas visits made by the Member or the Member's spouse or partner relating to or in any way arising out of membership of the House where the cost of the visit was not wholly borne by the Member or by United Kingdom public funds.

35. The Member should enter in the Register the date, destination and purpose of the visit and the name of the Government, organisation, company or individual which met the cost. Where only part of the cost was borne by an outside source (for example the cost of accommodation but not the cost of travel), those details should be stated briefly. When an overseas visit was arranged by a registered All-Party or parliamentary group or by a party backbench group, it is not sufficient to name the group as the sponsor of the visit: the Government, organisation, company or person ultimately meeting the cost should be specified.

36. The following categories of visit, which are mainly paid for from United Kingdom public funds or which involve reciprocity of payment with other Governments or Parliaments, together with any hospitality associated with such a visit and available to all participants, are exempt from registration:—

(i) Visits which are paid for by, or which are undertaken on behalf of, Her Majesty's Government or which are made on behalf of an international organisation to which the United Kingdom Government belongs;

(ii) Visits abroad with, or on behalf of, a Select Committee of the House or undertaken under a Resolution of the House;

(iii) Visits undertaken on behalf of, or under the auspices of, the Commonwealth Parliamentary Association, the Inter-Parliamentary Union (or the British-Irish Parliamentary Body), the British American Parliamentary Group, the Council of Europe, the Western European Union, the Westminster Foundation for Democracy, the North Atlantic Assembly, the OSCE Parliamentary Assembly, the Armed Forces Parliamentary Scheme, the Police Service Parliamentary Scheme, or the National Council for Voluntary Organisations' MP Secondment Scheme;

(iv) Visits arranged and paid for wholly by a Member's own political party;

(v) Visits paid for wholly by an institution of the European Union or by a political group of the European Parliament;

(vi) Visits as part of an Industry and Parliament Trust fellowship.

Similar categories of visit may be added to this list from time to time by the Committee on Standards and Privileges. Visits which are entirely unconnected with membership of the House, or the cost of which does not exceed 1 per cent of the current parliamentary salary, are also exempt from registration.

37. The financial limits and guidelines which apply to Category 5 also apply here. Members should enter a cross-reference under this Category where an interest already entered in Categories 1, 2 or 3 entails the receipt of payments from abroad. There are legal restrictions on Members' accepting benefits from abroad in connection with their political activities, about which they may wish to take advice.

Category 8

Land and property: Any land or property—

(a) which has a substantial value (unless used for the personal residential purposes of the Member or the Member's spouse or partner), or

(b) from which a substantial income is derived.

The nature of the property should be indicated.

38. Property used for the personal residential purposes of the Member or the Member's spouse or partner (that is, homes and second homes) does not need to be registered under Category 8(a). It *may* need to be registered under Category 8(b), but only if the Member derives an income from it *and* derives a *substantial* income from his total property portfolio (see paragraph 40). A property, such as a farm, on which the Member has a residence should be registered if it has a substantial value aside from the residential use.

39. "Substantial value" means a value greater than the current parliamentary salary. If a Member's total property portfolio (*excluding* homes and second homes) has a substantial value it should be registered.

40. "Substantial income" means an income greater than 10 per cent of the current parliamentary salary. If the income from a Member's total property portfolio (*including* homes and second homes) is substantial, all the properties from which any income is derived should be registered.

41. Entries should be reasonably specific as to the nature of the property and its general location, for example:-

"Woodland in Perthshire"

"Dairy farm in Wiltshire"

"3 residential rented properties in Manchester".

Category 9

Shareholdings: Interests in shareholdings held by the Member, either personally, or with or on behalf of the Member's spouse or partner or dependent children, in any public or private company or other body which are:

(a) greater than 15 per cent of the issued share capital of the company or body; or

(b) 15 per cent or less of the issued share capital, but greater in value than the current parliamentary salary.

The nature of the company's business in each case should be registered.

42. When determining whether or not shareholdings are registrable under the criteria set out above, Members should include not only holdings in which they themselves have a beneficial interest but also those in which the interest is held with, or on behalf of, their spouse or partner or dependent children. Members should also include identifiable holdings of overseas trusts of which they are actual or potential beneficiaries.

43. For each registrable shareholding, the entry should state the name of the company or body, briefly indicate the nature of its business, and make clear which of the criteria for registration is applicable.

44. The value of a shareholding is determined by the market price of the share on the preceding 5th April; but if the market price cannot be ascertained (e.g. because the company is unquoted and there is no market in the shares), the nominal value of the shareholding should be taken instead. Interests in shareholdings include share options.

45. In considering whether to register any shareholdings falling outside (a) and (b) Members should have regard to the definition of the main purpose of the Register: "to provide information of any

pecuniary interest or other material benefit which a Member receives which might reasonably be thought by others to influence his or her actions, speeches or votes in Parliament, or actions taken in his or her capacity as a Member of Parliament". If a Member considers that any shareholding which he or she holds falls within this definition, the Member should register the shareholding either in this Category or under Category 10.

Category 10

Miscellaneous: Any relevant interest, not falling within one of the above categories, which nevertheless falls within the definition of the main purpose of the Register which is "to provide information of any pecuniary interest or other material benefit which a Member receives which might reasonably be thought by others to influence his or her actions, speeches, or votes in Parliament, or actions taken in his or her capacity as a Member of Parliament", or which the Member considers might be thought by others to influence his or her actions in a similar manner, even though the Member receives no financial benefit.

46. The main purpose of this Category is to enable Members to enter in the Register any interests which they consider to be relevant to the Register's purpose, but which do not obviously fall within any of the other Categories. As the Select Committee on Members' Interests pointed out in its First Report of Session 1991–92: "it is a cardinal principle that Members are responsible for making a full disclosure of their own interests in the Register; and if they have relevant interests which do not fall clearly into one or other of the specified Categories, they will nonetheless be expected to register them". (Op cit, para 29.)

47. Members should register under this category potential or actual interests in overseas trusts, except where these have been registered under Category 9.

48. The general principle of the Register is that the requirement to register is limited to interests entailing remuneration or other material benefit. (Ibid, para 31.) Members are not, therefore, required by the rules to register unremunerated directorships (eg directorships of charitable trusts, professional bodies, learned societies or sporting or artistic organisations) and the Category should not be used to itemise these or other unremunerated interests. However, when a Member considers that an unremunerated interest which the Member holds might be thought by others to influence his or her actions in a similar manner to a remunerated interest, such an interest may be registered here.

Agreements for the provision of services

"Any Member proposing to enter into an agreement which involves the provision of services in his capacity as a Member of Parliament shall conclude such an agreement only if it conforms to the Resolution of the House of 6th November 1995 relating to Conduct of Members; and a full copy of any such agreement including the fees or benefits payable in bands of: up to £5,000, £5,001–£10,000, and thereafter in bands of £5,000, shall be deposited with the Parliamentary Commissioner for Standards at the same time as it is registered in the Register of Members' Interests and made available for inspection and reproduction by the public.

Any Member who has an existing agreement involving the provision of services in his capacity as a Member of Parliament which conforms to the Resolution of the House of 6 November 1995 relating to Conduct of Members, but which is not in written form, shall take steps to put the agreement in written form; and no later than 31 March 1996 a full copy of any such agreement including the fees or benefits payable in bands of: up to £5,000, £5,001–£10,000, and thereafter in bands of £5,000 shall be deposited with the Parliamentary Commissioner for Standards and registered in the Register of Members' Interests and made available for inspection and reproduction by the public.

Provided that the requirement to deposit a copy of an agreement with the Commissioner shall not apply—

(a) if the fees or benefits payable do not exceed 1 per cent of the current parliamentary salary; nor

(b) in the case of media work (but in that case the Member shall deposit a statement of the fees or benefits payable in the bands specified above)."

(Part of a Resolution of the House of 6 November 1995, amended on 14 May 2002)

49. Under a Resolution of the House of 6 November 1995 the House agreed that Members should deposit certain employment agreements with the Parliamentary Commissioner for Standards. The two Resolutions set out above have continuing effect. Any Member who has an existing agreement or proposes to enter into an agreement which involves the provision of services in his or her capacity as a Member of Parliament should:

— ensure that the agreement does not breach the ban on lobbying for reward or consideration (see paras 71–82 below);

— put any such agreement in written form;

— deposit a full copy of the agreement with the Parliamentary Commissioner for Standards. The agreement should indicate the nature of the services to be provided and specify the fees or benefits the Member is to receive in bands of (1) up to £5,000; (2) £5,001–£10,000 (and thereafter in bands of £5,000).

— make the appropriate entry in the Register of Members' Interests; and

— declare the interest when it is appropriate to do so (see paras 55–70).

Deposited agreements may be inspected in the Committee Office of the House of Commons. The terms of the Resolution of the House do not permit the taking of copies.

50. If the fees or benefits the Member is to receive do not exceed 1 per cent of the current parliamentary salary, the Member is not required to deposit a copy of the agreement with the Commissioner. Nor is the Member required to specify the fees or benefits, or to register the interest.

51. The Select Committee on Standards in Public Life (Select Committee on Standards in Public Life, Second Report, Session 1994–95, HC 816, p. xi) gave the guidance in respect of their application of the rule:—

"The present rule is that all remunerated outside employment must be included in the Register, irrespective of whether it has any bearing on a Member's actions in Parliament. We have no doubt that this discipline should continue to be observed.

If our recommendation that paid advocacy in Parliament should be prohibited altogether is adopted by the House, it is essential that no future agreements should require Members to take part in activities which can be described as advocacy.

The new requirement for employment agreements to be put in writing will apply principally to any arrangement whereby a Member may offer advice about parliamentary matters. We think it right, however, that it should also include frequent, as opposed to merely occasional, commitments outside Parliament which arise directly from membership of the House. For example, a regular, paid newspaper column or television programme would have to be the subject of a written agreement, but ad hoc current affairs or news interviews or intermittent panel appearances would not.

It may not always be immediately obvious whether a particular employment agreement arises directly from, or relates directly to, membership of the House. At one end of the spectrum are those Members whose outside employment pre-dates their original election, whilst at the other extreme are those who have taken up paid adviserships since entering the House. In between there will be many cases which are difficult to classify. Some Members, for example, may provide advice on

Parliamentary matters incidentally as part of a much wider employment agreement covering matters wholly unrelated to the House. In these circumstances, it would be for an individual Member to decide how far it would be proper to isolate the Parliamentary services within a separate, depositable agreement; in reaching that decision he may wish to consult the Commissioner."

52. On the basis of this guidance the Committee on Standards and Privileges has agreed that disclosing the remuneration for parliamentary services separately from remuneration for other services would be justified only in exceptional circumstances; eg where the parliamentary services are separately identifiable and form only a small proportion of the services as a whole. In any such case the entry in the Register should make it clear that the remuneration is for parliamentary services as part of a wider agreement.

53. The scope of the Resolutions is not limited to employment registered under Category 2 (remunerated employment, office, profession, etc.) but includes other forms of employment, such as directorships (including non-executive directorships), when these involve the provision of services by the Member in his or her capacity as a Member of Parliament.

54. The following provisions apply to media work (journalism, broadcasting, speaking engagements, media appearances, training, &c.):

a. The deposit of an agreement for the provision of services is not required.

b. Instead Members who register any form of media work under Category 2 (Remunerated employment, office, profession, etc.) should declare the remuneration, or value of the reward, they receive for each commitment, or group of commitments for the same organisation or audience in the same calendar year, in bands of (1) up to £5,000; (2) £5,001–£10,000 (and thereafter in bands of £5,000).

c. But such declarations are not required—
   i) for media work which is wholly unrelated to parliamentary affairs, such as a sports column in a newspaper, or
   ii) in any case where in the course of a calendar year total remuneration received from an employer or client, or through an agency, does not exceed 1 per cent of the current parliamentary salary.

Declaration of Members' interests

Rules of the House

"In any debate or proceeding of the House or its Committees or transactions or communications which a Member may have with other Members or with Ministers or servants of the Crown, he shall disclose any relevant pecuniary interest or benefit of whatever nature, whether direct or indirect, that he may have had, may have or may be expecting to have."

(Resolution of the House of 22 May 1974)

"For the purposes of the Resolution of the House of 22 May 1974 in relation to disclosure of interests in any proceeding of the House or its Committees,

(i) Any interest declared in a copy of the Register of Members' Interests shall be regarded as sufficient disclosure for the purpose of taking part in any division of the House or in any of its Committees.

(ii) The term 'proceeding' shall be deemed not to include the asking of a supplementary question."

(Resolution of the House of 12 June 1975, amended on 19 July 1995)

"This House takes note of the First Report from the Select Committee on Members' Interests, Session 1990–91 (House of Commons Paper No 108), relating to the interests of Chairmen and members of Select Committees, and approves the recommendations of the Committee relating to declaration of interest in Select Committees (paras 8 to 16), withdrawal from Committee proceedings (para 24) and procedures prior to the election of a Chairman (para 25)."

(Resolution of the House of 13 July 1992: Members' Interests (Interests of Chairmen and members of Select Committees)

55. In 1974 the House replaced a long standing convention with a rule that any relevant pecuniary interest or benefit of whatever nature, whether direct or indirect, should be declared in debate, or other proceeding. The same rule places a duty on Members to disclose to Ministers, or servants of the Crown, all relevant interests. The term "servants of the Crown" should be interpreted as applying to the staff of executive agencies as well as to all staff employed in government departments.

Past and potential interests

56. The rule relating to declaration of interest is broader in scope than the rules relating to the registration of interests in two important respects. As well as current interests, Members are required to declare both relevant past interests and relevant interests which they may be expecting to have. In practice only interests held in the recent past, ie those contained in the current printed edition of the Register, need normally be considered for declaration. Expected future interests, on the other hand, may be more significant. Where, for example, a Member is debating legislation or making representations to a Minister on a matter from which he has a reasonable expectation of personal financial advantage, candour is essential. In deciding when a possible future benefit is sufficiently tangible to necessitate declaration, the key word in the rule which the Member must bear in mind is 'expecting'. Where a Member's plans or degree of involvement in a project have passed beyond vague hopes and aspirations and reached the stage where there is a reasonable expectation that a financial benefit will accrue, then a declaration explaining the situation should be made.

Relevance

57. It is the responsibility of the Member, having regard to the rules of the House, to judge whether a pecuniary interest is sufficiently relevant to a particular debate, proceeding, meeting or other activity to require a declaration. The basic test of relevance should be the same for declaration as it is for registration of an interest; namely, that a pecuniary interest should be declared if it might reasonably be thought by others to influence the speech, representation or communication in question. A declaration should be brief but sufficiently informative to enable a listener to understand the nature of the Member's interest.

58. The House has endorsed the following advice on the occasions when such a declaration of interest should be made: "no difficulty should arise in any proceeding of the House or its Committees in which the Member has an opportunity to speak. Such proceedings, in addition to debates in the House, include debates in Standing Committees, the presentation of a Public Petition, and meetings of Select Committees at which evidence is heard. On all such occasions the Member will declare his interest at the beginning of his remarks . . . it will be a matter of judgement, if his interest is already recorded in the Register, whether he simply draws attention to this or makes a rather fuller disclosure." [Select Committee on Members' Interests (Declaration), First Report, Session 1974–75, HC 102, para 43; approved by the House, 12 June 1975.] Any declaration "should be sufficiently informative to enable a listener to understand the nature of the Member's pecuniary interest . . .". [Select Committee on Members' Interests, First Report, Session 1991–92, op cit, para 80.]

59. In a debate in the House the Member should declare an interest briefly, usually at the beginning of his or her speech. If the House is dealing with the Committee or Consideration stages of a Bill it will normally be sufficient for the Member to declare a relevant interest when speaking for the first time. In Standing Committee Members should declare relevant interests at the first meeting of the Committee or on the first occasion on which they address the Committee. It will not be necessary for a declaration to be repeated at subsequent meetings except when the Member speaks on an Amendment to which the interest is particularly relevant. When giving notice of an Amendment or a Motion (including a Motion for leave to introduce a "Ten Minute Rule" Bill), giving notice of the presentation of a Bill or adding a name to an Amendment or Motion, Members should declare any relevant interest in the appropriate manner (see paras 60–63 below).

Declaration of interest in respect of written notices

60. On 19 July 1995 the House agreed, with effect from the beginning of Session 1995–96, to extend the rules relating to declaration of interest by abolishing the exemption granted to the giving of written notices in the Resolution of 22 May 1974. Declaration of relevant interest is required on the Order Paper (or Notice Paper) when tabling any written notice, ie:

(a) Questions (for oral or written answer, including Private Notice Questions);

(b) Early Day Motions, Amendments to them, or any names added in support of such Motions or Amendments;

(c) a notice of a Motion for leave to introduce a "Ten Minute Rule" Bill;

(d) a notice for the presentation of a Bill (including a "Ballot" Bill);

(e) any other Motions, Amendments, or added names in support of them;

(f) Amendments to Bills (whether to be considered in the House or in a Committee) and any names added in support of them.

61. Whenever such an interest is declared, the symbol "[R]" is printed after the Member's name on the Notice Paper or Order Paper. The office accepting the written notice (including any written notice of a Member adding his or her name to a Motion or an Amendment) assumes that no interest is declarable unless the notice clearly indicates a declaration: this should be done by inserting "[R]" after the Member's name on the Motion or Amendment, as the case may be, or filling in the appropriate box which appears on the form for parliamentary Questions.

62. "Relevant interests" which should be declared include any interest which the Member is required to register in the Register of Members' Interests, or which the Member should declare in debate. It will therefore usually be the case that the interest to which the Member is drawing the attention of the House will already be entered in the Register. Provided it is readily apparent which of the Member's registered interests are applicable, the Member need take no further action. If this is not the case, or if the interest is a new interest which is not yet available for inspection in the Register, then the Member when giving notice should attach to that notice a brief written description of the interest which is being declared. This will then be available for inspection by Members in the Office where the notice was given: viz; the Table Office, the Public Bill Office, or the Private Bill Office. In the case of Private Notice Questions which are allowed, a Member with a relevant interest should declare that interest when the Question is formally asked in the House.

63. All Members need to exercise particular care when invited to add their names to any EDMs or other Motions or Amendments and to ensure that they have considered whether they have a relevant declarable interest. Given the informal way in which support for Motions and Amendments is often sought, the need for declaration may not be foremost in Members' minds, but great care needs to be exercised by Members in these circumstances.

Declaration of interest in applications for adjournment or emergency debates

64. Requests for emergency debates under Standing Order No 24 and applications for daily adjournment debates and adjournment debates in Westminster Hall are made to the Speaker. Such applications should be accompanied by a declaration of any relevant interest. When a Member is notified that he or she had been successful in obtaining an adjournment debate it is the Member's responsibility to notify the Table Office and to ensure that an indication of the relevant interest appears at the earliest opportunity on the Notice Paper or Order Paper. The procedure will be similar to that for written notices described in paragraph 60. If the Speaker allows a Member to present an application to the House for an emergency debate under Standing Order No 24 a Member with a relevant interest should begin his or her remarks to the House with a declaration of that interest.

Declaration of interest in Select Committees

65. Members of Select Committees on any matter or Bill are bound by the Resolution of the House of 13 July 1992 which approved certain paragraphs of a Report by the Select Committee on Members' Interests relating to the financial interests of Chairmen and Members of Select Committees. [Select Committee on Members' Interests, First Report, Session 1990–91, HC 108. The paragraphs which the House specifically approved were: 8–16, 24 and 25. The references in square brackets relate to the paragraphs in that Report.] The main provisions are:

— before the Committee proceeds to the election of a Chairman all Members nominated to serve upon a Select Committee are required to send to the Clerk of the Committee details of any pecuniary interests for circulation to the Committee under the authority of the senior Member before its first meeting. The procedure is not necessary in the case of Select Committees of a wholly procedural nature. [Para 25]

— "when a member of a Committee, particularly the Chairman, has a pecuniary interest which is directly affected by a particular inquiry or when he or she considers that a personal interest may reflect upon the work of the Committee or its subsequent Report, the Member should stand aside from the Committee proceedings relating to it". [Para 24]

— "before proceeding to business after the election of the Chairman, the Chairman of the Committee should invite all members of the Committee to declare any interests they may have which relate to the terms of reference of that Committee, or which are likely to be relevant to a substantial part of the work which the Committee may be expected to undertake". [Para 13]

— "A Member should make a declaration of interest at an early stage in any inquiry to which that interest particularly relates. If the interest is especially relevant to one witness or group of witnesses appearing before the Committee, the interest should be declared again at the appropriate session of evidence." [Para 13]

— A Member is required to "declare an interest when asking any questions which relate directly, or which might reasonably be thought by others to relate directly, to the pecuniary interest he or she holds . . . Such a declaration must be made irrespective of any declaration having been made at an earlier meeting of the Committee". One such declaration is sufficient for any questions asked of the same witnesses during one evidence Session. [Para 13]

— "Although the main purpose of declaration of interest is to inform colleagues, it is right that witnesses and the public, if the Committee is meeting in public, should also be informed. When a Committee meets in public, declaration of interest should be in public Session. When a Committee meets in private and regularly takes oral evidence, declaration should be made when witnesses are present." [Para 13]

— "In making any declaration a Member should clearly identify the nature of the pecuniary interest. The form in which a declaration of interest is made, and its extent, must be primarily for the individual Member." A casual reference is not sufficient. "A Member should make a declaration in clear terms and should ensure that such a declaration is entered in the Minutes of Proceedings of the Committee." [Para 14]

— It is "perfectly acceptable for a Member, when declaring an interest which is registered in the Register of Members' Interests . . . to refer to his or her entry in the Register". [Para 16]

— "we stress the importance of declaration when relevant and of declaring a pecuniary interest at the moment when it is most appropriate to do so. We do not wish to create a situation where the proceedings of Committees are frequently interrupted by declarations of tangential relevance to what is being considered . . . the interests that a Member is required to register may not be at all relevant to his or her work on the Select Committee and consequently may never need to be declared during its proceedings." [Para 16]

66. Where the subject matter of an inquiry of a Select Committee is of direct concern to an outside body in which a Member has a pecuniary interest, the Member must consider whether on grounds of

conflict of interest it is proper to take part in the inquiry. The Member must also consider whether the relationship of his or her interest to the subject of the inquiry is so close that it is not possible to participate effectively in the inquiry without crossing the borderline into advocacy.

Rule on declaration of interests relating to Private Bills

67. Under Standing Order 120 relating to Private Business a Member nominated by the Committee of Selection to serve on a Committee on a Private Bill is required to sign a declaration "that my constituents have no local interest, and I have no personal interest, in the said Bill". To be disqualified the Member's interest must be a direct interest where there is a potential benefit or disadvantage to the Member arising from the matter in issue; or the constituency interest must be a local interest affecting the constituency as a whole or a significant number of constituents. Where a Member is in doubt, the Clerk of Private Bills should be consulted.

Other occasions when declaration of interest should be considered

68. The requirement to declare a relevant interest **at the appropriate time** covers almost every aspect of a Member's parliamentary duties extending to correspondence and meetings with Ministers and public officials. Frankness with colleagues is also important. In 1975 the House agreed to the report of the Select Committee on Members' Interests (Declaration) which contained these words: "it should be a matter of honour that a pecuniary interest is declared not only, as at present, in debate in the House and its Committees but also whenever a Member is attempting to influence his fellow Members, whether in unofficial committees and gatherings or at any kind of sponsored occasion, with or without entertainment, or simply in correspondence or conversation. Above all it should be disclosed when a Member is dealing with Ministers of the Crown and civil servants, and this obligation becomes of paramount importance when a foreign government is involved either directly or indirectly". [Select Committee on Members' Interests (Declaration), First Report, Session 1974–75, HC 102, para 40 (quoting the Report of the Select Committee on Members' Interests (Declaration), Session 1969–70, HC 57).]

69. In its application of the 1974 Resolution the House has always recognised that there are certain proceedings where declaration of interest is impracticable; eg during oral Questions or when asking a question in response to ministerial statement on a matter of public policy or supplementary to a Private Notice Question. (The Member asking the Question should, however, declare an interest; see paragraphs 42–44.) However, Members are advised to declare any relevant interest when such a declaration does not unduly impede the business of the House, for example in relation to a request for a debate made in response to a Business Question or statement.

Divisions

70. For the purpose of taking part in any division in the House or in Committee, it is sufficient for the relevant interest to be disclosed in the Register of Members' Interests. A Member should seek to ensure prior to a vote taking place that any relevant interest is registered, or, where it is not, should register the interest immediately after the vote.

Lobbying for reward or consideration

The 1947 and 1995 Resolutions

71. On 6 November 1995 the House agreed to the following Resolution relating to lobbying for reward or consideration:—

"It is inconsistent with the dignity of the House, with the duty of a Member to his constituents, and with the maintenance of the privilege of freedom of speech, for any Member of this House to enter into any contractual agreement with an outside body, controlling or limiting the Member's complete independence and freedom of action in Parliament or stipulating that he shall act in any way as the representative of such outside body in regard to any matters to be transacted in Parliament; the duty of a Member being to his constituents and to the country as a whole, rather than to any particular section thereof: and that in particular no Members of the House shall, in consideration of any remuneration, fee, payment, or reward or benefit in kind, direct or indirect, which the Member or any member of his or her family has received is receiving or expects to receive—

(i) advocate or initiate any cause or matter on behalf of any outside body or individual, or

(ii) urge any other Member of either House of Parliament, including Ministers, to do so,

by means of any speech, Question, Motion, introduction of a Bill or Amendment to a Motion or a Bill or any approach whether oral or in writing to Ministers or servants of the Crown."

. . .

72. This Resolution prohibits paid advocacy. It is wholly incompatible with the advocacy rule that any Member should take payment for speaking in the House. Nor may a Member, for payment, vote, ask a Parliamentary Question, table a Motion, introduce a Bill or table or move an Amendment to a Motion or Bill or urge colleagues or Ministers to do so.

73. The Resolution does not prevent a Member from holding a remunerated outside interest as a director, consultant, or adviser, or in any other capacity, whether or not such interests are related to membership of the House. Nor does it prevent a Member from being sponsored by a trade union or any other organisation, or holding any other registrable interest, or from receiving hospitality in the course of his or her parliamentary duties whether in the United Kingdom or abroad.

74. The Resolution extends and reinforces an earlier Resolution of the House in 1947 that a Member may not enter into any contractual arrangement which fetters the Member's complete independence in Parliament by any undertaking to press some particular point of view on behalf of an outside interest. (Committee of Privileges, Report, Session 1946–47, HC 118, paras 11 to 15.) Nor, by virtue of the same Resolution, may an outside body (or person) use any contractual arrangement with a Member of Parliament as an instrument by which it controls, or seeks to control, his or her conduct in Parliament, or to punish that Member for any parliamentary action. [Committee of Privileges, Second Report, Session 1974–75, HC 634, para 3.]

75. In addition to the requirements of the advocacy rule, Members should also bear in mind the long established convention that interests which are wholly personal and particular to the Member, and which may arise from a profession or occupation outside the House, ought not to be pursued by the Member in proceedings in Parliament.

Guidelines on the application of the ban on lobbying for reward or consideration

76. If a financial interest is required to be registered in the Register of Members' Interests, or declared in debate, it falls within the scope of the ban on lobbying for reward or consideration. The Committee on Standards and Privileges has provided the following Guidelines to assist Members in applying the rule:

1. *Parliamentary proceedings:* When a Member is taking part in any parliamentary proceeding or making any approach to a Minister or servant of the Crown, advocacy is prohibited which seeks to confer benefit exclusively upon a body (or individual) outside Parliament, from which the Member has received, is receiving, or expects to receive a pecuniary benefit, or upon any registrable client of such a body (or individual). Otherwise a Member may speak freely on matters which relate to the affairs and interests of a body (or individual) from which he or she receives a pecuniary benefit, provided the benefit is properly registered and declared.

2. *Constituency interests:* Irrespective of any relevant interest which the Member is required to register or declare, he or she may pursue any constituency interest in any proceeding of the House or any approach to a Minister or servant of the Crown, except that:

— where the Member has a financial relationship with a company in the Member's constituency the guidelines above relating to parliamentary proceedings shall apply;

— where the Member is an adviser to a trade association, or to a professional (or other representative) body, the Member should avoid using a constituency interest as the means by which to raise any matter which the Member would otherwise be unable to pursue.

77. The current Guidelines give effect to a recommendation from the Committee on Standards in Public Life in the following terms:

"In recommending in the First Report a ban on agreements between MPs and multi-client consultancies, we were concerned to avoid a situation in which MPs could be presented as participating in 'a hiring fair'. We retain that concern. On the other hand, we are anxious that the rules should not unnecessarily inhibit the ability of MPs to become well informed and to use their expertise and experience effectively. Bearing in mind the evidence that we have heard about the present guidelines on 'initiation' and the ban on paid advocacy, we believe that they are operating unnecessarily harshly and that they should be amended. We recommend that the ban on paid advocacy should remain in place, but that the restriction on initiation should be removed and the guidelines relating to participation extended to include both participation and initiation. The effect of this would be that an MP who had a personal interest would be permitted to initiate proceedings in the same way that he or she is able to participate in proceedings under the current guidelines, but that MP (a) would not be able to engage in 'paid advocacy' or seek to confer benefits exclusively on a particular individual or body and (b) would be required to register and declare the benefit in accordance with the guidelines. We recommend a further safeguard (c) that, reinforcing present practice regarding the declaration of interests when tabling a written notice, in addition to registration and oral declaration, the MP would also be required to identify his or her interest on the Order Paper (or Notice Paper) by way of an agreed symbol." [Sixth Report of the Committee on Standards in Public Life, *Reinforcing Standards*, Cm 4557–1, January 2000.]

78. The Committee on Standards and Privileges has made it clear that it would regard it as a very serious breach of the rules if a Member failed to register or declare an interest which was relevant to a proceeding he had initiated. [Fourth Report, Session 2001–02 on the Initiation of Parliamentary Proceedings: A Consultation Paper, HC 478, para 15.]

[Note: "Initiating a parliamentary proceeding" includes:

— *presenting a Bill*;

— *presenting a Petition*;

— *tabling and asking a Parliamentary Question*;

— *asking a supplementary question to one's own Question*;

— *initiating, or seeking to initiate an adjournment (or other) debate*;

— *tabling or moving any Motion (eg an "Early Day Motion" a Motion for leave to introduce a Bill under the "Ten Minutes Rule" or a Motion "blocking" a Private Bill*;

— *tabling or moving an Amendment to a Bill*;

— *proposing a draft Report, or moving an Amendment to a draft Report, in a Select Committee*;

— *giving any written notice, or adding a name to such notice, or making an application for and introducing a daily adjournment debate, or an emergency debate*.

A similar consideration applies in the case of approaches to Ministers or civil servants.]

Parameters to the operation of the ban on lobbying for reward or consideration

79. The Committee on Standards and Privileges has also agreed to the following parameters to the operation of the rule:—

1) *Registrable interests:* The ban on lobbying for reward or consideration is to apply with equal effect to any registrable or declarable pecuniary benefit irrespective of the source of that benefit (ie no distinction is drawn between financial benefits received from a company, a representative organisation, a charity, a foreign government or any other source). Similarly, no distinction should be drawn

in the application of the advocacy rule to different categories of registrable or declarable benefit (except for the provision below relating to ballot bills, to overseas visits, and to membership of other elected bodies). Non-pecuniary interests registered by Members do not fall within the scope of the Resolution agreed by the House on 6th November 1995 and the rule does not apply to them.

2) *Past, present, and future benefits:* Unlike the Register, which lists current benefits, or benefits received in the immediate past, the Resolution on lobbying of 6 November 1995 also refers, as does the rule on declaration, to past and expected future benefits. It is difficult to contemplate circumstances where any benefit received some time in the past, particularly an interest which is not in the current printed Register, could be sufficiently relevant to be taken into account under the rule (see (4) below). Expected future interests, on the other hand, may be more significant. For example, Members expecting to derive direct financial benefit from particular legislation should, as well as declaring the interest in debate as appropriate, not seek to move Amendments to advance the expected future interest. The same consideration applies to other proceedings.

3) *Continuing benefits:* Continuing benefits, i.e. directorships, other employment, and sponsorship, can be divested to release a Member with immediate effect from the restrictions imposed by the rule, providing that the benefit is disposed of and there is no expectation of renewal.

4) *"One-off" benefits:* The rule applies to "one-off" registrable benefits, both visits and gifts, from the day upon which the interest was acquired until one year after it is registered.

5) *Family benefits:* The rule includes relevant payments to a Member's family, but any payment to a member of the family of any Member which arises out of the family member's own occupation is not regarded as a benefit for the purposes of the Resolution.

6) *Ballot Bills:* Private Members successful in the Ballot for Bills are not prevented from introducing and proceeding with a Bill by reason of the fact that they receive free or subsidised assistance from an organisation connected with the purposes of the Bill provided the Member had no pre-existing financial relationship with the organisation which is registered, or is required to be registered.

7) *Overseas Visits:* Although, except as set out in paragraph 35, overseas visits must be registered and declared, such visits shall not be taken into account when applying the rule.

8) *Membership of other elected bodies:* Membership of the Scottish Parliament, the National Assembly for Wales, the Northern Ireland Assembly, the European Parliament and local authorities in the United Kingdom shall not be taken into account when applying the rule.

9) *Ministers:* The restrictions imposed by the rule do not apply to Ministers when acting in the House as Ministers.

80. **The financial interests of Members are extremely varied, as the Register demonstrates. Each Member will need to apply the rule and the Guidelines to his or her particular circumstances. When in doubt, Members will be able to seek the advice of the Commissioner, or the Committee on Standards and Privileges**. However, some illustrative examples of the application of the Guidelines may be of value:—

(a) A Member who is director of a company may not seek particular preference for that company (eg tax relief, subsidies, restriction of competition) in any proceeding of the House or any approach to Ministers or officials.

(b) In the case of trade associations, staff associations, professional bodies, charities (or any similar representative organisation):

(i) Membership alone of any representative organisation does not entail any restrictions under the rule.

(ii) A Member who is, for example, a remunerated adviser:

— may not, whether by initiating a proceeding or participating in debate, advocate measures for the exclusive benefit of that organisation; nor speak or act in support of a campaign exclusively for the benefit of the representative organisation or its membership (eg a campaign for special tax relief, or for enhanced pay and numbers);

— may speak or act in support of a campaign which is of particular interest to the representative organisation (eg in the case of an animal welfare organisation, a campaign to prohibit the importation of animal fur, or prohibit blood sports; in the case of a charity for cancer research, a campaign for the prohibition of smoking).

(c) When a Member has a problem involving a company within his or her constituency the Member may take any parliamentary action to resolve that problem, even though he or she may hold a remunerated position with a body representing the relevant sector of the industry regionally or nationally, or with another company outside the constituency in the same industrial sector. Similarly a Member who has a remunerated position with a representative association is not restricted in any way in taking up the case of a constituent who is a member of that association, or is employed by a member of that association. The only circumstances when the Member's actions are restricted are when the Member has a registrable interest with the company concerned when the guidelines provide that the Member forfeits the special position he or she has as a constituency Member.

(d) Members are reminded that when accepting foreign visits they should be mindful of the reputation of the House. However, the knowledge obtained by Members on such visits can often be of value to the House as a whole. While it is desirable that Members should be able to use that knowledge in debate in the House there is a point at which promoting the interests, of eg a foreign Government from which hospitality has been received, crosses the line between informed comment and advocacy. Members may not, for example, either initiate or advocate in debate increased United Kingdom financial assistance to a Government from which they have recently received hospitality. Nor may the Member initiate any proceeding in Parliament which seeks to bring specific and direct benefit to the host Government. Subject to this constraint Members could, having declared their interest, raise matters relating to their experiences in the country either in a speech or by initiating any other proceeding. Similarly they could raise matters relating to the problems of the country generally, or make use of any local insight they have obtained in to regional problems (eg the situation in the Middle East or in South East Asia, economic or social problems or an external threat) or information they have obtained on local developments or initiatives.

(e) A Member whose visit was funded by a non-governmental organisation (NGO) or other agency would not be inhibited in speaking about its work or the problems it was dealing with. Only a matter which was for the exclusive benefit of the NGO or agency: eg a request for a grant-in-aid to the particular organisation, could not be pursued.

(f) Under the rule, a Member who is receiving free office accommodation provided by a local authority should not advocate measures for the specific and direct benefit of the local authority itself (as distinct from the interests of those whom the local authority represents). In practice, since Members also have a paramount duty to represent their constituents there will be few occasions when the application of the rule will place a limit on a Member's parliamentary actions. In any event, accommodation provided solely for the purpose of holding constituency surgeries is exempt from registration and therefore from the application of the rule.

Responsibility of the Member

81. In common with the rules of the House relating to registration and declaration of interest the main responsibility for observation of the rule on advocacy lies with the individual Member. The Select Committee on Standards in Public Life stated in its Second Report that "it is important to make clear that it will not be the function of the Chair to enforce the ban on paid advocacy during speeches, either by interrupting a Member thought to be contravening it, or by declining to call him. Complaints will be a matter for the Commissioner to investigate in the first instance". [Select Committee on Standards in Public Life, Second Report, Session 1994–95, HC 816, para 26.] The Speaker has declined to receive points of order relating to registration or advocacy. [Eg HC Deb, 25 April 1996, col 605 and 14 May 1996, cols 767–68.]

Delegations

" . . . a Member with a paid interest should not initiate or participate in, including attendance, a delegation where the problem affects only the body from which he has a paid interest."

(Part of a Resolution of the House of 6 November 1995)

82. A further Resolution agreed by the House on 6 November 1995 restricts the extent to which any Member with a paid interest may participate in, or accompany, a delegation to Ministers or public officials relating to that interest. A Member should not initiate, or participate in, or attend any such delegation where the problem to be addressed affects only the body with which the Member has a relevant interest, except when that problem relates primarily to a constituency matter.

Procedure for complaints

83. Complaints, whether from Members or from members of the public, alleging that the conduct of a Member is incompatible with the Code of Conduct or with this Guide, should be addressed in writing to the Parliamentary Commissioner for Standards.

84. Both the Commissioner and the Committee on Standards and Privileges will be guided by the view of the former Select Committee on Members' Interests that "it is not sufficient to make an unsubstantiated allegation and expect the Committee to assemble the supporting evidence", and that it "would not normally regard a complaint founded upon no more than a newspaper story or television report as a substantiated allegation". [Select Committee on Members' Interests, First Report, Session 1992–93, HC 383, para 4.] The Commissioner will not entertain anonymous complaints. . . .

86. Communications between a member of the public and the Commissioner are not covered by Parliamentary privilege nor privileged at law unless and until the Commissioner decides the case has some substance to merit further inquiry. If he decides to the contrary, he may at his discretion reject the complaint without further reference to the Committee. The receipt of a complaint by the Commissioner is not to be interpreted as an indication that a *prima facie* case has been established.

87. If the Commissioner is satisfied that sufficient evidence has been tendered in support of the complaint to justify his taking the matter further, he will ask the Member to respond to the complaint and will then conduct a preliminary investigation. If he decides, after some inquiry, that there is no *prima facie* case, he will report that conclusion briefly to the Select Committee. If he finds that there is a *prima facie* case or that the complaint raises issues of wider importance, he will report the facts and his conclusions to the Committee.

88. In the case of admitted failure to register or declare interests where the interest involved is minor or the failure to register or declare was inadvertent, the Commissioner has discretion to allow the Member to rectify the matter. In the case of non-registration, rectification requires a belated entry in the current Register, with an appropriate explanatory note; in the case of non-declaration, it requires an apology to the House by means of a point of order. Any rectification is reported briefly to the Committee.

89. The Committee on Standards and Privileges will consider any matter relating to the conduct of Members, including specific complaints in relation to alleged breaches of the Code of Conduct or Guide to which the House has agreed and which have been drawn to the Committee's attention by the Commissioner.

90. The Committee has power under its Standing Order to send for persons, papers and records; to order the attendance of any Member before it; and to require that specific documents in the possession of a Member relating to its inquiries or to the inquiries of the Commissioner be laid before it.

91. While it is the practice of the Committee to deliberate in private, the Committee determines for itself whether sessions at which evidence is to be taken shall be held publicly or in private, and is empowered to refuse leave for the broadcasting of any public sessions.

92. On specific complaints for which the Commissioner has decided there is a *prima facie* case, the Committee will make recommendations to the House on whether further action is required. It may also report to the House on other complaints if it thinks fit.

93. The Committee has said that where it feels that a complaint from a Member was frivolous or had been made only for partisan reasons, it would expect to state that in any report it made about the complaint.'

(b) Do the rules work? Continuing allegations of sleaze

A number of issues continue to affect the composition and privileges of Parliament. In addition to the question of the future of the House of Lords, there are concerns about how peers may currently be appointed—a matter that has become uncomfortably linked with the funding of political parties and the question of patronage generally. The issue of lobbying also continues to give rise to concerns and it is convenient to deal with this first.

On 13 January 2006 *The Times* reported that while MPs are forbidden from working for political consultancies, there are informal bodies known as 'all party groups' (APGs) who have political authority in that, appearing to cross party boundaries, they are independent when making policy statements and suggestions. There are some 370 such groups in Parliament, mostly focusing on specific subjects, and the number of these financed in whole or part by commercial organisations is, allegedly, almost 100, of which 36 receive administrative and financial assistance from lobbyists.

The membership of the groups is drawn primarily from back benchers in both Houses of Parliament, but non-parliamentarians can be members where associates are allowed. An APG must, however, have at least five members from the government party and five from the opposition parties. Such groups have to be registered in Parliament, but they are not Select Committees and have no limit on the number of members or rules as to how often they may meet, though most meet at least twice a year. They have no power to compel the attendance of witnesses or the production of papers nor any formal authority to produce reports. They receive no public funding for their work and hence are dependent on funding from outside bodies such as trade associations, though APGs should declare the identity of any such body giving them administrative support or funding on the register of interests which is subject to the oversight of the Committee on Standards and Privileges.

The Times' allegations named the AP Beer Group as receiving £45,100 from brewing interests, the AP Pharmacy Group, where reports on behalf of the group have been written by lobbyists, the AP Small Shops Group which has received secretarial support from a lobbyist paid by the Independent Retailers Confederation, and the AP Nuclear Group which has received administrative assistance from a person connected with the UK nuclear industry. *The Times* further argued that the AP Pharmacy Group had helped to sway policy on the supply of emergency contraception while being given support by the Company Chemist Association, the National Pharmaceutical Association, the Pharmaceutical Services Negotiating Committee and the Royal Pharmaceutical Society, all bodies whose members could benefit from the policy change that had been made. It must also be pointed out, however, that this group's particular declared aim is to 'raise awareness of pharmacy and pharmacists and to promote pharmacy's current and potential contribution to the health of the nation'.

The Times also pointed to various types of support for the following APGs, *some* of it financial: film industry (British Film Industry and UK Film Council); financial markets and services (inter alia British Bankers' Association, Corporation of London, London Stock Exchange, etc.); health (inter alia AstraZeneca, BT Health, BUPA, Standard Life Healthcare, etc.); identity fraud (Fellows Inc); information technology (inter alia Institution of Electrical Engineers, IBM UK, 3M); media (inter alia BBC, BSkyB, Time Warner); oil and gas industry (UK Offshore Operators Association); scientific (inter alia Institute of Physics, Institution of Chemical Engineers, Royal Society of Chemistry, AstraZeneca); skin (the Skin Care Campaign and the British Association of Dermatologists); smoking and health (Action on Smoking and Health); transport safety (inter alia British Petroleum, Volvo Car UK, BMW (GB), Association of Train Operating Companies, Association of British Insurers, Norwich Union); water (Water UK, Wessex Water, Anglian Water, Yorkshire Water, South East Water); weight watchers (Weight Watchers).

Writing in *The Times* for 13 January 2006 the political commentator, Peter Riddell, pointed out that APGs are defensible institutions enabling issues to be ventilated outside the normal limits of party politics, and to enable the claims of particular interests to be advanced. Neither is there anything inherently wrong in interest groups seeking to influence the minds of legislators: that is all part of the political process in a pluralist democracy. Similarly there is nothing wrong in an interest group providing assistance to an APG. The fear, however, is that an APG may become the pawn or tool or mere extension of an interest group. This may lead to confusion in the public mind for the very title 'APG' suggests impartiality and bipartisan consensus, while 'insiders' at Westminster may come to regard particular APGs with scepticism as 'fronts' for highly organised commercial groupings. If APGs are to be regarded as legitimate organisations they must be scrupulously transparent in declaring on the House of Commons Register whence they derive support. It may well be that the names and identities of their external supporters should also be declared on any report or statement made by an APG.

On 25 May 2006 the Parliamentary Commissioner for Standards responded to these allegations by calling on all parliamentary lobbyists to reveal their list of clients and urging MPs to observe caution in dealing with those who do not. He further called on charities giving assistance to MPs to reveal the names of any companies making donations to them of more than £5,000. Complaints against three APGs were upheld on the basis they had failed to comply with a requirement that where a consultancy supplies benefits to the group such as secretarial services at the request of a client the names of both the consultancy and the client must be declared. It is expected that changes to the rules relating to APGs will take place in 2007 to implement the Commissioner's recommendations. His report further recommended that all press releases, reports and publications from APGs should carry the names of the author, the organisation providing secretarial support and of any relevant clients or sponsors. He accepted that APGs may not be neutral organisations and may act as pressure groups and argued they should clearly distinguish themselves from Select Committees and dispel notions they have an institutional status.

A rather more worrying issue concerns allegations that political parties may have been funded in some way by those who have received, or who hope to receive, honours, including peerages. There are two general awards of honours made each year, one at New Year and one in the summer for the Queen's Official Birthday. These may include awards of peerages, though often 'working peers' to bolster the strength of the House of Lords are created at other times. The Honours Lists include the award of knighthoods and appointments to various Orders, such as that of the British Empire. The direct sale of honours became a matter of acute political controversy during and after the First World War when some 1500 knighthoods were conferred and 91 peerages created. While some of these were in recognition of war service it was claimed that knighthoods could be purchased for £10,000, baronetcies for £30,000 and peerages for £50,000, with the proceeds going to the funds of a portion of the Liberal Party led by David Lloyd George, the then Prime Minister, and known as the Coalition Liberals. In 1922, following an investigation by a Royal Commission, a Political Honours Scrutiny Committee was appointed (since 2002 known as the Honours Scrutiny Committee) and the Honours (Prevention of Abuses) Act 1925 was passed making it an offence for any person to accept monetary awards in return for the grant of an honour. However, only one person has been convicted under the legislation and suspicion has continued that peerages have 'coincidentally' been awarded to certain donors to the major political parties.

In an attempt, inter alia, to dispel concerns, the Political Parties Election and Referendums Act 2000 was passed giving effect to recommendations from the Committee on Standards in Public Life made in 1998, Cm 4057. The legislation deals with the amount of money that can be spent by candidates for election and also the sums that political parties can themselves spend in promoting their cause. In addition the legislation deals with the funding of political parties by requiring them to publish their sources of funding. Donations to parties may only be received from 'permitted donors' who are generally restricted to individuals registered to vote in the UK or who are companies registered under the Companies Act 1985 and trading in the UK. Anonymous donations are forbidden as are donations above £200 pa from individuals not on UK electoral registers. Any donations over £200 from permitted sources have to be recorded by the receiving party and their accounts must be submitted annually to the Electoral Commission established under the 2000 Act, and made publicly available. While there are no limits on the size of permitted donations any donation over £5,000 made to a political party's main office has to be reported to the Electoral Commission, and also donations of more than £1,000 made to local party or constituency offices.

A problem exists, however, as the legislation applies to *donations*, not to *loans*.

With particular regard to the House of Lords this problem became apparent in March 2006 when the House of Lords Appointments Commission—a further non-statutory body established in 2000—rejected certain nominees put forward for Life Peerages. This followed the submission of a list of 28 nominees for so-called 'Working Peerages' in 2005 from the Labour, Conservative, Liberal Democrat, Democratic Unionist and Ulster Unionist parties. Certain nominees subsequently withdrew their names from the list when allegations were made that they had either donated money or loaned it to political parties. The implication, hotly denied by some of the nominees it must be noted, was that the nomination was connected with the financial assistance that had been offered. Loans made on commercial terms, ie at 1 to 3 per cent above bank base rate are outside the reporting requirements of the 2000 Act, and in March 2006 newspaper allegations revealed that some £13.95m had been loaned to the Labour Party in respect of its 2005 election campaign in the form of private loans from unnamed individuals, though the full list was subsequently made public by the Labour Party on 20 March 2006, followed by a similar disclosure on 31 March 2006 of loans worth £15.95m made to the Conservative Party.

Investigations were commenced following these disclosures by both the Public Administration Select Committee of the House of Commons and the Electoral Commission. These were suspended, however, when the Metropolitan Police commenced their investigations into the issue under the Honours (Prevention of Abuses) Act 1925, the Public Bodies Corrupt Practices Act 1889 and the Political Parties Elections and Referendum Act 2000, and arrests were made in connection with these investigations.

244 PARLIAMENT: COMPOSITION AND PRIVILEGES

For the future a further review of the future funding of political parties under Sir Hayden Phillips was announced by the Department for Constitutional Affairs on 16 May 2006 to examine, inter alia, whether there should be a cap placed on donations to political parties, and changes made to the current limits in general election expenditure. In addition the Review will also examine whether the current very limited state funding of political parties in the UK should be expanded. Currently opposition parties in both the House of Commons and the House of Lords receive some state funding to help them discharge their parliamentary duties, for example to run the Leader of the Opposition's Office, while all parties can receive policy development grants, though this is limited to £2m pa. Indirect support is also given by the free 'air time' given to political parties for political broadcasting and 'free post' for a single mailing to each elector in a constituency at election times. Election campaigning as such is not state funded, and the question is whether it should be, so as to ensure political parties do not rely on funding from individuals.

In addition on 13 July 2006 the House of Commons Public Administration Select Committee published its fourth report for the session 2005–06.[19] This made the following recommendations and endorsements:

- A welcome for the Prime Minister's announcement of 23 March 2006 that once the twice yearly honours lists have gone through independent committee scrutiny, he will no longer add further names.
- That the award of a peerage should not be made as an honour—rather it should be explicit that such an award makes its recipient a working member of the legislature.
- A welcome for the insistence by the Appointments Commission that it must be informed about any financial or other matters which might affect its consideration of a person's nomination for a peerage.
- There should be scrutiny of all awards of higher honours to assess the appropriateness of any financial or like connection which might exist between the candidate for the honour and a political party, which should be enforced by candidates having to make a declaration whether they have financial or other connections with a political party which might affect their awards at the time when they are first conditionally approached as to whether they would be prepared to accept the award of an honour, for example a knighthood.
- Where an individual is under consideration for an honour and that person has assisted government programmes in a material way, for example by sponsoring a particular City Academy School, that is no automatic bar to the receipt of the honour but there must be a patently transparent assessment of the individual's contribution to government programmes.
- All citations for honours should be published to ensure the system is transparent.
- Any honours awarded by an outgoing Prime Minister in his resignation honours list should be settled by the Appointments Commission.
- The practice of inducing particular MPs to announce their resignation in the run-up to a general election followed by their being granted peerages so that their seats may be contested by government nominees should cease.

Future reforms might well include the creation of a new Honours Commission to oversee the entire process of the award of public honours, while with regard to the House of Lords the Appointments Commission's role, powers and independence should be enshrined in statute as soon as an agreed scheme for reforming the Upper House can be put on the statute book.

---

[19] 'Propriety and Honours' HC 1119.

FURTHER READING

Crick B *The Reform of Parliament* (2nd edn, revised, Weidenfeld and Nicolson, London, 1970) chs 1, 3, 4, 5 and 6.

Gay O and Leopold P (eds) *Conduct Unbecoming: The Regulation of Parliamentary Behaviour* (Politico's, London, 2004).

Griffith JAG and Ryle M *Parliament: Functions, Practice and Procedures* (Sweet & Maxwell, London, 1989) chs 1, 2, 3.

Jennings Sir Ivor *Parliament* (2nd edn, Cambridge University Press, Cambridge, 1969) chs II, III, V, VI and XII.

Jowell J and Oliver D (eds) *The Changing Constitution* (5th edn, OUP, Oxford, 2004) ch 10.

Leopold PM 'Freedom of Speech in Parliament—Its Misuse and Proposals for Reform' [1981] PL 30.

Leopold PM 'Parliamentary Privilege and the Broadcasting of Parliament' (1989) 9 Legal Studies 53.

Leopold PM ' "Proceedings in Parliament": The Great Grey Area' [1991] Public Law 475.

Longford Earl of *A History of the House of Lords* (Collins, London, 1988) chs VIII–XI.

McDonald O *Parliament at Work* (Methuen, London, 1989) chs 4, 5, and 6.

Munro C *Studies in Constitutional Law* (Butterworth and Co (Publishers) Ltd, London, 1987) ch 7.

Oliver D 'Standards of Conduct in Public Life—What Standards?' [1995] Public Law 497.

Renton T. *Chief Whip: People Power and Patronage in Westminster* (Politico's, London, 2004) chs 6, 14 and 15.

Russell M *Reforming the House of Lords: Lessons from Overseas* (Oxford University Press, Oxford, 2000).

Ryle M and Richards PG (eds) *The Commons Under Scrutiny* (Routledge, London, 1988) chs 2, 5, 6 and 11.

Shell D *The House of Lords* (2nd edn, 1992, London, Harvester Wheatsheaf).

Turpin C *British Government and the Constitution* (Butterworths, London, 1999) chs 7 and 8.

6 PARLIAMENT: PROCEDURES AND FUNCTIONS

Parliament's overall task is to ensure that issues affecting the nation (eg proposals for new laws, voting taxation to finance the activities of government, scrutiny of policy, administration and expenditure proposals) are fully discussed and ventilated. This subdivides into, in *increasing* order of importance and *decreasing* order of effectiveness, redress of individual grievances, supervision of executive activities (including making delegated legislation), oversight of public expenditure, production of workable, understandable legislation, and ultimate control over ministers. To understand this, one must realise that government by party, where political power is achieved consequent on direct popular election, has reduced Parliament's role from that of an intermediary between ministers and people to being an agency through which ministers can operate—a forum for continuing political debate. The great divide in Parliament is not between ministers and non-ministers but between the government (and its supporters) and the Opposition. Taking up individuals' causes, often (though not always) on a constituency basis, by Members of Parliament—perhaps by asking questions of ministers—is the function least affected by the above change. A member takes up a grievance, irrespective of whether or not the complainant(s) voted for his/her party, and may pursue it with success. In this connection members are assisted by the work of the Parliamentary Commissioner or 'Ombudsman'.[1] Members are least likely to find party loyalties at risk in relation to grievances not raising issues of policy, though pressure can be put on ministers by combinations of members from all parties, as was the case in 1989 over enhanced pensions for war widows.

I. Questions of Ministers

'Questions' may be set down by members to be answered either orally or in written form and must either seek information or press for some action, and must *not* be disguised statements or debating issues. Likewise a question cannot be asked if it has no basis in fact or is designed to mock or annoy or is so vague as to be unanswerable. Furthermore a question cannot be asked if it reflects on the conduct of the monarch or the royal family or if it relates to a foreign government. Questions must relate to the responsibilities of government and must as a general rule be addressed only to ministers, and indeed must not be addressed to a minister in

[1] See chapter 8 below.

respect of a matter for which he/she is not responsible or for which another minister is more responsible. It is not possible to ask a minister a question about the conduct of individuals or companies unless this is in relation to some aspect of regulation for which ministers are responsible, nor in respect of matters for which, for example, a local authority is directly responsible, though, of course, a member may take up a constituent's case directly with such a body. A question once asked cannot be opened again in the same session of Parliament unless circumstances have altered. Ministers may also decline to answer questions where relevant information is not held centrally or where it would be unduly expensive to provide an answer, in which case the question cannot be raised again for three months. Ministers may also refuse answers on the basis of national security or commercial confidentiality. An oral question must not be asked in an 'open form' eg 'will he visit constituencies in Liverpool?' Thus if a supplementary question is asked it must relate to the same subject matter as the main question. However, an exception to this exists in relation to Prime Minister's Question Time, which takes place on Wednesdays, where the Prime Minister is frequently asked to 'list his engagements for the day', and then one other supplementary question on any issue falling within the Prime Minister's responsibilities or for which no other minister has responsibility may be asked. This device enables members to put the Prime Minister to the test across a whole range of issues. The Leader of the Opposition is allowed to put more than one supplementary question and this results in frequent opportunities for sustained oral debate between the two principal party leaders.

Question time for oral questions is fixed for Mondays to Thursdays. Members must give written notice of questions at the 'Table Office' of the House, and generally two full days' (excluding Friday, Saturday and Sunday) notice has to be given. Each of the major departments of state will take its turn in a rota for its ministers to be subject to questions first in the time allotted for questions, thus ensuring that each department can be subject to questions once a month while Parliament is sitting. Furthermore question time is not unlimited and effectively only between eight and twenty questions will have a chance of being orally answered, though a written answer will be given. Ministers may defer answering a question to the end of question time where the nature of either the answer or the question requires a more extended answer. Written questions are subject to fewer constraints and may be directed to any department for an answer on any day when Parliament is sitting, and there is no limit to the number of 'ordinary' written questions a member may ask, though if the question is 'for a written answer on a named day' the limit is five.

The Speaker has a discretion to allow an 'Urgent Question' to be raised at the end of question time, even though the normal rules for tabling have not been observed, though only where the matter is urgent and relates to a matter of public importance.

The changes that have overtaken Parliament, and *principally* the House of Commons, date from the late nineteenth century. Following the first reform of the franchise in 1832, with the Commons elected by a small electorate and containing many men of independent attitudes, ministries could fall as a result of adverse votes, as witness Russell (1852 and 1866), Aberdeen (1855), Palmerston (1858) and Gladstone (1885). Party discipline was weak: the Commons controlled its own timetable, members had great freedom to raise any items of business or to appoint investigative committees. Since the 1880s all this has changed, largely because of growing party cohesion. Since 1882 it has been possible to close debate by simple majority vote (see further on the 'Closure' below), and since 1902 ministers have been responsible for timetabling the House. Government and opposition whips (see chapter 5) in discussion ('the usual channels': see further below) agree much of the timetable of the House, usually ensuring that the opposition selects issues for debate for some 30 per cent of the time; this emphasises its nature as a political forum. The consequences are a decline in the corporate feeling of Parliament—the Commons in particular—and diminution in the ability of individuals to influence the progress of events. It is, however, fair to add that discussion between 'the usual channels' prevents the over-heavy use of unpopular devices such as the closure and the guillotine. Even so there are times when their use may be imposed, as in 1987–88 when twenty non-agreed closure motions were carried, or as in 1988–89 when ten Bills were guillotined. Such devices are, of course, founded on the government having a workable, compliant majority in the Commons. Pressure developed, however, over a number of years for the majority of legislation to be timetabled so that a degree of certainty is injected into the legislative process. The Select Committee on the Modernisation of the House of Commons produced a set of cross-party recommendations in 1997/98. These included measures more formal than the 'usual channels' (but also more flexible than the guillotine) for 'programme motions', which are in effect an 'agreed guillotine' fixing a date for the Report Stage of a Bill, and the amount of time to be devoted to that and the Third Reading Stage. The Commons approved the proposal and since 1998 a number of Bills have been selected via 'the usual channels' for programming and this is a matter to which we shall return subsequently with regard to legislative procedure.

II. Sittings of the House of Commons

In July 2001 the then Leader of the House of Commons, the late Robin Cook, proposed that the sitting hours of Parliament should be altered particularly to make them more attractive to women. In August 2002 the Commons Modernisation Committee suggested that from Tuesdays to Thursdays the Commons should begin to sit at 11.30 am, and should conclude its main business by 7.00 pm, thus expanding the experiment commenced in 1999 of 11.30 am to 7.00 pm sittings on Thursdays, while also retaining the traditional 2.30 to 10.00 pm sitting on Mondays and a 9.30 am start on Fridays, days when many members travel to and from Westminister. It was further proposed that some sittings should take place in September. These proposals were controversial but were implemented in January 2003. However, by January 2004 there were indications of a reaction against the changes, with more than one third of members apparently seeking a return to traditional hours, which the House of Lords had not given up. The calls for a review of the innovation came from all sides of the House of Commons, some pointing out that the new hours were not as 'family friendly' as might be thought, with members being unable to take their children to school because of early commencement, while others pointed to clashes between the work of Select Committees which sit in the mornings and debates in the Chamber of the House. It was also argued that the new hours made it difficult for MPs to pursue outside careers, and while it is arguable that a nation's laws should not be made by part-time legislators, it is equally arguable that a legislature consisting solely of full-time politicians is also not well equipped to stay in tune with the views of those outside its walls. By January 2005 244 MPs from all parties had called for the changes to be reversed, and on 26 January 2005 there was a clear vote to return to the older pattern. Standing Order 9 of the House of Commons now provides for sittings to commence on Mondays and Tuesdays at 2.30 pm with business ending at 10.00 pm, on Wednesdays the House sits between 11.30 am and 7.00 pm and on Thursdays between 10.30 am and 6.00 pm. The timing of Thursday sittings allows members from the further flung areas of the UK to travel back to their constituencies.

The current pattern of sittings appears to be a compromise between those seeking a more modern 'family friendly' image for the House of Commons and those who feel that such points of view are specious and undermine the ability of the Commons to maintain a feeling of corporate identity, irrespective of party affiliation, essential to its task of maintaining effective scrutiny over the work of government. It has to be remembered, however, that for that scrutiny to be most effective it needs the support of the media to report it. Late sittings and debates in Parliament are not always well covered by the press and television while the government's press outlets have the entire day in which to release their versions of events.

Standing Order 36 allows any member to rise during any debate and claim that 'the question be now put', ie that debate be ended and a vote taken—the 'closure'. It is up to the Speaker to decide whether to accept such a motion, and if it is accepted then the matter must be put to the House. The Speaker then asks for those in favour—who will call 'aye' and those against, who will call 'no'. Indeed this is the traditional means of setting the procedure in motion for any vote in the House. The Speaker may determine from the volume of responses that, for example, 'the ayes have it', but if that is then challenged by members the Speaker must call for a vote or 'division' by announcing 'clear the lobbies' and the 'division bells' are rung which warns members not in the Chamber of the House that a vote is to be taken and they should proceed to either the 'Aye' or 'No' lobby through which they will pass as the way of recording their vote. So far as a closure motion is concerned, where there is a division it will only be carried if the ayes not only have the majority but also have at least 100 members in their lobby. Should the Ayes succeed, then the substantive issue must be put to a division straightaway. The closure may also be applied in a standing committee on a Bill (see below). In addition the closure may be claimed at 'the moment of interruption', ie the pre-arranged time when the House closes its business (see above), which again effectively closes debate on the issue then under discussion unless *ministers* successfully move a motion to suspend the 'moment of interruption' for either a fixed or indefinite period of time. Ministers thus have available to them devices to control, shorten or extend the time for debate in support of which they will use their majority in the House, and these devices are denied to private members and the opposition parties.

The changed role of Parliament must now be examined with regard to each function outlined at page 246.

III. Delegated (or Subordinate) Legislation

Governing the United Kingdom would be impossible if Parliament did not give delegated powers to ministers (and other agencies such as local authorities—who may make by-laws; the judges—who make the various rules of civil and criminal procedure; and even parts of Parliament such as the House of Commons acting alone in certain very special circumstances) to make subordinate legislation on a whole range of technical, detailed issues. Parliament has neither time to make all legislation needed, or the expertise to understand what is required. Yet there remains concern whether there is sufficient oversight by Parliament of such legislation. Delegated legislation is law, and 'ignorance of the law is no excuse' for those who contravene it. Furthermore it is often the details of the law which affect the average citizen more than its grand design. The ordinary person, for example, is little concerned with the concept of 'development' of land contained in section 55 of the Town and Country Planning Act 1990, but may often be affected by rights to alter dwellings—for example, by erecting extensions or television aerials—contained in the General Permitted Development Order 1995, yet only the Act is made by Parliament. The Order, technically made by the Secretary of State under section 59 of the Act, emanates from the unelected ranks of the Civil Service. There is, additionally, a tendency for the delegated powers to be given in increasingly wide terms. It is not just detail that is encountered in delegated legislation, but also main issues, for example, powers actually to repeal or amend primary legislation itself. It is equally observable, however, that of late many Acts of Parliament have become mere outline measures, so skeletal in nature that from their mere words alone it is more than hard to predict what the effective form of the law as laid down in delegated legislation will be. Delegated legislation, however, unlike Acts of Parliament may be challenged in court on the basis that it goes beyond the powers ('*ultra vires*') given by Parliament, see further chapters 9 and 10 on the *ultra vires* concept.

The key to understanding the parliamentary system of control over delegated legislation is to realise that much depends upon the drafting of the enabling (or 'parent') Act—a matter largely for ministers and their advisers to determine. It is the parent Act that, for example, determines the type and extent of scrutiny over delegated legislation made under its powers. For example, most delegated legislation is nowadays made in the form of statutory instruments, in relation to which publicity requirements exist so that changes in the law can be made patent. However, whether or not the requirements of the Statutory Instruments Act 1946 apply, depends upon whether that is made obligatory by the parent Act.

Statutory Instruments Act 1946 (as amended)

1 (1) Where by this Act or any Act passed after the commencement of this Act power to make, confirm or approve orders, rules, regulations or other subordinate legislation is conferred on His Majesty in Council or on any Minister of the Crown then, if the power is expressed—

(a) in the case of a power conferred on His Majesty, to be exercisable by Order in Council;

(b) in the case of a power conferred on a Minister of the Crown, to be exercisable by statutory instrument,

any document by which that power is exercised shall be known as a 'statutory instrument' and the provisions of this Act shall apply thereto accordingly …

[1A The references in subsection (1) to a Minister of the Crown shall be construed as including references to the National Assembly for Wales.]

2 (1) Immediately after the making of any statutory instrument, it shall be sent to the King's printer of Acts of Parliament and numbered in accordance with regulations made under this Act, and except in such cases as may be provided by any Act passed after the commencement of this Act or prescribed by regulations made under this Act, copies thereof shall as soon as possible be printed and sold by [or under the authority of] the King's printer of Acts of Parliament . . .

3. . . (2) In any proceedings against any person for an offence consisting of a contravention of any such statutory instrument, it shall be a defence to prove that the instrument had not been issued by [or under the authority of] His Majesty's Stationery Office at the date of the alleged contravention unless it is proved that at that date reasonable steps had been taken for the purpose of bringing the purport of the instrument to the notice of the public, or of persons likely to be affected by it, or of the person charged . . .

4 (1) Where by this Act or any Act passed after the commencement of this Act any statutory instrument is required to be laid before Parliament after being made, a copy of the instrument shall be laid before each House of Parliament and, subject as hereinafter provided, shall be so laid before the instrument comes into operation.

Provided that if it is essential that any such instrument should come into operation before copies thereof can be so laid as aforesaid, the instrument may be made so as to come into operation before it has been so laid; and where any statutory instrument comes into operation before it is laid before Parliament, notification shall forthwith be sent to the Lord Chancellor and to the Speaker of the House of Commons drawing attention to the fact that copies of the instrument have yet to be laid before Parliament and explaining why such copies were not so laid before the instrument came into operation.

(2) Every copy of any such statutory instrument sold by [or under the authority of] the King's printer of Acts of Parliament shall bear on the face thereof—

(a) a statement showing the date on which the statutory instrument came or will come into operation; and

(b) either a statement showing the date on which copies thereof were laid before Parliament or a statement that such copies are to be laid before Parliament . . .

5 (1) Where by this Act or any Act passed after the commencement of this Act, it is provided that any statutory instrument shall be subject to annulment in pursuance of resolution of either House of Parliament, the instrument shall be laid before Parliament after being made and the provisions of the last foregoing section shall apply thereto accordingly, and if either House, within the period of forty days beginning with the day on which a copy thereof is laid before it, resolved that an Address be presented to His Majesty praying that the instrument be annulled, no further proceedings shall be taken thereunder after the date of the resolution, and His Majesty may by Order in Council revoke the instrument, so, however, that any such resolution and revocation shall be without prejudice to the validity of anything previously done under the instrument or to the making of a new statutory instrument . . .

6 (1) Where by this Act or any Act passed after the commencement of this Act it is provided that a draft of any statutory instrument shall be laid before Parliament, but the Act does not prohibit the making of the instrument without the approval of Parliament, then, in the case of an Order in Council the draft shall not be submitted to His Majesty in Council, and in any other case the statutory instrument shall not be made, until after the expiration of a period of forty days beginning with the day on which a copy of the draft is laid before each House of Parliament, or, if such copies are laid on different days, with the later of the two days, and if within that period either House resolves that the draft be not submitted to His Majesty or that the statutory instrument be not made, as the case may be, no further proceedings shall be taken thereon, but without prejudice to the laying before Parliament of a new draft . . .

8 (1) The Treasury may, with the concurrence of the Lord Chancellor and the Speaker of the House of Commons, by statutory instrument make regulations for the purposes of this Act . . .

Statutory Instruments Regulations 1947 (SI 1948/1)

1 . . . (2) In these Regulations

(1) 'Principal Act' means the Statutory Instruments Act 1946;

(b) 'responsible authority' means—

(i) in relation to an Order in Council, the Minister responsible for the preparation of the draft of the Order submitted to His Majesty in Council, and

(ii) in relation to any other instrument, the Minister by whom the instrument is made; . . .

(c) 'general instrument' and 'local instrument' mean, respectively, an instrument classified as such under these Regulations; and

(d) 'Reference Committee' means the Statutory Instruments Reference Committee provided for by these Regulations . . .

3 All statutory instruments received by the King's printer of Acts of Parliament under subsection (1) of section 2 of the Principal Act shall be allocated to the series of the calendar year in which they are made and shall be numbered in that series consecutively as nearly as may be in the order in which they are received . . .

4 (1) For the purpose of these Regulations, statutory instruments shall be classified as local or general according to their subject matter.

(2) Unless there are special reasons to the contrary in any particular case, a statutory instrument which is in the nature of a local and personal or private Act shall be classified as local, and a statutory instrument which is in the nature of a Public General Act shall be classified as general.

(3) The responsible authority shall, on sending a statutory instrument to the King's printer of Acts of Parliament, certify it as local or general as the case may be; and, unless the Reference Committee otherwise direct under these Regulations, the instrument shall be classified accordingly.

5 The following statutory instruments shall, unless the Reference Committee in any particular case otherwise direct under these Regulations, be exempt from the requirement of subsection (1) of section 2 of the Principal Act with respect to the printing and sale of copies, that is to say:

(a) any local instrument, and

(b) any general instrument certified by the responsible authority to be of a class of documents which is or will be otherwise regularly printed as a series and made available to persons affected thereby . . .

6 If the responsible authority considers that the printing and sale of copies of a statutory instrument in accordance with the requirements of subsection (1) of section 2 of the Principal Act is unnecessary having regard to the brevity of the period during which that instrument will remain in force and to any other steps taken or to be taken for bringing its substance to the notice of the public, he may, on sending it to the King's printer of Acts of Parliament, certify accordingly; and any instrument so certified shall, unless the Reference Committee otherwise direct under these Regulations, be exempt from the requirements aforesaid. [*A similar exemption exists in respect to bulky instruments certified as such by the responsible authority, see reg 7.*] . . .

8 If the responsible authority considers that the printing and sale of copies of a statutory instrument in accordance with the requirements of subsection (1) of section 2 of the Principal Act would, if effected before the coming into operation of that instrument, be contrary to the public interest, he may, on sending it to the King's printer of Acts of Parliament, certify accordingly and any instrument so certified shall, so long as it has not come into operation, be exempt from the requirements aforesaid . . .

11 (1) There shall be a Committee to be known as the Statutory Instruments Reference Committee consisting of such two or more persons as the Lord Chancellor and the Speaker of the House of Commons may nominate . . .

(3) Where, under Regulation 6 or 7 of these Regulations, the responsible authority gives any certificate in respect of a statutory instrument, that authority shall notify the Committee; and the Committee may, if they consider that the requirements of subsection (1) of section 2 of the Principal Act with respect to the printing and sale of copies ought to be complied with, direct that the instrument shall not be exempt from those requirements or, as the case may be, shall not be exempt therefrom so far as concerns the document specified in the certificate:

Provided that the Committee may direct that the notification required by this paragraph need not be given in respect of any specified class of instrument.

A degree of oversight over most statutory instruments is ensured by requirements that they must be 'laid' before Parliament: the legislature is thereby informed of their existence. However, where an instrument is simply laid, no further parliamentary action needs to be taken on it—the requirement is informatory only. Most instruments so laid are, however, further subject to requirements either that they shall not come into force if a negative resolution is passed against them, or that they shall only come into force if an affirmative resolution is passed; again, all depends on the wording of the parent Act. It is furthermore the general rule that Parliament is unable to amend proposed delegated legislation, it can only approve, disapprove or annul it.

Where 'negative resolution' procedure applies the instrument will come into force *unless* within 40 days a 'prayer' to annul the instrument is moved as a motion and is carried. Any member may 'put down' such a motion to annul, and this is done mainly by means of an 'early day motion' (EDM), ie one for which no formal debating time is fixed. Such a motion is unlikely to progress unless a large number of Members sign the EDM. Alternatively a motion may be put down by the Opposition. (See further below on EDMs.) This is unlikely to be successful in the face of government opposition reliant upon a compliant majority. Ministers may, however, move that the instrument be referred to a standing committee on delegated legislation (see below) and there it may be debated for up to one and a half hours before being reported back to the House where a motion to annul would then be voted on. In the case of 'affirmative resolution' procedure an instrument or, more usually, a draft instrument will not come into force without the approval of both Houses of Parliament (or, less often, the Commons) expressed in a resolution. There may be other procedures such as where an instrument is laid and has immediate effect but may only continue in force for a limited period unless affirmatively approved. Sometimes there will be a requirement that an instrument may be laid in a draft form subject to a resolution that no further steps are taken. Where 'affirmative resolution' procedure applies the department of state responsible for the delegated legislation will prepare the motion and relevant ministers will then lead debate. Such instruments will be automatically referred to a standing committee on delegated legislation (see below) for debate which may last for up to one and a half hours only. A further one and a half hours' debate in the House is allowed once the committee refers the instrument back 'on report.'

There are no rules or criteria laid down as to which of these procedures should be utilised when delegated powers are being included in a parent Act—or indeed whether there should be a requirement for laying at all. Much can depend on the precedent set by previous legislation. Clearly it would be *politically* unacceptable for there to be opportunities for ministers to make delegated legislation on controversial issues without Parliament having any chance of seeing the measures and being able to check them—but this does not mean that governments will refrain from choosing that mode of oversight most favourable to the freest progress of delegated legislation, and that is the negative resolution procedure.

Furthermore, while Colin Turpin claimed in *British Government and the Constitution* (4th edn at p. 381) that 'affirmative procedure is usually preferred for powers whose exercise will substantially modify Acts of Parliament, powers to impose financial charges and powers to create new offences of a serious nature', Bradley and Ewing in *Constitutional and Administrative Law* (12th edn, p. 725) pointed out that both 'Labour and Conservative governments have been criticised for choosing the negative procedure for important measures modifying Acts of Parliament'.

Where negative resolution procedure applies members of Parliament wishing to annul the legislation must be ready to spot when it has been laid if they are to seek annulment within the set period of 40 days, and this is done by means of a 'prayer' to annul the instrument, though this is no guarantee that the prayer will be debated, and if it is it will only be one and a half hours at the end of the parliamentary day. Alternatively the instrument may be referred to a standing committee, see below.

(a) Super affirmatory procedure under the Regulatory Reform Act 2001

In 2001 the Regulatory Reform Act gave ministers powers to amend or repeal Acts of Parliament which made no provision for their own amendment by means of delegated legislation. Such delegated legislation can impose or remove a burden and can repeal and reenact legislation. They may grant ministers further powers to amend by way of yet more subordinate legislation. Thus the whole of a statutory regime may be substantially changed. The Act, however, only applies to those statutes which impose regulatory burdens on companies, public bodies and individuals, and is restricted to changing only those statutes which are less than two years old, or which have not been substantially amended within the previous two years.

Because the powers conferred on ministers by this Act are so extensive, a particular procedure known as 'super affirmative' is applied to them which requires the use of 'proposals' which are subject to consultation procedures. Thus ministers are required to put forward their proposals before Parliament in a draft form and then a period of sixty days must elapse. During this period a special Regulatory Reform Committee, which functions somewhat as a Select Committee (see below) will examine the proposal and scrutinise it in detail. This Committee may meet jointly with a Committee of the House of Lords examining regulatory reform orders and may invite MPs who are not members to participate in the examination of witnesses called to explain and elucidate the proposals. The Committee has power, inter alia, to comment not only on whether the proposal is intra vires the power granted by the Act but also whether it is an appropriate use of the powers.

During the sixty-day period non-parliamentary bodies are also given the opportunity to comment on the proposal as part of a wider consultation exercise required under the 2001 Act.

Once the sixty-day period is elapsed, ministers may lay their draft before Parliament, and this may take account of any points made by the Committee and its counterpart in the House of Lords. The Committee then has a fifteen day period to recommend by report whether the draft order should or should not be approved, though where non approval is proposed the sponsoring department must be allowed to explain its case. Following the report from the Regulatory Reform Committee and its House of Lords counterpart ministers may move a motion on the floor of the House. If the Committee approved the draft but a division was forced on this a period of up to one and a half hours is allowed for debate: if the draft was not approved by the Committee a period of three hours' debate is allowed before a vote is taken.

A government sponsored review of the working of the 2001 Act in 2005 concluded that its provisions were too technical and limited and that it should be replaced by legislation which further extended the powers of ministers to introduce legislative proposals of a non-controversial nature for simplifying regulatory regimes. These proposals were then developed in the Legislative and Regulatory Reform Bill 2006 which is examined further below in the context of post-legislative scrutiny.

The House of Commons has a Select Committee on Statutory Instruments and this joins with a similar Lords' committee to form a Joint Committee on Statutory Instruments by virtue of Standing Order 151. Nearly all statutory instruments of general applicability required to be laid before Parliament are subject to oversight, and the Joint Committee can also consider general statutory instruments not required to be laid. The Committees' terms of reference enable Parliament's attention to be drawn to a statutory instrument if it: imposes a charge or tax; is immune, under the provisions of its parent Act, from challenge in court; claims retrospective effect *without* express parent Act authority; has been subject to unjustifiable delay in laying or publication; has come into force before being laid and there has been unjustifiable delay in explaining this to the Lord Chancellor and Mr Speaker as is required under the Act of 1946; is doubtful whether the instrument is within the powers ('intra vires') granted by the parent Act, or where unusual or unexpected use has been made of those powers; requires elucidation of form or purpose; appears to have defective drafting. It is not possible, however, for this committee to consider the merits of the proposals in an instrument. References on the basis of retrospective effect or delay in laying are rare in recent times, more likely are those based on the need for elucidation or doubts as to drafting. Even so, only 2 per cent of all instruments considered are subject to critical reports. This may be due to the high quality of drafting but, as St John Bates pointed out in 'Scrutiny of Administration' in Ryle and Richards *The Commons Under Scrutiny*,[2] an alternative explanation is that the committees are working against the clock, especially where instruments are subject to the negative resolution procedure which means, of course, that there is only 40 days in which to move a prayer of annulment. This is not a great deal of time to consider an instrument, call for and receive evidence and produce a report which could form the basis of a prayer.

These Committees may only consider whether ministers are exercising their powers in accordance with the terms of the parent Act. Government departments may be required to submit explanations orally or in writing, but evidence may not be taken from non governmental sources. Where the Committee proposes to draw the attention of the House to an instrument it must give the relevant department a chance to give an explanation. Though in recent years the number of pieces of delegated legislation considered by the Commons has risen, time for debate has not increased. Debate may take place on the floor of the House—but usually only at the end of the day, and usually only for an hour and a half. Where the Committee criticises an instrument the relevant department may withdraw it and make amendments, or may bear the criticism in mind in relation to future instruments.

If the controls relating to what are particularly procedural aspects of the making of delegated legislation leave something to be desired, what of controls over their merits?

Since 1973, it has been possible to create Standing Committees on Delegated Legislation in which the merits, ie the desirability and content, of a statutory instrument may be debated, see now Standing Order 118. Such Committees normally have about seventeen voting members, though any other MP may attend and speak. Ministers automatically move that instruments subject to affirmative resolution procedure are referred to a Standing Committee. Other instruments *may* be referred in which case the motion will be made by the Opposition or some other private member. Even if an instrument is referred there will only be one and a half hour's debate, and no amendment is permitted, while any subsequent vote will be taken on the floor of the House where the government will once again rely on its majority to save the instrument no matter what has occurred in the Committee. St John Bates (op cit) concludes the chief use of the procedure has been to save the government debating time on the floor of the House. In 1998/99 150 instruments subject to affirmative resolution procedure were

[2] At pp. 202–203.

considered in Committee, 21 instruments were considered on the floor of the House, but 1,266 instruments subject to negative resolution procedure were laid before the House of Commons, of which only 28 were considered in Committee and one on the floor.

The House of Lords has the Merits of Statutory Instruments Committee which also examines the merits of instruments subject to either the affirmative or negative resolution procedure. This may draw the attention of the Lords to any instrument it considers to be:

• politically or legally important or which gives rise to public policy issues likely to be of interest to the Lords;
• inappropriate in view of changes in circumstances since the parent act was passed;
• an inappropriate measure to implement European Union legislation;
• imperfectly achieving policy objectives.

Currently there is no regular mechanism for scrutinising delegated legislation, despite its bulk at around 3,000 instruments per annum and its modern importance in 'fleshing out' legislative schemes—for example by 2005 the Financial Services and Markets Act 2000 had given rise to over one hundred statutory instruments. In its 2005 Consultation Paper No 178: 'Post-Legislative Scrutiny' the Law Commission pointed to the problems caused for the public by the flow of delegated legislation, for example problems of determining the detail of the law where older instruments are amended by newer ones, and suggested that departments should devote more time to consolidating statutory instruments that have been subject to change. The Commission further canvassed the argument that some sorts of delegated legislation ought to be subject to 'sunset' clauses whereby they automatically cease to have effect at the end of a stated period unless renewed, while older instruments should be made subject to a requirement for automatic review after a period of time by one or other of the parliamentary scrutiny committees. Against this, however, it can be argued that Parliament currently does not have enough time to scrutinise instruments that are being made let alone those from the past.

---

iv. The Oversight of Public Finance

To appreciate here the changed role of Parliament (and that means effectively the Commons) it is necessary to understand that the functioning of executive and legislature are fundamentally disparate. The chief task of government is the long-term management of the national economy as a whole. Parliament's task, historically, is to vote for the raising and expenditure of a certain amount of finance on an annual basis, for that is how government used to function. The financial functioning of government is now exceptionally widespread throughout society—stretching, for example, from funding individuals via social security benefits to authorising the raising of capital by way of loans by local and other public authorities for building houses and other long-term projects. Parliament is ill-equipped, in terms of time, personnel and understanding, to control how all these forms of 'public money' are spent, nor, indeed, the total amount of such money.

The dislocation of function has developed over a long period, though it is inherent in the dichotomy between Crown and Parliament, whereby the former *makes* policy for which it must *account* to the latter. In financial matters this dichotomy was not apparent in days when Crown expenditure was limited to military, naval, administrative and 'law and order' issues.

Before 1787 specific purposes were financed by specifically dedicated taxes; on the Continental mainland this is known as 'hypothecated taxation'. There was an obvious link between raising and spending money. The link was lost, however, when all taxation revenue began to be paid into one fund—the Consolidated Fund, otherwise known as the Exchequer Account. The lack of 'hypothecated taxation' in our system of government gives ministers—and officials in the Treasury—enormous power to raise or lower spending on public services and to switch funding between services, enabling them to bask in a glow of apparent generosity when they have really robbed Peter to pay Paul. While any new proposed programme or scheme to be authorised by legislation will have its financial implications spelt out in its parent Act, the actual expenditure will still fall within the overall system of annual authorisation.

Nevertheless, this annual raising and spending of money still accorded with basic constitutional principles that it is for the Crown to demand money, while the Commons grant it and the Lords merely assent to its grant. Since 1713 only ministers have been able to propose new or increased forms of taxation and proposals for expenditure: all such proposals have to be considered first by the Commons, and, if approved, have to be embodied in legislation passed by Parliament as a whole. However, this method of control only applies to the annual expenditure falling within what is known as 'estimates procedure'. Government borrowing, the financing of the national debt and expenditure from the National Insurance Fund are not subject to annual statutory control, see further below.

The key to understanding the *basics* of public finance in the United Kingdom is thus to remember first of all that there are parallel procedures (legal and administrative) and that Parliament (primarily the House of Commons) is involved in the former. In other words Parliament has certain legal functions with regard to raising and spending of money (and auditing the accounts of what is spent) by government, and unless these legal functions are complied with the government acts illegally. Equally, however, the government has control over policy matters concerning what amounts of money shall be raised by way of taxes and borrowing, and the matters on which that money is spent. That distinction must always be borne in mind. Obviously the government must seek Parliament's approval for its policies when it needs *legal* authority to raise taxes and spend money but Parliament does not thereby acquire a policy-making role, and the government will in any case look to its supporters in Parliament to ensure that the necessary legal authority is given.

Gladstone, in the mid-nineteenth century, attempted to create a closed 'circle of control' over public finance on a yearly basis, in accord with the above principles, to ensure that taxation can neither be levied, nor can money raised be spent, without specific statutory authority; with an audit staff to ensure financial probity, and a powerful House of Commons Committee—the Public Accounts Committee (PAC)—to provide for ministers to be called to account for money spent. National finance operates, according to the above notions, annually as a 'closed cycle' with any deficit of expenditure over revenue made up by borrowing, and any surplus used to pay off borrowings (the 'national debt'). The examination of individual departmental estimates (the documents leading to annual statutory authorisation of expenditure) with each 'vote of finance' having to be moved separately, took up an increasing amount of time in the Commons, so that by the 1880s the House found it impossible to deal with the estimates on the floor of the House. In 1896 a limit was set on the number of days available for discussion, and the guillotine (see above) was applied in order to vote through all estimates not discussed. Time technically devoted to examining estimates was instead used as 'supply days' on which the Opposition would generally criticise particular areas of government spending. An Estimates Committee was set up in 1912 in order to ensure detailed examination of estimates though, after 1945 when the Committee was allowed to create sub-committees, it tended to concentrate on investigations of how far money spent on particular issues had achieved government policy objectives. The deficiencies in this system were subsequently recognised and have been partly alleviated by a package of changes over the last twenty years which will be examined below.

Further weaknesses in parliamentary oversight of finance arise from the fact that Parliament does not determine the total amount of expenditure of all public bodies: some have the power to raise revenue independently. Likewise, as stated above, Parliament does not determine the policy objectives on which money is spent. In addition, as already noted above, some items of public expenditure—the Consolidated Fund Services, which cover matters such as the cost of interest on, and the management charges for, the national debt, subsidies to Northern Ireland and payments to the European Community—are not voted for on an annual basis. By the mid 1990s some 33 per cent of all public expenditure was permanently authorised by the various Consolidated Fund Acts and needed no annual Parliamentary authorisation. Furthermore, a statutorily provided Contingencies Fund enables ministers to meet emergency expenditure in advance of parliamentary approval of estimates covering the item in question. Governments may also finance their activities, and those of other public bodies such as local authorities, by borrowing—issuing, for example, 'gilt-edged securities' (various forms of loan stock), or by encouraging private lending to the government via the National Savings System whereby private citizens are offered attractive rates of interest or tax incentives. Over the last 20 years or so the government has derived much income from the sales of publicly owned assets such as British Telecom and British Gas. Where public sector expenditure as a whole exceeds income in a year the deficit which is met by borrowing is known as 'Public Sector Borrowing Requirement' (PSBR).

Before examining how Parliament has attempted to deal with the matters considered above, and the changed role of government from an annual spender of limited amounts of money to long-term national financial manager, it is necessary to examine the annual system within which Parliament attempts to operate financial oversight. The 'financial year' is *not* a calendar year; it runs from April to March, and the *actual financial cycle* is much longer than twelve months (see below). Within that span the formalities of the old yearly statutory authorisation of expenditure, taxation and audit of money spent are still encountered.

From 1982 for a number of years, in November/December of each calendar year, the Chancellor of the Exchequer made an *Autumn Statement*. This contained a forecast on the economy, details of changes in national insurance and social security, and an outline of planned expenditure for the *financial* year to come. This expenditure had already been agreed by the Cabinet. Disputes between 'spending departments' and the Treasury as to the amount to be spent had been referred to a Cabinet committee nicknamed 'The Star Chamber' for decision. A one day debate on the statement took place, but no legislation flowed from it. However, the statement was analysed in detail by the Commons Treasury and Civil Service Select Committee which produced a report. The Autumn Statement also 'set the scene' for the next financial year's expenditure and taxation proposals.

The next event chronologically, occurring in the period January–March, was the Annual Public Expenditure White Paper. The raison d'être of this document derived from the dislocation between executive and legislative oversight of finance referred to above. In 1961 the Treasury began to plan *total* public expenditure on a five year rolling programme. In the summer of each year the Public Expenditure Survey Committee (PESC), *a body of civil servants*, reviewed public expenditure plans for the next five years. *Ministers* received this, together with the Treasury's Medium Term Economic Assessment showing anticipated levels of resources to meet expenditure commitments. Parliament did not receive any of this information. Following examination of the issue by the Select Committee on Procedure in 1968–69, it was agreed by the government that an annual white paper would be produced; the first appeared in the session 1969–70. The Public Expenditure White Paper (PEWP) stated exhaustively government spending plans for the forthcoming three financial years for both central departments and local authorities. PEWP detailed the aims and objectives of spending, and was subject to a one day debate, and investigation and analysis by the Commons Treasury and Civil Service Committee. The Public Accounts Committee in 1986/87 and the Treasury and Civil Service Committee in 1987/88 proposed changes in the PEWP system, and in May 1988 the government proposed rationalisation to be implemented between 1988 and 1991. The material in PEWP became divided between the Autumn Statement and a series of volumes detailing departmental reports and plans which appeared early each *calendar* year. The object was to ensure, first, that the Autumn Statement contained the principal elements of the PESC survey and Cabinet decisions thereon within a reasonably short time of those decisions and, secondly, that the departmental reports provided the necessary background for understanding the supply estimates of money to be devoted to individual government services.

(a) Reform or backtracking on financial procedures?

By late 1991, when it was clear that there could be only a few months to go to a general election, there was growing realisation that the classic British system of separating parliamentary scrutiny of *decisions on spending money* from *decisions on raising* it was utterly outmoded. The emergence of 'the autumn statement' which had laid down the spending decisions of government way in advance of the Spring Budget which then merely tackled the issue of adjusting taxation to pay for spending had completely hijacked the traditional understanding of parliamentary scrutiny of finance.

The unreality of separating spending and taxation decisions, however, also dawned on the government. In his March 1992 budget the Chancellor of the Exchequer announced for the future the autumn statement on spending and the spring taxation package would be merged and the entire package dealt with as a 'December budget'. In the past when the old 'yearly cycle' of parliamentary oversight of public finance applied the spring budget made sense. Near the end of each financial year the Chancellor presented accounts for that year and set tax rates for the year to come. It was a system that worked well while public spending was low. But those days finally departed in 1909 when Lloyd George was forced to increase income and other taxes massively to pay for the pre First World War naval arms race and the beginnings of what we now call the welfare state. Inevitably such a commitment of public funds forces governments to begin to *plan* their spending over a longer period than one year, while the very magnitude of the sums of money involved has led also to government spending decisions being of prime importance to the state of the economy—hence the emergence of government's role as the manager of the economy—a task now acknowledged as belonging especially to the Prime Minister, the Chancellor and the Chief Secretary to the Treasury. Thus the 1992 decision to merge the two made a deal of sense, and should have created a link in the parliamentary and public mind between taxation and spending—if the latter increases the former probably cannot decline and may even have to rise.

In late 1993 came the first of the new combined budgets with 'spending' and 'raising' all in one. A White Paper setting projected spending targets for the next three years was retained as part of this exercise.

The incoming Labour government of 1997, however, changed the overall system of presentation of public finance yet again, and in June 1998 produced its first 'comprehensive spending review'. This aimed to end certain practices and to enshrine certain financial principles:

- an end of annual spending and yet more emphasis on long term planning;
- strategic planning for all departmental expenditure, and an end to year-to-year bidding by departments;
- spending should be directed to achieving defined results;
- more attention to be paid to long term investment and spending plans;
- more attention to be paid to the economic relationships between the public and private sectors.

However, the government returned to the notion of the autumn pre-budget statement in the form of a 'green' budget. The government also adopted a 'Code for Fiscal Stability' which was based on two rules:

- there should be a clear distinction between current expenditure budgets and long term capital expenditure budgets;
- there should be a strict requirement that the ratio between public debt and the Gross Domestic Product (in effect the wealth the nation produces) should always be at a stable and prudent level. This led to a system of giving departments firm three year limits within which they have to plan expenditure and manage and plan ahead public expenditure, while government itself must spell out its overall plans on a three year basis.

This may arguably be seen as also representing a further shift of power towards Whitehall—specifically the Treasury—and away from Westminster, by restoring the old dichotomy between the Annual 'pre budget report' (PBR) (now falling in November each year) and the actual spring budget itself. Furthermore the actual significance of the budget was further diminished by mid calendar year statements by the Chancellor—as happened in 1998 and 2000—on forecasted levels of public spending. On the other hand there are arguments that the new system with its Economic and Fiscal Strategy report (containing the long term objectives of government) and the annual PBR will encourage wider discussion of, and consultation on, financial measures and will enable greater scrutiny of proposals by both Parliament and the Treasury Select Committee. However, the PBR has achieved a significance of its own as the policies and tax changes outlined there have an effect on the wider economy and on the fiscal policies of the Bank of England in setting lending rates.

It can be argued, of course, that the 1993 changes were only a 'tidying up' operation designed primarily to indicate a link between expenditure and taxation, no more, and certainly not with the purpose of giving Parliament more control over the financial functioning of government. Then, as now, there was no change in the way Parliament authorises the expenditure of those funds which are spent on an annual basis. In short there remains minimal direct control over public expenditure via debates and votes in the Commons. Furthermore under the present government's system of making financial statements it is very difficult to know whether each successive statement is one of enhanced public spending on services or whether it only rolls forward commitments already made, with the consequence that more appears to be being done by government than is actually the case. It is not just Parliament that lacks an understanding of public finance, it is the population as a whole. Individual sectors and services, such as the National Health Service or the universities, are furthermore dependent on translation of Treasury financial statements into understandable figures by supplementary statements made by the relevant departments of state—and even then the real implications of the fine details of statements may take time to be appreciated or to appear.

There remains a dislocation between 'spending' and 'raising money' decisions. The 'estimates' cycle nowadays runs from October/November in a calendar year to July in the following calendar year, but within that cycle there will be 'supplementary estimates', for example in October/November looking back to the start of the current financial year, ie April, while at that very same time there will also be 'votes on account' in respect to advance authorisation of expenditure in the next financial year. The 'estimates cycle' which concerns spending thus effectively relates to an eighteen month period. This itself is punctuated by the administrative 'reporting cycle' whereby departments now make their 'performance reports' (which look back to the *previous* financial year) in October/November time of the calendar year, and their spending plans for the current financial year and for two years ahead in the following April.

The core of the 'estimates cycle', however, are the 'main estimates' which are presented in March of each calendar year, and these set out the total resources required for each department, and take the form of a series of 'Requests for Resources'. However, there will, as has been outlined above, be *Summer* supplementary estimates in May/June of each year asking for further resources, and *Winter* supplementary estimates in October/November. Yet more *Spring* supplementary estimates are presented in February.

How much control does the house of Commons exercise over this confusing sequence of events? Estimates are laid before the House at least fourteen days before they are voted on to allow examination by departmentally related select committees (see below) who may propose that particular estimates should be debated. Three days only are now set aside for debates and these are known as 'Estimates Days', and these may be spread through a parliamentary session, and normally occur in December, March and June, which somewhat reflects the pattern of main and supplementary estimates. In practice estimates are selected for debate by the House of Commons Liaison Committee by reference to recent Departmental Select Committee reports, so that debate may be focused by reference to the content of the report or reports in question. Clearly therefore there is no debate of the estimates as a whole, and in practice there will be only two estimates examined on each of the three estimates days. It is furthermore not possible for the Commons to propose an increase in expenditure as this is a task for the government, and so any amendment in the Commons can only take the form of a proposal to *reduce* an estimate, usually by a token sum, simply to initiate a debate on the estimate in question in the light of the relevant Departmental Select Committee report. The rest of the estimates are simply voted through on a block basis with no opportunity at all to amend or negative them and no debate. We may conclude that the House of Commons exercises but little effective scrutiny control over the spending decisions of government, and the various Appropriation and Consolidated Fund Acts which authorise actual expenditure under the estimates are passed without amendment or debate.

To replace the days formerly allotted to considering the estimates since 1985 Standing Order 14 of the House of Commons allots 20 days in each session where the opposition parties choose the items of business to be debated—but these issues need not, of course, relate to matters involving spending. The distribution of these days is generally agreed between the party whips. The leader of the largest opposition party receives seventeen of these days with the remainder being at the disposition of the leader of the next largest party who takes into account the remaining minor parties. On these 'opposition days' the debate will normally now take the form of a critical debate on some aspect of government policy.

The next item chronologically was and still is the Budget but this will be considered below, and about this time, March each year, the actual 'Main Supply Estimates' are published. The estimates relate to the majority (about 70 per cent) of annual public expenditure, and cover money 'supplied' to the Crown for authorised spending. The Annual Appropriation Act, which is enacted by July/August each year, allocates maximum authorised sums to each of the 190 or so heads of expenditure or 'votes' into which the estimates are divided, and authorises the Bank of England to make the necessary payments from the Consolidated Fund. Subsequent changes will, as stated, be accommodated in supplementary estimates and excess votes.

In summary what may we say of the current system for oversight of public expenditure by the House of Commons? It is generally agreed that the Estimates Days do not provide a proper opportunity for thorough scrutiny of each year's estimates. But this, technically yearly, system, though lacking in rigorous scrutiny, is further complicated by events throughout a calendar year whereby 'Supplementary Estimates' for the *current* financial year are taken (usually in March, to enable further spending) together with 'excess votes' for the *previous* financial year (ie authorisation for expenditure undertaken but not covered by an estimate for the previous year). Any proceedings here are purely formal and lead to a Consolidated Fund (No 2) Act—and may be followed by further supplementary estimates later in the year. The result is that though there is a notional twelve month financial year the preparations for, and the financial 'mopping up after' that year may spread over a number of calendar years. For example for the financial year 1984–85 the actual time span ran from December 1983 (when a 'vote on account' was passed to enable spending before the formal approval of the estimates) until March 1986 when the final excess votes were passed—a period of some two and a half years.

(b) Supplementary parliamentary controls over expenditure

Following expenditure, however, comes audit; each department must prepare resource accounts. These are examined by the Comptroller and Auditor General (CAG), a post created in 1866, though since the National Audit Act of 1983 the CAG is an officer of the House of Commons; his staff, the National Audit Office, are not civil servants.

National Audit Act 1983 (as amended)

1 [*Section 1(1) provides that Her Majesty's power to appoint the Comptroller and Auditor General is to be exercised on an address presented by the Commons moved by the Prime Minister in agreement with the Chairman of the Public Accounts Committee.*]

(2) The Comptroller and Auditor General shall by virtue of his office be an officer of the House of Commons.

(3) Subject to any duty imposed on him by statute, the Comptroller and Auditor General shall have complete discretion in the discharge of his functions and, in particular, in determining whether to carry out any examination under Part II of this Act and as to the manner in which any such examination is carried out; but in determining whether to carry out any such examination he shall take into account any proposals made by the Committee of Public Accounts . . .

3 (1) There shall be a National Audit Office consisting of—

    (a) the Comptroller and Auditor General, who shall be the head of that Office; and

    (b) the staff appointed by him under this section.

(2) The Comptroller and Auditor General shall appoint such staff for the National Audit Office as he considers necessary for assisting him in the discharge of his functions.

(3) The staff shall be appointed at such remuneration and on such other terms and conditions as the Comptroller and Auditor General may determine . . .

6 (1) The Comptroller and Auditor General may carry out examinations into the economy, efficiency and effectiveness with which any department, authority or other body to which this section applies has used its resources in discharging its functions.

(2) Subsection (1) above shall not be construed as entitling the Comptroller and Auditor General to question the merits of the policy objectives of any department, authority or body in respect of which an examination is carried out.

(3) . . . this section applies to—

    (a) [any department which is required to prepare resource accounts under section 5 of the Government Resource and Accounts Act 2000;]

    [(aa) The National Assembly for Wales;]

    (b) any body required to keep accounts under section 98 of the National Health Service Act 1977 or section 86 of the National Health Service (Scotland) Act 1978;

    (c) any other authority or body whose accounts are required to be examined and certified by, or are open to the inspection of, the Comptroller and Auditor General by virtue of any enactment, including an enactment passed after this Act; and

    (d) any authority or body which does not fall within section 7 below and whose accounts are required to be examined and certified by, or are open to the inspection of, the Comptroller and Auditor General by virtue of any agreement made, whether before or after the passing of this Act, between that authority or body and a Minister of the Crown . . .

The CAG is charged, first, with examining accounts to ensure money has been spent as authorised and, secondly, to ensure economy, efficiency and effectiveness in departmental spending; one third of audits by the CAG now fall under this heading. In particular the CAG has investigated divergence between ministerial policy declarations and actual out-turns of expenditure, and has undertaken specific 'value for money' investigations. The CAG is concerned lest the absence of profit and loss constraints in the public sector should induce a lack of businesslike attitudes where these would be appropriate, for example: under-valued sales of public assets; poor maintenance records with regard to NHS buildings and defence equipment leading to subsequent large bills; poor stocktaking of defence stores. However, the CAG may not question the *merits* of a policy to which finance has been devoted, nor examine the working of local authorities and nationalised industries. The CAG's audit reports are laid before Parliament. These reports inform the work of the Commons' Public Accounts Committee (PAC), first set up in 1861 and now under Standing Order 148 consisting of fifteen members reflecting the party composition of the Commons. A senior opposition member chairs the PAC; its members are financial specialists. It meets annually from February to July after receiving reports from the CAG, then reporting to Parliament. The PAC acts as a check on extravagant and inefficient spending, and was notable in exposing overcharging in connection with the Bloodhound missile in the 1960s, and escalating costs of other defence projects in the 1980s, such as updating the Polaris missile and new torpedo systems. The PAC has also concerned itself with the adequacy of procedures for taking decisions involving public finance, and cost effectiveness in public administration. The reports of the PAC are the

264 • PARLIAMENT: PROCEDURES AND FUNCTIONS

subject of an annual debate, though this normally is not a great event in Parliament's year. More importantly, the Treasury takes notes of PAC reports, and Whitehall's practices *can* be changed in consequence. The PAC is of limited effectiveness, however, in that it does not concern itself with policy issues, and because it is concerned with past expenditure. Furthermore the PAC cannot appoint specialist advisers, and while it may send for persons, papers and records it normally only examines Departmental Accounting Officers, and even then it is not concerned with the merits of policies but rather, as with the CAG, the efficiency, economy and effectiveness of securing policy objectives.

(i) Modernisation of accounting controls

Under the Government Resources and Accounts Act 2000 older legislation such as the Exchequer and Audit Departments Acts of 1866 and 1921 was replaced with a view to introducing Resource Account Budgeting (RAB) and enabling the preparation and audit of consolidated accounts (Whole of Government Accounts—WGA) for the entire public sector so that a better understanding of public finance can be obtained. In particular RAB requires: statements of outturns of expenditure shown against estimates; operating cost statements, ie statements of financial performance; balance sheets, ie statements of a Department's financial position; cash flow statements and statements relating costs to policy objectives. Departments are also under section 7 of the Act required to produce for parliamentary audit by the CAG the accounts of executive agencies.

Government Resources and Accounts Act 2000
Departmental accounts

5. (1) A government department for which an estimate is approved by the House of Commons in respect of a financial year shall prepare accounts (to be known as resource accounts) for that year detailing—

(a) resources acquired, held or disposed of by the department during the year, and

(b) the use by the department of resources during the year.

(2) Resource accounts shall be prepared in accordance with directions issued by the Treasury. . . .

(5) A department which prepares resource accounts shall send them to the Comptroller and Auditor General not later than 30th November of the financial year following that to which the accounts relate.

(6) The Treasury shall, in the case of each department which is obliged to prepare accounts in accordance with subsection (1), appoint an official of the department as its accounting officer. . . .

6. (1) The Comptroller and Auditor General shall examine any resource accounts which he receives from a department under section 5(5) with a view to satisfying himself—

(a) that the accounts present a true and fair view,

(b) that money provided by Parliament has been expended for the purposes intended by Parliament,

(c) that resources authorised by Parliament to be used have been used for the purposes in relation to which the use was authorised, and

(d) that the department's financial transactions are in accordance with any relevant authority.

(2) If resource accounts appear to the Comptroller and Auditor General to suggest that a material use of resources required but did not receive the authority of the Treasury—

    (a) he shall inform the Treasury, and

    (b) if the treasury sanction the use of resources, he shall treat it as having had the Treasury's authority.

(3) Where the Comptroller and Auditor General has conducted an examination of accounts under subsection (1)—

    (a) he shall certify them and issue a report,

    (b) he shall send the certified accounts and the report to the Treasury not later than 15th January of the financial year following that to which the accounts relate, and

    (c) if he is not satisfied of the matters set out in subsection (1)(a) to (d), he shall report to the House of Commons.

(4) The Treasury shall lay accounts and reports received under subsection (3)(b) before the House of Commons not later than 31st January of the financial year following that to which they relate. . . .

7. (1) The Treasury may direct a government department to prepare for each financial year accounts in relation to any specified matter.

(2) Accounts under subsection (1) shall be prepared in accordance with directions issued by the Treasury.

(3) Where a department prepares accounts under subsection (1)—

    (a) it shall send them to the Comptroller and Auditor General not later than 30th November of the financial year following that to which the accounts relate,

    (b) the Comptroller and Auditor General shall examine and certify the accounts, issue a report on them and send the certified accounts and the report to the Treasury not later than 15th January of that year, and

    (c) the Treasury shall lay the certified accounts and the report before the House of Commons not later than 31st January of that year.

(4) The Comptroller and Auditor General shall carry out his examination of accounts under subsection (3)(b) with a view to satisfying himself—

    (a) that money provided by Parliament has been expended for the purposes intended by Parliament,

    (b) that resources authorised by Parliament to be used have been used for the purposes in relation to which the use was authorised, and

    (c) that the department's financial transactions are in accordance with any relevant authority. . . .

8. (1) For the purposes of an examination by the Comptroller and Auditor General of a government department's accounts—

    (a) he shall have a right of access at all reasonable times to any of the documents relating to the department's accounts, and

    (b) a person who holds or has control of any of those documents shall give the Comptroller and Auditor General any assistance, information or explanation which he requires in relation to any of those documents.

(2) Subsection (1) applies only in relation to documents which are held or controlled—

    (a) by a government department, or

    (b) in pursuance of arrangements made by a government department for the compiling or handling of any of its financial records. . . .

(c) Commons' controls over the raising of revenue

Turning from expenditure to raising revenue, the principal event is the Budget; this, as already noted under the Blair administration, has returned to its traditional spring delivery date, but, for the reasons outlined above on spending, has less importance than it historically enjoyed. Indeed the autumn 'green' Budget may be examined by the Treasury Select Committee and their report debated by the House which also shifts attention away from the main Budget. The chief features of the Budget, from a popular point of view, are declarations of the rates of income and corporation tax, national insurance contributions, and vehicle and liquor excise duties. Some four to five days are given over to debating the Budget via various 'Ways and Means' resolutions tabled by the government. Its proposals are incorporated into the Finance Bill which normally becomes law in July each year. Because finance needs to be raised in the interim period the Provisional Collection of Taxes Act 1968 enables tax changes to be implemented by the Commons passing 'Ways and Means' resolutions which the Finance Act subsequently subsumes. This device dates from 1913 when the first Provisional Collection of Taxes Act was passed to legalise a practice of the House of Commons whereby they approved the rate of income tax for each year without legislation. This was declared illegal in *Bowles v Bank of England*[3] which held that nothing less than legislation was needed to authorise taxation. The 1913 Act effectively provided a statutory scheme to obviate this difficulty.

Despite the move to a pre-Budget report, much secrecy still surrounds the actual preparation of the Budget. Most Budget debates in consequence concentrate on the general state of the economy—the Commons are ill-equipped to investigate the tax system and the economic and social effects of individual taxes. Pressure groups may brief MPs at the committee stage of the Finance Bill which, since 1969, has been divided, with issues of principle being debated by the House as a whole sitting in committee, while detailed issues are referred to a standing committee. Some concessions by the Crown may be made at this stage, but these will not normally be substantial. Ministers can usually rely on their majority to ensure that tax reductions proposed are limited: their supporters will hardly wish to challenge them on a major issue that could lead to resignation. Supporters will also realise that reduction of tax in one area may lead to Crown proposals to increase it elsewhere to make up shortfalls.

There are a number of supplementary means whereby the Commons may scrutinise spending and taxation issues. Since 1997, for example, it has been the practice of the Chancellor of the Exchequer to release in July, every other year, the outcome of the Treasury's 'Comprehensive Spending Review' which will broadly allocate resources to particular activities over the next three years. This may be supplemented by White Papers which set out the long-term objectives and spending plans of individual departments. In addition each department must, in the period April/May, publish an expenditure report setting out the next three financial years' spending plans. These plans will also contain views on how objectives will be prospectively achieved and also look back over the spending out turns of previous years. These reports will then be examined by relevant Departmental Select Committees (see further below), while the Treasury Select Committee will inquire each year into the Budget. October/November in each calendar year also see the publication of departmental 'performance reports' which examine the previous financial year to determine what was achieved with regard to performance indicators agreed between individual departments and the Treasury. These may also be reviewed by Departmentally Related Select Committees.

[3] [1913] 1 Ch 57.

Parliamentary oversight of finance, however, remains weak. The amounts involved defy comprehension, running into billions of pounds per annum. Increased numbers of long-term projects are taken on for which the annual cycle is an inappropriate means of oversight and large areas of regular public expenditure occur outside the annual cycle, as does raising revenue by borrowing. The Commons do not have the resources of the Treasury to assist them in understanding public finance, and most members are not interested in its management and tax implications. Financial procedure is also defective in that taxation and expenditure are still not considered globally—it is not possible to debate whether a particular item of estimates expenditure should be moderated so that a specific head of tax in the Budget may be commensurately reduced. Parliament's task is limited to ensuring that money is spent as statutorily appropriated, to publicising the financial consequences of Crown policies and to pressing for economy, efficiency and effectiveness in the spending of public money.

Questions of more or less spending on defence or public services, etc are no longer constitutional issues where Parliament the institution is interposed between Crown and people. They are political questions, and Parliament is a place where debate on them takes place between representatives of various interest groups. Furthermore most members are not expert in financial matters, and only a few specialise in them. The average member will only be interested when a financial issue touches on some matter in which he/she is otherwise interested, or which bears upon his/her constituents. This applies to spending issues, and generally also to taxation where members usually only speak to press some particular group's claim for tax reductions or exemptions.

---

v. Legislation

Legislation normally takes many months to pass through Parliament (though in an emergency a Bill can become an Act very quickly, as witness the Criminal Justice (Terrorism and Conspiracy) Act 1998 which took only two days).

Some 45–50 per cent of the Commons' time is devoted to legislation (some say as much as 60%), yet the legislative process begins long before Parliament is presented with a Bill. The impetus for new legislation comes largely from the Crown, and it is the Crown and its agents that implement and, in so far as the activity is undertaken, monitor legislation, an issue to which we shall return below. Where a White or Green Paper (outlining legislative proposals—White Paper—or thoughts about future proposals—Green Paper) is issued there may be an opportunity in debate for parliamentary voices to shape the development of a proposal, as well as for input from those outside Parliament voicing opinions. Less formal chances to press a point of view may arise in ministers' meetings with other members in party committees, on social occasions, and in encounters, by chance or otherwise, in the precincts of Westminster. Once a proposal is determined on by, for example, a government department it may still, however, have to wait its turn for parliamentary time (which is limited) while its actual drafting will have been affected by discussions within and between Department and Cabinet Committees. Bills may also grow considerably during passage through Parliament. The overwhelming reason for such growth will be ministerial 'second thoughts', either because the initial wording is seen to be inappropriate to meet desired purposes, or because new purposes are grafted onto proposals as they proceed. Sometimes quite important changes will be introduced while Bills, having passed the Commons, are before the Lords. Of course the Commons have the chance to see these, technically, Lords' amendments, and ministers announce their intentions to add clauses and schedules to bills. However, the initiative for such growth is ministerial, and Parliament's role in the legislative process is largely confined to the formal law-making stages.

(a) Legislative procedure in the Commons

The House of Commons debates many issues other than proposed legislation, and not all its debates take place in its chamber. The House of Commons may sit in Westminster Hall at the same time as the main chamber when it will debate issues selected by by backbench members or raised by Select Committees, though such debates do not reach decisions on substantive issues, and most issues debated in Westminister Hall are uncontentious matters which might otherwise not be debated in Parliament. Legislative proposals, however, will be debated in the main chamber.

During its parliamentary life a legislative proposal is known as a Bill, and this consists of clauses and schedules which, on enactment, become sections and schedules. The latter supplement the former, but often some of the most crucial detail of legislation is to be found in schedules. The various classifications of Bills are:

- Public Bills—those affecting the general law;

- Private Bills—those affecting only particular bodies or localities, such as an individual local authority, and personal Bills which relate solely to individuals and are now very rare;

- Hybrid Bills—a Public Bill with some private characteristics, eg because it will have a particular effect upon a defined group, for example a Bill to construct a transport link which will affect property owners along its route; again these are rare;

- Government Bills—these are Public Bills introduced by ministers;

- Private Members' Bills—these are introduced by members who are not ministers. Little time is available in the timetable for such Bills and members wising to promote such a Bill will normally seek to obtain an opportunity to do so by participating in the ballot held for this purpose each session. Twenty 'slots' for such Bills are made available and those who are successful are normally given a second reading debate (see below) on those Fridays on which the House sits. It is rare for a Private Member's Bill to reach the statute book unless it receives the support of the majority party in Parliament at the bidding of the ministers.

Private Members' Bills do, however, serve some useful purposes for governments because they can allow contentious and morally sensitive issues to be debated outside the government's legislative programme without the need to apply party discipline, for example the Abortion Act 1967, or because they enable measures to become law for which there is no time in the government's legislative programme, eg the Housing (Homeless Persons) Act 1977. Some members who secure a place in the ballot will have a specific legislative proposal in mind, but others may invite proposals from specific interest groups anxious to have their cause taken up in Parliament.

It is also possible for a private member to introduce a Bill under the Standing Orders of the House of Commons No 23 known as a 'ten minute rule Bill'. Members seeking to follow this procedure are allowed on Tuesdays and Wednesdays to make brief ('ten minute') speeches asking the House for leave to introduce their particular Bill. Such Bills will only proceed if the House gives leave and so, once again, they have little chance of success unless they receive the backing of ministers, and Bills of this sort are often introduced only to draw attention to the existence of a particular issue. In 1979–80 125 Private Members' Bills were introduced and ten received the Royal Assent; in 1992–93 the figures were 166 and sixteen, and in 1998–99 104 and eight.

In 1997 a Select Committee on Modernisation of the House of Commons was created to examine, and recommend changes to, the procedure of the House of Commons. Its chairman is the Leader of the House, and it has made a number of proposals concerning the reform of the legislative process, including the sittings in Westminister Hall referred to above. A further innovation has been the publication of certain bills in draft form before their formal introduction to Parliament to enable wider debate on the form and purpose of the proposal as opposed to its actual wording which is the usual subject of parliamentary debate. The common practice of late is for the House of Commons to refer draft Bills to specially created Joint Committees of both Houses for their report, though such Bills may also be referred to a Departmental Select Committee or another Select Committee. This is somewhat different from the initial proposal from the former Leader of the House, Robin Cook, in July 2001 for nearly all Bills to be published in a draft form on a two-year rolling programme with initial scrutiny by Select Committees designed to enable outside interests to make their comments. In practice therefore only a small number of Bills are subject to pre-legislative scrutiny. In the 2003–4 sessions only twelve draft Bills were published, ten of which were scrutinised, while 38 Bills became Acts. While those Bills that are scrutinised may be of major importance the late publication of a draft may prevent effective scrutiny. There is, however, since 2002 a Scrutiny Unit set up within the Committee Office of the House of Commons with a staff of clerks, economists, lawyers and statisticians to assist the ad hoc Select Committees who scrutinise draft Bills, and it seems to be generally agreed that while pre-legislative scrutiny is limited in terms of the number of bills examined it does provide a useful opportunity for Parliament to examine policy proposals.

Since 2002 Bills are normally 'programmed' through their various parliamentary stages. The purpose of programming is to ensure a more predictable passage for the proposal from the outset and to end protracted examinations at the committee stage of a Bill (see below). Programme Orders have, since changes to the House of Commons' Standing Orders in 2001, been the means for ensuring the passage of legislation through its various stages. They are put in place at the start of the progress of a Bill, a point of distinction from the older 'Guillotine' procedure, see below, which was imposed during that progress. A programme order will fix 'final dates' for the report stages (see below) of a Bill and fixing allotted days for the other proceedings in the Chamber of the House of Commons. These are overall time limits which are then supplemented by subsequent programming resolutions. This practice, which effectively sets a timetable for a Bill's progress is controversial in that, arguably, it reduces the time available for proposals to be scrutinised, though, equally arguably, it prevents needless obstruction by the opposition in the form of filibustering. Programming generally applies to Government Bills, and takes effect after the second reading of a Bill (see below). The use of programming is controversial in that it limits the amount of time available for debate. However, the practice is less crude than the (still theoretically available but now little used) 'Guillotine' under which procedure 'allocation of time' motions can be passed which set rigid timetables for all the stages of a Bill's progress. The use of the Guillotine now appears to be generally limited to those rare occasions where a Bill has to pass all its stages in one day, while programming does at least provide for a slightly more flexible allocation of debating time.

The general stages in the life of a Bill before Parliament, assuming it is presented in the House of Commons, which will be the rule for nearly all politically controversial measures, are as follows.

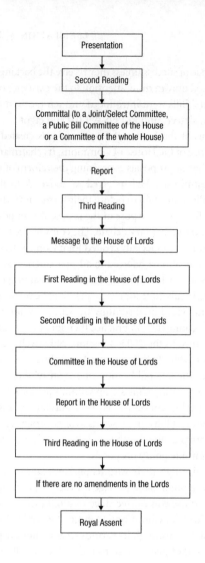

```
┌─────────────────────┐
│    Presentation     │
└─────────────────────┘
           │
┌─────────────────────┐
│   Second Reading    │
└─────────────────────┘
           │
┌───────────────────────────────────────┐
│  Committal (to a Joint/Select Committee, │
│     a Public Bill Committee of the House  │
│       or a Committee of the whole House)  │
└───────────────────────────────────────┘
           │
┌─────────────────────┐
│       Report        │
└─────────────────────┘
           │
┌─────────────────────┐
│    Third Reading    │
└─────────────────────┘
           │
┌─────────────────────────────────┐
│  Message to the House of Lords  │
└─────────────────────────────────┘
           │
┌─────────────────────────────────────┐
│ First Reading in the House of Lords │
└─────────────────────────────────────┘
           │
┌──────────────────────────────────────┐
│ Second Reading in the House of Lords │
└──────────────────────────────────────┘
           │
┌──────────────────────────────────┐
│  Committee in the House of Lords  │
└──────────────────────────────────┘
           │
┌──────────────────────────────────┐
│   Report in the House of Lords    │
└──────────────────────────────────┘
           │
┌─────────────────────────────────────┐
│  Third Reading in the House of Lords │
└─────────────────────────────────────┘
           │
┌───────────────────────────────────────────┐
│  If there are no amendments in the Lords   │
└───────────────────────────────────────────┘
           │
┌─────────────────────┐
│    Royal Assent     │
└─────────────────────┘
```

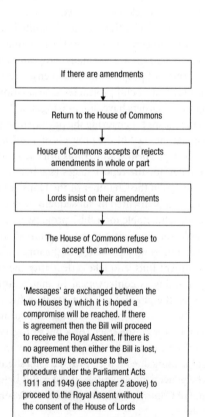

```
┌───────────────────────────────────────┐
│          If there are amendments       │
└───────────────────────────────────────┘
                    │
┌───────────────────────────────────────┐
│       Return to the House of Commons   │
└───────────────────────────────────────┘
                    │
┌───────────────────────────────────────┐
│  House of Commons accepts or rejects   │
│         amendments in whole or part    │
└───────────────────────────────────────┘
                    │
┌───────────────────────────────────────┐
│      Lords insist on their amendments  │
└───────────────────────────────────────┘
                    │
┌───────────────────────────────────────┐
│   The House of Commons refuse to       │
│        accept the amendments           │
└───────────────────────────────────────┘
                    │
┌───────────────────────────────────────┐
│ 'Messages' are exchanged between the   │
│ two Houses by which it is hoped a      │
│ compromise will be reached. If there   │
│ is agreement then the Bill will proceed │
│ to receive the Royal Assent. If there is │
│ no agreement then either the Bill is lost, │
│ or there may be recourse to the        │
│ procedure under the Parliament Acts    │
│ 1911 and 1949 (see chapter 2 above) to │
│ proceed to the Royal Assent without    │
│ the consent of the House of Lords      │
└───────────────────────────────────────┘
```

The First Reading of a Bill is purely formal and is taken to occur on Presentation. The 'member in charge of the Bill' who, traditionally, is the member who introduced it into Parliament, will have, inter alia, the privilege of naming days for the Bill's stages to be taken, though these may be altered, and may also withdraw the Bill from consideration between its stages. Ministers are usually named as those in charge of Government Bills and they will utilise programming measures outlined above. Printing of a Bill will be ordered by the House of Commons at Presentation and sessional numbers will be allocated. In the case of a Government Bill the printed version will contain the ministerial statement required under section 19 of the Human Rights Act 1998 that its provisions are compatible with European Convention Rights (see further chapter 13), and it is now the usual practice with such Bills for 'Explanatory Notes' to be published at the same time setting out the purpose of the proposals and details of what each clause is intended to achieve. Any likely affects on public sector manpower and funds will also be explained and the 'regulatory impact assessment' (eg cost implications) for the private sector, if any. An indication of the likely commencement of the new legislation may be given, as also may explanations of changes to existing statute law.

The Second Reading is concerned with obtaining assent to the principle of the Bill, hence debate may be wide ranging and can extend to what *should* be in the Bill. While actual amendment at this stage is not possible, a 'reasoned amendment' is possible which in giving an explanation of the reasoning of the House of Commons serves to prevent further progress on the Bill. Certain non-controversial Bills may be referred to a Second Reading Committee for their second reading, and this is the usual course of action for technical law reform proposals emanating from the Law Commission which also are normally introduced into Parliament via the House of Lords where they will in any case have been previously scrutinised by a special select committee of the Upper House.

The next phase, that of 'Committal', will see the Bill pass into Committee, and the general procedure is for that to be one of the Public Bill Committees ('Committees of Debate') of the House of Commons. These Committees normally sit in public and are required to reflect the composition of the House of Commons (ie the relative strengths of the parties) and its style of debate. Members are nominated—ranging in number from sixteen to fifty, though thirty is usually the upper limit—by the Committee of Selection, a body of nine members whose most active participants are the government and opposition 'whips', ie members whose task is to maintain party cohesion and discipline and to provide a means of communication between the 'back' and 'front' benches on each side of the House. The party whips also operate via what is known as 'the usual channels', whereby they can negotiate with their opposite numbers in other parties about the management of the business of the Commons. Each of the main parties will have a Chief Whip and a Deputy Chief Whip, while all governmental whips will also hold some form of ministerial rank. At all times when the House of Commons sits there will be government and opposition whips on duty, and those from the government side have particular responsibility for ensuring the smooth transaction of government business. Each party whip's office will indicate to its members the importance of their attendance by means of weekly bulletins 'requesting' members to vote in accordance with party policy on the items of business that are listed. These will be underlined to indicate their importance once, twice or three times.

The Committee of Selection will nominate any minister who wishes to sit on a Standing Committee, as well as the relevant opposition 'shadow ministers', while whips from the government and main opposition parties will also be nominated. The smaller parties in Parliament are also entitled to representation on such committees and they usually agree amongst themselves which of their members shall sit.

It is, however, possible for the House of Commons to agree to a Bill's committee stage being taken by a Committee of the Whole House, in which case all Members of the House will be members of the Committee; and this happens on a few occasions each year, or a Select Committee (see below) or a Joint Committee of both Houses, such occurrences are, however, very rare. The committal motion may additionally provide for a Bill to be split between a Committee of the Whole House and a Public Bill Committee so that each will debate particular clauses. This is the usual course of action for the annual Finance Bill, or for those Bills where ministers feel it is appropriate that the House of Commons as a whole should have the chance to examine, debate, and vote on particular clauses, such as those raising matters of conscience, for example the age of sexual consent.

At its committee stage a Bill will be examined in detail, subject to those constraints, if any, imposed by programming. Clauses and schedules can be examined and alternatives proposed, as may deletions, amendments and additions. These are unlikely to be accepted, however, unless they receive the support of ministers and their backbench members. In practice a proposed amendment will only be accepted for debate by the chair of the committee where at least two days' notice has been given. Putting forward such a proposal is known as 'tabling' because at one time motions, questions and reports to the House of Commons were delivered to its clerks who sit at the Table of the House between the Government and Opposition front benches: nowadays there is a 'Table Office' to receive such material. Where a number of proposed amendments are received they will be 'marshalled' into a list and will then be considered in the order in which they relate to the Bill, though subsequent amendments may be tabled throughout the committee stage. Amendments may be withdrawn before consideration. An amendment which goes outside the scope of a Bill, ie one that is not relevant to its subject matter, will not be considered if the chair of the committee comes to such a conclusion, relying on previous practice and his/her judgement. Similarly amendments that are contrary to the sense of a Bill, or which are incomplete because they require further consequential amendments or which are unintelligible or ungrammatical or are trivial or time wasting may not be taken for debate.

Any number of Public Bill Committees may be created. Such a Committee is appointed for every Bill going through Parliament, and each is named after the Bill which it is considering. Such Committees, unlike the former Standing Committees, may take written and oral evidence from civil servants and other experts. The object here is to ensure that Committees may have more objective information on which to base their deliberations and decisions.

The notion of programming the progress of a Bill has also been applied to the work of committees and this is achieved by each Public Bill Committee having a sub-committee—which will include the chairman and the relevant ministers and whips—which by resolution will determine a timetable to be debated and voted on by the committee as a whole. The chairman of the committee has, as stated above, powers with regard to amendments, including the selection of amendments for discussion, debate and consideration. This power is not subject to any form of appeal but is generally used with restraint, for example to prevent the reopening of an issue already fully discussed, or on the basis that an amendment is trivial. In practice amendments put forward by ministers are always considered, and it is common practice for additions and emendations to be made in committee on this basis. The chairman of a committee also has power to group proposed amendments so that they may be considered together, for example where mutually exclusive amendments have been proposed so that the merits of both arguments can be debated. The general rules of debate in the Chamber of the House of Commons that a member may only speak once on an issue (or 'Question') is relaxed in committee to ensure matters can be debated.

In committee a Bill may be examined clause by clause and schedule by schedule in the order in which they are printed with any added clauses and schedules being considered subsequently. However, this may be replaced by the programme order which may require a different order to be followed, and will require proceedings on the Bill in question to reach (and conclude consideration of) specified portions of the bill at particular points of the overall proceedings. However, each part of a Bill has to be separately considered.

The committee stage of a Bill may be short or long, but at the conclusion of deliberations the chairman will move that the Bill be 'reported' to the House of Commons, though where programming has been applied and the final deadline has arrived the report is automatic without any proposal.

It was mentioned earlier that the committee stage of a Bill may be taken in a Committee of the Whole House with every member therefore able to speak and vote. Such a proceeding is unusual but may occur for a variety of apparently mutually exclusive reasons, for example because the Bill is uncontroversial and no amendments are expected, or because the Bill is of major constitutional importance, or because it is controversial in some way transcending normal party divisions. Bills considered in a Committee of the Whole House do not have a report stage.

It is also possible for a Bill to be referred to a Select Committee. This is a rare occurrence for such a body is a committee 'of inquiry' not 'of debate' and has to be specifically created and given powers to call for documents and witnesses. Normally only hybrid Bills, ie those which affect the general law but which also impinge particularly on certain individuals or companies in a way not experienced by others in the same class, and draft Bills are referred to Select Committees.

The Report (or 'consideration on report') stage which takes place in the Chamber of the House of Commons enables all members to debate a Bill with the possibility of amendments and new additions. Normally a Bill at this stage will be dealt with in no more than two sittings of the House, though most Government Bills will be programmed in relation to this issue. The Speaker at this stage has the same powers as a Chairman in Committee with regard to selecting and grouping of amendments for debate. However, unless programming dictates otherwise, priority is given at this stage to considering any new clauses and schedules that are proposed.

The Third Reading of a Bill is normally quite brief as no amendments having a substantive effect may be made, thus confining the attention of the House to the Bill as it currently stands and the correction of any minor errors. It is possible for a 'reasoned amendment' to be proposed, as at the Second Reading, arguing why a bill should not be given a Third Reading, but so far as a Government Bill is concerned, provided the government's majority holds firm, such a proposal should be easily disposed of.

Following this stage a Bill is sent to the House of Lords, who will be invited in a 'message' to 'agree' with the Bill. The procedure of the House of Lords is broadly similar to that in the Commons. However, the committee stage is taken in a Committee of the Whole House, and any amendments proposed may be debated unlike the Commons where, as we have seen, Committee members may 'table' amendments only to find that the Chairman of the Committee does not select them for debate. Considerable use of this flexibility is made by ministers who may seek the inclusion of considerable new material in a Bill in the House of Lords, very often in furtherance of undertakings given in the House of Commons in response to misgivings expressed about a Bill there, or the realisation that initial proposals need to be further strengthened.

Where amendments are made to a Bill by the Lords these will be notified by 'message' to the Commons. These may be accepted or resisted, for the Commons has to reach a decision on every proposed amendment by the Lords whether to agree, disagree or agree with further amendments. The time available for the consideration of such matters may be limited when a Bill is subject to programming. If the Commons agree to the amendments made by the Lords without further amendment they will send the appropriate 'message' and the Bill may then proceed to receive the Royal Assent. Where such agreement is not possible the Bill will be returned to the Lords with the alterations made by the Commons who will explain what they have done. This may result in the Upper House accepting the proposals from the Lower and then the Bill may proceed to the Royal Assent. Where, however, the Lords do not accept this and 'insist' on their amendments or offer other compromise amendments the Bill returns once more to the Lower House. The Commons may concur at this point which will enable the Bill to receive the Royal Assent. If the Commons does not agree, however, and 'insist' on their original proposals the Bill returns once more to the Lords. Should the Lords make a 'double insistence' on their amendments there is an impasse between the Houses. In theory this means the Bill is 'lost' though in practice 'messages' can continue to pass between the Houses until the end of the parliamentary session in an attempt to save the Bill. Little legislation is ever 'lost', and should the Commons wish it they may impose their views on the Lords by resorting to the Parliament Act procedure which was examined in chapter 2.

Most Bills begin their life in the House of Commons and progress in the manner described above, and that is always the case with regard to any legislative proposals relating to taxation or expenditure. Some less politically controversial proposals, for example Law Reform measures, may be introduced to Parliament via the Lords. The legislative procedure outlined above will be followed in such a case though, obviously, with the Commons receiving what has first gone through the Lords.

A Parliament can last for up to five years, but will be divided into a number of sessions, generally running from November in one year to the following October. At the end of a session the Queen, on the 'request and advice' of the Prime Minister will bring it to an end by 'prorogation', though where a Parliament has expired in time or where a Prime Minister has advised a general election prorogation is replaced by 'dissolution', see further chapter 3 above. One effect of prorogation traditionally, however, was that any Bill that had not yet gained the Royal Assent was lost, and thus had to begin its progress *ab initio* in the next session. Since 2002 it has become more common to allow the previously rarely used device of 'carrying over'. Standing Order 80A now provides that ministers may move motions to allow Bills which do not complete their process in one session to resume again in the following one. Such a motion can only relate to one Bill at a time and can be moved either at the second reading or subsequently. Where a programme order applies to a Bill that is carried over so that order will continue to apply. However, it is also provided that proceedings on a carried over Bill must come to an end once twelve months have elapsed from its first reading in the House of Commons, and the Bill will then be 'laid aside' unless the House agrees to a motion put by a minister then proceedings may be extended for a further specified period.

(b) Criticisms of legislative procedure

The chief criticism has for long been that the Commons has little choice to consider alternatives to legislative proposals. Parliament has historically been confronted with a finished product when a Bill is introduced, and the various legislative stages represent no more than opportunities for debate on what has been introduced. The case for the Bill will be presented on a number of occasions as will the case against it, and while detailed changes may be made the reality is that most legislation will reach the statute book in a form recognisably the same as when it was first printed for the Second Reading debate. There is little room for a consideration of alternative ways of achieving an object, little chance for pressure groups to express their point of view unless they can secure the ear of sympathetic members, and little time for public opinion to form and express itself.

To meet this criticism, however, would be to require a fundamental restructuring of the philosophy of British government away from the present system whereby the legislative initiative lies with the government and towards a system in which Parliament became much more involved in policy making—a task for which it is currently not equipped. Perhaps, however, a change in the electoral system to one of proportional representation which could result in various parties having to collaborate together to form a government able to 'command the confidence' of the Commons might lead to a system where a wider range of views on the development of legislation would have to be sought.

One further criticism of Bill procedure remains, and that is that Parliament displays little interest in legislation once it has been enacted, and is lacking in procedures to enable it to examine how an Act is working in practice. The Select Committee on Procedure in the 1972–73 Session argued for the creation of 'post-legislative' committees to examine the immediate impact of new legislation with a view to making recommendations—for example as to the need for amending legislation to clarify issues of interpretation. However, this was not systematically adopted though there have been a number of Select Committees created to inquire into the working of particular pieces of legislation.

(c) Post-legislative scrutiny

It has, however, become increasingly recognised over the last thirty-five years that Parliament's involvement with legislation should not cease once proposals have reached the form of statute. Indeed the House of Lords Select Committee on the Constitution recommended in 2004 that post-legislative scrutiny should apply to nearly all legislation. The government was not opposed to this in principle and in 2005 requested the Law Commission to undertake a review of what such scrutiny could mean and what form it might take. The Law Commission then launched a staged consultation exercise on the issue. The Law Commission pointed to the growth in the use of Select Committees by both Houses of Parliament and the use of draft Bills (see above) as means whereby Parliament's involvement with the legislative process has altered. Post-legislative scrutiny, however, has not been similarly developed, with the result that where legislation is not found to be working well in the courts, for example, Parliament is often unaware for many years of the need for the law to be amended. There has been, however, no clear agreement about how such post-legislative scrutiny should operate, with some proposals favouring the creation of ad hoc individual select committees to examine the working of particular statutes, while others have proposed specialised standing committees with investigatory powers. Yet other proposals have argued for the post-legislative scrutiny task to be given to the Departmental Select Committees (see below). There has also been a range of views on the point of time at which scrutiny should take place with some favouring the monitoring of legislation once newly in place while others have suggested a review from two to three or up to six years after implementation. Views have also been expressed about how the post-legislative scrutiny system might operate, for example should the explanatory notes that now regularly accompany the publication of Government Bills also include criteria by which the legislation's subsequent impact can be judged, and should there be funding to enable scrutiny committees to commission research on the working of particular Acts?

As the Law Commission points out, there is in fact some post-legislative scrutiny but it is unsystematic. Some scrutiny is undertaken by government departments of particular Acts, usually in the context of a review of overall policy on a particular issue, while some is undertaken by House of Commons Select Committees monitoring the work of central departments, but again usually on an ad hoc basis and in response to perceived public concerns over the functioning of law and policy. The Joint Select Committee of the House of Commons and House of Lords on Human Rights has also been able to identify pieces of legislation whose functioning in practice could lead to incompatibilities with Convention Rights. Post-legislative scrutiny may also be undertaken by statutory organisations who have a remit to review particular areas of law and practice, for example the Commission for Racial Equality, a body which then reports to the Secretary of State, while the Information Commissioner set up under the Data Protection Act 1998 reports annually to Parliament. The National Audit Office investigates the question of law and policy where issues relating to the economy, efficiency and effectiveness of central departments and agencies are concerned and this body reports to Parliament, while yet other legislation is required by its drafting to be renewed by committees of privy counsellors. Post-legislative scrutiny exists but essentially in a patchy and uncoordinated fashion.

As the Law Commission point out each year sees a considerable amount of legislation reach the statute book, much of it resulting in further secondary or quasi legislation (see above, chapter 4). In 2003 there were 45 new Acts of Parliament, some 4000 pages of material, and 3,354 Statutory Instruments, some 11,977 pages. There are concerns that much of this legislation may have been amended during its parliamentary process with little consideration of the changes, while an even greater concern arises as to how new legislation works in practice and, where there are difficulties how to deal with these quickly and economically. It may also be argued that the possibility of post-legislative scrutiny may lead to better proposals at the pre-legislative and legislative stages, though the counter argument is that Parliament is already there to scrutinise legislative proposals.

Post-legislative scrutiny could, however, take many forms, such as a broad review of whether a statute is meeting its intended policy objectives and to what extent, and whether it has produced unintended economic, social or legal consequences; a narrower review might concentrate only on the legal effects of an Act of Parliament, such as whether there has been delay in implementing it, or whether its provisions have been interpreted and applied in particular ways. Both forms of scrutiny are commended by the Law Commission who point to a broad intra- and extra-parliamentary consensus on the desirability of such scrutiny, with most parliamentarians favouring the broader view of what scrutiny should be. The Law Commission argued that the benefits of post legislative scrutiny would be increased governmental accountability and better and more effective law. However, this does not mean that post-legislative scrutiny may be used as an opportunity for rehashing arguments against an Act deployed during its Bill stage: the concern must rather be with outcomes. Furthermore implementing post-legislative scrutiny will place further demands on parliamentary time, while different types of scrutiny may be needed for different types of legislation—eg for those Acts that are self contained as opposed to those heavily reliant on the issue of delegated legislation.

Furthermore because of the constraints on parliamentary time and resources, the Law Commission pointed out that it might be more desirable to review only a few pieces of legislation each year rather than conduct perfunctory reviews of too many, while in some cases it might be desirable only to review particular provisions in an Act, not its entirety. In addition it was argued that some sorts of legislation might be unsuitable for review, such as Finance and Appropriation Acts, Consolidation Acts and other legislation containing its own mode of analysis and reporting. In addition the Law Commission was somewhat sceptical of the need for early scrutiny of legislation once it comes into effect, and thought that a 'normal' requirement of review after three years might be excessive. Their initially preferred view was to let the issue of timing depend on the particular Act in question.

The Law Commission proposed two broad avenues of approach to the issue.

In a minority of cases a positive commitment to review could be made by the government to review before or during an Act's Bill stage. At a prefixed time the relevant department would then carry out a review which would then be received and considered by the relevant Select Committee who might then carry out its own scrutiny exercise. In most cases, however, review would be reactive and would occur post enactment on the occurrence of particular 'triggers'. These might include decisions by the government that a particular Act should be reviewed, or a decision by a Select Committee to undertake a review. In either case the initiative might be the result of inputs from external bodies.

Where there is a prior commitment to review a document(s) setting out the policy objectives to be achieved is/are needed. These *might* include 'purpose clauses' included in the Bill, explanatory notes (which are already an established feature of Government Bills) policy documents, Regulatory Impact Assessments, inputs from Scrutiny Committees. However, none of these is free from drawbacks, for example the presence of 'purpose clauses' in legislation might impede the process of interpretation of individual provisions by the courts. To this, however, it may be replied that a more 'purposive' style of interpretation already exists within the European Community and this inevitably affects UK law, while the courts have certainly become quite 'purposive' in interpreting issues under the Human Rights Act 1998.

If a commitment to review is given, it might take the form of a ministerial undertaking or a specific 'review clause' requiring scrutiny at a preset moment, such as section 14 of the Prevention of Terrorism Act 2005, in which case the requirement for review has the force of law, or a 'sunset clause'. This latter refers to the legislation automatically ceasing to have force unless a review is undertaken to keep it in place, for example where legislation is designed to deal with a time-limited problem, or where a particular measure impinges on civil liberties and the long term desirability of this needs to be kept under review, see for example section 16 of the Electronic Communications Act 2000.

A commitment to review should also, in the initial view of the Law Commission, involve a departmental review as this will acknowledge the initial policy input of a department, its knowledge, expertise and resources. This review should then be published and laid before Parliament which might then decide to utilise, for example, the services of relevant Select Committees or that of the House of Lords, or maybe a specially created Joint Post-Legislative Scrutiny Committee. Whatever route is taken at this stage the scrutinising body needs to be able to draw on expertise outside Parliament to assist its deliberations.

In those cases where there is no prior commitment to review, and they will, of course, be the majority, appropriate 'triggers' as mentioned above, have to be identified for initiating review. These could take the form of a rolling programme of review conducted by the government, or an independent initiative from a parliamentary committee, or a proposal from an external body such as the Judges' Council, the Law Commission, a consumer organisation, or the National Audit Office. The Law Commission considered that if a Joint Post-Legislative Scrutiny Committee were to be set up, it could play a role in considering such external initiatives.

Following post-legislative review a report with recommendations would need to be made to Parliament, which might include proposals for the law to be amended. The question then arises as to whether some 'fast track' mechanism is needed to implement such changes.

In this context the Law Commission's consultation was somewhat overtaken by the introduction into Parliament of the Legislative and Regulatory Reform Bill in January 2006. This was designed to replace the Regulatory Reform Act 2001 as part of an overall policy of improving, or making 'better', regulation under the overall 'banner' of reducing burdens while improving outcomes. The initial *scope* of the proposed legislation could then be considered as referring only to those Acts of Parliament which impose regulatory burdens on, for example, commerce and industry, while also seeking the improved enforcement of those regulatory burdens deemed necessary. However, the *form* of the Bill initially appeared to indicate that ministers would have power, *by order*, to reform (ie amend, repeal or replace), *virtually any* legislation, or to implement Law Commission recommendations. Ministers would thus have legislative powers equivalent to Parliament, and could, in relation to Law Commission proposals, amend or abolish or codify any rule of the Common Law. This extremely wide-ranging power was, however, subject to conditions which were:

- that ministers must first seek non-legislative solutions to the problem they seek to address and can only proceed if there are none found;
- that the effect of any provision made by order must be proportionate to the policy objective;
- that the provision made by the order must strike a fair balance between the public interest and the interests of those affected by the order;
- that the order must not remove any protection considered necessary by ministers;
- that the provision made will not prevent any person from continuing to exercise any right or freedom which he might reasonably expect to continue to exercise;
- that the minister must explain how the foregoing conditions are met to Parliament;
- that where an order is made which confers a further power to legislate on ministers, any legislation they make has to be in the form of a statutory instrument subject to either the negative or affirmative resolution procedure (see above);
- that an order may not impose or increase taxation;
- that there are strict limits to the extent to which an order may create new criminal offences or authorise forcible entries, searches and seizures;
- that orders made must be subject to parliamentary scrutiny, including the required use of draft orders and explanatory documents, these should indicate, inter alia, savings or increases in costs likely to result from the order and any other benefits/disbenefits and the identification of any reasons for any powers to legislate conferred;
- that where an order would simplify or modernise legislation, or make its overall effect less onerous or remove inconsistencies or anomalies, details of this must be included in the explanatory documents, with a similar requirement in relation to any order implementing Law Commission recommendations.

The scrutiny procedures applicable under the proposals would vary according to the nature of what changes ministers were proposing, their subject matter, and who is likely to be affected by them. In some cases orders made under the proposals would be subject to either the negative or affirmative resolution procedures considered earlier, while in some cases super affirmative resolution procedure would apply as under the Regulatory Reform Act 2001. In all cases ministers would be required to set drafts before Parliament together with explanatory documents explaining how ministers have come to a decision to make the proposals and the information about consultation they have undertaken. The document would also explain which of the three types of scrutiny procedure the ministers recommend should apply, though either House of Parliament or the relevant committees of either House could by vote require a more onerous procedure within a twenty one day period following the laying of the draft. Thus a ministerial recommendation of negative resolution procedure could be reversed and either affirmative or super affirmative procedure substituted. A lesser level of scrutiny, however, could not be required.

Thus while the initial proposals differed from the existing law in enabling ministers to *propose* a method of scrutiny and approval, either House of Parliament, or the relevant committees, ie the Commons Regulatory Reform Committee and the Lords Delegated Powers and Regulatory Reform Committee could require a more onerous form of scrutiny. Where the super affirmative procedure was to be used, this would be as described earlier in connection with delegated legislation scrutiny generally, with ministers being required to have regard to reports and resolutions made on draft proposals by either House of Parliament, though this would *not* extend to an *obligation* to redraft an order in line with such comments, though this might take place.

While it was clear from the overall content of the Legislative and Regulatory Reform Bill that its prime purpose was to deal with the creation of 'better' regulations—though even that expression was vague and open to debate as to what 'better' could possibly mean—the extreme theoretical width of the proposals drew forth adverse comment. Thus on 16 February 2006 a letter to *The Times* from a number of highly distinguished members of the Faculty of Law of the University of Cambridge pointed out that they considered the limiting conditions within the Bill as it stood to be too few and too weak as it would enable ministers to rewrite almost any law and to, inter alia:

- abolish trial by jury;
- permit the Home Secretary to introduce house arrest;
- allow the Prime Minister to dismiss judges;
- rewrite nationality and immigration law;
- finally displace what is left of Magna Carta.

What may have been intended as a simple regulatory reform measure could therefore have the effect of upsetting the balance of the constitution—and even if this were only to happen in theory it is to be deplored and runs counter to the philosophy of the separation of powers. Critics of the Bill further argued that explanations of the proposal on the basis that it was designed to create a pathway for Law Commission proposals despite the congested state of the parliamentary timetable, ignored the question of whether Parliament was being asked to pass too much legislation in the first place, and reiterated that the Bill would enable Parliament to be bypassed or railroaded into action. Other assurances from the government that the Bill would not be used to put through any matter of political controversy were, however, further countered by the arguments that (a) this was a political safeguard only, not a legal one, and (b) similar assurances were given in respect of the wide ministerial powers under section 2(2) of the European Communities Act 1972, but in practice those powers have been used to implement very wide ranging European measures. The decision in *Oakley Inc v Anima Ltd*[4]

---

[4] [2005] EWCA Civ 1191.

indicates that the powers of ministers to make delegated legislation under the 1972 Act are already exceptionally wide and extend into the area of policy making provided what they do relate closely to the purpose of a European Directive—a vague and imprecise notion which leaves it extremely unclear as to what can and cannot be achieved under this Act. It is moreover highly arguable that the use of even the super affirmative procedure is no substitute for effective parliamentary scrutiny of legislative proposals as it is generally accepted that the scrutiny of delegated legislation is never as strict and rigorous as that of primary legislation.

These criticisms drew a strong denial from the Parliamentary Secretary at the Cabinet Office writing to *The Times* on 1 March 2006 insisting that the Bill was no more than a 'response to repeated calls on government to tackle unnecessary regulations and red tape from sources as diverse as small businesses, industry leaders, charities and voluntary organisations, front line public sector staff, the Opposition and the media'. He reasserted that the object of the Bill was simply to provide a fast track procedure for regulatory reform with scrutiny by expert parliamentary committees in place of time-consuming primary legislative procedures. He repeated that 'no proposal will pass through Parliament without scrutiny' and added: 'all proposals can be debated if required, will have to undergo a thorough statutory public consultation and meet a set of preconditions to preserve existing rights, freedoms and protections. The relevant parliamentary select committee can reject any proposal.' (Such a rejection could, however, be overridden by a vote in the House of Commons where the government could mobilise its majority for that purpose.) That such a statement should be seen as necessary by the Cabinet Office was an indication of concern over the reaction to the Bill outlined above, and demonstrated how sensitive the issue was. Indeed this was confirmed when the following day, 2 March 2006, the Shadow Chancellor of the Duchy of Lancaster also wrote to *The Times* pointing out that the Bill was not restricted by its terms only to regulatory measures, while some of its procedures involved no parliamentary debate at all. The Conservative Party in Parliament undertook to press for amendments in the Bill making it clear that its fast track provisions applied only to non-controversial matters.

The extreme criticism engendered by the proposals led to the government tabling amendments to the Bill on 4 May 2006 to make it clear that the order making powers will only be used to deliver better regulatory outcomes, to enable relevant parliamentary committees to veto orders and to extend the period during which Parliament may determine which scrutiny procedure should apply to an order from 21 to 30 days.

The government declared it had listened to criticisms and had acted to satisfy critics. The history of this Bill indicates that concerted criticism of a legislative proposal from both within and outside of Parliament can lead to a ministerial change of mind.

In the meantime the principle of post-legislative scrutiny referred to earlier was accepted by the government in June 2006 in respect of the Family Court Bill whose operation once enacted will, after a period of time, be examined by both ministers and MPs. At the same time it was announced that the Coroners Reform Bill would be published in draft form with an explanation of each clause in so called 'plain' English running alongside each more traditionally phrased provision in an attempt to assist public understanding of proposed legislation. The problem with this innovation is, however, that 'plain' English is not necessarily the *precise* English that laws require and that in future litigation there could be a reliance by one party or the other on the explanation of the law as opposed to its exact wording. If, however, this experiment is successful it could be extended to other legislation in the future.

VI. Other Means of Parliamentary Oversight

(a) EDMs

Members may express their concern about issues by tabling a written motion, in the form of a resolution expressed as a single sentence, and less than 250 words in length, requesting debate 'at an early day' on the subject. EDMs express the view of the tabling member(s) and also allow other members to express their concern by adding their names—indeed this can occur on a cross-party basis in relation to a particular issue. Once an EDM has been tabled it will remain current throughout the parliamentary session. Any topic may be made the subject of an EDM provided it is not *sub judice* and provided the motion is kept within 250 words. However, debates rarely follow on from EDMs, and their use is primarily confined to showing the strength of parliamentary feeling on particular issues to which a government may feel impelled to respond should the pressure grow sufficiently great. EDMs may not be moved on issues not suitable for debate, or where they are designed to annoy or irritate, and multiple EDMs on effectively the same issue may be struck from the order paper by the Speaker. Within these limits, however, EDMs may be used to raise a very wide range of concerns from the conduct of war through to the pay prospects of University staff.

Select Committees are inquiring bodies and can be set up for a variety of fact finding purposes. They fall into a number of classes:

- the Departmentally Related Committees, considered at greater length below;
- the Public Administration and Environmental Audit Committees, whose work cuts across all departments;
- the Procedure Modernisation, Standards and Privileges and Liaison Committees are concerned with how the House of Commons functions;
- the Statutory Instruments, Regulatory Reform and European Scrutiny Committees are concerned with particular aspects of delegated legislation;
- the Public Accounts Committee (see above).

Some Committees sit jointly with members from the House of Lords, for example the Joint Committee on Human Rights.

Members are appointed to Select Committees by a resolution of the House of Commons following nomination by the Committee of Selection, which consists mainly of the party whips. Once a Committee is established its purpose is to take evidence from witnesses, to discuss the issue remitted to the Committee and to make a report on it to the House of Commons. Their deliberations are conducted in private though as a matter of practice the public is generally admitted to meetings.

Select Committees enjoy delegated powers from the House of Commons to send for persons, papers and records, ie to obtain evidence and information though they may not compel a member of either House of Parliament to give oral or written evidence, which privilege can be utilised by ministers, and it is further unclear whether this privilege extends to enable a minister to prevent the appearance of a named official before a committee. Where evidence is sought from a department it will normally be a decision for ministers to take as to which officials should represent that department. This is a matter we shall return to below in the specific context of considering the Departmentally Related Select Committees.

Once a Committee has agreed its report on an issue remitted to it that report will be published along with the formal minutes of the Committee and the Committee may also publish the oral and written evidence it has received, and that is normally done. These reports may be recommended by the Liaison Committee, ie all the chairmen of the various Select Committees sitting together, for debate, which may take place either on an Estimates Day (see above). The government at the request of a Committee may also indicate on the daily order paper listing the business of the House of Commons that a particular report is relevant to an issue to be debated that day, or, less usually, find time within government business to have a report debated.

(b) Select Committees

Long-term oversight over both public expenditure and the formulation and implementation of policy is exercised by the Select Committees related to the work of government departments set up in 1979 and now existing under Standing Order 152 to consider the expenditure, administration and policy of relevant departments and their associated public bodies, eg regulation of utilities such as water and gas. An impulse for their creation arose on perception of the dislocation between Parliament's annual financial cycle and government's rolling programme (see above). These Committees are concerned with the expenditure, administration and policy of 'their' departments. The amount of attention paid to expenditure proposals varies greatly. Most Committees concentrate on policy and administrative issues, seeing the financial side of their work as an ancillary activity. The Treasury Committee has in the past been an exception to this, having in the past initiated macro-economic inquiries to follow the former autumn statement, PEWP and the budget, and being involved in taking evidence from ministers and senior Treasury officials. However, this Committee did not create alternative economic policies to those of the Crown, nor did it trespass willingly on areas falling within the remit of other Committees. Traditionally the Departmental Select Committees have not been concerned with draft legislation, however, following recommendations by the Modernisation Committee they may now involve themselves in pre-legislative scrutiny of draft Bills, see further above.

Each Committee has a clerk and usually an assistant clerk and may have specialist inquiry staff to assist its inquiries with two to four administrative support staff. Further support is given by the Parliamentary Office of Science and Technology, and from the scrutiny unit established in the Central Committee Office of the House of Commons. This unit includes lawyers, accountants and other expert staff and may assist in examining draft bills or investigating the estimates. Specialist advisers may also be appointed by Committees on an ad hoc basis.

Since 2002 each Committee has had core illustrative tasks to pursue, as fixed by the House of Commons, including considering major policy initiatives, consideration of governmental responses to emerging issues, conducting pre-legislative scrutiny of bills, examining and reporting on estimates, monitoring performance targets in the public sector, taking evidence from relevant ministers on an annual basis, and taking evidence from regulatory and inspecting bodies, considering major appointments made by senior ministers, examining relevant treaties. Within these wide terms of reference, however, Committees set their own agendas, though they must consider the spending plans and budgets of 'their' departments on an annual basis. Committees also vary widely in the number of reports they produce each year, but each report will analyse and assess the information the Committee has received and will include a number of recommendations, to which the government will normally respond within two months—it does not necessarily accept all or any of the recommendations made.

Have these Committees actually enabled the Commons to exercise more effective oversight over the executive? Opinion has always been somewhat divided on this issue. However, in 1985 Gavin Drewry concluded in *The New Select Committees: A Study of the 1979 Reforms* that the Select Committee system was 'here to stay' in that the Committees offer 'something to everyone': backbench MPs may specialise in issues which interest them; ministers have an opportunity to explain themselves and their policies in an atmosphere which is inquiring rather than centred on debate; pressure groups may present their arguments in a public context, and even civil servants may 'recognise the benefits of arguing publicly a departmental case'.[5] However, Drewry concluded, the chief benefit flowing from the Select Committee system was the vastly increased flow of information resulting from their work—some of it information that would not otherwise have been discussed in Parliament. To that extent the Committees have made government more open and accountable. In 1989 in *Whitehall* Peter Hennessy concluded also that the new Committees had wrought a change in the relationship of the legislature and the executive. In particular every now and again articulate and intelligent questions by members on the Committees had forced officials to burn their lamps late 'thinking through the nuances of departmental policy' as they sought to ensure that 'their' ministers would be able to respond to questions effectively while under the public gaze of the press and the other media. Hennessy also records that ministers found that the Select Committees increased their own and their civil servants' workloads.[6]

By the end of the 1980s, therefore, there was something of a consensus that:

• the 'new' Select Committee system had contributed to the Commons having a more effective system for scrutinising the executive than previously, enabling an examination of the long-term development and implementation of policy, the discharge of functions and the allocation of resources;

• ministers and officials had come to accept a need to be able, at least on occasions, to explain and justify their activities;

• however, the Committees were unable to make policy nor to change it materially, nor to affect financial issues and the level of public expenditure;

• neither did the Committees much influence legislation, either in the pre-parliamentary or parliamentary stages;

• the Committees had not brought about any ministerial resignations, nor had they led to the disciplining of officials;

• they have not achieved a high 'public profile' and rarely 'make the news'.

• they do, however, ensure that there is a regular dialogue between the executive and the legislature in which criticisms can be voiced and explanations given.

We may now ask what has happened since then?

[5] (OUP, Oxford, 1985), p. 392.
[6] Hennessy, P, *Whitehall* (Secker & Warburg, London, 1989), pp. 330–336.

(i) Select Committees; their strengths and weaknesses

Departmental Committees have (as we have seen) powers under the Standing Orders of the House to 'send for persons, papers and records'. However, they cannot compel the attendance of a Member of Parliament—and that includes ministers. The Committees are in this respect forced to rely on a degree of voluntary co-operation—which is usually forthcoming. However, for example in 1991 the Ministry of Defence and the Secretary of State for Defence—Mr Tom King—declined to give information to the Defence Committee on proposed reductions in the size of the Army. It had been proposed in 1978/79 that the Committees should have much stronger powers to compel the attendance of witnesses, including ministers, but the government would only agree to a voluntary attendance by ministers, with a promise that if further powers were needed the matter would be considered at a later date. The Committees have formal powers to summon other individuals, including civil servants, but the powers are rarely resorted to.

If information requested is withheld the Committee in question must decide whether to use its 'persons and papers' powers. This involves a motion being put to the whole House of Commons for a resolution that the necessary 'persons and papers' are made available to the Committee. A failure to respond to such a resolution would be a contempt of Parliament. Such a motion has to be debated and voted on and this places the government's supporters in an acutely embarrassing position. By definition, the majority in the Committee reflects the majority in the House. The majority in the Committee, irrespective of party loyalty, however, believe that information needed for the functioning of the Committee, and hence the House of Commons, is being withheld. Where that information is being withheld by the government itself a clear conflict emerges: do the government's supporters in the Commons vote with their colleagues on the Committee and demand the information, or do they succumb to the pressures of the party whips? The whips will argue that the government should not be embarrassed by its own supporters and that party loyalty should be maintained.

In 1990 in *The Working of the Select Committee System*,[7] the efficiency and working of the Committees was examined. The 1990 report was a much more modest document than that of 1978/79 which led to the creation of the Committees, reflecting political realisation that what was accomplished in 1979 could not be repeated in 1990, especially with a government that had found itself frequently criticised over the years by the Committees. The report did, however, criticise the government for the delay it had shown in both 1983 and 1987 in setting up the Committees following the general elections of those years. One or two radical voices were raised, however. One Labour MP called for MPs to select the Committees by ballot as opposed to the present system whereby the party whips and the Committee of Selection make the choice.

So far as the relationship of Select Committees with the Civil Service is concerned, while the government has stated that as a matter of practice the Committees will be provided with such departmental information as is necessary to their investigations, 'The Civil Service Code' which was modelled on a draft actually put forward by the Commons Treasury and Civil Service Select Committee, and which came into force in January 1996 (being replaced in June 2006), stressed that civil servants are Crown servants and owe their loyalty to the Crown and government of the day. This is a term of employment of civil servants. The Code stressed that ministers are accountable to Parliament and that they have the duty to give information to

---

[7] Select Committee on Procedure: Session 1990, HC Paper 19–1.

Parliament and not to deceive or knowingly to mislead Parliament. Civil servants may not without authority disclose official information which has been communicated in confidence within government circles. The Code is supplemented by other relevant documents and understandings. The 'Armstrong Memorandum' was originally circulated in 1985, and was revised in 1987, and further revised in 1997. This 'Note by the Head of the Home Civil Service' repeats once more: 'Civil Servants are servants of the Crown', and exist 'to provide the Government of the day with advice on the formulation of the policies of the Government, to assist in carrying out the decisions of the Government, and to manage and deliver the services for which the Government is responsible.' With regard to the Select Committees, the note continued 'In [situations where they are required or expected to give evidence to a Parliamentary Select Committee] they should be guided by Government policies, codes and guidance issued from time to time . . . and by the requirements of security and confidentiality. . . . Thus, when a civil servant gives evidence to a Select Committee . . . he or she does so as the representative of the Minister . . . and subject to the Minister's instructions . . . The ultimate responsibility lies with Ministers . . . to decide what information should be made available, and how and when it should be released, whether it is to Parliament [or] to Select Committees . . .'

The basic weakness of the Select Committee system is that to a great extent they are dependent on *voluntary* disclosure of information by ministers, civil servants, and even private citizens, as the investigation into the collapse of the Maxwell media empire in January 1992 showed. The sons of the deceased Robert Maxwell were summoned to give evidence to the Committee then known as the Commons Social Security Committee, but both claimed a 'right to silence' and refused to answer questions. There was no legal justification for their claim, but the work of the Committee was hampered because to have forced disclosure would have required lengthy, and uncertain as to their outcome, procedures in Parliament.

The problem is that to enforce a Committee's right to obtain information the issue must, as stated earlier, be made subject to debate and vote before the whole house. The problems then are:

- will the issue be treated simply as a party political one with the whips being involved;
- does the Committee fear, however, setting a precedent so that a failure to pursue the matter indicates to others that they too may refuse to answer questions (and in the past *ministers* have got away with refusing to answer questions, eg Lord Young over the investigation into the sale of Rover to British Aerospace and Sir Leon Brittan over the Westland affair);
- does the Committee wish to press its claim if the consequence is that information is released that could prejudice possible future criminal proceedings, either for the defence or the prosecution;
- does the Committee wish to go so far as to press the whole House to pass a motion that the Committee's questions must be answered so that a further refusal constitutes contempt with imprisonment as a punishment for those in contempt?

Further debate on the role and functioning of the Select Committees arose after the 1992 general election. Anxious to avoid criticism that it had dragged its feet in 1983 and 1987 in setting up the Committees, the government got down to the task before the Commons' summer recess. However, a problem arose over the appointment of committee chairmen. The Commons do not select their own Select Committees, the selection is 'arranged' by the party whips and the Committee of Selection. The Conservatives changed their party's rules on selection for chairing Committees by introducing a new rule that any Conservative MP who had served continuously on select committees since 1979 should be ineligible to be a Select Committee member. The consequence of the change was that certain long-standing Conservative Committee chairmen were forced out of their chairs, for example Nicholas Winterton who had frequently been critical of his own party's ministers in relation to health service policy. The impression remained strong at Westminster that Mr Winterton together with another Conservative Committee chairman who had criticised government policy, Sir John Wheeler, had, in effect, been 'sacked', and that the whips had had a hand in the matter.

The new Conservative party 'three Parliament' rule (ie the rule that those who have served for three consecutive Parliaments on Select Committees shall no longer be eligible for membership) severely dented the image of the Committees as independent watchdogs. It must be remembered that the Committees were set up to provide backbench members on both sides of the Commons with a new means to probe and scrutinise the activities of government professionally and effectively away from the highly party political atmosphere of the Commons chamber itself. Accordingly the cross-party Committee on Selection was set up to choose who should sit on the Committees—though the whips were allowed some say in the matter. The three Parliament rule appeared to introduce an element of party political interference into the functioning of the Select Committee system. However, Standing Order 122A now provides that, unless the House otherwise orders, no Select Committee may have as its chairman any member who has served in that capacity for the two previous Parliaments, or for a continuous period of eight years, whichever is greater.

Currently, Committee chairmen are chosen by the Committees themselves from their ranks and an opposition member may take the chair—but there is no Standing Order of the House of Commons enshrining this. Since 1980 the Liaison Committee (see above) has met to consider all the work of the Committees and to make recommendations to the House. Its Report *Shifting the Balance*,[8] recommended that there should be a new system of Committee membership to avoid the suggestion of control by Party Managers. There should be a Chairman of Committees with two deputies, while members should have the freedom to propose themselves for Committee membership. The government was opposed to change, and in its response to the Report argued:

• Select Committees operate within a Constitutional framework which requires them to reflect the party composition of the House of Commons.

• The membership has to be endorsed by the Commons as a whole, and in the past the recommendations of the Committee of Selection have not always been accepted.

• The present selection system was itself recommended by the Select Committee on Procedure—in 1978.

• Some Committees are more popular than others and self selection might lead to competition for places on some and a dearth of candidates for others.

• Opposition parties are entitled to at least a proportion of Committee memberships—a feature guaranteed by the present system.

The government did, however, reaffirm the commitment of ministers to work with the Committees—though pointing out that the increase in Select Committee activity throughout the 1990s has put pressure on ministerial and departmental time. The government also reaffirmed its commitment to the pre-legislative scrutiny of Bills, but pointed out that this places pressure on departments and parliamentary draftsmen to speed up the advance drafting programme which enables Bills to be produced in draft. The government stated this

---

[8] House of Commons Liaison Committee: Session 1999/2000 HC 300.

programme would, however, continue to take second place to the drafting and redrafting of legislation actually before Parliament. The government also undertook to bring forward proposals to amend the Standing Orders of the Commons to enable the creation of ad hoc Select Committees to deal with issues cutting across departmental remits, and also to enable the existing Committees to meet together and to exchange papers, and this has in fact been done under, inter alia, Standing Order 137A.

For the moment, therefore, Select Committees retain the functions (though not the names which have regularly changed with the reorganisation of departments) conferred on them in 1980 to obtain information, to appoint specialist advisers, and to make reports to the Commons of their conclusions, and to make special reports on any matters they think it proper to bring to the Commons' notice. On the whole the Committees manage to present unanimous conclusions to the Commons, though where a highly controversial and divisive issue is examined this may lead to a split in a Committee and the issue of a minority report.

As there is an undertaking that the government will always respond to a Committee report, and thus there will be a reaction to criticisms made which can be taken up by members and the media, further publicity can be given to the work of Select Committees. However, it must be admitted that their reports rarely make 'headline news', and their chief value remains the eliciting and elucidation of information from government.

VII. Ultimate Control Over Ministers

Theoretically Parliament could refuse ministers' proposals for legislation or their 'requests' for supply. In fact, this is unlikely to happen. Between 1983 and 1987 only eight out of 165 Government Bills failed to be enacted within the session in which they were introduced. Four of these were 'hybrid' and were held over to the next session, and so did not actually 'fail'. Of the others: one was withdrawn to await the outcome of certain proceedings; the *principle* of a second was effectively incorporated in subsequent legislation; one concerned only limited technical issues of land law, and only the fourth, the Shops Bill 1985, represented a real defeat for the government, which even then did not resign for the issue was not sufficiently major. (See also chapter 4.) Likewise, Parliament is not always able to extract from either ministers or civil servants all the information it wishes as, for example, was the case with investigations by the Foreign Affairs Committee into the sinking of the *Belgrano* in 1982, and similarly, investigations by the Defence Committee into the Westland Affair in 1986 and into the future of the Brigade of Ghurkas in 1988–89. However, it is arguable that, as traditional means of debate and questions in Parliament are becoming less effective as checks on executive power, so the Departmental Select Committees have emerged as a new means, albeit imperfect, of producing, overall, an increased flow of information about the activities of government, and for holding ministers to account. And it remains true that a minister may be forced to resign as a result of criticism in the Commons (see also chapter 4). Likewise the House of Lords over the last few years has inflicted defeats on ministers, particularly where the Upper House has realised it has had the moral support of the government's own Commons backbenchers. Nevertheless such defeats are infrequent and the Upper House continues to lack legitimate political authority to oppose the will of the leaders of the elected majority in the Commons. A government with an effective and mobilised Commons majority has little reason to fear that its proposals will not proceed, changed only as ministers themselves wish, through Parliament.

VIII. Reform

Could parliamentary procedure be reformed to enhance control over the government? In 1999 the government was reported as having under consideration electronic voting systems to eliminate the need for members to go physically through the lobbies of the House to be counted—this was perhaps predictable from a government which arguably is obsessed with 'IT'. Such a system might at least enable MPs to register an abstention, which the present voting system does not allow. However, does new technology sit well with other current Commons procedures? We have already examined above the brief experiment with more 'family friendly' hours for sittings of the House, but whether any system enabling members to get to bed at a reasonable hour would increase its effectiveness is open to question. Are the real problems:

• the sheer volume of legislation put forward by government often in an ill-drafted initial form;

• the lack of formal pre-legislative scrutiny;

• a need for rearranged parliamentary year with shorter recesses;

• a tendency for ministers to bypass Parliament and make important policy announcements via the media or through their departmental press officers;

• a reluctance by ministers to answer parliamentary questions other than slowly and in a fashion giving away the least amount of information?

Despite all these problems, however, it is essential to remember that the chief role of Parliament is to hold the executive to account, and that ministers must explain and justify their policies there. Even so it is hard to escape the conclusions of Jowell and Oliver that: 'The House of Commons has had to struggle . . . to achieve some relatively modest modernizing reforms . . . since 1997. The dominance of party . . . serves to suppress any sense of a *corporate* House of Commons function or identity in holding government to account as opposed to sustaining it in power.'[9]

(a) Future reform?

In February 2006 the Joseph Rowntree Federation published *Power to the People*, the report of 'Power', an independent inquiry into Britain's democracy chaired by Baroness Helena Kennedy. This focused on what it concluded were malaises in our constitution and suggested certain reforming measures. It is certainly true that there has been a decline in voting at general elections and the report attributed much of this phenomenon to voter alienation with politicians and the main political parties. In more detail it was concluded, inter alia, that:

• voters do not feel that our democratic processes provide them with sufficient influence over political decision making;

• there appears to be too little difference in style or content between the policies of the major political parties;

---

[9] Jowell, J and Oliver, D, *The Changing Constitution* (5th edn, OUP, Oxford, 2004), p. xiii.

- there is a perception that elections depend on changes in control in a small number of marginal parliamentary constituencies so that the voters in those constituencies have a greater degree of power and influence than other citizens;
- there is a large body of people within British society who are well educated and affluent and who are accustomed to exercising control and choice with regard to consumer decisions, and they are impatient with not being able to exercise the same degree of choice and control with regard to political issues;
- there is much less deference to 'authority' within our society and not the same degree of class-based homogeneity which characterised much of the nineteenth and twentieth centuries during which our current political and constitutional structures were formed, and this leads to alienation from these traditional structures;
- there is a perception that too much political power is not subject to effective constitutional oversight.

With specific regard to Parliament the report, inter alia, recommended:

- there should be a concordat drawn up between ministers and Parliament which makes it clear who has the power to take decisions while providing Parliament with significant powers of scrutiny over ministers and the possibility of initiating policies itself;
- the powers of parliamentary Select Committees should be enhanced so that they have power to scrutinise and veto government appointments and to be able to subpoena witnesses to come before them;
- specialist Select Committees in the House of Lords should have power to co-opt expert non-members of the House to add specialist knowledge and experience where this is necessary when considering complex legislative or policy areas;
- limits should be placed on the powers of the party whips;
- in addition to powers to initiate legislation, Parliament should also have powers to set public inquiries in motion and to act on public petitions;
- there should be a Select Committee with overarching powers to scrutinise the activities of ministers when they deal with supra national bodies such as the European Union with the particular remit of ensuring that ministers are accountable for their actions and that their negotiations, etc are conducted in the best interests of the British people.

The picture painted by the report is one of a somewhat 'toothless' Parliament which needs not just a radical overhaul of its powers but almost a revolutionary change in its position with regard to the executive. Not only is such a change unlikely to occur, but it is uncertain whether Parliament is quite so toothless as it might be supposed, given its current role and functions, while many of the report's recommendations can be characterised as vague and too swayed by dissatisfaction with individual politicians as opposed to major weaknesses in constitutional and governing structures.

It cannot be too often stressed that Parliament is not a policy making body, and that the attachment of some thinkers to the notion that power is derived by Parliament from the people and then further sub-delegated to a committee known as 'the Cabinet' is historically incorrect and politically misleading. Parliament has neither the expertise nor the personnel to become a policy initiator. To provide it with such resources would be expensive and would simply duplicate much of the work of the Civil Service, while to give Parliament direct access to the expertise of the Civil Service would increase the work load of that body and would cause unacceptable conflicts of interest by creating a servant with two masters.

Ours is a system of representative democracy in which power is not derived from the people, rather its exercise is legitimised by their democratic involvement in electing central and local legislative bodies. There may well be a case for enhancing that degree of involvement by, for example, moving away from the current 'first past the post' system of electing Parliament and towards a system of proportional representation. Equally there is a case for enhancing the scrutiny powers of parliamentary Select Committees. However, there is much less of a case for arguing that the electorate should have direct legislative powers. To allow, for example, a powerful and well organised pressure group to have a direct influence in the initiations of policies by means of public petition to Parliament, could result in alienation on the part of those who do not share in the particular political vision of the pressure group, and anger on the part of those groups whose petitions having been debated are rejected.

The procedures and functioning of Parliament may well require reform, but there is little case for altering Parliament's current representational status and for giving it powers to initiate policies of its own motion.

FURTHER READING

Drewry G (ed) *The New Select Committees: A Study of the 1979 Reforms* (2nd edn, Clarendon Press, Oxford, 1989).

Englefield D (ed) *Commons Select Committees: Catalysts for Progress* (Longman, Harlow, 1984).

Erskine May *Treatise on the Law, Privileges, Proceedings and Usage of Parliament* (23rd edn, Butterworth Tolley, London, 2004).

Evans P *Dod's Handbook of House of Commons Procedure* (Dod's Parliamentary Communications, London, 2004).

Griffith JAG and Ryle M *Parliament: Functions Practice and Procedures* (Sweet and Maxwell, London, 1989) chs 6, 7, 8, 11 and 13.

Harden I 'Money and the Constitution: Financial Control, Reporting and Audit' (1993) 13 Legal Studies 16.

Harden I and Lewis N *The Noble Lie: The British Constitution and the Rule of Law* (Hutchinson, London, 1986) ch 4.

House of Commons *Standing Orders of the House of Commons: Public Business* (HMSO, London, 2005).

Jowell J and Oliver D (eds) *The Changing Constitution* (5th edn, OUP, Oxford, 2004) chs 6, 10 and 11.

Law Commission *Consultation Paper No 178, Post Legislative Scrutiny* (Law Commission, London, 2006).

Longley L and Davidson R *The New Roles of Parliamentary Committees* (Frank Cass, London, 1998).

Marsh D and Read M *Private Members' Bills* (Cambridge University Press, Cambridge, 1988).

Norton P *Parliament in British Politics* (Palgrave Macmillan, London 2005).

Power Inquiry *Power to the People: The report of Power: An Independent Inquiry into Britain's Democracy* (Joseph Rowntree Foundation, York, 2006).

Riddell P *Parliament Under Pressure* (Victor Gollancz, London, 1998).

Silk P *How Parliament Really Works* (5th edn, Longman, London, 2004).

7 THE UNITED KINGDOM AND THE EUROPEAN COMMUNITY AND UNION

I. The Creation and Development of the European Community and Union

(a) The origins of the European Communities

Any discussion of the European Communities must commence in a Europe devastated by war, devastated politically, socially and economically, and with the desire for political, social and economic reconstruction, together with the fervent wish that never again should there be war in Europe. To many, the solution lay in some form of inter-state action and in the immediate post-war years a number of organisations were created. The Organisation for European Economic Co-operation (later the Organisation for Economic Co-operation and Development: OECD) was established in 1948 and was aided by financial assistance ('Marshall Aid') from the United States. The North Atlantic Treaty Organisation (NATO) was established in 1949 as a military and defence alliance between the United States, Canada and several European states. The Council of Europe was established in 1949 to create closer links between the countries of Europe and to foster economic, social and cultural co-operation and, in particular, to foster the protection of human rights. To many, the solution lay in some form of unification or integration. In 1950, Robert Schuman, the French foreign minister, proposed that the way to provide for peace in Europe was to put the control of the principal raw materials of war, coal and steel, in the hands of a supranational organisation. The pooling of production of coal and steel, it was argued, would make the possibility of yet another conflict between France and Germany more unlikely, and would act as a basis for a common approach to the then perceived fears of Soviet aggression. Furthermore, coal and steel being also materials of reconstruction, this would act as a basis for reconstruction and economic expansion. The Schuman Plan was agreed to by Germany, Belgium, France, Italy, Luxembourg and the Netherlands and the Treaty creating the European Coal and Steel Community was signed in Paris in 1951. This provided for the elimination of tariffs and quotas on trade in iron ore, coal, coke, and steel within the community, there was a common external tariff on imports relating to the coal and steel industries from other countries, and controls on production and sales. To organise all this, the Paris treaty established supranational bodies: a high authority with executive powers, a council of ministers to safeguard the interests of the member states, a common assembly with advisory authority only, and a court of justice to settle disputes.

The members of the Coal and Steel Community gradually concluded that each country could improve its economic progress by the creation of a European trading area and that this would give them a firm base on which to establish export markets with the rest of the world. The Spaak Report (1956) emphasised that the individual states of Europe could not individually hope to emulate the vast industrial might of the United States of America, which comprised so many more millions of producers and buyers, and that a European unit of production should be established. Larger markets would promote competition and greater productivity. To achieve economies of scale and to find new customers, European businesses would need to operate in a larger market than each one's home nation. There should be a single European market, with obstacles to trade being abolished. The Treaty of Rome was signed in 1957 and the European Economic Community (EEC) came into existence on 1 January 1958. The Treaty of Rome provided for the gradual elimination of import duties and quotas on all trade between member states and for the institution of a common external tariff. Member nations agreed to implement common policies regarding transport and agriculture, and to permit the free movement of people and financial resources within the boundaries of the community. On 1 January 1958, there also came into existence the European Atomic Energy Community.

The United Kingdom had not played any positive part in these developments, but, fearing that the creation of the EEC might have harmful effects, by the elimination of trade barriers within the EEC and the creation by that Community of trade barriers against other countries, helped to create the European Free Trade Area in conjunction with Austria, Denmark, Norway, Portugal, Sweden and Switzerland. Europe was at sixes and sevens and gradually several of the seven decided to seek entry to the EEC. As the United Kingdom White Paper[1] put it: 'It is generally agreed that for advanced industrial countries the most favourable environment is one where markets are large and are free from barriers to [trade]. In particular, the development and exploitation of modern industrial technology, upon which so much of our employment and income increasingly depends, requires greater resources for research and development and wider markets than any one Western European nation can provide.' The United Kingdom, Ireland and Denmark joined the EEC on 1 January 1973. The United Kingdom's constitution was to be changed by a rather more abrupt and dramatic process than has hitherto been described in this work, because the aims of economic integration had resulted in the Treaty of Rome itself containing constitutional and legal implications which had had (and would continue to have) resounding effects on the constitutions of all the member states.

[1] 1971, Cmnd 4715.

(b) The constitutional implications of economic integration

Any organisation, including any organisation of states, which comes together with a common purpose, or a series of common purposes, will tend to create a formal, political, structure by which those purposes may be achieved and a general system according to which the members of the organisation agree to be governed. In one sense, concentrating on economic policies was not as innocuous as it might at first seem, because inherent in the methods and machinery designed to promote the desired economic integration is the surrender, in some part at least, of national sovereignty. Traditionally, states have taken measures to protect their own economies (tariffs, customs duties, import quotas, subsidies for domestic industry and the imposition of taxes on imported goods) and such measures are the antithesis of economic integration. Economic integration may be achieved by free trade areas (whereby member states eliminate restrictions relating to trade between those states on products originating in such states, leaving individual states free to impose restrictions on products originating from outside the area), customs unions (which take integration a stage further by the adoption by the member states of a common position with regard to uniform restrictions with regard to products originating outside the union) and common markets (which take the integration even further by eliminating all restrictions to free trade, by permitting free movement of such factors of production as labour and capital, and by harmonising the legislation and administrative practices of the states concerned).

There is a logical simplicity underpinning the infrastructure created by the Treaty of Rome. Economic agreement between states is not new but traditionally such co-operation has involved the reservation of national sovereignty in order to defend national interests and this immediately forms a barrier to economic integration and, if used only once by one member state, may lead to its use by all other member states. Therefore, the successful working of economic integration depended on the surrender of national sovereignty in favour of common and uniform rules imposed by the constituent states upon themselves. Traditionally, states enter into agreements by way of treaties and resolve disputes among themselves or by submission to international arbitration and judgment. Traditionally, such treaties are comprehensive and self-contained documents, designed to enact all matters contemplated by the parties involved and requiring amending treaties, agreed to by all parties concerned, should they not fulfil their purpose. A process of economic integration within Europe needed a different sort of treaty and a different sort of constitution. It was accepted that the process would be a continuing and developing one and that no one could predict all possible contingencies.

Although the main aims (for example, the customs union, the free movement of persons and capital, common policies in agriculture and transport) and many major principles (for example, fulfilment of Community obligations and non-discrimination on grounds of nationality) could be laid down in the founding treaty, the implementation of those aims and, in particular, the harmonisation of national laws in accordance with those aims, could only practicably be undertaken by an 'ongoing mechanism'. There had to be institutions to look after both day-to-day regulation of the system and the long-term developments. It was accepted that policies would need to be developed and that a 'policy initiating' authority would be necessary; it was accepted that secondary rule making would be needed in order to implement the Treaty and that a 'legislature' with the power to make binding decisions, creating legislation which would have legal force in each member state and take precedence over each member state's domestic laws, would be necessary; it was accepted that there might be divergent interpretations of those rules by the individual states and that an authority (such as a 'supreme court') to make binding decisions on questions of interpretation would be necessary; it was accepted that primary and secondary legislation might need also to be developed by reference to the legal principles which were then common to the member states; it was accepted that states might want to continue to protect domestic economies and might be slow to implement the rules or, indeed, to fail to implement those rules and that independent machinery to provide continuing supervision of member states and to make binding declarations as to whether a state had fulfilled or failed to fulfil a Community obligation would be necessary. In other words, it was accepted that the normal functions allocated by constitutions to organs within the state (legislative, executive and judicial) should be applied to the process of economic integration by the creation of Community institutions, with power to carry out the purposes of the Community independently of the member states, in which the national interests would be represented but would not be permitted to hinder the process of integration. The Treaty of Rome, albeit concluded in the form of an international agreement, nonetheless constituted the constitutional charter of a Community based on the rule of law.

That constitutional charter is also an integral part of the constitutions of the member states. Community law does not simply impose new benefits and obligations upon member states but (as will be seen) may create benefits and obligations for persons other than the member states within the domestic legal systems of all member states. The legal and constitutional implications of such a proposition follow with some logic. There is an 'all or nothing' situation: the Community is based on a principle of solidarity in that member states cannot act unilaterally and a share in the envisaged prosperity brings with it a duty to comply with obligations; the Community is based on a principle of cohesion in that economic forces are transnational and must be met, both inwardly and outwardly, by a common response; Community law must be implemented in all states and must be the same in all states, otherwise states might revert to national protection of domestic industry and services; all states must provide for this implementation or incorporation in accordance with their national constitutions and by the constitutional organs within the state; since Community law must be the same in all states, the law and administrative practices of those states cannot be different from, or conflict with, Community law and any differences or conflicts must be eliminated in each state; finally, if there is a difference or conflict which has not been eliminated within the state, such conflict must be resolved by the acceptance of the superiority of Community law; a state cannot opt out of any part of Community law which it finds burdensome and either surrenders all of its sovereignty in those areas where the Treaty provides for Community law to be created or surrenders nothing of its sovereignty and is no longer treated as a member of the Community.

(c) The Single European Act (SEA)

The Treaty of Rome referred to the establishment of a 'common market' and the progressive approximation of the 'economic policies of the member states', and the treaty contained measures to promote those aims, together with appropriate institutional and legislative machinery. During the early 1980s, it was accepted that the common market was not accomplished and that there were barriers which would prevent it from being accomplished. There was also pressure to widen the areas in which the Community was empowered to act (and, consequently, to limit individual member states) and to move towards a European Union based on more than just a common market. Furthermore, there was pressure to amend the institutional framework of the original treaty on the ground that the treaty did not provide an adequate constitutional framework within which the creation of the common market and further integration could effectively be carried out. These proposals culminated in the Single European Act (SEA), which came into force on 1 July 1987. According to the SEA, the member states are 'moved by the will [to] transform relations as a whole among their States into a European Union [and are] determined to improve the economic and social situation by extending common policies and pursuing new objectives and to ensure a smoother functioning of the Communities by enabling the Institutions to exercise their powers under conditions most in keeping with Community interests'. The SEA instituted radical reforms. The SEA required the member states to adopt more than 300 measures to remove physical, technical, and fiscal barriers in order to establish a single market, in which the economies of the member states would be completely integrated. There was a significant extension of the areas of competence of the Community. The principal extension related to the completion of the internal market and other extensions related to economic and monetary union, social policy, strengthening the scientific and technological basis of European industry and the protection of health and the environment. Finally, member states agreed to endeavour jointly to formulate and implement a European foreign policy with foreign ministers and the Commission meeting regularly through the framework of European political co-operation.

(d) The Treaty on European Union (TEU)

The Treaty on European Union (the 'Maastricht Treaty') (TEU) came into force on 1 November 1993. The member states resolved to mark a new stage in the process of European integration, resolved to promote economic and social progress for their peoples which is balanced and sustainable (in particular through the creation of an area without internal frontiers, through the strengthening and converging of their economies and through the establishment of economic and monetary union, ultimately including a single and stable currency), resolved to establish a citizenship of the Union common to nationals of their countries, resolved to implement a common foreign and security policy including the eventual framing of a common defence policy, which might in time lead to a common defence, reaffirmed their objective to facilitate the free movement of persons, while ensuring the safety and security of their peoples, by including provisions on justice and home affairs in the Treaty, resolved to continue the process of creating an ever closer union among the peoples of Europe, in which decisions are taken as closely as possible to the citizen in accordance with the principle of subsidiarity, and, in view of further steps to be taken in order to advance European integration, decided to establish a European Union.[2]

The Treaty of Rome, establishing the EEC, was significantly amended in order to establish a European Community and Union. Throughout that Treaty, the term 'European Economic

---

[2] TEU, Preamble.

Community' was replaced by the term 'European Community'. The TEU instituted the so-called 'three pillars' of the Union: the Community pillar, the common foreign and security pillar, and the police and judicial co-operation pillar. The Union is founded on the original European Communities, and the core of the Union is still the European Community (the 'first pillar' of the Union), with its supranational governing institutions. However, member states were enjoined to create an economic and monetary union. Now, the activities of the member states and the Community were to include the adoption of an economic policy based on the close co-ordination of member states' economic policies, on the internal market and on the definition of common objectives, and conducted in accordance with the principle of an open market economy with free competition; these activities would include the irrevocable fixing of exchange rates leading to the introduction of a single currency, and the definition and con-duct of a single monetary policy and exchange-rate policy the primary objective of both of which would be to maintain price stability and, without prejudice to this objective, to support the general economic policies in the Community, in accordance with the principle of an open market economy with free competition; these activities of the member states and the Community would entail compliance with the following guiding principles: stable prices, sound public finances and monetary conditions and a sustainable balance of payments. Responsibility for supervising the proposed single currency was given to the European Central Bank (ECB) (see head II(d) below). New competences were added. For example, the Community committed itself to the attainment of a high level of consumer protection through action which supports and supplements the policy pursued by the member states to protect the health, safety and economic interests of consumers and to provide adequate information to consumers and the Community committed itself to the pursuit of the following environmental objectives, namely, preserving, protecting and improving the quality of the environment, protecting human health, prudent and rational utilisation of natural resources, and promoting measures at international level to deal with regional or worldwide environmental problems. Citizenship of the Union was proclaimed loudly and inserted into the Community Treaty, but in no way reflects the normal attributes of citizenship of a sovereign state, and is really a cheap imitation of the genuine article.

Brief mention will be made of the provisions in the TEU for introducing inter-governmental activity in the sensitive fields of foreign policy and security and justice and home affairs (the other two 'pillars of the Union'). The emphasis here is on intergovernmen-tal co-operation and decision-making rather than a transfer of national competence and sovereignty to the Community institutions. The Union and its member states would define and implement a common foreign and security policy, to safeguard the common values, fundamental interests and independence of the Union, to strengthen the security of the Union and its member states in all ways, to preserve peace and strengthen international security, to promote international co-operation and to develop and consolidate democracy and the rule of law, and respect for human rights and fundamental freedoms. However, the fundamental principle of free movement of persons within the Community can conflict with the security and other policies of member states. Consequently, member states would regard the following areas as matters of common interest, namely, asylum policy, rules governing the crossing by persons, both legally and illegally, of the external borders of the member states and the exercise of controls thereon, immigration policy and policy regarding nationals of third countries, combating drug addiction, combating fraud on an international scale, judicial co-operation in civil matters, judicial co-operation in criminal matters, customs co-operation and police co-operation for the purposes of preventing and combating terrorism, unlawful drug trafficking and other serious forms of international crime (trade in stolen vehicles, people smuggling, pornography, the traffic in radioactive and nuclear materials, money laundering), in connection with the organisation of a Union-wide system for exchanging information within a European Police Office (Europol). These policies would be undertaken using inter-governmental action rather than the Community institutions, but those institutions would be consulted and kept informed of what has been determined.

(e) The Treaty of Amsterdam (TA)

All three pillars were amended and expanded by the Treaty of Amsterdam (TA), which came into force on 1 May 1999. In particular, some aspects of justice and home affairs were transferred from the third (inter-governmental) pillar to the first (supranational Community) pillar. The competence of the Community was expanded to include visas, asylum, immigration and other policies related to free movement of persons, appropriate action to combat discrimination based on sex, racial or ethnic origin, religion or belief, disability, age or sexual orientation, and work towards developing a co-ordinated strategy for employment and particularly for promoting a skilled, trained and adaptable work force and labour markets responsive to economic change. The TA introduced a procedure for suspending the membership rights of any country that might violate the fundamental rights of the citizen. Furthermore (see head III(c)), the TA fundamentally amended (almost destroyed) the autonomy of the member states in the decision making process (both policy making and legislating) by, first, extending the 'co-decision' legislative procedure to almost all areas of Community legislative competence (making it virtually the normal and practically exclusive procedure) and, second, by extending the system, of 'qualified majority' voting in the Council to almost all areas of Council competence (making it virtually the normal method of voting in the Council).

(f) Economic and Monetary Union

Economic and Monetary Union (EMU) was designed to take the single market, itself an extension of the original customs union, one step further towards economic integration among the member states. In particular, EMU involved the introduction of a single European currency, the euro, managed by a European Central Bank, and replacing currencies that were, for many of the countries concerned, part of their patrimony and symbols of national sovereignty. The TEU established criteria to be met by the member states if they were to qualify for EMU. The original Euroland countries were Austria, Belgium, Finland, France, Germany, Ireland, Italy, Luxembourg, Netherlands, Portugal, and Spain. The United Kingdom, Sweden, and Denmark met the EMU criteria but decided not to participate. Greece entered Euroland later, and in 2002, the ECB authorised euro coins and banknotes, and the former currencies of countries within the euro zone ceased to be legal tender. The ten newest member states were required to adopt the euro.

(g) Enlargement, the Treaty of Nice (TN) and the European Constitution

Over fifty years, the six became twenty-five. Denmark, Ireland and the United Kingdom joined in 1973, Greece in 1981, Spain and Portugal in 1986, and Austria, Finland and Sweden in 1995. By that time, all the former Communist countries of Eastern Europe had applied for membership. At the Copenhagen summit in 2002, the European Council decided to permit ten new countries (Cyprus, the Czech Republic, Estonia, Hungary, Latvia, Lithuania, Malta, Poland, Slovakia and Slovenia) to join the Community in 2004. Bulgaria and Romania joined in 2007, and Croatia and Turkey are waiting. Should the Community and Union cross the traditional geographical boundaries of Europe and absorb more and more countries, it will encompass the steppes and the Sahara. Community propaganda has promoted 'what it means to be European' and has applauded measures designed to enhance European integration of cultures in addition to economic and political integration. The Treaty of Nice (TN) came into force on 1 February 2003. Its purpose was to adapt, perhaps to streamline (a favourite piece of 'Eurospeak'), the institutions and decision-making processes with a view to preparing for enlargement. There was an enormous reduction in the cases where the Council was obliged to take decisions unanimously and a corresponding increase in the cases where the Council can now reach a decision by qualified majority; there were changes to the weighting of votes within the Council; there was a new distribution of seats in the European Parliament; France, Germany, the United Kingdom and Italy gave up their ancient prerogative of nominating two members of the Commission; and the organisation of the Courts of Justice was drastically changed. A system designed for six member nations had to meet the challenge of enlargement, whilst balancing the conflicting principles of supra-nationalism and inter-governmentalism. The sheer size of the 2004 enlargement posed fundamental questions as to the government of Europe and in June 2004 the European Council agreed the final text of the first European Union constitution, containing a number of propositions of a federal nature. Ratification of the new constitution required approval by all 25 member states. In May 2005, however, voters in France and the Netherlands rejected the proposed constitution, several member states reserved their positions and postponed their own ratification processes, and the original target date of ratification by November 2006 simply disappeared.

(h) Where do we go from here?

Although European integration has taken place with a rapidity which no one would have foreseen at the end of the Second World War, and although moves are being made towards something akin to a United States of Europe or a Federation, the current state of affairs is one of a surrender or delegation of national sovereignty in certain important economic and social issues (the 'first pillar' of the Union, to be governed by the Community, the member states and Community institutions) but a retention of national sovereignty in other issues of particular sensitivity to all states, namely, foreign and defence policy and justice and home affairs (the 'second and third' pillars of the Union, to be governed by inter-governmental activity). This chapter will concentrate on the first pillar of the Union, the Community and consequent effects on the constitutional laws of member states (with, of course, specific reference to the United Kingdom), rather than on the other two pillars of the Union. By the time of the Treaty of Amsterdam, the European Treaties had been amended many, many times. Consequently it was necessary to produce a consolidated version of both the Treaty of European Union and the Treaty Establishing the European Community. These consolidated texts have, in turn, been amended by the TN. References in the remainder of this chapter will be to article numbers of the EC Treaty as they now are (for example, now 234) and, occasionally when necessary, as enacted (for example, ex 177).

II. The European Political Institutions

(a) The European Parliament

The European Parliament represents the citizens of Europe.[3] The European Parliament does not play the same role as a national Parliament which is normally the principal legislator and to which the government is normally responsible. Parliament does not have the legislative powers of national Parliaments (these belong principally to the Commission, which has the sole power of initiative, and the Council, which plays the major role in taking decisions: see head III). However, a principal feature of the development of the Community constitution has been the development of the Parliament from an 'Assembly' (its original title), composed of designated members of national Parliaments, into a Parliament representative of the electorate, which has participated in direct elections since 1979, and claiming additional roles and powers based on that political legitimacy. In the legislative field, Parliament's role was originally simply to be consulted and, although failure to consult Parliament was and is a breach of the Treaty provision imposing that obligation, there was no corresponding obligation to take Parliament's opinion into account. However, subsequent treaties have enhanced the legislative powers of the Parliament and Parliament participates in the process leading up to the adoption of Community acts by exercising its powers under the procedures laid down in Articles 251 and 252 and by giving its assent or delivering advisory opinions (see head III).

The 'government' of the Community is not derived from the Parliament. There is nothing as yet in the constitutional scheme of things whereby the government consists of ministers chosen from the majority political party (or a coalition) or of ministers appointed with the approval of Parliament. Parliament exercises advisory and supervisory powers to hear members of the Commission and the Council, and to question members of the Commission. Parliament may, acting by a majority of its members, request the Commission to submit any appropriate proposal on matters on which it considers that a Community act is required for the purpose of implementing the Treaty. Parliament has a role in the appointment of the Commission and this role has become more dominant over the years (see head (c), below). However, since the power of appointment of the Commission is exercised by the member states in conjunction with the Parliament and since there is no constitutional mechanism to

---

[3] Articles 189–201, 214.

bring the Council to account, there is not the equivalent of the political accountability of the government to the Parliament which is normally found in a national constitution.

Apart from participation in the legislative process, Parliament's principal role is to discuss and to give opinion on major Community problems in committee and in plenary session. By means of debating the programmes and reports of the Commission and Council it adds an element of democratic supervision of those bodies and can achieve publicity for its views which, in turn, may influence the Council and Commission. The debates of Parliament are published and Parliament publicises its views in a number of ways, principally by issuing reports and briefing papers. Parliament holds an annual session and may meet in extraordinary session at the request of a majority of its members or at the request of the Council or Commission. Members of the Commission may attend all meetings and, at their request, are heard on behalf of the Commission. The Commission replies orally or in writing to questions put to it by the European Parliament or by its members. Parliament discusses in open session the annual report submitted to it by the Commission. Any citizen of the Union, and any natural or legal person residing or having its registered office in a member state, has the right to address, individually or in association with other citizens or persons, a petition to the European Parliament on a matter which comes within the Community's fields of activity and which affects him, her or it directly. The European Parliament appoints the European Ombudsman (see head (d), below) and has a role to play in the Ombudsman's effectiveness. Finally, Parliament has certain budgetary powers which allow it to take part in important decisions on Community expenditure in conjunction with the Council, but is unable to control effectively the mismanagement, waste and corruption revealed so often by the reports of the Court of Auditors (see head (d) below).

The European Parliament consists of representatives of the peoples of the member states and its members are elected every five years by universal suffrage. The number of representatives from each state is allocated roughly on the basis of population (ranging from 99 for Germany to 3 for Malta) but it is noticeable that the smaller states are more fully represented. The total number of United Kingdom MEPs is 78. There are twelve European Parliamentary electoral regions in the United Kingdom, one in each of Scotland, Wales and Northern Ireland and nine in England. The geographical composition of the nine English regions and the number of MEPs to be returned by each is: East Midlands (six); Eastern (seven); London (nine); North East (three); North West (nine); South East (ten); South West (which includes Gibraltar) (seven); West Midlands (seven); and Yorkshire and Humber (six). Scotland returns seven MEPS, Wales four MEPs and Northern Ireland three MEPs. European Parliamentary elections in Great Britain are conducted using a regional list electoral system designed to ensure that in each region parties will win a share of the seats which is broadly proportional to their share of the vote in that region. This system does not apply to Northern Ireland, which elects its three MEPs using the single transferable vote system.[4]

It must be noted that Members of Parliament do not normally act and vote on national lines, rather they form transnational political groups which are deemed 'important as a factor for integration' within the Union and 'contribute to forming a European awareness and to expressing the political will of the citizens of the Union' (for example, the Party of European Socialists, the European People's Party and the Greens Group). In addition, members may

---

[4] European Parliamentary Elections Act 2002; European Parliament (Representation) Act 2003; The European Parliament (Number of MEPs) (United Kingdom and Gibraltar) Order 2004 (SI 2004/1245); The European Parliamentary Elections (Combined Region and Campaign Expenditure) (United Kingdom and Gibraltar) Order 2004 (SI 2004/366).

form pressure groups to pursue particular aims. Parliament has its own officers and executive structure. The President of the Parliament is elected by the Parliament and directs all the activities of Parliament and of its bodies under the conditions laid down in the Rules of Procedure. The President opens, suspends and closes sittings, ensures observance of the Rules of Procedure, maintains order, calls upon speakers, puts matters to the vote and announces the results of votes. The European Parliament normally acts by an absolute majority of the votes cast. Parliament sets up standing committees which, in particular, give opinions on proposed legislation.

(b) The Council

The Council[5] is the institution which emphasises and perhaps represents the direct interests of the member states. It may be noted that, as a consequence of the TEU arranging the Union's activities into the three pillars of Community action, foreign and security policy, and justice and home affairs (see head I), the Council, formerly the Council of Ministers, adopted the title of Council of the European Union in 1993. The Council's functions and powers relate principally to the first pillar. With regard to the Community, the Council has the duty to ensure that the objectives of the Treaty are attained and to ensure the co-ordination of the general economic policies of the member states by taking the major policy decisions of the Community and by conferring on the Commission powers for the implementation of those decisions. The Council consists of a representative of each member state at ministerial level in that one minister, authorised to commit the government of that member state, from each member state government is delegated to the Council. The fact that each national minister is authorised to commit his or her government brings an element of democratic legitimacy into the Council's deliberations in that each national minister is responsible (in theory) to his or her national Parliament and, thence, to his or her electorate. The composition of the Council varies, depending on the subject matter to be discussed at a particular Council meeting. Normally, the national ministers take part in meetings in their respective fields (for example, agriculture ministers discuss agricultural policy, finance ministers discuss budgetary policy and transport ministers discuss transport policy).

The Council has laid down its own Rules of Procedure and much power lies in the hands of the President of the Council. The Presidency of the Council is held by each member state in turn for six months in order. Council meetings are chaired by the appropriate minister from the member state holding the Presidency. The current Presidency in Office will co-operate with the previous and following Presidencies in order to provide continuity and to achieve better organisation of the Council's work, but each Presidency (in other words, each member state holding the Presidency) announces a programme which it hopes to achieve during its term of office. Statements are made to the European Parliament on the Presidency programmes. The Council meets when convened by the President on his or her initiative or at the request of a member state or the Commission.

As will be seen (in head III), the Council plays a dominant role in the enactment of Community secondary legislation. Originally, its system of voting possessed characteristics of an international organisation of independent sovereign states, with decisions needing

---

[5] Articles 202–210.

unanimity. However, as the Community has passed the introductory or transitional stages of its development, a constant feature of the amending treaties has been the virtual elimination of the requirement for unanimity and its replacement by the system of 'qualified majority' voting designed to achieve some measure of weighting according to the population of the state. Members of the Council co-operate with the other institutions. They take part in the debates of Parliament, speak to Parliament on Council policy, and reply to questions raised by the Parliament. They also attend plenary sessions of the Economic and Social Committee (see head (d) below). The Council has a staff in Brussels. This is the General Secretariat, divided into a Legal Service and several Directorates General, responsible for specific sectors, such as agriculture and fisheries.

Ministers are busy people and are engaged in the politics and administration of their own member state. They cannot remain permanently in Council sessions and, in order to achieve an element of permanence and continuity of Community decision making, the Council is assisted by the Committee of Permanent Representatives of the Member States (COREPER) which is responsible for preparing the work of the Council. COREPER co-ordinates the preparatory work for Council decisions by means of meetings of senior civil servants from each member state, who are, in effect, rather like Ambassadors and diplomats to the Community. COREPER, together with a large number of working parties established to discuss specific matters, will draw up agenda for Council meetings, draft legislative texts and attempt to achieve an informal agreement on proposed policies in order to save the time of the Council. It would be normal for each member state to have in its Embassy or Chancery in Brussels, an Ambassador, together with Counsellors, Secretaries and Attachés from such Ministries as Finance, Inland Revenue, Agriculture, Fisheries, Labour and Social Affairs, Industry, Transport, Justice, Environment, Health, Energy, Education and Research, Cultural Affairs, Communications, together with a Press Office and Chancery officials.

(c) The Commission

The European Commission[6] is the institution which emphasises the supranational nature of the Community. It is the 'executive' of the Community, charged with ensuring the proper functioning and development of the common market by, inter alia, ensuring that the Treaty provisions and the measures taken by the institutions under the Treaty are applied, by formulating recommendations and delivering opinions, by participating in the legislative process by proposing to the Council measures likely to advance the development of Community policies. It will be seen (in head III) that, with regard to the enactment of Community secondary legislation, the Commission has the right of initiating such legislation and that the Council may only act on a proposal from the Commission. The Commission is often referred to as the 'guardian of the Treaties' and it will be seen (in head VI) that member states which fail to obey Treaty obligations may be taken before the Court of Justice. The Commission publishes an annual report on the activities of the Community and Bulletins on its work.

The Commission is composed of one national from each member state, but they are not appointees of that state. Commissioners are appointed, for a period of five years, by common accord of the governments of member states in conjunction with the Parliament (below), and

---

[6] Articles 211–219.

are chosen on the grounds of general competence and from persons whose independence is beyond doubt. Many of them have had an active political life (often at ministerial rank) in their respective member states. The Members of the Commission must, in the general interest of the Community, be completely independent in the performance of their duties. In the performance of these duties, they should neither seek nor take instructions from any government or from any other body. They should refrain from any action incompatible with their duties. Each member state undertakes to respect this principle and not to seek to influence the Members of the Commission in the performance of their tasks. The Members of the Commission may not, during their term of office, engage in any other occupation, whether gainful or not. When entering upon their duties they give a solemn undertaking that, both during and after their term of office, they will respect the obligations arising from that office. If any Member of the Commission no longer fulfils the conditions required for the performance of his or her duties or if he or she has been guilty of serious misconduct, the Court of Justice may, on application by the Council or the Commission, compulsorily retire him or her. The Council, meeting in the composition of Heads of State or Government and acting by a qualified majority, nominates the person it intends to appoint as President of the Commission. The nomination must be approved by the European Parliament. The Council, acting by a qualified majority and by common accord with the nominee for President, then adopts the list of the other persons whom it intends to appoint as Members of the Commission, drawn up in accordance with the proposals made by each member state. The President and the other Members of the Commission thus nominated are then subject as a body to a vote of approval by the European Parliament. After approval by the European Parliament, the President and the other Members of the Commission are appointed by the Council, acting by a qualified majority. In one sense, the Commission is responsible to the Parliament as this is the only body that can force them collectively to resign, following a motion of censure, as happened in 1999, when President Santer was forced to tender the Commission's resignation. However, as the Commission is not appointed by the Parliament from its members, it does not possess a direct political link to the European peoples.

The Commission works under the political guidance of its President. Commission decisions are taken on a collegiate basis, by majority voting if necessary, even though specific portfolios (such as competition policy, regional policy and budgetary policy) are allocated to each Commissioner by the President, and decisions are taken by a simple majority vote. The Commission has an administrative staff which is divided into specific departments (known as Directorates General) responsible for such matters as external affairs, economic and financial affairs, agriculture, transport, fisheries and regional policy.

(d) Others

The office of European Ombudsman[7] was created by the TEU. The European Parliament appoints the Ombudsman who is empowered to receive complaints concerning instances of maladministration in the activities of the Community institutions or bodies (with the exception of the Court of Justice and the Court of First Instance acting in their judicial role). The Ombudsman conducts inquiries, either on his or her own initiative or on the basis of

---

[7] Article 195.

complaints submitted direct or through a Member of the European Parliament, in order to establish if there has been maladministration. If the Ombudsman establishes an instance of maladministration, the matter is referred to the institution concerned for its comments. If the institution concerned does not accept the Ombudsman's recommendation, the Ombudsman can report to the institution concerned and to the European Parliament in order that Parliament can take whatever political action is necessary. The person lodging the complaint must be informed of the outcome of such inquiries. The Ombudsman submits an annual report to the European Parliament.

The Court of Auditors[8] consists of one national from each member state, chosen from among persons who belong or have belonged in their respective countries to external audit bodies or who are especially qualified for this office. Their independence must be beyond doubt. The Court examines the accounts of all revenue and expenditure of the Community and of all revenue and expenditure of all bodies set up by the Community. The Court examines whether all revenue has been received and all expenditure incurred in a lawful and regular manner and whether the financial management has been sound. In particular the Court reports on any cases of irregularity. The Court makes an annual report, often highly critical of both Community institutions and member states, at the close of each financial year and this is forwarded to the other institutions of the Community and published, together with the replies of these institutions to the observations of the Court, in the Official Journal.

The Economic and Social Committee[9] consists of representatives of producers, farmers, carriers, workers, dealers, craftsmen, professional occupations, consumers and the general public interest. The members of the Committee must be completely independent in the performance of their duties, in the general interest of the Community. The Committee has a consultative role and must be consulted on economic and social policy by the Council or by the Commission where the Treaty so provides. The Committee may be consulted by the institutions in all cases in which they consider it appropriate. It may issue an opinion on its own initiative in cases in which it considers such action appropriate.

The Committee of the Regions,[10] established by the TEU, consists of representatives of regional and local bodies who either hold a regional or local authority electoral mandate or are politically accountable to an elected assembly. The members of the Committee must be completely independent in the performance of their duties, in the general interest of the Community. The Committee has a consultative role and is consulted, where specific regional matters are involved, by the Council or by the Commission where the Treaty so provides, in particular with regard to cross-border cooperation. If the Economic and Social Committee is being consulted, the Committee of the Regions must be informed by the Council or the Commission of the request for an opinion. When it considers that specific regional interests are involved, the Committee of the Regions may issue an opinion on the matter.

The members of the European Investment Bank[11] are the member states. The task of the Bank is to contribute to the balanced and steady development of the common market in the interest of the Community. For this purpose, the Bank, operating on a non-profit-making basis, grants loans and gives guarantees which facilitate the financing of projects, especially industrial projects and projects supporting small businesses, for developing the less-developed regions.

A European System of Central Banks (ESCB) and a European Central Bank (ECB)[12] have been established to deal with monetary policy. They 'shall act within the limits of the powers

---

[8] Articles 246–248.   [9] Articles 257–262.   [10] Articles 263–265.
[11] Articles 9, 266–267.   [12] Articles 8, 105–115.

conferred upon them by this Treaty'. The ESCB is composed of the ECB and the national central banks. The ESCB is governed by the decision-making bodies of the ECB (the Governing Council and the Executive Board). The President of the Council and a member of the Commission may participate, without having the right to vote, in meetings of the Governing Council of the ECB. The primary objective of the ESCB is to define and implement the monetary policy of the Community. The ECB, based in Frankfurt, has exclusive authority for such matters, essential to economic and monetary union, as setting interest rates and regulating the money supply. The ECB has played a major role in overseeing the introduction and organisation of the euro as the single currency. In order to carry out the tasks entrusted to the ESCB, the ECB can make a regulation, which 'shall have general application [and] be binding in its entirety and directly applicable in all member states' and a decision, which 'shall be binding in its entirety upon those to whom it is addressed'. The ECB is also entitled to impose fines or periodic penalty payments on undertakings for failure to comply with obligations under its regulations and decisions.

III. Community Legislation

(a) Community competence to legislate

There are two principal forms of Community legislation. First, there is the 'primary legislation' created directly by the member states. It comprises the Community law contained in the treaties establishing and developing the European Community and Union. Examples are the Treaty of Rome, the SEA, the TEU, the TA, the TN, and the Accession Treaties providing for the accession to the Community of new member states. In addition to the main text of a treaty there may be additional annexes and protocols which have the same legal force as their parent treaty. Secondly, there is the 'secondary legislation' of the Community, the legal rules created by the Community institutions under the authority of the treaties.

The Community must act within the limits of the powers conferred upon it by the Treaty and of the objectives assigned to it in the Treaty and any action by the Community can not go beyond what is necessary to achieve the objectives of the Treaty.[13] Community secondary legislation can only be enacted if there is a treaty provision authorising this. The Treaty does not confer general powers but enacts, in the respective articles, individual powers to act. However, it may be noted that if 'action by the Community should prove necessary to attain, in the course of the operations of the common market, one of the objectives of the Community and this Treaty has not provided the necessary powers, the Council shall, acting unanimously on a proposal from the Commission and after consulting the European Parliament, take the appropriate measures'.[14] Furthermore (head I(c), (d), (e)), subsequent treaties have greatly extended the areas of competence reserved for Community legislative action. Whether there is authority to enact secondary legislation, therefore, depends on the existence of a provision of a treaty. Any question as to whether the Community has authority to act at all and to the exclusion of the member states, as to which institution has authority to

---

[13] Article 5.   [14] Article 308. See, eg, *Commission v Council* [1989] ECR 1425.

act on behalf of the Community, and as to whether that institution has acted in accordance with the correct procedures laid down may be referred to the Court of Justice (see head IV(a)).

(b) Secondary legislative measures

In order to carry out their task and in accordance with the provisions of the Treaty, the European Parliament acting jointly with the Council, the Council, and the Commission can make regulations and issue directives, take decisions, make recommendations or deliver opinions.[15] The principal secondary legislative measures are regulations and directives.

In some cases, secondary legislation may be drafted in such a way that its content can be translated directly and automatically into the domestic legal systems of each and every one of the member states in order that Community law is identical in each member state. The measure used here is the regulation. According to article 249 (ex 189), a regulation has 'general application', is 'binding in its entirety' in that a member state cannot opt out of any provision in a regulation of which that state disapproves, and is 'directly applicable' in all member states in that there is no need whatsoever for a member state to implement a regulation or transpose a regulation into its own domestic legal system. A regulation, therefore, is legislation created for each member state by the Community and replaces any existing and conflicting rule created by the domestic legal system of a member state. It is as though the exact words of a regulation automatically become part of the law of each member state in a uniform manner, and at the same time with no further action being required by the member state. Member states do not need to ratify a regulation as a regulation is, in effect, deemed to have been ratified, irrespective of the fact that any rules contained therein are not enacted by any of the national Parliaments. The consequence of this is that a regulation may confer rights and obligations within a member state on the member state, any organisation of that state, all organisations, and all individuals within that state.

On other occasions, it may be that the content of secondary legislation cannot be translated directly into the legal systems of the member states in a uniform manner because different member states may have different legislative and administrative mechanisms in their own systems for dealing with the relevant subject matter (for example, a written constitution, statute, delegated legislation, Royal or Presidential Decree). The measure used here is the directive. A directive is actually addressed to a member state or to some or all member states. According to article 249 (ex 189), such a directive is binding, 'as to the result to be achieved', upon each member state to which it is addressed, but leaves to the national authorities the choice of form and methods. A directive, being addressed to member states rather than directly applicable in member states, is an instruction to each member state to bring its legal system into exact conformity with the objectives specified in the directive (and within a specified time limit). It will usually impose this obligation by stating that 'Member states shall take the measures necessary to' achieve the purpose(s) intended and conveyed therein. The specified time limit may be months or years and this permits each member state to proceed at its own speed to repeal existing domestic laws, regulations and administrative practices and to enact new domestic laws, regulations and administrative practices. A directive differs from a

---

[15] Article 249 (ex 189).

regulation in that what creates its normative force is not (as it is with a regulation) the adoption by the Community institution of the directive but the entry into force of the national implementing measures (Act of Parliament or Ministerial or Royal Decree). Therefore the rule becomes 'law' in a member state when that member state implements or 'transposes' the directive (provided that it does so within the prescribed time limit). If a member state fails to fulfil the instruction, the omission may be rectified by the Commission (or another member state) bringing an action before the Court of Justice (see head VI(b)) or by an individual in the national courts of the member state under the principle of direct effect (see head VIII(c)), although it must be mentioned here that the principle of direct effect only has the result of imposing an obligation on the member state (or one of its organs) and not on private organisations or individuals, or in the national courts by the doctrine of positive interpretation (see head VIII(d)). Both the Commission and the Court of Justice have insisted that the obligation to implement a directive, where the wording of the directive so requires, be achieved to the very last letter.[16]

Sometimes the Community will wish to make a legally binding rule which only affects one or a limited number of member states or an identifiable organisation or even one individual. Sometimes the Community will wish to require a member state to take a course of action which does not directly concern individuals and which does not have to become in any direct way the law of the member state. Sometimes the Community makes what are more akin to administrative decisions (in particular in the organisation of agricultural matters). The measure here is a decision and a decision is binding on the addressee of the decision.

Regulations, directives and decisions adopted jointly by the European Parliament and the Council, and such acts adopted by the Council or the Commission, must state the reasons on which they are based and refer to any proposals or opinions which were required to be obtained pursuant to the Treaty.[17] Regulations, directives and decisions adopted in accordance with the 'co-decision' procedure (see head (c), below) must be signed by the President of the Parliament and by the President of the Council and published in the Official Journal of the European Communities. They enter into force on the date specified in them or, in the absence thereof, on the twentieth day following that of their publication. Regulations of the Council and of the Commission, as well as directives of those institutions which are addressed to all member states, must be published in the Official Journal of the European Communities. They enter into force on the date specified in them or, in the absence thereof, on the twentieth day following that of their publication. Other directives, and decisions, must be notified to those to whom they are addressed and will take effect upon such notification.[18] The Official Journal is published in each of the official languages of the Community.

(c) The Community legislator

In essence, the Community 'legislator' represents a balance of power between the representatives of the member states (the Council), the representative of the Community (the Commission), and the representatives of the people (the Parliament). The balance is achieved by the fact that the final affirmative decision belongs to the Council, and Treaty provisions will expressly state that regulations, directives and decisions are to be made, issued and taken by

---

[16] *Johnston*, p. 369.   [17] Article 253 (ex 190).   [18] Article 254 (ex 191).

the Council, but the Council can only act upon a proposal from the Commission, which, therefore, has a near monopoly in initiating legislative proposals, and if the Council acts on a proposal from the Commission unanimity in the Council is required for an act constituting an amendment to that proposal.[19] There is a further balance between the desire to allow member states to protect their national interests and the desire to limit the right of member states to veto matters on which there is overwhelming agreement by the majority of member states. This is achieved by provisions which provide for decisions to be taken by the Council by a simple majority of states, by unanimity, and by a 'qualified majority', designed to achieve some measure of weighting according approximately to the population of the state, although the system is weighted in favour of the smaller nations. For their adoption, acts of the Council require at least a prescribed minimum of votes to reach a qualified majority. In addition, a majority of member states (in some cases two-thirds) must approve the decision. A feature of the development of the Community has been a gradual change from the requirement of unanimity to the now almost normal requirement of qualified majority. A significant feature of the development of the Community has been a gradual change in the Parliament's role in the legislative process, from a very passive and somewhat dismissive position to one of very great activity and 'real teeth'. The Parliament now has a rejection power but not one of legislative initiative.

There is no single legislative procedure that is applied unwaveringly to the creation of all secondary legislation. In all cases the Council, as has been seen, can only act following a proposal from the Commission. The Commission may initiate a proposal of its own motion or it may be required by the Council to draw up a proposal. The proposal will be drafted within the appropriate Commission Directorate(s) General and the final text, if approved by the Commission, will be submitted to the Council for formal adoption. In practice, the Council, being in legal form simply a small group of representatives from each member state, cannot possibly undertake the vast amount of labour involved, or possess the complete expertise needed, in the enactment of secondary legislation. Consequently, the Council works through working parties composed of the administrative staff of the Council and COREPER (see head II(b)). COREPER will co-ordinate the work needed to prepare the Council for the formal adoption of secondary legislation and, in practice, unanimity achieved within COREPER will often result in speedy adoption by the Council. However, in addition to the Council and the Commission, a role may be played by the Parliament, by the Economic and Social Committee, and by the Committee of the Regions. The Council may simply be required to consult the Parliament, may be required to act in co-operation with the Parliament, or there may be no obligation to involve the Parliament. The Council may be required to consult the Economic and Social Committee or there may be no obligation to involve the Economic and Social Committee. One legislative procedure must be described in detail, namely, the 'co-decision procedure', now rapidly becoming the normal legislative procedure.

The 'co-decision procedure' is laid down in article 251. As its name suggests, this procedure is one in which the Council and the Parliament are equals and the Council cannot disregard the opinion of the Parliament, which can, therefore, veto proposed legislation. The co-decision procedure, introduced by the TEU in 1993, has been applied to more and more areas of Community competence by the TA and the TN and now applies to a whole series of important issues: non-discrimination on grounds of nationality (article 12), combating discrimination based on sex, racial or ethnic origin, religion or belief, disability, age or sexual orientation (article 13(2)), freedom of movement and of residence (article 18(2)), free

---

[19] Article 250 (ex 189a).

movement of workers (article 40), social security for migrant workers (article 42), establishment (articles 44(1), 46(2), 47), visas, asylum, immigration (article 67(4) and (5)), transport (article 71(1)), the internal market (article 95), employment (article 129), customs cooperation (article 135), social policy (article 137(2)), equal opportunities and equal treatment (article 141(3)), the European Social Fund (article 148), education (article 149(4)), culture (article 151(5)), public health (article 152(4)), consumer protection (article 153(4)), industry (article 157(3)), economic and social cohesion (article 159), research and technological development (article 166(1), 172), vocational training (article 150(4)), the environment (article 175(1), (3)), access to the institutions' documents (article 255(2)), and fraud (article 280).

If reference is made in the Treaty to article 251 for the adoption of an act, the following procedure will apply. First, the Commission submits a proposal to the Parliament and the Council. The Council must then obtain the opinion of the Parliament. If Parliament does not in fact propose any amendments, the Council, acting by a qualified majority may adopt the proposed act. If the Council approves all the amendments contained in Parliament's opinion, the Council, acting by a qualified majority, may adopt the proposed act thus amended. If the Council does not approve all the amendments contained in Parliament's opinion, the Council, acting by a qualified majority, must adopt a common position and communicate it to the Parliament. The Council must inform the Parliament fully of the reasons which led it to adopt its common position. The Commission must also inform the Parliament fully of its position. The Parliament may then do one of three things within three months of such communication (the period of three months can be extended by a maximum of one month at the initiative of the Parliament or the Council). If Parliament approves the common position or has not taken a decision, the act in question will be deemed to have been adopted in accordance with the common position of the Council; if Parliament rejects, by an absolute majority of its component members, the common position, the proposed act is deemed not to have been adopted; if Parliament proposes amendments to the common position by an absolute majority of its component members, the amended text must be forwarded to the Council and to the Commission, which will deliver an opinion on those amendments. If, within three months of the matter being referred to it (the period of three months can be extended by a maximum of one month at the initiative of the Parliament or the Council), the Council, acting by a qualified majority (below), approves all the amendments of the Parliament, the act in question is deemed to have been adopted in the form of the common position thus amended (it is important, however, to note that the Council must act unanimously on any amendments on which the Commission has delivered a negative opinion). If the Council does not approve all the amendments of the Parliament, the President of the Council, in agreement with the President of the European Parliament, must within six weeks convene a meeting of the Conciliation Committee (the period of six weeks can be extended by a maximum of two weeks at the initiative of the Parliament or the Council). The Conciliation Committee is composed of the members of the Council or their representatives and an equal number of representatives of the Parliament. The Committee has the task of reaching agreement on a joint text, by a qualified majority of the members of the Council or their representatives and by a majority of the representatives of the European Parliament. The Commission takes part in the Conciliation Committee's proceedings and is under a duty to take all the necessary initiatives with a view to reconciling the positions of the European Parliament and the Council. In fulfilling this task, the Conciliation Committee will address the common position on the basis of the amendments proposed by the European Parliament. If, within six weeks (this period can be extended by a maximum of two weeks at the initiative of the Parliament or the Council) of its being convened, the Conciliation Committee approves a joint text, the European Parliament, acting by an absolute majority of the votes cast, and the Council, acting by a qualified majority, will then each have a period of six weeks (this period can be extended by a maximum of two weeks at the initiative of the Parliament or the Council) from that approval in which to adopt the act in question in accordance with the joint text. If either of the two institutions fails to approve the proposed act within that period, the proposed act is deemed not to have been adopted. If in fact the Conciliation Committee does not approve a joint text, the proposed act again will be deemed not to have been adopted.

IV. The European Courts

(a) The judicial system

The Treaty of Rome created a self-contained judicial system to determine the different types of Community disputes which may arise and to ensure that Community law is implemented in a uniform manner by all concerned (institutions, member states, and all others affected by Community law).[20] This system has had to be developed over the years, as both the areas of Community competence and the number of member states (and their peoples) have expanded and this continually led to more and more cases being brought before the judicial system, such that sometimes the delay in determining cases amounted in reality to a denial of justice. The original Court of Justice was supplemented by the Court of First Instance in 1989. The TN provided for the creation of judicial panels attached to the Court of First Instance and these are specialist tribunals to hear at first instance certain classes of action or proceeding brought in specific areas. The first judicial panel, the European Union Civil Service Tribunal, was established in 2004[21] to hear and determine at first instance disputes involving the European Civil Service.

The Court of Justice consists of one judge for each member state. The Court of Justice sits in chambers consisting of three or five judges or in a Grand Chamber of eleven judges. The Court sits in a Grand Chamber when a member state or an institution that is party to the proceedings so requests. If the Court considers that a case before it is of exceptional importance, the Court may decide, after hearing the Advocate General, to refer the case to the full Court.

The Court of Justice is assisted by eight Advocates General. The duty of the Advocates General is to make, acting with complete impartiality and independence and in open court, reasoned submissions on cases which, in accordance with the Statute of the Court of Justice, require his or her involvement, in order to assist the Court in the performance of the Court's various tasks. The Advocate General will study the facts of the case, the contentions of the parties, the relevant Treaty and secondary legislative provisions, the previous decisions of the Court, and, of highest importance, relevant legal rules from the legal systems of the member states and from international law, in order to propose a solution to the given litigation. The Court is not bound to follow the advice of the Advocate General but it usually does so. Given the sometimes terse or laconic method of declaring judgments, the Court

---

[20] Articles 220–245; Protocol on the Statute of the Court of Justice.
[21] Council Decision of 2 November 2004.

preferring to limit its statement to a resolution of the case in hand and no more, the more detailed exposition of the Advocate General is often the more instructive.[22]

The Court of First Instance consists of one judge for each member state. The Members of the Court of First Instance may be called upon to perform the task of an Advocate General. It is the duty of the Advocate General, acting with complete impartiality and independence, to make, in open court, reasoned submissions on certain cases brought before the Court of First Instance in order to assist the Court of First Instance in the performance of its task. A Member called upon to perform the task of Advocate General in a case may not take part in the judgment of the case. The Court of First Instance sits in chambers of three or five judges. In certain cases, the Court of First Instance may sit as a full court or be constituted by a single judge.

The judges and Advocates General of the Court of Justice and the Members of the Court of First Instance are chosen from persons whose independence is beyond doubt and who possess the qualifications for appointment to high judicial office. They are appointed by common accord of the governments of the member states for a term of six years. The judges elect their President from among their number for a term of three years. Each court appoints its Registrar, who is responsible, under the authority of the President, for the acceptance, transmission and custody of documents and for effecting service. Other officials are attached to the court to enable it to function. They are responsible to the Registrar under the authority of the President. The court has established a translating service staffed by experts with adequate legal training and a thorough knowledge of the official languages of the court.

(b) Jurisdiction

The European Courts have been allocated a wider variety of jurisdictions than is normally given to a national court. There are three jurisdictions of particular constitutional importance to Community law and the member states (including, of course, the United Kingdom).

The first jurisdiction is to hear and determine disputes between Community institutions and member states and between member states and member states (see head VI(b)).

The second jurisdiction is to give preliminary rulings concerning the interpretation of the Treaty and the validity and interpretation of acts of the institutions of the Community (see head VI(c)).

The third jurisdiction is to pronounce upon the legality of acts of Community institutions and their compatibility with Treaty provisions and other legal rules. Member states have undertaken to be governed, at least in part, by Community institutions. The Community has jurisdiction to act to the exclusion of member states and the member states remain competent to act where they have not granted jurisdiction to the Community. The drawing up of the respective competences of the Community and the member states lies with the member states who agree and ratify the primary legislation of the Treaties and who, through the Council, take final decisions as to the adoption of secondary legislation. Although the developing nature of the Community and Union has seen a continuing devolution of national competence in favour of the Community institutions, the normal constitutional tensions within a national state are mirrored within the Community by the desire to ensure both political and

---

[22] *Transocean*, p. 317.

legal accountability of institutions to member states and a corresponding accountability of institutions to each other. Consequently, the Treaty provides that the Community 'shall act within the limits of the powers conferred upon it by this Treaty and of the objectives assigned to it therein', that 'any action by the Community shall not go beyond what is necessary to achieve the objectives of this Treaty',[23] and that each institution must 'act within the limits of the powers conferred upon it by this Treaty'.[24] Community acts, therefore, both legislative and administrative, must be adopted in accordance with the Treaty and its secondary legislation. In countries which have a written constitution it is normal to have some form of independent or judicial authority to examine and declare upon the constitutionality of acts of the legislature (to determine whether a statute contravenes or is in conformity with the constitution). Furthermore, it is normal, whether or not there is a written constitution, to have some form of independent or judicial authority to exercise an administrative law function designed to ensure that the administration's acts are executed in accordance with the legal powers granted to them. It was, therefore, entirely in keeping with general principles of constitutional law that the Treaty created both a constitutionality jurisdiction and an administrative law jurisdiction and, in order to ensure that both jurisdictions should act with one mind to produce a cohesive interpretation and application of the Treaty, granted both jurisdictions to the Court of Justice.[25]

The Court of Justice has jurisdiction to review the legality of acts adopted jointly by the European Parliament and the Council, of acts of the Council, of the Commission and of the ECB, other than recommendations and opinions, and of acts of the European Parliament intended to produce legal effects vis-à-vis third parties.[26] Article 249 (ex 189) provides that Community institutions may make regulations, issue directives, take decisions, make recommendations or deliver opinions (see head II(b)). A Community act is, prima facie, a regulation, directive or decision. This will include instruments ranging from the most far-reaching regulations to simple letters containing a decision against one person. A member state, the Council or the Commission has an automatic right to bring an action, as have the Court of Auditors, the Parliament and the European Central Bank for the purposes of protecting their prerogatives.[27] If, therefore, a member state alleges that a regulation or directive has been enacted 'unlawfully' (below), with the result that the regulation or directive purports to impose an obligation within that state which has no legal basis, the member state can bring the matter before the Court.[28]

The grounds on which an action for annulment may be brought are specified as lack of competence, infringement of an essential procedural requirement, infringement of the Treaty or of any rule of law relating to its application or misuse of powers.[29] Lack of competence, in essence, means that the Community act in question was not within the jurisdiction of the particular institution.[30] An infringement of an essential procedural requirement may relate to a breach of a written rule of procedure or a breach of a procedural rule enshrined in a general principle of law (such as the right to a fair hearing). The usual example of the former is the

---

[23] Article 5.   [24] Article 7.   [25] Article 230 (ex 173).
[26] Article 230(1).   [27] Article 230(2), (3).
[28] See *United Kingdom v Council* [1988] ECR 855 (successful) and *United Kingdom v Council* [1996] ECR 5755 (unsuccessful with regard to a directive relating to the organisation of working time). Problems have, however, arisen with regard to article 230(4), which, in limited circumstances, permits a natural or legal person to bring an action for annulment of acts which specifically concerns those persons but such matters are, however, best left to more substantive Community law studies and to its more specialist literature.
[29] Article 230(2).   [30] *Commission v Council* [1989] ECR 1425.

rule that regulations, directives and decisions must state the reasons on which they are based and refer to any proposals or opinions which were required to be obtained pursuant to the Treaty.[31] Another essential statutory procedural rule relates to the frequent stipulations in the Treaty that during the legislative process the Parliament or Economic and Social Committee must be permitted to play their part assigned by the Treaty and a breach of this obligation will be fatal.[32] As will be seen (head V(d)), the Court has developed general principles of law and these include the procedural requirement of a fair hearing.[33] An 'infringement of the Treaty' is to some extent tautological in that lack of competence and breach of a Treaty rule of procedure will also be infringements of the Treaty. More important is the use of the phrase 'of any rule of law relating to' the application of the Treaty. In particular, the development of general principles of law (see head V(d)) has been utilised to challenge Community acts which breach the principle of legitimate expectation, of proportionality and of non-discrimination. Consequently, in *Razzouk and Beydoun v Commission of the European Communities*,[34] it was held that the principle of equal treatment of both sexes formed part of the fundamental rights the observance of which the Court has a duty to ensure and any breach of that principle meant that a Commission decision had to be annulled. Misuse of powers reflects the general principle of administrative law known to the public law of most member states that a power, an admitted power, which is granted for one purpose may not be used for a purpose unconnected with the purpose for which the power was granted. This ground is rarely successful because Community institutions possess many specific powers on which to base their decisions, because the Court has often granted an institution a wide measure of discretion in what it does, and because it is very difficult to prove by objective evidence.[35]

(c) Division of jurisdiction

The Court of Justice has what could be called a common law jurisdiction to hear all matters granted to it by the Treaties. The Court of First Instance has jurisdiction to hear and determine at first instance actions or proceedings for annulment of Community acts,[36] failure of a Community institution to act,[37] compensation for damage caused by the Community,[38] disputes between the Community and its servants,[39] and disputes on arbitration clauses,[40] with the exception of those assigned to a judicial panel and those reserved for the Court of Justice. Decisions given by the Court of First Instance may be subject to a right of appeal to the Court of Justice. An appeal to the Court of Justice is limited to points of law (the grounds of lack of competence of the Court of First Instance, a breach of procedure before it which adversely affects the interests of the appellant, and the infringement of Community law by the Court of First Instance). If the appeal is well founded, the Court of Justice will quash the decision of the Court of First Instance. It may itself give final judgment in the matter or refer the case back to the Court of First Instance for judgment. When a case is referred back to the

---

[31] Article 253 (ex 190); *Germany v Commission* [1963] ECR 63; *Charles Lux v Court of Auditors of the European Communities* [1984] ECR 2447.

[32] *Roquette Frères v Council* [1980] ECR 3333; *European Parliament v Council* [1995] ECR I-1185.

[33] *Transocean*, p. 317.   [34] [1984] ECR 1509.

[35] *Charles Lux v Court of Auditors of the European Communities* [1984] ECR 2447 (unsuccessful); *Giuffrida v Council* [1976] ECR 1395 and *Gutmann v Commission* [1966] ECR 103 (both successful).

[36] Article 230.   [37] Article 232.   [38] Article 235.   [39] Article 236.   [40] Article 238.

Court of First Instance, that Court is bound by the decision of the Court of Justice on points of law. The Court of First Instance has jurisdiction to hear and determine actions or proceedings brought against decisions of the judicial panels. Such decisions may exceptionally be subject to review by the Court of Justice where there is a serious risk of the unity or consistency of Community law being affected. The Court of First Instance has a limited jurisdiction to hear and determine questions referred for a preliminary ruling,[41] in specific areas. When the Court of First Instance considers that the case requires a decision of principle likely to affect the unity or consistency of Community law, it may refer the case to the Court of Justice for a ruling. Decisions given by the Court of First Instance on questions referred for a preliminary ruling may exceptionally be subject to review by the Court of Justice, where there is a serious risk of the unity or consistency of Community law being affected.

If the Court of First Instance finds that it does not have jurisdiction to hear and determine an action in respect of which the Court of Justice has jurisdiction, it must refer that action to the Court of Justice; likewise, where the Court of Justice finds that an action falls within the jurisdiction of the Court of First Instance, it must refer that action to the Court of First Instance, whereupon that Court may not decline jurisdiction. Where the Court of Justice and the Court of First Instance are seised of cases in which the same relief is sought, the same issue of interpretation is raised or the validity of the same act is called in question, the Court of First Instance may, after hearing the parties, stay the proceedings before it until such time as the Court of Justice has delivered judgment. Where applications are made for the same act to be declared void, the Court of First Instance may also decline jurisdiction in order that the Court of Justice may rule on such applications.

(d) Procedure

The procedure before the Court is determined by the Statute of the Court and its Rules of Procedure. The procedure consists of two parts, namely, the written procedure and the oral procedure.

The written procedure consists of the communication to the parties and to the institutions of the Community whose decisions are in dispute, of applications, statements of case, defences and observations, and of replies, if any, as well as of all papers and documents in support. A case must be brought by a written application addressed to the Registrar. An expedited procedure makes it possible for the Court to give its ruling with the minimum of delay if the case is particularly urgent. As soon as the application has been lodged, the President will assign the case to one of the Chambers for any preparatory inquiries and will designate a judge from that Chamber to act as rapporteur. In essence the role of the Judge Rapporteur is to oversee the case from the beginning until the case comes to be determined by the Court or Chamber. One Advocate General is designated as the First Advocate General and the First Advocate General assigns each case to an Advocate General as soon as the Judge Rapporteur has been designated by the President. The Court may require the parties to produce all documents and to supply all information which the Court considers desirable.

---

[41] Article 234.

The Court, and note that it is the Court rather than the parties or their legal advisers, may at any time entrust any individual, body, authority, committee or other organisation it chooses with the task of giving an expert opinion and may determine that witnesses be heard in accordance with the rules of procedure, which emphasise that the nature and content of a witness's testimony is for the Court to decide. Actions brought before the Court of Justice do not have suspensory effect, but the Court may, if it considers that circumstances so require, order that application of the contested act be suspended. The Court of Justice may in any cases before it prescribe any necessary interim measures.

The dates and times of the sittings of the Court and Chambers are fixed by their respective Presidents. The oral procedure consists of the reading of the report presented by the Judge Rapporteur, which summarises the facts and arguments of the parties, the hearing by the Court of agents, advisers and lawyers, the hearing, if any, of witnesses and experts, together with the submissions of the Advocate General, although, if it considers that the case raises no new point of law, the Court may decide, after hearing the Advocate General, that the case should be determined without a submission from the Advocate General. The hearing is in public, unless the Court decides otherwise for serious reasons. During the hearing the Court may examine experts, witnesses and the parties themselves. The latter, however, may address the Court only through their representatives. The Court (and Chambers) deliberate in closed session. Their deliberations are and remain secret. Only those judges who were present at the oral proceedings may take part in the deliberation on that case. At the deliberation each judge taking part will state his or her opinion and the reasons for that opinion. The conclusions reached by the majority of the judges after final discussion determine the decision of the Court. There are no dissenting judgments. Votes are cast in strict order of precedence, the most junior judge voting first and the most senior judge voting last.

An important factor in the development of a coherent and consistent Community law has been the fact that litigation is not limited to the parties concerned and here there are two particular procedural features, namely intervention in a case and the reference for a preliminary ruling. Member states and institutions of the Community may intervene in cases before the Court in which they are not parties.[42] Although the Commission or the Council (and sometimes both) are so very often either plaintiff or defendant in direct actions before the Court, this is none the less an important right. The right is of course most valuable for the member states who may find that a dispute between, for example, the Commission and another member state could very well affect their own interest either immediately or in the future. If there is a reference for a preliminary ruling (see head VI(c)), the decision of the court or tribunal of a member state which suspends its proceedings and refers a case to the Court of Justice must be notified to the Court by the national court or tribunal concerned. The decision must then be notified by the Registrar to the parties, to the member states and to the Commission, and also to the Council if the act the validity or interpretation of which is in dispute originates from the Council. The parties, the member states, the Commission and, where appropriate, the Council, are entitled to submit their own written observations to the Court.

---

[42] *Commission v France*, p. 328; *van Gend*, p. 351.

v. Community Case Law

(a) Introduction

As stated in head IV, the Court of Justice has been allocated a wider variety of jurisdictions than is normally given to a court, principal of which is the seemingly innocuous statement[43] that the 'Court of Justice shall ensure that in the interpretation and application of this Treaty the law is observed'. The 'law' is derived ostensibly from the primary and secondary legislation discussed in head III, but the need to interpret that legislation has over the years resulted in the growing dominance of the Court as a legislator and a Treaty developer in its own right. Of paramount importance is the creation, by its case law, of doctrines of both interpretation and of substance which have welded Community activity into something approaching a cohesive and coherent whole. In particular, the Court has acted to ensure that the spirit of Community objectives is paramount and, sometimes with an apparent disregard for the literal wording of Treaty provisions and secondary legislation, has used those words to create the new legal order for the Community.

(b) Interpretation

Community legislation, both primary and secondary, is drafted in several ways, ranging from very wide (some might say deliberately vague) statements of principle to extremely detailed and minute and technical rules. In addition, Community legislation is drafted in the various official languages of the Community and may utilise, in diverse and sundry places, legal concepts which may be identical in each member state or which may exist in some member states and not in others. The Court, therefore, has faced problems of interpretation similar to those faced by the courts of member states, but accentuated by the fact that the Court is the court of last instance for both the Community institutions and the member states. The Court does not decline jurisdiction on the ground that the formal written sources do not provide an exact set of solutions for the legal problem at hand, since the Court has a positive duty to ensure that the law 'is observed'. As was argued early on, if a case involves a problem of law well known in the case law and legal theory of all the countries of the Community but for whose solution the Treaty does not contain any rules, the Court, on pain of perpetrating a denial of justice, is therefore obliged to resolve the problem by drawing on the rules recognised by the legislation, legal theory and case law of the member countries.[44]

When interpreting statutory rules, the Court has followed interpretative techniques common to all the member states' legal systems. The starting point is the literal interpretation of clearly defined Treaty and secondary legislative provisions and if the meaning of the words is clear, the statutory provision will be applied, unless so to do would achieve a result clearly absurd in relation to the objectives of the Treaty. Very often the spirit and purpose of the written provisions will be used to lay down certain presumptions or canons of interpretation,

---

[43] Article 220 (ex 164).   [44] *Algera v Common Assembly* [1957] ECR 39, at 55.

such as the fact that a provision creating what are called fundamental freedoms, such as free movement of goods or persons, must be interpreted broadly, whereas any statutory derogations from such fundamental freedoms must be interpreted narrowly.[45] These interpretative techniques, however, take on a new dimension when the primary sources are drafted and enacted in several languages by persons versed in different legal systems. There has to be a considerable element of comparative study in order to obtain an interpretation in accordance with the overriding purpose of achieving uniformity of application within the Community's internal legal order and the several legal orders of all the member states. Therefore, the interpretation of Treaty provisions and secondary legislation may well be aided by a comparative study and analysis of the vocabulary used in the written texts, together with further and similar analysis of the national legal systems from which that vocabulary may have been taken.[46]

The Court has, however, realised that the process of legal and linguistic semantics can be taken too far and has realised that the difficulties of providing an exact meaning to a word, phrase or principle are multiplied many-fold when working in more than one language and with more than one national legal system. On many occasions, the Court has been well advised by its Advocates General to think and determine in terms of principle, of the objectives and purposes of the treaties, and of the creation and development of Community legal terms and concepts which can transcend those of national legal systems.[47] Sometimes the Court has relied very heavily upon the legal system of one member state, but, in the main, the Court has searched for principles of Community law from all the national legal systems of the member states, together with principles from international law:

Transocean Marine Paint Association v Commission of the European Communities case 17/74 [1974] ECR 1063

In purported exercise of its powers, the Commission imposed a condition on the Association with regard to the provision to the Commission of certain information. The Association was composed of members established within the Community and members not so established and the condition was imposed on the Association as a whole. The Association claimed that the condition was too great a burden and might be impossible to perform with regard to its non-EEC members, some of whose laws would not permit the disclosure of such information. Failure to provide the information could be punished by fines imposed on the EEC members for a situation which was not their fault. There were fears that the EEC members might be dropped from the Association by the non-EEC members because of the condition. The Association claimed that they were not given the opportunity to state their case, to give their view as to what information should be communicated to the Commission and what dangers a too burdensome condition might await the EEC members of the Association. They argued that the written rules of procedure laid down in the appropriate regulation had been breached by the Commission. In addition, in anticipation of a ruling that the formal written statutory provisions did not impose on the Commission the duty to give a hearing to the Association, the Association pointed to another source of law imposing legal obligations on the Commission and claimed that the Commission had violated general principles of administrative procedure.

---

[45] *Levin v Staatssecretaris van Justitie* [1982] ECR 1035 and *van Duyn*, p. 353, paragraph 18 (on free movement of workers). [46] *Centre public d'aide sociale de Courcelles v Lebon* [1987] ECR 2811.
[47] *Jean Neu v Secrétaire d'État à l'Agriculture* [1991] ECR I-3617.

Advocate General Warner, at 1088–1089

'My Lords, [there] is a rule embedded in the law of some of our countries that an administrative author-ity, before wielding a statutory power to the detriment of a particular person, must in general hear what that person has to say about the matter, even if the statute does not expressly require it. "Audi alteram partem". [In] the law of England the rule is centuries old, firmly established and of daily application. It is considered to be a "rule of natural justice", a somewhat flamboyant and sometimes criticised phrase. [The] most often cited expression of the rule is in the judgment of Byles, J, in *Cooper v Wandsworth Board of Works* [p. 468], where he said that "although there are no positive words in a statute requiring that the party shall be heard, yet the justice of the common law will supply the omission of the legisla-ture". In England today there is no scope for controversy about the existence of the rule. [I] know, my Lords, of no exception to the rule, acknowledged in English law, which could have deprived the [Association] in the circumstances of the present case of the right to be heard before being subjected to an obligation such as that [at issue].

There can be no doubt that the rule forms part also of the law of Scotland (consider *Malloch v Aberdeen Corporation*) and of the laws of Denmark (see Anderson, *Dansk [Forvaltningsret]*), of Germany (see Forsthoff, *Lehrbuch des [Verwaltungsrechts]*) and of Ireland (see Kelly, *Fundamental Rights in the Irish Law and [Constitution]*). It appears that the principle here in question is of fairly recent origin in French law and that its scope is not yet settled. The decisions of the Conseil d'État evince three different approaches: the narrowest being to apply it only when the decision of the administrative authority concerned is in the nature of a sanction; a slightly wider approach which would apply it in any case where the decision of that authority is based on the character or on the behaviour of the person to be affected; and a third approach which is virtually as wide as that of the English common law. [The] position in Belgium and in Luxembourg is similar, though the Conseils d'État of those countries seem to have been less hesitant in developing the principle than that of France. [In] Italy the Consiglio di Stato has held that there is no general principle of law requiring an administrative authority to inform those concerned of its proposals so as to enable them to comment [and] it seems that the law of the Netherlands is similar, in this respect, to that of Italy.

[My Lords, that review of] the laws of the Member States, must, I think, on balance, lead to the conclusion that the right to be heard forms part of those rights which "the law" referred to in Article 164 [now 220] of the Treaty upholds, and of which, accordingly, it is the duty of this court to ensure the observance. I would therefore reject the contention of the Commission that it was under no duty to inform the [Association] of what it had in mind before imposing on them the obligation [to provide the information].'

The European Court of Justice

'15. It is clear [that the relevant regulation] applies the general rule that a person whose interests are perceptibly affected by a decision taken by a public authority must be given the opportunity to make his point of view known. This rule requires that an undertaking be clearly informed, in good time, of the essence of [the] conditions to which the Commission intends to [impose] and it must have the oppor-tunity to submit its observations to the Commission. This is especially so in the case of conditions which, as in this case, impose considerable obligations having far-reaching effects.'

Perhaps the Court has attempted to find and use principles well known and accepted by the legal systems of the member states in order to encourage the observance of Community law by the member states. The Court, however, is not content to draw its sources from a more or less arithmetical average of the various national solutions and will choose from each of the member countries those principles which, having regard to the Community objective, appear the best or the most progressive. 'That is the spirit which has hitherto guided the Court.'[48]

---

[48] *Hoogovens v High Authority* [1962] ECR 253, at 283–284, per Advocate General Lagrange.

This attitude has been of great importance in cases for preliminary rulings where there is a need for fruitful collaboration between the Court and the national courts which both refer questions to and receive replies from the Court (see head VI(c)). By drawing upon principles already established in the member states, the Court can at the same time guarantee that it will be employing methods of solving legal disputes that have already been proved in municipal law and yet, at the same time, the Court by choosing the most appropriate or progressive national solution(s) for the application of the Community objectives can develop supra-national concepts where these are considered necessary.[49]

(c) Community case law

Whether the Court has the power to make decisions which can form a source of Community law is not expressly stated in the Treaty. The 'interpretation' function of the Court of Justice has resulted, naturally, in decisions interpreting many specific written provisions. Two features stand out. First, as mentioned above, the Court has developed Community concepts when called upon to interpret words and phrases and, in so doing, the Court has undertaken at least a supplementary legislative function. Secondly, it would be very natural for a judicial body which interpreted a word or a phrase one way when the matter first came before it to accept that its original interpretation was correct when the matter was again raised and to repeat its earlier decision and the reasons therefor. In this way legal certainty, a principle of fundamental importance, is reinforced and the Court's decisions can provide a guide to the results of litigation before the Court and, in particular, can be applied by each and every national court. The Court in the early days did not act very overtly, preferring to refer to its earlier decisions by implication by simply repeating earlier words, phrases (and sometimes quite lengthy passages) without assigning any express citation to the earlier decision.[50] As the Court developed, the Court started actively to cite previous decisions, sometimes by using such phrases as 'as the Court has already stated' or 'settled case law'[51] and later the Court started to cite previous decisions rather in the manner used by common law jurisdictions.[52] Therefore, the Court has, on many occasions, built up a settled case law which since it will be followed in practice, even if not in legal theory, becomes a source of law in its own right because it is possible to predict the answer which will be handed down. The Court has not, however, erected a system of binding precedent which must be followed slavishly or unquestioningly in such a way that its rigidity might hinder the development of Community law and the objectives of the Treaty as these may change.

(d) General principles of law

These are principles which supplement the formal written sources of law when those sources are silent and which have created something akin to a series of fundamental freedoms against which may be measured the actions of the Community institutions and the member states.

---

[49] *Hoekstra v Bestuur der Bedrijfsvereniging voor Detailhandel en Ambachten* [1964] ECR 177 and *Levin v Staatssecretaris van Justitie* [1982] ECR 1035 (on the meaning of 'worker').

[50] Cf *Grad*, p. 352, and *van Duyn*, p. 353.   [51] *Ratti*, p. 356.

[52] *Commission v France*, p. 328, paragraphs 62, 63.

These general principles of law have been taken from the legal systems of the member states to assist in the process of the creation of an autonomous and separate legal order of Community law. General principles of law have achieved their legitimacy and normative force within the Community legal order by virtue of the fact that the Court of Justice has based them, sometimes very indirectly, upon Treaty provisions, albeit somewhat vague provisions: 'The Court of Justice shall ensure that in the interpretation and application of this Treaty the law is observed'; 'infringement of this Treaty or of any rule of law relating to its application'; 'in accordance with the general principles common to the laws of the Member States'.[53] The silence of the Treaty but for oblique references to some other 'law' has, argued the Court, imposed upon the Court itself the obligation to supplement the written law by a form of equity, albeit used in terms more familiar to the public lawyer. From the case law a number of principles may be discerned.

The principle of equality is sometimes written into Community law expressly. For example, article 12 (ex 6) states that within the scope of application of the Treaty 'any discrimination on grounds of nationality shall be prohibited'.[54] Furthermore, article 141 (ex 119) envisages equality between men and women in matters of equal pay for equal work. The principle of legal certainty means that an individual or organisation must be in a position to know where he, she or it stands with regard to Community rights and obligations.[55] The principle has been invoked by the Court in condemning member states for failure to implement directives in a manner which enables persons concerned to know their rights and obligations.[56] The Court has on numerous occasions stated that a general principle of legal certainty comprises the idea that a person should not be deprived of rights which that person was led to believe would be conferred, the principle of legitimate expectation[57] and that rights should not be interfered with retrospectively, the principle of non-retroactivity.[58] The principle that penal provisions may not have retroactive effect is one which is common to all the legal orders of the member states, is enshrined in the European Convention on Human Rights as a fundamental right, and takes its place among the general principles of law whose observance is ensured by the Court.[59] The principle of proportionality means that, given that a power to act exists and given that there is a choice of methods whereby to exercise that power, the method chosen must be suitable or appropriate to achieve the purpose of the power and the method chosen must not go further than is necessary in order to achieve that purpose.[60] There must be given a preference to that method which restricts the least those freedoms guaranteed by Community law. The principle is also applied to any sanctions imposed and the reaction of authority to the violation of a rule must be proportionate. In *R v Intervention Board for Agricultural Produce, ex p ED & Man (Sugar) Ltd*,[61] there was a scheme whereby companies could apply for permission to export sugar to third countries. Companies had to give a security to ensure that they actually exported the sugar and make a formal application for an export licence to the Commission. A regulation provided that if the application were late the whole security would be forfeit. Man applied for a licence and the application by telex was three to four hours late as the employee who normally sent such telexes was absent from work that day. The Commission declared that the £1,670,370 security should be forfeit. It was held

[53] Articles 220 (ex 164), 230(2) (ex 173(2)), 288(2) (ex 215(2)), respectively.

[54] *Cowan v Trésor Public* [1989] ECR 195 (United Kingdom national entitled under French criminal injuries compensation scheme).   [55] *Van Duyn*, p. 353, paragraph 13.

[56] *Commission v Denmark* [1985] ECR 427.

[57] *Commission v Council* [1973] ECR 575; *Merkur Außenhandel v Commission* [1977] ECR 1063.

[58] *Amylum v Council* [1982] ECR 3017.   [59] *R v Kent Kirk* [1984] ECR 2689.

[60] *Johnston*, p. 369, paragraph 39.   [61] [1985] ECR 2889.

that although the Commission was entitled to impose a time limit for applications, the penalty imposed, namely, the automatic forfeiture of the entire security, in the event of an infringement significantly less serious than the failure to fulfil the primary obligation to export, which the security was intended to guarantee, must be considered too drastic a penalty. The principle may he used against member states. For example, where Community law permits member states to make derogations from normally guaranteed freedoms, those derogations are subject to the principle, which has been applied with regard to free movement of persons,[62] goods,[63] and services.[64] A basic principle of public law is that of a fair administrative process. This may be statutory in that detailed procedural rules are laid down by the Community legislator. If, however, the legislation is silent or inadequate then the general principle of a fair hearing and the adequacy of legal remedies is applied both to Community institutions[65] and to member states.[66]

In most written constitutions it is normal to find a comprehensive statement of the rights and duties of the citizen. Such declarations of the rights of man arose in the seventeenth and eighteenth centuries and in modern times, especially following the violation of such rights during the Second World War, states of Europe incorporated express declarations into their written constitutions and ratified international conventions, such as the European Convention for the Protection of Human Rights and Fundamental Freedoms. The European Constitution, as established by the Treaty of Rome, did not possess an express Bill of Rights, and phrases such as 'human rights' and 'fundamental freedoms' were not contained therein. However, as the European Constitution developed from one governing an economic Community to one governing a European Union, references to human rights in Community documents emerged. The TEU made special reference to human rights, the TA introduced a procedure for suspending the Community membership rights of any country guilty of violating the fundamental rights of citizens, and in Nice in December 2000 the Charter of Fundamental Rights of the European Union was solemnly proclaimed. In the meantime, the Court took analogous provisions in the Treaty, the principles common to member states and the European Convention and incorporated the principle that the protection of human rights was indeed a part of Community law (which in turn was part of the law of the individual member states).[67] Principles such as non-discrimination on grounds of nationality[68] or sex,[69] rights to religion,[70] to property,[71] free movement,[72] the inviolability of the home,[73] have all been consecrated by the Court.

(e) Constitutional law

Outstanding amongst the creations of the Court's case law have been answers to fundamental questions which were very much not answered by express Treaty provisions. The Court has created constitutional doctrines which emphasise the autonomy of Community law and its

---

[62] *Watson and Belman* [1976] ECR 1185.

[63] *Rewe-Zentral v Bundesmonopolverwaltung für Branntwein (Cassis de Dijon)* [1979] ECR 649.

[64] *Commission v Greece* [1991] ECR I-727. [65] *Transocean*, p. 317. [66] *Johnston*, p. 369.

[67] *Stauder v City of Ulm* [1969] ECR 419; *Society for the Protection of Unborn Children Ireland Ltd v Grogan* [1991] ECR I-4685. For the Convention and Charter, see chapter 13. [68] *Cowan v Trésor Public* [1989] ECR 195.

[69] *Defrenne v SABENA* [1976] ECR 455. [70] *Prais v Council* [1976] ECR 1589.

[71] *Hauer v Land Rheinland-Pfalz* [1979] ECR 3727.

[72] *Rutili v Minister for the Interior* [1975] ECR 1219. [73] *Hoechst v Commission* [1989] ECR 2859.

supremacy over and within each member state and which, quite simply, cannot be found in any express way within the Treaty. Doctrines such as the supremacy of Community law and the granting of rights to individuals, in the absence of fulfilment of Community obligations by member states, by virtue of Community law itself have been based on the presumed (very presumed) intentions of the Treaty makers. These doctrines relate to the relationship between Community law and the member states, to which we now turn.

VI. Community Law and the Member States

(a) The supremacy of Community law

A number of crucial questions follow the discussion in previous heads with regard to the relationship between the member states and the primary and secondary legislation created by the member states and the Community institutions, respectively, and these lead, inevitably, to the proposition of the supremacy of Community law over the laws of the member states. First, what is the effect of the treaties on the legal systems of the member states? Secondly, with regard to regulations, what is the meaning of 'shall have general application [and] be binding in its entirety and directly applicable in all Member States'? Thirdly, what if a member state does not comply with a Treaty obligation imposed on it, in particular if a member state does not implement (or partially or imperfectly implements) a directive? The answers are not expressly provided for in the Treaty and come from the decisions of the Court of Justice interpreting the relevant provisions and inferring, deducing and applying an inevitable logical corollary to each provision and leading to the principle of the supremacy of Community law. This logical corollary has not simply been demonstrated with regard to disputes between Community institutions and member states (or between member states and member states) being resolved by some form of international arbitration. More significantly, the logical corollary has been directed to ensuring that the citizens of, or living or working in, member states are themselves, by the supremacy of Community law, the recipients of the rights granted and the obligations imposed by the Community in the achievement of the objectives of the Treaty.

The issue of the legal status of the Treaty in relation to the internal laws of a member state was first raised in *NV Algemene Transport-en Expeditie Onderneming van Gend & Loos v Nederlandse administratie der belastingen*,[74] where the European Court of Justice made its historic and often repeated statement: 'The conclusion to be drawn from this is that the Community constitutes a new legal order of international law for the benefit of which the states have limited their sovereign rights, albeit within limited fields, and the subjects of which comprise not only Member States but also their nationals. Independently of the legislation of Member States, Community law therefore not only imposes obligations on individuals but is also intended to confer upon them rights which become part of their legal heritage. These

---

[74] [1963] ECR 1, p. 351.

rights arise not only where they are expressly granted by the Treaty, but also by reason of obligations which the Treaty imposes in a clearly defined way upon individuals as well as upon the Member States and upon the institutions of the Community.' This was repeated and amplified in:

Flaminio Costa v ENEL case 6/64 [1964] ECR 585

Costa claimed, before the Giudice Conciliatore (an Italian court), that he was not obliged to pay his electricity bill on the ground that the Italian law nationalising the electricity industry was contrary to certain provisions of the EEC Treaty and was unconstitutional. The Giudice sought a preliminary ruling on the interpretation of those provisions. The Italian government argued that the reference was 'absolutely inadmissible' as the Giudice merely had to apply the national law which governed the question before it.

The European Court of Justice, at 592–599

'By contrast with ordinary international treaties, the EEC Treaty has created its own legal system which, on the entry into force of the Treaty, became an integral part of the legal systems of the Member States and which their courts are bound to apply. By creating a Community of unlimited duration, having its own institutions, its own personality, its own legal capacity and capacity of representation on the international plane and, more particularly, real powers stemming from a limitation of sovereignty or a transfer of powers from the states to the Community, the Member States have limited their sovereign rights, albeit within limited fields, and have thus created a body of law which binds both their nationals and themselves.

The integration into the laws of each Member State of provisions which derive from the Community, and more generally the terms and the spirit of the Treaty, make it impossible for the states, as a corollary, to accord precedence to a unilateral and subsequent measure over a legal system accepted by them on a basis of reciprocity. Such a measure cannot therefore be inconsistent with that legal system. The executive force of Community law cannot vary from one state to another in deference to subsequent domestic laws, without jeopardising the attainment of the objectives of the [Treaty]. The obligations undertaken under the Treaty establishing the Community would not be unconditional, but merely contingent, if they could be called in question by subsequent legislative acts of the [signatories]. The precedence of Community law is confirmed by Article 189 [now 249], whereby a regulation "shall be binding" and "directly applicable in all Member States". This provision, which is subject to no reservation, would be quite meaningless if a state could unilaterally nullify its effects by means of a legislative measure which could prevail over Community law.

It follows from all these observations that the law stemming from the Treaty, an independent source of law, could not, because of its special and original nature, be overridden by domestic legal provisions, however framed, without being deprived of its character as Community law and without the legal basis of the Community itself being called into question.

The transfer by the states from their domestic legal system to the Community legal system of the rights and obligations arising under the Treaty carries with it a permanent limitation of their sovereign rights, against which a subsequent unilateral act incompatible with the concept of the Community cannot prevail.'

The early case law was summed up cogently and concisely: the 'Treaty has established its own system of law, integrated into the legal systems of the Member States, and which must be applied by their courts. It would be contrary to the nature of such a system to allow Member States to introduce or to retain measures capable of prejudicing the practical effectiveness of the Treaty. The binding force of the Treaty and of measures taken in application of it must not differ from one state to another as a result of internal measures, lest the functioning of the Community system should be impeded and the achievement of the aims of the Treaty placed in peril.'[75]

With regard to regulations, the Court has constantly emphasised the wording of article 249 (ex 189). The inevitable logical corollary of the phrase 'shall have general application' is that regulations are general legislative acts of the Community and instruments for securing the uniformity of Community law. The inevitable logical corollary of the phrase 'be binding in its entirety' means that there is a fundamental rule requiring the uniform application of regulations throughout the Community and that a member state cannot disregard any part of a regulation or subject a regulation to implementing provisions other than those which might be required by the regulation itself. The inevitable logical corollary of the phrase 'directly applicable in all Member States' means that the legal effects occur without any further legislative activity by member states or their institutions and, indeed, the enactment of the words of a regulation in national legislation could distort the uniformity of the effect of the words in all member states. Regulations apply not only to, but also in, the member states and it is as though the exact words (and all the exact words) of the regulation enter the legal system of each member state automatically and contemporaneously.

The proposition that Community law becomes an integral part of the legal systems of all member states and takes precedence within those states has been consistently followed, the Court of Justice not permitting any exceptions to its stated position. This leads to the legal and constitutional consequence that any provision of national law which conflicts with Community law is invalid. Therefore, any conflict must be resolved by the national legal system of the member state withdrawing its national law so that the Community-derived law is the only one in existence within the member state. From this proposition follow four consequences:

(i) Member states are under a duty to fulfil all Treaty obligations and the Commission (or, more rarely, another state) may bring a defaulting member state before the Court of Justice (see head (b) below);

(ii) Since Community law must be fully and uniformly applied in all member states, article 234 (ex 177) provides that any court or tribunal of a member state is entitled or in certain situations obliged to make a reference to the Court of Justice whenever it considers that a preliminary ruling on a question of interpretation or validity relating to Community law is necessary to enable it to give judgment (see head (c) below);

(iii) The question has arisen on many occasions as to the position of the individual (person or company) who points to the fact that a national legal system has not been adjusted in order to comply with a Community obligation which grants that individual Community rights and that there are two rules, one emanating from the national legal system and one emanating from the Community, when it is the latter which is more favourable to the individual. The protection of Community rights granted to individuals, by means of the principle of direct effect, by positive interpretation by the national courts, and by the quest for adequate judicial remedies (including damages), is examined in the discussion relating to the reception of Community law by the United Kingdom (see heads VII and VIII);

(iv) The supremacy of Community law is, therefore, imposed on all member states' legislative, administrative and judicial organs and the validity of a Community measure or its

---

[75] *Walt Wilhelm v Bundeskartellamt* [1969] ECR 1.

effect within a member state cannot be affected by allegations that it runs counter to either fundamental rights as formulated by the constitution of that state or the principles of a national constitutional structure. All member states have, therefore, had to incorporate the principle of the supremacy of Community law into their own internal domestic legal and constitutional systems and this is discussed in relation to the reception of Community law by the United Kingdom (see heads VII and VIII).

(b) Enforcing Community obligations

Community obligations are imposed on the member states, principally by Treaty provisions, regulations, directives and decisions. Member states are enjoined to take all appropriate measures whether general or particular to ensure fulfilment of the obligations arising out of the Treaty or resulting from action taken by the institutions of the Community; they must facilitate the achievement of the Community's tasks; they must abstain from any measure which could jeopardise the attainment of the objectives of the Treaty.[76] In order to ensure the proper functioning and development of the common market, the Commission is under a duty to ensure that the provisions of the Treaty are applied[77] and the Court of Justice is enjoined to ensure that in the interpretation and application of the Treaty the law is observed.[78] The Commission and the Court, therefore, have, as one of their roles, the enforcement of Community obligations, either at the instance of the Commission (the usual case) or at the instance of another member state.

If the Commission considers that a member state has failed to fulfil a Treaty obligation, it must give the state concerned the opportunity to submit its observations and then deliver a reasoned opinion on the matter. If the state concerned does not comply with that opinion within the period laid down by the Commission, the Commission may bring the matter before the Court. Any member state which considers that another member state has failed to fulfil an obligation under the Treaty may bring the matter before the Court, but, before the accusing member state brings an action against another member state for an alleged infringement of such an obligation, it must bring the matter before the Commission. In such a case, the Commission must deliver a reasoned opinion after each of the states concerned has been given the opportunity to submit its own case and its observations on the other party's case (both orally and in writing).[79]

There are a number of means whereby allegations of a breach of a Community obligation may be brought to the Commission's notice, including complaints from members of the public and organisations and pressure groups (for example those concerned with equal opportunities, animal welfare and environmental protection), questions in the European Parliament and the Commission's own monitoring system. The primary responsibility for enforcing Community law lies with each member state and some Community measures impose very stringent duties upon the member state, together with policing powers being granted the Commission. Sometimes member states are enjoined to give the Commission

---

[76] Article 10 (ex 5).   [77] Article 211 (ex 155).   [78] Article 220 (ex 164).
[79] Articles 226 (ex 169) and 227 (ex 170); *Commission v Portugal* [1991] ECR I-3659.

information and if they fail to give the correct information the Commission may take action:

....

Commission of the European Communities v Ireland
case C-39/88 [1990] ECR I-4271

The Commission complained that Ireland had failed to notify to the Commission certain prices relating to the market in fish in order to fix an annual guide price for fish. A regulation required member states to notify the Commission of the prices recorded for fish on representative wholesale markets or in representative ports. The average price on the market day, the total quantities landed and marketed and the total quantity withdrawn from the market, had to be sent to the Commission by telex on the 10th and 25th day of each month and each market day if there was a threat of crisis or market disturbance.

The European Court of Justice:

'10. Ireland [submits] that, as it has already pointed out on several occasions during the discussions on the regulations in question, it is not possible for it to deploy its limited number of fisheries inspectors at the representative ports for the purpose of gathering the pricing information in question and submitting it to the Commission on a bi-monthly basis. Those inspectors are required to monitor some 900 ports and landing places in addition to the representative ports.

11. That submission cannot be accepted. It is well established in the case law of the court [that] a Member State may not plead internal circumstances in order to justify a failure to comply with obligations and time limits resulting from Community law. Moreover, it has been held on several occasions (see [Commission v Italy, p. 327]) that practical difficulties which appear at the stage when a Community measure is put into effect cannot permit a Member State unilaterally to opt out of fulfilling its obligations.

12. In those circumstances, it must be held that by its omission to notify certain prices relating to the market in fish, Ireland has failed to fulfil its obligations under [the regulation].'

The first stage in the process following a complaint, parliamentary question or an investigation by the Commission's staff is the administrative or pre-hearing stage. The Commission must give the state concerned the opportunity to submit its observations and the Commission must deliver a reasoned opinion on the failure, containing a formal statement of the existence of a breach of obligation. It is settled case law that the question whether a member state has failed to fulfil its obligations must be determined by reference to the situation prevailing in that state at the end of the period laid down in the reasoned opinion.[80] The Commission tries to settle as many cases as possible at this stage and the practice has arisen of holding package meetings, at regular intervals, in each member state with representatives of the government departments concerned. At such meetings, all the cases involving a member state are discussed. Pragmatic solutions in keeping with Community law can thus be sought jointly as early as the complaint stage. The procedure can be very protracted, taking several years.[81]

There must be a failure to fulfil a Community obligation and failures may be the result of a positive breach (for example, introducing legislative or administrative measures contrary to Community law) or a negative breach (for example, failing to transpose the provisions of a directive into national law, maintaining in force existing national provisions contrary to the results to be achieved by a directive, failing to obey a decision or failing to give the Commission sufficient information required by a directive). The failure must be on the part of the member state and this includes all those arms of the state which have, within the state,

---

[80] *Commission v France* [1997] ECR I-3827; *Commission v France* [1999] ECR I-1719.
[81] *Commission v France*, p. 328.

the jurisdiction to fulfil the obligation (legislature, administration both central and local, judiciary and whatever organ is entrusted with the power to make constitutional rules) (see head VIII(g)). In *Commission v Belgium*,[82] Belgium did not dispute the existence of discriminatory tax rules between home-grown and imported wood, and showed itself willing to take the necessary measures to eliminate the discriminatory provisions complained of by the Commission. A draft law was put before the Belgian Parliament but Parliament was dissolved and the Belgian government argued that this delay in enacting the law amounted to a 'force majeure' beyond its control. However, the Court held that the Treaty obligations 'devolve upon States as such and the liability of a Member State under [article 226 (ex 169)] arises whatever the agency of the State whose action or inaction is the cause of the failure to fulfil its obligations, even in the case of a constitutionally independent institution'. It may happen that the Commission considers that an alleged failure to comply with an obligation will cause irreparable harm during the time it takes to determine an article 226 (ex 169) application. In such a case the Commission may apply for a protective or interim measure.[83]

If the state concerned does not comply with the opinion within the period laid down by the Commission, the Commission may bring the matter before the Court for the judicial stage of the process. It is settled case law that, in proceedings under the Treaty for failure to fulfil an obligation, it is incumbent on the Commission to prove that the obligation has not been fulfilled and to place before the Court the information necessary to enable it to determine whether that is so.[84] In making use of article 226 (ex 169), the Commission enjoys a wide discretionary power.[85] Apprehension of internal difficulties cannot justify a failure by a member state to apply Community law correctly.[86] The defendant state cannot rely upon domestic difficulties or provisions of its national legal system, even its constitutional system, for the purpose of justifying a failure to comply with obligations resulting from Community directives.[87] The Court of Justice has taken a logically strict view of breaches of obligations:

Commission of the European Communities v Italian Republic
case 39/72 [1973] ECR 101

With a view to reducing the surpluses of milk and milk products, the Council introduced a system of premiums to encourage the slaughtering of dairy cows and the withholding of milk and milk products from the market. This was enacted by a Regulation. The Italian government implemented the system of slaughtering premiums very late and did not implement the system for paying non-marketing premiums.

The European Court of Justice

'With regard to the premiums for slaughtering

14. The [Regulation has] provided precise time limits for the carrying into effect of the system of premiums for slaughtering. The efficacy of the agreed measures depended upon the observation of these time limits, since the measures could only attain their object completely if they were carried out simultaneously in all the Member States at the time determined in consequence of the economic policy the Council was pursuing. [It] consequently appears that the delay on the part of [Italy] in performing the obligations imposed on it by the introduction of the system of premiums for slaughtering [constitutes] a default in its obligations.

[82] [1970] ECR 237.   [83] *Commission v Germany* [1990] ECR I-2715.
[84] *Commission v Netherlands* [1982] ECR 1791.   [85] *Commission v United Kingdom* [1988] ECR 3127.
[86] *Commission v France* [1995] ECR I-4443.   [87] *Commission v Italy* [1978] ECR 879.

As to the premiums for non-marketing

19. The default in putting into operation the provisions of [the Regulation] with regard to premiums for non-marketing is due to a deliberate refusal by the Italian authorities. The defendant justifies this refusal by the difficulty of providing an effective and serious inspection and control of the quantities of milk which are not marketed but destined for other use, taking into account both the special characteristics of Italian agriculture and the lack of adequate administration at a lower level. In any case, according to the Italian government, measures intended to restrict the production of milk were inappropriate to the needs of the Italian economy, which is characterised by insufficient food production. During the debate stages of [the Regulation the] Italian delegation made these difficulties known and expressed clear reservations at that time with regard to the carrying out of the Regulation. In these circumstances, complaint ought not to be made against [Italy] for having refused to put into effect on its national territory provisions passed in spite of the opposition which it has manifested.

20. [Under] the terms of Article 189 [now 249], the Regulation is binding "in its entirety" for Member States. In consequence, it cannot be accepted that a Member State should apply in an incomplete or selective manner provisions of a Community Regulation so as to render abortive certain aspects of Community legislation which it has opposed or which it considers contrary to its national interests.

21. In particular, as regards the putting into effect of a measure of economic policy intended to eliminate surpluses of certain products, the Member State which omits to take, within the requisite time limits and simultaneously with the other Member States, the measures which it ought to take, undermines the efficacy of the provision decided upon in common, while at the same time taking an undue advantage to the detriment of its partners in view of the free circulation of goods.

22. As regards the defence based on the preparatory work on [the Regulation], the objective scope of rules laid down by the common institutions cannot be modified by reservations or objections which Member States have made at the time the rules were being formulated. In the same way, practical difficulties which appear at the stage when a Community measure has to be put into effect cannot permit a Member State unilaterally to opt out of observing its obligations. The Community institutional system provides the Member State concerned with the necessary means to secure that its difficulties should be reasonably considered within the framework and principles of the Common Market and the legitimate interests of other Member [States].

24. In permitting Member States to profit from the advantages of the Community, the Treaty imposes on them also the obligation to respect its rules. For a state unilaterally to break, according to its own conception of national interest, the equilibrium between advantages and obligations flowing from its adherence to the Community brings into question the equality of Member States before Community law and creates discriminations at the expense of their nationals, and above all of the nationals of the state itself which places itself outside the Community rules.

25. This failure in the duty of solidarity accepted by Member States by the fact of their adherence to the Community strikes at the fundamental basis of the Community legal order. It appears therefore that, in deliberately refusing to give effect on its territory to one of the systems provided for by [the Regulation, Italy] has failed in a conspicuous manner to fulfil the obligations which it has assumed by virtue of its adherence to the European Economic Community.'

....

Commission of the European Communities v French Republic
case C-265/95 [1997] ECR I-441

For more than a decade, the Commission had regularly received complaints concerning the passivity of the French authorities in face of violent acts committed by private individuals and by protest movements of French farmers directed against agricultural products from other member states. Those acts consisted of the interception of lorries transporting such products in France and the destruction of their loads, violence against lorry drivers, threats against French supermarkets selling agricultural products originating in other member states, and the damaging of those goods when on display in shops in France. From 1993 to 1995, in particular, a vicious campaign was directed at strawberries originating in Spain and at tomatoes from Belgium. Violent incidents took place but the police who were present took no action to provide effective protection for the lorries and their loads. In 1995 the Commission therefore delivered a reasoned opinion stating that, by failing to take all necessary and proportionate measures in order to prevent the free movement of fruit and vegetables from being obstructed by actions by private individuals, the French Republic had failed to fulfil its obligations under the common organisations of the markets in agricultural products. A month later three lorries transporting fruit and vegetables from Spain were the subject of acts of violence in the south of France, without any intervention by the police. The Commission therefore brought an action against the French Republic and the Court granted the United Kingdom and Spain leave to intervene in support of the Commission.

The European Court of Justice

'16. In support of its application the Commission claims that Article 30 [now 28] of the Treaty and the common organisations of the markets in fruit and vegetables, which are based on the same principle of the elimination of obstacles to trade, prohibit quantitative restrictions on imports between the Member States and any measures having equivalent effect. Furthermore, in accordance with Article 5 [now 10] of the Treaty, the Member States are required to take all appropriate measures to ensure fulfilment of their obligations arising out of that Treaty.

17. Consequently, the interception of means of transport and the damaging of agricultural products originating in other Member States, and also the climate of insecurity caused by the threats made by various farmers' organisations against distributors of fruit and vegetables from those States, which have been found to have taken place in France, constitute an obstacle to intra-Community trade in those products, which the Member States are required to prevent by adopting appropriate measures, including measures against private individuals who imperil the free movement of goods.

18. In the present case, the fact that, year after year, serious incidents continued to hinder the importation and transit in France of fruit and vegetables originating in other Member States shows that the preventive and penal measures to which the French Government refers in defence are in practice neither adequate nor proportionate for the purpose of deterring the perpetrators of such offences from committing and repeating them. Moreover, it is clear from the factual evidence before the Commission that the French authorities have persistently abstained from taking effective action to prevent violent acts by farmers in France or to prosecute and punish them for the commission of such acts.

20. On the other hand, the French Government contends that there is no foundation for the Commission's action.

21. Thus, it claims that it put into effect, under conditions similar to those applicable to comparable breaches of domestic law, all necessary and appropriate means to prevent actions by private individuals that impeded the free movement of agricultural products and to prosecute and punish them for such actions. The surveillance measures implemented in 1993 enabled the number of acts of violence committed during subsequent years to be contained to a substantial degree.

22. However, in view of the large number of lorries transporting agricultural products in France and the wide variety of their destinations, on the one hand, and the unforeseeable nature of actions by farmers acting in small, commando-type groups, on the other, it is not possible to eliminate all risk of destruction. The latter reason also explains why it is very difficult to identify the perpetrators and to prove their individual participation in the acts of violence so as systematically to prosecute and punish such persons. Six more persons have, however, been convicted or placed under investigation since 1994. Moreover, the police must be allowed a discretion in deciding whether they should intervene in order to safeguard public order. In any event, the State compensates the victims of the offences on the

basis of liability without fault on the part of the public authorities. Thus, a sum in excess of FF 17 million was paid by way of damages in respect of the years 1993, 1994 and 1995.

23. The French Government adds that the dissatisfaction of French farmers is due to the considerable increase in exports of Spanish products since the accession of the Kingdom of Spain, which has led to a substantial fall in prices magnified by the competitive devaluation of the peseta and the dumping prices charged by Spanish producers. The French market for fruit and vegetables was seriously disrupted by the fact that the transitional period provided for on that accession had not been accompanied by any mechanism for monitoring the export prices charged by Spanish producers.

24. In order to determine whether the Commission's action is well founded, it should be stressed from the outset that the free movement of goods is one of the fundamental principles of the Treaty.

28. In particular, Article 30 provides that quantitative restrictions on imports and all measures having equivalent effect are prohibited between Member States.

29. That provision, taken in its context, must be understood as being intended to eliminate all barriers, whether direct or indirect, actual or potential, to flows of imports in intra-Community trade.

30. As an indispensable instrument for the realisation of a market without internal frontiers, Article 30 therefore does not prohibit solely measures emanating from the State which, in themselves, create restrictions on trade between Member States. It also applies where a Member State abstains from adopting the measures required in order to deal with obstacles to the free movement of goods which are not caused by the State.

31. The fact that a Member State abstains from taking action or, as the case may be, fails to adopt adequate measures to prevent obstacles to the free movement of goods that are created, in particular, by actions by private individuals on its territory aimed at products originating in other Member States is just as likely to obstruct intra-Community trade as is a positive act.

32. Article 30 therefore requires the Member States not merely themselves to abstain from adopting measures or engaging in conduct liable to constitute an obstacle to trade but also, when read with Article 5 of the Treaty, to take all necessary and appropriate measures to ensure that that fundamental freedom is respected on their territory.

37. As regards more specifically the present case, the facts which gave rise to the action brought by the Commission against the French Republic for failure to fulfil obligations are not in dispute.

38. The acts of violence committed in France and directed against agricultural products originating in other Member States, such as the interception of lorries transporting those products, the destruction of their loads and violence towards drivers, as well as threats to wholesalers and retailers and the damaging of goods on display, unquestionably create obstacles to intra-Community trade in those products.

39. It is therefore necessary to consider whether in the present case the French Government complied with its obligations under Article 30, in conjunction with Article 5, of the Treaty, by adopting adequate and appropriate measures to deal with actions by private individuals which create obstacles to the free movement of certain agricultural products.

40. It should be stressed that the Commission's written pleadings show that the incidents to which it objects in the present proceedings have taken place regularly for more than 10 years.

41. It was as long ago as 8 May 1985 that the Commission first sent a formal letter to the French Republic calling on it to adopt the preventive and penal measures necessary to put an end to acts of that kind.

42. Moreover, in the present case the Commission reminded the French Government on numerous occasions that Community law imposes an obligation to ensure de facto compliance with the principle of the free movement of goods by eliminating all restrictions on the freedom to trade in agricultural products from other Member States.

43. In the present case the French authorities therefore had ample time to adopt the measures necessary to ensure compliance with their obligations under Community law.

44. Moreover, notwithstanding the explanations given by the French Government, which claims that all possible measures were adopted in order to prevent the continuation of the violence and to prosecute and punish those responsible, it is a fact that, year after year, serious incidents have gravely jeopardised trade in agricultural products in France.

48. Moreover, it is not denied that when such incidents occurred the French police were either not present on the spot, despite the fact that in certain cases the competent authorities had been warned of the imminence of demonstrations by farmers, or did not intervene, even where they far outnumbered the perpetrators of the disturbances. Furthermore, the actions in question were not always rapid, surprise actions by demonstrators who then immediately took flight, since in certain cases the disruption continued for several hours.

49. Furthermore, it is undisputed that a number of acts of vandalism were filmed by television cameras, that the demonstrators' faces were often not covered and that the groups of farmers responsible for the violent demonstrations are known to the police.

50. Notwithstanding this, it is common ground that only a very small number of the persons who participated in those serious breaches of public order has been identified and prosecuted.

51. Thus, as regards the numerous acts of vandalism committed between April and August 1993, the French authorities have been able to cite only a single case of criminal prosecution.

52. In the light of all the foregoing factors, the Court, while not discounting the difficulties faced by the competent authorities in dealing with situations of the type in question in this case, cannot but find that, having regard to the frequency and seriousness of the incidents cited by the Commission, the measures adopted by the French Government were manifestly inadequate to ensure freedom of intra-Community trade in agricultural products on its territory by preventing and effectively dissuading the perpetrators of the offences in question from committing and repeating them.

53. That finding is all the more compelling since the damage and threats to which the Commission refers not only affect the importation into or transit in France of the products directly affected by the violent acts, but are also such as to create a climate of insecurity which has a deterrent effect on trade flows as a whole.

59. As regards the fact that the French Republic has assumed responsibility for the losses caused to the victims, this cannot be put forward as an argument by the French Government in order to escape its obligations under Community law.

60. Even though compensation can provide reparation for at least part of the loss or damage sustained by the economic operators concerned, the provision of such compensation does not mean that the Member State has fulfilled its obligations.

61. Nor is it possible to accept the arguments based on the very difficult socio-economic context of the French market in fruit and vegetables after the accession of the Kingdom of Spain.

62. It is settled case-law that economic grounds can never serve as justification for barriers prohibited by Article 30 of the Treaty (see, inter alia, Case 288/83 *Commission v Ireland* [1985] ECR 1761, paragraph 28).

63. As regards the suggestion by the French Government, in support of those arguments, that the destabilisation of the French market for fruit and vegetables was brought about by unfair practices, and even infringements of Community law, by Spanish producers, it must be remembered that a Member State may not unilaterally adopt protective measures or conduct itself in such a way as to obviate any breach by another Member State of rules of Community law (see, to that effect, Case C-5/94 *R v MAFF, ex p Hedley Lomas* [1996] ECR I-2553, paragraph 20).

64. This must be so a fortiori in the sphere of the common agricultural policy, where it is for the Community alone to adopt, if necessary, the measures required in order to deal with difficulties which some economic operators may be experiencing, in particular following a new accession.

65. Having regard to all the foregoing considerations, it must be concluded that in the present case the French Government has manifestly and persistently abstained from adopting appropriate and

adequate measures to put an end to the acts of vandalism which jeopardise the free movement on its territory of certain agricultural products originating in other Member States and to prevent the recurrence of such acts.

66. Consequently, it must be held that, by failing to adopt all necessary and proportionate measures in order to prevent the free movement of fruit and vegetables from being obstructed by actions by private individuals, the French Government has failed to fulfil its obligations under Article 30, in conjunction with Article 5, of the Treaty and under the common organisations of the markets in agricultural products.'

If the Court of Justice finds that a member state has failed to fulfil a Treaty obligation, the state is required to take the necessary measures to comply with the judgment of the Court of Justice. If, however, the Commission considers that the member state concerned has not taken such measures it will, after giving that state the opportunity to submit its observations, issue a reasoned opinion specifying the points on which the member state concerned has not complied with the judgment of the Court of Justice. If the member state concerned then fails to take the necessary measures to comply with the Court's judgment within the time-limit laid down by the Commission, the latter may bring the case before the Court of Justice. If the Court of Justice finds that the member state concerned has not complied with its judgment it may impose a lump sum or penalty payment on it.[88] In 1987, the Commission received a complaint drawing its attention to uncontrolled waste disposal in a river in Greece. In 1992 the Court of Justice held that Greece had failed to take the necessary measures for toxic and dangerous waste to be disposed of in the area while ensuring that human health and the environment were protected, as required by Community directives.[89] In 1997 the Commission applied to the Court of Justice for an order requiring Greece to pay a penalty. The Court held that, in the present case, a periodic penalty payment was the most appropriate means of ensuring that Community law was applied uniformly and effectively and of inducing Greece to comply with its obligations. The Court then fixed the amount of the fine. The basic criteria to be considered were the duration of the infringement, its degree of seriousness and the ability of the member state concerned to pay. In view of the particularly serious nature of the breaches of obligations, and of the duration of the infringement which was held to be considerable, the Court ordered Greece to pay a penalty payment of 20,000 euros for each day of delay in complying with the 1992 judgment, as from the date of the second judgment.[90]

(c) The reference procedure

The supranational characteristic of Community law means that Community law is part of the internal legal order of all member states. Therefore, a Community judicial function is carried on by all the courts and tribunals of the member states before whom arises a question of Community law. Criminal law courts may hear cases in which both prosecution and defence raise questions of Community law; actions for judicial review of administrative action by a

---

[88] Article 228 (ex 171).   [89] [1992] ECR I-2509.

[90] *Commission v Greece* [2000] ECR I-5047. See, also, *Commission v Spain* [2003] ECR I-14141; *Commission v France* [2005] ECR I-6263.

member state's public authorities may be raised in administrative courts; civil courts may have submitted to them actions for damages for loss allegedly caused by the non-implementation of a Community obligation; substantive rights granted in social security and employment protection situations by Community law may be enforced before social security and labour courts and tribunals. Within the member state, litigants may, therefore, find that their first encounter with Community law is when they come before their own domestic legal systems. National courts and tribunals will determine the facts and upon them is imposed the duty to make judicial determinations. However, during such litigation there may arise a question of interpretation of Community law which it is necessary to resolve before making a final determination. In view of the principle that Community law must be applied uniformly throughout the Community (including the national legal systems) and that national courts do not make different determinations on the same point of law, the definitive task of interpreting Community law is taken from the national courts and granted to the Court of Justice by article 234 (ex 177). Furthermore, that Court has emphasised that there is a corresponding constitutional obligation to abide by that Court's decisions. This applies not just to the court which referred the question but to all other national courts. Some of the fundamental rules of Community law have their origin in replies to requests for preliminary rulings as to interpretation.[91]

The Court of Justice has jurisdiction to give preliminary rulings concerning the interpretation of the Treaty, the validity and interpretation of acts of the institutions of the Community and of the European Central Bank, and the interpretation of the statutes of bodies established by an act of the Council, where those statutes so provide. A court or tribunal against whose decisions there is a judicial remedy under national law, has a power, if it considers that a decision on any question of interpretation or validity is necessary to enable it to give judgment, to request the Court to give a ruling on the question. As a matter of practice, courts and tribunals of quite minor rank in the judicial hierarchy of their respective member states have requested preliminary rulings, and fundamental rules of Community law have been proscribed in reply.[92] In seeking a preliminary ruling the national court must consider such a ruling to be 'necessary' to enable it to give judgment. If a question of interpretation or validity is raised in a case pending before a court or tribunal of a member state, against whose decisions there is no judicial remedy (such as appeal or judicial review) under national law, that court or tribunal must bring the matter before the Court of Justice. That Court has emphasised that there is an 'obligation'[93] which is established with a view to ensuring the proper application and uniform interpretation of Community law in all member states, by a partnership between national courts, in their capacity as courts responsible for the application of Community law, in cases upon which they are called to adjudicate, and the Court of Justice. Article 234 is thus an instrument of co-operation between the Court of Justice and the national courts, and, in the context of that co-operation, the national court which alone has the direct knowledge of the facts of the case and which is under a duty to give judgment in the case, is in the best position to assess both the need for a preliminary ruling and the wording of the question submitted.[94] Courts or tribunals are not obliged to refer questions concerning the interpretation of Community law if the answer to that question can in no way affect the outcome of the case and the correct application of Community law may sometimes be so obvious as to leave no scope for any reasonable doubt as to the manner in which the question

[91] *Van Gend*, p. 351; *Costa*, p. 323; *Marshall*, p. 357; *Johnston*, p. 369; *Francovich*, p. 383; and *Factortame*, p. 377.
[92] *Costa*, p. 323; *Francovich*, p. 383.   [93] *Cilfit v Ministry of Health* [1982] ECR 3415.
[94] *Schmidberger* [2003] ECR I-5659; *Mangold* [2005] ECR I-9981.

raised is to be answered. Before coming to the conclusion that the question is irrelevant or perfectly clear, the national court or tribunal must be convinced that the matter is equally obvious to the courts of the other member states and to the Court of Justice. Community legislation is drafted in several languages and an interpretation of a Community provision may involve a comparison of the different language versions and legal concepts do not necessarily have the same meaning in Community law and in the law of the various member states.[95]

VII. The Incorporation of Community Law in the United Kingdom—the Constitutional Mechanism

(a) A constitutional dilemma

The United Kingdom joined the Community on 1 January 1973. The United Kingdom's constitution was to be changed by a rather abrupt and dramatic process, because (see head I(b)) the aims of economic integration had resulted in the Treaty of Rome itself containing constitutional and legal implications which had had (and would continue to have) resounding effects on the constitutions of all member states. By the time the United Kingdom became a member state, the principle of supremacy of Community law had become an accepted fundamental constitutional part of Community law (the *acquis communautaire*).

'Whereas in joining the Communities the applicant states accept without reserve the Treaties and their political objectives, all decisions taken since their entry into force, and the action that has been agreed in respect of the development and reinforcement of the Communities; whereas it is an essential feature of the legal system set up by the Treaties establishing the Communities that certain of their provisions and certain acts of the Community institutions are directly applicable, that Community law takes precedence over any national provisions conflicting with it, and that procedures exist for ensuring the uniform interpretation of this law; and whereas accession to the Communities entails recognition of the binding force of these rules, observance of which is indispensable to guarantee the effectiveness and unity of Community law.'[96]

Therefore, the United Kingdom had to provide for the incorporation of an already well developed system of Community law which had provided for the rule-making capacity of the Treaties and of the secondary legislation created by Community institutions, the provisions for preliminary rulings, and, above all, the limited cessation of national sovereignty in favour of the supremacy of Community law.

The incorporation of Community law (as it had been created and developed by and within the original member states) presented two specific problems to the United Kingdom

---

[95] *Wörsdorfer v Raad van Arbeid* [1979] ECR 2717.

[96] Commission Opinion of 19 January 1972 on the application for Accession to the European Communities by Denmark, Ireland, Norway, and the United Kingdom.

constitution, namely, the incorporation of a Treaty into domestic law and the legislative supremacy of Parliament.

In some states, the written constitution will have a specific provision granting a Treaty, duly ratified by the Executive power, the force of law and, if desired, the force of law superior to that of an act of the legislative power.[97] However, of course, the United Kingdom has no written constitution and one cannot, therefore, talk of 'amending' the constitution by the insertion of a new article giving precedence to Community law. The traditional approach of United Kingdom constitutional law is that treaties do not automatically become part of United Kingdom law upon their making or even ratification. 'A treaty is an act of prerogative. In making, and negotiating, and perfecting that treaty the Crown acts of its own inherent authority, not by the authority, actual or supposed, of any subject. All that is done under that treaty is as much beyond the domain of municipal law as the negotiation of the treaty itself.'[98] Since the power to make a Treaty belongs to the monarch by virtue of the Royal Prerogative (although in reality this will be exercised by the Prime Minister or the Foreign Secretary), incorporation of a Treaty can only be performed by an Act of Parliament. For the rules and provisions contained in a Treaty to become part of United Kingdom domestic law, and, therefore, to bind the courts, public authorities and individual persons, those rules and provisions must be specifically enacted or incorporated by an Act of Parliament. Therefore the supremacy of Community law cannot result from the Treaty but can only result from an Act of Parliament. Therefore, the only way to incorporate the European Community Treaties and the developed system of Community law into the United Kingdom constitutional and legal system was to use an Act of Parliament, the European Communities Act 1972. This provides for the fulfilment of all 'Community obligations', which are obligations arising by or under 'the treaties'. The Act recognised the rule-making capacity of both the treaties and secondary legislation within the United Kingdom and incorporates the supremacy of Community law (past, present or future) over domestic law, but does not purport to bind the United Kingdom to everlasting membership of the Community (see head (b) below).

The traditional constitutional principle of the legislative supremacy of Parliament (see chapter 2), whereby any Act of Parliament may alter previous Acts of Parliament, with the consequence that no current Parliament may bind its successors as to the content of future Acts of Parliament, made it difficult to follow the principle laid down in *Costa*[99] that there is a new legal order whereby the member states have transferred some of their sovereignty to the Community on a permanent basis. As Lord Dunedin stated in *Mortensen v Peters*:[100]

'In this Court we have nothing to do with the question of whether the Legislature has or has not done what foreign powers may consider a usurpation in a question with them. Neither are we a tribunal sitting to decide whether an Act of the Legislature is ultra vires as in contravention of generally acknowledged principles of international law. For us an Act of Parliament duly passed by Lords and Commons and assented to by the King, is supreme, and we are bound to give effect to its terms.'

Not long after the United Kingdom's accession to the Community, the House of Lords strongly reaffirmed that no court is entitled to disregard a provision of an Act of Parliament (even where it was alleged that Parliament was fraudulently misled into enacting that Act), that any belief that an Act of Parliament could be disregarded was 'obsolete', and that the courts had no concern with the manner in which Parliament performed its legislative

---

[97] See, eg, article 55 of the French Constitution of 1958.
[98] *Rustomjee v The Queen* (1876) 2 QBD 69. On the Royal Prerogative, see chapter 3.
[99] See p. 323.   [100] (1906) 8 F 93.

functions. Lord Wilberforce stated bluntly that any idea that an Act of Parliament, public or private, could be declared invalid or ineffective in the courts on account of some irregularity in parliamentary procedure at its introduction or during its passage through Parliament, or on the ground that Parliament in passing it was misled, or on the ground that it was obtained by deception or fraud, 'has been decisively repudiated by authorities of the highest standing from 1842 onwards'.[101] He emphasised that the 'remedy for a Parliamentary wrong, if one has been committed, must be sought from Parliament, and cannot be gained from the courts'.[102]

(b) Incorporation of the *acquis communautaire*

As stated above, the incorporation of the European Community Treaties and the developed system of Community law (the *acquis communautaire*) into the United Kingdom constitutional and legal system was achieved by an Act of Parliament, the European Communities Act 1972:

....

The European Communities Act 1972

'2(1) All such rights, powers, liabilities, obligations and restrictions from time to time created or aris-ing by or under the Treaties, and all such remedies and procedures from time to time provided for by or under the Treaties, as in accordance with the Treaties are without further enactment to be given legal effect or used in the United Kingdom, shall be recognised and available in law, and be enforced, allowed and followed accordingly; and the expression "enforceable Community right" and similar expressions shall be read as referring to one to which this subsection applies.

(2) Subject to Schedule 2 to this Act, at any time after its passing Her Majesty may by Order in Council, and any designated Minister or department may by regulations, make provision—

(a) for the purpose of implementing any Community obligation of the United Kingdom, or enabling any such obligation to be implemented, or of enabling any rights enjoyed or to be enjoyed by the United Kingdom under or by virtue of the Treaties to be exercised; or

(b) for the purpose of dealing with matters arising out of or related to any such obligation or rights or the coming into force, or the operation from time to time, of subsection (1) above;

and in the exercise of any statutory power or duty, including any power to give directions or to legislate by means of orders, rules, regulations or other subordinate instrument, the person entrusted with the power or duty may have regard to the objects of the Communities and to any such obligation or rights as [aforesaid].

(4) The provision that may be made under subsection (2) above includes, subject to Schedule 2 to this Act, any such provision (of any such extent) as might be made by Act of Parliament, and any enactment passed or to be passed, other than one contained in this Part of this Act, shall be construed and have effect subject to the foregoing provisions of this section; but, except as may be provided by any Act passed after this Act, Schedule 2 shall have effect in connection with the powers conferred by this and the following sections of this Act to make Orders in Council and [regulations].

---

[101] *Edinburgh and Dalkeith Railway Co v Wauchope* (1842) 8 Cl & Fin 710; *Stead v Carey* (1845) 1 CB 496; *Waterford Railway Co v Logan* (1850) 14 QB 672; *Lee v Bude and Torrington Junction Railway Co* (1871) LR 6 CP 576.   [102] *British Railways Board v Pickin* [1974] AC 765. See, also, pp. 53 and 73.

3(1) For the purposes of all legal proceedings any question as to the meaning or effect of any of the Treaties, or as to the validity, meaning or effect of any Community instrument, shall be treated as a question of law (and, if not referred to the European Court, be for determination as such in accordance with the principles laid down by and any relevant decision of the European Court or any court attached thereto).

(2) Judicial notice shall be taken of the Treaties, of the Official Journal of the Communities and of any decision of, or expression of opinion by, the European Court or any court attached thereto on any such question as aforesaid; and the Official Journal shall be admissible as evidence of any instrument or other act thereby communicated of any of the Communities or of any Community institution.

Schedule 2

1(1) The powers conferred by section 2(2) of this Act to make provision for the purposes mentioned in section 2(2)(a) and (b) shall not include power —

(a) to make any provision imposing or increasing taxation; or

(b) to make any provision taking effect from a date earlier than that of the making of the instrument containing the provision; or

(c) to confer any power to legislate by means of orders, rules, regulations or other subordinate instrument, other than rules of procedure for any court or tribunal; or

(d) to create any new criminal offence punishable [by more than specified limits].

2(1) [Where] a provision contained in any section of this Act confers power to make regulations (otherwise than by modification or extension of an existing power), the power shall be exercisable by statutory instrument.

(2) Any statutory instrument containing an Order in Council or regulations made in the exercise of a power so conferred, if made without a draft having been approved by resolution of each House of Parliament, shall be subject to annulment in pursuance of a resolution of either House.'

It will be seen that reference is made in the Act to 'the Treaties' and that it is the Community law coming from the Treaties which is to enter the United Kingdom constitutional and legal system. 'The Treaties' include the basic Community Treaties, the Acts of Accession to the Community, the later Treaties such as the SEA, some of the TEU, some of the TA and some of the TN. Since the definition of 'the Treaties' is laid down in the European Communities Act, it is necessary to amend that Act if it is necessary to add another Treaty (such as the TA or the TN). However, certain Treaty provisions are excluded from the definition of 'the Treaties'. These relate principally to the provisions on foreign and security policy and co-operation in the field of justice and home affairs. These are the 'two pillars' which are subject to governmental action rather than Community institutions and the United Kingdom has excluded these from the definition of 'the Treaties' because in no way does the United Kingdom wish to face claims that rights arise from those two pillars.[103]

Section 2(1)[104] relates to particular features of the acquis communautaire, both 'created by' the Treaties, namely, the direct applicability of Treaty articles, which, by article 249 (ex 189), therefore, includes the direct applicability of Community Regulations, and arising 'under' the Treaties, namely, the creation of the doctrine of direct effect (see head VIII(c)) by the European Court of Justice. If, therefore, because of Community law a rule of Community law is deemed to be a rule in every member state, the United Kingdom Act of Parliament states that the rule is to be the law of the United Kingdom. Moreover, the use of the phrase

---

[103] Section 1(2); European Communities (Amendment) Act 1998; European Communities (Amendment) Act 2002.　　　　　　　　　　　　　　　　　　　　　　　　[104] See p. 336.

'from time to time' provides for the incorporation of future Community law. Section 2(1) does not use the terms 'direct applicability' or 'direct effect', even though those terms had been used and interpreted and applied within the Community before the United Kingdom's accession. The phrase 'are without further enactment to be given legal effect or used' relates to any right or obligation arising directly from Community law and, therefore, includes direct applicability and direct effect and also *Francovich* liability (see head VIII(g)), in that a breach of Community law is treated as a breach of United Kingdom law. Perhaps this use of words was very clever: if 'direct effect' had been used, it would have been necessary to add another formula, because *Francovich* liability arises even where, for example, a directive does not have direct effect. Until the enactment of section 2(1), obligations arising from the Treaties would be binding on the United Kingdom in international law only. Henceforth, Community law which is 'without further enactment to be given legal effect or used' is directly enforceable in the United Kingdom courts. These courts could not otherwise enforce a provision of a Treaty because of the United Kingdom's dualist attitude to international law. Now there is imposed an obligation on the courts so to do.

(c) The implementation of Community law

Section 2(1)[105] deals with the case where Community rights or obligations arise directly from Community imposed rules or norms. As has been seen (head III(b)), some Community law is created by Community regulations. Since a Community regulation is directly applicable, a regulation does not need to be enacted or transposed into domestic law. It is already domestic law. Indeed, a false domestic re-enactment might distort the Community rule. Within the United Kingdom, therefore, it has been accepted that a regulation, being directly applicable, would have the effect of superseding domestic law automatically and replacing the domestic rule. What the United Kingdom would do, however, would be to repeal the domestic rule so that there would be no confusion between, for example, a section of an Act which was still written down in the statute book and an article of a regulation which would be found in another part of the statute book. To take a very hypothetical example, if the United Kingdom had a Student Grants Act, which by section 1 stated that university students were to be given £10,000 a year; and if the Community enacted a Council regulation stating that university students were to be given £20,000 a year; the Council regulation would supersede section 1 of the Student Grants Act and to avoid any confusion, the United Kingdom would repeal section 1 of that Act.

However, as has been seen (head III(b)), much Community law is created by Community directives, which, by article 249 (ex 189), must be implemented by the member states. Incorporation or transposition of the ever-developing Community law within the United Kingdom could, of course, be achieved by a series of Acts of Parliament similar to the European Communities Act. However, incorporation is achieved in practical and pragmatic terms by giving power[106] to amend existing legislation (or to create new legislation) by means of statutory instruments. This means that the government can act quickly and without the need to pass an Act of Parliament every time legislative action is necessary to fulfil a Treaty obligation.

---

[105] See p. 336.   [106] Section 2(2) and 2(4), p. 336.

Under section 2(2),[107] the executive power may by regulations continue the process of incorporating Community law. There are two forms of legislative mechanism under section 2(2). First, there is the Order in Council, where the legislative instrument is drafted by the appropriate minister (such as the Foreign Secretary, the Chancellor of the Exchequer or the Minister of Agriculture) and is then submitted to the Queen for signature. Second, there is the act of a minister (including a Scottish minister) appointed to act in limited circumstances (such as the Minister of Agriculture for agriculture matters and the common agricultural policy). The provision that may be made under section 2(2) includes any such provision (of any such extent) as might be made by Act of Parliament (including an Act of the Scottish Parliament) and this includes a power to amend an Act of Parliament.[108] This is a power of constitutional importance, namely, permitting the executive to legislate and, subject to what is stated below, even to change what the legislature has enacted earlier.[109] Section 2(2)(a) concerns the primary purpose of the bringing into force of Community obligations arising from the Treaty and section 2(2)(b) concerns the taking of further measures which naturally arise from or closely relate to that primary purpose being achieved. This does not mean that the power to make subordinate legislation is virtually unlimited (a real Henry VIII clause). A minister cannot by statutory instrument change the whole law of contract just because of a directive related to some corner of contract law.[110] Furthermore, the executive power is not given complete legislative power, because, except as may be provided by any Act passed after the European Communities Act 1972, certain rules contained in Schedule 2 have effect in connection with the powers conferred by the Act to make Orders in Council and regulations. Therefore, the powers conferred by section 2(2) do not include power to impose or increase taxation (because for hundreds of years taxation has been for Parliament, and not the monarch or government), or to make any retrospective provision, or to confer any power to legislate by means of orders, rules, regulations or other subordinate instrument, other than rules of procedure for any court or tribunal, or to create any new criminal offence punishable by more than specified limits.[111] Both forms of legislative mechanism are subject to the, albeit limited, control of Parliament, in that the power to make regulations is exercisable by statutory instrument, which may be subject to approval by Parliament in draft or to annulment by Parliament.[112] Section 2(2), therefore, allows the United Kingdom to implement Community law according to the best ways of fitting in with domestic law on a particular topic.

(d) The European scrutiny system

The main purpose of the European scrutiny system in the House of Commons is to ensure that the House can seek to influence United Kingdom ministers on Community proposals and to hold those ministers to account for their activities in the Council of Ministers.

---

[107] See p. 336.   [108] Section 2(4), p. 336.

[109] See the statutory instrument in the *Factortame* litigation, p. 378, whereby the United Kingdom government gave effect to the order of the President of the European Court of Justice to suspend an Act of Parliament.

[110] *Oakley v Animal and The Secretary of State for Trade and Industry* [2005] EWCA (Civ) 1191. On the scope of section 2(2)(b), see the conflicting views expressed in *R v Secretary of State for Trade and Industry, ex p Unison* [1996] ICR 1003 and *Addison v Denholm Ship Management* [1997] ICR 770.

[111] Schedule 2, paragraph 1, p. 337.   [112] Schedule 2, paragraph 2, p. 337.

The system supplements the usual opportunities members have to examine and question government policies, such as parliamentary questions and select committee inquiries.[113] The key is the European Scrutiny Committee, an all-party select committee, consisting of sixteen members appointed to examine European Union documents (below) and to report its opinion on the legal and political importance of each such document. The expression 'European Union document' includes: (i) any proposal for legislation by the Council or the Council acting jointly with the European Parliament. This includes drafts of regulations, directives, and decisions of the Council, together with any amended proposal or amendments proposed by the European Parliament; (ii) any proposal for a common strategy, a joint action or a common position under the (second pillar) inter-governmental foreign and security policy; (iii) any proposal for a common position, framework decision, decision or a convention under the (third pillar) inter-governmental action relating to police and judicial co-operation in criminal matters; (iv) reports of the Court of Auditors, both the regular general reports and the special reports on particular areas of expenditure.[114] In an average year, some 1,000 documents come within these categories. All are considered by the Scrutiny Committee. About half are considered to be of political or legal importance. Legislation made by the Commission on its own authority is not routinely scrutinised, but may be investigated, if an issue of principle or political importance arises.[115]

The committee has a vital role to play in monitoring the the 'scrutiny reserve resolution'. The House has resolved[116] that no minister of the Crown should give agreement in the Council or in the European Council to any proposal for European Community legislation, or for a common strategy, joint action or common position under the (second pillar) inter-governmental foreign and security policy, or a common position, framework decision, decision or convention under the (third pillar) inter-governmental action relating to police and judicial co-operation in criminal matters, which either is still 'subject to scrutiny' (in other words, on which the European Scrutiny Committee has not completed its scrutiny) or is awaiting consideration by the House (in other words, which has been recommended by the European Scrutiny Committee for consideration but in respect of which the House has not come to a Resolution). However, the minister concerned may give agreement to a proposal which is still subject to scrutiny if he or she considers that it is confidential, routine or trivial or is substantially the same as a proposal on which scrutiny has already been completed or to a proposal which is awaiting consideration by the House, provided that the European Scrutiny Committee has indicated that agreement need not be withheld pending consideration. Furthermore, the minister concerned may also give agreement to a proposal which is still subject to scrutiny or awaiting consideration by the House if he or she decides that for 'special reasons' agreement should be given. In such a case, the minister should explain his or her reasons to the European Scrutiny Committee at the first opportunity after reaching his or her decision, and, in the case of a proposal awaiting consideration by the House, to the House at the first opportunity after giving agreement. The Scrutiny Committee monitors the operation of the resolution, and has a policy of calling ministers who override the resolution without what it regards as good cause to give oral evidence.[117]

[113] 'The European Scrutiny System in the House of Commons' (June 2005).
[114] Standing Order 143.   [115] See the Committee's Annual Report for 2004 (HC 38-vi of 2004–2005).
[116] Commons Hansard, 17 November 1998, column 803.
[117] See HC 3 of 2003–2004, paras 141–3. A similar scrutiny reserve was resolved by the House of Lords (Lords Hansard, 6 December 1999, columns 1019–1020).

The House of Lords Select Committee on the European Union has a similar role to its Commons counterpart. The Committee's primary purpose is to scrutinise Community law in draft before it is agreed by the Community institutions. Its terms of reference are 'To consider European Union documents and other matters relating to the European Union'. Most of its work is carried out through seven sub-committees: Economic and Financial Affairs and International Trade, Internal Market, Foreign Affairs, Defence and Development Policy, Environment and Agriculture, Law and Institutions, Home Affairs, Social Policy and Consumer Affairs. Whereas the Commons Scrutiny Committee deals with a wide range of documents, the Lords Committee tends to report on a much smaller number of documents, but in greater detail following longer inquiries.

(e) Ensuring the conformity of other legislation with the European Communities Act

It is typical of United Kingdom constitutional tradition that a constitutional feature of fundamental importance was inserted (almost in parentheses) in a section dealing with mechanical matters. Almost apologetically, it is stated, in section 2(4),[118] that 'any enactment passed or to be passed shall be construed [interpreted] and have effect subject to the forego-ing provisions of this section' (the 'foregoing provisions of this section' relating to the rights and obligations recognised by section 2(1)). What it means is that any past Act of Parliament can be amended by virtue of the European Communities Act 1972. Furthermore, what this means is that every future and subsequent Act of Parliament must be read as containing a clause (an interpretation clause) stating that that Act of Parliament must be interpreted in accordance with section 2(1) and in accordance with the rule of supremacy of Community law.[119] This is to deal with what is known as the principle of implied repeal and what one might term 'accidental' amendment of a provision of Community law (see head (g) below). Section 2(4) does not deprive Parliament of the power to enact legislation which is in conflict with Community law; it merely means that until the European Communities Act 1972 (or just section 2(4)) is repealed there is an interpretation clause stating that Parliament is presumed not to enact legislation contrary to Community law.

(f) The imposition of obligations on the United Kingdom courts

Community law is part of the internal legal order of all member states. Therefore, a Community judicial function is carried on by all the courts and tribunals of the United Kingdom before whom arises a question of Community law. Criminal courts may hear cases in which both prosecution and defence raise questions of Community law; actions for judicial review may be raised in the Administrative Court; civil courts may have submitted to them actions for damages for loss allegedly caused by the non-implementation of a Community

---

[118] See p. 336.   [119] Lord Bridge in *Factortame*, p. 379.

obligation; substantive rights granted in social security and employment protection may be enforced before social security and labour courts and tribunals.

Consequently, the European Communities Act 1972 stated that for 'any question as to the meaning or effect of any of the Treaties, or as to the validity, meaning or effect of any Community instrument, shall be treated as a question of law (and, if not referred to the European Court, be for determination as such in accordance with the principles laid down by and any relevant decision of the European Court)'.[120] This means that decisions of the European Court of Justice are given the force of binding precedents which must be followed by all the United Kingdom courts, including the House of Lords. The United Kingdom courts are expressly directed to interpret Community law in accordance with the principles laid down by the Court of Justice (and the other European Community courts) and, of course, the most significant of such principles are the uniform application of Community law and the supremacy of Community law over domestic law. Any failure to fulfil this obligation is a failure of the United Kingdom to comply with the United Kingdom's Treaty obligations.[121] Therefore, if there is a conflict between a Community rule and a United Kingdom rule, a United Kingdom court must interpret the United Kingdom rule in accordance with Community law. This will operate at two levels: first, where the European Communities Act 1972 is superior to the rule; second, where the European Communities Act 1972 is of the same status as the rule. A conflict between Community law and a United Kingdom rule which emanates from delegated legislation or administrative practice or judicial decision can be resolved in United Kingdom constitutional law terms by the superiority of the European Communities Act to that rule. A conflict between Community law and a United Kingdom rule created by an Act of Parliament raises two matters of fundamental constitutional importance, namely, the so called doctrine of implied repeal and the possibility of withdrawal from the Community.

(g) Implied repeal

The doctrine of implied repeal states that a provision in an earlier Act of Parliament may be repealed impliedly (as opposed to expressly) by the subsequent enactment of a provision in an Act of Parliament which is so inconsistent with the earlier provision that, in effect, it erases that earlier provision. For example: if an Act of Parliament of 1990, section 1, states that the maximum speed for cars is 60 miles per hour; then an Act of Parliament of 2000, section 1, states that the maximum speed for cars is 70 miles per hour; although the Act of 1990, section 1, is not expressly repealed, its effect is erased, the 60 miles per hour rule has no longer any validity and it is impliedly repealed. Parliament, being supreme at any time, can alter an Act previously enacted and cannot be bound by any statement in that earlier Act to the effect that a future Parliament cannot legislate in a manner inconsistent with that earlier Act. A 'repeal by implication is only effected when the provisions of a later enactment are so inconsistent with or repugnant to the provisions of an earlier one that the two cannot stand together. Unless two Acts are so plainly repugnant to each other that effect cannot be given to both at the same time a repeal will not be implied.'[122] Section 2(1) of the European Communities Act 197[123] states that the United Kingdom must, for example, enforce all rights directly resulting from the Treaties.

---

[120] Section 3(1), p. 337.   [121] See *Köbler v Austria*, p. 386.
[122] *Kutner v Phillips* [1891] 2 QB 267, per AL Smith J, at 271. See also, West *Ham Wardens v Fourth City* [1892] 1 QB 654; *Vauxhall Estates Ltd v Liverpool Corporation* [1932] 1 KB 733; *Ellen Streets Estates Ltd v Minister of Health* [1943] 1 KB 590 and pp. 57–58.   [123] See p. 336.

It can happen that there is a conflict between Community law and an Act of Parliament which is 'accidental' or 'non-deliberate' in that the Act was enacted in the belief that it conformed to Community law (or even that there was no Community law relevant to the appropriate subject matter). If, however, a United Kingdom law is enacted which denies a right directly resulting from the Treaties, such as that provided by article 119 (now 141) on equal pay for men and women, the constitutional question is whether the Act which denied the specific right also had the effect of impliedly repealing section 2(1) which states that Community rights must not be denied. If it is demonstrated by the European Court of Justice that, in fact, such a conflict exists, the normal response of the United Kingdom will be to amend the Act and to eliminate the conflict retrospectively. In the meantime (between determination of the existence of a conflict and corrective action), there is undoubtedly an inconsistency between the Act and the European Communities Act to which the implied repeal doctrine could, in theory, be applied. That theory has not been accepted. By the European Communities Act 1972, section 3(1), the United Kingdom Parliament has given a power and a duty to the United Kingdom courts to help the United Kingdom carry out its treaty obligations, and, in so doing, Parliament intended the courts to apply Community law. In the event of a conflict between Community law and an Act of Parliament, that conflict is presumed to be unintentional, an accident, an oversight or a mistake by the Parliamentary draftsman (not, of course, by the always infallible government or Parliament), and the courts can interpret the Act as if the mistake did not exist and was not present in the Act. There is no need for the courts to await the corrective action of the United Kingdom legislative machinery to implement a decision of the Court of Justice following an article 169 (now 226) action by the Commission. The courts are under a duty to give priority to Community law over inconsistent United Kingdom legislation and this duty is imposed by the European Communities Act. This does not infringe the legislative supremacy of Parliament, since Parliament, by its own act in the exercise of its sovereign powers has enacted that Community law should be enforced, allowed and followed in the United Kingdom. The 'implied repeal' argument was kicked into touch in:

Thoburn v Sunderland City Council [2002] EWHC 195 (Admin)

Thoburn was a greengrocer in Sunderland, who used weighing machines calibrated in pounds and ounces instead of the system promulgated by the European Union for metric weights and measures. He was convicted of offences under the Weights and Measures Act 1985. He appealed against conviction and one argument used to support his appeal was that the 1985 Act had impliedly repealed the European Communities Act (ECA) 1972.

Laws LJ

'37. [The] rule is that if Parliament has enacted successive statutes which on the true construction of each of them make irreducibly inconsistent provisions, the earlier statute is impliedly repealed by the later. The importance of the rule is, on the traditional view, that if it were otherwise the earlier Parliament might bind the later, and this would be repugnant to the principle of Parliamentary sovereignty.

. . .

59. [Parliament] cannot bind its successors by stipulating against repeal, wholly or partly, of the ECA. It cannot stipulate as to the manner and form of any subsequent legislation. It cannot stipulate against implied repeal any more than it can stipulate against express repeal. Thus there is nothing in the ECA which allows the Court of Justice, or any other institutions of the EU, to touch or qualify the conditions of Parliament's legislative supremacy in the United Kingdom. Not because the legislature chose not to

allow it; because by our law it could not allow it. That being so, the legislative and judicial institutions of the EU cannot intrude upon those conditions. The British Parliament has not the authority to authorise any such thing. Being sovereign, it cannot abandon its sovereignty. Accordingly there are no circumstances in which the jurisprudence of the Court of Justice can elevate Community law to a status within the corpus of English domestic law to which it could not aspire by any route of English law itself. This is, of course, the traditional doctrine of sovereignty. If it is to be modified, it certainly cannot be done by the incorporation of external texts. The conditions of Parliament's legislative supremacy in the United Kingdom necessarily remain in the United Kingdom's hands. But the traditional doctrine has in my judgment been modified. It has been done by the common law, wholly consistently with constitutional principle.

60. The common law has in recent years allowed, or rather created, exceptions to the doctrine of implied repeal: a doctrine which was always the common law's own creature. There are now classes or types of legislative provision which cannot be repealed by mere implication. These instances are given, and can only be given, by our own courts, to which the scope and nature of Parliamentary sovereignty are ultimately confided. The courts may say—have said—that there are certain circumstances in which the legislature may only enact what it desires to enact if it does so by express, or at any rate specific, [provision]. By this means, as I shall seek to explain, the courts have found their way through the impasse seemingly created by two supremacies, the supremacy of European law and the supremacy of Parliament.

61. The present state of our domestic law is such that substantive Community rights prevail over the express terms of any domestic law, including primary legislation, made or passed after the coming into force of the ECA, even in the face of plain inconsistency between the two. This is the effect of [*Factortame* I, p. 379, where Lord Bridge said]: "By virtue of section 2(4) of the [ECA], Part II of the [Merchant Shipping] Act of 1988 is to be construed and take effect subject to directly enforceable Community rights. This has precisely the same effect as if a section were incorporated in Part II of the Act of 1988 which in terms enacted that the provisions with respect to registration of British fishing vessels were to be without prejudice to the directly enforceable Community rights of nationals of any member state of the EEC". So there was no question of an implied pro tanto repeal of the ECA of 1972 by the later Act of 1988; on the contrary the Act of 1988 took effect subject to Community rights incorporated into our law by the ECA. In *Factortame* no argument was advanced by the Crown in their Lordships' House to suggest that such an implied repeal might have been effected. It is easy to see what the argument might have been: Parliament in 1972 could not bind Parliament in 1988, and section 2(4) was therefore ineffective to do so. It seems to me that there is no doubt but that in *Factortame* the House of Lords effectively accepted that section 2(4) could not be impliedly repealed, albeit the point was not argued.

62. [In] the present state of its maturity the common law has come to recognise that there exist rights which should properly be classified as constitutional or [fundamental]. And from this a further insight follows. We should recognise a hierarchy of Acts of Parliament: as it were "ordinary" statutes and "constitutional" statutes. The two categories must be distinguished on a principled basis. In my opinion a constitutional statute is one which (a) conditions the legal relationship between citizen and State in some general, overarching manner, or (b) enlarges or diminishes the scope of what we would now regard as fundamental constitutional rights; (a) and (b) are of necessity closely related: it is difficult to think of an instance of (a) that is not also an instance of (b). The special status of constitutional statutes follows the special status of constitutional rights. Examples are the Magna Carta, the Bill of Rights 1689, the Act of Union, the Reform Acts which distributed and enlarged the franchise, the [Human Rights Act], the Scotland Act 1998 and the Government of Wales Act 1998. The ECA clearly belongs in this family. It incorporated the whole corpus of substantive Community rights and obligations, and gave overriding domestic effect to the judicial and administrative machinery of Community law. It may be there has never been a statute having such profound effects on so many dimensions of our daily lives. The ECA is, by force of the common law, a constitutional statute.

63. Ordinary statutes may be impliedly repealed. Constitutional statutes may not. For the repeal of a constitutional Act or the abrogation of a fundamental right to be effected by statute, the court would apply this test: is it shown that the legislature's actual—not imputed, constructive or presumed—intention was to effect the repeal or abrogation? I think the test could only be met by express words in the later statute, or by words so specific that the inference of an actual determination to effect the result contended for was irresistible. The ordinary rule of implied repeal does not satisfy this test. Accordingly, it has no application to constitutional statutes. [A] constitutional statute can only be repealed, or amended in a way which significantly affects its provisions touching fundamental rights or otherwise the relation between citizen and State, by unambiguous words on the face of the later statute.

64. This development of the common law regarding constitutional rights, and as I would say constitutional statutes, is highly beneficial. It gives us most of the benefits of a written constitution, in which fundamental rights are accorded special respect. But it preserves the sovereignty of the legislature and the flexibility of our uncodified constitution. [Nothing] is plainer than that this benign development involves, as I have said, the recognition of the ECA as a constitutional statute.'

(h) A deliberate conflict

'I have assumed that our Parliament, whenever it passes legislation, intends to fulfil its obligations under the Treaty. If the time should come when our Parliament deliberately passes an Act with the intention of repudiating the Treaty or any provision in it or intentionally of acting inconsistently with it and says so in express terms then I should have thought that it would be the duty of our courts to follow the statute of our [Parliament]. Unless there is such an intentional and express repudiation of the Treaty, it is our duty to give priority to the Treaty. In the present case I assume that the United Kingdom intended to fulfil its obligations.'[124]

A 'deliberate' conflict between Community law and domestic United Kingdom law raises the question of withdrawal from the Community and Union. If the European Communities Act 1972 is removed, to use a neutral word, that priority is also removed. If the United Kingdom were to take the unlikely step of withdrawing from the Community, this would be accomplished in United Kingdom constitutional law by deliberately repudiating the Treaties and by expressly repealing the whole of the European Communities Act. In such a case, the courts would follow their traditional role, accept the repealing legislation and accept that there could now no longer be any conflicts between Community law and domestic law to worry about.

VIII. The Incorporation of Community Law in the United Kingdom—the Process

The European Communities Act 1972 has permitted the United Kingdom courts to react to the legislation and case law of the Community as and when that legislation was enacted and that case law developed. It is perhaps fortunate that the problems of incorporation of Community law have been posed in a sequence of situations which has permitted a pragmatic and gradualist series of solutions.

---

[124] *Macarthy's v Smith (No 1)* [1979] 3 All ER 325 (CA), per Lord Denning MR, at 328.

(a) The reference procedure

The reference procedure was a strange procedure for the United Kingdom. This procedure results in the case, in which is raised the question for interpretation being referred to the European Court of Justice, being suspended until the opinion of that Court is determined and received back. This is not the normal process of the several English and other United Kingdom courts. It was strange to leave a case half way through, because the court would normally consider both the facts and the law together, come to a determination of the facts and an application of the relevant law as stated or interpreted by the court leaving any further question of the law, if challenged, to be determined on appeal. Although strange, the reference procedure was accepted by the United Kingdom courts very early on. In *Bulmer v Bollinger*,[125] the Court of Appeal accepted that the Community Treaties were part of English law by virtue of section 2(1) of the European Communities Act, and, therefore, accepted that article 177 (now 234) was now part of English law, and that article 164 (now 220) was now part of English law. By a combination of articles 177 and 164, the true position was now that in the task of interpreting the Treaties and other Community law, the English and other United Kingdom judges are no longer the final authority, and the supreme tribunal for interpreting Community law was henceforward the European Court of Justice. That Court

'has a panoramic view of the Community and its institutions, a detailed knowledge of the Treaties and of much subordinate legislation made under them, and an intimate familiarity with the functioning of the Community market which no national judge denied the collective experience of the Court of Justice could hope to achieve. Where questions of administrative intention and practice arise the Court of Justice can receive submissions from the Community institutions, as also where relations between the Community and non-member states are in issue. Where the interests of Member States are affected they can intervene to make their views known. [Where] comparison falls to be made between Community texts in different languages, all texts being equally authentic, the multinational Court of Justice is equipped to carry out the task in a way which no national judge, whatever his linguistic skills, could rival. The interpretation of Community instruments involves [often] not the process familiar to common lawyers of laboriously extracting the meaning from words used but the more creative process of supplying flesh to a spare and loosely constructed skeleton. The choice between alternative submissions may turn not on purely legal considerations, but on a broader view of what the orderly development of the Community requires. These are matters which the Court of Justice is very much better placed to assess and determine than a national court.'[126]

Some years later, Sir Thomas Bingham MR was able to state[127] that

'if the facts have been found and the Community law issue is critical to the court's final decision, the appropriate course is to refer the issue to the Court of Justice unless the national court can with complete confidence resolve the issue itself. [The] national court must be fully mindful of the differences between national and Community legislation, of the pitfalls which face a national court venturing into what may be an unfamiliar field, of the need for uniform interpretation throughout the Community and of the great advantages enjoyed by the Court of Justice in construing Community instruments. If the national court has any real doubt, it should obviously refer.'

---

[125] [1974] Ch 401. See, also, *Macarthy's v Smith (No 1)* [1979] 3 All ER 325 (CA); *Macarthy's Ltd v Smith (No 2)* [1981] 2 QB 180.

[126] *Customs and Excise Commissioners v Samex* [1983] 1 All ER 1042, per Bingham J, at 1055–1056.

[127] *R v International Stock Exchange, ex p Else* [1993] QB 534.

What became known as the 'Else test' has been applied consistently, although with minor variations to meet particular circumstances.[128]

At first, there was an attitude, but not a rule, expressed by the Court of Appeal and the House of Lords, that it was advisable to leave references to the higher courts as they had the ability to draft the specific questions to be referred to the European Court of Justice more correctly and more efficiently than the lower courts. Later, although this advice was still made, the higher courts accepted the wide discretion allowed to lower courts. In *R v Plymouth Justices, ex p Rogers*,[129] the master of a French fishing boat was prosecuted before the magistrates' court for infringing certain regulations relating to the size of fishing nets. It was held that the magistrates' court in this case had jurisdiction to agree to refer questions to the European Court at the stage at which the case which was then before them had reached. The defendant was entitled to have a decision whether there was a case to answer before he was called on to bring evidence in his defence and a ruling on the questions of Community law raised by him was necessary to that decision. There was, however, added a word of caution to the effect that a higher court might usually be the more suitable forum and in a better position to assess whether any reference was necessary to the case and to formulate the form of the question referred.

It is important to note that in certain specialised fields the lower courts, such as the tribunals in social security and employment matters, both of which are courts of first instance, determine issues which dominate Community-law-based litigation, and may have as members persons who are not legally qualified, have in practice often referred questions of interpretation to the European Court of Justice. In general, the cases which have arisen before these tribunals have been relatively easy to decide and there has been an obvious question of law which is conclusive, when applied to the facts which the tribunal has found. In *Brack*,[130] the sole question of law was whether, on the facts as found and which were not disputed, a man, who had retired from employment, could benefit from Community rules relating to 'workers'. The Court of Justice held that the man could so benefit, and the tribunal applied the Community rules to the facts. In a case where there is no element of Community law present at all, an appeal from a social security tribunal would normally be taken on a point of law to a Social Security Commissioner, and from the Commissioner to the Court of Appeal and, sometimes, to the House of Lords. However, it is possible to by-pass the whole process of an appeal to the House of Lords, who, of course, have a duty to refer the case to the European Court of Justice. This is achieved by a practice that, in exceptional circumstances, the chairman of the tribunal can be, instead of the local chairman, a professionally qualified judge, the President of Appeal Tribunals, who has the status of a High Court judge. If it is seen that a question of interpretation of Community law may or will arise and that it is vital to the case, the President may sit as chairman and refer the question to the Court of Justice. This saves time and expense.[131]

So, it is safe to say that preliminary ruling requests are now regarded as a normal and necessary part of our legal procedures. In *Evans v The Secretary of State for the Environment, Transport and the Regions and Motor Insurers' Bureau*,[132] it was held with some reluctance that, although the overall costs of a protracted and expensive litigation had become wholly

---

[128] *Trinity Mirror* [2001] EWCA Civ 65; *R (on the application of Federation of Technological Industries) v Customs and Excise Commissioners* [2004] EWCA Civ 1020.   [129] [1982] QB 863.
[130] [1977] 1 CMLR 277 (R(S) 2/77).   [131] *Drake v Chief Adjudication Officer* [1986] ECR 1995.
[132] [2001] EWCA Civ 32.

disproportionate to the amounts in issue, if the 'interminable nightmare' had to be pursued to a conclusion, the opinion of the Court of Justice was, nevertheless, necessary to enable judgment to be given on a point of principle. *R v Secretary of State for Trade and Industry, ex p Trades Union Congress*[133] concerned the validity of a United Kingdom regulation on maternity and parental leave made to transpose into domestic law a Council directive. The TUC submitted that the regulation unlawfully restricted the scope of the directive to the detriment of its members. It was held that, although it was considered that the TUC's arguments were

'likely to [prevail], we are not persuaded that the position is clear, so that we should ourselves decide the point at issue without the benefit of guidance from the European Court of Justice. The point is one which concerns a number of other Member States. Although we only know of a reasoned opinion from the Commission in relation to Ireland, it may be that the Commission is or will be making similar approaches to other Member States, including the United Kingdom. Proceedings before the ECJ have the advantage that representations may be made by the Commission and other interested parties. One of the essential roles of the ECJ is to provide the Member States with judgments which have effect throughout the Community so as to ensure universality of approach. It would be inherently undesirable that this Court should give a ruling inconsistent with a judgment which might be given in another Member State or which, later, turned out to be inconsistent with an authoritative ruling of the ECJ.'[134]

Looking back, it is of great importance to note that a very high proportion of references to the European Court of Justice related to the application of Community law to individual persons who believed or complained that Community law granted them a right or an advantage, which had not been, or had not been completely, incorporated into domestic United Kingdom law. Of course, the United Kingdom was not alone in having to meet the problems posed by the obligation to transpose Community law into domestic law, and from the early days, the European Court of Justice imposed, by a series of replies to questions raised according to the reference procedure, upon the national courts of the member states what might be called the 'thesis of individual protection'.

(b) The protection of the individual by Community law

In *van Gend*,[135] the Court of Justice was faced with a claim by an individual seeking redress of a grievance caused by a member state. It was argued that such matters were best dealt with by the traditional international law methods of arbitration, incorporated into the Community legal system by the provisions for action to be taken by the Commission (see head VI(b)). The Court held otherwise, stating that Community law not only imposes obligations on individuals but is also intended to confer upon them rights which become part of their legal heritage. The Court has continued to emphasise that the subjects of Community law include individuals and organisations who may be affected by the law of a Community which is not merely an economic union of member states, but is at the same time intended to ensure social progress and seek the constant improvement of the living and working conditions of their people. There are individuals seeking the rights granted by Community law of entry and

---

[133] [2000] EWHC 345 (Admin).   [134] Per Morison J, at para 15.   [135] See p. 351.

residence, of equality in the labour market, together with their families and their employers, and there are business organisations (farmers, manufacturers, importers and exporters, and those engaged in a multiplicity of service industries) seeking the economic freedoms the Community was established to guarantee. The one thing all these people have in common is the wish to exercise the rights created by Community law. These rights are created by the Treaties and the secondary legislation discussed in head III and these rights depend for their effectiveness on the transposition of such rights into the national domestic legal systems of all the member states by national legislation, regulation or administrative practice.

If a member state adheres to article 10 (ex 5) (and the other Treaty and secondary legislative provisions which impose obligations on the member states), then the rights created by Community law are guaranteed. However, if the governments and legislatures of member states do not fulfil their Community obligations, the rights granted to individuals and organisations become merely illusory. There is no effective enjoyment of such rights if a national legislative, regulatory or administrative rule or practice hinders or, indeed, prevents the exercise of such a right. One method of ensuring that member states fulfil Community obligations is that provided for by article 226 (ex 169) (see head VI(b)). However, this has serious disadvantages to the individual. It is dependent on the Commission (or another member state) for its initiation, the Commission can be highly selective as to which states' failings should be prosecuted, there are many examples of member states not obeying the declarations of failure by the Court of Justice, and, probably of greatest importance to the citizen or the businessman, the process of prosecution by the Commission and the obtaining of a judgment of the Court takes such an inordinately long time that the result so often is, in fact, to deny justice. What the Court has done, therefore, has been to take article 10 (ex 5) to its logical conclusion and hold that if the government, legislature or administration of a member state fails in its Community obligations, the omissions of the member state should be remedied by the judicial organs of that state. After all, litigation designed to enforce rights in national law is determined by courts and tribunals and there should be no difference between the enforcement and protection of rights derived from national law and the enforcement and protection of such rights as are derived from Community law. Community provisions which are a direct source of rights and duties for all those affected thereby, whether member states or individuals, also concern the national courts. Their task, as an organ of a member state, is to protect, in a case within its jurisdiction, the rights conferred upon individuals by Community law:

....

Amministrazione delle Finanze dello Stato v Simmenthal SpA case 106/77 [1978] ECR 629

The European Court of Justice:

'13. The main purpose of the [question from an Italian court] is to ascertain what consequences flow from the direct applicability of a provision of Community law in the event of incompatibility with a subsequent legislative provision of a Member State.

14. Direct applicability in such circumstances means that rules of Community law must be fully and uniformly applied in all the Member States from the date of their entry into force and for so long as they continue in force.

15. These provisions are therefore a direct source of rights and duties for all those affected thereby, whether Member States or individuals, who are parties to legal relationships under Community law.

16. This consequence also concerns any national court whose task it is as an organ of a Member State to protect, in a case within its jurisdiction, the rights conferred upon individuals by Community law.

17. Furthermore, in accordance with the principle of the precedence of Community law, the relationship between provisions of the Treaty and directly applicable measures of the institutions on the one hand and the national law of the Member States on the other is such that those provisions and measures not only by their entry into force render automatically inapplicable any conflicting provision of current national law but—in so far as they are an integral part of, and take precedence in, the legal order applicable in the territory of each of the Member States—also preclude the valid adoption of new national legislative measures to the extent to which they would be incompatible with Community provisions.

18. Indeed any recognition that national legislative measures which encroach upon the field within which the Community exercises its legislative power or which are otherwise incompatible with the provisions of Community law had any legal effect would amount to a corresponding denial of the effectiveness of obligations undertaken unconditionally and irrevocably by Member States pursuant to the Treaty and would thus imperil the very foundations of the [Community].

. . .

21. It follows from the foregoing that every national court must, in a case within its jurisdiction, apply Community law in its entirety and protect rights which the latter confers on individuals and must accordingly set aside any provision of national law which may conflict with it, whether prior or subsequent to the Community rule.

22. Accordingly any provision of a national legal system and any legislative, administrative or judicial practice which might impair the effectiveness of Community law by withholding from the national court having jurisdiction to apply such law the power to do everything necessary at the moment of its application to set aside national legislative provisions which might prevent Community rules from having full force and effect are incompatible with those requirements which are the very essence of Community law.

. . .

24. The [question] should therefore be answered to the effect that a national court which is called upon, within the limits of its jurisdiction, to apply provisions of Community law is under a duty to give full effect to those provisions, if necessary refusing of its own motion to apply any conflicting provision of national legislation, even if adopted subsequently, and it is not necessary for the court to request or await the prior setting aside of such provisions by legislative or other constitutional means.'

The process of securing the protection of rights for individuals has been gradual but logical and inexorable, and parallels the development of general principles of law and the protection of human rights discussed in head V(d). The Court has started with the proposition that rights conferred by Community law must be enjoyed by those on whom the rights are conferred. The supremacy of Community law means that such rights must be uniformly enjoyed in their entirety within each member state. If a member state has not transposed into its own legal system those rights, the solidarity of Community achievement is jeopardised and if the cohesion of Community law is jeopardised so is the Community. As an inescapable consequence of membership of the Community, therefore, each member state will be deemed to have complied with Community obligations as from the moment that such obligations have binding force. The court has asked 'what would have been the legal situation within the member state had Community law been fully implemented by the member state' (a form of equity deeming that to have been done which was left undone). This has been achieved in three stages which have occurred in roughly chronological order.

(c) The doctrine of direct effect

The first stage in the development of effective protection of Community conferred rights was the application of the principle of direct effect, based upon the rationale that a member state which has not adapted its national law to meet Community obligations, whether imposed by Treaty articles, regulations or directive, may not rely, as against individuals, on its own failure to perform those obligations:

NV Algemene Transport-en Expeditie Onderneming van Gend & Loos v Nederlandse administratie der belastingen case 26/62 [1963] ECR 1

On 9 September 1960, van Gend imported into the Netherlands from Germany a quantity of ureaformaldehyde, a product which was classified under the current Netherlands import duties regulations (which had come into force on 1 March 1960) as being subject to an import duty of 8 per cent (which was duly imposed). Van Gend complained that on 1 January 1958 (the date on which the EEC Treaty came into force) the product had been classified under the Netherlands import duties regulations then in force as being subject only to an import duty of 3 per cent; that the current classification of the product as being subject to an import duty was an increase in the import duty on the product after the coming into force of the EEC Treaty; and that the Netherlands government, in so reclassifying the product, had infringed Treaty article 12, which stated that member states must refrain from introducing between themselves any new customs duties and from increasing those applied in their trade with each other. The Nederlandse administratie der belastingen (Netherlands Inland Revenue Administration) replied that, as a matter of fact, the product in question had, on 1 January 1958, not been charged with a duty of 3 per cent but with a duty of 10 per cent, so that there had not been any increase. Van Gend appealed to the Tariefcommissie (Netherlands revenue tribunal) which, without giving a formal decision on whether the product was subject to a 3 per cent, 8 per cent or 10 per cent duty, decided that it was necessary to determine, as a preliminary question, whether van Gend was entitled to rely on article 12.

The European Court of Justice, at 10–13

'The first question of the Tariefcommissie is whether Article 12 of the Treaty has direct application in national law in the sense that nationals of Member States may on the basis of this Article lay claim to rights which the national court must protect.

To ascertain whether the provisions of an international treaty extend so far in their effects it is necessary to consider the spirit, the general scheme and the wording of those provisions.

The objective of the EEC Treaty, which is to establish a common market the functioning of which is of direct concern to interested parties in the Community, implies that this Treaty is more than an agreement which merely creates mutual obligations between the contracting states. This view is confirmed by the preamble to the Treaty which refers not only to governments but to peoples. It is also confirmed more specifically by the establishment of institutions endowed with sovereign rights, the exercise of which affects Member States and also their [citizens].

In addition the task assigned to the Court of Justice under Article 177 [now 234], the object of which is to secure uniform interpretation of the Treaty by national courts and tribunals, confirms that the states have acknowledged that Community law has an authority which can be invoked by their nationals before those courts and tribunals.

The conclusion to be drawn from this is that the Community constitutes a new legal order of international law for the benefit of which the states have limited their sovereign rights, albeit within limited fields, and the subjects of which comprise not only Member States but also their nationals. Independently of the legislation of Member States, Community law therefore not only imposes obligations on individuals but is also intended to confer upon them rights which become part of their legal heritage. These rights arise not only where they are expressly granted by the Treaty, but also by reason of obligations which the Treaty imposes in a clearly defined way upon individuals as well as upon the Member States and upon the institutions of the [Community].

The wording of Article 12 contains a clear and unconditional prohibition which is not a positive but a negative obligation. This obligation, moreover, is not qualified by any reservation on the part of states which would make its implementation conditional upon a positive legislative measure enacted under national law. The very nature of this prohibition makes it ideally adapted to produce direct effects in the legal relationship between Member States and their subjects. The implementation of Article 12 does not require any legislative intervention on the part of the states. The fact that under this Article it is the Member States who are made the subject of the negative obligation does not imply that their nationals cannot benefit from this obligation.

In addition the argument based on Articles 169 [now 226] and 170 [now 227] of the Treaty put forward by the three governments which have submitted observations to the Court in their statements of case is misconceived. The fact that these Articles of the Treaty enable the Commission and the Member States to bring before the Court a state which has not fulfilled its obligations does not mean that individuals cannot plead these obligations, should the occasion arise, before a national court, any more than the fact that the Treaty places at the disposal of the Commission ways of ensuring that obligations imposed upon those subject to the Treaty are observed, precludes the possibility, in actions between individuals before a national court, of pleading infringements of these obligations.

A restriction of the guarantees against an infringement of Article 12 by Member States to the procedures under Article 169 and 170 would remove all direct legal protection of the individual rights of their [nationals].

The vigilance of individuals concerned to protect their rights amounts to an effective supervision in addition to the supervision entrusted by Articles 169 and 170 to the diligence of the Commission and of the Member States.

It follows from the foregoing considerations that, according to the spirit, the general scheme and the wording of the Treaty, Article 12 must be interpreted as producing direct effects and creating individual rights which national courts must protect.'

Franz Grad v Finanzamt Traunstein case 9/70 [1970] ECR 825

A German court asked the Court of Justice for a preliminary ruling on whether an article of a decision in conjunction with an article of a directive produced direct effects in the legal relationship between the member states and those subject to their jurisdiction in such a way that these provisions created rights for individuals which the national courts must protect.

The European Court of Justice

'4. The German government in its observations defends the view that by distinguishing between the effects of regulations on the one hand and of decisions and directives on the other, Article 189 [now 249] precludes the possibility of decisions and directives producing the effects mentioned in the question, which are reserved to regulations.

5. However, although it is true that by virtue of Article 189, regulations are directly applicable and therefore by virtue of their nature capable of producing direct effects, it does not follow from this that other categories of legal measures mentioned in that Article can never produce similar effects. In particular, the provision according to which decisions are binding in their entirety on those to whom

they are addressed enables the question to be put whether the obligation created by the decision can only be invoked by the Community institutions against the addressee or whether such a right may possibly be exercised by all those who have an interest in the fulfilment of this obligation. It would be incompatible with the binding effect attributed to decisions by Article 189 to exclude in principle the possibility that persons affected may invoke the obligation imposed by a decision. Particularly in cases where, for example, the Community authorities by means of a decision have imposed an obligation on a Member State or all the Member States to act in a certain way, the effectiveness (l'effet utile) of such a measure would be weakened if the nationals of that state could not invoke it in the courts and the national courts could not take it into consideration as part of Community law. Although the effects of a decision may not be identical with those of a provision contained in a regulation, this difference does not exclude the possibility that the end result, namely the right of the individual to invoke the measure before the courts, may be the same as that of a directly applicable provision of a regulation.

6. Article 177 [now 234], whereby the national courts are empowered to refer to the court all questions regarding the validity and interpretation of all acts of the institutions without distinction, also implies that individuals may invoke such acts before the national courts. Therefore, in each particular case, it must be ascertained whether the nature, background and wording of the provision in question are capable of producing direct effects in the legal relationships between the addressee of the act and third parties.'

Yvonne van Duyn v Home Office case 41/74 [1974] ECR 1337

The Church of Scientology was considered by the United Kingdom government to be socially harmful. There was no legal power to prohibit the practice of Scientology, the government allowed the Church to function through a college in East Grinstead and did not place restrictions on United Kingdom nationals wishing to become members of, or to take up employment with, the Church. However, with regard to foreign nationals, the government considered that the Church was so objectionable that steps would be taken to curb the Church's activities by refusing work permits for foreign nationals for work at a Scientology establishment. Miss van Duyn, a Netherlands national, was offered employment at the East Grinstead college but was refused entry to the United Kingdom on the ground that 'the Secretary of State considers it undesirable to give anyone leave to enter the United Kingdom on the business of or in the employment of' the Church. Miss van Duyn sought a declaration that she was entitled to enter and remain in the United Kingdom under article 48(3), which provides that workers who are Community nationals have the right, subject to limitations justified on grounds of public policy, public security or public health, inter alia, to accept offers of employment in any member state and that the public policy exceptions contained in Directive 64/221, article 3, cited in paragraph 10 below, did not apply as the refusal to grant entry was not based exclusively or at all on her personal conduct but on the general policy of refusal stated above. Since it was essential to seek whether Miss van Duyn could rely upon these provisions, Pennycuick, VC, stayed the action and referred three questions for a preliminary ruling. Note how the Court (paragraph 12) repeats its reasoning in *Grad* (paragraph 5).

The European Court of Justice

'First question

4. By the first question, the court is asked to say whether Article 48 [is] directly applicable so as to confer on individuals rights enforceable by them in the courts of a Member State.

5. It is provided, in Article 48(1) and (2), that freedom of movement for workers shall be secured [and] that such freedom shall entail "the abolition of any discrimination based on nationality between workers of Member States as regards employment, remuneration and other conditions of work and employment".

6. These provisions impose on Member States a precise obligation which does not require the adoption of any further measure on the part either of the Community institutions or of the Member States and which leaves them, in relation to its implementation, no discretionary power.

7. [Article 48(3)], which defines the rights implied by the principle of freedom of movement for workers, subjects them to limitations justified on grounds of public policy, public security or public health. The application of these limitations is, however, subject to judicial control, so that a Member State's right to invoke the limitations does not prevent the provisions of Article 48, which enshrine the principle of freedom of movement for workers, from conferring on individuals rights which are enforceable by them and which the national courts must protect.

8. The reply to the first question must therefore be in the affirmative.

Second question

9. The second question asks the Court to say whether [Directive 64/221] is directly applicable so as to confer on individuals rights enforceable by them in the courts of a Member State.

10. [The] only provision of the directive which is relevant is that contained in Article 3(1) which provides that "measures taken on grounds of public policy or public security shall be based exclusively on the personal conduct of the individual concerned".

11. The United Kingdom observes that, since Article 189 [distinguishes] between the effects ascribed to regulations, directives and decisions, it must therefore be presumed that the Council, in issuing a directive rather than making a regulation, must have intended that the directive should have an effect other than that of a regulation and accordingly that the former should not be directly applicable.

12. If, however, by virtue of the provisions of Article 189 regulations are directly applicable and, consequently, may by their very nature have direct effects, it does not follow from this that other categories of acts mentioned in that Article can never have similar effects. It would be incompatible with the binding effect attributed to a directive by Article 189 to exclude, in principle, the possibility that the obligation which it imposes may be invoked by those concerned. In particular, where the Community authorities have, by directive, imposed on Member States the obligation to pursue a particular course of conduct, the useful effect of such an act would be weakened if individuals were prevented from relying on it before their national courts and the latter were prevented from taking it into consideration as an element of Community law. Article 177, which empowers national courts to refer to the court questions concerning the validity and interpretation of all acts of the Community institutions, without distinction, implies furthermore that these acts may be invoked by individuals in the national courts. It is necessary to examine, in every case, whether the nature, general scheme and wording of the provision in question are capable of having direct effects on the relations between Member States and individuals.

13. By providing that measures taken on grounds of public policy shall be based exclusively on the personal conduct of the individual concerned, Article 3(1) of [Directive] 64/221 is intended to limit the discretionary power which national laws [confer] on the authorities responsible for the entry and expulsion of foreign nationals. First, the provision lays down an obligation which is not subject to any exception or condition and which, by its very nature, does not require the intervention of any act on the part either of the institutions of the Community or of Member States. Secondly, because Member States are thereby obliged, in implementing a clause which derogates from one of the fundamental principles of the Treaty in favour of individuals, not to take account of factors extraneous to personal conduct, legal certainty for the persons concerned requires that they should be able to rely on this obligation even though it has been laid down in a legislative act which has no automatic direct effect in its [entirety].

. . .

15. Accordingly, in reply to the second question, Article 3(1) of [Directive 64/221] confers on individuals rights which are enforceable by them in the courts of a Member State and which the national courts must protect.

Third question

16. By the third question the Court is asked to rule whether Article 48 [and] Article 3 of Directive No 64/221 must be interpreted as meaning that a Member State, in the performance of its duty to base a measure taken on grounds of public policy exclusively on the personal conduct of the individual concerned is entitled to take into account as matters of personal conduct: (a) the fact that the individual is or has been associated with some body or organisation the activities of which the Member State considers contrary to the public good but which are not unlawful in that State; (b) the fact that the individual intends to take employment in the Member State with such a body or organisation it being the case that no restrictions are placed upon nationals of the Member State who wish to take similar employment with such a body or organisation.

17. It is necessary, first, to consider whether association with a body or an organisation can in itself constitute personal conduct within the meaning of Article 3 of Directive 64/221. Although a person's past association cannot in general justify a decision refusing him the right to move freely within the Community, it is nevertheless the case that present association, which reflects participation in the activities of the body or of the organisation as well as identification with its aims and its designs, may be considered a voluntary act of the person concerned and, consequently, as part of his personal conduct within the meaning of [article 3].

18. The third question further raises the problem of what importance must be attributed to the fact that the activities of the organisation in question, which are considered by the Member State as contrary to the public good are not however prohibited by national law. It should be emphasised that the concept of public policy in the context of the Community and where, in particular, it is used as a justification for derogating from the fundamental principle of freedom of movement for workers, must be interpreted strictly, so that its scope cannot be determined unilaterally by each Member State without being subject to control by the institutions of the Community. Nevertheless, the particular circumstances justifying recourse to the concept of public policy may vary from one country to another and from one period to another, and it is therefore necessary in this matter to allow the competent national authorities an area of discretion within the limits imposed by the Treaty.

19. It follows from the above that where the competent authorities of a Member State have clearly defined their standpoint as regards the activities of a particular organisation and where, considering it to be socially harmful, they have taken administrative measures to counteract these activities, the Member State cannot be required, before it can rely on the concept of public policy, to make such activities unlawful, if recourse to such a measure is not thought appropriate in the circumstances.

20. The question raises finally the problem of whether a Member State is entitled, on grounds of public policy, to prevent a national of another Member State from taking gainful employment within its territory with a body or organisation, it being the case that no similar restriction is placed upon its own nationals.

21. In this connection, the Treaty, while enshrining the principle of freedom of movement for workers without any discrimination on grounds of nationality, admits, in Article 48(3), limitations justified on grounds of public policy, public security or public health to the rights deriving from this principle. Under the terms of [article 48(3)], the right to accept offers of employment actually made, the right to move freely within the territory of Member States for this purpose, and the right to stay in a Member State for the purpose of employment are, among others, all subject to such limitations. Consequently, the effect of such limitations, when they apply, is that leave to enter the territory of a Member State and the right to reside there may be refused to a national of another Member State.

22. Furthermore, it is a principle of international law, which the EEC Treaty cannot be assumed to disregard in the relations between Member States, that a state is precluded from refusing its own nationals the right of entry or residence.

23. It follows that a Member State, for reasons of public policy, can, where it deems necessary, refuse a national of another Member State the benefit of the principle of freedom of movement for workers in a case where such a national proposes to take up a particular offer of employment even though the Member State does not place a similar restriction upon its own nationals.

24. Accordingly, the reply to the third question must be that Article 48 [and] Article 3(1) of Directive No 64/221 are to be interpreted as meaning that a Member State, in imposing restrictions justified on grounds of public policy, is entitled to take into account, as a matter of personal conduct of the individual concerned, the fact that the individual is associated with some body or organisation the activities of which the Member State considers socially harmful but which are not unlawful in that state, despite the fact that no restriction is placed upon nationals of the said Member State who wish to take similar employment with these same bodies or organisations.'

Pubblico Ministero v Tullio Ratti case 148/78 [1979] ECR 1629

Dangerous substances contained in certain solvents, paints and varnishes were subject to different rules as regards labelling and packaging in different member states. The Council determined that the differences constituted a barrier to trade and to the free movement of goods and, in order to eliminate the differences, enacted Directive 73/173 (relating to solvents and to be implemented by 8 December 1974) and Directive 77/728 (relating to paints and varnishes and to be implemented by 9 November 1979). In particular, the directives made rules relating to the packaging and labelling of solvents, paints and varnishes, with regard to the information to be specified as to any harmful substances contained therein. Ratti was the legal representative of an Italian company which had already started to comply with the labelling provisions in anticipation of the implementation of the directives in Italy and in view of the fact that other member states had already implemented them. However, Italy had not implemented either directive and the relevant Italian statute differed from the directives (in some cases being less stringent and in others being more stringent) and laid down criminal penalties for persons failing to comply with it. Ratti was prosecuted in May 1978 and stated, by way of defence, that the directives, rather than the Italian statute, should be applied by the courts in Italy. The criminal court referred, inter alia, two questions: first, does Directive 73/173 'constitute directly applicable legislation conferring upon individuals personal rights which the national courts must protect?'; fifth, is Directive 77/728 'immediately and directly applicable with regard to the obligations imposed on Member States to refrain from action from the date of notification of that Directive in a case where a person, acting upon a legitimate expectation, has complied with the provisions of that Directive before expiry of the period within which the Member State must comply with the said Directive?' Note how the Court (paragraphs 18–21) follows its reasoning in *van Duyn* (paragraph 12).

The European Court of Justice:

'[18., 19. The first question raises the general problem of the legal nature of the provisions of a directive adopted under Article 189. In this regard, the settled case law of the court lays down that, whilst under Article 189 regulations are] directly applicable and, consequently, by their nature capable of producing direct effects, that does not mean that other categories of acts covered by that Article can never produce similar effects.

20. It would be incompatible with the binding effect which Article 189 ascribes to directives to exclude on principle the possibility of the obligations imposed by them being relied on by persons concerned.

21. Particularly in cases in which the Community authorities have, by means of directives, placed Member States under a duty to adopt a certain course of action, the effectiveness of such an act would be weakened if persons were prevented from relying on it in legal proceedings and national courts prevented from taking it into consideration as an element of Community law.

22. Consequently a Member State which has not adopted the implementing measures required by the directive in the prescribed periods may not rely, as against individuals, on its own failure to perform the obligations which the directive entails.

23. It follows that a national court requested by a person who has complied with the provisions of a directive not to apply a national provision incompatible with the directive not incorporated into the internal legal order of a defaulting Member State, must uphold that request if the obligation [is] unconditional and sufficiently precise.

24. Therefore the answer to the first question must be that after the expiration of the period fixed for the implementation of a directive a Member State may not apply its internal law—even if it is provided with penal sanctions—which has not yet been adapted in compliance with the directive, to a person who has complied with the requirements of the [directive].

. . .

43. It follows that, for the reasons expounded in the grounds of the answer to the national court's first question, it is only at the end of the prescribed period and in the event of the Member State's default that the directive [will] be able to have the effects described in the answer to the first question.

44. Until that date is reached the Member States remain free in that field.

45. If one Member State has incorporated the provisions of a directive into its internal legal order before the end of the period prescribed therein, that fact cannot produce any effect with regard to the other Member States.

46. In conclusion, since a directive by its nature imposes obligations only on Member States, it is not possible for an individual to plead the principle of "legitimate expectation" before the expiry of the period prescribed for its implementation.

47. Therefore the answer to the fifth question must be that Directive 77/728 [cannot] bring about with respect to any individual who has complied with the provisions of the said directive before the expiration of the adaptation period prescribed for the Member State any effect capable of being taken into consideration by national courts.'

Therefore, if the Community institutions have, by means of a directive, placed member states under a duty to adopt a certain course of action, the effectiveness of such a measure would be diminished if individuals and national courts were precluded from taking it into consideration as an element of Community law. Before the period for transposition of a directive has elapsed, a member state cannot be 'reproached' for not having adopted the national implementing measure.[136] Thus wherever the provisions of a directive appear, as far as their subject matter is concerned to be unconditional and sufficiently precise, those provisions may, in the absence of implementing measures adopted within the prescribed period, be relied upon as against any national provision which is incompatible with the directive or in so far as the provisions define rights which individuals are able to assert against the state.[137] Therefore, for there to be direct effect the provisions of a directive must be unconditional and sufficiently precise:

MH Marshall v Southampton and South West Hampshire Area Health Authority (Teaching) case 152/84 [1986] ECR 723

Miss Marshall worked for the Area Health Authority (AHA), which had a policy that the normal retirement age of its employees was the age at which the state retirement pension became payable (60 for a woman and 65 for a man). The AHA waived this policy for Miss Marshall for two years but when she was 62 the AHA dismissed her (although she wished to continue working until she was 65), the sole reason being that she was a woman who had passed retirement age. The AHA would not have ordinarily dismissed a man until he had attained the age of 65. In view of the fact that she had suffered

---

136 *Inter-Environment Wallonie* [1997] ECR I-7411.
137 *Becker v Finanzamt Munster-Innenstadt* [1982] ECR 53.

financial loss consisting of the difference between her earnings as an employee and the pension which she received on retirement and since she had lost the satisfaction derived from her work, Miss Marshall instituted proceedings against the AHA before an industrial tribunal and, on appeal, to the Court of Appeal, on the grounds of discriminatory treatment by the AHA on the ground of her sex, claiming that this was unlawful discrimination contrary to Directive 76/207 (the 'Equal Treatment Directive': below). The Court of Appeal referred the following questions to the Court of Justice:

'1. Whether the [AHA's] dismissal of [Miss Marshall] after she had passed her sixtieth birthday pursuant to the policy [followed by the AHA] and on the grounds only that she was a woman who had passed the normal retiring age applicable to women was an act of discrimination prohibited by the Equal Treatment Directive; 2. If the answer to 1 above is in the affirmative, whether or not the Equal Treatment Directive can be relied upon by [Miss Marshall] in the circumstances of the present case in national courts or [tribunals].'

The relevant provisions of the directive are as follows:

'Article 1(1)—The purpose of this directive is to put into effect in the Member States the principle of equal treatment for men and women as regards access to employment, including promotion, and to vocational training and as regards working [conditions]. This principle is hereinafter referred to as "the principle of equal treatment".

Article 2(1)—[The] principle of equal treatment shall mean that there shall be no discrimination whatsoever on grounds of sex either directly or indirectly by reference in particular to marital or family status.

Article 5(1)—Application of the principle of equal treatment with regard to working conditions, including the conditions governing dismissal, means that men and women shall be guaranteed the same conditions without discrimination on grounds of sex.

Article 5(2)—To this end, Member States shall take the measures necessary to ensure that: (a) any laws, regulations and administrative provisions contrary to the principle of equal treatment shall be abolished; (b) any provisions contrary to the principle of equal treatment which are included in collective agreements, individual contracts of employment, internal rules of undertakings or in rules governing the independent occupations and professions shall be, or may be declared, null and void or may be amended; (c) those laws, regulations and administrative provisions contrary to the principle of equal treatment when the concern for protection which originally inspired them is no longer well founded shall be revised; and that where similar provisions are included in collective agreements labour and management shall be requested to undertake the desired revision.'

The European Court of Justice

'[Is there discrimination?]

21. By the first question the Court of Appeal seeks to ascertain whether or not Article 5(1) of [Directive 76/207] must be interpreted as meaning that a general policy concerning dismissal, followed by a state authority, involving the dismissal of a woman solely because she has attained or passed the qualifying age for a state pension, which age is different under national legislation for men and for women, constitutes discrimination on grounds of sex, contrary to that directive.

22. [Miss Marshall] and the Commission consider that the first question must be answered in the affirmative.

23. According to [Miss Marshall], the said age limit falls within the term "working conditions" within the meaning of Articles 1(1) and 5(1) of [Directive 76/207]. A wide interpretation of that term is, in her opinion, justified in view of the objective of the EEC Treaty to provide for "the constant improving of the living and working conditions of [the Member States' peoples]".

. . .

26. The Commission emphasises that neither the [AHA's] employment policy nor the state social security scheme makes retirement compulsory upon a person's reaching pensionable age. On the contrary, the provisions of national legislation take into account the case of continued employment

beyond the normal pensionable age. In those circumstances, it would be difficult to justify the dismissal of a woman for reasons based on her sex and age.

27. The Commission also refers to the fact that the court has recognised that equality of treatment for men and women constitutes a fundamental principle of Community [law].

. . .

38. Consequently, the answer to the first question [must] be that Article 5(1) of [Directive 76/207] must be interpreted as meaning that a general policy concerning dismissal involving the dismissal of a woman solely because she has attained the qualifying age for a state pension, which age is different under national legislation for men [and] women, constitutes discrimination on grounds of sex, contrary to that directive.

[Is the directive capable of direct effect?]

39. Since the first question has been answered in the affirmative, it is necessary to consider whether Article 5(1) of [Directive 76/207] may be relied upon by an individual before national courts and tribunals.

40. [Miss Marshall] and the Commission consider that that question must be answered in the affirmative. They contend in particular, with regard to Articles 2(1) and 5(1) of [Directive 76/207], that those provisions are sufficiently clear to enable national courts to apply them without legislative intervention by the Member States, at least so far as overt discrimination is concerned.

41. [Miss Marshall] points out that directives are capable of conferring rights on individuals which may be relied upon directly before the courts of the Member States; national courts are obliged by virtue of the binding nature of a directive, in conjunction with Article 5 [now 10] of the EEC Treaty, to give effect to the provisions of directives where possible, in particular when construing or applying relevant provisions of national [law]. Where there is any inconsistency between national law and Community law which cannot be removed by means of such a construction, [Miss Marshall] submits that a national court is obliged to declare that the provision of national law which is inconsistent with the directive is inapplicable.

. . .

43. The [AHA] and the United Kingdom propose, conversely, that the second question should be answered in the negative. They admit that a directive may, in certain specific circumstances, have direct effect as against a Member State in so far as the latter may not rely on its failure to perform its obligations under the directive. However, they maintain that a directive can never impose obligations directly on individuals and that it can only have direct effect against a Member State qua public authority and not against a Member State qua employer. As an employer a state is no different from a private employer. It would not therefore be proper to put persons employed by the state in a better position than those who are employed by a private employer.

44. With regard to the legal position of the [AHA's] employees the United Kingdom states that they are in the same position as the employees of a private employer. Although according to United Kingdom constitutional law the health [authorities] are Crown bodies and their employees are Crown servants, nevertheless the administration of the National Health Service by the health authorities is regarded as being separate from the government's central administration and its employees are not regarded as civil servants.

45. Finally, both the [AHA] and the United Kingdom take the view that the provisions of [Directive 76/207] are neither unconditional nor sufficiently clear and precise to give rise to direct effect. The directive provides for a number of possible exceptions, the details of which are to be laid down by the Member States. Furthermore, the wording of Article 5 is quite imprecise and requires the adoption of measures for its [implementation].

. . .

48. With regard to the argument that a directive may not be relied upon against an individual, it must be emphasised that according to Article 189 [the] binding nature of a directive, which constitutes the

basis for the possibility of relying on the directive before a national court, exists only in relation to "each Member State to which it is addressed". It follows that a directive may not of itself impose obligations on an individual and that a provision of a directive may not be relied upon as such against such a person. It must therefore be examined whether, in this case, the [AHA] must be regarded as having acted as an individual.

49. In that respect it must be pointed out that where a person involved in legal proceedings is able to rely on a directive as against the state he may do so regardless of the capacity in which the latter is acting, whether employer or public authority. In either case it is necessary to prevent the state from taking advantage of its own failure to comply with Community law.

50. It is for the national court to apply those considerations to the circumstances of each case: the Court of Appeal has, however, stated in the order for reference that [the] Southampton and South West Hampshire Area Health Authority (Teaching) is a public authority.

51. The argument submitted by the United Kingdom that the possibility of relying on provisions of the directive against the [AHA] qua organ of the state would give rise to an arbitrary and unfair distinction between the rights of state employees and those of private employees does not justify any other conclusion. Such a distinction may easily be avoided if the Member State concerned has correctly implemented the directive in national law.

52. Finally, with regard to the question whether the provision contained in Article 5(1) of [Directive 76/207], which implements the principle of equality of treatment set out in Article 2(1) of the directive, may be considered, as far as its contents are concerned, to be unconditional and sufficiently precise to be relied upon by an individual as against the state, it must be stated that the provision, taken by itself, prohibits any discrimination on grounds of sex with regard to working conditions, including the conditions governing dismissal, in a general manner and in unequivocal terms. The provision is therefore sufficiently precise to be relied on by an individual and to be applied by the national [courts].

. . .

56. Consequently, the answer to the second question must be that Article 5(1) of [Directive 76/207], which prohibits any discrimination on grounds of sex with regard to working conditions, including the conditions governing dismissal, may be relied upon as against a state authority acting in its capacity as employer, in order to avoid the application of any national provision which does not conform to Article 5(1).'

It is of the greatest importance to note that a directive only imposes obligations on the 'state' and may not of itself impose obligations on an individual or private organisation and a provision of a directive may not be relied upon as such against such an individual or organisation.[138] The European Court of Justice has interpreted the words 'the state' very widely as including any 'emanation of the state' in order to minimise the effect of its decision in *Marshall* that directives can only be enforced vertically against the state and not horizontally against private bodies and organisations, such as private employers. The use of the word or concept of 'the state' is again rather strange to the United Kingdom legal system. Because of our history, we have tended to talk in terms of the legal personalities of 'the King', the King's 'ministers', individual government departments, such as the Department of Agriculture, and local authorities, such as Leicester City Council. Although, therefore, the use of the term 'the state' is strange, the United Kingdom courts have found no difficulty in accepting the decisions of the European Court of Justice and then applying them to determining whether a United Kingdom authority, body or organisation is or is not 'the state'.[139]

---

[138] *Marshall*, p. 359, paragraph 48; *El Corte Inglés SA v Cristina Blázquez Rivero* [1996] ECR I-1281.

[139] On the phrase 'public authority' for European Convention and Human Rights Act purposes, see pp. 501 and 858.

In *Foster v British Gas*,[140] the Court of Justice stated that it had held 'in a series of cases that unconditional and sufficiently precise provisions of a directive could be relied on against organisations or bodies which were subject to the authority or control of the state or had special powers beyond those which result from the normal rules applicable to relations between individuals'. More particularly, 'a body, whatever its legal form, which has been made responsible, pursuant to a measure adopted by the State, for providing a public service under the control of the State and which has for that purpose special powers beyond those which result from the normal rules applicable in relations between individuals is included in any event among the bodies against which the provisions of a directive capable of having direct effect may be relied on'. *Foster* was returned to the House of Lords. The House analysed the Gas Act 1972, which established the British Gas Corporation, and noted in particular that it was the duty of the Corporation to develop and maintain an efficient, co-ordinated and economical system of gas supply, the Corporation had the monopoly of gas supply, the Corporation reported to the minister, who could give Corporation directions for securing that the management of the activities of the Corporation and their subsidiaries was organised efficiently, it was the duty of the Corporation to give effect to any such directions, the Corporation had to make an annual report to the minister on the exercise and performance by the corporation of its functions during the year and on its policy and programmes. Accordingly, the House determined that the Corporation was a 'body which was made responsible, pursuant to a measure adopted by the state, for providing a public service under the control of the state and had for that purpose special powers beyond those which result from the normal rules applicable in relations between individuals'.[141]

National Union of Teachers v Governing Body of St. Mary's Church of England (Aided) Junior School[142] concerned the governors of a 'voluntary aided school', a school over which the Church of England has some measure of control. It was common ground that a local education authority was an emanation of the state, but the question arose as to whether the relationship of the governors of the school was sufficiently close to 'the state' so that the governors could be regarded as an emanation of 'the state'. An examination of the Education Acts demonstrated that, although such schools had the choice to be within the state system of education or not, once within the state system, they were subject to control and influence by the Secretary of State for Education and the local education authority with regard to matters, such as content of the curriculum, financial arrangements, employment rights of employees and central government defaults powers. Consequently, the governors of the schools were to be regarded as emanations of the state. In particular, the industrial disputes resolution system (industrial tribunal, Employment Appeal Tribunal, and Court of Appeal) has had to deal with a myriad of cases relating to employment protection directives. The following have been held (or assumed) to be emanations of the state: local authorities,[143] public utilities,[144] and various publicly funded educational establishments,[145] but not privatised companies such as British Airways,[146] commercial companies,[147] Lloyd's of London,[148] or the Motor Insurers' Bureau.[149]

---

[140] [1990] ECR 3313.   [141] *Foster v British Gas* [1991] 2 AC 306.   [142] [1996] EWCA Civ 1194.

[143] *Wilson and Others v St Helens Borough Council* [1998] UKHL 37.

[144] *Moase and Lomas v Secretary of State for the Environment, Transport and the Regions and South West Water* [2000] EWCA Civ 193.

[145] *The Governors of Highams Park School v Odger, Lamprell and Crudgington* (EAT) 21 January 1994; *Wills v London Guildhall University* (EAT) 18 March 1996; *Ralton v Havering College of Further and Higher Education* (EAT) 27 June 2001.   [146] *Reith v British Airways* (EAT) 30 October 1991.

[147] *Chessington World of Adventure v Reed* (EAT) 27 June 1997; *Iske v European Ferries* (EAT) 8 April 1997.

[148] *The Society of Lloyd's v Levy and Johnson* [2004] EWHC 1860 (Comm).

[149] *Mighell v Reading* [1998] EWCA Civ 1465.

The United Kingdom courts found it relatively easy to accept the doctrine of direct effect, provided that the words of Community legislation did not expressly conflict with domestic law. This was for three reasons. In the first place, section 2(1) of the European Communities Act permitted the reception of such a doctrine. Second, some of the first cases to affect the United Kingdom concerned regulations, as opposed to directives. Since a regulation was directly applicable in the United Kingdom and, indeed formed part of United Kingdom law, their direct effect was of the same legal status as the direct effect of United Kingdom legislation. Third, in the early cases the question of interpreting Community and domestic law did not present the courts with difficult decisions.

(d) The doctrine of positive interpretation

The second stage in the development of effective protection of Community conferred rights may be termed the 'doctrine of positive interpretation', which gave the United Kingdom courts much more difficulty:

Sabine von Colson and Elisabeth Kamann v Land Nordrhein-Westfalen
case 14/83 [1984] ECR 1891

This case (discussed further at p. 368) concerned the Equal Treatment Directive (p. 358). There was raised the question of effective enjoyment of a right conferred by Community law, in that there was a failure on the part of Germany to transpose a directive into national law sufficiently effectively so as to give the plaintiffs a real remedy against sex discrimination with regard to access to employment. However, the directive did not lay down any unconditional and sufficiently precise obligation to require the member state to adopt a sanction for the breach of the principle of equal treatment.

The European Court of Justice

'26. However, the member states' obligation arising from a directive to achieve the result envisaged by the directive and their duty under article 5 of the treaty to take all appropriate measures, whether general or particular, to ensure the fulfilment of that obligation, is binding on all the authorities of member states including, for matters within their jurisdiction, the courts. It follows that, in applying the national law and in particular the provisions of a national law specifically introduced in order to implement Directive No 76/207, national courts are required to interpret their national law in the light of the wording and the purpose of the directive in order to achieve the result referred to in the third paragraph of article [189].
. . .

28. It should, however, be pointed out to the national court that although [Directive No 76/207] leaves the member states free to choose between the different solutions suitable for achieving its objective, it nevertheless requires that if a member state chooses to penalise breaches of that prohibition by the award of compensation, then in order to ensure that it is effective and that it has a deterrent effect, that compensation must in any event be adequate in relation to the damage sustained and must therefore amount to more than purely nominal compensation such as, for example, the reimbursement only of the expenses incurred in connection with the application. It is for the national court to interpret and apply the legislation adopted for the implementation of the directive in conformity with the requirements of community law, in so far as it is given discretion to do so under national law.'

Von Colson, therefore, imposed the duty under article 5 (now 10) not only on the legislature and the executive but also on the judiciary. This duty applies to 'matters within their jurisdiction' and in so far as the national court is given discretion to do so under national law and has been imposed in particular where a provision of a directive lacks direct effect, either because that provision in not sufficiently clear, precise and unconditional or because the dispute is 'exclusively between individuals'.[150] The meaning of this was not crystal clear, especially in the context of the United Kingdom system. The question had to be raised as to whether it is within the jurisdiction of the United Kingdom courts to 'distort' the words of a statute by interpreting the words of a statute which are express and can have only one meaning in a way which contradicts that meaning. The duty of positive interpretation was originally to apply in particular to provisions of a national law specifically introduced in order to transpose a directive into national law. This caused grave problems in the United Kingdom with regard to national legislation on equal pay (the Equal Pay Act 1970) and sex discrimination (the Sex Discrimination Act 1975), which were enacted in the United Kingdom before the Community directives on equal pay and equal treatment were made by the Community institutions and which were not introduced specifically to transpose those directives:

....

Duke v GEC Reliance [1988] AC 618

The Sex Discrimination Act 1975 provided (section 1(1)) that a person discriminates against a woman if on the ground of her sex he or she treats her less favourably than he or she treats or would treat a man. Section 6 provided:

'6(1) It is unlawful for a person, in relation to employment by [him] to discriminate against a woman—

(a) in the arrangements he makes for the purpose of determining who should be offered that employment, or

(b) in the terms in which he offers her that employment, or

(c) by refusing or deliberately omitting to offer her that employment.

6(2) It is unlawful for a person, in the case of a woman employed by him [to] discriminate against her—

(a) in the way he affords her access to opportunities for promotion, transfer or training, or to any other benefits, facilities or services, or by refusing or deliberately omitting to afford her access to them, or

(b) by dismissing her, or subjecting her to any other detriment.

6(4) Subsections (1)(b) and (2) do not apply to provision in relation to death or retirement.'

Lord Templeman, at 629–642

'My Lords, this appeal raises a question of construction of an Act of the Parliament of the United Kingdom in the light of laws passed by the European Economic Community. The appellant, Mrs Duke, was employed by the respondent, GEC Reliance Ltd. The policy of the respondent was to enforce the retirement of employees when they reached the pensionable age of 60 in the case of women and 65 in the case of men. In conformity with this policy the respondent ceased to employ the appellant after she attained the age of 60 and before she attained the age of 65; if she had been a man her employment would not have been discontinued on account of age before the age of 65.

---

[150] *Adeneler* [2006] ECR I-6057.

The appellant claims that she was the victim of discrimination on the grounds of sex and that she is entitled to damages under the Sex Discrimination Act 1975 because the discriminatory retirement enforced on her was rendered unlawful by section 6(2) of that Act, which prohibits discrimination against a woman "by dismissing her". The respondent admits that the appellant was discriminated against by dismissal but denies that the discriminatory dismissal was unlawful because, by section 6(4) of the Act, section 6(2) does not "apply to provision in relation to death or [retirement]".

My Lords, section 6(4) makes lawful a dismissal which would otherwise be unlawful under section 6(2). The discriminatory dismissal made lawful by section 6(4) is confined to a dismissal for which provision is made in relation to retirement. If an employer dismisses a woman in order to replace her by a man, the dismissal will infringe section 6(2) and will not be saved by section 6(4). But, if an employer dismisses a woman because the employer has made provision for men and women alike to retire when they reach their retirement ages, then, if there are differential retirement ages, the dismissal is saved from being unlawful by section 6(4) because the dismissal is pursuant to provision relating to [retirement].

The United Kingdom government considered that the equal treatment directive (EC Council Directive 76/207) did not prohibit discriminatory ages of retirement. The argument of the government [was that] retirement provisions were conditioned by pension age. Women retired at 60 when they qualified for a pension. Men retired at 65 because they did not reach pensionable age until then. The discrimination under Community law permitted in pensionable ages must extend to discrimination in retirement ages; pensionable ages and retirement ages ran in harness. This argument was rejected by the Court of Justice [in *Marshall*, p. 359]. The Court decided:

> "38. Article 5(1) of Directive 76/207 must be interpreted as meaning that a general policy concerning dismissal involving the dismissal of a woman solely because she has attained the qualifying age for a state pension, which age is different under national legislation for men and for women, constitutes discrimination on grounds of sex, contrary to that directive."

The United Kingdom, pursuant to its obligations under the EEC Treaty to give effect to Community legislation as construed by the European court and following the decision in [*Marshall*], enacted the Sex Discrimination Act 1986 [which amended] section 6(4) of the Sex Discrimination Act 1975 so as to render unlawful discriminatory retirement ages as between men and women. The 1986 Act was not retrospective and does not avail the appellant.

[*Marshall*] decided that the equal treatment directive required member states to prohibit discrimination with regard to retirement or dismissal in accordance with an employer's policy. [But *Marshall*] also decided that the equal treatment directive did not possess direct effect as between individuals, so that the appellant cannot claim damages against the respondent simply for breach of the directive. In their decision the European court said [para 48: "the] binding nature of a directive, which constitutes the basis for the possibility of relying on the directive before a national court, exists only in relation to 'each Member State to which it is addressed'. It follows that a directive may not of itself impose obligations on an individual and that a provision of a directive may not be relied on as such against such a person".

Nevertheless, it is now submitted that the appellant is entitled to damages from the respondent because Community law requires [the] Sex Discrimination Act enacted on 12 November 1975 to be construed in a manner which gives effect to the equal treatment directive dated 9 February 1976 as construed by the European court in [*Marshall*] published on 26 February 1986.

Of course a British court will always be willing and anxious to conclude that United Kingdom law is consistent with Community law. Where an Act is passed for the purpose of giving effect to an obligation imposed by a directive or other instrument a British court will seldom encounter difficulty in concluding that the language of the Act is effective for the intended purpose. But the construction of a British Act of Parliament is a matter of judgment to be determined by British courts and to be derived from the language of the legislation considered in the light of the circumstances prevailing at the date of [enactment].

The [Sex Discrimination Act 1975 was] not passed to give effect to the equal treatment directive and [was] intended to preserve discriminatory retirement [ages. The] Sex Discrimination Act 1975 was not intended to give effect to the equal treatment directive as subsequently construed in [*Marshall*] and the words of section 6(4) are not reasonably capable of being limited to the meaning ascribed to them by the appellant. Section 2(4) of the European Communities Act 1972 does not in my opinion enable or constrain a British court to distort the meaning of a British statute in order to enforce against an individual a Community directive which has no direct effect between individuals. Section 2(4) applies and only applies where Community provisions are directly [applicable].

The submission that the Sex Discrimination Act 1975 must be construed in a manner which gives effect to the equal treatment directive as construed by the European court in [*Marshall*] is said to be derived from the decision of the European court in [*von Colson*, p. 362. *Von Colson* is no authority] for the proposition that a court of a member state must distort the meaning of a domestic statute so as to conform with Community law which is not directly [applicable].

It would be most unfair to the respondent to distort the construction of the 1975 Sex Discrimination Act in order to accommodate the 1976 equal treatment directive as construed by the European court in [*Marshall*]. As between the appellant and the respondent the equal treatment directive did not have direct effect and the respondent could not reasonably be expected to reduce to precision the opaque language which constitutes both the strength and the difficulty of some Community legislation. The respondent could not reasonably be expected to appreciate the logic of Community legislators in permitting differential retirement pension ages but prohibiting differential retirement ages. The respondent is not liable to the appellant under Community law. [I] would dismiss this appeal.'

Pickstone v Freemans [1989] AC 66

In *Commission v United Kingdom* [1982] ECR 2601, the European Court of Justice held that, by failing to transpose properly into its national legal system the provisions of Council Directive 75/117 (the Equal Pay Directive), the United Kingdom had failed to fulfil its obligations under the Treaty. The United Kingdom government immediately took steps to correct the defect in its equal pay legislation identified in the judgment of the European Court and made the Equal Pay (Amendment) Regulations 1983 (SI 1983 No 1794). A draft of the regulations had been approved by resolution of each House of Parliament. It was argued that one (and possibly the more literal) interpretation of the new regulations precluded Mrs Pickstone from claiming equal pay with a man, notwithstanding that she might be performing work of equal value with his and notwithstanding that the difference in pay might be the result of discrimination on grounds of sex.

Lord Keith of Kinkel, at 112

'[The argued interpretation] would leave a large gap in the equal work provision, enabling an employer to evade it by employing one token man on the same work as a group of potential women claimants who were deliberately paid less than a group of men employed on work of equal value with that of the women. This would mean that the United Kingdom had failed yet again fully to implement its obligations under article 119 of the Treaty and the Equal Pay Directive, and had not given full effect to the decision of the European [Court]. It is plain that Parliament cannot possibly have intended such a failure. The draft Regulations of 1983 were presented to Parliament as giving full effect to the decision in question. The draft Regulations were not subject to the Parliamentary process of consideration and amendment in Committee, as a Bill would have been. In these circumstances [I] consider it to be entirely legitimate for the purpose of ascertaining the intention of Parliament to take into account the terms in which the draft was presented by the responsible Minister and which formed the basis of its acceptance. The [words] must be construed purposively in order to give effect to the manifest broad intention of the maker of the Regulations and of Parliament.'

Lord Templeman, at 121–123

'The draft of the Regulations of 1983 was not subject to any process of amendment by Parliament. In these circumstances the explanations of the Government and the criticisms voiced by Members of Parliament in the debates which led to approval of the draft Regulations provide some indications of the intentions of Parliament. The debate on the draft Regulations in the House of Commons which led to their approval [was] initiated by the Under Secretary of State for Employment who [said]: "The Equal Pay Act allows a woman to claim equal pay with a man [if] she is doing the same or broadly similar work, or if her job and his have been rated equal through job evaluation in effort, skill and decision. However, if a woman is doing different work from a comparable man, or if the jobs are not covered by a job evaluation study, the woman has at present no right to make a claim for equal pay This is the gap, identified by the European Court, which we are closing". [In *Duke*, p. 363] this House declined to distort the construction of an Act of Parliament which was not drafted to give effect to a Directive and which was not capable of complying with the Directive as subsequently construed by the European Court of Justice. In the present case I can see no difficulty in construing the Regulations of 1983 in a way which gives effect to the declared intention of the Government of the United Kingdom responsible for drafting the Regulations and is consistent with the objects of the EEC Treaty, the provisions of the Equal Pay Directive and the rulings of the European Court of Justice.'

The facts of *Litster v Forth Dry Dock Co*[151] are complicated but provide an excellent illustration of effective protection of Community conferred rights by the doctrine of positive interpretation. Directive 77/187 (the Acquired Rights Directive (ARD)), article 3, provided that, in order to protect employees in the event of a change of employer and, in particular, to ensure that their rights were safeguarded, on the transfer of a business from one employer (the old owner) to another (the new owner), the benefit and burden of a contract of employment between the old owner and a worker in the business should both lie on the new owner. In the United Kingdom, ARD was transposed by the Transfer of Undertakings (Protection of Employment) Regulations 1981 (SI 1981 No 1794) (TUPE), and approved by a resolution of each House of Parliament for the express purpose of implementing ARD. TUPE, regulation 5(1), provided that 'a relevant transfer shall not operate so as to terminate the contract of employment of any person employed by the transferor [the old owner] in the undertaking or part transferred but any such contract which would otherwise have been terminated by the transfer shall have effect after the transfer as if originally made between the person so employed and the transferee [the new owner]'. On 6 February, at 3.30 pm, the appellants were dismissed by Forth Dry Dock and the business was transferred to Forth Estuary at 4.30 pm on the same day. TUPE, regulation 5(3) provided:

'Any reference in [regulation 5(1), above] to a person employed in an undertaking or part of one transferred by a relevant transfer is a reference to a person so employed immediately before the transfer, including, where the transfer is effected by a series of two or more transactions, a person so employed immediately before any of those transactions.'

It was argued that, since the appellants were dismissed at 3.30 pm by Forth Dry Dock, they were not employed 'immediately before the transfer' at 4.30 pm and therefore TUPE, regulation 5(1), did not transfer any liability for the workforce from Forth Dry Dock to Forth Estuary. In *P Bork International v Foreningen af Arbejdsledere i Danmark*,[152] the Court of Justice held that the

---

[151] [1990] AC 546.   [152] [1988] ECR 3057, paragraphs 17–18.

'question whether or not a contract of employment or employment relationship exists at the date of transfer must be assessed under national law, subject, however, to the observance of the mandatory rules of the Directive concerning the protection of workers against dismissal by reason of the transfer. It follows that the workers employed by the undertaking whose contract of employment or employment relationship has been terminated with effect on a date before that of the transfer [must] be considered as still employed by the undertaking on the date of the transfer with the consequence, in particular, that the obligations of an employer towards them are fully transferred from the transferor to the transferee, in accordance with Article 3(1) of the Directive.'

It was held that, on the authority of *von Colson* (p. 362), the courts of the United Kingdom were under a duty to give a purposive construction to directives and to regulations issued for the purpose of complying with directives. TUPE, regulation 5(3), was not intended to limit the operation of the employment protection provisions to persons employed immediately before the transfer in point of time and had to be interpreted as applying to a person employed immediately before the transfer or who would have been so employed if he or she had not been unfairly dismissed before the transfer for a reason connected with the transfer. *Litster* was followed in *Alderson v Secretary of State for Trade and Industry*,[153] again concerned with TUPE. TUPE used the phrase 'an undertaking in the nature of a commercial venture'. It was held that the national 'Court is under an obligation, in so far as the language of TUPE permits, to construe TUPE in a manner which accords with the ARD. If it is not possible to give the two the same scope, the Court must go as far towards this as is possible.' Since the European Court of Justice had interpreted 'undertaking' in the ARD as 'an organised grouping of resources which has the objective of pursuing an economic activity', it was quite possible, 'without stretching the meaning of the phrase to breaking point', to give the phrase 'an undertaking in the nature of a commercial venture' the same meaning as laid down by the Court of Justice, because the words 'in the nature of a commercial venture' were 'sufficiently imprecise and elastic'.[154]

So far, then, if there would be a clear distortion, the courts would not follow the rule of positive interpretation because they were not given discretion to do so under national law and must act within the confines of the United Kingdom constitution, but, if there would not be a clear distortion and the United Kingdom law was specifically introduced to transpose a directive, the courts would follow the *von Colson* rule of positive interpretation. The rule of positive interpretation was taken further in *Marleasing v La Comercial Internacional de Alimentación*,[155] where it was held that it followed from article 5 (now 10) that, in applying national law, whether the national law in question were adopted before or after the directive, the national court called upon to interpret that law is required to do so, as far as possible, in the light of the wording and the purpose of the directive in order to achieve the result pursued by the directive. Before the period for transposition of a directive has expired, the political institutions of a member state cannot be 'reproached' for not having adopted implementing domestic law, and, consequently, the obligation of national courts to interpret domestic law in conformity with the directive commences only once the period for its transposition has expired. Once the period for transposition has in fact expired, the national courts are bound to interpret domestic law, as far as possible, in the light of the wording and purposes of the directive.[156] One reaction to this was that if a court could not follow the rule of positive interpretation because there was a real doubt as to which way to go, then the solution is to refer the

---

[153] [2003] EWCA Civ 1767.   [154] Per Lord Phillips MR, at paras 25, 28.

[155] [1990] ECR I-4135. See, also, *Pfeiffer* [2004] ECR I-8855.

[156] *Inter-Environment Wallonie* [1997] ECR I-7411; *Adeneler* [2006] ECR I-6057.

doubt to the Court of Justice and then, if the Court of Justice says that the court must interpret the United Kingdom law in a specific manner, the United Kingdom court can follow that instruction, even if there is a distortion, because the United Kingdom court would be obeying section 3 of the European Communities Act.[157] In *Webb v EMO Air Cargo*,[158] Webb was engaged by EMO with a view to replacing a pregnant employee, during the latter's maternity leave. Then, Webb found that she too was pregnant and EMO dismissed her. She claimed that her dismissal constituted discrimination against her on the ground of her sex, contrary to section 1 of the Sex Discrimination Act 1975. The House of Lords requested a preliminary ruling from the Court of Justice in order to see whether the dismissal was contrary to the Equal Treatment Directive, and if so to consider whether it was possible to construe the relevant provisions of the 1975 Act so as to accord with the ruling of the Court of Justice. The ruling of the Court of Justice[159] was that the Equal Treatment Directive 'precludes dismissal of an employee who is recruited for an unlimited term with a view, initially, to replacing another employee during the latter's maternity leave and who cannot do so because, shortly after recruitment, she is herself found to be pregnant'. The House held that they were under a duty to endeavour to construe the Sex Discrimination Act 1975 so as to accord if at all possible with the ruling of the European Court. The Court of Justice has held on several occasions that, if the result prescribed by a directive cannot be achieved by way of the doctrine of positive interpretation and the relevant provisions of domestic law cannot be interpreted in conformity with that directive, the Community law doctrine of state liability (see head (g)) requires the member states to make good damage caused to individuals through failure to transpose a directive.[160]

(e) The doctrine of the right to a remedy

The third stage of the development of effective protection of Community conferred rights may be called the 'doctrine of the right to a remedy' or the 'principle of effective judicial control'. This was emphasised in:

Sabine von Colson and Elisabeth Kamann v Land Nordrhein-Westfalen
case 14/83 [1984] ECR 1891

Various questions were raised in the course of proceedings between two qualified social workers, Sabine von Colson and Elisabeth Kamann, and the land Nordrhein-Westfalen, because a prison, administered by Nordrhein-Westfalen and which catered exclusively for male prisoners, refused to engage the plaintiffs for reasons relating to their sex. The prison justified the refusal to engage the plaintiffs by citing the problems and risks connected with the appointment of female candidates and appointed instead male candidates who were, however, less well-qualified. The German labour court held that there had been discrimination and that under German law relating to compensation for discrimination,

---

[157] See p. 337.   [158] [1995] 1 WLR 1454. See, also, *Alabaster v Barclay's Bank* [2005] EWCA Civ 508.
[159] [1994] ECR I-3567.
[160] *Faccini Dori v Recreb* [1994] ECR I-3325; *El Corte Inglés SA v Cristina Blázquez Rivero* [1996] ECR I-1281; *Dillenkofer v Germany* [1996] ECR I-4845; *EvoBus Austria GmbH v Niederösterreichische Verkehrsorganisations GmbH (Növog)* [1998] ECR I-5411; *Carbonari v Università degli Studi di Bologna* [1999] ECR I-1103.

it could only order the reimbursement of the travel expenses incurred by the plaintiffs in applying for the posts.

The European Court of Justice

'8. [The labour court] asks essentially whether [the Equal Treatment Directive No 76/207, p. 358] requires discrimination on grounds of sex in the matter of access to employment to be penalized by an obligation, imposed on an employer who is guilty of discrimination to conclude a contract of employment with the candidate who was the victim of [discrimination].

. . .

16. It is therefore necessary to examine Directive No 76/207 in order to determine whether it requires member states to provide for specific legal consequences or sanctions in respect of a breach of the principle of equal treatment regarding access to [employment].

. . .

18. Article 6 [of the Directive] requires member states to introduce into their national legal systems such measures as are necessary to enable all persons who consider themselves wronged by discrimination "to pursue their claims by judicial process". It follows from the provision that member states are required to adopt measures which are sufficiently effective to achieve the objective of the directive and to ensure that those measures may in fact be relied on before the national courts by the persons concerned. Such measures may include, for example provisions requiring the employer to offer a post to the candidate discriminated against or giving the candidate adequate financial compensation, backed up where necessary by a system of fines. However the directive does not prescribe a specific sanction; it leaves member states free to choose between the different solutions suitable for achieving its [objective].

. . .

23. [Although, stated above], full implementation of the directive does not require any specific form of sanction for unlawful discrimination, it does entail that that sanction be such as to guarantee real and effective judicial protection. Moreover it must also have a real deterrent effect on the employer. It follows that where a member state chooses to penalize the breach of the prohibition of discrimination by the award of compensation, that compensation must in any event be adequate in relation to the damage sustained.

24. In consequence it appears that national provisions limiting the right to compensation of persons who have been discriminated against as regards access to employment to a purely nominal amount, such as, for example, the reimbursement of expenses incurred by them in submitting their application, would not satisfy the requirements of an effective transposition of the [directive].'

....

Marguerite Johnston v Chief Constable of the Royal Ulster Constabulary case 222/84 [1986] ECR 1651

Within Northern Ireland, the United Kingdom measures taken to implement the provisions of the Equal Treatment Directive (p. 358) were contained in the Sex Discrimination (Northern Ireland) Order 1976 (SI 1976 No 1042). Article 53(1) of the order provided that none of its provisions prohibiting discrimination 'shall render unlawful an act done for the purpose of safeguarding national security or of protecting public safety or public order' and article 53(2) provided that a 'certificate signed by or on behalf of the Secretary of State and certifying that an act specified in the certificate was done for the purposes mentioned in paragraph (1) shall be conclusive evidence that it was done for that purpose'. Because of the large number of police officers assassinated in Northern Ireland over a number of years, the Chief Constable of the Royal Ulster Constabulary (RUC) considered that he could not maintain the normal practice whereby police officers do not as a general rule carry firearms in the performance of their duties (a practice where no distinction was made between men and women). The Chief Constable decided that in the RUC and the RUC Reserve, men should carry firearms in the regular course of their duties but that women would not be equipped with firearms and would not receive training in the handling and use of firearms. He also decided, in 1980, that the number of women in the RUC was sufficient for the particular tasks generally assigned to women officers. He took the view that general police duties, frequently involving operations requiring the carrying of firearms, should no longer be assigned to women and decided not to offer or renew any more contracts for women in the RUC full-time Reserve, except where they had to perform duties assigned only to women officers. Mrs Johnston had been a member of the RUC Reserve from 1974 to 1980 and had efficiently performed the general duties of a uniformed police officer (acting as station duty officer, taking part in mobile patrols, driving patrol vehicles and assisting in searching persons brought to the police station). She was not armed when carrying out those duties and was ordinarily accompanied in duties outside the police station by an armed male officer. In 1980 the Chief Constable refused to renew her contract because of his new policy (above) with regard to female members of the RUC Reserve. Mrs Johnston brought an action before an industrial tribunal challenging the decision to refuse to renew her contract and to give her training in the handling of firearms. Before the industrial tribunal, the Chief Constable produced a certificate issued by the Secretary of State for Northern Ireland in which he certified, in accordance with article 53 (above) that 'the act consisting of the refusal of the Royal Ulster Constabulary to offer further full-time employment to [Mrs Johnston] in the Royal Ulster Constabulary Reserve was done for the purpose of: (a) safeguarding national security; and (b) protecting public safety and public order'. Article 6 of the Equal Treatment Directive provides that 'Member States shall introduce into their national legal systems such measures as are necessary to enable all persons who consider themselves wronged by failure to apply to them the principle of equal treatment [to] pursue their claims by judicial process after possible recourse to other competent authorities'. Mrs Johnston argued, inter alia, that article 53(2) of the Northern Ireland Order (above) was contrary to article 6 inasmuch as it prevented the industrial tribunal (and any higher appellate court) from exercising any effective judicial control over compliance with the provisions of the directive and with the national legislation intended to put into effect that directive. The Advocate General argued that, by removing measures taken by the member states from the ambit of Community law, this would in fact allow the national authorities to create a 'no-go area for the law' as and when they saw fit, thus calling in question the very foundations of that legal order.

The European Court of Justice

'The right to an effective judicial remedy

13. It is therefore necessary to examine [whether] Community law, and more particularly Directive 76/207, requires the Member States to ensure that their national courts and tribunals exercise effective control over compliance with the provisions of the directive and with the national legislation intended to put it into effect.

14. In Mrs Johnston's view, a provision such as [article 53(2)] is contrary to Article 6 of the directive inasmuch as it prevents the competent national court or tribunal from exercising any judicial control.

15. The United Kingdom observes that Article 6 [does] not require the Member States to submit to judicial review every question which may arise in the application of the directive, even where national security and public safety are involved. Rules of evidence such as the rule laid down in [article 53(2)] are quite common in national procedural law. Their justification is that matters of national security and public safety can be satisfactorily assessed only by the competent political authority, namely the minister who issues the certificate in question.

16. The Commission takes the view that to treat the certificate of a minister as having an effect such as that provided for in [article 53(2)] is tantamount to refusing all judicial control or review and is therefore contrary to a fundamental principle of Community law and to Article [6].

17. As far as this issue is concerned, it must be borne in mind first of all that Article 6 [requires] Member States to introduce into their internal legal systems such measures as are needed to enable all persons who consider themselves wronged by discrimination "to pursue their claims by judicial process". It follows from that provision that the Member States must take measures which are sufficiently effective to achieve the aim of the directive and that they must ensure that the rights thus conferred may be effectively relied upon before the national courts by the persons concerned.

18. The requirement of judicial control stipulated by [article 6] reflects a general principle of law which underlies the constitutional traditions common to the Member States. That principle is also laid down in Articles 6 and 13 of the European Convention for the Protection of Human Rights and Fundamental [Freedoms and] as the Court has recognised in its decisions, the principles on which that Convention is based must be taken into consideration in Community law.

19. By virtue of Article [6], interpreted in the light of the general principle stated above, all persons have the right to obtain an effective remedy in a competent court against measures which they consider to be contrary to the principle of equal treatment for men and women laid down in the directive. It is for the Member States to ensure effective judicial control as regards compliance with the applicable provisions of Community law and of national legislation intended to give effect to the rights for which the directive provides.

20. A provision which, like [article 53(2)], requires a certificate such as the one in question in the present case to be treated as conclusive evidence that the conditions for derogating from the principle of equal treatment are fulfilled allows the competent authority to deprive an individual of the possibility of asserting by judicial process the rights conferred by the directive. Such a provision is therefore contrary to the principle of effective judicial control laid down in Article [6].

21. The answer to [the question] put by the industrial tribunal must therefore be that the principle of effective judicial control laid down in Article [6] does not allow a certificate issued by a national authority stating that the conditions for derogating from the principle of equal treatment for men and women for the purpose of protecting public safety are satisfied to be treated as conclusive evidence so as to exclude the exercise of any power of review by the [courts].

. . .

[On the role of the national court]

39. By reason of the division of jurisdiction provided for in Article 177 of the EEC Treaty, it is for the national court to say whether the reasons on which the Chief Constable based his decision are in fact well founded and justify the specific measure taken in Mrs Johnston's case. It is also for the national court to ensure that the principle of proportionality is observed and to determine whether the refusal to renew Mrs Johnston's contract could not be avoided by allocating to women duties which, without jeopardising the aims pursued, can be performed without [firearms].

. . .

[On the question of interpretation]

53. [It should be observed that] the Member States' obligation under a directive to achieve the result envisaged by that directive and their duty under Article 5 of the Treaty [is] binding on all the authorities of Member States including, for matters within their jurisdiction, the courts. It follows that, in applying national law, and in particular the provisions of national legislation specifically introduced in order to implement Directive 76/207, national courts are required to interpret their national law in the light of the wording and purpose of the directive in order to achieve the result referred to in [article 189(3)]. It is therefore for the industrial tribunal to interpret the provisions of the [Northern Ireland] Order, and in particular Article 53(1) thereof, in the light of the provisions of the directive [in] order to give it its full [effect].

Remedies provide for redress in a wide variety of circumstances. In *UNECTEF v Heylens*,[161] the Court held that, since free access to employment is a fundamental right which the Treaty confers individually on each worker in the Community, the existence of a remedy of a judicial nature against any decision of a national authority refusing the benefit of that right is essential in order to secure for the individual effective protection for his or her rights and that this included an obligation to give the person concerned the reasons for an administrative authority's decision. One remedy can be the quashing of an unlawful rule or administrative act. Delegated legislation is the making of rules, usually called 'regulations', under the direct authority of an Act of Parliament (see p. 249). Regulations must be made in conformity with the authority of the 'parent' Act of Parliament. If a regulation is *ultra vires* an Act of Parliament, the courts can declare the regulation to be invalid and quash it. The same principle could be applied to any regulation which is contrary to Community law. For example, free movement of workers is a very important part of Community law and some of the rights of migrant workers are laid down in Council Regulation 1612/68. Article 7(2) of Regulation 1612/68 provides that migrant workers shall have the same 'social advantages' as home workers. In the United Kingdom scheme of things many rules relating to the granting of social advantages are laid down by an Act of Parliament which grants the appropriate government department the power to implement the Act of Parliament in the form of delegated legislation. If, and this is purely hypothetical, the Minister of Social Security made a regulation denying Community workers the right to be awarded a particular social security benefit, this regulation would be declared to be invalid or *ultra vires* by the United Kingdom courts, by the combined effect of Regulation 1612/68, which is directly applicable, and section 2(1) of the European Communities Act (see p. 336). In administrative law (see chapters 9 and 10), the courts will quash an administrative act which has been taken contrary to a statute or declare that a proposed administrative act would be unlawful because of being contrary to statute. If the statute happens to be the European Communities Act, then no conceptual or practical problem arises. One example of administrative action is the activity of immigration officers who make individual decisions applying United Kingdom law, which incorporates, in relation to those persons governed by Community law, Community law, to persons entering the United Kingdom. Directive 90/364 grants the right of residence in a member state to certain persons who are not economically active. This is something akin to a citizen's right to reside in his or her country. However, persons wishing to use this Directive must have 'adequate resources' so that they are not a burden on the host member state. It has been held that an immigration officer cannot ask the person to prove that he or she has adequate resources at the point of entry into the member state.[162] Therefore, if a United Kingdom immigration official took an individual decision preventing a Community national from entering the United Kingdom until that person had proved that he or she possessed adequate resources, that individual decision would be quashed by the United Kingdom court to which the case was brought. In *Hockenjos v Secretary of State for Social Security*,[163] it was held that a regulation relating to jobseeker's allowance (a social security benefit providing financial relief against unemployment) was contrary to the prohibition against indirect discrimination on the basis of sex in relation to social security schemes as laid down in the Equal Treatment Directive, and that that indirect discrimination could not be objectively justified according to Community law. The regulation 'must, therefore, be disapplied'.[164]

---

[161] [1987] ECR 4097.   [162] *Commission v Netherlands* [1991] ECR I-2637.
[163] [2004] EWCA Civ 1749.   [164] Per Ward LJ, at para 189.

Another form of remedy may be financial compensation:

Marshall v Southampton and South-West Hampshire Area Health Authority case C-271/91 [1993] ECR I-4367

In *Marshall I* (p. 357), the Court of Justice held that the policy to dismiss women because they have passed the qualifying age for a state pension was contrary to the Equal Treatment Directive (p. 358). The case, therefore, was returned to the industrial tribunal to consider the question of a remedy, namely, financial compensation for unlawful dismissal. The industrial tribunal assessed her financial compensation at £19,000, including elements for loss of earnings, interest on loss of earnings from her dismissal to the time the compensation was paid, and injury to feelings. At that time, the maximum financial compensation under the domestic United Kingdom labour legislation (which was in the form of delegated legislation) was £6,250. Article 6 of the Directive stated that member states 'shall introduce into their national legal systems such measures as are necessary to enable [persons discriminated against] to pursue their claims by judicial process'. By this time *von Colson* (p. 368) had been determined by the Court of Justice, which held that article 6 does not prescribe a specific measure to be taken in the event of discrimination, that there is no 'Euro-remedy', that member states are free to choose the most suitable remedy available in national law, and that that remedy must guarantee real and effective judicial protection and have a real deterrent effect on the employer. By this time *Johnston* (p. 369) had been decided and the Court of Justice had held that article 6 was directly effective and could be relied upon by persons in the national courts. The industrial tribunal, therefore, considered what had been stated in *von Colson* and *Johnston* and held that article 6 of the Directive could be relied on as it was directly effective, that on the facts and in accordance with the principle that the remedy must guarantee real and effective judicial protection and have a real deterrent effect on the employer, Miss Marshall should be awarded the £19,000, and that the maximum limit imposed by the United Kingdom delegated legislation was in breach of article 6 of the Directive and should be ignored in favour of the £19,000 awarded. The Area Health Authority appealed and the House of Lords referred the compatibility of United Kingdom law on maximum awards by industrial tribunals with the provisions of article 6 of the Directive to the Court of Justice.

The European Court of Justice

'11. In essence, the questions put by the House of Lords ask whether it follows from [Directive 76/207] that a victim of sex discrimination on the part of an authority which is an emanation of the State is entitled to full reparation for the loss and damage he or she has sustained and whether Article 6 of the Directive enables such a person to contest the applicability of national legislation which is intended to give effect to the Directive but sets limits to the compensation recoverable. The fundamental problem is therefore to determine the meaning and scope of Article 6 having regard to the principles and aims of the [Directive].

. . .

17. As the Court has consistently held, [article 189 (now 249)] of the Treaty requires each Member State to which a directive is addressed to adopt, in its national legal system, all the measures necessary to ensure that its provisions are fully effective, in accordance with the objective pursued by the directive, while leaving to the Member State the choice of the forms and methods used to achieve that objective.

18. It is therefore necessary to identify the objectives of the Directive and in particular to see whether, in the event of a breach of the prohibition of discrimination, its provisions leave Member States a degree of discretion as regards the form and content of the sanctions to be applied.

19. The purpose of the Directive is to put into effect in the Member States the principle of equal treatment for men and women as regards the various aspects of employment, in particular working conditions, including the conditions governing [dismissal].

. . .

22. Article 6 of the Directive puts Member States under a duty to take the necessary measures to enable all persons who consider themselves wronged by discrimination to pursue their claims by judicial process. Such obligation implies that the measures in question should be sufficiently effective to achieve the objective of the Directive and should be capable of being effectively relied upon by the persons concerned before national courts.

23. As the Court held in [von Colson, p. 368, at paragraph 18], Article 6 does not prescribe a specific measure to be taken in the event of a breach of the prohibition of discrimination, but leaves Member States free to choose between the different solutions suitable for achieving the objective of the Directive, depending on the different situations which may arise.

24. However, the objective is to arrive at real equality of opportunity and cannot therefore be attained in the absence of measures appropriate to restore such equality when it has not been observed. As the Court stated [in paragraph 23 of von Colson], those measures must be such as to guarantee real and effective judicial protection and have a real deterrent effect on the [employer].

. . .

26. Where financial compensation is the measure adopted in order to achieve the objective indicated above, it must be adequate, in that it must enable the loss and damage actually sustained as a result of the discriminatory dismissal to be made good in full in accordance with the applicable national rules.

The first and second questions

27. In its first question, the House of Lords seeks to establish whether it is contrary to Article 6 of the Directive for national provisions to lay down an upper limit on the amount of compensation recoverable by a victim of discrimination.

28. In its second question, the House of Lords asks whether Article 6 requires (a) that the compensation for the damage sustained as a result of the illegal discrimination should be full and (b) that it should include an award of interest on the principal amount from the date of the unlawful discrimination to the date when compensation is paid.

29. The Court's interpretation of Article 6 as set out above provides a direct reply to the first part of the second question relating to the level of compensation required by that provision.

30. It also follows from that interpretation that the fixing of an upper limit of the kind at issue in the main proceedings cannot, by definition, constitute proper implementation of Article 6 of the Directive, since it limits the amount of compensation a priori to a level which is not necessarily consistent with the requirement of ensuring real equality of opportunity through adequate reparation for the loss and damage sustained as a result of discriminatory dismissal.

31. With regard to the second part of the second question relating to the award of interest, suffice it to say that full compensation for the loss and damage sustained as a result of discriminatory dismissal cannot leave out of account factors, such as the effluxion of time, which may in fact reduce its value. The award of interest, in accordance with the applicable national rules, must therefore be regarded as an essential component of compensation for the purposes of restoring real equality of treatment.

32. Accordingly, the reply to be given to the first and second questions is that the interpretation of Article 6 of the Directive must be that reparation of the loss and damage sustained by a person injured as a result of discriminatory dismissal may not be limited to an upper limit fixed a priori or by excluding an award of interest to compensate for the loss sustained by the recipient of the compensation as a result of the effluxion of time until the capital sum awarded is actually paid.'

The Court of Justice had, therefore, come to the same conclusion as the industrial tribunal. The House of Lords restored the decision of the industrial tribunal.[165] Miss Marshall received the money awarded to her. The United Kingdom then changed the law on upper limits for compensation for unfair dismissal by the Sex Discrimination and Equal Pay (Remedies) Regulations 1993,[166] which removed the statutory limit on awards in sex discrimination cases and granted a power to award interest on awards in sex discrimination cases.

Another form of 'remedy' comes from what have become known in Community law as the principle of equivalence and the principle of effectiveness. Early on the Court of Justice stated:

'it is the national courts which are entrusted with ensuring the legal protection which citizens derive from the direct effect of the provisions of Community Law. Accordingly, in the absence of Community rules on this subject, it is for the domestic legal system in each Member State to designate the courts having jurisdiction and to determine the procedural conditions governing actions at law intended to ensure the protection of rights which citizens have from the directive effect of Community Law, it being understood that such conditions cannot be less favourable than those relating to similar actions of a domestic nature. The right conferred by Community Law must be exercised before the national courts in accordance with the conditions laid down by national rules. The position would be different only if the conditions and time limits made it impossible in practice to exercise the rights which the national courts are obliged to protect. This is not the case where reasonable periods of limitation of actions are fixed.'[167]

Later it was opined that:

'[Each] case which raises the question whether a national procedural provision renders application of Community law impossible or excessively difficult must be analysed by reference to the role of that provision in the procedure, its progress and its special features, viewed as a whole, before the various national instances. In the light of that analysis the basic principles of the domestic judicial system, such as protection of the rights of the defence, the principle of legal certainty and the proper conduct of procedure, must, where appropriate, be taken into consideration.'[168]

In *Palmisani*,[169] the Court of Justice stated that

'it is on the basis of the rules of national law on liability that the State must make reparation for the consequences of the loss or damage caused; further, the conditions, in particular time-limits, for reparation of loss or damage laid down by national law must not be less favourable than those relating to similar domestic claims (principle of equivalence) and must not be so framed as to make it virtually impossible or excessively difficult to obtain reparation (principle of effectiveness).'

The reference to time limits is of immense importance. It is usual for a legal system to have procedural rules limiting the time in which to apply for a remedy for the infringement of a right in order to attain legal certainty. The principle of legal certainty may permit an individual to act without fear of legal nemesis but the time limits laid down by the member state must, on principle, be reasonable and give the individual asserting the infringement of a right

---

[165] [1994] 1 AC 530.   [166] SI 1993/2798.

[167] *Rewe v Zentral Finanz eg Landwirtschaftskammer* [1976] ECR 1989, at 1998.

[168] *Rewe-Handelsgesellschaft Nord mbH and Rewe-Markt Steffen v Hauptzollamt Kiel* [1981] ECR 1805, at paragraph 44; *Peterbroeck van Campenhout & Cie v Belgium* [1994] ECR I-4599, at paragraph 14.

[169] [1997] ECR I-4025.

granted by Community law:

....

Emmott v Minister for Social Welfare and Attorney General case No 208/19 [1991] ECR I-4269

The European Court of Justice

'16. As the Court has consistently [held], in the absence of Community rules on the subject, it is for the domestic legal system of each Member State to determine the procedural conditions governing actions at law intended to ensure the protection of the rights which individuals derive from the direct effect of Community law, provided that such conditions are not less favourable than those relating to similar actions of a domestic nature nor framed so as to render virtually impossible the exercise of rights conferred by Community law.

. . .

19. In this regard it must be borne in mind that the Member States are required to ensure the full application of directives in a sufficiently clear and precise manner so that, where directives are intended to create rights for individuals, they can ascertain the full extent of those rights and, where necessary, rely on them before the national [courts].

21. So long as a directive has not been properly transposed into national law, individuals are unable to ascertain the full extent of their rights. That state of uncertainty for individuals subsists even after the Court has delivered a judgment finding that the Member State in question has not fulfilled its obligations under the directive and even if the Court has held that a particular provision or provisions of the directive are sufficiently precise and unconditional to be relied upon before a national court.

22. Only the proper transposition of the directive will bring that state of uncertainty to an end and it is only upon that transposition that the legal certainty which must exist if individuals are to be required to assert their rights is created.

23. It follows that, until such time as a directive has been properly transposed, a defaulting Member State may not rely on an individual's delay in initiating proceedings against it in order to protect rights conferred upon him by the provisions of the directive and that a period laid down by national law within which proceedings must be initiated cannot begin to run before that time.'

Since then it has become apparent 'that national courts may have to alter their procedure and remedies, and even their jurisdiction, in order to meet the demands of the principle of effectiveness: the areas in which national courts may have to adapt their rules include limitation periods and other time limits, monetary limits to awards of compensation, interest and costs, and rules of evidence'.[170]

In *Metallgesellschaft Ltd v Inland Revenue Commissioners* and *Hoechst AG v Inland Revenue Commissioners*,[171] the Court of Justice held that United Kingdom rules relating to advance corporation tax were contrary to Community law and that certain companies, which had been required to pay, and had paid, the tax earlier than should have been the case were entitled to compensation. They

'should have an effective legal remedy in order to obtain reimbursement or reparation of the financial loss which they have sustained and from which the authorities of the member state concerned have benefited as a result of the advance payment of [tax. While] in the absence of Community rules, it is for the domestic legal system of the member state concerned to lay down the detailed procedural rules governing such actions, including ancillary questions such as the payment of interest, those rules must

---

[170] *Autologic Holdings v Her Majesty's Commissioners of Inland Revenue* [2005] UKHL 54, per Lord Walker, at paras 92 and 94.　　　　　　　　　　　　　　　　　　　　　　[171] [2001] ECR I-1727.

not render practically impossible or excessively difficult the exercise of rights conferred by Community law.'

Following this, in *Sempra Metals Ltd v Commissioners of Inland Revenue, Her Majesty's Attorney-General*,[172] the Court of Appeal held that the

'national court is required to give a remedy, whether by way of restitution or as compensation, in respect of the breach of Community law. It is not open to the national court to deny restitution or compensation on the ground that no remedy would lie under domestic law. If necessary, Community law demands an autonomous remedy in respect of the breach of Community law which has occurred. [The] remedy to be given by the national court must be a "full" remedy; in the sense that it must be such as will restore the equality of treatment guaranteed by [the] EC Treaty. Nothing less will do. A full remedy for the loss of the use of money over a specified period may be measured by reference to the interest "accrued" on the amount of the tax paid prematurely. The task of the national court is to ascertain the amount which the member state must pay to the claimant in order to restore the claimant to the position that it would have been in if it had not been required to pay an amount of corporation tax prematurely.'

At first instance, the judge, contrary to the normal approach under domestic law, had held that the computation should be on the basis that interest was compounded as that would provide full, rather than partial, recompense for the loss sustained. The Court of Appeal held

'that the judge was right to reach the conclusion that he did. Community law requires full compensation for the loss of the use of money; and full compensation for the loss of the use of money requires that interest is [compounded]. The English domestic rules as to interest fail to provide the remedy which Community law requires. Those rules must yield to the overriding requirement that the domestic court gives full compensation.'[173]

The right to an effective remedy, in this case adequate interlocutory relief, was maintained in the earlier *Factortame* litigation, where the United Kingdom courts were led to overturn a long standing (centuries old) constitutional principle that that an injunction did not lie against the Crown:

....

R v Secretary of State for Transport, ex p Factortame [1990] 2 AC 85

Proceedings were brought against the Secretary of State for Transport by Factortame and other companies and also by the directors and shareholders of those companies, most of which were Spanish nationals. The companies were the owners or operators of 95 fishing vessels registered in the register of British vessels under the Merchant Shipping Act 1894. The Community common fisheries policy, established, inter alia, to regulate the over-fishing in the North Sea and Atlantic Ocean, determined the allocation of the quotas of fish between the member states. At first, the United Kingdom had the naïve belief that the common fisheries policy's system of quotas would result in the quotas allocated to the United Kingdom being assigned to the benefit of United Kingdom fishermen and the United Kingdom fish and chips-eating population. Subsequently, the United Kingdom decided to amend the 1894 legislation in order to put a stop to the practice known as 'quota-hopping', whereby, according to the United Kingdom, its fishing quotas were 'plundered' by vessels flying the British flag but lacking any genuine link with the United Kingdom. In order to implement this part of the common fisheries policy and to define the fishing boats which could benefit from the quotas assigned to the United Kingdom, the United Kingdom decided in 1987 to introduce in the Merchant Shipping Act 1988,

---

[172] [2005] EWCA Civ 389.   [173] Per Chadwick LJ, at paras 25 and 53.

certain provisions relative to the conditions for registration of fishing boats, submitting, inter alia, the owners and operators of the boats to two conditions: a nationality condition and a residence condition.

Consequently, Parliament enacted the Merchant Shipping Act 1988, Part II, which, together with the Merchant Shipping (Registration of Fishing Vessels) Regulations 1988 (SI 1988/1926), radically altered the registration system of British fishing vessels, with effect from 1 December 1988. The 1988 Act provided for the establishment of a new register in which all British fishing vessels were to be registered, including those which were already registered in the old register maintained under the 1894 Act. However, only fishing vessels fulfilling the conditions laid down in section 14 of the 1988 Act could be registered in the new register.

Section 14(1) provided that a fishing vessel was eligible to be registered in the new register only if '(a) the vessel is British-owned; (b) the vessel is managed, and its operations are directed and controlled, from within the United Kingdom; and (c) any charterer, manager or operator of the vessel is a qualified person or company'. Section 14(2) provided that a fishing vessel is deemed to be British-owned if the legal title is vested wholly in one or more qualified persons or companies and if the vessel is beneficially owned by one or more qualified companies or, as to not less than 75 per cent, by one or more qualified persons. Section 14(7) provided that a 'qualified person' means a person who is a British citizen resident and domiciled in the United Kingdom and 'qualified company' means a company incorporated in the United Kingdom and having as its principal place of business there, at least 75 per cent of its shares being owned by one or more qualified persons or companies and at least 75 per cent of its directors being qualified persons.

The United Kingdom Government informed the European Commission of its proposal in 1987, but the Commission did nothing. Then, on 28 March 1988, the Commission warned the United Kingdom that the conditions 'appeared' incompatible with article 52 of the Treaty (the right of establishment). In 1989, the Commission stated that, in its opinion, the nationality condition was incompatible with both articles 7 (no discrimination on grounds of nationality) and 52 (the right of establishment) of the Treaty. On 4 August 1989 the Commission brought an action before the Court of Justice under article 169 for a declaration that, by imposing the nationality requirements laid down in section 14 (above), the United Kingdom had failed to fulfil its obligations under articles 7 and 52 of the Treaty. The Commission also applied to the Court of Justice for an interim order requiring the United Kingdom to suspend the application of the nationality requirements as regards the nationals of other member states and in respect of fishing vessels which until 31 March 1989 were carrying on a fishing activity under the British flag and under a British fishing licence. On 10 October 1989, the President of the European Court of Justice made an order ordering the United Kingdom to suspend the nationality condition (see [1989] ECR 3125) and, on 1 November 1989, that is to say three weeks later (an important point for *Factortame V* (p. 392)), the Secretary of State made an Order in Council, suspended the operation of the nationality condition and amended section 14 of the 1988 Act (see the Merchant Shipping Act 1988 (Amendment) Order 1989 (SI 1989/2006), which came into force on 2 November 1989).

At the time, the 95 fishing vessels of the companies in question could not satisfy one or more of the conditions for registration under section 14 and, therefore, could not be registered in the new register. Since those vessels were to be deprived of the right to engage in fishing as from 1 April 1989, the companies, by means of an application for judicial review, challenged the compatibility of Part II of the 1988 Act with Community law. They also applied for the grant of interim relief until such time as final judgment was given on their application. On 10 March 1989, the Divisional Court decided to stay the proceedings and to make a reference for a preliminary ruling on the issues of Community law thus raised and ordered that, by way of interim relief, the application of Part II of the 1988 Act and the 1988 Regulations should be suspended as regards the applicants. On 22 March 1989, the Court of Appeal held that under United Kingdom law the courts had no power to suspend, by way of interim relief, the application of Acts of Parliament. It therefore set aside the order of the Divisional Court. The case came before the House of Lords and the House of Lords referred the interim relief question to the European Court of Justice on 18 May 1989.

Lord Bridge, at 134–151

'The applicants sought [to] challenge the legality of the relevant 1988 legislation on the ground that it contravened the provisions of the EEC Treaty and other rules of law given effect thereunder by the European Communities Act 1972 by depriving the applicants of rights of the kind referred to in section 2(1) of the 1972 Act as enforceable Community [rights].

It is estimated that the preliminary ruling requested by the Divisional Court from the ECJ will not be given for two years from the date when the reference is made. The applicants claim that unless they are protected during this period by an interim order which has the effect of enabling them to continue to operate their 95 vessels as if they were duly registered British fishing vessels (which would be necessary to enable them to continue to hold licences to fish against the British quota of controlled stocks of fish) they will suffer irreparable damage. The vessels are not eligible to resume the Spanish flag and fish against the Spanish quota. To lay the vessels up pending the ruling of the ECJ would be prohibitively expensive. The only practical alternative would be to sell the vessels or the Spanish holdings in the companies owning the vessels in what would be a glutted market at disastrously low prices. In addition many of the individual applicants are actively engaged in the operation and management of the vessels and would lose their livelihood. No doubt has been cast on the factual accuracy of these claims and I approach the question of interim relief on the footing that they are well [founded].

By virtue of [the European Communities Act 1972, section 2(1), (4), p. 336], Part II of the 1988 Act is to be construed and take effect subject to directly enforceable Community rights and those rights are [to] be "recognised and available in law, and enforced, allowed and followed accordingly". This has precisely the same effect as if a section were incorporated in Part II of the 1988 Act which in terms enacted that the provisions with respect to registration of British fishing vessels were to be without prejudice to the directly enforceable Community rights of nationals of any Member State of the EEC. Thus it is common ground that, in so far as the applicants succeed before the ECJ in obtaining a ruling in support of the Community rights which they claim, those rights will prevail over the restrictions imposed on registration of British fishing vessels by Part II of the 1988 [Act].

[An] order granting the applicants the interim relief which they seek will only serve their purpose if it declares that which Parliament had enacted to be the law from 1 December 1988, and to take effect in relation to vessels previously registered under the 1894 Act from 31 March 1989, not to be the law until some uncertain future date. Effective relief can only be given if it requires the Secretary of State to treat the applicants' vessels as entitled to registration under Part II of the 1988 Act in direct contravention of its provisions. Any such order, unlike any form of order for interim relief known to the law, would irreversibly determine in the applicants' favour for a period of some two years rights which are necessarily uncertain until the preliminary ruling of the ECJ has been given. If the applicants fail to establish the rights they claim before the ECJ, the effect of the interim relief granted would be to have conferred on them rights directly contrary to Parliament's sovereign will and correspondingly to have deprived British fishing vessels, as defined by Parliament, of the enjoyment of a substantial proportion of the United Kingdom's quota of stocks of fish protected by the common fisheries policy. I am clearly of opinion that, as a matter of English law, the court has no power to make an order which has these consequences.

It follows that this appeal must fall to be dismissed unless there is, as the applicants contend, some overriding principle derived from the jurisprudence of the ECJ which compels national courts of Member States, whatever their own law may provide, to assert, and in appropriate cases to exercise, a power to provide an effective interlocutory remedy to protect putative rights in Community law once those rights have been claimed and are seen to be seriously arguable, notwithstanding that the existence of the rights is in dispute and will not be established unless and until the ECJ so [rules].

The basic propositions of Community law on which the applicants rely [may] be quite shortly summarised. Directly enforceable Community rights are part of the legal heritage of every citizen of a Member State of the EEC. They arise from the Treaty itself and not from any judgment of the ECJ declaring their existence. Such rights are automatically available and must be given unrestricted retroactive effect. The persons entitled to the enjoyment of such rights are entitled to direct and immediate protection against possible infringement of them. The duty to provide such protection rests with the national court. The remedy to be provided against infringement must be effective, not merely symbolic or illusory. The rules of national law which render the exercise of directly enforceable Community rights excessively difficult or virtually impossible must be overridden.

[I] do not think that it is open to your Lordships' House to decide one way or the other whether, in relation to the grant of interim protection in the circumstances of the instant case, Community law overrides English law and either empowers or obliges an English court to make an interim order protecting the putative rights claimed by the applicants. It follows, I think, that your Lordships are obliged under Article 177 of the Treaty to seek a preliminary ruling from the ECJ. I would propose that the questions to be referred should read as follows:

1. Where: (i) a party before the national court claims to be entitled to rights under Community law having direct effect in national law ("the rights claimed"), (ii) a national measure in clear terms will, if applied, automatically deprive that party of the rights claimed, (iii) there are serious arguments both for and against the existence of the rights claimed and the national court has sought a preliminary ruling under Article 177 as to whether or not the rights claimed exist, (iv) the national law presumes the national measure in question to be compatible with Community law unless and until it is declared incompatible, (v) the national court has no power to give interim protection to the rights claimed by suspending the application of the national measure pending the preliminary ruling, (vi) if the preliminary ruling is in the event in favour of the rights claimed, the party entitled to those rights is likely to have suffered irremediable damage unless given such interim protection, does Community law either (a) oblige the national court to grant such interim protection of the rights claimed or (b) give the court power to grant such interim protection of the rights claimed?

2. If question 1(a) is answered in the negative and question 1(b) in the affirmative, what are the criteria to be applied in deciding whether or not to grant such interim protection of the rights claimed?'

R v Secretary of State for Transport, ex p Factortame [1991] 1 AC 603

In *R v Secretary of State for Transport, ex p Factortame* ([1990] ECR 1-2433), the European Court of Justice on 19 June 1990 held (at paragraphs 19 to 21) in reply to the two questions posed by the House of Lords that it

'is for the national courts, in application of the principle of co-operation laid down in Article 5 of the EEC Treaty, to ensure the legal protection which persons derive from the direct effect of provisions of Community law[; that] any provision of a national legal system and any legislative, administrative or judicial practice which might impair the effectiveness of Community law by withholding from the national court having jurisdiction to apply such law the power to do everything necessary at the moment of its application to set aside national legislative provisions which might prevent, even temporarily, Community rules from having full force and effect are incompatible with those requirements, which are the very essence of Community law[; that] the full effectiveness of Community law would be just as much impaired if a rule of national law could prevent a court seised of a dispute governed by Community law from granting interim relief in order to ensure the full effectiveness of the judgment to be given on the existence of the rights claimed under Community law. It follows that a court which in those circumstances would grant interim relief, if it were not for a rule of national law, is obliged to set aside that rule.'

Lord Bridge, at 658–660

'My Lords, when this appeal first came before the House in last year [p. 377] your Lordships held that, as a matter of English law, the courts had no jurisdiction to grant interim relief in terms which would involve either overturning an English statute in advance of any decision by the European Court of

Justice that the statute infringed Community law or granting an injunction against the Crown. It then became necessary to seek a preliminary ruling from the European Court of Justice as to whether Community law itself invested us with such jurisdiction. [It] will be remembered that, on that occasion, the House never directed its attention to the question how, if there were jurisdiction to grant the relief sought, discretion ought to be exercised in deciding whether or not relief should be granted.

In June [1990] we received the judgment of the Court of Justice [above] replying to the questions we had posed and affirming that we had jurisdiction, in the circumstances postulated, to grant interim relief for the protection of directly enforceable rights under Community law and that no limitation on our jurisdiction imposed by any rule of national law could stand as the sole obstacle to preclude the grant of such relief. In the light of this judgment we were able to conclude the hearing of the appeal in July and unanimously decided that relief should be granted in terms of the orders which the House then made, indicating that we would give our reasons for the decision [later].

Some public comments on the decision of the Court of Justice, affirming the jurisdiction of the courts of member states to override national legislation if necessary to enable interim relief to be granted in protection of rights under Community law, have suggested that this was a novel and dangerous invasion by a Community institution of the sovereignty of the United Kingdom Parliament. But such comments are based on a misconception. If the supremacy within the European Community of Community law over the national law of member states was not always inherent in the EEC Treaty it was certainly well established in the jurisprudence of the European Court of Justice long before the United Kingdom joined the Community. Thus, whatever limitation of its sovereignty Parliament accepted when it enacted the European Communities Act 1972 was entirely voluntary. Under the terms of the Act of 1972 it has always been clear that it was the duty of a United Kingdom court, when delivering final judgment, to override any rule of national law found to be in conflict with any directly enforceable rule of Community law. Similarly, when decisions of the European Court of Justice have exposed areas of United Kingdom statute law which failed to implement Council directives, Parliament has always loyally accepted the obligation to make appropriate and prompt amendments. Thus there is nothing in any way novel in according supremacy to rules of Community law in those areas to which they apply and to insist that, in the protection of rights under Community law, national courts must not be inhibited by rules of national law from granting interim relief in appropriate cases is no more than a logical recognition of that supremacy.

[If] the applicants were to succeed after a refusal of interim relief, the irreparable damage they would have suffered would be very great. That is now beyond dispute. On the other hand, if they failed after a grant of interim relief, there would have been a substantial detriment to the public interest resulting from the diversion of a very significant part of the British quota of controlled stocks of fish from those who ought in law to enjoy it to others having no right to it. In either case, if the final decision did not accord with the interim decision, there would have been an undoubted injustice. But the injustices are so different in kind that I find it very difficult to weigh the one against the other.

[Unlike] the ordinary case in which the court must decide whether or not to grant interlocutory relief at a time when disputed issues of fact remain unresolved, here the relevant facts are all ascertained and the only unresolved issues are issues of law, albeit of Community law. Now, although the final decision of such issues is the exclusive prerogative of the European Court of Justice, that does not mean that an English court may not reach an informed opinion as to how such issues are likely to be resolved.'

Their Lordships were prepared to put their collective shirts on the firm favourite, namely, that the applicants had a sufficiently strong case to justify the granting of interim relief. The House, therefore, ordered that, pending final judgment the Secretary of State (whether by himself, his servants or agents, or otherwise howsoever) be restrained from withholding or withdrawing registration in the register of British fishing vessels maintained by him in respect of certain specified vessels which might be accorded protection and be granted fishing rights by Community law by the forthcoming decision of the Court of Justice. On 11 October 1990 (an important date for 'Factortame III', p. 392, and 'Factortame V', p. 392), therefore, the House of

Lords changed the United Kingdom constitution, and the Lords made an injunction against the Crown forbidding the Secretary of State to apply the Merchant Shipping Act 1988.[174]

(f) Disapplication of an Act of Parliament

The *Factortame* litigation, commencing with the seemingly innocuous matter of interim relief, led, inevitably and inexorably, to the acceptance of the fundamental rule of supremacy of Community law in that, in order to grant interim relief, the United Kingdom courts had to disapply an Act of Parliament. Once this step had been taken, it was followed as a matter of course. In *R v Secretary of State for Employment, ex p Equal Opportunities Commission*,[175] it was held that certain provisions of the Employment Protection (Consolidation) Act 1978 resulted in indirect discrimination against women and were not based upon objectively justified grounds in accordance with the test propounded by the Court of Justice[176] for determining whether or not measures involving indirect discrimination were an infringement of article 119 of the Treaty. Consequently, it was agreed that declarations should be made that the provisions of the Employment Protection (Consolidation) Act 1978 whereby employees working for fewer than 16 hours per week were, in respect of qualification for redundancy pay or in respect of the right to compensation for unfair dismissal, treated less favourably than employees working for 16 hours per week or more were incompatible with article 119 of the Treaty, the Equal Pay Directive, and the Equal Treatment Directive. Some years later, in *Lawrence v Regent Office Care*[177] it was accepted as common ground that article 141 (ex 119) on equal pay conferred directly enforceable rights on citizens of member states and that its effect, read with the European Communities Act 1972, was to require the disapplication of any incompatible provisions of the Equal Pay Act 1970.

(g) State liability

One judicial remedy which is common to the public law of all member states is that of awarding damages for wrongful acts of the state and its agents. Therefore, the question had to be raised whether an individual may claim damages for any pecuniary or other loss the person may have suffered as a result of a failure by a member state to fulfil a Community obligation. If the intention of Community legislation is to confer rights on individuals then, in one sense, direct effect is irrelevant. The fact that a provision of a directive is not unconditional or sufficiently precise has the result that the directive cannot be directly effective and asserted against the member states, but, on principle, does not negate the intention to confer those

---

[174] See Sir John Laws [1995] PL 72. On interim measures, injunctions and the adequacy of damages, see *R v Secretary of State for Health, ex p Generics and Squibb* [1997] EWCA Civ 1058; *R v Social Security Commissioner, ex p Snares*, Decision R(DLA) 4/99, [1997] EWHC 317 (Admin); *The International Transport Workers' Federation and The Finnish Seamen's Union v Viking Line* [2005] EWCA Civ 1299.

[175] [1995] 1 AC 1.   [176] *Bilka-Kaufhaus GmbH v Weber von Hartz* [1986] ECR 1607.

[177] [2000] EWCA Civ 196. See also *Imperial Chemical Industries v Colmer* [1999] UKHL 48; *Perceval Price, Davey and Brown v Department of Economic Development, Department of Health and Social Services and Her Majesty's Attorney-General for Northern Ireland* [2000] NICA 9.

rights. Furthermore, should the Commission (or another member state) bring an action under article 169 (now 226) (or 170 (now 227)) and the Court of Justice finds against the member state, a further obligation is imposed on the defaulting member state by article 171 (now 228) (see head VI(b)). In these cases the obligation is to take the necessary measures to carry out the obligations to the full and it may happen that until those obligations are in fact carried out, individuals who should have benefited from a correct implementation by the member state have been caused pecuniary or other loss by that failure. This issue was faced in:

Francovich, Bonifaci v Republic of Italy cases **C-6, 9/90** [1991] ECR 1–5357

Directive 80/987 was adopted in order to provide employed workers with a Community minimum level of protection in the event of the insolvency of their employer and, in particular, it provided for specific guarantees of payments of workers' outstanding claims relating to remuneration and the establishment of bodies (guarantee institutions) liable to meet those claims. Member states were obliged to implement the directive by 23 October 1983. As Italy, once again, did not fulfil the obligation, the Commission finally brought an action under article 169 and the Court of Justice once again found that Italy had failed to comply with a Treaty obligation (*Commission v Italy* [1989] ECR 143). Francovich had been employed by a company in Vicenza and had only received part payment of his salary at sporadic intervals. He sued the company before the Pretura di Vicenza which found the company liable for the sum of some 6m lire. The Vicenza court was unable to enforce judgment against the company and Francovich, therefore, relied on his entitlement provided for by Directive 80/987 to obtain the guarantee payment. Bonifaci and other workers brought an action before the Pretura di Bassano del Grappa, stating that they had been employed by a company which had been declared bankrupt on 5 April 1985. When the employment relationship came to an end, the plaintiffs were owed more than 253m lire. More than five years after the bankruptcy they had received no payment and the official dealing with the bankruptcy stated that payment of even part of the sum owed was utterly improbable. Consequently, the plaintiffs brought proceedings against Italy requesting, in the light of the obligation imposed on Italy to implement Directive 80/987 as from 23 October 1983, that Italy be ordered to pay the claimed payments of unpaid remuneration, at least for the last three months, or failing that, that Italy be ordered to pay them monetary compensation. Both national courts referred, inter alia, to the Court of Justice the following question, identical in both cases, for a preliminary ruling:

'By virtue of the Community law in force, can an individual who has suffered harm as a result of the failure by the State to implement Directive 80/987, which failure has been established by a judgment of the Court of Justice, call for the implementation by the State of those provisions contained in the directive which are sufficiently precise and unconditional by invoking directly, against the Member State in default, the Community rules in order to obtain the guarantees which that Member State has to ensure, and, in any event, to claim compensation for the damage suffered in respect of provisions which do not have that character?'

The Court stated in reply to the first part of the question that the provisions of Directive 80/987 which define the rights of workers were not sufficiently precise and unconditional to pass the 'direct effect test' (see p. 357) and that the parties could not rely on those rights against the member state before the national courts, when the state had failed to take the necessary measures to implement the directive within the prescribed period.

The European Court of Justice:

'28. In the second part of the [question] the national court seeks to determine whether a Member State is obliged to make good loss and damage suffered by individuals as a result of the failure to transpose Directive 80/987.

29. The national court thus raises the issue of the existence and scope of a State's liability for loss and damages resulting from breach of its obligations under Community law.

30. That issue must be considered in the light of the general system of the Treaty and its fundamental principles.

(a) The existence of State liability as a matter of principle

31. It should be borne in mind at the outset that the EEC Treaty has created its own legal system, which is integrated into the legal systems of the Member States and which their courts are bound to apply. The subjects of that legal system are not only the Member States, but also their nationals. Just as it imposes burdens on individuals, Community law is also intended to give rise to rights which become part of their legal patrimony. Those rights arise not only where they are expressly granted by the Treaty but also by virtue of obligations which the Treaty imposes in a clearly defined manner both on individuals and on the Member States and the Community institutions (see [*van Gend*, p. 351 and *Costa*, p. 323]).

32. Furthermore, it has been consistently held that the national courts whose task it is to apply the provisions of Community law in areas within their jurisdiction must ensure that those rules take full effect and must protect the rights which they confer on individuals (see in particular [*Simmenthal*, p. 349]).

33. The full effectiveness of Community rules would be impaired and the protection of the rights which they grant would be weakened if individuals were unable to obtain redress when their rights are infringed by a breach of Community law for which a Member State can be held responsible.

34. The possibility of obtaining redress from the Member State is particularly indispensable when, as in this case, the full effectiveness of Community rules is subject to prior action on the part of the State and where, consequently, in the absence of such action, individuals cannot enforce before the national courts the rights conferred upon them by Community law.

35. It follows that the principle whereby a State must be liable for loss and damage caused to individuals as a result of breaches of Community law for which the State can be held responsible is inherent in the system of the Treaty.

36. A further basis for the obligation of Member States, to make good such loss and damage is to be found in Article 5 [now 10] of the Treaty, under which the Member States are required to take all appropriate measures, whether general or particular, to ensure fulfilment of their obligations under Community law. Among these is the obligation to nullify the unlawful consequences of a breach of Community [law].

37. It follows from all the foregoing that it is a principle of Community law that the Member States are obliged to make good loss and damage caused to individuals by breaches of Community law for which they can be held responsible.

(b) The conditions for State liability

38. Although State liability is thus required by Community law, the conditions under which that liability gives rise to a right to reparation depend on the nature of the breach of Community law giving rise to the loss and damage.

39. When, as in this case, a Member State fails to fulfil its obligation under [Article 189 (now 249)] to take all the measures necessary to achieve the result prescribed by a directive, the full effectiveness of that rule of Community law requires that there should be a right to reparation provided that three conditions are fulfilled.

40. The first of these conditions is that the result prescribed by the directive should entail the grant of rights to individuals. The second condition is that it should be possible to identify the content of those rights on the basis of the provisions of the directive. Finally, the third condition is the existence of

a causal link between the breach of the State's obligation and the loss and damage suffered by the injured parties.

41. Those conditions are sufficient to give rise to a right on the part of individuals to obtain reparation, a right founded directly on Community law.

42. Subject to that reservation, it is on the basis of the rules of national law on liability that the State must make reparation for the consequences of the loss and damage caused. In the absence of Community legislation, it is for the internal legal order of each Member State to designate the competent courts and lay down the detailed procedural rules for legal proceedings intended fully to safeguard the rights which individuals derive from Community [law].

. . .

44. In this case, the breach of Community law by a Member State by virtue of its failure to transpose Directive 80/987 within the prescribed period has been confirmed by a judgment of the Court. The result required by that directive entails the grant to employees of a right to a guarantee of payment of their unpaid wage claims. As is clear from the examination of the first part of the [question], the content of that right can be identified on the basis of the provisions of the directive.

45. Consequently, the national courts must, in accordance with the national rules on liability, uphold the right of employees to obtain reparation for the loss and damage caused to them as a result of failure to transpose the directive.

46. The answer to be given to the national court must therefore be that a Member State is required to make good loss and damage caused to individuals by failure to transpose Directive 80/987.'

It is now well settled that the 'state' must make reparation for the consequences of the loss and damage caused. The principle holds good for any breach by a 'member state', whatever be the national public authority organ (legislative, executive or judicial) whose act or omission was responsible for the breach. It is for each member state to ensure that individuals obtain reparation for loss and damage caused to them by non-compliance with Community law, whichever public authority is responsible for the breach and whichever public authority is in principle, under the law of the member state concerned, responsible for making reparation. Member states cannot escape that liability either by pleading the internal distribution of powers and responsibilities as between the bodies which exist within their national legal order or by claiming that the public authority responsible for the breach of Community law did not have the necessary powers, knowledge, means or resources. As regards member states with a federal structure, if the procedural arrangements in the domestic system enable the rights which individuals derive from the Community legal system to be effectively protected and it is not more difficult to assert those rights than the rights which they derive from the domestic legal system, reparation for loss and damage caused to individuals by national measures taken in breach of Community law need not necessarily be provided by the federal state in order for the Community law obligations of the member state concerned to be fulfilled.[178] The application of what is stated above to the judicial authority of the state is considered in *Köbler* (p. 386) and *Traghetti* (p. 387) and raises the (hopefully hypothetical) scenario of the House of Lords determining, without requesting a preliminary ruling, that a directive was not sufficiently clear, precise and unconditional as to be directly effective, that, therefore, individuals could not rely on the directive, that those individuals were not entitled to the benefits conferred by the directive, and that the House's determination was subsequently followed by a ruling by the

[178] *Konle v Austria* [1999] ECR I-3099.

Court of Justice that the directive was in fact directly effective:

....

Köbler v Austria case C-224/01 [2003] ECR I-10239

Köbler brought an action against Austria for breach of a provision of Community law by a judgment of the *Verwaltungsgerichtshof* (Supreme Administrative Court).

The European Court of Justice

'Principle of State liability

30. First, as the Court has repeatedly held, the principle of liability on the part of a Member State for damage caused to individuals as a result of breaches of Community law for which the State is responsible is inherent in the system of the [Treaty].

31. The Court has also held that that principle applies to any case in which a Member State breaches Community law, whichever is the authority of the Member State whose act or omission was responsible for the [breach].

32. In international law a State which incurs liability for breach of an international commitment is viewed as a single entity, irrespective of whether the breach which gave rise to the damage is attributable to the legislature, the judiciary or the executive. That principle must apply a fortiori in the Community legal order since all State authorities, including the legislature, are bound in performing their tasks to comply with the rules laid down by Community law which directly govern the situation of [individuals].

33. In the light of the essential role played by the judiciary in the protection of the rights derived by individuals from Community rules, the full effectiveness of those rules would be called in question and the protection of those rights would be weakened if individuals were precluded from being able, under certain conditions, to obtain reparation when their rights are affected by an infringement of Community law attributable to a decision of a court of a Member State adjudicating at last instance.

34. It must be stressed, in that context, that a court adjudicating at last instance is by definition the last judicial body before which individuals may assert the rights conferred on them by Community law. Since an infringement of those rights by a final decision of such a court cannot thereafter normally be corrected, individuals cannot be deprived of the possibility of rendering the State liable in order in that way to obtain legal protection of their rights.

35. Moreover, it is, in particular, in order to prevent rights conferred on individuals by Community law from being infringed that [a] court against whose decisions there is no judicial remedy under national law is required to make a reference to the Court of Justice.

36. Consequently, it follows from the requirements inherent in the protection of the rights of individuals relying on Community law that they must have the possibility of obtaining redress in the national courts for the damage caused by the infringement of those rights owing to a decision of a court adjudicating at last [instance].

37. Certain of the governments which submitted observations in these proceedings claimed that the principle of State liability for damage caused to individuals by infringements of Community law could not be applied to decisions of a national court adjudicating at last instance. In that connection arguments were put forward based, in particular, on the principle of [the] independence and authority of the [judiciary].

. . .

42. As to the independence of the judiciary, the principle of liability in question concerns not the personal liability of the judge but that of the State. The possibility that under certain conditions the State may be rendered liable for judicial decisions contrary to Community law does not appear to entail any particular risk that the independence of a court adjudicating at last instance will be called in question.

. . .

50. It follows from the foregoing that the principle according to which the Member States are liable to afford reparation of damage caused to individuals as a result of infringements of Community law for which they are responsible is also applicable where the alleged infringement stems from a decision of a court adjudicating at last instance. It is for the legal system of each Member State to designate the court competent to adjudicate on disputes relating to such reparation.

Conditions governing State liability

51. As to the conditions to be satisfied for a Member State to be required to make reparation for loss and damage caused to individuals as a result of breaches of Community law for which the State is responsible, the Court has held that these are threefold: the rule of law infringed must be intended to confer rights on individuals; the breach must be sufficiently serious; and there must be a direct causal link between the breach of the obligation incumbent on the State and the loss or damage sustained by the injured [parties].

52. State liability for loss or damage caused by a decision of a national court adjudicating at last instance which infringes a rule of Community law is governed by the same conditions.

53. With regard more particularly to the second of those conditions and its application with a view to establishing possible State liability owing to a decision of a national court adjudicating at last instance, regard must be had to the specific nature of the judicial function and to the legitimate requirements of legal certainty, as the Member States which submitted observations in this case have also contended. State liability for an infringement of Community law by a decision of a national court adjudicating at last instance can be incurred only in the exceptional case where the court has manifestly infringed the applicable law.

54. In order to determine whether that condition is satisfied, the national court hearing a claim for reparation must take account of all the factors which characterise the situation put before it.

55. Those factors include, in particular, the degree of clarity and precision of the rule infringed, whether the infringement was intentional, whether the error of law was excusable or inexcusable, the position taken, where applicable, by a Community institution and non-compliance by the court in question with its obligation to make a reference for a preliminary [ruling].

56. In any event, an infringement of Community law will be sufficiently serious where the decision concerned was made in manifest breach of the case-law of the Court in the [matter].

59. In the light of all the foregoing, the reply to [the] questions must be that the principle that Member States are obliged to make good damage caused to individuals by infringements of Community law for which they are responsible is also applicable where the alleged infringement stems from a decision of a court adjudicating at last instance where the rule of Community law infringed is intended to confer rights on individuals, the breach is sufficiently serious and there is a direct causal link between that breach and the loss or damage sustained by the injured parties. In order to determine whether the infringement is sufficiently serious when the infringement at issue stems from such a decision, the competent national court, taking into account the specific nature of the judicial function, must determine whether that infringement is manifest. It is for the legal system of each Member State to designate the court competent to determine disputes relating to that reparation.'

Traghetti v Italy case C-173/03 [2006] ECR I-5177

The European Court of Justice

'30. [It should be noted that, in *Köbler*, p. 386], the Court held that the principle that a Member State is obliged to make good damage caused to individuals as a result of breaches of Community law for which it is responsible applies to any case in which a Member State breaches Community law, whichever is the authority of the Member State whose act or omission was responsible for the [breach].

31. Basing its reasoning in that respect, inter alia, on the essential role played by the judiciary in the protection of the rights derived by individuals from Community rules and on the fact that a court adjudicating at last instance is by definition the last judicial body before which individuals may assert the rights conferred on them by Community law, the Court infers that the protection of those rights would be weakened—and the full effectiveness of the Community rules conferring such rights would be brought into question—if individuals were precluded from being able, under certain conditions, to obtain reparation when their rights are affected by an infringement of Community law attributable to a decision of a court of a Member State adjudicating at last [instance].

32. It is true that, having regard to the specific nature of the judicial function and to the legitimate requirements of legal certainty, State liability in such a case is not unlimited. As the Court has held, State liability can be incurred only in the exceptional case where the national court adjudicating at last instance has manifestly infringed the applicable law. In order to determine whether that condition is satisfied, the national court hearing a claim for reparation must take account of all the factors which characterise the situation put before it, which include, in particular, the degree of clarity and precision of the rule infringed, whether the infringement was intentional, whether the error of law was excusable or inexcusable, the position taken, where applicable, by a Community institution and non-compliance by the court in question with its obligation to make a reference for a preliminary [ruling].

33. Analogous considerations linked to the need to guarantee effective judicial protection to individuals of the rights conferred on them by Community law similarly preclude State liability not being incurred solely because an infringement of Community law attributable to a national court adjudicating at last instance arises from the interpretation of provisions of law made by that court.

34. On the one hand, interpretation of provisions of law forms part of the very essence of judicial activity since, whatever the sphere of activity considered, a court faced with divergent or conflicting arguments must normally interpret the relevant legal rules—of national and/or Community law—in order to resolve the dispute brought before it.

35. On the other hand, it is not inconceivable that a manifest infringement of Community law might be committed precisely in the exercise of such work of interpretation if, for example, the court gives a substantive or procedural rule of Community law a manifestly incorrect meaning, particularly in the light of the relevant case law of the Court on the [subject], or where it interprets national law in such a way that in practice it leads to an infringement of the applicable Community law.

36. As the Advocate General observed [in] his Opinion, to exclude all State liability in such circumstances on the ground that the infringement of Community law arises from an interpretation of provisions of law made by a court would be tantamount to rendering meaningless the principle laid down by the Court in [Köbler]. That remark is even more apposite in the case of courts adjudicating at last instance, which are responsible, at national level, for ensuring that rules of law are given a uniform interpretation.

37. An analogous conclusion must be drawn with regard to legislation which in a general manner excludes all State liability where the infringement attributable to a court of that State arises from its assessment of the facts and evidence.

38. On the one hand, such an assessment constitutes, like the interpretation of provisions of law, another essential aspect of the judicial function since, regardless of the interpretation adopted by the national court seised of a particular case, the application of those provisions to that case will often depend on the assessment which the court has made of the facts and the value and relevance of the evidence adduced for that purpose by the parties to the dispute.

39. On the other hand, such an assessment—which sometimes requires complex analysis—may also lead, in certain cases, to a manifest infringement of the applicable law, whether that assessment is made in the context of the application of specific provisions relating to the burden of proof or the weight or admissibility of the evidence, or in the context of the application of provisions which require a legal characterisation of the facts.

40. To exclude, in such circumstances, any possibility that State liability might be incurred where the infringement allegedly committed by the national court relates to the assessment which it made of

facts or evidence would also amount to depriving the principle set out in [*Köbler*] of all practical effect with regard to manifest infringements of Community law for which courts adjudicating at last instance were [responsible].

. . .

46. [The answer to the question referred by the national court for a preliminary ruling] must be that Community law precludes national legislation which excludes State liability, in a general manner, for damage caused to individuals by an infringement of Community law attributable to a court adjudicating at last instance by reason of the fact that the infringement in question results from an interpretation of provisions of law or an assessment of facts or evidence carried out by that court. Community law also precludes national legislation which limits such liability solely to cases of intentional fault and serious misconduct on the part of the court, if such a limitation were to lead to exclusion of the liability of the Member State concerned in other cases where a manifest infringement of the applicable law was [committed].'

Three conditions must be satisfied for a member state to be required to make reparation for loss and damage caused to individuals as a result of breaches of Community law for which the state can be held responsible. First, the rule of law infringed must be intended to confer rights on individuals. Second, the breach must be sufficiently serious in that the member state has 'manifestly and gravely disregarded' the limits on the exercise of its powers. A mere infringement of Community law by a member state may, but does not necessarily, constitute a sufficiently serious breach. If the member state fails to take any steps to achieve the results laid down by a directive within the prescribed time limit, that member state per se manifestly and gravely disregards the law. In order to determine whether such an infringement of Community law constitutes a sufficiently serious breach, a national court hearing a claim for reparation must take account of all the factors which characterise the situation put before it. If a member state takes steps to achieve the results laid down by a directive but those are found to be incorrect and incomplete, the factors which the Court may take into consideration include the clarity and precision of the rule breached (if the rule is imprecisely worded and is reasonably capable of bearing the interpretation given to it by the member state in good faith and on the basis of arguments which are not entirely devoid of substance, that may not be considered a serious breach), the measure of discretion left by the rule on the national authority, whether the infringement and the damage caused was intentional or involuntary, whether any error of law was excusable or inexcusable, and the fact that the position taken by a Community institution may have contributed towards the omission by not raising doubts as to the member state's implementing measures. The application of those criteria must be applied by the national courts. The fact that there is a prior judgment of the Court of Justice finding an infringement will certainly be determinative, but it is not essential for the second condition because that would make effective protection dependent on Commission action. Third, there must be a causal link between the breach of the obligation imposed on the State and the damage sustained by the injured party (it is for the national courts to determine whether there is such a link). If the conditions are met, the State must make reparation for the consequent loss or damage in accordance with the domestic rules on civil liability (and these rules must be not less favourable than those relating to similar domestic claims).[179]

---

[179] *Brasserie du Pêcheur v Germany* and *R v Secretary of State for Transport, ex parte Factortame* ('*Factortame III*') [1996] ECR I-1029; *R v HM Treasury, ex p British Telecommunications plc* [1996] ECR I-1631; *R v Ministry of Agriculture, Fisheries and Food, ex p Hedley Lomas* [1996] ECR I-2553; *Dillenkofer and Others v Germany* [1996] ECR I-4845; *Norbrook Laboratories v MAFF* [1998] ECR I-1531; *Haim* [2000] ECR I-5123; *Larsy* [2001] ECR I-5063.

Henceforth, the United Kingdom must make reparation for the consequences of any loss and damage caused in accordance with the domestic rules on liability. The first question for the courts of the United Kingdom was to decide how it would be possible, in domestic law, to establish the liability of the state for the non-implementation of an obligation imposed by Community law, especially an obligation imposed by a Treaty article. In the common law, there is no general theory of the liability of the state, and the causes of action for the non-fulfilment of a duty (the action for breach of statutory duty, where a duty is imposed on a public authority by statute or regulation, and an action for misfeasance in public office, where there is a complaint that a public authority has abused its power) were not entirely suitable, especially when the claim for damages was alleged to be the result of primary legislation. There was a need to look for a remedy or cause of action imposed by Community law, which by virtue of the European Communities Act 1972, became part of domestic law. The answer of the common law was simple. The two causes of action and remedies, breach of statutory duty and misfeasance in public office, as is the case with the majority of actions in civil liability (the law of torts, both public and private), were created, over the centuries, by the judges of the common law. Why not create a new cause of action, analogous to breach of statutory duty, to take account of the *Francovich* and *Factortame* case law, that cause of action being a claim for damages for breach of a statutory duty, that duty being imposed by Community law, or for the infringement of a right, that right being created by Community law, the Community law involved being rendered part of domestic law by virtue of the European Communities Act 1972.[180]

For there to be state liability, the breach must be sufficiently serious in that the member state has 'manifestly and gravely disregarded' the limits on the exercise of its powers:

....

R v Ministry of Agriculture, Fisheries and Food, ex p Lay and Gage
[1998] EWHC 1 (Admin)

The applicants had claimed that the Ministry had misinterpreted a Council Regulation on milk quota and thereby had reduced the quota allocated to the applicants. Questions on interpretation were referred to the European Court of Justice. Although the Commission and the Council supported the United Kingdom's interpretation, the Court of Justice agreed with the applicant (*R v Ministry of Agriculture, Fisheries and Food, ex p Lay and Gage* [1997] ECR I-1195). The United Kingdom had, therefore, been in breach of a Community obligation.

Latham J

'14. [The] debate is over the meaning to be given to the phrase "sufficiently serious" and its application to the facts of this case. The respondent argues that the United Kingdom's misinterpretation, as found by the Court, of the Regulation was an inadvertent excusable error of law in relation to an unclear and imprecise provision of Community law as to which there was no judgment of the Court or previous settled case law, and that it accorded with the view of the proper meaning to be given to the Regulation by both the Commission and the Council. The [respondent] submits its misinterpretation of the

---

[180] *Bourgoin v Ministry of Agriculture, Fisheries and Food* [1986] QB 716; *Three Rivers District Council v Governor and Company of the Bank of England* [1977] 3 CMLR 429; *R v Secretary of State for Transport, ex p Factortame* [1999] EWHC 755 (Admin).

Regulation cannot on any sensible basis be described as a manifest and grave breach of Community law so as to satisfy the second [condition].

. . .

22. A serious fault, defined as a breach of a clear provision of Community law (or of a provision already interpreted by the Court) or a repeated breach—or a breach in which a Member State persists despite a judgment declaring that it has failed to fulfil its obligations—ought, without any doubt, to render the State [liable].

. . .

28. The respondent, on the other hand, points out that the Advocate General acknowledged that the applicable legislation was somewhat complex [and acknowledged] that the definitions provided for "areas under forage" and "producer" were not such as to make clear once and for all what was meant by the phrase "areas under forage". [Further], the fact that the Commission and Council supported the respondent's interpretation establishes that the respondent's view was not an aberrant or irrational one.

29. In my view the respondent's argument is correct. The respondent acted bona fide, and made an excusable mistake as to the interpretation of a legislative provision which was not clear or [precise].

30. For these reasons the applicants do not have any rights to claim damages for the breach of Community law which has been committed by the respondent in these cases.'

....

Re Burns [1999] NIQB 5

Burns sought, inter alia, a declaration that the United Kingdom was in breach of its obligation to transpose into domestic law the Directive on the Organisation of Working Time (Directive 93/104/EC) whereby each member state was required to adopt the laws, regulations and administrative procedures necessary to implement the Directive by 23 November 1996. She sought damages for the harm (including loss of employment) which she claimed to have suffered as a result of the failure of the United Kingdom to enact legislation giving effect to the Directive. In March 1994, the United Kingdom had applied to the European Court of Justice requesting that the Directive be annulled in whole or in part. On 12 November 1996, that application was dismissed (*United Kingdom of Great Britain and Northern Ireland v Council of the European Union* [1996] ECR I-5755). Thereafter, proposals for the implementation of the Directive were made and the Working Time Regulations 1998 (SI 1998/1833) were made on 30 July 1998 and came into force on 1 October 1998.

Kerr J

'25. The applicant relied on the decision in [*Dillenkofer v Bundesrepublik Deutschland* [1996] ECR I-4845]. It was submitted that this established that the failure to transpose a Directive in order to achieve the result it prescribes is per se a serious breach of Community [law].

. . .

27. [In *Dillenkofer* the Court said, at para 29]: "failure to take any measure to transpose a directive in order to achieve the result it prescribes within the period laid down for that purpose constitutes per se a serious breach of Community law and consequently gives rise to a right of reparation for individuals suffering injury if the result prescribed by the directive entails the grant to individuals of rights whose content is identifiable and a causal link exists between the breach of the state's obligation and the loss and damage suffered".

28. I consider that this passage is clear in its effect. If a member state does not transpose a directive within the proscribed period, it is in automatic and serious breach of Community law and, therefore, liable for an injury suffered by an individual who suffers loss and damage in consequence.

R v Secretary of State for Transport, ex p Factortame ('Factortame V')
[2000] 1 AC 524

On 25 July 1991, in *R v Secretary of State for Transport, ex p Factortame ('Factortame II')* [1991] ECR I-3905 and *Commission v United Kingdom* [1991] ECR I-4607, it was held that the member state cannot stipulate that a certain percentage of owners, shareholders and directors be nationals of that member state or that owners, shareholders and directors be resident and domiciled in that member state. Therefore both the nationality and the residence conditions (see p. 378) were incompatible with Community law, and, in particular, article 52 (right of establishment). In *Brasserie du Pêcheur SA v Federal Republic of Germany, R v Secretary of State for Transport, ex p Factortame ('Factortame III')* [1996] ECR I-1029, the Court held that, in the event of infringement of a right directly conferred by a Community provision upon which individuals are entitled to rely before the national courts, 'the right to reparation is the necessary corollary of the direct effect of the Community provision whose breach caused the damage sustained' (paragraph 22). Furthermore, 'Community law confers a right to reparation where three conditions are met: the rule of law infringed must be intended to confer rights on individuals; the breach must be sufficiently serious; and there must be a direct causal link between the breach of the obligation resting on the State and the damage sustained by the injured parties' (paragraph 51). The Court held that the first condition was 'manifestly satisfied' in the case of article 52 of the Treaty. 'The essence of article 52 is to confer rights on individuals' and this article has direct effect in the sense that it confers 'on individuals rights upon which they are entitled to rely directly before the national courts' (paragraphs 23 and 54). It was common ground between the government of the United Kingdom and the plaintiffs that article 52 conferred on the plaintiffs rights upon which they were entitled to rely directly before the United Kingdom courts. The Court held that, as 'for the third condition, it is for the national courts to determine whether there is a direct causal link between the breach of the obligation borne by the State and the damage sustained by the injured parties' (paragraph 65). In *Factortame*, there were 97 plaintiffs. The determination whether there was a direct causal link between the breach of the obligation and the losses claimed to have been sustained by the 97 plaintiffs, the calculation of any damages and costs, all depend on the individual circumstances of each plaintiff. Therefore the Divisional Court, the Court of Appeal and the House of Lords decided to postpone judgment with regard to the third condition. It was more important to give judgment on the second condition. The Divisional Court and the Court of Appeal were unanimous. They made four important rulings:

With regard to the nationality condition, it was held that such a condition was a direct violation of a fundamental principle of the Treaty, a direct discrimination manifestly contrary to Community law, 'almost inevitably' creating a liability for damages. With regard to the nationality condition, therefore, there was a liability to pay damages from the coming into force of the Merchant Shipping Act 1988 until 1 November 1989, when the nationality condition was abolished (p. 378).

With regard to the residence condition it was held that this 'indirect discrimination' must be regarded as a manifest and grave disregard, thus creating a liability for damages. With regard to the residence condition, therefore, there was a liability to pay damages from the coming into force of the Merchant Shipping Act 1988 until 11 October 1990, the date of the injunction against the Crown by the House of Lords (p. 381).

With regard to the opinion of the European Commission, it was held that, even though it is for the European Court of Justice to determine questions of community law, the role of the Commission must be given very serious respect.

With regard to the failure to adopt immediately the measures needed to comply with the order of the President of the Court of 10 October 1989 (p. 378), that order being mandatory and having immediate effect, the Secretary of State accepted and it was held that this failure should be regarded as constituting in itself a manifest and, therefore, sufficiently serious breach of Community law to give rise to liability for any damage caused.

Lord Slynn, at 530–549

'[The] question on this appeal is whether the appellant's breaches of Community law were sufficiently serious to give rise under Community law to a right to compensatory damages to those who can show that the breach caused them damage. Any question of causation has been left over pending a determination as to the seriousness of the breach for the purpose of Community law. The Divisional Court and the Court of Appeal unanimously held that the breaches were sufficiently serious for that [purpose].

The appellant contends, however, that the Divisional Court and the Court of Appeal were wrong in their conclusions that there had been a sufficiently serious breach of Community law. In summary it is said that here the United Kingdom was adopting legislation to deal with a serious economic problem. In deciding what to do it had a wide measure of discretion and damages can only be awarded if there is a manifest and grave disregard of its powers; to impose liability otherwise would be to inhibit legislative action which was necessary. Even where there is a breach of Community law there can be no liability to compensate where the breach was excusable. Here the breach was excusable since the law was not clear until the judgment in *Factortame II* [and] there were substantial objective grounds to justify what was done when regard is had both to the existence of the common fisheries policy, which is intended to provide national quotas which member states are entitled to protect, and to a state's rights under international law to decide who should be entitled to register a vessel on its register and to fly its national [flag].

[The] basic approach is clear. Before a member state can be held liable, a national court must find (i) that the relevant rule of Community law is one which is intended to confer rights on individuals; (ii) the breach must be sufficiently serious; (iii) there must be a direct causal link between the breach and the loss or damage complained of. That condition (i) is satisfied is rightly accepted by the appellant; (iii) is deferred if the respondents succeed on (ii). The question, therefore, is what constitutes being "sufficiently serious" and whether the Divisional Court and the Court of Appeal were right to hold that the breaches here were sufficiently [serious].

In *Factortame III* [paragraphs 55 and 56 the Court said:]

"55. As to the second condition, as regards both Community liability [and] member state liability for breaches of Community law, the decisive test for finding that a breach of Community law is sufficiently serious is whether the member state or the Community institution concerned manifestly and gravely disregarded the limits on its discretion. 56. The factors which the competent court may take into consideration include the clarity and precision of the rule breached, the measure of discretion left by that rule to the national or Community authorities, whether the infringement and the damage caused was intentional or involuntary, whether any error of law was excusable or inexcusable, the fact that the position taken by a Community institution may have contributed towards the omission, and the adoption or retention of national measures or practices contrary to Community [law]."

More recent cases show the working out of these rules. Thus in *R v HM Treasury, ex p British Telecommunications* [[1966] ECR I-1631], the court held that where the interpretation adopted by the United Kingdom was arguable on the basis of an imprecisely worded article of the relevant directive and where there was no case law to give guidance the state was not liable in damages. In *R v Ministry of Agriculture Fisheries and Food, ex p Hedley Lomas* [[1996] ECR I-2553], where there was no or very little room for discretion in granting a licence, that could in itself be a sufficiently serious breach. In *Dillenkofer v Germany* [[1996] ECR I-4845], it was held that a failure to implement a directive, where no or little question of legislative choice was involved, the mere infringement may constitute a sufficiently serious breach. In *Denkavit Internationaal BV v Bundesamt für Finanzen* [[1996] ECR I-5063], the court held that other member states, after discussion with the Council had adopted the same interpretation of the directive as Germany and as there was no relevant case law of the court it was held that the breach was not sufficiently serious. It was also clear from the cases that it is not necessary to establish fault or negligence on the part of the member state going beyond what is relevant to show a sufficiently serious breach.

In the present case, the United Kingdom was entitled to consider how it would exercise the margin of discretion left to it under Community law in the application of the common fisheries policy and in particular of the quota system and also, subject to those limits, how it would exercise its rights under international law to provide for registration as a British fishing vessel. Although the [nationality and residence conditions held in *Factortame II* to] be a breach of the Treaty taken in conjunction reflect what the British government was seeking to do, for the purposes of liability to compensate, the conditions have been considered separately. The first question is, therefore, whether in imposing a nationality requirement the United Kingdom committed a sufficiently serious breach in that it had manifestly and gravely disregarded the limits of its discretion.

In the first place it is to be noted that the relevant rule of Community law is not to be found in an ambiguous directive but in a clear and fundamental provision of the Treaty. By article 7 it is provided: "Within the scope of application of this Treaty and without prejudice to any special provision contained therein, any discrimination on the grounds of nationality shall be [prohibited]". It is obvious that what was done here by the government was not done inadvertently. It was done after anxious consideration and after taking legal advice. I accept that it was done in good faith and with the intention of protecting British fishing communities rather than with the deliberate intention of harming Spanish fishermen and those non-British citizens with financial stakes in British registered fishing vessels. The inevitable result of the policy adopted, however, was to take away or seriously affect their rights to fish against the British quota. The nationality condition was obviously discriminatory and in breach of article 52 as *Factortame II* [decided]. Although the question whether this was a sufficiently serious breach justifying the award of damages is a matter for the national courts, and therefore for your Lordships, to decide it is to be noted that in *Factortame III* [paragraph 61] the European Court stated bluntly that the nationality condition constituted direct discrimination which was manifestly contrary to Community law.

Can it be said that, even if the Act was deliberately adopted, it was an unintentional and "excusable" breach which should prevent what was done being "a sufficiently serious breach" in that it was a manifest and grave disregard of the limits of the United Kingdom's discretion?

The appellant relies on the history of the discussions leading up to the enactment of the 1988 Act and the making of regulations under it. He explains the problem and the understandable aim of seeking to protect British fishing communities and the British quota. Licensing rules having not been adequate, the only solution they felt was to change the rules on registration by primary [legislation]. They were, however, aware from the beginning of the legal problems [involved]. Officials and ministers were clearly aware that there was a risk that if the legislation was adopted it would be held to be contrary to Community [law].

On 31 March 1987 the Law Officers advised: "that there is a reasonably good prospect that the proposed legislation would be upheld by the European Court". On 18 November 1988 Mr Advocate-General Mischo gave his opinion [in *Jaderow* [1989] ECR 4509, at paragraph 7] that: "Community law does not therefore restrict the power which each member state has under public international law to determine the conditions on which it allows a vessel to fly its [flag]".

On the other hand, it is to be remembered that the power of member states in this area is subject to the extensive control exercised by the Community institutions under the common fisheries policy. On 28 March 1988, before the Bill received the royal assent, the Commission (DG XV) told the United Kingdom government that the proposed conditions were prima facie contrary to the right of establishment under article 52. The Commission continued to state its opposition to the nationality condition and subsequently to the domicile and residence conditions. The article 169 proceedings against the United Kingdom in respect of the nationality condition, led to the president's order of 10 October 1989 as an interim measure suspending that [condition].

How far the views of the Commission ought to be taken into account has been much debated in argument. The Divisional Court [said]: "Where there is a doubt about the legality of any proposal, a failure by a member state to seek the views of the Commission or, if it receives them, to follow them is likely to lead to any breach being regarded as inexcusable and so manifest". The Court of Appeal [added]: "If a member state [proceeds on its course despite the opinion of the Commission] and it subsequently transpires that this was a course which should not have been followed, the fact that the Commission's advice has not been followed, strengthens the case of those who seek damages for the loss that they have suffered". The appellant contends that the Court of Appeal and the Divisional Court have overstated the importance of the Commission's role.

It is in my view clear that the views of the Commission are not conclusive (a) as to whether there has been a breach of Community law and (b) as to whether the breach is a sufficiently serious breach to justify an award of damages. The former is as a last resort for the European Court in proceedings under article 169 or on a reference under article 177 and the latter is for the national court. The considered view of the Commission in a case of this kind, where the Community has a substantial role, is however of importance. Indeed in an area so closely subject to Community control as is the common fisheries policy, it is not only wise but often a necessary step to consult the Commission. The government did here consult the Commission. A member state may choose to ignore the advice given but if it does so, it incurs the risk that, if it proves to be wrong and the Commission to be right, the member state will be found to have gone ahead deliberately, well aware of the Commission's views, and that a court will be more likely to find that the breach has been manifest and grave and thus sufficiently serious. In the present case, the Commission's view was firm, consistent and hostile to the [government].

Accordingly, despite the arguments of the United Kingdom and the advice it received, it seems to me clear that the deliberate adoption of legislation which was clearly discriminatory on the ground of nationality and which inevitably violated article 52 of the Treaty (since it prevented establishment in the United Kingdom) was a manifest breach of fundamental treaty obligations. It was a grave breach of the Treaty both intrinsically and as regards the consequences it was bound, or at the least was most likely, to have on the respondents. It has not been shown to have been excusable. The Commission opposed it and [there] was no decision of the European Court to support the government. What was done, therefore, in regard to nationality plainly constituted a sufficiently serious breach for the purposes of the second condition of [liability].

As to residence, the European Court said in [*Factortame III*]:

"62. The latter conditions are prima facie incompatible with article 52 of the Treaty in particular, but the United Kingdom sought to justify them in terms of the objectives of the common fisheries policy. In the judgment in *Factortame II*, the Court rejected that justification.

63. In order to determine whether the breach of article 52 thus committed by the United Kingdom was sufficiently serious, the national court might take into account, inter alia, the legal disputes relating to particular features of the common fisheries policy, the attitude of the Commission, which made its position known to the United Kingdom in good time, and the assessments as to the state of certainty of Community law made by the national courts in the interim proceedings brought by individuals affected by the Merchant Shipping Act."

I have had some doubt about the condition as to residence. If the aim of protecting the livelihood of British fishing communities, including allied trades such as preparing and processing landed fish, is justified then it is arguable that to require active fishermen to live in these communities might be excusable. The condition here was not, however, limited to such fishermen or to such areas. It covered shareholders and directors of companies owning fishing vessels. It allowed the fishermen to live anywhere. It seems to me that this condition cannot be justified where the discrimination is, as it is here, [clear].

I, therefore, conclude that the United Kingdom's breach of its Community obligations by imposing and applying the conditions of nationality, domicile and residence in and pursuant to the Merchant Shipping Act 1988 was a sufficiently serious breach so as to entitle the respondents to compensation for damage directly caused by that breach. I consider also that the United Kingdom was in breach of Community law by failing to give effect to the order of the president of the European Court of 10 October 1989 until 2 November 1989 and that this also constituted a serious breach of community [obligations].'

Lord Hoffmann, at 547–549

'In passing the Merchant Shipping Act 1988 the United Kingdom (acting by its legislature) took a calculated risk. It knew that there was, to put the matter at its lowest, doubt over whether the legislation contravened fundamental principles of Community law. The European Commission had expressed the clear view that it infringed the rights of establishment of citizens of other member states and their right to invest in United Kingdom companies. The U.K. government knew that the effect of the legislation would be to cause substantial losses to the owners of boats which they could no longer use for fishing under the British flag. It could have delayed implementation of the legislation until there had been an authoritative ruling on whether it was [lawful. In] the end, the United Kingdom was held to have been [wrong. The] question is now whether they are entitled to compensation. [There] is no doubt that in discriminating against non-U.K. Community nationals on the grounds of their [nationality], the legislature was prima facie flouting one of the most basic principles of Community law. The responsible Ministers considered, on the basis of the advice they had received, that there was an arguable case for holding that the United Kingdom was entitled to do so. In that sense, the Divisional Court has held that the Government acted bona fide. But they could have been in no doubt that there was a substantial risk that they were wrong. Nevertheless, they saw the political imperatives of the time as justifying immediate action. In these circumstances, I do not think that the United Kingdom, having deliberately decided to run the risk, can say that the losses caused by the legislation should lie where they fell. Justice requires that the wrong should be made good. The Solicitor-General argued that the breach of Community law was excusable on the grounds that the government acted upon legal advice. He relied in particular on the written opinion given by Mr. Francis Jacobs Q.C. and others in February 1987. I do not think that a member state can rely simply upon the fact that its relevant organ of government acted upon legal advice. It is a basic principle of Community law that in considering the liabilities of a member state, all its various organs of government are treated as a single aggregate entity. It does not matter how their responsibilities are divided under domestic law or what passed between them. Likewise, as it seems to me, the process of advice and consultation undertaken within a member state by its responsible organs of government is [irrelevant]. I would dismiss the appeal.'

Lord Hope, at 550–552

'[It] is a novel task for the courts of this country to have to assess whether a breach is sufficiently serious to entitle a party who has suffered loss as a result of it to damages. The general rule is that where a breach of duty has been established and a causal link between the breach and the loss suffered has been proved the injured party is entitled as of right to damages. In the present context however the rules are different. The facts must be examined in order that the court may determine whether the breach of Community law was of such a kind that damages should be awarded as compensation for the loss. The phrases "sufficiently serious" and "manifestly and gravely" which the European Court has used indicate that a fairly high threshold must be passed before it can be said that the test has been [satisfied].

The Solicitor General laid great stress on the point made by the European Court that one of the factors which could be taken into account in the assessment of seriousness was whether or not the breach was excusable. Much importance was attached by him to the legal advice which had been taken and received. But I was not impressed by this argument. The good faith of the Government is not in question. It is not suggested that it proceeded without taking advice, or that it acted directly contrary to the advice which it received. Nor is it suggested that there was a lack of clarity in the wording of the relevant provisions of the Treaty or that there was some other point which might reasonably have been overlooked. So this case cannot, I think, be described as one which went wrong due to inadvertence, misunderstanding or oversight. The meaning of the relevant articles was never in doubt. The critical issue related to the interaction between these articles and the Common Fisheries Policy. On this matter there was clearly a serious issue to be resolved. Different views had been expressed within government, and the Commission was known to have taken a view contrary to that which the Government decided to adopt. I do not wish to be taken as suggesting that the Government should have deferred to the views of the Commission on this matter. It was clearly entitled to take a different view and to decide upon its own course. But the Commission's role, while not conclusive, was important. It was seized of the matter, and it had stated its position in terms which were unequivocal. The decision to legislate was taken by the Government in full knowledge of the risks. I find it impossible to describe that decision as having been based on an oversight or an error of law which was excusable.'

Post scriptum: when Her Majesty's Government was asked how 'they intend to meet expenditure relating to payment of claims following judgment against the UK in the *Factortame* case', the minister for the Ministry of Agriculture, Fisheries and Food replied that 'Parliamentary approval to expenditure arising from the *Factortame* case is being sought in the Main Estimate for the Ministry of Agriculture, Fisheries and Food. Pending that approval, urgent expenditure estimated at £9,735 million is being met by repayable advances from the Contingencies Fund.'[181]

---

[181] Commons *Hansard*, 4 July 2000, column 105W; Lords *Hansard*, 4 July 2000, column WA132.

8 THE PARLIAMENTARY COMMISSIONER FOR ADMINISTRATION

---

1. Government, Administration and Political Redress

As was seen in chapter 1, a modern government assumes a very full responsibility for the welfare of the nation, and, from the nineteenth century through to the present day, the role of the state has expanded enormously with regard to such matters as employment protection, housing, environmental protection, income maintenance, education, health, social services, control of the economy, transport, and so on. It may be appropriate simply to refer to the many central government departments and authorities subject to the jurisdiction of the Parliamentary Commissioner (see head IV below). Increased governmental responsibility, functions, and regulation naturally provide opportunities for conflict between the state and the citizen. The creation of public works, such as airports, reservoirs, nuclear power stations and motorways may result in the individual losing his or her land, or the creation of nuisances such as noise; the decision to locate a hostel for drug addicts in a residential area may cause immense outcries; a person may wish to appeal against refusal of planning permission; there are often disputes relating to income tax and social security benefits; there may be complaints about the standard and service of education; restrictions may be placed on how we drive, on what we do with our property and money, and we may need a licence to operate a market stall, a bingo hall or a sex shop. The modern administration may make decisions which the citizen wishes to challenge. Therefore, there must be opportunity to obtain redress against wrong decisions. The first step will almost always be to approach the relevant authority which made the original decision, giving reasons why that decision is perceived as being wrong, and seeking to persuade the authority to alter the decision in whole or in part. It can often happen that a second attempt to resolve a particular problem will be based on a clearer perspective of the issues, factual, legal and policy, than the first time round. If the authority is not minded to alter the original decision, the citizen may seek aid and comfort from two forms of independent dispute settlement.

First, and more traditional, there are the courts and tribunals which may hear appeals against administrative decisions or may pronounce upon the legality of administrative action (see chapters 9 and 10).

Second, there is the political machinery provided by the administration itself, the elected representatives of the citizen and a series of Ombudsmen, specially constructed over the last fifty years to investigate complaints and to propose a suitable remedy. In the beginning was the Parliamentary Commissioner for Administration, established following the Whyatt Report (see head II below) to deal with complaints of maladministration by central government departments. Then came the Health Service Commissioner, followed, for local and regional government, by the Commissions for Local Administration for England, Wales and Scotland, and the Northern Ireland Parliamentary Commissioner and Commissioner for Complaints. Finally, there are Ombudsmen established to deal with complaints in specific areas of modern administration, and these include the Advertising Standards Authority, the Estate Agents Ombudsman, the Financial Ombudsman, the Independent Housing Ombudsman, the Independent Review Service for the Social Fund, the Information Commissioner, the Independent Police Complaints Commission, the Legal Services Ombudsman, the Pensions Ombudsman or the Prisons and Probation Ombudsman.

This chapter concentrates on the activities of central government departments and other public authorities and redress through Parliament and the Parliamentary Commissioner for Administration. Redress through Parliament is traditionally channelled through a Member of Parliament (usually the member for the area in which the aggrieved person lives). Many members hold periodic 'surgeries' to hear complaints and many local newspapers publish the times and places where such surgeries are to be held. Conscientious members are prepared to guide people through the complicated machinery of central government decision-making and members can take up constituents' cases with the appropriate minister. If a grievance is not redressed, the member may refer the matter to the Parliamentary Commissioner for Administration.

II. The Whyatt Report

In 1959, JUSTICE, the British section of the International Commission of Jurists, set up a committee to investigate grievances against the administration of the modern administrative and welfare state in cases in which the courts had no role to play, namely, official maladministration which did not amount to an illegal exercise of power (as discussed in chapters 9 and 10). This committee published its report[1] in 1961. The Report was concerned, inter alia, with

'complaints against acts of maladministration. These are, broadly speaking, complaints aimed at official misconduct. In this type of complaint, it is a question, not of appealing from, but making accusations against, authority. [These were] complaints of official misconduct in the sense that the administrative authority responsible for the act or decision complained of has failed to observe proper standards of conduct and behaviour when exercising his administrative powers.'

The Report recommended that any inquiry into such complaints 'should be conducted by some outside authority free from the real or apparent influence of the Department'.[2] The Report considered that the administration of most government departments was satisfactory, there being few major mistakes made. However, there was a 'continuous flow of relatively minor complaints, not sufficient in themselves to attract public interest but, nevertheless, of great importance to the individuals concerned, which give rise to feelings of frustration and resentment because of the inadequacy of the existing means of seeking redress'.[3] The Report

---

[1] 'The Citizen and the Administration', the Whyatt Report.   [2] Paras 10, 72, 74–75.
[3] Paras 76–77.

considered the existing means of redress provided by the political machinery of redress through Members of Parliament. It was felt that the Parliamentary Question was inadequate since the machinery was already overloaded; the department itself did the investigating; a complainant did not have full access to documents; the MP did not have full access to documents; 'controversial matters of detail cannot be discussed satisfactorily in the short space of a single answer' and 'any attempt to prove the issues by means of supplementary questions rarely resolves the dispute and frequently heightens the atmosphere of controversy'; the Parliamentary Question was not an adequate means of redressing this type of complaint of an individual.[4] The adjournment debate procedure was inadequate since there was not much time to have many debates; again the complainant and MP did not have full access to documents; and adjournment debates were really machinery for attacking broad policy and party political matters.[5] The Report investigated complaints machinery in Sweden, Denmark, and Norway[6] and proposed the creation of a Parliamentary Commissioner for Administration to receive and investigate complaints of maladministration against government departments[7] and after some vacillation the government proposed the institution of a Parliamentary Commissioner.[8] Following this, there was enacted the Parliamentary Commissioner Act 1967, which was largely based on the Whyatt Report, and which created the office of Parliamentary Commissioner for Administration (referred to below as 'the Commissioner') 'for the purpose of conducting investigations'.

III. The Commissioner and the Select Committee

The Commissioner is appointed by Her Majesty during good behaviour and may be removed by Her Majesty in consequence of Addresses from both Houses of Parliament. The office of Commissioner may be declared vacant if the current Commissioner is incapable for medical reasons of performing the duties of the office and pending the appointment of a new Commissioner an acting Commissioner may be appointed. These provisions are similar to those relating to the appointment and security of tenure of High Court judges and are designed to ensure the Commissioner's independence from the government.[9] The Commissioner appoints the officers who will aid the Commissioner and the Commissioner may authorise any such officer to perform any of the Commissioner's functions.[10] The officers are appointed mainly, but not exclusively, from the civil service, as being the best sort of person to understand the internal workings and insider dealings of the departments to be investigated. The staff act under the close supervision of the Commissioner, visiting government departments and agencies, interviewing complainants, collecting materials and preparing documents and reports for the Commissioner.

---

[4] Paras 79–84, and see pp. 246–248.   [5] Paras 85–87.   [6] Paras 92–108, 109–127, 126–133.
[7] Paras 146–156.   [8] 1965, Cmnd 2767.
[9] Section 1, as amended by the Parliamentary and Health Service Commissioner Act 1987, section 2(1); section 3A, as inserted by the Parliamentary and Health Service Commissioner Act 1987, section 6(1).
[10] Section 3, as amended by the Parliamentary and Health Service Commissioner Act 1987, section 3.

The intention was that the Commissioner would not replace traditional question time and debates, but would give backbenchers a new and powerful weapon. The Commissioner would have powers far in excess of members and would be aided by a Select Committee of the House of Commons. First, there was the Select Committee on the Parliamentary Commissioner for Administration and, in 1997, this Committee was merged with the Public Services Committee to form the Public Administration Select Committee. The Select Committee consists of a dozen or so backbenchers (together with secretarial and other support staff). The terms of reference of the Select Committees are to examine the Commissioner's reports laid before the House of Commons. When the Committee meets, the Commissioner normally attends to hear the evidence produced and to assist the Committee. There has been a real partnership between an investigator armed with extensive powers of investigation but possibly limited powers of redress (see head VII below) and a committee of backbenchers able to raise matters in the House itself. On occasions, the Select Committee has been most supportive of the Commissioner.[11] What the Commissioner has done in the majority of situations has been to indicate to the Select Committee cases where there has been found some element of dissatisfaction (eg, rules made without any maladministration where none the less hardship was caused, where a department had not given an appropriate remedy, where there might be a need for extra publicity). The Select Committee can call the Commissioner and civil servants, such as the permanent secretary of a department or the chief executive of an agency, before it to give evidence and the evidence of these hearings is published.[12] More recently, the Committee has taken evidence from the appropriate minister in addition to the permanent secretary or chief executive. This occurred first when the Committee considered an inquiry into the Child Support Agency, as a result of a special report by the Commissioner on that agency.[13] The Committee accepted that it would be the permanent secretary or chief executive who in reality would make the important administrative decisions but followed the traditional doctrine that ministers are responsible and must be held to account for those administrative actions.[14] Furthermore, the Select Committee pressed[15] for a system whereby the government would reply to their reports (whether agreeing or rejecting them) and this system has, somewhat sporadically, been implemented.[16] The Select Committee sometimes produces general or 'thematic' reports on both wider issues and specific aspects of the Parliamentary Commissioner scheme of things.[17]

[11] 'There is ample evidence to support the Ombudsman's finding of maladministration' (Public Administration Select Committee, A Debt of Honour (HC 735 of 2005–2006)); 'The Parliamentary Commissioner is Parliament's Ombudsman: Government must respect her' (Select Committee on Public Administration, Sixth Report (HC 1081 of 2005–2006), para 79.

[12] See HC 258 of 1967–1968, Minutes of Evidence on the *Sachsenhausen* Case, 21 and 28 February 1968; HC 234 of 1971–1972, Minutes of Evidence following a Report on War Pensions (HC 587 of 1970–1971), 29 March 1972.   [13] HC 135 of 1994–1995.

[14] Report of the Select Committee on the Parliamentary Commissioner for Administration: the Child Support Agency (HC 199 of 1994–1995). On the doctrine of ministerial responsibility and the Parliamentary Commissioner, see head VIII below, and on the role of the Select Committee in the occupational pensions débâcle, see pp. 452–460.   [15] HC 513 of 1970–1971.

[16] See 1971, Cmnd 4661 in reply to HC 127 of 1969–1970 (rejecting the Select Committee's views on the extension of the Commissioner's jurisdiction); 1971, Cmnd 4729 in reply to HC 240 of 1970–1971 (accepting the Select Committee's views on the need for changes in practices by the Inland Revenue); HC 819 of 1994–95 (Response to the Report from the Select Committee on the Channel Tunnel rail link and exceptional hardship (p. 423)).

[17] See 'The Powers, Work and Jurisdiction of the Ombudsman' (HC 33 of 1993–1994); 'Maladministration and Redress' (HC 112 of 1994–1995) and Government Reply (HC 316 of 1994–1995); 'Open Government' (HC 84 of 1995–1996); 'Ombudsman Issues' (HC 448 of 2002–2003) and Government Response (Cm 5890).

IV. Jurisdiction

There is a long list of government departments and other authorities which come under the Commissioner's jurisdiction.[18] Any reference to a government department includes a reference to any of the ministers or officers of such a department and any reference to an authority includes a reference to any members or officers of such an authority.[19] The Select Committee on the Commissioner pressed for extensions to the original list of departments and bodies which were subject to the Commissioner's jurisdiction, especially with regard to non-departmental public bodies or quangos. This was accepted by the then government with regard to bodies which have executive or administrative functions which directly affect individual citizens or groups of citizens (including companies) and which would be within the Commissioner's jurisdiction if carried out by a government department and which are subject to some degree of ultimate ministerial accountability to Parliament in that they are dependent for their financing and continued existence on government policy.[20] This major extension was implemented by the Parliamentary and Health Service Commissioner Act 1987. The Select Committee maintains pressure on the government to extend the Commissioner's jurisdiction.[21] When an existing department or body is abolished (or changes its name), the appropriate reference is deleted from the Schedule.[22] When a decision is made to establish a new department or body, a decision has to be made as to whether it should come within the Commissioner's jurisdiction. If it is, the department or body is added to the Schedule.[23] The Parliamentary Commissioner Order 1999[24] added no less than 149 bodies to the Commissioner's jurisdiction.

The central government departments currently within the Commissioner's jurisdiction include the Board of Trade, Cabinet Office (in part), Department for Constitutional Affairs (including the Lord Chancellor's Department and the Public Trustee), Department for Communities and Local Government, Department for Culture, Media and Sport, Department for Education and Skills, Department for Environment, Food and Rural Affairs, Department of Health, Department for International Development, Department of Trade and Industry, Department for Transport, Department for Work and Pensions, Foreign and Commonwealth Office, Her Majesty's Revenue and Customs, Her Majesty's Treasury, Home

---

[18] Section 4, as amended by the Parliamentary and Health Service Commissioner Act 1987, section 1(1), together with Schedule 2, as substituted by the Parliamentary and Health Service Commissioner Act 1987, section 1(2), as consolidated in SI 2005/3430, and as amended by SI 2006/1926. [19] Section 4(8).

[20] Report of the Select Committee on Access to and Jurisdiction of the Commissioner (HC 615 of 1977–1978), together with the Government's Reply (Cmnd 7449); Fourth Report from the Select Committee on the Parliamentary Commissioner: 'Non-Departmental Public Bodies' (HC 619 of 1983–84); White Paper: 'Observations by the Government on the Fourth Report from the Select Committee on the Parliamentary Commissioner' (Cmnd 9563 (1985)).

[21] 'The Powers, Work and Jurisdiction of the Ombudsman' (HC 33 of 1993–1994); 'Open Government' (HC 84 of 1995–1996).

[22] The Countryside Commission for Scotland was deleted by the National Heritage (Scotland) Act 1991.

[23] The Human Fertilisation and Embryology Authority was added by the Human Fertilisation and Embryology Act 1990; the Legal Aid Board was added by the Legal Aid Act 1988; the Office of the Director of the National Lottery was added by the National Lottery Act 1993; the Director of Passenger Rail Franchising was added by the Railways Act 1993. [24] SI 1999/277.

Office, Ministry of Defence, Northern Ireland Office, Office of the Secretary of State for Scotland, and Wales Office.

Other public or quasi-governmental organisations currently within the Commissioner's jurisdiction include Advisory, Conciliation and Arbitration Service, Agricultural Wages Board for England and Wales, Boundary Commissions for England, Northern Ireland, Scotland and Wales, British Potato Council, British Tourist Authority, Central Office of Information, Charity Commission, Civil Aviation Authority, Commission for Racial Equality, Commissioner for Victims and Witnesses, Committee on Standards in Public Life, Countryside Agency, Crown Estate Office, Disability Rights Commission, Electoral Commission, English Sports Council, Environment Agency, Equal Opportunities Commission, The Director of Fair Access to Higher Education, Food Standards Agency, Football Licensing Authority, Forestry Commission, Gambling Commission, Gangmasters Licensing Authority, Government Actuary's Department, Health and Safety Commission, Health and Safety Executive, Her Majesty's Stationery Office, Higher Education Funding Council for England, Horserace Betting Levy Board, Housing Corporation, the Information Commissioner, Land Registry, Law Commission, Legal Services Commission, the Legal Services Complaints Commissioner, Low Pay Commission, National Forest Company, National Lottery Commission, Office of Her Majesty's Chief Inspector of Schools in England, Office of the Children's Commissioner, the Official Solicitor, Ordnance Survey, Parole Board, the Pensions Regulator, Royal Mint, Small Business Council, Standards Board for England, the Treasury Solicitor, United Kingdom Atomic Energy Authority, Wine Standards Board, Zoos Forum.

In addition, there are many advisory bodies relating to science (including Human Fertilisation and Embryology Authority, Human Genetics Commission and Human Tissue Authority), certain Research Councils (Alcohol Education and Research, Arts and Humanities, Biotechnology and Biological Sciences, Economic and Social, Engineering and Physical Sciences, Medical, Natural Environment, Particle Physics and Astronomy Research Council), certain consumers' organisations (Consumer Councils for Postal Services, Water, Gas and Electricity, National Consumer Council, Office of the Director General of Water Services, Office of Fair Trading, Office of Rail Regulation, Rail Passengers' Council), and certain organisations concerned with the protection and promotion of our heritage (Advisory Councils on Historical Manuscripts, Libraries, Public Records, Arts Council, British Council, British Film Institute, British Library Board, British Museum, Historic Royal Palaces, Imperial War Museum, National Gallery, National Maritime Museum, National Portrait Gallery, Natural History Museum, Public Record Office, Railway Heritage Committee, Royal Botanic Gardens, Kew, Tate Gallery, and Victoria and Albert Museum).

Certain matters are not subject to investigation.

There is a borderline between the jurisdiction of the Commissioner and that of courts and tribunals. As a general rule, the Commissioner cannot conduct an investigation in respect of any action in respect of which the person aggrieved has or had a right of appeal, reference or review to or before a tribunal constituted by or under any enactment or by virtue of Her Majesty's prerogative and any action in respect of which the person aggrieved has or had a remedy by way of proceedings in any court of law. However, the Commissioner may conduct an investigation notwithstanding that the person aggrieved has or had such a right or remedy if satisfied that, in the particular circumstances, it is not reasonable to expect that person to resort or to have resorted to it (for example, because the legal process is expensive and disproportionate to the case in question).[25] The Commissioner's way of thinking was considered in:

'A debt of honour': the ex gratia scheme for British groups interned by the Japanese during the Second World War (HC 324 of 2005–2006)

The Commissioner

'16. The 1967 Act also provides, in section 5(2)(b), that I may not conduct an investigation into any action in respect of which the person aggrieved has or had a remedy by way of proceedings in any court of law unless I am satisfied that, in the particular circumstances of the case, it is not reasonable to expect the person aggrieved to resort to such a remedy.

. . .

18. [While] my predecessor was considering whether to investigate Professor Hayward's complaint, he was informed that the Association of British Civilian Internees Far Eastern Region (ABCIFER) had initiated an application for judicial review impugning the legality of the scheme [see p. 610]. In that context, my predecessor decided to defer consideration of Professor Hayward's complaint until the ABCIFER litigation had been concluded.

. . .

21. Following the conclusion of the ABCIFER court proceedings in April 2003, I gave careful consideration as to whether it was reasonable to expect Professor Hayward to resort to legal proceedings as an alternative to my investigating his complaint.

22. In doing so, I first considered whether Professor Hayward had already exercised an alternative remedy.

23. Professor Hayward was not party to the judicial review proceedings concerned with the position of civilian internees and he had never been a member of the organisation which initiated them. It was my conclusion that he had not exercised an alternative remedy through ABCIFER's actions.

24. I next considered whether it would have been reasonable to expect him to initiate legal proceedings on his own behalf.

25. Professor Hayward's complaint, which my predecessor had received prior to the initiation of any proceedings, was not directed at whether the scheme was lawful but concerned the injustice he claimed to have suffered in consequence of maladministration. His complaint was in my view therefore not one that was wholly amenable to an application for judicial review, as maladministration is not synonymous with acting unlawfully. Thus I considered that in this case the availability of an alternative remedy was limited.

26. In any event, having regard to the circumstances of his case I did not consider it reasonable to expect Professor Hayward to exercise any alternative remedy—to the limited extent that he might have had such a remedy—by means of proceedings before a court of law. I believed that such proceedings might well have been costly to him—in both emotional and financial terms.

27. I also had regard to the fact that court proceedings are adversarial in nature and, given the particular circumstances of Professor Hayward's case, I did not consider it reasonable to expect him to have to resort to such a process when that could have been distressing and as he had firmly indicated that instead he wished me to investigate his complaint.

[25] Section 5(2). For examples, see the Commissioner's report on compensation for losses arising from feeding denatured sugar to bees (HC 261 of 1970–1971, Case No 433/S), together with the comment of the Select Committee (HC 513 of 1970–1971, paras 12–14); the Commissioner's report on revocation of television licences (HC 680 of 1974–1975), later the subject of *Congreve v Home Office* (p. 565); the Commissioner's Annual Report for 1980 (HC 148 of 1980–1981); the Commissioner's report on compensation for slaughtering poultry during the salmonella crisis (HC 519 of 1992–1993).

28. In addition, I considered that it would have been difficult for Professor Hayward to have obtained the evidence necessary to pursue legal proceedings as he did not have access to official files. I have considerable powers in relation to access to evidence. That being so, in the circumstances of this case I considered that my fact-finding powers made an investigation by me more appropriate than expecting Professor Hayward to initiate legal proceedings.

. . .

34. For the reasons set out above, I decided that I should investigate Professor Hayward's complaint.'

Although courts and tribunals are not within the Commissioner's jurisdiction (as they are not listed in Schedule 2), the administrative functions of the administrative staff of courts and of certain tribunals which affect many individuals by relating to child support and social security are subject to investigation, except if the action taken is taken at the direction (or on the express or implied authority) of any person acting in a judicial capacity or as a member of the tribunal.[26]

The Commissioner cannot conduct an investigation in respect of certain actions, which mainly relate to the exercise of prerogative power, including: action taken in matters certified by a Secretary of State or other minister of the Crown to affect relations or dealings between the government of the United Kingdom and any other government or any international organisation of states or government; action taken in connection with the administration of the government of any country or territory outside the United Kingdom which forms part of Her Majesty's dominions or in which Her Majesty has jurisdiction; action taken by the Secretary of State with regard to extradition; action taken by or with the authority of the Secretary of State for the purposes of investigating crime or of protecting the security of the State (including action so taken with respect to passports); the commencement or conduct of civil or criminal proceedings; any exercise of the prerogative of mercy; action taken in matters relating to contractual or other commercial transactions, whether within the United Kingdom or elsewhere (being transactions of a government department or a specified authority and not being transactions for or relating to the acquisition of land compulsorily or in circumstances in which it could be acquired compulsorily or the disposal as surplus of land acquired compulsorily or in circumstances in which it could be acquired compulsorily); action taken in respect of appointments or removals, pay, discipline, superannuation or other personnel matters, in relation to service in any of the armed forces of the Crown (including reserve and auxiliary and cadet forces) or service in certain public office or employment; the grant of honours, awards or privileges within the gift of the Crown, including the grant of Royal Charters.[27]

The Commissioner cannot conduct an investigation into matters within the jurisdiction of the Health Service Commissioner or the Local Government Commissioners. A complaint may of course, on being analysed, relate to both central and local government, especially in planning, health and social services matters, where statutory powers may overlap. In such a case, the two Commissioners may produce a joint report and, if maladministration is found,

---

[26] Section 5(6), as added by the Courts and Legal Services Act 1990, section 110(1); section 5(7)–(9), as added by the Parliamentary Commissioner Act 1994, section 1(1); Schedule 3, paragraph 6A, as added by the Courts and Legal Services Act 1990, section 110(2); Schedule 3, paragraph 6B, as added by the Parliamentary Commissioner Act 1994, section 1(2); Schedule 4, as added by the Parliamentary Commissioner Act 1994, section 1(3).

[27] Section 5(3) and Schedule 3, as amended by SI 1983/1707, by the Extradition Act 1989, section 36(1), by the Parliamentary and Health Service Commissioner Act 1987, section 1(3), and by SI 2005/3430.

determine an equitable division of responsibility and remedial action.[28] The Cabinet Office are currently proposing much closer co-ordination and collaboration between the Parliamentary, Health Service and Local Government Commissioners to provide a more efficient and streamlined service to complainants in the future.[29]

Finally,

'it is not for me to question the adequacy of legislation enacted by Parliament or of European law. While, in any investigation, I will have regard to the relevant legislative framework and—at its end— may draw Parliament's attention to situations where I consider that the relevant legislation has had a direct bearing on the injustice claimed by complainants, I do not have the power to investigate complaints that legislation itself is inadequate, unfair or has caused injustice to an individual.'[30]

---

v. Procedure

The Whyatt Report[31] considered it very important that the additional Parliamentary Commissioner procedure should not disturb the basic position of Parliament as a channel for complaints against the executive and should not appear to interfere with the relations between individual Members of Parliament and their constituents. The essence of the Commissioner's role is that of a supplement to the rights and powers of Members of Parliament and not a substitute for them. The Commissioner may conduct an investigation only where a written complaint is duly made to a member of the House of Commons by a member of the public who claims to have sustained injustice in consequence of maladministration and the complaint is referred to the Commissioner, with the consent of the person who made it, by a member of that House with a request to conduct an investigation into the complaint.[32] Complaints, therefore, must be channelled through Members of Parliament. It is usual to use one's own constituency member but there is no obligation so to do. There is no direct access to the Parliamentary Commissioner (as there is with equivalents in other countries and, indeed, in the case of the Health Service and Local Government Commissioners) and it should be noted that complaints cannot be channelled through members of the House of Lords. Successive Commissioners have developed the practice of referring complaints made directly to the Commissioner to an appropriate Member of Parliament for re-referral to the Commissioner.

A complaint may be made by any individual or by any body of persons whether incorporated or not, not being either a local authority or other authority or body constituted for purposes of the public service or of local government or for the purpose of carrying on under national ownership any industry or undertaking or part of an industry or undertaking or any other authority or body whose members are appointed by Her Majesty or any minister of the

---

[28] See 'Redress in the round; remedying maladministration in central and local government' (HC 475 of 2005–2006).

[29] See 'Review of the Public Sector Ombudsmen In England', Cabinet Office Consultation Papers April 2000, June 2000, August 2005.

[30] 'Trusting in the pensions promise: government bodies and the security of final salary occupational pensions' (HC 984 of 2005–2006), para 1.47. See also: 'State earnings-related pension scheme (SERPS) inheritance provisions' (HC 35 of 1999–2000), para 42.   [31] Para 156.

[32] Section 5(1).

Crown or government department, or whose revenues consist wholly or mainly of moneys provided by Parliament.[33] If the person by whom a complaint might have been made has died or is for any reason unable to act for him or herself, the complaint may be made by the person's personal representative or by a member of the person's family or any other individual suitable to represent him or her. Apart from this, however, a complaint cannot be entertained unless made by the person aggrieved him or herself.[34] There is a time limit in that a complaint cannot be entertained unless it is made to a member of the House of Commons not later than twelve months from the day on which the person aggrieved first had notice of the matters alleged in the complaint. However, the Commissioner may conduct an investigation into a complaint not made within that twelve month period if the Commissioner considers that there are special circumstances which made it proper to do so,[35] such as where a person has been prevented by illness from presenting the complaint or has pursued an alternative course of action in the reasonable expectation of finding a remedy. Note that, although the Commissioner may be sympathetic to complaints out of time, the Commissioner has to be practical in that the person who made the impugned decision might not now be identifiable or might have been moved to another department, the relevant papers or files might not be in existence, and an administrative action taken a long time ago might have been taken in circumstances far different than at the present.[36] As a general rule, a complaint cannot be entertained unless the person aggrieved is resident in the United Kingdom (or was so resident at the time of his or her death) or the complaint relates to action taken in relation to the person while he or she was present in the United Kingdom (or on an installation such as an oil rig, or on a ship or aircraft registered in the United Kingdom) or in relation to rights or obligations which accrued or arose in the United Kingdom (or on such an installation, ship or aircraft). However, if the complaint relates to action in any country or territory outside the United Kingdom by an officer exercising certain consular functions on behalf of the United Kingdom government and the person aggrieved is a United Kingdom citizen with the right of abode in the United Kingdom, the complaint may nevertheless be entertained.[37]

In determining whether to initiate, continue or discontinue an investigation, the Commissioner acts in accordance with the Commissioner's own discretion.[38] The procedure is contradictory. The emphasis is on informality and the avoidance of an adversarial or litigation-style process which can be costly for all but the lawyers involved. The process is free. If the Commissioner proposes to conduct an investigation following a complaint, the Commissioner must give to the principal officer of the department or authority concerned (the permanent secretary of a department or the chief executive of an agency) (and to any other person who is alleged in the complaint to have taken or authorised the action complained of) an opportunity to comment on any allegations contained in the complaint.[39] Occasionally, the actions of individual officials will be called into question, in which case the principal officer of the authority is enjoined to make them aware of the nature of the complaint and to give them an opportunity to explain their position. Any official who is said to have been at fault during the course of an investigation must be given an opportunity to comment to the Commissioner.[40] Any investigation will be conducted in private, which can be helpful to all concerned. Apart from the above two rules, the procedure for conducting an

---

[33] Section 6(1).   [34] Section 6(2).   [35] Section 6(3).   [36] HC 134 of 1967–1968, paras 27, 29.
[37] Section 6(4), as amended by the Parliamentary Commissioner (Consular Complaints) Act 1981, section 1; section 6(5), as added by the Parliamentary Commissioner (Consular Complaints) Act 1981, section 1.
[38] Section 5(5).   [39] Section 7(1).
[40] 'Handling of Parliamentary Ombudsman Cases' (Cabinet Office), paras 21–28.

investigation is such as the Commissioner considers appropriate in the circumstances of the case (but note *Dyer*, p. 492, and *Balchin*, p. 494). If the Commissioner receives many (sometimes in the hundreds) complaints from people in similar situations who all claim to have suffered injustice due to the same administrative action, the Commissioner will usually conduct one investigation, using a small number of complainants as representative of all those who had complained.[41] The Commissioner may determine whether any person may be represented, by counsel or solicitor or otherwise, in the investigation and may pay the expenses of the complainant and any other person who attends or furnishes information for the purposes of an investigation. As a matter of practice, members of the Commissioner's staff will often interview the complainant at the complainant's home where the complainant will usually be more at ease. One possible defect in simply using a Member of Parliament to redress grievances is that Members of Parliament may not have sufficient powers to obtain relevant, and often crucial, information and it is expressly stated that the Commissioner may obtain information from such persons and in such manner, and may make such inquiries as the Commissioner thinks fit. The conduct of an investigation does not affect any action taken by the department or authority concerned, or any power or duty of that department or authority to take further action with respect to any matters subject to the investigation. However, if the person aggrieved has been removed from the United Kingdom under the immigration legislation, the Commissioner may direct that the person aggrieved be allowed to re-enter and remain in the United Kingdom for the purposes of the investigation.[42]

For the purposes of an investigation, the Commissioner may require any minister, officer or member of the department or authority concerned or any other person who, in the opinion of the Commissioner, is able to furnish information or produce any document relevant to the investigation to furnish any such information or to produce any such document.[43] For the purposes of any such investigation, the Commissioner has the same powers as the High Court in respect of the attendance and examination of witnesses (including the administration of oaths or affirmations and the examination of witnesses abroad) and in respect of the production of documents.[44] No obligation to maintain secrecy or other restrictions upon the disclosure of information obtained by or furnished to persons in Her Majesty's service applies to the disclosure of information for the purposes of an investigation and the Crown will not be entitled in relation to any investigation to any such privilege in respect of the production of documents or the giving of evidence as is allowed by law in legal proceedings, but, subject to this, no person can be compelled for the purposes of an investigation to give any evidence or produce any document which he or she could not be compelled to give or produce in civil proceedings before the High Court.[45] However, no person can be required or authorised to furnish any information or answer any question relating to proceedings of the Cabinet or of any committee of the Cabinet or to produce so much of any document as relates to such proceedings (and for these purposes a certificate issued by the Secretary of the Cabinet with the approval of the Prime Minister and certifying that any information, question, document or part of a document so relates is conclusive).[46] The above provisions are probably the most important of the Act, since it would be absurd to pretend that the Commissioner

---

[41] See 'Trusting in the pensions promise: government bodies and the security of final salary occupational pensions' (HC 984 of 2005–2006), para 2.3. [42] Section 7(2), (3), (4).

[43] Section 8(1). [44] Section 8(2).

[45] Section 8(3), 8(5), as amended by the Civil Evidence Act 1988, section 17(1). On the Crown and the giving and withholding of evidence, see p. 117.

[46] Section 8(4). This provision has caused some concern to the Select Committee (HC 615 of 1977–1978, para 34; HC 84 of 1995–1996, para 113) but governments have stood firm (HC 75 of 1996–1997, p. vii).

could do the job properly if the Commissioner were to be denied access to any relevant departmental papers. Whyatt accepted that in proposing that the Commissioner should have access to departmental files they were suggesting a procedure which marked a further departure from the established practice of the Civil Service 'which traditionally favours secrecy and anonymity in its activities', but a trend in recent years had 'rightly been towards more openness and less secrecy in administration in order to meet the reasonable demands of the public for more information as to how Government Departments conduct their business'.[47] If any person without lawful excuse obstructs the Commissioner or any officer of the Commissioner in the performance of the Commissioner's functions or is guilty of any act or omission in relation to any investigation which, if that investigation were a proceeding in the High Court, would constitute contempt of court, the Commissioner may certify the offence to the High Court.[48] Finally, as a compromise between the desire to prevent security leaks and the desire to give the Commissioner the full means of investigation, a minister of the Crown may give notice in writing to the Commissioner, with respect to any document or information specified in the notice, or any class of documents or information specified in the notice, that in the opinion of the minister the disclosure of that document or information, or of documents or information of that class, would be prejudicial to the safety of the state or otherwise contrary to the public interest.[49]

Sometimes the investigation is very long and complicated. It is always thorough:

Trusting in the pensions promise: government bodies and the security of final salary occupational pensions (HC 984 of 2005–2006)

The Commissioner

'3.2. [I] should explain that, as the matters which formed the subject of this investigation are complex and were often technical, I have treated Dr Ros Altmann—an investment expert, investment banker and economist, adviser to the pensions industry, and Governor of the London School of Economics—as the advocate for complainants. Complainants had requested that I do so and she had also been mandated to act on behalf of the action group representing a large number of individuals affected by the wind-up of their schemes.

3.3. The further enquiries I made as part of this investigation had the following key elements: (i) we conducted a survey of every individual complainant registered with us to establish what their detailed position [was. I] received 198 responses to that [survey]; (ii) Dr Ros Altmann submitted a considerable amount of evidence on behalf of complainants and provided comments on the main aspects of the response to their complaints by the bodies under investigation; (iii) my investigator interviewed the four representative complainants, who provided valuable insight into their [complaints]; (iv) we asked the bodies under investigation for further evidence and for their views on some of the more detailed allegations made by Dr Altmann and complainants during the investigation, which the Government provided on several occasions; (v) we scrutinised the other written submissions of complainants which were held on our [files]; (vi) my investigator also visited NICO [the National Insurance Contributions Office] on site, scrutinised a random sample of their files, and obtained detailed reports on action taken by NICO on the pension schemes of which the four representative complainants had been members and also on a random selection of other schemes with which other complainants were associated; (vii) in addition, my investigator interviewed independent trustees responsible for winding-up pension

---

[47] Whyatt Report, para 152.   [48] Section 9.
[49] Section 11(3). For a rare use of this power, see HC 116 of 1971–1972, paras 18–21, and the comments of the Select Committee (HC 334 of 1971–1972), paras 4–6.

schemes to obtain an insight into their experience; (viii) we met office-bearers of the all-party groups on Occupational Pensions and on Insurance and Financial Services and scrutinised many submissions by other Members of Parliament made on behalf of their constituents. These have been helpful in establishing the wider context in which the complaints are placed; (ix) I sought the comments of the Association of British Insurers and of the National Association of Pension Funds, some of whose members administer occupational pension schemes, on matters related to the alleged delays in winding-up final salary [schemes]; (x) I sought actuarial advice on some of the issues raised by the [complaints]; and (xi) finally, I also sought the comments of the actuarial profession on the same matters, which were provided by the Faculty and Institute of Actuaries.

3.4. In addition to the above, we scrutinised a considerable number of Government files, official publications and other documentary sources to establish the factual context in which the complaints were [placed].'

The Commissioner has placed emphasis on achieving speedier resolutions of complaints without embarking on a formal investigation and has pursued the policy of settling cases by informal enquiries whenever possible. During 1999–2000 for example, the Commissioner's staff did so in 400 cases, and in 121 cases that 'led to a satisfactory conclusion in the form of prompt and appropriate action by the body concerned'.[50]

If the Commissioner conducts an investigation or decides not to conduct an investigation, the Commissioner must send to the member of the House of Commons by whom the request for an investigation was made (or, if he or she is no longer a member of that House, to such member of that House as the Commissioner thinks appropriate) a report of the results of the investigation, or, as the case may be, a statement of the reasons for not conducting an investigation. If the Commissioner conducts an investigation, the Commissioner must also send a report of the results of the investigation to the principal officer of the department or authority concerned and to any other person who is alleged in the relevant complaint to have taken or authorised the action complained of.[51] Whyatt considered that when submitting reports, the Commissioner should, in one important respect, follow the practice already adopted by the then Comptroller and Auditor-General who criticised the department but did not mention any individual civil servant by name. This was 'a sound practice and the question of taking disciplinary or other appropriate action against particular civil servants should properly be left to the higher authorities in the civil service'.[52]

'When the investigation is complete, the Ombudsman nearly always sends the draft report to the Principal Officer of the body for comments, and invariably does so if it involves criticisms of identifiable individuals. The Ombudsman will require the draft report to be shown to anyone who has been criticised in the report. There is no specific deadline for comments on a draft report, but there is a general expectation that comments should be provided in about three weeks. When responding to a draft report, the Principal Officer is expected, where appropriate, to give some indication of the action that will be taken to implement the Ombudsman's recommendation and may discuss with the Ombudsman at that stage any financial or other remedy that may have been recommended. The Ombudsman's recommendations are not legally binding, but Ministers have made clear to Parliament that they will be accepted. In the very rare case where a body proposes not to accept the Ombudsman's recommendation, the department should notify the Cabinet Office as soon as possible.'[53]

'In the light of investigation of a case, the Parliamentary Ombudsman will decide whether complainants have suffered injustice because of maladministration; and whether any injustice has

[50] HC 593 of 1999–2000, para 1.2.   [51] Section 10(1), (2).   [52] Whyatt Report, para 153.
[53] 'Handling of Parliamentary Ombudsman Cases' (Cabinet Office), paras 38, 42, 45, 48.

been, or will be, remedied. The Parliamentary Ombudsman's findings on maladministration are final; there is no established avenue of appeal.'[54]

If after an investigation it appears to the Commissioner that injustice has been caused to the person aggrieved in consequence of maladministration and that the injustice has not been, or will not be, remedied, the Commissioner may, if the Commissioner thinks fit, lay before each House of Parliament a special report on the case.[55] The Commissioner may from time to time lay before each House of Parliament such other reports as the Commissioner thinks fit.[56] The constitutional consequences of the, few, 'special reports' are considered in head VIII below. The Commissioner must annually lay before each House of Parliament a general report on the performance of the Commissioner's functions[57] and regularly reports to Parliament anonymised summaries of typical cases, with the facts, the department's actions, whether there was injustice, what maladministration was found and what action the department intended to take to try to ensure that the injustice would not be repeated. Several of these are extracted below.

The fact that both annual and special reports are laid before each House of Parliament brings the House of Lords into the Parliamentary Commissioner scheme of things. Ministerial statements on the reports are made to both Houses, the reports are debated in both Houses, responsible ministers are questioned in both Houses, and, softly be it said, the House of Lords, having the attributes of time available, expertise and experience, and, even now, an independence of approach, can be a very effective supporter of the Commissioner and the Select Committee.

VI. Maladministration

The Commissioner may investigate any action taken by or on behalf of a government department or other authority to which the Parliamentary Commissioner Act applies (see head IV above), being action taken in the exercise of administrative functions of that department or authority in any case where a complaint is duly made by a member of the public who claims to have sustained injustice in consequence of maladministration in connection with the action so taken. Nothing, however, authorises or requires the Commissioner to question the merits of a decision taken without maladministration by a government department or other authority in the exercise of a discretion vested in that department or authority.[58] It must be emphasised that 'administrative functions', 'injustice' and 'maladministration' are not defined in the Act and this was deliberate policy. Mr Crossman, introducing the second reading of the Parliamentary Commissioner Bill, was obviously mindful of the fact that the moulding of a new institution into the British constitution must take time and that the powers and functions of the Commissioner should not be unduly restricted by precise definitions of 'injustice' and

---

[54] 'Government Accounting' (1996, revised 2005), chapter 18: 'Financial Redress—Maladministration and Charter Standards'.

[55] Section 10(3). See the Report of the Select Committee on the Channel Tunnel rail link and exceptional hardship (HC 270 of 1994–1995), p. 419; 'Trusting in the pensions promise: government bodies and the security of final salary occupational pensions' (HC 984 of 2005–2006), p. 446.

[56] Section 10(4). See *Sachsenhausen*, p. 412, and *Barlow Clowes*, p. 428.   [57] Section 10(4).

[58] Section 5(1); section 12(3).

'maladministration' which might well include 'bias, neglect, incompetence, perversity, arbitrariness' and that 'we can let the meaning of the word be filled out by the practical application of case work'.[59]

The early approach to maladministration and the initial cases referred to the Commissioner were explained in the Commissioner's first report:

'The Act does not define maladministration. I have to identify instances of it in the course of my casework. So far it has not been my practice to require the complainant to specify the maladministration. The Act only requires that he should claim to have sustained injustice in consequence of maladministration: and while he is naturally specific about the injustice he has sustained, he may tell me very little about the alleged maladministration. My investigation, on the other hand, must be directed to identifying the maladministration. Accordingly I proceed by enquiring into the administrative action that the department took in relation to the complainant in order to see if there was any element of maladministration by the department in connection with that action. If there was, I go on to form an opinion on whether that maladministration caused any, and if so what, injustice to the person aggrieved.'[60]

At this early stage, the cases brought out the distinction between maladministration connected with the executive actions of government ('defects or failings on the part of the departmental operator or in the procedures he has to operate', where 'the nature of the maladministration (if any) in the departmental action is relatively easy to establish, and, if the maladministration caused injustice, the appropriate remedy to the aggrieved person is usually apparent') and maladministration connected with the discretionary decisions of government. Here, what

'the complainant usually wants, and the Member for that matter, is a review of the decision. Often I am asked to question a discretionary decision because the minister's finding in that decision is alleged by the complainant to be "biased" or "perverse", and bias and perversity were listed as types of maladministration in the debates on the Bill. My practice so far is to regard the area for my investigation to be the administrative processes attendant on the discretionary decision: collection of the evidence on which the decision was taken, the presentation of the case to the minister, and so on. If I find there has been a defect in these processes, detrimental to the complainant, then I do enquire into the prospects of a remedy by way of review of the decision. But if I find no such defect, then I do not regard myself as competent to question the quality of the decision, even if, in an extreme case, it has resulted in manifest hardship to the complainant.'[61]

The first major investigation by the Commissioner resulted in the Report of the Commissioner on the *Sachsenhausen* case:

....

Report of the Commissioner on the *Sachsenhausen* case (HC 54 of 1967–68)

The complainants alleged that they suffered injustice as a result of maladministration by the Foreign Office who refused to pay compensation under an Anglo-German Agreement which provided £1 million for the benefit of United Kingdom nationals who were victims of Nazi persecution. Certain men had been held within a special camp (Sonderlager A) or in a cell block (Zellenbau) which were attached to the Sachsenhausen Cencentration Camp. They had their claims rejected by the Foreign Office who had applied two tests in order to see if a person had been the victim of Nazi persecution. First, was the

<hr/>

[59] 734 HC Official Report (5th series) col 51: the 'Crossman catalogue'.
[60] First Report of the Commissioner (HC 6 of 1967–1968), para 31.
[61] First Report of the Commissioner (HC 6 of 1967–1968), paras 32–34.

victim detained in a concentration camp? If so, that made the victim eligible without regard to degrees of severity of treatment. If not, the claim might be eligible if the person passed a second test, namely, was it detention in an institution where the conditions were comparable to those in a concentration camp? The complainants' case was that Sonderlager A and the Zellenbau were within the concentration camp, under the same SS management and that the severity of treatment of some of them exceeded the severity of treatment of some of the inmates of the main concentration camp. The complaint of injustice caused by maladministration was that in the procedures by which the Foreign Office reached the decision to refuse their claims and subsequently persisted in that refusal, the Foreign Office made unfair use of, or failed to use, the evidence provided by the complainants that they had been detained in the concentration camp and that they had suffered treatment comparable with that suffered by persons accepted by the Foreign Office as detained in Sachsenhausen. The Foreign Office defined concentration camp conditions as meaning severe forms of Nazi persecution and the Foreign Office advised that the complainants' account of their conditions was 'fantastic'. The Commissioner had full access to documentary evidence, was able to question the complainants and civil servants orally, and he thought it right to extract from the Foreign Office records the particulars of the Sachsenhausen claimants registered by the Foreign Office in order to make the comparison between the complainants' cases and those which the Foreign Office had actually accepted as having been victims of Nazi persecution by being detained in the Sachsenhausen concentration camp.

The Commissioner

'53. I am obliged to report that there have been defects in the administrative procedure by which the decisions on these claims were reached in the first place, and defended when subsequently [challenged].

. . .

57. [In] dealing with the complainants' claims to have been held in Sachsenhausen concentration camp it seems to me that the Foreign Office procedure was biased against the complainants in two respects. My first criticism is that the Foreign Office decision that Sonderlager A and the Zellenbau were not part of Sachsenhausen concentration camp was taken on partial evidence. The Foreign Office gave insufficient weight to the fact that at all times the Sachsenhausen SS Commandant was in control of both Sonderlager A and the Zellenbau as parts of the whole Sachsenhausen complex and that the Zellenbau cells, while physically separated, were within the main camp, were operated in conjunction with the main compound and were indeed an integral part of the concentration camp [organisation]. The Zellenbau were indeed graded, from the so-called "luxury cells" to the lowest form of punishment cell. But likewise these were gradations of living and working conditions in the main compound. While there is doubt as regards Sonderlager A, it does seem to me that the Foreign Office were at fault in disregarding the weight of evidence in favour of the Zellenbau being classed as part of the Sachsenhausen concentration camp [complex].

. . .

59. Having determined that these claimants had not been in Sachsenhausen concentration camp, the Foreign Office applied to them the rule that as non-camp claimants they were only eligible if the detention conditions in Sonderlager A and in the Zellenbau [were] "comparable with those in a concentration camp". Here as elsewhere the Foreign Office defined concentration camp conditions as meaning severe forms of Nazi persecution [treatment].

60. The Foreign Office have made it plain to me that this was a policy rule which applied to the compensation scheme as a whole. Indeed the Notes for Guidance imply that this was the standard by which the Foreign Office intended to admit all claims to compensation when they made detention in a concentration camp the first test of eligibility. The practical effect, it seems to me, has been to make the second test more exacting than the first. For a claimant who had been held in what the Foreign Office ruled to be a "concentration camp proper", had only to establish his physical presence there: a

claimant who had not been so held, had to pass a treatment test of extreme severity. Sachsenhausen, with a wide range of living conditions and treatment in the main compound, has provided evidence that presence in the main compound did not necessarily mean concentration camp treatment as generally understood. Apart from evidence offered by the complainants, there is the evidence of the treatment received by the Norwegians [and] the further evidence obtained by me from the Foreign Office case files of Sachsenhausen main compound claimants. There were only two British servicemen survivors from the main compound. Both were compensated for the full period of their detention there. The one, Sergeant Kemp, was brutally [treated]; the other, Captain Starr, after two weeks in the punishment company, was transferred to painting huts and lived comparatively well for six [months].

61. The Foreign Office, aware of evidence of gradations of treatment that I have mentioned, maintained the policy of testing those they ruled to be non-camp claimants by reference to the concept of concentration camp treatment as generally understood. The Foreign Office have represented to me, I think correctly, that as Parliamentary Commissioner I am not authorised to question the merits of the rule. But I record as fact the result of applying the rule at Sachsenhausen, including the actual case of the main compound claimant awarded compensation who was more leniently treated than Zellenbau claimants refused compensation.

62. My other criticism relates to the treatment given by the Foreign Office to the evidence adduced by the complainants in support of their claims. The complainants' evidence was of two kinds: (a) descriptions of the location in which they were detained and the treatment they received; (b) statements from their own experience and from other sources about conditions in the main compound of Sachsenhausen.

63. The Foreign Office tested the complainants' descriptions of their own treatment against the information recorded in their 1945 interrogation reports and against other accounts of conditions in Sonderlager A. The decision to maintain the refusal of their claim was based inter alia upon a Foreign Office judgment that in important matters the 1945 reports did not bear out the claims of severe treatment they made in 1965. The evidence I have taken from the complainants has led me to the [conclusion] that generally the discrepancies are minor ones and that their evidence of ill treatment is [sustained].

64. The complainants' evidence about more lenient treatment in the main compound of Sachsenhausen was based upon their own observation and supporting evidence from the Norwegian and other [sources]. The Foreign Office also had the experience of Captain Starr, of which the complainants did not know. In presenting this part of the case to the Secretary of State, the Foreign Office confined their description of conditions in Sachsenhausen main camp to Sergeant Kemp's account [and] advised that the complainants' account of the main camp conditions in Sachsenhausen was "fantastic". In later evidence to me, the Foreign Office officials concerned have said that they thought it right to dismiss the complainants' statements because Sergeant Kemp's account was typical of the mass evidence they had for conditions in concentration camps generally. But my investigation of the departmental record has established that in this part of their brief to the Secretary of State in December 1966 they were dealing with the reliability of the complainants' accounts of conditions in the main compound of [Sachsenhausen].

66. Summarising my conclusions:

(i) I criticise the process by which the Foreign Office decided against Sonderlager A and Zellenbau being part of Sachsenhausen Concentration Camp, because in my view the original decision was based on partial and largely irrelevant information, and the decision was maintained in disregard of additional information and evidence, particularly as regards Zellenbau.

(ii) I may not question the merits of the general ruling as applied throughout the compensation scheme that claimants judged not to have been held in a concentration camp had to establish detention in conditions comparable with those in a concentration camp "as generally understood", meaning severe forms of Nazi persecution treatment. I record that this ruling could mean that a non camp claimant had to pass a more severe test than a camp claimant, and that this actually happened at Sachsenhausen.

(iii) I criticise the treatment by the Foreign Office of the evidence submitted by the complainants in support of their claims as regards their own conditions under detention in Zellenbau and as regards conditions in the main compound of Sachsenhausen.

The Report of the Commissioner on the *Sachsenhausen* case[62] and the First Report of the Commissioner[63] were later considered by the Select Committee:

Report of the Select Committee on the Parliamentary Commissioner
(HC 350 of 1967–8)

'9. In his First Report the Commissioner described the process by which he identifies maladministration in his casework. He proceeded to distinguish between maladministration in the executive actions of Government (meaning defect or failings on the part of the departmental operator or in the procedures he has to operate), and the more difficult area of maladministration attendant on discretionary decisions in [government].

10. [Your] Committee feel able to offer guidance to the Commissioner as regards the definition of maladministration. For the reasons given below, they think that within the terms of the Act the Commissioner can concern himself with the two matters that so far he has regarded as outside his scope: the bad decision, and the bad rule.

The bad decision

11. Your Committee agree that, in the absence of a legal definition, there is no alternative to the practical course adopted by the Commissioner of proceeding by example, ie identifying instances which appear to him to partake of the nature of maladministration in the course of his casework, and building up the definition from those cases. In doing so he presumably has regard to the types of administrative action which were mentioned in debate in Parliament as instances of maladministration—particularly the so called "Crossman [catalogue]".

12. Your Committee note that for the most part the administrative defects actually found and reported to Members by the Commissioner, though often important to the aggrieved persons and significant to the Departments investigated, have so far been relatively trivial in relation to the types of maladministration described in the House and elsewhere as the likely subject matter of investigation by a Parliamentary Commissioner.

13. These results may be read as confirming the high standards of administration practised by Government Departments, and Your Committee appreciate their importance in this respect. At the same time, they feel that the instances of maladministration found by the Commissioner might have been more in number and less trivial in content if he had allowed himself to find on occasion that a decision had been taken with maladministration because it was a bad decision.

14. Your Committee are fully seized of the importance of section 12(3) of the [Act, p. 411]. The object of this provision was to declare that it is not the function of the Commissioner to substitute his decision for that of the Government, and Your Committee are giving him no encouragement to do this. They do suggest, however, that if he finds a decision which, judged by its effect upon the aggrieved person, appears to him to be thoroughly bad in quality, he might infer from the quality of the decision itself that there had been an element of maladministration in the taking of it and ask for its review. In such cases the distinction drawn by the Commissioner in his First Report, between the quality of the procedures attending the decision and the quality of the decision itself, would tend to be blurred. Your Committee

62 HC 54 of 1967–1968, p. 412.   63 HC 6 of 1967–1968, p. 412.

think that the Commissioner will then be able to act in some types of case where, judging by the legislative history, it was clearly the intention of Parliament that he should operate, in particular, decisions alleged by the complainant and found by the Commissioner to be biased or perverse, for bias and perversity were listed as types of maladministration in the debates on the Bill.

The bad rule

15. The other area in which Your Committee wish to encourage the Commissioner to extend his scope is the class of case where the aggrieved person is found to sustain hardship and indeed injustice through the correct application in his case of an administrative [rule. A striking] instance was provided by the "Butler rules" in the Commissioner's [Report on *Sachsenhausen*, p. 412].

16. [The] Commissioner decided that he was not authorised to call the rule in question. He recorded as fact the result to the complainant of applying the rule, but did not go on to consider whether there was maladministration on the part of the Department in continuing to operate a rule which the aggrieved person, judging by the result for him, claimed to be defective. In [their Report on Sachsenhausen (HC 258 of 1967–68), para 16], Your Committee gave notice of their feeling that "the Commissioner may have taken too narrow a view of his authority here. His findings of fact make it clear that the application of the 'Butler Rules' produced results at Sachsenhausen which were anomalous and indeed unfair as between individual claimants". Having now given the matter further consideration, Your Committee have concluded that it would be appropriate and consistent with the provisions of the Act for the Commissioner to extend his authority in such cases.

17. Clearly the extension must be defined with care. For just as it is not for the Commissioner to substitute his administrative decisions for the Government's, so also it is not for the Commissioner to rewrite the Government's administrative rules. Nor is it for the Commissioner to judge a rule only on the strength of its result in the particular case that he has investigated. The fact that a rule causes hardship to an individual complainant does not necessarily prove that the rule is defective. For example, there may be grounds of public need which in the judgment of the Department override the hardship to the individual. But in the opinion of Your Committee it would be proper for the Commissioner to enquire whether, given the effect of the rule in the case under his investigation, the Department had taken any action to review the rule. If found defective and revised, what action had been taken to remedy the hardship sustained by the complainant ? If not revised, whether there had been due consideration by the Department of the grounds for maintaining the rule ? It would then be open to the Commissioner to find that the complainant had sustained injustice in consequence of maladministration, if these enquiries showed that there had been deficiencies in the departmental process of reviewing the [rule].'

In response to the Select Committee, the Commissioner extended the meaning to be given to maladministration. Many of the cases discussed in this chapter are cases where the Commissioner, in effect, investigates all the circumstances surrounding the decision, including both procedural faults and decisions which are manifestly not supported by the facts:

Report of the Commissioner (HC 118 of 1988–89, case no 475/87: delay and mishandling of an application for a full driving licence)

'1. Mr A, who had been a provisional licence holder since 1 February 1986, complained of delay and mishandling by the Driver and Vehicle Licensing Centre (DVLC) of the Department of Transport in dealing with his application for a full driving licence. [The] solicitors acting on the complainant's behalf said that he had passed his driving test on 3 April 1987 and that, on the same day, he had sent DVLC his provisional licence and the certificate showing that he had passed his driving test. A few weeks later he had received a letter from DVLC saying that he was ineligible for a licence because he had been disqualified from driving. Mr A had replied [that] this was not the case as he had successfully appealed against the conviction in question. DVLC had eventually responded by sending him a provisional licence. On 16 July the solicitors had written to DVLC explaining that the convictions recorded against their client had been overturned on appeal and that he should therefore be issued with a full licence which did not show any endorsements. The solicitors had enclosed the provisional licence and had asked that a full licence be issued without delay so as to enable their client to take up offers of employment which he had received. The solicitors had subsequently telephoned DVLC on a number of occasions but had been transferred from one section to another without satisfactory response. When the complainant had still not received a full licence by 13 August, the solicitors had written asking you [the Member of Parliament] to refer the matter to me. The complainant contended that DVLC's inefficiency in failing to supply him with a full driving licence had severely hampered his job prospects and had caused him difficulties with the police.

2. My investigation has shown that the delay and inefficiency about which Mr A complains stemmed initially from DVLC's not receiving notification from the Crown Court of the successful outcome of two of Mr A's appeals against convictions for driving offences. On 4 July 1986 he had appealed successfully against his conviction at a magistrates' court (Court X) on 9 April 1986 for using a vehicle (on 11 February 1985) uninsured against third party risks. And on 25 November 1986 he had appealed successfully against his conviction at another magistrates' court (Court Y) on 17 July 1986 (and subsequent sentence on 11 September 1986 of disqualification for two years) for driving, on 5 February 1986, uninsured and without a licence. Thus, when Mr A's application of 3 April 1987 for a full driving licence was received at DVLC on 7 April these two convictions—along with an earlier conviction (at a third magistrates' court (Court Z) on 17 March 1986) against which he had successfully appealed and which DVLC had tried, but failed (because of processing mistakes on their part), to erase—remained on the computer [record].

. . .

9. [The] initial difficulties in dealing with this case stemmed from DVLC's not receiving notification from the Crown Court of Mr A's successful appeal on 25 November 1986. Nevertheless, when confirmation of the successful appeal was received in May 1987 it should have been a simple matter to amend Mr A's record by removing the disqualification details and then to issue him with a full driving licence. But a series of clerical errors occurred when attempts were made to clear the application for issue. These first delayed the issue of any licence at all and later resulted in the issue, mistakenly, of a provisional licence. Previous clerical errors made by DVLC in December 1986 when dealing with a notification about a successful appeal against Mr A's conviction on 17 March [1986], together with the non-receipt of timely notification from the Crown Court of the result of Mr A's appeal against the conviction on 9 April 1986 led to the erroneous retention of endorsements on Mr A's record and eventually to the issue of a full licence containing these endorsements.

10. Allowing for the non-receipt, until mid May 1987, of notification from the Crown Court of the outcome of the appeals against Mr A's convictions at both magistrates' courts X and Y, there was no reason why, given appropriate handling by DVLC, the complainant should not have been issued with a full licence by the end of May. That this was not achieved was due entirely to gross mishandling of his application by [DVLC].'

Of course, in so many cases there is no finding of maladministration. A complaint arose from the decision to close the Museum of British Transport at Clapham and to open a new Railway Museum at York. Various interest groups contested the decision and considered that the merits of the decision should be thoroughly investigated at a public inquiry before the move took place. There had been an investigation by the department, which had come to the view that the best solution was to transfer the existing railway materials from Clapham to York to make a national Railway Museum. The Commissioner stated that all the decisions taken by the department fell within the category of 'discretionary decisions' and the question was whether such decisions were taken without maladministration and on a fair consideration of all the relevant facts. There had been three decisions. The first decision was: why leave Clapham? There was a general government policy to develop cultural attractions outside London and, several years before, the experts of the Science Museum had advised that the Clapham site was thoroughly unsuitable, in that the Clapham Museum had no rail connections with any railway system and that, in the absence of a turntable, the heavy objects exhibited could not easily be moved round inside the building in order to develop the collection. (It may be noted that the York site would provide nearly twice the area for exhibitions than the Clapham site.) The Commissioner accepted the factual evidence that the present site at Clapham could not be expanded and that it would be impossible to add any more large exhibits to the collection (thereby rendering the collection gradually more out of date and more incomplete). The first decision was, therefore, not arbitrary or perverse. The second decision was: if Clapham could not be developed, why go to York? The department had considered over thirty sites but only two were worth serious consideration, one at Harrow, on an existing railway goods yard, and one at York. Both met the major requirements of being connected by rail to an existing railway system and both could provide more exhibition space than that at Clapham. However, the Harrow site would prove vastly more expensive than the York site, because of the need to build a new museum building and to purchase the land, whereas to convert the York site would be much cheaper. Consequently, the Commissioner accepted this factual evidence and considered that the second decision was based on firm evidence. The third decision was: what about a public inquiry? The Commissioner stated that he did not think that any proposal which raised controversy must automatically be referred to a public inquiry before the proposal can be implemented. He found as a fact that the interested groups had, in any case, had a full opportunity to present their views to the department and that those views had been adequately considered. Consequently, he did not feel that the refusal of a further and more public opportunity for discussion necessarily constituted maladministration.[64] The York museum is fabulous—go there if you can.

In recent years, the Commissioner has made a significant addition to the Crossman catalogue. In his Annual Report for 1993,[65] the then Ombudsman, wrote:

'To define maladministration is to limit it. Such a limitation could work to the disadvantage of individual complainants with justified grievances which did not fit within a given definition. However I suggest an expanded list of examples going beyond those recounted in what has become known as the Crossman catalogue. When the Parliamentary Commissioner Bill was being taken through Parliament, the examples with Mr Crossman as Leader of the House of Commons then gave were bias, neglect, inattention, delay, incompetence, ineptitude, perversity, turpitude, arbitrariness and so on. In the language of the 1990s I would add: rudeness (though that is a matter of degree); unwillingness to treat the complainant as a person with rights; refusal to answer reasonable questions; neglecting to inform a complainant on request of his or her rights or entitlement; knowingly giving advice which is misleading or inadequate; ignoring valid advice or overruling considerations which would produce an uncomfortable result for the overruler; offering no redress or manifestly disproportionate redress; showing bias whether because of colour, sex, or any other grounds; omission to notify those who thereby lose a right of appeal; refusal to inform adequately of the right of appeal; faulty procedures; failure by management to monitor compliance with adequate procedures; cavalier disregard of guidance which is intended to be followed in the interest of equitable treatment of those who use a service; partiality; and failure to mitigate the effects of rigid adherence to the letter of the law where that produces manifestly inequitable treatment.'

[64] HC 261 of 1970–1971, Case 564/L.   [65] HC 290 of 1993–1994.

The phrase 'failure to mitigate the effects of rigid adherence to the letter of the law where that produces manifestly inequitable treatment' is examined with regard to complaints of 'blighting' of property during the planning of the Channel Tunnel, the investigation of the Commissioner, the response of the Select Committee and the government's reply:

Report of the Select Committee on the Parliamentary Commissioner for Administration—the Channel Tunnel rail link and exceptional hardship
(HC 270 of 1994–95)

'Introduction

. . .

2. In February 1995 the Ombudsman laid a special report before the House: "The Channel Tunnel Rail Link and Blight: Investigation of complaints against the Department of Transport" [HC 193 of 1994–1995]. The Report was laid under section 10(3) of the Parliamentary Commissioner Act 1967 [which] provides for the Ombudsman to lay a special report before the House where it appears to him that injustice has been caused to a person in consequence of maladministration and that the injustice has not been, or will not be, remedied.

3. This is only the second time in the history of the Office that such a report has been laid and we must view its appearance with concern. The first occasion was in Session 1977–78 and also involved the Department of Transport [see p. 443]. This Committee then recommended that the Government remedy the injustice which the Ombudsman had identified and "the Government agreed to amend legislation and that compensation should be paid to those affected in that case".

4. Another notorious case was that of *Barlow Clowes* [p. 428]. The Government did not accept the Ombudsman's conclusion that maladministration had taken place. It nevertheless agreed to pay compensation to investors "without admission of fault or liability". This decision was made in the light of the extent of the financial hardship suffered, the investors' expectations of security and "out of respect for the Office of the Parliamentary Commissioner" [p. 430]. The Government did not, however, believe it right "for this case to be seen as a precedent". Thus, as in the earlier case, redress was finally awarded despite initial Government [opposition].

. . .

The Ombudsman's Report

6. The Ombudsman's Report recounts in some detail the history of the Channel Tunnel Rail Link ["CTRL"] project. He concludes, in brief, that CTRL was an exceptional project subject to exceptional delay. It was important to understand that blight resulted from the "perception of those members of the public who fear that they may be affected by [CTRL]". Mr Reid listed his reasons for considering CTRL to be exceptional, "The project is to build the first major railway in this country this century. That alone, again rightly or wrongly, has caused it to be seen differently. The effects of major new road schemes or the scheme to build an airport are at least known in the sense that it is known in relatively recent times that there has been some comparable [development]. The Department may argue that the effects of this scheme will be no greater or even lesser than those of other schemes. I believe that there are good reasons why the public have not seen it that way. Until the project is completed and the line is up and running there can be no absolute assurance about its effects, however soundly based the forecasts may be. From the outset the project generated widespread blight for which no arrangements had been made."

7. CTRL was perceived by the public to be an exceptional project and it generated exceptional fears. This situation was exacerbated by significant delay. The Department wished the construction of CTRL to be funded by the private sector. However, the

"necessary financial commitment was not forthcoming, so the project could not proceed, although a preferred route, announced in March 1989, appeared to have been settled. That was the position when, in June 1990, the then Secretary of State announced that the route was to be further considered, leaving open the possibility that it would change. As I see matters it could not be funded, so no line could be built, but the project was kept alive. That prolonged the uncertainty and associated blight for a period of unknown duration, with no certainty that the position would change. It did change, but only after a very significant change of policy to the effect that a public subsidy would be paid towards the project. That was in December 1993."

The route was finally determined in April 1994. The Ombudsman considered the maladministration of the Department to have occurred between June 1990 and April 1994. In all the circumstances the Ombudsman believed that the Department

"should have considered whether something exceptional was needed to cater for those exceptionally affected by the results of their policy [and] the Department should have considered the possible need to provide redress for persons suffering extreme or exceptional hardship who were not covered by the various compensation schemes."

8. The Ombudsman argued that the DOT "had a responsibility to consider the position of [persons] suffering exceptional or extreme hardship and to provide for redress where appropriate". This is because "Good administration means having due regard at all times to the position of the citizen, not just to the position of the Government and the taxpayer, but to the individual citizen [no] specific consideration was given to that aspect of good administration and it is on that basis that I criticise the Department". Compensation [schemes] were in place but they extended only to the proximity of proposed routes. The "generalised blight", that is, the widespread blight caused by the uncertainties of the planning and consultation process, remained. It was Government policy not to compensate those affected by such generalised blight.

9. Mr Reid emphasised that compensation would be "for an isolated number of cases of exceptional suffering and exceptions are by definition few in number". It was for the Department to decide who might and who might not qualify for such relief and, while difficult, he did "not accept at all that it is technically beyond a government department's capabilities". He considered that

"any applicant for redress and compensation of this kind would have to show that he or she was experiencing the most severe hardship or distress because they could not sell their property and move. I accept that exceptional hardship does not fall into neat categories which can be tightly defined and it is not possible to list all the circumstances which might merit compensation. It appears to me that such cases are likely to be highly individualistic with features of hardship going far beyond that suffered by reason of blight by the generality of those affected by [it]. If there were a scheme it would need to say what would not qualify. That might encompass cases of persons wishing to move for entirely valid reasons, who may very well have suffered significant loss and stress but whose circumstances do not include that additional element of extreme personal distress. Thus, cases of persons wishing to move because of retirement or loss of employment or marital breakdown would not in themselves qualify, however much one might sympathise with those concerned."

Mr Reid stressed that he was not "asking for a scheme" but for ex gratia payments on a non-statutory basis.

10. The Ombudsman's conclusions [are:

"[The] effect of DOT's policy was to put the project in limbo, keeping it alive when it could not be funded. That increased uncertainty and blight in the period from June 1990. The position was not the same as that pertaining when a road scheme is introduced—the project raised exceptional difficulties and exceptional measures were called for. Persons not covered by the compensation schemes may have suffered as a result of the delay in settling the route. DOT had a responsibility to consider the position of such persons suffering exceptional or extreme hardship and to provide for redress where appropriate. They undertook no such consideration. That merits my criticism."

The Department's disagreement

Exceptional uncertainty?

12. The Department argued that it was quite normal for funding not to be committed even in a wholly public sector funded major project. Indeed the "promise of funding is not the sole or even a normal test of whether it is reasonable to continue with any project". Even after June 1990, when the EuroRail study failed to provide a wholly private sector option, "working on finding alternative routes and funding structures continued". The direct result of this continuing activity "was that it was decided to seek a different sort of private sector joint venture and the result of that work is the present competition for a joint venture Channel Tunnel Rail Link and the Bill which was approved in principle without division by the House of Commons in January". From the start of planning to the opening of CTRL would be around 14 years "which is the average for major trunk road schemes and a good deal better than the 20 or more years taken by the more controversial ones". It was therefore unreasonable to claim that the project had been delayed.

Exceptional project?

13. CTRL was, in the Government's view, unexceptional in its funding and in the uncertainty generated. It was also unexceptional in the area affected and in its environmental impact. The study of future airport needs in the South East was cited as an example of wide localised blight. There had also been considerable experience of high speed railways in France and mitigation of the effects of noise had been planned with French experience in mind. There was therefore "no reason to assume that the noise impact would be worse than existing roads and railways and new roads". Sir Patrick [Brown, Permanent Secretary] summarised "In my judgement, and that of Ministers at the time, the generalised blight effects of CTRL were not materially different from those of many other projects and as such it did not fall outside the scope of the national policy, which is not to compensate for generalised [blight]."

. . .

Exceptional hardship?

15. The policy of the Government has been not to compensate for generalised blight. [To] come to Mr Reid's charge of maladministration, Sir Patrick argued "that the reluctance of successive governments to deal with generalised blight and continuing Ministerial agreement to that policy meant that officials were not under an obligation to propose a new scheme which, in any case, they knew that Ministers had just [rejected]".

. . .

17. Mr Reid has emphasised that he was arguing only for compensation in a few cases of exceptional suffering. Sir Patrick found "it difficult to contemplate the creation of a scheme only for exceptional hardship which could be properly managed". It was impossible to establish criteria

"which would single out a small number of extreme or exceptional cases and which would be equitable and command general public acceptance. Health problems, inability to afford the existing mortgage, the need to care for infirm relatives, divorce, a job outside commuting distance, overcrowding due to an expanding family can all potentially make compelling hardship cases. There is no public consensus that any of these categories is more deserving than the rest."

Conclusions of the Committee

18. The Department argued that there was a clear Government policy not to compensate in cases of generalised blight. It had been recently and actively considered by Ministers. We are in no doubt that both civil servants and Ministers were clear on the policy towards compensation for generalised blight. This does not, however, address the Ombudsman's criticism [that]

"they did not produce for my information any submission to Ministers which comprehensively considered whether steps needed to be taken to mitigate the severest effects of generalised blight caused by prolonging the uncertainty about the options for the line of the railway. [I] have been shown no material to suggest that the Department then sought to ask themselves whether the prolongation of blight in the particular circumstances of this project called for different treatment of the householders affected by it; whether it was desirable to provide a remedy for a small number of such cases; and whether it was possible to distinguish those who might qualify for a remedy."

19. We agree with the Ombudsman's assessment of the evidence. The Department failed to provide any material to contradict this finding when invited to do so by the Committee. At no point was direct and comprehensive consideration given to the question of whether it was either desirable or possible to offer ex gratia compensation to those exceptionally afflicted by the generalised blight of the CTRL project.

20. The Ombudsman has specifically and repeatedly disclaimed any intention to question the policy not to compensate for generalised blight: "it was put to me in the course of our discussion that I was criticising government [policy]. I am well aware of the boundaries of my jurisdiction. I comment on the effects of policy and a failure to consider the possible need for action to address those effects. That is not the same thing at all". We would also disclaim any attempt to question government policy. Our purpose is rather to establish how any policy should be administered. At the heart of this debate is a definition of maladministration found in the Parliamentary Ombudsman's Annual Report for 1993: "failure to mitigate the effects of rigid adherence to the letter of the law where that produces manifestly inequitable treatment". [The] definition, which we fully support, implies an expectation that when an individual citizen is faced with extraordinary hardship as a result of strict application of law or policy, the Executive must be prepared to look again and consider whether help can be given. That the Department did not do. It never considered the possibility of distinguishing cases of extreme hardship from the mass of those affected adversely by blight. It is not the same thing at all merely to respond to particular cases and complaints along the lines of the general policy agreed by [government].

. . .

22. We consider the Department's argument against the exceptional nature of the project to rely too heavily on the benefit of hindsight and to ignore the extent, however misplaced, of public anxiety. This is particularly true with regard to the period when consideration continued of possible alternative routes while there seemed no possibility of funding being made available which would meet the Government's clear requirement of a largely privately funded project. The exceptional nature of the project, in particular the uncertainty as to funding, deprives the Department of any excuse for not having considered the possibility of ex gratia redress for extreme hardship. It should have caused the Department to reconsider the adequacy of its compensation policy. Indeed, Sir Patrick admitted as much when asked what he had learned from the Ombudsman's Report: "it is clear to me that from time to time it is appropriate for the Department to consider with Ministers whether, where there are serious effects of a policy on individuals, Ministers might reconsider whether they wish to maintain the policy in explicit terms". The Ombudsman asked "How could responsible administration not have recognised that a decision which meant keeping those fears alive for a period of uncertain duration, at a time when a resolution of the funding problem was imponderable, should have been followed by at least consideration of whether interim action was called for to address those effects, certainly in exceptional cases". It was at that point that the Department should have considered whether any ex gratia payments might be due to those placed in impossible positions by the continuing [uncertainty].

. . .

Summary of conclusions and recommendations

26. We conclude

(i) That the Department of Transport should have considered whether any ex gratia payments were due when the Channel Tunnel Rail Link project entered the period of uncertainty caused by problems of funding between June 1990 and April 1994.

(ii) That it is desirable to grant redress to those affected to an extreme and exceptional degree by generalised blight, in line with the principle that maladministration includes a "failure to mitigate the effects of rigid adherence to the letter of the law where that produces manifestly inequitable treatment".

(iii) That it should be possible to distinguish a small number of cases of exceptional hardship.

27. We recommend that the Department of Transport reconsider its response to the Ombudsman's findings, accept his conclusion that maladministration has occurred and consider arrangements to determine whether there are householders who merit compensation on the grounds of exceptional hardship. That is very much a matter for the Department's judgement, a point the Ombudsman emphasised. It would be most regrettable if the Department were to remain [obdurate].'

Response to the Report from the Select Committee on the Parliamentary Commissioner for Administration on the Channel Tunnel rail link and exceptional hardship (HC 819 of 1994–95)

Letter from Sir George Young, MP, Secretary of State for Transport, to the Chairman of the Select Committee

'[I] said that the Government would respond to the Select Committee's report on this subject when we had considered the detail. This letter is the Government's formal response. It follows consideration of your Committee's report and of the evidence which was published with [it].

My predecessor and my Permanent Secretary set out very fully in evidence provided to the Commissioner, and subsequently to the Select Committee, why the Department could not accept the finding of maladministration. I have looked again at the arguments and discussed them with Ministerial colleagues in the light of the Select Committee endorsement of the Commissioner's findings. However, the Government has concluded that it must continue to resist the finding of maladministration against the Department of Transport. The reasons for the Government maintaining its position have been set out fully already, and I will not rehearse them in detail here. Suffice it to say that our view remains that:

(i) there was nothing "exceptional" about the planning and funding of the rail link project;

(ii) the project was never "in limbo" as suggested by the Commissioner; and

(iii) we cannot accept that officials should have considered and proposed to Ministers that something should have been done for cases of exceptional hardship when there was a clear Government policy, endorsed by Parliament during the period of alleged "maladministration", that there should be no remedy for generalised blight.

Taken to their logical conclusion, the arguments set out in your Committee's report appear to advocate (particularly in paragraph 20) a fundamental new principle of [administration]. It would imply that if a new policy is adopted, or a new circumstance arises which affects an existing policy, the Government has a duty to identify those individuals who would be particularly adversely affected and to provide financial redress. If this was your Committee's intention, then it would be a new, general principle of administration that the Government could not accept, since its adoption would make government unworkable.

Finally, I appreciate that, as the Committee report notes, there has only been one previous instance of a report under Section 10(3) of the 1967 Act, and that in that case the Government eventually agreed to provide redress "without admission of fault or liability". We have considered the Committee's concerns about CTRL against that background very carefully. Despite the doubts recorded earlier, the Government is prepared to consider afresh whether a scheme might be formulated to implement the Committee's recommendation that redress should be granted to those affected to an extreme and exceptional degree by generalised blight from CTRL during the period June 1990 and April 1994 and how it might operate [see p. 436]. The Government would of course consult the Committee as proposals are being developed. I should add that in agreeing to look again at a compensation scheme, the Government does so out of respect for the PCA Select Committee and the office of the Parliamentary Commissioner, and without admission of fault or liability.'

Delay by administrative authorities in dealing with cases has become a dominant basis of complaint. Both the citizen and the administrative authorities are faced with more and more complexities in their lives; seemingly unnecessary and certainly never-ending changes by 'reforming' governments result in extensive but often merely cosmetic amendment to an existing situation (but a nice new logo may arrive); more and more people seek aid and comfort from the administration in matters such as child support, immigration status, land use, passports, social security and taxation; proposed solutions of departmental reorganisation (a euphemism for a plague of senior management and redundancies at the workplace), the introduction of costly computers which are not properly programmed to do the required tasks, and reduction in staff who do the real work, mean, inevitably and inexorably, that the citizen has to wait far longer than should be necessary for the requested answer. As one Commissioner commented:

'there are areas of the public service where unreasonable delay is seen as a denial of justice. It may become more common for departments to say that greater delays are inevitable if resources are limited. I have been troubled about the validity of this argument. Taken literally, it seems to say that because of shortage of staff the volume of demand at a particular point in the public service exceeds the output which that point is capable of delivering. If this is what is meant, the position can only grow steadily worse, to the point where delays become intolerable.'[66]

In his Annual Report for 1999–2000, the Commissioner stated:

'Despite the frequent expression of a contrary intention, the schemes and systems which departments and agencies administer tend to become ever more complex; and the resources which they can deploy on administration are under constant downward pressure. As my predecessor, Sir William Reid, said in his Annual Report for 1995:

"I surmise that the further reductions in the number of civil servants which are planned to take place will lead to an increased level of complaints. There is a risk that fewer staff will lead both to slower service to the public and to more mistakes. I doubt whether automation and technology will compensate fully for cuts in human resources. I foresee more, not less, maladministration, despite the reference to efficiency savings."

The underlying policy issues are, of course, matters for government and Parliament; and it is not for me to express a view on them. But, like my predecessor, I believe that greater complexity, with fewer resources to administer it, will lead to more maladministration occasioning more injustice; and that is a matter of legitimate concern to me. The injustice will be visited on a random selection of those within the scope of the scheme or the system, without regard to circumstances or desert. It is inequitable that they alone should suffer detriment while the generality of taxpayers enjoy the benefits of savings on administrative costs.'[67]

That year, the Commissioner gave many examples of delays causing injustice. For example, in one case, the Benefits Agency had failed to reassess the complainant's entitlement to an increase to incapacity benefit for an adult dependant, following new earnings rules for that benefit, at the correct time with the result that the complainant had not been afforded the opportunity of reducing the relevant earnings before a transitional period had elapsed. The

[66] HC 322 of 1983–1984, para 6. See 'Dealing with the Complexity of the Benefits System', Comptroller and Auditor General (HC 592 of 2005–2006).   [67] HC 593 of 1999–2000, paras 1.23, 1.24.

Chief Executive said that when the new regulations had come into force the Agency had taken a policy decision not to trawl through the hundreds of thousands of incapacity benefit cases where such an increase was payable. Instead, Agency offices had been required to identify relevant cases when carrying out yearly reviews or when a change of circumstances had arisen. Although the complainant's yearly review had been 'undertaken' in March 1997, owing to an administrative oversight it had not been referred to an adjudication officer for decision until October 1997. The Commissioner stated that claimants affected in this way were clearly put into a different position than that they would have been in had the Agency dealt with their cases on time. They learned of the Agency's decision too late to adjust their earnings so as to retain the adult dependency increase. The Chief Executive was wrong to suggest that it had been solely the new regulations which had been responsible for the complainant's loss. The most direct cause was rather the Agency's delay in implementing the new regulations in the complainant's case since there was little doubt that, if the Agency had dealt with his case within the correct time, his wife would have been able to adjust her earnings so as to retain, or re-qualify for, an adult dependency increase.[68] In that same report, the Commissioner cited, from many, a failure on the part of the Immigration and Nationality Directorate to make a timely offer to the complainant of an extension of leave to remain in the United Kingdom to enable her to travel, which had resulted in having to cancel a holiday (Case C.1526/99), a delay on the part of that Directorate in processing an application for permanent residence in the United Kingdom, preventing the complainant from travelling at various important times (Case C.290/00), and a delay on the part of that Directorate in processing an application for indefinite leave to remain in the United Kingdom, which meant that the complainant was not allowed to visit his father before he died and to attend his funeral (Case C.378/00).

In recent years, many complaints have emphasised the obsession of government departments with complicated schemes over-reliant on technology which has gone wrong. For years, complaint after complaint was levelled at the Child Support Agency. When the Commissioner investigated that Agency, he thought it fair to record the comments of the Agency's Chief Executive:

'It has been evident for some time that the task set for the Agency has proven to be more difficult in practice than had been anticipated when the scheme was devised. In particular, I do not think it was fully appreciated that the Agency's intervention into the most personal and sensitive areas of people's lives would make such a negative impact; nor was it realised how many people would actively resist or reject prioritising child maintenance above nearly all other financial commitments. As a new organisation [operating] new procedures, implementing new Government policy, with new computer systems, many new staff, and with no opportunity to do any piloting prior to our operational start date in April 1993, it has taken much longer than anticipated for both our clients and staff to get used to the new arrangements. That said, I am acutely aware that there have been shortcomings in the Agency's performance, both in the time taken to progress applications for maintenance generally, and in the way we have handled individual cases. My predecessor acknowledged [that] performance has not always measured up to the high standards the Agency set out to achieve. Despite these difficulties, the Agency managed to take on over 858,000 child maintenance cases in its first year, almost 60% of which involved clients not already receiving maintenance. Over 200,000 assessments were made and, as a result, many of these parents will be entitled to maintenance for the first time or will receive more than they did previously. I have already emphasised to our senior managers that we must now put greater emphasis on quality, and they in turn have passed on this message to their staff. We all accept we have a responsibility to ensure that when we enter into people's private lives, we get it right and act with the highest degree of efficiency, accuracy and responsiveness.'

[68] HC 592 of 1999–2000, Case C.463/99.

The Commissioner wisely commented:

'Maladministration leading to injustice is likely to arise when a new administrative task is not tested first by a pilot project; when new staff, perhaps inadequately trained, form a substantial fraction of the work force; where procedures and technology supporting them are untried; and where quality of service is subordinated to sheer throughput. If the misfortunes described in the following reports [see p. 433] are to be avoided, great care should be applied by public servants and those who instruct them whenever a policy decision is taken to devise a fresh administrative task which affects large numbers of the public.'[69]

On 24 July 2006, John Hutton (Secretary of State, Department for Work and Pensions) announced the demise of the Child Support Agency and 'an entirely new system for child support that will be simpler to use and administer, will be tougher on parents who do not face up to their responsibilities and will make a bigger impact on the reduction in child poverty, while delivering value for money for the taxpayer'. Tell us the old, old story.

Probably the most notorious (of many) IT fiascos related to tax credits, when, following years of criticism from Parliamentary Committees,[70] the Commissioner issued a damning report:

Tax credits: putting things right (HC 124 of 2005–2006)

'1.4. [The] influx of complaints on tax credits has risen dramatically. In the year to 31 March 2004 I had received 37 complaints; at the end of the following year I had received a further 216 complaints. From being just 3% of the workload of the Parliamentary Ombudsman in 2003–04, in 2004–05 complaints about tax credits rose to form over 9% of total complaints to the Parliamentary Ombudsman. During this business year, tax credits complaints currently account for over 23% of all Parliamentary Ombudsman business. Of the tax credit investigations concluded, the rate of complaints upheld has been far higher than is usual, some 78% of them having been upheld at least in part in the last business year, compared to the general rate of complaints upheld last year by the Parliamentary Ombudsman, which was around a third.

. . .

3.1. [The] processing of tax credit applications is wholly IT based. Although the intention was thereby to create a more efficient processing service, the wholly automated system has been plagued with significant and extensive technical problems which have impeded performance.

3.2. The Revenue assured Parliament as long ago as December 2003 that the system was now stable and working well. The Revenue's Annual Report in October 2004 repeated these assurances. The Minister told Parliament in February 2005, that "the system has been stable and performing very well in terms of availability and speed for well over a year". But the cases I have investigated lead me to the conclusion that such reassurances did not give a complete picture of what has been happening, and the devastating effects the IT problems have had on some individuals' lives, in terms of stress, financial hardship and living with continuous uncertainty regarding their awards. It may only have been a

[69] Report of the Commissioner on the investigation of complaints against the Child Support Agency (HC 135 of 1994–1995), paras 4, 5. See also the highly critical Report by the Comptroller and Auditor General (HC 1174 of 2005–2006).

[70] 'Inland Revenue: Tax Credits and Tax Debit Management' (Committee of Public Accounts) (HC 332 of 2002–2003); 'Inland Revenue: Tax Credits' (Committee of Public Accounts) (HC 89 of 2003–2004); 'Inland Revenue standard report: new Tax Credits' (Committee of Public Accounts) (HC 782 of 2005–2006); 'Tax Credits: putting things right' (Select Committee on Public Administration) (HC 577 of 2005–2006), together with the government's response (HC 1076 of 2005–2006).

minority of tax credit recipients who were affected in this way; but they amount to many tens of thousands of [families].

. . . .

3.4. When the Revenue gets tax credits wrong, it can have significant consequences for people's lives. It can lead to uncertainty and loss of confidence in tax credits, with people unsure whether they can trust the accuracy of award they are getting and therefore rely on the money as part of their household budget. It can plunge the family finances into crisis. There is also the sheer stress of having repeatedly to contact the Revenue to sort out the consequences—both getting mistakes rectified, and then, if overpaid, challenging the recovery of any overpayment which has [resulted].

. . .

3.9. In early 2004–05 the Revenue identified an isolated system problem, which during 2003–04 and early 2004–05 caused 60,000 customers to be overpaid a total of around £45 [million].

3.10. Although from the Revenue's point of view, these problems were successfully fixed over a year ago, for the customers affected the consequences have been long-lasting. The reduction in tax credit payments to recover the overpayment has caused major financial difficulties for families, affecting their ability to pay for childcare and household bills. It has caused immense [stress].

. . .

3.15. There were also processing delays caused by IT problems, which meant that changes of circumstances, notified to the Revenue by customers were not processed for weeks if not months. This led to much confusion for customers in understanding their awards, and in some cases, errors going [unspotted].

3.16. Although described by the Revenue as "isolated difficulties", these technical glitches—mixed with staff mistakes—have had devastating consequences for the families affected. In some cases they have led to overpayments of tax credits; in others, to an award being halted [altogether].'

VII. Remedies

It is important to note that, according to the strict wording of the Parliamentary Commissioner Act, the Commissioner is not a tribunal or an appeal court and has no statutory power to enforce any findings or to redress grievances. The Commissioner cannot award damages, quash decisions, substitute a new decision for that of the administrative authority, or order the administrative authority to follow a particular course of action. The Commissioner has been appointed 'for the purpose of conducting investigations'.[71] However, the Parliamentary Commissioner scheme of things has developed such that a remedy may be given to a complainant in circumstances where there is no unlawful interference with a legal right and where the judicial review scheme of things (discussed in chapters 9 and 10), therefore, might leave the complainant without any remedy. Courts can of course, enforce their decisions. The Commissioner may, however, have to rely on the political tactic of using the 'esteem' of the office of Parliamentary Commissioner to cause political embarrassment which has to be swept under the carpet by the (often grudging) bestowal of a remedy. If mal-administration is found, that fact, together with the department's response, is reported to the referring Member of Parliament, who may then take the matter further. Early on, a Commissioner said that he did not think it appropriate to 'recommend' a remedy.[72]

---

[71] Section 1.   [72] HC 49 of 1969–1970, Select Committee on the *Duccio* case, questions 25–30.

Nevertheless, in a later case,[73] a student complained that the Scottish Education Department, at short notice, refused her a grant for an educational course. Maladministration was found in that the student had not been given clear advice as to her circumstances and the rules relating to grants and the department issued an apology. However, the Commissioner felt that an apology was not a sufficient remedy where the complainant was faced with expenditure that she might otherwise not have incurred, and 'suggested' that financial compensation might be awarded, with the result that an ex gratia payment was made. The Commissioner said that this was a satisfactory outcome of his investigation. For an example of 'suggesting' an appropriate (and expensive) remedy, see the *Barlow Clowes* case[74] and for an example of 'asking' for an appropriate remedy, see the passport case.[75]

Report of the Commissioner on the *Barlow Clowes* case (HC 76 of 1989–1990)

In May 1988, the Barlow Clowes group of companies collapsed and many, many Members of Parliament referred complaints to the Commissioner from members of the public who had lost their investments in Barlow Clowes, and who alleged that their financial loss had been caused by the acts or omissions of the Department of Trade and Industry in respect of the Department's regulatory functions with regard to the surveillance and licensing of Barlow Clowes.[76] The Commissioner conducted a long detailed investigation and identified five findings of maladministration and considered that there was a strong case for compensation for those investors who had suffered as a result of Barlow Clowes being allowed to continue in business.

The Commissioner

'8.13 Before addressing the matter of compensation in detail, it is right that I should say something about what might be represented as the harshness of a conclusion that compensation should be paid on account of, it might be said, some minor oversights. For my part, however, I would not look at the matter in that way. A regulatory agency—which is what the Department were, at the time, in relation to the protection of investors—ought, to my mind, by definition to adopt a rigorous and enquiring approach as regards material coming into its possession concerning an undertaking about which suspicions have been aroused, and also as regards representations made to it on the part of the undertaking in [question].

. . .

8.15 A matter which it seemed to me would need to be taken into account, in some manner or other, was the possible blameworthiness of others besides the Department. [It] is not part of my function to consider questions of blameworthiness of persons or organisations other than the governmental organisations to which my jurisdiction extends. On the other hand I could not ignore the fact that accusations had been levelled by investors at others besides the Department, to the effect that those others should in some sense or another bear part of the blame for what occurred in the Barlow Clowes affair and for the losses suffered by investors and those representing them to the possibility of legal proceedings in various directions with a view to recouping the losses which investors have suffered, or some part of them. In that connection, it had been represented to me on behalf of investors that if I were to find that a case for compensation by the Department had been made out, the solution to the problem of compensation would be for the Department, in effect, to bear the cost of compensating investors in full, while being "subrogated to", and taking the benefit of, any claims which investors, and the receivers and liquidators [might] have against third [parties].

[73] HC 190 of 1983–1984, Case 752/82.   [74] P. 429.   [75] P. 430.
[76] See Gregory R and Drewry G, 'Barlow Clowes and the Omdusman' [1991] PL 192–214 and 408–442.

8.16 It seemed to me, certainly, that matters ought to be arranged in a manner which, while securing a just result for investors, enabled recoupment action to be taken against any persons who might have been at fault. It also seemed to me that, while fairness required that the investors affected should be left, at the end of the day, in the position of having had the great bulk of their losses made good to them, it would not be unfair or inappropriate if, bearing in mind the inherent risks of high return investments, the ultimate settlement left them a modest way short of being compensated in full.

8.17 When I put to the Principal Officer of the Department my recommendation that the injustice which I had found investors to have suffered as a result of the Department's administrative failings ought to be remedied by the payment of compensation on a basis which took account of the considerations set out above, he indicated to me that the Government disagreed with a number of my specific findings and proposed to set out its views on those matters in a separate document to be published at the same time as my report [HC 99 of 1989–1990]. The Principal Officer also indicated that in the Government's view my report raised a number of important issues about the responsibilities of regulators, and said that the Government proposed to set out its views on these issues in the same document. However, the Principal Officer told me that the Government recognised that this case had created very great hardship, and involved a unique combination of unusual features. In the light of that the Government was, in the exceptional circumstances, and without admission of fault or liability, prepared to make a substantial payment to investors who had suffered loss. This payment would be made to investors in [return] for their assigning to the Secretary of State their rights, in the liquidation and against third parties, and giving an undertaking to provide reasonable assistance in the pursuit of those [rights].

. . .

8.19 The Principal Officer summarised the basis for calculating the payments to investors as follows:

"First, a calculation would be made of the basic claim attributable to each investor at the date of the liquidation of the relevant company. This calculation would take into account not only the amount originally invested but also interest which would have been earned had the amount invested been deposited and earned compound interest in a long-term UK deposit account. The amounts thus calculated would then be abated on the following basis. Where the basic claim as calculated was not greater than £50,000 it would be abated by 10%. Where the basic claim was greater than £50,000 but not greater than £100,000 the first £50,000 would be abated by 10% and the remainder would be abated by 20%. Where the basic claim was over £100,000 the first £50,000 would be abated by 10%, the next £50,000 by 20% and the remainder by 40%. Where an investor had more than one account his or her accounts would be aggregated for this purpose. The amount to be paid would then be calculated by applying compound interest (up to the end of 1989) at an appropriate rate to the abated sum thus calculated, taking account of the interest which investors could have earned on sums which have already been paid in the liquidation or by third parties. This would give a gross figure, from which would be deducted the amounts already paid to investors in the liquidation or by third parties to give the total amount to be paid."

8.20 The Principal Officer explained to me the reasons why the Government proposed that claims should be abated in this way. First, he said, the Government considered it important for investors to understand that no investment is entirely free of all risk, and that investors must be expected to bear part of the risk themselves. Secondly, investors who have large sums at their disposal might also be expected to be better placed to take proper care before committing their funds, and should accept a greater degree of responsibility for the consequences of their own decisions: the payment to them should reflect [this].

8.21 I was, of course, disappointed that the Government was not willing to give its unreserved acceptance to the findings I had made as the result of my investigation. Such indications as I had seen of the grounds for questioning my findings had left me altogether unconvinced. The Government had however—with whatever reservations—proposed making substantial payments to Barlow Clowes [investors]. In that I saw ground for satisfaction. It remained, however, for me to consider whether the quantum of the proposed payments would be such as to enable me to say [that] the injustice which I had found that investors had suffered in consequence of the Department's maladministration would be remedied by the payments. As to that, it seemed to me not unsatisfactory that those with investments of £50,000 or less would end up having received 90 per cent—and those with investments of up to £100,000 at least 85 per cent—of their capital and, in addition, compensation in the form of interest for loss of income on that amount since the collapse. Those investors, with £100,000 or less invested, constitute, I understand, over 99.5 per cent of the number of investors involved. As to the larger investors, they would certainly be left with a greater percentage loss. [In] the result I concluded that I could not say, in all the circumstances, that the Government's proposals would not constitute a fair remedy for the injustice which had been suffered.'

Statement by the Secretary of State for Trade and Industry (164 HC Official Report (6th series) cols 207–212)

'Mr Ridley: [The] House will be pleased to know that, after very careful consideration, the Government have decided, in the exceptional circumstances of this case and out of respect for the office of the Parliamentary Commissioner, to make substantial ex gratia payments to all investors who have suffered loss. I shall give the details later. Equally, I want to make it clear that the Government do not accept the Parliamentary Commissioner's main findings, nor are the Government legally [liable]. There are, however, a number of unusual features which taken altogether distinguish this case from other business failures. Although at the relevant time the Government had started on the process of overhauling the legislative background, before April 1988 the regulatory machinery was inadequate. It is also true that a large number of investors, many of them elderly, have suffered hardship. Many believed, although wrongly, that they were investing in gilts. They were led to believe that their investment was safer than it was. When disagreeing with the findings in the PCA's report, the Government are not asserting that the conduct of the Department was beyond criticism, given the benefit of hindsight, but in the Government's view, the Department's handling of the case was within the acceptable range of standards reasonably to be expected of a regulator. For the reasons that I have given, the Government have decided to offer substantial payments, without admission of fault or liability, to investors who have suffered loss. The Government have decided that investors who invested up to £50,000, including reinvested interest calculated at building society rates, should be able to recover 90 per cent of their investment. It is important to maintain the principle, which the PCA recognises, that investors should bear some of the loss themselves. This is particularly so for larger investors, who must be expected to bear a greater part of the responsibility for their own decisions. To reflect this, the Government have decided that investors should be able to recover 80 per cent of their investments between £50,000 and £100,000 and 60 per cent of investments over [£100,000].'

Report of the Commissioner (HC 592 of 1999–00, case no C.1500/99)

The Commissioner upheld a complaint by Mr A that the Immigration and Nationality Directorate (IND) of the Home Office had delayed for five months in transferring his stepson's conditions of stay in the United Kingdom from his wife's Russian passport to his stepson's new Russian passport. The Commissioner criticised IND for their poor handling of letters and telephone calls from Mr A and the Member of Parliament's office chasing progress on the matter. As a result, the family had been unable to visit relatives in Russia and Mr A's wife, who acted as his interpreter, had been unable to accompany him abroad, thereby preventing him from carrying out his business activities. Mr A sought redress for his business losses and for the stress and inconvenience suffered by his family as a result of IND's delay.

The Commissioner

'6.21. There remains the question of compensation for Mr A. What unremedied injustice has been caused to Mr A and his family by IND's maladministration? [It] seemed to me that, had it not been for IND's maladministration, [Mr] A could reasonably have expected to have received the passports back by the beginning of November 1998; in the event he did not receive them back until the end of March 1999. It therefore seemed to me that in that respect the effect of IND's maladministration was to prevent Mr A's family from using their passports for five months between November 1998 and March 1999, and that therefore for that period they lost the benefit of freedom to travel, on business and for other [reasons].

6.22. The Permanent Under Secretary has said that he would consider further whether to offer an ex gratia payment to Mr A if he were to provide an explanation of how he incurred business-related financial loss as a result of returning his wife's and stepson's passports, and of how his losses were quantified. What business loss did Mr A unavoidably incur? Mr A has said that he suffered business losses as he was unable to travel to Russia on business without his wife as his translator. I am satisfied from Mr A's account that he needed to travel to Russia in order to do business there; that it would have been virtually impossible, and wholly impractical, for him to have done so unaccompanied by a Russian translator; and further, that in all the circumstances it was reasonable for him to conclude that he could not do so if his wife could not travel with him to perform that function.

6.23. Mr A has been unable to provide the audited accounts of his actual earnings that the Permanent Under Secretary has said that IND would usually require; neither, because of the sporadic and unpredictable nature of his business, can he provide accurate forecasts of the sums he may have lost as a result of being unable to travel to Russia with his wife between November 1998 and March 1999. I have seen sufficient evidence to convince me both that Mr A carried out extensive business in Russia of the type he has described prior to returning to the UK, and that he had lined up business commitments in Russia which he was unable to undertake because of IND's delay. However, it also seems likely that Mr and Mrs A would not have taken full-time employment in the UK in February 1999 and November 1998 respectively had they been able to resurrect their business in Russia in late 1998 as they had intended. Therefore at least some of the potential business income that they have lost as a result of being unable to travel to Russia for five months will have been offset by the money they earned instead during that period from full-time employment in the UK. It is impossible to calculate whether such earnings will have fully offset the potential losses of the A family. Nevertheless, I asked the Permanent Under Secretary whether he would agree in principle to make an ex gratia payment to the A family in respect of business loss, less their total income from employment for the period from November 1998 to March 1999. In reply he said that he was prepared, in principle, to consider paying such compensation. However, his difficulty was that, despite the best efforts of the Ombudsman's staff who had visited Mr A, he did not have sufficient evidence on the basis of which, as accounting officer, he could justify such expenditure. The Permanent Under Secretary recognised that by the nature of Mr A's business his income was not a regular one, and he noted that he had no audited accounts, but he said that it would be right for IND to have some firm existing evidence on which to rely before making such a payment. He said that IND would be willing to consider further the issue of making a payment to Mr A in respect of business loss if he could provide them with the information that he had supplied to the tax authorities in his country of residence in the past two years, or some other firm evidence of his income for the last two years of trading. In the circumstances, I accept the Permanent Under Secretary's reasoning for requiring such firm evidence before IND can consider further the matter of compensation for Mr A's potential business loss.

6.24. I turn finally to the stress and anxiety which Mr A says he and his family have undergone. Mr A has described a number of ways in which the overall effect of IND's maladministration was to put tremendous strain on him and his family. Chief among those effects was to prevent Mrs A and her son both from visiting their family for Christmas and New Year, and from visiting Mrs A's father and taking medicine to him when he became dangerously ill. The illness of Mrs A's father would have been distressing enough for her and her family in itself, but IND's failures served only to compound that distress. It is only in exceptional circumstances that the Ombudsman considers it appropriate to seek recompense for anything other than quantifiable financial loss. I regard this as such a case. I therefore asked the Permanent Under Secretary to consider making an ex gratia payment to the A family in recognition of the considerable distress and anxiety that IND had caused them. In reply IND said that they were prepared to make Mr A an ex gratia payment of £1,000. I welcome that.'

Is there now a constitutional convention or a legitimate expectation that a finding of injustice caused by maladministration will be remedied by the department or authority concerned?

Nowadays, once maladministration has been identified, the almost invariable practice of the department or authority is to give an 'appropriate' remedy. A typical series of everyday situations, complaints and remedial action may be found in the Annual Report of the Commissioner for 1983:[77] arrears of sickness benefit were paid and national insurance contributions refunded and a benefit, which had been overlooked, was also paid; after an unnecessarily prolonged investigation of a person's tax affairs, a contribution was made to the complainant's accountancy costs; when recovery of overpaid supplementary benefit was mishandled, there was a review of local office procedures and organisation; after a delay in providing a girocheque for a claimant, the local office payment arrangements were improved; after an unreasonable delay in handling an appeal against non-payment of unemployment benefit, arrears were paid and procedures examined with a view to making them more effective; after a Home Office failure to act on receipt of information led to the improper issuing of a visa to enter the United Kingdom, a review of procedures was undertaken; following the failure to review the decision to reduce level of war pension, arrears, plus compensation, were paid; when procedures relating to an overpayment of supplementary benefit were mishandled, the recovery of an overpayment was not pursued.

The constant approach taken by successive Commissioners has been that a person who has suffered injustice as a result of maladministration should as far as possible be put back in the position in which he or she would have been had the maladministration not occurred. Initially, this tended to concentrate on making good financial loss and to financial compensation which could be quantified (for example, arrears of benefits, payment of interest, the costs of engaging a solicitor or debt counselling fees):

....

Report of the Commissioner (HC 118 of 1988–89, case no 475/87: delay and mishandling of an application for a full driving licence, p. 416)

'11. In regretting the confusion and inconvenience caused by DVLC's handling of Mr A's case, the Principal Officer of the Department, through me, offers his apologies to Mr A. The Principal Officer also accepted that an ex gratia payment would be justified to meet Mr A's expenses in trying to obtain his licence. I am pleased to note that in February 1988 the parties reached agreement and that DVLC made payments of £57.50 in settlement of legal costs and £30 in settlement of telephone costs incurred by Mr [A].'

---

[77] HC 322 of 1983–1984, para 13.

Gradually, however, other forms of injustice have been emphasised, such as the causing of distress, stress and physical illness. This probably commenced with:

....

Report of the Commissioner on the investigation of complaints against the Child Support Agency (HC 135 of 1994–95), case no C.31/94: erroneous identification of complainant as father of a child for child support maintenance purposes

'1. A man complained that the Child Support Agency (CSA) wrongly identified him as the father of a [child].

. . .

4. Before April 1993, a man (Mr H) of the same name as the complainant and also living in the same town was maintaining his son under an attachment of earnings order through the local Magistrates' Court. The boy's mother, Miss A, is receiving income support and the court order was collected by DSS [Department of Social Security]. The collection was handled by the Benefits Agency Finance Office (BAFO). After the introduction of the Child Support Act, such cases were taken on by CSA for assessment under the new legislation. Miss A's case was referred to the CSA Centre at Dudley (the Centre) in April 1993.

5. On 19 April 1993 Miss A completed a maintenance application form which was received at the Centre on 27 April. She named Mr H as the father of her son and gave his address as the one previously held by BAFO. She did not give Mr H's national insurance number or his date of birth. She pointed out that Mr H was paying maintenance for their son to DSS. The Centre obtained a printout from the BAFO computer system which confirmed the address given by Miss A but did not give a national insurance number or a date of birth for Mr H. The Centre consulted the Departmental Central Index (DCI) looking for a national insurance number for the absent parent. They found an entry for the complainant and, believing him to be the absent parent and the listed address to be out of date, they recorded the complainant's national insurance number and date of birth on the BAFO printout as being those of the absent parent. On 19 May the Centre issued a maintenance enquiry form, together with notes on its completion, an explanatory leaflet about child maintenance and a standard covering letter, to the address recorded on the BAFO printout which had also been given by Miss A. No reply was received and on 3 June the Centre issued a reminder. On 11 June the reminder was returned by the Royal Mail marked "Gone away".

6. On 17 June the Centre sent a form to the Inland Revenue asking them to try to trace Mr H through their records. The Centre quoted the complainant's national insurance number on the form. On 29 June the Inland Revenue returned the form showing Mr H's address as that of the complainant. On 26 July the Centre issued the maintenance enquiry form and accompanying correspondence to the complainant. On 2 August the complainant telephoned the Centre about the correspondence which had been sent to him. He said that he did not know Miss A and was not the father of her child. According to the Centre's contemporary note of the conversation, the officer to whom the complainant spoke apologised for the mistake and promised to investigate the matter further. In his complaint to the Commissioner, however, the complainant said that the officer had expressed the view that he "must be the right Mr H" because his national insurance number tallied with that of the absent parent. The officer refused to disclose the national insurance number but promised to make further enquiries and contact the complainant again. Also on 2 August the Centre telephoned the local office of the Benefits Agency (BA) who were responsible for paying Miss A's income support about the case. Their records showed no current address and no national insurance number for Mr H the absent parent but his date of birth was recorded as 28 January 1961. The Centre checked DCI records but there was no trace of a Mr H with that date of birth.

7. On 23 August the Centre received a letter from the complainant in which he again said that he was not the father of Miss A's child and complained about the failure of the Centre to withdraw their imputation. He said that the pain and anguish which the accusation had caused had been such that he was on medication for insomnia and his wife on medication for depression. He said that they might have sown seeds of doubt in his wife's mind as to his trustworthiness and honesty and that their relationship might never be the same again. The complainant asked for an immediate statement from the Centre admitting their error and an assurance that the matter would not be pursued. On 26 August the Centre wrote to the BA office asking them to interview Miss A to obtain as much information as possible about her child's father. On 31 August the Centre wrote to the complainant telling him that a full investigation was taking place to identify the absent parent. They said that it was inevitable that the investigation might take some time and they expressed the hope that the delay in resolving the matter would not cause any more anguish and distress for him and his wife. The Centre promised to write again as soon as the matter had been resolved.

8. On 2 September the BA office obtained the name of the absent parent's employers from the Magistrates' Court. On 3 September Miss A called at the BA office and confirmed that the absent parent's date of birth was January 1960 or 1961. On 6 September the office telephoned the absent parent at his employers. He confirmed that he was the father of Miss A's child and supplied his date of birth and current address. On the same day the BA office passed the information to the Centre.

9. On 15 October the Centre wrote to the complainant telling him that they had identified the correct absent parent. They apologised for any inconvenience and distress which the incident might have caused him and his wife and assured him that the matter was closed. On 21 October the Centre received an enquiry from the Member about the progress of their investigation. On 1 November the Centre acknowledged the Member's enquiry and promised a reply within ten days. On 26 November the Centre wrote to the Member saying that an error had been made and that a letter of apology had been sent to the complainant. The complainant was dissatisfied with that response and asked the Member to refer his complaint to me and he did so. I received it on 10 January 1994. The complainant said that the Centre's ineptitude had damaged his marriage to such an extent that it would be a long time before the relationship recovered.

10. In his comments to me on the case the Deputy Secretary added his apologies to those already given by the Centre for their mistake in sending a maintenance enquiry form to the complainant and for the distress it had caused. He also apologised for the delays by the Centre in writing to the complainant once the identity of the absent parent had been established, and in sending a substantive reply to the Member's enquiry. The Deputy Secretary said that staff at the Centre had been told during initial training about the importance of matching records very carefully and that that had been reinforced once the Centre had become operational. The mistake had happened very soon after the Centre had opened and had been made by an inexperienced officer who had relied too heavily on computer records and had failed to test the validity of the information obtained. The Deputy Secretary told me that procedures at Dudley and at other Centres were being tightened up to reduce the margin of error in such cases and that CSA were also examining the forms used in specialist tracing action to see what improvements could be made to avoid similar errors.

11. The man's complaint against CSA is the second which I have accepted for investigation involving mistaken identity. I regard such errors as very serious. The mistake made in the complainant's case was inexcusable. When a check was made with the DCI the only points of similarity between the complainant and the absent father of Miss A's child were the name and the area in which they lived (paragraph 5). To assume on that basis that they were the same man was irresponsible. The purpose of the enquiry and the consequences of getting it wrong make it inconceivable that action should have been taken on such scant evidence. Moreover, the information necessary to trace the correct absent parent was already held by the BA office (paragraphs 6 and 8) as the Centre should have realised. I severely criticise the Centre's actions.

12. The effect on the complainant and his wife of receiving correspondence about child mainten-ance was clearly—and understandably—traumatic (paragraphs 7 and 9). It was made worse by the

Centre's slow and lackadaisical approach to putting right their mistake. There is some dispute about what took place during the telephone conversation on 2 August 1993 (paragraph 6) but in any event the Centre ought to have made immediate enquiries to find out what had happened. The matter could, and should, have been resolved that day. Instead, after a half-hearted attempt to investigate, the Centre let matters slide until they received a letter from the complainant three weeks later (paragraph 7). Even then, despite the contents of the letter, the Centre showed no sense of urgency. They were content to place enquiries in the hands of the local BA office and let matters take their course; the Centre's reply to the complainant was insensitive and inadequate. Then the Centre took more than five weeks to let the complainant know that the absent father had been identified and formally to acknowledge that they had made a mistake (paragraphs 8 to 9). That was unforgivable. The Centre's handling of the Member's correspondence on the case also left something to be desired. The Centre's maladministration deserves my strongest criticism.

13. The distress and anxiety which the Centre caused the complainant and his wife over a period of some eleven weeks and the effect on their relationship was such that in my view the Department's apologies did not provide adequate redress. I therefore invited the Permanent Secretary, in the exceptional circumstances of the case, to make the complainant an ex gratia payment as well. The Permanent Secretary added his apologies to those already given for CSA's error, but said that he did not agree that the circumstances of the case were so exceptional as to warrant compensation for distress. He said that he was prepared to consider reimbursing the complainant for any out-of-pocket expenses which he had necessarily incurred in his dealings with [CSA].

14. I was dissatisfied with the Permanent Secretary's response and on 23 September wrote asking him to reconsider the matter. I pointed out that he has a clear duty to afford equitable relief against injustice which is shown to have arisen directly from maladministration by a government department. I remained of the view that the distress and anxiety to which the complainant had been subjected, by the receipt of enquiries about a child of whom he was not the father, was sufficiently serious to justify financial recompense. On 12 December the Permanent Secretary replied that his legal advice was that there is no liability in respect of anxiety and distress without proof of either injury to health or bad faith on the part of the Agency. He said that it was the view of DSS that such mistakes should be treated as broadly comparable to legal challenges and similar principles applied in order that there should be consistency of outcome and ease of resolution. In the light of those considerations he accepted that, if the complainant were able to provide medical evidence to support his contention that he had suffered insomnia and depression as a direct consequence of CSA's actions, he would be prepared to reconsider the question of making some compensatory payment to him. After very careful consideration I decided to accept that proposition.

15. The complainant suffered entirely unnecessarily at the hands of CSA. CSA have admitted their error and have apologised to him. In addition the Permanent Secretary has agreed to consider compensating him should he be able to provide evidence of illness resulting from the actions of CSA. I find that to be an acceptable response to a fully justified complaint.'

The wide variety of remedies given as a result of the Commissioner's investigations may be illustrated by a report on, inter alia, the Immigration and Nationality Directorate:[78] a failure to make a timely offer to the complainant of an extension of leave to remain to enable her to travel had resulted in having to cancel a holiday, the Home Office offered apologies to the complainant and agreed to make an ex gratia payment in respect of deposits that were lost on the holiday (Case C.1526/99); a delay in processing an application for permanent residence was compensated by ex gratia payments in respect of an unpaid day off work that had to be taken to visit the Directorate in an attempt to sort out the matter, and in respect of the distress that had been caused by being prevented from travelling at various important times (Case C.290/00); a delay in processing an application for indefinite leave to remain which prevented

[78] HC 592 of 1999–2000.

the complainant from visiting his father before he died and to attend his funeral was compensated by an ex gratia payment in recognition of the severe distress caused (C.378/00); a delay in processing an application for leave to remain was compensated by an ex gratia payment in recognition of distress and uncertainty caused to them (Case C.733/00).

Sometimes findings of maladministration may result in the introduction of special compensation schemes. This happened in the case of the Channel Tunnel link (again, see p. 419):

The Channel Tunnel link

(a) Commons *Hansard* 9 January 1996: column 120, 121

'The Minister for Railways and Roads (Mr John Watts): [The] House is aware of the Parliamentary Commissioner for Administration's report on the channel tunnel rail link and blight, which relates to the generalised blight phase of the rail link project. [On] this occasion, I simply reiterate that, in the response to the Select Committee given by my right hon. Friend the Secretary of State for Transport on 1 November [p. 423], the Government concluded that they had to continue to resist the Parliamentary Commissioner's finding of maladministration in this case, and that any new principle of administration implied in the Committee's report was unacceptable, but that the Government were prepared to consider afresh whether a scheme might be formulated to implement the Committee's recommendation that redress should be granted to those affected to an extreme and exceptional degree by generalised blight from the channel tunnel rail link during the period June 1990 to April 1994, and how such a scheme might operate. The Government agreed to look again at the possibility of a compensation scheme out of respect for the Select Committee and the office of the Parliamentary Commissioner, and without admission of fault or liability. We also made it clear that the Government would have to consider seriously the possible costs of such a scheme, which cannot yet be established, and that we could not make an open-ended commitment on an uncosted basis, in view of the Government's responsibilities to the taxpayer.'

(b) Commons *Hansard* 4 December 1997: column 285

'Mr Rowe: To ask the Secretary of State for the Environment, Transport and the Regions what steps he has taken to notify households likely to be eligible for the exceptional compensation payable as a result of Channel Tunnel Rail Link blight on their properties; and if he will make a statement.

Ms Glenda Jackson: The arrangements for the Scheme of Redress for Exceptional Hardship were advertised in a range of local newspapers selected to cover the various route options. In addition, details were sent to Members of Parliament, local authorities and Citizens Advice Bureaux for the areas concerned. As a reminder prominent newspaper advertisements have recently been re-published. Furthermore, the initial announcement of the Scheme attracted wide coverage including on local television news.'

(c) Lords *Hansard* 17 December 1998: column WA166

'Lord Ponsonby of Shulbrede asked Her Majesty's Government: Whether decisions will be issued to applicants under the scheme of redress for extreme and exceptional hardship for those affected by blight from Channel Tunnel Rail Link (CTRL) route options between 1990 and 1994.

The Parliamentary Under-Secretary of State, Department of the Environment, Transport and the Regions (Lord Whitty): We have today announced that 28 applicants demonstrated that they suffered extreme and exceptional hardship as a result of past CTRL blight and will be receiving £10,000 each. This is an ex gratia scheme which is additional to normal compensation arrangements for those directly affected by the CTRL. The scheme originated from a finding of maladministration against the then Department of Transport by the Parliamentary Commissioner for Administration.'

The convention of financial remedies for injustice caused by maladministration has resulted in specific instructions from the Cabinet Office to departments, authorities and agencies. Guidance on compensation payments in cases where maladministration has occurred is set out in detail in:

Government Accounting (1996, revised 2005), chapter 18: 'Financial Redress—Maladministration and Charter Standards'

'18.7.5 If the department concerned accepts that maladministration has occurred and that financial redress is appropriate, the general principle should be to provide redress which is fair and reasonable in the light of all the facts and circumstances of the case. Where the complainant has suffered actual financial loss as a result of the maladministration, or faced costs which would otherwise not have been incurred (and which are reasonable in the circumstances), the general approach should be to restore the complainant to the position he or she would have enjoyed had the maladministration not occurred. Where there is not an actual financial loss or cost, careful judgement will be needed to decide whether financial redress is appropriate and, if so, what constitutes fair and reasonable financial [redress]. Payment for non-financial loss should be [exceptional]; in all cases, the normal requirements for the proper care and use of public funds apply.

18.7.6 Where, following a complaint or the discovery of a case, departments conclude that other individuals or bodies may have suffered in the same way, they should seek to identify (wherever reasonably practicable) all those affected and consider whether, in the interests of equity, they should offer [redress].

. . .

18.7.11 Cases involving actual financial loss or costs are likely to fall into three broad categories: where the complainant has lost in whole or in part an entitlement to a government grant, subsidy, benefit payment, allowance or other payment; where the complainant has been put to additional expense; and where payment of a grant or benefit [has] been delayed and compensation has been sought on account of the delay.

18.7.12 Loss of entitlement to a payment or an allowance might occur, for example, because of misleading advice by the department about closing-date rules, with the result that an application was not submitted in time. Where the department is satisfied that failure to comply with the rules was a direct result of official failure, the redress should restore the complainant to the position he or she would have enjoyed had the maladministration not [occurred].

18.7.13 [Where] an individual or body has, as a result of maladministration, incurred extra expenditure (for example, out-of-pocket expenses in having to go through an administrative procedure which otherwise would not have been necessary, in order to obtain a proper decision, or having to employ professional advice or representation to do so), departments may reimburse such additional costs to the extent that they were reasonably and legitimately incurred. Reimbursement of costs would not, however, be appropriate, where a department had properly made a decision (i.e. there was no maladministration) which was subsequently altered through some appeals mechanism.

18.7.14 Claims may also be made for lost earnings or income, through having to spend time to pursue complaints, or for out-of-pocket expenses incurred in the process, e.g. expenditure on travel, post, photocopying or telephone calls. Similar questions should be asked: was the time spent to sort things out excessive; was the expenditure beyond what would normally have been necessary and reasonable in the light of the circumstances of the case?

. . .

18.7.16 Consideration of compensation for fruitless expenditure may arise where a complainant has incurred, as a direct result of a department's maladministration, expenditure which he or she would not have incurred if the case had been handled correctly at the outset. (For example, where an individual had been told he or she would qualify for assistance under a scheme and, in the light of that assurance, incurred expenditure, only to be told subsequently that the original assurance was incorrect). Departments may pay compensation for reasonable expenditure which would not otherwise have been incurred.

18.7.17 Delay falls within the working definition of maladministration. Moreover, claims for compensation payments can give rise to difficult issues and consequently extensive consultation, within departments and between departments and the Treasury. Claims for compensation should therefore be handled as promptly as possible at all stages.

18.7.18 Although there is no comprehensive entitlement in law to interest for a period during which individuals or bodies may have been denied money to which they are entitled, delay is among the examples of maladministration quoted during the passage of legislation relating to the Parliamentary Ombudsman. Compensation payments in Parliamentary Ombudsman cases may include an element for [delay].

18.7.19 In considering compensation for delay, relevant factors include: the need, when assessing the amount of such compensation, to allow for normal delay—[the] test is whether the delay is excessive or unreasonable; any contribution to the delay by the claimant's own conduct—his or her actions or inaction—which may be a material factor; and the degree to which the claimant can be considered to have suffered financially as a result of the delay.

18.7.20 If the compensation for delay is to be calculated as if it were an interest payment, it should usually, for administrative simplicity, be on the basis of simple [interest].

. . .

18.7.24 Claims for compensation may arise on grounds other than actual financial loss or costs. These include the following: (a) inconvenience, annoyance, frustration, worry, distress, suffering or anguish: these may include claims made on the grounds of "time and trouble" (as distinct from lost earnings or out-of-pocket expenses) or "botheration", that is, maladministration in the process of dealing with a complaint. The Parliamentary Ombudsman has said that he or she recommends such "consolatory" payments (also described sometimes as "solace" payments) only in exceptional cases and for exceptional reasons; (b) hardship: where maladministration has resulted in some form of privation, for example where an official error had led to loss of employment for a period, causing a substantial deterioration in standards of living. Such claims may cover both loss of income and compensation for the effects of the loss; (c) the loss of an opportunity to make a gain: for example, where a delay in granting planning permission as a result of maladministration has delayed the setting-up of a business, with the result that the complainant claims loss of income; (d) compensation for the loss of a physical or financial asset, or a reduction in its [value].

. . .

18.7.26 In considering claims of the types listed in 18.7.24, departments should take the following points into account:

(a) the fact that some degree of inconvenience, frustration, worry or distress, etc. may necessarily be involved in the administrative process which has caused the complaint (for example, in the establishment of an entitlement to benefit) and may also be unavoidable in the investigation of the complaint—in short, the occurrence of inconvenience [does] not of itself constitute grounds for payment, and departments should look at the degree and the reasons for its occurrence;

(b) the effects of the [inconvenience];

(c) the complainant's own contribution to the situation—for example, the amount claimed may represent a loss which the complainant could have taken reasonable steps to reduce or avoid;

(d) whether the loss may have been caused wholly or partly by the fault of a third party rather than a government body;

(e) whether the inconvenience [was] caused by the wilful action of, or improper behaviour by, a member of the department's staff—this might be regarded differently from the results of a genuine error;

(f) any legal analogies which might help inform the decision; and

(g) whether the amounts claimed are realistic, taking into consideration the position in which the complainant would be likely to have been if the maladministration had not occurred.

In claims of financial hardship as a result of maladministration, the complainant's financial circumstances may also be a relevant consideration.'

In some circumstances, material compensation is not the adequate remedy:

Report of the Commissioner on the *Sachsenhausen* case (HC 54 of 1967–68)

'67. Having found evidence of maladministration it is my practice [to] proceed to identify the injustice so caused and to consider whether any such injustice has been or will be remedied.

68. I have no doubt about the sincerity of the complaint that has been made to me by certain of the complainants I have seen, that the rejection of their claim and the terms in which the rejection has been defended by the Foreign Office have done harm to their standing and reputation. For these men it is an essential part of a distinguished and gallant war record that they were held in a concentration camp and suffered Nazi persecution there. If it is denied that they were so held, their reputation is impaired and their veracity called in question. This is an injustice which in my opinion will be remedied by the publication, and I hope acceptance, of my finding that they were all held by the SS in premises which were part of the Sachsenhausen complex; as regards those detained in the Zellenbau, that they were held in premises which while structurally separated within the main compound were an integral part of the Sachsenhausen concentration camp organisation and were operated in conjunction with the main camp; and that as regards Nazi persecution, all the complainants suffered loss of identity, risk of liquidation and constant anxiety over their fate, while certain Zellenbau detainees sustained further persecution in the form of different degrees of physical hardship and degradation, with mental suffering from isolation, proximity to the execution of others, and the constant threat that they themselves would be executed without warning. Further, this was exceptional treatment which they incurred because of the exceptional bravery and resource that they had shown in working for their country and damaging the German war [effort].'

Report of the Select Committee on the Parliamentary Commissioner on the *Sachsenhausen* case (HC 258 of 1967–68)

'9. The other finding of maladministration by the Commissioner relates to the treatment by the Foreign Office of the evidence submitted by the complainants in support of their claims as regards their own conditions under detention in the Zellenbau and as regards conditions in the main compound of [Sachsenhausen].

10. As regards the complainants' evidence of more lenient treatment received by others held in Sachsenhausen, the Foreign Office were no doubt justified in regarding this as irrelevant to the men's claims because in their view the right comparison was with "concentration camp treatment as generally understood", which they alone could define and which they defined as the worst forms of Nazi brutality. But the fact remains [that ministers were advised that the] complainants' account of

conditions in the main compound of Sachsenhausen was "fantastic", when in fact there was corroboration for it ([paragraph 64, p. 414]). Under this head the Commissioner makes it clear, and Your Committee agree with him, that the criticism relates to the action of officials. No attempt has been made to single out the names of officials for criticism. The advice given to ministers in this matter was the collective responsibility of Foreign Office officials, and there is no evidence or suggestion of personal bias or animosity on the part of any official in the chain. Indeed it is clear that the attention of Foreign Office officials was fixed on the irrelevance to the success of the complainants' claim of their evidence of instances of lenient treatment in the Sachsenhausen main compound. It seems to have escaped their notice that they were providing ministers with an assessment of the evidence that reflected upon the reputation and veracity of the [complainants]. Your Committee think it unfortunate that the Foreign Office, by disputing the findings of the Commissioner, might be thought to be reviving the question of the veracity of these complainants. In order to remove any doubts upon this score, Your Committee put it on record that they for their part accept the findings of the Commissioner [and] regard the standing and reputation of these Zellenbau complainants as completely vindicated.'

A finding of maladministration may result in administrative changes designed to ensure that maladministration will not occur in future (or at least that the opportunities for maladministration will be reduced). Where

'schemes are the subject of large numbers of complaints alleging [maladministration], I believe that it is good administrative practice to review the relevant scheme. An early recognition that lessons can be learned from complaints and other feedback can prevent systemic failure or a situation in which public resources are expended on remedial action, which would not have been necessary had a thorough review taken place at the appropriate time and had any corrective action been carried out proactively.'[79]

Early on, the Commissioner considered it appropriate to examine general changes in administrative practice, of general benefit to the public or sections of the public, which could be shown to have derived wholly or in part from the Commissioner's investigations, typical examples being: the Department of Employment issued clearer leaflets relating to unemployment benefit and people going on holiday; the Department of Health and Social Security, when one claimant successfully appealed against a decision, automatically reviewed all other similar claimants whose claims had been rejected but who had not appealed; the Home Office revised their prison rules to allow prisoners to consult a solicitor and institute proceedings against the prison authorities; the Inland Revenue issued clearer tax forms.[80] A Home Office policy to pay on an ex gratia basis compensation to members of the public who suffered damage to property as a result of offences committed by borstal absconders only where the damage occurred in the neighbourhood of the borstal was changed (or at least extended) by interpreting the concept of 'neighbourhood' more liberally;[81] in addition to paying the individual complainant arrears of war pension, the DHSS undertook to review the cases of 24 other retired officers in a similar situation to that of the complainant and, where appropriate, to pay arrears of pension to them, plus compensation for delay in paying those arrears;[82] three complaints relating to motor licensing renewal reminder forms were upheld against the Department of Transport and, as a result of a review, small refunds (amounting in total to over £1 million), were made in over 100,000 other cases;[83] the DHSS changed their written instructions to staff as the previous instructions had resulted in an inordinate delay in a claim

---

[79] 'A debt of honour': the ex gratia scheme for British groups interned by the Japanese during the Second World War (HC 324 of 2005–2006), para 226. [80] HC 72 of 1971–1972.
[81] HC 42 of 1973–1974. [82] HC 312 of 1977–1978. [83] HC 247 of 1978–1979.

for attendance allowance;[84] finally in the delay and mishandling of an application for a full driving licence case (p. 416):

'The Principal Officer of the Department has acknowledged that the mishandling arose essentially as a result of human error and has told me that it has been drawn to the attention of the clerk mainly concerned and that the consequences of her actions have been explained to her. He said that the complaint had also highlighted the delay in letters reaching the correct destination and that, as a result, DVLC were reviewing their distribution arrangements with a view to ensuring that correspondence was circulated with the minimum possible delay. I understand that procedures are also being reviewed and steps taken to ensure that staff at executive officer level become involved where correspondence received indicates that the case is not being correctly handled or is giving cause for complaint and communication between the courts and generalist teams within Clerical Drivers Branch are improved.'[85]

Sometimes the finding of maladministration may result in a fundamental change to government policy:

State earnings-related pension scheme (SERPS) inheritance provisions: redress for maladministration (HC 271 of 2000–2001)

'1. Additional pension, more commonly known as SERPS, is the earnings-related part of the state retirement pension. [Widows] and widowers were to receive the full additional pension earned by their [spouse. However], the inheritance rules were [subsequently changed] so that widows and widowers would inherit only one-half of the amount of additional pension payable to their [spouse].

2. [I] received 344 individual complaints referred to me by 170 Members of Parliament. Their common basis was that the change had not been mentioned in DSS [Department of Social Security] and BA [Benefits Agency] leaflets purporting to explain SERPS [entitlements] nor had DSS and BA staff drawn the future reduction to the attention of those making enquiries about pensions. Several of those who complained to me said that they had made financial provisions for the future of their spouse on a misinformed basis. They contended that, if they and their spouse had been made aware of the true position, they would have made different provision more suited to their circumstances and which would have better secured the financial position of the survivor.

3. [In] my report to Parliament [HC 305 of 1999–2000], I found DSS and BA guilty of maladministration. I strongly criticised their failure to make their leaflets accurate and complete, and commented that they had compounded that mistake by not recognising the need to check that staff were aware of the change in the law. I said publicly that many thousands of people were very concerned both that they had not provided sufficiently for their spouses, and that they had still not been advised of the correct position. Those who had received oral advice also feared they would not be able to prove they had been misled. I emphasised in my report that, in those circumstances, the burden of proof rested on DSS and BA to show that citizens claiming to have been misled would not have acted differently had they not been misinformed, rather than on those citizens to show that they would have acted differently.

. . .

5. [On 15 March 2000, the Secretary of State for Social Security in a statement to Parliament said that he accepted my] recommendations. He said that the change to the inheritance provisions due to come into force in April 2000 would be postponed until 6 October 2002; and that the Government would set up a scheme whereby those who had been misinformed and who would have acted differently had they been correctly advised would have their former inheritance rights [protected].

. . .

---

[84] HC 585 of 1985–1986, Case 697/85.   [85] HC 118 of 1988–89, Case No 475/87, para 10.

8. On 29 November 2000 the Secretary of State made a further statement to Parliament in which he announced that the proposal for a protected rights scheme was to be abandoned. Instead, the surviving spouse of anyone reaching, or due to reach, state pension age before 6 October 2002 would inherit up to 100% of their SERPS [entitlement].

. . .

12. I therefore welcome the Government's proposals that the widow or widower of anybody who reaches state pension age before 6 October 2002 will be able to inherit up to 100% of his or her late spouse's SERPS [entitlement].'

So, there may be a constitutional convention of accepting the Commissioner's findings of injustice caused by maladministration and the appropriate ways to remedy that injustice. Cabinet Office pronouncements have taken the moral high road: 'The Ombudsman's recommendations are not legally binding, but Ministers have made clear to Parliament that they will be accepted. In the very rare case where a body proposes not to accept the Ombudsman's recommendation, the department should notify the Cabinet Office as soon as possible.'[86] 'In the light of investigation of a case, the Parliamentary Ombudsman will decide whether complainants have suffered injustice because of maladministration; and whether any injustice has been, or will be, remedied. The Parliamentary Ombudsman's findings on maladministration are final; there is no established avenue of appeal.'[87] But, what if the convention is disregarded and the high moral tone demonstrates a veneer of hypocracy? Quis custodiet?

VIII. Ministerial Responsibility

When the institution of Parliamentary Commissioner was being proposed, there was considerable debate as to the relationship between the advocated institution and the traditional doctrine of individual ministerial responsibility and the equally traditional doctrine that an aggrieved citizen applies for redress to his or her Member of Parliament, who will use the doctrine of ministerial responsibility to Parliament to achieve that redress (see chapter 6). The Whyatt Report took pains to emphasise that the new institution would not conflict with those doctrines.[88] The then government's attitude was expressed as being that the proposed institution could not be reconciled 'with the principle of Ministerial Responsibility to Parliament [and that] the appointment of a Parliamentary Commissioner would seriously interfere with the prompt and efficient dispatch of public business. In the Government's view there is already adequate provision under our constitution and Parliamentary practice for the redress of any genuine complaint of maladministration, in particular by means of the citizen's rights of access to Members of Parliament.'[89] JUSTICE replied (in a memorandum) that

'the Commissioner would help to make ministerial responsibility more effective. He would penetrate the screen which ministers interpose between members of Parliament and government departments, and he would keep Parliament informed about administrative practices which were open to criticism. [The] Commissioner would be concerned with maladministration, ie, with exactly the class of acts for

---

[86] 'Handling of Parliamentary Ombudsman Cases' (Cabinet Office), paras 38, 42, 45, 48.
[87] 'Government Accounting'(1996, revised 2005), Chapter 18: 'Financial Redress—Maladministration and Charter Standards'.   [88] Paras 155, 156.
[89] The Attorney-General, 666 HC (5th series) col 1125.

which the full rigour of the doctrine of ministerial responsibility is relaxed. The only possibility of conflict would be if the Commissioner criticised something which the Minister wanted to defend. In that case the Minister could perfectly well make his defence in Parliament in the ordinary way. It would be quite wrong to suggest that the responsibility of the Minister for what is done in his Department would be reduced if a Commissioner investigated complaints. The responsibility would remain the same as at present, neither more nor less.'

As has been seen, the Parliamentary Commissioner was established (perhaps rather cautiously) as an arm of Parliament (principally, the House of Commons, since complaints are received from, and results reported to, Members of the House of Commons and, in addition, the Commissioner is supervised and supported by a select committee of the House of Commons). Since the establishment of the office, the Commissioner has indeed penetrated the screen interposed between Members of Parliament and government departments, has kept Parliament informed about administrative practices which were open to criticism, the class of acts for which the full rigour of the doctrine of ministerial responsibility is relaxed, namely, minor and relatively non-political acts of maladministration, have been remedied. However, in the relatively few politically important and sometimes emotive situations where the Commissioner has criticised something which the minister wanted to defend, the minister has made his or her defence in Parliament in the ordinary way and the responsibility has remained in accordance with tradition. As one Commissioner commented:

'There is no appeal or review procedure for my investigation reports or recommendations and the power of enforcement quite properly rests with Parliament and not with me. If a department or authority found my recommendation for a remedy unacceptable and refused to grant it, I would report the fact to Parliament that an injustice had gone unremedied. It would be for Parliament then to decide what to do about it. The constitutional wisdom of this arrangement is self-evident. But so, I think, is the fact of its effectiveness. [The] "teeth" are therefore where they belong in a parliamentary democracy: in Parliament itself.'[90]

The Commissioner was, of course, referring to the provision that if 'after an investigation it appears to the Commissioner that injustice has been caused to the person aggrieved in consequence of maladministration and that the injustice has not been, or will not be, remedied, the Commissioner may, if the Commissioner thinks fit, lay before each House of Parliament a special report on the case'.[91] The purpose of this provision was and is, in circumstances where the department, authority, agency, or government as a whole refuses to give a remedy or proposes an inadequate remedy, for Parliament (and here the House of Lords has an often crucial role to play) to sit in judgment (often relying on the aid and comfort provided by the select committee) on the Commissioner's findings of injustice, maladministration, and redress and the department's, authority's, or government's response. In addition, 'the Commissioner may from time to time lay before each House of Parliament such other reports as the Commissioner thinks fit'.[92] Section 10(4) reports may raise issues analogous to section 10(3) reports. To date, there have been four section 10(3) reports[93] and two section 10(4)

---

[90] HC 322 of 1983–84, para 12.   [91] Section 10(3).   [92] Section 10(4).

[93] Rochester Way Bexley (Complaint about late claims for compensation from the Department of Transport: HC 598 of 1977–1978); 'The Channel Tunnel rail link and exceptional hardship' (HC 270 of 1994–95), pp. 419 and 423; 'A Debt of Honour: the ex gratia scheme for British groups interned by the Japanese during the Second World War' (HC 324 of 2005–2006), where the Commissioner's finding of maladministration was upheld by the Select Committee on Public Administration (HC 735 of 2005–2006, para 37); 'Trusting in the pensions promise: government bodies and the security of final salary occupational pensions' (HC 984 of 2005–2006), p. 446.

reports,[94] where the Commissioners findings were originally disputed by the department concerned or the government as a whole. The constitutional consequences of a 'special report' are considered below:[95]

Statement of the Foreign Secretary on the *Sachsenhausen* case
(758 HC Official Report (5th series) cols 107–117)

'[I] find myself dealing with the Report of the Parliamentary Commissioner with mixed feelings. On the one hand, I applaud the office which he holds and would like to take some credit for having helped to bring it into existence. On the other hand, I now find myself dealing with a Report which is critical of the Department for which I am responsible. I have strong feelings about Ministerial responsibility which I would like to touch upon later. Hon. Members will have read the Report, so I will not go over it or try to recapitulate it. I would, however, ask the House to spend a few minutes looking at the case through the eyes of the Ministers in the Foreign Office who have had to deal with it over a large number of years. The case did not begin with me. I came to it, and I admit it quite frankly, predisposed towards the view of the [claimants]. I wished to be generous and I questioned at that point whether the Foreign Office was being over-legalistic but, having started from that position, I am prepared to accept the responsibility for being satisfied that all the information I needed was supplied to me. This is one of the grounds on which I disagree with the Parliamentary Commissioner. I was satisfied that all the information I needed was supplied to me. I read every piece of paper on the file and I came to my conclusions by my own processes of judgment. That these conclusions were the same as the Department's does not, of course, invalidate them, and that they were the same as every previous Minister's does not invalidate them. I want to make it quite clear that every Minister who has looked at these things has come by his own processes of judgment to the same [conclusion].

This difficult problem was further complicated by the need imposed upon us by [the] "Butler" rules—the rules which the then Foreign Secretary laid down which arose from the Anglo-German Agreement which obliged us to distinguish between, on the one hand, those who were held to have suffered the full brutality of Nazi persecution and, on the other hand, those many gallant men and women who were ill treated, and grievously ill treated, as prisoners of war or civilian internees but were not under the rules so [regarded]. In order to distribute the money in this country, the term "Nazi persecution" had to be defined, and Lord Butler [decided] then that a claimant must satisfy one of two conditions: either he must have been detained in a concentration camp or he must have been in an institution where the conditions were [comparable]. Cases of Nazi persecution outside concentration camps were also provided for. The Notes for Guidance which the then Foreign Secretary, Lord Butler, approved in 1964 [provided] that anybody who had been in an institution where the conditions were comparable with those of a concentration camp would be eligible. Claimants from such institutions had to justify their claims by detailing the actual conditions in their place of detention. Claimants who were held in a concentration camp did not have to do [this].

Having filled in that background, I come to the Parliamentary Commissioner's Report. I would like first to deal with the allegation that there were defects in the procedure by which the Foreign Office reached its decisions on these claims. I have examined this with all the thoroughness at my command and I say quite frankly that I do not believe that I was misled by officials. I regard it as a minister's job to see that he has all the necessary information. If he does not have it, that is a very severe mark against him. If, having got it, he does not take it aboard, that is an even severer mark against him, and I reject completely the Parliamentary Commissioner's allegation that officials did not submit the evidence that ministers right up to and including me should have had.

---

[94] *Sachsenhausen*, pp. 412 and 439, and *Barlow Clowes*, pp. 428 and 430.   [95] P. 446.

I want to say something else, and I think that the House had better accept this. [Interruption.] I said I think the House should accept this. Of course, it may accept what it likes but I am entitled to say what I think. Hon. Members are entitled to disagree with me, but I must say what I think. I think that the House had better accept this, and before it disagrees with me it had better think seriously about it. It is that we will breach a very serious constitutional position if we start holding officials responsible for things that are done wrong. In this country, ministers are Members of Parliament. That is not true of many countries. I think that we have the best Parliamentary democratic system in the world and one of the reasons for this is that our ministers are responsible to Parliament. If things are wrongly done, then they are wrongly done by ministers and I think that it is tremendously important to hold to that principle. If things have gone wrong, then ministers have gone wrong and I accept my full share of the responsibility in this case. It happens that I am the last of a series of ministers who have looked at this matter and I am the one who got caught with the ball when the lights went up. But I accept, I repeat, my share of the responsibility. I could not possibly do other. I read every page of all the information. It is ministers who must be attacked, not officials.

The Office of Parliamentary Commissioner was intended to strengthen our form of democratic Government, but let me say that if that Office were to lead to changing this constitutional position so that officials got attacked and ministers escaped, then I think that the whole practice of ministers being accountable to Parliament would be undermined. I think that the morale of the Civil and Diplomatic Services would be undermined and I am sure that many experienced [Members] want to think twice about that [situation]. Ministers are responsible to the House, and must be: officials in Departments are responsible to their ministers, and must be. I assure the House that in so far as there are lessons to be learned from this case, I have ensured that the Foreign Office has learned them. I have issued to the Department the instructions which seemed to me to follow. They will be carried out. It is for the House to hold me responsible for that and not try to hold responsible any officials for whom I speak in the [House].

What the Parliamentary Commissioner has not found is that the conditions of these men, bad as they were, were as bad as those suffered by many other gallant men in many other German camps. The Parliamentary Commissioner concentrated exclusively on Sachsenhausen—[HON. MEMBERS: "Those were his terms of reference."] Those were the terms of reference, but because he concentrated on that, he, unlike me and unlike my predecessors, did not have also to take into account the thousands of other cases of other people who suffered even more than these gallant men suffered. He concentrated his report on the narrow issue, the very much narrower issue, and that I was not allowed to do. I had to take into account the wider issue.

He concentrated his attention on the very much narrower issue of whether the special camp, the Sonderlager, or the Zellenbau, the cell block, formed part of the concentration [camp]. Whether the Sonderlager or the Zellenbau were inside the perimeter of Sachsenhausen was always an arguable issue. All the [ministers] who have dealt with this case—and I ask the House to understand that it has been dealt with with the utmost compassion and the utmost desire to do the right thing and the fair thing—all the ministers who have dealt with this case on the basis of the "Butler Agreement" have come to one conclusion, which was that technically speaking they were not inside the [perimeter. All] the ministers who have looked at this quite separately have come to one conclusion and the Parliamentary Commissioner has come to another. I repeat that no one has ever disputed that this was a borderline case. I am bound to say that I do not see any reason for thinking that the judgment of the Parliamentary Commissioner is necessarily better than that of all of us. [HON. MEMBERS: "Then why appoint him?"]. I must be allowed to make my own [case].

I have issued the required instructions in the office as to how cases like this should be dealt with in the future. I hope that the House will agree with me that there is no useful purpose to be served by prolonging a controversy which has caused distress and resentment to some very honourable, very gallant and most deserving people. I hope too, that the House will feel that justice has been done to them by the decision I have made and that I have taken all the care I can to ensure that we do not have another problem like this.

Before I sit down let me say this. Newspapers talk about bungling and blundering. It is imperative for me to say that no one has blundered or bungled. This was an issue of judgment. The Parliamentary Commissioner's view is that our judgment was wrong. I am willing to accept that. I have therefore reviewed and revised my decision, but this remains a matter of judgment and on a matter of judgment on an issue as narrow as this anyone can be wrong. I would have wished, since it has come out this way, that I had taken this decision earlier. I did not, but there it is. I have taken the decision now, and I hope on this basis we can end what for me is a very unhappy story.'

An idealistic view was presented by the Select Committee early on:

'The doctrine of ministerial responsibility [is] as follows: The minister in charge of the Department is answerable to Parliament for the workings of the Department. The action of the Department is action for which the Department is collectively responsible and for which the minister in charge is alone answerable to Parliament. It is only in exceptional cases that blame should be attached to the individual civil servant: and it follows from the principle that the minister alone has responsibility for the actions of his Department that the individual civil servant who has contributed to the collective decision of the Department should remain [anonymous].'[96]

Whether or not ministerial responsibility following a report from the Parliamentary Commissioner now has any real effective meaning in the modern constitutional scheme of things is debatable, particularly in view of the high level of incompetence from central government and the ascendancy of political spin-doctors in recent years:

The security of final salary occupational pensions

(a) Trusting in the pensions promise: government bodies and the security of final salary occupational pensions (HC 984 of 2005–2006)

'The injustice claimed

2.38. The representative complainants complained that members of schemes had not been able to make informed decisions about whether to diversify their pension and savings provision, about whether to remain in schemes when they left the employment of the sponsoring company, and when making other choices such as seeking new employment with a more secure employer, taking early retirement, or agreeing to stay at work beyond normal scheme retirement age.

. . .

2.40. Others who have complained to me have told me of the significant losses they have suffered, of the outrage they feel that this has been allowed to happen, and of the effects that these events have had on their health, their financial security, their future plans, and on the other members of their families. They have also told me of their loss of faith in Government, in their employer, and in the wider pension system.

. . .

2.45. However, complainants have told me that the injustice they feel is not "merely" such financial loss, enormous though such financial loss is in most cases. There are three other aspects of the injustice they claim.

2.46. The first is a deep sense of outrage at the way that their pensions, in words that have been used to me on many occasions, "have been stolen". A common theme among the many letters and other communications I have received was anger, directed both at Government and at employers, that the pension system had failed scheme members.

. . .

---

[96] Report of the Select Committee on the Parliamentary Commissioner (HC 350 of 1967–68), para 24.

2.48. The second additional aspect of the injustice claimed relates to a sense that individual members of final salary schemes had been prevented from making informed choices about their provision for retirement and about their other financial planning.

2.49. Many individuals told me that, in a context in which Government, employers, and the pensions industry were all promoting membership of occupational pension schemes and where those responsible for the legal, regulatory and administrative frameworks that underpinned the security of such schemes were encouraging membership without mention of risk, they had been misled into making extremely critical financial decisions without any knowledge of the right questions to ask. This, in the view of complainants, amounted to misdirection and a dereliction of a duty on public bodies to provide balanced information about the statutory regime for pensions protection which they had introduced, which they operated and for which they were wholly responsible.

2.50. The final additional aspect of the injustice claimed by individuals was the profound effects that the loss of their pension rights had had on their self-respect and their family life.

2.51. Many individuals told me that the uncertainty and distress that they had suffered was compounded by a sense that they as individuals had failed their families by having been lulled into a sense of false security by official statements about their pensions. This also had been reinforced by the effects that the loss of their pension had had on other members of their families, many of whom had had to make a larger financial contribution to family income than expected, had had their own plans ruined, or who had had to deal with the stress and anxiety caused to the scheme member.

2.52. All of the above constitutes the injustice claimed by complainants.

. . .

Findings

5.19. There is no general statutory or common law obligation on public bodies to provide information or advice to members of the public. However, it was recognised by legal advice provided to DWP [Department for Work and Pensions] in May 2000 that, where DWP or another public body chooses to provide information, this should be correct and complete. Such advice constituted, along with other things such as its public statements, the "internal" standards to which DWP should have had regard.

5.20. In addition, [previous] Ombudsmen have held that a public body may be deemed to have acted with maladministration either where it had knowingly provided information or advice which was misleading or inadequate or where it had failed to follow its own procedures or policies in relation to the provision of such information or advice. I concur with that view.

. . .

5.68. [I] consider that the official information given to the public about the degree of security provided by a scheme being funded to the MFR [the Minimum Funding Requirement, which prescribed the level of contributions that a scheme had to hold] level (i) was, prior to September 2000, misleading, incomplete and inaccurate, in that it gave assurances which were incompatible with the design and purpose of the MFR as prescribed by Government, and with its practical operation. These assurances were that the MFR was designed to ensure that schemes had sufficient assets to meet their liabilities and that a scheme funded to the MFR level would be able to pay cash transfers of accrued rights to non-pensioners. In addition, no disclosure or even mention was made of risks to accrued rights or of the potential effects of statutory priority orders on wind-up; (ii) was, between September 2000 and April 2004, deficient, in that it lacked any degree of consistency as to what might be expected from the MFR. Some official statements and publications, especially those aimed at the general public continued not to mention risk and to give a misleading impression as to the security of pension rights, while others began to explain the true position; and (iii) was only broadly accurate from April 2004 onwards.

. . .

5.74. [I] consider that the deficiencies in the relevant official information that I have identified constituted maladministration.

. . .

Have individuals suffered injustice?

5.167. It is clear to me from the evidence I have reviewed about the personal circumstances of all those who have complained to me that they and their families have suffered financial loss, a sense of outrage, and considerable distress, anxiety and uncertainty.

5.168. I am also satisfied that they have suffered injustice through an inability to make informed choices or to take remedial action. It is not in dispute that scheme members were not provided with full information about the degree of security afforded by the MFR; what this investigation has sought to establish was whether the information provided about these matters by official sources constituted maladministration.

. . .

Has this injustice been remedied?

5.180. It seems to me that, had individuals had all the information they needed, they would have been able to make properly informed choices about the options—whether in relation to membership of their scheme or to seek to remedy funding issues concerning their scheme—that were open to them.

. . .

5.186. Taking all of the above into account, I am satisfied that this form of injustice, these lost opportunities, was caused by the incomplete, inconsistent, unclear, and often inaccurate information given to scheme members, trustees and sponsoring employers through official sources.

. . .

5.226. Where I identify maladministration, it is my usual practice to seek to put individuals back into the position they would have been in had that maladministration not [occurred].

5.227. That is why my assessment which follows is restricted to considering the impact of the failure by public bodies to disclose risk and to properly inform scheme members of the degree of security they could expect from their scheme being covered up to the MFR level.

5.228. Had the members of schemes known fully the risks to their pensions, I consider that many of their financial decisions would unquestionably have been different.

. . .

5.234. I have found that Government provided incomplete, inconsistent, misleading or inaccurate information about the degree of protection that the law provided.

. . .

5.236. These lost opportunities were the result of the maladministration I have identified in this report and, in my view, contributed directly, with other factors, to the situation in which the loss of pensions and other benefits which were to be derived from the members' contributions to their scheme were able to occur.

. . .

5.242. They were also unable to consider what action they could take to remedy the financial weakness of their scheme, as the official information given to them was deficient.

5.243. Official information effectively distorted the reality of the position in which scheme members found themselves. As a result, they were wholly unaware that their pension rights were dependent on the ongoing security of the employer sponsoring their scheme.

5.244. That constitutes an injustice which was caused by maladministration. While I cannot say that maladministration alone caused the financial loss suffered by complainants, I do consider that it was a significant factor in creating the environment in which those losses were crystallised.

. . .

Recommendations

6.14. My first recommendation relates to remedying the financial injustice suffered by those who have complained to me and also those in a similar position as those individuals.

6.15. I recommend that the Government should consider whether it should make arrangements for the restoration of the core pension and non-core benefits promised to all those whom I have identified above are fully covered by my recommendations—by whichever means is most appropriate, including if necessary by payment from public funds, to replace the full amount lost by those individuals.

6.16. I recognise that this would be a significant commitment, although it seems to me that it would be a commitment that could be discharged over a number of years if the right means were identified and that this would be a commitment that would decline over the years.

6.17. I recognise that it may be felt by the Government that it is possible to mitigate the cost to the taxpayer of pension replacement from monies due from other bodies—particularly any that they consider played a significant role in the relevant events. If that is so, I consider that the Government should reflect on whether it would be more appropriate for it to take action itself—rather than to expect individual scheme members or trustees to do so to recoup such sums using the considerable collection and enforcement powers that Government has.

6.18. I am aware, in addition, that the relevant pension schemes have assets that could assist pension replacement and that alternatives to securing pension liabilities for members of the affected schemes through the purchase of annuities have been suggested. These alternatives, as I understand matters, would still require Government action.

6.19. I recognise that asking the taxpayer to meet part or all of the cost of this recommendation raises significant public policy questions. However, I believe that the Government should consider whether its response to my recommendations should have regard to what might be considered by many—and certainly by some of the people who have complained to me to be a [precedent].

. . .

6.23. My second and third recommendations relate to the recognition of the effects of the maladministration on those who have suffered as a result—and are directed in different ways at scheme members and scheme trustees.

6.24. I recommend that the Government should consider whether it should provide for the payment of consolatory payments to those scheme members fully covered by my recommendations—as a tangible recognition of the outrage, distress, inconvenience and uncertainty that they have endured.

6.25. I also recommend that the Government should consider whether it should apologise to scheme trustees for the effects on them of the maladministration I have identified, particularly for the distress that they have suffered due to the events relevant to this investigation.

6.26. I recognise that it may not be possible to make a personal apology to every trustee concerned, not least because it would be very difficult to identify them. However, I consider that those people rightly feel that their professional reputations have suffered and I believe that official regret for this should be publicly stated.'

(b) Commons *Hansard* 15 March 2006: column 1449, 1450

'Sir Menzies Campbell: [The] former Secretary of State for Work and Pensions [said] that if someone lost out because of inaccurate information, the Government should offer redress as a matter of principle. What happened to that principle?

The Prime Minister: [I] accept and understand entirely the sense of loss, anger and anxiety of those who have lost pensions for which they have paid for many, many years, but we have been asked to give, on behalf of the taxpayer, a £15 billion commitment and we simply cannot do that in circumstances where the reason for the loss is the collapse of the pension schemes themselves.

Sir Menzies Campbell: What is the point of an independent ombudsman and a report which makes recommendations when the Government will not accept the conclusions? Does not the Prime Minister understand that if the Government fail to offer compensation it will operate only as a further diminution of public confidence in pensions?

The Prime Minister: Except that, as I said to the right hon. and learned Gentleman, although of course we must and do treat seriously the ombudsman's findings, we are being asked as a consequence of them to give, on behalf of general taxpayers £15 billion-worth of commitment. We simply cannot do [that].'

(c) Commons *Hansard* 16 March 2006: column 1620–1635

'The Secretary of State for Work and Pensions (Mr. John Hutton): With permission, I should like to make a statement on the ombudsman's report on the security of final salary occupational pensions published yesterday. The Parliamentary Commissioner's report is a detailed piece of work and, of course, deserves a proper, full and formal response. It is my intention to publish such a response in the next few weeks. However, I would like today to set out the reasons why, after very careful consideration, we have reached the view that we cannot accept any of the findings of maladministration and why we have therefore decided to reject all but one of her [recommendations].

Turning to the individual findings: first, the ombudsman found that official information about the security that members of final salary occupational pension schemes could expect from the minimum funding requirement, introduced in the Pensions Act 1995, was sometimes inaccurate, incomplete, inconsistent and therefore potentially misleading, and that that constituted maladministration. We do not accept that the Department's leaflets were inaccurate, incomplete, inconsistent or misleading. It is true that some were more detailed than others, but that was because they were designed for different audiences. All the leaflets covered by the report carried very specific statements that they were not a full explanation of the law and were for general guidance only. The leaflets themselves make that [clear].

Against this background, the Government have considered carefully the ombudsman's [recommendations], which involve considering whether to restore the lost pension rights of affected scheme members, making consolatory payments and apologising to scheme trustees. As I have already made clear, the Government are unable to accept the findings on which those recommendations are based. We do not believe that the findings of maladministration can be supported by the facts. It simply cannot be right that the losses from the schemes that have collapsed should be met by the taxpayer without establishing any causal connection between the actions criticised in the ombudsman's report and the losses that people have incurred. The report fails to establish that connection.

[I] do not consider that it would be in the wider public interest for Government to accept that very substantial liability on behalf of taxpayers. We calculate that liability as being in the range of £13 billion and £17 billion in cash terms over the next 60 years. We estimate that the administration costs would be in the region of a further £20 million each year. We do not therefore intend to take the actions recommended by the ombudsman. The taxpayer cannot be asked to accept the responsibility for effectively underwriting the value of private investments in the way the report [suggests].

I would like to finish by making two things absolutely clear. First, this Government have been the first to accept the moral and social obligation to make sure that as many as possible of those who have suffered hardship and distress in these circumstances receive financial support. That is why this Government have set up the financial assistance scheme, with £400 million of public money. The scheme is designed to provide help to those who have lost the most and who are in the greatest need—those closest to retirement and who are therefore least able to make alternative provision. The scheme will currently help up to 15,000 people who have faced significant occupational pension losses. [The] financial assistance scheme will top up those people's pensions with financial support, to give a maximum income of up to £12,000 a [year].

Mr. Philip Hammond (Runnymede and Weybridge) (Con): May I start with the bit that the Secretary of State missed out? On behalf of Opposition Members, I should like to express my sympathy for the 85,000 people who have lost their pensions through occupational pension scheme failures. Those are decent people who set out to do the right thing to try to ensure a decent retirement for themselves, and they have seen their dreams of a comfortable and secure retirement cruelly shattered. Their plight is not only a series of personal tragedies, but a tragedy for the cause of increased pension saving as confidence in the system is further undermined.

The ombudsman's report specifically addresses misleading information by [Government. On] the first count the ombudsman, an official of Parliament charged with the task of reporting to Parliament on claims of maladministration, has investigated and found that maladministration has occurred. What is the Government's response? A direct challenge to the authority of Parliament. The accused in the dock has decided that he will be judge and jury in his own case. He has just spent 10 minutes of his 15-minute statement going over the case again and telling us that the ombudsman, an Officer of the House, got her findings wrong.

The ombudsman rightly replies to the right hon. Gentleman that "Parliament has decided that it is my role—and not that of any party to a complaint—to determine what constitutes maladministration". The House must insist that the Government bow to the decision arrived at by the due process which the House put in place in respect of the factual finding of maladministration by the ombudsman. While they are at it, the Government could also comply with the ombudsman's recommendation that they apologise. I do not know whether the right hon. Gentleman's mother ever taught him this, but my mother always taught me that an apology costs nothing.

The real problem for the Government is that the right hon. Member for Edinburgh, South-West (Mr. Darling), then Secretary of State for Social Security, and the present Secretary of State for Transport, has already committed the Government to the principle of redress. In March 2000 he told the House that: "As a matter of principle, we believe that when someone loses out because they were given the wrong information by a Department, they are entitled to redress".

Surprisingly, yesterday at Prime Minister's questions, the right hon. Gentleman was rather more honest about the situation. He did not say the ombudsman was wrong. He did not question her findings of maladministration. He simply told the House that the Government could not pay what he claimed would be a £15 billion bill. However, the ombudsman's principal recommendation was that the Government should consider whether they should make arrangements for the restoration of the pensions and other benefits of those who had lost out, in her words "by whichever means is most appropriate". [The] obvious way, to which the Secretary of State alluded, is the financial assistance scheme, which was put in place to help people who lost their pensions or suffered diminished pensions because their pension funds had failed. [Will] the Secretary of State as a matter of urgency look at how the financial assistance scheme can be reconstructed to help a much wider group of people who have suffered loss of pension rights through no fault of their own? He said in his statement that it would be wrong for the whole burden to fall on the taxpayer. With that thought in mind, will he consider the possible use of unclaimed assets, in particular unclaimed pension and insurance assets, to see whether those could be used to support an expanded financial assistance [scheme]?

Both the Prime Minister and the Secretary of State have used the figure of £15 billion. The Secretary of State today spoke of £13 billion to £17 billion. That is a cash figure and it is meaningless. Will he make a commitment today to put in the Library for the benefit of all Members a properly worked out net present value figure for the cost of making good the pension funds, so that Members can understand what the real figure is, not the hyped-up figure that he and the Prime Minister have been using?

The Government must accept without further delay the ombudsman's factual finding of maladministration. If they do not, the authority of Parliament and the credibility of the ombudsman's office will be critically undermined. The right hon. Member for Edinburgh, South-West had already committed them to the principle of redress in these circumstances, but the ombudsman's recommendations leave scope for examining various ways to deliver that [redress]. The commitment to redress, in whichever form, has already been made by the right hon. Gentleman on behalf of the Government, so Ministers cannot duck it by refusing to accept the ombudsman's finding of fact. It is for the Government to deliver on that commitment, and a great deal is at [stake].

Mr. David Laws (Yeovil) (LD): [As] I understand it, the essence of his statement is that he believes that the Government have got more or less everything right and that the ombudsman has got more or less everything wrong. [If] the Government are going to trample over the ombudsman's report, what is the point in having a parliamentary ombudsman and giving her those [responsibilities?].

Does the Secretary of State agree that those people who have lost their pensions will now feel doubly betrayed, not only because of what originally happened, but because of the way in which the Government have dealt with the report, which comprehensively condemns the Government and states that they provided information that was "inaccurate, incomplete, unclear and inconsistent"? Is the defence in the DWP response to the ombudsman's report—that many people will not have bothered to read those leaflets or that those who have read them will not have paid any attention to them—good enough? One wonders why the Government bother to distribute such leaflets, if people are not supposed to read them or pay attention to them. The Secretary of State's statement was peppered with the excuse that people should have read the small print in the leaflets, but that is the approach of a dodgy second-hand car dealer, which one would not expect from a Secretary of State charged with regulating such [matters].

Mr. Iain Duncan Smith (Chingford and Woodford Green) (Con): The Secretary of State's statement is shameful. It is an outrage to come to the House and systematically attack an independent arbiter who was set up by this House independently to investigate accusations of difficulties. His defence that those people had a let-out clause at the bottom of their advice is utter nonsense. Does he not realise that when lawmakers offer advice, it is categorically different from advice offered by second-hand car dealers who then opt out by saying "You didn't read the small print"? Surely he should accept that his responsibility now is to shoulder the burden of the difficulties that have happened as a result of his advice and deal with it instead of attacking the messenger.

Mr. Hutton: I absolutely reject what lies behind the right hon. Gentleman's comments. They are not accurate and they are not a proper reflection of my [statement].

Miss Anne Begg (Aberdeen, South) (Lab): [Will] my right hon. Friend take this opportunity to reiterate that the Government will stand behind those individuals who have lost large amounts of money and savings? The Government are the only body who can reimburse them for their loss, whether through the financial assistance scheme or any other mechanism. I am looking to the Secretary of State to reiterate that these people will be reimbursed in [future].

Mr. Hutton: That is why the financial assistance scheme was established: to provide financial assistance and support for people who find themselves in those terrible circumstances. As I keep saying, we are re-examining the scheme to ascertain what further scope there might be for providing additional help. [I] have made it clear that no Government can take responsibility for underwriting the total value of people's private savings. That is impossible and [untenable].

Steve Webb (Northavon) (LD): The Secretary of State appears to say one of two things: either the ombudsman is ill informed and has not done a proper job, or she is well informed but her views are irrelevant. Which is it?

Mr. Hutton: The ombudsman has prepared a thorough report and reached conclusions. We disagree with them.'

(d) House of Commons Minutes of Evidence taken before the Public Administration Select Committee (HC 1081-I of 2005–2006)

Witness: Ms Ann Abraham, Parliamentary and Health Service Ombudsman, gave evidence

'Q13 Jenny Willott: There are a number of issues raised about the difference between policy decisions made by the Government and administration by the Government as to what is your remit and what is [not].

Ms Abraham: [I] have been very concerned, and it is one of the points, really, about the manner of the Government's response, about the way in which the Government's response has asserted that the report said things and then challenged them when the report never said those things. If you go back to the judge and jury metaphor, it is almost as if not content with wanting to be judge and jury in its own case it also wants to rewrite the judgment and criticise it on the basis of the rewritten version. If you go to the heart of this report, which is all about the official information that was published and the statements that were made, the findings there, I have been told, were unsustainable. Well, I have looked very carefully at the Department's own standards for official information, in terms of accuracy and completeness, clarity and consistency, and I have looked at the official information against those standards. It [fails].

Q14 Jenny Willott: One of the main issues of dispute with the Government is the fact that the Government says it is going to cost £15 billion to do what you are asking them to do, and that is clearly being disputed by a lot of people. Have you done any estimates about what you think the potential costs of your recommendations are?

Ms Abraham: No, because I do not make recommendations that had any sort of cost to them. Again, if you look at the assertions, the assertions that have been made talk about the causal connection between the leaflets and people's decisions, and then this is Lord Hunt in the Lords: "The Ombudsman's recommendation is that the Government should pay £15 billion over 60 years". I never said that. The report does not say that. The recommendations do not make recommendations of any figures, and I have not done the estimates.

. . .

Q25 Julie Morgan: You are able to make a clear link between the maladministration and the losses that people suffered?

Ms Abraham: I would make it clear that again a lot has been said about what the report does not say. I would like to be clear about what it does say. There were a number of illustrations of injustice that we identified. First of all, we talked about the lost opportunities to make informed choices. As a result of relying on information that was produced by government bodies, people had no idea of the risks that there were to their schemes and how reliant they were on the security of the employer. There were lost opportunities to make informed choices about their pension options. Very simply, if you were aware that your pension was only as secure as your employer was, you might not have chosen to put additional, voluntary contributions into the pension scheme. You might have put that money somewhere else. People simply were not aware and could not make those informed choices. We talked about injustice in terms of outrage and distress and then we talked about the hard financial losses in terms of loss of considerable portions of pensions. That is where we said that the Government maladministration was a significant factor amongst others. We did not say it was exclusively the consequence of the maladministration. The fact was that we identified it as a significant contributory factor amongst others. I said very clearly, I thought, in the report that I was not saying that the Government had sole responsibility here. I could not see how the Government could say it had no responsibility [here].

. . .

Q33 Paul Flynn: What John Hutton said in his parliamentary statement was that the leaflets were general and introductory in nature. They were not a full statement of the law. They made both these points clear. Did they?

Ms Abraham: I do not think they did. I would quote back to DWP its own standards for official information: "Information should be correct and complete"—DWP's own public information policy statement—"Information should be appropriate, relevant, correct, up to date, clear, concise. Any information we provide must be timely, complete and correct". I would also quote back to DWP its own Secretary of State on issues of burden of proof and redress. This is a response to a previous report by one of my predecessors: "The giving of wrong information by government departments is inexcusable. There is a clear responsibility to ensure that the information provided is accurate and complete. As a matter of principle, we believe that when someone loses out because they were given the wrong information by a government department they are entitled to redress". This is not some standard or test that the Ombudsman has dreamed up. This is me assessing the department against the test that it set itself.

. . .

Q41 Mr Prentice: Why do you think the Government has rubbished your report and why did they do it within 24 hours of your report's publication?

Ms Abraham: There are two questions there. In a funny way, I am not sure it has rubbished my report. I think it has rubbished a different report. I was trying to do this all along in relation to the investigation, certainly in the latter stages. I was trying to get the department to address what the report did say rather than attack what it did not say. So far I seem to have singularly failed to do that. That may be something to do with my powers of persuasion. Why so quickly? The response that is in the report which I had from the Permanent Secretary was that they did not want two months to think about it because that would only raise expectations unreasonably and they did not want to do that. Equally, the Secretary of State has said subsequently that the report does deserve a considered and full response so I am waiting for that.

. . .

Q69 Chairman: I got the impression reading your report and your response to the Government's response that you would not have minded nearly so much if the Government had said, "we think she has got a point but we do not agree with her recommendations". In ombudsman terms, you would have found that much more acceptable, would you not?

Ms Abraham: Yes, I would.

Q70 Chairman: What really irked you was the fact that in rejecting the recommendation, they felt they had to go on and reject your finding of maladministration?

Ms Abraham: I think what really "irked me", if that is the term, were statements like "The Government rejects the findings of maladministration. The Government does not accept that maladministration occurred. The Government does not believe the report makes a sustainable case that maladministration occurred. We cannot accept any of the findings of maladministration". Actually that is interesting but unacceptable from the prisoner in the dock, as it has been described by a Member in Parliament, that actually it is not for governments to reject findings of maladministration. If they want to say that no reasonable ombudsman could have reached these findings and these conclusions, there is a place to say that and it is a court of law. I do not want to spend a lot of time in court responding to judicial reviews by Government, but that is the only place to make that challenge properly it seems to me. I think the other thing that irked me was the comment that "The report fails to demonstrate that decisions taken by individual scheme members were influenced by the information that Government did or did not make available". That did seem to me to be a serious challenge to my judgment, but more importantly to the credibility of the people who had complained to me. I think that is where, as I said, my sense of outrage was developed. Then, they went on to rewrite the judgment and made all sorts of assertions about things it did not say. All I would expect in these circumstances is an engagement with what the report says and an acceptance that the Government has some responsibility here and it should treat my findings seriously and it should consider my recommendations seriously. So far, I have not seen that. I think Parliament deserves a better response. I think these complainants deserve a better response.'

(e) Memorandum to the Public Administration Select Committee by the Parliamentary and Health Service Ombudsman, 26 June 2006

'1. The purpose of this Memorandum is to assist the Committee in its inquiry in relation to the Government's response to the [occupational pensions] report.

2. The Memorandum is in three parts: (i) This main section sets out my concerns about the wider implications of the Government's response to my report [in] relation to the constitutional position of the Ombudsman's office, and the role that Parliament has determined the Ombudsman should play in investigating complaints about the administrative actions of public [bodies]. (ii) Annex A sets out my detailed observations on the Government's response to my [report]. In summary my observations are that the Government's response: fails to address the basis on which I found that maladministration had occurred; makes selective use of the comprehensive and detailed evidence set out in my report; provides an unbalanced view of the role of Government in the system of final salary occupational pension provision; and misrepresents what my report says about the causes of financial loss. (iii) Annex B

provides information about [special report] cases in the past [including *Sachsenhausen*, pp. 412 and 439, *Barlow Clowes*, pp. 428 and 430, and *Channel Tunnel*, pp. 419 and 436]. In some cases Government initially rejected findings but remedied the injustice; in others it accepted findings but did not, at first, provide an appropriate remedy. However, in no case did Government both reject findings of malad-ministration and refuse to consider righting the injustice that had been sustained in consequence of that maladministration. Nor has an injustice remained unremedied in any previous case. There is, therefore, no precedent for the Government's response to my report.

. . .

7. In its response, the Department for Work and Pensions (DWP) continues to assert that it can be the final arbiter of complaints about its own actions. As the Committee will understand, this position goes to the heart of the system of independent scrutiny of executive action that Parliament has established; and to the confidence that citizens can have that they will receive an effective scrutiny of and outcome to their complaints.

8. The Government's own rule book, Government Accounting, [says]: "In the light of the investigation of a case, the Parliamentary Ombudsman will decide whether complainants have suffered injustice because of maladministration; and whether any injustice has been, or will be, remedied. The Parliamentary Ombudsman's findings on maladministration are final; there is no established avenue of appeal".

. . .

12. It is not only in relation to this report that I have concerns. There appears to be an emerging atti-tude amongst Government departments that they can properly, and with impunity, reject my independ-ent assessment of their actions, and my findings of maladministration.

13. As the Committee knows, the Chairman of Her Majesty's Revenue and Customs told another Parliamentary Committee that he did not accept my judgement that maladministration had occurred in relation to the administration of tax credits.

14. The Permanent Secretary of the Home Office has recently informed me that he does not accept my findings of maladministration in relation to a number of immigration cases.

15. It would appear that DWP's response to this report has given permission for a wider pattern of behaviour to develop. If this becomes a general pattern, or a culture, I am sure the Committee will agree that this can only undermine the confidence and credibility that is necessary to ensure that the Ombudsman's office can fulfil its role and purpose.

16. Whilst I remain concerned that everything possible is done to secure whatever Parliament considers to be appropriate redress for the people who have lost their pensions, I am also concerned about the implications of the Government's response for the constituents of Members who might wish to complain to me in the future.

17. Since publication of my report, I have received many letters from people with complaints about the loss of their pension, and also from other members of the public.

18. One such correspondent asked me: "what was the point of me coming with my complaint to you if, whatever you say, the Government can still refuse to accept that my complaint was justified? Can the Government ignore the courts, too?"

19. Another said: "I thought you were an independent investigator who could decide on the facts whether my complaint was well founded. If the Government refuses to accept the verdict of Parliament's own Ombudsman, what hope is there for other people who have suffered injustice because of Government action?"

20. Such a loss of confidence is inevitable if Government creates the impression that it is prepared to pick and choose which of my findings it is willing to accept.

. . .

28. I am deeply disappointed that the Government's response to my report has rejected my findings and misrepresented my recommendations. My report does not suggest that the redress for the undoubted injustice suffered by many thousands of pension scheme members should be paid for

wholly by the taxpayer. However, for the reasons given in my report, I do believe that only the Government can organise a proper remedy for the losses sustained by those who complained to me. I remain concerned that everything possible is done to secure whatever Parliament considers to be appropriate redress for the people who have lost their pensions.

29. In addition, I am concerned that the Government's response to my report, together with what appears to me to be an emerging attitude amongst Government officials and Ministers in relation to my findings of maladministration, has serious implications for the constitutional position of my Office.'

(f) Minutes of Evidence taken before House of Commons Public Administration Select Committee (HC 1081-iii, 28 June 2006)

'Q128 Chairman: [Why] has the Government decided to trigger a constitutional crisis?

Mr Hutton [Secretary of State for Work and Pensions]: We have not.

Q129 Chairman: Let me try again. Why has the Government repudiated uniquely an Ombudsman report in the way that it has?

Mr Hutton: Well, let me say two things on that, Chairman. I do not think this is unique. I think there have been previous occasions where governments have not been able to accept a finding of maladministration. We do so with extreme regret and extreme [reluctance]. If you look at the Department's record in relation to working with the Ombudsman, this is the first time in nearly 40 years that we have felt obligated to respond to the Ombudsman's report in the way that we have and, as I said, we have done that with extreme reluctance and having looked very carefully at the arguments that she presented to us. We have not rushed into this [lightly]. Let me also say one other thing: prior to the establishment of the Ombudsman's inquiry into the allegations of maladministration, we had already decided to look at the situation and see to what extent we could provide ex gratia payments to those who have suffered loss in these circumstances. We have the very greatest of sympathy for people who have been caught up in this situation. That is why the Government 18 months ago or so set up a Financial Assistance [Scheme]. We do not accept there is a responsibility on the Government to compensate in the way that she recommended that we should, but we have tried to respond to the financial plight that many people have found themselves in with a very substantial scheme of financial assistance.

Q130 Chairman: Thank you for that but let us just be clear about the constitutional territory that we are in. The Government has cited various previous cases of government disagreement with the Ombudsman [*Barlow Clowes*, pp. 428 and 430], which does not sustain the current position because remedy was provided [and *Channel Tunnel Rail Link*, pp. 419 and 436], where again initially the Government sought to reject but finally accepted and paid remedy. So when the Ombudsman writes to us in her recent memorandum [p. 454], having reviewed the whole recent history of her office and says: "However, in no case did Government both reject findings of maladministration and refuse to consider righting the injustice that had been sustained in consequence of that maladministration. Nor has an injustice remained unremedied in any previous case. There is, therefore, no precedent for the Government's response to my report".

Mr Hutton: I think in the Barlow Clowes case, if I am right, the Secretary of State made it clear, he said: "I want to make it clear the Government do not accept the Parliamentary Commissioner's main findings. Nor are the Government legally liable". It then went on to make an offer of financial assistance available. We have done the same in this case. We have a financial assistance scheme available which is designed to provide some measure of compensation. I accept that it is not the full compensation that the Parliamentary Commissioner recommended that we take but we have, nonetheless, tried to respond to the predicament that many people have found themselves in, whilst reserving the right and I think the Government must always be able to express a view on Parliamentary Commissioners' reports and findings of maladministration. I think it would be very odd if the Government were not able to express a view in these [cases].

. . .

Q132 Chairman: The Government clearly is a party to the dispute and that is why Parliament decided 40 years ago to set up its own independent office who would investigate the actions of government to see whether maladministration had taken place. If you look at the government's own official guidance on all of this from this document called, excitingly, Government Accounting, it could not be clearer. It says: "In the light of investigation of a case, the Parliamentary Ombudsman will decide whether complainants have suffered injustice because of maladministration and whether any injustice has been or will be remedied. The Parliamentary Ombudsman's findings on maladministration are final". It is categorical about the authority of the Ombudsman's position in relation to maladministration.

Mr Hutton: I would simply ask the Committee whether it is also the view of the Committee that that is properly reflected in the legislation. I would say it is not. [If] Parliament intended anything different, it would have made that quite clear in the legislation. I think it is perfectly proper for government to take a view on these matters, but I think we have always tried to take full and proper account, showing full respect to the Office of the Ombudsman in responding to her reports. As I said, I think on this occasion although we were not able to accept her main findings (and that has happened before) we were able to take her report fully into account in the deliberations that took place across government in deciding to what extent we could further extend the Financial Assistance [Scheme].

. . .

Q134 Chairman: This is quite unprecedented in terms of rejection of the findings and refusal of a remedy. Never before have those two conditions not been met in the way that has happened in this case. That is why the Ombudsman says, quite rightly, we are in extremely serious constitutional territory here. We feel that we are. Let me ask you this: is this a decision that the DWP took or is it something that was raised within Government and therefore became a collective Government position?

Mr Hutton: Yes, it was raised in discussion across Government.

Q135 Chairman: Right, so we can take it that the Government has now developed a new view on the position of the Ombudsman?

Mr Hutton: No, we have not developed a new view on the relationship with the Ombudsman. We have found ourselves in a position where we have, I am afraid on this occasion, not agreed with her in relation to the main finding on maladministration, and that has happened [before].

Q136 Chairman: People will say and indeed are already saying what on earth is the point of going to the Ombudsman with complaints about public bodies if government can reject the findings out of hand? Is not the problem here that it would have been possible for you to accept the findings in relation to maladministration that she found? Indeed nobody reading the Ombudsman's report—and we will come on to this in a moment—and reading all the literature that has been produced at the time could possibly doubt that there was maladministration here. It would have been possible for the Government to have accepted that but still have taken issue with the recommendations about redress. Is not the problem because the Government was so anxious not to accept the recommendations about redress, that it felt it had to repudiate what the Ombudsman said about maladministration? Does that go to the heart of it?

Mr Hutton: No, I do not think it [does]. With respect to the Committee and obviously to the Ombudsman, we have I think tried to discharge our responsibilities properly and fully in this case. We have not sought in the Department for Work and Pensions to sit down one night and say "How can we generate a constitutional crisis?" Absolutely not. We have nothing but respect for the work of the Ombudsman. In the last year she looked at something like 600 cases involving the Department for Work and Pensions and we accepted every single one of her recommendations in those cases. This is, as I said, the first time ever we have not been able to reach an agreement with the Parliamentary [Commissioner].

. . .

Q164 Mr Hutton: [The] issue for government and taxpayers is were the leaflets maladministrative? The Ombudsman says yes. We disagree strongly. And even if they were maladministrative, were they the cause of people's financial loss? Again, I am afraid, on that occasion too we do disagree with the causal argument that is contained in the report. It is for the combination of those two reasons that we have not been able, as I said, to accept her recommendations.

Q165 Chairman: Ann Abraham?

Ms Abraham: Only to say that the causal argument is not in the report and the report does not say that the maladministration which has been talked about in terms of the leaflets caused the financial losses. It did not say that.

Chairman: Thank you for that.

. . .

Q186 Grant Shapps: Who then, tell me, made the decision to ignore the ruling of the Ombudsman about maladministration: you, the Prime Minister or perhaps the Chancellor?

Mr Hutton: It was a collective decision of ministers.

Q187 Grant Shapps: So it was not, as we might assume, the Secretary of State of the DWP?

Mr Hutton: Of course I was involved in that decision because this primarily affects my Department's responsibilities but this was, as I said again, a collective decision of ministers.

Q188 Grant Shapps: That is quite interesting. Was it a Cabinet decision? Was it discussed in the Cabinet?

Mr Hutton: It was discussed by ministers in the normal way through correspondence.

Q189 Grant Shapps: Yes, but "ministers" could just mean you and your junior ministers. I am trying to understand at what point in Government this was discussed.

Mr Hutton: It was a cross government decision involving ministers from other departments in a way that normally decisions are made in government.

. . .

Q252 David Heyes: [It] seems to me this is an appropriate point to ask the Commissioner if she wants to take up the opportunity to comment on what has just been said.

Q253 Chairman: I was going to do that. I was going to ask in particular about the suggestion that the Government seems to have made that she has suggested that somehow the Government took the entire responsibility for what happened and, therefore, it should pick up the entire bill from public funds. I think the Ombudsman believes quite strongly that is a misrepresentation of what she has said. I think you may like to say something on that, Ann?

Ms Abraham: [I] would just like to say a couple of things about precedent and respect, if I may. It has been suggested that somehow the Barlow Clowes case is a precedent here. I really find it very difficult to understand how that could be the case because although in the Barlow Clowes case it is true that the Government did not accept the Ombudsman's findings, they did remedy the injustice to the Barlow Clowes investors. Therefore, the entire population of those complainants in that case were included in the [remedy]. I have reflected on whether I should say this, but I think I should. It is this phrase "respect for the office" and, of course, I take at face value what is said about respect for the office, but it is very hard to feel respect for the office when the Government's report says that the report says things it does not say and that is repeated and has been repeated in the House yesterday and [today]. I hope the Committee will come back to the constitutional issues which have been discussed today because I do think they are important. I do think they are important because although this may be a one-off, as has been described, it does encourage the others, and when I say "the others" I mean departments and other parts of government. It does go to the heart of public and parliamentary confidence in the office and that, it seems to me, is very serious. The urgent issue that I think is before us is about what can be done to get these people's pensions back. The central recommendation of my report was that because the Government was not a bystander here, that it had some responsibility—not all the responsibility, some responsibility—to organise a [remedy.] I will just read a bit about what I said about maladministration: "Maladministration, I have identified, was a significant and contributory factor in the creation of financial losses suffered by individuals along with other systemic issues". Somehow to suggest that

I said it was the sole responsibility of Government or that the taxpayer should pick up the tab was not what I said. What I was trying to ask the Government to do was consider what it could do to help these people who had lost their pensions. I did not say, "Write a blank cheque", but to organise a remedy. This is a general point, and I think it goes to the heart really of the relationship between my office and Government, and certainly what I have seen in recent months, the response is defensive, legalistic and it uses words like "liability". I do not use words like "liability". I do not talk about "causal links". It is unimaginative and does nothing to help these people. I suppose, as has been said, I was looking, maybe naïvely, for Government to put its brightest and best people on to thinking about how can we organise a remedy that will do whatever Government and Parliament thinks is appropriate to provide redress for these people who suffered these injustices. I said they should do that by whichever means is most appropriate including, if necessary, payment from public [funds]. I did not expect the Government to get out its chequebook, but I also did not expect the Government to refuse to even think about what could be done. I did not expect it to put all its energy into defending its position. I suppose, fundamentally, what I am looking for in this report and in everything I do is I want a response which is not about defensiveness and denial, it is about constructive engagement and putting things right to whatever extent Parliament thinks is appropriate, not into defending what has gone wrong.'

(g) Annual Report of the Commissioner for 2005–06: Making a difference
(HC 1363 of 2005–2006)

'4. Government departments may legitimately contest recommendations, having properly considered the public interest and the cost of implementing them. However, it is inappropriate for a body under investigation to seek to override the judgment of the independent arbiter established by Parliament to act on its behalf.'

(h) Select Committee on Public Administration, Sixth Report (HC 1081 of 2005–2006)

'21. We have made our own investigations. We believe the Government is being, at best, naïve, and, at worst, misleading.

. . . .

33. We agree with the Parliamentary Ombudsman that the Government itself prescribed the regulatory framework for occupational pension schemes and, as such, was not a bystander. Once the Government had chosen to give information about the pensions system, that information should have been complete and accurate. Any limitations should have been made clear. A reasonable reader would have expected the official leaflets on pensions to have covered all the important points about occupational pensions. In fact, they did not mention one of the greatest risks. This is clearly maladministration.

. . .

66. [We take it extremely seriously what the Ombudsman has now told us in the Commissioner's Memorandum, paras 12–15, p. 454].

67. We share the Ombudsman's concerns. It is not unprecedented for governments to reject findings of maladministration. However, it is extremely rare. Moreover, precedent has shown that, even when departments have denied that maladministration has occurred, they have ultimately been willing to offer some recompense out of respect for the Ombudsman's office. The series of rejections of Ombudsman's reports is deeply [troubling].

68. We also consider that this series of rejections of Ombudsman's reports has been taken in a way which suggests the Government is paying only lip service to the principle that the Ombudsman's findings should be [respected].

69. Throughout our discussions with the Ombudsman she has shown a willingness to distinguish between findings of maladministration, and recommendations about redress. While the Ombudsman does not make recommendations lightly, it is clear that she understands that the Government may

"reject recommendations that I may make, after proper consideration of the public interest, and other calls on the public purse, and any other relevant matters. That is a decision that it is entitled to [take".] We believe that such rejections should be rare, but what causes the Ombudsman, and us, most concern, is the Government's increasing willingness not just to dispute her recommendations, but her findings of maladministration as well.

70. It is not unprecedented for the Government to contest an Ombudsman's finding of maladministration. It is, however, unprecedented for there to be so many problems, in such a short space of time. Our scrutiny leads us to conclude that the fault lies with the Government, not the Ombudsman.

71. [We] agree that if the Government routinely rejects the Ombudsman's findings without good cause, public confidence in the system will be undermined. The Government has recently been too ready simply to reject findings of maladministration, apparently without proper study of the Ombudsman's reports.

. . .

75. [We] believe that when there are disputes between Government and the Ombudsman, Parliament is the proper place for them to be debated.

76. However, this system will only work if the Parliamentary Ombudsman, the Government and Parliament share a broad common understanding of what maladministration might be and who should properly identify it. If it became clear that the Government routinely considered rejection of a finding of maladministration, then that common understanding would no longer exist. The first step towards resolving such difficulties would be for the House to debate these matters. However, if that failed, new legislation might be needed, or the Government could attempt to use judicial review to establish where current boundaries lie. We hope it will not come to that.

. . .

78. We share the Ombudsman's concern that the Government has been far too ready to dismiss her findings of maladministration. Our investigations have shown that these findings were sound. It would be extremely damaging if Government became accustomed simply to reject findings of maladministration, especially if an investigation by this Committee proved there was indeed a case to answer. It would raise fundamental constitutional issues about the position of the Ombudsman and the relationship between Parliament and the Executive.

79. We trust that this Report will act as a warning to the Government. We will continue to monitor the Government's responses to the Parliamentary Commissioner's reports. If necessary we will seek a debate on the floor of the House, so that all Members can discuss these issues, and re-establish the Parliamentary Commissioner's role. The Parliamentary Commissioner is Parliament's Ombudsman: Government must respect her.'

9 THE AVAILABILITY OF JUDICIAL REVIEW

1. The Development of the Jurisdictions of Courts and Tribunals

(a) The Court of King's Bench

The present jurisdiction of the High Court extends in an unbroken line from the earliest periods of the English common law, starting with the gradual splitting up of the King's Council around 1200, when the growing expansion of royal business demanded some form of delegation of routine business away from that Council. Taxation matters were given to the Exchequer and assize judges dealt with serious crimes in the provinces. Other important matters which concerned the King were left to certain judge-members of the Council and who became known as the King's Bench. King's Bench could hear cases concerning serious crimes, actions for trespass and contract, and disputes over feudal land (especially where the King had a personal interest in the matter). King's Bench was also granted a jurisdiction of greater importance to the development of administrative law in that the King empowered King's Bench to supervise and correct the actions of inferior courts and officials. There were two significant features from this early period. First, King's Bench had a jurisdiction 'in error'. Anyone wishing to challenge any judicial decision would ask for a writ of error directing the judge to produce to King's Bench the record (of proceedings) of the case. King's Bench would decide if the alleged error existed. If there was an error on the record (but only on the record), the decision would be quashed. Second, King's Bench used powers, which it possessed when it was still part of the King's Council, known as 'prerogative writs' (instruments whereby the King would issue commands to his subjects, such as habeas corpus, which ordered the attendance of a person before the King).

(b) The justices of the peace

The justices of the peace had performed governmental tasks in relation to the preservation of law and order almost since antiquity. By the Justices of the Peace Act 1361, 'one lorde and with him three or four of the most worthy in the county, with some [quorum] learned in the law' were to be appointed to keep the peace. The justices of the peace also performed other governmental functions. Probably the best known was implementing the early series of Industrial Relations Acts, then known as the Statutes of Labourers, introduced after the ravages of the Black Death in 1349. At the end of the fifteenth century, it was important for the Tudor monarchs to have strong government and strong central control over the emerging national state after the Wars of the Roses. Some means of ensuring that the royal will was carried out in the provinces was needed and the King's chosen representatives were the justice of the peace and the borough magistrate. Above came the Council and the Star Chamber (head (c) below). By the middle of the sixteenth century, the justices were the administrators of a very complex scheme of local government. Books on the law and duties of the justices of the peace were becoming very large. Lambard's *Eirenarcha*, first published in 1581, cites over three hundred statutes relating to their duties and powers.

(c) The Council, the Star Chamber, and back to King's Bench

The Tudor monarchs were particularly concerned with the means whereby the royal will could oversee the actions of the justices of the peace and other administrative bodies, such as the Commissioners of Sewers, which possessed powers of local taxation and rule-making.[1] King's Bench could exercise legal control over justices of the peace sitting in their judicial capacity by the writ of error.

'What was most urgently needed was a change in the character of the control exercised by the central government. It must be a constant, a minute and a regular control which should gradually enforce upon the units of local government conformity to the newer and higher standards of government demanded by the modern state. This requisite was supplied by the Tudor Council. [Thus] if we take our stand in the sixteenth century, it might appear that the English state, like the continental state, was travelling along the road which led to centralised government founded upon royal absolutism and supported by a system of administrative law.'[2]

Although the Council was mainly an executive body (almost a Cabinet) formulating policy and ensuring that that policy was carried out, the Council was often petitioned by aggrieved persons to ask for justice against alleged unlawful or unfair administrative action. The body to perform this 'judicial business' was established as the Court of Star Chamber. It was, to coin a phrase, a judicial committee of the Privy Council. Various statutes gave Star Chamber wide powers of control and punishment of offenders and Star Chamber exercised an inquisitorial procedure (occasionally made more efficient by the rack, and other forms of obtaining confessions). The other courts had no jurisdiction over Star Chamber. Star Chamber became such an efficient court that instead of using its wide and undefined powers in exceptional cases, the Stuart monarchs began to use it and to rely on it as a matter of course. During the seventeenth century struggles between King and Parliament (and between the common law courts and the special jurisdictions established by the King), King's Bench laid down certain principles and rules which otherwise would have been created by a constituent assembly and written down in a written constitution. The extent of prerogative power was laid down. King's Bench (backed up by the House of Commons) intervened to place restrictions on the

---

[1] Bill of Sewers, 1531.   [2] Holdsworth, *History of English Law*, vol IV, 105–106.

existence of prerogative power.[3] This was the common law at work (sometimes with the aid and comfort of references to divine or natural law), although the claim by Coke in *Bonham's Case*[4] that 'in many cases the common law will control acts of Parliament and sometimes adjudge them to be utterly void; for when an act of Parliament is against common right or reason, or repugnant or impossible to be performed, the common law will control it and adjudge such act to be void' was somewhat exaggerated and overtaken by events. The seventeenth century was, of course, the scene for the emergence of parliamentary power and the development of a constitutional monarchy. One of the first stages was to abolish Star Chamber. 'The tyrannical proceedings of the Star Chamber aroused popular feeling against it. It was, it is true, an efficient court where the case before it was not political. But the political cases, though they were the smallest part of its daily business, made the most noise at the time, and have given to it its reputation in history.'[5] It may well be that had Parliament merely abolished the more 'political' jurisdiction of Star Chamber, such as its powers to punish conspiracy, offences against the established church, and treason, and abolished its somewhat draconian methods of obtaining evidence and punishment, there could have developed a separate system of administrative law in that a court composed of judges experienced in government and administration would have exercised a jurisdiction separate from that of the common law courts. However, Star Chamber was abolished and there was a need to fill the vacuum left. In the middle of the seventeenth century and in the confusion of the impending civil struggles there was an even greater need for an administrative court to supervise the justices of the peace and various administrative authorities established to deal with such matters as highways and sewers. King's Bench had, as has been seen, exercised a supervisory jurisdiction over the work of the justices and other local authorities and the 'ordinary' citizens of the seventeenth century seemed to see in King's Bench some form of stable legal machinery for the redress of grievances in the chaotic political scene of the time. Note that King's Bench did not assume all the powers of the Council and Star Chamber and did not become a constitutional court with power over all governmental activity, including legislative activity. King's Bench accepted the constitutional monarchy which emerged at the end of the seventeenth century and, in particular, accepted the legislative supremacy of Parliament and Parliament's control over governmental policy-making, leaving control of the King's ministers to Parliament.[6] King's Bench remained essentially a court of common law dealing with litigation, albeit litigation concerned with government. The instrument by which grievances should be redressed appears to have been settled not by any planned settlement, but by those who complained of unlawful administration and King's Bench set about devising suitable remedies.

(d) The development of remedies

The development of an 'administrative law series of remedies' in the second half of the seventeenth century showed the genius of the common law. What was needed was for some convenient and simple method of reviewing alleged unlawful administrative action. What

---

[3] *Case of Proclamations* (1611), 12 Co Rep 74, p. 82. See, also, *Bates' Case* (1606) 2 St. Tr. 357; *Case of Prohibitions del Roy* (1607) 12 Co. Rep. 63; *Case of the King's Prerogative in Saltpetre* (1607) 12 Co. Rep. 12; *R v Hampden (Ship Money)* (1637) 3 St. Tr. 825.   [4] See p. 51.

[5] Holdsworth, *History of English Law*, vol I, 514–515.   [6] See pp. 8–15.

happened was the development by King's Bench of the use of the prerogative writs of certiorari, prohibition and mandamus. King's Bench would pronounce upon the legality of administrative action in two main circumstances. First, where a body acted in excess of the jurisdiction granted to it and, second, where a body, acting within the jurisdiction granted to it, made an error of law which was apparent on the face of the record. The writ of certiorari would lie to quash (or annul) any unlawful action and the writ of prohibition would lie to prevent a body from acting outside its jurisdiction. By the end of the seventeenth century, Holt CJ was able to proclaim, with some justification: 'It is a consequence of all jurisdictions to have their proceedings returned here by certiorari to be examined here.'[7] In addition, King's Bench also developed a means of compelling a body to perform a duty imposed on it by law. This was the writ of mandamus, which, as its name would indicate, was a writ ordering a body, such as a borough corporation, to perform public duties which had not been performed. By the end of the seventeenth century King's Bench had achieved a supreme position in matters relating to the judicial review of governmental activity. It must be emphasised that this was not a question of King's Bench assuming powers and jurisdiction of Star Chamber which were novel and alien to King's Bench. It was a question of adaptation and continuity; people went for remedies to the court which they thought would best grant them redress of grievances; and King's Bench did its best to adapt old ideas, old forms of action and their old connections with government to meet the new situations they were called upon to deal with (see, further, head IV).

(e) The nineteenth century

At the beginning of the nineteenth century, public administration (at least at the local level) was still mainly in the hands of the justices of the peace and the magistrates of the boroughs and King's Bench exercised the same powers of control over their 'administrative' functions as over their more 'judicial' functions. Two things then happened to the justices: first, the greater part of their administrative functions were handed over to newly organised local authorities (supervised by newly created central government departments, which were being created to administer the ever-widening regulatory powers of government); second, the still remaining judicial functions of their criminal summary jurisdiction were reorganised. Both events affected the development of judicial supervision of administrative activity.

With regard to the administrative functions which were handed over to the new local authorities and statutory boards, it must be admitted that these bodies bore little resemblance to the justices. The municipal and county councils, and their various committees, were elected (albeit on a limited franchise) and their discussions were deliberative rather than those of court-like proceedings. In many cases express rights of appeal against their decisions were granted to the courts and to the new central government departments (see (g) below). Where no appellate jurisdiction was created by Parliament, King's/Queen's Bench had to decide how far they should continue their centuries-old supervision with regard to the new authorities and, in doing so, they chose to look at the functions performed rather than the specific body which performed those functions. Where, previously, the courts had held that a function was judicial, judicial not necessarily in the sense of a 'discharge of duties exercisable by a judge or

---

[7] *Groenvelt v Burwell* (1700) 1 Ld. Raym. 454, at 469. See, also, the *Cardiff Bridge Case* (1700) 1 Ld. Raym. 580. See E Henderson, *Foundations of English Administrative Law* (1963).

by justices in court [but] to administrative duties which need not be performed in court, but in respect of which it is necessary to bring a judicial mind—that is, a mind to determine what is fair and just in respect of matters under consideration',[8] then King's/Queen's Bench would hold that the same function when performed by a local authority or a central government department was still to be exercised judicially, and the court would retain and exercise their powers of supervision. It was a matter of emphasis. Instead of claiming jurisdiction over all the functions of the new administrative authorities (and possibly run the risk of having such an exaggerated claim taken away), the court simply claimed to continue to exercise a jurisdiction which they had possessed since antiquity, namely, to keep inferior bodies acting judicially within the bounds of the powers given to such bodies by the law. Certiorari would lie to quash the decisions of licensing authorities because this was the same sort of judicial function exercised by the justices of the peace. It all depended on what the justices were doing: 'It has been repeatedly held that licensing powers are administrative as distinct from judicial functions. The fact that at some time a body is a court of summary jurisdiction does not make it always a court of summary jurisdiction.'[9] There was a progression from retaining supervisory powers over bodies acting 'judicially'; then changing 'judicially' to 'having a duty to act judicially'; and then by construing the duty to act judicially in a very wide fashion.[10] As a result, Atkin LJ was able to sum up centuries of judicial activity and to make his much quoted contribution to administrative jurisprudence that 'Whenever any body of persons having legal authority to determine questions affecting the rights of subjects, and having the duty to act judicially, act in excess of their legal authority they are subject to the controlling jurisdiction of the King's Bench Division exercised in [the] writs of [certiorari and prohibition].'[11]

As mentioned above,[12] one of the two grounds for intervention by King's Bench was to correct errors of law which appeared on the face of the record. Before 1848, the justices had to give very full statements as to the facts and reasons for their decisions. There was, therefore, very adequate opportunity for finding out whether the justices had made an error of law. Unfortunately, it appears that many convictions were quashed by certiorari on minor matters of procedure, rather than on real matters of substance and the 1848 Summary Jurisdiction Act provided that the record of a summary conviction should omit all the evidence and the reasons for the decision. There was thus very little for the superior courts to get their teeth into. '[The Act] did not stint the jurisdiction of the Queen's Bench, or alter the law of certiorari. What it did was to disarm its exercise. The effect was not to make that which had been error error no longer, but to remove nearly all opportunity for its detection. The face of the record "spoke" no longer; it was the inscrutable face of a sphinx.'[13] Often when new statutory authorities were established, the same trend continued. Some bodies had to give reasons, but, in the main, all that was necessary was the decision. The intervention of the courts to correct errors of law on the face of the record therefore decreased. This meant that if the superior courts wanted to intervene, they had to base their decisions on the alternative basis for intervention. Consequently, the High Court developed a supervisory jurisdiction based almost exclusively on excess of or want of jurisdiction and this will be discussed in outline in head III and in detail in chapter 10. The error jurisdiction was not abolished, but the

---

[8] *Royal Aquarium v Parkinson* [1892] 1 QB 431, per Lopes J, at 452.
[9] *Huish v Liverpool Justices* [1914] 1 KB, per Scrutton J, at 116, 117. See, also, *Hagmaier v Willesden Overseers* [1904] 2 KB 316; *R v Southampton Justices* [1906] 1 KB 446.   [10] *Cooper*, p. 468.
[11] *R v Electricity Commissioners* [1924] 1 KB 171.   [12] See p. 464.
[13] *R v Nat Bell Liquors* [1922] 2 AC 128, per Lord Sumner, at 159.

use of the error jurisdiction was really again rendered minimal by the development of granting statutory rights of appeal from a wide variety of public bodies to courts, tribunals, and to other administrative authorities (see (g) below) and by the development of judicial control based, from the 1850s onwards, on that of lack of or excess of jurisdiction.

(f) The development of lack of or excess of jurisdiction

As has been seen,[14] it is normal to point to the second half of the nineteenth century as the period when matters traditionally left in private hands (landowners, merchants, factory owners, speculative builders, rail, docks, gas and electricity companies) came within the portfolio of 'government' and when, inter alia, intolerable housing conditions, diseases such as cholera and typhoid, water pollution, and industrial pollution, meant that laissez-faire freedom of property and freedom of contract had to be subordinated to humanitarian reform. Parliament enacted statute after statute relating to working conditions, building controls, the suppression of nuisances and noxious trades, powers of compulsory acquisition of property for street widening, paving, sewers and drains, and slum clearance. Employers had to take part in (pay for) compensation schemes for those injured at work, the Poor Laws had to be organised and paid for out of the rates, the dreadful scourge of intoxicating liquor had to be controlled. All this (the interference with property rights for the general commonwealth) was abhorrent to the principle of laissez faire, and there is a vast and fascinating nineteenth century jurisprudence[15] emanating from challenges to the exercise of wide powers of discretion granted to the new regulatory bodies.

The nineteenth century regulatory bodies, local authorities and government boards, were created by statute. Their composition, powers and procedures were, in varying degrees of completeness, detailed by Parliament and this enabled the courts to continue their controlling role by basing that control on the interpretation, the courts' interpretation naturally, of the will of Parliament as expressed in those statutes. The jurisdiction of those regulatory bodies being statutory and Parliament's will being supreme, contravention of that will could be *ultra vires* and could be supervised by the courts.[16] So very often, a court would base a decision on the fact that a proposition had been 'expressly enacted by the legislature'. Sometimes a statute might be incomplete in the way the extent of delegated power was phrased. Consequently, the doctrine of *ultra vires* 'ought to be reasonably, and not unreasonably, understood and applied, and that whatever may fairly be regarded as incidental to, or consequent upon, those things which the legislature has authorised, ought not (unless expressly prohibited) to be held by judicial construction to be *ultra vires*'.[17] Therefore, an authority could not act in excess of its statutory powers or decline to follow a pre-ordained procedure. 'It is well settled that a public body invested with statutory powers such as those conferred upon the corporation must take care not to exceed or abuse its powers. It must keep

---

[14] See pp. 17–20.   [15] What follows is only a taste of favourite lollipops.
[16] *Bunbury v Fuller* (1853) 9 Ex 111.
[17] *AG v Great Eastern Railway* (1880) 5 App Cas 473, per Lord Selborne LC, at 478. See, also, *Wenlock v River Dee Co* (1887) 36 ChD 675.

within the limits of the authority committed to it.'[18] Much was made of the words actually used by Parliament. In *Sharp v Wakefield*,[19] the question was raised as to the extent of the discretionary power of licensing justice to refuse a licence for the sale of intoxicating liquor, when the refusal was on the ground of remoteness from police supervision and the character and necessity of the locality and neighbourhood in which the inn was situated (the wilds of the Lake District). It was held that the justices had jurisdiction to base their decision on such grounds. 'By the express language of the statute, the grant of a licence is expressly within the discretion of the magistrates. [It] surely must have been in the contemplation of the legislature that the circumstances of the neighbourhood might change, a population might diminish or increase.'[20]

Many statutes granted, according to the words used, a discretion to act. 'Discretion' means 'when it is said that something is to be done within the discretion of the authorities, that that something is to be done according to the rule of reason and justice, not according to private opinion, according to law and not humour. It is to be not arbitrary, vague and fanciful, but legal and regular. And it must be exercised within the limit, to which an honest man competent to the discharge of his office ought to confine himself.'[21] 'Without meaning to deny that it is confided to the discretion of the magistrates to determine what particular localities require other hours for opening and closing than those specified, it is obvious that such discretion as they have is not an arbitrary discretion to define any localities they please, but they must be such localities as they consider, in the honest and bona fide exercise of their own judgment, to require a difference to be made.'[22]

Often the statute granting a discretionary power would also indicate, expressly or by necessary implication, the matters which the authority should take into consideration when exercising that discretion. Consequently, if 'people who are to exercise a public duty by exercising their discretion take into account matters which the Courts consider not to be proper for the guidance of their discretion, then in the eye of the law they have not exercised their discretion'.[23] In *R v Sylvester* [24] it was held that licensing justices, who were required by statute only to certify whether applicants for beer licences were real residents and ratepayers of the parish, were not entitled to refuse the certificate on the ground that in their opinion there were already too many public houses. Furthermore, it was held that to grant beer licences only to those applicants who were prepared also to apply for and take out a licence for the sale of spirits was a fetter on their discretion. In *R v Lord Leigh*,[25] K, the former Chief Constable of Warwick, had fled to Portugal in order to defraud his creditors and to evade the bankruptcy laws. He took with him his 'golden handshake' in the form of a substantial pension paid on account of his poor health. The police committee did not approve of this payment to such a rogue and ordered K to submit himself for medical examination at the Chief Constable's office at Warwick. The key issue was whether the order to submit to medical examination was made for the purpose of satisfying the committee as to his then state of health, in which case it would have been an order made by the committee within the jurisdiction conferred upon them by the Police Act 1890, or whether the order was made, not for that purpose, but for some other purpose, in which case it would not be within the jurisdiction of

---

[18] *Mayor of Westminster v London and North Western Railway Co* [1905] AC 426, per Lord Macnaghton, at 427. See p. 472. [19] [1891] AC 173.

[20] Per Lord Halsbury LC, at 178. [21] *Sharp v Wakefield* [1891] AC 173, per Lord Selborne, at 179.

[22] *Macbeth v Ashley* (1874) LR 2 HL, Sc, 352, per Lord Selborne, at 380.

[23] *R v The Vestry of St Pancras* (1890) 24 QBD 371, per Lord Esher MR, at 375–376.

[24] (1862) 32 LJMC 93. [25] [1897] 1 QB 132.

the committee to make the order, and, further, in which case the refusal of K to comply with the order would afford no ground for cancelling K's pension. It was held, on the facts, that: 'What the police authority [did] was to order [K] over here not in reality for the purpose of examining him to see if his incapacity had ceased, but for the purpose of supporting the Court of Bankruptcy. [This] was without jurisdiction and cannot be upheld in a court of law.'[26] Where the justices imposed as a condition for the grant of a liquor licence that applicants should pay over a sum of money, which money the justices intended to divert to the reduction of the rates of the borough, this was held to be irrelevant to the licensing system and invalid, however laudable was the idea of reducing the rates. 'If the justices allow themselves to take into consideration matters which have no bearing upon the merits of the case before them and which influence their minds in arriving at their decision, it cannot be said that [the person aggrieved] has been heard according to law.'[27]

The courts, could not, however, rely on using the 'will of Parliament' argument when, as sometimes happened, Parliament had not actually spoken its will. The common law took over in emphasising that decision makers must not be influenced by outside factors:

'No one can suppose that Lord Cottenham could be, in the remotest degree, influenced by the interest that he had in this concern; but, my Lords, it is of the last importance that the maxim that no man is to be a judge in his own cause should be held sacred. And that is not to be confined to a cause in which he is a party, but applies to a cause in which he has an interest. Since I have had the honour to be Chief Justice of the Court of Queen's Bench, we have again and again set aside proceedings in inferior tribunals because an individual, who had an interest in a cause, took a part in the decision. And it will have a most salutary influence on these tribunals when it is known that this high Court of last resort, in a case in which the Lord Chancellor of England had an interest, considered that his decree was on that account a decree not according to law, and was set aside. This will be a lesson to all inferior tribunals to take care not only that in their decrees they are not influenced by their personal interest, but to avoid the appearance of labouring under such an influence.'[28]

In addition, the common law imposed canons of fairness with regard to the procedures to be followed by the new authorities when they were granted wide powers to interfere with the traditional values of property owners:

Cooper v Wandsworth Board of Works (1863) 14 CBNS 180

Erle CJ, at 189

'This was an action for trespass by the plaintiff against the Wandsworth district board [a local government authority] for pulling down and demolishing his house; and the ground of defence that has been put forward by the defendants has been under [the Metropolis Management Act 1855, section 76, where] it is enacted that, before any person shall begin to build a new house, he shall give seven days notice to the district board of his intention to build; and it provides at the end that, in default of such notice, it shall be lawful for the district board to demolish the house. The district board here say that no notice was given by the plaintiff of his intention to build the house in question, wherefor they demolished it. The contention on the part of the plaintiff has been that, although the words of the statute, taken in their literal sense, without any qualification at all, would create a justification for the act which the district board has done, the powers granted by that statute are subject to a qualification

---

[26] Per AL Smith LJ, at 142–143.

[27] *R v Bowman* [1898] 1 QB 663, per Wills J, at 666. See, also, *R v Cotham* [1898] 1 QB 802.

[28] *Dimes v The Proprietors of the Grand Junction Canal Co* (1852) 3 HLC 759, per Lord Campbell, at 793.

which has been repeatedly recognised, that no man is to be deprived of his property without his having an opportunity of being [heard]. It is a power carrying with it enormous consequences. [The] board ought to have given notice to the plaintiff and to have allowed him to be heard. The default in sending notice to the board of the intention to build is a default which may be explained. There may be a great many excuses for the apparent default. The party may have intended to conform to the law. He may have actually conformed to all the regulations which they would wish to impose, though by accident his notice may have [miscarried]. I cannot conceive any harm that could happen to the district board from hearing the party but I can conceive a great many advantages which might arise in the way of public order, in the way of doing substantial justice, and in the way of fulfilling the purpose of the statute, by the restriction which we put upon them, that they should hear the party before they inflict upon him such a heavy loss.'

Willes J, at 190

'I apprehend that a tribunal which is by law invested with power to affect the property of one of Her Majesty's subject, is bound to give such subject an opportunity of being heard before it proceeds: and that that rule is of universal application, and founded upon the plainest principles of justice.'

Byles J, at 194

'[Although] there are no positive words in a statute requiring that the party shall be heard, yet the justice of the common law will supply the omission of the legislature.'

The reference to the 'justice of the common law' was based on many early authorities.[29] *Cooper* was followed:

'No doubt, in the absence of special provisions as to how the person who is to decide is to proceed, the law will imply no more than that substantial requirements of justice shall not be violated. He is not a judge in the proper sence of the word; but he must give the parties an opportunity of being heard before him and stating their case and their view. He must give notice when he will proceed with the matter and he must act honestly and impartially and not under the dictation of some other person or persons to whom the authority is not given by law. There must be no malversation of any kind. There would be no decision within the meaning of the statute if there were anything of that sort done contrary to the essence of justice.'[30]

In *R v Sykes*,[31] the liquor licensing legislation stated that an application for an off-licence to sell beer could only be refused on one or more of four grounds specified. It was held that the practice of licensing justices to refuse such applications without giving any indication as to their reasoning was wrong.

'The legislature has expressly enacted that such a licence as this shall be refused on four grounds only. The justices by refusing a licence sub silentio and refusing to state on which of the grounds they acted, might practically evade the enactment altogether, and refuse licences arbitrarily and on other grounds than the four mentioned in the section. They cannot be said to have "heard and determined" the application until they have stated on which ground their refusal was based.'[32]

Similarly, if licensing justices 'decide against the applicant, they must state the grounds of their decision, so that she may know what she has to meet on appeal if she desires to appeal'.[33] The case law was summed up in:

---

[29] *Bagg's Case* (1613) 11 Co Rep 93b; *R v University of Cambridge* (1723) 1 Stra. 557.

[30] *Spackman v Plumstead District Board of Works* (1885) 10 App Cas 229, per Lord Selborne LC, at 240. See, also, *Wood v Woad* (1874) LR 9 Ex 190, per Kelly, CB, at 196; *Hopkins v Smethwick Local Board of Health* [1890] 24 QBD 712, per Wills J, at 714.   [31] (1875) 1 QBD 52.

[32] Per Quain J, at 54.   [33] *R v Thomas* [1892] 1 QB 426, per Wills J, at 431.

Board of Education v Rice [1911] AC 179

There was an inquiry by the Board of Education (a central government department) into an allegation by the managers of a church school that a local education authority had failed to maintain the efficiency of the school.

Lord Loreburn, at 182

'[Comparatively] recent statutes have extended, if they have not originated, the practice of imposing upon departments or officers of state the duty of deciding or determining questions of various kinds. In the present instance, as in many others, what comes for determination is sometimes a matter to be settled by discretion, involving no law. It will, I suppose, usually be of an administrative kind: but sometimes it will involve matter of law as well as matter of fact, or even depend upon matter of law alone. In such cases the Board of Education will have to ascertain the law and also to ascertain the facts. I need not add that in doing either they must act in good faith and fairly listen to both sides, for that is a duty lying upon every one who decides anything. But I do not think they are bound to treat such a question as though it were a trial. They have no power to administer an oath, and need not examine witnesses. They can obtain information in any way they think best, always giving a fair opportunity to those who are parties in the controversy for correcting or contradicting any relevant statement prejudicial to their [view].'

'There are some principles of justice which it is impossible to disregard.'[34] One 'principle of justice which it is impossible to disregard' was that of reasonableness (perhaps the forerunner of 'irrationality'[35]): 'It is well settled that a public [body] must act in good faith. And it must act reasonably.'[36]

For example, local and other authorities were granted the power to make rules or bye-laws which bound the individual just as much as an Act of Parliament. Queens' Bench applied the litmus test not of an appellate court but of the 'reasonable individual or subject of Her Majesty'. In *Kruse v Johnson*,[37] a bye-law enacted that 'No person shall sound or play upon any musical or noisy instrument or sing in any public place or highway within fifty yards of any dwelling-house after being required by any constable or by an inmate of such house person-ally, or by his or her servant, to desist.' It was emphasised that what was important was not the views of the court as to whether a bye-law was desirable, but whether the bye-law was within the reasonable range of responses which Parliament could have intended the local authority to make to the grant of the bye-law making power. In a famous passage from the annals of common law jurisprudence, it was stated:

'I do not mean to say that there may not be cases in which it would be the duty of the Court to condemn by-laws, made under such authority as these were made, as invalid because unreasonable. But unreasonable in what sense? If, for instance, they were found to be partial and unequal in their operation as between different classes; if they were manifestly unjust; if they disclosed bad faith; if they involved such oppressive or gratuitous interference with the rights of those subject to them as could find no justification in the minds of reasonable men, the Court might well say: "Parliament never intended to give authority to make such rules; they are unreasonable and *ultra vires*". But it is in this sense, and in this sense only, as I conceive, that the question of unreasonableness can properly be

---

[34] *Andrews v Mitchell* [1905] AC 78, per Lord Halsbury LC, at 80.   [35] See p. 561.
[36] *Mayor of Westminster v London and North Western Railway Co* [1905] AC 426, per Lord Macnaghton, at 427.   [37] [1898] 2 QB 91.

regarded. A byelaw is not unreasonable merely because particular judges may think that it goes further than is prudent or necessary or convenient, or because it is not accompanied by a qualification or an exception which some judges think ought to be there.'[38]

Furthermore, 'In my opinion, judged by the test of reasonableness, [this is a reasonable bye-law and] I am clearly of opinion that no court of law can properly say that it is invalid.'[39] However, a bye-law prohibiting, in effect, the playing of music other than military music in the streets of the borough on Sunday was declared unreasonable on the grounds that it did not require evidence of annoyance being caused.[40] In *Scott v Lord Provost, Magistrates and Town Council of Glasgow*,[41] local authorities had power to make bye-laws under the Diseases of Animals Act 1894 to 'regulate' markets and fairs. Glasgow Town Council made a bye-law, in order to stop the widespread practice of rigging (ringing) cattle auctions, to the effect that a public market should not be used for private sales and for sales where the sellers did not accept bids from everyone present. This raised the question 'whether the administration of a public market, under statutory authority, given to them to make regulations or by-laws for regulating the use of the market, are entitled to impose conditions which shall have the effect of preventing sellers of goods from limiting the class of purchasers with whom they mean to deal, as they undoubtedly can do in premises of their own'.[42] To the Earl of Halsbury LC:

'It seems to me that the by-law means that a place intended for the public sale of cattle by auction shall be sanctioned and that the public and every member of it shall be permitted to go to that place, and upon equal terms with his neighbour be permitted to buy and to have his bid treated on equal terms [with] that of everyone else. [What] they have simply done is to make this particular place a place for public auctions with all the incidents which, according to ordinary practice, are attached to a public auction and to prohibit its use for any other purpose.'[43]

This was well within the meaning of 'regulate' and the bye-law was valid.

As stated above, nineteenth century statutes granted, almost as a matter of course, powers of compulsory acquisition of property, often in terms so wide that the authority could seemingly do what it liked. Here, however, the courts applied the presumption that Parliament did not intend the authority to gain ownership of property belonging to another unless that acquisition was expressly authorised. In *Gard v Commissioner of Sewers of the City of London*,[44] under an Act 'for better paving, improving and regulating the streets of the Metropolis and removing and preventing nuisances and obstructions thereon', the Commissioners were empowered to widen streets and to purchase compulsorily land and houses for that purpose. The Commissioners determined to acquire the whole of a property which was in a ruinous state following a fire. They stated that they wanted $5\frac{1}{2}$ feet of land for street widening purposes and that they would sell the remainder for commercial profit. It was held that they could not take the whole of the property when they wanted 'only an infinitesimal part of it' and that a large site of valuable building ground could not be taken away from the owner 'because a part happens to be wanted for a kerb-stone'.[45] Furthermore, a determination that a particular property was required for the purpose of widening streets had to be supported by evidence in

---

[38] Per Lord Russell of Killowen, at 99.   [39] Per Lord Russell of Killowen, at 103.
[40] *Johnson v Mayor of Croydon* (1887) 16 QBD 708. Of many bye-law cases, see *Wanstead Local Board v Wooster* (1885) 37 JP 403 (prohibition on keeping pigs within 100 feet of a dwelling house held reasonable) and *Alty v Farrell* [1896] 1 QB 636 (bye-law giving a policeman an unqualified right to require sellers of coal to weigh the coal in the policeman's presence held unreasonable because the power might be used oppressively).
[41] [1899] AC 470.   [42] Per Lord Shand, at 480–481.   [43] At 474, 477.
[44] (1885) 28 ChD 486.   [45] Per Bowen LJ, at 512–513.

order to be valid, and such a determination could not be supported if there were no grounds on which a reasonable person could come to the conclusion that it was so required.[46]

The requirement that power must be exercised reasonably was interpreted by the courts as meaning that if an authority was granted a power to act for a specific purpose, that power could not be exercised for a different purpose:

Mayor of Westminster v London and North Western Railway [1905] AC 426

Westminster Corporation had power (under the Public Health Act 1891, section 44), to provide and maintain public conveniences and had constructed public lavatories and other conveniences for the use of persons of both sexes.

'These conveniences are placed under the ground in the middle of the [street]. On each side of the roadway there is an entrance, five feet nine inches wide, protected by railings and leading by a staircase of the same width to a passage or subway, ten feet wide and eight feet high, which runs the whole way across on a level with the underground conveniences. Out of this subway there are openings—two for men and one for women—into spacious chambers, where the usual accommodation (politely described as lavatories and cloakrooms) is provided on a large and liberal scale. All the arrangements seem to have been designed and carried out with due regard to decency and with every possible consideration for the comfort of wayfarers in need of such accommodation'

(per Lord Macnaghton, at 428–429). The railway company (owners of a large and valuable block of buildings opposite the entrance to the conveniences) objected to the sanitary works and sought to have them removed. Their argument was that what the corporation had constructed 'is not a public sanitary convenience at all. It is a subway, and none the less a subway because, owing to the way in which it has been constructed, it can be utilised as a means of access to a convenience. It is really a crossing for foot-passengers, with conveniences communicating therewith' (per Younger, KC). In other words, it was claimed that a power for the provision and maintenance of public conveniences had been used for an improper purpose, namely, that of constructing a subway, for which there was no statutory authority.

The Earl of Halsbury LC, at 427–428

'My Lords, it seems to me that the power of the local authority to erect certain public conveniences cannot be disputed. The shape, site, and extent of them are left to the discretion of the authority in question, and so far as regards the things themselves, which, under this discretion, have been erected, I do not understand that any objection can be made. The objections, so far as they assume the force of legal objections, refer to the access to them, and to the supposed motives of the local authority in the selection of the [site]. It appears to me impossible to contend that these conveniences are not the things authorised by the Legislature. It seems to me that the provision of the statute itself contemplates that such conveniences should be made beneath public roads, and if beneath public roads some access underneath the road level must be provided; and if some access must be provided, it must be a measure simply of greater and less convenience, when the street is a wide one, whether an access should be provided at only one or at both sides of the street. That if the access is provided at both sides of the street, it is possible that people who have no desire or necessity to use the convenience will nevertheless pass through it to avoid the dangers of crossing the carriageway seems to me to form no objection to the provision itself; and I decline altogether to sit in judgment upon the discretion of the local authorities upon such materials as are before us. I quite agree that if the power to make one kind of building was fraudulently used for the purpose of making another kind of building, the power given

---

[46] *Lynch v Commissioner of Sewers for the City of London* (1866) 32 ChD 72.

by the Legislature for one purpose could not be used for another: but I have endeavoured to shew that the Legislature did contemplate making subterranean works under the roadway and also access to them.'

Lord Macnaghton, at 430–433

'[The corporation were not to be blamed for making a passage wider than might be needed for a mere convenience] in order to obviate crushing and jostling in a place where crowding is (to say the least) not convenient. [It] was not suggested that there was any notice or any intention of putting up a notice, directing the public to this subway as a means of crossing. The entrance, which was of the usual limited dimensions, did not of itself offer any invitation to the public to enter for the purpose of crossing the roadway. [Then] I come to the question of want of good faith. That is a very serious charge. It is not enough to show that the corporation contemplated that the public might use the sub-way as a means of crossing the street. That was an obvious possibility. It cannot be otherwise if you have an entrance on each side and the communication is not interrupted by a wall or a barrier of some sort. In order to make out a case of bad faith it must be shown that the corporation constructed this subway as a means of crossing the street under colour and pretence of providing public conveniences which were not really wanted at that particular [place]. The primary object of the council was the construction of the conveniences with the requisite and proper means of approach thereto and exit therefrom.'

Much of the content of jurisdictional control of public authorities, by using the doctrine of *ultra vires* and the justice of the common law, was, therefore, more or less mapped out during the late nineteenth and early twentieth century. The supervisory jurisdiction is introduced in head III and discussed in detail in chapter 10.

(g) The development of appellate jurisdictions

As mentioned earlier (head (b) above), the King's chosen local representative was the justice of the peace. A citizen might feel aggrieved at being convicted for an offence by the justices. Gradually a system was established of appeals to specially constituted benches of justices, which as they met four times a year became known as Quarter Sessions. A specified number of justices at Quarter Sessions had to be learned in the law and many of these had at some time studied the law at the Inns of Court. Indeed, in 1846, a Select Committee of the House of Commons proposed that law students be taught 'Administrative Law in its connection with magisterial and official duty'. When, in the nineteenth century, more and more governmental matters were given to the newly constituted local authorities, the system of appeals to Quarter Sessions was maintained, as providing a speedy and local appellate structure. For example, the Public Health Acts gave powers to public authorities to provide sanitary systems and to control the use to which landowners might put their property. Those Acts provided comprehensive rights of appeal.[47] Later, when the modern welfare state was being developed with regard to social security, provision had to be made for appeals against decisions refusing to grant unemployment benefit. It was determined that such appeals should not go to the ordinary courts because the subject matter concerned people who might be intimidated by courts and lawyers. Therefore, a specially constituted appellate body was created—a Court of Referees, composed of a chairman, one representative of employees and one representative of

---

[47] Public Health Act 1875, section 268. See *R v Local Government Board* (1882) 10 QBD 309.

the employers. This was the forerunner of the modern tribunal system. There is nowadays a wide variety of appellate jurisdictions (such as the magistrates' courts, the county court and statutory tribunals) and these are discussed in head II.

II. The Appellate Jurisdiction

An appellate jurisdiction means that the appellate authority has the power to reconsider the decision of an administrative authority or of an inferior tribunal and that the decision of the appellate authority is substituted for that of the inferior body. It is a means of giving an aggrieved party, whether an individual or an administrative authority, a second opportunity of presenting submissions on the merits of a particular decision and/or the legal rules to be applied to that situation. So often, what an individual person wants is that 'second bite at the cherry' in the hope of having an adverse decision amended, withdrawn or annulled. If that adverse decision is in fact abolished, it matters little to that individual that the agency performing the task has exercised an appellate or a supervisory jurisdiction, apart from the all important factors that the forum of an appellate jurisdiction generally tends to be in closer proximity to the individual's habitat, there is a swifter and cheaper process, and, in so many cases, the issue is disposed of by experts.

For example, the current scheme for social security provides for a wide range of benefits payable to the unemployed, the elderly, the disabled and those with family responsibilities. An unsuccessful claimant for benefit has a right to appeal to an appeal tribunal, and this takes the form of a complete re-hearing of the case. Then, an appeal lies to a specially qualified Social Security Commissioner from any decision of an appeal tribunal on the ground that the decision of the tribunal was erroneous in point of law. If the Commissioner holds that the decision appealed against was erroneous in point of law, he or she will set it aside and may give the decision which the tribunal should have given or refer the case to another tribunal with directions for its determination. Finally, an appeal on a question of law lies to the appropriate court (the Court of Appeal, the Court of Session or the Court of Appeal in Northern Ireland) from any decision of a Commissioner.[48] For example, a local education authority must make arrangements for enabling the parent of a child in the area of the authority to express a preference as to the school at which the parent wishes education to be provided for his or her child in the exercise of the authority's functions. If the local education authority or school governing body do not comply with any preference expressed in accordance with these arrangements, the parent of a child may appeal to an appeal committee against any decision made by or on behalf of the authority as to the school at which education is to be provided for the child in the exercise of the authority's functions and any decision made by or on behalf of the school governing body refusing the child admission to such a school. The decision of an appeal committee on any such appeal is binding on the local education authority or school governing body.[49] For example, a person aggrieved by certain decisions of licensing justices (a decision granting or refusing to grant a new licence or any decision as to the conditions of a licence) may appeal to the Crown Court against the decision. On such an appeal, the Crown Court may confirm or reverse the decision appealed against. Where on any such appeal the Crown Court grant or confirm the grant of a licence or where

---

[48] Social Security Act 1998, sections 12, 14, 15.   [49] Education Act 1996, sections 411, 423.

such an appeal is against a decision as to the conditions of a licence, the Crown Court may make any provision as to the attachment of conditions which the licensing justices might have done.[50]

Sometimes, an appellate jurisdiction may be created in order to reduce the number of actions for judicial review in a specific subject area. For example, the Housing Act 1996, sections 202–203, introduced, as a filter mechanism, a statutory review procedure to be operated by local housing authorities for certain decisions relating to homelessness and with a right of appeal to the county court from that statutory review.

There is no general right of appeal from the decisions of administrative authorities. Each and every right depends on statute. It is a fundamental common law rule that a person only has a right of appeal to a court or tribunal if Parliament has granted such a right of appeal by statute. Unless a statute gives a right of appeal, there cannot be an appeal.[51] The courts, therefore, have always held that they must look at the words of the relevant statute in order to see if those words have granted them any appellate jurisdiction. Therefore, the words of the statute must be construed with care in each case. It must be emphasised that the grounds on which an appeal lie may vary according as to the statute. Sometimes the statute may grant an appeal on a point of law only and sometimes the statute grants an appeal on both the law and the facts. In the latter case, this means that the appeal is a complete rehearing of the original application to the administrative authority. For example, the liquor licensing appeal to the Crown Court referred to above is just as if the hearing before the Crown Court were taking place before the licensing justices and the Crown Court may decide the appeal on any of the grounds which could have been used by the licensing justices, even on grounds not considered in the original hearing. In *Stepney Borough Council v Joffe*,[52] Joffe, a street trader licensed by Stepney Borough Council, was convicted of selling goods above the maximum prices allowed by the law and the Council revoked his street trader's licence on the grounds that he was unsuitable to hold such a licence. The appropriate statute[53] allowed an appeal to the local magistrate and 'on any such appeal the court may confirm, revise or vary the decision of the Borough Council'. It was argued that on an appeal against a refusal on the ground of miscon-duct or for any other sufficient reason rendering the applicant unsuitable to hold a licence, the magistrate was not entitled to substitute his or her opinion for that of the Borough Council, but all the magistrate can decide is whether there was evidence on which the Council could come to that conclusion. It was held that there was an unrestricted right of appeal, and, if there is an unrestricted right of appeal, it is for the court of appeal, in this case the metropolitan magistrate, to substitute its opinion for the opinion of the Borough Council. That did not mean to say that the court of appeal ought not to pay great attention to the fact that the duly constituted and elected local authority had come to an opinion on the matter and ought not lightly to reverse their opinion, but the magistrate, given power to 'confirm, reverse or vary' the decision of the Council, was 'bound to form an opinion on the matter and "confirm, reverse or vary the decision of the Borough Council" according to the judgment which he forms'.[54]

It must be emphasised that, if an appellate jurisdiction has been provided by Parliament, that jurisdiction must be used first by the person aggrieved by an administrative authority's

[50] Licensing Act 1964, sections 21 and 23.

[51] *R v East Riding Quarter Sessions, ex p Newton* [1968] 1 QB 32; *Healey v Minister of Health* [1955] 1 QB 221; *R v Cornwall Quarter Sessions Appeal Committee, ex p Kersley* [1956] 1 WLR 906.

[52] [1949] 1 KB 199.   [53] London County Council (General Powers) Act 1947, section 21(3).

[54] Per Lord Goddard CJ, at 201.

decision, rather than the supervisory jurisdiction. An applicant for judicial review should first exhaust whatever other rights he or she has by way of appeal. It was a long-standing principle that the prerogative orders of certiorari and mandamus (discussed in head IV(b)) will lie only where there is no other equally effective, beneficial and convenient remedy.[55] Furthermore, if 'application is made for judicial review but an alternative remedy is available, an applicant should normally be left to pursue that remedy. Judicial review in such a case should only be granted in exceptional circumstances.'[56] It has been referred to as 'a cardinal principle' that, except in the most exceptional circumstances, the supervisory jurisdiction will not be exercised where other remedies were available and have not been used.[57] The rationale for the principle was explained in *Preston v IRC*[58] as being that, since judicial review is a collateral challenge and is not an appeal, if Parliament has provided by statute appeal procedures, those procedures should be used, and consequently, it will only be very rarely that the courts will allow the collateral process of judicial review to be used to attack an appealable decision. The factors which the courts will take into account when deciding whether to grant relief by way of judicial review, when an alternative remedy is available, are whether the alternative statutory appeal remedy will resolve the question at issue fully and directly, whether the statutory procedure would be quicker, or slower, than by way of judicial review, whether the matter depends on some particular fact-finding process or technical knowledge which is more readily available to the alternative appellate body, and the desirability of an authoritative ruling on any point of law arising.[59]

R v Birmingham City Council, ex p Ferrero[60] concerned the Consumer Protection Act 1987. If an enforcement authority had reasonable grounds for suspecting that any safety requirement had been contravened in relation to any goods, the authority could serve a 'suspension notice', inter alia prohibiting the person on whom it was served from supplying the goods to the public.[61] Any person having an interest in any goods in respect of which a suspension notice was in force could apply for an order setting aside the notice to a magistrates' court. Birmingham City Council issued a suspension notice which prohibited Ferrero for a period of six months from supplying chocolate eggs containing a plastic capsule containing a kit from which a small toy could be made. Ferrero decided to apply for judicial review. It was held that in such cases, it was necessary to look carefully at the suitability of the statutory appeal in the context of the particular statute. Section 14 was 'aimed at providing enforcement authorities with a means of swift, short-term action to prevent goods which have come to their notice from endangering the public'. The appeal (under section 15) did not require leave, as was the case with judicial review, was capable of being heard quickly, was heard before justices, who could deal with the essential facts as to whether the goods were in contravention of a safety requirement on oral evidence (whereas judicial review normally proceeded on affidavit evidence). Therefore, 'there was available an appeal specifically provided by Parliament to enable a party aggrieved by a suspension notice to challenge it. The appeal was at least as expeditious, if not more so, than judicial review. It was more suited than judicial review to the resolution of issues of fact.'[62]

---

[55] *R v Paddington Valuation Officer, ex p Peachey Property Ltd* [1966] 1 QB 380.

[56] *R v Chief Constable of the Merseyside Police, ex p Calveley* [1986] QB 424, per Glidewell LJ, at 43.

[57] *R v Epping and Harlow General Commissioners, ex p Goldstraw* [1983] 3 All ER 257, per Donaldson MR, at 262.   [58] [1985] AC 835.

[59] *R v Hallstrom, ex p W* [1986] QB 824; *R v Falmouth and Truro Port Health Authority, ex p South West Water Ltd* [2000] 3 All ER 306 (CA).   [60] [1993] 1 All ER 530.

[61] Section 14.   [62] Per Taylor LJ, at 540.

THE SUPERVISORY JURISDICTION: AN INTRODUCTION · 477

III. The Supervisory Jurisdiction: An Introduction

The supervisory jurisdiction of the High Court differs from an appellate jurisdiction in three very important ways. First, the supervisory jurisdiction is a means of review, at least in theory, of the law that has been applied by the body under review and it is not an investigation into the facts. Second, the supervisory jurisdiction, being to investigate the legality of a decision, is limited to a decision of the supervisory court that the body under review either acted lawfully or did not act lawfully. If the body acted lawfully, nothing further is needed and the original decision stands. If the body acted unlawfully, the original decision is nullified (to use a non-legal word) and the body has to make its original investigation and determination all over again. Third, the legal basis of the supervisory jurisdiction is not that of statute but is based on the inherent common law powers of the courts to see that justice is done (as developed in accordance with head I). Therefore, in contrast to an appellate jurisdiction, one does not need to find a statute to give a right to apply for the supervisory jurisdiction, although the exercise of that right is governed by statutory rules.[63]

What has to be done is to attempt to draw up the lines which mark off the area of power and to identify the conditions on which the right of a body to act depends. The grounds for judicial review will be analysed in detail in chapter 10, but, since in heads IV to VIII references will be made to cases which, naturally, relate to the grounds for judicial review as well as the matters discussed in those heads, the conditions on which the right of a body to act are summarised here as being that: the body must possess the qualifications laid down in the appropriate statute; the body's decision must not be vitiated by illegality (ie the body must not misunderstand or misapply the relevant law, the case in which the decision is made must be one of the kind of subject matter described in the appropriate statute and the decision-maker must not have misconstrued the statute giving it power to act so that it failed to deal with the question remitted to it and decided some question which was not remitted to it); the body's decision must not be vitiated by irrationality (ie where the decision is outrageously absurd, or utterly illogical or perversely defies accepted standards to such an extent that no rational person could have taken it); and the body's decision must not be vitiated by procedural impropriety (ie a failure to observe procedural rules and practices laid down by the appropriate statute or a failure to observe the rules of natural justice (or to act fairly)).

However, before discussing in chapter 10 the grounds on which a decision is vitiated by a failure to comply with one or more of the above factors, further preliminary considerations are necessary, namely, whether the courts will even entertain an application for the exercise of the supervisory jurisdiction. The question of the availability of judicial review today is essentially whether a person has raised before the courts an issue which is triable in proceedings for judicial review or, as is increasingly being stated, an issue which is 'justiciable'. Justiciability involves an analysis of four questions, namely, what bodies will the courts supervise, at the behest of whom and with the granting of what remedies and to what extent can the supervisory jurisdiction be restricted or ousted by the clear words of Parliament expressed in a statute? The last question is discussed in head VIII and, since it will be seen that much of the current law relating to the first two questions is of recent origin, those

[63] See p. 481.

questions are discussed in heads VI and VII, respectively, leaving for heads IV and V a discussion of the earlier developed principles relating to those judicial remedies which the courts will grant.

IV. The Availability of a Judicial Remedy

(a) Judicial remedies

As explained in head I(d), King's Bench developed over the centuries a series of remedies which the courts would grant the citizen whose complaint of administrative illegality has been successful in accordance with the principles discussed in the next chapter. The citizen may wish to have a decision rescinded or annulled so that the decision no longer has any legal force; to prevent illegal administrative action from taking place so that damage may be prevented; for an authority to perform a duty which the authority refuses to perform; to have a statement that administrative activity is (or will be) illegal, so that the administrative authority knows that if the activity is continued, this illegal activity may give rise to further illegal action; or to obtain monetary compensation for damage caused by illegal administrative action. All these remedies are available to the citizen and may be granted by the superior courts. However, these remedies have arisen in a spasmodic manner and what the courts have done has been to take existing remedies and to adapt them to the modern administrative and welfare state. Traditionally, there have been two categories of remedy, namely, 'prerogative remedies' and 'equitable remedies', and these are discussed first, but in 1977 those remedies were subsumed under the general heading of 'an application for judicial review', governed by RSC Order 53. Further (and somewhat cosmetic) changes in nomenclature were made in 2000 and judicial review is now governed by the Civil Procedure Rules, Part 54. In that Part an order of mandamus is called a 'mandatory order', an order of prohibition is called a 'prohibiting order', and an order of certiorari is called a 'quashing order'. The judicial review procedure is described in head (d) below.

(b) Prerogative remedies

The term 'prerogative' is given to remedies which have developed from the prerogative powers of the King, which were originally used by the King to control (through the courts) his servants, and which have now been developed to provide redress for the citizen against the administration generally.

Certiorari and prohibition were originally writs (now orders) which King's Bench issued in order to protect the King's interest. Certiorari was, as its Latin name suggests, a writ whereby the King asked to be informed of a matter, had the case brought to Westminster before his court of King's Bench, and if the King (or rather the court) did not approve of the matter, the decision was annulled or quashed. This is why the older cases were reported as 'R v X, ex parte Y'— the King or Queen against X on the application of Y. The modern terminology refers to 'R (on the application of X) v Y'. Plus ça change. Prohibition, as its name suggests, was an order of

King's Bench to prohibit another court from acting in a particular matter. Prohibition is very rare. We are really only concerned with the quashing order (the former certiorari), quashing an action of an administrative authority, government department, local authority, statutory tribunal or inferior court. Note that certiorari is discretionary and that the courts will not grant the remedy if no substantial injustice has been caused, if the remedy would not be of use to the citizen or if the citizen delays seeking redress[64] or if by his or her conduct a person has precluded him or herself from relief by way of judicial review.[65]

Mandamus, as its name suggests, was originally a royal command from the King to an inferior body telling that body to perform a duty. When King's Bench took over the supervision of local authorities, they used mandamus to order recalcitrant local authorities to perform such duties as the provision of street paving and other amenities and the correct operation of the poor law. The mandatory order (the former mandamus) may be used to compel a wide variety of public authorities to perform a public duty imposed by law. In particular, the court, having in its judgment determined 'what the law is', may order the authority to reconsider the decision that has been challenged and to act in accordance with that judgment. Mandamus was granted in several cases discussed in chapter 10.[66] In *R v London Borough of Hounslow, ex p Pizzey*,[67] Errin Pizzey was the director of an association devoted to helping battered wives and she applied for premises to be registered as a common lodging house. The authority refused to register the premises. It was held that the authority could only refuse to register the premises on grounds listed in the appropriate statute, such as an unsuitable applicant, unsuitable premises, or premises causing a nuisance,[68] and that the authority must register the premises unless satisfied as to one of those matters. As there was no evidence as to any of the above matters, mandamus was granted ordering the authority to register the premises.

(c) Equitable remedies

Essentially the injunction is a stopping remedy, a prohibitory injunction being used to prevent future interference with the complainant's rights, a mandatory injunction being used to remove an interference with the complainant's rights, an interlocutory injunction to prevent a change in the status quo until the substantive matter is determined, and a perpetual injunction to be used at the end of proceedings.[69] Sometimes, an injunction may be claimed by the Attorney-General to enforce the general right of the public against a private citizen if existing remedies are insufficient. *A-G v Harris*[70] concerned a bye-law prohibiting the obstruction of the highway outside the entrance to a cemetery. Harris established a flower stall outside the cemetery, causing an obstruction. He was convicted of a breach of the bye-law and fined; the next day he set up his stall outside the cemetery, causing an obstruction, was convicted and fined and found it profitable to pay the fine and continue to flout the law. The Attorney General, on the application of Manchester Corporation, sought an injunction to restrain

[64] *Everett*, p. 93.
[65] R (*on the application of Barwise) v Chief Constable of West Midlands Police* [2004] EWHC 1876 (Admin).
[66] *Rotherham Justices*, p. 559, *Cowan*, p. 619. See, also, *R v Woodbury Licensing Justices, ex p Rouse* [1960] 1 WLR 461; *R v Paddington Rent Tribunal, ex p Millard* [1955] 1 All ER 691; *R v Bristol Corporation, ex p Hendy* [1974] 1 WLR 498. Note that mandamus was refused in *Tameside*, p. 572.
[67] [1977] 1 WLR 58. [68] Housing Act 1985, sections 402, 403 and 404(1), (3).
[69] *Bradbury*, p. 613. [70] [1961] 1 QB 74.

Harris from continuing. In *A-G v Chaudry,*[71] Mr and Mrs Chaudry acquired three houses and converted them into an hotel. The Greater London Council made an inspection and found that there was a very serious risk of fire. Under the London Building Acts (Amendment) Act 1939, section 34(5), the magistrates' court could issue a prohibition order prohibiting the occupation of the building. However, the enforcement proceedings would not commence for two months. Consequently, the Council, by leave of the Attorney-General, brought proceedings for an injunction to restrain Mr and Mrs Chaudry from using the hotel buildings for occupation in breach of the law. It was held that there were

'many statutes which provide penalties for breach of them—penalties which are enforceable by means of a fine—or even imprisonment—but this has never stood in the way of the High Court granting an injunction. Many a time people have found it profitable to pay a fine and go on breaking the law. In all such cases the High Court has been ready to grant an [injunction]. In this particular case it is plain that the magistrates' court has not sufficient powers at its command. It cannot act for several weeks. It cannot make any order until there is a conviction. I ask, what is to happen in the meanwhile? Is the law to be defied? Is this house to be occupied when there is a serious fire risk? If a fire should catch hold, it may mean serious loss of life. This risk must not be allowed. The High Court must act to stop it. We are told that Mr and Mrs Chaudry do not mean to use the house pending the proceedings: and that they have not taken any more bookings for the hotel. But they have not given any undertaking to the court. In the circumstances it seems to me quite plain that an injunction must issue.'[72]

It must be emphasised that an injunction is a discretionary remedy. Although a plaintiff may have a strictly legal case, the court may refuse the remedy if the injury is trivial, damages would be an adequate remedy, or the plaintiff has delayed too much. In *Glynn v Keele University,*[73] the plaintiff had decided to contribute to the cultural life of the University of Keele by taking his clothes off. He was excluded from residence on University precincts. It was held that, although there had been a breach of the rules of natural justice in that Glynn had not been given a proper hearing, an injunction would not be granted, because there was no dispute as to the facts and the penalty was entirely 'proper'.

A declaration (or a declaratory judgment) is a statement by the court as to the existing basis of parties' rights and obligations and the courts may make binding declarations of right whether or not any consequential relief is or could be claimed. It may appear surprising to call a mere exposition of what the legal position is a remedy and yet very often the exposition of what the law is on a given matter is what an individual and an administrative authority may want to know. Once the existing state of the law is declared, the parties know their position and can act or not act accordingly.[74]

A useful case is *Price v Sunderland Corporation.*[75] Sunderland Corporation wanted to compel its school teachers to collect school milk and school meals money and intended to serve notice of dismissal on those school teachers who did not comply with the instruction. It was held that this was illegal, as not being part of the teachers' terms of employment, and that a declaration was the most appropriate remedy because the other method of testing the legality of the instruction would have been for the teachers to have been dismissed and then to raise the illegality of the instructions as part of an action for unfair dismissal. This would have caused much more bother than the simplicity of a statement as to the parties' rights and obligations. Cases where binding declarations of rights have been made include complaints

---

[71] [1971] 3 All ER 938 (CA).   [72] Per Lord Denning MR, at 946–947.

[73] [1971] 1 WLR 487.

[74] *Dyson v AG* [1911] 1 KB 410 (CA). See *Barnard*, p. 533, *Hillingdon*, p. 577, *Aylesbury Mushrooms*, p. 614, and *Ridge*, p. 616.   [75] [1956] I WLR 1253.

that a Corporation's travel concession scheme[76] and conditions relating to the use of caravan sites[77] were unlawful. Local authorities may also seek declarations in order to find the true legal extent of their powers and duties, such as the power to apportion costs of local authority works,[78] powers to grant pensions to employees,[79] the power to demolish temporary buildings,[80] payments for fares for travel for school children,[81] and the legality of a council's housing policy in relation to the Race Relations legislation.[82]

Not all problems can be solved by a declaration. Where there is an alternative remedy, the courts may refuse to make a binding declaration.[83] Of great importance is the fact that a declaration merely declares rights and does not quash an *ultra vires* exercise of power.[84]

(d) The judicial review procedure

The application for judicial review is a process whereby the remedies discussed in heads (b) and (c) above may be applied for[85] and lies to a specialist part of the High Court to deal with public and administrative law cases, the Administrative Court. In what follows, a 'claim for judicial review' means a claim to review the lawfulness of either an enactment or a decision, action or failure to act in relation to the exercise of a public function. An application to the High Court for one or more of the following forms of relief, namely, a mandatory order (mandamus), a prohibiting order (prohibition) or a quashing order (certiorari) and a declaration or injunction (in specified circumstances: below) must be made in accordance with the procedure known as an application for judicial review. A declaration may be made or an injunction granted in any case where an application for judicial review, seeking that relief, has been made and the High Court considers that, having regard to the nature of the matters in respect of which relief may be granted by an order of mandamus, prohibition or certiorari, to the nature of the persons and bodies against whom relief may be granted by such an order, and to all the circumstances of the case, it would be just and convenient for the declaration to be made or the injunction to be granted, as the case may be. A claim for judicial review may include a claim for damages but may not seek damages alone. On an application for judicial review the High Court may award damages to the applicant if the applicant has joined with the application a claim for damages arising from any matter to which the application relates and the court is satisfied that, if the claim had been made in an action begun by the applicant at the time of making the application, the applicant would have been awarded damages.

There is a 'pre-action protocol', which has the purpose of encouraging and facilitating the settlement of cases, to avoid burdening the Administrative Court with cases which do not need to go there and to reduce the cost to all concerned. Litigation is expensive and the public

---

[76] *Prescott v Birmingham Corporation* [1955] Ch 210.

[77] *Mixnam's Properties Ltd v Chertsey UDC* [1965] AC 735.

[78] *Sunderland Corporation v Gray* [1928] Ch 756.

[79] *Wimbledon and Putney Commons Conservators v Tuely* [1931] 1 Ch 190.

[80] *Ruislip Northwood UDC v Lee* (1931) 145 LT 208.

[81] *Surrey CC v Ministry of Education* [1953] 1 WLR 516.

[82] *Ealing LBC v Race Relations Board* [1972] AC 342.

[83] *Watt v Kesteven CC* [1955] 1 QB 408, education policy of local authority to be supervised by Secretary of State; *Re Croydon Development Plan* [1967] 2 All ER 589, questions relating to compensation for compulsory acquisition of land to be determined by the Lands Tribunal.

[84] *Punton v Ministry of Pensions and National Insurance (No 2)* [1964] 1 WLR 226.

[85] Supreme Court Act 1981, section 31, Civil Proceedings Rules, Part 54, and appropriate practice directions.

purse can well be spent elsewhere. Before making the claim for judicial review, the claimant should send a 'letter before claim' identifying the decision challenged, the issues in dispute and the facts relied upon. The defendant should send a 'letter of response' either conceding the claim or giving a fuller explanation of the decision, addressing the issues in dispute. The claim form provides for the giving of full information as to the grounds of challenge and the facts on which the challenge is based. This is important in view of the 'permission stage' (below).

No application for judicial review can be made unless the leave (or 'permission to proceed') of the High Court has first been obtained. If the court refuses permission, the court must give reasons for the refusal. The claimant cannot appeal against a refusal but may ask the court to reconsider the decision. The court will normally consider the question of permission without a hearing.

It is expressly stated that the court must not grant leave to make an application for judicial review unless it considers that the applicant has a sufficient interest in the matter to which the application relates. This question of 'sufficient interest', or *locus standi*, is discussed in head VII.

The claim form for judicial review must be filed promptly and, in any event, not later than three months after the grounds to make the claim first arose. This time limit can not be extended by agreement between the parties. If the High Court considers that there has been undue delay in making an application for judicial review, the court may refuse to grant leave for the making of the application or any relief sought on the application, if it considers that the granting of the relief sought would be likely to cause substantial hardship to, or substantially prejudice the rights of, any person or would be detrimental to good administration.[86] The above provisions are without prejudice to any statutory provision or rule of court which has the effect of limiting the time within which an application for judicial review may be made (ie, when any other enactment specifies a shorter time limit for making the claim for judicial review).

If, on an application for judicial review seeking an order of certiorari, the High Court is satisfied that there are grounds for quashing the decision to which the application relates, the High Court may, in addition to quashing it, remit the matter to the decision-maker (the court, tribunal or authority concerned), with a direction to reconsider it and reach a decision in accordance with the findings of the High Court. If the High Court considers that there is no purpose to be served in remitting the matter to the decision-maker it may, subject to any statutory provision, take the decision itself.

v. The Principle of Procedural Exclusivity

It is of utmost importance to note that if the matter is one of public law, whatever that may mean but where, in essence, the case concerns the rights of the citizen against the state, the case must be brought by way of judicial review. This fundamental proposition was laid down in:

O'Reilly v Mackman [1983] 2 AC 237

The appellants had had forfeited some of the remission of sentence by the Board of Prison Visitors on the grounds that they had taken part in riots at Hull Prison. They sought to establish that the Board had acted contrary to natural justice and sought to establish this by an originating summons, in the case of

---

[86] On delay, see *R v Stratford on Avon District Council, ex p Jackson* [1985] 1 WLR 1319; *R v Dairy Produce Quota Tribunal, ex p Caswell* [1990] 2 AC 728.

one appellant and by writ in the case of the other appellants. It was not contested that if the facts alleged were true, they would have been able to seek judicial review under what was then Order 53 because rights granted to them by public law (under the Prison Rules) would have been curtailed by a public authority (the Board of Visitors) and that if they had used Order 53 they would have had to follow that procedure, including an application for leave to appeal, a procedure which was not obligatory by way of originating summons. The sole question was whether in 1980 (after RSC Order 53 in its new form had come into operation) it was an abuse of the process of the court to apply for a declaration by way of writ or originating summons instead of by way of Order 53 for an application for judicial review.

Lord Diplock, at 275–285

'It is not, and it should not be, contended that the decision of the [Board] had infringed or threatened to infringe any right of the appellants derived from private law, whether a common law right or one created by a statute. [Therefore] none of the appellants had any remedy in private law. In public law, as distinguished from private law, [each] of the appellants, if he established the facts alleged in the action, was entitled to a remedy in public law which would have the effect of preventing the decision of the board from having any adverse consequences on him.

My Lords, the power of the High Court to make declaratory judgments is conferred by [RSC Order 15, rule 16, which does not] draw any distinction between declarations that relate to rights and obligations under private law and those that relate to rights and obligations under public law. Indeed the appreciation of the distinction in substantive law between what is private law and what is public law has itself been a latecomer to the English legal system. It is a consequence of the development that has taken place in the last thirty years of the procedures available for judicial control of administrative action. This development started with the expansion of the grounds on which orders for certiorari could be obtained as a result of the decisions [in, inter alia, *Ridge*, p. 616, and *Anisminic*, p. 514]. Although the availability of the remedy of orders to quash a decision by certiorari had in theory been widely extended by these developments, the procedural disadvantages under which applicants for this remedy laboured remained substantially unchanged until the alteration of Order 53 in [1977].

[As] compared with an action for a declaration commenced by writ or originating summons, the procedure under Order 53 [provided for the decision-making public] authority against which the remedy of certiorari was sought protection against claims which it was not in the public interest for courts of justice to entertain.

Those [procedural] disadvantages, which formerly might have resulted in an applicant's being unable to obtain justice in an application for certiorari under Order 53, have all been removed by the new Order introduced in [1977]. So Order 53 since 1977 has provided a procedure by which every type of remedy for infringement of the rights of individuals that are entitled to protection in public law can be obtained in one and the same proceeding by way of an application for judicial review, and whichever remedy is found to be the most appropriate in the light of what has emerged upon the hearing of the application, can be granted to him. If what should emerge is that his complaint is not of an infringement of any of his rights that are entitled to protection in public law, but may be an infringement of his rights in private law and thus not a proper subject for judicial review, the court has [power], instead of refusing the application, to order the proceedings to continue as if they had begun by [writ].

The position of applicants for judicial review has been drastically ameliorated by the new Order 53. It has removed all those disadvantages [that] were manifestly unfair to them and had, in many cases, made applications for prerogative orders an inadequate remedy if justice was to be done. This it was that justified the courts in not treating as an abuse of their powers resort to an alternative procedure by way of action for a declaration or injunction (not then obtainable on an application under Order 53), despite the fact that this procedure had the effect of depriving the defendants of the protection to statutory tribunals and public authorities for which for public policy reasons Order 53 provided.

Now that those disadvantages to applicants have been removed and all remedies for infringements of rights protected by public law can be obtained upon an application for judicial review, as can also remedies for infringements of rights under private law if such infringements should also be involved, it would in my view as a general rule be contrary to public policy, and as such an abuse of the process of the court, to permit a person seeking to establish that a decision of a public authority infringed rights to which he was entitled to protection under public law to proceed by way of an ordinary action and by this means to evade the provisions of Order 53 for the protection of such authorities.

My Lords, I have described this as a general rule: for though it may normally be appropriate to apply it by the summary process of striking out the action, there may be exceptions, particularly where the invalidity of the decision arises as a collateral issue in a claim for infringement of a right of the plaintiff arising under private law, or where none of the parties objects to the adoption of the procedure by writ or originating summons. Whether there should be other exceptions should, in my view, at this stage in the development of procedural public law, be left to be decided on a case to case basis.

In the instant cases where the only relief sought is a declaration of nullity of the decisions of a statutory tribunal, the Board of Visitors of Hull Prison, as in any other case in which a similar declaration of nullity in public law is the only relief claimed, I have no hesitation, in agreement with the Court of Appeal, in holding that to allow the actions to proceed would be an abuse of the process of the court. They are blatant attempts to avoid the protections for the defendants for which Order 53 provides.'

The decision that an application for a declaration or injunction in what was an 'essentially public law' matter must be by way of judicial review has become known as the 'principle of procedural exclusivity'.[87] There have been a number of cases since *O'Reilly* in which it has been necessary for the courts to consider the distinction between public and private law and in many of them, it has been argued by the defendant body that in seeking a remedy in private law, instead of public law, the plaintiff has attempted to deprive the defendant body of the special protection afforded by the judicial review process which was referred to in *O'Reilly*. There will be many situations where the position is clear and a challenge to the legality of an administrative decision will be easily classified as public or private. It was, however, accepted in *O'Reilly* that there might be cases where private law rights were being asserted in a way which incidentally also raised issues of illegality of administrative action so that there is a combination of both public and private law issues. According to *O'Reilly*, it is important to maintain the principle that an issue which depends exclusively on the existence of a purely public law right should be determined in judicial review proceedings and not otherwise. However, it is also important that if a person asserts his or her entitlement to a right in private law, the fact that the existence and extent of the private right asserted may incidentally involve the examination of a public law issue should not prevent that person from seeking to establish the private right by a private law action or prevent him or her from setting up the private law right in proceedings brought against him or her:

Wandsworth LBC v Winder [1985] AC 461

Winder was a tenant of a local authority which gave notice that his rent was to be raised. Winder contended that the rent increase was unreasonable, as it was contrary to the housing legislation then in force, refused to pay the increase and paid only what he considered 'reasonable'. The authority brought an action against Winder for possession of the premises on the ground that rent had not been paid. Winder defended the action on the ground that the rent increase was ultra vires and void as being unreasonable.

[87] Law Commission Consultation Paper No 126 (1993).

Lord Fraser, at 504–510

'My Lords, the question in this appeal is whether it is an abuse of process for an individual, who claims that his existing rights under a contract have been infringed by a decision of a public authority, to challenge the decision in defence to an action at the instance of the public authority for payment, instead of by judicial review under RSC Order [53].

The respondent seeks to show in the course of his defence in these proceedings that the appellants' decisions to increase the rent were such as no reasonable man could consider justifiable. But your Lordships are not concerned in this appeal to decide whether that contention is right or wrong. The only issue at this stage is whether the respondent is entitled to put forward the contention as a defence in the present proceedings. The appellants say that he is not because the only procedure by which their decision could have been challenged was by judicial review under RSC Order 53. The respondent was refused leave to apply for judicial review out of time and (say the appellants) he has lost the opportunity to challenge the decisions. [The] respondent accepts that judicial review would have been an appropriate procedure for the purpose, but he maintains that it is not the only procedure open to him, and that he was entitled to wait until he was sued by the appellants and then to defend the proceedings, as he has done.

[The question raised in *O'Reilly*] was the same as that in the present case, although of course, the circumstances were [different]. In that case four prisoners in Hull prison had started proceedings, in three cases by writ and in one case by originating summons, each seeking to establish that a disciplinary award of forfeiture of remission of sentence made by the Board of Visitors of Hull Prison was void because the board had failed to observe the rules of natural justice. This House held that the proceedings were an abuse of the process of the court, and that the only proper remedy open to the prisoners was by way of judicial review under Order 53. There are two important differences between the facts in *O'Reilly* and those in the present case. First, the plaintiffs in *O'Reilly* had not suffered any infringement of their rights in private law; their complaint was that they had been ordered to forfeit part of their remission of sentence but they had no right in private law to such a remission, which was granted only as a matter of indulgence. Consequently, even if the board of visitors had acted contrary to the rules of natural justice when making the award, the members of the board would not have been liable in damages to the prisoners. In the present case what the respondent complains of is the infringement of a contractual right in private law. Secondly, in *O'Reilly* the prisoners had initiated the proceedings, and Lord Diplock, throughout in his speech, treated the question only as one affecting a claim for infringing a right of the plaintiff while in the present case the respondent is the defendant. The decision on *O'Reilly* is therefore not directly in point in the present [case].

[*Cocks v Thanet District Council* [1983] 2 AC 286] was an action by a homeless person claiming that the local housing authority had a duty to provide permanent accommodation for him. The council resolved that the plaintiff had become homeless "intentionally" in the sense of the Housing (Homeless Persons) Act 1977. Consequently the plaintiff had no right in private law to be provided with permanent housing accommodation by the authority. The plaintiff raised an action in the county court claiming, inter alia, a declaration that the council were in breach of their duty to him in not having provided him with permanent accommodation. In order to proceed in his action he had to show as a condition precedent that the council's decision was invalid. This House held that the plaintiff was not entitled to impugn the council's decision in public law otherwise than by judicial review, notwithstanding that the effect of the decision was to prevent him from "establishing a necessary condition precedent to the statutory private law right which he [was seeking to enforce"]. The essential difference between that case and the present is that the impugned decision of the local authority did not deprive the plaintiff of a pre-existing private law right: it prevented him from establishing a new private law [right].

Although neither *O'Reilly* nor *Cocks* [is] an authority which directly applies to the facts of the instant appeal, it is said on behalf of the appellants that the principle underlying those decisions applies here, and that, if the respondent is successful, he will be evading that principle. My Lords, I cannot agree. The principle underlying those decisions, as Lord Diplock explained in *O'Reilly* [is] that there is a "need, in the interests of good administration and of third parties who may be indirectly affected by the decision, for speedy certainty as to whether it has the effect of a decision that is valid in public law". The main argument urged on behalf of the appellants was that this is a typical case where there is a need for speedy certainty in the public interest. I accept, of course, that the decision in this appeal will indirectly affect many third parties including many of the appellants' tenants, and perhaps most if not all of their ratepayers because if the appellants' impugned decisions are held to be invalid, the basis of their financial administration [will] be upset. That would be highly inconvenient from the point of view of the appellants, and of their ratepayers, and it would be a great advantage to them if persons such as the respondent who seek to challenge their decision were limited to doing so by procedure under Order 53. Such procedure is speedy and avoids prolonged uncertainty about the validity of decisions. An intending applicant for judicial review under Order 53 has to obtain leave to apply, so that unmeritorious applications can be dismissed in limine and an application must normally be made within a limited period of three months after the decision which has impugned, unless the court allows an extension of time in any particular case. Procedure under Order 53 [affords protection to public authorities]. It may well be that such protection to public authorities tends to promote good administration. [In] any event, the arguments for protecting public authorities against unmeritorious or dilatory challenges to their decisions have to be set against the arguments for preserving the ordinary rights of private citizens to defend themselves against unfounded claims.

It would in my opinion be a very strange use of language to describe the respondent's behaviour in relation to this litigation as an abuse or misuse by him of the process of the court. He did not select the procedure to be adopted. He is merely seeking to defend proceedings brought against him by the appellants. In so doing he is seeking only to exercise the ordinary right of any individual to defend an action against him on the ground that he is not liable for the whole sum claimed by the plaintiff. [I] find it impossible to accept that the right to challenge the decision of a local authority in course of defending an action for non payment can have been swept away by Order 53, which was directed to introducing a procedural [reform].

If the public interest requires that persons should not be entitled to defend actions brought against them by public authorities, where the defence rests on a challenge to a decision by the public authority, then it is for Parliament to change the law.'

The application of the principle of procedural exclusivity has not been without difficulties. *Davy v Spelthorne BC*[88] related to the circumstances in which a person, with a cause of action against a public authority 'connected with' the performance of the authority's public duty, is entitled to proceed against the authority by way of an ordinary action, as distinct from an application for judicial review. Davy claimed damages from the authority on the ground that the authority, or their officers, had purported to advise him as to his rights under the planning legislation and that this advice had been negligent. It was held that the proceedings, so far as they consisted of a claim for damages for negligence, appeared to be simply an ordinary action for tort. They did not raise any issue of public law. The negligence claim was not concerned with the infringement of rights to which the plaintiff was entitled to protection under public law. It was concerned with the alleged infringement of Davy's rights at common law, which were not even peripheral to a public law claim. They were the essence of the entire claim (so far as negligence was concerned) and they did not fall within the scope of the general rule laid down in *O'Reilly*. In *Roy v Kensington and Chelsea Family Practitioner Committee*,[89] Roy was a doctor providing general medical services in the area administered by a family practitioner committee and his entitlement to payment for the services provided was established by certain National Health Service Regulations. In certain instances the amount

---

[88] [1984] AC 262.   [89] [1992] 1 AC 624.

of remuneration depended on a determination by the committee involving some element of subjective or discretionary judgment, making the doctor's entitlement to the full rate of basic practice allowance conditional on the opinion of the family practitioner committee that the doctor was devoting 'a substantial amount of time' to his or her national health service practice. The family practitioner committee, in purported reliance on this provision, decided to withhold 20 per cent of Roy's full rate of basic practice allowance and Roy brought an action claiming that this was a breach of his contract with the committee. The committee alleged that this was an abuse of process because, according to the committee, the correct procedure for challenging their decision was by way of an application for judicial review. It was held that the terms which governed the obligation of Roy as to the services he was to provide and of the family practitioner committee as to the payments which it was required to make were prescribed in the Regulations and those statutory terms were just as effective as they would be if they were contractual to confer upon Roy an enforceable right in private law to receive the remuneration to which the terms entitled him. It followed that, in any case of dispute, Roy was entitled to claim and recover in an action commenced by writ the amount of remuneration which he was able to prove as being due to him. Whatever remuneration he was entitled to under the Regulations was remuneration he had duly earned by the services rendered. The fact that the amount of that remuneration was affected by a discretionary decision made by the committee could not deny Roy his private law right of recovery or subject him to the constraints which the necessity to seek judicial review would impose upon that right. *Davey*, *Roy* and many similar cases led to strong expressions of judicial displeasure:

'The old forms of action have doubtless long been laid to rest, but others have sprung up in their place, giving rise once again to litigation which is devoted to the question whether the right form of action has been used, rather than addressing and resolving the real dispute between the parties. The present proceedings are of this nature, for the question is whether the claim is properly brought by ordinary action or should first have been advanced by way of judicial review. [Over] the last decade or so there has been a stream of litigation on this subject, much of it proceeding to the House of Lords. The cases raise and depend upon the most sophisticated arguments, such as the distinction and difference between what is described as "public" as opposed to "private" law, whether rights are of a "private" or "public" nature, whether "private" rights depend upon the exercise of "public" obligations and so on; as well as seeking to decide, in the context of legislation which does not make the position clear, whether or not Parliament did or did not intend to limit or exclude rights that might otherwise exist under common law. [The] cost of this litigation, borne privately or through taxation, must be immense, with often the lawyers the only people to gain. Such litigation brings the law and our legal system into disrepute.'[90]

However, a more recent and perhaps more flexible approach may be found in:

Steed v Home Office [2000] UKHL 32

The Secretary of State was empowered to make arrangements to secure the orderly surrender of legally held large calibre hand guns and ammunition and to make payments in respect of firearms surrendered 'in accordance with a scheme made by him'. Firearms had to be surrendered by 30 September 1997 and claims for compensation made to the police for transmission to the Firearm Compensation Section of the Home Office (FCS) for them to check. Steed surrendered firearms and ammunition to the police on 29 July 1997. On 27 October 1997, he issued a county court summons

---

[90] *British Steel v HM Commissioners of Customs and Excise* [1997] 2 All ER 366, per Saville LJ, at 379.

claiming, in view of the inordinate delay in settling the claim under the scheme, the immediate payment of the value of the surrendered items, together with interest at the statutory rate from 30 days after the date of such surrender, together with costs. His claims were paid on 26 November 1997 and on 25 September 1998, respectively. Therefore, the outstanding claim in respect of all items was only for interest. The Home Office contended that any complaint was solely justiciable in judicial review proceedings. The Home Office contended that if claimants could proceed by summons they would be able to jump the queue and have their claims processed before others who were prepared to wait without beginning legal proceedings.

Lord Slynn

'The first question [is] whether a person who has handed in his guns has any right to compensation. The answer in my view is plainly that once all the conditions laid down in the Scheme have been satisfied the claimant is entitled to the sum [specified. There] is no fixed period in which FCS's consideration and approval of the claim must take place or of the period within which the payment must be [made. It] seems to me to be plain or at least to be plainly arguable [that] when a person is obliged to surrender his property and is to be compensated for it his claim will be considered, approved or rejected within a reasonable [time. The] second question is whether the citizen who has given in his gun can challenge in the court what he considers unreasonable delay in the consideration of his claim or the failure to pay in due time. It is again to my mind plain that he must be able to bring such a challenge by one means or another. The Home Office contends that this can only be done by judicial review at any rate until all the scheme's procedures have been gone through and his entitlement and the value decided by the F.C.S. At that stage if the agreed sum due is not paid a claim by summons is possible. Before that stage is reached it is an abuse of process to raise the matter by such a summons.

The starting point for this contention is [*O'Reilly*, p. 482] and in particular the passage in the speech of Lord [Diplock]: "it would in my view as a general rule be contrary to public policy, and as such an abuse of the process of the court, to permit a person seeking to establish that a decision of a public authority infringed rights to which he was entitled to protection under public law to proceed by way of an ordinary action and by this means to evade the provisions of Order 53 for the protection of such authorities". That [case] attached particular importance to the protection given to public authorities by Order 53 [to] the extent that leave to bring proceedings was required and a time limit imposed subject to good reason for extending it. *O'Reilly* [has] had an important influence on the regulation of court proceedings where an individual seeks to assert his rights against a public authority. But even in the passage cited, Lord Diplock sets out the position "as a general rule". Earlier [he] said that Parliament and the Rules Committee had been "content to rely upon the express and the inherent power of the High Court, exercised upon a case to case basis, to prevent abuse of its process whatever might be the form taken by that abuse. Accordingly I do not think that your lordships would be wise to use this as an occasion to lay down categories of cases in which it would necessarily always be an abuse to seek in an action begun by a writ or originating summons a remedy against infringement or rights of the individual that are entitled to protection in public law". He accepted [that] although striking out may be appropriate "normally", "there may be exceptions, particularly where the invalidity of the decision arises as a collateral issue in a claim for infringement of a right of the plaintiff arising under private law, or where none of the parties objects to the adoption of the procedure by writ or originating summons". Other exceptions, if any, should be decided on a case to case basis.

One such exception is to be found in *Roy Kensington and Chelsea and Westminster Family Practitioner Committee* [p. 486] when it was accepted that a claim for private rights could be made by action even if that involved a challenge to a "public law act or decision". Another is to be found in *Mercury Communications Ltd v Director General of Telecommunications* [1996] 1 WLR 48, at 57, when, in a speech with which other members of the House agreed, I said:

> "The recognition by Lord Diplock that exceptions exist to the general rule may introduce some uncertainty but it is a small price to pay to avoid the over-rigid demarcation between procedures

reminiscent of earlier disputes as to the forms of action and of disputes as to the competence of jurisdictions apparently encountered in civil law countries where a distinction between public and private law has been [recognized]. The experience of other countries seems to show that the working out of this distinction is not always an easy matter. In the absence of the single procedure allowing all remedies, quashing, injunctive and declaratory relief, damages, some flexibility as to the use of different procedures is necessary. It has to be borne in mind that the overriding question is whether the proceedings constitute an abuse of the process of the court."

In *Trustees of the Dennis Rye Pension Fund v Sheffield City Council* [1998] 1 WLR 840, at 849, Lord Woolf said that the guidelines he gave involved: "not only considering the technical questions of the distinctions between public and private rights and bodies but also looking at the practical consequences of the choice of procedure which has been made. If the choice has no significant disadvantage for the parties, the public or the court, then it should not normally be regarded as constituting an abuse."

In the present case, if there had been a general challenge to the *vires* of the scheme—a question as to whether it complies with the statutory intention—it would no doubt be right to begin by an application for judicial review. But here essentially this claimant says that money was due to him; it was not paid when it was due; he has accordingly suffered damage (valued in terms of interest) because of the delay. I do not see that any of the questions which might arise here cannot be dealt with by a judge on the hearing of the summons or that answering such questions usurps the province of the administration where a discretionary decision is reserved to the administration. Here there are largely either objective questions of fact as to whether the gun is a listed gun and whether the procedures have been completed or they depend on valuation on which evidence can be given and a decision arrived at by a judge. As a matter of procedure it seems to me that it was more convenient to begin by summons and to deal with a particular claim (and if a real question of law arose to appeal) than by application for judicial review, perhaps followed by an appeal. As I have said, the Home Office stresses the large number of claims which might be affected by a decision in this case and is concerned by the possibility of one or more claimants being able to jump the queue by commencing court proceedings. I understand this concern, but I am not persuaded that this points to judicial review being the only remedy. Indeed, even allowing for the risk of "jumping the queue" it might in an analogous situation be better for a summons like this one to be adjourned for a short period to enable the claim to be dealt with by the administrative authority. [This] summons was not an abuse of the process of the court.'

One important question that has had to be faced has been to what extent a person may challenge, by way of collateral defence to a criminal prosecution, the rule (statutory instrument or bye-law) on which the prosecution against that person is based on grounds which could have been raised upon an application for judicial review? This is most relevant, since the first time that person may know of the rule and its effect on him or her is when he or she is charged with an offence under the rule. In *Boddington v British Transport Police*,[91] Boddington was charged and convicted of an offence contrary to a bye-law, which prohibited smoking in a train where there was a notice to that effect. He raised the defence that the bye-law was *ultra vires* the appropriate parent Act and the House of Lords held that he could so raise the legality of the 'No Smoking' notices by way of defence to the charge against him. This was something of a Pyrrhic victory, as the Lords also held that the bye-law was not *ultra vires* and the notices were perfectly lawful.[92]

---

[91] [1999] 2 AC 143.
[92] See also, *Quietlynn Ltd v Plymouth City Council* [1988] QB 114; *R v Wicks* [1998] AC 92; *Palacegate Properties v London Borough of Camden* [2000] EWHC 372 (Admin).

vi. What Bodies are Amenable to Judicial Review?

(a) A presumption

Certiorari and mandamus were historically always connected with bodies performing a 'public duty'. What bodies perform a public duty? If the defendant body is created by statute and is granted power by statute to affect 'the rights of citizens', there should normally be no problem and the intervention of the courts by way of judicial review is based on the premise that Parliament intended the defendant body to act in accordance with the will of Parliament. In recent years, much attention has been placed on the extent to which bodies whose existence and powers are not statutory but which have the right to determine questions affecting the rights or legitimate expectations of the citizen, namely, bodies which exercise the common law prerogative power of the Crown and bodies which exercise neither statutory nor prerogative power. The case law of those years has demonstrated almost a presumption of judicial intervention and that few bodies should now escape judicial review.

(b) Prerogative power

Chapter 3 is devoted to the Royal Prerogative, where it was seen that prerogative power may be 'subject to law'[93] or, to use the language of judicial review, 'justiciable'. With regard to prerogative power, there has been mild controversy as to whether the term 'prerogative' should be limited to those acts which only a head of state or government may perform (such as declaration of war or dissolution of Parliament) (the 'strict' interpretation), or whether the term 'prerogative' should include all exercise by head of state or government of non statutory power (such as regulating the employment of Crown servants and the provision of non statutory forms of compensation by way of bounty) (the 'wide' interpretation). That controversy seems to have been settled by the courts in that they have labelled the exercise of any common law power by government as 'prerogative'.[94] GCHQ concerned an area of law where a common law power was exercised in circumstances analogous to those where the source of power was statutory, namely the employment of Crown servants, where the common law still deems such servants to hold office during the pleasure of the Crown.[95] At one time no one would have considered that point of view remarkable, because for so long most people who were employed (as distinct from holding an office) were also dismissible at the will of the steel master, domestic service employer or landowner. Today, extensive employment protection rights are granted by statute and, occasionally, statute has intervened to grant to civil servants legal rights analogous to those employed in service other than under the Crown (such as statutory maternity pay). The House of Lords treated the relevant Order in Council relating to trade union membership and issued under the prerogative as being on a par with the

---

[93] See p. 82.   [94] GCHQ, p. 86; Fire Brigades Union, p. 101; Burmah Oil, pp.100–101.
[95] Riordan v War Office [1959] 1 WLR 1046.

employment protection legislation applicable to persons employed otherwise than under the Crown and held that, if no question of national security had arisen, the decision making process would have been unfair. One part of the 'employment protection system' for civil servants is the Civil Service Appeals Board, established under the prerogative. The courts have resisted claims that the Board is immune from judicial review, at least as far as the obligation to follow a fair procedure is concerned.[96]

R v Criminal Injuries Compensation Board, ex p Lain[97] concerned an organisation described as 'a servant of the Crown charged by the Crown, by executive instruction, with the duty of distributing the bounty of the Crown'. That description did not prevent the court from determining that the Board was not immune from judicial review as it was exercising a public law function directly affecting the interests of victims of criminal acts. Since then, decisions of the Compensation Board have been subjected to judicial review where it has been found that the Board incorrectly interpreted the individual rules of the compensation scheme[98] or applied those rules in a manner which was unreasonable.[99] In *R v Criminal Injuries Compensation Board, ex p P*,[100] the court was faced with a bolder proposition. Under the compensation scheme, compensation for offences committed against a member of the offender's family living with him or her at the time of the offence was originally excluded. Subsequent revision to the scheme removed the exclusion of claims in respect of family violence incurred on or after 1 October 1979 (the date of the revision). The applicants claimed compensation for acts of sexual abuse committed by their stepfathers when they were children, but the Board rejected the claims which related to acts occurring before 1 October 1979. The applicants alleged that the decision of the Home Secretary to continue the time-bar was irrational, was unjust to women and children and was based on no objective evidence. The court, naturally, accepted jurisdiction, reaffirming that the distribution of bounty on behalf of the Crown did not preclude the courts from exercising their 'constitutional powers' of judicial review, but, with regard to the substantive claim of irrationality, categorised the issue as non justiciable because the issue involved a balance of competing claims on the public purse and the allocation of economic resources with which the court was ill-equipped to deal.[101]

At one time in the past the decision to grant a passport to a citizen (or rather a subject of the monarch) would have been regarded as a high matter of state. Monarchs wanted to monitor the presence of influential citizens within the realm and a personal application to the monarch or Secretary of State was needed. Furthermore, in times past, the monarch could use the high prerogative writ of *ne exeat regno*. Today, the monarch's interest in those going on package tours is minimal and the passport application process has been automated. However, when counsel for the Secretary of State 'sought to put the grant of passports under the umbrella of foreign affairs and thereby elevate it to that level of high policy which would preclude the intervention of the courts', because it involved a request in the name of the Queen to a foreign power to grant free passage, that argument was rejected.[102]

R v Ministry of Defence, ex p Smith, which is discussed in the next chapter[103] as it relates to 'irrationality', is a case of great significance. It related to the claimed defence interests of the

[96] *R v Civil Service Appeals Board, ex p Cunningham* [1991] 4 All ER 310.
[97] [1967] 2 QB 864.　　[98] *R v Criminal Injuries Compensation Board, ex p Clowes* [1977] 1 WLR 1353.
[99] *R v Criminal Injuries Compensation Board, ex p Thompstone and Crowe* [1984] 1 WLR 1234.
[100] [1995] 1 All ER 870.
[101] See, also, *R v Secretary of State for the Home Office, ex p Harrison* [1988] 3 All ER 86.
[102] *Everett*, p. 93.　　[103] See p. 579.

state and national security; to the growing recognition of 'fundamental human rights' and the influence on that recognition of standards laid down by international conventions. Unlike *Bentley*[104] or *Everett*,[105] it related to a direct attack on the creation of government policy and not merely to the manner of exercise of a policy with whose formulation the courts would not interfere. The applicants had been discharged, in accordance with Ministry of Defence policy, from the armed forces because of their homosexual orientation and claimed that, even though the operation of such a policy had as its source the prerogative power, that policy was reviewable and should be reviewed on the grounds of irrationality. The Divisional Court had no hesitation in holding the challenge to the policy justiciable and stated that, today, only the rarest cases will be held outside the courts' review jurisdiction. Although *Smith* related to the armed forces, it did not relate to the 'disposition of the armed forces', a matter still excluded by *China Navigation v Attorney-General*,[106] because no operational considerations were involved in the policy. The Court of Appeal agreed that the issue was justiciable but held that the Ministry policy was not irrational.[107] However, even if the courts are prepared to entertain judicial review proceedings against a body exercising prerogative power, there will be certain exceptions, such as the conduct of foreign affairs, making treaties, the declaration of war, the operational deployment of the armed forces, and decisions whether or not to prosecute, and there is consistent case law as to self-denial of both jurisdiction and justiciability.[108]

(c) Parliamentary matters

Chapter 5 told of the privileges of Parliament, the law and custom of Parliament and the immunity from suit of 'proceedings in Parliament'. Proceedings in Parliament and analogous matters have traditionally raised 'No Entry' signs to the courts. As has been seen in chapter 8, the Parliamentary Commissioner for Administration makes many, many decisions affecting the rights of citizens each year. In *Re Fletcher*,[109] Fletcher appealed against the refusal of a Divisional Court to grant him leave to apply for an order of mandamus requiring the Commissioner to investigate an allegation of neglect of duty against the Official Receiver acting as liquidator of a company. The appeal failed and leave to appeal to the House of Lords was refused by the House of Lords on the ground that there was no jurisdiction to order the Commissioner to investigate a complaint because the Parliamentary Commissioner Act 1967 conferred a discretion whether to investigate or not. More recently, the increasing willingness of the courts to extend the principle of justiciability has been applied to the Commissioner:

R v Parliamentary Commissioner, ex p Dyer [1994] 1 WLR 621

Miss Dyer applied for judicial review of a decision of the Commissioner not to reopen his investigation into her complaints against the Department of Social Security, with regard to the department's mishandling of her claims for various social security benefits. The Commissioner regarded his investigation as at an end when he sent a detailed report of its results to Roy Hattersley MP (who had referred the complaint to him) and to the department. The report found Miss Dyer's complaint to be

[104] See p. 98.   [105] See p. 93.   [106] [1932] 2 KB 197.   [107] See p. 579.

[108] *Rustomjee v R* (1876) 2 QBD 69; *Blackburn v A-G* [1971] 1 WLR 1037; *Mighell v Sultan of Johore* [1894] 1 QB 149; *Chandler v Director of Public Prosecutions* [1962] AC 763; *R v Bottrill, ex p Kuechenmeister* [1947] KB 41; *Gouriet v Union of Post Office Workers* [1978] AC 435.   [109] [1970] 2 All ER 527.

justified. It criticised the department for maladministration and in particular the local office for mishandling various aspects of her benefit claims. In several instances where the report identified matters of justified complaint it noted that the Permanent Secretary offered his apologies to the applicant. The Commissioner stated that he regarded the Permanent Secretary's apologies and an ex gratia payment of £500 sent to Miss Dyer by way of reimbursement for a proportion of her claim for the expenses incurred in pursuing her claim as a satisfactory outcome. The report did not, however, satisfy Miss Dyer, who criticised the Commissioner: first, that he investigated some only of her original complaints, omitting several which she regarded as of importance; second, that although he gave the department an opportunity to comment upon the report in draft, he gave her no such opportunity; third, that he refused to reopen the investigation when, after reading the final report, she pointed out his failure to consider a number of her complaints.

Simon Brown LJ, at 623–629

'This is the first substantive application for judicial review of the Commissioner to come before the [courts]. The first question raised for decision upon it concerns the proper ambit of this court's supervisory jurisdiction over the Commissioner. Mr [Richards] submits to us that, certainly so far as the Commissioner's discretionary powers are concerned, this court has no review jurisdiction whatever over their exercise. In the alternative he submits that the court should intervene only in the most exceptional cases of abuse of [discretion]. The resolution of this initial jurisdictional issue clearly depends essentially on the legislation which created the Commissioner's office and governs the discharge of his [functions]. As to his wider proposition, that this court has literally no right to review the Commissioner's exercise of his discretion under the Act of 1967 (not even, to give the classic illustration, if he refused to investigate complaints by red-headed complainants), Mr Richards submits that the legislation is enacted in such terms as to indicate an intention that the Commissioner should be answerable to Parliament alone for the way he performs his functions. The Commissioner is, he suggests, an officer of the House of Commons, and, the argument runs, the parliamentary control provided for by the statute displaces any supervisory control by the [courts. I] would unhesitatingly reject this argument. Many in government are answerable to Parliament and yet answerable also to the supervisory jurisdiction of this court. I see nothing about the Commissioner's role or the statutory framework within which he operates so singular as to take him wholly outside the purview of judicial [review].

[However], it does not follow that this court will readily be persuaded to interfere with the exercise of the Commissioner's discretion. Quite the contrary. The intended width of these discretions is made strikingly clear by the legislature: under section 5(5), when determining whether to initiate, continue or discontinue an investigation, the Commissioner shall "act in accordance with his own discretion"; under section 7(2), "the procedure for conducting an investigation shall be such as the Commissioner considers appropriate in the circumstances of the case". Bearing in mind too that the exercise of these particular discretions inevitably involves a high degree of subjective judgment, it follows that it will always be difficult to mount an effective challenge on what may be called the conventional ground of *Wednesbury* unreasonableness [see p. 563].

[In] my judgment, the Commissioner was entitled in the exercise of his discretion to limit the scope of his investigation, to be selective as to just which of Miss Dyer's many detailed complaints he addressed, to identify certain broad categories of complaint (the six main aspects as he called them) and investigate only those. Inevitably such an approach carried the risk that some of the problems which Miss Dyer complained of having experienced with the local office would continue, and that indeed is what Miss Dyer says has occurred. But no investigation should be expected to solve all problems for all time and it cannot in my judgment be said that the approach adopted here by the Commissioner was not one properly open to him.

Turning to Miss Dyer's complaint that the draft report was sent to the department for comment on the facts but not to her, the Commissioner's evidence indicates that this is a practice which has existed for 25 years, and is known to and acquiesced in by the select committee. The reasons for it are explained as follows. First, that it is the department rather than the complainant who may subsequently be called upon to justify its actions before the select committee and, if it is shown the draft report and does not point out any inaccuracy, it will then be unable to dispute the facts stated in it. Second, the practice affords the department an opportunity to give notice in writing to the Commissioner [of] any document or information the disclosure of which, in the opinion of the relevant minister, would be prejudicial to the safety of the state or otherwise contrary to the public interest. Third, sight of the draft report gives the department the opportunity to propose the remedy it is prepared to offer in the light of any findings of maladministration and injustice contained in it. The Commissioner can then include in his final report what that proposed remedy is and indicate whether he finds that it satisfactorily meets the need.

[To] graft on to the existing practice a need to show the draft report to complainants too would introduce a further stage into the process. Does natural justice require this? I do not think so. As Lord Bridge said in *Lloyd v McMahon* [[1987] AC 625 at 702]: "My Lords, the so-called rules of natural justice are not engraved on tablets of stone. To use the phrase which better expresses the underlying concept, what the requirements of fairness demand when any body, domestic, administrative or judicial, has to make a decision which will affect the rights of individuals depends on the character of the decision-making body, the kind of decision it has to make and the statutory or other framework in which it operates". Assuming, as I do, and indeed as Mr Richards concedes, that the Commissioner makes "a decision which will affect the rights of" Miss Dyer, it should nevertheless be borne in mind that it is the department and not her who is being investigated and who is liable to face public criticism for its acts. I cannot conclude that fairness here demanded that she too be shown the draft report. Rather it seems to me that the Commissioner, in determining the procedure for conducting his investigation as provided for by section 7(2), was amply entitled to consider it appropriate to follow his long-established practice.

I come finally to Miss Dyer's complaint about the Commissioner's refusal to reopen this investigation. [It] seems to me that the Commissioner is clearly correct in his view that, once his report had been sent to Mr Hattersley and the [DSS], he was functus officio and unable to reopen the investigation without a further [referral]. Section 5(5), as already indicated, confers a wide discretion indeed; it does not, however, purport to empower the PCA to reopen an investigation once his report is submitted. It would seem to me unfair to the department and outside the scheme of this legislation to suppose that the Commissioner could do as Miss Dyer wished. That apart, however, it is plain that even if the Commissioner had had the power to reopen his investigation he would inevitably have refused to do so: he had long since decided not to investigate Miss Dyer's further complaints and I have already held that he was entitled to limit his investigations in that way.

It follows that, in my judgment, none of Miss Dyer's grounds of challenge can be made good and this application accordingly fails.'

In *R v Parliamentary Commissioner for Administration, ex p Balchin*,[110] Sedley J

'hesitated long before concluding that, notwithstanding the very wide area of judgment and discretion given to the [Commissioner], he has been led by a scrupulous regard for his jurisdictional remit, excluding as it does local government, into a failure to consider the relevant fact of [the attitude of a local government authority, Norfolk County Council] in order to decide, as his own findings made it necessary for him to do, whether the Department of Transport ought in response to have drawn the council's attention to its new power to acquire blighted property and perhaps also to its obligation to consider exercising it. [Whether] the Department's undoubted failure to tender such advice amounted to maladministration and whether, if it did, it caused injustice to the [complainants] remains entirely a question for the Commissioner. My decision is limited to holding that in declining to consider the

[110] [1996] EWHC 152 (Admin).

ostensible propriety of Norfolk County Council's negative attitude to its compensatory powers and its amenability to correction by the Department, the Commissioner omitted a potentially decisive element from his consideration of whether the Department of Transport had caused injustice [by] maladministration in its dealings with the county council.'[111]

In *R v Parliamentary Commissioner for Administration, ex p Balchin*,[112] it was

'clear that the issue of injustice was one of the principal controversial issues, and the Commissioner was required to give reasons in relation to it, which were sufficient to enable the parties to know what he decided, and why. [It] is particularly unfortunate that, for a second time, a decision of the Commissioner on this affair has been quashed. I am extremely conscious of the constraints that are placed on a court in reviewing decisions of a Commissioner. It is, however, common ground that the decisions of the Commissioner are susceptible to judicial review, and that a reasons challenge will succeed in circumstances such as I have found to exist in the present case, namely where there has been a failure to give reasons for findings on a principal controversial issue.'[113]

(d) The grey area

Difficulties have arisen with regard to defendant bodies which exercise neither statutory power nor prerogative power and where there is an element of submission by the individual to 'authority' which is technically that of contract. Private or 'domestic' bodies or tribunals have traditionally been outside the scope of certiorari, because their authority is derived solely from contract, from the agreement of the parties concerned, and they may have remedies for breach of contract. In *R v BBC, ex p Lavelle*,[114] Woolf J emphasised that, although applications for judicial review are not confined to those cases where relief could be granted by way of prerogative order, he regarded the wording of what was then Order 53 as making it clear that the application for judicial review is confined to reviewing activities of a public nature as opposed to those of a purely private or domestic character (and held that as a disciplinary appeal procedure set up by the BBC depended purely on the contract of employment between the applicant and the BBC it was a procedure of a purely private or domestic character). In *R v Derbyshire County Council, ex p Noble*,[115] the Court of Appeal held that the termination of appointment as a police surgeon relates to a contract of employment, with no real element of public law. However, in some situations a régime which is technically based on contract or even voluntary submission may have substantial consequences for many members of the public. The issue was faced in:

....

R v Panel on Take-overs and Mergers, ex p Datafin [1987] QB 815 (CA)

Sir John Donaldson MR, at 824–839

'The Panel on Take-overs and Mergers is a truly remarkable body. Perched on the 20th floor of the Stock Exchange building in the City of London, both literally and metaphorically it oversees and regulates a very important part of the United Kingdom financial market. Yet it performs this function without visible means of legal [support]. It has no statutory, prerogative or common law powers and it is not in

---

[111] At paras 40, 41. [112] [1999] EWHC 484 (Admin). [113] Per Dyson J, at paras 47, 49.
[114] [1983] 1 WLR 23. [115] [1990] IRLR 332.

contractual relationship with the financial market or with those who deal in that market. According to the introduction to the City Code on Take-overs and Mergers, which it promulgates:

> "The code has not, and does not seek to have, the force of law, but those who wish to take advantage of the facilities of the securities markets in the United Kingdom should conduct themselves in matters relating to take-overs according to the code. Those who do not so conduct themselves cannot expect to enjoy those facilities and may find that they are withheld. The responsibilities described herein apply most directly to those who are actively engaged in all aspects of the securities markets, but they are also regarded by the Panel as applying to directors of companies subject to the code, to persons or groups of persons who seek to gain [control] of such companies, and to all professional advisers (insofar as they advise on the transactions in [question)]."

The panel [exercises] immense power de facto by devising, promulgating, amending and interpreting the City Code on Take-overs and Mergers, by waiving or modifying the application of the code in particular circumstances, by investigating and reporting on alleged breaches of the code and by the application or threat of sanctions. These sanctions are no less effective because they are applied indirectly and lack a legally enforceable base. Thus, to quote again from the introduction to the code:

> "If there appears to have been a material breach of the code, the executive invites the person concerned to appear before the panel for a hearing. He is informed by letter of the nature of the alleged breach and of the matters which the director general will [present]. If the panel finds that there has been a breach, it may have recourse to private reprimand or public censure or, in a more flagrant case, to further action designed to deprive the offender temporarily or permanently of his ability to enjoy the facilities of the securities markets. The panel may refer certain aspects of a case to the Department of Trade and Industry, the Stock Exchange or other appropriate body. No reprimand, censure or further action will take place without the person concerned having the opportunity to appeal to the appeal committee of the [panel]."

The principal issue in this [appeal] is whether this remarkable body is above the law. Its respectability is beyond question. So is its bona fides. I do not doubt for one moment that it is intended to and does operate in the public interest and that the enormously wide discretion which it arrogates to itself is necessary if it is to function efficiently and effectively. While not wishing to become involved in the political controversy on the relative merits of self-regulation and governmental or statutory regulation, I am content to assume for the purposes of this appeal that self-regulation is preferable in the public interest. But that said, what is to happen if the panel goes off the rails? Suppose, perish the thought, that it were to use its powers in a way in which was manifestly unfair. What then? [Counsel for the panel] submits that the panel would lose the support of public opinion in the financial markets and would be unable to continue to operate. Further or alternatively, Parliament could and would intervene. Maybe, but how long would that take and who in the meantime could or would come to the assistance of those who were being oppressed by such conduct?

[The] picture which emerges is clear. As an act of government it was decided that, in relation to take-overs, there should be a central self-regulatory [body]. No one could have been in the least surprised if the panel had been instituted and operated under the direct authority of statute law, since it operates wholly in the public domain. Its jurisdiction extends throughout the United Kingdom. Its code and rulings apply equally to all who wish to make take-over bids or promote mergers, whether or not they are members of bodies represented on the panel. Its lack of a direct statutory base is a complete anomaly, judged by the experience of other comparable markets [world wide].

The issue is thus whether the historic supervisory jurisdiction of the Queen's courts extends to such a body discharging such functions, including some which are quasi-judicial in their nature, as part of such a system. [Counsel for the panel] submits that it does not. He says that this jurisdiction only extends to bodies whose power is derived from legislation or the exercise of the prerogative. [Counsel for the applicants] submits that this is too narrow a view and that regard has to be had not only to the source of the body's power, but also to whether it operates as an integral part of a system which has a public law character, is supported by public law in that public law sanctions are applied if its edicts are ignored and performs what might be described as public law functions.

[The Take-over Panel] is without doubt performing a public duty and an important one. This is clear from the expressed willingness of the Secretary of State for Trade and Industry to limit legislation in the field of take-overs and mergers and to use the panel as the centrepiece of his regulation of that market. The rights of citizens are indirectly affected by its decisions, some, but by no means all of whom, may in a technical sense be said to have assented to this situation, eg the members of the Stock Exchange. At least in its determination of whether there has been a breach of the code, it has a duty to act judicially and it asserts that its raison d'être is to do equity between one shareholder and another. Its source of power is only partly based on moral persuasion and the assent of institutions and their members, the bottom line being the statutory powers exercised by the Department of Trade and Industry and the Bank of England. In this context I should be very disappointed if the courts could not recognise the realities of executive power and allowed their vision to be clouded by the subtlety and sometimes complexity of the way in which it can be exerted.'

Lloyd LJ, at 846–849

'[Counsel for the panel argues that] the sole test whether the body of persons is subject to judicial review is the source of its power [and] that there has been no case where that source has been other than legislation, including subordinate legislation, or the prerogative. I do not agree that the source of the power is the sole test whether a body is subject to judicial [review]. Of course the source of the power will often, perhaps usually, be decisive. If the source of power is a statute, or subordinate legislation under a statute, then clearly the body in question will be subject to judicial review. If, at the other end of the scale, the source of power is contractual, as in the case of private arbitration, then clearly the arbitrator is not subject to judicial [review]. But in between these extremes there is an area in which it is helpful to look not just at the source of the power but at the nature of the power. If the body in question is exercising public law functions, or if the exercise of its functions have public law consequences, then that [may] be sufficient to bring the body within the reach of judicial review. It may be said that to refer to "public law" in this context is to beg the question. But I do not think it does. The essential distinction, which runs through all the [cases], is between a domestic or private tribunal on the one hand and a body of persons who are under some public duty on the other. [So] I would reject [counsel for the panel's] argument that the sole test whether a body is subject to judicial review is the source of its power. So to hold would in my judgment impose an artificial limit on the developing law of judicial [review].

But suppose I am wrong; suppose that the courts are indeed confined to looking at the source of the power, as [counsel for the panel] submits. Then I would accept the submission of [counsel for the applicants] that the source of the power in the present case is indeed governmental, at least in part. Counsel for the panel argued that, so far from the source of the power being governmental, this is a case where the government has deliberately abstained from exercising power. I do not take that view. I agree with [counsel for the applicants] when he says that there has here been an implied devolution of power. Power exercised behind the schemes is power none the less. The express powers conferred on inferior tribunals were of critical importance in the early days when the sole or main ground for intervention by the courts was that the inferior tribunal had exceeded its powers. But those days are long since past. Having regard to the way in which the panel came to be established, [I] am persuaded that the panel was established "under authority of [the government]". If in addition to looking at the source of the power we are entitled to look at the nature of the power, as I believe we are, then the case is all the stronger.'

The fact that a decision-making authority is undoubtedly a 'public' body is apparently not conclusive:

R (Tucker) v Director General of the National Crime Squad [2003] EWCA Civ 57

Tucker was a police officer. As an office holder, he did not have a contract of employment. He was seconded for five years to the National Crime Squad ('NCS'). His secondment was terminated and he was summarily returned to his local force, but without any disciplinary implications. He was told that the 'National Crime Squad Professional Standards Unit has received information that you have failed to maintain the professional standards required by a Detective Inspector on the National Crime Squad. The Deputy Director General no longer has confidence in your ability to carry out your responsibilities.'

Scott Baker LJ

'32. [It] seems to me that this was an entirely operational decision similar to the kinds of decision that are made with officers up and down the country every day of the week. Examples are transferring officers from uniform to CID or from traffic to other duties. These, to my mind, are run of the mill management decisions involving deployment of staff or running the force. They are decisions that relate to the individual officer personally and have no public element. They are, if you like, the nuts and bolts of operating a police force, be it the NCS or any other. It is, in my judgment, quite inappropriate for the courts to exercise any supervisory jurisdiction over police operational decisions of this kind. There is, quite simply, no public law element to them. The position is different where, however, disciplinary proceedings have been taken against an officer and the ordinary principles of fairness have been breached.

. . .

35. [In] my judgment there is a clear line between disciplinary issues where an officer has the right to public law safeguards such as fairness, and operational or management decisions where the police are entitled to run their own affairs without the intervention of the [courts].

. . .

37. The fact that the NCS is a public body [does] not turn what was essentially a managerial decision in relation to the Appellant into one with a sufficient public law element to trigger the jurisdiction of the Administrative Court. It is true this is not a case in which the Appellant can invoke a private law remedy. That is a factor, but not in this case determinative. What is critical is whether the dispute has a sufficient public law [element].

38. In my judgment the decision impugned in the present case does not have a sufficient element of public law to be subject to judicial review. It was of purely domestic nature.'

Datafin[116] extended judicial review to a non-statutory body which regulated an important aspect of national life and did so with the support of the state in that, but for its existence, the state would create a public body to perform its functions (in other words where there was potentially a government interest in the decision-making power in question). In subsequent cases, the scalps of other bodies have been claimed by the courts: the Advertising Standards Authority,[117] the Code of Practice Committee of the Association of the British Pharmaceutical Industry,[118] the Professional Conduct Committee of the Bar Council,[119] certain decisions of the Legal Aid Board,[120] and, if they act outside their jurisdiction, abuse their power or act in

---

[116] See p. 495.   [117] *R v Advertising Standards Authority Ltd, ex p Insurance Services* (1989) 9 Tr LR 169.
[118] *R v Code of Practice Committee of the Association of the British Pharmaceutical Industry, ex p Professional Counselling Aids* (1991) 3 Admin LR 697.   [119] *R v Bar Council, ex p Percival* [1990] 3 All ER 137.
[120] *R v Legal Aid Board, ex p Bateman* [1992] 1 WLR 711.

breach of the rules of natural justice, University and other Visitors.[121] In these cases, had there been no self-regulatory authority in existence, it was argued that Parliament would almost inevitably have had to intervene to control the activity in question. However, certain decisions of Lloyd's of London, categorised as being governed by contract, have been held non-justiciable,[122] as have those of the Medical Defence Union.[123]

Certain 'private bodies' are of a monopolistic character, in that if anyone wants to undertake a particular activity, in particular a popular sporting activity, that person must join the society and abide by its rules, and, in practice, there is no difference between a private body and the state. The case law was examined in:

R v Disciplinary Committee of the Jockey Club, ex p Aga Khan
[1993] 1 WLR 909 (CA)

Sir Thomas Bingham MR, at 912–924

'On 10 June 1989 the filly Aliysa, owned by His Highness the Aga Khan, won the Oaks at Epsom. In a routine examination after the race, a metabolite of camphor was said to be found in a sample of the filly's urine. Under the Jockey Club's Rules of Racing camphor was a prohibited substance and the disciplinary committee of the Jockey Club held an inquiry. On 20 November 1990 the committee ruled that the urine contained a metabolite of camphor, that the source of the metabolite was camphor, that the filly should be disqualified for the race in question and that the filly's trainer should be fined £200.

[The Aga Khan] sought leave to move for judicial review of the committee's decision. In granting leave Macpherson J suggested trial of a preliminary issue whether the committee's decision was susceptible to judicial review. [The] issue squarely raised before this court is whether the Jockey Club's decision here in issue can be challenged by judicial [review].

For purposes of this appeal I must attempt to describe, necessarily in very general terms, the salient features of the British racing industry and the role of the Jockey Club within it. The evidence before the court makes plain that racing is aptly described as an industry. There are 59 active racecourses in Great Britain which in 1990 attracted nearly five million racegoers to over 1,000 meetings with some 7,000 races, 69,000 runners and prize money of nearly £48m. The turnover of off-course betting subject to the levy on horserace betting in 1989–90 was some £4bn. In the same period general betting duty (not all derived from bets on horse racing) yielded revenue of some £327m. It has been estimated that over 100,000 people depend for their livelihood on racing and betting. There were (at the end of 1990) some 19,000 owners, 6,500 stable lads, 550 trainers and 1,000 jockeys registered with or licensed by the Jockey [Club].

The powers which the Jockey Club exercised in the present case (to order the taking of samples, to fine and to disqualify) are among those assumed by the Jockey Club to safeguard the integrity of British [racing].

The Rules of Racing are a skilfully drafted, comprehensive and far-reaching code of rules through which the Jockey Club exercises its control over racing in this country. So far as relevant for present purposes, the effect of the rules is broadly speaking as follows. (1) The stewards have power to license racecourses and allocate fixtures. Any meeting not held at a licensed racecourse is unrecognised. (2) The stewards have power to license clerks of the course, jockeys, trainers and others and issue permits to trainers, amateur riders and others. (3) No one may act as a clerk of the course, trainer or

---

[121] *Page v Hull University Visitor* [1993] AC 682; *R v Visitors to the Inns of Court, ex p Calder and Persaud* [1993] 3 WLR 287.

[122] *R v Lloyd's of London, ex p Briggs* [1993] 1 Lloyd's Rep 176; *R (West) v Lloyd's of London* [2004] EWCA Civ 506.   [123] *R (on the application of Mareton) v Medical Defence Union* [2006] EWHC 1948 (Admin).

jockey under the rules unless he holds an appropriate licence or permit. (4) A horse may not (subject to certain exceptions) be entered for a race by any owner whose name is not registered with the Jockey Club. (5) A horse is not qualified to run in any race if it has run at any unrecognised meeting. (6) A trainer may not employ any person whose name has not been registered with the Jockey Club and may not employ any person to work in his stable who has previously been employed in a training stable without referring to the last trainer to employ him and receiving a reply. A person thus prevented from obtaining employment has a right of appeal to the stewards. (7) Where any person subject to the Rules of Racing has committed a breach thereof the stewards have power (among other penalties) to declare him a disqualified person. (8) A person reported by the Committee of Tattersalls is a disqualified person or subject to exclusion from any premises owned, licensed or controlled by the Jockey Club. A person disqualified by a sister authority abroad is a disqualified person here unless the stewards decide otherwise. (9) Any person who owns, trains or rides a horse at an unrecognised meeting in Great Britain or Ireland or who acts in any official capacity in connection with such a meeting is liable to be declared a disqualified person. (10) A disqualified person may not act as a steward or official at any recognised meeting, enter, run, train, or ride a horse in any race at any recognised meeting, enter any racecourse, stand, enclosure or other premises owned, used, or controlled by the stewards of any meeting, be employed (without the permission of the stewards) in any racing stable, or deal in any capacity with a racehorse. Any person (whether subject to the rules or not) may be excluded from any premises owned, licensed or controlled by the [stewards].

No serious racecourse management, owner, trainer or jockey can survive without the recognition or licence of the Jockey Club. There is in effect no alternative market in which those not accepted by the Jockey Club can find a place or to which racegoers may resort. Thus by means of the rules and its market domination the Jockey Club can effectively control not only those who agree to abide by its rules but also those—such as disqualified or excluded persons seeking to participate in racing activities in any capacity—who do not. For practical purposes the Jockey Club's writ runs in the British racing world, to the acknowledged benefit of British racing.

[The] central thrust of the applicant's case is this. The Jockey Club is the effective de facto controller of a significant national activity. Its functions are essentially public. Its powers are of a nature and scope which affect the public. It matters not that it is a private body: that is an accident of history. What matters is that if it or some other private body did not perform the functions it does the government would be obliged to create a body to perform those functions. It makes no difference that it exerts control in the main by contract, since those who contract with it have no effective alternative to accepting the obligations thus imposed, and authority is effectively exerted over those not bound by contract. [The] decision here in question was an exercise of power public in character and of serious consequence to the applicant and is as such susceptible to judicial review, by which means alone he can obtain the decision he wants, an order that the decision be quashed.

The Jockey Club takes radical issue with this argument. On its argument, it is a private body independent of government in origin, constitution and function and forming no part of any governmental system of regulation. Its relationship with those who, like the applicant, agree to be bound by the Rules of Racing is an essentially private law relationship based on contract. A duty to conduct any inquiry fairly would be implied into this contract and if the applicant could establish a breach of that duty he could recover appropriate private law remedies by way of declaration, injunction and damages. Remedies developed to curb abuses and excesses of power by government and public tribunals cannot appropriately be applied to a private body exercising a domestic jurisdiction pursuant to [contract].

We were referred to a considerable body of authority relied on as relevant in determining the scope of judicial review and identifying the bodies and decisions which are susceptible to judicial [review. In *Law v National Greyhound Racing Club Ltd* [1983] 1 WLR 1302, at 1307, Lawson LJ stated]:

"In my judgment, such powers as the stewards had to suspend the plaintiff's licence were derived from a contract between him and the defendants. This was so for all who took part in greyhound racing in stadiums licensed by the defendants. A stewards' inquiry under the defendants' rules of racing concerned only those who voluntarily submitted themselves to the stewards' jurisdiction. There was no public element in the jurisdiction itself. [Consequences] affecting the public generally can flow from the decisions of many domestic tribunals. In the past the courts have always refused to use the orders of certiorari to review the decisions of domestic [tribunals]."

[Fox LJ, at 1309, stated]:

"Accordingly, in my view, the authority of the stewards to suspend the licence of the plaintiff derives wholly from a contract between him and the defendants. I see nothing to suggest that the defendants have rights or duties relating to members of the public as such. What the defendants do in relation to the control of greyhound racing may affect the public, or a section of it, but the defendants' powers in relation to the matters with which this case is concerned are [contractual]."

In [*Datafin*, p. 495, the Court of Appeal] held that the panel was in principle amenable to judicial review. The decision was novel, because the panel was not created by statute or by any exercise of prerogative or governmental power. [The] effect of this decision was to extend judicial review to a body whose birth and constitution owed nothing to any exercise of governmental power but which had been woven into the fabric of public regulation in the field of take-overs and [mergers].

I have little hesitation in accepting the applicant's contention that the Jockey Club effectively regulates a significant national activity, exercising powers which affect the public and are exercised in the interest of the public. I am willing to accept that if the Jockey Club did not regulate this activity the government would probably be driven to create a public body to do so. [It] has not been woven into any system of governmental control of horse racing, perhaps because it has itself controlled horse racing so successfully that there has been no need for any such governmental system and such does not therefore exist. This has the result that while the Jockey Club's powers may be described as, in many ways, public they are in no sense [governmental].

I would accept that those who agree to be bound by the Rules of Racing have no effective alternative to doing so if they want to take part in racing in this country. It also seems likely to me that if, instead of Rules of Racing administered by the Jockey Club, there were a statutory code administered by a public body, the rights and obligations conferred and imposed by the code would probably approximate to those conferred and imposed by the Rules of Racing. But this does not, as it seems to me, alter the fact, however anomalous it may be, that the powers which the Jockey Club exercises over those who (like the applicant) agree to be bound by the Rules of Racing derive from the agreement of the parties and give rise to private rights on which effective action for a declaration, an injunction and damages can be based without resort to judicial review. It would in my opinion be contrary to sound and long-standing principle to extend the remedy of judicial review to such a case.'

(e) The Human Rights Act and a 'public authority'

Under the Human Rights Act 1998, it is unlawful, in certain circumstances, for a 'public authority' to act in a way which is incompatible with a Convention right. 'Public authority' is not really defined. A 'public authority' includes a court or tribunal. Furthermore, there is a Delphic statement that a 'public authority' includes 'any person certain of whose functions are functions of a public nature' but, in relation to a particular act, a person is not a public authority by virtue only of that statement if the nature of the act is 'private'.[124] An early attempt to

---

[124] Human Rights Act 1998, section 6. See p. 858.

answer the riddle posed by the oracle was:

....

Poplar Housing and Regeneration Community Association Ltd v Donoghue
[2001] EWCA Civ 595

Lord Woolf CJ

'2. The proceedings started in the Bow County Court as a straightforward claim for possession of [a house] of which the defendant was the tenant and which is owned by the claimant housing association ("Poplar"). On the day of the hearing, [the] proceedings were in the ordinary housing list. It had not been appreciated that the defendant wished to raise the issue that to make an order for possession would contravene her rights to respect for her private and family life and respect for her home contrary to [the Human Rights Act 1998].

. . .

36. Part IV of the 1996 [Housing] Act governs the allocation of housing accommodation by local housing authorities. A housing authority can select someone to be a secure tenant, or an introductory tenant, or nominate someone to be an assured tenant of [registered social landlord ("RSL") stock].

37. Part VII of the 1996 Act places obligations on local housing authorities to assist homeless applicants. The level of assistance depends on the circumstances of the applicant and his or her household. The extent of the duty depends upon whether the applicant is or is not intentionally [homeless].

. . .

41. The role of housing associations in providing accommodation has [been] affected by government policy.

42. [Originally], many were small local charities, though others were large entities endowed by wealthy employers or philanthropists. The legal definition of a housing association [makes] it clear that a housing association may be a charity, an industrial and provident society, or a company which does not trade for profit and which has among its objects the provision of housing accommodation. [Throughout] the 20th century many housing associations were funded by grants or loans usually through local authorities. In 1964, the Housing Corporation ("the Corporation") was created and thereafter most of the public funding was channelled through the [Corporation. There] are now 4,000 housing associations, of which approximately 2,200 are registered with the Corporation as RSLs. [The] other major development has been the growth in the transfer of housing stock from local authorities to RSLs. Both under the previous and the present government, some 500,000 dwellings have been transferred in this way. Today, there are 1.5 million dwellings in the ownership of RSLs.

43. Under Part I of the 1996 Act, the Corporation is given two basic roles. These are to provide funding to RSLs and to regulate them. [Regulations cover] the area of governance, finance and housing management. If performance fails, the Corporation can exercise a number of powers: it can withdraw funding; make appointments to the governing body of the RSL and remove employees or governing body [members].

44. Section 170 of the 1996 [Housing] Act importantly provides: "Where a local housing authority so request, a registered social landlord shall co-operate to such extent as is reasonable in the circumstances in offering accommodation to people with priority on the authority's housing [register]."

. . .

46. Many local authorities have transferred some or all of their housing stock to one or more RSLs. This has happened so far as Poplar is concerned. Poplar was created for the purpose of taking over part of the housing stock of the borough of Tower [Hamlets].

. . .

55. The importance of whether Poplar was at the material times a public body or performing public functions is this: the Human Rights Act 1998 will only apply to Poplar if it is deemed to be a public body or performing public functions. Section 6(1) of the Human Rights Act 1998 makes it unlawful for a public

authority to act in a way which is incompatible with a Convention right. Section 6(3) states that a "public authority" includes "(b) any person certain of whose functions are functions of a public nature". Section 6(5) provides: "In relation to a particular act, a person is not a public authority by virtue only of subsection (3)(b) if the nature of the act is [private]."

. . .

58. We agree [that] the definition of who is a public authority, and what is a public function, for the purposes of section 6, should be given a generous interpretation. However, [the] fact that a body performs an activity which otherwise a public body would be under a duty to perform cannot mean that such performance is necessarily a public function. A public body in order to perform its public duties can use the services of a private body. Section 6 should not be applied so that if a private body provides such services, the nature of the functions are inevitably public. If this were to be the position, then when a small hotel provides bed and breakfast accommodation as a temporary measure, at the request of a housing authority that is under a duty to provide that accommodation, the small hotel would be performing public functions and required to comply with the Human Rights Act 1998. This is not what the Human Rights Act 1998 intended. The consequence would be the same where a hospital uses a private company to carry out specialist services, such as analysing blood samples. The position under the Human Rights Act 1998 is necessarily more complex. Section 6(3) means that hybrid bodies, who have functions of a public and private nature are public authorities, but not in relation to acts which are of a private nature. The renting out of accommodation can certainly be of a private nature. The fact that through the act of renting by a private body a public authority may be fulfilling its public duty, does not automatically change into a public act what would otherwise be a private [act].

59. The purpose of section 6(3)(b) is to deal with hybrid bodies which have both public and private functions. It is not to make a body, which does not have responsibilities to the public, a public body merely because it performs acts on behalf of a public body which would constitute public functions were such acts to be performed by the public body itself. An act can remain of a private nature even though it is performed because another body is under a public duty to ensure that that act is performed.

60. A useful illustration is provided by the decision of the European Court of Human Rights in *Costello-Roberts v United Kingdom* (1993) 19 EHRR 112. The case concerned a seven-year-old boy receiving corporal punishment from the headmaster of an independent school. The Court of Human Rights made it clear that the state cannot absolve itself of its Convention obligations by delegating the fulfilment of such obligations to private bodies or individuals, including the headmaster of an independent school. However, if a local authority, in order to fulfil its duties, sent a child to a private school, the fact that it did this would not mean that the private school was performing public functions. The school would not be a hybrid body. It would remain a private body. The local authority would, however, not escape its duties by delegating the performance to the private school. If there were a breach of the Convention, then the responsibility would be that of the local authority and not that of [the school].

. . .

65. In coming to our conclusion as to whether Poplar is a public authority within the Human Rights Act 1998 meaning of that term, we regard it of particular importance in this case that:

(i) While section 6 of the Human Rights Act 1998 requires a generous interpretation of who is a public authority, it is clearly inspired by the approach developed by the courts in identifying the bodies and activities subject to judicial review. The emphasis on public functions reflects the approach adopted in judicial review by the courts and textbooks since the decision of the Court of Appeal [in *Datafin*, p. 495].

(ii) Tower Hamlets, in transferring its housing stock to Poplar, does not transfer its primary public duties to Poplar. Poplar is no more than the means by which it seeks to perform those duties.

(iii) The act of providing accommodation to rent is not, without more, a public function for the purposes of section 6 of the Human Rights Act 1998. Furthermore, that is true irrespective of the section of society for whom the accommodation is provided.

(iv) The fact that a body is a charity or is conducted not for profit means that it is likely to be motivated in performing its activities by what it perceives to be the public interest. However, this does not point to the body being a public authority. In addition, even if such a body performs functions, that would be considered to be of a public nature if performed by a public body, nevertheless such acts may remain of a private nature for the purpose of sections 6(3)(b) and 6(5).

(v) What can make an act, which would otherwise be private, public is a feature or a combination of features which impose a public character or stamp on the act. Statutory authority for what is done can at least help to mark the act as being public; so can the extent of control over the function exercised by another body which is a public authority. The more closely the acts that could be of a private nature are enmeshed in the activities of a public body, the more likely they are to be public. However, the fact that the acts are supervised by a public regulatory body does not necessarily indicate that they are of a public nature. This is analogous to the position in judicial review, where a regulatory body may be deemed public but the activities of the body which is regulated may be categorised private.

(vi) The closeness of the relationship which exists between Tower Hamlets and Poplar. Poplar was created by Tower Hamlets to take a transfer of local authority housing stock; five of its board members are also members of Tower Hamlets; Poplar is subject to the guidance of Tower Hamlets as to the manner in which it acts towards the defendant.

(vii) The defendant, at the time of transfer, was a sitting tenant of Poplar and it was intended that she would be treated no better and no worse than if she remained a tenant of Tower Hamlets. While she remained a tenant, Poplar therefore stood in relation to her in very much the position previously occupied by Tower Hamlets.

66. While these are the most important factors in coming to our conclusion, it is desirable to step back and look at the situation as a whole. As is the position on applications for judicial review, there is no clear demarcation line which can be drawn between public and private bodies and functions. In a borderline case, such as this, the decision is very much one of fact and degree. Taking into account all the circumstances, we have come to the conclusion that while activities of housing associations need not involve the performance of public functions, in this case, in providing accommodation for the defendant and then seeking possession, the role of Poplar is so closely assimilated to that of Tower Hamlets that it was performing public and not private functions. Poplar therefore is a functional public authority, at least to that extent. We emphasise that this does not mean that all Poplar's functions are public. We do not even decide that the position would be the same if the defendant was a secure tenant. The activities of housing associations can be ambiguous. For example, their activities in raising private or public finance could be very different from those that are under consideration here. The raising of finance by Poplar could well be a private [function].'

Donoghue was distinguished in:

Heather v The Leonard Cheshire Foundation [2001] EWHC 429 (Admin)

The Leonard Cheshire Foundation ('Leonard Cheshire') provides care and support services for the disabled. One of its homes was Le Court Cheshire Home ('Le Court'), with some 42 long-stay residents. The majority of the residents at the home (including the claimants) had been placed there, and their places were funded, either by the local authority social services department or by a health authority. In either case, placement and funding resulted from the exercise of statutory powers by the local authority or the health authority. The Trustees of Leonard Cheshire decided to close Le Court and residents who could not be kept at Le Court would be relocated. The claimants sought judicial review of that decision. They argued that Leonard Cheshire, in relation to them, exercised functions of a public nature within the meaning of section 6(3)(b) of the Human Rights Act 1998; that Leonard Cheshire was a public authority within the meaning of section 6; that by virtue of section 6(1) Leonard Cheshire owed them a duty to comply with the Articles of the European Convention on Human Rights; and that the Trustees' decision to close Le Court was made in contravention of article 8, which conferred on them the right to respect for their home, which was Le Court.

Stanley Burnton J

'[17] The principal issue between the parties [is] whether Leonard Cheshire is for any relevant purpose a public [authority].

. . .

[19] The decision on [the] jurisdictional issue does not, of course, merely go to jurisdiction. It goes also to the duties owed by Leonard Cheshire in making its decisions and to the standing of the Claimants to challenge them. It is only if Leonard Cheshire is a public authority in relation to them that it could have owed them a duty under section 6(1) of the Human Rights Act to comply with the Convention; and it is only if it is a public authority that it could have owed the duties imposed by public law on such [authorities].

[20] If the Claimants' submissions on [this issue] are not well-founded, [the] increased privatisation of formerly governmental functions may involve the loss of judicial review of those functions and of the decisions made when exercising [them].

. . .

[44] Until the decision of the Court of Appeal [in *Datafin*, p. 495], judicial review had been confined to decisions made by bodies exercising governmental authority, either under statute or under the Royal [Prerogative. In] *Datafin*, for the first time a body exercising authority under neither statute nor the Prerogative was held amenable to judicial review at the instance of a party affected by its [decisions]. It, and the subsequent decision of the Court of Appeal [in *Aga Khan*, p. 499], are landmark [decisions].

[45] Any thoughts that the decision in *Datafin* meant that all bodies exercising regulatory functions under systems of so-called self-regulation were thenceforth amenable to judicial review were dispelled by the decision of the Court of Appeal in [*Aga Khan*]. *Datafin* was explained by Sir Thomas Bingham, MR, [as] follows: "The effect of this decision was to extend judicial review to a body whose birth and constitution owed nothing to any exercise of governmental power but which had been woven into the fabric of public regulation in the field of take-overs and mergers".

[46] [In *R v Servite Housing Association and Wandsworth LBC, ex p Goldsmith and Chatting* [2001] LGR 55, a] charitable housing association was the provider of residential accommodation to disabled persons in need of residential care pursuant to arrangements made by a local authority. Apart from the nature of the provider, in relation to the questions of public law obligations and amenability to judicial review, the facts of that case were indistinguishable from the present. In that case too the provider of accommodation and services for the disabled had decided to close its home. Residents at the home sought to challenge that decision by judicial review on public law grounds. Moses J held that the housing association was not amenable to judicial review. He held: (i) That the housing association was not acting as the local authority's agent in providing community care services. Arrangements made by a local authority with third parties [result in the local authority discharging its obligations under the National Assistance Act 1948]. Such arrangements do not constitute the third parties as agents of the local authority for the performance of their [National Assistance Act] duties. (ii) That there was not the statutory underpinning or statutory penetration of the housing association's functions which would result in its being amenable to judicial review. (iii) The relationship between the local authority and the housing association was purely commercial. The source of the housing association's power was solely contractual, and this was inconsistent with a public law jurisdiction. (iv) Accordingly "in providing residential accommodation, Servite (the housing association) was not performing a public function and is not under any public law duty to the [applicants]".

[47] I so entirely agree with Moses J's analysis of the authorities and his conclusions that it is unnecessary for me to comment on [them].

[48] My comments on the Claimants' submissions [are] as follows:

(i) The presence of State funding does not in my judgment indicate that a body exercises public functions, whether the funding is by grant or by payment for goods or services supplied pursuant to [contract]. Bodies such as fringe theatres often benefit from State funding by way of grants. This does not mean that they are public authorities. Where funding is by payment pursuant to contract, the inference of a public function is even weaker. Contracting by public authorities cannot make public authorities of the otherwise private provider of services or goods. It is only if there is a true delegation or sharing of functions that this may occur; and true delegation or sharing, to a body which but for such delegation or sharing would not be a public authority, is a rarity, if it occurs at all, and where the original function is exercised pursuant to statute, requires statutory [authority].

(ii) State regulation if anything points against the body regulated being a public authority. Increased privatisation has led to increased regulation, because of the need for activities that have passed from the public sector to the private sector to be subject to a measure of public control. It is the regulator, not the regulated, who exercises a public function. On this, see paragraph 65(v) of the judgment in [*Donoghue*, p. 503].

(iii) The origin of the criterion that if the body in question were not exercising its function, the government would step in, is, I believe, the judgment of Simon Brown J in *R v Chief Rabbi of the United Hebrew Congregations of Great Britain and the Commonwealth, ex p Wachmann* [1993] 2 All ER 249, [1992] 1 WLR 1036, where the learned Judge referred [to] the applicability of judicial review in cases where, if there were no self-regulatory body, "Parliament would almost inevitably intervene to control the activity in question". [The] difficulty with this criterion is that the proper ambit of government intervention is a matter of political controversy at any time, and a matter on which opinions change from time to time. [Where] statute has already conferred regulatory or other powers on a non-governmental body, or involved the body in a statutory framework, the "if the body did not exist Parliament would intervene" test may seem less [political]. I also point out that in [*Aga Khan*, p. 501], Sir Thomas Bingham MR [accepted] that "if the Jockey Club did not regulate this activity the government would probably be driven to create a public body to do so". Nonetheless, the Jockey Club was held not to be amenable to judicial review.

(iv) It does not follow from the proposition that public authorities' activities are governed by public law that all bodies carrying on some of those activities are subject to public law. This is the fallacy of the undistributed middle. It is only if the activity itself involves a public function that public law [applies].

[49] [Parliament] has permitted local authorities to provide mandatory services either themselves or by contracting with third parties. This does not of itself make the third parties public authorities. It does not of itself mean that the third parties exercise public functions. The third parties are simply contractors to the local authorities. Were it otherwise, proprietors of bed-and-breakfast homes who provide accommodation pursuant to arrangements with local authorities would be public authorities, as would contractors building roads for central government, or repairing roads for local government, or building homes for local authorities who are housing [authorities].

. . .

[55] [The matters referred to above] do not either individually or collectively lead to the conclusion that at common law Leonard Cheshire owed administrative law obligations or was amenable to judicial [review].

. . .

[66] A purely functional test would be concerned solely with the nature of the function in question. The nature of the body exercising the function in question, and the source of its authority, would be irrelevant. If there is a purely functional [test], the scope of judicial review and of the subjects of public law obligations has indeed been revolutionised by the [Human Rights] Act. The provision of education is a core governmental function: are all private schools exercising a "public function"? [What] about a teacher giving private lessons in his spare time? Or a retired teacher giving private lessons? The provision of health care is another core governmental function. Are all private hospitals exercising a "public function"? What about a single doctor providing private medical [care?]

. . .

[68] It is apparent, therefore, that the public authority criterion cannot be purely functional. The function must be "public", and that requirement may mean more than that a significant number of people are involved or are affected. I do therefore propose to consider the purpose of the Human Rights Act and the ambit of the European Convention on Human Rights, in order to arrive at a "purposive" interpretation of section 6.

[69] Article 1 of the Convention [is] as follows: "The High Contracting Parties shall secure to everyone within their jurisdiction the rights and freedoms defined in Section 1 of this Convention."

[70] It is generally recognised that the object of the Convention was to grant to (or to confirm for) citizens the specified rights and freedoms as against governments and governmental authorities. In general, these rights are in the nature of freedoms rather than positive rights to social or economic [benefits].

. . .

[75] [*Costello-Roberts v United Kingdom* (1995) 19 EHRR 112 concerned] corporal punishment in a private school. The Court held that the United Kingdom would be liable for any breach of [the Convention] resulting from the acts of the headmaster of the school. The Court [observed]: "the State cannot absolve itself of responsibility by delegating its obligations to private bodies or [individuals. In] the present case, which relates to the particular domain of school discipline, the treatment complained of, although it was the act of a headmaster of an independent school, is none the less such as may engage the responsibility of the United Kingdom under the Convention if it proves to be incompatible with [the Convention]."

. . .

[77] [In] *Costello-Roberts*, the Court held that the United Kingdom, as a High Contracting Party, was responsible for conferring and protecting [rights], if necessary by appropriate [legislation]:

"The Court has consistently held that the responsibility of a State is engaged if a violation of one of the rights and freedoms defined in the Convention is the result of non-observance by that State of its obligation under Article 1 to secure those rights and freedoms in its domestic law to everyone within its jurisdiction. Indeed, it was accepted by the Government for the purposes of the present proceedings that such an obligation existed as regards securing the rights guaranteed [to] pupils in independent schools."

The Government referred to is of course that of the United Kingdom.

[78] The party which would have been liable in *Costello-Roberts* if there had been an infringement of a Convention right was the United Kingdom government. If a State party to the Convention fails to secure such rights, if necessary by domestic [legislation], it incurs responsibility to its citizens under the Convention, irrespective of the status of the person or body under its jurisdiction infringing the Convention right in question. It therefore does not follow that the Convention was intended to make non-governmental bodies, acting in accordance with their (on this hypothesis non-Convention-compliant) domestic law, directly liable for breach of a right that the government had failed to secure under domestic law.

[79] In *Costello-Roberts*, the Court held that the United Kingdom would be responsible for any failure to secure [rights], irrespective of the nature of the body providing education, governmental or otherwise. It therefore does not follow that an independent school is a governmental or public author-ity. Indeed, the very wording of the above extract from judgment of the Court, referring to "private bodies or individuals", contradicts any such interpretation of the decision. Nor does it follow that under English Law a non-public authority is liable under our domestic law for breach of a Convention right that is not part of our domestic law. In such a case, the party responsible is the State, which has failed to secure the Convention right under its domestic [law].

[80] The above analysis of *Costello-Roberts* seems to be consistent with the approach of the Court of Appeal in [*Donoghue*, para 60].

. . .

[83] Doubtlessly because Convention rights are rights against government and governmental bodies, the Human Rights Act was intended to incorporate into English Law Convention rights as against government and governmental authorities. It is for that reason that the unlawfulness created by section 6 is restricted to public authorities and bodies exercising public [functions].

. . .

[88] My original conclusion was that the Human Rights Act had not altered the status of Leonard Cheshire, and that it does not exercise public functions, in the sense of governmental functions. If this conclusion is to stand, it is necessary to distinguish it from Poplar. It is not difficult to do so. There are the following differences between them:

(i) Whereas Poplar was created by the local authority that provided all its tenants, Leonard Cheshire was established by private individuals.

(ii) Poplar is registered with the Housing Corporation as a social landlord ("RSL"). RSLs are under statutory duties to co-operate with local housing [authorities]. In most local authority areas the housing authority has nomination agreements with RSLs, enabling them to nominate tenants to whom the RSL should grant tenancies from the housing [registers].

(iii) In contrast, no purchasing authority is able to compel Leonard Cheshire to accept a particular person as a service user or resident of Leonard Cheshire.

(iv) As an RSL, Poplar is subject to supervision and regulation by the Corporation as to its governance, finance and housing management. The Corporation's powers in relation to an unsatisfactory RSL include the withdrawal of funding, the making of appointments to its governing body, and the removal of employees or governing body members.

(v) The registration of Leonard Cheshire under the Registered Homes Act 1984 does not involve the kind or extent of regulation that applies to an RSL. The conduct of Leonard Cheshire is subject to statutory regulation; but there are no powers under that Act for any statutory authority to impose members on the governing body of Leonard Cheshire or to interfere in the running of Leonard Cheshire as an [organisation].

(vi) Poplar was created by Tower Hamlets to take a transfer of local authority housing stock; five of its board members are also members of Tower Hamlets; and Poplar was subject to the guidance of Tower Hamlets as to the manner in which it acted towards Ms Donoghue.

(vii) Leonard Cheshire does not have with any statutory authority the kind of closely integrated relationship that Poplar has with Tower Hamlets. The residents of Leonard Cheshire do not come from one local authority, but from several, and also include privately funded residents and those funded by local health authorities. In no sense can Leonard Cheshire be said to be dependent on any single public authority.

[89] In my judgment, the decision in *Donoghue* that Poplar is a public authority depended on the close assimilation of its role to that of Tower Hamlets, and its integration with the functions of Tower [Hamlets].

[90] As indicated above, therefore, my conclusion remains that Leonard Cheshire does not, in relation to the Claimants, exercise a public function. It is not subject to the duty imposed by section 6(1) of the Human Rights Act. Equally, it is not amenable to judicial review.'

The story of *Donoghue* and *Cheshire* and the Human Rights Act concept of 'public authority' is continued in *Wallbank v Parochial Church Council of Aston Cantlow and Wilmcote with Billesley, Warwickshire*[125] and *Johnson v London Borough of Havering.*[126]

---

[125] See p. 860.   [126] See pp. 866–869.

VII. Locus Standi

Even if a body is amenable to judicial review, not every citizen can make an application for such review. The courts in exercising their power to grant prerogative orders, have always reserved the right to be satisfied that the applicant had some genuine standing in the case. It has long been held that a 'mere busybody', a 'crank' or a 'mischief maker' does not have sufficient interest. However, the problem arises of distinguishing between preventing a busybody from interfering with other people's affairs and the person who has no specific legal right to protect but who has a genuine and reasonable concern with the matter at issue and its alleged illegality, especially where there may be no other effective remedy. The meaning of standing has been expressed in a number of different ways. Sometimes it was stated that, in an application for certiorari, the applicant must be 'a person aggrieved' or have 'a particular grievance'[127] and, in an application for mandamus, that the applicant must have 'a specific legal right'[128] and, occasionally, the phrase 'a sufficient interest' was used.[129] In 1977, the rule on standing (now in the Supreme Court Act 1981, section 31(3)) used, for the first time in a statute, the words 'sufficient interest', presumably a phrase which 'could sufficiently embrace all classes of those who might apply and yet permit sufficient flexibility in any particular case to determine whether or not "sufficient interest" was in fact shown'.[130]

The question as to whether standing could belong to a group of people has caused some problems.[131] It has been held that there are a number of 'factors of significance': the importance of vindicating the rule of law, the importance of the issue raised, the likely absence of any other responsible challenger, the nature of the breach of duty against which relief is sought, and the prominent role of applicants in giving advice, guidance and assistance with regard to the particular subject matter.[132] Sometimes an organisation will be granted almost automatic locus standi in certain matters because of the purposes for its establishment. The Equal Opportunities Commission has, inter alia, duties to work towards the elimination of discrimination and to promote equality of opportunity between men and women generally.[133] In a number of cases the Commission has been the initiating party to proceedings designed to secure the elimination of discrimination.[134] In *R v Secretary of State for Employment, ex p Equal Opportunities Commission*,[135] the issue was whether certain provisions of the employment protection legislation were compatible with Community law regarding equal pay and equal treatment and the question was raised as to whether the Commission had a sufficient interest in that matter? It was held that steps taken by the Commission towards securing that these provisions are changed might very reasonably be regarded as taken in the course of working towards the elimination of discrimination. In a number of earlier decisions the locus

---

[127] *R v Thames Magistrates' Court, ex p Greenbaum* (1957) 55 LGR 129.

[128] *R v Guardians of Lewisham Union* [1897] 1 QB 498.

[129] *R v Cotham* [1898] 1 QB 802; *R v Metropolitan Police Commissioner, ex p Blackburn* [1968] 1 All ER 763; *R v Customs and Excise Commissioners, ex p Cooke and Stevenson* [1970] 1 All ER 1068.

[130] *Inland Revenue Commissioners v National Federation of Self-Employed and Small Businesses Ltd* [1982] AC 617, per Lord Roskill, at 117.

[131] *R v Secretary of State for Social Services, ex p Child Poverty Action Group* [1989] 1 All ER 1047.

[132] *R v Secretary of State for Foreign Affairs, ex p World Development Movement Ltd* [1995] 1 All ER 611, per Rose LJ, at 620.   [133] Sex Discrimination Act 1975, section 53(1).

[134] *Equal Opportunities Commission v Birmingham City Council* [1989] AC 1155, where the EOC successfully challenged the policy of the council as regards the relative availability of grammar school places for girls and for boys.   [135] [1995] 1 AC 1.

standi of the Commission had not been challenged and it would be a very retrograde step now to hold that the Commission had no locus standi to agitate in judicial review proceedings questions related to sex discrimination which are of public importance and affect a large section of the population. The Commission, therefore, had sufficient interest to bring the proceedings and hence the necessary locus standi.

It can happen that one action for judicial review brought by one or a limited number of persons can raise issues which are of importance to a much wider range of persons. The courts have sometimes permitted a 'third party intervention' from a group or organization which is not specifically involved in the case but which can at the same time bring forward specialist expertise and further the general interest of those whom the group or organisation represent. In *Pinochet*,[136] Amnesty International, in *Coughlan*,[137] the Royal College of Nursing, and in *Johnson v Havering*,[138] the Secretary of State for Constitutional Affairs and the Disability Rights Commission, were, respectively, given permission to intervene.

The authorities on both individual and group standing are conveniently extracted in:

R v North Somerset District Council, ex p Garnett and Pierssene
[1997] EWHC 318 (Admin)

This was an application for leave to challenge a decision of the North Somerset District Council to grant planning permission relating to an extension to a quarry at Ashton Court, Bristol. The applicants described themselves as local residents and environmentalists.

Popplewell J

'13. I turn to what was said in [*Inland Revenue Commissioners v National Federation of Self-Employed and Small Businesses* [1982] AC 617] as to the proper approach of the court in this type of [case. Lord Wilberforce said, at 630]:

"There may be simple cases in which it can be seen at the earliest stage, that the person applying for judicial review has no interest at all or no sufficient interest to support the application. Then it would be quite correct at the threshold to refuse him leave to apply. In other cases this will not be so. In these it will be necessary to consider the powers or the duties in law of those against whom the relief is sought, the position of the applicant in relation to those powers or duties and to the breach of those said to have been committed. In other words the question of sufficient interest cannot in such cases, be considered in the abstract or as an isolated point, it must be taken together with the legal and factual content. The rule requires sufficient interest in the matter to which the application relates. This in the present case necessarily involves the whole question of the duties of the Inland Revenue and the breaches or failure of those duties of which the respondents [claim]."

. . .

15. [Lord Fraser said, at 645]:

"The question whether the respondents have a sufficient interest to make the application at all is a separate and logically prior question which has to be answered affirmatively before any question on the merits arises. Refusal of the application on its merits therefore, implies the prior question has been answered affirmatively. I recognise that in some cases perhaps it may be impractical to decide whether an applicant has sufficient interest or not without having evidence from both parties as to the matter to which the application relates and that in such cases the court before whom the matter comes in the first instance cannot refuse leave to the applicant at the ex parte [stage, but] where

---

[136] See. p. 541.   [137] See. p. 586.   [138] See. p. 868.

after seeing the evidence of both parties the proper conclusion is that the applicant did not have a sufficient interest to make the application the decision ought to be made on that ground."

16. [Lord Fraser said, at 646]:

"The correct approach in such a case is in my opinion, to look at the statute under which the duty arises and see whether it gives any express or implied right to persons in the position of the applicant to complain of the alleged unlawful act or [omission]."

. . .

18. My attention was drawn to a number of authorities described by Counsel as setting out principles. They can I think more properly, be described merely as illustrations depending on the particular facts of the case. In *Covent Garden Community Association Limited v Greater London Council* [1981] JPL 183, [Woolf J said, at 184]:

"However, the fact that leave was required in judicial review proceedings and was required before prerogative orders prior to the new rule [in 1977, p. 509], was a significant factor to be taken into account in the approach to locus standi, since the requirement of leave provided a necessary filter to prevent frivolous actions by persons who had no sufficient interest in the result of the proceedings . . . Here the court was concerned with the right of local residents, who had incorporated themselves, to be heard in respect of the manner in which a local authority reached a decision in a planning matter affecting the locality. That such decisions on planning matters could materially affect residents was recognised by their being allowed to appear and be heard at public inquiries when they were held into such matters, and the fact that their representations would in any event be taken into account in considering whether planning permission should be granted. It was true that, as the respondents pointed out, there was another body which was democratically elected which also represented persons in the locality."

[Woolf J was] quite satisfied that the applicants had sufficient interest and that it would be out of accord with the general approach to questions of locus standi in prerogative proceedings to decide that the applicants had no right to make the application.

19. In *R v Secretary of State for the Environment, ex p Rose Theatre Trust* [1990] 1 QB 505, [Schiemann J said, at 519]: "There is no doubt that, in the early part of this decade, the High Court was fairly liberal in its interpretation of who had 'a sufficient interest' to be able to apply for judicial [review]."

. . .

23. [Schiemann J said, at 533]:

"I do not consider that an interested member of the public who has written and received a reply in relation to a decision not to schedule a site as an ancient monument has sufficient interest in the decision to enable him to apply for judicial review. [The] law does not see it as the function of the courts to be there for every individual who is interested in having the legality of an administrative action litigated. Parliament could have given such a wide right of access to the court but it has not done so. The challenger must show that he 'has a sufficient interest in the matter to which the application relates'. The court will look at the matter to which the application relates—in this case the non-scheduling of a monument of national importance—and the statute under which the decision was [taken] and decide whether the statute gives that individual expressly or impliedly a greater right or expectation than any other citizen of this country to have that decision taken lawfully. We all expect our decision makers to act lawfully. We are not all given by Parliament the right to apply for judicial [review]."

24. The final authority which was cited to me was *R v Inspectorate of Pollution, ex p Greenpeace* [[1994] 4 All ER 329, where Otton J said, at 333]: "Greenpeace [is] a well-known campaigning organisation which has as its prime object the protection of the natural [environment]."

. . .

27. [Otton J said, at 349]:

"In reaching my conclusions I adopt the approach indicated by Lord Donaldson, MR in *R v Monopolies and Mergers Commission, ex p Argyll Group* [1986] 1 WLR 763, at 773: 'The first stage test, which is applied on the application for leave, will lead to a refusal if the applicant has no interest whatsoever and is, in truth, no more than a meddlesome busybody. If, however, the application appears to be otherwise arguable and there is no other discretionary bar, such as dilatoriness on the part of the applicant, the applicant may expect to get leave to apply, leaving the test of interest or standing to be re-applied as a matter of discretion on the hearing of the substantive application. At this second stage, the strength of the applicant's interest is one of the factors to be weighed in the [balance].'"

. . .

29. [Otton J said, at 349]:

"Thus I approach this matter primarily as one of discretion. I consider it appropriate to take into account the nature of Greenpeace and the extent of its interest in the issues raised, the remedy Greenpeace seeks to achieve and the nature of the relief sought."

30. [Otton J said, at 350]:

"[British Nuclear Fuels (BNFL)] rightly acknowledges the national and international standing of Greenpeace and its integrity. So must I. I have not the slightest reservation that Greenpeace is an entirely responsible and respected body with a genuine concern for the environment. That concern naturally lead to a bona fide interest in the activities carried on by BNFL at Sellafield and in particular the discharge and disposal of radioactive waste from its premises to which the respondents' decision to vary relates. The fact that there are 400,000 supporters in the United Kingdom carries less weight than the fact that 2,500 of them come from the Cumbria region. I would be ignoring the blindingly obvious if I were to disregard the fact that those persons are inevitably concerned about (and have a genuine perception that there is) a danger to their health and safety from any additional discharge of radioactive waste even from testing. I have no doubt that the issues raised by this application are serious and worthy of determination by this court. It seems to me that if I were to deny standing to Greenpeace, those it represents might not have an effective way to bring the issues before the court. There would have to be an application either by an individual employee of BNFL or a near neighbour. In this case it is unlikely that either would be able to command the expertise which is at the disposal of Greenpeace. Consequently, a less well-informed challenge might be mounted which would stretch unnecessarily the court's resources and which would not afford the court the assistance it requires in order to do justice between the parties. Further, if the unsuccessful applicant had the benefit of legal aid it might leave the respondents and BNFL without an effective remedy in costs."

31. [Otton J said, at 351]:

"I also take into account [the] fact that Greenpeace has been treated as one of the consultees during the consultation [process]. It follows that I reject the argument that Greenpeace is a 'mere' or 'meddlesome busybody'. I regard the applicant as eminently respectable and responsible and its genuine interest in the issues raised is sufficient for it to be granted locus standi. It must not be assumed that Greenpeace (or any other interest group) will automatically be afforded standing in any subsequent application for judicial review in whatever field it (and its members) may have an interest. This will have to be a matter to be considered on a case by case [basis]."

. . .

36. [It was submitted, on behalf of the applicants, that the following factors supported their application: they lived locally; they had used and enjoyed the site; they had taken an active part in the objections before the planning decision; there was no other body which had challenged the planning

decision and if they did not have standing, an unlawful act would have been committed; although they were members of the Friends of the Earth, the local branch of the Friends of the Earth was an unincorporated body which could not bring proceedings; sport and recreation were important components of civilised life; it was "impossible to describe these applications as being no more than meddlesome busybodies"].

37. [The respondents emphasised the following contrary factors: the applicants lived several miles from the site; there were other significant parks much closer to the applicants, which provided the opportunity for walking, recreation and ecological study, some of which were designated as sites of importance for nature conservation; the public had no right of access to the area of the extension; there was still a substantial portion of the area available as an open space; being "a protestor however persistent does not of itself give sufficient interest"].

38. As I indicated the general approach of the Courts is set out in the various authorities to which reference has been made. In the end the Court has to do a balancing act between the various factors and exercise its discretion in deciding whether the applicants have [shown a sufficient interest]. I have looked at the various factors which have been advanced on both sides and stood back. In the end I come to the firm conclusion that a sufficient interest has not been made out by either of these applicants. Accordingly for that reason in the exercise of my discretion I should not grant leave.'

VIII. Statutory Exclusion of Judicial Review

(a) The context

We are here concerned with a balancing operation between two crucial features of the modern state, namely, the balance of control of legality of administrative action (more specifically directed towards protecting the individual) and the efficiency of the administration of the modern state (more specifically directed towards the protection of the public interest). Here we are concerned with the extent to which the courts will submit themselves to the will of Parliament when Parliament uses statutory machinery designed to limit the interference of the courts in the interest of administrative efficiency by inserting into the relevant statutory provisions sections designed to 'oust' the supervisory jurisdiction of the courts. Note that any discussion of ouster clauses is only relevant to the supervisory jurisdiction: in order to prevent the courts from exercising an appellate jurisdiction, Parliament simply needs to omit to grant such a jurisdiction.

The thesis behind statutory ouster clauses is as follows. Whilst we need to be able to control the unlawful exercise of power, it would be administratively inefficient if every decision of every administrative body were subject to complete control by the courts, so that in effect the courts became the final decision-maker in place of the administration in every case. If every single decision which is needed to be taken in the modern state were to be subject to judicial review as to the relevant facts, the appropriate public policies and as to the law, the administration would be redundant and the judicial system would be overwhelmed. Consequently, Parliament has designed ouster clauses in order to limit the supervisory jurisdiction. Ouster clauses have traditionally taken three distinct forms.

(b) Final clauses

Sometimes, Parliament has given a right of appeal to a higher court or to a higher tribunal and then states that the decision of that court or tribunal is 'final'. Here, there is the desire of Parliament that there should not be an unrestricted series of rights of appeal in what are often relatively minor matters and which can normally be settled definitively at the lower level of adjudication in order that both the administrative process and the courts system should not be overwhelmed. The question is how far the use of the finality clause can oust the supervisory jurisdiction, as opposed to any appellate jurisdiction, and this question was answered definitively in *R v Medical Appeal Tribunal, ex p Gilmore*.[139] Under the then industrial injuries social security scheme, compensation was granted to persons suffering an accident at work. A person losing one eye was entitled to 30 per cent of a set sum and a person who lost both eyes was entitled to 100 per cent of the set sum. Gilmore lost the sight of both eyes, in successive accidents, and a medical appeal tribunal assessed the disablement at 20 per cent. It was conceded by the (then) Ministry of Pensions and National Insurance that this was an error of law. However, there was at that time no right of appeal on a point of law from a medical appeal tribunal. The statute stated that 'the decision on any medical question by a medical appeal tribunal is final'. The question was whether those words precluded the court from issuing certiorari to quash what was obviously a very wrong decision. It was stated: 'I find it very well settled that the remedy by certiorari is never to be taken away by any statute except by the most clear and explicit words. The word "final" is not enough. That only means "without appeal". It does not mean "without recourse to certiorari". It makes the decision final on the facts, but not final on the law. Notwithstanding that the decision is by a statute made "final", certiorari can still issue for excess of jurisdiction or for error of law on the face of the record.'[140]

(c) Shall not be questioned clauses

Parliament has on rare occasions inserted provisions which state, quite simply and baldly, that a decision 'shall not be questioned in any legal proceedings whatsoever'. The purpose here is usually to keep the decision within the jurisdiction of a specially created decision-maker and to prevent 'excessive' interference by the courts. The principal question is whether this form of ouster clause should be interpreted by the courts literally, as ousting their review jurisdiction when the decision-maker makes what may be described as a 'very bad' decision, or whether the courts will go beyond the very plain words of Parliament in order to remedy that 'very bad' decision. The extent of the courts' willingness to act as a final review body may be seen in:

....

Anisminic v Foreign Compensation Commission [1969] 2 AC 147

Anisminic owned mining property in Egypt worth over £4 million. Egypt nationalised considerable properties and Anisminic's property was sequestrated and sold to an Egyptian organisation named TEDO. In November 1957, Anisminic made an agreement with TEDO selling to TEDO their whole

---

[139] [1957] 1 QB 574.   [140] Per Denning LJ, at 583.

business for £500,000, but this did not include any claim which Anisminic might be entitled to assert against any government authority other than the Egyptian Government. In 1959, a treaty between the United Kingdom and Egypt agreed that certain properties (listed in Annex E of the treaty) were to continue to be sequestrated and that Egypt paid to the United Kingdom £27.5 million as full settlement of properties listed in Annex E. Anisminic had no legal right to claim to participate in that sum. The disposal of that sum was in the discretion of the United Kingdom Government. The Foreign Compensation Commission was given the task of disposing of the money to claimants under an Order made under the Foreign Compensation Act 1950. Article 4(1) of the Order stated that 'the Commission shall treat a claim [as] established if the applicant satisfies them of the following matters'. First, 'that his application relates to property in Egypt which is referred to in Annex E'. Anisminic's property was listed in Annex E and the first condition was, therefore, satisfied. Second, 'that the applicant [is] the owner of the property or is the successor in title of such person'. Anisminic was the owner of the property and the second condition, therefore, was satisfied. Third, 'that the [owner] and any person who became successor in title of [the owner] were British nationals on [certain specified dates]'. The third (nationality) condition (contained in article 4(1)(b)(ii)) was to cause not a little difficulty, especially when it must be noted that the Foreign Compensation Act 1950 provided that 'the determination by the Commission of any application made to them under this Act shall not be called in question in any court of law' (section 4(4)). It may be convenient to list in logical order (as opposed to the chronological sequence of their Lordships' speeches), the key factors and questions to be answered by the House of Lords.

(1) What was the meaning of the third, nationality, condition according to the majority of the House of Lords? (see Lords Reid and Wilberforce, where it will be seen that one only has to consider the nationality of the successor in title if the successor is the claimant, that the successor (TEDO) was not the claimant, that the claimant was Anisminic and Anisminic was of British nationality at the time). What was the meaning of the third, nationality, condition according to the Foreign Compensation Commission? (see Lords Reid and Pearson, where it will be seen that the Commission had held that even where the applicant was the original owner, they had to enquire whether there was a successor in title, that TEDO was the successor in title to Anisminic, and that since TEDO was not a British national, Anisminic's claim had to be rejected). The majority of the House of Lords and the Commission came to contradictory conclusions and the Commission were in error as to the meaning of the third condition.

(2) Which view was to prevail? Parliament had not included in the 1950 Act a right of appeal, since it was considered that the advantages of securing finality of decisions outweighed any disadvantages that might possibly result from having no appeal procedure. Therefore, the question was whether the courts could exercise their supervisory jurisdiction. Had Parliament decided that the conclusive decision as to the meaning of the third condition should be made by the courts or the Commission and what was the effect of the Foreign Compensation Act 1950, section 4(4), on, first, errors of law on the face of the record (errors within jurisdiction) and, second, jurisdictional errors (errors going to jurisdiction or errors in excess of jurisdiction)? (Lords Reid, Morris, Wilberforce and Pearson all agreed that a tribunal must keep within its jurisdiction and cannot add to or subtract from its jurisdiction, that errors are divided into two categories (errors within jurisdiction and errors going to jurisdiction), that section 4 ousted the courts jurisdiction and deprived the court of any power to correct a determination of the Commission which was within jurisdiction, but that section 4 did not oust the jurisdiction of the courts to enquire and determine whether the Commission had acted within or without jurisdiction.)

(3) The Commission had made an erroneous interpretation of the third, nationality, condition, but was that error committed by the Commission an error of law on the face of the record (error within jurisdiction) or a jurisdictional error (error going to jurisdiction)? This is where we come to the decisive part of the case, where the Court of Appeal and two members of the House of Lords (Lords Morris and Pearson) disagreed with three members of the House of Lords (Lords Reid, Pearce and Wilberforce), whose majority decision, that the Commission had acted outside their jurisdiction and made a jurisdictional error, prevailed.

As the Iron Duke might have commented, it was a very close thing.

It is important to note that, in subsequent case law, the distinction between errors within jurisdiction and errors going to or in excess of jurisdiction, a distinction vital to the legal solution of the specific problem raised in *Anisminic* by a combination of a very bad decision and an ouster clause, has been drastically modified (nay abolished) with regard to the supervisory jurisdiction in the normal situation where there is no 'shall not be questioned' clause. Confused? You may be, but help is forthcoming (see p. 527).

Lord Reid, at 169–175

'[With regard to the Foreign Compensation Act 1950, section 4(4), cited above, the Foreign Compensation Commission maintains] that these are plain words only capable of having one meaning. Here is a determination which is apparently valid: there is nothing on the face of the document to cast any doubt on its validity. If it is a nullity, that could only be established by raising some kind of proceedings in court. But that would be calling the determination in question, and that is expressly prohibited by the statute. The appellants maintain that that is not the meaning of the words of this provision. They say that "determination" means a real determination and does not include an apparent or purported determination which in the eyes of the law has no existence because it is a nullity. Or, putting it in another way, if you seek to show that a determination is a nullity you are not questioning the purported determination—you are maintaining that it does not exist as a determination. It is one thing to question a determination which does exist: it is quite another thing to say that there is nothing to be [questioned].

Statutory provisions which seek to limit the ordinary jurisdiction of the court have a long history. No case has been cited in which any other form of words limiting the jurisdiction of the court has been held to protect a nullity. If the draftsman or Parliament had intended to introduce a new kind of ouster clause so as to prevent any inquiry even as to whether the document relied on was a forgery, I would have expected to find something much more specific than the bald statement that a determination shall not be called in question in any court of law. Undoubtedly such a provision protects every determination which is not a nullity. But I do not think that it is necessary or even reasonable to construe the word "determination" as including everything which purports to be a determination but which is in fact no determination at [all].

I can now turn to the provisions of the Order under which the commission [acted.] The meaning of the important parts of this Order is extremely difficult to discover, and, in my view, a main cause of this is the deplorable modern drafting practice of compressing to the point of obscurity provisions which would not be difficult to understand if written out at rather greater [length]. The main difficulty in this case springs from the fact that the draftsman did not state separately what conditions have to be satisfied (1) where the applicant is the original owner and (2) where the applicant claims as the successor in title of the original owner. It is clear that where the applicant is the original owner he must prove that he was a British national on the dates stated. And it is equally clear that where the applicant claims as being the original owner's successor in title he must prove that both he and the original owner were British nationals on those dates, subject to later provisions in the article about persons who had died or had been born within the relevant period. What is left in obscurity is whether the provisions with regard to successors in title have any application at all in cases where the applicant is himself the original owner. If this provision had been split up as it should have been, and the conditions to be satisfied where the original owner is the applicant had been set out, there could have been no such obscurity.

This is the crucial question in this case. It appears from the commission's reasons that they construed this provision as requiring them to inquire, when the applicant is himself the original owner, whether he had a successor in title. So they made that inquiry in this case and held that TEDO was the applicant's successor in title. As TEDO was not a British national they rejected the appellants' claim. But if, on a true construction of the Order, a claimant who is an original owner does not have to prove anything about successors in title, then the commission made an inquiry which the Order did not empower them to make, and they based their decision on a matter which they had no right to take into account. If one uses the word "jurisdiction" in its wider sense, they went beyond their jurisdiction in considering this matter. It was argued that the whole matter of construing the Order was something remitted to the commission for their decision. I cannot accept that argument. I find nothing in the Order to support it. The Order requires the commission to consider whether they are satisfied with regard to the prescribed matters. That is all they have to do. It cannot be for the commission to determine the limits of its powers. Of course if one party submits to a tribunal that its powers are wider than in fact they are, then the tribunal must deal with that submission. But if they reach a wrong conclusion as to the width of their powers, the court must be able to correct that—not because the tribunal has made an error of law, but because as a result of making an error of law they have dealt with and based their decision on a matter with which, on a true construction of their powers, they had no right to deal. If they base their decision on some matter which is not prescribed for their adjudication, they are doing something which they have no right to do and, if the view which I expressed earlier is right, their decision is a nullity. So the question is whether on a true construction of the Order the applicants did or did not have to prove anything with regard to successors in title. If the commission were entitled to enter on the inquiry whether the applicants had a successor in title, then their decision as to whether TEDO was their successor in title would I think be unassailable whether it was right or wrong: it would be a decision on a matter remitted to them for their decision. The question I have to consider is not whether they made a wrong decision but whether they inquired into and decided a matter which they had no right to consider.

I have great difficulty in seeing how in the circumstances there could be a successor in title of a person who is still in existence. This provision is dealing with the period before the Order was made when the original owner had no title to anything: he had nothing but a hope that some day somehow he might get some compensation. The rest of the article makes it clear that the phrase (though inaccurate) must apply to a person who can be regarded as having inherited in some way the hope which a deceased original owner had that he would get some compensation. But "successor in title" must I think mean some person who could come forward and make a claim in his own right. There can only be a successor in title where the title of its original possessor has passed to another person, his successor, so that the original possessor of the title can no longer make a claim, but his successor can make the claim which the original possessor of the title could have made if his title had not passed to his [successor]. In themselves the words "successor in title" are, in my opinion, inappropriate in the circumstances of this Order to denote any person while the original owner is still in existence, and I think it most improbable that they were ever intended to denote any such person. There is no necessity to stretch them to cover any such person. I would therefore hold that the words "and any person who became successor in title to such person" in article 4(1)(b)(ii) have no application to a case where the applicant is the original owner. It follows that the commission rejected the appellants' claim on a ground which they had no right to take into account and that their decision was a nullity.'

Lord Morris of Borth y Gest, at 181–194

'The provisions of section 4(4) of the Act do not, in my view, operate to debar any inquiry that may be necessary to decide whether the commission has acted within its authority or jurisdiction. The provisions do operate to debar contentions that the commission while acting within its jurisdiction has come to wrong or erroneous conclusions. The control which is exercised by the High Court over inferior tribunals (a categorising but not a derogatory description) is of a supervisory but not of an appellate nature. It enables the High Court to correct errors of law if they are revealed on the face of the record. The control cannot, however, be exercised if there is some provision (such as a "no certiorari" clause) which prohibits removal to the High Court. But it is well settled that even such a clause is of no avail if the inferior tribunal acts without jurisdiction or exceeds the limit of its [jurisdiction].

So the question is raised whether in the present case the commission went out of bounds. Did it wander outside its designated area? Did it outstep the confines of the territory of its inquiry? Did it digress away from its allotted task? Was there some preliminary inquiry upon the correct determination of which its later jurisdiction was dependent?

For the reasons which I will endeavour to explain it seems to me that at no time did the commission stray from the direct path which it was required to [tread]. It seems to me that the words which stated that it was for the commission to be satisfied of certain matters, and defined those matters, inevitably involved that any necessary interpretation of words within the compass of those matters was for the commission. They could not come to a conclusion as to whether they were satisfied as to the specified matters unless and until they gave meaning to the words which they had to follow. Unless such a phrase as "successor in title" was defined in the Order—and it was not—it was an inescapable duty of the commission to consider and to decide what the phrase [signified]. In the present case the commission could be controlled if being "satisfied" of the matters referred to "them" they failed to obey the mandatory direction of the Order in Council. But in deciding whether or not they were satisfied of the matters they were working within the confines of their denoted delegated and remitted jurisdiction. In the exercise of it very many questions of construction were inevitably bound to arise. At no time was the commission more centrally within their jurisdiction than when they were grappling with those problems. If anyone could assert that in reaching honest conclusions in regard to the questions of construction they made any error, such error would, in my view, be an error while acting within their jurisdiction and while acting in the discharge of their function within it.'

Lord Pearce, at 194–195

'My Lords, the courts have a general jurisdiction over the administration of justice in this country. From time to time Parliament sets up special tribunals to deal with special matters and gives them jurisdiction to decide these matters without any appeal to the courts. When this happens the courts cannot hear appeals from such a tribunal or substitute their own views on any matters which have been specifically committed by Parliament to the tribunal. Such tribunals must, however, confine themselves within the powers specially committed to them on a true construction of the relevant Acts of Parliament. It would lead to an absurd situation if a tribunal, having been given a circumscribed area of inquiry, carved out from the general jurisdiction of the courts, were entitled of its own motion to extend that area by misconstruing the limits of its mandate to inquire and decide as set out in the Act of Parliament.

If, for instance, Parliament were to carve out an area of inquiry within which an inferior domestic tribunal could give certain relief to wives against their husbands, it would not lie within the power of that tribunal to extend the area of inquiry and decision, that is, jurisdiction, thus committed to it by construing "wives" as including all women who have, without marriage, cohabited with a man for a substantial period, or by misconstruing the limits of that into which they were to inquire. It would equally not be within the power of that tribunal to reduce the area committed to it by construing "wives" as excluding all those who, though married, have not been recently co-habiting with their husbands. Again, if it is instructed to give relief wherever on inquiry it finds that two stated conditions are satisfied, it cannot alter or restrict its jurisdiction by adding a third condition which has to be satisfied before it will give relief. It is, therefore, for the courts to decide the true construction of the statute which defines the area of a tribunal's jurisdiction. This is the only logical way of dealing with the situation and it is the way in which the courts have acted in a supervisory capacity.'

Lord Wilberforce, at 207–214

'Although, in theory perhaps, it may be possible for Parliament to set up a tribunal which has full and autonomous powers to fix its own area of operation, that has, so far, not been done in this country. The question, what is the tribunal's proper area, is one which it has always been permissible to ask and to answer, and it must follow that examination of its extent is not precluded by a clause conferring conclusiveness, finality, or unquestionability upon its decisions. These clauses in their nature can only relate to decisions given within the field of operation entrusted to the tribunal. They may, according to the width and emphasis of their formulation, help to ascertain the extent of that field, to narrow it or to enlarge it, but unless one is to deny the statutory origin of the tribunal and of its powers, they cannot preclude examination of that [extent].

The courts, when they decide that a "decision" is a "nullity", are not disregarding the preclusive clause. For, just as it is their duty to attribute autonomy of decision of action to the tribunal within the designated area, so, as the counterpart of this autonomy, they must ensure that the limits of that area which have been laid down are [observed]. In each task they are carrying out the intention of the legislature, and it would be misdescription to state it in terms of a struggle between the courts and the executive. What would be the purpose of defining by statute the limit of a tribunal's powers if, by means of a clause inserted in the instrument of definition, those limits could safely be [passed?].

In my opinion, therefore, article 4 should be read as if it imposed three conditions only on satisfaction of which the applicant was entitled, under statutory direction, to have his claim admitted, namely—(a) that his application relates to property in Egypt referred to in Annex E; (b) that he was the person referred to in Annex E paragraph (1)(a) as the owner of the property; (c) that he was a British national at the specified dates. As, ex concessis, all these conditions were fulfilled to the satisfaction of the commission, the appellants' claim was in law established: the commission by seeking to impose another condition, not warranted by the Order, was acting outside its remitted powers and made no determination of that which alone it could [determine].

Lord Pearson, at 215 and 223

'[I agree that] what has been called the "ouster provision" in section 4(4) of the Foreign Compensation Act 1950, does not exclude the court's intervention in a case where there is a merely purported determination given in excess of jurisdiction. [I] would join with my noble and learned friends to this extent, that if the appellants' contentions as to the true construction of the relevant Order in Council are upheld, it must follow that the commission have acted in excess of jurisdiction and the court should intervene in the exercise of its supervisory [function].

I am, however, not able to agree that the commission misunderstood the Order in Council, or made any error affecting their [jurisdiction]. It seems to me that the provisions of [article 4(b)] can and should be read quite literally as meaning what they appear to say. "Successor in title" means a person, whether an individual or a corporation, to whom the claim for restitution or compensation (being all that was left of the owner's interest in the property) has passed by any mode, whether by testamentary disposition or by devolution on intestacy or by assignment or otherwise. [The] applicant may be the initial owner claiming on his own behalf, or the initial owner claiming for the benefit of a successor in title, or he may be the successor in [title]. The stringent requirement that each of them must have been a British national on both of the dates (so that an initial owner would have to remain a British national after he had parted with the beneficial interest in the claim and a successor in title would need to have been a British national before he acquired any interest in the claim), though prima facie surprising, was entirely natural because it was following the requirements of the treaty under which the compensation money for meeting such claims had been [paid].

I would say therefore that the commission construed the article correctly and did not ask themselves any wrong question or exceed their jurisdiction in any way. Having so construed the article, the commission had to make a decision as to the effect of the November agreement. They decided that by that agreement the claim passed to TEDO, and so was at the date of the treaty foreign-held and therefore it was excluded by the provisions of article 4(b)(ii) from participation in the fund. The decision as to the effect of the November agreement, whether right or wrong, was plainly within their jurisdiction, and therefore by virtue of section 4(4) of the Foreign Compensation Act 1950, it cannot be called in question in any [court].'

(d) Time limit clauses

Here Parliament has given the aggrieved citizen a right to apply to the superior courts within a specified time limit (usually the relatively short period of six weeks), but once the time limit has expired Parliament has used words designed to oust the supervisory jurisdiction of the courts altogether. This device is used almost exclusively with regard to provisions relating to an interference with a citizen's rights to property in the public interest, especially with regard to compulsory acquisition of land, where it is necessary for the acquiring authority to have the legal certainty of title to the land acquired before setting in motion the necessary plans, contracts and financial arrangements for building a motorway, airport, housing estate or Olympic village. The thesis behind time limit clauses is that there has to come a point at which the public interest must outweigh the private interest and that even if the public interest is unfair to the private citizen and administrative action might otherwise be declared a nullity, the public interest against overturning the administrative action far outweighs the private interest. A whole series of time limit clauses, illustrating the increasing use of such devices, may be found in the Water Resources Act, 1991:

Water Resources Act, 1991, schedule 14

'5(1) If any person aggrieved by an order [transferring certain functions to the National Rivers Authority] desires to question its validity on the ground (a) that it is not within the powers of this Act; or (b) that any requirement of this Act has not been complied with, he may, within six weeks of the date of the publication of the notice [relating to the order] make an application for the purpose to the High Court.

(2) Where an application is duly made to the High Court under this paragraph, the High Court, if satisfied (a) that the order is not within the powers of this Act; or (b) that the interests of the applicant have been substantially prejudiced by any requirements of this Act not having been complied with, may quash the order either generally or in so far as it affects the applicant.

(3) Except by leave of the Court of Appeal, no appeal shall lie to the House of Lords from a decision of the Court of Appeal in proceedings under this paragraph.

(4) Subject to the preceding provisions of this paragraph [a transfer order] shall not at any time be questioned in any legal proceedings whatsoever.'

Water Resources Act, 1991, schedule 16

'8(1) If any person aggrieved by an [order imposing special drainage charges] desires to question its validity on the ground (a) that it is not within the powers of this Act or (b) that any requirement of this Act has not been complied with, he may, within six weeks of the relevant date, make an application for the purpose to the High Court.

(2) Where an application is duly made to the High Court under this paragraph, the High Court, if satisfied (a) that the order is not within the powers of this Act; or (b) that the interests of the applicant have been substantially prejudiced by any requirements of this Act not having been complied with, may quash the order either generally or in so far as it affects the applicant.

(3) Except by leave of the Court of Appeal, no appeal shall lie to the House of Lords from a decision of the Court of Appeal in proceedings under this paragraph.

(4) Subject to the preceding provisions of this paragraph an [order imposing special drainage charges] shall not at any time be questioned in any legal proceedings whatsoever.'

Water Resources Act, 1991, schedule 19

'6(2) [If] any person aggrieved by a compulsory works order containing powers of compulsory acquisition [desires] to question the validity of the order, or of any provision of the order, on the grounds that any powers of compulsory acquisition conferred by the order are not authorised by this Act to be so conferred, or that any of the relevant requirements have not been complied with in relation to the [order], he may make an application for the purpose to the High Court at any time before the end of the period of six weeks beginning with the date on which notice of the making of the order is first [published].

(3) On any application under sub-paragraph (2) above with respect to any [order], the High Court (a) may by interim order suspend the operation of the order, or any provision of the order, [(either] generally or in so far as it affects any property of the applicant to the High Court) until the final determination of the proceedings; and (b) if satisfied (i) that any powers of compulsory acquisition conferred by the order are not authorised by this Act to be so conferred; or (ii) that the interests of that applicant have been substantially prejudiced by a failure to comply with any of the relevant requirements in relation to the [order], may quash the order, or any provision of the order, [(either] generally or in so far as it affects any property of that applicant).

(4) Except as provided by sub-paragraph (2) above, the validity of any such order [as] is mentioned in that sub-paragraph shall not, either before or after the order [has] been made or given, be questioned in any legal proceedings whatsoever.

(5) Subject to any order of the High Court under sub-paragraph (3) above, any such order [as] is mentioned in sub-paragraph (2) above shall become operative [on] the date on which notice of the making or giving of the order [is] published as mentioned in the said sub-paragraph (2).'

One fundamental question to be answered was whether *Anisminic*[141] could override a time limited ouster clause. The traditional, pre-*Anisminic*, view of the courts was stated in:

Smith v East Elloe Rural District Council [1956] AC 736

A statute relating to compulsory acquisition of land granted an aggrieved person the right to question the validity of a compulsory purchase order within six weeks of the date of the confirmation or making of the order. Subject to that right, 'a compulsory purchase order [shall not] be questioned in any legal proceedings whatsoever' (this is referred to below as 'paragraph 16'). A compulsory purchase order was made of Smith's property. Smith did not question the validity of the order within the six weeks time limit. Six years later, Smith alleged that the order had been wrongly confirmed and in bad faith and that the time limit clause could not apply in cases of bad faith and should be interpreted as if the words 'made in good faith' were added to the clause. The House (by a majority of Viscount Simonds, Lords Morton and Radcliffe to Lords Reid and Somervell) concluded that the court could not entertain the action so far as it impugned the validity of the compulsory purchase order. The House of Lords unanimously held that Smith could continue her claim against the clerk to the council, which alleged that the clerk had knowingly acted wrongfully and in bad faith in procuring the compulsory purchase order.

[141] See p. 514.

Viscount Simonds (majority), at 750–752

'My Lords, I think that anyone bred in the tradition of the law is likely to regard with little sympathy legislative provisions for ousting the jurisdiction of the [court]. But it is our plain duty to give the words of an Act their proper meaning and, for my part, I find it quite impossible to qualify the words of [paragraph 16] in the manner suggested. It may be that the legislature had not in mind the possibility of an order being made by a local authority in bad faith or even the possibility of an order made in good faith being mistakenly, capriciously or wantonly challenged. This is a matter of speculation. What is abundantly clear is that words are used which are wide enough to cover any kind of challenge which an aggrieved person may think fit to make. I cannot think of any wider words. Any addition would be mere [tautology]. It was argued by learned counsel for [Smith] that there is a deep-rooted principle that the legislature cannot be assumed to oust the jurisdiction of the court, particularly where fraud is alleged, except by clear words. [But paragraph 16 is unambiguous]; there is no alternative construction that can be given to it; there is, in fact, no justification for the introduction of limiting words such as "if made in good faith", and there is the less reason for doing so when those words would have the effect of depriving the express words "in any legal proceedings whatsoever" of their full meaning and [content]. I come, then, to the conclusion that the court cannot entertain this action so far as it impugns the validity of the compulsory purchase order. It is no part of my present duty to attack or defend such a provision of an Act of Parliament, but two things may, I think, fairly be said. First, if the validity of such an order is open to challenge at any time within the period allowed by the ordinary Statute of Limitations with the consequence that it and all that has been done under it over a period of years may be set aside, it is not perhaps unreasonable that Parliament should have thought fit to impose an absolute bar to proceedings even at the risk of some injustice to individuals. Second, the injustice may not be so great as might appear. For the bad faith or fraud upon which an aggrieved person relies is that of individuals, and this very case shows that, even if the validity of the order cannot be questioned and he cannot recover the land that has been taken from him, yet he may have a remedy in damages against those individuals.'

Lord Reid (minority), at 764–765

'[Paragraph 16 uses] words which are general and emphatic, and, to my mind, the question is whether this use of general words necessarily leads to the conclusion that the jurisdiction of the court is entirely excluded in all cases of misuse of powers in mala fide where those acting in mala fide have been careful to see that the procedure was in order and the authority granted by the order was within the scope of the Act under which it was made. A person deliberately acting in bad faith would naturally be careful to do this. In my judgment, paragraph 16 is clearly intended to exclude, and does exclude entirely, all cases of misuse of power in bona fide. But does it also exclude the small minority of cases where deliberate dishonesty, corruption or malice is involved? In every class of case that I can think of the courts have always held that general words are not to be read as enabling a deliberate wrongdoer to take advantage of his own [dishonesty].

  There are many cases where general words in a statute are given a limited meaning. That is done, not only when there is something in the statute itself which requires it, but also where to give general words their apparent meaning would lead to conflict with some fundamental principle. Where there is ample scope for the words to operate without any such conflict it may very well be that the draftsman did not have in mind and Parliament did not realise that the words were so wide that in some few cases they could operate to subvert a fundamental principle. In general, of course, the intention of Parliament can only be inferred from the words of the statute, but it appears to me to be well established in certain cases that, without some specific indication of an intention to do so, the mere generality of words used will not be regarded as sufficient to show an intention to depart from fundamental principles. So, general words by themselves do not bind the Crown, they are limited so as not to conflict with international law, they are commonly read so as to avoid retrospective infringement of rights, and it appears to me that they can equally well be read so as not to deprive the court of jurisdiction where bad faith is [involved].'

R v Secretary of State for the Environment, ex p Ostler [1977] QB 122 (CA)

The Highways Act 1959, provided that if a person aggrieved by a compulsory purchase order relating to the building of roads desired to question the validity of the order on the ground that it was not within the powers of the Act or on the ground that any requirement of the Act had not been complied with, that person might, within six weeks from the date on which notice of publication of the order was first published, make an application for the purpose to the High Court. Subject to this, the order 'shall not be questioned in any legal proceedings whatsoever'. An inner relief road was proposed for Boston and was planned in two stages: first, the acquisition of land for the main road; second, the acquisition of land for side roads giving access to the main road. There was a public inquiry for both stages. At the first inquiry (relating to the main road) a firm objected on the ground that the road would cut off access to its premises. It was alleged that there was a secret assurance given to the firm by an officer of the Department of the Environment that access would be given for their lorries by widening another road and this would take place during the second stage. The firm withdrew their objection. The widening of the other road would have the effect of interfering with Ostler's business premises, but as he did not know of the alleged secret assurance, he did not object at the first stage, although he would have so objected had he known of the assurance. A compulsory purchase order was made and confirmed. The second stage involved the widening of the road and Ostler objected at this stage as he realised that his business would be affected. At the second inquiry, he wanted to give evidence that he would have objected at the first stage if he had known that the whole project would affect his property. But he was not allowed to give such evidence as the inquiry was only concerned with the second stage. Some months later, Ostler got to know of the secret agreement and applied to quash the compulsory purchase order on the ground that the order had been wrongly confirmed for want of natural justice and in bad faith verging on fraud in that there had bean a secret agreement between the Department of the Environment and other business interests. It was accepted that if Ostler had come to the court within the six weeks time limit, his complaint could and would have been considered by the court. But he had not commenced his action within the time limit. The key question was whether *Smith* (p. 521) had been affected by *Anisminic* (p. 514). It was held that *Smith* was still a binding decision. *Anisminic* was distinguished on a number of grounds.

Lord Denning MR, at 95–96

'[First, in *Anisminic*] the Foreign Compensation Act ousted the jurisdiction of the court altogether. It precluded the court from entertaining any complaint at any time about the determination. Whereas in [*Smith*] the statutory provision has given the court jurisdiction to inquire into complaints so long as the applicant comes within six weeks. The provision is more in the nature of a limitation period than of a complete [ouster. Second in *Anisminic*] the House was considering a determination by a truly judicial body, the Foreign Compensation Tribunal, whereas in [*Smith*] the House was considering an order which was very much in the nature of an administrative [decision]. There is a great difference between the two. In making a judicial decision the tribunal considers the rights of the parties without regard to the public interest. But in an administrative decision (such as a compulsory purchase order) the public interest plays an important part. The question is, to what extent are private interests to be subordinated to the public interest. Third in [*Anisminic*] the House had to consider the actual determination of the tribunal, whereas in [*Smith*] the House had to consider the validity of the process by which the decision was reached. Looking at it broadly, it seems to me that the policy underlying the 1959 Act is that when a compulsory purchase order has been made, then if it has been wrongly obtained or made, a person aggrieved should have a remedy. But he must come promptly. He must come within six weeks. If he does so, the court can and will entertain his complaint. But if the six weeks expire without any application being made, the court cannot entertain it afterwards. The reason is because, as soon as that time has elapsed, the authority will take steps to acquire property, demolish it and so forth. The public interest demands that they should be safe in doing so.'

In *R v Secretary of State for the Environment, ex p Kent*,[142] a company applied to the London Borough of Ealing (the council) for planning permission to construct a cellular radio base station near to flats occupied by Kent (and others). The council wrote, giving notice of the application, to occupants of many of the flats but not to Kent. Later the council refused planning permission. The company appealed to the Secretary of State. The proceedings were conducted in writing, an inspector was appointed to determine the appeal and the Secretary of State wrote to the council stating that the council should notify local residents and others who might be affected, telling them of the form of the appeal procedure and inviting them to make their views known to the inspector. The council wrote to many occupants of the flats but, again, failed to write to Kent, erroneously believing that there were 28 such occupants whereas, in fact, there were 46 flats. The inspector determined that planning permission should be granted. Two months later, Kent found out about the original application, the original refusal, the appeal and the decision to grant permission. One month later Kent applied for judicial review of the Secretary of State's decision to grant permission, on the ground of want of natural justice. The relevant statutory provision, the Town and Country Planning Act 1971, sections 242 and 245, provided for the traditional right of an aggrieved person to question the validity of the Secretary of State's decision before the High Court, the traditional six weeks time limit and the traditional ouster clause that the validity of any decision on the part of the Secretary of State could not be questioned in any legal proceedings whatsoever. It was held that reliance on *Anisminic* (p. 514) was misconceived as in that case, although there was a total ouster provision, the Foreign Compensation Commission had misinterpreted the limits of its jurisdiction, as conferred by Parliament, and Parliament could not have intended to protect decisions made without jurisdiction. In the present case, by contrast, having barred all attack, subject to qualifications, Parliament had specifically provided for jurisdictional challenges to be made, albeit only within a limited time. Although, owing to a failure on the part of the council the applicants not only had no opportunity to make representations but also were wholly unaware of what had happened until long after the time limit for challenging the decision in the only way it could be challenged had expired, it was clear that *Ostler* was conclusive against the appellant unless it could be distinguished and the Court of Appeal could not so distinguish. The intention of Parliament, therefore, in enacting an 'Anisminic clause' is that questions as to jurisdiction or validity are not excluded but the intention of Parliament in enacting an 'Ostler clause' is that questions as to jurisdiction or validity may be raised on the specified grounds in the prescribed time and manner, but that otherwise the courts' supervisory jurisdiction is excluded in the interests of certainty.[143]

By way of postscript, attention should be drawn to the Interception of Communications Act 1985, section 7(8), which states that the decisions of the Interception of Communications Tribunal '(including any decisions as to their jurisdiction) shall not be subject to appeal or liable to be questioned in any court'. How far such decisions are immune from judicial review is for the future. Watch this space.

---

[142] [1990] JPL 124 (CA).   [143] *R v Cornwall CC, ex p Huntingdon* [1994] 1 All ER 694 (CA).

10 GROUNDS FOR JUDICIAL REVIEW

I. Introduction

As stated in chapter 9, the supervisory jurisdiction of the High Court differs from an appellate jurisdiction of a court or tribunal in three very important ways. First, the supervisory jurisdiction is a means of review, at least in theory, of the law that has been applied by the body under review and it is not an investigation into the facts. Second, the supervisory jurisdiction, being to investigate the legality of a decision, is limited to a decision of the supervisory court that the body under review either acted lawfully or did not act lawfully. If the body acted lawfully, nothing further is needed and the original decision stands. If the body acted unlawfully, the original decision is nullified (to use a non-legal word) and the body has to make its original investigation and determination all over again. Third, the legal basis of the supervisory jurisdiction is not that of statute but is based on the inherent common law powers of the courts to see that justice is done.

The supervisory jurisdiction of the courts is based on the common law powers of the courts to keep bodies within their jurisdiction. In essence 'jurisdiction' means 'authority to decide'. If a body has jurisdiction, it has authority to decide a given matter; it is acting '*intra vires*' (or within its powers). If a body has no jurisdiction, it has no authority to decide the given matter; it is acting '*ultra vires*' (or outside its powers). In the modern state, jurisdiction, the power to decide, is given to various kinds of administrative authorities by common law (sometimes) and by statute (in most cases). First, and it is suggested, foremost we are concerned with the powers granted by Parliament.

Since the seventeenth century, the courts have accepted that Parliament is supreme in the field of legislative power. There is no written constitution with a built-in system of fundamental rights and principles which, as in other countries, can be used to declare as invalid enactments of the legislature or royal, presidential and ministerial decrees.

'Parliamentary sovereignty means Parliament can, if it chooses, legislate contrary to fundamental principles of human rights. The Human Rights Act 1998 will not detract from this power. The constraints upon its exercise by Parliament are ultimately political, not legal. But the principle of legality means that Parliament must squarely confront what it is doing and accept the political cost. Fundamental rights cannot be overridden by general or ambiguous words. [In] the absence of express language or necessary implication to the contrary, the courts, therefore presume that even the most general words were intended to be subject to the basic rights of the individual. In this way the courts of the United Kingdom, though acknowledging the sovereignty, apply principles of constitutionality little different from those which exist in countries where the power of the legislature is expressly limited by a constitutional document.'[1]

---

[1] *R v Home Secretary, ex p Simms* [2000] 2 AC 115, per Lord Hoffman, at 131.

The courts must accept the will of Parliament but, as the will of Parliament is presumed to be that administrative authorities will act according to law, as enforcers of that parliamentary will, the courts will apply certain canons of interpretation and certain presumptions.

We are therefore, first of all, concerned with the statutory interpretation and common law presumptions which the courts will make as to Parliament's intentions. These are common law rules and they do not depend on statute for their existence or validity. The following are basic presumptions which will underlie many of the grounds for judicial review which will be discussed in this chapter. Unless the contrary is clearly expressed by Parliament, the courts will presume that there shall be no deprivation of property rights, of goods, land, or money, and no deprivation of a legitimate expectation that a current situation will continue; there shall be no alteration of clear principles of the common law, especially of the courts' powers to inquire into a matter and to redress a grievance; there shall be no exclusion of the rules of natural justice (which we will see are basic roles of procedural fairness).[2] The basic rule is that any change must be expressly ordered by Parliament. One hundred years ago, women graduates, who, by reason of their status as graduates, were members of the general council of their university, claimed that they were entitled to the parliamentary franchise under a statutory provision,[3] which provided that 'every person' whose name was on the register of the general council of a university, was of full age, and was not subject to any legal incapacity, was to be entitled to vote for the Member of Parliament for that university. This was too progressive. The statutory provision did not give 'Votes for Women'. 'It would require a convincing demonstration to satisfy me that Parliament intended to effect a constitutional change so momentous and far-reaching by so furtive a process.'[4]

....

R v The Lord Chancellor, ex p Witham [1997] EWHC 237 (Admin)

Witham sought a declaration that an Order relating to Supreme Court fees was unlawful. He alleged that he was being denied access to the courts because he could not afford to pay the appropriate fee.

Laws J

'12. The common law does not generally speak in the language of constitutional rights, for the good reason that in the absence of any sovereign text, a written constitution which is logically and legally prior to the power of legislature, executive and judiciary alike, there is on the face of it no hierarchy of rights such that any one of them is more entrenched by the law than any other. And if the concept of a constitutional right is to have any meaning, it must surely sound in the protection which the law affords to it. Where a written constitution guarantees a right, there is no conceptual difficulty. The State authorities must give way to it, save to the extent that the constitution allows them to deny [it].

13. In the unwritten legal order of the British State, at a time when the common law continues to accord a legislative supremacy to Parliament, the notion of a constitutional right can in my judgment inhere only in this proposition, that the right in question cannot be abrogated by the State save by specific provision in an Act of Parliament, or by regulations whose vires in main legislation specifically confers the power to abrogate. General words will not suffice. And any such rights will be creatures of the common law, since their existence would not be the consequence of the democratic political process but would be logically prior to [it].

. . .

[2] *R v Secretary of State for the Home Department, ex p Pierson* [1997] UKHL 37.
[3] Representation of the People (Scotland) Act 1868, section 27.
[4] *Nairn v University of St Andrews* [1909] AC 147, per Lord Loreburn LC, at 161.

24. It seems to me, from all the authorities to which I have referred, that the common law has clearly given special weight to the citizens's right of access to the courts. It has been described as a constitutional right, though the cases do not explain what that means. In this whole argument, nothing to my mind has been shown to displace the proposition that the executive cannot in law abrogate the right of access to justice, unless it is specifically so permitted by Parliament; and this is the meaning of the constitutional [right].

. . .

27. In my judgment [the Order's] effect is to bar absolutely many persons from seeking justice from the courts. [Access] to the courts is a constitutional right; it can only be denied by the government if it persuades Parliament to pass legislation which specifically—in effect by express provision—permits the executive to turn people away from the court door. That has not been done in this case.'

One historical conumdrum should be laid to rest. It has been seen[5] that the court of King's Bench developed two methods of control over inferior bodies: errors 'in excess of' or 'going to' jurisdiction and errors 'within jurisdiction', and that in *Anisminic*,[6] the House of Lords decided that a decision of the Foreign Compensation Commission was a very bad decision and since the only possible way to proceed was to maintain the distinction, for which there was considerable authority, between errors 'in excess of' or 'going to' jurisdiction and errors 'within jurisdiction' and to label the decision of the Foreign Compensation Commission as going to jurisdiction (and that is what they did). However, there was no answer at all to the question: how do you recognise an error 'in excess of' or 'going to' jurisdiction and an error 'within jurisdiction', and what is the difference between errors 'in excess' or 'going to' jurisdiction and errors 'within jurisdiction'. There was a reaction.

In *Pearlman v Keepers and Governors of Harrow School*,[7] the Leasehold Reform Act 1967 gave certain tenants the right to buy the houses they lived in, provided that, inter alia, the rateable value of the house was not more than £1,500. In calculating the rateable value there was to be disregarded the increase in rateable value resulting from an 'improvement' by the tenant made by the execution of works amounting to 'structural alteration, extension or addition'. Pearlman had installed central heating to his house and this had the result of raising the rateable value to above £1,500. He asked the county court for a ruling that the installation of the central heating was an 'improvement' amounting to 'structural alteration, extension or addition'. The county court judge held that the installation of the central heating was not such an improvement. The Court of Appeal disagreed, unanimously, with this and held that the judge was wrong. According to the Leasehold Reform Act, the decision of the county court judge was 'final and conclusive' of the matter. The Court of Appeal could have treated this as just another example of a 'final' clause,[8] but they decided to consider the question of error within and error going to jurisdiction and a majority (Lord Denning MR and Eveleigh LJ, Geoffrey Lane LJ dissenting) held that the error of the judge was an error going to jurisdiction. The dilemma raised as a consequence of *Anisminic* was succinctly put by Lord Denning MR:[9]

'[The] distinction between an error which entails absence of jurisdiction and an error made within jurisdiction is very fine. So fine indeed that it is rapidly being eroded. Take this very case. When the judge held that the installation of a full central heating installation was not a "structural alteration or addition", we all think, all three of us, that he went wrong in point of law. He misconstrued those words. That error can be described on the one hand as an error which went to his jurisdiction. [On] the other hand, his error can equally well be described as an error made by him within his jurisdiction. [So] fine is the distinction that in truth the High Court has a choice before it whether to interfere with an inferior

---

[5] See p. 464.   [6] See p. 514.   [7] [1979] 1 All ER 365.   [8] See p. 514.   [9] At 371–372.

court on a point of law. If it chooses to interfere, it can formulate its decision in the words "The court below had no jurisdiction to decide this point wrongly as it did". If it does not choose to interfere, it can say "The court had jurisdiction to decide it wrongly, and did so". Softly be it stated but that is the reason for the difference between the decision of the Court of Appeal in *Anisminic* and the House of Lords. I would suggest that this distinction should now be discarded. The High Court has, and should have, jurisdiction to control the proceedings of inferior courts and tribunals by way of judicial review [and] no court or tribunal has any jurisdiction to make an error of law on which the decision of the case depends.'

To this rejoined Geoffrey Lane LJ:[10]

'I am, I fear, unable to see how that determination, assuming it to be an erroneous determination, can properly be said to be a determination which he was not entitled to make. The judge is considering the words in the [statute] which he ought to consider. He is not embarking on some unauthorised or extraneous or irrelevant exercise. All he has done is to come to what appears to this court to be a wrong conclusion on a difficult question. It seems to me that, if this judge is acting outside his jurisdiction, so then is every judge who comes to a wrong decision on a point of law.'

There is a certain logic in stating that no body can have jurisdiction to make an error of law. But the corollary of this would, as Geoffrey Lane LJ admitted, be to call every error of law an error going to jurisdiction and this was against the long tradition summarised in *Anisminic*. The *Anisminic* view that there is a distinction between errors within jurisdiction and errors going to jurisdiction, whatever that might mean, was then confirmed by the Privy Council in *South East Asia Firebricks v Non-metallic Mineral Products Manufacturing Employees' Union*.[11] It was robustly stated:

'The decision of the House of Lords [in *Anisminic*] shows that, when words in a statute oust the power of the High Court to review decisions of an inferior tribunal by certiorari, they must be construed strictly, and that they will not have the effect of ousting that power if the inferior tribunal has acted without jurisdiction or if "it has done or failed to do something in the course of the inquiry which is of such a nature that its decision is a nullity" [(see Lord Reid)]. But if the inferior tribunal has merely made an error of law which does not affect its jurisdiction, and if its decision is not a nullity for some reason such as breach of the rules of natural justice, then the ouster will be effective. In [*Pearlman*, p. 527], Lord Denning MR suggested that the distinction between an error of law which affected and one which did not should now be "discarded". Their Lordships do not accept that suggestion. They consider that the law was correctly applied to the circumstances of that case in the dissenting opinion of Geoffrey Lane LJ when he said "[the] only circumstances in which this court can correct what is to my mind the error of the [county court] judge is if he was acting in excess of his jurisdiction as opposed to merely making an error of law in his judgment by misinterpreting the meaning of structural alteration or addition".'[12]

In *O'Reilly v Mackman*,[13] Lord Diplock, in a speech approved by the other members of the House, stated that *Anisminic*:

'has liberated English public law from the fetters that the courts had theretofore imposed upon themselves so far as determinations of inferior courts and statutory tribunals were concerned, by drawing esoteric distinctions between errors of law committed by such tribunals that went to their jurisdiction, and errors of law committed by them within their jurisdiction. The breakthrough that

---

[10] At 376.   [11] [1981] AC 363 (PC).

[12] Per Lord Fraser, at 369–374. See, also, *Re Racal Communications Ltd* [1981] AC 374, where Lord Diplock, together with Lord Keith, dissented, pronouncing that the 'breakthrough made by *Anisminic* was that, as respects administrative tribunals and authorities, the old distinction between errors of law that went to jurisdiction and errors of law that did not was for practical purposes abolished'.   [13] See p. 482.

Anisminic made was the recognition by the majority of this House that if a tribunal whose jurisdiction was limited by statute or subordinate legislation mistook the law applicable to the facts as it had found them, it must have asked itself the wrong question, ie one into which it was not empowered to inquire and so had no jurisdiction to determine. Its purported "determination", not being "a determination" within the meaning of the empowering legislation, was accordingly a nullity.'[14]

The House of Lords and other courts fell into line: The decision in *Anisminic* 'rendered obsolete the distinction between errors of law on the face of the record and other errors of law';[15] *Anisminic* 'made obsolete' the historic distinction between errors of law on the face of the record and other errors of law;[16] 'Modern public law has progressively discarded the distinction between error of law within and outwith jurisdiction, starting with [*Anisminic* and culminating with *Page*]. Inferior tribunals are today subject in principle to judicial review for all errors of law.'[17]

There is, as mentioned above, no constitutional document which sets out with clarity and precision a list of conditions on which the right of a body to act depends and there is no universally accepted list in the textbooks or the decisions of the judges. For the purposes of this chapter (and for clarity of exposition), the grounds for judicial review are founded on several major propositions taken from the analysis of Lord Diplock in *GCHQ*.[18] The conditions on which the right of a body to act are that:

(a) The decision-maker must possess the qualifications laid down in the appropriate statute and, unless otherwise provided in the statute either expressly or by implication, the presumed intention of Parliament is absence of bias. This is discussed in head II.

(b) The decision-maker's decision must not be vitiated by illegality. The decision-maker must not misunderstand or misapply the relevant law. The case in which the decision is made must be one of the kind of subject matter described in the appropriate statute and the decision-maker must not have misconstrued the statute giving it power to act so that it failed to deal with the question remitted to it and decided some question which was not remitted to it. This is discussed in head III.

(c) The decision-maker's decision must not be vitiated by irrationality, where the decision is outrageously absurd, or utterly illogical or perversely defies accepted standards to such an extent that no rational person could have taken it. This is discussed in head IV.

(d) The decision-maker's decision must not be vitiated by procedural impropriety, by a failure to observe procedural rules and practices laid down by the appropriate statute or a failure to observe the rules of natural justice (or to act fairly). This is discussed in head V.

It may be noted that heads (a) to (d) are not themselves clear-cut divisions (logically a decision by an unqualified decision-maker is illegal and could be irrational) and that a decision may be vitiated by more than one of those heads.

'Challenge to the lawfulness of subordinate legislation or administrative decisions and acts may take many forms, compendiously grouped [in *GCHQ*] under the headings of illegality, procedural impropriety and irrationality. Categorisation of types of challenge assists in an orderly exposition of the principles underlying our developing public law. But these are not water tight compartments because the various grounds for judicial review run together. The exercise of a power for an improper

---

[14] [1983] 2 AC 237, at 278.

[15] *Page v Hull University Visitor* [1993] AC 682, per Lord Brown-Wilkinson, at 701–702.

[16] *Boddington v British Transport Police* [1999] 2 AC 143. See, also, *Palacegate Properties v London Borough of Camden* [2000] EWHC 372 (Admin), per Laws LJ, at para 25.

[17] *Carter v Ahsan* [2005] EWCA Civ 990, per Sedley LJ, at para 28.   [18] See pp. 86, 90–92.

purpose may involve taking irrelevant considerations into account, or ignoring relevant consider-ations; and either may lead to an irrational result. The failure to grant a person affected by a decision a hearing, in breach of principles of procedural fairness, may result in a failure to take into account relevant considerations.'[19]

Furthermore, the list is neither exclusive nor exhaustive. Indeed, Lord Diplock had in mind 'particularly the possible adoption in the future of the principle of proportionality'.[20] Finally, it is suggested that, over and above the four-fold classification (which corresponds to a large extent with analogous classifications in civil law systems and the system practised by the European Court of Justice) lie certain fundamental principles, in that all forms of power should be exercised fairly and in no way abused.

II. A Qualified Decision-Maker

The first condition precedent to an exercise of authority within jurisdiction listed in head I is that the decision must be taken by the proper authority. In the vast majority of situations, the authority will be created and invested with power by a statutory provision.

(a) General

When a statutory provision gives power to an authority, it will usually specify the constitution of the authority and will usually state that a particular power is to be vested in a local author-ity (for example, a housing or social services authority), a minister of the Crown, an appellate court or tribunal, a quango, or any other public authority. Sometimes, there may be special attributes designated, for example the Appeal Committee hearing appeals relating to parental preferences for school admissions:

....

Education Act 1996, schedule 33

'Constitution of Appeal Committees

1 (1) An appeal pursuant to arrangements made by a local education authority [relating to parental preferences for school admissions] shall be to an appeal committee constituted in accordance with this paragraph.

(2) An appeal committee shall consist of—

    (a) one person nominated by the authority from among persons who are eligible to be lay members [see paragraph 5];

    (b) two, four or six other members nominated by the authority from among persons appointed by the authority under sub-paragraph 3.

---

[19] *Boddington v British Transport Police* [1999] 2 AC 143, per Lord Irvine LC, at 152.
[20] *GCHQ*, at 410. For proportionality, see p. 597.

(3) The persons appointed by the authority under this sub-paragraph shall comprise—

    (a) members of the authority; and

    (b) persons who are not members of the authority but who have experience in education, are acquainted with the educational conditions in the area of the authority or are parents of registered pupils at a school, but shall not include any person employed by the authority otherwise than as a teacher.

(4) Sufficient persons may be appointed by the authority under sub-paragraph (2) to enable two or more appeal committees to sit at the same time.

(5) The authority shall not nominate a person under sub-paragraph (2)(a) if he is a member of the authority or is employed by them.

(6) The members of an appeal committee who are members of the authority shall not outnumber the others.

(7) A person who is a member of the authority or employed by the authority shall not be chairman of an appeal committee.

(8) A person shall not be a member of an appeal committee for the consideration of an appeal against a decision if he was among those who made the decision or took part in discussions as to whether the decision should be made.

(9) A person who is a teacher at a school shall not be a member of an appeal committee for the consideration of an appeal involving a question whether a child is to be admitted to that [school].

. . .

5 (1) A person is eligible to be a lay member for the purposes of [paragraph 1(2)(a)] if—

    (a) he is a person without personal experience in the management of any school or the provision of education in any school (disregarding any such experience as a governor or in any other voluntary capacity); and

    (b) he satisfies the conditions in sub-paragraph 2.

(2) Those conditions are—

    (a) in the case of a person to be nominated as a lay member for the purposes of paragraph 1(2)(a), that he does not have, and has not at any time had, in connection with—

        (i) the local education authority in question, or

        (ii) any person who is a member of, or employed by, that authority, of a kind which might reasonably be taken to raise doubts about his ability to act impartially in relation to the [authority].'

Cases of unqualified persons making determinations are rare. *In R v Aston University Senate, ex p Roffey,*[21] two students failed their examinations. The University Regulations, regulation 3, stated that 'any student who fails to satisfy the examiners may at the discretion of the examiners be permitted to take a referred examination'. The students claimed that there had been a breach of the rules of natural justice. It was held that the only body invested by the regulations with the power and discretion to decide whether or not the students should be sent down or not was 'the examiners'. In *Adams v Adams,*[22] Mrs Adams lived and was married in what was then Southern Rhodesia. She wanted a divorce and, in 1970, was granted a divorce by Macaulay J. Under the 1961 Southern Rhodesian Constitution, which was the only lawful constitution of Southern Rhodesia according to United Kingdom law, section 54(3), a judge could not enter on his duties unless he had taken an oath of allegiance to the Queen and a judicial oath before the Governor of Southern Rhodesia. In 1965, the governing politicians declared

---

[21] [1969] 2 QB 538.   [22] [1971] P 188.

the Unilateral Declaration of Independence. Macaulay J was 'appointed' a judge in 1966 under the illegal constitution established after UDI. It was held that as Macaulay J had not taken the oaths in accordance with section 54(3), he was not a judge and could not, according to United Kingdom law, grant a valid decree of divorce in Southern Rhodesia. It must be emphasised that the decision-making must be exercised by the proper authority on his, her or their own and not in conjunction with other unauthorised persons or bodies.[23] This brings us to the problem raised by the administrative practice of delegating decision-making.

(b) Delegation

As mentioned in head (a) above, a statute will usually state that a particular power is to be vested in a local authority, a minister of the Crown, an appellate court or tribunal, or any other administrative authority. At one time it was possible for the named authority to take decisions vested in it or to supervise very closely the few civil servants it employed. In modern times, it is a fact of life that the named authority may simply not be able individually to take all the decisions under the statutory authority. In modern times, administrative authorities employ many, many people who take individual decisions. In modern times, it would be impossible for each statute vesting power in an administrative body to name the human being who will actually exercise the power. For example, a large number of decisions relating to social security are vested in 'the Secretary of State' and a large number of decisions relating to housing and social services are vested in local housing and social services authorities, respectively. Sometimes, there is an express provision permitting delegation of power:

Local Government Act 1972

'101 (1) Subject to any express provision in this Act or any Act passed after this Act, a local authority may arrange for the discharge of any of their functions [by] a committee, a sub-committee or an officer of the [authority].

(2) Where by virtue of this section any functions of a local authority may be discharged by a committee of theirs, then, unless the local authority otherwise direct, the committee may arrange for the discharge of any of those functions by a sub-committee or an officer of the authority and where by virtue of this section any functions of a local authority may be discharged by a sub-committee of the authority, then, unless the local authority or the committee otherwise direct, the sub-committee may arrange for the discharge of any of those functions by an officer of the [authority].

. . .

(4) Any arrangements made by a local authority or committee under this section for the discharge of any functions by a committee, sub-committee, officer or local authority shall not prevent the authority or committee by whom the arrangements are made from exercising those functions.'

If there is no express power to delegate in the enabling statute, then it depends on the interpretation of the statute by the courts as to whether and as to how far delegation is

---

[23] See *Birmingham City Magistrates*, p. 623.

permitted. Delegation is not a complete giving up of power and the delegating authority may always re-take its power from the delegate. The constitutional propriety of delegation to members of the Civil Service was approved in *Carltona v Commissioners of Works*.[24] The Commissioners of Works (a body headed by the then Minister of Works and Planning) were given power under wartime regulations to requisition property, and Carltona's factory was requisitioned. The actual requisition notice was made by a civil servant of the rank of assistant secretary, for and on behalf of the Commissioners. Lord Greene MR pronounced that in the

'administration of government in this country the functions which are given to ministers (and constitutionally properly given to ministers because they are constitutionally responsible) are functions so multifarious that no minister could ever personally attend to [them]. It cannot be supposed that [the particular statutory provision] meant that, in each case, the minister in person should direct his mind to the matter. The duties imposed upon ministers and the powers given to ministers are normally exercised under the authority of the ministers by responsible officials of the department. Public business could not be carried on if that were not the case. Constitutionally the decision of such an official is of course the decision of the minister, the minister is responsible. It is he who must answer before Parliament for anything his officials have done under his authority, and, if for an important matter he selected an official of such junior standing that he could not be expected competently to perform the work, the minister would have to answer for that in Parliament.'[25]

Since the actual official making the decision to requisition was a senior official, it was held that there was a proper delegation of the power. In *Liversidge v Anderson*,[26] it was stated that certain matters were so important that they must be determined personally by the minister. The Anderson concerned was Sir John Anderson, the then Home Secretary, whose name achieved immortality when it was given to the air-raid shelter which he introduced. The Liversidge concerned was not really Liversidge. His real name was Perlzweig, and he was a German national living in this country at the outbreak of the Second World War. As an 'enemy alien' he was detained under emergency regulations, which permitted detention of persons if the Minister 'had cause to believe that' they were a danger to the state. It was shown that Sir John Anderson personally looked at the papers relating to Perlzweig, he did not delegate such an important decision to his officials, and, moreover, he reported personally to the House of Commons at regular intervals as to the exercise of such an important power. The detention of Perlzweig was therefore lawful. Generally speaking, decisions on liberty, such as imprisonment and release, deportation and grant of citizenship will be taken by very senior officials and often by the minister personally. As a general rule, judicial decisions should not be delegated. In *Barnard v National Dock Labour Board*,[27] the Board was established to run the docks. It had disciplinary powers (which included the power to suspend a dock worker). The London Dock Labour Board delegated this power to the local port manager. Barnard and a number of fellow dockers refused to unload a cargo of sugar because of a change in the industrial practices for unloading cargoes, and was suspended. He sought a declaration that this was unlawful.

'[It] was urged on us that the local board had power to delegate their functions to the port manager on the ground that the power of suspension was an administrative and not a judicial function. [I do not accept this view. The] board are put in a judicial position between the men and the employers; they are to receive reports from the employers and investigate them; they have to inquire whether the man has been guilty of misconduct, such as failing to comply with a lawful order, or failing to comply with the provisions of the scheme; and if they find against him they can suspend him without pay, or can even dismiss him summarily. In those circumstances they are exercising a judicial [function]. While an

[24] [1943] 2 All ER 560 (CA).   [25] At 563.   [26] [1942] AC 206.   [27] [1953] 2 QB 18 (CA).

administrative function can be delegated, a judicial function rarely can be. No judicial tribunal can delegate its functions unless it is enabled to do so expressly or by necessary [implication].'[28]

(c) Bias

It is one of the so-called principles of natural justice that a person or authority which makes a determination must be fair and unbiased.

'It has long been regarded as essential that judicial decision-makers should, so far as reasonably possible, resolve disputes coming before them on their legal and factual merits, uninfluenced by extraneous prejudice or predilection or personal interest. The qualification "so far as reasonably possible" is necessary because judicial decision-makers are human beings upon whom multifarious experiences and influences inevitably leave a mark. The decision-maker should consciously shut out of his decision-making process any extraneous prejudice or predilection of which he is aware; but he cannot shut out an extraneous prejudice or predilection of which he is unaware. The name given by the law to extraneous prejudice or predilection or personal interest in this context is bias. Injustice will have occurred as a result of bias if the decision-maker unfairly regarded with disfavour the case of a party to the issue under consideration and "unfairly regarded with disfavour" means "was pre-dis-posed or prejudiced against one party's case for reasons unconnected with the merits of the issue".'[29]

The entitlement to a fair hearing by an impartial tribunal is guaranteed, insofar as it applies to the determination of a person's 'civil rights and obligations or of any criminal charge against him', by the European Convention on Human Rights, article 6, now a 'Convention right' under the Human Rights Act 1998.[30]

Obviously the most important disqualifying interest is that of a pecuniary or proprietorial interest (whether directly the concern of the decision-maker or the concern of someone close to the decision-maker). In *Dimes v Grand Junction Canal Co*,[31] the Lord Chancellor held shares in the canal company. It was held that he could not hear a case involving the company, as he had a pecuniary interest which invalidated his sitting to hear the case. There was no evidence that Lord Cottenham was biased in favour of the company, but it would simply not be fair for there to be any suspicion of a biased judge. In *Metropolitan Properties v Lannon*,[32] tenants lived in a block of flats (Oakwood Court) owned by Metropolitan Properties (part of a group of companies owned by the Freshwater Group). Metropolitan Properties proposed to raise the tenants' rents. The case was heard by the rent assessment committee, which made drastic reductions in the rents and put the fair rent at figures which were far lower than the tenants themselves had offered. Metropolitan Properties naturally wanted to challenge the decisions of the committee. They alleged that the committee chairman (Lannon) was biased. Lannon was a solicitor whose flat was owned by the parent company (the Freshwater Group),

---

[28] Per Denning LJ, at 39–41.

[29] *R v Inner West London Coroner, ex p Dallaglio* [1994] 4 All ER 139, per Simon Brown LJ, at 151.

[30] See p. 771. On the application of the Convention's insistence on an 'independent and impartial tribunal', see *R (on the application of Bono) v Harlow DC* [2002] EWHC 423 (Admin) and *Begum v London Borough of Tower Hamlets* [2003] UKHL 5 (housing benefit review board); *R (on the application of the Chief Constable of Lancashire) v Preston Crown Court* [2001] EWHC 928 (Admin) (composition of Crown Court for licensing matters); *R (on the application of Beeson) v Dorset CC* [2001] EWHC 986 (Admin) (composition of panel assessing means for residential care purposes).   [31] (1852) 3 HLC 759.

[32] [1969] 1 QB 577.

the tenant of this flat was Lannon's father who was disputing the rent for the flat on grounds similar to those raised by the Oakwood Court tenants. Lannon's firm acted both for his father and for other tenants in the same block of flats. His father's dispute was pending when he sat as chairman in the Oakwood Court case, to which the same landlords were parties. It was held that Lannon should not have sat as chairman in that particular case. 'If he was himself a tenant in difference with his landlord about the rent of his flat, he clearly ought not to sit on a case against the self same landlord, also about the rent of a flat, albeit another flat. In this case he was not a tenant, but the son of a tenant. But that makes no difference. No reasonable man would draw any distinction between him and his father, seeing he was living with him and assisting him with his case.'[33]

In practice, there are often statutory rules designed to eliminate, by way of a priori control, such interests and certain codes of administrative best practice have been introduced. Following publication of two reports: 'The Conduct of Local Authority Business'[34] and 'Standards of Conduct in Local Government in England, Scotland and Wales, by the Committee on Standards in Public Life',[35] the Secretary of State made the Local Authorities (Model Code of Conduct) (England) Order.[36] Consequently, a 'member must regard himself as having a personal interest in any matter if a decision upon it might reasonably be regarded as affecting to a greater extent than other council tax payers, ratepayers, or inhabitants of the authority's area, the well-being or financial position of himself, a relative or a [friend]'; 'a member with a personal interest in a matter also has a prejudicial interest in that matter if the interest is one which a member of the public with knowledge of the relevant facts would reasonably regard as so significant that it is likely to prejudice the member's judgement of the public [interest]'; 'a member with a prejudicial interest in any matter must (a) withdraw from the room or chamber where a meeting is being held whenever it becomes apparent that the matter is being considered at that meeting, unless he has obtained a dispensation from the authority's standards committee; (b) not exercise executive functions in relation to that matter; and (c) not seek improperly to influence a decision about that matter'.[37] *R (on the application of Paul Richardson and Another) v North Yorkshire County Council*[38] concerned the grant of planning permission by North Yorkshire County Council for the extension of quarrying of sand and gravel. The Council's Planning and Regulatory Functions Committee had resolved that permission be granted, but it was alleged that a councillor, Richardson, was unlawfully excluded from the meeting at which the resolution was adopted, on the ground that he had a 'prejudicial interest' (within the meaning of paragraph 12). It was held that it was 'plain' that he did have a prejudicial interest. It was not in dispute that he had a 'personal interest', in that the planning decision might reasonably be regarded as affecting his well-being and financial position to a greater extent than other relevant persons. His home was very close to the proposed extension of the quarry and was one of a handful of properties liable to be most affected by the development. Consequently,

'a member of the public with knowledge of the relevant facts would reasonably have regarded Mr Richardson's personal interest as so significant that it was likely to prejudice his judgement of the public interest. I reject [the] submission that a knowledgeable member of the public would reasonably have regarded him as simply putting forward the views of the people he represented, or making a contribution to the debate based on his perception of the public interest, rather than being influenced

[33] Per Lord Denning MR, at 598–600.   [34] Chaired by David Widdicombe QC, 1986, Cmnd. 9860.
[35] Chaired by Lord Nolan, 1997, Cm. 3702.
[36] SI 2001/3575. All the provisions of the Model Code are mandatory (article 2(2)). See, also, pp. 154–159 (Ministers) and pp. 219–244 (MPs).   [37] Paras 8(1), 10(1), 12(1), respectively.
[38] [2003] EWHC 764 (Admin).

by the potential impact of the development on his own home. However conscientious a councillor might be in his representative role and his concern to protect the public interest, the personal interest was a highly material additional consideration.'

Since paragraph 12 did apply to Richardson in his capacity as a councillor, that paragraph required him to withdraw from the meeting.[39]

Another type of disqualifying interest is what may be called a 'personal interest' in the case being determined and the rule may be applied even in cases where an adjudicator might be influenced by the personal interest of another person. The leading case is:

R v Sussex Justices, ex p McCarthy [1924] 1 KB 256

McCarthy was charged with dangerous driving and was also sued for damages as a result of the accident. The acting clerk of the magistrates' court was a solicitor whose firm was representing the person who was suing McCarthy for damages. The clerk retired with the justices when they considered their verdict. It was proved that the magistrates did not consult the clerk and the clerk did not give them any advice.

Lord Hewart CJ, at 259

'It is said, and, no doubt, truly, that when [the clerk] retired in the usual way with the justices, taking with him the notes of the evidence in case the justices might desire to consult him, the justices came to a conclusion without consulting him, and that he scrupulously abstained from referring to the case in any way. But while that is so, a long line of cases shows that it is not merely of some importance but is of fundamental importance that justice should not only be done, but should manifestly and undoubtedly be seen to be done. The question therefore is not whether in this case the deputy clerk made any observation or offered any criticism which he might not properly have made or offered; the question is whether he was so related to the case in its civil aspect as to be unfit to act as clerk to the justices in the criminal matter. The answer to that question depends not upon what actually was done but upon what might appear to be done. Nothing is to be done which creates even a suspicion that there has been an improper interference with the course of justice. [I] accept the statements contained in the justices' affidavit, but they show very clearly that the deputy clerk was connected with the case in a capacity which made it right that he should scrupulously abstain from referring to the matter in any way, although he retired with the justices; in other words, his one position was such that he could not, if he had been required to do so, discharge the duties which his other position involved. His twofold position was a manifest contradiction. In those circumstances I am satisfied that this conviction must be [quashed].'

It is a fact of life, that persons involved in public life as magistrates, tribunal members, local authority officials, local councillors, school governors, members of public authorities and ministers are bound to have some opinions with regard to the proper conduct of the modern state and, indeed, may be chosen to serve precisely because of their experience. We cannot eliminate all opinions on matters of current interest from the minds of the great and the good who are set above us. Consequently, it was held early on in *R v Handsley*,[40] that a member of the prosecuting local authority was not disqualified from sitting as a justice to hear a

---

[39] Per Richards J, at para 84. See, also, *R v Secretary of State for the Environment, ex p Kirkstall Valley Campaign* [1996] 3 All ER 304; *R (on the application of Liverpool City Council) v Local Commissioner for North and North East England* [2000] EWCA Civ 54.   [40] (1881) 8 QBD 383.

summons against a ratepayer in arrears. Similarly, in *R v Deal Justices*,[41] it was held that a magistrate who was a member (but not an overtly active member) of a society devoted to preventing cruelty to animals was not disqualified from hearing a prosecution by that society. The position with regard to persons called on to adjudicate in a superior judicial capacity was succinctly described: People

'who are called on to adjudicate will often have substantial experience in the relevant field and will therefore be familiar with the background issues which they may have encountered previously in various roles. Indeed, the individuals concerned will often be particularly suited to adjudicate on the matter precisely because of the experience and wisdom on the topic which they have accumulated in those other roles. [Judges] draw on their previous work, whether as advocates, legal civil servants or academic lawyers. [The] knowledge and expertise developed in these ways can only help, not hinder, their judicial work.'[42]

Decisions of great importance are taken by local authorities with regard to licensing, planning, social services, education, and development. The members, whether elected or un-elected, of such bodies will usually have definite, publicly stated, and often party political, opinions on a variety of policy issues. Furthermore, local councillors, who often live in the area which they represent, will often have an intimate knowledge of the area, its recent history, its communities, its characters, and the divergent opinions as to what is best for the area. There are two ways of approaching this. First to use the rule against bias and to ask whether on the facts now known there was bias in one or more members of the decision-making body. Second, to ask whether the body as a whole can be shown to have predetermined a particular course and to have fettered its own discretion (see head III(b)). 'In this way the necessary involvement of local elected councillors in matters of public controversy, and the probability that they will have taken a public stand on many of them, limits the range of attack which can properly be made upon any decision in which even a highly opinionated councillor has taken part. [This being so, the] decision of a body, albeit composed of disinterested individuals, will be struck down if its outcome has been predetermined whether by the adoption of an inflexible policy or by the effective surrender of the body's independent [judgment].'[43] In *R v Amber Valley DC, ex p Jackson*,[44] it was held that the principles of natural justice were not violated by a decision of the majority political party that it supported a particular planning application.

'The rules of fairness or natural justice cannot be regarded as being rigid. They must alter in accordance with the context. Thus in the case of highways, the department can be both the promoting authority and the determining authority. When this happens, of course any reasonable man would regard the department as being predisposed towards the outcome of the inquiry. The department is under an obligation to be fair and to carefully consider the evidence given before the inquiry but the fact that it has a policy in the matter does not entitle a court to intervene. So in this case I do not consider the fact that there is a declaration of policy by the majority group can disqualify a district council from adjudicating on a planning application. It may mean that the outcome of the planning application is likely to be favourable to an applicant and therefore unfavourable to objectors. However, Parliament has seen fit to lay down that it is the local authority which have the power to make the [decision].'[45]

---

[41] (1881) 45 LT 439.

[42] *R v Secretary of State for the Home Department, ex p Al-Hasan* [2005] UKHL 13, per Lord Rodger, at para 9.

[43] *R v Secretary of State for the Environment, ex p Kirskstall Valley Campaign Ltd* [1996] 3 All ER 304, per Sedley J, at 321.   [44] [1984] 3 All ER 501.

[45] Per Woolf J, at 509.

The two approaches often intertwine. In a case when a panel of councillors refused to license premises as a sex establishment, and when it was shown that two of the members belonged to the majority group which had previously decided that it was not in favour of sex establishments, and, furthermore, when one of them had written to the local press saying that sex shops should be banned, it was held that Parliament had entrusted to local authorities the task of deciding whether or not to grant licences and that it was only to be expected that the local authority would use their local knowledge.[46] In *R v Crown Court at Bristol, ex p Cooper*,[47] it was accepted that licensing justices not only will have considerable knowledge, but will be expected to have a considerable knowledge of the licensing circumstances, policy and premises in the area for which they are responsible.

It has often been alleged that, because people are appointed to authorities, committees and appeal and other tribunals because of their expertise in the subject matter under discussion, such persons have automatically prejudged the issues and are, therefore, guilty of bias. Certainly, one aspect of the bias rule is that someone sitting to decide a case or an application must not already be prejudiced one way or another so as to have prejudged the issues involved. There has been much clutching at straws here. There are many examples of judicial approval of what is, after all, a desire to promote effective decision-making. In describing a person's qualification to sit on the Professional Conduct Committee of the General Medical Council as one of its lay members, it was opined: 'She brought to that membership an extensive knowledge of the health service in Wales, as a result of having worked there for many years as a nurse and midwife and her period of service as director of the South East Wales Institute. It is in the public interest that those who serve as lay members on disciplinary bodies of this kind should be well-informed and have experience of working in the area within which cases are likely to arise on which they may be called upon to adjudicate.'[48] In *Modahl v British Athletics Federation*,[49] an allegation of drug-taking was heard by a Disciplinary Committee the members of which were chosen (by the independent Drugs Advisory Committee) 'in order to provide a spread of expertise'. Some had been former athletes and three had competed at the highest level, one was appointed because of his medical knowledge, one for his legal knowledge, and one because he came from a different national athletic federation. The Court of Appeal commented:[50] 'The evidence was [that] there was no bias in the appointment or selection of membership of the five-person Disciplinary Committee. On the contrary, appropriate care had been taken to ensure a well-balanced and appropriately experienced committee in what was known to be a high profile case.' In *Flaherty v National Greyhound Racing Club*,[51] there was a complaint of bias in the composition of a stewards' inquiry for regulating the sport of greyhound racing. Scott Baker LJ emphasised[52] that one member 'was the veterinary steward and was appointed to the inquiry because of his expertise. [In] my judgment his expertise was a qualification rather than a disability. Although there does not appear to be any obligation for the veterinary steward to sit on an inquiry, there are many circumstances where his expertise is likely to prove invaluable and it is to be remembered that

---

[46] *R v Reading BC, ex p Quietlynn Ltd* (1986) 85 LGR 387.   [47] [1990] 2 All ER 193 (CA).
[48] *Nwabueze v General Medical Council* [2000] 1 WLR 1760, per Lord Hope, at 1771.
[49] [2001] EWCA Civ 1447.   [50] Per Mance LJ, at para 126.   [51] [2005] EWCA Civ 1117.
[52] At para 39.

animal welfare issues are likely to arise as well as doping issues.' The issue was confronted in:

Gillies v Secretary of State for Work and Pensions [2006] UKHL 2

Lord Hope

'2. In this case it is alleged that there was a reasonable apprehension that the medical member of a disability appeal tribunal was [biased].

3. [The] test which this House approved in *Porter v Magill* [p. 550] [is] whether the fair-minded and informed observer, having considered the facts, would conclude that there was a real possibility that the tribunal was biased. The issue for determination in this case therefore is whether, on the facts of the case, this test has been satisfied.

. . .

8. The factual background to this question can be stated quite simply. The medical member of the tribunal was Dr J F Armstrong. She [was appointed] to the panel of medical practitioners [from] which medical members of disability appeal tribunals were [drawn].

9. For a number of years Dr Armstrong had been providing reports for the Benefits Agency as an examining medical practitioner ("EMP"). [In] 1998 the Benefits Agency contracted out the provision of EMP reports in respect of a number of types of benefit to [a company] which subcontracted part of that work to another company [Nestor].

10. During the period from 1990 to 2000 Dr Armstrong provided an average of four EMP reports each month in disability living allowance cases. She carried out her examination of the claimants for the purposes of these reports in the claimants' own homes. [At] the time of the hearing of the appellant's appeal, Dr Armstrong was spending the majority of her working week either examining claimants and preparing reports on them for Nestor on behalf of the Benefits Agency, or sitting as a tribunal member hearing appeals relating to disability living allowance and other [benefits]. She was sitting as a tribunal member at an average of one session per [week].

11. The tribunal which heard the appellant's appeal was constituted in the usual way. There was a legally qualified chairman, and there were two panel members, one of whom was Dr Armstrong. Its decision to refuse the appeal was [unanimous].

. . .

17. The critical issue is whether the fair-minded and informed observer would conclude, having considered the facts, that there was a real possibility that Dr Armstrong would not evaluate reports by other doctors who acted as EMPs objectively and impartially against the other evidence. The fair-minded and informed observer can be assumed to have access to all the facts that are capable of being known by members of the public generally, bearing in mind that it is the appearance that these facts give rise to that matters, not what is in the mind of the particular judge or tribunal member who is under [scrutiny].

18. It is important to stress at the outset that the facts do not support the appellant's primary argument that Dr Armstrong was to be seen as a Benefits Agency doctor or that she was in some other way aligned with the Benefits Agency. [Her] relationship with the Benefits Agency was as an independent expert adviser. Her advice was sought and given because of the skills that she was able to bring to bear on medical issues in the exercise of her professional judgment. A fair-minded observer who had considered the facts properly would appreciate that professional detachment and the ability to exercise her own independent judgment on medical issues lay at the heart of her relationship with the Agency. He would also appreciate that she was just as capable of exercising those qualities when sitting as the medical member of a disability appeal tribunal. So there is no basis for a finding that there was a reasonable apprehension of bias on the ground that Dr Armstrong had a predisposition to favour the interests of the Benefits Agency. Nor, it must be emphasised, is there any suggestion that she did

or said anything in the course of her work which might be thought to cast doubt on her impartiality or her integrity.

19. The question then is whether there were grounds for thinking that Dr Armstrong was likely to be unconsciously biased when she was examining the medical evidence because of a predisposition to prefer the EMP report as against any contrary evidence due simply to her current involvement in providing reports as an EMP. Doctors holding current engagements to provide these reports can be assumed, no doubt, to have a special interest and experience in this kind of work. [But] why should these facts be said to lead to the conclusion that there was a real possibility that she was biased in favour of the views expressed by the EMP?

20. The weakness of the argument that this was a real possibility is exposed as soon as the task that Dr Armstrong was performing as an EMP is compared with the task which she was performing on the tribunal. In each of these two roles she was being called upon to exercise an independent professional judgment, drawing upon her medical knowledge and her experience. The fair-minded observer would understand that there is a crucial difference between approaching the issues which the tribunal had to decide with a predisposition in favour of the views of the EMP, and drawing upon her medical knowledge and experience when testing those views against the other evidence. He would appreciate, looking at the matter objectively, that her knowledge and experience could cut both ways as she would be just as well placed to spot weaknesses in these reports as to spot their strengths. He would have no reason to think, in the absence of any other facts indicating the contrary, that she would not apply her medical knowledge and experience in just the same impartial way when she was sitting as a tribunal member as she would when she was acting as an EMP.

21. [The] observer would appreciate that Dr Armstrong's experience of working as an EMP would be likely to be of benefit to her, and through her to the other tribunal members, when she was evaluating the EMP report. The exercise of her independent judgment, after all, was the function that she was expected to perform as the tribunal's medical member. Her experience in the preparation of these reports was an asset which was available, through her, for the other tribunal members to draw upon when they were considering the whole of the evidence.

22. One of the strengths of the tribunal system as it has been developed in this country is the breadth of relevant experience that can be built into it by the use of lay members to sit with members who are legally qualified. [The] panel system provided for the appointment of persons to act as members of disability appeal [tribunals] gives effect to that principle. There [are] two panels for each area, one composed of medical practitioners and the other composed of persons experienced in dealing with the needs of disabled persons in a professional or voluntary capacity or because they themselves are disabled. It would greatly undermine the practical utility of this system if panel members were to be disabled from sitting on cases because their experience was likely to give them an advantage when examining the evidence over those who did not have the same background.

23. The fact is that the bringing of experience to bear when examining evidence and reaching a decision upon it has nothing whatever to do with bias. [Impartiality] consists in the absence of a predisposition to favour the interests of either side in the dispute. Therein lies the integrity of the adjudication system. But its integrity is not compromised by the use of specialist knowledge or experience when the judge or tribunal member is examining [the evidence].

. . .

27. In my opinion the idea that Dr Armstrong was likely to be predisposed in favour of reports by EMP practitioners simply because she had a special interest in and experience of the preparation of these reports has no objective basis in the evidence. The test for her disqualification on the ground of apparent bias has not been made [out].'

A traditional question is: how much bias must be shown for a decision to be invalidated? Actual bias causes no problem if it can be proved. These are cases in which a decision-maker is shown, in fact and for whatever reason, to have been influenced in his or her decision-making by 'prejudice, predilection or personal interest'. Here, 'the law is very clear and very emphatic: where a decision is shown to have been tainted by actual bias it cannot stand'.[53] However, in practice no administrator, gravy train dependant, minister or magistrate is going to be silly enough to provide evidence of actual bias, even in today's sleaze-ridden society. Therefore the test had to be a lesser one. But which one?

There is the 'automatic disqualification' principle. Here, the existence of bias is presumed. In this category of case, the mere fact of being a party to the action or having a financial, proprietary, or other relevant interest in its outcome, including the active (and the emphasis is on 'active') promotion of the same particular cause as a party, is sufficient to cause the person's 'automatic' disqualification, without any investigation into whether there was a danger, likelihood or suspicion of bias. As stated above, the most important disqualifying interest is that of a pecuniary or proprietorial interest[54] and the rule against bias in the case of an alleged pecuniary interest is strict. 'There is no doubt that any direct pecuniary interest, however small, in the subject of inquiry, does disqualify a person from acting as a judge in the matter.'[55] 'It is, of course, clear that any direct pecuniary or proprietary interest in the subject-matter of a proceeding, however small, operates as an automatic disqualification.'[56] With regard to non-pecuniary interest 'a long line of cases shows that it is not merely of some importance, but is of fundamental importance, that justice should not only be done but should manifestly and undoubtedly be seen to be done'.[57] What has been considered as Lord Hewart's finest hour was considered in:

Re Pinochet [1999] UKHL 1

Lord Browne-Wilkinson

'Background facts

Senator Pinochet was the Head of State of Chile from [1973 until 1990]. It is alleged that during that period there took place in Chile various crimes against humanity (torture, hostage taking and murder) for which he was knowingly responsible. In October 1998 Senator Pinochet was in this country receiving medical treatment. In October and November 1998 the judicial authorities in Spain issued international warrants for his arrest to enable his extradition to Spain to face trial for those alleged [offences]. Senator Pinochet was arrested. He immediately applied to the Queen's Bench Divisional Court to quash the [arrest warrant. This raised the question] as to "the proper interpretation and scope of the immunity enjoyed by a former Head of State from arrest and extradition proceedings in the United Kingdom in respect of acts committed while he was Head of [State]".

The court proceedings

The Divisional Court [unanimously quashed the warrant] on the ground that Senator Pinochet was entitled to [immunity. The] matter proceeded to your Lordships' House with great speed. It was heard [by] a committee consisting of Lord Slynn of Hadley, Lord Lloyd of Berwick, Lord Nicholls of Birkenhead, Lord Steyn and Lord Hoffmann. However, before the main hearing of the appeal, there was an interlocutory decision of the greatest importance for the purposes of the present application. Amnesty International ("AI") [petitioned for leave to intervene in the appeal and] AI accordingly became an intervener in the [appeal].

---

[53] *R v Inner West London Coroner, ex p Dallaglio* [1994] 4 All ER, per Sir Thomas Bingham, at 162.
[54] *Dimes v The Proprietors of the Grand Junction Canal Co* (1852) 3 HLC 759.
[55] *R v Rand* (1866) LR 1 QB 230, per Blackburn J, at 232.
[56] *R v Camborne Justices, ex p Pearce* [1955] 1 QB 41.   [57] *Sussex Justices*, p. 536.

The hearing of this case [produced] an unprecedent degree of public interest not only in this country but worldwide. The case raises fundamental issues of public international law and their interaction with the domestic law of this country. The conduct of Senator Pinochet and his régime have been highly contentious and emotive matters. There are many Chileans and supporters of human rights who have no doubt as to his guilt and are anxious to bring him to trial somewhere in the world. There are many others who are his supporters and believe that he was the saviour of Chile. Yet a third group believe that, whatever the truth of the matter, it is a matter for Chile to sort out internally and not for third parties to interfere in the delicate balance of contemporary Chilean politics by seeking to try him outside [Chile].

The decision and afterwards

Judgment in your Lordships' House was given on 25 November 1998. The appeal was allowed by a majority of three to two and your Lordships' House restored the [arrest warrant]. Of the majority, Lord Nicholls and Lord Steyn each delivered speeches holding that Senator Pinochet was not entitled to immunity: Lord Hoffmann agreed with their speeches but did not give separate reasons for allowing the appeal. Lord Slynn and Lord Lloyd each gave separate speeches setting out the reasons for their dissent. As a result of this decision, Senator Pinochet was required to remain in this country to await the decision of the Home Secretary whether to authorise the continuation of the proceedings for his [extradition].

The link between Lord Hoffmann and AI

[On] 10 December 1998, Senator Pinochet lodged the present petition asking that the order of 25 November 1998 should either be set aside completely or the opinion of Lord Hoffmann should be declared to be of no effect. The sole ground relied upon was that Lord Hoffmann's links with AI were such as to give the appearance of possible bias. It is important to stress that Senator Pinochet makes no allegation of actual bias against Lord Hoffmann; his claim is based on the requirement that justice should be seen to be done as well as actually being [done].

Amnesty International and its constituent parts

[AI] itself is an unincorporated, non profit making organisation founded in 1961 with the object of securing throughout the world the observance of the provisions of the Universal Declaration of Human Rights in regard to prisoners of [conscience]. AI consists of sections in different countries throughout the world and its International Headquarters in London. [The] work of the International Headquarters is undertaken through two United Kingdom registered companies Amnesty International Limited ("AIL") and Amnesty International Charity Limited ("AICL"). AIL is an English limited company incorporated to assist in furthering the objectives of AI and to carry out the aspects of the work of the International Headquarters which are not charitable. AICL is a company limited by guarantee and also a registered [charity]. It appears that AICL was incorporated [to] carry out such of the purposes of AI as were [charitable].

I can give one example of the close interaction between the functions of AICL and AI. The report of the Directors of AICL for the year ended 31 December 1993 records that AICL commissioned AIL to carry out charitable activities on its behalf and records as being included in the work of AICL certain research publications. One such publication related to Chile and referred to a report issued as an AI report in 1993. Such 1993 report covers not only the occurrence and nature of breaches of human rights within Chile, but also the progress of cases being brought against those alleged to have infringed human rights by torture and otherwise in the courts of Chile. It records that "no one was convicted during the year for past human rights violations. The military courts continued to claim jurisdiction over human rights cases in civilian courts and to close cases covered by the 1978 Amnesty law." It also records "Amnesty International continued to call for full investigation into human rights violations and for those responsible to be brought to justice. The organisation also continued to call for the abolition of the death penalty." Again, the report stated that "Amnesty International included references to its concerns about past human rights violations against indigenous peoples in Chile and the lack of accountability of those responsible." Therefore AICL was involved in the reports of AI urging the punishment of those guilty in Chile for past breaches of human rights and also referring to such work as being part of the work that it supported.

The Directors of AICL do not receive any remuneration. Nor do they take any part in the policy-making activities of AI. Lord Hoffmann is not a member of AI or of any other body connected with [AI].

[Conclusion—Apparent bias]

[Senator] Pinochet does not allege that Lord Hoffmann was in fact biased. The contention is that there was a real danger or reasonable apprehension or suspicion that Lord Hoffmann might have been biased, that is to say, it is alleged that there is an appearance of bias not actual bias.

The fundamental principle is that a man may not be a judge in his own cause. This principle, as developed by the courts, has two very similar but not identical implications. First it may be applied literally: if a judge is in fact a party to the litigation or has a financial or proprietary interest in its outcome then he is indeed sitting as a judge in his own cause. In that case, the mere fact that he is a party to the action or has a financial or proprietary interest in its outcome is sufficient to cause his automatic disqualification. The second application of the principle is where a judge is not a party to the suit and does not have a financial interest in its outcome, but in some other way his conduct or behaviour may give rise to a suspicion that he is not impartial, for example because of his friendship with a party. This second type of case is not strictly speaking an application of the principle that a man must not be judge in his own cause, since the judge will not normally be himself benefiting, but providing a benefit for another by failing to be impartial.

In my judgment, this case falls within the first category of case, where the judge is disqualified because he is a judge in his own cause. In such a case, once it is shown that the judge is himself a party to the cause, or has a relevant interest in its subject matter, he is disqualified without any investigation into whether there was a likelihood or suspicion of bias. The mere fact of his interest is sufficient to disqualify him unless he has made sufficient [disclosure]. I will call this "automatic disqualification".

[The starting-point was *Dimes*, p. 534] in which a judge was indeed purporting to decide a case in which he was a party. This was held to be absolutely prohibited. That absolute prohibition was then extended to cases where, although not nominally a party, the judge had an interest in the outcome. The importance of this point in the present case is this. Neither AI, nor AICL, have any financial interest in the outcome of this litigation. We are here confronted, as was Lord Hoffmann, with a novel situation where the outcome of the litigation did not lead to financial benefit to anyone. The interest of AI in the litigation was not financial; it was its interest in achieving the trial and possible conviction of Senator Pinochet for crimes against humanity.

By seeking to intervene in this appeal and being allowed so to intervene, in practice AI became a party to the appeal. Therefore if, in the circumstances, it is right to treat Lord Hoffmann as being the alter ego of AI and therefore a judge in his own cause, then he must have been automatically disqualified on the grounds that he was a party to the appeal. Alternatively, even if it be not right to say that Lord Hoffmann was a party to the appeal as such, the question then arises whether, in non financial litigation, anything other than a financial or proprietary interest in the outcome is sufficient automatically to disqualify a man from sitting as judge in the cause.

Are the facts such as to require Lord Hoffmann to be treated as being himself a party to this appeal? [I] do not think it would be right to identify Lord Hoffmann personally as being a party to the appeal. He is closely linked to AI but he is not in fact AI. Although this is an area in which legal technicality is particularly to be avoided, it cannot be ignored that Lord Hoffmann took no part in running AI. Lord Hoffmann, AICL and the Executive Committee of AI are in law separate people.

Then is this a case in which it can be said that Lord Hoffmann had an "interest" which must lead to his automatic disqualification? Hitherto only pecuniary and proprietary interests have led to automatic disqualification. But, as I have indicated, this litigation is most unusual. [Most] unusually, by allowing AI to intervene, there is a party to a criminal cause or matter who is neither prosecutor nor accused.

That party, AI, shares with the Government of Spain and the [Crown Prosecution Service], not a financial interest but an interest to establish that there is no immunity for ex-Heads of State in relation to crimes against humanity. The interest of these parties is to procure Senator Pinochet's extradition and trial— a non-pecuniary interest. So far as AICL is concerned, [one] of its objects is "to procure the abolition of torture, extra-judicial execution and disappearance". [In] my opinion, therefore, AICL plainly had a non-pecuniary interest, to establish that Senator Pinochet was not immune.

That being the case, the question is whether in the very unusual circumstances of this case a non-pecuniary interest to achieve a particular result is sufficient to give rise to automatic disqualification and, if so, whether the fact that AICL had such an interest necessarily leads to the conclusion that Lord Hoffmann, as a Director of AICL, was automatically disqualified from sitting on the appeal? My Lords, in my judgment, although the cases have all dealt with automatic disqualification on the grounds of pecuniary interest, there is no good reason in principle for so limiting automatic disqualification. The rationale of the whole rule is that a man cannot be a judge in his own cause. In civil litigation the matters in issue will normally have an economic impact; therefore a judge is automatically disqualified if he stands to make a financial gain as a consequence of his own decision of the case. But if, as in the present case, the matter at issue does not relate to money or economic advantage but is concerned with the promotion of the cause, the rationale disqualifying a judge applies just as much if the judge's decision will lead to the promotion of a cause in which the judge is involved together with one of the parties. Thus in my opinion if Lord Hoffmann had been a member of AI he would have been automatically disqualified because of his non-pecuniary interest in establishing that Senator Pinochet was not entitled to [immunity].

Can it make any difference that, instead of being a direct member of AI, Lord Hoffmann is a Director of AICL, that is of a company which is wholly controlled by AI and is carrying on much of its work? Surely not. The substance of the matter is that AI, AIL and AICL are all various parts of an entity or movement working in different fields towards the same goals. If the absolute impartiality of the judiciary is to be maintained, there must be a rule which automatically disqualifies a judge who is involved, whether personally or as a Director of a company, in promoting the same causes in the same organisation as is a party to the [suit].

Since, in my judgment, the relationship between AI, AICL and Lord Hoffmann leads to the automatic disqualification of Lord Hoffmann to sit on the hearing of the appeal, it is unnecessary to consider [other factors, such as] the fact that Lord Hoffmann was involved in the recent appeal for funds for Amnesty. Those factors might have been relevant if Senator Pinochet had been required to show a real danger or reasonable suspicion of bias. But since the disqualification is automatic and does not depend in any way on an implication of bias, it is unnecessary to consider these factors. I do, however, wish to make it clear (if I have not already done so) that my decision is not that Lord Hoffmann has been guilty of bias of any kind: he was disqualified as a matter of law automatically by reason of his Directorship of AICL, a company controlled by a party, [AI].'

It will happen that a decision-maker is not a party to the suit, does not have a financial or other relevant interest in its outcome, and cannot derive any benefit from that outcome (and, therefore, may not be automatically disqualified), but in some other way his or her conduct or behaviour may give rise to a suspicion that he or she is not impartial, for example because of his or her friendship or other relationship with a party. There were, for a long time, two approaches: the 'real likelihood or real danger' test and the 'sufficient that a reasonable person would think or suspect that an authority might be biased' test. The argument is illustrated by the following dicta: 'We have not to inquire what impression might be left on the minds [of] the public generally. We have to satisfy ourselves that there was a real likelihood of bias, and not merely satisfy ourselves that that was the sort of impression which might reasonably get abroad. [Bias] is or may be an unconscious thing and a man may honestly say that he was not actually biased and did not allow his interest to affect his mind, although, nevertheless, he may have allowed it unconsciously to do so. The matter must be determined on the probabilities to be inferred from the circumstances in which the justices sit.'[58] In 'considering whether there was a real likelihood of bias, the court does not look at the mind of the [person] who sits in a judicial capacity. It does not look to see if there was a real likelihood that he would, or did, in fact favour one side at the expense of the other. The court looks at the impression which would be given to other people. Even if he was as impartial as could be, nevertheless if right-minded persons would think that, in the circumstances, there was a real likelihood of bias on his part, then he should not sit. And if he does sit, his decision cannot stand.'[59] 'With profound respect to those who have propounded the "real likelihood" test, I take the view that the requirement that justice must manifestly be done operates with undiminished force in cases where bias is alleged and that any development of the law which appears to emasculate that requirement should be strongly resisted.'[60]

'To my mind, there really is little (if any) difference between the two tests which are propounded in the cases which have been cited to us. If a reasonable person who has no knowledge of the matter beyond knowledge of the relationship which subsists between some members of the tribunal and one of the parties would think that there might well be bias, then there is in his opinion a real likelihood of bias. Of course, someone else with inside knowledge of the characters of the members in question might say: "Although things don't look very well, in fact there is no real likelihood of bias." That, however, would be beside the point, because the question is not whether the tribunal will in fact be biased, but whether a reasonable man with no inside knowledge might well think that it might be biased.'[61]

At one time, the House of Lords decreed *ex cathedra* that henceforth the 'Gough real danger' test was sacrosanct, infallible, and must be universally applied:

R v Gough [1993] AC 646

Robert Gough was convicted of conspiracy with his brother, David Gough, to commit certain robberies and was sentenced to 15 years' imprisonment. After the trial it was found that a member of the jury was David Gough's next door neighbour. The defence case was based, inter alia, on the premise that David Gough was one of the robbers. Both brothers had a record of previous convictions and, during the trial, photographs of both brothers had been produced to the jury, and retained by them. In addition, the vehicle alleged to have been used in one robbery was owned by Elaine Gough, David Gough's wife, and her statement including her address was read to the jury. Robert Gough claimed that, because of the presence on the jury of David Gough's next door neighbour, there was a serious irregularity in the conduct of the trial and, therefore, his conviction should be quashed. The Court of Appeal held that the test was 'whether there was a real danger that Gough might not have had a fair trial and not whether a reasonable and fair-minded person sitting in court and knowing all the facts would have had a reasonable suspicion that a fair trial for Gough had not been possible'. The Court of Appeal held that there was no real danger and the House of Lords agreed.

Lord Goff, at 670

'The argument [was] presented on the basis that there were two rival, alternative tests for bias to be found in the authorities, and that the result in the present case depended on the choice made by your Lordships' House between them. The first test, [was] whether a reasonable and fair-minded person

58 *R v Barnsley Justices* [1960] 2 QB 167 (CA), per Devlin LJ, at 186–187.
59 *Metropolitan Properties v Lannon* [1969] 1 QB 577 (CA), per Lord Denning MR, at 598–600.
60 *Metropolitan Properties v Lannon* [1969] 1 QB 577 (CA), per Edmund Davies LJ, at 504.
61 *Hannam v Bradford Corporation* [1970] 1 WLR 937 (CA), per Cross LJ, at 949.

sitting in the court and knowing all the relevant facts would have had a reasonable suspicion that a fair trial by the defendant was not possible. The second test, [was] whether there was a real likelihood of bias. I shall for convenience refer to these two tests respectively as the reasonable suspicion test and the real likelihood test. It was recognised [that], if the real likelihood test is to be preferred, the appeal must fail. [At] the heart of the present inquiry lies the need to identify the precise nature of these tests, and to consider what, if any, are the differences between [them].

[I] wish to express my understanding of the law as follows. I think it possible, and desirable, that the same test should be applicable in all cases of apparent bias, whether concerned with justices or members of other inferior tribunals, or with [jurors]. Furthermore, I think it unnecessary, in formulating the appropriate test, to require that the court should look at the matter through the eyes of a reasonable man, because the court in cases such as these personifies the reasonable man; and in any event the court has first to ascertain the relevant circumstances from the available evidence, knowledge of which would not necessarily be available to an observer in court at the relevant time. Finally, for the avoidance of doubt, I prefer to state the test in terms of real danger rather than real likelihood, to ensure that the court is thinking in terms of possibility rather than probability of bias. Accordingly, having ascertained the relevant circumstances, the court should ask itself whether, having regard to those circumstances, there was a real danger of bias on the part of the relevant member of the tribunal in question, in the sense that he might unfairly regard (or have unfairly regarded) with favour, or disfavour, the case of a party to the issue under consideration by [him].'

Locabail (UK) v Bayfield Properties Ltd [1999] EWCA Civ 3004

Lord Bingham CJ

'2. In determination of their rights and liabilities, civil or criminal, everyone is entitled to a fair hearing by an impartial tribunal. That right, guaranteed by the European Convention on Human Rights, is properly described as fundamental. The reason is obvious. All legal arbiters are bound to apply the law as they understand it to the facts of individual cases as they find them. They must do so without fear or favour, affection or ill-will, that is, without partiality or prejudice. Justice is portrayed as blind not because she ignores the facts and circumstances of individual cases but because she shuts her eyes to all considerations extraneous to the particular case.

3. Any judge (for convenience, we shall in this judgment use the term "judge" to embrace every judicial decision-maker, whether judge, lay justice or juror) who allows any judicial decision to be influenced by partiality or prejudice deprives the litigant of the important right to which we have referred and violates one of the most fundamental principles underlying the administration of justice. Where in any particular case the existence of such partiality or prejudice is actually shown, the litigant has irresistible grounds for objecting to the trial of the case by that judge (if the objection is made before the hearing) or for applying to set aside any judgment given. Such objections and applications based on what, in the case law, is called "actual bias" are very [rare].

4. There is, however, one situation in which, on proof of the requisite facts, the existence of bias is effectively presumed, and in such cases it gives rise to what has been called automatic disqualification. That is where the judge is shown to have an interest in the outcome of the case which he is to decide or has [decided].

. . .

7. The basic rule is not in doubt. Nor is the rationale of the rule: that if a judge has a personal interest in the outcome of an issue which he is to resolve, he is improperly acting as a judge in his own cause;

and that such a proceeding would, without more, undermine public confidence in the integrity of the administration of [justice].

. . .

16. In practice, the most effective guarantee of the [rule against bias is afforded not] by the rules which provide for disqualification on grounds of actual bias, nor by those which provide for automatic disqualification, because automatic disqualification on grounds of personal interest is extremely rare and judges routinely take care to disqualify themselves, in advance of any hearing, in any case where a personal interest could be thought to arise. The most effective protection of the right is in practice afforded by a rule which provides for the disqualification of a judge, and the setting aside of a decision, if on examination of all the relevant circumstances the court concludes that there was a real danger (or possibility) of bias. Until 1993 there had been some divergence in the English authorities. Some had expressed the test in terms of a reasonable suspicion or apprehension of [bias. Others] had expressed the test in terms of a real danger or likelihood of [bias. Whatever] the merits of these competing tests, the law was settled in England and Wales by the House of Lords' decision in [*Gough*, p. 545].

17. [We] need not debate whether the substance of the two tests is [different]. Nor need we consider whether application of the two tests would necessarily lead to the same outcome in all cases. For whatever the merit of the reasonable suspicion or apprehension test, the test of real danger or possibility has been laid down by the House of Lords and is binding on every subordinate court in England and [Wales]. In the overwhelming majority of cases we judge that application of the two tests would anyway lead to the same outcome. Provided that the court, personifying the reasonable man, takes an approach which is based on broad common sense, without inappropriate reliance on special knowledge, the minutiae of court procedure or other matters outside the ken of the ordinary, reasonably well-informed member of the public, there should be no risk that the courts will not ensure both that justice is done and that it is perceived by the public to be [done].

. . .

25. It would be dangerous and futile to attempt to define or list the factors which may or may not give rise to a real danger of bias. Everything will depend on the facts, which may include the nature of the issue to be decided. We cannot, however, conceive of circumstances in which an objection could be soundly based on the religion, ethnic or national origin, gender, age, class, means or sexual orientation of the judge. Nor, at any rate ordinarily, could an objection be soundly based on the judge's social or educational or service or employment background or history, nor that of any member of the judge's family; or previous political associations; or membership of social or sporting or charitable bodies; or Masonic associations; or previous judicial decisions; or extra-curricular utterances (whether in text books, lectures, speeches, articles, interviews, reports or responses to consultation papers); or previous receipt of instructions to act for or against any party, solicitor or advocate engaged in a case before him; or membership of the same Inn, circuit, local Law Society or [chambers]. By contrast, a real danger of bias might well be thought to arise if there were personal friendship or animosity between the judge and any member of the public involved in the case; or if the judge were closely acquainted with any member of the public involved in the case, particularly if the credibility of that individual could be significant in the decision of the case; or if, in a case where the credibility of any individual were an issue to be decided by the judge, he had in a previous case rejected the evidence of that person in such outspoken terms as to throw doubt on his ability to approach such person's evidence with an open mind on any later occasion; or if on any question at issue in the proceedings before him the judge had expressed views, particularly in the course of the hearing, in such extreme and unbalanced terms as to throw doubt on his ability to try the issue with an objective judicial [mind]; or if, for any other reason, there were real ground for doubting the ability of the judge to ignore extraneous considerations, prejudices and predilections and bring an objective judgment to bear on the issues before [him].

There was a reaction, nay rebellion:

....

Director General of Fair Trading v Proprietary Association of Great Britain
[2000] EWCA Civ 350

The Restrictive Practices Court heard an application by the Director General of Fair Trading. Lightman, J, was the presiding judge and, since the application raised issues of accountancy and economics, Mr James Scott (an accountant) and Dr Rowlatt (an economist) were appointed as the two other members. The application related to resale price maintenance and branded medicaments. The case was contested by two trade associations who represented a large number of the manufacturers and retailers of branded medicaments. Mr Zoltan Biro, a co-founder and Director of Frontier Economics (an economic consultancy firm), was a principal expert witness in the proceedings for the Director General. His report concerned the impact on small independent community pharmacies if resale price maintenance were to be abolished. The trade associations contended that the analysis carried out by Mr Biro was methodologically unsound, employed inappropriate techniques and reasoning and drew erroneous conclusions. The case was almost over when Dr Rowlatt admitted that she had, while the hearing was actually going on, decided to ring Frontier Economics to ask them if they would consider her for a part time post. Frontier Economics replied that there were no vacancies 'for a person of your experience and are unlikely to [be] so for the foreseeable future'. Later she stated that 'If I had had in mind the involvement of Frontier Economics in the case, I would never have made the application in the first [place]. I am confident that I retain [the] essential independence of mind required of a member of the Court and [I] do not consider that I ought to recuse myself.' It was submitted that the test was not to evaluate the likelihood or danger that Dr Rowlatt was actually biased; the Court should consider whether the factual situation was one which gave rise to a reasonable apprehension of the possibility of bias; the test in law was whether the facts of the case were such as to raise a reasonable apprehension in the mind of the objective onlooker that Dr Rowlatt might be affected by bias, whether conscious or unconscious, when performing her judicial duties. Lord Phillips, MR, referred to article 6 of the European Convention on Human Rights and the obligation under the Human Rights Act 1998 to give effect to the right to a fair trial as embodied in Article 6, and stated that this was an occasion to review *Gough* (p. 545) to see whether the test it laid down was, or was not, in conflict with the case law of the European Court of Human Rights in Strasbourg.

Lord Phillips MR

'37. Bias is an attitude of mind which prevents the Judge from making an objective determination of the issues that he has to resolve. A Judge may be biased because he has reason to prefer one outcome of the case to another. He may be biased because he has reason to favour one party rather than another. He may be biased not in favour of one outcome of the dispute but because of a prejudice in favour of or against a particular witness which prevents an impartial assessment of the evidence of that witness. Bias can come in many forms. It may consist of irrational prejudice or it may arise from particular circumstances which, for logical reasons, predispose a Judge towards a particular view of the evidence or issues before him.

38. The decided cases draw a distinction between "actual bias" and "apparent bias". The phrase "actual bias" has not been used with great precision and has been applied to the situation 1 where a Judge has been influenced by partiality or prejudice in reaching his decision and 2 where it has been demonstrated that a Judge is actually prejudiced in favour of or against a party. "Apparent bias" describes the situation where circumstances exist which give rise to a reasonable apprehension that the Judge may have been, or may be, biased.

39. Findings of actual bias on the part of a Judge are rare. The more usual issue is whether, having regard to all the material circumstances, a case of apparent bias is made [out].

40. It has long been held that where a Judge has a pecuniary interest in the outcome of a case, he is automatically [disqualified].

. . .

63. The decision in *Gough* received critical analysis by the High Court of Australia in *Webb v The Queen* [(1994) 181 C.L.R. 41 at 50–52]:

"[This Court prefers] the reasonable suspicion or apprehension test. [In] the light of the decisions of this Court which hold that the reasonable apprehension or suspicion test is the correct test for determining a case of alleged bias against a judge, it is not possible to use the 'real danger' test as the general test for bias without rejecting the authority of those decisions. [There] is a strong reason why we should continue to prefer the reasoning in our own cases to that of the House of Lords. In *Gough*, the House of Lords rejected the need to take account of the public perception of an incident which raises an issue of bias except in the case of a pecuniary interest. Behind this reasoning is the assumption that public confidence in the administration of justice will be maintained because the public will accept the conclusions of the judge. But the premise on which the decisions in this Court are based is that public confidence in the administration of justice is more likely to be maintained if the Court adopts a test that reflects the reaction of the ordinary reasonable member of the public to the irregularity in question. References to the reasonable apprehension of the 'lay observer', the 'fair-minded observer', the 'fair-minded, informed lay observer', 'fair-minded people', the 'reasonable or fair-minded observer', the 'parties or the public', and the 'reasonable person' abound in the decisions of this Court and other courts in this country. They indicate that it is the court's view of the public's view, not the court's own view, which is determinative. If public confidence in the administration of justice is to be maintained, the approach that is taken by fair-minded and informed members of the public cannot be [ignored]. "

64. These comments presuppose that the "real danger" test may lead the Court to reach a conclusion as to the likelihood of bias which does not reflect the view that the informed observer would form on the same facts—and this because the viewpoint of the Judge may not be the same as that of members of the [public].

. . .

67. What is the Court to do where, although inclined to accept a statement about what the Judge under review knew at any material time, it recognises the possibility of doubt and the likelihood of public scepticism? It is invidious for the reviewing Court to question the word of the Judge in such circumstances, but less so to say that the objective onlooker might have difficulty in accepting it.

68. Such a situation highlights a wider consideration. [A] finding that in a particular case there is a real danger that a particular Judge was biased inevitably carries with it a slur on the Judge in question, albeit that the reviewing Court may take pains to emphasise that the bias may have been [unconscious].

69. The problem with the "real danger" test is particularly acute where a Judge is invited to recuse himself. In such a situation it is invidious to expect a Judge to rule on the danger that he may actually be influenced by partiality. The test of whether the objective onlooker might have a reasonable apprehension of bias is manifestly more satisfactory in such circumstances.

70. [We] turn to consider the Strasbourg [jurisprudence].

. . .

84. [The Strasbourg] approach comes close to that in *Gough*. The difference is that when the Strasbourg Court considers whether the material circumstances give rise to a reasonable apprehension of bias, it makes it plain that it is applying an objective test to the circumstances, not passing judgment on the likelihood that the particular tribunal under review was in fact biased.

85. When the Strasbourg jurisprudence is taken into account, we believe that a modest adjustment of the test in *Gough* is called for, which makes it plain that it is, in effect, no different from the test applied in most of the Commonwealth and in Scotland. The Court must first ascertain all the

circumstances which have a bearing on the suggestion that the Judge was biased. It must then ask whether those circumstances would lead a fair-minded and informed observer to conclude that there was a real possibility, or a real danger, the two being the same, that the tribunal was biased.

. . .

The material circumstances in the present case

95. What concerns would the remarkable facts that we have set out above raise in the mind of a fair-minded observer? The Restrictive Practices Court is, in this case, going to have to resolve a fundamental conflict of economic analysis between rival economic consultants. [Counsel] stated that her clients considered that Dr Rowlatt had, by making her application for employment to one of these consultants, indicated a partiality to them which could not be undone. We consider that the fair-minded observer would be concerned that, if Dr Rowlatt esteemed Frontier sufficiently to wish to be employed by them, she might consciously or unconsciously be inclined to consider them a more reliable source of expert opinion than their rivals.

96. [Counsel] advanced a more basic contention—that an objective bystander would conclude that Dr Rowlatt might still harbour hopes that, sooner or later, she might find employment with Frontier and that this might induce in her, whether consciously or unconsciously, a reluctance to reject as unsound evidence advanced by Frontier's experts.

97. We agree [that] the fair-minded observer would not be convinced that all prospects of Dr Rowlatt working for Frontier at some time in the future had been destroyed, nor that she might not still hope, in due course, to work for [Frontier].

98. It is for these reasons that we concluded that a fair-minded observer would apprehend that there was a real danger that Dr Rowlatt would be unable to make an objective and impartial appraisal of the expert evidence placed before the Court by Frontier and that, on objection being taken, she should have recused herself.

99. Having reached this decision, we then had to consider the position of the other two members of the Court. The trial had reached an advanced stage by the time that it was [interrupted]. Dr Rowlatt must have discussed the economic issues with the other members of the Court. We concluded that it was inevitable that the decision that Dr Rowlatt should be disqualified carried with it the consequence that the other two members of the Court should stand down.

100. We reached our decision with great regret. Its consequence is that an immense amount of industry will have gone for nothing, and very substantial costs will be thrown [away].'

Magill v Porter [2001] UKHL 67

The case concerned alleged political corruption (and this aspect will be considered in detail at p. 566). Mr Magill was an auditor appointed by the Audit Commission to audit the accounts of Westminster City Council. As part of the process, he issued a preliminary provisional report and invited those concerned to indicate whether they wished him to hold an oral hearing. He made a public statement which representatives of the media were invited to attend and which attracted widespread publicity on television news, in the press and in Parliament. The statement raised questions about his impartiality. There was a request to the Audit Commission to replace Mr Magill but the Audit Commission refused to do so. An application was made that Mr Magill should disqualify himself from further consideration of the process but Mr Magill decided that he should not disqualify himself.

Lord Hope

'95. [The] respondents submit that the way in which the auditor conducted himself when he made his statement [indicated] an appearance of bias on his part which affected all stages of his investigation both before and after that [date].

. . .

101. The English courts have been reluctant, for obvious reasons, to depart from the test which Lord Goff of Chieveley so carefully formulated in [*Gough*, p. 545].

102. In my opinion however it is now possible to set this debate to rest. The Court of Appeal took the opportunity in [*Director General*, p. 548] to reconsider the whole question. Lord Phillips [observed] that the precise test to be applied when determining whether a decision should be set aside on account of bias had given rise to difficulty, reflected in judicial decisions that had appeared in conflict, and that the attempt to resolve that conflict in [*Gough*] had not commanded universal approval. [He] said that, as the alternative test had been thought to be more closely in line with Strasbourg jurisprudence which [the] English courts were required to take into account, the occasion should now be taken to review [*Gough*] to see whether the test it lays down is, indeed, in conflict with Strasbourg jurisprudence. Having conducted that review he summarised the court's [conclusions]: "When the Strasbourg jurisprudence is taken into account, we believe that a modest adjustment of the test in [*Gough*] is called for, which makes it plain that it is, in effect, no different from the test applied in most of the Commonwealth and in Scotland. The court must first ascertain all the circumstances which have a bearing on the suggestion that the judge was biased. It must then ask whether those circumstances would lead a fair-minded and informed observer to conclude that there was a real possibility, or a real danger, the two being the same, that the tribunal was biased."

103. I respectfully suggest that your Lordships should now approve the modest adjustment of the test in [*Gough*]. It expresses in clear and simple language a test which is in harmony with the objective test which the Strasbourg court applies when it is considering whether the circumstances give rise to a reasonable apprehension of bias. It removes any possible conflict with the test which is now applied in most Commonwealth countries and in Scotland. I would however delete from it the reference to "a real danger". Those words no longer serve a useful purpose here, and they are not used in the jurisprudence of the Strasbourg court. The question is whether the fair-minded and informed observer, having considered the facts, would conclude that there was a real possibility that the tribunal was biased.

. . .

105. I think that it is plain [that] the auditor made an error of judgment when he decided to make his statement in public at a press conference. The main impression which this would have conveyed to the fair-minded observer was that the purpose of this exercise was to attract publicity to himself, and perhaps also to his firm. It was an exercise in self-promotion in which he should not have indulged. But it is quite another matter to conclude from this that there was a real possibility that he was biased. [The] question is what the fair-minded and informed observer would have thought, and whether his conclusion would have been that there was real possibility of bias. The auditor's conduct must be seen in the context of the investigation which he was carrying out, which had generated a great deal of public interest. A statement as to his progress would not have been inappropriate. His error was to make it at a press conference. This created the risk of unfair reporting, but there was nothing in the words he used to indicate that there was a real possibility that he was biased. He was at pains to point out to the press that his findings were provisional. There is no reason to doubt his word on this point, as his subsequent conduct demonstrates. I would hold, looking at the matter objectively, that a real possibility that he was biased has not been demonstrated.'

Taylor v Lawrence [2002] EWCA Civ 90

Lord Woolf CJ

'60. [Fortunately, in *Magill v Porter*, p. 550], the House of Lords has put to rest the conflicting views as to how the test in cases of apparent bias should be expressed. It can now be said that the approach should be: "The court must first ascertain all the circumstances which have a bearing on the suggestion that the judge was biased. It must then ask whether those circumstances would lead a fair-minded and informed observer to conclude that there was a real possibility that the tribunal was [biased]."

. . .

64. [Judges] should be circumspect about declaring the existence of a relationship where there is no real possibility of it being regarded by a fair minded and informed observer as raising a possibility of bias. If such a relationship is disclosed, it unnecessarily raises an implication that it could affect the judgment and approach of the judge. If this is not the position no purpose is served by mentioning the relationship. On the other hand, if the situation is one where a fair minded and informed person might regard the judge as biased, it is important that disclosure should be made. If the position is borderline, disclosure should be made because then the judge can consider, having heard the submissions of the parties, whether or not he should withdraw. In other situations disclosure can unnecessarily undermine the litigant's confidence in the judge.

65. If disclosure is made, then full disclosure must be made. [If] there has been partial disclosure and the litigant learns that this is the position, this is naturally likely to excite suspicions in the mind of the litigant concerned even though those concerns are unjustified.'

Lawal v Northern Spirit Limited [2003] UKHL 35

Lord Bingham

'14. In *Porter v Magill* [p. 550] the House of Lords approved a modification of the common law test of bias enunciated in [*Gough*, p. 545]. The House unanimously endorsed this proposal. In the result there is now no difference between the common law test of bias and the requirements under Article 6 of the Convention of an independent and impartial tribunal, the latter being the operative requirement in the present [context. Public] perception of the possibility of unconscious bias is the key. It is unnecessary to delve into the characteristics to be attributed to the fair-minded and informed observer. What can confidently be said is that one is entitled to conclude that such an observer will adopt a balanced [approach].'

It has been emphasised that it is 'clear both as a matter of principle and authority that once proceedings have been successfully impugned for want of independence and impartiality on the part of the tribunal, the decision itself must necessarily be regarded as tainted by unfairness and so cannot be permitted to stand'.[62] In other words, the original decision is a nullity, the case must start all over again with all the disadvantages to all concerned, except for those looking to redouble their claims to legal costs. The comment in *Director General of Fair Trading*[63] says all: 'We reached our decision with great regret. Its consequence is that an immense amount of industry will have gone for nothing, and very substantial costs will be thrown away.'[64] Advice on the timing of raising issues of bias and the response with regard to recusal by the decision-maker has been given in:

Sir Alexander Morrison v AWG Group [2006] EWCA Civ 6

When the judge was preparing for the case, he noticed that it was intended to call as a witness for AWG Group a Richard Jewson, who was formerly a director of AWG and chairman of the audit sub-committee of its board. Jewson was well known to the judge, lived in the next village, they had played tennis together, their families had known each other for at least 30 years, their children were friends, the families had dined together on a number of occasions. The judge admitted, most honestly, that he 'would have the greatest difficulty in dealing with a case in which Mr Jewson was a witness where a challenge was to be made as to the truthfulness of his evidence'. AWG decided that, in order to avoid

---

[62] *R v Secretary of State for the Home Department, ex p Al-Hasan* [2005] UKHL 13, per Lord Brown, at 43.
[63] See p. 550.   [64] [2000] EWCA Civ 350, per Lord Phillips MR, at para 100.

the judge's embarrassment and rather than risk his withdrawal and the consequent delay in obtaining another judge and his completing the pre-reading process, not to call Mr Jewson to give evidence, since they did not regard him as other than a relatively peripheral witness. The defendants did not agree, because they would be denied the opportunity to cross-examine Mr Jewson, they would be unable to ask the judge to draw inferences from his failure to give evidence, as he was chairman of the audit committee, any criticism of his fellow directors to discharge their duties was likely to constitute a criticism of Mr Jewson, and the defendants might even wish to call him as a witness, even if AWG did not.

Mummery LJ

'21. In my judgment, the judge ought to have recused himself in the unfortunate circumstances in which, through no fault of his own or of anyone else, he was placed. [My] assessment of the circumstances bearing on the issue of apparent judicial bias is as follows.

22. First, the judge knew Mr Jewson and Mr Jewson knew the judge. It was not a fleeting acquaintance. They had known each other for 30 years. The judge recognised that this fact alone was potentially a valid ground of objection to his trying the case when he acknowledged that he would have "the greatest difficulty" if he had to deal with a challenge to Mr Jewson's evidence.

. . .

29. [In] terms of time, cost and listing it might well be more efficient and convenient to proceed with the trial, but efficiency and convenience are not the determinative legal values: the paramount concern of the legal system is to administer justice, which must be, and must be seen by the litigants and fair-minded members of the public to be, fair and impartial. Anything less is not worth having.

30. [Adjourning] the trial now is bad enough for all concerned, but an even worse disaster, such as having to abort the trial several months into the hearing and to start all over again, may be waiting to happen. That would be inefficient, as well as unjust. It is a potential disaster that can be avoided. A decision must be made now one way or the other. By far the safer course is to remove all possibility of apparent bias by the recusal of the judge before the trial even begins. There will be other judges available to try this case and there will be other cases available for this judge to try.'

Finally, one question arises frequently in practice. Many authorities, boards, committees and tribunals are composed of several members, and, in order to preclude over-frequent 'draws', there is an odd number of members. The question which arises is: given that one member of the decision-making body is biased, actually or presumed, does that invalidate the decision of the majority of (unbiased) members. As is so often the case, it all depends on the facts, the extent to which the biased member participated in the proceedings, influenced them and his or her fellow member, and even dominated those proceedings either by reason of being the chairman or by reason of a domineering personality. In *Director General of Fair Trading*,[65] the Court of Appeal determined: 'Having reached this decision, we then had to consider the position of the other two members of the Court. The trial had reached an advanced stage by the time that it was [interrupted]. Dr Rowlatt must have discussed the economic issues with the other members of the Court. We concluded that it was inevitable that the decision that Dr Rowlatt should be disqualified carried with it the consequence that the other two members of the Court should stand down.'[66] In *Modahl*,[67] having held that 'Dr Lucking was tainted by apparent bias. An informed person, that is a person knowing, as the judge found, that Dr Lucking had in 1991, albeit in the heat of the moment, asserted that athletes were guilty unless they were able to prove that they were innocent of doping, would consider that there was a risk that he might, albeit unconsciously, be affected by that attitude', the court continued: 'If this, of itself, produced [unfairness], the judge's findings of fact however conclusively

[65] See p. 550.   [66] [2000] EWCA Civ 350, per Lord Phillips MR, at para 99.   [67] See p. 538.

establish that that breach caused no loss. Whatever Dr Lucking's state of mind, the evidence of the other three members of the Committee who gave evidence satisfied the judge that they were not in anyway infected by Dr Lucking, and came to a wholly independent judgment on the evidence which was fully justified by the material before them.'[68]

III. Illegality

(a) The general principle

The second condition precedent to an exercise of authority within jurisdiction listed in head I is that the decision-maker must not misunderstand or misapply the appropriate law. 'The case must be one of the kind mentioned in the [statute]. If the inferior tribunal, as a result of its misconstruing the statutory description of the kind of case in which it has jurisdiction to enquire, makes a purported determination in a case of a kind into which it has not jurisdiction to inquire, its purported determination is a nullity.'[69]

Very often this depends on the meaning of simple words, which then turn out not to be so simple. Examples to be considered are 'laundry', 'park', 'house'. Such words sometimes have to be construed with great care. Fulham Corporation was once empowered by statute to establish wash-houses so that persons could wash their own clothes. The Corporation decided to establish a municipal laundry, where clothes were washed by corporation employees. The court, therefore, had to interpret the statute to determine whether a power to establish a 'wash-house' included a power to establish a 'laundry'. It was held that 'wash-house' had a specific meaning of a place where people washed clothes for themselves and a 'laundry' had a specific meaning of a place where people took their clothes to be washed by someone else. Therefore, the Corporation had acted illegally.[70] In *R v Paddington and St Marylebone Rent Tribunal, ex p Bell, London and Provincial Properties*,[71] the court was concerned with methods of controlling the rents that landlords could charge their tenants. The system of rent control had been reintroduced after the war because there was a scarcity of privately owned property and this had the tendency to put up the rents in a sellers' market. The system, at that time, only related to 'furnished lettings' (where the tenant both occupied the property and had the use of furniture provided by the landlord) under the Furnished Houses (Rent Control) Act 1946. One feature of the system was that as well as permitting tenants to apply to the rent tribunal, local authorities were also empowered to refer cases to the rent tribunal, in order that some tenants might be protected without the fear that an application to the tribunal would prejudice them in the eyes of their landlords. The local authority, empowered, therefore, to refer 'furnished lettings' to rent tribunals, was held to have no jurisdiction to refer a large number (300) of flats in one block of flats, some of which were 'unfurnished'. More recently, there have been numerous cases on whether a piece of land was a 'town or village green',

---

[68] [2001] EWCA Civ 1447, per Latham LJ, at para 68.
[69] *Anisminic v Foreign Compensation Commission* [1968] 2 QB 862, per Diplock LJ, at 890–891.
[70] *A-G v Fulham Corporation* [1921] 1 Ch 440.   [71] [1949] 1 KB 666.

defined as including 'land on which the inhabitants of any locality have indulged in [lawful] sports and pastimes as of right for not less than 20 years'.[72]

Often, of course, a claim of illegality will fail. For example, in *Ashbridge Investments Ltd v Minister of Housing and Local Government*,[73] Stalybridge Borough Council wanted to clear an area of land for redevelopment as part of their slum clearance programme. They had power to do so if there were 'houses unfit for human habitation'. They drew up a map determining a clearance area, which included two terraced houses which were in a tumble down condition. After a public inquiry, the inspector concluded that one 'property' was an unfit house but the second 'property' had lost its identity as a house. The minister accepted this and removed the second property from the map. The owner of the properties objected to the inclusion of the first property on the map (because, if it was included as a 'house', he would not have received as much compensation as if it were not a 'house'). He claimed that because of the standard of the property, it was not a 'house'. It was held that the decision whether a property was an unfit house, a fit house or not a house was entrusted by the relevant legislation to the minister, that the inspector had taken into account all relevant considerations, that, on the facts before the minister, there was plenty of evidence that the building was a house and that it was unfit for human habitation. The courts would not substitute their decision for that of the minister in such circumstances and would only interfere if there was absolutely no such evidence or the building was undoubtedly not a 'house'.

White and Collins v Minister of Health [1939] 2 KB 838 (CA)

Local authorities were empowered to acquire by compulsory acquisition land for housing purposes (Housing Act 1936, section 74). However, nothing was to authorise the compulsory acquisition of 'any land which forms part of any park, garden or pleasure ground' (section 75). Ripon Borough Council made a compulsory purchase order of 23 acres of land forming part of the grounds of a large house called Highfield (35 acres in all) on the outskirts of Ripon. There was a public inquiry at which considerable emphasis was placed on the fact that the land in question was not used by the occupiers but was let on a yearly tenancy to a farmer for grazing cattle. The inquiry inspector reported to the minister, who confirmed the compulsory purchase order and (in an affidavit to the Court of Appeal) stated: 'it was considered that the [land] did not form part of the park, garden or pleasure ground of Highfield'.

Mackinnon LJ, at 847

'It is true that thirty-five acres is not a very large piece of ground. But I see no reason why it should not be a park, if perhaps a small [one]. Upon the evidence before us I am satisfied that this land was part of a park within the meaning of section 75 of the Act of 1936, that its compulsory purchase was therefore not within the powers of the Act, and that therefore the order of the minister ought to be quashed.'

Luxmore LJ, at 852–856

'[What] is meant by the word "park"? Is it used here in its strict legal sense, or is it used in its wider and more popular meaning? In its strict legal significance the word "park" means "a tract of land enclosed and privileged for wild beasts of chase by the Monarch's grant or by prescription"; while in its popular sense (see the second definition in the Oxford English Dictionary) it is used to describe "a large

---

[72] Commons Registration Act 1965, section 22(1). See *R v Oxfordshire County Council, ex p Sunningwell Parish Council* [2000] 1 AC 335; *R v City of Sunderland, ex p Beresford* [2003] UKHL 60; *Oxfordshire County Council v Oxford City Council* [2006] UKHL 25. Note, also, *Anisminic*, p. 514 ('successor in title'), and *Pearlman*, p. 527 ('structural alteration, extension or addition').   [73] [1965] 1 WLR 1320 (CA).

ornamental piece of ground usually comprising woodland and pasture, attached to or surrounding a country house or mansion and used for recreation, and often for keeping deer, cattle or sheep". The word "park" has frequently been held to have been used in its popular sense in Acts of [Parliament]. I have no hesitation in holding that in the Housing Act 1936, the word "park" is used in its popular [meaning]. The evidence in the affidavits in support of the application is uncontradicted, and leads only to the conclusion that the land is part of the park. [The] most important matter to bear in mind is that the jurisdiction to make the order is dependent on a finding of fact: for, unless the land can be held not to be part of a park or not to be required for amenity or convenience, there is no jurisdiction in the borough council to make, or in the minister to confirm, the order. In such a case it seems almost self-evident that the court which has to consider whether there is jurisdiction to make or confirm the order must be entitled to review the vital finding on which the existence of the jurisdiction relied upon depends. If this were not so, the right to apply to the court would be illusory.'

(b) Failure to act

Sometimes a citizen will complain that the law grants a power to act but the public authority has not acted. We are not so much concerned with cases where there is a duty to act clearly laid down in the statute which is deliberately disobeyed by the public authority (for example should a local authority cancel their refuse collection service or close all their schools), but with circumstances where there has been a sort of decision or determination which (on closer examination) turns out not to be a proper exercise of power. Delegation has already been discussed (head II(b)). Two further matters need to be examined.

'Surrendering discretion' occurs when a public authority invested with a decision-making power will appear to take a decision itself, and prima facie not seem to be delegating the actual decision-making power, when in reality this is not so. It may be that the authority is obeying the will of another body in whom Parliament has not vested the particular decision-making power:

Ellis v Dubowski [1921] 3 KB 621

Under the Cinematograph Act 1909, a local authority 'may grant licences to such persons as they think fit to use the premises [for the purpose of showing films] on such terms and conditions and under such restrictions as the [authority] may by the respective licences determine'. The local authority attached to the grant of the licence the following condition: 'That no film be shown which is likely to be injurious to morality or to encourage or incite to crime, or lead to disorder, or be in any way offensive in the circumstances to public feeling or which contains any offensive representations of living persons or which has not been certified for public exhibition by the British Board of Film Censors.' Dubowski, the proprietor of the Gaiety Theatre, Twickenham, had shown a film called 'Auction of Souls' which had not been certified for public exhibition by the British Board of Film Censors.

Lawrence CJ, at 625

'[The] requirement under the condition that a film should be certified by the British Board of Film Censors before it can be shown is bad and *ultra vires* the licensing committee. The condition sets up an authority whose *ipse dixit* is to control the exhibition of films. The effect is to transfer a power which belongs to the County Council and can be delegated to committees of the Council or to district councils or to justices sitting in petty sessions alone. I think that such a condition is unreasonable, and that the committee had no power to impose [it]. I am prepared to assume that the powers of the Board are exercised wisely and discreetly. But the committee have no power to create an absolute body from which no right of appeal exists [and] a condition putting the matter into the hands of a third person or body not possessed of statutory or constitutional authority is *ultra vires* the committee.'

Avory J, at 626

'[I] also agree, although with considerable doubt and hesitation, that [the] condition as to the certificate of the British Board of Film Censors is so unreasonable as to be *ultra vires* the licensing authorities. I do so solely because, as the condition stands, the Board could prohibit the exhibition of a film, although it might be neither injurious to morality, nor an encouragement to crime or disorder, nor contain offensive representations of living persons. The Board are thus given absolute power to prohibit for reasons which may be private or may be influenced by trade considerations. I do not say that they are likely so to be influenced, but I think that this possibility is sufficient to render the condition *ultra vires*.'

Mills v London County Council [1925] 1 KB 213

Harry Mills was the owner of the Nelson Electric Theatre, Camberwell. He was granted by the local authority under the Cinematograph Act 1909 a licence subject to the following condition: 'That no film which has not been passed for universal exhibition by the British Board of Film Censors shall be exhibited in the premises without the express consent of the Council during the time that any child under or appearing to be under the age of sixteen is therein.' He was prosecuted for allowing the showing of a film (entitled 'Woman to Woman') which had been classed by the British Board of Film Censors as an 'A' film (ie unsuitable for children and not for universal exhibition) when unaccompanied children under sixteen were present. His defence was that the condition was *ultra vires*.

Lord Hewart CJ, at 219–221

'[It] is important to remember that under the Cinematograph Act, 1909, the licensing authority is given, and no doubt most deliberately given, very wide [powers]. As was said by Lord Alverstone CJ in *London County Council v Bermondsey Bioscope* [[1911] 1 KB 445, at 551]: "The language of [the statute] seems to me to be quite clear and we must therefore construe it according to its plain meaning. In my opinion that section is intended to confer on the County Council a discretion as to the conditions which they will impose, so long as those conditions are not unreasonable." [It is said that] this condition is bad, because it means that the London County Council have delegated, or transferred, to the British Board of Film Censors no small part of the duties of the London County Council under the Act, and reference is made to *Ellis v Dubowski* [p. 556]. In that case the condition which was attached to the licence was in these terms: "That no film be [shown] which has not been certified for public exhibition by the British Board of Film Censors." It was held with some doubt that that condition was unreasonable and *ultra vires*. In the present case that mischief is avoided. This condition with which we are now concerned provides an exception where the express consent of the Council is given. In other words, there is an appeal in the matter from the decision of the British Board of Film Censors to the Council itself.'

H Lavender & Son Ltd v Minister of Housing and Local Government [1970] 1 WLR 1231

Lavender applied for planning permission to extract sand and gravel from land which was high class agricultural land and included in an 'agricultural reservation'. The local planning authority refused the permission and Lavender appealed to the minister. The Ministry of Agriculture objected to the application in order to conserve agricultural land. The minister dismissed the appeal, stating in the decision letter: 'It is the minister's present policy that land in the reservations should not be released for mineral working unless the Minister of Agriculture is not opposed to the working. In the present case the agricultural objection has not been waived, and the minister has therefore decided not to grant planning permission for the working of the appeal site.'

Willis J, at 1236–1241

'It is those last two sentences in the decision letter which lie at the heart of the matter in issue: and it is submitted [by counsel for Lavender] that they show, in this case, that the minister had so fettered his own discretion to decide the appeal by the policy which he had adopted that the decisive matter was not the exercise of his own discretion upon a consideration of the report and other material considerations, but the sustained objection of the Minister of Agriculture. In effect he says that the decision was not that of the Minister of Housing and Local Government, the authority entrusted with the duty to decide, but of the Minister of Agriculture, who had no status save perhaps in a consultative capacity and certainly no status to make the effective [decision]. He really puts his argument in two ways— (1) that the minister has fettered his discretion by a self-created rule of policy, and (2) that the minister, who has a duty to exercise his own discretion in determining an appeal, has in this case delegated that duty to the Minister of Agriculture, who has no such duty and is, statutorily, a stranger to any decision.

It is, of course, common [ground] that the minister is entitled to have a policy and to decide an appeal in the context of that policy. He can also differ from the inspector on any question of fact, and disagree with the inspector's conclusions and recommendations. He can, and no doubt should, reject any recommendation of an inspector which runs counter to his policy, [since] it is of the very essence of the [statutory duties laid upon the minister] that he should secure consistency and continuity in the framing and execution of a national policy with respect to the use and development of [land].

[It seems to me that the minister] has said in language which admits of no doubt that his decision to refuse permission was solely in pursuance of a policy not to permit minerals in [the] agricultural reserve to be worked unless the Minister of Agriculture was not opposed to their [working]. How can his mind be open to persuasion, how can an applicant establish an "exceptional case" in the face of an inflexible attitude by the Minister of Agriculture? That attitude was well known before the inquiry, it was maintained during the inquiry, and presumably thereafter. The inquiry was no doubt, in a sense, into the Minister of Agriculture's objection, since, apart from that objection, it might well have been that no inquiry would have been necessary, but I do not think that the minister after the inquiry can be said in any real sense to have given genuine consideration to whether on planning (including agricultural) grounds this land could be worked. It seems to me that by adopting and applying his stated policy he has in effect inhibited himself from exercising a proper discretion (which would of course be guided by policy considerations) in any case where the Minister of Agriculture has made and maintained an objection to mineral working in an agricultural reservation. Everything else might point to the desirability of granting permission, but by applying and acting on his stated policy I think the minister has fettered himself in such a way that in this case it was not he who made the decision for which Parliament made him responsible. It was the decision of the Minister of Agriculture not to waive his objection which was decisive in this case, and while that might properly prove to be the decisive factor for the minister when taking into account all material considerations, it seems to me quite wrong for a policy to be applied which in reality eliminates all the material considerations save only the consideration, when that is the case, that the Minister of Agriculture objects. That means, as I think, that the minister has by his stated policy delegated to the Minister of Agriculture the effective decision on any appeal within the agricultural reservations where the latter objects to the working. I am satisfied that [Lavender] should succeed. I think the minister failed to exercise a proper or indeed any discretion by reason of the fetter which he imposed upon its exercise in acting solely in accordance with his stated policy: and further, that upon the true construction of the minister's letter the decision to dismiss the appeal, while purporting to be that of the minister was in fact, and improperly that of the Minister of [Agriculture].'

'Fettering discretion' occurs when a public authority lays down general principles as to how it will exercise its discretion and in applying such a general principle refuses to consider each case on the merits and within the boundaries of its discretion. Very often we are concerned with general principles applying a discretionary power to local conditions, and this is almost a legislative power. London County Council had power to make bye-laws relating to the parks in their area. They made a bye-law which prohibited the sale of any article in their parks without the consent of the council. The council later passed a resolution—a resolution and not another bye-law—that existing consents to sell articles in the parks would be withdrawn and that no new consents would be given in future. It was held that the existence of the bye-law seemed to indicate that there was a legitimate expectation that some consents would be given—otherwise why make the bye-law, why not simply prohibit all sales in the parks. While the bye-law had a legal existence, it conferred a discretion on the council, namely to give consideration to all applications for consent, and the council's resolution could not empower the council not to exercise this discretion.[74] Licensing justices had power to grant 'occasional' licences (licences outside the normal system where the application is for the sale of alcohol at premises not normally licensed for the sale of alcohol and beyond the normal licensing hours). The Rotheram Justices decided to make it a general policy that the number of occasional licences to be granted to any individual would be limited to two per year and that an interval of at least three months must elapse before the granting of a second licence to an individual. It was held that the rule or principle which was to define for the future the limits within which alone applications for an occasional licence would be granted 'seems plainly designed to prevent the application of an unfettered judgment to the individual case, and to prescribe in advance a hard-and-fast [rule]. That seems to me to be an abdication of the duty of the justices impartially to consider upon the particular facts and merits of each individual application.'[75] In *Sagnata Investments v Norwich Corporation*,[76] the 1963 Betting, Gaming and Lotteries Act provided that the granting or renewal of a permit to run amusement arcades was to be 'at the discretion of the local authority'. Sagnata applied for a permit to operate an amusement arcade, but this was refused because the Norwich council had passed a general policy decision not to grant permits for any such amusement places in Norwich. There was no objection to Sagnata on the normal grounds of suitability of site, premises and management. In other words no application to the local authority, however suitable, would have succeeded. It was held that 'the Council had not exercised any form of discretion. They had simply dismissed this application after going through the necessary motions without regard to its individual merits or demerits.'[77] Although the Prison Service may legitimately have a policy that children should normally cease to reside with their mothers in prison when they became 18 months old, the service cannot fetter its discretion by operating the policy rigidly, insisting that all children should leave their mothers, however catastrophic the effect of separation might be.[78]

Stringer v Minister of Housing and Local Government [1970] 1 WLR 1281

Stringer applied to Congleton Rural District Council for outline planning permission to build houses on 'the appeal site' (as it is called). The application was refused and the council gave as their principal reason for refusing: 'The site is in close proximity to the Jodrell Bank Authority Research Station and the

[74] *R v LCC, ex p Corrie* [1918] 1 KB 68.
[75] *R v Rotherham Licensing Justices* [1939] 2 All ER 710, per Lord Hewart CJ, at 713.
[76] [1971] 2 QB 614 (CA).   [77] Per Phillimore LJ, at 639.
[78] *R (P and Q) v Secretary of State for the Home Department* [2001] EWCA Civ 1151.

development if approved, would be likely to seriously interfere with the efficient running of the radio telescope.' Stringer appealed to the minister who appointed an inspector to hold a public inquiry. The minister, following the recommendation of the inspector, upheld the refusal to grant planning permission.

Cooke J, at 1284–1298

'The site of the proposed development is an area of some four and three-quarter acres [and] is just over four miles from the Nuffield Radio Astronomy Laboratories at Jodrell Bank. These laboratories are a department of Manchester University, and they are, of course, nationally and internationally famous as being the seat of the Jodrell Bank telescope, the world's largest radio telescope. This department of the university is under the direction of Professor Sir Bernard Lovell FRS, who has been the moving spirit in the conception and birth of the telescope and in the growth and development of the important scientific activities which depend upon [it]. Electrical sparks and other forms of disturbance from terrestrial sources in the neighbourhood of the telescope produce signals which bear a remarkable similarity to the signals which the telescope receives from outer space. Signals from terrestrial sources can thus interfere with the work of the telescope, but the danger of interference from such sources tends to diminish as their distance from the telescope increases. [The] telescope was built in the knowledge that certain towns and villages existed in the [neighbourhood]. It has always been a matter of anxiety to Sir Bernard Lovell that there should be as little further development as possible within a radius of two miles from the telescope on the north side and within a radius of some six miles from the telescope on the eastern, western and southern sides. Outside, but adjacent to a zone thus roughly delimited, certain forms of development might be a source of concern as giving rise to the kind of activities and incidents which produce [interference]. Sir Bernard's evidence at the inquiry, in addition to demonstrating his impatience with terrestrial interference in any form whatsoever, dealt in the most cogent and authoritative manner with the anticipated effect of the proposed development on the work of the telescope. He said that if Mr Stringer's appeal were allowed a very serious danger would arise to the continued operation of the telescope. That evidence was uncontradicted.

After making his findings of fact, the inspector set out his conclusions: "[The] strength of the arguments made at the inquiry in support of this reason for refusal are overwhelming. On the evidence I must accept that the erection of 23 dwellings on the appeal site, no matter how phased, would constitute a serious danger to the continued satisfactory operation of the Jodrell Bank telescope." The inspector then recommended that the appeal be dismissed. The minister issued his [decision]: "The minister agrees with the inspector's conclusions and accepts his recommendation. He is satisfied on the evidence put forward, and in particular having regard to the inspector's conclusions quoted above, that the development proposed might interfere to a serious extent with the working of the Jodrell Bank telescope [and] that as a result planning permission should not be granted."

[The] minister's anxiety that proper provision should be made for protecting the interests of the telescope is clear from many years of history. He has encouraged the definition by agreement of areas in which development is likely to interfere with the work of the telescope. He has encouraged arrangements for consultation between local authorities and the Jodrell Bank directorate about applications for planning permission in those areas. All that appears to me to be perfectly proper and in no way inconsistent with the proper performance of the minister's quasi-judicial duties when occasion arises to perform them. The matter, however, may be said to go further than that, because it appears that the minister has a policy for the area around Jodrell Bank, [a] policy of discouraging development which would interfere with the efficient working of the telescope. It is not, however, as it seems to me, a policy which is intended to be pursued to the disregard of other relevant considerations. The question is whether the existence of such a policy disables the minister from acting fairly on the consideration of an appeal.

There are obviously many matters in the field of planning legislation on which the minister is entitled and indeed bound to have a policy. The relationship between a minister's functions in formulating and giving effect to a policy and his functions in making a decision of a quasi-judicial nature have been considered in many [cases]. It seems to me that the general effect of the many relevant authorities is that a minister charged with the duty of making individual administrative decisions in a fair and impartial manner may nevertheless have a general policy in regard to matters which are relevant to those decisions, provided that the existence of that general policy does not preclude him from fairly judging all the issues which are relevant to each individual case as it comes up for decision.

I think that in this case the minister was entitled to have a policy in regard to Jodrell Bank, and I think that his policy is not such as to preclude him from fairly considering a planning appeal on its merits. I do not think that it precluded him from fairly considering Mr Stringer's appeal. I do not think that the minister has prejudged the case, or tied his own hands, or abdicated any of his [functions].'

IV. Irrationality

The third condition precedent to an exercise of authority within jurisdiction listed in head I is that the decision-maker's decision must not be vitiated by irrationality, where the decision is outrageously absurd, or utterly illogical or perversely defies accepted standards to such an extent that no rational person could have taken it.

(a) The context

Cases where the courts are called upon to adjudicate on the rationality of administrative action most frequently arise where public authorities are given by statute wide powers to act according to their own discretion and are not bound by detailed rules. However, sometimes an irrationality challenge may be made to the policy on which administrative action or statutory enactment is based. For the moment, let us take a few examples of discretion-giving statutes: 'If the Secretary of State is satisfied [that any local education authority] have acted or are proposing to act unreasonably with respect to the exercise of any power conferred or the performance of any duty imposed by or under this Act, he may give such directions as to the exercise of the power or the performance of the duty as appear to him to be expedient.'[79] 'A local housing authority may make such reasonable charges for the tenancy or occupation of the houses as they may determine.'[80] 'A local authority may make bye-laws for the good rule and government of the whole or any part of their area and for the prevention or suppression of nuisances therein.'[81]

There are several noticeable features in discretion-giving statutes such as are cited above. First, the use of subjective language ('if X is satisfied', 'thinks fit', and 'deem expedient'). Second, there are limited rights of appeal, and this might suggest a deliberate decision by Parliament that the arbiter (and final arbiter) on matters of fact, and inferences to be drawn from fact, and matters of policy, should be the public authority concerned. Third, the statutes predominantly (but not exclusively) relate to the exercise of power within a particular locality where the public authority's appreciation of the local situation (by means of opportunity for

---

[79] Education Act 1996, section 496.   [80] Housing Act 1985, section 24.
[81] Local Government Act 1972, section 235.

inquiry and objection or by presumed views expressed through the ballot box) may be a decisive factor.[82] Fourth, the public authority may be constrained in the exercise of its discretion not by motives of irrationality of its own creation but by economic constraints,[83] especially those imposed on local government by central government, and physical factors beyond its control:

R v London Borough of Barnet, ex p G, R v London Borough of Lambeth, ex p W, R v London Borough of Lambeth, ex p A [2003] UKHL 57

Lord Nicholls

'1. These three appeals concern the responsibilities of local authorities for the accommodation of children who are in [need].

. . .

10. Behind the legal questions arising in these appeals is the seemingly intractable problem of local authorities' lack of resources. Local authorities discharge a wide range of functions, from education to housing, upkeep of roads to disposal of waste. All these activities call for money, of which there is never enough to go round. Often there is also a shortage, sometimes acute, of other resources such as trained staff.

11. The financial resources of local authorities are finite. The scope for local authorities to increase the amount of their revenue is strictly limited. So, year by year, they must decide what priority to give to the multifarious competing demands on their limited resources. They have to decide which needs are the most urgent and pressing. The more money they allocate for one purpose the less they have to spend on another. In principle, this decision on priorities is entrusted to the local authorities themselves. In respect of decisions such as these council members are accountable to the local electorate.

12. The ability of a local authority to decide how its limited resources are best spent in its area is displaced when the authority is discharging a statutory duty as distinct from exercising a power. A local authority is obliged to comply with a statutory duty regardless of whether, left to itself, it would prefer to spend its money on some other purpose. A power need not be exercised, but a duty must be discharged. That is the nature of a duty. That is the underlying purpose for which duties are imposed on local authorities. They leave the authority with no choice.

13. The extent to which a duty precludes a local authority from ordering its expenditure priorities for itself varies from one duty to another. The governing consideration is the proper interpretation of the statute in question. But identifying the precise content of a statutory duty in this respect is not always easy. This is perhaps especially so in the field of social welfare, where local authorities are required to provide services for those who need them. As a general proposition, the more specific and precise the duty the more readily the statute may be interpreted as imposing an obligation of an absolute character. Conversely, the broader and more general the terms of the duty, the more readily the statute may be construed as affording scope for a local authority to take into account matters such as cost when deciding how best to perform the duty in its own area. In such cases the local authority may have a wide measure of freedom over what steps to take in pursuance of its duty.'

In many cases, the High Court (not normally being granted direct appellate jurisdiction, not being local, and not being faced with inescapable problems of resources—but being entrusted with using its age-old common law jurisdiction of ascertaining, interpreting and applying the will of Parliament) is forced to tread a path not of primroses but of thorns. If, for example, the

---

[82] See *Thameside*, p. 572.   [83] See the dilemma in *Coughlan*, p. 586.

courts say to a public authority that the authority have acted illegally over introducing comprehensive education, imposing conditions to the grant of planning permission, deciding not to give students a liquor licence, deciding to pay their officers higher than average wages, deciding to charge their tenants an uneconomic rent, determining not to allocate health service funds to certain categories of person, defining its community care parameters, operating its anti-terrorist programmes, so often the immediate reaction of the public authority (especially ministers found to have been economical with the truth) is to counter-attack by accusing the judges of being political.

It is almost axiomatic to commence with *Associated Provincial Picture Houses v Wednesbury Corporation*. This is the key case and one which is cited so very often that the compendium of principles taken from centuries of common law administrative justice and developed in the nineteenth century[84] which is enumerated in the judgment of Lord Greene, MR, is now called the '*Wednesbury* principles' and it is normal to refer to '*Wednesbury* unreasonableness'.

Associated Provincial Picture Houses v Wednesbury Corporation
[1948] 1 KB 223 (CA)

The Corporation had power to grant licences for the opening of cinemas on Sundays 'subject to such conditions as the authority think fit to impose'. The Corporation, when granting a Sunday licence, imposed a condition that no children under fifteen should be admitted.

Lord Greene MR, at 227–234

'Mr Gallop, for the plaintiffs, argued that it was not competent for the Wednesbury Corporation to impose any such condition and he said that if they were entitled to impose a condition prohibiting the admission of children, they should at least have limited it to cases where the children were not accompanied by their parents or a guardian or some adult. His argument was that the imposition of that condition was unreasonable and that in consequence it was *ultra vires* the corporation. The plaintiffs' contention is based, in my opinion, on a misconception as to the effect of this Act in granting this discretionary power to local authorities. The courts must always, I think, remember this: first, we are dealing with not a judicial act, but an executive act; secondly, the conditions which, under the exercise of that executive act, may be imposed are in terms, so far as language goes, put within the discretion of the local authority without limitation. Thirdly, the statute provides no appeal from the decision of the local authority.

What, then, is the power of the courts? They can only interfere with an act of executive authority if it be shown that the authority has contravened the law. It is for those who assert that the local authority has contravened the law to establish that proposition. On the face of it, a condition of the kind imposed in this case is perfectly lawful. It is not to be assumed prima facie that responsible bodies like the local authority in this case will exceed their powers: but the court, whenever it is alleged that the local authority have contravened the law, must not substitute itself for that authority. It is only concerned with seeing whether or not the proposition is made good. When an executive discretion is entrusted by Parliament to a body such as the local authority in this case, what appears to be an exercise of that discretion can only be challenged in the courts in a strictly limited class of case. As I have said, it must always be remembered that the court is not a court of appeal. When discretion of this kind is granted the law recognises certain principles upon which that discretion must be exercised, but within the four corners of those principles the discretion, in my opinion, is an absolute one and cannot be questioned in any court of law. What then are those principles? They are well understood. They are principles which

[84] See p. 466.

the court looks to in considering any question of discretion of this kind. The exercise of such a discretion must be a real exercise of the discretion. If, in the statute conferring the discretion, there is to be found expressly or by implication matters which the authority exercising the discretion ought to have regard to, then in exercising the discretion it must have regard to those matters. Conversely, if the nature of the subject-matter and the general interpretation of the Act make it clear that certain matters would not be germane to the matter in question, the authority must disregard those irrelevant collateral [matters]. I am not sure myself whether the permissible grounds of attack cannot be defined under a single head. It has been perhaps a little bit confusing to find a series of grounds set out. Bad faith, dishonesty—those of course, stand by themselves—unreasonableness, attention given to extraneous circumstances, disregard of public policy and things like that have all been referred to, according to the facts of individual cases, as being matters which are relevant to the question. If they cannot all be confined under one head, they at any rate, I think, overlap to a very great extent. For instance, we have heard in this case a great deal about the meaning of the word "unreasonable". It is true the discretion must be exercised reasonably. Now what does that mean? Lawyers familiar with the phraseology commonly used in relation to exercise of statutory discretions often use the word "unreasonable" in a rather comprehensive sense. It has frequently been used and is frequently used as a general description of the things that must not be done. For instance, a person entrusted with a discretion must, so to speak, direct himself properly in law. He must call his own attention to the matters which he is bound to consider. He must exclude from his consideration matters which are irrelevant to what he has to consider. If he does not obey those rules, he may truly be said, and often is said, to be acting "unreasonably". Similarly, there may be something so absurd that no sensible person could ever dream that it lay within the powers of the [authority].

In the present case, it is said by Mr Gallop that the authority acted unreasonably in imposing this condition. It appears to me quite clear that the matter dealt with by this condition was a matter which a reasonable authority would be justified in considering when they were making up their mind what condition should be attached to the grant of this licence. Nobody, at this time of day, could say that the well-being and the physical and moral health of children is not a matter which a local authority, in exercising their powers, can properly have in mind when those questions are germane to what they have to consider. Here Mr Gallop did not, I think, suggest that the council were directing their mind to a purely extraneous and irrelevant matter, but he based his argument on the word "unreasonable", which he treated as an independent ground for attacking the decision of the authority; but once it is conceded, as it must be conceded in this case, that the particular subject-matter dealt with by this condition was one which it was competent for the authority to consider, there, in my opinion, is an end of the case. Once that is granted, Mr Gallop is bound to say that the decision of the authority is wrong because it is unreasonable, and in saying that he is really saying that the ultimate arbiter of what is and is not reasonable is the court and not the local authority. It is just there, it seems to me, that the argument breaks down. It is clear that the local authority are entrusted by Parliament with the decision on a matter which the knowledge and experience of that authority can best be trusted to deal with. The subject-matter with which the condition deals is one relevant for its consideration. They have considered it and come to a decision upon it. It is true to say that, if a decision on a competent matter is so unreasonable that no reasonable authority could ever have come to it, then the courts can interfere. That, I think, is quite right: but to prove a case of that kind would require something overwhelming, and, in this case, the facts do not come anywhere near anything of that kind. I think Mr Gallop in the end agreed that his proposition that the decision of the local authority can be upset if it is proved to be unreasonable, really meant that it must be proved to be unreasonable in the sense that the court considers it to be a decision that no reasonable body could have come to. It is not what the court considers unreasonable, a different thing altogether. If it is what the court considers unreasonable, the court may very well have different views to that of a local authority on matters of high public policy of this kind. Some courts might think that no children ought to be admitted on Sundays at all, some courts might think the reverse, and all over the country I have no doubt on a thing of that sort honest and sincere people hold different views. The effect of the legislation is not to set up the court as an arbiter of the correctness of one view over another. It is the local authority that are set in that position and, provided they act, as they have acted, within the four corners of their jurisdiction, this court, in my opinion, cannot [interfere].

In the result, this appeal must be dismissed. I do not wish to repeat myself but I will summarise once again the principle applicable. The court is entitled to investigate the action of the local authority with a view to seeing whether they have taken into account matters which they ought not to take into account, or, conversely, have refused to take into account or neglected to take into account matters which they ought to take into account. Once that question is answered in favour of the local authority, it may be still possible to say that, although the local authority have kept within the four corners of the matters which they ought to consider, they have nevertheless come to a conclusion so unreasonable that no reasonable authority could ever have come to it. In such a case, again, I think the court can interfere. The power of the court to interfere in each case is not as an appellate authority to override a decision of the local authority, but as a judicial authority which is concerned, and concerned only, to see whether the local authority have contravened the law by acting in excess of the powers which Parliament has confided in [them].'

From the *Wednesbury* principles and the decided cases, irrationality may be considered under a number of sub-headings. This is not an exhaustive list. There has been an explosion of judicial activity with regard to irrationality, especially following the entry into force of the Human Rights Act. What follows, albeit in a possibly unorthodox or even heretical exposition, represents case law in a state of flux.

(b) Misuse of power

A power granted for one purpose (purpose A) must not be used for the wrong purpose (purpose B). In *Hanson v Radcliffe UDC*,[85] local authorities had power to dismiss teachers 'on educational grounds'. Hanson was an uncertificated teacher and was earning more than the appropriate rate for such teachers. The council asked all uncertificated teachers to resign and if they did this they would be offered new contracts, but on the lower scale. Hanson refused and was dismissed. It was held that the dismissal was not on educational grounds, but rather to save money. The statute had been used for a wrong purpose. In *Grice v Dudley Corporation*,[86] Dudley Corporation had, in 1937, made a compulsory purchase order on Grice's shop for the purposes of widening a road. Compensation was agreed but the scheme fell through because of the war. After the war, the Corporation wanted to use the compulsory purchase order to acquire the shop for a completely new redevelopment of the area. It must be noted that the property if used for city centre redevelopment would have had a vastly increased value. It was held that a power to acquire compulsorily property for road widening purposes could not be used for compulsory acquisition for city centre redevelopment. In *Congreve v Home Office*,[87] under the Wireless Telegraphy Act 1949, section 1, a television licence could be issued subject to such terms, provisions and limitations as the minister might think fit and could be revoked on giving written notice to the recipient. It was known that the television licence was going to be increased from £12 to £18, and Congreve decided to take out a new licence while there was still some time of his old licence to run. So did some 20,000 other people. The Home Office, fearing the loss of a great deal of revenue, decided to revoke the

---

[85] [1922] 2 Ch 490 (CA).   [86] [1958] Ch 329.   [87] [1976] QB 629 (CA).

licence after eight months in order to make Congreve take out a new licence for £18 at the end of that time. It was held (per Lord Denning MR) that 'the licence is granted for 12 months and cannot be revoked simply to enable the minister to raise more money. Want of money is no reason for revoking a licence' and (per Geoffrey Lane LJ) that 'the revocation is an improper use of a discretionary power to use a threat to exercise that power as a means of extracting money which Parliament has given the executive no mandate to demand'. In *R v Lewisham LBC, ex p Shell*,[88] the council decided to boycott Shell as Shell had commercial interests in South Africa. The council organised a campaign to persuade other organisations to follow suit. It was held that it was not contrary to law to have links with South Africa and that a power to ensure good race relations could not be used for the purpose of forcing Shell to sever economic links with South Africa. In *R v Ealing LBC, ex p Times Newspapers*,[89] the court had to consider the Public Libraries Act 1964, section 7, which empowered local authorities to provide a 'proper' library service. Several newspaper groups were in industrial disputes with the printing trade unions. The trade unions asked local authorities to ban that national institution *The Times* from being displayed in local authority libraries. It was held that local authorities could not use their powers to provide a library service (which naturally involved some discretion in choosing materials to be bought and displayed in libraries) as a weapon in a trade dispute to which the local authority was not a party.

Magill v Porter [2001] UKHL 67

Lord Scott

'132. This is a case about political corruption. The corruption was not money corruption. No one took a bribe. No one sought or received money for political favours. But there are other forms of corruption, often less easily detectable and therefore more insidious. Gerrymandering, the manipulation of constituency boundaries for party political advantage, is a clear form of political corruption. So, too, would be any misuse of municipal powers, intended for use in the general public interest but used instead for party political advantage. Who can doubt that the selective use of municipal powers in order to obtain party political advantage represents political corruption? Political corruption, if unchecked, engenders cynicism about elections, about politicians and their motives and damages the reputation of democratic [government].

133. When detected and exposed it must be expected, or at least it must be hoped, that political corruption will receive its just deserts at the polls. Detection and exposure is, however, often difficult and, where it happens, is usually attributable to determined efforts by political opponents or by investigative journalists or by both in tandem. But, where local government is concerned, there is an additional very important bulwark guarding against [misconduct].

. . .

136. The statutory [system of audit of local government finance provides] an institutional means whereby political corruption consisting of the use of municipal powers for party political advantage might be detected and cauterised by public [exposure].'

Lord Bingham

'2. Magill [was the auditor appointed by the Audit Commission to audit the accounts of Westminster City Council. He certified that] three councillors and three officers had, by wilful misconduct, jointly and severally caused a loss of approximately £31m to the council which they were liable to make [good].

. . .

---

[88] [1988] 1 All ER 938. See, also, *Wheeler*, p. 573.   [89] (1987) 85 LGR 316.

4. The council comprised 60 [councilors]. As a result of the local government elections in May 1986, the overall Conservative party majority was reduced from 26 to 4. The close results of those elections prompted leading members of the council to consider how council policies could be developed in order to advance the electoral prospects of the Conservative party in the next local government election to be held in 1990. Dame Shirley Porter [reorganized] the party's administrative and decision-making structure and herself chaired a group of committee chairmen. This body comprised herself as leader, Mr Weeks, the deputy leader, the majority party's chief whip and the chairmen of the council's committees. It was not a committee or sub-committee appointed by the council. It met on a regular basis, sometimes with officers in attendance. It developed and promoted policy. One of these concerned the designation of council-owned properties for sale.

5. The council first introduced a policy of designated sales in 1972. Under this policy, blocks of council dwellings were designated and, when a dwelling in a designated block became vacant, it was not re-let but offered for sale to an approved applicant with the intention that all dwellings in designated blocks would become owner-occupied. Under the [scheme], 10 to 20 sales per annum were generated from the 300 dwellings then designated. With a view to achieving greater success in the 1990 elections, the chairmen's group formulated a [policy]. This included targets for increasing the numbers of Conservative voters in each of eight key wards, the target voter figures for those wards adding up to a total of 2,200. [Those] eight wards were chosen in mid-February 1987 by some members of the majority party on the council (including Dame Shirley Porter and Councillor Weeks), and were known as the "key wards". [The] references in contemporary documents to "new residents", "more electors" and "new electors" in many instances were euphemisms for "more potential Conservative voters", particularly in marginal wards. A major element [was] to increase designated sales of council properties in the eight key wards to potential owner-occupiers. It was believed that owner-occupiers would be more likely to vote Conservative. [The] intention of the majority party was to develop council policies which would target marginal wards, including such housing policies as could affect the make-up of the electorate in those wards.

. . .

12. On 13 May 1987, Dame Shirley Porter was re-elected leader and Mr Weeks deputy leader of the majority [party].

. . .

14. [Dame] Shirley Porter and Mr Weeks hoped to increase the Conservative vote in marginal wards by selling each year 250 council properties in those [wards. The housing] committee resolved to designate a number of specific properties for sale which were expected to produce 500 sales per [annum]. 20,697 properties had been identified [as] eligible for designation. Of these, 5,912 dwellings (29%) were in the eight key wards, 13,633 dwellings (66%) were in the other fifteen [wards]. The list of properties to be designated was not recommended by officers; it was presented by the chairman of the Housing Committee. 9,360 dwellings were [designated]. 74% of all eligible dwellings in the eight key wards were designated; only 28% of all eligible properties in the other wards were [designated].

. . .

16. At a meeting on 29 July 1987 the council received a report from the Housing Committee. The city solicitor informed the council that a report on designated sales had been prepared following a consultation with leading counsel and that it had been seen and approved by leading counsel before it went to the Housing Committee. The council voted to receive the report.

. . .

18. [The] auditor was appointed following objections made by a number of local government [electors].

19. [The principal legal principles at issue were summarized as "Powers conferred on a local authority may be exercised for the public purpose for which the powers were conferred and not. It is

misconduct in a councillor to exercise or be party to the exercise of such powers otherwise than for the public purpose for which the powers were conferred. Powers conferred on a local authority may not lawfully be exercised to promote the electoral advantage of a political party"].

20. Counsel for Dame Shirley Porter and Mr Weeks urged [what] were said to be the realities of party politics. Councillors elected as members of a political party and forming part of that party group on the council could not be expected to be oblivious to considerations of party political advantage. So long as they had reasons for taking action other than purely partisan political reasons their conduct could not be [impugned].

21. Whatever the difficulties of application which may arise in a borderline case, I do not consider the overriding principle to be in doubt. Elected politicians of course wish to act in a manner which will commend them and their party (when, as is now usual, they belong to one) to the electorate. Such an ambition is the life blood of democracy and a potent spur to responsible decision-taking and administration. Councillors do not act improperly or unlawfully if, exercising public powers for a public purpose for which such powers were conferred, they hope that such exercise will earn the gratitude and support of the electorate and thus strengthen their electoral position. The law would indeed part company with the realities of party politics if it were to hold otherwise. But a public power is not exercised lawfully if it is exercised not for a public purpose for which the power was conferred but in order to promote the electoral advantage of a political party. The power at issue in the present case is [the] Housing Act 1985, which conferred power on local authorities to dispose of land held by [them]. Thus a local authority could dispose of its property [to] promote any public purpose for which such power was conferred, but could not lawfully do so for the purpose of promoting the electoral advantage of any party represented on the council.

. . .

24. [The decision of the auditor and the Divisional Court adverse to Dame Shirley Porter and Mr Weeks rested, first of all, on the finding] that the Westminster City Council adopted a policy the object of which was to achieve a specified annual level of sales of properties owned by the council in the eight marginal wards with the intention that the properties thus vacated should be sold to new residents who, as owner-occupiers, might reasonably be expected to vote Conservative and so increase the electoral strength of the Conservative Party in those wards in the 1990 council elections. The auditor [stated]:

> "both the decision to increase the number of designated sales and the selection of the properties designated for sale were influenced by an irrelevant consideration, namely the electoral advantage of the majority party. I have found that the electoral advantage of the majority party was the driving force behind the policy of increased designated sales and that that consideration was the predominant consideration which influenced both the decision to increase designated sales by 500 per annum and the selection of properties designated for sale. My view is that the Council was engaged in gerrymandering, which I have found is a disgraceful and improper purpose, and not a purpose for which a local authority may act."

The Divisional Court [accepted this conclusion].

25. Nothing that the House has heard gives any ground for doubting the correctness of the conclusion of the auditor and the Divisional Court on this point. It follows from the legal principles already summarised that the council's policy was unlawful because directed to the pursuit of electoral advantage and not the achievement of proper housing objectives.

. . .

48. The Divisional Court's findings adverse to Dame Shirley Porter and Mr Weeks, reached on a mass of evidence, were fully justified, if not inevitable. The [passage] of time and the familiarity of the accusations made against Dame Shirley Porter and Mr Weeks cannot and should not obscure the unpalatable truth that this was a deliberate, blatant and dishonest misuse of public power. It was a

misuse of power by both of them not for the purpose of financial gain but for that of electoral advantage. In that sense it was corrupt. The auditor may have been strictly wrong to describe their conduct as gerrymandering, but it was certainly unlawful and he was right to stigmatise it as disgraceful.'

It may be noted that if an authority can act under two or more statutory powers (power A and power B), the authority may validly choose the power more favourable to the authority:

Westminster Bank v Minister of Housing and Local Government
[1971] AC 508

It may be necessary to restrict building in order to keep land available for road widening. Under the system then pertaining, there were two courses open. A highway authority could prescribe an 'improvement line' when owners of property adjoining the street could no longer build on that part of the property lying between the street and the improvement line, but had a right to compensation from the authority. A planning authority could refuse planning application, but the unsuccessful applicant did not receive any compensation and 'if planning permission is refused on the ground that the proposed development conflicts with a scheme for street widening, the unsuccessful applicant is in exactly the same position as other applicants whose applications are refused on other grounds' (per Lord Reid, at 529). Westminster Bank had a branch on a site between the Market Place and Lairgate, Beverley. They wanted to extend their premises by building on an open space which adjoined Lairgate. The council refused planning permission on the ground that 'the proposed development might prejudice the possible future widening of Lairgate'. The council had not prescribed an improvement line and the bank was not, therefore, entitled to compensation.

Lord Reid, at 529–530

'In the present case the same authority is both the local planning authority and the highway authority for Lairgate. So they could if they had so chosen have achieved their object by the alternative method of prescribing an improvement line and thereby entitling the appellants to compensation. At one stage the appellants put their case so high as to say that the only reason they proceeded by way of refusal of planning permission was in order to avoid having to pay compensation. This is denied by the local [authority. But], even if the sole reason for the authority proceeding in the way it did had been the desire to save public money, it does not follow that they were not entitled to do that. The appellants say that this was "unreasonable". The [word "unreasonable" as used in *Wednesbury*, p. 563] requires, I think, a little expansion. The decision of any authority can be attacked on the ground that it is in excess of its powers or on the ground that it is an abuse of its powers. The word "unreasonable" is not at all an apt description of action in excess of power, and it is not a very satisfactory description of action in abuse of [power]. Here the authority did not act in excess of power in deciding to proceed by way of refusal of planning permission rather than by way of prescribing an improvement line. Did it then act in abuse of power? I do not think so.

Parliament has chosen to set up two different ways of preventing development which would interfere with schemes for street widening. It must have been aware that one involved paying compensation but the other did not. Nevertheless, it expressed no preference, and imposed no limit on the use of either. No doubt there might be special circumstances which make it unreasonable or an abuse of power to use one of these methods but here there were none. Even if the appellants' view of the facts is right, the authority had to choose whether to leave the appellants without compensation or to impose a burden on its ratepayers. One may think that it would be most equitable that the burden should be shared. But the Minister of Transport had made it clear in a circular sent to local authorities [that] there would be no grant if a local authority proceeded in such a way that compensation would be payable, and there is nothing to indicate any disapproval of this policy by Parliament and nothing in any of the legislation to indicate that Parliament disapproved of depriving the subject of compensation. I cannot in these circumstances find any abuse of power in the local authority deciding that the appellants and not its ratepayers should bear the burden.'

(c) Relevant and irrelevant considerations

It is irrational to take 'irrelevant matters' into consideration or fail to take 'relevant matters' into consideration. Sometimes, this rather meaningless statement presents little or no problem when the statute granting power to an authority specifically states that in making a particular decision, the authority shall take into consideration factor A, factor B and factor C. In the absence of such specific statutory instructions, the courts must determine what is relevant and what is irrelevant from the context or deemed purpose of the enabling statute.

In *Coleen Properties Ltd v Minister of Housing and Local Government*,[90] local authorities had power to declare an area to be a clearance area on the ground that houses therein were unfit for human habitation and then to redevelop the area. They also had power to acquire compulsorily 'any adjoining land the acquisition of which is reasonably necessary for the satisfactory development or use of the clearance area'. The purpose of acquiring adjoining lands is to facilitate the development of the area as a whole. Tower Hamlets Council declared two rows of houses in two streets to be a clearance area and wanted to acquire, as adjoining land, a house (owned by Coleen Properties) on the corner of the two streets. This house was in good condition and Coleen Properties objected to its acquisition. There was a public inquiry, at which the council asserted that the acquisition was necessary but gave no evidence in support of the assertion. The inspector stated that the house was 'a first class property and I am of the opinion that its acquisition by the council is not reasonably necessary for the satisfactory development or use of the cleared area'. The minister disagreed. It was held that 'the minister was in error in reversing the inspector's recommendation. The minister had before him only the report of the inspector. He did not see the premises himself. [What] is "reasonably necessary" [is] an inference of fact on which the minister should not overrule the inspector's recommendation unless there is material evidence sufficient for the purpose. There is none here.'[91] In *R v Port Talbot Borough Council, ex p Jones*,[92] a councillor (K) applied to Port Talbot Borough Council for housing accommodation as she was in the process of divorce. The housing tenancy committee of the council resolved that K's application should be accorded priority status. Later, K was granted the tenancy of a council house in Aberavon. She represented Aberavon ward on the council but was at that time living outside the ward. The reasons for the house being allocated to K were that: to effectively carry out her council duties, that is members of the public calling on her, she should be given a house rather than a flat; there was no prospect of a two-bedroomed house being available; and K needed to return to the ward that she represented in sufficient time to establish her presence for the next election. It was held that there 'could hardly be a clearer case of a decision which, to adopt one test propounded in [*Wednesbury*, p. 563] was based on irrelevant considerations and ignored relevant considerations. To put it more simply, the decision was unfair to others on the housing list and was an abuse of power.'[93]

---

[90] [1971] 1 WLR 433 (CA).   [91] Per Lord Denning MR, at 437.
[92] [1988] 2 All ER 207.   [93] Per Nolan J, at 214.

Of course, it may be held that an authority took into account completely relevant matters in making a decision:[94]

Stringer v Minister of Housing and Local Government [1970] 1 WLR 1281

This was the case of the Jodrell Bank telescope (p. 559).

Cooke J, at 1298

'The first point taken on behalf of the applicant is that the likelihood that the development would interfere with the work of the telescope is not a material consideration in determining whether permission for the development should be given. The interests of the telescope, it is said, are interests of a private character. It is said that the purpose of the planning legislation is to protect only the public interest, and indeed only the public interest in a particular sphere, namely, the sphere of amenity. Therefore it is said that in this case the minister has exercised his powers for a purpose not authorised by the Planning Acts, and reliance is placed on the judgment of Lord Denning in *Pyx Granite Co Ltd v Ministry of Housing and Local Government* [1958] 1 QB 554, where he said, at 572: "Although the planning authorities are given very wide powers to impose 'such conditions as they think fit', nevertheless the law says that those conditions, to be valid, must fairly and reasonably relate to the permitted development. The planning authority are not at liberty to use their powers for an ulterior object, however desirable that object may seem to them to be in the public [interest]."

It may be conceded at once that the material considerations to which the minister is entitled and bound to have regard in deciding the appeal must be considerations of a planning nature. I find it impossible, however, to accept the view that such considerations are limited to matters relating to amenity. So far as I am aware, there is no authority for such a proposition, and it seems to me to be wrong in principle. In principle, it seems to me that any consideration which relates to the use and development of land is capable of being a planning consideration. Whether a particular consideration falling within that broad class is material in any given case will depend on the circumstances. However, it seems to me that in considering an appeal the minister is entitled to ask himself whether the proposed development is compatible with the proper and desirable use of other land in the area. For example, if permission is sought to erect an explosives factory adjacent to a school, the minister must surely be entitled and bound to consider the question of safety. That plainly is not an amenity [consideration]. I find it equally difficult to accept that the local planning authority and the minister on appeal must have regard only to the public interest as opposed to private interests. It is, of course, [true] that the scheme of the legislation is to restrict development for the benefit of the public at large. But it seems to me that it would be impossible for the minister and local planning authorities to carry out their duties as custodians of the public interest if they were precluded from considering the effect of a proposed development on a particular use of land by a particular occupier in the neighbourhood. The public interest, as I see it, may require that the interests of individual occupiers should be considered. The protection of the interests of individual occupiers is one aspect, and an important one, of the public interest as a whole. The distinction between public and private interests appears to me to be a false distinction in this [context].'

As stated above, many discretion-giving statutes relate to the exercise of power within a particular locality where the public authority's appreciation of the local situation (by means of opportunity for inquiry and objection or by presumed views expressed through the ballot

---

[94] See *Wednesbury*, p. 563; *Prescott v Birmingham Corporation* [1955] Ch 210; *Hanks v Minister of Housing and Local Government* [1953] 1 QB 999; *Bromley LBC v Greater London Council* [1983] 1 AC 768; *R v Broadcasting Complaints Commission, ex p Owen* [1985] QB 1153; *R v Cambridge Health Authority, ex p B* [1995] 1 WLR 898.

box) may be a decisive factor. In *Roberts v Hopwood*,[95] Poplar Borough Council were empowered to pay their employees 'such salaries and wages as [they] think fit'. In 1920 the wages of both men and women were increased to £4 per week because of an increase in the cost of living. In 1923 these wage levels were maintained even though there had been a reduction in the cost of living, comparable wages in the private sector were lower, and there had been a reduction in the number of hours worked by the council employees. It was held that a public authority should act in a businesslike manner and that what is a reasonable wage at any time must depend on the circumstances which exist in the labour market. A public authority should take into consideration not only the general principle of paying fair wages but also the interests of the ratepayers, some of whom were on lower wages. The council had not taken into consideration the relationship between the authority and the ratepayers. The relationship between the public authority and the electorate was crucial in:

Secretary of State for Education v Tameside Metropolitan Borough Council
[1997] AC 1014

In March 1975, Tameside was Labour controlled and the local education authority proposed a scheme of comprehensive education to come into effect in September 1976. In March 1976, a Conservative council was elected and the Conservatives' opposition to the planned reorganisation was given great emphasis in their election manifesto. The new council decided to continue five grammar schools and a number of secondary modern schools and to continue the completion of three new purpose built comprehensive schools started by the previous council. In June 1976 the Secretary of State issued a direction under the Education Act 1944, section 68, ordering the Conservative council to implement the 1975 Labour proposals. Section 68 provided: 'If the Secretary of State is satisfied [that any local education authority] have acted or are proposing to act unreasonably with respect to the exercise of any power conferred or the performance of any duty imposed by or under this Act he may give such directions as to the exercise of the power or the performance of the duty as appear to him to be expedient.' The council gave evidence that the 1975 proposals were not completed; the schools were not ready for their changing role; building works were not completed and not in most cases begun; complete implementation of the 1975 proposals in September 1976 would itself have caused great disruption to the children's education; the continuation of the five grammar schools would mean that of some 3,000 places to be allocated for September 1976, over 90 per cent would remain unaltered but that there would be some 240 places available for allocation at the grammar schools and if the number of applicants to the grammar schools exceeded the number of places, there would have to be a process of selection based on school reports, records and interviews (there would be no 11-plus examination). It was emphasised that the local elections had been fought, inter alia, on the platform that some selective basis would be preserved and it was held that the Secretary of State had failed to take into account that the council was entitled to carry out the policy on which it was elected.

Lord Wilberforce, at 1046–1051

'[The] matters with which the action is concerned are primarily matters of educational administration. The action, which the Secretary of State is entitled to stop, is unreasonable action with respect to the exercise of a power or the performance of a duty [and section 68] does not enable the Secretary of State to require them to abandon or reverse a policy just because the Secretary of State disagrees with it. Specifically the Secretary of State cannot use power under [section 68] to impose a general policy of comprehensive education on a local education authority which does not agree with the [policy].

---

[95] [1925] AC 578.

The Secretary of State, under section 68, is not merely exercising a discretion: he is reviewing the action of another public body which itself has discretionary powers and duties [and] must take account of what the authority, under the statute, is entitled to do. [Owing] to the democratic process involving periodic elections, abrupt reversals of policy may take place, particularly where there are only two parties and the winner takes all. Any reversal of policy if at all substantial must cause some administrative disruption. [So] the mere possibility or probability of disruption cannot be a ground for issuing a direction to abandon the policy. What the Secretary of State is entitled, by a direction if necessary, to ensure is that such disruptions are not "unreasonable". [After] all, those who voted for the new programme, involving a change of course, must also be taken to have accepted some degree of disruption in implementing it. The ultimate question in this case [is] whether the Secretary of State has given sufficient, or any, weight to this particular factor in the exercise of his [judgment].

What the Secretary of State was entitled to do, under his residual powers, was to say something to the effect that: "the election has taken place; the new authority may be entitled to postpone the comprehensive scheme; this may involve some degree of selection and apparently the parents desire it. Nevertheless from an educational point of view, whatever some parents may think, I am satisfied that in the time available this, or some part of it, cannot be carried out and no reasonable authority would attempt to carry it out". Let us judge him by this test, though I do not think that this was the test he himself applied. Was the procedure to be followed for choosing which of the applicants were to be allotted the 240 selective places such that no reasonable authority could adopt it? [His Lordship held that a selection process based on reports, records and interviews, to be carried out over three months for a small number of places, was not such that no reasonable authority would carry it out.]

The authority's selection plans were opposed by a number of the teachers' unions, and there was a likelihood of non-cooperation by some of the head teachers in the primary schools in production of records and [reports]. Is this a fact on which the Secretary of State might legitimately form the judgment that the authority were acting unreasonably? [He held that it could not be unreasonable for the authority to put forward a plan on their approved procedures.] The teachers, after all, are public servants, with responsibility for their pupils. They were under a duty to produce reports. These reports and records in the primary schools are public property. I do not think that it could be unreasonable for the authority to take the view that [the] teachers would cooperate in working the authority's procedure—a procedure which had, in similar form, been operated in part of this very area.

[The] Secretary of State, real though his difficulties were, fundamentally misconceived and misdirected himself as to the proper manner in which to regard the proposed action of the authority after the local election of May 1976: that if he had exercised his judgment on the basis of the factual situation in which this newly elected authority were placed—with a policy approved by the electorate, and massively supported by the parents—there was no ground, however much he might disagree with the new policy, and regret such administrative dislocation as was brought about by the change, on which he could find that the authority were acting or proposing to act [unreasonably].'

It may happen that factors peculiar to one locality may be of decisive importance to the decision-maker but not the referee:

Wheeler v Leicester City Council [1985] AC 1054

In 1984, the Rugby Football Union (RFU) announced that they were to take a touring side to South Africa and in the team were, naturally, members of Leicester Football Club (The Tigers). The club Secretary was asked to meet with the leader of Leicester City Council (Mr Soulsby) to discuss the tour and the participation of the club's members. At that meeting, Mr Soulsby read out four questions: 'Does the Leicester Football Club support the Government opposition to the tour; does the Leicester Football Club agree that the tour is an insult to the large proportion of the Leicester population; will the Leicester

Football Club press the RFU to call off the tour; and will the Leicester Football club press the players to pull out of the tour?' It was made plain that 'the club's response would only be acceptable if in effect all four questions were answered in the affirmative'. The club replied:

'Leicester Football Club have always enjoyed cordial relations with Leicester City Council on a strictly non-political basis and seek to continue that relationship. The club join with the council in condemning apartheid but recognise that there are differences of opinion over the way in which the barriers of apartheid can be broken down. The government have not declared sporting contacts illegal or even applied sanctions against those involved in [tours]. Rugby Union players as amateur sportsmen have individual choice as to when and where they play, subject only to the constraints of RFU rules and club loyalty. However, the club [have] supplied copies [of a document on apartheid] to the tour players and asked them seriously to consider the contents before finally reaching a decision whether to tour. The club are and always have been multi-racial and will continue that principle for the benefit of Leicester and rugby football.'

The city council resolved 'that the Leicester Football Club be suspended from using [a local recreation ground owned by the council, and now named after Nelson Mandela] for a period of 12 months and that the situation be reviewed at the end of that period in the light of the club's attitude to sporting links with South Africa.'

Lord Roskill, at 1076–1079

'The reasons for the imposition of the ban are clearly set out [in an affidavit by Mr Soulsby]:

"I refute any suggestion that the purported sanction against the club was imposed in response to the actions of their players. I wish to make it clear that the action taken by the council was in response to the attitude taken by the club in failing to condemn the tour and to discourage its members from playing. The council has taken its steps therefore because of what the club did or did not do. It was always recognised that the club were not in the position of employers and could not instruct their players. However, the club is [a] premier rugby football club and an influential member of the Rugby Football Union. At no time was the club asked to do anything by the city council which was beyond their powers to do. The steps taken by the city council have not been taken in order to penalise the club for having members who went to South Africa, still less, to penalise the club in order to penalise the players."

It is important to emphasise that there was nothing illegal in the action of the [players] in joining the tour. The government policy recorded in [the] Gleneagles agreement has never been given the force of law at the instance of any government, whatever its political complexion, and a person who acts otherwise than in accordance with the principles of that agreement, commits no offence even though he may by his action earn the moral disapprobation of large numbers of his fellow citizens. That the club condemns apartheid, as does the council, admits of no doubt. But the council's actions against the club were not taken, as already pointed out, because the club took no action against its three members. They were taken, according to Mr Soulsby, because the club failed to condemn the tour and to discourage its members from [playing]. Thus, so the argument ran, the council, legitimately bitterly hostile to the policy of apartheid, were justified in exercising their statutory discretion to determine by whom the recreation ground should be used so as to exclude those, such as the club, who would not support the council's policy on the council's [terms].

The council's main defence rested on section 71 of the Race Relations Act [1976]: "[It] shall be the duty of every local authority to make appropriate arrangements with a view to securing that their various functions are carried out with due regard to the need—(a) to eliminate unlawful racial discrimination; and (b) to promote equality of opportunity, and good relations, between persons of different racial groups."

My Lords, it was strenuously argued on behalf of the club that this section should be given what was called a "narrow" construction. It was suggested that the section was only concerned with the actions of the council as regards its own internal behaviour and was what was described as "inward looking". The section had no relevance to the general exercise by the council or indeed of any local authority of their statutory functions, as for example in relation to the control of open spaces or in determining who should be entitled to use a recreation ground and on what [terms. I] unhesitatingly reject this argument. I think the whole purpose of this section is to see that in relation to matters other than those specifically dealt with, for [example, employment and education], local authorities must in relation to "their various functions" make "appropriate arrangements" to secure that those functions are carried out "with due regard to the need" mentioned in the section. It follows that I do not doubt that the council were fully entitled in exercising their statutory discretion under, for example, the Open Spaces Act 1906 and the various Public Health Acts, [to] pay regard to what they thought was in the best interests of race relations.

The only question is, therefore, whether the action of the council of which the club complains is susceptible of attack by way of judicial review. It was forcibly argued by [counsel] for the council, that once it was [accepted] that section 71 bears the construction for which the council contended, the matter became one of political judgment only, and that by interfering the courts would be trespassing across that line which divides a proper exercise of a statutory discretion based on a political judgment, in relation to which the courts must not and will not interfere, from an improper exercise of such a discretion in relation to which the courts will [interfere]. To my mind the crucial question is whether the conduct of the council in trying by their four questions, whether taken individually or collectively, to force acceptance by the club of their own policy (however proper that policy may be) on their own terms, as for example, by forcing them to lend their considerable prestige to a public condemnation of the tour, can be said either to be so "unreasonable" as to give rise to "*Wednesbury* unreasonableness" [or] to be so fundamental a breach of the duty to act fairly which rests upon every local authority in matters of this kind and thus justify interference by the courts.

I do not for one moment doubt the great importance which the council attach to the presence in their midst of a 25 per cent population of persons who are either Asian or of Afro-Caribbean origin. Nor do I doubt for one moment the sincerity of the view expressed in Mr Soulsby's affidavit regarding the need for the council to distance itself from bodies who hold important positions and who do not actively discourage sporting contacts with South Africa. Persuasion, even powerful persuasion, is always a permissible way of seeking to obtain an objective. But in a field where other views can equally legitimately be held, persuasion, however powerful, must not be allowed to cross that line where it moves into the field of illegitimate pressure coupled with the threat of [sanctions].

[I] am clearly of the opinion that the manner in which the council took that decision was in all the circumstances [unfair]. The council formulated those four questions in the manner of which I have spoken and indicated that only such affirmative answers would be acceptable. They received reasoned and reasonable answers which went a long way in support of the policy which the council had accepted and desired to see accepted. The views expressed in these reasoned and reasonable answers were lawful views and the views which, as the evidence shows, many people sincerely hold and believe to be correct. If the club had adopted a different and hostile attitude, different considerations might well have arisen. But the club did not adopt any such attitude. In my view, therefore, this is a case in which the court should interfere because of the unfair manner in which the council set about obtaining its [objective].'

Lord Templeman, at 1079–1081

'My Lords, in my opinion the Leicester City Council were not entitled to withdraw from the Leicester Football Club the facilities for training and playing enjoyed by the club for many years on the council's recreation ground for one simple and good reason. The club could not be punished because the club had done nothing [wrong]. My Lords, the laws of this country are not like the laws of Nazi Germany.

A private individual or a private organisation cannot be obliged to display zeal in the pursuit of an object sought by a public authority and cannot be obliged to publish views dictated by a public authority.

The club having committed no wrong, the council could not use their statutory powers in the management of their property or any other statutory powers in order to punish the club. There is no doubt that the council intended to punish and have punished the club. When the club were presented by the council with four questions it was made clear that the club's response would only be acceptable if, in effect, all four questions were answered in the affirmative. When the club committee made their dignified and responsible response to these questions, a response which the council find unsatisfactory to the council, the council commissioned a report on possible sanctions that might be taken against the club. That report suggested that delaying tactics could be used to hold up the grant of a lease then being negotiated by the club. It suggested that land could be excluded from the new lease as it was "thought that this could embarrass the club because it had apparently granted [subleases]". It was suggested that the council's consent, which had already been given for advertisements by the club's sponsors, could be withdrawn although according to the report "the actual effect of this measure on the club is difficult to assess". It was suggested that "a further course is to insist upon strict observance of the tenant's covenants in the lease. However, the city estates surveyor, having inspected the premises, is of the opinion that the tenant's covenants are all being complied with". Finally, it was suggested that "the council could terminate the club's use of the recreation ground". This might cause some financial loss to the council and might "form the basis of a legal challenge to the council's decision. The club may contend that the council has taken an unreasonable action against the club in response to personal decisions of members of its team over which it had no control". Notwithstanding this warning the council accepted the last suggestion and terminated the club's use of the recreation ground. In my opinion, this use by the council of its statutory powers was a misuse of power. The council could not properly seek to use its statutory powers of management or any other statutory powers for the purposes of punishing the club when the club had done no [wrong].'

(d) Unreasonableness

Probably the most difficult 'Wednesbury principle' relates to 'acting reasonably', as this is where there may be a temptation for the courts to substitute their own values for those of the decision-maker. It has been held that 'Fairness and reasonableness (and their contraries) are objective concepts; otherwise there would be no public law, or if there were it would be palm tree justice. But each is a spectrum, not a single point, and they shade into one another. It is now well established that the Wednesbury principle itself constitutes a sliding scale of review, more or less intrusive according to the nature and gravity of what is at stake.'[96] Reasonableness (and the opposite of reasonableness would appear to be unreasonableness or irrationality) is of particular importance in relation to local authority action, where the decision-maker is so often called upon to balance the conflicting interest of the private individual and various local, community and national interests. In Hall & Co Ltd v Shoreham-by-Sea Urban District Council,[97] local planning authorities could grant planning permission subject to such conditions as the council 'think fit'. Hall was granted planning permission to develop land for a sand and gravel business, subject to the following condition: 'The applicants shall construct an ancillary road over the entire frontage of the site at their

---

[96] R v Secretary of State for Education and Employment, ex p Begbie [1999] EWCA Civ 2100, per Laws LJ, at para 78.
[97] [1964] 1 WLR 240 (CA).

own expense, as and when required by the local planning authority, and shall give right of passage over it to and from such ancillary roads as may be constructed on the adjoining land.' Hall would suffer in two ways, in that the road that they would have to pay for themselves would carry a vastly increasing amount of traffic from a quickly developing area and they would not be able to obtain compensation for the damage caused to the road, and, when the council so decided, the road that they had paid for would be closed and they would have to seek other access to the main roads themselves, and might be barred from so doing by other developments. It was held that planning conditions 'must fairly and reasonably relate to the permitted development [and] must not be so unreasonable that it can be said that Parliament clearly cannot have intended that they should be imposed'.[98] Since the council would obtain the benefit of having the road constructed for them at Hall's expense, on Hall's land, and without the necessity for paying any compensation, this result would be utterly unreasonable and such as Parliament could not possibly have intended. Similarly, in *R v Hillingdon London Borough Council, ex p Royco Homes Ltd*,[99] Royco wanted to develop land for housing purposes and applied for planning permission to Hillingdon Council. The Council granted planning permission, subject to conditions. Royco objected to two conditions, namely, that the houses should be occupied by persons who were on the council's waiting list for council houses and that for ten years the houses should be occupied by persons who were under the provisions of the Rent Acts relating to security of tenure and rent restriction. It was accepted that the council had wide power to grant planning permission 'subject to such conditions as they think fit'. However, such a power was clearly too wide to be given a literal meaning. And it was held that the conditions required Royco to take on at their own expense a significant part of the duty of the council as a housing authority, and, although well intentioned, were unreasonable. Sometimes, allegations of impropriety and bad faith may be made. In *Cannock Chase District Council v Kelly*,[100] it was held that such an allegation must be proved rather than inferred. 'Bad faith' means 'dishonesty' and 'always involves a grave charge. It must not be treated as a synonym for honest, though mistaken, taking into consideration a factor which is in law irrelevant.'

The balancing of local and national interests with regard to who should pay for a socially desirable purpose is illustrated by:

Luby v Newcastle-under-Lyme Corporation [1964] 2 QB 64

Under the Housing Act 1957, section 111, 'a local housing authority may make such reasonable charges for the tenancy or occupation of the houses as they may determine'. It was claimed by Luby that the council had acted unreasonably in that they had not taken into account the fact that some tenants had less money than others and that they should be charged less rent than persons in similar houses but who had more money and, therefore, the council should operate a differential rent scheme.

Diplock LJ, at 72–73

'[The] court's control over the exercise by a local authority of a discretion conferred upon it by Parliament is limited to ensuring that the local authority has acted within the powers conferred. It is not for the court to substitute its own view of what is a desirable policy in relation to the subject matter of the discretion so conferred. It is only if it is exercised in a manner which no reasonable man could consider justifiable that the court is entitled to interfere. In determining the rent structure to be applied to houses provided by a local authority the local authority is applying what is, in effect, a social policy upon which reasonable men may hold different views. Since any deficit in the housing revenue account has to be made good from the general rate fund, the choice of rent structure involves weighing the interest of the tenants as a whole and of individual impoverished tenants against those of the general body of ratepayers. [Because of the system of National Assistance, which was in operation at the time, for paying some of the rent of poor tenants] there is also involved a choice as to whether the individual impoverished tenant should be assisted at the expense of the general body of ratepayers by a reduction in the rent or at the expense of the general body of taxpayers by way of National Assistance. The evidence shows that the defendant corporation has directed its mind to this problem and to the desirability or otherwise of applying a differential rent scheme. It has determined that the burden of assisting individual tenants who cannot afford to pay the rents which the corporation has fixed as appropriate for the type of house which they occupy ought to fall upon the general body of tax payers and not upon the general body of ratepayers in the district. It is in my view quite impossible for this court to say that this choice, which is one of social policy, is one which no reasonable man could have made, and is therefore ultra vires, any more than it could be said that the opposite choice would have been ultra vires. The policy which the defendant corporation has adopted was, I think, within the discretion conferred upon them.'

One question raised in recent years has been, given that a body exercising common law prerogative power or wide discretionary statutory power is, prima facie subject to judicial review by the courts, how far will the courts intervene, on the grounds of 'irrationality', to control the exercise of that power when that power is used to create the policies whereby that power is exercised. In such a situation, there is no Act of Parliament demonstrating, expressly or by implication, the 'will of Parliament' against which can be measured the '*ultra vires*' or '*intra vires*' categorisation of what a public authority has done. In some cases, it has been held that the formulation and implementation of national political and economic policy are entirely dependent on political judgement, the decisions to take are for politicians and the proper forum where such policies should be debated, approved or disapproved is the House of Commons. In *R v Criminal Injuries Compensation Board, ex p P*,[101] the court was faced with an application for judicial review designed to overturn the actual policy rules relating to the compensation scheme. The court reaffirmed that the distribution of bounty on behalf of the Crown did not preclude the courts from exercising their 'constitutional powers' of judicial review, but categorised the issue as non-justiciable because the issue involved a balance of competing claims on the public purse and the allocation of economic resources with which the court was ill-equipped to deal.[102] In *GCHQ*,[103] the House of Lords was, understandably as the issue was not relevant, hesitant to pronounce unequivocally on the question of irrationality. While noting no a priori reason to rule out irrationality as a ground for review, Lord Diplock found it 'difficult to envisage in any of the various fields in which the prerogative remains the only source of the relevant decision-making powers a decision of a kind that would be open to attack through the judicial process on this ground. The decisions will generally involve the application of government policy. The reasons for the decision-maker taking one course rather than another do not normally involve questions which, if disputed, the judicial process is adapted to provide the right answer.' There is a risk, in exercising judicial review of imprecisely defined common law and statutory powers by means of the *Wednesbury* principles, in that certain of the powers may relate to matters of government policy based on

---

[101] [1995] 1 All ER 870.

[102] A similar approach had been taken in *R v Home Secretary, ex p Harrison* [1988] 3 All ER 86.

[103] See p. 86.

government ideology in the fields of foreign affairs and economic strategy and the courts may be accused of, and indeed seen to be, interfering with matters which are claimed by politicians to be within the province of political persona and institutions. Because of this risk, it has been asserted that in order to review an undoubted prerogative power on the ground of irrationality, the irrationality must be a very extreme case of abuse of power, something outrageously aberrant, and that the application for judicial review must pass a 'super-*Wednesbury* test'. In the context of statute based exercises of power, this view has been given an element of support.[104] The 'super-*Wednesbury*' question was raised and rejected in *Smith*, which, unlike *Everett*,[105] related to a direct attack, on the grounds of irrationality, on the creation of government policy on the sexual orientation of members of the armed forces.

R v Ministry of Defence, ex p Smith [1996] QB 517

Note that this case is of great importance to the discussion of proportionality (see p. 599).

Sir Thomas Bingham MR

'The policy which currently governs homosexuals (male and female) in the British armed forces is clear: "The Ministry of Defence's policy is that homosexuality is incompatible with service in the Armed Forces. Service personnel who are known to be homosexual or who engage in homosexual activity are administratively discharged from the Armed Forces". As this statement makes plain, proof of homosexual activity is not needed. A reliable admission of homosexual orientation is enough. Where homosexual orientation or activity is clear, the service authorities give themselves no choice but to discharge the member involved without regard to the member's service record or character or the consequences of discharge to the member personally.

These four appellants, three men and one woman, were administratively discharged from the armed forces because they were homosexual. None of them had committed any offence against the general criminal law, nor any offence against the special law governing his or her service. None of them had committed any homosexual act on service premises nor (save in one instance, said to be unwitting) any act involving another member of the service. All of them had shown the qualities required of loyal and efficient service personnel. All of them had looked forward to long service careers, now denied them. Their lives and livelihoods have been grossly disrupted by their involuntary discharge.

The appellants challenge the lawfulness of their discharge and thus, indirectly, of the policy which required them to be discharged. They say that the policy is [irrational]. They accept without reservation that any member of the armed services who acts inappropriately towards any other member, or who is guilty of any harassment, or who commits any offence or breach of service discipline, may be discharged administratively, if not on disciplinary grounds. So too, if a member's sexual orientation undermines that member's efficiency as a member of the service or is shown to cause demonstrable damage to the service. They claim no right or liberty to commit homosexual acts or to make homosexual advances on the mess-deck or in the barrack-room or in any other service setting. They accept that membership of a disciplined fighting force involves a curtailment of freedoms enjoyed by others in civilian employments, and recognise that the exigencies of service life may properly justify restrictions on homosexual activity and manifestations of homosexual orientation. Their challenge is, and is only, to the blanket, non-discretionary, unspecific nature of the existing [policy].

There can be no doubt that public attitudes to homosexuals and homosexuality have in the past varied widely from country to country, and within the same country at different times, and among different social groups in the same country. [But] there has in this country been a discernible trend,

---

[104] *Nottinghamshire County Council v Secretary of State for the Environment* [1986] AC 240; *Hammersmith and Fulham LBC v Secretary of State for the Environment* [1991] 1 AC 521.   [105] See p. 93.

over the last half century or so, towards greater understanding and greater tolerance of homosexuals by heterosexuals, and towards greater openness and honesty by [homosexuals]. The routine quinquennial review of the statutes governing the armed forces has the effect that issues such as the treatment of homosexuals are reconsidered periodically. In 1986 a Select Committee of the House of Commons [concluded] that the law should remain as it then stood. But opinion did not stand still. In 1991 another House of Commons Select Committee returned to the subject. Submissions were then made that service law should be brought into line with civilian law and that homosexual orientation alone should not be a bar to membership of the armed forces. The Select Committee accepted the first of these submissions, seeing "no reason why Service personnel should be liable to prosecution under Service law for homosexual activity which would be legal in civilian [law]". But they rejected the second submission, concluding that there was "considerable force to MoD's argument that the presence of people known to be homosexual can cause tension in a group of people required to live and work sometimes under great stress and physically at very close quarters, and thus damage its cohesion and fighting [effectiveness]". The Select Committee were not persuaded in 1991 that the time had yet come to permit the armed forces to accept homosexuals or homosexual [activity]. In upholding the existing policy that homosexual activity or orientation should be an absolute bar to membership of the armed forces, the 1991 Select Committee undoubtedly reflected the overwhelming consensus of service and official opinion in this country. It does not appear that the Select Committee required or received any evidence of actual harm done by sexual orientation alone or by private homosexual activity outside the context of service life. Nor does the Select Committee appear to have considered whether the objectives of the existing policy could be met by a rule less absolute in its effect than that which was then applied.

In other areas of national life opinion has shifted. In July 1991 the Prime Minister announced that neither homosexual orientation nor private homosexual activity should henceforth preclude appointment even to sensitive posts in the home civil service and the diplomatic service. [The Lord Chancellor] has made similar announcements in relation to judicial office. In July 1994 the Royal Fleet Auxiliary introduced an equal opportunities policy stating that it did not discriminate on grounds of homosexuality. A majority of police forces now follow the same policy. Outside the United Kingdom also, opinion has not stood still. Very few NATO countries bar homosexuals from their armed forces. This practice does not appear to have precluded the closest co-operation between such forces and our own. In the course of 1992–93 Australia, New Zealand and Canada relaxed their ban on homosexuals in their armed services but, importantly, introduced codes of conduct which defined the forms of homosexual conduct which were judged to be unacceptable. In the United States, on the other hand, as an authoritative report in 1993 made plain, military opinion remained overwhelmingly against allowing homosexuals to [serve].

I regard the progressive development and refinement of public and professional opinion at home and abroad, here very briefly described, as an important feature of this case. A belief which represented unquestioned orthodoxy in Year X may have become questionable by Year Y and unsustainable by Year Z. Public and professional opinion are a continuum. The four appellants were discharged towards the end of 1994. The lawfulness of their discharge falls to be judged as of that date.

[On irrationality]

Mr David Pannick [submitted] that the court should adopt the following approach to the issue of irrationality: "The court may not interfere with the exercise of an administrative discretion on substantive grounds save where the court is satisfied that the decision is unreasonable in the sense that it is beyond the range of responses open to a reasonable decision-maker. But in judging whether the decision maker has exceeded this margin of appreciation the human rights context is important. The more substantial the interference with human rights, the more the court will require by way of justification before it is satisfied that the decision is reasonable in the sense outlined above." This submission is in my judgment an accurate distillation of the principles laid down by the House of Lords in *Bugdaycay v Secretary of State for the Home Dept* [[1987] AC 514] and *Brind v Secretary of State for the Home Dept* [[1991] 1 AC 696].

It was argued for the ministry, in reliance on *Nottinghamshire CC v Secretary of State for the Environment* [[1986] AC 240] and *Hammersmith and Fulham London BC v Secretary of State for the Environment* [[1991] 1 AC 521], that a test more exacting than *Wednesbury* was appropriate in this [case]. The Divisional Court rejected this argument and so do I. The greater the policy content of a decision, and the more remote the subject matter of a decision from ordinary judicial experience, the more hesitant the court must necessarily be in holding a decision to be irrational. That is good law and, like most good law, common sense. Where decisions of a policy-laden, esoteric or security-based nature are in issue, even greater caution than normal must be shown in applying the test, but the test itself is sufficiently flexible to cover all situations.

The present cases do not affect the lives or liberty of those involved. But they do concern innate qualities of a very personal kind and the decisions of which the appellants complain have had a profound effect on their careers and prospects. The appellants' rights as human beings are very much in issue. It is now accepted that this issue is justiciable. This does not of course mean that the court is thrust into the position of the primary decision-maker. It is not the constitutional role of the court to regulate the conditions of service in the armed forces of the Crown, nor has it the expertise to do so. But it has the constitutional role and duty of ensuring that the rights of citizens are not abused by the unlawful exercise of executive power. While the court must properly defer to the expertise of responsible decision-makers, it must not shrink from its fundamental duty to "do right to all manner of [people]".

The reasons underlying the present policy were given in an affidavit sworn by Air Chief Marshal Sir John Willis KCB CBE, the vice-chief of the defence staff, an officer of great seniority and [experience]. Sir John advanced three reasons. The first related to morale and unit effectiveness, the second to the role of the services as guardian of recruits under the age of 18, and the third to the requirement of communal living in many service situations. Sir John described the ministry's policy as based not on a moral judgment but on a practical assessment of the implications of homosexual orientation on military life. By "a practical assessment" Sir John may have meant an assessment of past experience in practice, or he may have meant an assessment of what would be likely to happen in practice if the present policy were varied. His affidavit makes no reference to any specific past experience, despite the fact that over the years very many homosexuals must have served in the armed forces. He does, however, make clear the apprehension of senior service authorities as to what could happen if the existing policy were revoked or varied, and the grounds upon which he relies were the subject of consideration by the House of Commons Select Committees to which reference has already been made.

[In addition to specific and detailed criticisms of the MOD policy, above] all, Mr Pannick criticised the blanket nature of the existing rule. He placed great emphasis on the practice of other nations whose rules were framed so as to counter the particular mischiefs to which homosexual orientation or activity might give rise. He pointed out that other personal problems such as addiction to alcohol, or compulsive gambling, or marital infidelity were dealt with by the service authorities on a case by case basis and not on the basis of a rule which permitted no account to be taken of the peculiar features of the case under [consideration].

The existing policy cannot in my judgment be stigmatised as irrational at the time when these appellants were discharged. It was supported by both Houses of Parliament and by those to whom the ministry properly looked for professional advice. There was, to my knowledge, no evidence before the ministry which plainly invalidated that advice. Changes made by other countries were in some cases very recent. The Australian, New Zealand and Canadian codes had been adopted too recently to yield much valuable experience. The ministry did not have the opportunity to consider the full range of arguments developed before us. Major policy changes should be the product of mature reflection, not instant reaction. The threshold of irrationality is a high one. It was not crossed in this case.'

....

Smith and Grady v The United Kingdom (27 December 1999)

The applicants complained that the investigations into their homosexuality and their subsequent discharge from the Royal Air Force on the sole ground that they were homosexual, in pursuance of the Ministry of Defence's absolute policy against homosexuals in the British armed forces, constituted a violation of their right to respect for their private lives. The European Court of Human Rights agreed and held that neither the investigations conducted into the applicants' sexual orientation nor their discharge on the grounds of their homosexuality were justified under the Convention. The applicants further complained of a violation of Article 13 of the Convention, in that they had no 'effective remedy before a national authority' in respect of the violation of their Convention right.

The European Court of Human Rights

'135. The Court recalls that Article 13 guarantees the availability of a remedy at national level to enforce the substance of Convention rights and freedoms in whatever form they may happen to be secured in the domestic legal order. Thus, its effect is to require the provision of a domestic remedy allowing the competent national authority both to deal with the substance of the relevant Convention complaint and to grant appropriate relief. However, Article 13 does not go so far as to require incorporation of the Convention or a particular form of remedy, Contracting States being afforded a margin of appreciation in conforming with their obligations under this provision. Nor does the effectiveness of a remedy for the purposes of Article 13 depend on the certainty of a favourable outcome for the [applicant].

136. [As] was made clear by the High Court and the Court of Appeal in [*Smith*, p. 579], since the Convention did not form part of English law, questions as to whether the application of the policy violated the applicants' [Convention rights] and, in particular, as to whether the policy had been shown by the authorities to respond to a pressing social need or to be proportionate to any legitimate aim served, were not questions to which answers could properly be offered. The sole issue before the domestic courts was whether the policy could be said to be "irrational".

137. The test of "irrationality" applied in the present case was that explained in the judgment of Sir Thomas Bingham MR: a court was not entitled to interfere with the exercise of an administrative discretion on substantive grounds save where the court was satisfied that the decision was unreasonable in the sense that it was beyond the range of responses open to a reasonable decision-maker. In judging whether the decision-maker had exceeded this margin of appreciation, the human rights context was important, so that the more substantial the interference with human rights, the more the court would require by way of justification before it was satisfied that the decision was reasonable. It was, however, further emphasised that, notwithstanding any human rights context, the threshold of irrationality which an applicant was required to surmount was a high one. [The] Court notes that the main judgments in both courts commented favourably on the applicants' submissions challenging the reasons advanced by the Government in justification of the policy. Simon Brown LJ [in the High Court] considered that the balance of argument lay with the applicants and that their arguments in favour of a conduct-based code were [powerful]. Sir Thomas Bingham MR found that those submissions of the applicants were of "very considerable cogency" and that they fell to be considered in depth with particular reference to the potential effectiveness of a conduct-based [code]. Furthermore, while offering no conclusive views on the Convention issues raised by the case, Simon Brown LJ expressed the opinion that "the days of the policy were numbered" in light of the United Kingdom's Convention [obligations], and Sir Thomas Bingham MR observed that the investigations and the discharge of the applicants did not appear to show respect for their private lives. He considered that there might be room for argument as to whether there had been a disproportionate interference with their rights under Article 8 of the [Convention]. Nevertheless, both courts concluded that the policy could not be said to be beyond the range of responses open to a reasonable decision-maker and, accordingly, could not be considered to be "irrational".

138. In such circumstances, the Court considers it clear that [the] threshold at which the High Court and the Court of Appeal could find the Ministry of Defence policy irrational was placed so high that it effectively excluded any consideration by the domestic courts of the question of whether the interference with the applicants' rights answered a pressing social need or was proportionate to the national security and public order aims [pursued].

139. In such circumstances, the Court finds that the applicants had no effective remedy in relation to the violation of their right to respect for their private lives guaranteed by Article 8 of the Convention. Accordingly, there has been a violation of Article 13 of the Convention.'

Post scriptum: On January 12, 2000, the Minister of Defence announced that the then existing ban would be lifted and that homosexuality was no longer a bar to serving in the armed forces.[106]

(e) Legitimate expectation

Legitimate expectation refers to the principle of good administration or administrative fairness that, if a public authority leads a person or body to expect that the public authority will, in the future, continue to act in a way either in which it has regularly (or even always) acted in the past or on the basis of a past promise or statement which represents how it proposes to act, then, prima facie, the public authority should not, without an overriding reason in the public interest, resile from that representation and unilaterally cancel the expectation of the person or body that that state of affairs will continue. This is of particular importance if an individual has acted on the representation to his or her detriment. The principle does not appear in the original Diplock classification,[107] but, it is suggested, should be included as an element of irrationality because the principle is based on administrative 'fairness' and, although not amounting to an enforceable legal right, is capable of being protected in public law.[108] The denial of a legitimate expectation created by a public authority may, therefore, amount to an abuse of power, which is a useful phrase which 'catches the moral impetus of the rule of law'.[109]

The principle of legitimate expectation, therefore, exists as yet another common law control on the exercise of powers by a public authority. It is one of a number of attempts to pin point vague concepts of unfairness and often the departure from a promise made or a policy promulgated could equally be struck down on the *Wednesbury* sub-principle that the decision-maker has failed to have regard to material considerations or has had regard to immaterial considerations. The principle involves the simplistic statement that promises should be kept, that good administration requires adherence by public authorities to their promises, but that statement is limited in accordance with the principles stated earlier in this chapter that, first, a public authority cannot fetter the exercise of its discretion and, second, cannot act illegally.

The public authority must create an expectation in the mind of an individual. The current state of judicial creativity is that there are recognised three types of expectation: 'adopt a fair procedure', 'conform to stated policy criteria', and 'confer a substantive benefit'.

It may happen that a public authority, by an express undertaking or past practice or a combination of the two, has represented to those concerned that it will give them a right to be

---

[106] Commons *Hansard* 12 January 2000 column 287–301.   [107] See p. 529.
[108] *R v Secretary of State for the Home Department, ex p Behluli* [1998] EWCA Civ 788.
[109] *Nadarajah v Secretary of State for the Home Department* [2005] EWCA Civ 1363, per Laws LJ, at para 67.

heard before it makes any change in its policy upon a particular issue which affects them. If so, it will have created a legitimate expectation that it will consult before making changes, and in *GCHQ*,[110] it was held that the trade unions would have had a legitimate expectation that they would be consulted before the terms of employment were changed, but for the fact that considerations of national security prevailed. Similarly, it was held that the Home Secretary was under a duty to exercise his discretion with regard to immigration matters fairly and, if he undertook to allow in persons on certain conditions, he should not resile from that undertaking without affording interested persons a hearing and even then only if the overriding public interest demanded it.[111] In *R v Watford Borough Council, ex p Incorporated West Herts Golf Club*,[112] the club challenged the council's decision refusing to renew the club's lease of council-owned property which was used by the club as a golf course. The club's lease was due to expire and the council wanted to alter the terms by which the land was used (in particular to obtain more access to the land by the general public). The council gave an express promise to enter into negotiations but did not do so and determined that the land should be used as a municipal golf course. It was held that, having promised that there would be negotiations over the future use of the land, the Council could not unilaterally decide not to continue with those negotiations. In one sense, an expectation that a public authority will follow a fair procedure, especially with regard to giving an individual an adequate hearing or allowing a consultation process, is an aspect of procedural fairness discussed in head V. The main characteristic of a procedural expectation is that the expectation derives from the public authority's statement and not from statutory provision or the common law principle of natural justice. However, if there is in fact no clear and unambiguous statement promising an advantageous procedure, legitimate expectation is not the end of the story and the more general concept of 'unfairness amounting to an abuse of power', in which the doctrine of legitimate expectation is rooted may take over.[113]

It is a common feature of modern public administration that, for the day to day operation of a particular governmental policy, the relevant administrative authority will lay down guidance which is both publicly available and which gives to the individual likely to be affected thereby an indication of the criteria which the decision maker will take into consideration when determining a matter within that policy. This is important to the individual, who will then be able to arrange his or her affairs, to present his or her case with those policy criteria in mind, and to build a case based on his or her circumstances. Obviously the individual who then finds that those criteria have not been followed will claim that the decision is unfair. This 'conform to its stated policy criteria' expectation is somewhat analogous to creating a substantive benefit, because if the individual can prove that he or she comes within the criteria laid down for the conferment of an advantage or benefit, a substantive benefit is more likely (or even certain) to be granted. In *Ruddock*,[114] Taylor J concluded that the doctrine of legitimate expectation in essence imposes a duty to act fairly and to keep promises, but that the doctrine is not confined to the right to be consulted or heard. He held that, since the practice had been to publish the current policy, it was incumbent on the Secretary of State, in dealing fairly, to publish the new policy, unless that would conflict with his duties relating to national security. As to the strength of the legitimate expectation, the policy had been consistently repeated publicly in similar terms and it would be hard to imagine a stronger case of an expectation arising either from an express promise given on behalf of a public authority or from the existence of a regular practice which the claimant could reasonably expect to

---

[110] See p. 86.   [111] *R v Secretary of State for the Home Department, ex p Khan* [1985] 1 All ER 40.
[112] [1990] 1 EGLR 263.   [113] See *Camelot*, p. 624.   [114] See p. 95.

continue. In *R v Inland Revenue Commissioners, ex p Unilever*,[115] the Income and Corporation Taxes legislation provided for a two-year time limit within which to make a tax claim. For twenty years, the final tax computations had been submitted more than two years after the end of the relevant accounting period to which they related and this had been accepted by the Revenue. Then the Revenue refused to allow Unilever to claim loss relief against profits on the ground that the tax computations for those accounting periods had been submitted more than two years after the end of each respective accounting period. Unilever applied for judicial review of this decision on the grounds that the Revenue could not, having regard to its past conduct, treat the claim as time-barred. It was held that, although there had been no clear unambiguous and unqualified representation by the Revenue, on the unique facts of Unilever's case, to reject their claims in reliance on the time limit, without clear and general advance notice, was so unfair as to amount to an abuse of power. It has sometimes been argued, especially with regard to applications for asylum, that if the United Kingdom enters into an international treaty, that may give rise to a legitimate expectation on the part of individuals that the executive arm of government will act in accordance with the terms of the treaty. Furthermore, it may happen that, following ratification of a treaty, the executive arm of government may implement the terms of the treaty in the domestic sphere, by means of publicly stated policies or codes of practice and, again on principle, such implementation should be recognized as a statement capable of creating an expectation. It has been held 'that the entering into a Treaty by the Secretary of State could give rise to a legitimate expectation on which the public in general are entitled to rely. Subject to any indication to the contrary, it could be a representation that the Secretary of State would act in accordance with any obligations which he accepted under the Treaty. This legitimate expectation could give rise to a right to relief, as well as additional obligations of fairness, if the Secretary of State, without reason, acted inconsistently with the obligations which this country had undertaken.'[116]

There was, for some time, a debate as to whether the principle of legitimate expectation was limited to an insistence upon fair procedure or to an insistence of conformity to stated policy criteria or whether the principle could confer a substantive benefit on an individual. Against the latter, was raised the argument that public authorities were vested by the legislature with powers and duties to act and could not be estopped from using those powers in the public interest by a promise given earlier (and sometimes in different circumstances than those currently pertaining).

Initial decisions were mixed with regard to the claim of the individuals who reacted to an administrative decision refusing a benefit: 'but you promised me I would get the benefit'. One judge had difficulty in seeing how the concept of legitimate expectation 'can properly provide the basis in the law relating to immigration for any substantive right'.[117] In *R v Devon County Council, ex p Baker*,[118] the Court of Appeal accepted that the phrase 'legitimate expectation' could be used to denote, in additional to procedural rights, a substantive right or an entitlement. The doctrine was somewhat akin to an estoppel. In *R v Ministry of Agriculture Fisheries and Food, ex p Hamble Fisheries*,[119] Sedley J held that the

---

[115] [1996] STC 681.

[116] *R v Secretary of State for the Home Department, ex p Ahmed and Patel* [1998] INLR 570, per Lord Woolf MR, at 583. See, also, *Zeqiri v Secretary of State for the Home Department* [2001] EWCA Civ 342; *Rashid*, p. 594.

[117] *R v Secretary of State for the Home Department ex p Golam Mowla* [1992] 1 WLR 70, per Ralph Gibson LJ, at 87, 88.   [118] [1995] 1 All ER 73.

[119] [1995] 2 All ER 715, at 731.

'real question is one of fairness in public administration. It is difficult to see why it is any less unfair to frustrate a legitimate expectation that something will or will not be done by the decision-maker than it is to frustrate a legitimate expectation that the applicant will be listened to before the decision-maker decides whether to take a particular step. Such a doctrine does not risk fettering a public body in the discharge of public duties because no individual can legitimately expect the discharge of public duties to stand still or be distorted because of that individual's peculiar [position. It] is the court's task to recognise the constitutional importance of ministerial freedom to formulate and to reformulate policy; but it is equally the court's duty to protect the interests of those individuals whose expectation of different treatment has a legitimacy which in fairness out tops the policy choice which threatens to frustrate [it].'

However, in *R v Secretary of State for the Home Department, ex p Hargreaves*,[120] it was held that the only legitimate expectation of certain prisoners whose hopes of home leave and early release were claimed to have been frustrated because of a change in official policy was to have their applications individually considered in light of whatever official policy was currently in force. That legitimate expectation now applies, as a general principle of fairness, to 'substantive rights' in addition to merely 'procedural rights' or 'conform to criteria rights' was strongly endorsed by the Court of Appeal in:

R v North and East Devon Health Authority, ex p Coughlan [2000] QB 213 (CA)

Lord Woolf MR

'3. Miss Coughlan was grievously injured in a road traffic accident in 1971. [In] 1993 she and seven comparably disabled patients were moved with their agreement from Newcourt Hospital, which it was desired to close, to a purpose-built facility, Mardon House. It is a decision of the Health Authority [to] close Mardon House which is the immediate cause of the present litigation.

. . .

6. [The] Health Authority does not dispute that Miss Coughlan and her fellow long-term patients accepted the move from Newcourt Hospital to Mardon House in 1993 on the basis of a clear promise that Mardon House would be their home for [life].

. . .

53. [Mardon] House was a purpose built NHS facility costing £1.5m. It was designed to house young, long term, severely disabled, residential patients. [There] were 20 beds. There were 17 purpose built, individual flatlets each designed to have a bedroom, sitting room, inter-connecting bathroom and a designated kitchenette area. They were individually tailored for the needs of those moving into them. The residents of Newcourt had been involved in discussions about the nature and design of the building and its services. They chose their flatlets and the decor. Intensive reablement services and respite care were also to be provided there. There was a mix of residential/nursing home care and active acute treatment. The Newcourt patients were persuaded to move to Mardon House by representations on behalf of the Health Authority that it was more appropriate to their needs. The patients relied on an express assurance or promise that they could live there "for as long as they chose". Nursing care was to be provided for them in Mardon House. It was the "new [Newcourt]".

. . .

---

[120] [1996] EWCA Civ 1006.

Legitimate expectation—the court's role

55. [It] is necessary to begin by examining the court's role where what is in issue is a promise as to how it would behave in the future made by a public body when exercising a statutory [function].

56. What is still the subject of some controversy is the court's role when a member of the public, as a result of a promise or other conduct, has a legitimate expectation that he will be treated in one way and the public body wishes to treat him or her in a different way. Here the starting point has to be to ask what in the circumstances the member of the public could legitimately [expect. Where] there is a dispute as to this, the dispute has to be determined by the [court]. This can involve a detailed examination of the precise terms of the promise or representation made, the circumstances in which the promise was made and the nature of the statutory or other discretion.

57. There are at least three possible outcomes. (a) The court may decide that the public authority is only required to bear in mind its previous policy or other representation, giving it the weight it thinks right, but no more, before deciding whether to change course. Here the court is confined to reviewing the decision on *Wednesbury* [grounds]. (b) On the other hand the court may decide that the promise or practice induces a legitimate expectation of, for example, being consulted before a particular decision is taken. Here it is uncontentious that the court itself will require the opportunity for consultation to be given unless there is an overriding reason to resile from [it] in which case the court will itself judge the adequacy of the reason advanced for the change of policy, taking into account what fairness requires. (c) Where the court considers that a lawful promise or practice has induced a legitimate expectation of a benefit which is substantive, not simply procedural, authority now establishes that here too the court will in a proper case decide whether to frustrate the expectation is so unfair that to take a new and different course will amount to an abuse of power. Here, once the legitimacy of the expectation is established, the court will have the task of weighing the requirements of fairness against any overriding interest relied upon for the change of [policy].

. . .

59. [Most] cases of an enforceable expectation of a substantive benefit (the third category) are likely in the nature of things to be cases where the expectation is confined to one person or a few people, giving the promise or representation the character of a contract. We recognise that the courts' role in relation to the third category is still controversial; but, as we hope to show, it is now clarified by authority.

60. We consider that [the facts of this case as coming into the third category]. Our reasons are as follows. First, the importance of what was promised to Miss [Coughlan]; second, the fact that promise was limited to a few individuals, and the fact that the consequences to the Health Authority of requiring it to honour its promise are likely to be financial only.

. . .

The authorities

64. It is axiomatic that a public authority which derives its existence and its powers from statute cannot validly act outside those powers. This is the familiar ultra vires [doctrine]. Since such powers will ordinarily include anything fairly incidental to the express remit, a statutory body may lawfully adopt and follow policies [and] enter into formal undertakings. But since it cannot abdicate its general remit, not only must it remain free to change policy; its undertakings are correspondingly open to modification or abandonment. The recurrent question is when and where and how the courts are to intervene to protect the public from unwarranted harm in this [process].

65. The court's task in all these cases is not to impede executive activity but to reconcile its continuing need to initiate or respond to change with the legitimate interests or expectations of citizens or strangers who have relied, and have been justified in relying, on a current policy or an extant promise. The critical question is by what standard the court is to resolve such conflicts. It is when one examines the implications for a case like the present of the proposition that so long as the decision-making

process has been lawful, the court's only ground of intervention is the intrinsic rationality of the decision, that the problem becomes apparent. Rationality, as it has developed in modern public law, has two faces: one is the barely known decision which simply defies comprehension; the other is a decision which can be seen to have proceeded by flawed logic (though this can often be equally well allocated to the intrusion of an irrelevant factor). The present decision may well pass a rationality test [but] to limit the court's power of supervision to this is to exclude from consideration another aspect of the decision which is equally the concern of the [law].

. . .

71. Fairness in such a situation, if it is to mean anything, must [include] fairness of outcome. This in turn is why the doctrine of legitimate expectation has emerged as a distinct application of the concept of abuse of power in relation to substantive as well as procedural [benefits]. Legitimate expectation may play different parts in different aspects of public law. The limits to its role have yet to be finally determined by the courts. Its application is still being developed on a case by case basis. Even where it reflects procedural expectations, for example concerning consultation, it may be affected by an overriding public interest. It may operate as an aspect of good administration, qualifying the intrinsic rationality of policy choices. And without injury to the *Wednesbury* doctrine it may furnish a proper basis for the application of the now established concept of abuse of power.

. . .

76. [In this case it is contended that fairness] required the Health Authority, as a matter of fairness, not to resile from their promise unless there was an overriding justification for doing [so]. Here the decision can only be justified if there is an overriding public interest. Whether there is an overriding public interest is a question for the court.

. . .

78. It is from the revenue cases that, in relation to the third category, the proper test emerges. Thus in [*Unilever*, p. 585], this court concluded that for the Crown to enforce a time limit which for years it had not insisted upon would be so unfair as to amount to an abuse of power. As in other tax cases, there was no question of the court's deferring to the Inland Revenue's view of what was fair. The court also concluded that the Inland Revenue's conduct passed the "notoriously high" threshold of irrationality; but the finding of abuse through unfairness was not dependent on this.

. . .

82. The fact that the court will only give effect to a legitimate expectation within the statutory context in which it has arisen should avoid jeopardising the important principle that the executive's policy-making powers should not be trammelled by the [courts]. Policy being (within the law) for the public authority alone, both it and the reasons for adopting or changing it will be accepted by the courts as part of the factual data, in other words, as not ordinarily open to judicial review. The court's task [is] then limited to asking whether the application of the policy to an individual who has been led to expect something different is a just exercise of power. In many cases the authority will already have considered this and made appropriate exceptions [or] resolved to pay compensation where money alone will suffice. But where no such accommodation is made, it is for the court to say whether the consequent frustration of the individual's expectation is so unfair as to be a misuse of the authority's power.

Fairness and the decision to close

83. How are fairness and the overriding public interest in this particular context to be judged? The question arises concretely in the present case. [The] Health Authority voted for closure in spite of the promise. The propriety of such an exercise of power should be tested by asking whether the need which the Health Authority judged to exist to move Miss Coughlan to a local authority facility was such as to outweigh its promise that Mardon House would be her home for life.

84. That a promise was made is confirmed by the evidence of the Health Authority that: "the Applicant and her fellow residents were justified in treating certain statements made by the Authority's predecessor, coupled with the way in which the Authority's predecessor conducted itself at the time of the residents' move from Newcourt Hospital, as amounting to an assurance that, having moved to Mardon House, Mardon House would be a permanent home for [them]".

. . .

86. [This] was an express promise or representation made on a number of occasions in precise terms. It was made to a small group of severely disabled individuals who had been housed and cared for over a substantial period in the Health Authority's predecessor's premises at Newcourt. It specifically related to identified premises which it was represented would be their home for as long as they chose. It was in unqualified terms. It was repeated and confirmed to reassure the residents. It was made by the Health Authority's predecessor for its own purposes, namely to encourage Miss Coughlan and her fellow residents to move out of Newcourt and into Mardon House, a specially built substitute home in which they would continue to receive nursing care. The promise was relied on by Miss Coughlan. Strong reasons are required to justify resiling from a promise given in those circumstances. This is not a case where the Health Authority would, in keeping the promise, be acting inconsistently with its statutory or other public law duties. A decision not to honour it would be equivalent to a breach of contract in private law.

. . .

88. It is, however, clear from the Health Authority's evidence and submissions that it did not consider that it had a legal responsibility or commitment to provide a home, as distinct from care or funding of care, for the Applicant and her fellow residents. It considered [that] the provision of care services to the current residents had become "excessively expensive", having regard to the needs of the majority of disabled people in the Authority's area and the "insuperable problems" involved in the mix of long term residential care and reablement services at Mardon House. Mardon House had, contrary to earlier expectations, become "a prohibitively expensive white elephant. The unit was not financially viable. Its continued operation was dependent upon the Authority supporting it at an excessively high cost. This did not represent value for money and left fewer resources for other services." The Health Authority's attitude was that "It was because of our appreciation of the residents' expectation that they would remain at Mardon House for the rest of their lives that the Board agreed that the Authority should accept a continuing commitment to finance the care of the residents of Mardon for whom it was responsible." But the cheaper option favoured by the Health Authority misses the essential point of the promise which had been given. The fact is that the Health Authority has not offered to the Applicant an equivalent facility to replace what was promised to her. The Health Authority's undertaking to fund her care for the remainder of her life is substantially different in nature and effect from the earlier promise that care for her would be provided at Mardon House. That place would be her home for as long as she chose to live there.

89. We have no hesitation in concluding that the decision to move Miss Coughlan against her will and in breach of the Health Authority's own promise was in the circumstances unfair. It was unfair because it frustrated her legitimate expectation of having a home for life in Mardon House. There was no overriding public interest which justified it.'

....

R v The London Borough of Newham, ex p Bibi [2001] EWCA Civ 607

Two families had been provided by a housing authority with housing for the last ten years or so but they never had security of tenure. However, in the erroneous (but at the time widely held) belief that the Housing Act 1985 imposed a duty to provide accommodation with security of tenure, the authority in

the early 1990s promised to each of them and to others in a similar position legally secure accommodation within eighteen months. The authority did not fulfil its promise although many years had passed.

Schiemann LJ

'19. In all legitimate expectation cases, whether substantive or procedural, three practical questions
arise. The first question is to what has the public authority, whether by practice or by promise, committed itself; the second is whether the authority has acted or proposes to act unlawfully in relation to
its commitment; the third is what the court should [do].

. . .

44. In very broad terms what has happened to each of the applicants is this. At a time when the
Authority had the power but also erroneously thought that it was obliged under the law to provide
secure accommodation to the applicants suitable for their families it promised to do so within 18
months. The letter sent out was, we understand, in standard form and regularly sent out at that time to
those unintentionally homeless[.]

. . .

To what has the authority committed itself?

46. We accept [that] Newham's letter and subsequent conduct will have generated an expectation in
each applicant, as in others in their situation, that Newham would be providing them with secure
housing in the relatively near future. We agree too that such an expectation was legitimate, both in the
sense that it was entirely reasonable for the applicants to entertain it and in the sense [that] it lay within
the powers of the local authority both to make the representation and to fulfil [it].

. . .

48. We proceed therefore on the basis that the Authority has lawfully committed itself to providing
the applicants with suitable accommodation with secure [tenure].

. . .

Has the authority acted unlawfully?

50. The Authority should when considering the position of the applicants have borne in mind that a
promise was made to each of them that they would be given secure tenancies and that these promises
have to this day, many years after they were made, not been fulfilled. There is no indication that the
Authority has ever come to a judgment as to what weight should be given to the fact that the promises
were made. There is no reason why the applicants should be disadvantaged by the fact that the
promises were made as a result of the Authority's misunderstanding of the law.
51. The law requires that any legitimate expectation be properly taken into account in the decision
making process. It has not been in the present case and therefore the Authority has acted [unlawfully].

. . .

54. The present case is one of reliance without concrete detriment. We use this phrase because
there is moral detriment, which should not be dismissed lightly, in the prolonged disappointment
which has [ensued]. In our view these things matter in public law, even though they might not found an
estoppel or actionable misrepresentation in private law, because they go to fairness and through
fairness to possible abuse of power. To disregard the legitimate expectation because no concrete
detriment can be shown would be to place the weakest in society at a particular disadvantage. It would
mean that those who have a choice and the means to exercise it in reliance on some official practice or
promise would gain a legal toehold inaccessible to those who, lacking any means of escape, are
compelled simply to place their trust in what has been represented to [them].

. . .

59. [When] the Authority looks at the matter again it must take into account the legitimate expectations. Unless there are reasons recognised by law for not giving effect to those legitimate expectations

then effect should be given to them. In circumstances such as the present where the conduct of the Authority has given rise to a legitimate expectation then fairness requires that, if the Authority decides not to give effect to that expectation, the Authority articulate its reasons so that their propriety may be tested by the court if that is what the disappointed person requires.

. . .

What should the court do?

63. The present case illustrates a potential conflict between the "legitimate aspirations" of those who have been told where they are on the housing waiting list and what the Authority's allocation scheme is on the one hand and the "legitimate expectations" of those to whom promises have been made by the Authority the fulfilment of which conflicts with the priorities contained in the allocation scheme on the other.

64. In an area such as the provision of housing at public expense where decisions are informed by social and political value judgments as to priorities of expenditure the court will start with a recognition that such invidious choices are essentially political rather than judicial. In our judgment the appropriate body to make that choice in the context of the present case is the Authority. However, it must do so in the light of the legitimate expectations of the respondents.

. . .

69. We [make] a declaration that the Authority is under a duty to consider the applicants' applications for suitable housing on the basis that they have a legitimate expectation that they will be provided by the Authority with suitable accommodation on a secure tenancy.'

From the authorities extracted above and from other authority, a number of sub-principles have emerged over the last few decades.

The expectation must on principle be 'legitimate', a word capable of a number of meanings. 'Legitimate' is not the same as 'lawful', but, as we are concerned with 'public law equity', perhaps those ancient maxims prohibiting a right to arise from an unlawful action and relating to the clean hands of the applicant may be applied, albeit with suitable modifications. Therefore, certain shopkeepers, who had been trading illegally in breach of the Sunday trading law, had no legitimate expectation that they would not be prosecuted for so doing.[121] When it was alleged that a temporary licensing scheme for portrait artists in Leicester Square had been introduced without consultation despite a claimed legitimate expectation of consultation, Maurice Kay J rejected that argument:

'The present case is concerned with unlicensed street trading, a repeated criminal [offence. The] law should be slow to extend to persons acting unlawfully a legitimate expectation of consultation because their expectation does not have a basis in legitimacy and their interest is not one that the law holds protected. [Whilst] I do not say that there can never be circumstances in which persons acting unlawfully may successfully invoke a legitimate expectation, the circumstances of this case do not give rise to a legitimate expectation of consultation.'

The Court of Appeal refused permission to appeal from that decision.[122]

The simplistic statement that promises should be kept is limited in accordance with the fundamental principle stated earlier that a public authority cannot act illegally. The party seeking to invoke the principle must demonstrate that it was within the powers of the public authority both to make the representation relied upon and to fulfil its content. 'Neither legitimate expectation nor estoppel can override a statutory prohibition. [An] erroneous

---

[121] *R v South Somerset DC, ex p DJB* (1989) 1 Admin LR 11.

[122] *R (On the Application of Dinev) v The City of Westminster Council* [2001] EWCA Civ 80. See, also, *R, on the Application of Thompson v Secretary of State for the Home Department* [2003] EWHC 2382 (Admin).

statement made by or on behalf of the Secretary of State purporting to recognise a status which, upon a correct interpretation of the relevant statutory provisions, could not exist cannot have the effect of bringing that status into existence.'[123] This is illustrated by:

....

R v Secretary of State for Education and Employment, ex p Begbie
[1999] EWCA Civ 2100

The 'Assisted Places Scheme' (APS) was a scheme whereby some pupils at independent schools had their school fees paid out of public funds. The Labour Party, then the Opposition, stated that if it regained power it would dismantle the scheme, but assurances were made 'that Labour will honour those existing places which have already been given; your child will not be forced to move school'. Heather Begbie was offered a place at an independent school under the APS. After the May 1997 election, Labour came to power and quickly abolished the scheme. The effect for Heather 'was that she was entitled to keep her assisted place until the end of the year in which she completed her primary education, but thereafter she would not be so entitled unless the Secretary of State could be persuaded that on the individual merits of her case it was reasonable for her to continue to hold her assisted place while she was receiving secondary education' (a 'discretionary extension'). Later, the Prime Minister in an article in the *Evening Standard* newspaper wrote: '[N]o child currently at private school under the scheme or who has already got a place has lost out. They will be able to continue their education.' An application was made on Heather's behalf for a discretionary extension but the Secretary of State would not exercise his discretion in her favour and the application was formally refused. An application for judicial review of that refusal was made on the ground that the statements made by or on behalf of the Government gave rise to a legitimate expectation that Heather would retain her assisted place until she completed her education at her school.

Peter Gibson LJ

'52. [No] doubt statements such as those made by the Leader of the Opposition before May 1997 did give rise to an expectation that children already on the APS, from which group children at "all through" schools were not excepted, would continue to receive support in their education until it was [completed], but the question for the court is whether those statements give rise to a legitimate expectation, in the sense of an expectation which will be protected by [law].

. . .

54. [Reliance] on the pre-election statements founders on the fact that such statements were not made on behalf of a public [authority].

55. An opposition spokesman, even the Leader of the Opposition, does not speak on behalf of a public authority. A further difficulty relates to the effect in law of a pre-election promise by politicians anxious to win the votes of electors. [No] case has been shown to us of the court treating such a promise as of binding effect or otherwise as having legal consequences. There are good practical reasons why this should be so. As was explained on behalf of the Labour [Party]: "Only once the new Government had full access to information on APS numbers and projected spending, was it possible to present more details on our policy of phasing out the APS."

56. It is obvious that a party in opposition will not know all the facts and ramifications of a promise until it achieves office. To hold that the pre-election promises bound a newly elected Government could well be inimical to good government. I intend no encouragement to politicians to be extravagant in

[123] *R v Secretary of State for the Home Department, ex p Nawal Khan* [1997] EWHC 455 (Admin), per McCullough J, at para 13. See, also, *R (on the application of Theophilus) v London Borough of Southwark* [2002] EWHC 1371 (Admin) (Borough had power to grant financial support to a student); *Rowland v The Environment Agency* [2003] EWCA Civ 1885 (Agency had no power to treat as private water a stretch of river over which the public had rights of navigation).

their pre-election promises, but when a party elected into office fails to keep its election promises, the consequences should be political and not legal.

. . .

74. I cannot conclude without expressing my considerable sympathy with Heather and her parents and indeed all others in a similar position. Few things matter more to properly concerned parents with children of school age than that their children should have the best possible chance in life through the best education that can be arranged for them. The hopes of many of seeing their children complete their education under the APS were raised by the general statements made by politicians in opposition and have been cruelly disappointed by the policy adopted by the same politicians when in government, and their aggrieved feelings will not have been lessened by the erroneous, confused and contradictory statements made by the Government while they were trying to obtain clarification of the [policy. I] regret that I can see no way in which redress in law can be given them for their [grievance].'

Laws LJ

'84. If there had been reliance and detriment in consequence, I would have been prepared to hold that it would be abusive for the Secretary of State not to make the earlier representations good. But there has not. Bitter disappointment, certainly; but I cannot see that this, though it excites one's strongest sympathy, is enough to elevate the Secretary of State's correction of his error into an abuse of power. We do not sit here to punish public authorities for incompetence, though incompetence may most certainly sometimes have effects in public law.'

It is settled law that a public authority can only be bound by acts and statements of its employees and agents if and to the extent that they had actual or ostensible authority to bind the public body by their acts and statements:

Bloggs 61 v Secretary of State for the Home Department
[2003] EWCA Civ 686

Auld LJ

'1. This is an appeal by a serving prisoner against the order [dismissing] his challenge by way of judicial review of the Secretary of State's decision to remove him from a protected witness unit to a "mainstream" prison régime.

. . .

3. A protected witness unit is an internally secure part of a prison. It provides segregated accommodation for prisoners who have committed serious criminal offences [and] who have provided information and/or given evidence against others involved in serious crime and who, for that reason, would be at particular risk if held under "mainstream" prison conditions. [To] preserve their anonymity within the prison system, protected witnesses are all given the name of Bloggs followed by a number; it is known colloquially within the Prison Service as "the Bloggs system".

4. [The issue in the appeal was] whether representations allegedly made by police officers to the appellant could and did give him a legitimate expectation as against the Prison Service that it would retain him within one of its protected witness units for the length of his prison [service].

. . .

30. It is plain from the legal framework [that] the Police had neither actual authority to make the alleged representations on which the appellant relies, nor the authority to implement any such as might have been made. As to the latter, not even the Prison Service had authority to grant him the status of a protected witness for the duration of his [sentence].

. . .

38. The starting point [is] that the Police could not bind the Prison Service to treat the appellant as a protected witness unless they, the Police, had actual or ostensible authority to do so. There [was neither actual authority nor ostensible authority].'

The statement of the public authority must be 'clear', 'unambiguous', 'unequivocal'.[124] There are many dicta to this effect. 'It is settled law that for such an expectation to arise, an applicant has to prove that there has been representation that was "clear, unambiguous and devoid of relevant qualification"' and a mere 'statement of enthusiasm is a long way short of the clear and unambiguous representation"' referred to, as it does not amount to a commitment on the part of the public authority.[125] Legitimate expectation 'has only a limited effect. It applies where there has been an express promise which is unqualified and upon which the promisee is entitled to rely.'[126] If, of course, the statement is not communicated to the person concerned, and, consequently, that person does not know of it, there can not be any sensible expectation based upon it.[127]

If a legitimate expectation is established, it must be unfair for the public authority to resile from giving effect to that expectation, unless the wider interests of the public require that the public authority resiles in order properly to protect those wider interests. On principle, since the individual citizen will always be subordinate to the commonwealth as a whole, the question whether it would be so unfair as to amount to an abuse of power for a public authority to resile from the position which it (and, perhaps, its predecessors) have allowed to arise is determined by the court. The court must consider not just the interests of the parties (such as any detrimental reliance by the claimant and the impact on his or her interests), but also the wider interest which the public authority serves and which may need to be protected by permitting the public body to resile from its previous position. The 'court must decide whether having regard to all the relevant circumstances including the reliance by the citizen, the impact on the interests of the citizen and the public and considerations of proportionality for the public body to resile would in all the circumstances and applying the criteria referred to be so unfair as to constitute an abuse of power':[128]

R (on the application of Rashid) v Secretary of State for the Home Department [2005] EWCA Civ 744

Rashid was an Iraqi Kurd who sought asylum. According to the departmental policy in force at the date of his application for asylum, Rashid was entitled to asylum. His claim was, however, rejected by the Secretary of State. Later, the existence of the policy was revealed to Rashid's advisers who requested a reconsideration of the asylum application. It was claimed that, if at any time after his arrival the asylum policy which ought to have been applied had been applied, Rashid would have been granted asylum. The Secretary of State agreed to reconsider the case in the light of the policy. By the time the decision on the reconsideration was taken, the situation in Iraq had changed considerably as a result of

[124] *R v IRC, ex p MFK Underwriting Agencies* [1991] 1 WLR 1545; *R v Jockey Club, ex p RAM Racecources* [1993] 2 All ER 225. Note, however, *Rowland v The Environment Agency* [2003] EWCA Civ 1885, per Peter Gibson LJ, at para 68.
[125] *R (on the application of Hilary Wainwright) v Richmond upon Thames London Borough Council* [2001] EWHC 310 (Admin), per Silber J, at para 60.
[126] *R v London Borough of Brent, ex p Mary Jerker* [1998] EWHC 509 (Admin), per Latham J, at para 24, 25.
[127] *R (on the application of Toovey) v Law Society* [2002] EWHC 391 (Admin).
[128] *Rowland v The Environment Agency* [2003] EWCA Civ 1885, per Peter Gibson LJ, at para 67; *R (on the application of Jones) v The Environment Agency* [2005] EWHC 2270 (Admin), per Ouseley J, at para 77.

the invasion by coalition forces and the removal of Saddam Hussein's régime. The policy was withdrawn and the Secretary of State once again refused the claim for asylum. In a letter, the Secretary of State admitted 'that there was a failure to follow the terms of the previous (but now redundant) policy that would, while Saddam Hussein's régime was still in power, have resulted in the grant of refugee status to Mr Rashid' and 'that prior to the military intervention to remove that régime', two applicants (M and A) 'whose position, in all material respects, was identical to that of' Rashid had been granted refugee status in accordance with the policy.

Pill LJ

'25. [There] plainly is a legitimate expectation in a claimant for asylum that the Secretary of State will apply his policy on asylum to the claim. Whether the claimant knows of the policy is not in the present context relevant. It would be grossly unfair if the court's ability to intervene depended at all upon whether the particular claimant had or had not heard of a policy, especially one unknown to relevant Home Office [officials].

. . .

33. Eventually, the correct policy emerged in the cases of M and A. The claimant's case had been "stacked" behind them. Aware as they must, or should, have been that the point involved in the three cases was identical, and of the possibility of a change of circumstances in Iraq, fairness required that the same treatment be given to the [claimant].

34. [It is] a claim of unfairness amounting to an abuse of power, of which legitimate expectation is only one application. The abuse is based on an expectation that a general policy for dealing with asylum applications will be applied and will be applied [uniformly].

. . .

36. [The] degree of unfairness was such as to amount to an abuse of power requiring the intervention of the [court]. This was far from a single error in an obscure field. A state of affairs was permitted to continue for a long time and in relation to a country which at the time would have been expected to be in the forefront of the respondent's deliberations. I am very far from saying that administrative errors may often lead to a finding of conspicuous unfairness amounting to an abuse.'

Dyson LJ

'49. [The] facts of the case, viewed always in their statutory context, will steer the court to a more or less intrusive quality of review. In some cases, a change of tack by a public authority, though unfair from the applicant's stance, may involve questions of general policy affecting the public at large: in such cases the judges may not be in a position to adjudicate save at most on a bare *Wednesbury* [basis. In] other cases, where, for example, there are no wide-ranging policy issues, the court may be able to apply a more intrusive form of review to the decision. The more the decision which is challenged lies in the field of pure policy, particularly in relation to issues which the court is ill-equipped to judge, the less likely it is that true abuse of power will be found.

50. The nature of the decision will, therefore, always be relevant to the question whether the frustration of an expectation is an abuse of power. The court will not only have regard to whether wide-ranging issues of policy are involved, but also whether holding the public body to its promise or policy has only limited temporal effect and whether the decision has implications for a large class of persons. The degree of unfairness is also material. [The] more extreme the unfairness, the more likely it is to be characterised as an abuse of power. If the frustration of a legitimate expectation is made in bad faith, then it is very likely to be regarded as an abuse of power and, therefore, unlawful.

. . .

52. [In] my judgment it is clear that there has been conspicuous unfairness in this case. It is true that [there] is no evidence that the failure to apply or even reveal the existence of the policy [during the

relevant period] was deliberate and the result of bad faith. But it is a remarkable feature of this case that, despite repeated requests for clarification and direct instructions from the interviewing officer, the caseworker and the presenting officer who were party to the original and appellate consideration of the claimant's case as to their state of knowledge of the policy, no response has ever been provided; not even after the grant of permission to apply for judicial review, when the Secretary of State had a duty of full and frank [disclosure].

53. In the absence of any explanation, I consider that the court is entitled at the very least to infer that there has been flagrant and prolonged incompetence in this case. This is a far cry from the case of a mistake which is short-lived and the reasons for which are fully explained. The unfairness in this case has been aggravated by the fact that [the] claimant was not treated in the same way as M and A, with whose cases his case had been linked procedurally. Had he been so treated, he would have had the benefit of the policy and been accorded full refugee status.

54. Accordingly, the [Secretary] of State acted unlawfully in choosing to ignore his policy. In so doing, he acted with conspicuous unfairness amounting to an abuse of power.'

R v Beatrix Potter School, ex p Kanner [1996] EWHC Admin 397

The headmaster of the Beatrix Potter primary school decided to offer a place at that school to the applicant, in a letter to her mother, stating: 'your child will enter school on the morning of September 9' and ending: 'May I formally welcome you to the school and wish you a long and happy association with us'. The applicant and the mother went shopping and bought a school uniform. Later that day, the headmaster telephoned to say that the offer was withdrawn. Then, he wrote a letter, withdrawing the offer and offering an apology. The reasoning behind the withdrawal was set out in the affidavit of an official of the education department: the school was oversubscribed and extra admissions would result in two classes needing to be provided over the next six years, which was 'clearly an inefficient use of resources given the vacancies in neighbouring schools. [The] application for places in primary schools is a stressful and emotional experience for some parents, particularly when the school is heavily over-subscribed. For this and other reasons I consider it absolutely fundamental that places are allocated as and when they properly arise and to the child who, according to a strict application of the criteria, has the highest priority for that place. Any other system would justifiably cause many parents to perceive the system as unjust and arbitrary. When the extraordinary occurs, as in this case, I consider the only correct approach is to rectify the error and withdraw the place with a minimum of delay.'

Popplewell J

'15. That was the clearest possible offer to the parents of a place in the school. It was submitted on behalf of the respondent that the headmaster did not have either actual or ostensible authority to make that [offer. I] am satisfied he had ostensible authority and any parent receiving that letter [was] entitled to take the view that their child had now been admitted to the school.

. . .

24. [All] the factors necessary [to] give rise to legitimate expectation are there. There has been a clear express promise. It has been relied on and there has been some detriment. It is not only to the detriment in the cost of buying clothes, but the upset that was caused to the mother and child. That is more particularly so when one has regard to the fact that there is in the school a brother of this applicant, and the family unit would be upset in the broadest sense from the withdrawal of this application. Legitimate expectation is in my view a fact to be take into account in deciding whether the respondents have acted *Wednesbury* unreasonably. In some cases it may be the only factor and would therefore be wholly decisive in an applicants's claim. In other cases it may be no more than one of the

matters to be taken into account. It is really an aspect of the general public law obligation and the obligation on the respondents not to act unreasonably.

. . .

32. The way that it is put by the respondents is that this was a genuine mistake; that albeit of some detriment to the parents because of the upset that it caused and the money that was spent on clothes, nevertheless it was not unreasonable for them to withdraw the offer in order to have regard to proper entry criteria and the administration of education in the area.

. . .

44. I therefore turn to consider the *Wednesbury* principle and if the withdrawal by the respondents of this offer was unreasonable. I look at the policy behind the respondent's decision. I look at the effect that it had on the applicant and the length of it and I come to the clearest possible conclusion that it is impossible to categorise the decision to withdraw as *Wednesbury* unreasonable. If there were a test of fairness I would also take the same view, that given the short period of time in which these parents were mistakenly of the view that the child had a place is of itself extremely irrelevant. Nothing that I can say of course should encourage the idea that an offer is other than a very serious matter. Parents who receive an offer are likely to treat it very seriously and I entirely accept that the upset which was caused to the child and to the parents was a very real one. But given all the circumstances of this case this application must fail.'

Of course, the appropriate decision-maker authority can always change its policy. If a public body makes a lawful policy and subsequently makes a second lawful policy, the legal authority which empowers the making of the original policy will logically also permit the making of the changed policy. *R (on the application of Aggregate Industries) v English Nature*[129] concerned the duty under the Wildlife and Countryside Act of English Nature to notify a site if it was of the opinion that the site was of special scientific interest. It was held that any legitimate expectation created by one decision of English Nature was subordinate to the Wildlife and Countryside Act and English Nature could not estop itself from discharging its statutory functions in the public interest. Those statutory functions involved both short-term and long-term considerations of forestry management and its effects on the bird-life, a continuing programme, necessarily involving change. Therefore, once the current council of English Nature was of opinion that a previous decision about a site having special interest was wrong, their statutory duty was to act in accordance with their current opinion. Therefore, English Nature was entitled to change that decision and the policy on which it had been based, 'unless it was irrational to do so'.[130]

(f) Proportionality

The principle of proportionality in essence means that there must be a proportionate relationship between the objective which is sought to be achieved by a public authority and the method used by the public authority to achieve that objective. In more common parlance, you should not use a sledge-hammer to crack a nut. Proportionality is relied on or asserted when an individual considers that an administrative decision is harsh or excessive in comparison with what should have happened. If the decision is in the nature of a sanction and an

---

[129] [2002] EWHC 908 (Admin).   [130] Per Forbes J, at paras 117–119.

interference with an existing or claimed right, the common law has long applied a sliding scale of intervention.[131] For proportionality to be an appropriate means of challenge, the public authority must have the power to act, there must be no error of law, the correct procedure must have been followed, and, most important, there must be open to the authority a choice of several actions, a discretion to operate on a sliding scale. To take some illustrative and hypothetical examples, a person who has contravened immigration rules may face deportation, imprisonment, a fine; a person who has parked caravans on a local authority recreation ground rather than on a legal caravan site may face destruction of the caravans, imprisonment, an order to remove the caravans to take effect immediately or within time to fund another site; a person who owns an unfit house which is a nuisance and a danger may face compulsory acquisition, demolition, an order to repair at his or her own expense; a person who is disqualified from a social security benefit for leaving an employment without good case may face a period of disqualification ranging from one day to six months, depending on the circumstances. In English law, the principle probably first saw light as a ground on which the superior courts would quash unreasonable penalties, imposed by inferior courts and public authorities, which were disproportionate to the gravity of the offence committed and the purpose of granting power to impose those penalties. In *Commins v Massam*,[132] Commins did not like a penalty which had been imposed on him by a public authority called the Commissioners of Sewers. Branston CJ stated: 'and I conceive in some clearness that [a remedy] may be granted where any fine is imposed upon any man by commissioners, which they have authority to do by their commission, as appeareth by the statute, to moderate it in case that it be excessive'. In *Hook*,[133] the principle was applied in that it was stated that the penalty (revoking Hook's means of earning his livelihood) was excessive when compared with Hook's offence. Eighty years before, Lord Russell of Killowen had opined:[134]

'I do not mean to say that there may not be cases in which it would be the duty of the Court to condemn by-laws [as] invalid because unreasonable. But unreasonable in what sense? If, for instance, they were found to be partial and unequal in their operation as between different classes; if they were manifestly unjust; if they disclosed bad faith; if they involved such oppressive or gratuitous interference with the rights of those subject to them as could find no justification in the minds of reasonable men, the Court might well say "Parliament never intended to give authority to make such rules; they are unreasonable and *ultra vires*".'

Although the philosophy of the principle may have been used over the centuries by the common law, the modern terminology ('proportionality', 'proportionate', 'disproportionate') has not. The terminology is changing. When a committee of a London Borough resolved to ban a man, who had been involved in a fracas and had made offensive remarks to two councillors, from visiting any of the Borough's properties and to remove him from his appointment as a governor of a school, the authority's response was held to be wholly out of proportion to the offences. Such a lack of proportion was itself held to be indicative of unreasonableness in a *Wednesbury* sense.[135] In *GCHQ*,[136] Lord Diplock referred to 'the possible adoption in the future of the principle of proportionality'. Later, Schiemann J referred to proportionality as 'one aspect of reasonableness'.[137] The relationship between *Wednesbury* unreasonableness and the increasing, and possibly indiscriminate, use of

---

[131] See p. 617.　　[132] (1643) March 196.　　[133] See p. 621.
[134] *Kruse v Johnson* [1898] 2 QB 91, at 99.
[135] *R v Brent London Borough Council, ex p Assegai* (1987) 151 LGR 891.　　[136] See p. 86.
[137] *R v Secretary of State for Transport, ex p Pegasus Holdings* [1988] 1 WLR 990, at 1001.

proportionality was originally treated with caution and, perhaps suspicion by the House of Lords. In *R v Secretary of State for the Home Department, ex p Brind*,[138] the Home Secretary had issued directives to the Independent Broadcasting Authority and BBC requiring them, in the public interest, to refrain from broadcasting the direct statements of persons involved in terrorist organisations in Northern Ireland. Certain journalists argued that proportionality meant that the courts could balance objective and method and, if the courts determined that the method was disproportionate, they could quash the decision of the public authority. The House did not see how, in this particular case, proportionality could assist the journalists. The particular circumstances of the case were not very appropriate for that principle in that the public authority took decision 'A' and by quashing decision 'A' the court would be substituting its view for that of the public authority, exercising in effect an appellate jurisdiction, which took *Wednesbury* too far. The 'primary judgment' as to whether the public interest of prohibiting direct statements of persons involved with terrorist organisations justified the particular restriction imposed was entrusted by Parliament to the Secretary of State. The courts could exercise their traditional role by asking whether a reasonable Secretary of State, on the material before him, could reasonably make that primary judgment. The House held that, applying the conventional (*Wednesbury*) principles of judicial review, the Secretary of State could not be said to have acted so unreasonably that no reasonable Secretary of State could have made such a decision.

However, the principle of proportionality was given greater acknowledgement and support, where the issue involved what were termed 'constitutional', 'basic' or 'fundamental' rights. 'The more substantial the interference with human rights, the more the court will require by way of justification before it is satisfied that the decision is reasonable.'[139] 'In all these cases the importance of the right was directly relevant to the lawfulness of what had been done to interfere with its enjoyment.'[140] Finally, the

'intensity of review in a public law case will depend on the subject-matter in hand; and so in particular any interference by the action of a public body with a fundamental right will require a substantial objective [justification. There is] what may be called a sliding scale of review; the graver the impact of the decision in question upon the individual affected by it, the more substantial the justification that will be required. It is in the nature of the human condition that cases where, objectively, the individual is most gravely affected will be those where what we have come to call his fundamental rights are or are said to be put in jeopardy.'[141]

The principle of proportionality has achieved considerable recognition in European Community law and the European Court of Justice has based decisions against Community institutions and member states on the principle.[142] The principle is also one which is well developed in European Human Rights law and it would be normal for the European Court of Human Rights to apply the principle of proportionality in determining whether an undoubted interference with a protected right was justifiable.[143] The case law of both those

---

[138] [1991] 1 AC 696.

[139] *R v Ministry of Defence, ex p Smith* [1996] QB 517, per Sir Thomas Bingham MR, at 554, p. 579. See, also, *R v Secretary of State for the Home Department, ex p Simms* [1999] UKHL 33; *R v Home Secretary, ex p Leech*, [1994] QB 198; *R v Secretary of State for the Home Department, ex p Pierson* [1998] AC 539; *R v Lord Chancellor, ex parte Witham* [1998] QB 575, p. 526; *R v Secretary of State for the Home Department, ex p Daly* [2001] UKHL 26, p. 603.   [140] *Watkins v Home Office* [2006] UKHL 17, per Lord Bingham, at para 24.

[141] *R v Secretary of State for the Home Department, ex p Mahmood* [2000] EWCA Civ 315, per Laws LJ, at paras 18, 19.   [142] See p. 320.

[143] See pp. 789–790.

courts has produced four principal considerations: whether the policy objective is sufficiently important to the public welfare to justify limiting a fundamental right of an individual; whether the measure designed and taken to meet the policy objective is suitable for that purpose; whether the measure which limits the right is necessary in that the policy objective could not have been accomplished by some other less burdensome means; whether the decision-maker has properly weighed and balanced the competing burdens imposed on the individual by the measure which limits the right and the competing benefits to the public welfare in determining whether the exercise of the power is or is not proportionate to the object to be accomplished. These principles were raised in:

....

R v Chief Constable of Sussex, ex p International Trader's Ferry Limited [1999] 2 AC 418

It will be seen that that case was argued on both 'domestic' grounds (where 'reasonableness' was the benchmark) and on 'European Community' grounds (where 'proportionality' was the benchmark). The end result in both cases was the same. International Trader's Ferry Ltd (ITF) was incorporated for the purpose of carrying live animals across the Channel. ITF chose Shoreham as being the most convenient port. ITF were met by protests and demonstrators from those opposing the trade. On 2 January 1995, when the first ship sailed, the police had 74 officers at the port to protect the lorries. They were met by between 500 and 600 demonstrators, some of whom were violent to drivers and to the police, damaging the vehicles. Others blocked the road by sitting down. On 2 and 3 January 1995 the lorries could not get through. Between 4 and 14 January the average number of demonstrators was the same as on 2 January and the Chief Constable arranged for some 1,125 officers to be present for each sailing. For these few days the sum of £1,252,000 had to be paid for assistance from other police forces. The police made many arrests. By 14 January 1995, 67 demonstrators had been arrested. Between 15 January and 23 April, 183 persons were arrested. On 10 April 1995 the Chief Constable wrote to ITF:

'The policing operation demands considerable resources to be deployed. Whilst I would not seek to impose a cost threshold on the policing of any dispute the resources being utilised at present are of such a scale that they significantly impact upon my ability to deliver policing services in other areas. I now have the gravest concerns that the balance between what is being committed to policing the Port Authority area and the policing needs, expectations and rights of the remainder of the community throughout East and West Sussex is no longer equitable. I have decided that there is no alternative but to reduce the frequency of policing in the port area. With effect from Monday, 24 April 1995 I will intro-duce one of the following two policies in respect of policing the port area which essentially involve my being prepared to police an operation on either two consecutive days per week or alternatively four consecutive days per fortnight. Either option would involve policing on days between Monday and Thursday. We are not prepared to provide policing on either a Friday, Saturday or Sunday or, indeed, any public holiday. Please consider which of these two options is the more suitable for you [so] that the necessary policing arrangements may be [made].'

On 24 April, the Assistant Chief Constable confirmed the decision of 10 April. Thereafter, ITF sailed twice a week, and later sailed from Dover with regular sailings, though during this period they encountered sharp competition from another trader in Dover which made their business less prof-itable. Because of the BSE crisis, regular sailings ceased in March 1996 and ITF went out of business in mid-June 1996. ITF applied to quash the Chief Constable's decisions of 10 April 1995 to provide no policing, save on two consecutive days a week or on four days consecutively a fortnight, excluding Fridays, weekends and bank holidays, and also his decision of 24 April 1995 refusing to change that decision or to review its implementation. These decisions were claimed by ITF to be so unreasonable as to justify the court quashing them on *Wednesbury* grounds.

Lord Slynn, at 429–440

'Domestic law

As a matter of domestic law ITF's case in essence is that the Chief Constable had an overriding duty to make it possible for lawful activities to be carried out and that he could not lawfully allow the illegal acts of violent demonstrators to deflect him from that duty. Alternatively if he had a discretion as to how he dealt with the problem then he failed adequately to take into account relevant matters and gave too much weight to other matters; in any event his decisions in the letters of 10 and 24 April 1995 were those to which no Chief Constable could reasonably come. My Lords, it is clear that, although the duty to keep the peace is that of the Chief Constable, what he does may be reviewed by the courts; if his act is clearly unlawful it will be quashed and he may be ordered to do something else; he may have to pay damages. As I see it, however, a right of the kind claimed—here to trade lawfully—is not an absolute right by which the Chief Constable owes a duty to protect the trader at whatever cost and in whatever way necessary, any more than is the right to protest lawfully an absolute right owed by the Chief Constable to protestors which he must protect at whatever cost. [In] a situation where there are conflicting rights and the police have a duty to uphold the law the police may, in deciding what to do, have to balance a number of factors, not the least of which is the likelihood of a serious breach of the peace being committed. That balancing involves the exercise of judgment and discretion.

The courts have long made it clear that, though they will readily review the way in which decisions are reached, they will respect the margin of appreciation or discretion which a Chief Constable has. He knows through his officers the local situation, the availability of officers and his financial resources, the other demands on the police in the area at different times [*Chief Constable of the North Wales Police v Evans* [1982] 1 WLR 1155, 1174].

Here although on occasions lorries got through with few demonstrators and a small number of police, it is plain that, particularly in the early months, there was no possibility of the lorries getting through without damage when large numbers of demonstrators were present. [The] Chief Constable provided a large number of men at great cost in January but in my view he was entitled to consider whether in all the circumstances the use of so many officers and such costs were justified on a continuing basis even without imposing a total ban on shipment. On the evidence it is clear that in coming to his decisions the Chief Constable took into account in the present case (a) the number of men available to him, (b) his financial resources to provide police officers, (c) the rights of others in his area and their protection, (d) the risk of injury during the demonstration to the drivers, to the police and to others; he took into account no less the competing rights of ITF to trade and of those who objected to the trade peacefully to [demonstrate].

As to the availability of officers and finance the Chief Constable emphasises that the first problem was that of providing officers. It seems obvious that if the normal strength was in the region of 2,929 officers for the whole police area then to use in the region of 1,125 of these officers for the supervision of these lorries was not realistically possible. [The] Chief Constable was entitled to take the view that the amount of money available was not sufficient to cover the cost of continuing the heavy police coverage at Shoreham. [The] Chief Constable gave evidence of the areas where other policing was [required. It was his view that the 1995 crime] figures were an increase on 1994 both in relation to overall crime, and to residential burglary, to crimes of violence and to vehicle crime. He attributed in part these increases to the "disproportionately high level of policing which was allocated to the port between January and March 1995". [There] were fewer searches of premises to investigate crime [and] the crime strategy in his view was adversely affected in other areas such as traffic control and training, in the maintenance of public order and in community assistance. In all these areas there was an adverse effect which he attributed in part to the police services he provided at Shoreham. [It] is not possible to say that this is something that he could not reasonably have taken into account in deciding the level of policing at Shoreham.

[The Chief Constable did] carry out a balancing exercise as he was required to do. He allocated his men on a carefully considered basis. He has not been shown to have ignored relevant facts or taken account of irrelevant factors in a way which vitiates his overall decisions. These decisions have not been shown to be unreasonable in a *Wednesbury* [sense].

Community law

[Lord Slynn referred to the judgment of the European Court of Justice in *Commission v France* [1997] ECR I-441, p. 328, and continued: The Court] made it clear that when it comes to taking all necessary and appropriate measures to ensure that the fundamental freedom [of movement of goods] is respected on its territory:

> "The Member States, which retain exclusive competence as regards the maintenance of public order and the safeguarding of internal security, unquestionably enjoy a margin of discretion in determining what measures are most appropriate to eliminate barriers to the importation of products in a given [situation. It] is for the Member State concerned, unless it can show that action on its part would have consequences for public order with which it could not cope by using the means at its disposal, to adopt all appropriate measures to guarantee the full scope and effect of Community law so as to ensure its proper implementation in the interests of all economic operators."

I do not accept that the Court is here saying that in every case where steps have to be taken by a Member State a court must consider whether, somehow, the Member State could have found, somewhere, the money necessary to take steps which could theoretically have been taken. If that were so the State could always in theory call upon moneys allocated for education or health or defence and use them for this kind of purpose. That cannot have been intended. It would in any event require an investigation as to whether other competing claims for money allocated allowed moneys to be taken away from other areas of government. That is an impossible inquiry for the court to undertake and I think is an unreasonable exercise for the Member State itself to be required to undertake.

What is required in a case like the present where the Chief Constable has statutory and common law duties to perform is to ask whether he did all that proportionately and reasonably he could be expected to do with the resources available to him. He is after all dealing with an emergency situation and there is no question of funds being deliberately withheld by the State to hamper his work. The budget for the Authority was a very large one and it was for him to decide how he would use the moneys apportioned to [him].

In [*Brind*, p. 599] the House treated *Wednesbury* reasonableness and proportionality as being different. So in some ways they are though the distinction between the two tests in practice is in any event much less than is sometimes suggested. The cautious way in which the European Court usually applies this test, recognising the importance of respecting the national authority's margin of appreciation, may mean that whichever test is adopted, and even allowing for a difference in onus, the result is the same.

I am satisfied [that] the Chief Constable has shown here that what he did in providing police assistance was proportionate to what was required. To protect the lorries, in the way he did, was a suitable and necessary way of dealing with potentially violent demonstrators. To limit the occasions when sufficient police could be made available was, in the light of the resources available to him to deal with immediate and foreseeable events at the port, and at the same time to carry out all his other police duties, necessary and in no way disproportionate to the restrictions which were involved. Unlike the authorities in the case of France he was controlling and arresting violent offenders. He was, moreover, not dealing with a situation where no other way of exporting the animals was available. Dover was available and there were, and might be, other occasions when the lorries could get through. Far from failing to protect the appellants' trade he was seeking to do it in the most effective way available to him with his finite resources. It was only on rare and necessary, even dangerous, occasions that lorries were turned [back].'

Lord Cooke, at 452–454

'[I agree with the proposition that] on the particular facts of this case the European concepts of proportionality and margin of appreciation produce the same result as what are commonly called the *Wednesbury* principles. Indeed in many cases that is likely to be so.

[It] is said by the European Court of Justice in *Commission v France* [that] "The Member States, which retain exclusive competence as regards the maintenance of public order and the safeguarding of internal security, unquestionably enjoy a margin of discretion in determining what measures are most appropriate." For practical purposes in this case I think that the Chief Constable must enjoy a margin of discretion that cannot differ according to whether its source be found in purely domestic principles or superimposed European principles. [*Wednesbury* itself confirms that] the administrative authority must direct himself properly in law. In the field now relevant he must therefore give weight both to his duty to enforce the rule of law as far as reasonably practicable and to the principle that, as stressed by the European Court in *Commission v [France]*, the free movement of goods is one of the fundamental principles of the Treaty. [Under] both the ordinary United Kingdom and the broader European systems, public policy or public security may justify restrictions on a lawful trade. Whatever the rubric under which the case is placed, the question here reduces, as I see it, to whether the Chief Constable has struck a balance fairly and reasonably open to [him. I conclude] that the Chief Constable struck a fair and reasonable balance which survives scrutiny under purely domestic law and European-originating domestic law [alike].'

The coming into force of the Human Rights Act and the consequent incorporation of the case law of the European Court of Human Rights, at least where a case concerned a now protected 'Convention right', took the story much further:

R v Secretary of State for the Home Department, ex p Daly [2001] UKHL 26

Daly, a long-term prisoner, challenged the lawfulness of the policy that a prisoner could not be present when his legally privileged correspondence was examined by prison officers. It was held that, although a 'custodial order inevitably curtails the enjoyment, by the person confined, of rights enjoyed by other citizens [the] order does not wholly deprive the person confined of all rights enjoyed by other [citizens, especially]: the right of access to a court; the right of access to legal advice; and the right to communicate confidentially with a legal adviser under the seal of legal professional privilege. Such rights may be curtailed only by clear and express words, and then only to the extent reasonably necessary to meet the ends which justify the curtailment.' Those ends were 'to prevent the conceal-ment of material likely to endanger prison security, or the safety of others or which would contribute to criminal activity within the prison'. Lord Bingham stated (at paras 5, 14, 23) that the 'policy cannot in my opinion be justified in its present blanket form. The infringement of prisoners' rights to maintain the con-fidentiality of their privileged legal correspondence is greater than is shown to be necessary to serve the legitimate public objectives already identified. I accept Mr Daly's submission on this [point]. I have reached the conclusions so far expressed on an orthodox application of common law principles derived from the authorities and an orthodox domestic approach to judicial review.'

Lord Steyn

'27. The contours of the principle of proportionality are familiar. In *de Freitas v Permanent Secretary of Ministry of Agriculture, Fisheries, Lands and Housing* [[1999] 1 AC 69, at 80], the Privy Council adopted a three stage test. Lord Clyde observed [that] in determining whether a limitation (by an act, rule or decision) is arbitrary or excessive the court should ask itself: "whether: (i) the legislative objective is sufficiently important to justify limiting a fundamental right; (ii) the measures designed to meet the legislative objective are rationally connected to it; and (iii) the means used to impair the right or freedom are no more than is necessary to accomplish the objective". Clearly, these criteria are more precise and more sophisticated than the traditional grounds of review. [The] starting point is that there is an overlap between the traditional grounds of review and the approach of proportionality. Most cases would be decided in the same way whichever approach is adopted. But the intensity of review is somewhat greater under the proportionality approach. [I] would mention three concrete differences without suggesting that my statement is exhaustive. First, the doctrine of proportionality may require the reviewing court to assess the balance which the decision maker has struck, not merely whether it is within the range of rational or reasonable decisions. Secondly, the proportionality test may go further than the traditional grounds of review inasmuch as it may require attention to be directed to the relative weight accorded to interests and considerations. Thirdly, even the heightened scrutiny test developed in [*Smith*, p. 579] is not necessarily appropriate to the protection of human rights [see *Smith* and *Grady*, p. 582].

28. The differences in approach between the traditional grounds of review and the proportionality approach may therefore sometimes yield different results. It is therefore important that cases involving convention rights must be analysed in the correct way. This does not mean that there has been a shift to merits [review].'

Proportionality quickly became a designer accessory to any challenge by way of judicial review. The reported cases have demonstrated the validation of the statutory scheme of the Child Support Agency as providing a reasonable relationship of proportionality between the legitimate aims of the legislation and the means employed,[144] the eviction of caravan dwellers when 'the legitimate aim of maintaining a planning regime really does make it necessary to interfere with the [family and home rights of the dwellers]',[145] the deportation, following conviction for drug trafficking, of a man settled in the United Kingdom with a family,[146] the imposition of an exclusion zone on the movements of a convicted murderer, in order to minimise the risk of accidental contact between him and the family of his victim,[147] regulations restricting the advertising and promotion of tobacco sales in order to meet the objective of promoting health,[148] the restriction of prisoner telephonic communication with the community at large in a manner that would be calculated to encourage or promote illegal drug use in prison and communication with the outside community in areas that would foster crime in other outside circumstances,[149] emergency action taken to restrict distribution of cheese during a serious outbreak of food poisoning,[150] the length of a period of disqualification imposed by the Jockey Club proportionate to the seriousness of the offence,[151] and ordering a group of protesters to disperse as being the least restrictive and least intrusive method of dealing with an inflammatory situation.[152]

---

[144] *R (on the application of Denson) v Child Support Agency* [2002] EWHC 154 (Admin).

[145] *Coates v South Bucks District Council* [2004] EWCA Civ 1378, per Lord Phillips MR, at para 24.

[146] *Samaroo v Secretary of State for the Home Department* [2001] EWCA Civ 1139.

[147] *R (on the application of Craven) v The Parole Board* [2001] EWHC 850 (Admin).

[148] *R, on the application of British American Tobacco v Secretary of State for Health* [2004] EWHC 2493 (Admin).

[149] *R (on the application of Taylor) v Governor of HM Prison Risley* [2004] EWHC 2654 (Admin).

[150] *R v Secretary of State for Health, ex p Eastside Cheese Co and Duckett & Co* [1999] EWCA Civ 1739.

[151] *Bradley v The Jockey Club* [2005] EWCA Civ 1056.

[152] *R (on the application of Singh) v Chief Constable of West Midlands Police* [2006] EWCA Civ 1118.

An illuminating illustration of the working of the principle is:

....

R, on the application of Baker v First Secretary of State
[2003] EWHC 2511 (Admin)

Baker, the owner and occupier of land, appealed against the decision of the Secretary of State upholding a decision of the London Borough of Ealing to purchase compulsorily the claimant's land pursuant to a clearance order made under the Housing Act 1985.

Nicholas Blake QC

'4. The debate in this case hinges on whether the Secretary of State, in adopting and endorsing the decision of the planning inspector, who in turn was satisfied of the council's case for compulsory purchase, has identified and explained the decision with sufficient clarity to enable the public authority to discharge the burden of justifying what is undoubtedly an interference with these rights, respectively of home and private life, and possession, occupation, and ownership of land, for compelling reasons of the public interest.

. . .

16. There is no doubt that the house is unfit for human [habitation]. It is also clear that both the structural condition of the property and the continued accumulation of rubbish in the premises have an adverse effect on adjoining residential occupiers. The state of the property was such that [if] the clearance and compulsory purchase order was the only way of returning the property to a state of fitness for human habitation, and preventing it from continuing to pose a serious threat to the health of both the occupant and the immediate environment, it would have been amply justified in the public interest on compelling grounds.

17. The real debate is whether there were practical alternatives to the compulsory purchase route that could have been used to achieve the same result. The claimant suggests that there were, that they were not [used].

. . .

43. [If] the Secretary of State was simply faced with one means to achieve the highly desirable result of preventing the premises of the claimant from being statutorily unfit, preventing it from being the source of a nuisance to adjoining occupiers and returning the premises to residential housing in proper repair for the benefit of at least some future occupier, then, manifestly, those laudable ends would justify the means of acquiring property compulsorily from the owner. But was it the only alternative, or [was] it the least intrusive means of securing the public interest?

. . .

45. [Proportionality] is not simply whether at the end result the balance is fair, but whether, in getting there, it has been decided that the most appropriate course of conduct is also the least interfering with human rights, having regard to the public benefit to be achieved and the different means of achieving it.

. . .

50. So the question is whether [read] as a whole the decision did examine, and carefully examine, whether there was a less intrusive [alternative].

. . .

57. In my judgment, read as a whole, the inspector's report, accepting the case for compulsory purchase made by the council, [amply] meets the requirements of the Human Rights Act and the European Convention of Human Rights, that there are relevant and adequate reasons to justify why a compulsory purchase order was the necessary and proportionate way of giving effect to the public

interest in this case. Once that stage is reached there is very little debate about the justification overall, as a fair balance, given the benefits that the public would achieve by the compulsory purchase of these premises.'

According to Lord Steyn in *Daly*,[153] proportionality involves a greater 'intensity of review' than under the 'traditional grounds of review'. Furthermore, 'even the heightened scrutiny test' in *Smith*[154] is not necessarily appropriate to the protection of human rights. The case law has dutifully followed suit. 'It has now been recognised that, although there is an overlap between them, a greater intensity of review is available under the proportionality approach to issues relating to alleged breaches of Convention rights than is the case where the review is conducted on the traditional *Wednesbury* [grounds. It] is now clear that, if the approach which was explained and approved in [*Daly*] is adopted, the more precise method of analysis which is provided by the test of proportionality will be a much more effective safeguard.'[155]

It has been held in a deportation case that the 'Secretary of State must show that he has struck a fair balance between the individual's right to respect for family life and the prevention of crime and disorder. How much weight he gives to each factor will be the subject of careful scrutiny by the court. The court will interfere with the weight accorded by the decision-maker if, despite an allowance for the appropriate margin of discretion, it concludes that the weight accorded was unfair and unreasonable. In this respect, the level of scrutiny is undoubtedly more intense than it is when a decision is subject to review on traditional Wednesbury grounds, where the court usually refuses to examine the weight accorded by the decision-maker to the various relevant factors.'[156] If government 'policy perpetrates an apparent violation of a Convention right so that the government must demonstrate proportionality, the court will not be satisfied merely upon its being shown that a reasonable decision maker might consider the policy proportionate. It will require a substantial reasoned justification of the [policy]. The difference between this approach and *Wednesbury* is plain to see. *Wednesbury* review consigned the relative weight to be given to any relevant factor to the discretion of the decision maker. In the new world, the decision maker is obliged to accord decisive weight to the requirements of pressing social need and proportionality.'[157]

However, an ostensible application of proportionality may some times produce echoes of *Wednesbury*. In *R (on the application of Nayley Mitchell) v Horsham District Council*,[158] it was clear that the Council was fully aware that direct action to remove the claimants' caravans from land would be incompatible with the claimants' (Convention) right to family life, unless proportionate and justified. Since 'the Council, through its officers, carefully took into account all relevant and material matters that required its consideration when striking the balance between the relevant competing interests and deciding whether the taking of direct action [would] be proportionate and, therefore, [justified, the] Council came to the

---

[153] See p. 603.   [154] See p. 579.   [155] *R v Shayler* [2002] UKHL 11, per Lord Hope, at para 75.

[156] *Samaroo v Secretary of State for the Home Department* [2001] EWCA Civ 1139, per Dyson LJ, at para 39.

[157] *Huang v Secretary of State for the Home Department* [2005] EWCA Civ 105, per Laws LJ, at para 54. See, also, *R (on the application of Ponting) v Governor of HM Prisons Whitemoor* [2002] EWCA Civ 224, per Arden LJ, at para 108; *R (on the application of Farrakhan) v Secretary of State for the Home Department* [2002] EWCA Civ 606, per Lord Phillips MR, at para 64; *R, on the application of Nilsen v Governor of HMP Full Sutton and The Secretary of State for the Home Department* [2003] EWHC 3160 (Admin), per Maurice Kay J, at para 24; *R (on the application of Taylor) v Governor of HM Prison Risley* [2004] EWHC 2654 (Admin), per McCombe J, at para 28.

[158] [2003] EWHC 234 (Admin).

conclusion that direct action was so justified in the circumstances of this case and, therefore, would be lawful. In my view, that conclusion was clearly one that was open to the Council on the material that its officers considered. I am satisfied that it is a conclusion that cannot possibly be stigmatised as irrational or *Wednesbury* unreasonable.'[159]

Lord Steyn emphasised that the '*Daly* approach' did 'not mean that there has been a shift to merits review'. This is important, because the more an unelected judge, by way of judicial review, substitutes his or her version of the merits of the case for that of the original lawfully appointed decision-maker, the more that judge will be exercising a jurisdiction akin to that of an appeal of fact and law, which has been denied that judge by the legislature. 'When applying a test of proportionality, the margin of appreciation or discretion accorded to the decision maker is all important, for it is only by recognising the margin of discretion that the court avoids substituting its own decision for that of the decision maker':[160]

....

Claire F v Secretary of State for the Home Department
[2004] EWHC 111 (Fam)

Under the Prison Rules: 'The Secretary of State may, subject to any conditions he thinks fit, permit a woman prisoner to have her baby with her in prison, and everything necessary for the baby's maintenance and care may be provided there.' Claire F was a long sentence prisoner; she was pregnant when sentenced; gave birth to a daughter, currently with her, in the mother and baby unit. There was disagreement between the parties as to the proper role of the court and as to the approach the court should adopt when addressing the argument that the Secretary of State's decision was wrong on the merits. One counsel submitted that the judge was 'exercising a merits-based best interests jurisdiction' and that he must decide for himself whether it was in the daughter's best interests to be separated from her mother; the other counsel submitted that the judge's function was 'limited to reviewing the Secretary of State's decision in the manner indicated in [*Daly*]'.

Munby J

'22. In this case what the claimant seeks to challenge is a decision taken by the Secretary of State in pursuance of the statutory powers conferred on him by [the Prison Rules. Such] a case raises issues of public law to be determined, whether in the Family Division or in the Administrative Court, by reference to the appropriate principles of public law. It follows from this that the primary decision maker is the Secretary of State and not the court. The court's function in this type of dispute is essentially one of review—review of the Secretary of State's decision—rather than one of primary judicial decision making. It is not the function of the court itself to come to a decision on the merits.

23. The fact is that in the present context Parliament has chosen to confer the relevant power on the Secretary of State: not on the court or on anyone else. There is nothing in that which is in any way incompatible with the Convention. My duty is to recognise the will of Parliament and not to seek to usurp a power which Parliament, compatibly with the Convention, has chosen to confer on an accountable minister rather than on an unaccountable judge.

. . .

31. [The] court is not concerned to come to its own assessment of what is in the child's best interests. The court is concerned only to review the Secretary of State's decision, and that is not a review of the merits of the Secretary of State's decision but a *Daly* type [review].'

---

[159] Per Forbes J, at para 48.

[160] *R (on the application of Farrakhan) v Secretary of State for the Home Department* [2002] EWCA Civ 606, per Lord Phillips MR, at para 67.

The case law has identified a number of factors which made it appropriate to accord a particularly wide margin of discretion to the decision-maker and, therefore, a high level of deference. These are reminiscent of earlier discussion on justiciability[161] and include the defence of the realm, the right of a state to control immigration into its territory, the fact that the decision maker is often far better placed to reach an informed decision as to the situation than a court (especially so in the area of macro-economic policy and the macro-political field), and the fact that decision-makers, such as ministers or local authorities, are democratically accountable for their decisions.[162] The modern law of deference may be illustrated by:

Alconbury [2001] UKHL 23

Lord Clyde

'139. [Planning] is a matter of the formation and application of policy. The policy is not matter for the courts but for the Executive. Where decisions are required in the planning process they are not made by judges, but by members of the [administration].

140. Planning and the development of land are matters which concern the community as a whole, not only the locality where the particular case arises. They involve wider social and economic interests, considerations which are properly to be subject to a central supervision. By means of a central authority some degree of coherence and consistency in the development of land can be secured. National planning guidance can be prepared and promulgated and that guidance will influence the local development plans and policies which the planning authorities will use in resolving their own local [problems].

141. Once it is recognised that there should be a national planning policy under a central supervision, it is consistent with democratic principle that the responsibility for that work should lie on the shoulders of a minister answerable to [Parliament].

. . .

159. [Parliament], democratically elected, has entrusted the making of planning decisions to local authorities and to the Secretary of State with a general power of supervision and control in the latter. Thereby it is intended that some overall coherence and uniformity in national planning can be achieved in the public interest and that major decisions can be taken by a minister answerable to Parliament. Planning matters are essentially matters of policy and expediency, not of law. They are primarily matters for the executive and not for the courts to [determine].'

Huang v Secretary of State for the Home Department [2005] EWCA Civ 105

Laws LJ

'51. [Because the] Secretary of State acts for the elected government, the court should accord him that margin of discretion, or discretionary area of judgment, often said to be properly enjoyed by the democratic decision maker. The principle here is respect for the democratic powers in our [constitution].

---

[161] See p. 490. On judicial deference in a HRA context, see pp. 805–814, 856.

[162] *R (on the application of Farrakhan) v Secretary of State for the Home Department* [2002] EWCA Civ 606, per Lord Phillips MR, at paras 71–74; *International Transport Roth GmbH & Ors v Secretary of State for the Home Department* [2002] EWCA Civ 158, per Laws LJ, at paras 72–74, 83–87; *R v The Department of Education and Employment, ex p Begbie* [1999] EWCA Civ 2100, per Laws LJ, at paras 78, 79.

52. [The] principle of law by which respect for the democracy requires a margin of discretion to be accorded to the democratic decision maker primarily applies where the subject of decision is the formation of policy. We accept there are other cases where the courts will [defer] to government: cases where for practical reasons the courts are in no position to arrive at an autonomous decision. Historically, the most familiar instance arose where the question was whether the interests of national security required this or that particular action to be [taken].

53. [In] deciding whether a policy (whether enshrined in legislation or not) of itself entails violations of the Convention rights, or whether by contrast it represents no more than a proportionate response to the problem in hand, the courts will generally recognise that the democratic powers in the State have a special responsibility. Policy making is their territory, and not that of the judges. Hence the margin of discretionary judgment accorded to the government policy-maker on democratic grounds. The courts are also likely to recognise that government is better equipped than the court to judge how needful the policy is to achieve the aim in view. So where policy is the subject-matter in hand, principle and practicality alike militate in favour of an approach in which the court's role is closer to review than appeal: where a degree of deference does no more than respect the balance to be struck between the claims of democratic power and the claims of individual rights.'

....

Secretary of State for the Home Department v Akaeke [2005] EWCA Civ 947

Carnwath LJ

'29. [The] courts of course retain a vital role as final arbiters in relation to genuine issues of law, such as the interpretation of the relevant statutes, and in relation to the overall fairness of the procedures. However, they should, in my view, be cautious before interfering with decisions on matters within the special expertise and competence of the [immigration appeal] Tribunal. In this field, such matters include, not only the evaluation of the difficult and often harrowing evidence produced in support of individual claims, but more generally questions of general principle relating to the conditions in particular categories of claimant or particular [countries].

30. [The] tribunal, against the background of its day-to-day experience, is much better placed than the courts to judge whether the circumstances of a particular case are sufficiently exceptional to justify a departure from the ordinary policy approach. That applies not only to the assessment of the circumstances of a particular applicant, but also to judgments about the management of the system by the Secretary of State. In my view, the making of such judgments in exceptional cases is well within the proper boundaries of the supervisory role given to the tribunal by [Parliament].'

All this sounds conspicuously like a list of the restrictions imposed by the self-same courts on *Wednesbury* grounds which trendy judges (and academics) have been so ready to criticise. Where is the much lauded intensity of review when there is so much deference? Where, therefore, does this leave *Wednesbury* unreasonableness?

In recent years, the principle of *Wednesbury* unreasonableness (but not the other *Wednesbury* principles stated above) has been subject to much comment, ranging from 'Good old *Wednesbury* irrationality'[163] to 'an unfortunately retrogressive decision in English administrative law'.[164] In practice, since the incorporation of the European Convention of Human Rights into domestic law by the Human Rights Act, the reported cases demonstrate that the principle of proportionality has been loudly trumpeted to the detriment of *Wednesbury* unreasonableness. There are still fundamental questions; first, is proportionality a ground for judicial review in its own right or, at the moment, one (albeit extremely important) aspect of

---

[163] *O'Connor v Chief Adjudication Officer* [1999] 1 FLR 1200, per Auld LJ, at 1210.

[164] *R v Secretary of State For The Home Department, ex p Daly* [2001] UKHL 26, per Lord Cooke, at para 32.

irrationality; second, is proportionality now an ordinary (even traditional) part of the common law of judicial review or is it yet limited to 'European Community Law' cases and 'European Human Rights' cases; third, if proportionality is now an ordinary (even traditional) part of the common law of judicial review which will be applied equally to 'domestic' cases, 'European Community Law' cases and 'European Human Rights' cases, to what extent, if any, has it superseded or replaced *Wednesbury* unreasonableness? In *Alconbury*,[165] Lord Slynn considered that 'the time has come to recognise that this principle is part of English administrative law, not only when judges are dealing with Community acts but also when they are dealing with acts subject to domestic law. Trying to keep the *Wednesbury* principle and proportionality in separate compartments seems to me to be unnecessary and confusing.' In *R (on the application of Medway Council) v Secretary of State for Transport*,[166] the claimants challenged a decision which would involve expansion at Heathrow and Stansted airports but not at Gatwick airport. It was held

'that Convention rights are not engaged in this case. Nor does any issue of Community Law arise. Thus for the proportionality challenge to succeed it must do so purely within the confines of domestic law. The question therefore arises as to whether proportionality has a discrete part to play in domestic [law]. In my judgment, the greater intensity of review which is required by the proportionality test does not arise in domestic law where there is no engagement of a Convention right and no fundamental right is in play. The test remains *Wednesbury*. There is no room for a proportionality challenge in the present case. It is important that proportionality is confined to its proper role and is not allowed to run amok as the "unruly horse" of the new era.'[167]

Whether the reported demise of *Wednesbury* is premature is debatable:

....

R (Association of British Civilian Internees Far East Region) v Secretary of State for Defence [2003] EWCA Civ 473

The Association of British Civilian Internees Far Eastern Region represented a substantial number of individuals (and their surviving spouses) who were interned by the Japanese during the Second World War as British civilians. The government had announced the introduction of a non-statutory compensation scheme under which a single ex-gratia payment of £10,000 would be made to certain persons who were held prisoner by the Japanese, in recognition of the unique circumstances of their captivity. British subjects whom the Japanese interned and who were born in the United Kingdom, or had a parent or grandparent born there were to be eligible for the payment. It was alleged that, in refusing to make payments unless a claimant who was a British subject at the time of internment was born in the UK or had a parent or grandparent who was born in the UK ('the birth criteria'), the government had acted unlawfully.

Dyson LJ

'32. [A] preliminary question that arises is whether proportionality exists as a separate ground of review in a case which does not concern Community law or human rights protected by the European Convention on Human Rights (ECHR).

33. It is true that the result that follows will often be the same whether the test that is applied is proportionality or *Wednesbury* unreasonableness. This is particularly so in a case in the field of social

---

[165] [2001] UKHL 23, at para 51.   [166] [2002] EWHC 2516 (Admin).
[167] Per Maurice Kay J, at paras 45–47.

PROCEDURAL IMPROPRIETY · 611

and economic policy. But the tests are [different]. It follows that the two tests will not always yield the same [results].

34. [As] Lord Slynn points out, trying to keep the *Wednesbury* principle and proportionality in separate compartments is unnecessary and confusing. The criteria of proportionality are more precise and [sophisticated]. It is true that sometimes proportionality may require the reviewing court to assess for itself the balance that has been struck by the decision-maker, and that may produce a different result from one that would be arrived at on an application of the *Wednesbury* test. But the strictness of the *Wednesbury* test has been relaxed in recent years even in areas which have nothing to do with fundamental [rights]. The *Wednesbury* test is moving closer to proportionality, and in some cases it is not possible to see any daylight between the two [tests]. Although we did not hear argument on the point, we have difficulty in seeing what justification there now is for retaining the *Wednesbury* test.

35. But we consider that it is not for this court to perform its burial rites. The continuing existence of the *Wednesbury* test has been acknowledged by the House of Lords on more than one occasion. The obvious starting point is [*Brind*, p. 599. Counsel] submits that *Brind* does not stand in the way of this court holding that proportionality has supplanted the *Wednesbury* test in English domestic law, even where no human right or Community Law issues are raised. We do not agree. It is true [that] Lord Bridge and Lord Roskill left the door open for the possible future introduction and development of the doctrine of proportionality into English domestic law. But all of their Lordships rejected the proportionality test in that case, and applied the traditional *Wednesbury* test. In other words, they closed the door to proportionality in domestic law for the time being.

36. In [*International Trader's Ferry*, p. 600], the House of Lords was asked to apply both tests in the context of a case about what was alleged by the applicant to be the inadequate response by the police to the obstruction by protesting animal rights groups of shipments of livestock. The applicant said in relation to domestic law that the police response was unreasonable (ie in the *Wednesbury* sense). In relation to Community law (the enforcement of the EU Treaty which prohibits restrictions), the applicant's case was that the police response was disproportionate. The challenge failed on both grounds. Separate consideration was given to the two grounds and to the application of the two tests, although Lord Slynn pointed [out] that "the distinction between the two tests in practice is in any event much less than is sometimes suggested". The suggestion that it is open to this court to hold that the *Wednesbury* test is no longer part of English domestic law is entirely at odds with the approach of the House of Lords in *Brind* and in *International Trader's Ferry*.

37. [We] therefore approach the issues in the present appeal on the footing that the *Wednesbury* test does survive, and that this is the correct test to apply in a case such as the present which does not involve Community law, and does not engage any question of rights under the ECHR.'

v. Procedural Impropriety

The fourth condition precedent to an exercise of authority within jurisdiction listed in head I is that the decision must not be vitiated by procedural impropriety. In other words, the public authority must act in accordance with the correct procedure. In many situations, Parliament has provided that certain procedures must be followed by an authority in exercising its power and by the citizen when the citizen uses the administrative machinery of the modern state. If Parliament has not laid down statutory procedural rules, the courts may infer that long accepted common law standards of fair procedures shall apply. These common law standards are usually referred to as the right to a fair hearing.

(a) Statutory rules of procedure

One typical example of statutory procedural rules is given, relating to the appeal committee established to determine parental choice in education:

Education Act 1996, schedule 33 Admission Appeals

'9. An appeal shall be by notice in writing setting out the grounds on which it is made.

10. An appeal committee shall give the appellant an opportunity of appearing and making oral representations, and may allow him to be accompanied by a friend or to be represented.

11. The matters to be taken into account by an appeal committee in considering an appeal shall include—(a) any preference expressed by the appellant in respect of the [child], and (b) the arrangements for the admission of pupils published by the local education authority or the governing [body].

12(1) Appeals shall be heard in private except when the local education authority or governing body [direct otherwise]. . . .

13. In the event of disagreement between the members of an appeal committee, the appeal under consideration shall be decided by a simple majority of the votes cast, and in the case of an equality of votes the chairman of the committee shall have a second or casting vote.

14. The decision of an appeal committee and the grounds on which it is made shall be communicated by the committee in writing to—(a) the appellant and the local education [authority].'

Sometimes statutory rules may relate to time limits within which a citizen or the administration must act. Sometimes the rules may relate to the giving of adequate notice to the citizen of the proposed action to be taken by the administrative body. Sometimes the rules may relate to the matters which must be produced by the citizen or by the administrative authority. Sometimes the rules may relate to the right of the citizen to appear before an administrative body, to give evidence before that body, to address argument to that body or to be represented (whether by a legally qualified person or not) before that body. Sometimes, the rules may lay down that before taking a particular decision, the administrative authority must consult with appropriate persons or bodies. The purpose here is, as with delegated legislation, to ensure that persons likely to be affected by administrative action and, indeed, who may have considerable expertise of the subject matter under consideration, can give their views before the taking of action.

Often, statutory rules may state that the administrative authority must give reasons for the decision. A duty to give reasons can serve both individual and decision maker. On the one hand, the individual will abhor a system whereby administrative decisions are rendered immune from judicial review by reason of a veil of silence raised by a refusal to give reasons; on the other hand, a decision appearing prima facie irrational may be justified when the reasons are published. The principle of fairness demands that the parties, especially the losing party, should know exactly why they have won or lost. Furthermore, as anyone who has acted as a decision-maker will testify, a requirement to give reasons concentrates the mind of the decision-maker. Finally, the duty is very important in that if the authority has made a mistake, the mistake will appear on the record of the authority's decision and may be subsequently corrected. In *Mountview Court Properties Ltd v Devlin*,[168] it was held that if there is an

---

[168] (1970) 21 P & CR 689.

obligation to state the reasons for a decision, those reasons must be adequate and if the reasons are not adequate then this is an error of law which can be corrected by the superior courts. 'Parliament provided that reasons shall be given, and in my view that must be read as meaning that proper, adequate reasons must be given. The reasons that are set out must be reasons which will not only be intelligible, but which deal with the substantial points that have been raised.'[169] The following passage relating to planning decisions provides a useful general summary:

South Bucks District Council v Porter [2004] UKHL 33

Lord Brown

'36. The reasons for a decision must be intelligible and they must be adequate. They must enable the reader to understand why the matter was decided as it was and what conclusions were reached on the "principal important controversial issues", disclosing how any issue of law or fact was resolved. Reasons can be briefly stated, the degree of particularity required depending entirely on the nature of the issues falling for decision. The reasoning must not give rise to a substantial doubt as to whether the decision-maker erred in law, for example by misunderstanding some relevant policy or some other important matter or by failing to reach a rational decision on relevant grounds. But such adverse inference will not readily be drawn. The reasons need refer only to the main issues in the dispute, not to every material consideration. They should enable disappointed developers to assess their prospects of obtaining some alternative development permission, or, as the case may be, their unsuccessful opponents to understand how the policy or approach underlying the grant of permission may impact upon future such applications. Decision letters must be read in a straightforward manner, recognising that they are addressed to parties well aware of the issues involved and the arguments advanced. A reasons challenge will only succeed if the party aggrieved can satisfy the court that he has genuinely been substantially prejudiced by the failure to provide an adequately reasoned decision.'

Failure to comply with statutory rules of procedure may result in the citizen forfeiting his or her rights or expectations and, more important, may result in a decision being nullified. The principle is illustrated by *Rayner v Stepney Corporation*.[170] A statute stated that when the local authority served notice of their intention to acquire a person's land for slum clearance purposes, they should in the notice state that the person had a statutory right of appeal to the courts. It was held that failure to give the owner of property about to be the subject of a clearance order due notice of his rights of appeal to the courts as was required by the statute was *ultra vires*:

Bradbury v Enfield London Borough Council [1967] 1 WLR 1311 (CA)

Section 13 of the Education Act 1944 provided that if a local education authority intended to establish a new school or cease to maintain an existing school, they were required to submit proposals to the minister, and then to give public notice of the proposals, after which, the managers, governors, or any ten or more local government electors could submit to the minister objections to the proposals. The Enfield Borough Council wished to introduce comprehensive education and decided to submit proposals relating to eight schools which included the changing of 11 to 18 schools into 11 to 14 and

[169] *Re Poyser and Mills' Arbitration* [1964] 2 QB 467, per Megaw J, at 478.
[170] [1911] 2 Ch 312.

14 to 18 schools and the changing of a girls' school to a mixed school. They did not submit the appropriate notice for public examination. The plaintiffs sought an injunction.

Lord Denning MR, at 438–440

'[Ought] an injunction to be granted against the council? It has been suggested by the chief education officer that, if an injunction is granted, chaos will supervene. All the arrangements have been made for the next term, the teachers appointed to the new comprehensive schools, the pupils allotted their places, and so forth. It would be next to impossible, he says, to reverse all these arrangements without complete chaos and damage to teachers, pupils and the public. I must say this: if a local authority does not fulfil the requirements of the law, this court will see that it does fulfil them. It will not listen readily to suggestions of "chaos". The department of education and the council are subject to the rule of law and must comply with it, just like everyone else. Even if chaos should result, still the law must be obeyed; but I do not think that chaos will result. The evidence convinces me that the "chaos" is much over-stated. If an injunction is granted now, there will be much less chaos than if it were sought to reverse the situation in a year or so. After all, the injunction will only go as to the eight schools, and not as to the remaining twenty or so schools in the borough. Moreover in regard to these eight schools, it will only affect the new intake coming in at the bottom forms. I see no reason why the position should not be restored, so that the eight schools retain their previous character until the statutory requirements are fulfilled. I can well see that there may be a considerable upset for a number of people, but I think it far more important to uphold the rule of law. Parliament has laid down these requirements so as to ensure that the electors can make their objections and have them properly considered. We must see that their rights are [upheld].'

Agricultural, Horticultural and Forestry Industry Training Board v Aylesbury Mushrooms Ltd [1972] 1 WLR 190

Donaldson J, at 192–195

'The Industrial Training Act 1964 makes provision for the establishment of industrial training boards which [arrange] industrial training for those employed in the industries concerned. The expenses of the boards are defrayed out of a levy imposed on employers in the [industry]. Section 1(4) of the Act provides: "Before making an industrial training order the minister shall consult any organisation or association of organisations appearing to him to be representative of substantial numbers of employers engaging in the activities concerned and any organisation or association of organisations appearing to him to be representative of substantial numbers of persons employed in those [activities]."

[In 1965 the] Minister of Labour was minded to set up the plaintiff board and, as is customary, officials of his Ministry held preliminary consultations with the largest representative body concerned, namely the National Farmers' Union. By April 1966 a draft Order had been prepared. An advance copy of the schedule to the Order, which defined the industry to which the order related, was sent to the National Farmers' Union on 15 April 1966. On 26 April 1966, copies of this document were circulated to a large number of addressees, including the Mushroom Growers' Association, inviting comments. Simultaneously there was a press notice summarising the activities which it was proposed should be covered by the new board and advising any organisation which considered that it had an interest in the draft schedule and which had not received a copy to apply to the Ministry of Labour. No comments were received from the Mushroom Growers' Association and no application was made by them for a copy of the schedule. The Minister of Labour made the order constituting the board on 2 August 1966, it was laid before Parliament on 11 August and came into operation on 15 August of that [year].

In subsequent correspondence it emerged for the first time that the Mushroom Growers' Association had never received a copy of the draft schedule and had no knowledge of the consultations which took place between the Minister and the National Farmers' Union, between September 1965 and April 1966. It is implicit in the evidence [filed] that the Mushroom Growers' Association were also unaware of the contents of the press [notice].

Both parties are agreed that under the terms of section 1(4) of the Act, some consultation by the minister is mandatory and that in the absence of any particular consultation which is so required, the persons who should have been but were not consulted are not bound by the Order, although the Order remains effective in relation to all others who were in fact consulted or whom there was no need to [consult].

Both parties are also agreed that the organisations required to be consulted are those which appear to the minister [to] be representative of substantial numbers of employers engaging in the activities concerned or persons employed therein and nationalised industries which engage in those activities to a substantial extent. Thus whether any particular organisation has to be consulted depends upon a subjective test, subject always to bona fides and reasonableness which are not in [question]. Mr Gettleson for the board submitted that "any" in the phrase "the minister shall consult any organisation" imposed a duty to consult not more than one organisation, that posting the letter of 26 April 1966 constituted consultation with the Mushroom Growers' Association despite the fact that it was never received, that the Mushroom Growers' Association was not an organisation which had to be consulted and that consultation with the National Farmers' Union involved consultation with all its branches including the Mushroom Growers' Association. I have no doubt that Mr Gettleson's first point is without foundation. "Any" must mean "every" in the context of section 1(4). There is a little more to be said for his submission that the mere sending of the letter of 26 April 1966 constituted consultation in that the Shorter Oxford English Dictionary gives as one definition of the verb "to consult" "to ask advice of, seek counsel from, to have recourse to for instruction or professional advice". However, in truth the mere sending of a letter constitutes but an attempt to consult and this does not suffice. The essence of consultation is the communication of a genuine invitation, extended with a receptive mind, to give [advice]. If the invitation is once received, it matters not that it is not accepted and no advice is proffered. Were it otherwise organisations with a right to be consulted could, in effect, veto the making of any order by simply failing to respond to the invitation. But without communication and the consequent opportunity of responding, there can be no consultation.'

(b) Common law principles

The common law principles of 'natural justice' have been developed by the courts where there are no or inadequate statutory roles to provide for fair procedures. Fundamental to any action taken by someone in authority is the attitude of those who may be affected by such action that such action should be 'fair' or 'correct' or 'just', words scarcely any of which can be succinctly formulated by the person in the street, but which add up to a sense of fairness or justice (and 'fairness' has been a common theme of this chapter). Underlying the processes of administration of the state is the fact that the ordinary citizen, who may be asking for a particular benefit, asking the state's permission to carry out a particular form of activity or who may be having his or her property or livelihood harmfully affected by the state, will be face to face in most cases with a complicated rule structure and a monolithic bureaucracy. There ought not to be added to whatever other grievance he or she may feel, the grievance of being treated unfairly. What we are concerned with is an attempt to take these vague sentiments of fairness and to see how the courts have developed procedural rules, which may be original in the sense that they are the only rules of law applicable or may be supplementary in that there are already in existence some statutory rules applicable, but the courts hold that those rules do not themselves reach the required standard of fairness. It may well be that the citizen who believes that he or she has been unfairly treated in that a statutory rule of fair practice has not been observed will ground the case on 'procedural *ultra vires*' as this may be easier to prove. What must be emphasised is that if there is no statutory rule, or if the statutory rule is insufficient, then the courts have created rules, or at least principles, which are an attempt to instil procedural fairness or justice into the actions of public authorities. These rules are known as the rules of natural justice and, as developed in English law, comprise two fundamental rules (each with a variety of sub-rules), namely that no one shall be condemned unheard (*audi alteram partem*) and that no one shall be a judge in his own cause (*nemo judex in causa sua potest*) (the rule against bias discussed in head II(c)). It is a fundamental presumption of interpretation of statutes that no statute excludes natural justice unless the exclusion is expressly stated.[171] The rules of natural justice had been applied to the criminal, common law and chancery courts for a long time. As we have seen in chapter 9, for a long time administration was in the hands of the justices of the peace, King's Bench exercised the same powers of control over their administrative activities as it did over their criminal law activities, and the new local authorities and statutory boards established in the nineteenth century did not at all resemble the justices of the peace. An important question in the second half of the nineteenth century was that of controlling the new public authorities and how to ensure that these authorities acted in the fair and just way of the justices of the peace and the other courts. *Cooper* (p. 468) and *Rice* (p. 470) provided an answer.

Ridge v Baldwin [1964] AC 40

Ridge, the chief constable of Brighton, and two other officers were tried for conspiracy to pervert the course of justice. Ridge was acquitted but the others were convicted. In sentencing them, the judge stated that the evidence established 'that neither of you had that professional and moral leadership which both of you should have had and were entitled to expect from the chief constable'. The Brighton Watch Committee dismissed Ridge without giving him a chance to appear before them. They acted under the Municipal Corporations Act 1882, section 191(4): 'The Watch Committee may at any time suspend and dismiss any borough constable whom they think negligent in the discharge of his duty or otherwise unfit for the same.' Ridge appealed against the dismissal. His main reason was that he wanted to be allowed to resign instead of being dismissed, because, if he were allowed to resign, his pension rights would not be affected, whereas a dismissal would lead to forfeiture of pension rights.

Lord Reid, at 64–79

'The appellant's case is that in proceeding under the Act of 1882 the watch committee were bound to observe what are commonly called the principles of natural justice. Before attempting to reach any decision they were bound to inform him of the grounds on which they proposed to act and give him a fair opportunity of being heard in his own [defence]. The principle *audi alteram partem* goes back many centuries in our law and appears in a multitude of judgments of judges of the highest authority. In modern times opinions have sometimes been expressed to the effect that natural justice is so vague as to be practically meaningless. But I would regard these as tainted by the perennial fallacy that because something cannot be cut and dried or nicely weighed or measured therefore it does not exist. The idea of negligence is equally insusceptible of exact definition, but what a reasonable man would regard as fair procedure in particular circumstances and what he would regard as negligence in particular circumstances are equally capable of serving as tests in law, and natural justice as it has been

[171] *R v Secretary of State for the Home Department, ex p Pierson* [1997] UKHL 37. See, also, *Cowan*, p. 619.

PROCEDURAL IMPROPRIETY · 617

interpreted in the courts is much more definite than that. It appears to me that one reason why the authorities on natural justice have been found difficult to reconcile is that insufficient attention has been paid to the great difference between various kinds of cases in which it has been sought to apply the principle. What a minister ought to do in considering objections to a scheme may be very different from what a watch committee ought to do in considering whether to dismiss a chief [constable]. I find an unbroken line of authority to the effect that an officer cannot lawfully be dismissed without first telling him what is alleged against him and hearing his defence or [explanation].

It may be convenient at this point to deal with an argument that, even if as a general rule a watch committee must hear a constable in his own defence before dismissing him, this case was so clear that nothing that the appellant could have said could have made any difference. It is at least very doubtful whether that could be accepted as an excuse. But, even if it could, the respondents would, in my view, fail on the facts. It may well be that no reasonable body of men could have reinstated the appellant. But as between the other two courses open to the watch committee the case is not so clear. Certainly on the facts, as we know them, the watch committee could reasonably have decided to forfeit the appellant's pension rights, but I could not hold that they would have acted wrongly or wholly unreasonably if they had in the exercise of their discretion decided to take a more lenient course.

[So] I would hold that the power of dismissal in the Act of 1882 could not then have been exercised and cannot now be exercised until the watch committee have informed the constable of the grounds on which they propose to proceed and have given him a proper opportunity to present his case in defence.'

(c) The content of the *audi alteram partem* rule

The content of the *audi alteram partem* rule must be deduced from the decided cases. It must be emphasised that the courts have not set down a detailed code of good administrative behaviour. Their function is to decide the case before them and to ask whether the authority's conduct was correct and fair in the circumstances of the case. Two general principles emerge from the cases. First, the more serious the effect of the administrative action (for example, if the administrative action is in the nature of a sanction), the more the courts will insist on a full, almost court-like, process; the less serious the effect of the administrative action, the more the courts will only insist on 'fairness' (whatever that might mean). This is another example of the 'sliding scale' approach to judicial review. Second, if a person has an existing right (for example, the right to property, to an office or to earn one's livelihood) or a legitimate expectation that an existing right will continue, the courts will be more strict than if a person only has a claim to a right (for example, a claim to exercise for the first time the privilege of running a gaming establishment, or to use one's property in a particular way or to be allowed as a matter of grace to enter the country).

·····

R v Gaming Board for Great Britain, ex p Benaim and Khaida
[1970] 2 QB 417 (CA)

Under the Gaming Act 1968 a person wishing to run a gaming establishment had to apply for a 'certificate of consent' from the Gaming Board, which had the duty to inquire whether he or she was a fit person to run a gaming establishment. The Act enacted guidelines on 'fitness', taking into account the applicant's character, reputation and financial standing. Obviously some of the evidence that might come to the Board would be of a confidential nature. To deal with this, the Board laid down the following: 'In cases where the source or content of this information is confidential, the Board accept that they are obliged to withhold particulars the disclosure of which would be a breach of confidence inconsistent with their statutory duty and the public [interest]. In the course of the interview the applicant will be made aware, to the greatest extent to which this is consistent with the board's statutory duty and the public interest of the matters that are troubling the board.' The applicants wished to run the famous London gambling club Crockford's. Their application was refused and the Board did not give the reason for the refusal or the matters which caused the refusal.

Lord Denning MR, at 429–432

'What they are really seeking is a privilege [to] carry on gaming for [profit]. It is for them to show that they should be trusted with it. [The] Gaming Board are bound to observe the rules of natural justice. [The] board have a duty to act fairly. They must give the applicant an opportunity of satisfying them of the matters specified in the [Act]. They must let him know what their impressions are so that he can disabuse them. But I do not think that they need quote chapter and verse against him as if they were dismissing him from an office as in [*Ridge*, p. 616] or depriving him of his property as in [*Cooper*, p. 468]. After all they are not charging him with doing anything wrong. They are simply inquiring as to his capability and diligence and are having regard to his character, reputation and financial standing. [Seeing] the evils which led to this legislation the board can and should investigate the credentials of those who make application to them. They can and should receive information from the police in this country or abroad. [Much] of it will be confidential. But that does not mean that the applicants are not to be given a chance of answering it. They must be given the chance subject to this qualification: I do not think they need tell the applicant the source of their information if that would put the informant in peril or otherwise be contrary to the public interest. [The] Board was set up by Parliament to cope with disreputable gaming clubs and to bring them under control. By bitter experience it was learned that these clubs had a close connection with organised crime, often violent crime, with protection rackets and strong-arm methods. If the Gaming Board were bound to disclose the sources of information no one would "tell" on those clubs for fear of reprisals. Likewise with the details of the information. If the board were bound to disclose every detail that might itself give the informer away and put him in peril. But without disclosing every detail I should have thought that the board ought in every case to be able to give to the applicant sufficient indication of the objections raised against him such as to enable him to answer [them. The Board] acted with complete fairness. They put before the applicants all the information which led them to doubt their suitability. They kept the sources secret, but disclosed all the information. [The] Board gave the applicants full opportunity to deal with the information. [There] was nothing whatever at fault with their [decision].'

There are a number of detailed sub-principles of the *audi alteram partem* principle. As a general rule, the authority must give the individual concerned a fair opportunity of dealing with the matters raised in the case, including evidence raised by the authority or others, and to give the individual sufficient indication of any objections or any allegations raised against him or her such as to enable him or her to answer them. As a general rule, the individual must be given adequate time within which to prepare a case, to study the case and to seek evidence and witnesses. Note that in so many situations, an adequate opportunity will be assured by a time limit laid down by statutory provisions. As a general rule, the authority must give to each of the parties the opportunity of adequately presenting the case made. However, there is no obligation to follow the strict and exact procedures of a court of law and administrative authorities need not all follow the same procedure and should not regard themselves as being bound by strict rules of evidence as they are applied in a court of law. The authority must consider such evidence relevant to the question to be determined as any person concerned wishes to put, inform every such person of any evidence which the authority proposes to take into consideration, allow each person concerned to comment upon any such evidence and, where the evidence is given orally by witnesses, to put questions to these witnesses, and allow each person concerned to address argument on the whole of the case. Browse through the following: *Cooper* (p. 468), *Gaming Board* (p. 617), *Cowan* (p. 619), *Moore* (p. 620), *Hull Prison* (p. 620), *Barnsley Metropolitan Borough Council* (p. 621), *Birmingham City Magistrates* (p. 623), *Camelot* (p. 624), and *Q* (p. 625).

R v Huntingdon District Council, ex p Cowan [1984] 1 WLR 501

Glidewell J, at 502–508

'This is an application by way of judicial review for an order of certiorari to quash the decision of the Huntingdon District Council refusing to grant a licence for public entertainment for [a discotèque known as "Cuddles"] and for mandamus directed to the council requiring them to hear the application according to [law].

On 14 March 1983, the Local Government (Miscellaneous Provisions) Act 1982, which now governs the grant of what are called "public entertainment licences", had come into force. On that date, Whitbreads applied, through Mr Cowan, for an entertainment licence for these premises. The district council, whose function it now is to consider and make a decision upon that application, received observations upon it from the chief officer of police and the fire [authority]. They also received a petition from a number of members of the public, presumably in opposition either to the licence being granted or to the hours at which the premises were open for public entertainment, I know not which. Whitbreads were not informed by the local authority that any objections had been received. They were not informed that there was opposition. It follows that they were not informed of the substance of the observations or of the terms or substance of the petition. They were given no opportunity to comment upon what objectors had said either by way of oral hearing or in writing. On 22 June 1983 the application was [refused].

Mr Richardson, for the applicants, submits that where an objector has made representations to the local authority, or where the local authority itself has some reason to believe that there is doubt about whether it should grant the [application,] then it is under a duty to give notice to the applicant, either by sending a copy of the representations or objections. Or at least giving the substance of them, or if it is its own point, telling the applicant what the point is. Then it must, says Mr Richardson, give the applicant the opportunity to make representations in answer, to seek to deal with the objection or the point, and it may be that this needs to be by way of oral [hearing]. Mr Richardson's basic point is that the rules of natural justice require an authority charged with the decision such as this, whether or not to grant a licence, to give to the applicant an opportunity to know of the objections and, if he can, to answer them.

[Mr] Steel for the district council, accepts that the authority has a duty to act fairly but he does not accept that that extends to disclosing the objections or giving any opportunity for reply. He maintains that the authority is perfectly entitled to act as it has [done]. What seems to me to be Mr Steel's strongest argument, however, is this, that the other Parts of the Act of 1982, which are dealing with different sorts of licensing, do provide detailed procedures for the making of objections; the notification of objections to the applicant; for representations to be made by the applicant; and, indeed, for a [hearing]. What Mr Steel submits, with a great deal of force, is that this is one Act, and a normal principle of statutory construction is that an Act must be construed as a whole. It follows, he says, that where you have in relation to two similar subjects dealt with by the Act, detailed provisions providing for objections, notification, representations by an applicant and a hearing, and no such provisions in relation to entertainment licences, that can only be because Parliament intended that those provisions should not apply to entertainment licences, and thus the Act, in effect, is expressly excluding the necessity for those [provisions].

The question which has exercised my mind is, does the fact that in the other Parts of the Act to which I have referred, specific provision is made for those features, whereas no such provision is made in [the Schedule dealing with public entertainment licences], mean that Parliament intended that that rule of natural justice should not here apply? I have come to the conclusion that I ought not to draw that [deduction].

Accordingly, in my judgment, a local authority is under a duty, when dealing with entertainment licences, first, to inform the applicant of the substance of any objection or of any representation in the nature of any objection (not necessarily to give him the whole of it, nor to say necessarily who has made it, but to give him the substance of it), and, secondly, to give him an opportunity to make representations in reply. '

R v Deputy Industrial Injuries Commissioner, ex p Moore [1965] 1 QB 456 (CA)

Mrs Moore, a lady crane-driver, claimed industrial injuries benefit in that she had suffered a slipped disc while working. The Social Security Commissioner took into account two earlier Commissioners' decisions in which medical opinion on slipped discs was cited. He gave Mrs Moore and the insurance officer (acting on behalf of the Department) an opportunity of commenting on those opinions.

Diplock LJ, at 488

[Held that natural justice demanded, following *Rice* (p. 470), that the Commissioner must listen fairly to both sides. This had been done. Natural justice also demanded that any decision must be based on 'evidence'.]

'["Evidence"] is not restricted to evidence which would be admissible in a court of law. For historical reasons, based on the fear that juries who might be illiterate would be incapable of differentiating between the probative values of different methods of proof, the practice of the common law courts has been to admit only what the judges then regarded as the best evidence of any disputed fact, and thereby to exclude much material which, as a matter of common sense, would assist a fact-finding tribunal to reach a correct conclusion. These technical rules of evidence, however, form no part of the rules of natural justice. The requirement that a person exercising quasi-judicial functions must base his decision on evidence means no more than it must be based upon material which tends logically to show the existence or non-existence of facts relevant to the issue to be determined, or to show the likelihood or unlikelihood of the occurrence of some future event the occurrence of which would be relevant. It means that he must not spin a coin or consult an astrologer, but he may take into account any material which, as a matter of reason, has some probative value in the sense mentioned above. If it is capable of having any probative value, the weight to be attached to it is a matter for the person to whom Parliament has entrusted the responsibility of deciding the issue. The supervisory jurisdiction of the High Court does not entitle it to usurp this responsibility and to substitute its own view for [his].'

R v Hull Prison Board of Visitors, ex p St Germain [1979] 1 WLR 1401

There were riots at Hull Prison and serious damage was caused. It was decided to deal with prisoners accused of rioting under the prison disciplinary procedure, whereby a Board of Visitors operates a procedure similar to that of a magistrates' court and has power to impose penalties (including the power to order forfeiture of remission of sentence). The Board acted under the Prison Rules, made under the Prison Act 1952, section 47(2), which stated that the rules 'shall make provision for ensuring that a person who is charged with any offence under the rules shall be given a proper opportunity of presenting his case'. Rule 49(2) provided that 'at any inquiry into a charge against a prisoner he shall be given a full opportunity of hearing what is alleged against him and of presenting his case'. In essence, the applicants maintained that by being subject to the Board of Visitors, they had not had the same procedural safeguards as they would have had in a criminal court in that the Board had refused to allow the applicants to call certain witnesses to support their case, and the Board had admitted and acted on hearsay evidence supplied by the Prison Governor.

Geoffrey Lane LJ, at 1406–1410

'Clearly in the proper exercise of his discretion a chairman may limit the number of witnesses, either on the basis that he has good reason for considering that the total number sought to be called is an attempt by the prisoner to render the hearing of the charge virtually impracticable or where quite simply it would be quite unnecessary to call so many witnesses to establish the point at issue. But mere administrative difficulties, simpliciter, are not in our view [enough. The] right to be heard will include, in appropriate cases, the right to call evidence. It would in our judgment be wrong to attempt an exhaustive definition as to what are appropriate cases, but they must include proceedings whose function is to establish the guilt or innocence of a person charged with serious misconduct. In the instant cases, what was being considered was alleged serious disciplinary offences, which, if established, could and did result in very substantial loss of liberty. In such a situation it would be a mockery to say that an accused had been "given a proper opportunity of presenting his case" (section 47(2) of the Prison Act 1952) or "a full opportunity of presenting his own case" (rule 49(2) [of the Prison Rules 1964]), if he had been denied the opportunity of calling evidence which was likely to assist in establishing the vital facts at [issue].

It is of course common ground that the board of visitors must base their decisions on evidence. But must such evidence be restricted to that which would be admissible in a criminal court of law? [It] is clear that the entitlement of the Board to admit hearsay evidence is subject to the overriding obligation to provide the accused with a fair hearing. Depending on the facts of the particular case and the nature of the hearsay evidence provided to the board, the obligation to give the accused a fair chance to exculpate himself, or a fair opportunity to controvert the charge [or] a proper or full opportunity of presenting his [case] may oblige the board not only to inform the accused of the hearsay evidence but also to give the accused a sufficient opportunity to deal with that evidence. Again, depending on the nature of that evidence and the particular circumstances of the case, a sufficient opportunity to deal with the hearsay evidence may well involve the cross-examination of the witness whose evidence is initially before the board in the form of hearsay.

We [take] by way of example the case in which the defence is an alibi. The prisoner contends that he was not the man identified on the roof. He, the prisoner, was at the material time elsewhere. In short the prisoner has been mistakenly identified. [The] prisoner may well wish to elicit by way of questions all manner of detail, eg the poorness of the light, the state of confusion, the brevity of the observation, the absence of any contemporaneous record, etc., all designed to show the unreliability of the witness. To deprive him of the opportunity of cross-examination would be tantamount to depriving him of a fair hearing. We appreciate that there may well be occasions when the burden of calling the witness whose hearsay evidence is readily available may impose a near impossible burden on the board. However, it has not been suggested that hearsay evidence should be resorted to in the total absence of any first-hand evidence. In the instant cases hearsay evidence was only resorted to to supplement the first-hand evidence and this is the usual practice. Accordingly where a prisoner desires to dispute the hearsay evidence and for this purpose to question the witness, and where there are insuperable or very grave difficulties in arranging for his attendance, the board should refuse to admit that evidence, or, if it has already come to their notice, should expressly dismiss it from their [consideration].'

R v Barnsley Metropolitan Borough Council, ex p Hook [1976] 1 WLR 1052 (CA)

Lord Denning MR, at 1055–1058

'To some this may appear to be a small matter, but to Mr Harry Hook it is very important. He is a street trader in the Barnsley market. He has been trading there for some six years without any complaint being made against him; but, nevertheless, he has now been banned from trading in the market for life. All because of a trifling incident. On Wednesday, 16 October 1974, the market closed at 5.30. So were all the lavatories, or "toilets" as they are now called. They were locked up. Three-quarters of an hour [later], Harry Hook had an urgent call of nature. He wanted to relieve himself. He went into a side street near the market and there made water, or "urinated", as it is now said. No one was about except one or two employees of the council, who were cleaning up. They rebuked him. He said: "I can do it here if I like." They reported him to a security officer who came up. The security officer reprimanded Harry Hook. We are not told the words used by the security officer. I expect they were in language which street traders understand. Harry Hook made an appropriate reply. Again we are not told the actual words, but it is not difficult to guess. I expect it was an emphatic version of "You be off." At any rate, the security officer described them as words of abuse. Touchstone would say the security officer gave the "reproof valiant" and Harry Hook gave the "countercheck quarrelsome": *As You Like It*, Act V, Scene IV.

On the Thursday morning the security officer reported the incident. The market manager thought it was a serious matter. So he saw Mr Hook the next [day]. Mr Hook admitted it and said he was sorry for what had happened. The market manager was not satisfied to leave it there. He reported the incident to the chairman of the amenity services committee of the council. He says that the chairman agreed "that staff should be protected from such abuse". That very day the market manager wrote a letter to Mr Hook, banning him from trading in the market. It read: "[I] have to give you notice that you are no longer considered to be a suitable tenant of this authority. The stalls and pitch at present reserved for you each market day will cease to be available for your use after Wednesday [next]. Please arrange to clear stock from your cupboards by this date." So there he [was] dismissed as from the next Wednesday, banned for life.

He was, however, granted a further hearing. [Mr] Hook went there with a young articled clerk from his solicitors and the trade union representative. The committee met at 10 a.m. but Mr Hook and his representatives had to wait for an hour before they were allowed in. Then the articled clerk and the union representative went in. But Mr Hook himself did not go in. He stayed outside in the corridor. The articled clerk and the union representative were allowed to address the committee, but they were not given particulars of the charge or of the evidence against Mr Hook. At that meeting the market manager was present and was in a position to tell the committee his view of the evidence. After Mr Hook's representatives had been heard, that subcommittee discussed the case (with the market manager still present) and decided to adhere to the original [decision].

[The right of a stall holder] is not to be taken away except for just cause and in accord with natural justice. [The hearing was] vitiated by the fact that the market manager was there all the time. He was the one who gave evidence—the only one who did—and hearsay evidence, too. His evidence was given privately to the committee, not in the presence of Mr Hook or his representatives. Mr Hook was not himself in the room. His representatives were there, and they were heard. But when the committee discussed the case and came to their decision, the market manager was there all the time. His presence at all their deliberations is enough to vitiate the proceedings. It is contrary to natural justice that one who is in the position of a prosecutor should be present at the deliberations of the adjudicating [committee].

But there is one further matter: and that is that the punishment was too severe. It appears that there had been other cases where men had urinated in a side street near the market and no such punishment had been inflicted. Now there are old cases which show that the court can interfere by certiorari if a punishment is altogether excessive and out of proportion to the occasion. In one case the Commissioners of Sewers imposed an excessive fine: and it was quashed by the Court of King's Bench on the ground that in law their fines ought to be [reasonable]. So in this case if Mr Hook did misbehave, I should have thought the right thing would have been to take him before the magistrates under the byelaws, when some small fine might have been inflicted. It is quite wrong that the Barnsley Corporation should inflict upon him the grave penalty of depriving him of his livelihood. That is a far more serious penalty than anything the magistrates could inflict. He is a man of good character, and ought not to be penalised thus. On that ground alone, apart from the others, the decision of the Barnsley Corporation cannot [stand].'

R v Birmingham City Magistrates, ex p Chris Foreign Foods Ltd
[1970] 1 WLR 1428

Under the Food and Drugs Act 1955, it was forbidden to add certain colouring matters to certain imported products if the addition occurred when the product was in a raw or unprocessed state. Local authority enforcement officers could seize such products, which were then liable to be condemned by a magistrate as unfit for human consumption and destroyed. This case concerned a quantity of sweet potatoes. The magistrate inspected the potatoes at the premises of the local authority health department where he met the senior food inspector and the chief veterinary officer. He took and cut open a sample of the potatoes, which appeared to be raw. He was given a certificate from the public analyst which stated that the potatoes appeared unprocessed. The magistrate, following the normal statutory procedure, held a hearing at which Chris was invited to give evidence as to why the potatoes should not be condemned as unfit. Chris gave evidence and his counsel addressed the magistrate. Then the magistrate retired to make his decision, but he retired with the chief veterinary officer and the public analyst in order, as he put it to 'take advice'. The three of them came back some minutes later and the magistrate announced his decision that he upheld the public analyst's certificate that the sweet potatoes in question did appear to be unprocessed and that the potatoes must be destroyed, without giving Chris any opportunity of knowing what the 'advice' (if any) was and of commenting on that 'advice'.

Lord Parker CJ, at 1433–1434

'[The] point where I feel the rules of natural justice in their limited application to such a case as this, limited to openness, impartiality and fairness, have been broken, is when the justice retired with the two officials in order, as he puts it, "to take advice", and the three of them came back and he announced his decision. It seems to me that in a case such as this a justice must be very careful not to take any fresh advice or hear any fresh evidence in the absence of the objectors, unless he returns and enables the objectors to know what the advice is that he has received, thus enabling them to deal with it. To give an illustration of the present case, the public analyst has said that the highest he had put it was that the potatoes appeared to be unprocessed. Supposing that when the justice retires with him he says "I was being very cautious, I think it is quite clear they were unprocessed". One asks: should not the objectors have an opportunity of meeting that, and probably meeting it by cross examination, to which in the ordinary way, this not being a trial, there would be no right? One looks to see what is fair. But the matter does not end there, because this is, as [the] Act of 1955 says, a decision of the justice. It is not a decision of the justice together with the public analyst and the chief veterinary officer, any more than the decision of a justice when he is sitting in a court of summary jurisdiction is the decision of himself and his [clerk].'

James J, at 1434

'[To] leave the room with the protagonists of the applicants, the man who had brought in the justice to adjudicate, with the person who has provided the evidence, namely, the certificate of analysis, and then to return and announce a decision without indicating to the applicants what, if any, further advice had been given by those persons, in my judgment was a breach of the requirements that the procedure should be carried out seemingly openly and with [fairness].'

R v National Lottery Commission, ex p Camelot Group [2000] EWHC 391 (Admin)

The National Lottery was operated under a seven year licence by Camelot. The licence was due to expire on 30 September 2001. The National Lottery Commission established a competitive invitation to apply (ITA) procedure for the award of the new licence and bids were received from Camelot and The People's Lottery (TPL). The Commission announced on 23 August 2000 that it had decided that neither of the bidders' plans met the statutory criteria for granting a licence and that they would proceed on the basis of a new procedure under which it would negotiate exclusively with TPL for one month. It did so for very different reasons in the case of the two applicants. In the case of Camelot, the reasons related to their fitness and propriety. In the case of TPL, the Commission was not satisfied that adequate arrangements had been made for the protection of the interests of every participant in the National Lottery and the Commission had significant concerns about the financial viability of TPL. In a press release issued on 23 August, the Commission Chairman stated:

'Both bids had many merits. We met the bidders and gave them every chance to make improvements to their applications. But they also had important failings. We are disappointed about that, but we would fail in our statutory duty if we granted a seven-year licence based on either bid in its present form. The question now, of course, is what happens in the light of this decision. The Commission has been advised that it can proceed on the basis of a new process. This would be with one bidder only and would take place over a short period. This we propose to do as quickly as possible. We propose to negotiate with The People's Lottery and hope that we can reach a satisfactory solution within the deadline we have set of one month from today.'

Richards J

'34. Mr Pannick [on behalf of Camelot] submits that it was grossly unfair to abandon the ITA procedure and then to give only one of the bidders an opportunity to allay the Commission's concerns even though the Commission had decided that each bid had many merits as well as important failings. To be prepared to listen to one bidder but not the other is unprecedented.

. . .

39. Thus it is submitted that the Commission has adopted an unfair [procedure]. Having received two bids, each of which has defects, the Commission has unfairly decided to give one bidder the opportunity to improve its bid, while denying the opportunity to Camelot, even though, if each were given the same opportunity, Camelot's improved bid might be found by the Commission to be the better [bid].

. . .

67. [It] is common ground that the Commission acted lawfully in declining to accept either bid under the competitive procedure established by the ITA and in bringing that procedure to an end. The Commission had made clear provision for that possibility in the ITA itself. The court is concerned only with the lawfulness of the Commission's further decision as to the procedure to be followed once the ITA procedure was at an end. The 1993 [Lottery] Act does not lay down the procedure to be [followed]. The Commission is left with a wide discretion. The question is whether the Commission has exercised that discretion in a way that offends the general principles of public law.

68. [At] bottom the case is about fairness: whether, in the circumstances existing on the termination of ITA procedure, the decision to carry on an exclusive negotiation with TPL for one month, thereby giving TPL an opportunity to allay the Commission's concerns but denying a similar opportunity to Camelot, was so unfair as to amount to an unlawful exercise of [discretion].

. . .

72. I find it remarkable that in those circumstances the Commission chose to allow TPL the opportunity to allay its concerns but to deny a similar opportunity to Camelot. Such a marked lack of

even-handedness between the rival bidders calls for the most compelling justification, which I cannot find in the reasons advanced by the Commission in support of its decision.

. . .

74. It is no answer to say that Camelot's new proposals will take longer than one month to evaluate. Whether that is so must depend not on the estimate given in the consultants' report, but on what actually happens in the course of negotiations conducted in good faith between the Commission and Camelot. Camelot believes that it can satisfy the Commission on the point. It is entitled to a fair opportunity to do [so].

. . .

79. One of the individual strands to Camelot's case is that it had a legitimate expectation of consultation before the Commission reached its decision on the way forward following the termination of the ITA procedure. In my view the conditions for a legitimate expectation [were] not made out. Although there had been consultation at every stage of the ITA procedure, there was no clear and unambiguous representation that there would be consultation in the different circumstances that prevailed at the end of that procedure. Consultation would certainly have been the prudent course and could perhaps be considered a necessary course in order that the Commission could take a properly informed decision. Had there been consultation, it is difficult to believe that the Commission would have adopted the procedure it did; but that does not of itself make the absence of consultation unlawful. On the other hand, [legitimate] expectation is not the end of the matter. The absence of consultation is an additional factor to be taken into account in assessing the overall position. Where the actual procedure decided on is very unfair to Camelot, as it is, the fact that it was decided on without giving Camelot any opportunity to make representations about it serves to increase the degree of unfairness overall.

. . .

84. [The] essence of the judgment is, however, clear. The Commission, while intending to be fair, has decided on a procedure that results in conspicuous unfairness to Camelot—such unfairness as to render the decision unlawful. That broad point is perhaps more important than the precise legal analysis. [The] ultimate question is whether something has gone wrong of a nature and degree which requires the intervention of the court. In my judgment it has.'

....

R (On the Application of Q) v Secretary of State for the Home Department
[2003] EWCA Civ 364

Section 55 of the Nationality, Immigration and Asylum Act 2002 provided that the Secretary of State 'may not provide or arrange for the provision of support' to a person making a claim for asylum where he 'is not satisfied that the claim was made as soon as reasonably practicable after the person's arrival in the United Kingdom'. Collins, J, heard applications for judicial review by six asylum seekers whose claims for support had been refused on the ground that they had failed to satisfy the Secretary of State that they had advanced their claims for asylum as soon as reasonably practicable. Collins, J, allowed those applications and quashed the decisions, primarily on the grounds that the procedure adopted in each case was not fair. The Secretary of State appealed.

Lord Phillips MR

'The principle of fairness

69. It is common ground that [the] burden of satisfying the Secretary of State that the claim for asylum was made as soon as reasonably practicable after arrival in the United Kingdom is on the applicant. [It is] common ground that in deciding whether the applicant has so satisfied him the Secretary of State

must act fairly, which means both that he must set up a fair system to enable the decisions to be made and that he must operate the system [fairly].

. . .

The system

74. The system [may] be summarised in this way.

75. A person applying for asylum was interviewed by an administrative officer ("an AO"), who was given a screening form to help him decide what questions to [ask].

. . .

78. Although there are a large number of questions on the form, very few of them seem to us to be related directly to the key [question], namely whether the applicant applied for asylum as soon as reasonably practicable after [arrival].

79. There are then questions about means and assets which complete the first part of the form. There follows what is described as a level two form, of which there are two types. They are a long version and a shorter [version]. The shorter version asks whether the interviewee passed through immigration control when he reached the UK and, if so, what reasons he gave [for] his visit, how long he said he planned to stay and on what conditions he entered the UK, and, if not, how he entered the UK. If the interviewee entered by lorry it further asks what type of lorry, what its cargo was, how long he was in the lorry and where in the UK he was dropped off. Finally it asks what evidence he has to support the statements made in the interview and whether he has anything else to add. The longer form asks one or two more questions, including what documentation the interviewee has and concludes with this warning: "It is vital that you tell us everything you know which is relevant to the questions I have asked you or to which you think you should tell us. It may affect your entitlement to support if you fail to provide full [details]."

. . .

Is the system fair?

84. As we understand it, the decisions as to whether the applicant claimed asylum as soon as reasonably practicable [are] taken (at least in the first instance) on the basis of the answers given as part of the general screening process described above. In these circumstances fairness requires that the applicant be told what the purpose of the interview is in clear terms. Further thought should be given to an appropriate formulation. It might include a statement that an important purpose of the interview is to enable the Secretary of State to decide whether he is eligible for [support and that] he may not be eligible unless he persuades the Secretary of State that he had good reason for not applying for asylum [earlier].

85. Quite apart from the adequacy or otherwise of the information given to the applicant before the interview begins, we have reached the conclusion that the system operated to date by or (more accurately) on behalf of the Secretary of State is not fair in a number of respects.

86. First it seems to us to be important that the interviewer and the decision maker should be properly instructed as to what is meant by "reasonably [practicable]". Otherwise the issue is most unlikely to be properly investigated on the [facts].

87. We have already expressed our view that in order to decide whether the applicant applied for asylum "as soon as reasonably practicable after [his] arrival in the United Kingdom" the Secretary of State should ask himself the question: on the premise that the purpose of coming to this country was to claim asylum and having regard both to the practical opportunity for claiming asylum and to the asylum seeker's personal circumstances, could the asylum seeker reasonably have been expected to claim asylum earlier? We have also expressed the view that in answering that question the Secretary of State should have in mind the asylum seeker's state of mind including his state of mind resulting from any information or instructions given by the agent who facilitated his entry.

88. It is clear that the decision makers were not given instructions to that effect. If they had been, we have no doubt that the questions asked in interview would have been more extensive than there were in [fact].

89. It [seems] to us to be important for the interviewer to probe the facts of each case in order to ensure that he has a reasonably full picture so that the Secretary of State's decision can be properly informed. Few, if any, asylum seekers have advice at the time of the interview, so that (at any rate without a much clearer explanation of the purpose of the interview) it is insufficient for the Secretary of State to contend that the burden of proof is on the applicant and that he has only himself to blame if he does not provide the interviewer with the whole picture.

90. We do not think that the questions asked at present enable the interviewer (let alone the decision maker) to have a sufficiently full picture for a fair decision to be made. [Fairness] requires the interviewer to try to ascertain the precise reason that the applicant did not claim asylum, say, at the airport or immediately after being let out of a lorry. This calls for interviewing skills and a more flexible approach than simply completing a standard form [questionnaire].

. . .

98. [There] are two further serious defects in the system [adopted], at any rate until now. The first is that the decision maker is not in the ordinary course of events the same person as the interviewer. This means that a view has to be formed as to the credibility of the applicant's account by a person who has not seen the applicant but only read the answers noted on the screening form by someone else. We understand from the Attorney-General that that aspect of the system is to be changed and that the interviewer and the decision maker will be the same person. In our view that will be a most welcome change for the future.

99. [Collins, J] stressed that it was important that the applicant should be given a reasonable opportunity to deal with and to explain any matter which was to be relied on against him. We agree. Before the decision maker concludes that the applicant is not telling the truth he must be given the opportunity of meeting any concerns [or] he should be informed of the gist of the case against him. We should add that we also [agree] that at the very least the applicant must be given the chance to rebut a suggestion of incredibility and to explain himself if he [can].

100. The system as operated to date does not afford the applicant such an opportunity, although it will no doubt be much easier for it to do so once the interviewer and the decision taker are the same [person].

. . .

Postscript

120. We dismiss these appeals because Collins J was correct to conclude that each of the six decisions under consideration was vitiated as a result of deficiencies in the procedure. We were told by the Attorney-General that these procedures are being radically overhauled. When they have been put in order we can see no reason why section 55 should not operate [effectively].'

(d) A common law duty to give reasons?

It has often been asked whether there is a general common law duty to give reasons and that question has consistently received a negative answer.[172] In recent years, a possibly more subtle (and possibly more effective) question asked has been whether, in certain circumstances, the duty to provide a fair hearing or to act fairly includes a duty to give reasons. After all,

---

[172] *Doody v Secretary of State for the Home Department* [1994] 1 AC 531.

'the so-called rules of natural justice are not engraved on tablets of stone [and] what the requirements of fairness demand when any body, domestic, administrative or judicial, has to make a decision which will affect the rights of individuals depends on the character of the decision-making body, the kind of decision it has to make and the statutory or other framework in which it operates. In particular, it is well established that when a statute has conferred on any body the power to make decisions affecting individuals, the courts will not only require the procedure prescribed by the statute to be followed, but will readily imply so much and no more to be introduced by way of additional procedural safeguards as will ensure the attainment of fairness.'[173]

The prevailing trend of the law in recent times has been towards an increased recognition of the duty upon decision-makers of many kinds to give reasons.[174] At present, there are probably three categories of case emerging. First, where there is something odd or aberrant in the decision and where fairness demands that reasons need to be given. In *R v Civil Service Appeal Board, ex p Cunningham*,[175] Cunningham was unfairly dismissed from a post in the Prison Department of the Home Office and had to seek compensation from the Civil Service Appeal Board, a body established under prerogative powers, rather than from an industrial tribunal. The Board awarded him compensation of £6,500, giving no reasons for this amount, whereas had he been able to go to an industrial tribunal, his compensation would have been somewhere near £15,000. The Court of Appeal held that Cunningham succeeded upon the ground 'that fairness requires a tribunal such as the board to give sufficient reasons for its decision to enable the parties to know the issues to which it addressed its mind and that it acted lawfully'.[176]

'In default of explanation [the applicant's] award was so far below what, by analogy with the award of an industrial tribunal, he was entitled to expect as [to] compel the inference that the assessment was irrational, if not perverse. Because there was no general duty to give reasons, the absence of reasons does not by itself entitle the court to hold that the award was not supportable. But the unexplained meagreness of the award does compel that inference. In my judgment the duty to act fairly in this case extends to an obligation to give reasons. Nothing more onerous is demanded of the board than a concise statement of the means by which they arrived at the figure awarded.'[177]

Second, where the subject matter of the decision forms a serious interference with liberty. *Doody v Secretary of State for the Home Department*[178] related to imprisonment. When a person is sentenced to life imprisonment, one factor to be taken into consideration before deciding whether the prisoner should be released is a determinate number of years appropriate to the nature and gravity of the offence (the 'penal' element). Once the penal element is over, the case may be reviewed. Doody and others were each convicted of murder and sentenced to life imprisonment. They alleged that the Home Secretary had increased the penal element of the sentence recommended by the judiciary, thereby delaying the date of their review. It was held that the common law presumption that a power will be exercised in a fair manner will very often require that a person who may be adversely affected by the decision

---

[173] *Lloyd v McMahon* [1987] AC 625, per Lord Bridge, at 702–703.

[174] *R v The Mayor and Commonalty and Citizens of the City of London, ex p Matson* [1997] 1 WLR 765; *Stefan v The General Medical Council* [1999] UKPC 10.

[175] [1991] 4 All ER 310. See, also, *R v Higher Education Funding Council, ex p Institute of Dental Surgery* [1994] 1 WLR 242.   [176] Per Lord Donaldson MR, at 320.

[177] Per Leggatt LJ, at 326.   [178] [1994] 1 AC 531.

should have an opportunity to make representations on his or her own behalf, and that, since the person affected usually cannot make worthwhile representations without knowing what factors may weigh against his or her interests, fairness will very often require that he or she is informed of the gist of the case which he or she has to answer. In a case where freedom was at stake and the decision of the Home Secretary on the penal element was susceptible to judicial review, the only effective way to challenge that decision necessitated that the reasoning of the Home Secretary should be disclosed. Third, 'fairness' may require the giving of reasons when a decision casts a shadow on the reputation of a person.[179]

---

[179] *R v The Mayor and Commonalty and Citizens of the City of London, ex p Matson* [1997] 1 WLR 765; *Stefan v The General Medical Council* [1999] UKPC 10.

11 PUBLIC ORDER

1. Introduction

The inherent power of the protest or the demonstration to bring about change is clearly apparent from the pages of history books and modern day experience. Those who seek to reform the political system of a nation, such as the Suffragettes who chained themselves to railings in their campaign to see the franchise extended to women, or indeed to overthrow the system altogether, have long since appreciated that the protest is a powerful weapon at their disposal. If the demand for reform acquires widespread support and hence an unstoppable momentum, weak governments who have lost the support of the military may well be compelled to meet the demands of the protesters if they wish to remain in power. History is replete with examples of successful military coups d'état, revolutions and uprisings where the incumbent ruler or government has been removed from office and has been replaced by another. Equally there are many examples of protests and demonstrations which have ended in disaster for those who were involved. An example of such a protest in England was a meeting held on St Peter's Field in Manchester on 16 August 1819, which resulted in the infamous Peterloo Massacre, in which 11 people were killed in clashes between the protesters and, among others, the Manchester Yeomanry.

The complete overthrow of the political system by way of revolution inevitably involves, for however limited a period, the breakdown of public order. Protests which have as their motive force more limited objectives, such as the end of an unpopular government policy or the improvement of conditions in the workplace, may actually achieve those objectives without seriously impinging upon public order. More often than not, however, some form of disturbance is a corollary of the protest. In more recent times, we in Britain have witnessed protests which have resulted in rather different outcomes. The demonstrations which were held against the levying of the Community Charge or 'poll tax' clearly played a significant part in the decision of the government of the day to dispense with what had been a flagship policy and replace it with the less politically controversial council tax as a means of raising local taxation. By contrast, the treetop protesters against the construction of the Newbury by-pass received a great deal of media attention for their cause, but ultimately they were unsuccessful in their attempt to prevent work from commencing on the project.

Whether or not it can be said that there is a right to protest or demonstrate in this country is, however, a moot point. In his report into the Red Lion Square disorders,[1] Lord Scarman ventured the opinion that:

'Amongst our fundamental human rights, there are, without doubt, the rights of peaceful assembly and public protest and the right to public order and tranquillity. Civilised living collapses—it is obvious—if

[1] Cmnd 5919 (1974).

public protest becomes violent protest or public order degenerates into the quietism imposed by successful oppression. But the problem is more complex than a choice between two extremes—one, a right to protest whenever and wherever you will and the other, a right to continuous calm upon our streets unruffled by the noise and obstructive pressure of the protesting procession. A balance has to be struck, a compromise found that will accommodate the exercise of the right to protest within a framework which enables ordinary citizens, who are not protesting, to go about their business and pleasure without obstruction or inconvenience . . .'[2]

Clearly Lord Scarman's use of rights language when discussing protests and demonstrations implied some positive entitlement on the part of the individual to engage in this type of activity when he or she feels that there is a need to do so. Lord Denning ascribed a similarly positive nature to the 'right' to protest in *Hubbard v Pitt*[3] where he referred to a 'right to demonstrate and the right to protest on matters of public concern'. Continuing on the same theme, he observed that: 'These are rights which it is in the public interest that individuals should possess; and indeed that they should exercise without impediment so long as no wrongful act is done.'[4]

The traditional approach when discussing civil liberties in this country has been to talk in terms of the individual having the freedom to do that which is not prohibited by law, either in its statutory or common law form. Seen in this light, the 'right' to protest assumes a more residual form, consisting only of a freedom to do that which does not conflict with legal obligations, such as the requirement in section 137 of the Highways Act 1980 not to wilfully obstruct free passage along the highway.[5] In chapter VII of his seminal work *An Introduction to the Study of the Law of the Constitution*,[6] Professor A V Dicey emphasised this point in the following terms:

'No better instance can indeed be found of the way in which in England the constitution is built up upon individual rights than our rules as to public assemblies. The right of assembling is nothing more than a result of the view taken by the courts as to individual liberty of person and individual liberty of speech. There is no special law allowing A, B and C to meet together either in the open air or elsewhere for a lawful purpose, but the right of A to go where he pleases so that he does not commit a trespass, and to say what he likes to B so that his talk is not libellous or seditious, the right of B to do the like, and the existence of the same rights of C, D, E and F, and so on *ad infinitum*, lead to the consequence that A, B, C, D and a thousand or ten thousand other persons, may (as a general rule) meet together in any place where otherwise they each have a right to be for a lawful purpose and in a lawful manner.'[7]

Following the enactment of the Human Rights Act 1998[8] it is now possible, however, to talk in terms of the rights of the individual in a far more positive manner given that the Act has incorporated certain of the rights contained in the European Convention and its protocols into English law. Thus in the context of public order and the right to protest, when such a right is interfered with, the courts will hear arguments relating to articles 10 (freedom of expression) and 11 (freedom of assembly) of the Convention. As we shall see, however, very few Convention rights are absolute. There may be circumstances where a public authority is entitled to act in such a way as to interfere with an individuals' rights and yet still remain within the bounds of the law because the action falls within a prescribed exception and is proportionate to the legitimate aim which is being pursued, i.e. maintaining public order.

---

[2] At para 5.   [3] [1975] 3 All ER 1.   [4] Ibid., at 10.
[5] In determining whether or not the offence has been committed, the reasonableness of the use of the highway is an important factor: see *Nagy v Weston* [1965] 1 All ER 78 and *Hirst and Agu v Chief Constable of West Yorkshire* (1987) 85 Cr App R 143.   [6] (10th edn, 1959).
[7] Ibid., at p. 271.   [8] See chapter 13.

In the present context, English law has long wrestled with a conundrum in the form of a lawful protest or demonstration which provokes or occasions a breach of the peace or some other unlawful activity by another party. In these circumstances, the crucial issue is whether the police are entitled to intervene to prevent the lawful activity from taking place on the grounds that past experience has shown that it will inevitably lead to unlawful activity committed by another party.

II. Preventive Action

The question of preventive action was the matter at issue in an important nineteenth century case.

....

Beatty v Gillbanks (1882) 9 QBD 308

The appellants, who were members of the Salvation Army, had been bound over to keep the peace by magistrates for unlawfully and tumultuously assembling in the public streets of Weston-super-Mare so as to cause a breach of the public peace. On several previous occasions, the Salvation Army had encountered a rival organisation known as the Skeleton Army and the antagonism between these two groups had resulted in fighting, uproar, tumult, stone throwing, and general disorder. Accordingly, on the particular occasion in question, the police stopped the advance of the Salvation Army procession and issued a direction that they must disperse at once or be arrested. When the leader of the procession refused to do so, he was arrested as were the other appellants who persisted in leading the procession. The question for the Divisional Court to determine was whether the appellants had been properly charged with participating in an unlawful assembly.

Field J, at 313–315

'The appellants have, with others, formed themselves into an association for religious exercises among themselves, and for a religious revival, if I may use that word, which they desire to further among certain classes of the community. No one imputed to this association any other object, and so far from wishing to carry that out with violence, their opinions seem to be opposed to such a course, and, at all events in the present case, they made no opposition to the authorities. That being their lawful object, they assembled as they had done before and marched in procession through the streets of Weston-super-Mare. No one can say that such an assembly is in itself an unlawful one . . . There is no doubt that they and with them others assembled together in great numbers, but such an assembly to be unlawful must be tumultuous and against the peace. As far as these appellants are concerned there was nothing in their conduct when they were assembled together which was either tumultuous or against the peace. But it is said that the conduct pursued by them on this occasion was such as, on several previous occasions, had produced riots and disturbance of the peace and terror to the inhabitants, and the appellants knowing when they assembled together that such consequences would again arise are liable to this charge.

Now I entirely concede that everyone must be taken to intend the natural consequences of his own acts, and it is clear to me that if this disturbance of the peace was the natural consequence of acts of the appellants they would be liable, and the justices would have been right in binding them over. But the evidence set forth in the case does not support this contention; on the contrary, it shows that the disturbances were caused by other people antagonistic to the appellants, and that no acts of violence were committed by them . . .

What has happened here is that an unlawful organisation has assumed to itself the right to prevent the appellants and others from lawfully assembling together, and the finding of the justices amounts to this, that a man may be convicted for doing a lawful act if he knows that his doing it may cause another to do an unlawful act. There is no authority for such a proposition, and the question of the justices whether the facts stated in the case constituted the offence charged in the information must therefore be answered in the negative.'

If the magistrates had been correct in their decision to issue a notice banning assemblies in the public streets of Weston-super-Mare, such a course of action would have had serious implications for those who gather peacefully and, more importantly, lawfully, in order to make their views known, for it would in effect have prevented those persons from doing so on the basis that, by their own lawful actions, they had brought about or caused the unlawful conduct of others. Indeed, the Law Commission has suggested in its Report *Binding Over*[9] that one possible interpretation of the events in *Beatty v Gillbanks* is that the Salvation Army could be said to have ' "caused" the breaches of the peace by providing the occasion and temptation for the Skeleton Army to react, knowing as it did from previous encounters that such breaches were likely to occur'. Clearly, however, to prevent a lawful protest from taking place on the basis that it will be met by unlawful opposition is to give into lawlessness. As a general rule, the correct approach must be for the law enforcement agencies to deal with those who are breaking the law rather than to act against those who are seeking to comply with its dictates during the course of a peaceful protest. In the case of *Verrall v Great Yarmouth Borough Council*,[10] the Court of Appeal upheld the earlier decision of Watkin J to order specific performance of a contract between the council and the National Front for the hire of a hall in which the latter was to hold its annual conference. Lord Denning MR stressed that such a ruling was necessary 'in the interests of our fundamental freedoms—freedom of speech, freedom of assembly, and the importance of holding people to their contracts'. Dealing with the question of the opposition which was likely to arise from organisations which campaign against the activities of the National Front, Lord Denning observed that:

'The evidence is that if there is any trouble it will not be at the meeting at all. If it does occur, it will be outside caused by opponents of the National Front. There are societies such as the Anti-Nazi League who object to all the goings on of the National Front. Their members may threaten or assault the members of the National Front: or try to stop their meeting. It would then be those interrupters who would be the destroyers of freedom of speech. They cannot be allowed to disrupt the meeting by mass pickets, or by violent demonstrations, and the like. The police will, I hope, be present in force to prevent such disruptions.'[11]

The foregoing discussion and the decision in *Verrall* reflect Professor Dicey's remarks in *An Introduction to the Study of the Law of the Constitution*, where he opined that: ' . . . checks and preventive measures are inconsistent with the pervading principle of English Law, that men are to be interfered with or punished, not because they may or will break the law, but only when they have committed some definite assignable legal offence'.[12] However, despite this 'pervading principle', the law has recognised that there may be circumstances in which it will be necessary to take action in relation to someone who is not acting unlawfully in order to prevent subsequent unlawfulness by another.[13] The difficulty in such circumstances lies in

---

[9] Law Com No 222 (1994).   [10] [1981] QB 202.   [11] Ibid., at 217.
[12] *An Introduction to the Study of the Law f the Constitution* (10th edn, 1959), at 249.
[13] See, for example, *Wise v Dunning* [1902] 1 KB 167.

determining at what point an individual's freedom of expression should be curtailed in the interests of preserving the peace.

Two cases separated by some 70 years serve to illustrate the point. In the first of these, *Humphries v Connor*,[14] a Protestant walked through a predominantly Catholic area wearing a party emblem, an orange lily, with the result that she was threatened with personal violence by a number of people who felt provoked by the emblem. In order to protect the plaintiff from such violence, a police constable removed the lily from her, in respect of which conduct the plaintiff sued for assault. The defence that the prima facie assault was necessary in order to prevent a breach of the peace was accepted by an Irish court on the basis that: 'When a constable is called upon to preserve the peace, I know of no better mode of doing so than that of removing what he sees to be the provocation to the breach of the peace; and, when a person deliberately refuses to acquiesce in such removal, after warning so to do, I think the constable is authorised to do everything necessary and proper to enforce it.'[15] However, while Fitzgerald, J did not actually dissent from the judgment of the court, he nevertheless expressed his 'very serious doubt' as to the correctness of the decision for the reason that he was reluctant to sanction a constable's interference with another who was neither about to commit a breach of the peace nor perform an illegal act. His assertions about the propriety of the constable's actions were expressed in the following manner:

'I do not see where we are to draw the line. If a constable is at liberty to take a lily from one person, because the wearing of it is displeasing the others, who may make it an excuse for a breach of the peace, where are we to stop? It seems to me that we are making, not the law of the land but the law of the mob supreme, and recognising in constables a power of interference with the rights of the Queen's subjects, which, if carried into effect to the full extent of the principle, might be accompanied by constitutional danger.'

The second case highlights how the preventive powers may be used to restrain a person's freedom of assembly and freedom of expression.

Duncan v Jones [1936] 1 KB 218

The appellant was about to address a meeting in a street, opposite to the entrance of an unemployed training centre, when she was told by the chief constable of the district that the meeting would have to be held some 175 yards away in a different street. A similar meeting addressed by the appellant had been held in the same position the previous year, and a disturbance which had occurred later the same day inside the training centre had been attributed to the meeting by the superintendent of the centre. The appellant refused to comply with the chief constable's request and accordingly she was charged with wilfully obstructing a police officer in the execution of his duty contrary to section 2 of the Prevention of Crimes Amendment Act 1885. The appellant's appeal against her conviction was dismissed by the Divisional Court.

Lord Hewart CJ, at 221–223

'There have been moments during the argument in this case when it appeared to be suggested that the Court had to do with a grave case involving what is called the right of public meeting. I say "called", because English law does not recognise any special right of public meeting for political or other purposes. The right of assembly, as Professor Dicey puts it, is nothing more than a view taken by the

[14] (1864) 17 ICLR 1.   [15] Per Hayes J.

Court of the individual liberty of the subject. If I thought that the present case raised a question which has been held in suspense by more than one writer on constitutional law—namely, whether an assembly can properly be held to be unlawful merely because the holding of it is expected to give rise to a breach of the peace on the part of persons opposed to those who are holding the meeting—I should wish to hear much more argument before I expressed an opinion. This case, however, does not even touch that important question.

Our attention has been directed to the somewhat unsatisfactory case of *Beatty v Gillbanks*. The circumstances of that case and the charge must be remembered, as also must the important passage in the judgment of Field J, in which Cave J concurred. Field J said: "I entirely concede that every one must be taken to intend the natural consequences of his own acts, and it is clear to me that if this disturbance of the peace was the natural consequence of acts of the appellants they would be liable, and the justices would have been right in binding them over. But the evidence set forth in the case does not support this contention; on the contrary, it shows that the disturbances were caused by other people antagonistic to the appellants, and that no acts of violence were committed by them" . . . In my view, *Beatty v Gillbanks* is apart from the present case. No such question as that which arose there is even mooted here . . .

The case stated which we have before us indicates clearly a causal connection between the meeting of May 1933, and the disturbance which occurred after it—that the disturbance was not only post the meeting but was also propter the meeting.'

Humphreys J, at 223

'I regard this as a plain case. It has nothing to do with the law of unlawful assembly. No charge of that sort was even suggested against the appellant. The sole question raised by the case is whether the respondent, who was admittedly obstructed, was so obstructed when in the execution of his duty.

It does not require authority to emphasize the statement that it is the duty of a police officer to prevent apprehended breaches of the peace. Here it is found as a fact that the respondent reasonably apprehended a breach of the peace. It then, as is rightly expressed in the case, became his duty to prevent anything which in his view would cause that breach of the peace. While he was taking steps so to do he was wilfully obstructed by the appellant. I can conceive no clearer case within the statutes than that.'

The decision in *Duncan v Jones* met with contemporary criticism in academic quarters, most notably from Professor ECS Wade who opined:

'The case thus leaves the law in the unsatisfactory position that it is for the police to decide whether a political party can organise a meeting in a district where its opponents are known to be hostile. The apprehension of a single policeman based upon the fears of somebody else may apparently be decisive.'[16]

It may be argued that *Duncan v Jones* represents a high water mark in terms of the courts' acceptance of the police use of their preventive powers. After all, it is difficult to attach much blame to Mrs Duncan who was merely seeking to express her views on a Bill which was before Parliament at the time. This is the sort of behaviour which one would expect and which ought to be encouraged in a country which purports to be a democracy. In more recent times, the courts have shown a greater willingness to ensure that police preventive action is targeted at the right individuals, i.e. those whose actions are most likely to transgress the law. Whilst this does not mean that *Duncan v Jones* has been overruled, it does cast doubt on whether the case would be decided in the same way were its facts to arise again.

[16] See 'Police Powers and Public Meetings' (1936) 6 CLJ 175.

In *Redmond-Bate v DPP*,[17] the appellant was preaching to passers-by whilst standing on the steps of Wakefield Cathedral when she was approached by a police officer. Acting on a complaint the officer informed those preaching that they were not to stop members of the public. However, since he observed that this was not happening, he left. On his return, he found that a crowd of more than one hundred people had gathered and that some of its members were behaving in a hostile manner towards the preachers. In order to prevent what he considered to be an imminent breach of the peace, he requested that the preachers cease preaching. They refused to do so and were duly arrested for causing a breach of the peace. The appellant was subsequently charged and convicted of wilfully obstructing a police officer in the execution of his duty contrary to section 89(2) of the Police Act 1996. On appeal, the Divisional Court took a rather different view of the matter. In its opinion, it defied logic to proceed, as the Crown Court had done, from the fact that the women were preaching about God, morality and the Bible to the view that there was a reasonable apprehension that violence would erupt if preventive action were not taken. Given that freedom of speech was at issue, the Divisional Court considered that it also amounted to an illiberal construction of events. In short, there was nothing in the situation as perceived by the officer which entitled him to reasonably apprehend a breach of the peace, much less a breach of the peace for which the appellant would be responsible.

The decision in *Redmond-Bate v DPP* is important for a number of reasons, not least of which is that it represents a salient reminder to the police that when taking preventive action, they must seek to ensure that they take it against the correct party. Although the Divisional Court had sympathy for the police when faced with situations like the present which called for 'difficult on-the-spot judgments' to be made, that sympathy did not extend to allowing the police to prevent the preachers from doing that which they were lawfully entitled to do. Thus in the words of Sedley LJ:

'The one critical question for the constable, and in turn for the Court, is where the threat is coming from, because it is there that the preventive action must be directed. It is only if otherwise lawful conduct gives rise to a reasonable apprehension that it will, by interfering with the rights or liberties of others, provoke violence which, though unlawful, would not be entirely unreasonable that a constable is empowered to take steps to prevent it.'[18]

These remarks were subsequently approved by the Court of Appeal in *Bibby v Chief Constable of the Essex Police*.[19] In that case, where a bailiff had been arrested at a debtors shop for refusing to leave the property when requested to do so by a police officer who believed that there would be a breach of the peace otherwise, the Court of Appeal held that the arrest had been unlawful. Schiemann LJ, who gave the leading judgment, explained the court's reasoning as follows:

'I have sympathy for the constable faced with an explosive situation which required fast judgments. No one criticises him for coming to the conclusion that a breach of the peace was imminent. . . . But as it seems to me PC O'Hare made the same mistake as the constable in *Redmond-Bate*. He failed to consider where the threat was coming from. True it is that had the bailiff not been seeking to exercise his rights there would have been no threat to the peace. But in circumstances such as these, the threat, in so far as there was one, of violence should have been perceived as coming from the debtor rather than the bailiff.'

---

[17] (1999) 163 JP 789; [1999] Crim LR 998; [2000] HRLR 249.
[18] At [16].   [19] (2000) 164 JP 297.

III. Breach of the Peace

(a) Definition

The concept of a breach of the peace is a long-established and important feature of what is commonly termed 'preventive justice'. Where a breach of the peace has been committed or, alternatively, where such a breach is reasonably believed to be imminent, a police officer, or for that matter a member of the public, has the power at common law to arrest without warrant the individual or individuals who have either committed or are about to commit that breach of the peace even though no offence has actually been committed. In essence, therefore, the power to arrest for a breach of the peace arises not only where such an event has occurred, but also in order to prevent such an event from occurring. It follows, therefore, that precisely what is a breach of the peace is a crucial matter which, in view of the antiquity of the concept, would seem likely to have long since been established. However, this is not so. Writing in 1954, Professor Glanville Williams commented that: 'The expression "breach of the peace" seems clearer than it is and there is a surprising lack of authoritative definition of what one would suppose to be a fundamental concept in criminal law.'[20] Thus while section 40(4) of the Public Order Act 1986 provides that 'Nothing in this Act affects the common law powers in England and Wales to deal with or prevent a breach of the peace', no attempt is made by the statute to define what is meant by a 'breach of the peace'. The statutory silence on this matter is not altogether surprising given the common law nature of the concept. Accordingly, it has fallen to the courts to define what constitutes a breach of the peace.

R v Howell [1982] QB 416

A house party had been taking place in the early hours of the morning when some of the guests spilled out onto the street and proceeded to make a disturbance. The police arrived at the scene following complaints made by residents and informed some of the more boisterous partygoers that they would be arrested for breach of the peace unless they returned to their own homes. The police officers in question were verbally abused by the appellant who was warned once again that he would be arrested if he persisted in this conduct. He failed to heed this warning and while a police officer was in the process of informing him that he was under arrest for breach of the peace, the appellant struck the officer and a struggle ensued. The appellant was convicted of an assault occasioning actual bodily harm. He appealed against his conviction on several grounds, including that he had been acting in a lawful manner when he struck the police officer since he was merely attempting to free himself from an arrest which was unlawful because there had been no breach of the peace. The Court of Appeal dismissed the appellant's appeal. In delivering the judgment of the Court, Watkins LJ, who had been referred to the decision in R v Podger [21] in which case it was held that the power to arrest for a breach of the peace at common law only arose where the breach was either committed in the presence of the arresting party, or where a breach had taken place and its renewal was threatened, stated

[20] 'Arrest for Breach of the Peace' [1954] Crim LR 578.   [21] [1979] Crim LR 524.

the following:

Watkins LJ, at 426–428

'We entertain no doubt that a constable has a power of arrest where there is reasonable apprehension of imminent danger of a breach of the peace; so for that matter has the ordinary citizen. *R v Podger* involved the examination, by the recorder who tried it, of a number of authorities, including *Light's* case, all of which we have perused. *R v Podger* was in our opinion wrongly decided. We hold that there is power of arrest for breach of the peace where (1) a breach of the peace is committed in the presence of the person making the arrest, or (2) the arrestor reasonably believes that such a breach will be committed in the immediate future by the person arrested although he has not yet committed any breach, or (3) where a breach has been committed and it is reasonably believed that a renewal of it is threatened.

The public expects a policeman not only to apprehend the criminal but to do his best to prevent the commission of crime, to keep the peace in other words. To deny him, therefore, the right to arrest a person whom he reasonably believes is about to breach the peace would be to disable him from preventing that which might cause serious injury to someone or even to many people or property. The common law, we believe, whilst recognising that a wrongful arrest is a serious invasion of a person's liberty, provides the police with this power in the public interest.

In those instances of the exercise of this power which depend on a belief that a breach of the peace is imminent it must, we think we should emphasise, be established that it is not only an honest, albeit mistaken belief but a belief which is founded on reasonable grounds.

A comprehensive definition of the term "breach of the peace" has very rarely been formulated so far as, with considerable help from counsel, we have been able to discover from cases which go as far back as the 18th century. The older cases are of considerable interest but they are not a sure guide to what the term is understood to mean today, since keeping the peace in this country in the latter half of the 20th century presents formidable problems which bear up on the evolving process of the development of this branch of the common law. Nevertheless, even in these days when affrays, riotous behaviour and other disturbances happen all too frequently, we cannot accept that there can be a breach of the peace unless there has been an act done or threatened to be done which either actually harms a person, or in his presence his property, or is likely to cause such harm, or which puts someone in fear of such harm being done. There is nothing more likely to arouse resentment and anger in him, and a desire to take instant revenge, than attacks or threatened attacks on a person's body or property.

In 11 *Halsbury's Laws* (4th edn) para 108 it is stated:

"For the purpose of the common law powers of arrest without warrant, a breach of the peace arises where there is an actual assault, or where public alarm and excitement are caused by a person's wrongful act. Mere annoyance and disturbance or insults to a person or abusive language, or great heat and fury without personal violence, are not generally sufficient."

That is an amalgam of opinions expressed in various old cases which is principally criticised by counsel for the appellant for its failure to attach the actual commission of violence to all acts which are said to be capable of causing a breach of the peace.

He makes a similar criticism of the crisp definition provided by the Attorney General, referred to in *Geldberg v Miller* [1961] 1 All ER 291 at 295, [1961] 1 WLR 153 at 158 with reference to the word disturbance. Lord Parker CJ said:

"The Attorney General, to whom the court is grateful for his assistance, has appeared and has told the court that he feels unable to contend that a constable is entitled to arrest somebody for obstructing him in the course of his duty—which, of course, is a misdemeanour under s 2 of the Prevention of Crimes Amendment Act, 1885—unless the circumstances show that a breach of the peace or an apprehended breach of the peace is involved, meaning by that some affray or violence or possibly disturbance."

The statement in *Halsbury's Laws of England* is in parts, we think, inaccurate because of its failure to relate all the kinds of behaviour there mentioned to violence. Furthermore, we think, the word 'disturbance' when used in isolation cannot constitute a breach of the peace.

We are emboldened to say that there is a breach of the peace whenever harm is actually done or is likely to be done to a person or in his presence to his property or a person is in fear of being so harmed through an assault, an affray, a riot, an unlawful assembly or other disturbance. It is for this breach of the peace when done in his presence or the reasonable apprehension of it taking place that a constable, or anyone else, may arrest an offender without warrant.

The recorder in the present case in ruling on the submission clearly regarded violence as of the essence of a breach of the peace. So we find that neither in that nor in any other way did he misdirect himself on the associated matters of the power of arrest and the definition of a breach of the peace. Furthermore, as to the appellant's knowledge of why he was arrested he correctly applied the principles laid down in *Christie v Leachinsky* [1947] 1 All ER 567, [1947] AC 573. The evidence at the end of the prosecution showed plainly that either the appellant knew without being told at the moment of arrest the reason for it or, by striking PC Hammersley when he did, he made it impossible for that officer to tell him why he was being arrested. In this connection we should make it clear, since the point was argued, that a constable makes a valid arrest when he reasonably believes a breach is about to be committed if he says merely: "I am arresting you for a breach of the peace." It is ridiculous to expect him to give, in what may be for him very trying circumstances, some such incantation as : "I am arresting you because I reasonably believe you are about to commit a breach of the peace." In speaking merely of a "breach of the peace" on arrest the arrestor is not, as counsel for the appellant seemed to suggest, to be taken as referring only to the actual commission of a breach and, therefore, forbidden from giving evidence the effect of which would be that he had in fact carried out the arrest for an apprehended breach.'

In *R v Howell* the Court of Appeal believed that harm or the threat of harm to either a person or property was a central feature or ingredient of a breach of the peace. However, this approach is not easily reconciled with that which was taken by one member of a differently constituted Court of Appeal in *R v Chief Constable of the Devon and Cornwall Constabulary, ex p Central Electricity Generating Board.*[22] In that case, in which the CEGB sought an order of mandamus (now a mandatory order) to compel the Chief Constable to remove protesters from a site which was being surveyed for the purposes of determining where to construct a power station, Lord Denning took a rather different view as to the type of conduct which was capable of amounting to a breach of the peace. He opined:

'I think that the conduct of these people, their criminal obstruction, is itself a breach of the peace. There is a breach of the peace wherever a person who is lawfully carrying out his work is unlawfully and physically prevented by another from doing it. He is entitled by law peacefully to go on with his work on his lawful occasions. If anyone unlawfully and physically obstructs the worker, by lying down or chaining himself to a rig or the like, he is guilty of a breach of the peace. Even if this were not enough, I think that their unlawful conduct gives rise to a reasonable apprehension of a breach of the peace. . . . But in deciding whether there is a breach of the peace or the apprehension of it, the law does not go into the rights or wrongs of the matter, or whether it is justified by self-help or not. Suffice it that the peace is broken or is likely to be broken by one or another of those present. With the result that any citizen can, and certainly any police officer can, intervene to stop breaches.

If I were wrong on this point, if there was here no breach of the peace or apprehension of it, it would give a licence to every obstructer and every passive resister in the land. He would be able to cock a snook at the law as these groups have done. Public works of the greatest national importance could be held up indefinitely. This cannot be. The rule of law must prevail.'[23]

[22] [1981] 3 All ER 826.   [23] At 833.

Thus the law had developed from a position where there was no satisfactory definition of a breach of the peace to one where there were now two Court of Appeal definitions of the concept. It should be noted, however, that in delivering their opinions in *Ex p CEGB*, neither Lawton LJ nor Templeman LJ endorsed the earlier remarks of Lord Denning in the same case. Thus it would seem that the test for a breach of the peace as laid down in *R v Howell* is the one to be preferred. Certainly this was the view taken by the Divisional Court in *Parkin v Norman*,[24] where it was held that in order for a disturbance to constitute a breach of the peace, it was necessary for there to be actual or threatened violence. Moreover, in *Percy v DPP*,[25] Lord Denning's dicta were further doubted by a Divisional Court which held that a civil trespass could not amount to a breach of the peace. In delivering the judgment of the court, Collins J remarked that:

'In our judgment, breach of the peace is limited to violence or threats of violence as set out in *R v Howell* and any observations which may indicate something wider ought not to be followed.'[26]

It is also worth noting that on the basis of the *Howell* definition, the European Court of Human Rights held in *Steel v UK*[27] that the concept of a breach of the peace is sufficiently clear in English law to satisfy the requirements of article 5(1)(c) of the European Convention on Human Rights (ECHR). In the later case of *Hawkes (R on the application of) v DPP*,[28] Newman J opined:

'I have no doubt that conduct involving . . . extreme abuse and aggression, and an aggressive demeanour may cross the threshold and constitute a breach of the peace. The absence of verbal threats and the absence of actual threats, for example, by the shaking of a fist, will not be determinative.'[29]

(b) Is breach of the peace an offence?

The decision in *R v County of London Quarter Sessions Appeals Committee ex p Metropolitan Police Commissioner*[30] is authority for the proposition that a breach of the peace does not amount to an offence in English law. In that case, Lord Goddard CJ observed:

'There is no suggestion to be found . . . that before sureties can be required a person must have committed a criminal offence or that by ordering him to enter into sureties the court either expressly or impliedly convicts him of a criminal offence. Where a magistrate merely requires a person brought before him, not for having committed a criminal offence, but for having acted in a way that may cause a breach of the peace to enter into a recognizance, there is no pretence of saying that he has convicted him of anything. He is merely taking a precaution against the defendant committing an offence . . . *There is no such offence known to the law as blemishing the peace* . . . and by offence I mean an offence known to the law for which a person can be brought before a court and punished.'[31]

Despite the fact that this opinion was expressed nearly 60 years ago, it remains good law. This was confirmed by the recent Court of Appeal decisions in *Addison v Chief Constable of the West*

---

[24] [1982] 2 All ER 583.   [25] [1995] 3 All ER 124.   [26] At 132.   [27] (1998) 28 EHRR 603.
[28] [2005] EWHC 3046 (Admin). See further p. 648.
[29] At [11]. In the earlier cases of *Jarrett v Chief Constable of West Midlands Police* [2003] EWCA Civ 397, it had been held that agitation or excitement, including the hysterical waving of a handbag in front of a police officer, did not constitute a breach of the peace.   [30] [1948] 1 KB 670.
[31] At 676.

Midlands Police[32] and *Williamson v Chief Constable of the West Midlands Police.*[33] In the latter case, the claimant had been arrested by police officers at his home address for a breach of the peace. He had been taken to a police station and the circumstances of his arrest had been recorded. The officers concerned believed that the provisions of the Police and Criminal Evidence Act 1984 (PACE) relating to detention in police custody did not apply to the claimant because a breach of the peace did not amount to an 'offence' under PACE. Accordingly, he was detained overnight and brought before the magistrates the following morning. The claimant subsequently sought damages from the police for an alleged wrongful arrest and unlawful detention. At the original trial, the trial judge concluded that the ECHR required him to interpret 'offence' as it appeared in section 34(1) of PACE as including a breach of the peace. On appeal, however, the Court of Appeal construed 'offence' differently.

The leading judgment was delivered by Dyson LJ. Looking at the construction point from a purely domestic position without reference to the ECHR, his Lordship expressed approval for what Lord Goddard had said in the *Metropolitan Commissioner* case and sought to emphasise that whether or not a breach of the peace amounted to an offence depended upon whether it exhibited 'two of the hallmarks of a criminal offence': whether it was conduct which was capable of forming the basis of a charge; and, if that charge were proved, whether a conviction would follow. Testing breach of the peace by the standard of these 'hallmarks', Dyson LJ observed:

'But a person arrested for breach of the peace is not charged, and even if the magistrates find that there has been a breach of the peace, no conviction results. An order binding a person over to be of good behaviour and keep the peace is not a conviction.'[34]

His Lordship also considered that the wording of some of the provisions in PACE[35] confirmed that Parliament had not intended breach of the peace to be an offence for the purposes of the Act. Turning to consider the effect of the ECHR on the case, it will be remembered that in *Steel v UK*,[36] the European Court of Human Rights decided, amongst other things, that the common law rules relating to a breach of the peace conformed with article 5(1)(c) of the ECHR. However, in the opinion of Dyson LJ, it was:

'impermissible to reason that since (a) breach must be regarded as an "offence" within the meaning of art.5(1)(c), therefore (b) it must also be an "offence" within the meaning of PACE'.[37]

The decision in *Williamson* thus serves to confirm that a breach of the peace does not amount to an offence for the purposes of PACE. Strictly speaking, therefore, a person detained at a police station in respect of a breach of the peace does not enjoy the same measure of protection against an unlawful detention as the person who has been arrested for an offence. However, although the provisions of Part IV of PACE do not apply as matter of law to the person detained for a breach of the peace, it would seem likely, as a matter of good practice, for the police to treat such persons in the same way as those who have been arrested for an offence. In any case, a person detained for a breach of the peace does have some protection at common law in that they must either be released unconditionally or taken to a magistrates' court as soon as reasonably practicable.

[32] [2004] 1 WLR 29. Although the case was reported in 2004 it was actually decided on 10 March 1995. It would appear to have been finally reported because it was followed in *Williamson v Chief Constable of the West Midlands Police* [2003] EWCA Civ 337; [2004] 1 WLR 14.
[33] [2003] EWCA Civ 337; [2004] 1 WLR 14.   [34] At [11].
[35] In particular, sections 17, 25 (now repealed), 39 and 47.   [36] (1998) 28 EHRR 603.   [37] At [27].

(c) Location

Although breaches of the peace are more likely to occur in public places such as the street,[38] it is a misconception to believe that they can only occur in public. Harm or the threat of harm can take place on private premises as well as in the public domain.

Thomas v Sawkins [1935] 2 KB 249

A public meeting was arranged to be held in a hall in order to protest against the Incitement to Disaffection Bill which was then before Parliament, and to demand the dismissal of the Chief Constable of Glamorgan. Stewards had been appointed in order to assist in the ejection of any police officers who might attend. Between 500 and 700 members of the public attended following an extensive advertising campaign by the convenors of the meeting. Three police officers presented themselves at the entrance to the hall and requested admission. They were denied entrance by one of the convenors but they nevertheless insisted on entering the hall and seated themselves in the front row. The officers were repeatedly requested to leave and a complaint was lodged at the local police station to this effect. Nevertheless they remained in the hall and thus Thomas took hold of one of the officers for the purpose of ejecting him. He was accordingly charged with unlawfully assaulting the officer contrary to section 42 of the Offences Against the Person Act 1861. On appeal, the Divisional Court upheld his conviction on the basis that the police officers were entitled to remain on the premises where they apprehended that an offence or a breach of the peace was likely to be committed.

Lord Hewart CJ, at 254–255

' . . . it is said that it is an unheard-of proposition of law, and that in the books no case is to be found which goes the length of deciding that, where an offence is expected to be committed, as distinct from where an offence has been committed, there is a right in the police to enter on private premises and to remain there against the will of those who, as hirers or otherwise, are for the time being in possession of the premises. When, however, I look at the passages which have been cited from Blackstone's Commentaries, and from the judgments in *Humphries v Connor* (1864) 17 ICLR 1 and *O'Kelly v Harvey* (1883) 14 LR Ir 105 and certain observations of Avory J, in *Lansbury v Riley* [1914] 3 KB 229, I think that there is quite sufficient ground for the proposition that it is part of the preventive power and, therefore, part of the preventive duty, of the police in cases where there are such reasonable grounds of belief as the justices have found in the present case, to enter and remain on private premises. It goes without saying that the powers and duties of the police are directed, not to the interests of the police, but to the protection and welfare of the public.

It was urged in one part of the argument of counsel for the appellant that what was done here was really a trespass. It seems somewhat remarkable to speak of trespass when members of the public who happen to be police officers attend a public meeting which has been publicly advertised, a meeting to which the public has been invited, and which is to discuss as one part of its business a proposal to demand the dismissal of the chief constable of the county. It is elementary that a good defence to an action for trespass is to show that the act complained of was done by authority of law, or by leave and licence.

I am not at all prepared to accept the doctrine that it is only where an offence has been, or is being, committed that the police are entitled to enter and remain on private premises. On the contrary,

---

[38] See, for example, *R v Howell* [1982] QB 416, p. 637.

it seems to me that a police officer has ex virtue officii full right so to act when he has reasonable ground for believing that an offence is imminent or is likely to be committed.

I think, therefore, that the justices were right and that this appeal should be dismissed.'

Avory J, at 255–257

'With regard to the general question regarding the right of the police to attend the meeting notwithstanding the opposition of the promoters, I cannot help thinking that that right follows from the passage which counsel for the appellants relies on in Stone's Justices' Manual, where it is said that if a constable hears an affray in a house he may break in to suppress it, and may, in pursuit of an affrayer, break in to arrest him. If he can do that, I cannot doubt that he has a right to break in to prevent an affray which he has reasonable cause to suspect may take place on private premises . . .

I am not impressed by the fact that many statutes have expressly given to police constables in certain circumstances the right to break open or to force an entrance into premises. Those are all cases in which a breach of the peace is not necessarily involved and express statutory authority is, therefore, required to empower the police to enter. In my opinion, no express statutory authority is necessary in a case where the police have reasonable ground to apprehend a breach of the peace, and in the present case I am satisfied that the justices had before them material on which they could properly hold that the police officers in question had reasonable ground for believing that, if they were not present, seditious speeches would be made and (or) that a breach of the peace would take place. To prevent any such breach of the peace the police were entitled to enter and to remain on the premises . . .'

The later case of *McLeod v Metropolitan Police Commissioner*[39] involved a situation where the former husband of the plaintiff had obtained a county court order for the possession of certain articles of furniture and other effects from the former marital home. Three days before the expiry of the time limit for complying with the order, he had arrived at the plaintiff's house accompanied by his brother and sister, a solicitor's clerk and two police officers. The plaintiff's elderly mother let them into the house and they proceeded to load a van with the furniture. While they were in the process of loading the van for the second time, the plaintiff returned and demanded that the furniture be unloaded. At this point one of the police officers intervened insisting that this should not happen and that any disputes between the parties ought to be resolved between the parties' solicitors. The plaintiff subsequently instituted a number of proceedings against several of the parties involved in the affair, including proceedings in the High Court against the police for damages in respect of trespass and breach of duty. The action was dismissed by the judge on the basis that the police officers had been acting throughout in the performance of their duty to prevent an apprehended breach of the peace from occurring. In dismissing the plaintiff's subsequent appeal, the Court of Appeal held that at common law the police have the power to enter private premises to prevent a breach of the peace from occurring where they reasonably believed that such a breach was likely to occur. Central to this finding was that the power to enter private premises without a warrant had been expressly retained by section 17(6) of the Police and Criminal Evidence Act 1984. Thus Neill LJ opined:

'Having had the benefit of argument, I am satisfied that Parliament in section 17(6) has now recognised that there is a power to enter premises to prevent a breach of the peace as a form of preventive justice. I can see no satisfactory basis for restricting that power to particular classes of premises such as those where public meetings are held. If the police reasonably believe that a breach of the peace is likely to take place on private premises, they have the power to enter those premises to prevent it. The apprehension must, of course, be genuine and it must relate to the near future.'[40]

---

[39] [1994] 4 All ER 553.   [40] At 560.

Having regard to the practical exercise of this common law power of entry Neill LJ further observed:

'It seems to me it is important that when exercising his power to prevent a breach of the peace a police officer should act with great care and discretion; this will be particularly important where the exercise of his power involves entering on private premises contrary to the wishes of the owners or occupiers. The officer must satisfy himself that there is a real and imminent risk of a breach of the peace, because, if the matter has to be tested in court thereafter there may be scrutiny not only of his belief at the time but also of the grounds for his belief.'[41]

McLeod is of particular interest in that it highlights how the power to enter a person's property without their consent must be exercised with care. The courts clearly have an important role to play in ensuring that the power is not abused. Mere assertions that a police officer apprehended an imminent breach of the peace are insufficient to justify the exercise of preventive powers. There must be an evidential basis for the officers reasonable belief and it is the task of the courts to ensure that this is so. If the courts are too relaxed about this requirement, there is a danger that the proprietary rights and liberties of the individual may be infringed. When Ms Mcleod took her case to the European Court of Human Rights, alleging that the entry into her property had constituted a violation of article 8 of the ECHR, that Court concluded, amongst other things, that the police officers ought not to have entered the former matrimonial home. Once it became apparent that Ms McLeod was not actually at home at the relevant time, the Court took the view that there was little or no risk of disorder or crime occurring and that entry had thus been unnecessary. Accordingly, the Court held by a majority of seven votes to two that the police officers' actions had been disproportionate to the legitimate aim which they had pursued and that they therefore amounted to a breach of article 8.[42] In more recent times it would appear that the English courts have taken a more robust approach to the requirement of reasonable apprehension. This is illustrated by *Redmond-Bate v DPP* (discussed above) and the decision in *Foulkes v Chief Constable of the Merseyside Police*.[43]

(d) Restriction on movement

The police may be entitled to impose restrictions on a person's freedom of movement where it is done in order to prevent a breach of the peace occurring. Thus in *Moss v McLachlan*,[44] the Divisional Court was concerned with action taken by the police to prevent a convoy of 'flying pickets' making their way to various collieries in the Nottinghamshire coalfield to protest in the form of a mass picket. The pickets had been stopped as they turned off at a motorway junction and informed by the inspector in charge to turn round since he apprehended a breach of the peace if they were allowed to continue to their intended destination. Some of the pickets who attempted to break through the police cordon were charged and convicted by magistrates of the offence of wilfully obstructing a police officer in the execution of his duty contrary to section 51(3) of the Police Act 1964.[45] On appeal, the Divisional Court upheld the pickets' convictions, since the facts of the case were such that 'anyone with knowledge of the current strike would realise that there was a substantial risk of an outbreak of violence'.

[41] Ibid.   [42] See *McLeod v UK* [1998] 2 FLR.   [43] [1998] 3 All ER 705. See further p. 647.
[44] [1985] IRLR 76.   [45] Now section 89(2) of the Police Act 1996.

Moreover, the potential outbreak of violence was imminent in that it was proximate both in terms of time and place; the distance from the roadblock to the collieries was between one and half miles and five miles, a distance which could be rapidly travelled in a car. Accordingly, the exercise of the police's common law preventative powers had therefore been justified by the circumstances of the case.

It is therefore apparent from *Moss v McLachlan* and *R v Howell* that where a police officer reasonably apprehends a breach of the peace, that officer is 'not only entitled but is under a duty to take reasonable steps to prevent that breach occurring'. With regard to the need for the breach of the peace to be imminent in terms of being proximate in both time and place, the fact that the collieries in question were anything between one and a half and five miles from the police cordon was dismissed by the court on the basis that it would not take long to reach these sites by car. However, while the particular facts of the case do serve to suggest that the Divisional Court was correct in its finding, the decision does have important implications for the individual's freedom of movement. Although the court considered in the present case that the apprehension of a breach of the peace justified police intervention, undoubtedly there must be a distance at which it would be unacceptable for the police to take similar preventative action. Thus if the police prevented an individual continuing on a journey where he or she was some 30 miles from the site of an apprehended breach of the peace, while an officer's belief may be reasonably and honestly held, the breach of the peace would clearly not be sufficiently imminent to justify preventative action.

The decision in *Moss v McLachlan* was recently approved by the Court of Appeal in a case involving a restriction on the freedom of movement of protesters heading for an air base.

Laporte (R on the application of) v Chief Constable of Gloucestershire Constabulary [2005] 2 WLR 789

RAF Fairford is an air base used by the American Air Force. Towards the end of 2002, with a war against Iraq becoming increasingly likely, the airbase became the subject of a number of protests during which the perimeter fence was damaged and a number of trespassers were ejected. On 23 February 2003, there was serious public disorder at the air base after protesters had managed to force open the main gate. Twelve arrests were made. Two groups, the White Overalls Movement Building Libertarian Effective Struggles (WOMBLES) and the Gloucestershire Weapons Inspectors, advertised on their respective websites that 22 March 2003 was to be 'Judgment Day—a National day of action at Fairford'. The police accordingly put into place a tactical plan to deal with the threat of public disorder. A statutory stop and search authorisation was made pursuant to section 60 of the Criminal Justice and Public Order Act 1994. Three coaches and a van were stopped and boarded by the police in a lay-by some 5km from RAF Fairford. A search of the vehicles resulted in a haul which included masks and protective clothing, spray paint, shields, a smoke bomb and two pairs of scissors. None of the passengers on the vehicles accepted responsibility for what had been found. The officer in charge concluded that if the vehicles were permitted to proceed to their intended destination, some or all of the occupants would either cause or contribute to a breach of the peace. Accordingly, he gave instructions that the vehicles and their occupants be escorted back to London. The journey took some two and a half hours to complete. During its duration, none of the vehicles were permitted to stop at any motorway service station.

The claimant sought judicial review of the police officer's actions. It was claimed that she had been unlawfully detained by the police. At first instance, the Administrative Court[46] was of the opinion that on the facts, the officer in charge had been entitled to reach the conclusion that if the vehicles were

---

[46] [2004] 2 All ER 874.

allowed to continue on their journey, a breach of the peace would follow and that such a belief was honestly and reasonably held. Accordingly, the officer had been under a duty to give the instructions which he gave. In the judgment of the court, however, the enforced return to London had been unlawful for a number of reasons which included that there had been no immediately apprehended breach of the peace sufficient to justify even a transitory detention. The defendant appealed and the claimant cross-appealed. The Administrative Court's decisions were affirmed by the Court of Appeal.

Lord Woolf CJ

'44. On this aspect of the case [the "imminence point"], we would adopt a very similar approach to that of May LJ. We agree with him that it is necessary to distinguish between arrest and preventive action short of arrest, including temporary detention. We regard what is sufficiently "imminent" to justify taking action to prevent a breach of the peace as dependent on all the circumstances. As in *Moss's* case, so here, it is important that the claimant was intending to travel in a vehicle if the preventive action had not taken place. The distance involved did not mean that there was no sufficient imminence. What preventive action was necessary and proportionate, however, would be very much influenced by how close in proximity, both in place and time, the location of the apprehended breach of the peace was. The greater the distance and the greater the time involved, the more important it is to decide whether preventive action is really necessary and, if it is necessary, the more restrained the action taken should usually be as there will be time for further action if the action initially taken does not deter. It may be that as the police thought, arrest at the lay-by would have been a disproportionate level of action, but this does not necessarily mean that no action was appropriate.

45. We would see the instant case as being very much on all fours with the decision in *Moss's* case which we would endorse. If the police had done no more than direct the passengers to reboard the coach and instructed the driver not to proceed to Fairford, this would have been an appropriate response that was both necessary and proportionate . . .

46. Like May LJ, we would regard the "real risk" or "close proximity" test and the "imminence" test as not being in conflict. Action should not be taken until it is necessary and reasonable to take the action on the facts of the particular circumstances. In the present case, on the evidence before us, the alternatives were either taking the preventive action at the lay-by or waiting until the coaches had arrived at Fairford, the site at which the disturbance was feared. To have delayed taking action until the coach passengers reached the air base could have provoked the very disturbance which the preventive action was intended to avoid.

The "blanket" point

47. Mr Fordham [counsel for the Chief Constable] here relies upon the fact that the information that was available did not enable Mr Lambert to do more than reasonably conclude that some, but not all, of the passengers in the claimant's coach were likely to be responsible for performing acts which would constitute a breach of the peace. He relies on the statement of Sedley LJ in *Redmond-Bate v Director of Public Prosecutions* (1999) 163 JP 789, 791 [p. 636]:

> "a judgment as to the imminence of a breach of the peace does not conclude the constable's task. The next and critical question for the constable, and in turn for the court, is where the threat is coming from, because it is there that the preventive action must be directed."

Again, in our judgment, the answer to Mr Fordham's point is provided by the need for the police to act reasonably. In view of the attitude adopted generally by the passengers in the coaches, it is difficult to see how it would be possible to distinguish between the occupants. The occupants were clearly committed to seeking to proceed to the base and, being realistic, it is most unlikely that it would have been possible to identify passengers who would not play a part in provoking a breach of the peace. The important feature to note about the ability to take preventive action is that its justification is not derived from the person against whom the action is taken having actually committed an offence, but based upon a need to prevent the apprehended breach of the peace. In some situations, preventing a breach of the peace will only be possible if action is taken which risks affecting wholly innocent individuals. In other situations, it will be possible to identify precisely which individuals are the likely troublemakers and when this is the position, the type of action taken will be determined by what is necessary to prevent the apprehended breach of the peace. Again, we would agree with the approach of the court below.'

This extract from the judgment in *Laporte* makes clear that where the police have used their common law powers in order to prevent a breach of the peace from occurring, the courts will carefully scrutinize the actions of officers in any subsequent legal challenge. Since the Human Rights Act 1998 was enacted, a finding that an officer's actions were reasonable need not necessarily defeat the claim that they were unlawful. It is also important now to consider whether those actions were proportionate. In *Laporte*, the police officer's actions had been lawful up until the enforced return of the passengers. It was then that they went beyond what was necessary, reasonable and proportionate for the purposes of preventing a breach of the peace since there were other less intrusive courses of action which were open to the officer. Interestingly, the Court of Appeal did 'not consider it necessary to decide that it would never be justifiable to take action of this nature'.[47] In other words, although the circumstances of this case did not justify the full extent of the preventive action taken by the police, there may be other occasions when such action may be justified. In any event, the Court of Appeal felt that such action would be 'very much a matter of last resort'.[48]

(e) Power to arrest or detain

Although as we have noted previously, a breach of the peace does not amount to the commission of a criminal offence, the police nevertheless have a power at common law to arrest persons who are or whom they reasonably believe are about to breach the peace.[49] This power was expressly preserved by section 40(4) of the Police and Criminal Evidence Act 1984. It is, however, a power which ought to be used in a circumspect manner given that it authorises the arrest of a person who is not acting unlawfully at the material time. Thus in *Foulkes v Chief Constable of the Merseyside Police*,[50] in responding to a report of a domestic dispute, two officers arrived at an address and found the claimant sitting on the front doorstep, locked out of the property. One of the officers remained with the plaintiff whilst the other went inside the house to talk with the plaintiff's family. It appeared to the officer outside the house that the plaintiff was nervous and jittery and not completely coherent as he gave the officer an account of the incident. When the other officer returned, he informed the plaintiff that his wife, son and daughter did not want him to go back into the house. It was suggested to the plaintiff that he ought to go and have a cup of tea or go to a relative's house until tempers had cooled. The plaintiff, however, demanded to get back into the house which he jointly owned with his wife. After rejecting several more requests to move away from the front of the house, the plaintiff was arrested by one of the officers in order to prevent what he perceived to be an imminent breach of the peace. He was taken to a police station and detained overnight before being released. The plaintiff brought a claim for damages against the Chief Constable in which he alleged that his arrest had been unlawful, that he had been falsely imprisoned, and that the

---

[47] At [54].   [48] Ibid.
[49] See, for example, the remarks of May LJ in the Divisional Court judgment in *R (on the application of Laporte) v Chief Constable of Gloucestershire* [2004] 2 All ER 874 at [20].   [50] [1998] 3 All ER 705.

duration of his detention was unreasonable. That claim was rejected by the Liverpool County Court and the plaintiff accordingly appealed. The success or failure of his appeal thus turned upon the lawfulness of his arrest. In concluding that an arrest had not been justified by the circumstances of the case, Beldam LJ remarked:

' . . . although I am prepared to accept that a constable may exceptionally have power to arrest a person whose behaviour is lawful but provocative, it is a power which ought to be exercised by him only in the clearest of circumstances and when he is satisfied on reasonable grounds that a breach of the peace is imminent.'[51]

Turning to the facts of the present case, Beldam LJ continued:

' . . . Pc McNamara acted with the best of intentions. He had tried persuasion but the plaintiff refused to be persuaded or to accept the sensible guidance he had been given but in my judgment that was not a sufficient basis to conclude that a breach of the peace was about to occur or was imminent. There must, I consider, be a sufficiently real and present threat to the peace to justify the extreme step of depriving of his liberty a citizen who is not at the time acting unlawfully.'[52]

In a shorter judgment in the same case, Thorpe LJ commented:

'In my opinion the husband was both the injured party and the detained person. That is a manifestly unsatisfactory result. I accept it is a possible result under the law as it has evolved to prevent breach of the peace. But I would hope that only in the rarest of cases would domestic dispute and the rights of occupation of the matrimonial home be subject to the breach of the peace regime.'[53]

This latter observation is of particular interest in the context of the reform of the police powers of arrest which has been effected by the Serious Organised Crime and Police Act 2005.[54] When contemplating the extent of that reform, the Home Office was initially in favour of abolishing the common law power of arrest in relation to a breach of the peace. However, the power was ultimately retained in the light of representations from the Police Federation which made it clear that it continued to be useful in the context of domestic violence, where it was evident that an offence had been committed but where the victim refused to lodge a complaint, and for dealing with persons who were likely to be detained under the provisions of the Mental Health Act 1983.

Where a police officer does decide to exercise the common law power of arrest, it is important that the officer is clear as to whether the arrest relates to an actual or threatened breach of the peace. Thus in *Hawkes (R on the application of) v DPP*,[55] where the appellant had been arrested for having committed a breach of the peace and had subsequently assaulted the arresting officer, her conviction for an offence contrary to section 89(1) of the Police Act 1996[56] was quashed on appeal on the ground that although her behaviour towards the officer[57] prior to the arrest may well have suggested an imminent *threat* of a breach of the peace, crucially it was insufficient to amount to an *actual* breach of the peace. Accordingly, since the officer had had no basis for arresting the appellant for an actual breach of the peace, he was not acting in the execution of his duty at the time of the assault.

The decision in *Hawkes* thus confirms that breach of the peace cases turn on their own particular facts and that an error of judgment made by a police officer in the heat of the moment may have important legal consequences. Had the officer arrested the appellant on the ground that her conduct gave rise to a reasonable belief that a breach of the peace was about to occur, it is likely that her arrest would have been lawful.

---

[51] At 711.   [52] Ibid.   [53] At 713.   [54] For a discussion of these reforms, see chapter 12.
[55] [2005] EWHC 3046 (Admin).   [56] See p. 754 for a discussion of this offence.
[57] The appellant had verbally abused rather than verbally threatened the officer.

In addition to the power of arrest, the police (and the private citizen) also have the power to detain a person who is committing or is about to commit a breach of the peace.

Albert v Lavin [1982] AC 546

The appellant had attempted to 'jump the queue' at a bus stop when he was prevented from doing so by Lavin, an off-duty police officer. Lavin's reason for obstructing the appellant was that he had reasonable grounds for believing that if he failed to deal with the situation, a breach of the peace would occur. He informed the appellant that he was an off-duty police officer but, nevertheless, Albert struck Lavin on a number of occasions. The appellant was charged in respect of this conduct with the offence of assaulting a police officer in the execution of his duty contrary to section 51(1) of the Police Act 1964.[58] Albert was convicted by magistrates of the offence in part on the basis that though he had honestly believed that Lavin was not a police officer, that belief was unreasonably held. His appeal against conviction was dismissed by both the Divisional Court and the House of Lords. In the Divisional Court, Hodgson J had referred to what he termed 'the well-established principle that to detain a man against his will without arresting him is an unlawful act and serious interference with a citizen's liberty'. However, in the opinion of the House of Lords, there was a well-established exception to this principle.

Lord Diplock, at 565

'What had been overlooked in the argument in the Divisional Court and in the written cases of both parties that were lodged in this House is that to the well-established principle referred to by the learned judge there is an equally well-established exception, not confined to constables, that is applicable to the instant case. It is that every citizen in whose presence a breach of the peace is being, or reasonably appears to be about to be, committed has the right to take reasonable steps to make the person who is breaking or threatening to break the peace refrain from doing so; and those reasonable steps in appropriate cases will include detaining him against his will. At common law this is not only the right of every citizen, it is also his duty, although, except in the case of a citizen who is a constable, it is a duty of imperfect obligation . . . Even if Albert's belief that Lavin was a private citizen and not a constable had been correct, it would not have made his resistance to Lavin's restraint of him lawful.'

It will be noted that in the case of the private citizen, detaining a person in respect of a breach of the peace was what Lord Diplock termed a 'duty of imperfect obligation'. In other words, there may be circumstances where such an obligation would not apply. Thus a person suffering from a disability ought not to be expected to comply with the common law duty. Similarly it could be argued that a person with childcare responsibilities could not be expected to abandon those in order to detain a person in respect of a breach of the peace.

The power to detain a person for a breach of the peace is used by the police from time to time in the context of public marches or demonstrations. Persons who appear likely to cause a breach of the peace may, for example, be detained in a police van until they have 'calmed down'. However, as the decision in *Laporte*[59] makes clear, a detention will only be permitted to last for as long as the threat of a breach of the peace remains real. Detaining a person in respect of a threatened breach of the peace may also be an appropriate course of action to take in the context of domestic violence for the reason stated previously.[60]

---

[58] Now section 89(1) of the Police Act 1996.   [59] See p. 645.

[60] For examples of where this happened, see *McGrogan v Chief Constable of Cleveland Constabulary* [2002] EWCA Civ 86 and *R (on the application of Wragg) v DPP* [2005] EWHC 1389 (Admin).

(f) Binding over

Where an individual has been found by magistrates to have caused a breach of the peace or to have engaged in conduct likely to have caused a breach of the peace, he or she will be bound over to keep the peace and/or be of good behaviour. Essentially the process of binding over involves the individual agreeing to keep the peace for a fixed period on pain of forfeiting the whole or part of a fixed sum or bond in the event that they act in breach of the peace during that period. The power to bind over is of great antiquity though it seems to be unclear as to exactly when it originated. In its report *Binding Over*,[61] the Law Commission commented that the power can be traced back as far as the tenth century, and it is worth noting that the magistracy retains statutory powers under the still extant Justices of the Peace Act 1361 as well as common law powers to bind over to keep the peace.

The power to bind over is also exercisable by magistrates where an individual has acted *contra bonos mores*, ie in a manner which is wrong in the judgment of the majority of his or her fellow citizens. In *Hashman and Harrup v UK*,[62] the European Court of Human Rights held that a binding over order was too imprecise to comply with the terms of article 10(2) of the Convention. This judgment has some significance in the present context in that binding over orders granted in respect of a breach of the peace may also fall foul of the Convention (and now the Human Rights Act 1998) if they are worded in such a way that it is not clear to those to whom they apply what it is that they must refrain from doing in order not to transgress the order.

IV. Statutory Powers

In addition to the powers which the police possess at common law for dealing with public disorder, there are also statutory powers available to them which may be used in conjunction with or as an alternative to the common law powers. In the sections which follow, therefore, the relevant provisions of the Public Order Act 1986 will be discussed. Attention will also focus upon the Public Processions (Northern Ireland) Act 1998 and the Protection From Harassment Act 1997.

V. Public Order Act 1986

(a) Background

The Public Order Act 1986 owes its existence to a combination of events and circumstances which collectively generated the impetus for reform.

In terms of significant instances of the breakdown of public order prior to the enactment of the 1986 legislation, we need look no further than the Red Lion Square disorders of 1974 and

---

[61] Law Com No 222 (1994).   [62] (1999) 30 EHRR 241.

the Brixton riots of 1981, both of which resulted in the establishment of inquiries chaired by Lord Scarman. However, while the subsequent reports contained a number of recommendations as to how to prevent a repetition of events, including the need for more sensitive policing in inner city areas, these recommendations were not immediately put into effect. A further impetus for reform came in 1983 with the publication of the Law Commission's Report *Criminal Law: Offences Relating to Public Order*[63] in which that body conducted an extensive review of the existing common law public order offences as part of its programme of codifying the criminal law of England and Wales. Foremost among the Law Commission's recommendations was the abolition of the four common law offences of affray, riot, rout and unlawful assembly[64] and the enactment of a number of new statutory offences including riot, affray and acts and threats of group violence. The Report, together with an earlier government Green Paper[65] and a later White Paper[66] had a significant influence upon the content of the Public Order Act 1986, especially with regard to the creation of a set of new statutory offences of varying degrees of seriousness. It should be noted, however, that the 1986 legislation does not amount to a codification of the law on public order. One or two provisions of its predecessor, the 1936 Public Order Act, remain in force. The most notable of these, section 1, provides that it is an offence for a person to wear a 'uniform signifying his association with any political organisation or with the promotion of any political object' in any public place or at any public meeting. The absence of a statutory definition of 'uniform' in the 1936 Act was overcome by the Divisional Court in *O'Moran v DPP* and *Whelan v DPP*,[67] where it was held that the wearing of a black beret could, by itself, amount to a 'uniform' for the purposes of the Act. In the words of Lord Widgery CJ:

'Whether or not a particular article of dress is to be described as a uniform must depend on all the circumstances of the case . . . I see no difficulty whatever in saying that a uniform can consist of nothing more than a black beret. When one looks at the circumstances of this case, of 300 people forming up to march, carrying banners with political slogans, and being issued with black berets which were clearly intended to be worn to show an association between the marchers and those who carried the banners, it seems to me in those circumstances that there can be no doubt that an offence under the Public Order Act 1936 was committed.'[68]

In addition, as we have already seen, the 1986 Public Order Act has not affected the common law powers of both the police and the ordinary citizen to deal with breaches of the peace.

(b) The offences

Part I of the 1986 Act is concerned with the enactment of the statutory offences of riot,[69] violent disorder,[70] affray,[71] fear or provocation of violence,[72] harassment, alarm or distress,[73] and intentional harassment, alarm or distress.[74] The first two offences in this Part of the Act share some common characteristics both in terms of the substance of the offences and the way in which they are set out in the statute. Accordingly, in the discussion which follows, they are considered together.

[63] Law Com No 123 (1983).
[64] This was subsequently given statutory effect by section 9 of the Public Order Act 1986.
[65] *Review of the Public Order Act 1936 and related legislation,* Cmnd 7891, (1980).
[66] *Review of Public Order Law,* Cmnd 9510, (1985).   [67] [1975] 2 WLR 413.   [68] At 424.
[69] Section 1.   [70] Section 2.   [71] Section 3.   [72] Section 4.   [73] Section 5.
[74] Section 4A.

(c) Riot and violent disorder

'1 Riot

(1) Where 12 or more persons who are present together use or threaten unlawful violence for a common purpose and the conduct of them (taken together) is such as would cause a person of reasonable firmness present at the scene to fear for his personal safety, each of the persons using unlawful violence for the common purpose is guilty of riot.

(2) It is immaterial whether or not the 12 or more use or threaten unlawful violence simultaneously.

(3) The common purpose may be inferred from conduct.

(4) No person of reasonable firmness need actually be, or be likely to be, present at the scene.

(5) Riot may be committed in private as well as in public places.

(6) A person guilty of riot is liable on conviction on indictment to imprisonment for a term not exceeding ten years or a fine or both.

2 Violent disorder

(1) Where 3 or more persons who are present together use or threaten unlawful violence and the conduct of them (taken together) is such as would cause a person of reasonable firmness present at the scene to fear for his personal safety, each of the persons using or threatening unlawful violence is guilty of violent disorder.

(2) It is immaterial whether or not the 3 or more use or threaten unlawful violence simultaneously.

(3) No person of reasonable firmness need actually be, or be likely to be, present at the scene.

(4) Violent disorder may be committed in private as well as in public places.

(5) A person guilty of violent disorder is liable on conviction on indictment to imprisonment for a term not exceeding 5 years or a fine or both, or on summary conviction to imprisonment for a term not exceeding 6 months or a fine not exceeding the statutory maximum or both.'

In order to be guilty of the offence of riot or violent disorder, it is necessary that a specified number of persons, twelve in the case of riot and three in the case of violent disorder, are present together and that they use or threaten unlawful violence.[75] Both offences are committed in a group context, and this should be specified as part of an indictment, along with the actual offence itself.[76] In *R v Fleming and Robinson*,[77] the Court of Appeal held that where three or more defendants had been indicted for the offence of violent disorder contrary to section 2, and the only persons against whom there was evidence of using or threatening violence were those named in the indictment, a jury should be directed to acquit every defendant where it was not sure that three or more of the defendants were using or threatening violence. It would seem to follow, therefore, that where two persons were using or threatening violence they may still be convicted of a section 2 offence provided that the prosecution is able to convince a jury that a person or persons not named in the indictment were also present and that they too were using or threatening unlawful violence.[78]

---

[75] 'Violence' is defined in section 8, see further p. 670.
[76] See, for example, *R v Jefferson* [1994] 1 All ER 270; (1994) 99 Cr App R 13.   [77] [1989] Crim LR 658.
[78] On this point see *R v Mahroof* (1989) 88 Cr App R 317 and *R v Morris* [2005] EWCA Crim 609.

In the case of the offence of riot, it is also necessary for the prosecution to establish that the use or threat of violence occurred 'for a common purpose'. In its Report *Criminal Law: Offences Relating to Public Order*, the Law Commission observed that 'it is the possession of a common purpose by a number of people which constitutes the particular danger of riot'. Accordingly, the Law Commission sought to stress that a common purpose was something distinct from motive and that it was unnecessary to establish for the purposes of the offence that the rioters had planned what action was to be taken, although, of course, if there was evidence of some prior planning, it would be a clear indication of the existence of a common purpose. It would appear that the common purpose, which may, for example, take the form of an attack on the police or the use of violence to celebrate a victory in a football match as in *R v Jefferson*,[79] will often be capable of being inferred from the conduct of the rioters when considered as a whole. A parenthetical reference to this very point which was included in clause 1(1) of the Law Commission's Draft Bill (annexed to their Report) appears as section 1(3) of the 1986 Act.

A further common feature of both riot and violent disorder is that there will be no offence committed unless the use or threat of unlawful violence is such as would cause 'a person of reasonable firmness present at the scene to fear for his personal safety'. Moreover, in both cases, no such person need actually be, or be likely to be present at the scene. The 'person of reasonable firmness' is therefore a notional person, a hypothetical bystander, and the objective test is thus concerned with how that notional person would have responded to the events which are alleged to have constituted a riot or violent disorder given that they are possessed of reasonable firmness. It is only if the relevant events would have caused such a person to fear for their personal safety (assuming that all the other ingredients of the offence are made out) that a person could be convicted of riot or violent disorder. The 'person of reasonable firmness' is also the standard which is applied to assess the degree of violence used for the purposes of determining whether an affray has taken place contrary to section 3 of the 1986 Act.[80]

Riot, violent disorder and affray may all be committed in private as well as public places. Although it was argued in some quarters that this amounted to an undue extension of police powers, the Law Commission considered that it was unnecessary to draw a distinction between public and private places so as to avoid anomalies, such as that to be found in:

'the example of a large-scale fight which has broken out at a social gathering on private premises, for example a dance hall or discotheque to which on the occasion in question admission is by invitation only; the fight spills out onto the adjacent roadside. Were a new offence to be restricted to conduct in public places, only those in this overspill would be liable to be penalised; those engaged in the more serious fighting within would escape such liability, and if no-one volunteered evidence, they might escape liability altogether.'[81]

The most notable difference between riot and violent disorder is that in the case of riot, only those who actually use unlawful violence are guilty of the offence, whereas a person may be guilty of violent disorder where they use *or* threaten to use unlawful violence. In both cases, however, it is necessary to establish intention on the part of the defendant. Thus to be guilty of riot, a defendant must have intended to use violence or to have been aware that his or her conduct may be violent, and in the case of violent disorder, a defendant is required to have intended to use or threaten violence, or to have been aware that his or her conduct may be violent or threaten violence.[82] It is apparent from the maximum sentence of ten years'

---

[79] [1994] 1 All ER 270; (1994) 99 Cr App R 13.   [80] See further p. 654.
[81] *Criminal Law: Offences relating to Public Order*, at para 3.25.
[82] Section 6(1) and (2) of the 1986 Act (see p. 669).

imprisonment for riot that it is a more serious offence than violent disorder, for which the maximum penalty is five years' imprisonment. In *Criminal Law: Offences relating to Public Order*, the Law Commission justified this disparity in maximum sentences on the ground that: 'Substantially more must be proved under the offence of riot by way of numbers and of common purpose.'[83] Thus since riot is designed to deal with the most serious instances of public disorder, it is not likely to be charged as often as the less serious offence of violent disorder. Indeed, a prosecution for an offence of riot or incitement to riot is only capable of being instituted either by or with the consent of the Director of Public Prosecutions.[84] The Law Commission considered that this requirement was desirable for the reason that 'charges of riot may in some cases raise issues of some sensitivity which may in a broad sense be regarded as "political"'. Therefore, by the inclusion of the consent provision, it is possible for the DPP to prevent a prosecution from taking place even where there appears to be sufficient evidence to secure a conviction. An additional noteworthy feature of riot and violent disorder, and for that matter the other offences created in Part I of the 1986 Act, is that they may be committed by aiders and abetters as well as by principals.[85]

(d) Affray

'3 Affray

(1) A person is guilty of an affray if he uses or threatens unlawful violence towards another and his conduct is such as would cause a person of reasonable firmness present at the scene to fear for his personal safety.

(2) Where 2 or more persons use or threaten the unlawful violence, it is the conduct of them taken together that must be considered for the purposes of subsection (1).

(3) For the purposes of this section a threat cannot be made by the use of words alone.

(4) No person of reasonable firmness need actually be, or be likely to be, present at the scene.

(5) Affray may be committed in private as well as in public places.

(6) . . .[86]

(7) A person guilty of an affray is liable on conviction on indictment to imprisonment for a term not exceeding 3 years or a fine or both, or on summary conviction to imprisonment for a term not exceeding 6 months or a fine not exceeding the statutory maximum or both.'

Section 3 of the 1986 Act creates the statutory offence of affray, which replaces the old common law offence of the same name. In its report *Criminal Law: Offences relating to Public Order*, the Law Commission noted that the common law offence of affray had been widely considered to be obsolete although it had re-emerged in 1957 with the decision in *R v Sharp and Johnson*,[87] which was apparently the first reported affray case for over 100 years.[88] Since

---

[83] *Criminal Law: Offences relating to Public Order*, para 6.32.   [84] Section 7(1) of the 1986 Act.
[85] See *R v Jefferson* [1994] 1 All ER 270.
[86] This subsection, which provided for a power of arrest, was repealed by sections 111 and 174(2) and Schedule 7 to the Serious Organised Crime and Police Act 2005.   [87] [1957] 1 QB 552.
[88] See para 3.1 of the Law Commission's report. This lack of use of the common law offence of affray can be contrasted with the use which has been made of its statutory successor. In *I v DPP, M v DPP and H v DPP* [2002] 1 AC 285 (see further p. 655), in giving judgment Lord Hutton referred to 'an increasing tendency to charge the

that date, it had generally been charged in conjunction with offences against the person such as manslaughter or assault occasioning actual bodily harm, primarily in cases involving fights and attacks either on individuals or between rival gangs. However, while it was apparent that the facts of a particular case would often reveal the commission of an offence other than affray, the Law Commission took the view that it would create a vacuum in the law to abolish the common law offence without making provision for a statutory replacement. In its *Offences against Public Order*,[89] the Law Commission stressed the very essence of the offence of affray in the following manner:

'Affray is designed to deal with a type of conduct in which, by contrast with offences against the person, both the identity of the victim and the extent of his injury are immaterial . . . [W]hile the fact that serious injuries are inflicted in the course of an affray may affect the general level of sentences imposed, it is not necessary to show that the particular defendant inflicted those particular injuries on a particular victim. The essence of affray lies rather in the fact that the defendant participates in fighting or other acts of violence inflicted on others of such a character as to cause alarm to the public: it is essentially an offence against public order.'

It is clear, therefore, that an individual who participates in a street fight may be charged with the offence of affray even though the circumstances in which the fight took place, such as the numbers involved or the time of day at which it occurred, may make it impossible to identify and hence to charge that same person with a particular offence committed against another person. In response to the argument that if there is insufficient evidence to charge an individual with an offence against the person then that individual should not be charged with any offence at all, the Law Commission observed that to charge a person with affray in respect of a street fight would be an entirely appropriate course of action on account of the 'seriousness of the behaviour and the alarm which it causes to the public'. It is this latter feature of affray, the fact that it causes alarm to the public, which justifies its classification as a public order offence. The views of the Law Commission were cited extensively by the House of Lords when it was required to determine an appeal involving a conviction for the statutory offence of affray.

I v DPP; M v DPP; H v DPP [2002] 1 AC 285

Following an anonymous tip off that approximately thirty Asian youths armed with sticks were gathering in an area in the East End of London, a marked police carrier containing seven officers arrived at the scene. The officers saw some forty to fifty youths milling around, eight or nine of whom were carrying petrol bombs. The youths dispersed as soon as the police carrier came into view. None of the youths had therefore shown any violence towards the police. The police gave chase and a number of the youths, including the three appellants, were captured and arrested. Prior to their capture, each of the appellants had thrown away a petrol bomb. They were charged with and convicted of the offence of affray contrary to section 3(1) of the 1986 Act. A subsequent appeal to the Divisional Court was unsuccessful.[90] The appellants therefore appealed to the House of Lords.

The appeal raised three questions for their Lordships' consideration: (1) whether the overt possession of a weapon constituted a threat of violence for the purposes of affray when it was not used or brandished in a violent manner; (2) whether the threat of unlawful violence had to be towards a person or persons present at the scene in order to constitute an affray; and (3) whether, in order to constitute a threat for the purposes of affray, the threat must be perceived as such by a person against whom it is

offence of affray' which had meant that in 2000, there had been '1,891 offences of affray charged in the Metropolitan Police area' (at [28]).

[89] Working Paper No. 82 (1982).   [90] See (2000) 1 Cr App R 251.

addressed. Their Lordships held unanimously that the appeals should be allowed. The opinion of the court was delivered by Lord Hutton.

'10. My Lords, the issue which arises on the first certified question is whether, as a matter of law, the carrying of petrol bombs by a group of persons can constitute a threat of violence where those petrol bombs are not being waved or brandished. I consider that giving the words "threatens unlawful violence" in section 3(1) their ordinary and natural meaning the carrying of dangerous weapons, such as petrol bombs by a group or persons can, in some circumstances, constitute the threat of violence, without those weapons being waved or brandished.'

[Lord Hutton then proceeded to consider the authorities on the common law offence of affray which supported this view.[91]]

'17. The offence of affray, both at common law and now under statute, was primarily intended to punish a person or persons who engaged in a face to face confrontation where violence was used or threatened and where reasonably firm-minded members of the public would be put in fear. As Lord Bingham of Cornhill CJ said in *R v Smith (Christopher)*: "It typically involves a group of people who may well be shouting, struggling, threatening, waving weapons, throwing objects, exchanging and threatening blows and so on."

18. The appellants submit that the offence of affray requires three persons: a person who uses or threatens unlawful violence, a person at whom he directs the violence or threat (the victim), and a hypothetical bystander of reasonable firmness. The appellants further submit that the victim must be present at the scene. In support of this submission they rely on the words "towards another" in section 3(1). They contend that unlawful violence cannot be threatened towards another unless that other is present. They rely on the judgment of Taylor LJ in *Atkin v Director of Public Prosecutions* . . . where in considering the words in section 4(1) of the 1986 Act, he said: "The phrase 'uses towards another person' means, in the context of section 4(1)(a) 'uses in the presence of and in the direction of another person directly'." '

[Lord Hutton then proceeded to have regard to what the Law Commission had said about the elements of a proposed statutory offence of affray in its report, *Offences Relating to Public Order Law*.[92]]

'24. Therefore it is apparent that the Law Commission and Parliament intended that the offence set out in section 3 should penalise those who engage in a fight, whether they are landing blows, or attempting to land blows, or threatening to land blows, but it is also clear that in such circumstances the victim or victims are bound to be present with the offender or offenders. Accordingly I regard it as clear that the section does not make guilty of an affray a person whose conduct constitutes a threat of violence to persons who are not present. This conclusion also derives support from the requirement in subsection (1) that the conduct of the offender is such that it would cause a bystander "present at the scene" to fear for his personal safety. The concept of presence at the scene suggests that the notional bystander would be in the presence of both the offender and the victim. It is also relevant to observe that there is no reported case of affray where the victim was not present at the scene where the accused threatened violence.

. . .

26. . . . In order to constitute an offence under section 3 there must be a threat of violence towards another person. Whilst the carrying of petrol bombs can constitute a threat of violence, it does not necessarily follow that because a person is present at a location where a gang are carrying petrol bombs there is a threat of violence towards that person. Whether there is a threat of violence towards a person present at the scene constituted by the carrying of a weapon or weapons will depend on the

---

[91] See *R v Sharp and Johnson* [1957] 1 QB 552, and *R v Taylor* [1973] AC 964.
[92] Law Com No 123 (1983).

facts of the actual case, but that issue does not arise in the present case because, apart from the police officers towards whom there were was no threat, no one was present at the scene.'

The decision in *I v DPP* makes it clear that in order to be guilty of the statutory offence of affray, it must be shown that the defendant threatened violence towards another person and that the victim was present at the material time. Moreover, the threat must be such as would cause a person of reasonable firmness also present at the scene to fear for his personal safety. On the facts of the case however, there was no victim of an affray to justify a conviction. It is worth noting in passing that although their Lordships upheld the appeal, this did not mean that they considered the appellants behaviour to be blameless. Rather, although they considered them to be 'clearly guilty of criminal conduct', the case was an example of the prosecuting authorities having framed the wrong charge. In the opinion of Lord Hutton, it would have been open to those authorities to have charged the appellants with carrying an offensive weapon contrary to section 1 of the Prevention of Crime Act 1953[93] or with possession of explosives contrary to section 4 of the Explosive Substances Act 1883.

As with riot and violent disorder, affray involves the use or threat of unlawful violence.[94] However, in spite of the example of street fighting where large numbers of people are involved, it is not necessary that the offence should be committed in a group context. Additional common features with riot and violent disorder are the need for the conduct causing the affray to be intended by the defendants,[95] and for the conduct to be such as to 'cause a person of reasonable firmness present at the scene to fear for his personal safety'. One interesting feature of affray is that the threat of unlawful violence 'cannot be made by the use of words alone'.[96] This subsection therefore reflects what was said by the House of Lords in relation to the old common law offence of affray in *Taylor v DPP*.[97]

Finally, it is worth noting that if a person is found not guilty of either affray or violent disorder at their trial, a jury may nevertheless find them guilty of an offence contrary to section 4 of the 1986 Act.[98] This possibility of convicting a defendant of an alternative offence is not confined to circumstances where the jury has of its own volition found the defendant not guilty of a section 2 or section 3 offence. It also arises where the trial judge has directed the jury to find the defendant not guilty of the offence charged.[99] Moreover, where a defendant pleads not guilty to a section 2 or section 3 offence but is prepared to plead guilty to a section 4 offence, the Court of Appeal has held that such a plea may be accepted by a trial judge thus avoiding the unnecessary time and expense of empanelling a jury.[100]

(e) Fear or provocation of violence

'4 Fear or provocation of violence

(1) A person is guilty of an offence if he—

(a) uses towards another person threatening, abusive or insulting words or behaviour, or
(b) distributes or displays to another person any writing, sign or other visible representation which is threatening, abusive or insulting,

---

[93] In *R v Kane* [1965] 1 All ER 705, several of the accused were charged with the common law offence of affray and with an offence contrary to section 1 of the 1953 Act.
[94] 'Violence' is defined in section 8, see further p. 670.   [95] Section 6(2) (see p. 669).
[96] Section 3(3) of the 1986 Act.   [97] [1973] AC 964.   [98] See section 7(3) of the 1986 Act.
[99] See *R v Carson* (1991) 92 Cr App R 236.   [100] See *R v O'Brien* [1993] Crim LR 70.

with intent to cause that person to believe that immediate unlawful violence will be used against him or another by any person, or to provoke the immediate use of unlawful violence by that person or another, or whereby that person is likely to believe that such violence will be used or it is likely that such violence will be provoked.

(2) An offence under this section may be committed in a public or a private place, except that no offence is committed where the words or behaviour are used, or the writing, sign, or other visible representation is distributed or displayed, by a person inside a dwelling and the other person is also inside that or another dwelling.

(3) . . .[101]

(4) A person guilty of an offence under this section is liable on summary conviction to imprisonment for a term not exceeding 6 months or a fine not exceeding level five on the standard scale or both.'

Section 4 of the 1986 Act is concerned with criminalising the use of words or behaviour or the distribution or display of signs or other visible representations which are 'threatening, abusive or insulting' to another person. In addition, it is necessary that the defendant who uses such words or behaviour etc. either intends to cause that person to fear that immediate unlawful violence will be used against either himself or another; or, to provoke the immediate use of unlawful violence by that person or another; or, that as a consequence of the defendant's actions, it is likely that that person will believe that such violence will either be used or provoked.

The phrase 'threatening, abusive or insulting' is not defined by the statute. Accordingly, in the light of a House of Lords decision on the statutory predecessor of section 4, section 5 of the Public Order Act 1936, it would seem that these words should be accorded their ordinary and natural meaning.

....

Brutus v Cozens [1973] AC 854

During the course of a tennis match which was being played on No 2 Court at the Wimbledon tennis championships, the appellant and a number of other anti-apartheid demonstrators stepped onto the court. A whistle was blown, leaflets were distributed and banners and placards, on which various slogans were written, were displayed in front of the crowd. Play was accordingly brought to a halt for two to three minutes while the police removed the demonstrators, to the applause of the crowd. The appellant was charged with using insulting behaviour whereby a breach of the peace was likely to be occasioned contrary to the now repealed section 5 of the Public Order Act 1936. The insult in question was said to have been directed at the match spectators. Following a consideration of the evidence, the justices arrived at the conclusion that the appellant's behaviour was not insulting within section 5 of the 1936 Act and thus the information against him was dismissed. A subsequent appeal by the respondent was allowed by the Divisional Court[102] and thus the case ultimately came before the House of Lords. In allowing the appellant's appeal, it was necessary for the House of Lords to consider the meaning of 'insulting' in the statute.

---

[101] This subsection, which provided for a power of arrest, was repealed by sections 111 and 174(2) and Schedule 7 to the Serious Organised Crime and Police Act 2005.

[102] [1972] 1 WLR 484; [1972] 2 All ER 1.

Lord Reid, at 861–863

'The meaning of an ordinary word of the English language is not a question of law. The proper construction of a statute is a question of law. If the context shows that a word is used in an unusual sense the court will determine in other words what the unusual sense is. But here there is in my opinion no question of the word 'insulting' being used in any unusual sense. It appears to me, for reasons which I shall give later, to be intended to have its ordinary meaning. It is for the tribunal which decides the case to consider, not as law but as fact, whether in the whole circumstances the words of the statute do or do not as a matter of ordinary usage of the English language cover or apply to the facts which have been proved. If it is alleged that the tribunal has reached a wrong decision then there can be a question of law but only of a limited character. The question would normally be whether their decision was unreasonable in the sense that no tribunal acquainted with the ordinary use of language could reasonably reach that decision.

Were it otherwise we should reach an impossible position. When considering the meaning of a word one often goes to a dictionary. There one finds other words set out. And if one wants to pursue the matter and find the meaning of those other words the dictionary will give the meaning of those other words in still further words which often include the word for whose meaning one is searching.

No doubt the court could act as a dictionary. It could direct the tribunal to take some word or phrase other than the word in the statute and consider whether that word or phrase applied to or covered the facts proved. But we have been warned time and again not to substitute other words for the words of a statute. And there is very good reason for that. Few words have exact synonyms. The overtones are almost always different.

Or the court could frame a definition. But then again the tribunal would be left with words to consider. No doubt a statute may contain a definition—which incidentally often creates more problems than it solves—but the purpose of a definition is to limit or modify the ordinary meaning of a word and the court is not entitled to do that.

So the question of law in this case must be whether it was unreasonable to hold that the appellant's behaviour was not insulting. To that question there could in my view be only one answer—No.

But as the Divisional Court [1972] 1 WLR 484, have expressed their view as to the meaning of 'insulting' I must, I think, consider it. It was said, at p. 487:

"The language of section 5, as amended, of the Public Order Act 1936, omitting words which do not matter for our present purpose, is: 'Any person who in any public place . . . uses . . . insulting . . . behaviour, . . . with intent to provoke a breach of the peace or whereby a breach of the peace is likely to be occasioned, shall be guilty of an offence.' It therefore becomes necessary to consider the meaning of the word 'insulting' in its context in that section. In my view it is not necessary, and is probably undesirable, to try to frame an exhaustive definition which will cover every possible set of facts that may arise for consideration under this section. It is, as I think, quite sufficient for the purpose of this case to say that behaviour which affronts other people, and evidences a disrespect or contempt for their rights, behaviour which reasonable persons would foresee is likely to cause resentment or protest such as was aroused in this case, and I rely particularly on the reaction of the crowd as set out in the case stated, is insulting for the purpose of this section."

I cannot agree with that. Parliament had to solve the difficult question of how far freedom of speech or behaviour must be limited in the general public interest. It would have been going much too far to prohibit all speech or conduct likely to occasion a breach of the peace because determined opponents may not shrink from organising or at least threatening a breach of the peace in order to silence a speaker whose views they detest. Therefore vigorous and it may be distasteful or unmannerly speech or behaviour is permitted so long as it does not go beyond any one of three limits. It must not be threatening. It must not be abusive. It must not be insulting. I see no reason why any one of these should be construed as having a specially wide or a specially narrow meaning. They are all limits easily recognisable by the ordinary man. Free speech is not impaired by ruling them out. But before a man can be convicted it must be clearly shown that one or more of them has been disregarded.

We were referred to a number of dictionary meanings of "insult" such as treating with insolence or contempt or indignity or derision or dishonour or offensive disrespect. Many things otherwise unobjectionable may be said or done in an insulting way. There can be no definition. But an ordinary sensible man knows an insult when he sees or hears it.

Taking the passage which I have quoted, "affront" is much too vague a word to be helpful; there can often be disrespect without insult, and I do not think that contempt for a person's rights as distinct from contempt of the person himself would generally be held to be insulting. Moreover, there are many grounds other than insult for feeling resentment or protesting. I do not agree that there can be conduct which is not insulting in the ordinary sense of the word but which is "insulting for the purpose of this section." If the view of the Divisional Court was that in this section the word "insulting" has some special or unusually wide meaning, then I do not agree. Parliament has given no indication that the word is to be given any unusual meaning. Insulting means insulting and nothing else.

If I had to decide, which I do not, whether the appellant's conduct insulted the spectators in this case, I would agree with the magistrates. The spectators may have been very angry and justly so. The appellant's conduct was deplorable. Probably it ought to be punishable. But I cannot see how it insulted the spectators.'

In the earlier case of *Jordan v Burgoyne*,[103] where the defendant had been convicted of an offence contrary to section 5 of the 1936 Act in respect of an address that he made as leader of the National Socialist Movement at a rally in Trafalgar Square, Lord Parker LJ observed that:

'A man is entitled to express his own views as strongly as he likes, to criticise his opponents, to say disagreeable things about his opponents and about their policies, and to do anything of that sort. But what he must not do is—and these are the words of the section—he must not threaten, he must not be abusive and he must not insult them, "insult" in the sense of "hit by words".'[104]

The use of the word 'immediate' prior to 'unlawful violence' in section 4 does not mean that the violence should instantly follow the act which is held to be threatening, abusive or insulting. However, were the violence to take place after more than a relatively short period of time following the relevant act, during which there had been an intervening occurrence, it would seem that it would not be 'immediate' for the purposes of the section.

R v Horseferry Road Metropolitan Stipendiary Magistrate, ex p Siadatan
[1991] 1 QB 260

The applicant sought judicial review by way of an order of certiorari to quash the decision of a stipendiary magistrate to refuse to issue a summons on the information laid by the applicant before the magistrates' court. In the information, it was alleged that Viking Penguin Books Ltd had committed an offence contrary to section 4(1) of the Public Order Act 1986 by distributing a book entitled *The Satanic Verses* written by the author Salman Rushdie. The book was, it was claimed, offensive to the Islamic faith since it contained abusive and insulting writing whereby it was likely that unlawful violence would be provoked. The Divisional Court was invited by counsel for the applicant to interpret section 4(1) in such a way that where the words 'such violence' appeared in that subsection, they could mean 'unlawful violence' as well as 'immediate unlawful violence', thus broadening the scope of the offence. However, for the following reasons, the Divisional Court felt that the phrase 'such violence' in section 4(1) meant only 'immediate unlawful violence' and thus the application was dismissed.

[103] [1963] 2 QB 744.   [104] At 749.

Watkins LJ, at 267–269

[Following a consideration of the short history of the legislation referred to by counsel for the applicant, the judgment of the court continued thus:]

'We were referred to the Law Commission's report entitled *Criminal Law Offences Relating to Public Order* (1983) (Law Com No 123). The content and structure of section 4(1) is foreshadowed in the very clearly expressed para 5.43 of that paper thus:

"Fear of violence and provoking violence

5.43 The offence requires that each defendant use threatening etc words or behaviour which is intended or is likely—(a) to cause another person to fear immediate unlawful violence, or (b) to provoke the immediate use of unlawful violence by another person."

That the parliamentary draftsman, when drafting the last part of section 4(1), did not achieve the same clarity and precision found in that paragraph is, we think, most regrettable.

The context in which section 4(1) appears in the 1986 Act is the first matter which leads to our conclusion. The title to the Act recounts that it is "An Act to abolish . . . certain statutory offences relating to public order; to create new offences relating to public order . . ." Section 4 appears in the first part of the Act together with the creation of new offences, namely riot by section 1, violent disorder by section 2, affray by section 3, harassment, alarm or distress by section 5. The provisions of those sections are such that the conduct of the defendants must produce in an actual or notional person of reasonable firmness fear in relation to sections 1, 2 and 3 which is contemporaneous with the unlawful violence being used by the defendants or harassment, alarm or distress which is contemporaneous with the threatening, abusive or insulting conduct under section 5. We consider it most unlikely that Parliament could have intended to include, among sections which undoubtedly deal with conduct having an immediate impact on bystanders, a section creating an offence for conduct which is likely to lead to violence at some unspecified time in the future.

The second reason is that, in our view, by itself a proper reading of section 4(1) leads to this conclusion. We accept . . . that the words "immediate unlawful violence" and the words "the immediate use of unlawful violence" have precisely the same meaning. The change in the phraseology used by Parliament is simply a matter of style. The only violence mentioned in section 4(1) is "immediate unlawful violence". The words "such violence" refer back to the earlier use or uses of the word "violence" in the subsection as qualified by the other words which appear in the same phrases as the word "violence". On the first occasion that the word "violence" is used it is qualified by the words "immediate unlawful" and on the second it is qualified by the words "the immediate use of unlawful". In our opinion . . . it is not possible in construing the words "such violence" in part (iv), which reads "it is likely that such violence will be provoked", to return to part (ii) and ignore the words "the immediate use". Parts (iii) and (iv) must have been intended by Parliament to be mirror images of parts (i) and (ii) of the subsection.

A third and very compelling reason for our conclusion on the correct construction of this subsection is that here we are construing a penal statute, of which there are, or may be, two possible readings. It is an elementary rule of statutory construction that, in a penal statute where there are two possible readings, the meaning which limits the scope of the offence thus created is that which the court should adopt. It would surely be strange indeed, if, where it could be shown that a defendant had an intent to provoke unlawful violence by another person, Parliament required the prosecution to establish an intent to provoke the immediate use of unlawful violence, but in a situation where a defendant had no such intent, but nevertheless it was likely that violence would be provoked, there was no requirement that such violence be immediate.

For these reasons we hold that the magistrate was right to refuse to issue a summons.

Finally, we consider it advisable to indicate our provisional view on the meaning of the word "immediate". In the Law Commission's report to which reference has already been made, at para 5.46 the Law Commission indicated that in their opinion the new offence to replace that created by section 5 of the 1936 Act should include the element of immediacy; in the case of behaviour provoking the use of violence, it must be the immediate use of such violence. Nevertheless, the Law Commission in para 5.44 gave an example of a gang in one part of a town uttering threats directed at persons, for example, of a particular ethnic or religious group resident in another part, and stated that that would be an offence, although the threat would not be capable of being performed until the gang arrived in the other part of the town. So the Law Commission recommended there that Parliament enact a law to create an offence of the making of threats which lead to the fear of violence to the person simpliciter as opposed to an offence of the making of threats, causing fear of violence to the person hearing the threats.

It seems to us that the word "immediate" does not mean "instantaneous", that a relatively short time interval may elapse between the act which is threatening, abusive or insulting and the unlawful violence. "Immediate" connotes proximity in time and proximity in causation, that it is likely that violence will result within a relatively short period of time and without any other intervening occurrence.'

In *DPP v Ramos*,[105] Kennedy LJ stressed that it is the state of mind of the victim which is the crucial factor in determining whether an offence has been committed under this section rather than the statistical risk of violence actually occurring within a very short space of time. Thus if the receipt of a threatening letter led the recipient to believe that immediate unlawful violence would be used, the offence would have been committed. Similarly in *Valentine v DPP*,[106] it was held that a verbal threat to burn a house down the next time that a prison officer went on duty did constitute a section 4(1) offence. The Divisional Court rejected the argument that the delay between the threat and the officer's next duty period meant that the victims could not have feared immediate unlawful violence. Instead, the Court accepted the magistrates findings that the victims did fear that such violence would be used on them during the course of the night on which the threats were made.

It is necessary that the threatening, abusive or insulting words or behaviour etc are directed at another person in order for a section 4 offence to be committed, but since that person need only fear violence to the person in general rather than violence to his own person, the offence is consequently wider in scope than if it were restricted to fear of violence to one's own person alone. The point was illustrated in the Law Commission's *Criminal Law: Offences relating to Public Order* by the use of the following example:

'If a gang in one part of a town were to utter threats directed at persons of, for example, a particular ethnic or religious group resident in another part, an offence restricted to causing another to fear violence to his person could not be committed until the gang arrived in the latter part; it would however be capable of being committed wherever the gang happened to be if the offence were to penalise, as we recommend, causing another to fear violence to the person simpliciter.'[107]

In some respects, therefore, it can be argued that section 4 of the 1986 Act, and for that matter the now repealed section 5, constitute a limitation upon the freedom of speech of the individual which is justified on the basis that the conduct caught by the section exceeds the bounds of that which is acceptable in modern day society. The second point to note about section 4 is that despite the fact that the offence may be committed in a public as well as a private place, no offence is actually committed where the relevant words or behaviour etc are used by one person towards another when both persons are inside either the same or different dwellings. Thus in *Atkin v DPP*,[108] two customs officers and a bailiff had gone to the defendant's farm in order to recover value added tax which was owed. The bailiff remained outside the farmhouse

---

[105] [2000] Crim LR 768.   [106] [1997] COD 339.   [107] At para 5.44.
[108] (1989) 89 Cr App R 199.

in a car where he could hear none of the conversation between the customs officers and the defendant. It became apparent during this conversation that the defendant was unable to pay the outstanding sum, and thus he was informed that the bailiff would have to enter the farmhouse in order to distrain on his goods. At this point the defendant became angry and declared: 'If the bailiff gets out of the car he's a dead un.' These threats were repeated on two further occasions and one of the customs officers noticed that there was a gun in the corner of the room. The bailiff was subsequently informed by a customs officer that the farmer had issued threats against him and the three left the farm. In respect of this conduct the defendant was charged with an offence contrary to section 4 of the Public Order Act 1986. Following his conviction by magistrates, he appealed by way of case stated on the basis that the phrase 'uses towards another person' in section 4(1) required that the person against whom the threatening words and behaviour were used must actually be physically present to personally witness such words and behaviour. In quashing his conviction, Taylor LJ sitting in the Divisional Court remarked that: '. . . when one construes in the context of this case section 4(1)(a) and the phrase "uses towards another person" it cannot be right to regard the bailiff as being that other person because he was not in earshot and the words were not directed towards him'.[109] Accordingly, the only persons to whom the words could have been directed were the Customs and Excise Officers but since they were in the appellant's dwelling at the relevant time, no offence had been committed as a consequence of the exception set out in section 4(2) of the 1986 Act. In commenting on the rationale underpinning the statutory exception, Henry J observed:

'. . . it is clear that the intention of Parliament was to exclude domestic quarrels conducted within the home even in circumstances where such words or behaviour would, if repeated outside the dwelling, create an offence. It also seems to me to follow from the clear words of the statute that it was the intention to exclude such domestic quarrels from criminal liability attaching to such domestic quarrels, even where the threat uttered, though spoken to the person sharing the dwelling was related to violence against someone who was not in the dwelling at the time.'[110]

(f) Harassment, alarm or distress

'5 Harassment, alarm or distress

(1) A person is guilty of an offence if he—
    (a) uses threatening, abusive or insulting words or behaviour, or disorderly behaviour, or
    (b) displays any writing, sign or other visible representation which is threatening, abusive or insulting,
within the hearing or sight of a person likely to be caused harassment, alarm or distress thereby.

(2) An offence under this section may be committed in a public or a private place, except that no offence is committed where the words or behaviour are used, or the writing, sign or other visible representation is displayed, by a person inside a dwelling and the other person is also inside that or another dwelling.

(3) It is a defence for the accused to prove—
    (a) that he had no reason to believe that there was any person within hearing or sight who was likely to be caused harassment, alarm or distress, or

[109] At 205.   [110] At 205–206.

(b) that he was inside a dwelling and had no reason to believe that the words or behaviour used, or the writing, sign or other visible representation displayed, would be heard or seen by a person outside that or any other dwelling, or

(c) that his conduct was reasonable.

(4) . . .

(5) . . .[111]

(6) A person guilty of an offence under this section is liable on summary conviction to a fine not exceeding level 3 on the standard scale.'

Section 5 of the 1986 Act differs from section 4 in a number of important respects. Unlike section 4, the threatening, abusive or insulting words or behaviour etc need not be used towards a person; it is enough that the conduct in question takes place 'within the hearing or sight of a person likely to be caused harassment, alarm or distress thereby'. For the purposes of section 5, it would appear that a police officer is a person capable of being caused harassment, alarm or distress by the words or behaviour of another.

Director of Public Prosecutions v Orum [1989] 1 WLR 88

The defendant and his girlfriend were engaged in an argument in a residential area when they were approached by two police officers. In view of the early hour and the disturbance being caused to neighbours by the abusive language which was being used, the officers asked the defendant to quieten down. However, when he failed to do so, he was arrested for causing a breach of the peace. The defendant was placed in the rear of a police vehicle, from which position he attacked one of the officers, kicking him and hitting him about the head and body. He was charged with two offences: using threatening, abusive or insulting words or behaviour contrary to section 5(1)(a) of the Public Order Act 1986; and assaulting a police officer in the execution of his duty contrary to section 51(1) of the Police Act 1964 (now section 89(1) of the Police Act 1996). The charges were dismissed by magistrates, but on appeal by the prosecutor, the Divisional Court set aside the defendant's acquittal for the section 5(1)(a) offence and remitted the matter back to the magistrates with regard to the section 51(1) offence with a direction that they should convict the respondent. The views of the Divisional Court were expressed as follows:

Glidewell LJ, at 92–93

'The main question which we have to answer is: can a police officer be a person who is likely to be caused harassment, alarm or distress by the threatening, abusive or insulting words or behaviour? It is apparent, as counsel who appears for the defendant sensibly concedes, that in the first part of the passage in which they set out their opinion, the magistrates had firstly taken the view that they can discount any question of harassment, alarm or distress to people living in and presumably mostly asleep in the nearby dwelling houses, because there is no evidence that any such person was likely to be caused harassment. Secondly, they appear to have totally discounted the effect of the defendant's conduct on his girlfriend. What they concerned themselves with, and what we are asked to concern ourselves with, is the impact of that conduct on either or both of the two police constables.

The magistrates seem to have been advised by their clerk that they could not properly, presumably as a matter of law, conclude that either of the constables was likely to be caused harassment, alarm or distress by the words or behaviour of the respondent . . .

[111] Subsections (4) and (5), which provided for a power of arrest, were repealed by sections 111 and 174(2), and Schedule 7 to the Serious Organised Crime and Police Act 2005.

I find nothing in the context of the Act of 1986 to persuade me that a police officer may not be a person who is caused harassment, alarm or distress by the various kinds of words and conduct to which section 5(1) applies. I would therefore answer the question in the affirmative, that a police officer can be a person who is likely to be caused harassment and so on. However, that is not to say that the opposite is necessarily the case, namely it is not to say that every police officer in this situation is to be assumed to be a person who is caused harassment. Very frequently, words and behaviour with which police officers will be wearily familiar will have little emotional impact on them save that of boredom. It may well be that, in appropriate circumstances, magistrates will decide (indeed, they might decide in the present case) as a question of fact that the words and behaviour were not likely to cause harassment, alarm or distress to either of the police officers. That is a question of fact for the magistrates to decide having regard to all the circumstances: the time, the place, the nature of the words used, who the police officers are and so on . . .

Counsel for the prosecution poses for our consideration a second question: if in fact a police officer is not likely to be caused harassment etc does he then have any power to arrest under section 5(4)? Theoretically, the answer to that question must be Yes, but in practice, in my view, it must almost invariably be No. The reason is this. If an officer is not caused harassment alarm or distress, it is difficult to see how he can reasonably suspect, if he is the only person present, that an offence against section 5(1) has been committed since such causation is a necessary element in the offence. If he does not reasonably suspect that such an offence has been committed, then he has no power of arrest under section 5(4).'

McCullough J, at 95

'In enacting section 5 of the Public Order Act 1986 in place of section 5 of the Public Order Act 1936, Parliament advisedly deleted the requirement that a breach of the peace was either intended by the defendant or was likely to result from his conduct. In its place was put the requirement that someone within sight or sound of the defendant at the material time would be likely to be caused harassment, alarm or distress by his conduct. Thus, what matters now is not the likely physical reaction to the conduct complained of, but the likely mental reaction to it. It is improbable in the extreme that any police officer would ever be provoked by threatening, abusive or insulting words or behaviour to cause a breach of the peace, but it is by no means impossible that such an officer may not feel harassed, alarmed or distressed as a result of such words or behaviour.'

In *Holloway v DPP*,[112] the Divisional Court was required to determine whether it was necessary for conduct potentially amounting to a section 5 offence to be actually witnessed by a third party before a defendant could be convicted or whether it was sufficient that such conduct could have been seen by a third party. The conduct in question involved the appellant standing naked in front of a video camera in a countryside location. Behind him schoolchildren were visible playing on the nearby school field. Significantly, however, no one saw the appellant in his naked state. A district judge found at first instance that the appellant's behaviour was 'insulting' within the meaning of section 5 and he was therefore convicted of the offence. On appeal, however, although the Divisional Court agreed that the appellant's behaviour had indeed been insulting, it concluded that the appeal should be allowed. Silber J took the view that the relevant behaviour must be 'within the . . . sight of a person' in order for the offence to have been committed. In his opinion: 'These words mean that some person must have actually seen the abusive or insulting words or behaviour. It is not enough that somebody merely might have seen or could possibly have seen that behaviour.'[113] In support of this view Silber J drew a distinction between section 5 and section 3(1) of the 1986 Act. In the case of the latter, it will be remembered that the concept of the notional person of reasonable firmness is introduced with the result that the prosecution do not need to adduce

[112] [2004] EWHC 2621 (Admin).   [113] At [17].

evidence from someone who actually feared for their own safety in order to obtain a conviction for the section 3 offence. In the opinion of Silber J:

' . . . if Parliament had intended that an offence under section 5 would have been committed if the offensive behaviour could have been seen by somebody (even if not actually seen), then it would have inserted in section 5 a provision to that effect or perhaps wording similar to that used in section 3'.[114]

Interestingly, although Collins J agreed with Silber J that the appeal should be allowed, he was prepared to accept that a defendant might be convicted of a section 5 offence where a court had 'properly and safely' drawn the inference that there were people who could have seen or heard what was going on even though, for whatever reason, they may not actually have done so. Collins J described this as being 'perhaps a slight gloss' on what Silber J had said. Might it be argued, however, that in so doing he was understating the difference between himself and Silber J on this point?

In the later case of *Taylor v DPP*,[115] both members of the Divisional Court commented on the difference of approach taken by the members of the differently constituted Divisional Court in *Holloway*. In the opinion of Keene LJ (with which Jack J agreed), the conflict between the two judges 'comes down to a question of what evidence the prosecution is required to call to prove the offence'. In his judgment, the approach advocated by Collins J was to be preferred. Accordingly, although there had to be evidence that there was someone able to hear or see the defendant's conduct, the prosecution did not need to prove that the person actually heard the words or saw the behaviour in order to secure a conviction for the section 5 offence. Commenting on the meaning of 'within the hearing or sight of a person' in section 5(1), Jack J observed:

'There is a distinction between something which it is established was said or done within the hearing or sight of a person and something which it is established the person in fact heard or saw. The draftsman of the section elected for the former.'[116]

Two further distinctions may be made between section 4 and section 5. First, the less severe nature of the section 5 offence is evidenced by the fact that a defendant does not need to intend to cause the belief that violence will either be used or provoked as a consequence of his words or behaviour for an offence to have been committed. Secondly, 'disorderly behaviour' is capable of being the actus reus of a section 5 offence but not a section 4 offence. 'Disorderly behaviour' is not actually defined in the statute and thus it seems likely that as with 'threatening, abusive or insulting', the words ought to be accorded their ordinary and natural meaning for the purposes of establishing whether an offence has been committed. Bonner and Stone have argued that 'noisy singing after closing time' might be rightly described as disorderly behaviour.[117] In *Chambers v DPP*,[118] the defendants were jointly charged with an offence under section 5 where they held their hands in front of and walked in front of a theodolite which was being used to take measurements on land being developed as a motorway link road. On appeal against their convictions, the Divisional Court held that such conduct constituted 'harassment' within the meaning of section 5. Moreover, as to whether the behaviour could be said to be 'disorderly', the Divisional Court took the view that this was a question of fact for a trial court to determine. It did not follow that where a person harassed another that behaviour was itself disorderly. The use of separate and different terminology clearly indicated that the

---

[114] At [20].   [115] [2006] EWHC 1202 (Admin).   [116] At [21].
[117] 'The Public Order Act 1986: Steps in the Wrong Direction?' [1987] PL 202 at 208.
[118] [1995] Crim LR 896.

words 'harassment' and 'disorderly' should not be conflated or deemed to have an equivalent meaning. In the opinion of Keene J, for there to be disorderly behaviour, there need not be any element of violence, present or threatened. On the facts, a reasonable tribunal could have held that the appellant's behaviour was disorderly.

While an offence may be committed under section 4(1)(b) of the 1986 Act by the distribution or display of a sign or other visible representation which is threatening, abusive or insulting, the corresponding offence under section 5(1)(b) only relates to the display of a sign or other visible representation with these characteristics. Accordingly, the handing out of leaflets which have printed on them a threatening, abusive or insulting visible representation would not be an offence under section 5 of the Act whereas the same conduct would constitute an offence under section 4.

It is a necessary ingredient of the offences under both section 4 and section 5 that the defendant either intended his words or behaviour etc to be threatening, abusive or insulting, or that he was aware that they may be so.[119] In *Vigon v DPP*,[120] the defendant ran a market stall on which swimwear was sold. He set up a partially concealed video camera to film customers trying on the swimwear in the changing room. He was convicted of using insulting behaviour within the sight of a person likely to be caused harassment, alarm or distress thereby contrary to section 5. On appeal, the Divisional Court concluded that the attempt to conceal the camera was clear evidence that the appellant was aware that his behaviour may be insulting. Accordingly, since filming could be equated with peeping through the curtains with his own eyes (which would have fallen within the scope of section 5), the appellant had been rightly convicted by justices.

Section 5(3) provides additional means by which a defendant may escape conviction for an offence contrary to that section in the form of three statutory defences. Thus, for example, if a defendant is able to establish, on the balance of probabilities, that although his conduct amounted to a prima facie offence, such conduct was in the circumstances reasonable, he will have a valid defence to the offence charged. In determining whether his conduct was reasonable, the court will apply an objective rather than a subjective test of reasonableness. Thus in *DPP v Clarke*,[121] where a group of protesters outside an abortion clinic had shown police officers and passers-by a photograph of an aborted foetus and had been arrested and charged with an offence contrary to sections 5 and 6 of the 1986 Act, the Divisional Court confirmed that 'the question whether the defendant's conduct is reasonable so as to entitle him to invoke the defence provided by section 5(3)(c) can only be answered by reference to objective standards of reasonableness'.[122] The burden of proof in relation to section 5(3) rests upon the defendant. He or she will therefore have to prove on the balance of probabilities that the conduct in question was reasonable in order to be able to successfully avail themselves of the section 5(3) defence.

(g) Intentional harassment, alarm or distress

'4A Intentional harassment, alarm or distress

(1) A person is guilty of an offence if, with intent to cause a person harassment, alarm or distress, he—
  (a) uses threatening, abusive or insulting words or behaviour, or disorderly behaviour, or
  (b) displays any writing, sign or other visible representation which is threatening, abusive or insulting,

[119] See section 6(3) and (4) of the 1986 Act.   [120] [1998] Crim LR 289.
[121] (1992) 94 Cr App R 359.   [122] At 365.

thereby causing that or another person harassment, alarm or distress.

(2) An offence under this section may be committed in a public or a private place, except that no offence is committed where the words or behaviour are used, or the writing, sign or other visible representation is displayed, by a person inside a dwelling and the person who is harassed, alarmed or distressed is also inside that or another dwelling.

(3) It is a defence for the accused to prove—

    (a) that he was inside a dwelling and had no reason to believe that the words or behaviour used, or the writing, sign or other visible representation displayed, would be heard or seen by a person outside that or any other dwelling, or

    (b) that his conduct was reasonable.

(4) . . .[123]

(5) A person guilty of an offence under this section is liable on summary conviction to imprisonment for a term not exceeding 6 months or a fine not exceeding level 5 on the standard scale or both.'

This particular provision was inserted into the Public Order Act 1986 by section 154 of the Criminal Justice and Public Order Act 1994. The wording of section 4A largely mirrors that of section 5 save in two important respects. First, it is a requirement of the section 4A offence that the defendant intended to cause a person harassment, alarm or distress. Secondly, the victim of the offence must actually be caused such harassment, alarm or distress; it is not enough that they were a person 'likely' to be caused harassment etc as in section 5. It would seem that the purpose underlying the enactment of section 4A was to provide a means of dealing with racial harassment which is both persistent and serious. Accordingly, it should be noted that a person guilty of an offence under section 4A may receive a prison sentence of up to six months, whereas section 5 only provides for the imposition of a fine on conviction.

In *Rogers and others v DPP*,[124] the Divisional Court was required to consider whether the appellants had been rightly convicted of offences contrary to section 4A(1) where they had been in a crowd of some 200 to 250 people which had gathered outside a farm licensed to breed cats for scientific research. The protesters had pulled down a security fence and had tried to breach a police line in order to enter the farm. The farm's owner, who was on the premises at the time, heard the demonstration becoming noisier and watched the events unfold on a close circuit television. He stated that he was concerned for the safety of himself, his family and the police and was alarmed, distressed and terrified. A number of questions were posed for the opinion of the court. These included whether the offence could be committed in a group context and, whether a person can be said to have been caused harassment alarm or distress where they have chosen to observe the protest on CCTV. With regard to the first of these questions, the Divisional Court held that it could be properly and reasonably inferred that the appellants intended to cause harassment, alarm or distress by their actions committed in the context of a large group which had gathered to protest at the farming of cats for scientific research. Moreover, the fact that the owner watched the protest on CCTV did not constitute a break in the causal connection between the appellant's activities and the distress which he suffered; he was still present at the scene at the material time.

As with sections 4 and 5 of the 1986 Act, following the enactment of the Human Rights Act 1998[125] the courts will be assiduous in ensuring that freedom of expression is not interfered

---

[123] This subsection, which provided for a power of arrest, was repealed by sections 111 and 174(2), and Schedule 7 to the Serious Organised Crime and Police Act 2005.
[124] (unreported), CO/4041/98, 22 July 1999.   [125] See chapter 13.

with unless it is established that the conduct which is the subject of the charge amounts to such a threat to public order as to justify the bringing of a prosecution. Thus in *Dehal v CPS*,[126] where the appellant had been convicted of an offence contrary to section 4A(1) for posting a notice in a Sikh Guruwarda which accused the President of the Temple of being, amongst other things, a hypocrite and a liar, it was held in the Administrative Court that even though the Crown Court had found the notice to be abusive and insulting and that it had been posted with intent to cause harassment, alarm or distress, the criminal prosecution was nevertheless unlawful. This conclusion was reached on the basis that it had not been established that a prosecution was necessary in order to prevent public disorder. The Crown Court had erred by concluding that a prosecution was a proportionate response to the appellant's conduct without explaining the reasoning underpinning its decision.

(h) Mental element of the sections 1–5 offences and interpretation

'6 Mental element: miscellaneous

(1) A person is guilty of riot only if he intends to use violence or is aware that his conduct may be violent.

(2) A person is guilty of violent disorder or affray only if he intends to use or threaten violence or is aware that his conduct may be violent or threaten violence.

(3) A person is guilty of an offence under section 4 only if he intends his words or behaviour, or the writing, sign or other visible representation, to be threatening, abusive or insulting, or is aware that it may be threatening, abusive or insulting.

(4) A person is guilty of an offence under section 5 only if he intends his words or behaviour, or the writing, sign or other visible representation, to be threatening, abusive or insulting, or is aware that it may be threatening, abusive or insulting or (as the case may be) he intends his behaviour to be or is aware that it may be disorderly.

(5) For the purposes of this section a person whose awareness is impaired by intoxication shall be taken to be aware of that of which he would be aware if not intoxicated, unless he shows either that his intoxication was not self-induced or that it was caused solely by the taking or administration of a substance in the course of medical treatment.

(6) In subsection (5) "intoxication" means any intoxication, whether caused by drink, drugs or other means, or by a combination of means.

(7) subsections (1) and (2) do not affect the determination for the purposes of riot or violent disorder of the number of persons who use or threaten violence.'

Section 6 of the 1986 Act makes provision in respect of the mental element of the various offences set out in sections 1–5 of the Act. Since it is stated separately from the actus reus of those offences, there is a danger that it may be overlooked. It is, however, an important section which should be read in conjunction with the appropriate parts of sections 1–5.

---

[126] [2005] EWHC 2154 (Admin).

'8 Interpretation

In this Part—

"dwelling" means any structure or part of a structure occupied as a person's home or as other living accommodation (whether the occupation is separate or shared with others) but does not include any part not so occupied, and for this purpose "structure" includes a tent, caravan, vehicle, vessel or other temporary or movable structure;

"violence" means any violent conduct, so that—

  (a) except in the context of affray, it includes violent conduct towards property as well as violent conduct towards persons, and
  (b) it is not restricted to conduct causing or intended to cause injury or damage but includes any other violent conduct (for example, throwing at or towards a person a missile of a kind capable of causing injury which does not hit or falls short).'

Section 8 defines 'dwelling' and 'violence' for the purposes of Part I of the 1986 Act. It will be noted that the definition of 'violence' is wide and that since it includes violence to property as well as violence towards persons (other than in the context of affray), there are clear parallels between the statute and the accepted definition of a breach of the peace in *R v Howell.*[127]

(i) Racially or religiously aggravated public order offences

Section 31 of the Crime and Disorder Act 1998 has created a number of racially or religiously aggravated public order offences. It is therefore a distinct offence to commit an offence under either sections 4, 4A or 5 of the 1986 Act which is racially/religiously aggravated. For the purposes of section 31 (and for the other racially/religiously aggravated offences created in sections 29, 30 and 32 of the 1998 Act), an offence is racially/religiously aggravated if:

'(a) at the time of committing the offence, or immediately before or after doing so, the offender demonstrates towards the victim of the offence hostility based on the victim's membership (or presumed membership) of a racial or religious group; or

(b) the offence is motivated (wholly or partly) by hostility towards members of a racial or religious group based on their membership of that group.'[128]

Unlike the basic offences under sections 4, 4A and 5 of the 1986 Act, which are summary offences, the racially aggravated equivalents are triable either way. Accordingly, whereas the maximum sentence for the commission of a section 4 or section 4A offence is six months' imprisonment, if D were to commit the racially aggravated equivalent offence, he may be sentenced to a maximum of two years' imprisonment if convicted on indictment.[129] The introduction of specific racially or religiously aggravated public order offences thus emphasises the unacceptable nature of the conduct which they cover. Rather than the racial/religious element being something which is merely reflected in sentencing, sections 28 and 31 make it part of the offence itself. The burden of proof lies with the prosecution to show, beyond reasonable doubt, that either section 28(1)(a) or (b) is satisfied. If, in a trial on

---

[127] [1982] QB 416, extracted at p. 637. [128] Section 28(1) of the 1998 Act.
[129] Section 31(4)(b) of the 1998 Act.

indictment, the jury find D not guilty of the racially/religiously aggravated version of sections 4 or 4A, they may nevertheless find him guilty of the basic offence.[130] This specific provision therefore displaces the general rule regarding conviction for alternative offences provided for in section 6(3) of the Criminal Law Act 1967. There is no corresponding provision which permits a magistrate to do likewise.[131]

For the purposes of section 28 of the 1998 Act , the phrase 'racial group' means 'a group of persons defined by reference to race, colour, nationality (including citizenship) or ethnic or national origins'.[132] The courts have subsequently held that expressions such as 'African bitch', 'jungle bunny', 'black bastard', 'wog', 'fucking Islam', 'bloody foreigners' and 'immigrant doctor' are all capable of denoting hostility to a victim based on the victim's membership of a racial group.[133] Although the victim of a racially aggravated public order offence is unlikely to be a member of the same racial group as the defendant, it has been held that a person may show hostility towards a member of the same racial group as himself sufficient for the purposes of the offence.[134]

Section 28(5) of the Crime and Disorder Act 1998 defines 'religious group' to mean 'a group of persons defined by reference to religious belief or lack of religious belief'. In Norwood v DPP,[135] the defendant had displayed a poster in the window of his flat which contained the words 'Islam out of Britain' and 'Protect the British People' on a reproduction of a photograph of one of the twin towers of the World Trade Centre in flames on 11 September 2001. In upholding his conviction for the offence of causing alarm or distress in a manner which was religiously aggravated, the Divisional Court took the view that:

'The poster was a public expression of attack on all Muslims in this country, urging all who might read it that followers of the Islamic religion here should be removed from it and warning that their presence here was a threat or danger to the British people. In my view, it could not, on any reasonable basis be dismissed as merely an intemperate criticism or protest against the tenets of the Muslim religion, as distinct from an unpleasant and insulting attack on its followers generally.'

The appellant subsequently took his case to the European Court of Human Rights. His chief argument was that the prosecution brought against him had violated his right to freedom of expression as protected by article 10 of the ECHR. The court, however, rejected his application as inadmissible.[136] In so doing, the court agreed with the domestic court's assessment that the public order offence and the prosecution had amounted to a justifiable interference with the appellant's right. It also took the view that its conclusion was in accordance with article 17 of the ECHR which precludes individuals or groups who espouse totalitarian views from exploiting the principles of the ECHR for their own purposes.[137]

The consequences in terms of sentencing of committing a public order offence which is either racially or religiously aggravated can be demonstrated with the aid of two examples from the case law. In R v Miller,[138] the appellant was travelling on a train without a ticket. When confronted by a senior conductor, he claimed that he had lost his ticket. When pressed by the conductor he became abusive and referred to the conductor as, amongst other things,

[130] Section 31(6).   [131] See DPP v McFarlane [2002] EWHC 485 (Admin).   [132] Section 28(4).
[133] See R v White [2001] 1 WLR 1352, R v Duffy (unreported) 21 November 2000, DPP v McFarlane [2002] EWHC 485 (Admin), DPP v Humphrey [2005] EWHC 822 (Admin), DPP v M [2004] 1 WLR 2758 and R v Rogers [2005] EWCA Crim 2863.   [134] See DPP v Pal [2000] Crim LR 756.
[135] [2003] Crim LR 888.
[136] See pp. 787–788 for a consideration of the admissibility criteria which the court applies when determining whether or not an application ought to proceed.   [137] See Norwood v UK (2005) 40 EHRR SE11.
[138] [1999] Crim LR 590.

a 'fucking Paki'. In respect of this conduct, he was convicted by the Crown Court of having committed a section 31 offence and sentenced to eighteen months' imprisonment. On appeal, the Court of Appeal noted that this was a bad example of this type of offence and that the sentence had therefore been fully justified. In *R v Duffy*,[139] however, the Court of Appeal quashed a sentence of twelve months imprisonment and substituted a sentence of six months where D had been convicted of a section 31 offence after having racially abused a store detective who suspected that he had stolen several bottles of wine. In the Court's opinion, although the offence was unpleasant and deserving of a custodial sentence, the fact that D had pleaded guilty and that the Crown Court had accepted that he did not harbour racist views meant that the original term of imprisonment had been excessive.

The Sentencing Advisory Panel, which was originally established under the Crime and Disorder Act 1998 for the purpose of advising the Criminal Division of the Court of Appeal on the drawing up of sentencing guidelines or the amendment of those already in existence,[140] published an Advice in July 2000 recommending that the Court should frame a sentencing guideline on racially aggravated offences.[141] Where a sentencer is dealing with one of the specifically racially aggravated offences created by the 1998 Act (such as a racially aggravated public order offence), the Panel proposed that he or she should first decide and publicly state what would have been the appropriate sentence for the corresponding basic offence and then add an enhancement in the range of 40 per cent to 70 per cent according to the seriousness of the racial aggravation. This enhancement would apply whether the sentence was a fine or imprisonment. Although the Court of Appeal subsequently approved of the first stage in this process, it rejected the suggestion that there should be a percentage enhancement for racially aggravated offences. In its judgment, it was neither possible nor necessary to evaluate the level of aggravation. Rather, the correct approach was for a trial judge to determine the total appropriate sentence having regard to all the circumstances of the case.[142]

(j) Processions and assemblies

Part II of the Public Order Act 1986 is concerned with the regulation of processions and assemblies, and, as a consequence of insertions made by the Criminal Justice and Public Order Act 1994, the prohibition of trespassory assemblies. To a large extent the provisions relating to processions and assemblies reflect the proposals which appeared in the government White Paper, *Review of Public Order Law*.[143] In that publication, the government expressed its determination to 'uphold the right of peaceful protest, including the right to march'.[144] Continuing on the same theme, however, the White Paper stressed that:

'Marches and processions will be accepted by the wider community if they are satisfied that the police have adequate powers to prevent and control disorder, and to ensure that marches are held without causing undue inconvenience to the rights of others.'[145]

---

[139] (Unreported), 21 November 2000.

[140] Although the Panel still exists, its revised task is to provide advice for the consideration of the Sentencing Guidelines Council which was established under section 167 of the Criminal Justice Act 2003.

[141] See *http://www.sentencing-guidelines.gov.uk/docs/offences_racially.pdf*.

[142] See *R v Kelly* and *R v Donnelly* [2001] 2 Cr App Rep (S) 73.   [143] (1985) Cmnd 9510.

[144] At para 4.1 (p. 21).   [145] Ibid.

'Part II Processions and assemblies

11 Advance notice of public processions

(1) Written notice shall be given in accordance with this section of any proposal to hold a public procession intended—

    (a) to demonstrate support for or opposition to the views or actions of any person or body of persons,

    (b) to publicise a cause or campaign, or

    (c) to mark or commemorate an event,

unless it is not reasonably practicable to give any advance notice of the procession.

(2) Subsection (1) does not apply where the procession is one commonly or customarily held in the police area (or areas) in which it is proposed to be held or is a funeral procession organised by a funeral director acting in the normal course of his business.

(3) The notice must specify the date when it is intended to hold the procession, the time when it is intended to start it, its proposed route, and the name and address of the person (or of one of the persons) proposing to organise it.

(4) Notice must be delivered to a police station—

    (a) in the police area in which it is proposed the procession will start, or

    (b) where it is proposed the procession will start in Scotland and cross into England, in the first police area in England on the proposed route.

(5) If delivered not less than 6 clear days before the date when the procession is intended to be held, the notice may be delivered by post by the recorded delivery service; but section 7 of the Interpretation Act 1978 (under which a document sent by post is deemed to have been served when posted and to have been delivered in the ordinary course of post) does not apply.

(6) If not delivered in accordance with subsection (5), the notice must be delivered by hand not less than 6 clear days before the date when the procession is intended to be held or, if that is not reasonably practicable, as soon as delivery is reasonably practicable.

(7) Where a public procession is held, each of the persons organising it is guilty of an offence if—

    (a) the requirements of this section as to notice have not been satisfied, or

    (b) the date when it is held, the time when it starts, or its route, differs from the date, time or route specified in the notice.

(8) It is a defence for the accused to prove that he did not know of, and neither suspected nor had reason to suspect, the failure to satisfy the requirements or (as the case may be) the difference of date, time or route.

(9) To the extent that an alleged offence turns on a difference of date, time or route, it is a defence for the accused to prove that the difference arose from circumstances beyond his control or from something done with the agreement of a police officer or by his direction.

(10) A person guilty of an offence under subsection (7) is liable on summary conviction to a fine not exceeding level 3 on the standard scale.'

Section 11 of the Public Order Act 1986 requires that advance written notice be given of a proposed public procession unless it is not reasonably practicable to do so. 'Public processions' are defined rather unhelpfully by the Act as being 'a procession in a public place'.[146]

---

[146] Section 16.

It would seem, however, in the light of the decision in *Flockhart v Robinson*,[147] that 'a procession is not a mere body of persons: it is a body of persons moving along a route'.[148]

The requirement of advance notice was a key recommendation made by the House of Commons Select Committee on Home Affairs in its report, *The Law Relating to Public Order*.[149] Essentially the Select Committee considered that it was a desirable inclusion in the public order legislation for several reasons. First, by requiring the organisers of a procession or march to notify the police of their intention to hold such an event, a dialogue is immediately established between both parties 'thus enabling agreements to be reached without recourse to formal directions or bans'. Secondly, the Select Committee was of the opinion that the requirement served as a means of reinforcing the organiser's responsibility for the safety, welfare and good behaviour of all those who are participating in the march. Indeed, section 11(3) dictates that the notice must specify, amongst other things, the name and address of the person or persons organising the procession. Thirdly, the nature of the information which the organisers are required to give to the police, relating to the date, time and proposed route of the procession[150] enables those responsible for the disposition of police resources to ensure that the procession is properly policed and that public order is accordingly preserved. Importantly, an organiser who fails to comply with the requirements of section 11 is guilty of an offence, and an offence is also committed if the date, time or route of the procession does not correspond with that stated in the notice.[151]

It is not necessary to comply with the advance written notice requirement where it is 'not reasonably practicable'[152] to give the requisite information. This may occur where, for example, a procession amounts to a spontaneous response to an unforeseeable event. In the Green Paper[153] which was published a number of years before the Public Order Bill, the following were identified as examples of spontaneous demonstrations:

'a march to the embassy of a foreign power which has announced that one of its political prisoners was to be executed within 24 hours, or, on a more local level, a march against a factory closure or in favour of a pedestrian crossing outside a school after a fatal road accident'.[154]

Section 11(2) provides for further exemptions from the advance written notice requirement. Although it refers to processions which are 'commonly or customarily held', that expression is not defined in the Act. Following the passage of the 1986 Act, it was thought that the exemption applied to events such as Remembrance Day or May Day processions.[155] In *Kay (R on the application of) v Commissioner for Metropolitan Police Service*,[156] the Administrative Court was required to determine, amongst other things, whether or not a group of cyclists who met on the last Friday of every month for a period of almost twelve years and who rode through the streets of London could be said to amount to a commonly or customarily held procession. In the judgment of the court, the gathering did amount to a public procession which was entitled to the exemption from the notice requirement. Of course, as the court noted in passing, 'no event can initially be either common or customary'.[157] Thus whether or not a procession has acquired a common or customary character will depend upon the particular facts of the case.

---

[147] [1950] 2 KB 498.   [148] Per Lord Goddard CJ, at 502.   [149] HC 756 I and II, August 1980.
[150] Section 11(3).   [151] Section 11(7).   [152] Section 11(1).
[153] *Review of the Public Order Act 1936 and related legislation*, Cmnd 7891 (1980).   [154] Ibid., at para 68.
[155] See Bonner and Stone, 'The Public Order Act 1986: Steps in the Wrong Direction?' [1987] PL 202 at 214.
[156] [2006] EWHC 1536 (Admin).   [157] At [24].

'12 Imposing conditions on public processions

(1) If the senior police officer, having regard to the time or place at which and the circumstances in which any public procession is being held or is intended to be held and to its route or proposed route, reasonably believes that—

    (a) it may result in serious public disorder, serious damage to property or serious disruption to the life of the community, or

    (b) the purpose of the persons organising it is the intimidation of others with a view to compelling them not to do an act they have a right to do, or to do an act they have a right not to do,

he may give directions imposing on the persons organising or taking part in the procession such conditions as appear to him necessary to prevent such disorder, damage, disruption or intimidation, including conditions as to the route of the procession or prohibiting it from entering any public place specified in the directions.

(2) In subsection (1) "the senior police officer" means—

    (a) in relation to a procession being held, or to a procession intended to be held in a case where persons are assembling with a view to taking part in it, the most senior in rank of the police officers present at the scene, and

    (b) in relation to a procession intended to be held in a case where paragraph (a) does not apply, the chief officer of police.

(3) A direction given by a chief officer of police by virtue of subsection (2)(b) shall be given in writing.

(4) A person who organises a public procession and knowingly fails to comply with a condition imposed under this section is guilty of an offence, but it is a defence for him to prove that the failure arose from circumstances beyond his control.

(5) A person who takes part in a public procession and knowingly fails to comply with a condition imposed under this section is guilty of an offence, but it is a defence for him to prove that the failure arose from circumstances beyond his control.

(6) A person who incites another to commit an offence under subsection (5) is guilty of an offence.

(7) . . . [158]

(8) A person who is guilty of an offence under subsection (4) is liable on summary conviction to imprisonment for a term not exceeding 3 months or a fine not exceeding level 4 on the standard scale or both.

(9) A person guilty of an offence under subsection (5) is liable on summary conviction to a fine not exceeding level 3 on the standard scale.

(10) A person guilty of an offence under subsection (6) is liable on summary conviction to imprisonment for a term not exceeding 3 months or a fine not exceeding level 4 on the standard scale or both, notwithstanding section 45(3) of the Magistrates' Courts Act 1980 (inciter liable to same penalty as incited).

(11) . . . '

Section 12 of the 1986 Act confers upon the police the power to impose conditions on public processions. This power may be exercised either in advance of the procession by the chief officer of police[159] in which case any directions that are issued must be in writing,[160] or, where

---

[158] This subsection, which provided for a power of arrest, was repealed by sections 111 and 174(2), and Schedule 7 to the Serious Organised Crime and Police Act 2005.   [159] Section 12(2)(b).

[160] Section 12(3).

the procession is actually underway, by the most senior police officer present at the scene.[161] However, the power to impose conditions on a public procession is not without restrictions. It is only exercisable where the relevant police officer reasonably believes that the procession may result in: serious public disorder; serious damage to property; serious disruption to the life of the community; or, where the purpose of those organising the procession is the intimidation of others.[162] Provided that grounds for forming the relevant reasonable belief exist, the police officer may issue directions to the organisers of the procession relating to, amongst other things, the route of the procession or requiring it to refrain from entering a specified public place. 'Serious public disorder' and 'serious damage to property' are self-explanatory terms. 'Serious disruption to the life of the community' appears to justify the imposition of a condition or conditions where, for example, the proposed route of the march would bring a town's traffic to a standstill and would therefore prevent the delivery of goods and produce to the town's shops. Perhaps the most interesting of the grounds justifying the exercise of the power to impose conditions on a procession is where it is considered necessary in order to prevent the intimidation of others. In its White Paper,[163] the government stated that this provision amounted to 'a libertarian safeguard designed to prevent demonstrations whose overt purpose is to persuade people from being used as a cloak by those whose real purpose is to intimidate or coerce'.[164] The power to impose conditions to prevent intimidation or coercion is thus a particularly useful weapon in the police armoury for dealing with processions organised by those espousing racist views who propose to march through areas with large ethnic populations. However, it is not only racist marches which have a coercive or intimidatory effect. The White Paper expressed the view that a march may be coercive 'simply by reason of the number of marchers compared with its objective' and went on to give the example of a thousand people marching on the home of a local councillor or an inquiry inspector.[165] As with section 11, section 12 also creates offences; on this occasion in relation to persons who fail to observe the conditions which have been imposed on a procession. Thus an organiser who knowingly fails to comply with a condition so imposed is guilty of an offence,[166] as is a participant who does likewise.[167] Additionally, it is an offence to incite a participant to fail to comply with a condition.[168]

'13 Prohibiting public processions

(1) If at any time the chief officer of police reasonably believes that, because of particular circumstances existing in any district or part of a district, the powers under section 12 will not be sufficient to prevent the holding of public processions in that district or part from resulting in serious public disorder, he shall apply to the council of the district for an order prohibiting for such period not exceeding 3 months as may be specified in the application the holding of all public processions (or of any class of public procession so specified) in the district or part concerned.

(2) On receiving such an application, a council may with the consent of the Secretary of State make an order either in the terms of the application or with such modifications as may be approved by the Secretary of State.

(3) Subsection (1) does not apply in the City of London or the metropolitan police district.

(4) If at any time the Commissioner of Police for the City of London or the Commissioner of Police for the Metropolis reasonably believes that, because of particular circumstances existing in his police

---

[161] Section 12(2)(a). [162] Section 12(1)(a) and (b).
[163] *Review of Public Order Law*, Cmnd 9510, (1985). [164] Ibid., at para 4.1.
[165] Ibid., at para 4.23. [166] Section 12(4). [167] Section 12(5). [168] Section 12(6).

area or part of it, the powers under section 12 will not be sufficient to prevent the holding of public processions in that area or part from resulting in serious public disorder, he may with consent of the Secretary of State make an order prohibiting for such period not exceeding 3 months as may be specified in the order the holding of all public processions (or of any class of public procession so specified) in the area or part concerned.

(5) An order made under this section may be revoked or varied by a subsequent order made in the same way, that is, in accordance with subsections (1) and (2) or subsection (4), as the case may be.

(6) An order under this section shall, if not made in writing, be recorded in writing as soon as practicable after being made.

(7) A person who organises a public procession the holding of which he knows is prohibited by virtue of an order under this section is guilty of an offence.

(8) A person who takes part in a public procession the holding of which he knows is prohibited by virtue of an order under this section is guilty of an offence.

(9) A person who incites another to commit an offence under subsection (8) is guilty of an offence.

(10) . . .[169]

(11) A person guilty of an offence under subsection (7) is liable on summary conviction to imprisonment for a term not exceeding 3 months or a fine not exceeding level 4 on the standard scale or both.

(12) A person guilty of an offence under subsection (8) is liable on summary conviction to a fine not exceeding level 3 on the standard scale.

(13) A person guilty of an offence under subsection (9) is liable on summary conviction to imprisonment for a term not exceeding 3 months or a fine not exceeding level 4 on the standard scale or both, notwithstanding section 45(3) of the Magistrates' Courts Act 1980.'

Section 13, which is concerned with the power to ban processions, is a provision of last resort. It is exercisable only where the chief officer of police reasonably believes that the powers available under section 12 are not sufficient to prevent a public procession from resulting in serious public disorder.[170] The power to ban processions, which originally stems from the 1936 Public Order Act, does not therefore arise where it is believed that the procession will give rise to either serious damage to property, or serious disruption to the life of the community, or the intimidation of others. In the Home Affairs Select Committee report it was suggested that processions should be banned on the basis that the views which were to be expressed would be seriously offensive. However, such a proposal was rejected by the government on the basis that it 'would place an impossible task upon the police and be an unacceptable infringement of freedom of speech'.[171] In addition, a further proposal to ban processions where there was a likelihood that they would incite racial hatred was also rejected in the White Paper for several reasons, including the suggestion that such a provision would lead to 'insuperable problems of enforcement'.

Several other features of section 13 are worthy of note. First, the retention of the power to ban processions in the 1986 Act appears to have been justified in part on the basis of its increasing use in the years immediately prior to the passage of the Act. The White Paper notes, for example, that between the years 1970 and 1980 only eleven banning orders were issued in

[169] This subsection, which provided for a power of arrest, was repealed by sections 111 and 174(2), and Schedule 7 to the Serious Organised Crime and Police Act 2005. [170] Section 13(1).
[171] Review of Public Order Law, Cmnd 9510 (1985), at para 4.8.

England and Wales and yet in the troubled year of 1981, which saw both riots and demonstrations, including those in Brixton, forty-two such orders were issued in the space of twelve months. Secondly, as with the power to impose conditions under section 12, the power to ban processions under section 13 is conditional upon the chief officer of police reasonably believing that it is a necessary step. Accordingly, the exercise of both powers is subject to judicial review by the courts but, in practice, it may not be an easy task to establish that those powers have actually been exercised unlawfully. Thus in *Kent v Metropolitan Police Commissioner*,[172] the Court of Appeal refused to declare *ultra vires* a 28-day ban on processions (save for the May Day procession and those of a religious character customarily held) in the Commissioner's area despite Ackner LJ's observation that:

'Blanket bans on all marches for however short a time are a serious restriction of a fundamental freedom, and the courts will always be vigilant to see that the power to impose such a ban has not been abused.'

Thirdly, a ban on processions in a particular area which is issued under section 13 can remain in force for a maximum of three months, and in order to avoid allegations of political bias on the part of the police in seeking the ban, 'blanket bans' applying to all public processions in the area are permissible under the section, as illustrated by *Kent v Metropolitan Police Commissioner*.[173] Fourthly, the identity of the party granting a banning order will depend upon where the order was sought. In all areas other than the City of London or the metropolitan police district, it is the council of the relevant district which grants the banning order, although the consent of the Secretary of State is required before such an order can be made.[174] In the City of London and the metropolitan police district, the power to grant a banning order is conferred upon the Commissioner of Police for the City of London or the Metropolitan Police Commissioner provided that the consent of the Secretary of State has been obtained.[175] Finally, offences are committed where: a person organises a procession which is subject to a banning order;[176] or where a person takes part in a banned procession;[177] or where a person incites another to take part in a banned procession.[178]

'14 Imposing conditions on public assemblies

(1) If the senior police officer, having regard to the time or place at which and the circumstances in which any public assembly is being held or is intended to be held, reasonably believes that—

  (a) it may result in serious public disorder, serious damage to property or serious disruption to the life of the community, or

  (b) the purpose of the persons organising it is the intimidation of others with a view to compelling them not to do an act they have a right to do, or to do any act they have a right not to do,

he may give directions imposing on the persons organising or taking part in the assembly such conditions as to the place at which the assembly may be (or continue to be) held, its maximum duration, or the maximum number of persons who may constitute it, as appear to him necessary to prevent such disorder, damage, disruption or intimidation.

(2) In subsection (1) "the senior police officer" means—

  (a) in relation to an assembly being held, the most senior in rank of the police officers present at the scene, and

---

[172] *The Times*, 15 May 1981. [173] See above. [174] Section 13(1) and (2).
[175] Section 13(4). [176] Section 13(7). [177] Section 13(8). [178] Section 13(9).

(b) in relation to an assembly intended to be held, the chief officer of police.

(3) A direction given by a chief officer of police by virtue of subsection (2)(b) shall be given in writing.

(4) A person who organises a public assembly and knowingly fails to comply with a condition imposed under this section is guilty of an offence, but it is a defence for him to prove that the failure arose from circumstances beyond his control.

(5) A person who takes part in a public assembly and knowingly fails to comply with a condition imposed under this section is guilty of an offence, but it is a defence for him to prove that the failure arose from circumstances beyond his control.

(6) A person who incites another to commit an offence under subsection (5) is guilty of an offence.

(7) . . .[179]

(8) A person guilty of an offence under subsection (4) is liable on summary conviction to imprisonment for a term not exceeding 3 months or a fine not exceeding level 4 on the standard scale or both.

(9) A person guilty of an offence under subsection (5) is liable on summary conviction to a fine not exceeding level 3 on the standard scale.

(10) A person guilty of an offence under subsection (6) is liable on summary conviction to imprisonment for a term not exceeding 3 months or a fine not exceeding level 4 on the standard scale or both, notwithstanding section 45(3) of the Magistrates' Courts Act 1980.'

A public assembly was originally defined by the Public Order Act 1986 as an assembly of twenty or more persons in a public place which is wholly or partly open to the air. Now, however, as a result of an amendment made to section 16 of the 1986 Act by section 57 of the Anti-social Behaviour Act 2003,[180] a public assembly exists where *two* or more persons are gathered together in a public place. This seemingly innocuous amendment in fact has some rather important consequences in terms of policing public gatherings of people. Under the previous definition, the numerical threshold of twenty made it necessary for police to 'count heads' in order to determine whether the gathering amounted to a 'public assembly' and hence whether their power to impose conditions pursuant to section 14 was exercisable. If nineteen people were present the gathering may have amounted to an assembly, but crucially it was not a 'public assembly' for the purposes of the 1986 Act. Now, however, the new threshold of two has rendered head counts a thing of the past. From a practical point of view, it means that the police are now able to use statutory powers to control the activities of far smaller groups of people with the result that they are less likely to use their common law powers in respect of actual or threatened breaches of the peace unless, that is, the disturbance is on private premises rather than in a public place.

In contrast to public processions, assemblies are not subject to a requirement to give advance notice of an intention to hold them, and neither can they be banned. The Select Committee on Home Affairs[181] advocated treating public assemblies on a par with public

[179] This subsection, which provided for a power of arrest, was repealed by sections 111 and 174(2), and Schedule 7 to the Serious Organised Crime and Police Act 2005.

[180] The clause which became section 57 of the 2003 Act did not appear in the Bill as originally drafted. Accordingly, its effect was not considered in the government White Paper, *Respect and responsibility—taking a stand against anti-social behaviour*, Cmnd 5778.

[181] See *The Law Relating to Public Order*, HC 756 (1979–80).

processions, but such an approach was rejected by the government. It was felt that it would be inappropriate to introduce statutory provisions under which assemblies could be banned due to the fact that:

'Meetings and assemblies are a more important means of exercising freedom of speech than are marches: a power to ban them, even as a last resort, would be potentially a major infringement of speech (especially at election time).'[182]

Accordingly, section 14 only confers upon the police the power to impose conditions on public assemblies. As with the power to impose conditions on public processions under section 12 of the 1986 Act, the section 14 power is exercisable where the senior police officer reasonably believes that the assembly *may* result in either serious public disorder, or serious damage to property, or serious disruption to the life of the community, or the intimidation of others, and that the condition or conditions are necessary in order to prevent these outcomes from occurring. In *Brehony (R on the application of) v Chief Constable of Greater Manchester Police*,[183] Bean J stressed the importance of the word 'may' in the present context. Thus it is not necessary for a Chief Constable to reasonably believe that the consequences outlined in either section 14(1)(a) or (b) will result, or that they are more likely than not, in order for him to be able to exercise the power to impose conditions on a public assembly. In that case, Bean J sought to draw a distinction between the three triggers in subsection (1)(a) which he described as being 'not fault based' and the trigger in subsection (1)(b), which was 'fault based'. In other words, the imposition of conditions under section 14(1)(a) is not dependent upon the purpose of those organising the assembly whereas in relation to section 14(1)(b), it is.

The decision in *Brehony* is of further interest for what it says about the distinction which section 14 makes between conditions imposed prospectively and those imposed at the time when an assembly is actually taking place. In the case of the former, Bean J was of the opinion that a Chief Constable[184] is under a duty to give reasons for the conditions which have been imposed. Such a duty extends beyond merely identifying the relevant trigger for imposing the condition. It entails explaining, not necessarily in any great detail, why the directions are being imposed so as to enable the demonstrators to understand the Chief Constable's thinking and, in the event of a legal challenge, for a court to determine whether his belief was reasonable.

Guidance is given in section 14 as to the nature of the conditions which may be imposed. Thus they may relate to the place at which the assembly is held, or its maximum duration, or the maximum number of persons who may attend the event.[185] In the White Paper, the government stressed that limiting the nature of the conditions capable of being imposed to those specified in section 14 was a means of ensuring that conditions 'tantamount to a ban' would not be imposed. Moreover, emphasis was placed upon the utility of section 14 where, for example, a march has been banned and a rally has been proposed as an alternative, or as a means of controlling pickets on sites where industrial disputes are taking place. With regard to pickets and other forms of assembly, it must be remembered that in addition to the statutory powers available to them, the police may also control such gatherings of people by having recourse to their power at common law for preventing breaches of the peace.[186]

There is no statutory right of appeal against a condition which has been imposed upon an assembly in the exercise of the section 14 power. However, given that the power is subject to

---

[182] *Review of Public Order Law*, Cmnd 9510 (1985), at para 5.3.   [183] [2005] EWHC 640 (Admin).
[184] By virtue of section 15(1) of the 1986 Act, the chief officer of police is able to delegate any of his functions under sections 12–14A of the Act.   [185] Section 14(1).
[186] See *Piddington v Bates* [1961] 1 WLR 162.

the requirement that the officer 'reasonably believes' that conditions are necessary in order to prevent any of the four 'triggers' from occurring (eg serious public disorder), it follows that the exercise of this power is subject to judicial review. However, challenging the legality of a section 12 or section 14 condition will only really be effective where the condition has been imposed by the Chief Constable, ie prior to the procession or assembly. Conditions imposed at the time of a procession or assembly will already have restricted individual freedom even if they are subsequently held to have been unlawful. Nevertheless, a judicial declaration to this effect may at least influence the way in which the power is exercised in the future.[187] Moreover, in the light of the Human Rights Act 1998, the courts are more likely to seek to ensure that the legitimate aim of maintaining public order is not allowed to automatically trump the rights under articles 10 (freedom of expression) and 11 (freedom of assembly) of the ECHR. Faced with a legal challenge, therefore, it will be necessary for a court to strike a balance between the rights of protestors and the rights of those who wish to go about their daily business with the minimum amount of disruption.

In practice, it is not uncommon for a notice imposing conditions on a public assembly to refer to more than one of the four 'triggers' as justification for this course of action. Thus in *Broadwith v Chief Constable of Thames Valley Police Authority*,[188] the Chief Constable imposed a number of conditions on a public assembly due to be held outside a farm where cats were bred for scientific purposes on the basis that he believed that the demonstration might result in: serious public disorder; serious damage to property; or, serious disruption to the life of the community. It is a moot point whether the holding of a public assembly could give rise to genuine concerns that all three eventualities may occur. To frame a conditions notice as broadly as this might be a way of ensuring that the decision to impose conditions is relatively review-proof.

A person charged with having knowingly failed to comply with a section 12 or section 14 condition may of course raise the alleged invalidity of the relevant condition as a defence. It is clear from the House of Lords decision in *Boddington v British Transport Police*,[189] that the general rule of procedural exclusivity established by the same court in *O'Reilly v Mackman*,[190] has not deprived a defendant of such a right. Judicial review is therefore not the only means by which the lawfulness of a section 12 or section 14 condition may be challenged. In *Police v Reid*,[191] a successful collateral challenge was made upon the validity of a condition imposed upon a group of demonstrators outside South Africa House. The Chief Inspector who verbally imposed a condition upon the assembly requiring the demonstrators to move away from the Embassy did so in the belief that it was necessary to prevent them from intimidating those who were entering the building. The defendant was charged with a section 14(5) offence where she failed to comply with the condition. The Metropolitan Stipendiary Magistrate accepted the argument that the Chief Inspector had wrongly equated intimidation with discomfort. Causing someone to feel uncomfortable was not the same as intimidating them. For the intimidation 'trigger' to be activated, it was necessary for the officer to believe that the demonstrators were acting with a view to compelling visitors not to enter South Africa House. Since the Chief Inspector had not believed this at the material time, there had been no ground for imposing the condition and therefore no offence had been committed.[192]

---

[187] Professor DGT Williams has expressed the view that: 'Review after the event can be significant as a guide for future conduct . . .': see 'Processions, Assemblies and the freedom of the individual' [1987] Crim LR 167 at 179.   [188] CO/4073/99, 22 February 2000.
[189] [1999] 2 AC 143, p. 489.   [190] [1983] 2 AC 237, p. 482.   [191] [1987] Crim LR 702.
[192] See also *DPP v Baillie* [1995] Crim LR 426.

In the later case of *DPP v Jones*,[193] where the respondent also sought to challenge the lawfulness of conditions imposed under section 14 as a defence to proceedings brought against her, the Divisional Court was required to consider, amongst other things, whether if some of the conditions in a notice were *ultra vires* they could be severed from those which were not. It was argued on behalf of the respondent that notices issued under sections 12 and 14 of the 1986 Act were unique and that any lack of clarity or any inaccuracy in them thereby rendered the entire notice invalid since it would be unfair on a demonstrator to discover months afterwards that part of the notice was valid and the other part was not. This argument was rejected by the Divisional Court:

'If a person taking part in an assembly breaches a condition which is clear and properly severable from conditions which are not valid, for my part I can see nothing unfair in him or her being prosecuted for their breach.'[194]

The test to be applied for severability was that laid down by the House of Lords in *DPP v Hutchinson*.[195] Applying that test the Divisional Court concluded that the *ultra vires* conditions were capable of being severed without invalidating the entire notice. The decision in *Jones* therefore illustrates that although the police ought to be careful when imposing conditions on public assemblies under section 14, if they do stray beyond location, duration or numbers, this will not necessarily invalidate the notice. Severance may later take place provided that a court is satisfied that the remaining portion of the notice retains its grammatical sense.

An alternative to a collateral challenge is to simply contend that a section 14 condition did not apply to the defendant. In *Broadwith*, the defendant appealed against his conviction for an offence contrary to section 14(5) of the 1986 Act. He argued, amongst other things, that the conditions imposed upon the assembly in the Chief Constable's written notice did not apply to him because he had not been present at the original assembly which moved to a different location where the assembly to which the conditions applied was held. In other words, by arriving direct, he claimed to be beyond the reach of a condition which stated that at the relevant location, 'a further assembly will be held commencing no sooner than 1.30 p.m. and finishing no later than 4 p.m.' The Divisional Court was not prepared to construe the Chief Constable's notice so narrowly. In the opinion of Rose LJ (with which Alliott J agreed):

'The circumstances of the appellant's arrival . . . in a bus, with others intent upon demonstrating in relation to this matter, the fact that he chose to cover his face, the fact that he had, immediately prior to being stopped, been in conversation with a larger group of persons whom it is conceded were in excess of 20, some distance away, all supported, as it seems to me, the Stipendiary's findings in relation to this matter.'

The appellant's second contention, that at the material time he was not part of an assembly, also received short shrift from the Divisional Court. In the opinion of Rose LJ, a group consisted of individuals and it was therefore necessary, on occasion, for the police to take action to control the movements of an individual (as in the present case) rather than the group as a whole. Although the appellant had been walking away from the group, this did not mean that he had ceased to be part of the assembly to which the Chief Constable's notice applied.

---

[193] [2002] EWHC 110 (Admin).   [194] Per Gage J at [31].
[195] [1990] 2 All ER 836. Although the test was designed for legislation and legislative instruments, both parties in *Jones* accepted that it should also be applied to the facts of the case.

'14A Prohibiting trespassory assemblies

(1) If at any time the chief officer of police reasonably believes that an assembly is intended to be held in any district at a place on land to which the public has no right of access or only a limited right of access and that the assembly—

    (a) is likely to be held without the permission of the occupier of the land or to conduct itself in such a way as to exceed the limits of any permission of his or the limits of the public's right of access, and

    (b) may result—

        (i) in serious disruption to the life of the community, or

        (ii) where the land, or a building or monument on it, is of historical, architectural, archaeological or scientific importance, in significant damage to the land, building or monument,

he may apply to the council of the district for an order prohibiting for a specified period the holding of all trespassory assemblies in the district or a part of it, as specified.

(2) On receiving such an application, a council may—

    (a) in England and Wales, with the consent of the Secretary of State make an order either in the terms of the application or with such modifications as may be approved by the Secretary of State; or

    (b) in Scotland, make an order in the terms of the application.

(3) Subsection (1) does not apply in the City of London or the metropolitan police district.

(4) If at any time the Commissioner of Police for the City of London or the Commissioner of Police of the Metropolis reasonably believes that an assembly is intended to be held at a place on land to which the public has no right of access or only a limited right of access in his police area and that the assembly—

    (a) is likely to be held without the permission of the occupier of the land or to conduct itself in such a way as to exceed the limits of any permission of his or the limits of the public's right of access, and

    (b) may result—

        (i) in serious disruption to the life of the community, or

        (ii) where the land, or a building or monument on it, is of historical, architectural, archaeological or scientific importance, in significant damage to the land, building or monument,

he may with the consent of the Secretary of State make an order prohibiting for a specified period the holding of all trespassory assemblies in this area or a part of it, as specified.

(5) An order prohibiting the holding of trespassory assemblies operates to prohibit any assembly which—

    (a) is held on land to which the public has no right of access or only a limited right of access, and

    (b) takes place in the prohibited circumstances, that is to say, without the permission of the occupier of the land or so as to exceed the limits of any permission of his or the limits of the public's rights of access.

(6) No order under this section shall prohibit the holding of assemblies for a period exceeding 4 days or in an area exceeding an area represented by a circle with a radius of 5 miles from a specified centre.

(7) An order made under this section may be revoked or varied by a subsequent order made in the same way, that is, in accordance with subsection (1) and (2) or subsection (4), as the case may be.

(8) Any order under this section shall, if not made in writing, be recorded in writing as soon as practicable after being made.

(9) In this section and sections 14B and 14C—

"assembly" means an assembly of 20 or more persons;

"land", means land in the open air;

"limited", in relation to a right of access by the public to land, means that their use of it is restricted to use for a particular purpose (as in the case of a highway or road) or is subject to other restrictions;

"occupier" means—

(a) in England and Wales, the person entitled to possession of the land by virtue of an estate or interest held by him; or

(b) in Scotland, the person lawfully entitled to natural possession of the land,

and in subsection (1) and (4) includes the person reasonably believed by the authority applying for or making the order to be the occupier;

"public" includes a section of the public; and

"specified" means specified in an order under this section.

(10), (11) . . .

14B Offences in connection with trespassory assemblies and arrest therefor

(1) A person who organises an assembly the holding of which he knows is prohibited by an order under section 14A is guilty of an offence.

(2) A person who takes part in an assembly which he knows is prohibited by an order under section 14A is guilty of an offence.

(3) In England and Wales, a person who incites another to commit an offence under subsection (2) is guilty of an offence.

(4) . . .[196]

(5)–(8) . . .

14C Stopping persons from proceeding to trespassory assemblies

(1) If a constable in uniform reasonably believes that a person is on his way to an assembly within the area to which an order under section 14A applies which the constable reasonably believes is likely to be an assembly which is prohibited by that order, he may, subject to subsection (2) below—

(a) stop that person, and

(b) direct him not to proceed in the direction of the assembly.

(2) The power conferred by subsection (1) may only be exercised within the area to which the order applies.

(3) A person who fails to comply with a direction under subsection (1) which he knows has been given to him is guilty of an offence.

(4) . . .[197]

(5) A person guilty of an offence under subsection (3) is liable on summary conviction to a fine not exceeding level 3 on the standard scale.'

These sections were inserted into the Public Order Act 1986 by sections 70 and 71 of the Criminal Justice and Public Order Act 1994. They are important statutory provisions in the

---

[196] This subsection, which provided for a power of arrest, was repealed by sections 111 and 174(2), and Schedule 7 to the Serious Organised Crime and Police Act 2005.

[197] This subsection, which provided for a power of arrest, was repealed by sections 111 and 174(2), and Schedule 7 to the Serious Organised Crime and Police Act 2005.

context of the civil liberties of the individual. Section 14A confers upon the police the right to apply to a council for the issue of an order banning a trespassory assembly. In many respects, therefore, section 14A is similar to section 13 of the 1986 Act which relates to public processions. It was noted above that the government rejected submissions that a power to impose bans on assemblies ought to be provided for in the 1986 Act on the basis that it would constitute an unwarranted incursion into freedom of speech. However, no such concerns arose in relation to trespassory assemblies which, unlike public assemblies, are prima facie unlawful. Accordingly, a power to impose conditions on this type of assembly was not required. Interestingly, the concept of a 'trespassory assembly' is not expressly defined in the provisions, but by reading section 14A(1)(a) in conjunction with subsection(9) of the same section, its nature becomes apparent.

In *R v Tunbridge Wells Borough Council & another, ex p The Gypsy Council for Education, Culture, Welfare and Civil Rights and another*,[198] the applicants sought judicial review of a decision by the Borough Council to make an order under section 14A in respect of the Horsmonden Horse Fair, an annual event held on the Horsmonden Village Green in Kent. The Chief Constable for Kent had sought the order on the basis that he reasonably believed that were the fair to take place, it would result in serious disruption to the life of the community.[199] His justification for this belief was that fairs held in previous years had involved, amongst other things: incidents between feuding groups of travellers; the racing of horses on the highway; the illegal and indiscriminate parking of vehicles; concerns over public health due to poor hygiene etc.; necessary road closures; fear expressed by residents; and a background level of increased crime. The order itself was to prohibit the holding of all trespassory assemblies in the area for a period of four days. Sitting as a Deputy High Court Judge, David Pannick QC dismissed the application. In his opinion, the concerns of the Chief Constable did amount to a reasonable belief that the fair might result in serious disruption to the life of the community. Moreover, he also drew attention to the fact that the adverse impact of the order on the Romany community was lessened by the existence of an alternative venue for the fair some 20 miles distant which had the support of both the local authority and the public.

Section 14B also borrows from section 13 in that it makes it an offence to: organise a prohibited trespassory assembly; or take part in such an assembly; or incite another to take part in a trespassory assembly. In an important case, the House of Lords overturned an earlier ruling by the Divisional Court that the offence of taking part in a trespassory assembly was committed where the respondent had taken part in a peaceful, non-obstructive and static demonstration on part of the public highway which was the subject of a section 14A order.

....

Director of Public Prosecutions v Jones and another [1999] 2 AC 240

An order had been made under section 14A(2) of the Public Order Act 1986 prohibiting the holding of trespassory assemblies within a four mile radius of Stonehenge between 29 May and 1 June inclusive. On 1 June 1995, a number of persons gathered on a grass verge on the roadside adjacent to the perimeter fence. The police took the view that they numbered more than twenty persons and that they were therefore a trespassory assembly within the meaning of the Act. They informed the gathering of their belief that they fell within the scope of the order and asked them to disperse. The group refused to disperse and the appellants were arrested and charged with offences contrary to section 14B(2) of the 1986 Act. They were convicted by magistrates. On appeal to the Crown Court, their convictions

[198] (Unreported), 7 September 2000.   [199] Section 14A(1)(b)(i).

were quashed on the basis that they had not exceeded the public's limited right of access to the highway. The DPP's appeal against that decision was upheld by the Divisional Court.[200] The appellants convictions were therefore restored. They appealed to the House of Lords. By a majority of three to two (Lords Slynn and Hope dissenting), the House of Lords concluded that a peaceful, non-obstructive assembly of more than twenty persons did not exceed the public's right of user so as to constitute a trespassory assembly within the terms of section 14A of the 1986 Act.

Lord Irvine LC, at 254–258

'The question to which this appeal gives rise is whether the law today should recognise that the public highway is a public place, on which all manner of reasonable activities may go on. For the reasons I set out below in my judgment it should. Provided these activities are reasonable, do not involve the commission of a public or private nuisance, and do not amount to an obstruction of the highway unreasonably impeding the primary right of the general public to pass and repass, they should not construe a trespass. Subject to these qualifications, therefore, there would be a public right of peaceful assembly on the public highway.'

[Lord Irvine then went on to consider the decision of the Court of Appeal in *Hickman v Maisey* [1900] 1 QB 752. He continued:]

'I do not, therefore, accept that, to be lawful, activities on the highway must fall within a rubric incidental or ancillary to the exercise of the right of passage. The meaning of Lord Esher's judgment in *Harrison's* case [1893] 1 QB 142 at 146–147, [1891–4] All ER Rep 514 at 517 is clear: it is not that a person may use the highway only for passage and repassage and acts incidental or ancillary thereto; it is that any "reasonable and usual" mode of using the highway is lawful, provided it is not inconsistent with the general public's right of passage. I understand Collins LJ's acceptance in *Hickman v Maisey* [1900] 1 QB 752 at 757–758, of Lord Esher's judgment in *Harrison's* case in that sense.

   To commence from a premise, that the right of passage is the only right which members of the public are entitled to exercise on a highway, is circular: the very question in this appeal is whether the public's right is confined to the right of passage. I conclude that the judgments of Lord Esher MR and Collins LJ are authority for the proposition that the public have the right to use the public highway for such reasonable and usual activities as are consistent with the general public's primary right to use the highway for purposes of passage and repassage.

   Nor can I attribute any hard core of meaning to a test which would limit lawful use of the highway to what is incidental or ancillary to the right of passage. In truth very little activity could accurately be described as "ancillary" to passing along the highway; perhaps stopping to tie one's shoe lace, consulting a street-map, or pausing to catch one's breath. But I do not think that such ordinary and usual activities as making a sketch, taking a photograph, handing out leaflets, collecting money for charity, singing carols, playing in a Salvation Army band, children playing a game on the pavement, having a picnic, or reading a book, would qualify. These examples illustrate that to limit lawful use of the highway to that which is literally "incidental or ancillary" to the right of passage would be to place an unrealistic and unwarranted restriction on commonplace day-to-day activities. The law should not make unlawful what is commonplace and well accepted.

   Nor do I accept that the broader modern test which I favour materially realigns the interests of the general public and landowners. It is no more than an exposition of the test Lord Esher proposed in 1892. It would not permit unreasonable use of the highway, nor use which was obstructive. It would not, therefore, afford carte blanche to squatters or other uninvited visitors. Their activities would almost certainly be unreasonable or obstructive or both. Moreover the test of reasonableness would be strictly applied where narrow highways across private land are concerned, for example, narrow footpaths or bridle paths, where even a small gathering would be likely to create an obstruction or a nuisance.

[200] [1997] 2 All ER 119.

Nor do I accept that the "reasonable user" test is tantamount to the assertion of a right to remain, which right can be acquired by express grant, but not by user or dedication. That recognition, however, is in no way inconsistent with the "reasonable user" test. If the right to use the highway extends to reasonable user not inconsistent with the public's right of passage, then the law does recognise (and has, at least since Lord Esher MR's judgment in *Harrison*'s case, recognised) that the right to use the highway goes beyond the minimal right to pass and repass. That user may in fact extend, to a limited extent, to roaming about on the highway, or remaining on the highway. But that is not of the essence of the right. That is no more than the scope which the right might in certain circumstances have, but always depending on the facts of the particular case. On a narrow footpath, for example, the right to use the highway would be highly unlikely to extend to remain, since that would almost inevitably be inconsistent with the public's primary right to pass and repass.'

[Lord Irvine then went on to consider how a highway may be created by the common law doctrine of dedication, and how the common law might impose constraints on the public's right of user of the highway. He continued:]

'I conclude therefore the law to be that the public highway is a public place which the public may enjoy for any reasonable purpose, provided the activity in question does not amount to a public or private nuisance and does not obstruct the highway by unreasonably impeding the primary right of the public to pass and repass; within these qualifications there is a public right of peaceful assembly on the highway.

Since the law confers this public right, I deprecate any attempt artificially to restrict its scope. It must be for the magistrates in every case to decide whether the user of the highway under consideration is both reasonable in the sense defined and not inconsistent with the primary right of the public to pass and repass. In particular, there can be no principled basis for limiting the scope of the right by reference to the subjective intentions of the persons assembling. Once the right to assemble within the limitations I have defined is accepted, it is self-evident that it cannot be excluded by an intention to exercise it. Provided an assembly is reasonable and non-obstructive, taking into account its size, duration and the nature of the highway on which it takes place, it is irrelevant whether it is premeditated or spontaneous; what matters is its objective nature. To draw a distinction on the basis of anterior intention is in substance to reintroduce an incidentality requirement. For the reasons I have given, that requirement, properly applied, would make unlawful commonplace activities which are well accepted. Equally, to stipulate in the abstract any maximum size or duration for a lawful assembly would be an unwarranted restriction on the right defined. These judgments are ever ones of fact and degree for the court of trial.

Further, there can be no basis for distinguishing highways on publicly owned land and privately owned land. The nature of the public's right of use of the highway cannot depend upon whether the owner of the sub-soil is a private landowner or a public authority. Any fear, however, that the rights of private landowners might be prejudiced by the right as defined, are unfounded. The law of trespass will continue to protect private landowners against unreasonably large, unreasonably prolonged or unreasonably obstructive assemblies upon these highways.

Finally, I regard the conclusion at which I have arrived as desirable, because it promotes the harmonious development of two separate but related chapters in the common law. It is neither desirable in theory nor acceptable in practice for commonplace activities on the public highway not to count as breaches of the criminal law of wilful obstruction of the highway, yet to count as trespasses (even if intrinsically unlikely to be acted against in the civil law), and therefore form the basis of a finding of trespassory assembly for the purposes of the 1986 Act. A system of law sanctioning these discordant outcomes would not command respect.'

Lord Slynn (dissenting), at 263–265

'The right of assembly, of demonstration, is of great importance, but in English law it is not an absolute right which requires all limitations on other rights to be set aside or ignored . . .

On existing authority, I consider that the law is clear. The right [of user of the highway] is restricted to passage and reasonable incidental uses associated with passage.

It seemed to be suggested or at least implicit in argument that demonstrations and assemblies are a new development of the late twentieth century and cannot have been in the mind of judges when they defined the law in the nineteenth century. . . [T]his is plainly wrong as the two Trafalgar Square cases [*R v Graham* (1888) 16 Cox CC 420 and *Ex p Lewis* (1888) 21 QBD 191] (and nineteenth century contemporary conditions) show, even though the extent, nature, size and object of such demonstrations and assemblies have changed. I am willing to assume that more people are now more conscious of the importance of assembly and demonstration than they were in previous centuries, but I do not see that this, in itself, is enough to justify changing the nature and scope of the public's right to use the highway. That it cannot in itself justify as of right assemblies or demonstrations on private land is obvious. The defendants' argument in effect involves giving to members of the public the right to wander over or to stay on land for such a period and in such numbers as they choose so long as they are peaceable, not obstructive, and not committing a nuisance. It is a contention which goes far beyond anything which can be described as incidental or ancillary to the use of a highway as such for the purposes of passage; nor does such an extensive use in my view constitute a reasonable, normal or usual use of the highway as a highway. If the defendants' claim is right, it seems to me to follow that other uses of the highway than assembly would be permitted—squatting, putting up a tent, selling and buying food or drinks—so long as they did not amount to an obstruction or a nuisance. To get over the fence from adjoining land (as could have happened here) and to sit or stand on the highway, including the verge, in order to demonstrate does not seem to me to be a normal or usual use of the highway as such and has nothing to do with passing and repassing.

The fact that the purpose of the demonstration or assembly is one which most or many people would approve does not change what is otherwise a trespass into a legal right. Nor does the fact that an assembly is peaceful or unlikely to result in violence, or that it is not causing an obstruction at the particular time when the police intervene, in itself change what is otherwise a trespass into a legal right of access.

It is objected that very often people on the highway singly or in groups take part in activities which go beyond passage and repassage and are not stopped. That is no doubt so, but reasonable tolerance does not create a new right to use the highway and indeed may make it unnecessary to create such a right which in its wider definition goes far beyond what is justified or needed. It may well be that in the situation with which your Lordships are concerned that, but for section 14 of the 1986 Act, nothing would have been done to a peaceful non-obstructive group like the one in which the defendants took part. But Parliament in 1994 has enabled action over and above existing remedies to deal with trespass on the highway, or on land for entry on which the landowner's permission is required, to be taken to deal with what was seen as a growing problem. If Parliament wants to take away that form of control, it can obviously do so. I do not consider that disapproval of this power justifies a change in the law as to the public's rights over the highway, which is what at times seems to be one of the bases of the defendants' arguments.'

Lord Clyde, at 279–281

'The fundamental purpose for which roads have been accepted to be used is the purpose of travel, that is to say passing and repassing along it. But it has also been recognised that the use comprises more than the mere movement of persons or vehicles along the highway. The right to use a highway includes the doing of certain other things subsidiary to the user for passage. It is within the scope of the right that the traveller may stop for a while at some point along the way. If he wishes to refresh himself, or if there is some particular association with the place which he wishes to keep alive, his presence on the road for that purpose is within the scope of the acceptable user of the road . . . .'

[Lord Clyde then briefly considered the decisions in *Hickman v Maisey* and *Harrison v Duke of Rutland* before he continued as follows:]

'But it must immediately be noticed that the public's right is fenced with limitations affecting both the extent and the nature of the user. So far as the extent is concerned the user may not extend beyond the physical limits of the highway. That may often include the verges. It may also include a lay-by. Moreover, the law does not recognise any jus spatiendi which would entitle a member of the public simply to wander about the road, far less beyond its limits, at will. Further, the public has no jus manendi on a highway, so that any stopping and standing must be reasonably limited in time. While the right may extend to a picnic on the verge, it would not extend to camping there.

So far as the manner of the exercise of the right is concerned, any use of the highway must not be so conducted as to interfere unreasonably with the lawful use by other members of the public for passage along it. The fundamental element in the right is the use of the highway for undisturbed travel. Certain forms of behaviour may of course constitute criminal actings in themselves, such as a breach of the peace. But the necessity also is that travel by the public should not be obstructed. The use of the highway for passage is reflected in all the limitations, whether on extent, purpose or manner. While the right to use the highway comprises activities within those limits, those activities are subsidiary to the use for passage, and they must be not only usual and reasonable but consistent with that use even if they are not strictly ancillary to it. As was pointed out in M'Ara v Edinburgh Magistrates 1913 SC 1059 and in Aldred v Miller 1924 JC 117, the use of a public street for free unrestricted passage is the most important of all the public uses to which public streets are legally dedicated. No issue regarding the nature of the user arises in the present case. It appears that everyone was behaving with courtesy and civility and restraint. Moreover there was no obstruction at all to any traffic.

In the generality there is no doubt that there is a public right of assembly. But there are restrictions on the exercise of that right in the public interest. There are limitations at common law and there are express limitations laid down in art 11 of the European Convention for the Protection of Human Rights and Fundamental Freedoms (Rome, 4 November 1950; TS 71 (1953); Cmnd 8969). I would not be prepared to affirm, as a matter of generality, that there is a right of assembly on any place on a highway at any time and in any event I am not persuaded that the present case has to be decided by reference to public rights of assembly. If a group of people stand in the street to sing hymns or Christmas carols they are in my view using the street within the legitimate scope of the public right of access to it, provided of course that they do so for a reasonable period and without any unreasonable obstruction to traffic. If there are shops in the street and people gather to stand and view a shop window, or form a queue to enter the shop, that is within the normal and reasonable use which is matter of public right. A road may properly be used for the purposes of a procession. It would still be a perfectly proper use of the road if the procession was intended to serve some particular purpose, such as commemorating some particular event or achievement. And if an individual may properly stop at a point on the road for any lawful purpose, so too should a group of people be entitled to do so. All such activities seem to me to be subsidiary to the use for passage. So I have no difficulty in holding that in principle a gathering of people at the side of a highway within the limits of the restraints which I have noted may be within the scope of the public's right of access to the highway.

In my view the argument for the defendants, and indeed the reasoning of the Crown Court, went further than it needed to go in suggesting that any reasonable use of the highway, provided that it was peaceful and not obstructive, was lawful, and so a matter of public right. Such an approach opens a door of uncertain dimensions into an ill-defined area of uses which might erode the basic predominance of the essential use of a highway as a highway. I do not consider that by using the language which it used Parliament intended to include some distinct right in addition to the right to use the road for the purpose of passage.

I am not persuaded that in any case where there is a peaceful non-obstructive assembly it will necessarily exceed the public's right of access to the highway. The question then is, as in this kind of case it may often turn out to be, whether on the facts here the limit was passed and the exceeding of it established. The test then is not one which can be defined in general terms but has to depend upon the circumstances as a matter of degree. It requires a careful assessment of the nature and extent of the activity in question. If the purpose of the activity becomes the predominant purpose of the occupation of the highway, or if the occupation becomes more than reasonably transitional in terms of either time or space, then it may come to exceed the right to use the highway.'

Section 14C confers a power upon the police to stop persons whom it is reasonably believed are on their way to attend a trespassory assembly. This provision therefore shares a common characteristic with section 65 of the Criminal Justice and Public Order Act which gives the police a similar power in relation to raves.

VI. Public Processions (Northern Ireland) Act 1998

Given that there is a 'marching season' in Northern Ireland when members of the Protestant and Catholic communities march to commemorate events in their respective histories, and that these marches often lead to confrontation and a threat to the maintenance of public order, it is no surprise that Parliament has from time to time made special legislative provision for this part of the UK. The most recent legislative initiative has been the Public Processions (Northern Ireland) Act 1998[201] which, amongst other things, provides for the establishment of a Parades Commission.[202] The duties of the Commission include promoting greater understanding by the general public of issues concerning 'public processions' (defined by the Act as being a procession in a public place whether or not involving the use of vehicles or other conveyances)[203] and promoting and facilitating mediation as a way of resolving disputes relating to public processions.[204] The organisers of public processions in Northern Ireland are also subject to the requirement to give advance written notice to the police of their intentions.[205] However, unlike the six-day requirement under the Public Order Act 1986 (POA), the notice must be given at least twenty-eight days before the date of the procession or, if that is not reasonably practicable, as soon as it is reasonably practicable to give such notice.[206]

The information to be given by the organiser is broadly similar to that which is required under the POA. However, the particular circumstances of Northern Ireland are reflected in the requirement that the names of any bands which are to take part in the procession must be specified.[207] Moreover, the organiser must also specify the arrangements which he or she has made for the control of the procession.[208] The potential for confrontation and disorder is further addressed within the Act by the requirement that those who wish to organise a protest meeting in respect of a public procession must also give the police advance written notice (14 days) of their intention to hold such a meeting.[209] For the purposes of the Act, a 'protest

---

[201] As amended by the Public Processions (Amendment) (Northern Ireland) Order 2005, SI 2005/857 (NI 2).
[202] Section 1 and Schedule 1. A legal challenge to the way in which several members of the Commission were appointed and the final composition of the Commission, which was claimed to be unrepresentative of the community, was rejected in *Re White's Application for Judicial Review* [2000] NI 432.   [203] Section 17(2).
[204] Section 2.   [205] Section 6.   [206] Section 6(2)(a) and (b).
[207] Section 12 of the Act provides for the registration of such bands.
[208] Section 6(4)(d) and (e).   [209] Section 7.

meeting' is an open air public meeting (within the meaning of the Public Order (Northern Ireland) Order 1987):

'(a) which is, or is to be, held—

  (i) at a place which is on or in the vicinity of the route or proposed route of a public procession; and

  (ii) at or about the same time as the procession is being or is to be held; and

(b) the purpose (or one of the purposes) of which is to demonstrate opposition to the holding of that procession on that route or proposed route.'[210]

Originally the Parades Commission had the power to impose such conditions on a public procession as it considered necessary.[211] Additionally it now has a corresponding power to impose conditions on a protest meeting.[212] Conditions imposed on a public procession may therefore relate to matters such as the route of the procession or, they may prohibit it from entering any place. In considering whether or not to impose conditions, the Commission is required to have regard to a set of guidelines which it will itself have issued in respect of its functions under section 8.[213] In addition to the 'triggers' for imposing conditions under the POA (see p. 675), the Commission must have regard to matters such as: any impact which the procession may have on relationships within the community; and the desirability of allowing a procession customarily held along a particular route to be held along that route.[214] An exercise of the power to impose conditions is subject to the judicial review jurisdiction of the courts.[215]

Although the Parades Commission can impose conditions on public processions and protest meetings, it does not have the power to prohibit public processions in Northern Ireland. This power belongs to the Secretary of State.[216] It is exercisable where it is necessary in the public interest to prohibit a procession, having regard to factors such as: serious public disorder or serious damage; any serious impact which the procession may have on relationships within the community; and any undue demands which the procession may cause to be made on the police or military forces. The same factors will also be taken into account where the Secretary of State is of the opinion that it is necessary in the public interest to prohibit all processions of a particular class in an area or all processions generally in that area.[217] Where a prohibition order is made under section 11(2) or (3), it shall not last for more than twenty-eight days. Moreover, any procession or class of procession may be exempted from the scope of either order.[218]

Like the POA, the Public Processions (Northern Ireland) Act 1998 creates various offences. Thus, for example, it is an offence to organise or take part in a public procession which has not satisfied the written notice requirement or which does not comply with matters specified in the notice, such as the route.[219] Corresponding offences may be committed in respect of protest meetings.[220] It is also an offence to organise or take part in a public procession which has been prohibited under section 11.[221] Section 14 of the 1998 Act is concerned with behaviour the

[210] Section 17(1).   [211] Section 8.

[212] See section 9A as inserted by article 4(1) of the Public Processions (Amendment) (Northern Ireland) Order 2005.   [213] See section 5 and section 8(5).

[214] Section 8(6)(c) and (e).

[215] In Re Tweed's Application for Judicial Review [2001] NI 165, the court rejected a legal challenge to a condition imposed under the authority of section 8 of the 1998 Act which prevented an Orange Order parade from entering a specified village. In the judgment of the court, the condition was in accordance with article 11(2) of the ECHR in that it had been imposed to deal with the risk of public disorder.

[216] Section 11.   [217] Section 11(2) and (3).   [218] Section 11(4).

[219] Section 6(7)(a) and (b).   [220] Section 7(6)(a) and (b).   [221] Section 11(8).

purpose of which is to prevent or hinder lawful public processions from taking place or to annoy persons participating in such processions. The actus reus of the offence is committed where D:

'(a) hinders, molests or obstructs those persons or any of them;

(b) acts in a disorderly way towards those persons or any of them; or

(c) behaves offensively and abusively towards those persons or any of them.'[222]

Two further aspects of the 1998 Act need to be noted. First, the common law powers of the police to deal with an actual or apprehended breach of the peace are expressly preserved by the Act.[223] Secondly, a power of arrest without warrant is conferred upon a police officer where he reasonably suspects that an offence has been committed under the Act.[224]

VII. Protection from Harassment Act 1997

(a) Background

This Act, as its short title implies, was passed in order to protect persons from harassment and similar conduct. During the course of its second reading, the then Home Secretary, Michael Howard MP, observed that the impetus for reform had been 'a number of highly publicised stalking cases' which had come to public attention during the course of 1996. Moreover, the House of Commons was informed that the Bill would not only give the courts more effective powers to deal with stalkers, but that it would also apply to 'disruptive neighbours and those who target people because of the colour of their skin'.[225]

(b) The offences

'1 Prohibition of harassment

(1) A person must not pursue a course of conduct—

    (a) which amounts to harassment of another, and

    (b) which he knows or ought to know amounts to harassment of the other.

  [(1A) A person must not pursue a course of conduct—

    (a) which involves harassment of two or more persons, and

    (b) which he knows or ought to know involves harassment of those persons, and

    (c) by which he intends to persuade any person (whether or not one of those mentioned above)—

      (i) not to do something that he is entitled or required to do, or

      (ii) to do something that he is not under any obligation to do.][226]

---

[222] Section 14(1).   [223] Section 10.   [224] Section 15.

[225] HC Vol 287, col 781, 17 December 1996. In *Majrowski v Guy's and St Thomas's NHS Trust* [2006] 3 WLR 125, Lord Nicholls commented that: 'The Act seeks to provide protection against stalkers, racial abusers, disruptive neighbours, bullying at work and so forth' (at [18]).

[226] This subsection was inserted by section 125(1) and (2)(a) of the Serious Organised Crime and Police Act 2005.

(2) For the purposes of this section, the person whose course of conduct is in question ought to know that it amounts to [or involves] harassment of another if a reasonable person in possession of the same information would think the course of conduct amounted to [or involved] harassment of the other.[227]

(3) Subsection (1) [or (1A)][228] does not apply to a course of conduct if the person who pursued it shows—

    (a) that it was pursued for the purpose of preventing or detecting crime,

    (b) that it was pursued under any enactment or rule of law or to comply with any condition or requirement imposed by any person under any enactment, or

    (c) that in the particular circumstances the pursuit of the course of conduct was reasonable.

2 Offence of harassment

(1) A person who pursues a course of conduct in breach of [section 1(1) or (1A)][229] is guilty of an offence.

(2) A person guilty of an offence under this section is liable on summary conviction to imprisonment for a term not exceeding six months, or a fine not exceeding level 5 on the standard scale, or both.

(3) . . .

4 Putting people in fear of violence

(1) A person whose course of conduct causes another to fear, on at least two occasions, that violence will be used against him is guilty of an offence if he knows or ought to know that his course of conduct will cause the other so to fear on each of those occasions.

(2) For the purposes of this section, the person whose course of conduct is in question ought to know that it will cause another to fear that violence will be used against him on any occasion if a reasonable person in possession of the same information would think the course of conduct would cause the other so to fear on that occasion.

(3) It is a defence for a person charged with an offence under this section to show that—

    (a) his course of conduct was pursued for the purpose of preventing or detecting crime,

    (b) his course of conduct was pursued under any enactment or rule of law or to comply with any condition or requirement imposed by any person under any enactment, or

    (c) the pursuit of his course of conduct was reasonable for the protection of himself or another or for the protection of his or another's property.

(4) A person guilty of an offence under this section is liable—

    (a) on conviction on indictment, to imprisonment for a term not exceeding five years, or a fine, or both, or

    (b) on summary conviction, to imprisonment for a term not exceeding six months, or a fine not exceeding the statutory maximum, or both.

(5) If on the trial on indictment of a person charged with an offence under this section the jury find him not guilty of the offence charged, they may find him guilty of an offence under section 2.

---

[227] The words in square brackets were inserted by section 125(1) and (2)(b) of the 2005 Act.
[228] The words in square brackets were inserted by section 125(1) and (2)(c) of the 2005 Act.
[229] The words in square brackets were inserted by section 125(1) and (3) of the 2005 Act.

(6) The Crown Court has the same powers and duties in relation to a person who is by virtue of subsection (5) convicted before it of an offence under section 2 as a magistrates' court would have on convicting him of the offence.

. . .

7 Interpretation of this group of sections

(1) This section applies for the interpretation of sections 1 to 5.

(2) References to harassing a person include alarming the person or causing the person distress.

[(3) A "course of conduct" must involve—

    (a) in the case of conduct in relation to a single person (see section 1(1)), conduct on at least two occasions in relation to that person, or

    (b) in the case of conduct in relation to two or more persons (see section 1(1A)), conduct on at least one occasion in relation to each of those persons.][230]

[(3A) A person's conduct on any occasion shall be taken, if aided, abetted, counselled or procured by another—

    (a) to be conduct on that occasion of the other (as well as conduct of the person whose conduct it is); and

    (b) to be conduct in relation to which the other's knowledge and purpose, and what he ought to have known, are the same as they were in relation to what was contemplated or reasonably foreseeable at the time of the aiding, abetting, counselling or procuring.][231]

(4) "Conduct" includes speech.

[(5) References to a person, in the context of the harassment of a person, are references to a person who is an individual.]'[232]

Section 1(1) of the Act imposes a prohibition on a person pursuing a 'course of conduct' which amounts to harassment of another and which he knows or ought to know amounts to harassment of that other. For the purposes of sections 1–5 of the Act, 'harassment' includes alarming a person or causing them distress.[233] There are clear parallels, therefore, between this provision and sections 4 and 5 of the Public Order Act 1986.

A person is taken to know that his course of conduct amounts to or involves the harassment of another 'if a reasonable person in possession of the same information would think that the course of conduct amounted to harassment of the other'.[234] It will be noted, therefore, that intention is not an ingredient of the offence. The prosecution do not need to prove that D intended to harass another; it is enough that he knew or ought to have known that his conduct would have that effect.[235] Thus in *Majrowski v Guy's and St Thomas's NHS Trust*,[236] Baroness Hale observed:

'If prevention and protection were the aim [of the 1997 Act], it is also easy to see why the mental element was framed as it was . . . There is no requirement that harm, or even alarm or distress, be

---

[230] This subsection was substituted by section 125(1) and (7)(a) of the Serious Organised Crime and Police Act 2005.

[231] This subsection was inserted by section 44 of the Criminal Justice and Police Act 2001.

[232] This subsection was inserted by section 125(1) and (7)(b) of the Serious Organised Crime and Police Act 2005.

[233] Section 7(2).

[234] Section 1(2).

[235] The stalker whose mental illness precludes him from appreciating the import of his conduct would therefore fall within the scope of the Act: see Finch, 'Stalking the perfect stalking law: an evaluation of the efficacy of the Protection from Harassment Act 1997' [2002] Crim LR 702 at 710.

[236] [2006] 3 WLR 125. See further p. 699.

actually foreseeable, although in most cases it would be. This broad formulation helps the courts to intervene to warn the perpetrator and encourage him to mend his ways.'[237]

In the 1997 Act as originally enacted, a 'course of conduct' was stated to involve conduct on at least two occasions. This definition still applies where the conduct is in relation to a single individual. Thus isolated one-off incidents do not fall within the scope of section 1(1), though they may amount to offences under the Public Order Act 1986. Now, however, as a consequence of an amendment made by the Serious Organised Crime and Police Act 2005, a 'course of conduct' may also involve conduct on one occasion provided that the conduct is in relation to two or more persons.[238]

'Conduct' itself may involve a variety of things such as a threat, a slap, following a person, sending abusive letters or making abusive telephone calls. It is possible, therefore, that the harassment offence may be committed by a person who is already serving a prison sentence for a similar or unconnected offence. In *Thomas v News Group Newspapers Ltd*,[239] Lord Phillips MR stated:

'Section 7 of the 1997 Act does not purport to provide a comprehensive definition of harassment. There are many actions that foreseeably alarm or cause a person distress that could not possibly be described as harassment. It seems to me that section 7 is dealing with that element of the offence which is constituted by the effect of the conduct rather than with the types of conduct that produce that effect. The Act does not attempt to define the type of conduct that is capable of constituting harassment. "Harassment" is, however, a word which has a meaning which is generally understood. It describes conduct targeted at an individual which is calculated to produce the consequences described in section 7 and which is oppressive and unreasonable.'[240]

Similarly in the later case of *Majrowski*, Baroness Hale commented:

'All sorts of conduct may amount to harassment. It includes alarming a person or causing her distress: section 7(2). But conduct might be harassment even if no alarm or distress were in fact caused. A great deal is left to the wisdom of the courts to draw sensible lines between the ordinary banter and badinage of life and genuinely offensive and unacceptable behaviour.'[241]

The Act is silent as to whether there must be temporal proximity between the incidents which collectively constitute a 'course of conduct' for the purposes of section 1(1). This begs the question whether incidents separated by a number of days, months or even years may amount to a course of conduct for the purposes of the Act. In *Lau v DPP*,[242] where the appellant had slapped his girlfriend across the face and had also, some four months later, threatened her new boyfriend in her presence, the Queen's Bench Division quashed his conviction for an offence contrary to section 2(1) of the 1997 Act on the basis that this did not amount to the necessary course of conduct. In the words of Schiemann LJ (with whom Silber J agreed):

'I fully accept that the incidents which need to be proved in relation to harassment need not exceed two incidents, but, as it seems to me, the fewer occasions and the wider they are spread the less likely it would be that a finding of harassment can reasonably be made. One can conceive of circumstances where incidents, as far apart as a year, could constitute a course of conduct and harassment. In argument Mr Laddie [counsel for the appellant] put the context of racial harassment taking place outside a synagogue on a religious holiday, such as the day of atonement, and being repeated each year as the day of atonement came round. Another example might be a threat to do something once a year on a person's birthday. Nonetheless the broad position must be that if one is left with only two

---

[237] At [67].   [238] Section 1(1A).   [239] *The Times*, 25 July 2001.   [240] At [29]–[30].
[241] [2006] 3 WLR 125 at [66].   [242] [2000] Crim LR 799.

incidents you have to see whether what happened on those two occasions can be described as a course of conduct.'

In *Baron v Crown Prosecution Service*,[243] the course of conduct in question amounted to the sending of two letters to a Benefits Agency employee by a person who was in dispute with the Agency. In one of the letters, the appellant referred to previous legal proceedings for an offence contrary to the Malicious Communications Act 1988 in which he had personally cross-examined the victim who was a work colleague of the recipient of the letters. The time interval between receipt of the letters was four and a half months. Nevertheless, on appeal, the Divisional Court upheld the appellant's conviction for an offence contrary to section 2(1) of the 1997 Act. In the judgment of Morison J:

'. . . it is plain . . . that a line must be drawn between legitimate expression of disgust at the way a public agency has behaved and conduct amounting to harassment. The right to free speech requires a broad degree of tolerance in relation to communications. It is a legitimate exercise of that right to say things which are unpleasant or possibly hurtful to the recipient. Persons in the public service, in my view, are used to rudeness, aggression and unpleasantness of every form and the courts are likely in my judgment to expect of them a degree of robustness and fortitude beyond that which other members of the public may be expected to show . . . [B]ut if the line is crossed an offence will have been committed because there is, in my judgment, a limit to that which it is lawful to say in written communications.'

There are clear echoes here of the sentiments expressed by Glidewell LJ in *DPP v Orum*,[244] where it was necessary to consider whether a police officer could be the victim of an offence contrary to section 5(1) of the Public Order Act 1986. In *Baron*, Morison J went on to observe that citizens are entitled to use the courts to resolve disputes which may arise, and to conduct proceedings in a forceful manner. However, he continued:

'On the other hand, if proceedings are being used for an ulterior purpose, namely not to air legitimate grievances but to cause distress to those involved in the process, then the line may be crossed and the acts may become unlawful under the Protection from Harassment Act 1997.'

Although the cases referred to thus far reflect harassment which did not really impinge upon public order, harassment can occur in this context. Persons who protest outside the home of a person who, for example, runs a mink farm or who is believed to be a paedophile, may commit offences contrary to the 1997 Act as a consequence of their actions. Where protesters have been charged with harassment, they may seek to rely upon the defence provided by section 1(3) of the 1997 Act i.e. that the pursuit of the course of conduct was reasonable. If this is the case, a court will be required to strike a balance between the interests of the victim of the harassment and the rights of the protesters to engage in conduct which amounts to harassment.[245] The Act does not elaborate upon what might make a course of conduct which amounts to harassment reasonable. In *DPP v Moseley*, the Divisional Court held that the conduct of protesters outside the victim's mink farm amounted to harassment which was not reasonable since it was in breach of an injunction. In the words of Collins J: 'It cannot be right for an individual to say to him or herself, that he or she will ignore the terms of the injunction because he or she believes that the conduct in question is reasonable.' The appropriate course of action would, therefore, have been to apply to have the injunction set aside.

---

[243] (Unreported), 13 June 2000.   [244] [1989] 1 WLR 88, extracted at p. 664.
[245] See *DPP v Moseley, The Times*, 23 June 1999.

To pursue a course of conduct contrary to section 1 of the 1997 Act is a summary offence.[246] In addition, an actual or apprehended breach of section 1 may form the basis of a civil action.[247] It should be noted, however, that the 1997 Act also provides for the commission of a more serious offence, where D's course of conduct causes another to fear on at least two occasions that violence will be used against him.[248] In *R v Henley*,[249] the Court of Appeal made it clear that the section 4 offence does not include fear of violence to a member of a person's family. In other words, the victim must fear that violence will be used against himself. A person guilty of a section 4 offence may be sentenced to up to five years' imprisonment where they are convicted on indictment.[250] Where D is found not guilty of the section 4 offence in a trial on indictment, the jury may nevertheless find him guilty of the less serious offence under section 2.[251]

In determining the sentence for an offence contrary to either section 2 or section 4 of the 1997 Act, a court will of course have to take a number of considerations into account. In *R v Liddle* and *R v Hayes*,[252] the Court of Appeal indicated that these factors would include:

- the seriousness of the defendant's conduct;
- whether there had been persistent misconduct;
- the physical and psychological effect upon the victim;
- the defendant's mental health; and
- the defendant's reaction to the court proceedings, particularly whether he has pleaded guilty, whether there is remorse and whether there is a recognition of the need for help.[253]

In *Daiichi Pharmaceuticals UK Ltd and others v Stop Huntingdon Animal Cruelty and others*,[254] the Queen's Bench Division was required to determine whether on its proper construction the term 'person' in sections 1 and 7(2) of the 1997 Act was capable of embracing a corporate entity. The defendants were various campaigning groups who were opposed to the use of live animals for experimentation in the manufacture of pharmaceutical products. They had embarked upon conduct which had included threatening letters and telephone calls, criminal damage, fire-bombings and hoax bombings, intimidatory home visits, demonstrations, and physical assaults on employees leaving the claimants' premises. The evidence revealed, therefore, that the claimant companies, their directors and employees had 'unquestionably been subjected to harassment of a very serious nature intended to intimidate and terrify'.[255] In the judgment of Owen J, however, whilst 'person' in section 1 of the Act covered the directors and employees of the companies, it did not embrace the companies themselves. A company could not therefore be the victim of harassment for the purposes of the 1997 Act. In reaching such a conclusion Owen J agreed with the following words uttered by Rose LJ in *DPP v Dziurzynski*:[256]

'I accept of course that the word "person", unless the contrary intention is shown is . . . to be understood, by virtue of the Interpretation Act 1978, as including a body of persons corporate or incorporate. But that said, it seems to me that the legislative history to which, in my view, reference can properly be made when construing what is meant by the word "person" in section 1 of the Act, points against person here meaning a corporation. It is to my mind also significant that in section 4(1) the word "him" is used, and in section 5(2) the word "victim" is used . . . As it seems to me, as a matter of

---

[246] Section 2(1). [247] Section 3. See further p. 698. [248] Section 4.
[249] [2000] Crim LR 582. [250] Section 4(4)(a). [251] Section 4(5).
[252] [1999] 3 All ER 816. [253] At 819. [254] [2004] 1 WLR 1503.
[255] Per Owen J, at [9]. [256] [2002] EWHC 1380 (Admin).

statutory construction, this Act was not intended by Parliament to embrace, within the ambit of a criminal offence, conduct amounting to harassment directed to a limited company rather than to an individual human being.'[257]

(c) Civil remedies and injunctive relief

'3 Civil remedy

(1) An actual or apprehended breach of [section 1(1)][258] may be the subject of a claim in civil proceedings by the person who is or may be the victim of the course of conduct in question.

(2) On such a claim, damages may be awarded for (among other things) any anxiety caused by the harassment and any financial loss resulting from the harassment.

(3) Where—

(a) in such proceedings the High Court or a county court grants an injunction for the purpose of restraining the defendant from pursuing any conduct which amounts to harassment, and

(b) the plaintiff considers that the defendant has done anything which he is prohibited from doing by the injunction,

the plaintiff may apply for the issue of a warrant for the arrest of the defendant.

(4) An application under subsection (3) may be made—

(a) where the injunction was granted by the High Court, to a judge of that court, and

(b) where the injunction was granted by a county court, to a judge or district judge of that or any other county court.

(5) The judge or district judge to whom an application under subsection (3) is made may only issue a warrant if—

(a) the application is substantiated on oath, and

(b) the judge or district judge has reasonable grounds for believing that the defendant has done anything which he is prohibited from doing by the injunction.

(6) Where—

(a) the High Court or county court grants an injunction for the purpose mentioned in subsection (3)(a), and

(b) without reasonable excuse the defendant does anything which he is prohibited from doing by the injunction,

he is guilty of an offence.

(7) Where a person is convicted of an offence under subsection (6) in respect of any conduct, that conduct is not punishable as a contempt of court.

(8) A person cannot be convicted of an offence under subsection (6) in respect of any conduct which has been punished as a contempt of court.

(9) A person guilty of an offence under subsection (6) is liable—

(a) on conviction on indictment, to imprisonment for a term not exceeding five years, or a fine, or both, or

(b) on summary conviction, to imprisonment for a term not exceeding six months, or a fine not exceeding the statutory maximum, or both.

---

[257] At [32]–[33]. Cited in *Daiichi Pharmaceuticals* [2004] 1 WLR 1503 at [15].
[258] The words in square brackets were inserted by section 125(1) and (4) of the 2005 Act.

[3A Injunctions to protect persons from harassment within section 1(1A)

(1) This section applies where there is an actual or apprehended breach of section 1(1A) by any person ('the relevant person').

(2) In such a case—

(a) any person who is or may be a victim of the course of conduct in question, or

(b) any person who is or may be a person falling within section 1(1A)(c),

may apply to the High Court or a county court for an injunction restraining the relevant person from pursuing any conduct which amounts to harassment in relation to any person or persons mentioned or described in the injunction.

(3) Section 3(3) to (9) apply in relation to an injunction granted under subsection (2) above as they apply in relation to an injunction granted as mentioned in section 3(3)(a).]' [259]

Section 3 provides for the award of a remedy in civil proceedings in respect of the actual or apprehended breach of section 1(1). In other words, it provides for a civil remedy where a person has been or may be the victim of harassment. In *Majrowski v Guy's and St Thomas's NHS Trust,*[260] where it was accepted that an employee of the Trust had bullied and intimidated a fellow employee on account of the victim being a gay man, the House of Lords was required to decide whether an employer could be vicariously liable for harassment committed by an employee in the course of her employment. The House of Lords held unanimously that the principle of vicarious liability did apply to the Protection from Harassment Act 1997 since there was nothing in the statute which expressly or impliedly excluded such liability. During the course of argument, counsel for the Trust had submitted that the word 'may' in section 3(2) indicated that the award of damages was a discretionary matter for the courts. In other words, a claimant was not entitled to damages as of right. In rejecting this argument, Lord Nicholls noted that 'by section 3 Parliament created a new cause of action, a new civil wrong'.[261] In his judgment:

'The effect of section 3(1) is to render a breach of section 1 a wrong giving rise to the ordinary remedies the law provides for civil wrongs. This includes an entitlement to damages for any loss or damage sustained by a victim by reason of the wrong.'[262]

The decision in *Majrowski* thus confirms that an employer may be held vicariously liable for a course of conduct by one of its employees which amounts to harassment for the purposes of the 1997 Act. As such, it highlights the fact that the reach of the legislation goes far beyond criminalising the actions of those whose protests and campaigns have exceeded the limits of the right to freedom of expression or of freedom of assembly or association. Employers must therefore be careful to ensure that they provide appropriate training and that they have harassment policies in place so as to identify and deal with conduct which has crossed the divide between 'the ordinary banter and badinage of life' and 'genuinely offensive and unacceptable behaviour'.[263]

Section 3A provides for the grant of an injunction where a person either has or may pursue a course of conduct which involves the harassment of two or more persons. Its purpose is to prevent a person from becoming a victim of harassment or to prevent someone who has

---

[259] This new section was inserted by section 125(1) and (5) of the Serious Organised Crime and Police Act 2005.   [260] [2006] 3 WLR 125.

[261] At [25].   [262] At [22].   [263] Per Baroness Hale, at [66].

already been a victim from being a victim once again. Seeking an injunction may be an appropriate course of action to follow in the case of a person who is being harassed in order to persuade them not to work for a company whose activities are the subject of criticism and ill-feeling.

(d) Restraint

'5 Restraining orders

(1) A court sentencing or otherwise dealing with a person ("the defendant") convicted of an offence under section 2 or 4 may (as well as sentencing him or dealing with him in any other way) make an order under this section.

(2) The order may, for the purpose of protecting the victim of the offence, or any other person mentioned in the order, from further conduct which—

    (a) amounts to harassment, or
    (b) will cause fear of violence,

prohibit the defendant from doing anything described in the order.

(3) The order may have effect for a specified period or until further order.

(4) The prosecutor, the defendant or any other person mentioned in the order may apply to the court which made the order for it to be varied or discharged by a further order.

(5) If without reasonable excuse the defendant does anything which he is prohibited from doing by any order under this section, he is guilty of an offence.

(6) A person guilty of an offence under this section is liable—

    (a) on conviction on indictment, to imprisonment for a term not exceeding five years, or a fine, or both, or
    (b) on summary conviction, to imprisonment for a term not exceeding six months, or a fine not exceeding the statutory maximum, or both.'

Where a defendant has been convicted of either the section 2 or the section 4 offence, when sentencing or otherwise dealing with him, a court has a discretion to also make the defendant the subject of a restraining order.[264] The order, which is granted to protect the victim or any other person mentioned from further harassment or fear of violence, prohibits the defendant from behaving in such a way. A failure to mention in the order the names of those in respect of whom protection is sought would thereby render the order unsustainable.[265] In the absence of a reasonable excuse, it is an offence to do anything prohibited by a section 5 order.[266]

The scope of a restraining order may be very wide indeed. Thus in *R v Debnath*,[267] where the appellant had harassed her victim over a period of approximately twelve months by conduct which included interfering with his email account and making accusations about his sexuality, the restraining order to which she was subject prohibited her from making either direct or indirect contact with the complainant, his fiancée or other specified persons, and publishing any information concerning the complainant and his fiancée whether or not the information was true. In appealing against that order, it was argued on her behalf that it was

---

[264] Section 5.   [265] See *R v Mann* 144 SJ LB 149.   [266] Section 5(5).
[267] [2006] 2 Cr App R(S) 25.

too wide since it went beyond protecting against gratuitous personal attacks and instead amounted to an infringement of her right to freedom of expression as protected by article 10 of the ECHR. However, in upholding the order, the Court of Appeal was of the view that the 'exceptional circumstances' of the case merited such an order which was, despite its breadth: (a) prescribed by law; (b) furthering a legitimate aim; (c) necessary in a democratic society; and (d) proportionate.[268] In delivering the judgment of the Court, Cresswell J identified the following five principles as being applicable to restraining orders under section 5:

'(1) The purpose of a restraining order is to prohibit particular conduct with a view to protecting the victim or victims of the offence and preventing further offences under section 2 or 4 of the Act. (2) A restraining order must be drafted in clear and precise terms so there is no doubt as to what the defendant is prohibited from doing. (3) Orders should be framed in practical terms (for example it may be preferable to frame a restriction order by reference to specific roads or a specific address). A radius restriction will not necessarily invalidate an order. If necessary a map should be prepared . . . (4) In considering the terms and extent of a restraining order the court should have regard to considerations of proportionality . . . (5) The power of the court to vary or discharge the order in question by a further order under section 5(4) is an important safeguard to defendants. The Court of Appeal Criminal Division is unlikely to interfere with the terms of a restraining order, if an application to the court which imposed the restraining order to vary or discharge was in the circumstances the appropriate course.'[269]

Section 5(4) provides that the terms of a restraining order may be varied or discharged by a further order following an application from a specified party. In *Shaw v DPP*,[270] the High Court made it clear that there had to be a good reason in the form of a change of circumstances to justify the variation of a restraining order. In the later case of *DPP v Hall*,[271] it was argued on behalf of the defendant that the section 5(4) power to vary could not be used to extend an order's expiry date even though the order had been breached on several occasions. This submission was, however, rejected by the Queen's Bench Division. In its judgment, the duration of an order was just as much a term of the order as any other provision. Accordingly, since the purpose of a restraining order was to protect the victim, section 5(4) should be construed so as to enable the period of an order to be extended.

VIII. Serious Organised Crime and Police Act 2005

(a) Introduction

Much of this Act is beyond the scope of this chapter.[272] For present purposes, therefore, the discussion will focus on those provisions in Part IV of the 2005 Act which provide the Metropolitan Police with new and specific powers for dealing with demonstrations in the vicinity of Parliament.

[268] At [26]. All these characteristics were necessary if the restraining order was to amount to a justifiable interference with the right to freedom of expression in accordance with article 10(2) of the ECHR.
[269] At [20].   [270] [2005] EWHC 1215 (Admin).   [271] [2006] 1 WLR 1000.
[272] The amendments which the Act makes to police powers of arrest will be considered in the next chapter.

(b) Demonstrations in the vicinity of Parliament

Demonstrating outside the Westminster Parliament has, over the years, proved to be a most effective means of bringing matters of concern and importance to the attention of the nation's legislature and the wider general public. Thus, for example, those who are opposed to the present government's policies in Iraq have displayed banners and camped out on the pavement opposite Parliament in order to make their point. In *Westminster City Council v Haw*,[273] the council failed in its attempt to secure an injunction to force a protestor to leave an area outside Parliament because it was held that the demonstration neither caused an obstruction nor did it give rise to any fear that a breach of the peace might occur. Now, however, the position regarding demonstrations in the vicinity of Parliament is covered by new statutory provisions laid down in the Serious Organised Crime and Police Act 2005.

Section 132 of the 2005 Act makes it an offence to organize, take part in, or carry on a demonstration in a public place in the designated area where there is no authorisation in place at the time when the demonstration starts. The power to designate the area for the purposes of sections 132–137 of the 2005 Act is exercisable by the Secretary of State.[274] Essentially the 'designated area' involves an area incorporating Parliament Square and the surrounding streets.[275] It is a defence to show that the person accused of an offence reasonably believed that an authorisation had been given.[276]

The power to authorise a demonstration in the vicinity of Parliament vests in the Metropolitan Police Commissioner. He must give authorisation where he is in receipt of a notice which satisfies the requirements of section 133 of the 2005 Act. These requirements are broadly the same as those which apply in relation to public processions under section 11 of the Public Order Act 1986.[277] They include the date and start time of the demonstration, its location and its duration.[278] The notice must be given at least six days before the day on which the demonstration is to be held, unless it is not reasonably practicable to do so. Where this is the case, it must be given as soon as it is reasonably practicable and in any event not less than twenty-four hours before the demonstration is due to start. There is therefore no exemption for spontaneous demonstrations in the vicinity of Parliament.

When authorising a demonstration, the Metropolitan Police Commissioner has the power to impose conditions on those organising or taking part. The exercise of the power is triggered by the Commissioner's reasonable opinion that conditions are necessary in order to prevent any of a number of specified outcomes. These outcomes include those which apply in relation to public processions and public assemblies for the purposes of sections 12 and 14 of the Public Order Act 1986. However, they also include the following: hindrance to any person wishing to enter or leave the Palace of Westminster; hindrance to the proper operation of Parliament; and, a security risk in any part of the designated area. The conditions themselves may in particular relate to: the place where the demonstration may, or may not, be carried on; the times at which it may be carried on; its duration; the number of persons taking part; the number and size of banners or placards used; or maximum permissible noise levels.[279] A power to impose additional conditions or to vary those which have already been imposed under section 134 is exercisable whilst a demonstration is taking place by the most senior

---

[273] [2002] EWHC 2073 (QB).   [274] Section 138.
[275] See the Serious Organised Crime and Police Act 2005 (Designated Area) Order 2005, SI 2005/1537.
[276] Section 138(2).   [277] See p. 673.   [278] Section 133(4).   [279] Section 134(4)(a)–(f).

police officer present at the scene.[280] Any breach of a condition imposed under either section 134 or 135 is a criminal offence.[281]

In *R (on the application of Haw) v Secretary of State for the Home Department and the Commissioner of the Metropolitan Police Service*,[282] the respondent sought a declaration that the regime set out in sections 132–138 of the 2005 Act did not apply to his demonstration (which had begun in June 2001) on the basis that it predated the coming into force of the provisions. The Divisional Court had previously held, by a majority, in favour of the respondent.[283] On appeal, the Court of Appeal reached a different conclusion. In the judgment of the court (delivered by Sir Anthony Clarke MR), the case turned on the construction of the Act. It concluded that the intention of Parliament was clear; 'to regulate all demonstration within the designated area, whenever they began'.[284] In reaching such a conclusion, the Court of Appeal took into account the fact that section 132(6) of the 2005 Act disapplies section 14 of the Public Order Act 1986 so that demonstrations within the vicinity of Parliament are subject to sections 132–138 of the 2005 Act rather than the earlier legislation. In the judgment of the Court of Appeal, it was 'inconceivable that Parliament would have repealed section 14 with respect to demonstrations which had already started, if it did not intend to apply the provisions of sections 132 to 138 of the Act to such demonstrations'.[285] Accordingly, it was held that the respondent was not exempt from the requirement to seek authorisation from the Commissioner for his demonstration.

FURTHER READING

Bailey SH, Harris DJ and Jones BL *Civil Liberties: Cases and Materials* (5th edn, Butterworths, London, 2001).

Barendt E *Free Speech* (2nd edn, OUP, Oxford, 2005).

Bonner D and Stone R 'The Public Order Act 1986: Steps in the Wrong Direction?' [1987] PL 202.

Burney E 'Using the Law on Racially Aggravated Offences' [2003] Crim LR 28.

Card R *Public Order Law* (Jordans, Bristol, 2000).

Finch E 'Stalking the Perfect Stalking Law: An Evaluation of the Efficacy of the Protection from Harassment Act 1997' [2002] Crim LR 703.

Geddis A 'Free Speech Martyrs or Unreasonable Threats to Social Peace? "Insulting" Expression and Section 5 of the Public Order Act 1986' [2004] PL 853.

Kerrigan K 'Breach of the Peace and Binding Over—Continuing Confusion' (1997) 2(1) J Civ Lib 30.

McCabe S and Wallington P *The Police, Public Order and Civil Liberties: Legacies of the Miners' Strike* (Routledge, London, 1988).

Mead D 'The Human Rights Act—A Panacea for Peaceful Public Protest?' (1998) 3(3) J Civ Lib 206.

Stone R 'Breach of the Peace: The Case for Abolition' [2001] Web JCLI.

Stone R *Textbook on Civil Liberties and Human Rights* (6th edn, OUP, Oxford, 2006).

Thornton P *Public Order Law* (Blackstone Press, London, 1987).

---

[280] Section 135.   [281] Section 136.   [282] [2006] EWCA Civ 532.
[283] [2005] EWHC 2061 (Admin).   [284] [2006] EWCA Civ 532, at [18].   [285] Ibid., at para 21.

Townshend C *Making the Peace: Public Order and Public Security in Modern Britain* (Oxford University Press, Oxford, 1993).

Tromans S and Thomann C 'Environmental Protest and the Law' [2003] JPL 1367.

Waddington PAJ *Liberty and Order: Public Order Policing in a Capital City* (UCL Press, London, 1994).

Wade ECS 'Police Powers and Public Meetings' (1936) 6 CLJ 175.

Williams D *Keeping the Peace: The Police and Public Order* (Hutchinson, London, 1967).

Williams DGT 'Processions, Assemblies and the Freedom of the Individual' [1987] Crim LR 167.

Williams G 'Arrest for Breach of the Peace' [1954] Crim LR 578.

12 POLICE POWERS

I. Introduction

In order to carry out their manifold tasks, which include, amongst others, the maintenance of law and order and the prevention and investigation of crime, the police have been endowed with significant and wide-ranging powers. Such powers are derived from either the common law or statute. In the discussion which follows, it will be necessary to consider the Police and Criminal Evidence Act 1984 since it is the chief source of police powers in the present context. It empowers the police to do many things which interfere with the rights of the individual, such as to stop a person and carry out a search in a public place. However, for present purposes, we will be concerned with the powers of the police to: enter and search premises without a warrant; seize articles; and, arrest persons.

Prior to examining the relevant statutory provisions contained in PACE and the associated case law, it is first necessary to deal with two important issues which are connected with these powers. What we may term 'police discretion' merits separate consideration for the reason that every time that a police officer makes a decision as to whether or not to exercise a statutory power in PACE, or their common law powers for that matter, they are exercising a discretion. In other words, whether or not to exercise a statutory power is a matter of choice rather than an obligation. However, police discretion is not without its limits. We must therefore consider how the courts have responded to invitations to review the legality of police actions in judicial review proceedings. Turning to the second issue, while it will become apparent that PACE is the source of a number of legal powers entitling the police to enter property without a warrant, it must not be forgotten that the police enjoy, along with the ordinary citizen, an implied licence to enter premises. This concept will also be discussed in the early stages of this chapter.

II. Police Discretion

Every police officer, from the rank of chief constable down, is daily concerned with the exercise of discretionary power. Thus the decision as to whether or not to arrest a person involves the exercise of discretion, as does a chief constable's disposition of those police officers who are available for duty. Decisions such as these may involve a great deal of thought and deliberation. Alternatively, it may be necessary that they are made on the spot because the circumstances require a rapid response on the part of an officer. The discretionary powers which the police exercise are wide but, importantly, they are not unfettered. The general principle that the exercise of discretionary powers is subject to the supervisory jurisdiction of the courts applies as much to the exercise of police discretionary powers as it does to any other discretionary powers that are exercised. Thus an applicant for judicial review of a decision made by, for example, the chief constable of a police force, may request the grant of one or more of the remedies which are available under Civil Procedure Rule 54.[1] Whether or not the court grants the remedy sought will of course depend upon the particular circumstances of the case, and whether these indicate that there has been a transgression of the *Wednesbury* principles.[2]

Holgate-Mohammed v Duke [1984] AC 437

The appellant was suspected of having stolen jewellery while living in a house as a lodger. On the basis of a description received from a jeweller concerning the identity of the person who sold the jewellery to him, the police officer investigating the crime believed that he had reasonable cause for suspecting that the appellant had stolen the jewellery. However, since he did not believe that the jeweller's evidence would be enough to secure a conviction in the absence of further evidence, the officer decided to arrest the plaintiff in the belief that she would be more likely to confess to the crime at a police station than if she were questioned in her own home. Accordingly the appellant was arrested under section 2(4) of the Criminal Law Act 1967 but, after a fruitless interrogation, she was released without charge. In a subsequent civil action, the appellant was awarded £1,000 damages for false imprisonment. On appeal by the chief constable, the Court of Appeal held that where a police officer has reasonable grounds for suspecting that a person had committed an arrestable offence, he was entitled to use his section 2(4) power of arrest in order to determine whether his suspicions were correct. On a further appeal by the appellant, the House of Lords affirmed the Court of Appeal's decision.

Lord Diplock, at 441–446

'The word "arrest" in section 2 is a term of art. First, it should be noted that arrest is a continuing act: it starts with the arrester taking a person into his custody (sc by action or words restraining him from moving anywhere beyond the arrester's control), and it continues until the person so restrained is either released from custody or, having been brought before a magistrate, is remanded in custody by the magistrate's judicial act. In practice, since the creation of organised police forces during the course of the nineteenth century an arrested person, on being taken into custody by a constable, is brought to a police station and it is there that he is detained until he is either brought before a magistrate or released, whether unconditionally or on police bail. In modern conditions any other way of dealing with an arrested person once he has been taken into custody would be impracticable . . .

. . . it should be noted that the mere act of taking a person into custody does not constitute an "arrest" unless that person knows, either at the time when he is first taken into custody or as soon thereafter as it is reasonably practicable to inform him, on what charge or on suspicion of what crime he is being arrested: see *Christie v Leachinsky* [1947] 1 All ER 567, [1947] AC 573 . . .

So the condition precedent to Det Con Offin's power to take the appellant into custody and the power of the other constables at Southsea police station to detain her in custody was fulfilled; and, since the wording of the subsection under which he acted is "*may* arrest without warrant", this left him with an executive discretion whether to arrest her or not. Since this is an executive discretion expressly conferred by statute on a public officer, the constable making the arrest, the lawfulness of the way in which he has exercised it in a particular case cannot be questioned in any court of law except on those

---

[1] See pp. 481–482 for a discussion of the judicial review procedure.
[2] See pp. 563–565 for a discussion of the *Wednesbury* principles.

principles laid down by Lord Greene MR in *Associated Provincial Picture Houses Ltd v Wednesbury Corpn* [1948] 1 KB 223 [p. 563], that have become too familiar to call for repetitious citation. The *Wednesbury* principles, as they are usually referred to, are applicable to determining the lawfulness of the exercise of the statutory discretion of a constable under section 2(4) of the 1967 Act, not only in proceedings for judicial review but also for the purpose of founding a cause of action at common law for damages for that species of trespass to the person known as false imprisonment, for which the action in the instant case is brought.

The first of the *Wednesbury* principles is that the discretion must be exercised in good faith. The county court judge expressly found that Det Con Offin in effecting the initial arrest acted in good faith. He thought that he was making a proper use of his power of arrest. So his exercise of that power by arresting the appellant was lawful unless it can be shown to have been "unreasonable" under *Wednesbury* principles, of which the principle that is germane to the instant case is "he [sc the exerciser of the discretion] must exclude from his consideration matters which are irrelevant to what he has to consider" . . .

. . . Det Con Offin and his fellow police officers concerned in the inquiries thought (with obvious justification) that, even if the jeweller were to succeed in picking out the appellant on a properly conducted identification parade, such evidence would be too weak to justify convicting her of committing the crime of burglary in December 1979. In these circumstances, if she had in fact committed the offence of which there were reasonable grounds at the time of her arrest for suspecting her to be guilty, the only kind of admissible evidence probative of her guilt that would be likely to be procurable would be a confession obtained from the appellant herself.

Det Con Offin thought that she would be more likely to confess to what he had reasonable cause to believe to be the truth if she were arrested and taken for questioning to the police station. In other words, the reason why Det Con Offin arrested her was that he held the honest opinion that the police inquiries were more likely to be fruitful in clearing up the case if the appellant was compelled to go to the police station to be questioned there. It is relevant to add that officers who had been concerned, as Det Con Offin had not, in the original investigations in December 1979 would have been available, and there would have been facilities for recording any statements that the appellant decided to make.

The county court judge, however, described Det Con Offins' reason for making the arrest in some-what emotive phraseology (for which I have myself supplied the emphasis) as being "to subject her to the *greater stress and pressure* involved in arrest and deprivation of liberty in the belief that if she was going to confess she was more likely to do so in a state of arrest". Yet, despite his use of the expressions "stress" and "pressure", the judge went on to find that the questioning to which the appellant was subjected at the police station was conducted with complete propriety. "There was not," he said, "any suggestion of verbal bullying at the police station or anything approaching it". Indeed, it would appear that the appellant's solicitor, who had been sent for at her request, was present for part of the time at least and made no complaint of the arrest or the nature of the questioning or the length of time for which she was being detained.

So, applying *Wednesbury* principles, the question of law to be decided by your Lordships may be identified as this: was it a matter that Det Con Offin should have excluded from his consideration, as irrelevant to the exercise of his statutory power of arrest, that there was a greater likelihood (as he believed) that the appellant would respond truthfully to questions about her connection with or knowledge of the burglary, if she were questioned under arrest at the police station, than if, without arresting her, questions were put to her by Det Con Offin at her own home from which she could peremptorily order him to depart at any moment, since his right of entry under section 2(6) of the Criminal Law Act 1967 was dependent on his intention to arrest her?

My Lords, there is inevitably the potentiality of conflict between the public interest in preserving the liberty of the individual and the public interest in the detection of crime and the bringing to justice of those who commit it. The members of the organised police forces of the country have, since the mid-nineteenth century, been charged with the duty of taking the first steps to promote the latter public interest by inquiring into suspected offences with a view to identifying the perpetrators of them and of obtaining sufficient evidence admissible in a court of law against the persons they suspect of being the perpetrators as would justify charging them with the relevant offences before a magistrates' court with a view to their committal for trial for it . . .

That arrest for the purpose of using the period of detention to dispel or confirm the reasonable suspicion by questioning the suspect or seeking further evidence with his assistance was said by the Royal Commission on Criminal Procedure in England and Wales (Cmnd 8092) in 1981, at para 3.66 "to be well established as one of the primary purposes of detention upon arrest". That is a fact that will be within the knowledge of those of your Lordships with judicial experience of trying criminal cases, even as long ago as I last did so, more than 20 years before the Royal Commission's report. It is a practice which has been given implicit recognition in r 1 of successive editions of the Judges' Rules (see Practice Note [1964] 1 All ER 237, [1964] 1 WLR 152) since they were first issued in 1912. Furthermore, parliamentary recognition that making inquiries of a suspect in order to dispel or confirm the reasonable suspicion is a legitimate cause for arrest and detention at a police station was implicit in section 38(2) of the Magistrates' Courts Act 1952 (which is now reproduced in section 43(3) of the Magistrates' Courts Act 1980, with immaterial amendments consequent on the passing of the Bail Act 1976).'

[Lord Diplock then proceeded to state that part of the subsection which was relevant in the context of his general point, before continuing as follows:]

'So whether or not to arrest the appellant and bring her to the police station in order to facilitate the inquiry into the case of the December burglary was a decision that it lay within the discretion of Det Con Offin to take.

In my opinion the error of law made by the county court judge in the instant case was that, having found that Det Con Offin had reasonable cause for suspecting the appellant to be guilty of the burglary committed in December 1979 to which he rightly applied an objective test of reasonableness, the judge failed to recognise that the lawfulness of the arrest and detention based on that suspicion did not depend on the judge's own view whether the arrest was reasonable or not, but on whether Det Con Offin's action in arresting her was an exercise of discretion that was ultra vires under *Wednesbury* principles because he took into consideration an irrelevant matter. For the reasons that I have given and in agreement with the Court of Appeal, I do not think that in the circumstances Det Con Offin or any other police officers of the Hampshire Constabulary acted unlawfully in the way in which they exercised their discretion.

I would dismiss this appeal.'

In some instances, although there is merit in an applicant's case, it may nevertheless be unnecessary to grant a remedy because a change in police policy prior to or during the course of the judicial review proceedings makes a remedy otiose. This is what happened in an important case heard by the Court of Appeal.

R v Commissioner of Police of the Metropolis, ex p Blackburn [1968] 2 QB 118

The Commissioner of Police of the Metropolis issued a policy decision in April 1966 to the effect that the police under his control were not to attempt to enforce section 32(1)(a) of the Betting, Gaming and Lotteries Act 1963. The policy decision was in part based on the uncertain state of the law at the time, together with concerns at the expense and manpower which was involved in keeping gaming clubs under observation. The applicant, a private citizen, sought an order of mandamus directing the Commissioner to reverse his policy decision. While the Court of Appeal were of the opinion that the police have a wide discretion in terms of the way in which they exercise their powers, nevertheless such discretion was not beyond the review of the courts. However, in the present case, it was unnecessary to grant the order which the applicant sought since the Commissioner had given an undertaking to the court that the policy decision would be revoked.

Lord Denning MR, at 135–138

'The office of the Commissioner of Police within the Metropolis dates back to 1829 when Sir Robert Peel introduced his disciplined force. The commissioner was a justice of the peace specially appointed to administer the police force in the metropolis. His constitutional status has never been defined either by statute or by the courts. It was considered by the Royal Commission on the Police in their Report in 1962 (Cmnd 1728). But I have no hesitation in holding that, like every constable in the land, he should be, and is, independent of the executive. He is not subject to the orders of the Secretary of State, save that under the Police Act 1964, the Secretary of State can call upon him to give a report, or to retire in the interests of efficiency. I hold it to be the duty of the Commissioner of Police of the Metropolis, as it is of every chief constable, to enforce the law of the land. He must take steps so to post his men that crimes may be detected; and that honest citizens may go about their affairs in peace. He must decide whether or not suspected persons are to be prosecuted; and, if need be, bring the prosecution or see that it is brought. But in all these things he is not the servant of anyone, save of the law itself. No Minister of the Crown can tell him that he must, or must not, keep observation on this place or that; or that he must, or must not, prosecute this man or that one. Nor can any police authority tell him so. The responsibility for law enforcement lies in him. He is answerable to the law and to the law alone. That appears sufficiently from *Fisher v Oldham Corpn* [1930] 2 KB 364, and *A-G for New South Wales v Perpetual Trustee Co Ltd* [1955] 1 All ER 846.

Although the chief officers of police are answerable to the law, there are many fields in which they have a discretion with which the law will not interfere. For instance, it is for the Commissioner of Police of the Metropolis, or the chief constable, as the case may be, to decide in any particular case whether inquiries should be pursued, or whether an arrest should be made, or a prosecution brought. It must be for him to decide on the disposition of his force and the concentration of his resources on any particular crime or area. No court can or should give him direction on such a matter. He can also make policy decisions and give effect to them, as, for instance, was often done when prosecutions were not brought for attempted suicide. But there are some policy decisions with which, I think, the courts in a case can, if necessary, interfere. Suppose a chief constable was to issue a directive to his men that no person should be prosecuted for stealing any goods less than £100 in value. I should have thought that the court could countermand it. He would be failing in his duty to enforce the law . . .

. . . I turn to see whether it is shown that the Commissioner of Police of the Metropolis has failed in his duty. I have no doubt that some of the difficulties have been due to the lawyers and the courts. Refined arguments have been put forward on the wording of the statute which have gained acceptance by some for a time. I can well understand that the commissioner might hesitate for a time until those difficulties were resolved; but, on the other hand, it does seem to me that his policy decision was unfortunate. People might well think that the law was not being enforced, especially when the gaming clubs were openly and flagrantly being conducted as they were in this great city. People might even go further and suspect that the police themselves turned a blind eye to it. I do not myself think that was so. I do not think that the suggestion should even be made. But nevertheless the policy decision was, I think, most unfortunate.

The matter has, I trust, been cleared up now. On 19 December 1967, the House of Lords in *Kursaal Casino v Crickitt (No 2)* [1968] 1 WLR 53, made it quite clear that roulette with a zero was not rendered lawful simply by the "offer of the bank". Following that decision, on 30 December 1967, the commissioner issued a statement in which he said: "it is the intention of the Metropolitan Police to enforce the law as it has been interpreted". That implicitly revoked his policy decision of 22 April 1966; and the commissioner by his counsel gave an undertaking to the court that that policy decision would be officially revoked. We were also told that immediate steps are being taken to consider the "goings-on" in the big London clubs with a view to prosecution if there is anything unlawful. That is all that Mr Blackburn or anyone else can reasonably expect.'

Salmon LJ, at 138–139

'The chief function of the police is to enforce the law. The Divisional Court left open the point as to whether an order of mandamus could issue against a chief police officer should he refuse to carry out that function. Constitutionally it is clearly impermissible for the Secretary of State for Home Affairs to issue any order to the police in respect of law enforcement. In this court it has been argued on behalf of the commissioner that the police are under no legal duty to anyone in regard to law enforcement. If this argument were correct it would mean that insofar as their most important function is concerned, the police are above the law and therefore immune from any control by the court. I reject that argument. In my judgment the police owe the public a clear legal duty to enforce the law—a duty which I have no doubt they recognise and which generally they perform most conscientiously and efficiently. In the extremely unlikely event, however, of the police failing or refusing to carry out their duty, the court would not be powerless to intervene. For example, if, as is quite unthinkable, the chief police officer in any district were to issue an instruction that as a matter of policy the police would take no steps to prosecute any housebreaker, I have little doubt but that any householder in that district would be able to obtain an order of mandamus for the instruction to be withdrawn. Of course, the police have a wide discretion as to whether or not they will prosecute in any particular case. In my judgment, however, the action I have postulated would be a clear breach of duty. It would be so improper that it could not amount to an exercise of discretion.'

In other cases, however, the court may take the view that it would be inappropriate to grant the particular remedy sought, as was the case in *R v Chief Constable of Devon and Cornwall Constabulary, ex p Central Electricity Generating Board*.[3] In this case, the Court of Appeal refused to grant an order of mandamus[4] to compel the Chief Constable to have his officers remove or assist in the removal of persons who were obstructing the CEGB's work. Lord Denning MR expressed the view that: 'The decision of the chief constable not to intervene in this case was a policy decision with which I think the courts should not interfere.'[5] His fellow judges, Lawton and Templeman LJJ, stressed that the facts of the case were such as to indicate the need for co-operation between the two parties rather than the granting of an order of mandamus. In the words of Templeman LJ, the role of the court in the present case was as follows:

'The Court cannot tell the police how and when their powers should be exercised, for the court cannot judge the explosiveness of the situation or deal with the individual problems which will arise as a result of the activities. This court can and does confirm that the police have powers to remove and arrest passive resisters in the circumstances which prevail at the site when the board resume their work to complete the survey. This court can and does indicate that the time has come for the board and the police to exercise their respective powers so that the survey may be completed.'[6]

While an exercise of the discretionary powers of the police is therefore subject to judicial review, it does not follow that the exercise of all such powers falls within the supervisory jurisdiction of the courts. There may be certain aspects of policing, such as a chief constable's decision as to the concentration of the available resources in order to deal with a particular crime or public order situation, with which the courts will be reluctant to interfere.[7] Nevertheless, it is patently the case that an improper exercise of discretion or indeed a complete failure to exercise a discretion will result in the relevant police officer being called to account before the courts.

---

[3] [1982] QB 458.   [4] Now a mandatory order (see p. 478).   [5] At 472.   [6] At 481.
[7] See, for example, *R v Chief Constable of Sussex, ex p International Trader's Ferry Ltd* [1999] 2 AC 418, extracted at p. 600.

Lindley v Rutter [1980] 3 WLR 660

The defendant was arrested for disorderly behaviour while drunk and taken to a police station. At the station she was placed in a cell and a woman police officer (WPC Fry) unsuccessfully attempted to search her. In view of the fact that WPC Fry had been kicked and scratched by the defendant, assistance was called for and together with a female colleague, the two police women succeeded in removing the defendant's brassiere. Both officers believed that this course of action was necessary in order to comply with standing orders issued by the chief constable which required the removal of this article of clothing for the defendant's own protection. In respect of her struggles in the cell, the defendant was charged with the offence of assaulting a police officer in the execution of her duty contrary to section 51(1) of the Police Act 1964. On appeal, the Divisional Court held that the police officer had failed to properly exercise her discretion in removing the defendant's brassiere. Her failure to consider the circumstances of the defendant's case before exercising her discretion meant that her conduct was not justified and that she was therefore acting outside the execution of her duty at the time of the assault.

Donaldson LJ, at 663–666

'The wording of this offence is liable to be misunderstood by the public, but it is difficult to suggest an alternative form of words. However, I must make it clear that there is no suggestion that WPC Fry was acting otherwise than in accordance with what she believed to be her duty. The issue is whether what she did was justifiable in law. Police constables of all ranks derive their authority from the law and only from the law. If they exceed that authority, however slightly, technically they cease to be acting in the execution of their duty and have no more rights than any other citizen. This is a most salutary principle upon which all our liberties depend and it is not to be eroded merely because, as in this case, the limits of the constable's authority may not have been clearly defined and WPC Fry was acting in the bona fide belief that she was authorised to act as she did. These considerations may well provide an answer to criticism of the officer concerned. They do not deprive the aggrieved citizen of any of her rights. . . .'

[The court then considered the limits of the common law power to search a person who is in custody.]

'It is the duty of the courts to be ever zealous to protect the personal freedom, privacy and dignity of all who live in these islands. Any claim to be entitled to take action which infringes these rights is to be examined with very great care. But such rights are not absolute. They have to be weighed against the rights and duties of police officers, acting on behalf of society as a whole. It is the duty of any constable who lawfully has a prisoner in his charge to take all reasonable measures to ensure that the prisoner does not escape or assist others to do so, does not injure himself or others, does not destroy or dispose of evidence and does not commit further crime such as, for example, malicious damage to property. This list is not exhaustive, but it is sufficient for present purposes. What measures are reasonable in the discharge of this duty will depend upon the likelihood that the particular prisoner will do any of these things unless prevented. That in turn will involve the constable in considering the known or apparent disposition and sobriety of the prisoner. What can never be justified is the adoption of any particular measures without regard to all the circumstances of the particular case.

That is not to say that there can be no standing instructions. Although there may always be special features in any individual case, the circumstances in which people are taken into custody are capable of being categorised and experience may show that certain measures, including searches, are prima facie reasonable and necessary in a particular category of case. The fruits of this experience may be passed on to officers in the form of standing instructions. But the officer having custody of the prisoner must always consider, and be allowed and encouraged to consider, whether the special circumstances of the particular case justify or demand a departure from the standard procedure either by omitting what would otherwise be done or by taking additional measures. So far as searches are concerned, he should appreciate that they involve an affront to the dignity and privacy of the individual. Furthermore, there are degrees of affront involved in such a search. Clearly going through someone's pockets or handbag is less of an affront than a body search. In every case a police officer ordering a search or depriving a prisoner of property should have a very good reason for doing so.

In the instant case, WPC Fry might have been justified in searching the defendant if she had doubts whether she was suffering from the effects of drink or drugs and thought that a search might have resolved that doubt. But, of course, there was no reason whatsoever to believe that the defendant's condition was attributable to anything other than intoxication. Again, a search would have been justified if, bearing in mind the defendant's condition, including her reaction to being in custody, WPC Fry or the station officer had had any reason for thinking that the defendant might have some object on her with which she might accidentally or intentionally injure herself or others.

The forcible removal of her brassiere was understandably regarded by the defendant as peculiarly offensive. Such conduct would require considerable justification. It was inherently unlikely that possession of the brassiere could lead to accidental injury. If it was to be used intentionally for this purpose, other clothing would probably have served as well. Indeed, there would have had to have been some evidence that young female drunks in general were liable to injure themselves with their brassieres or that the defendant had shown a peculiar disposition to do so. It would obviously be a justification if the defendant had by words or conduct threatened to do so. But that is not this case.

The justices have found that WPC Fry was acting in accordance with the standing orders of the chief constable which applied to any female person arrested and placed in a cell in whatever circumstances and for whatever reason. They have made no finding that the constable gave any consideration to whether the search was necessary for any lawful purpose or whether the removal of the brassiere was in fact necessary for the defendant's own protection. It is impossible to justify such a standing instruction or WPC Fry's conduct if based upon it. Accordingly, WPC Fry was not acting in the execution of her duty and the defendant was entitled to use reasonable force to resist. In fact, she used more force than was necessary and so was guilty of a common assault upon WPC Fry. However, she was not guilty of the very much more serious offence of assaulting WPC Fry in the execution of her duty, since the constable was exceeding her duty. It follows that this conviction must be quashed.'

In the recent case of *Joseph v DPP*,[8] the issue for the court to consider was the discretion afforded to a police officer with regard to the obtaining of evidence to show that a person had been drinking with an excess amount of alcohol in their blood. Section 7(4) of the Road Traffic Act provides that:

'If the provision of a specimen other than a specimen of breath may be required in pursuance of this section the question whether it is to be a specimen of blood or a specimen of urine shall be decided by the constable making the requirement, but if a medical practitioner is of opinion that for medical reasons a specimen of blood cannot or should not be taken the specimen shall be a specimen of urine'.

It is therefore evident from section 7(4) that the decision as to which sample should be provided, blood or urine, rests with the police officer. In *Joseph*, a suspected drink-driver, a Rastafarian man, claimed that it would be contrary to his religious beliefs to provide a specimen of blood. However, the police officer who was dealing with the matter was of the view that unless there were medical reasons for not supplying a blood sample, then section 7(4) required that such a sample should be supplied. In the judgment of the Divisional Court, this amounted to a failure to properly exercise his discretion. The police officer had misunderstood the legal position. He had believed that the discretion afforded to him by the statute was narrower than it in fact was; medical reasons were not the only basis on which he might decide not to require a sample of blood.

---

[8] [2003] EWHC 3078 (Admin).

III. Implied Licence to Enter Premises

In addition to the statutory powers to enter premises provided for under PACE (discussed at pp. 720–729), the police enjoy along with ordinary citizens what the law of tort terms an 'implied licence' to enter premises. The importance of this implied licence, which may exist in addition to an express licence to enter, is that it authorises a presence on land or property which would otherwise be a trespass. Thus a person delivering newspapers clearly has an implied licence to open the gate of a house and to walk up a garden path in order to put a newspaper through a letter-box. So to the police officer conducting house-to-house inquiries in respect of a crime recently committed in the locality. In both of these instances:

'The path or driveway is . . . held out by the occupier as the bridge between the public thoroughfare and his or her private dwelling upon which a passer-by may go for a legitimate purpose that in itself involves no interference with the occupier's possession nor injury to the occupier, his or her guests or his, her or their property.'[9]

This passage from a judgment in an Australian case highlights the fact that an implied licence to be on private property is restricted to those persons who have a 'legitimate purpose' for being on such property. Evidently, the newspaper deliverer and the police officer mentioned above both have a legitimate or lawful purpose for being on the property and for going up to the front door of the house. However, if either were to attempt to do more than this by, for example, entering an adjoining garage or seeking to gain access to the back door of the house, they would be acting beyond the scope of their implied licence and would thus need express consent from the householder to justify this further action. In the New Zealand case *Edwards v A-G*,[10] Eichelbaum J stated the position in the following manner:

' . . . the concept of an implied licence does not take the visitor beyond the door of the house. No authority has been cited to suggest that there is any licence to enter a house or even a garage uninvited. One has only to ask what might reasonably be in the mind of the ordinary householder, who would willingly accept that by virtue of an unlocked gate or the equivalent he had assented to any person entering his property on lawful business and knocking on the door. In most cases he would I believe reject any suggestion that this entitled the visitor to wander through his garage or outbuildings or enter the house itself, notwithstanding that doors may have been left unlatched or even open. Scrutton LJ's famous dictum that when you ask a person into your house to use the staircase, you do not invite him to slide down the banisters can readily be adapted to this situation (see *The Carlgarth* [1927] P 93, 110).'[11]

The implied licence to enter premises is precisely what it purports to be. It exists by way of implication, but the licence itself is capable of being revoked either verbally or by way of a sign or notice. Thus a person who is verbally requested to leave premises by the owner must do so since otherwise, he or she will become a trespasser. In the case of a police officer who is requested to leave premises, a failure to do so will also therefore take that officer outside the execution of their duty. In *Lambert v Roberts*,[12] the Divisional Court held that informing a police officer that he was on private property and therefore a trespasser was sufficient to revoke his implied licence to enter the defendant's property. Accordingly, the officer was acting

---

[9] Per Gibbs CJ, Mason, Wilson and Deane JJ in *Halliday v Nevill* (1984) 155 CLR 1 at 7–8.
[10] [1986] 2 NZLR 232.   [11] At 237–238.   [12] [1981] 2 All ER 15.

outside the execution of his duty from that point onward and thus his subsequent arrest of the defendant was unlawful. Where an implied licence is revoked by words, the person requested to leave the premises must be given a reasonable opportunity to do so. It is only when such an opportunity has been given and the person has still not left the premises that the owner would be entitled to use reasonable force to remove that person from the premises on the basis that they have now become a trespasser.

Robson v Hallet [1967] 2 QB 939

Three police officers, a sergeant and two constables, were in the process of making enquiries about the commission of an offence when they went to the appellant's house. The two constables went to the front door of the house and knocked on it while the sergeant parked the car. The door was opened by the appellant and the officers proceeded to ask him where he had been the previous night. The sergeant joined the two officers at the front of the house and was invited in by the appellant while the other officers remained outside. Once inside the house, the appellant's father told the sergeant to leave, but as he reached the threshold of the door, the appellant jumped on the sergeant's back and punched him. The tussle spilled out onto the doorstep of the house and one of the officers went to the assistance of the sergeant. At this point, the appellant's brother appeared from the back of the house and started to kick and punch the other police officer. On appeal against their convictions for assaulting a police officer in the execution of his duty contrary to section 51(1) of the Police Act 1964, the Divisional Court found that all three officers were lawfully on the premises at the time of the assaults and that therefore they had been acting in the execution of their duty at the time when they were assaulted. Accordingly, the appellants had been rightly convicted.

Lord Parker CJ, at 950–953

'What is said in this case, and this is really the foundation of counsel for the appellants' argument, is that all three police officers were trespassers ab initio; having arrived at the garden gate, although up till then they were acting in the execution of their duty, making inquiries into an offence committed that night, yet the moment when they set foot onto the steps leading up to the front door they were all three trespassers. For my part, it is no doubt true that the law is sometimes said to be an ass, but I am happy to think that it is not an ass in this respect, because I am quite satisfied that these three police officers, like any other members of the public, had implied leave and licence to walk through that gate up those steps and to knock on the door of the house. We are not considering for this purpose the entering of private premises in the form of a dwelling-house, but of the position between the gate and the front door. There, as it seems to me, the occupier of any dwelling-house gives implied licence to any member of the public coming on his lawful business to come through the gate, up the steps, and knock on the door of the house . . .

What happened then was, as I have said, that Sgt McCaffrey was allowed to enter the house by the permission of the occupier's son. It was not suggested that the occupier's son had no authority to do so, and, accordingly, when Sgt McCaffrey was in the house he was lawfully in the house and was still acting in the execution of his duty.

What counsel for the appellants says in regard to Sgt McCaffrey is this, that the moment Mr Robson senior said "Get out" he at once became a trespasser and at once, instanter, ceased to be acting in the execution of his duty. That proposition, which I confess sounds remarkable, is based as I understand it on the last sentence in the judgment of Goddard, J in *Davis v Lisle* [p. 715], where he said: "He had no right to be on the premises once he had been asked to leave." In my judgment, it is quite wrong to read those words as words of a statute; they were in relation to a case where the police officer, having been plainly told to leave, was remonstrating and asserting his right to stay. In the present case, Sgt McCaffrey was doing all he could to leave, and was not asserting any right to stay.

It seems to me that, when a licence is revoked as a result of which something has to be done by the licensee, a reasonable time must be implied in which he can do so, in this case to get off the premises; no doubt it will be a very short time, but he was doing here his best to leave the premises.

Looked at in a slightly different way, it is argued that he was acting in the execution of his duty up to the very moment he was told to get out, and one asks oneself what was he doing when he was assaulted? He was surely carrying on his duty, which was a duty to get out.'

Diplock LJ, at 953–954

'These appeals raise three simple points on the law of trespass on land which affect all members of the public as well as the police officers with whom this appeal is concerned. The points are so simple that the combined researches of counsel have not revealed any authority on them. There is no authority because no one has thought it plausible up till now to question them. The first is this, that when a householder lives in a dwelling-house to which there is a garden in front and does not lock the gate of the garden, it gives an implied licence to any member of the public who has lawful reason for doing so to proceed from the gate to the front door or back door, and to inquire whether he may be admitted and to conduct his lawful business. Such implied licence can be rebutted by express refusal of it, as in this case the Robsons could no doubt have rebutted the implied licence to the police officers by putting up a notice on their front gate "No admittance to police officers"; but that was not done in this case.

The second proposition is this, that when, having knocked at the front door of the dwelling-house, someone who is inside the dwelling-house invites the person who has knocked to come in, there is an implied authority in that person, which can be rebutted on behalf of the occupier of the dwelling-house, to invite him to come in and so licence him to come into the dwelling-house itself. In the present case, it was the son, the appellant Thomas Robson, and not the father who was the occupier who invited Sgt McCaffrey to come in. In those circumstances, Sgt McCaffrey, whilst in the dwelling-house on the invitation of the son, was no trespasser. The licence, however, could be withdrawn by the father who was the person entitled to give it. He withdrew it and, on its being withdrawn, the sergeant had a reasonable time to leave the premises by the most appropriate route for doing so, namely, out of the front door, down the steps and out of the gate, and, provided that he did so with reasonable expedition, he would not be a trespasser while he was so doing . . .

In the case of PC Paxton and PC Jobson, once a breach of the peace was taking place under their eyes, they had not only an independent right but a duty to go out and stop it, and it matters not from that moment onwards whether they started off on their journey to stop it from outside the premises or from inside the premises. They were entitled, once the breach of the peace occurred, to be on the premises for the purpose of preventing it or stopping it.'

With regard to the words which are used to revoke an implied licence, whether they are sufficient to achieve that purpose will depend upon the particular circumstances of the case. Clearly to declare to a police officer that he or she may not enter premises without a search warrant is a revocation of that officer's implied licence to be on the premises.

....

Davis v Lisle [1936] 2 QB 434

Two on-duty police officers noticed that a lorry parked outside a garage was causing what they believed to be an obstruction of the highway contrary to section 54(6) of the Metropolitan Police Act 1839. The officers went along the street and on their return, it became apparent that the lorry had been moved into a garage. Accordingly the officers entered the garage in order to make inquiries as to the identity of the person responsible for the obstruction. They did so despite the fact that they had not requested permission to enter the garage. Moreover, neither officer was in possession of a search warrant. Two men who had previously been seen working on the lorry when it was parked in the street were once again at work on the lorry in the garage. As one of the officers spoke to them the appellant entered the garage and on being informed that the questioner was a police officer, he said: "Get outside—you can't come here without a search warrant." The police officer to whom he spoke was in the act of producing his warrant card when he was attacked by the appellant. In respect of this conduct the appellant was convicted of having: (a) assaulted a police officer in the execution of his duty contrary to section 18 of the Metropolitan Police Act 1839; (b) wilfully obstructed a police officer in the execution of his duty contrary to section 2 of the Prevention of Crimes Amendment Act 1885; and (c) unlawfully, wilfully and maliciously damaged a police tunic contrary to section 14 of the Criminal Justice Administration Act 1914. On appeal, the Divisional Court upheld the conviction for offence (c) but allowed the appeal against convictions (a) and (b).

Lord Hewart CJ, at 437–439

'The point which is raised here with regard to the appellant's first two convictions is whether the officers were at the material time acting in the execution of their duty. In my opinion, they were not, and there are no grounds on which they can be held to have been so acting. The only ground which is put forward in support of the contention that they were so acting seems to me to be quite beside the point. I feel a difficulty in envisaging the legal proposition that because the police officers had witnessed an offence being committed on the highway they were acting in the execution of their duty in entering and remaining on private premises because the offenders then were on those premises. Admittedly, the officers had no warrant entitling them to search the premises. It is one thing to say that the officers were at liberty to enter this garage to make an inquiry, but quite a different thing to say that they were entitled to remain when, not without emphasis, the appellant had said: "Get outside. You cannot come here without a search warrant." From that moment on, while the officers remained where they were, it seems to me that they were trespassers and it is quite clear that the act which the respondent was doing immediately before the assault complained of was tantamount to putting forward a claim as of right to remain where he was. The respondent was in the act of producing his warrant card. That was after the emphatic order to "get out" had been made. Mr Raphael [counsel for the police officer], with his usual candour, has admitted that, if the finding in the case that the respondent was in the act of producing his warrant card is fairly to be construed as meaning that he was asserting his right to remain on the premises, it is not possible to contend that at that moment the respondent was acting in the execution of his duty. I think it is quite clear that the act of producing his warrant card constituted the making of such a claim. I cannot think that there was any ambiguity about it . . .

In my opinion, it is not possible to maintain the conclusion that at the material time the respondent was acting in the execution of his duty as a constable. But that conclusion by no means disposes of everything contained in this case. It does not dispose of the question whether the assault which was in fact committed was justified. We have not the materials before us which would enable us to determine that question. Nor was the appellant prosecuted for assault. He was prosecuted for assaulting and obstructing a police officer in the execution of his duty. Furthermore, the conclusion to which I have come does not affect the third conviction—that of damaging a tunic by "wilfully and maliciously tearing" it. On that part of the case no question arises whether at that moment the officer was acting in the execution of his duty and I see no reason why we should interfere with that conviction. With regard to the first two convictions, I think that the conclusion of quarter sessions was erroneous and that, with regard to those two convictions, which are the real pith and substance of this case, the appeal ought to be allowed and the case go back to the court of quarter sessions with the direction that at the material time the respondent was not acting in the execution of his duty.'

The position is less straightforward, however, where a revocation of an implied licence is purported to have been effected by the use of strong language. Thus in *Snook v Mannion*,[13] the

---

[13] [1982] RTR 321.

Divisional Court held that justices were entitled to find that telling police officers to 'Fuck off' did not amount to a revocation of their implied licence to be on the defendant's driveway. In the circumstances of the case, which involved the defendant's refusal to submit to a breathalyser test where he was suspected of having driven with excess alcohol in his blood, the justices had treated his words merely as a vulgar expletive.[14]

It would seem in the light of the decision in *Fullard and Roalfe v Woking Magistrates' Court*,[15] that where there is a misunderstanding between the person making the request to leave and the person to whom the request is directed as to the meaning of what has been said, the test to be applied is an *objective* test. That is to say, were the relevant words such as would have caused an objective bystander (had he been present) to have concluded that permission to be on the premises had been withdrawn? In *Fullard and Roalfe* itself, it was held that the words 'you can fucking get out of my house' were sufficient to revoke an implied licence to enter. Crucially, however, the police officer in question was assaulted before he was given a reasonable opportunity to leave. Accordingly at the time of the assault, he was acting in the execution of his duty and the appellant had therefore been rightly convicted of an offence contrary to section 89(1) of the Police Act 1996.[16]

A clearly visible sign or notice may be sufficient to revoke a person's implied licence to be on property, especially where it is specifically directed at the persons who seek to rely upon an implied licence to be on the land. Thus the legend 'No door-to-door salesmen' affixed to the front gate of a house will have served to revoke the implied licence of such persons to enter the premises and, if they disregard the sign, they will become trespassers once they step on to the property. If the implied licence of police officers to be on property has been revoked in a similar manner, it will be necessary for those officers to seek some other authority, perhaps in the form of a warrant (but certainly not in the form of a warrant card as in *Davis v Lisle*), which will make their presence on the property lawful.

IV. Police and Criminal Evidence Act 1984

(a) Background

The enactment of PACE was by no means a smooth process. The original version of the Bill was lost as a consequence of the calling of a general election in May 1983, and its replacement which ultimately became the 1984 Act differed from its predecessor in a number of respects, thus highlighting, inter alia, a difference in approach between successive Home Secretaries. In introducing the revised and amended Bill before the House of Commons in November 1983, the then Home Secretary, Leon Brittan, declared that the measure was necessary for the following reasons:

'First, the present state of the law is unclear and contains many indefensible anomalies. Secondly, the police need to have adequate and clear powers to conduct the fight against crime on our behalf and the public need to have proper safeguards against any abuse of such powers if they are to have confidence in the police. Thirdly, these measures play an essential part in an overall strategy designed to create

---

[14] See also *Gilham v Breidenbach* [1982] RTR 328.   [15] [2005] EWHC 2922 (Admin).
[16] For a further discussion of this particular offence, see pp. 754–766.

more effective policing. They do not solve, or pretend to solve, all the problems of policing in Britain today, but they have an important part to play alongside administrative and other measures needed or being dealt with already to ensure that the police can operate efficiently, fairly and with the active support of the public.'[17]

Despite the fact that the second version of the Bill took account of the amendments which had been made to its predecessor and the views which had been expressed during the course of the process of consultation and review which had preceded its own introduction, the completion of the various parliamentary stages prior to enactment was not without its difficulties. Indeed, the fifty-nine sittings which were necessary in order to complete the committee stage in the House of Commons exceeded the previous record. The process of enactment was, however, as Professor Zander has argued, 'an example of the democratic system working'.[18] Amendments which were made to the second Bill were done so on the basis that they were necessary in order to secure a better, more workable piece of legislation. Interested groups such as the Law Society, the Police Federation, the British Medical Association and the National Council for Civil Liberties all had a part to play in this process, as of course did the opposition parties in Parliament. Indeed, the initial impetus for reform had come not from the Conservative government of the day but from the previous Labour government which had announced in June 1977 that it intended to establish a Royal Commission on Criminal Procedure in order to consider, inter alia, whether changes were needed in England and Wales to 'the powers and duties of the police in respect of the investigation of criminal offences and the rights and duties of suspect and accused persons, including the means by which these are secured'. In the report which followed,[19] the Royal Commission emphasised the fact that in conducting their review, their central challenge had lain in striking a balance between the interests of the wider community and the rights and liberties of the individual citizen. While the fact that the report was generally supported by the police and the legal profession and opposed by the political left, including what was by then the Labour Opposition, appeared to indicate that for some, the Royal Commission had not met their central challenges, the report did serve as an important source of recommendations on which a Bill could originally be fashioned.

(b) Codes of practice

The provisions of PACE which are considered in this chapter are concerned with the powers that the police have to arrest people and to search the premises of those who have been arrested or premises where such persons were either at the time of their arrest or immediately prior to their arrest. However, the relevant sections of PACE are but part of the overall picture for they provide little guidance as to how these statutory powers are to be exercised in practice. Accordingly, in compliance with sections 60 and 66 of PACE, the Secretary of State has from time to time issued Codes of Practice (and revised versions of Codes). The most recent version of the Codes generally came into effect after midnight on 31 December 2005. They deal with: the exercise by police officers of statutory powers of stop and search (Code A); the searching of premises by police officers and the seizure of property found by police officers on persons or premises (Code B); the detention, treatment and questioning of persons by police officers

---

[17] *Hansard*, HC Debates, Vol 48, cols 25–26.
[18] *The Police and Criminal Evidence Act 1984* (5th edn, 2005), at p. xiii.   [19] Cmnd 8092.

(Code C); the identification of persons by police officers (Code D); the tape recording of police interviews (Code E); the visual recording with sound of interviews (Code F); the statutory power of arrest by police officers (Code G); and the detention of terrorist suspects (Code H). Codes G[20] and H are new rather than revised versions of previous Codes.[21] It is a requirement of each of the Codes that they must be readily available at all police stations in order that they may be consulted by police officers, persons who have been detained and members of the public.

The legal status of the Codes of Practice is dealt with by a number of supplementary provisions in section 67 of PACE. Thus the Codes are admissible in evidence in all criminal and civil proceedings, and if any provision of a Code is relevant to any question in those proceedings, a court or tribunal is entitled to take it into account in determining that particular question.[22] A failure to comply with any provision of any of the Codes will not of itself result in civil or criminal proceedings against a police officer.[23] Neither will it necessarily result in disciplinary proceedings as was once the case.[24] An interesting feature of the Codes is that they govern not only the actions of the police but also the actions of those persons 'who are charged with the duty of investigating offences or charging offenders'.[25] Thus in the discharge of their duties, such persons are required to have regard to any relevant provision in any of the Codes. In *R v Bayliss*,[26] the Court of Appeal held that a store detective could be a person 'charged with the duty of investigating offences' within the meaning of section 67(9), since 'at the present day the duty of investigating offences is not restricted to the officers of central government or to other persons acting under statutory powers'. However, the Court of Appeal emphasised that whether a person came within the scope of section 67(9) was a question of fact to be determined in each case. In addition, it was thought that a question of law may arise where the duty under consideration involved the construction of a statute or some other document. In the present case, the Court of Appeal was not prepared to overturn the trial judge's decision to admit a store detective's evidence in a theft trial. Its reason for so finding was that the evidence as to the store detective's employment and the scope of her duties was not sufficiently clear to suggest that she ought to have complied with the Code of Practice and cautioned the appellant when she became convinced that he had committed a theft.

Interestingly, a matter of a few days after the judgment in *R v Bayliss*, a Court of Appeal consisting of the same three judges held in *R v Smith*,[27] that a supervising manager at the Bank of England whose responsibility it was to ensure that minimum criteria for authorisation as a Bank were met and maintained in accordance with Schedule 3 to the Banking Act 1987 was not a person 'charged with the duty of investigating offences' within the meaning of section 67(9) of PACE. Accordingly, the manager had not been required to comply with the terms of Code C in an interview with the appellant during which the appellant admitted that he had committed a fraud. In the course of delivering the judgment of the court, Neill LJ observed that:

'The question whether a person is charged with the duty of investigating offences involves an examination of the statute, contract or other authority under which he carries out his functions and a consideration of his actual work. It is a question of mixed law and fact.'[28]

[20] See pp. 737, 745–746.   [21] Code H came into effect as from midnight on 24 July 2006.
[22] Section 67(11) of PACE.   [23] Section 67(10).
[24] Section 67(8) of PACE was repealed by section 37(a) of the Police and Magistrates' Courts Act 1994.
[25] Section 67(9).   [26] (1994) 98 Cr App R 235.   [27] [1994] 1 WLR 1396.   [28] At 1405.

Customs officers[29] and officers of the Serious Fraud Office[30] are further examples of persons who must have regard to the PACE Codes of Practice when exercising their powers.

(c) Entry and search without warrant

'17 Entry for purpose of arrest etc

(1) Subject to the following provisions of this section, and without prejudice to any other enactment, a constable may enter and search any premises for the purpose—

    (a) of executing—

       (i) a warrant of arrest issued in connection with or arising out of criminal proceedings; or

       (ii) a warrant of commitment issued under section 76 of the Magistrates' Courts Act 1980;

    (b) of arresting a person for an [indictable] offence;

    (c) of arresting a person for an offence under—

       (i) section 1 (prohibition of uniforms in connection with political objects) . . . of the Public Order Act 1936;

       (ii) any enactment contained in sections 6 to 8 or 10 of the Criminal Law Act 1977 (offences relating to entering and remaining on property);

      [(iii) section 4 of the Public Order Act 1986 (fear or provocation of violence)];

      [(iiia) section 4 (driving etc. when under the influence of drink or drugs) or 163 (failure to stop when required to do so by a constable in uniform) of the Road Traffic Act 1988];

      [(iiib) section 27 of the Transport and Works Act 1992 (which relates to offences involving drink or drugs)]; [;or

      (iv) section 76 of the Criminal Justice and Public Order Act 1994 (failure to comply with an interim possession order);]

    [(ca) of arresting, in pursuance of section 32(1A) of the Children and Young Persons Act 1969, any child or young person who has been remanded or committed to local authority accommodation under section 23(1) of that Act;

    (cb) of recapturing any person who is, or is deemed for any purpose to be, unlawfully at large while liable to be detained—

       (i) in a prison, remand centre, young offender institution or secure training centre, or

       (ii) in pursuance of [section 92 of the Powers of Criminal Courts (Sentencing) Act 2000] (dealing with children and young persons guilty of grave crimes), in any other place;]

    (d) of recapturing [any person whatever] who is unlawfully at large and whom he is pursuing; or

    (e) of saving life or limb or preventing serious damage to property.

(2) Except for the purpose specified in paragraph (e) of subsection (1) above, the powers of entry and search conferred by this section—

    (a) are only exercisable if the constable has reasonable grounds for believing that the person whom he is seeking is on the premises; and

    (b) are limited, in relation to premises consisting of two or more separate dwellings, to powers to enter and search—

      (i) any parts of the premises which the occupiers of any dwelling comprised in the premises use in common with the occupiers of any other such dwelling; and

---

[29] See *R (Hoverspeed Ltd) v Customs and Excise Commissioners* [2003] 2 All ER 533.
[30] See *R v Director of Serious Fraud Office, ex p Saunders* [1988] Crim LR 837.

(ii) any such dwelling in which the constable has reasonable grounds for believing that the person whom he is seeking may be.

(3) The powers of entry and search conferred by this section are only exerciseable for the purposes specified in subsection (1)(c)(ii) [or (iv)] above by a constable in uniform.

(4) The power of search conferred by this section is only a power to search to the extent that is reasonably required for the purpose for which the power of entry is exercised.

(5) Subject to subsection (6) below, all the rules of the common law under which a constable has power to enter premises without a warrant are hereby abolished.

(6) Nothing in subsection (5) above affects any power of entry to deal with or prevent a breach of the peace.'

Section 17 of PACE confers a power upon police officers to enter and search premises without first obtaining a search warrant from a magistrate. The power is exerciseable primarily for the purpose of executing a warrant of arrest or a warrant of commitment;[31] or for the purpose of arresting a person for an indictable offence;[32] or for arresting a person for one of a number of specified offences.[33]

The section 17(1)(b) power of entry is now broader than when originally enacted. Formerly it was exercisable in respect of arrestable offences. Now, however, as a consequence of the reforms made to PACE by the Serious Organised Crime and Police Act 2005, the power of entry can be exercised in order to arrest for an indictable offence, which is a wider category of offences than arrestable offences.

The power conferred by section 17 also entitles a police officer to enter premises without a warrant for the purpose of recapturing a person who is unlawfully at large,[34] or in an emergency situation in order to save life or limb or to prevent serious damage to property.[35] With regard to the section 17(1)(d) power of entry, it should be noted that in addition to being unlawfully at large, the person whom the officer is seeking to recapture must be being pursued by the officer in order for the power to be exercisable. Thus in *D'Souza v DPP*,[36] the House of Lords was required to consider whether the police were entitled to rely on section 17(1)(d) as justification for a forcible entry into premises in order to return to hospital a patient who had been admitted for psychiatric assessment under section 6(2) of the Mental Health Act 1983. The facts of the case were that the patient's husband and daughter had visited her in hospital and had taken her back to the family home where she arrived at 3.55 p.m. At 7.00 p.m. two police officers accompanied by two nurses went to the house with the intention of returning the patient to hospital. In compliance with section 17(2)(a) of PACE, the police officers had reasonable grounds for believing that the patient was in the house. They requested and were denied entry to the house and accordingly they effected an entry by the use of force. A struggle ensued and the patient's daughter and husband were arrested and charged with assaulting a police officer in the execution of his duty contrary to section 51(1) of the Police Act 1964.[37] The correctness or otherwise of the appellant's and her father's convictions depended on whether the police officers had been acting in the execution of their duty at the time of the assault. This in turn depended on whether the police had been entitled to forcibly enter the house without a warrant when the assaults were committed.

In order for the police to be entitled to rely on section 17(1)(d) in the present case, it was necessary that: the patient was unlawfully at large; and that the patient was a person whom the

[31] Section 17(1)(a).　　[32] Section 17(1)(b), as amended.　　[33] Section 17(1)(c) and (ca).
[34] Section 17(1)(cb) and (d).　　[35] Section 17(1)(e).　　[36] [1992] 1 WLR 1073.
[37] Now section 89(1) of the Police Act 1996.

police were pursuing. Dealing with the first of these issues, Lord Lowry, with whom all their Lordships agreed, arrived at the conclusion that the patient had been unlawfully at large in that she had absconded from her lawful detention in the mental hospital. However, the appeals against conviction were allowed on the basis that the facts of the case failed to disclose that the police officers had actually pursued the patient prior to the break-in at the house. Indeed, the time lapse between the patient's arrival at her home and the arrival of the police was of a sufficient length to imply that there had been no pursuit. Accordingly, the police officers could not justify their entry into the house on the basis of section 17(1)(d) and thus they were acting outside the execution of their duty when they were assaulted. In the opinion of the House of Lords, the pursuit element of section 17(1)(d) should be interpreted in the following manner:

'The verb in the clause "whom he is pursuing" is in the *present continuous* tense and therefore, give or take a few seconds or minutes—this is a question of degree—the pursuit must be almost contemporaneous with the entry into the premises. There must, I consider, be an act of pursuit, that is a chase, however short in time and distance. It is not enough for the police to form an intention to arrest, which they put into practice by resorting to the premises where they believe that the person whom they seek may be found.'[38]

A common feature of most of the powers of entry provided for in section 17 is that they cannot be exercised unless a police officer has reasonable grounds for believing that the person whom he is seeking is on the premises in question.[39] The section 17(1)(e) power of entry is, however, an exception. Thus an entry for the purpose of 'saving life or limb or preventing serious damage to property' is not conditional on an officer reasonably believing that an entry is necessary for any of these purposes although in practice, it is likely that he will have a reasonable belief at the relevant time. There are few authorities on section 17(1)(e). In *Friswell v Chief Constable of Essex*,[40] a police officer had entered a house following a report of a non-violent domestic incident at the claimant's house during the course of which the claimant had taken an overdose of tablets. In the subsequent civil proceedings for damages for trespass to land, false imprisonment and assault, it was contended on behalf of the officer that his entry had been justified on any of the following grounds: the consent of the owner; a fear of an imminent breach of the peace;[41] or section 17(1)(e). It was held, however, that none of these justifications applied in the present case and that the police officer had therefore been a trespasser. In reaching her conclusion on the section 17(1)(e) point, Cox J referred to the decision in *Murgatroyd v Chief Constable of West Yorkshire Police*.[42] In that case, the Court of Appeal had held that there had been no immediate and present threat to justify entering the claimant's house under section 17(1)(e) even though the claimant had cut one of his wrists and had been 'threatening to do himself in' due to the apparent break-up of a relationship.

Patently, section 17(1)(e) cases turn on their own particular facts. Thus in *Blench v DPP*,[43] where police officers had attended at a house in response to a 999 telephone call and had been met with shouts of abuse and aggressive conduct from the appellant on their arrival, the Divisional Court was of the opinion that section 17(1)(e) 'provides a complete answer to the submission that the officers were trespassers either ab initio or when they attempted to enter

---

[38] [1992] 1 WLR 1073 at 1085.   [39] Section 17(2).   [40] [2004] EWHC 3009 (QB).
[41] See chapter 11 for a discussion of the common law power of entry onto private premises which a police officer has in order to deal with an actual or reasonably apprehended breach of the peace.
[42] (Unreported), November 8, 2000.   [43] [2004] EWHC 2717 (Admin).

the house'. Indeed, in the judgment of Fulford J, the facts of the case were such as to not only justify the officers' entry into the house under section 17(1)(e) but also to suggest that had they instead 'meekly turned on their heels and walked away', they would have been 'in grave dereliction of their duty'.

The decision in *Blench* is of further interest because it highlights the potential overlap which exists between the power of entry under section 17(1)(e) and a police officer's common law power of entry in respect of an actual or threatened breach of the peace.[44] Where an entry is necessary in order to save life or limb, it is also likely that those same circumstances will have given rise to a breach of the peace.[45] Where this is the case, *Blench* suggests that it does not matter if the police were to claim that they were entering the relevant premises pursuant to their common law power when in fact they were doing so under the authority of the statutory power. Thus having regard to the facts of *Blench* itself, Fulford J observed: 'They [the police] explained substantively why they were at the house and any technical mistake, such as reference to the common law rather than statute, would not render their actions unlawful or take them outside the execution of their duty.'[46]

Practical guidance for the police relating to the exercise of, amongst other things, the section 17 power is contained in Code of Practice B. This makes it clear to the police (if it was not already clear) that section 17 'does not create or confer any powers of arrest'.[47] Code B also impresses upon the police that the officer in charge of a section 17 entry and search should first try to communicate with the occupier or person entitled to grant access to the premises, explain the authority under which the search is to be carried out and ask the occupier to allow the entry.[48] It may not be necessary to comply with these formalities, however, where, for example, 'there are reasonable grounds for believing that alerting the occupier or any other person entitled to grant access would frustrate the object of the search or endanger officers or other people'.[49] Code B further provides that 'reasonable and proportionate force' may be used to effect an entry under section 17 where, for example, the occupier or other person entitled to grant access has refused entry or it is impossible to communicate with the person entitled to grant access.[50] Thus in *D'Souza*, the police officers' breaking of a glass panel in a front door would have been a use of reasonable force fully within the scope of Code B had the officers actually been in pursuit of Mrs D'Souza.

On a more general note concerning the use of force, section 117 of PACE provides that a police officer may use reasonable force in the exercise of a power under the Act where it is necessary to do so and where the power in question is not one which may only be exercised with the consent of a person other than a police officer. Thus section 117 clearly applies to the power contained in section 17 of PACE and to a number of other powers considered in this chapter concerning: the entry and search of premises following arrest for an indictable offence;[51] the seizure of evidence;[52] and, the search of a person on arrest.[53] Whether or not the degree of force used was 'reasonable' will depend upon an objective consideration of the facts of the case. In the case *Swales v Cox*,[54] where a police officer used force by opening a door and entering a house in order to arrest a person in accordance with section 2(6) of the Criminal Law Act 1967, Donaldson LJ defined what was meant by 'force'. Accordingly, where a police

---

[44] This was the only common law power of entry preserved by PACE: see section 17(5) and (6).
[45] The test for a breach of the peace is that laid down in *R v Howell* [1982] QB 416, see p. 637.
[46] [2004] 2717 (Admin) at [29].   [47] Para 4.1.   [48] Para 6.4.   [49] Para 6.4.(iii).
[50] Para 6.6.   [51] Section 18.   [52] Section 19.   [53] Section 32.   [54] [1981] QB 849.

officer is confronted by an obstacle:

'. . . then he uses force if he applies any energy to the obstacle with a view to removing it. It would follow that, if my view is correct, where there is a door which is ajar but it is insufficiently ajar for someone to go through the opening without moving the door and energy is applied to that door to make it open further, force is being used. A fortiori force is used when the door is latched and you turn the handle from the outside and then ease the door open. Similarly, if someone opens any window or increases the opening in any window, or indeed dislodges the window by the application of any energy, he is using force to enter, and in all those cases a constable will have to justify the use of force.'[55]

Although the police may therefore enter premises by force, the circumstances in which they may do so are limited. Given that such an entry involves an interference with the property rights of another, it seems only right that limitations exist. In *Swales v Cox*, Donaldson LJ remarked that for a police officer to be able to justify the use of force:

'The first hurdle which he will have to overcome . . . will be by providing an answer to the question: "Why did you not ask to be allowed in?" That "an Englishman's home is his castle"[56] is perhaps a trite expression, but it has immense importance in the history of this country, and it still has immense importance. Anybody who seeks to enter by force has a very severe burden to displace.'[57]

The dicta of Donaldson LJ in *Swales v Cox* were later applied in *O'Loughlin v Chief Constable of Essex*.[58] Here the majority of the Court of Appeal held that when exercising the section 17 power of entry, the police were under an obligation to give reasons for the entry. Moreover, it was considered that the refusal of a request to enter to carry out an investigation did not render the use of force necessary. In commenting on the passages cited above from the judgment of Donaldson LJ, Roch LJ observed in *O'Loughlin* that:

'It would, in my view, be quite wrong to read those passages in that judgment as saying that the simple refusal of a request by the constable to be allowed to enter the premises of itself rendered the use of force necessary. It cannot be right that an officer in plain clothes who has good grounds for entering a house under section 17 can simply ask to enter the house and if refused then use force, or that the householder who tries to prevent entry in those circumstances finds that he is committing offences such as those of obstructing or assaulting a police officer in the execution of his duty.'[59]

It would seem, therefore, in the light of the decision in *O'Loughlin*, that a police officer would only be entitled to effect a forced entry to premises where he has first stated: (i) the authority under which he is acting; and (ii) the proper reason why entry is required, and yet entry has been refused. A failure to comply with either (i) or (ii) would thereby render the entry unlawful even though a police officer may have both the authority and a valid reason for requiring entry.

---

[55] At 854–855. In a recent case it was held, amongst other things, that opening a closed but unlocked backdoor constituted the use of force to effect an entry: see *Friswell v Chief Constable of Essex* [2004] EWHC 3009 (Admin).

[56] The same phrase was used by Donaldson LJ in *McLorie v Oxford* [1982] QB 1290 at 1296.

[57] [1981] QB 849 at 855. In *Entick v Carrington* (1765) 19 State Tr 1029, Lord Camden CJ stated the following legal principle which has been much quoted ever since: 'No man can set his foot upon my ground without my licence, but he is liable to an action, though the damage be nothing? . . . If he admits the fact, he is bound to show by way of justification, that some positive law has empowered or excused him' (at 1066).

[58] [1998] 1 WLR 374.   [59] At 383.

(d) Entry to search for evidence following arrest

'18 Entry and search after arrest

(1) Subject to the following provisions of this section, a constable may enter and search any premises occupied or controlled by a person who is under arrest for an [indictable] offence, if he has reasonable grounds for suspecting that there is on the premises evidence, other than items subject to legal privilege, that relates—

    (a) to that offence; or

    (b) to some other [indictable] offence which is connected with or similar to that offence.

(2) A constable may seize and retain anything for which he may search under subsection (1) above.

(3) The power to search conferred by subsection (1) above is only a power to search to the extent that is reasonably required for the purpose of discovering such evidence.

(4) Subject to subsection (5) below, the powers conferred by this section may not be exercised unless an officer of the rank of inspector or above has authorised them in writing.

(5) A constable may conduct a search under subsection (1) above—

    (a) before the person is taken to a police station or released on bail under section 30A, and

    (b) without obtaining an authorisation under subsection (4),

if the condition in subsection (5A) is satisfied.

(5A) The condition is that the presence of the person at a place (other than a police station) is necessary for the effective investigation of the offence.

(6) If a constable conducts a search by virtue of subsection (5) above, he shall inform an officer of the rank of inspector or above that he has made the search as soon as practicable after he has made it.

(7) An officer who—

    (a) authorises a search; or

    (b) is informed of a search under subsection (6) above, shall make a record in writing—

        (i) of the grounds for the search; and

        (ii) of the nature of the evidence that was sought.

(8) If the person who was in occupation or control of the premises at the time of the search is in police detention at the time the record is made, the officer shall make the record as part of the custody record.

. . .

32 Search upon arrest

(1) A constable may search an arrested person, in any case where the person to be searched has been arrested at a place other than a police station, if the constable has reasonable grounds for believing that the arrested person may present a danger to himself or others.

(2) Subject to subsections (3) to (5) below, a constable shall also have power in any such case—

    (a) to search the arrested person for anything—

        (i) which he might use to assist him to escape from lawful custody; or

        (ii) which might be evidence relating to an offence; and

    (b) if the offence for which he has been arrested is an indictable offence, to enter and search any premises in which he was when arrested or immediately before he was arrested for evidence relating to the offence.

(3) The power to search conferred by subsection (2) above is only a power to search to the extent that is reasonably required for the purpose of discovering any such thing or any such evidence.

(4) The powers conferred by this section to search a person are not to be construed as authorising a constable to require a person to remove any of his clothing in public other than an outer coat, jacket or gloves [but they do authorise a search of a person's mouth].

(5) A constable may not search a person in the exercise of the power conferred by subsection (2)(a) above unless he has reasonable grounds for believing that the person to be searched may have concealed on him anything for which a search is permitted under that paragraph.

(6) A constable may not search premises in the exercise of the power conferred by subsection (2)(b) above unless he has reasonable grounds for believing that there is evidence for which a search is permitted under that paragraph on the premises.

(7) In so far as the power of search conferred by subsection (2)(b) above relates to premises consisting of two or more separate dwellings, it is limited to a power to search—

(a) any dwelling in which the arrest took place or in which the person arrested was immediately before his arrest; and

(b) any parts of the premises which the occupier of any such dwelling uses in common with the occupiers of any other dwellings comprised in the premises.

(8) A constable searching a person in the exercise of the power conferred by subsection (1) above may seize and retain anything he finds, if he has reasonable grounds for believing that the person searched might use it to cause physical injury to himself or to any other person.

(9) A constable searching a person in the exercise of the power conferred by subsection (2)(a) above may seize and retain anything he finds, other than an item subject to legal privilege, if he has reasonable grounds for believing—

(a) that he might use it to assist him to escape from lawful custody; or

(b) that it is evidence of an offence or has been obtained in consequence of the commission of an offence.

(10) Nothing in this section shall be taken to affect the power conferred by [section 43 of the Terrorism Act 2000].'

Section 18 of PACE confers upon a police officer the power to enter and search any premises, which are either occupied or controlled by a person under arrest for an indictable offence, where that officer has reasonable grounds for believing that there is evidence on the premises relating to that offence or some other indictable offence.[60] In short, section 18 authorises a post-arrest search for evidence. As originally enacted, this power of entry was exercisable only in respect of 'arrestable' offences.[61] Now, however, the power of entry relates to indictable offences as a consequence of the reforms made to the police powers of arrest by the Serious Organised Crime and Police Act 2005.[62] Although an arrest for an indictable offence is a condition precedent of the section 18 power, a statement by a police officer that a search was carried out under this section does not lead to the inference that a person has been arrested for an indictable offence.[63]

---

[60] Section 18(1).   [61] See p. 734 for an explanation of the concept of an 'arrestable' offence.
[62] See further p. 735.
[63] See R (on the application of Odewale) v DPP (unreported), 28 November 2000.

An additional power to search premises following an arrest is provided for in section 32 of PACE. However, the section 32 power differs from section 18 in a key aspect in that it entitles the police to search a potentially different class of premises to those which can be searched in accordance with section 18 since it authorises the search of any premises (including a vehicle) in which the arrested person was either at the time of their arrest or immediately prior to their arrest.[64] Accordingly, the power contained in section 32 may entitle the police to search the premises of an innocent third party if that was where the arrested person was immediately prior to being arrested. However, the section 32 power must not be used as a cover to hide the real reason for wishing to enter and search premises.

In *R v Beckford*,[65] police officers had kept premises consisting of three flats under surveillance because they suspected that they were being used in connection with drug dealing. In the early hours of one morning, officers intercepted a man who had just left the premises carrying a package which he dropped when he was confronted. The package was subsequently established to have contained heroin. The police's previous searches of the premises had been conducted under warrant but, on this occasion, the officers entered the premises under the power conferred on them by section 32 of PACE. Once inside the premises, the officers arrested the appellant for being in possession of heroin, a Class A prohibited drug. On appeal against conviction, the Court of Appeal was required to consider both the effect of section 32 in the instant case, and, the trial judge's direction to the jury in which he had withdrawn from them the question whether the police were being truthful in relation to their dealings with the first arrested person and their stated reasons for entering the premises. In finding that the conviction was unsafe and unsatisfactory and should therefore be quashed, the Court of Appeal ruled that the question whether the first arrested person's arrest had merely been used by the police as a pretext for entering the premises without a warrant was a matter that ought to have been left to the jury. In delivering the judgment of the court, Watkins LJ observed that: 'It must be a question of fact in every case where the power in section 32 has been used whether that genuinely is the reason why police officers made their entry and search.'[66] Clearly, therefore, if the police were to enter premises in the purported exercise of the section 32 power when their real purpose was not to search for evidence relating to an indictable offence for which a person had been arrested, their presence on those premises would be unlawful. The decision in *R v Beckford* is also of interest for an additional reason. Section 32(7) provides that where premises consist of two or more dwellings, the police may only search the dwelling where the arrest took place or where the person was immediately prior to their arrest, or any common parts of the premises. However, if the police officers did not see exactly which dwelling the person now arrested was in prior to their arrest, *R v Beckford* seems to suggest that they may nevertheless be entitled to use their previous knowledge of the premises to properly assume where the arrested person had been.

Further distinctions between the powers in sections 18 and 32 were made apparent in *R v Badham*.[67] In this case, the appellant was convicted of wilfully obstructing a police officer in the execution of his duty when he refused to allow police officers to enter his house. The appellant's two sons had been arrested at approximately 11.00 a.m. and 12.00 p.m. in separate incidents outside the appellant's house. They had been taken to a police station and, at about 2.00 p.m., the arresting officer obtained authorisation from a police inspector to search the appellant's house in accordance with the requirement laid down in section 18(4) of PACE. A search of the relevant premises was attempted at about 3.00 p.m., at which point the

[64] Section 32(2)(b).   [65] (1992) 94 Cr App R 43.   [66] At 49.   [67] [1987] Crim LR 202.

appellant refused to let the officers enter his house after having demanded to see the authorisation for the search. In allowing the appeal against conviction, the Crown Court made several observations. First, the requirement in section 18(4) that the authorisation of a search under the section must be made in writing by an officer of the rank of inspector or above had not been properly complied with in the present case. The recording of a verbal authorisation by a police inspector in the arresting officer's notebook was insufficient for the purposes of section 18(4); what was needed was an independent document in which the authorisation was stated in writing.[68] Secondly, before the magistrates the prosecution had argued that the facts of the present case were such that the police officers were empowered to search the appellant's house in accordance with section 32(2)(b) of PACE. The Crown Court rejected this submission, however, on the basis that although there are no temporal restrictions on the exercise of the section 32 power expressed in the statute itself, nevertheless the power is immediate in nature and it therefore could not be exercised several hours after the sons' arrests had taken place. It was suggested by the court that in the circumstances, section 18(1) was the only power entitling the officers to return and conduct a search of the premises.

In the later case of *R v Heap*,[69] however, the Court of Appeal rejected the argument that an officer who arrests a person is able initially to use the powers set out in section 32, and thereafter only to use the powers set out in section 18. On the facts of the case, a search of a vehicle at a police station which took place approximately an hour and a half after the arrest of the defendants was held to have been authorised by the terms of section 32.

It is a moot point whether or not the requirements in section 18 are mandatory or directory. To take a specific example, does a failure by an officer to comply with the requirement to make a written record of the ground for a search and the nature of the evidence that was sought[70] thereby render the search invalid? In *Krohn v DPP*,[71] the Divisional Court held that on the facts of the case before it, the requirement was directory and that the failure of an Acting Inspector to record the relevant information relating to a search which he had authorised did not invalidate that search. However, both judges who heard the case (Brooke LJ and Blofeld J) were anxious to stress that their ruling should not be treated as a binding authority that the requirements of section 18 are directory.

The power provided for in section 18 is of particular importance in relation to the nature of the evidence for which a search can be undertaken. While a search under section 32 must be confined to looking for evidence relating to the indictable offence for which the person has been arrested, section 18 entitles a police officer to search for evidence relating to the relevant indictable offence or, alternatively, some other indictable offence which is connected with or similar to that offence.[72] Thus if a person has been arrested under section 24 of PACE[73] for the offence of rape, a police officer would not be entitled to search premises which are either occupied or controlled by that person for evidence relating to the offence of arson. However, where the relevant indictable offence is the publication of obscene matter contrary to section 2 of the Obscene Publications Act 1959, a police officer may well be entitled to search the arrested person's premises for evidence relating to the offence of the taking and distribution of indecent photographs of children, contrary to section 1 of the Protection of Children Act 1978, since the two indictable offences are certainly similar in nature and may even be connected.

---

[68] It does not seem necessary, however, for a copy of a section 18 authorisation to be produced as evidence in court where the issue is whether the authorisation was granted: see *Linehan v DPP* [2000] Crim LR 861.

[69] (Unreported) 13 October 1994.   [70] Section 18(7).   [71] [1997] COD 345.

[72] Section 18(1).   [73] See p. 735.

Five further points are worth noting in respect of the powers of search conferred upon the police by section 18 and 32. First, the exercise of both powers is dependent on the requirement that the officer carrying out the search has reasonable grounds for suspecting[74] or believing[75] that there is evidence on the premises for which he is entitled to search under the authority of the relevant power. Thus neither section 18 nor section 32 entitles the police to carry out routine searches of arrested person's premises (or those of others) in the vague hope that evidence relating to criminal activity will be found. Secondly, although a search which does not comply with the terms of one or other of these provisions and which has not been authorised in another way, eg under a warrant, is therefore unlawful, it does not necessarily follow that the evidence obtained as a consequence of an illegal search will be inadmissible in court. A court retains a discretion as to whether or not to admit such evidence.[76] Thirdly, the power to enter and search premises conferred by section 18 is accompanied by a power to seize and retain evidence which an officer finds as a result of that search.[77] Fourthly, unlike section 17 which, as has already been noted, expressly abolishes common law powers of entry without warrant, section 18 makes no corresponding provision in respect of powers of entry and search following an arrest. Thus it would seem that the police retain a power at common law to search for and seize evidence.[78] This common law power was referred to by Lord Denning MR in *Ghani v Jones*[79] in the following terms:

'I would start by considering the law where police officers enter a man's house by virtue of a warrant, or arrest a man lawfully, with or without a warrant, for a serious offence. I take it to be the settled law, without citing cases, that the officers are entitled to take any goods which they find in his possession or in his house which they reasonably believe to be material evidence in relation to the crime for which he is arrested or for which they enter. If in the course of their search they come on any other goods which show him to be implicated in some other crime, they may take them provided they act reasonably and detain them no longer than is necessary.'[80]

Finally, it should be noted that guidance on the exercise of the section 18 and section 32 search powers is provided by Code of Practice B. Much of that guidance applies generally to statutory and common law search powers and some of it has already been referred to in the context of section 17 of PACE, eg the use of reasonable force in the conduct of a search.[81] For present purposes, therefore, it should be noted that Code B makes it clear that an officer of the rank of inspector or above should only authorise a section 18 search where he is satisfied that the necessary grounds for the search exist. The Code states that if possible, the authority should be recorded on the Notice of Powers and Rights.[82] It is more prescriptive in relation to the recording of the grounds for the search and the nature of the evidence sought as required by section 18(7). Such information has to be recorded in the custody record, if there is one,[83] and otherwise in the officer's pocket book or the search record.[84]

---

[74] Section 18(1).   [75] Section 32(6).

[76] See section 78 of PACE and, for example, *Jeffrey v Black* [1978] 1 All ER 555.

[77] Section 18(2).   [78] See *Cowan v Condon* [2000] 1 WLR 254, p. 731.   [79] [1970] 1 QB 693.

[80] At 706. In uttering these words, Lord Denning relied on the previous authorities of *Pringle v Bremner and Stirling* (1867) 5 Macph., HL 55, 60 and *Chic Fashions (West Wales) Ltd v Jones* [1968] 2 QB 299.

[81] See pp. 723–724.

[82] Para 4.3. This document will, amongst other things, summarise the extent of the PACE search and seizure powers, explain the rights of the occupier and the owner of any property seized, and explain that compensation may be payable in appropriate cases for damage caused entering and searching premises: see Code B, para 6.7.

[83] A custody record will not exist if the section 18 power of search has been exercised prior to taking the arrested person to a police station under the authority of section 18(5) and (5A).   [84] Code B, para 4.3.

(e) General power of seizure

'19 General power of seizure etc

(1) The powers conferred by subsection (2), (3) and (4) below are exercisable by a constable who is lawfully on any premises.

(2) The constable may seize anything which is on the premises if he has reasonable grounds for believing—

(a) that it has been obtained in consequence of the commission of an offence; and

(b) that it is necessary to seize it in order to prevent it being concealed, lost, damaged, altered or destroyed.

(3) The constable may seize anything which is on the premises if he has reasonable grounds for believing—

(a) that it is evidence in relation to an offence which he is investigating or any other offence; and

(b) that it is necessary to seize it in order to prevent the evidence being concealed, lost, altered or destroyed.

(4) The constable may require any information which is [stored in electronic form] and is accessible from the premises to be produced in a form in which it can be taken away and in which it is visible and legible if he has reasonable grounds for believing—

(a) that—

(i) it is evidence in relation to an offence which he is investigating or any other offence; or

(ii) it has been obtained in consequence of the commission of an offence; and

(b) that it is necessary to do so in order to prevent it being concealed, lost, tampered with or destroyed.

(5) The powers conferred by this section are in addition to any power otherwise conferred.

(6) No power of seizure conferred on a constable under any enactment (including an enactment contained in an Act passed after this Act) is to be taken to authorise the seizure of an item which the constable exercising the power has reasonable grounds for believing to be subject to legal privilege.'

Section 19 of PACE confers upon police officers[85] a general power of seizure in relation to anything which they find on premises for which there are reasonable grounds for believing that it has either been obtained in consequence of the commission of an offence or that it is evidence in relation to an offence which is being investigated, or any other offence.[86] In both cases, the seizure must be necessary in order to prevent the article being concealed, lost, altered or destroyed,[87] although in the case of a seizure made under section 19(2)(a), additional provision is made for seizure in order to prevent the article being damaged.[88] Professor Zander has suggested that this difference between section 19(2)(b) and (3)(b) may be due to a drafting oversight which seems to be the only plausible explanation for the omission of 'damage' from section 19(3)(b).[89]

---

[85] The power may also be exercised by investigating officers where a relevant designation has been made: see Schedule 4, Part 2, para 19(a) of the Police Reform Act 2002.　　　　[86] Section 19(2)(a) and (3)(a).

[87] See also Code of Practice B, para 7.1(b).　　　[88] Section 19(2)(b).

[89] *The Police and Criminal Evidence Act* 1984 (5th edn, 2005) at para 2–68 (p. 83).

The power in section 19 is a general power of seizure and thus it exists as a supplement to specific statutory seizure powers such as those to be found in section 26 of the Theft Act 1968 or section 23 of the Misuse of Drugs Act 1971, or for that matter section 18(2) and section 32(8) of PACE itself. Importantly the power to seize is only exercisable where a police officer is lawfully on premises.[90] Thus a police officer whose presence on premises has been consented to by the owner may exercise the section 19 power as may an officer who is on premises by virtue of a warrant issued by magistrates. In addition, the section 19 power may be exercised by an officer whose presence on premises is not authorised by warrant but by virtue of sections 17, 18 or 32 of PACE.

In *Cowan v Condon*,[91] the Court of Appeal was required to consider whether the powers of seizure conferred on the police by sections 18(2) and 19(3) of PACE entitled the police to seize the whole of a 'premises' in the form of a vehicle. The appellant had been charged with and subsequently convicted of a number of sexual offences against children which were alleged to have been committed in his car. The car had therefore been seized for finger-printing and to prevent it being interfered with by others, such as the parents of the alleged victims or those close to the appellant. The Court of Appeal held that the seizure had been lawful. In the words of Roch LJ, with whom Butler-Sloss LJ and Sir Oliver Popplewell agreed:

'Neither section gives a constable power to seize and retain the premises as a whole. On the other hand neither section prohibits the constable from seizing and retaining the premises as a whole. A constable will not be able to seize and retain premises when they are immovable property because of the physical impossibility of doing so. That practical barrier does not exist where the premises are readily movable such as a vehicle or a tent or a caravan. In my judgment there is no reason why the word "anything" contained in sections 18(2) and 19(2) and (3) should not include "everything" where the nature of the premises makes it physically possible for the totality of the premises to be seized and retained by the police, and where practical considerations make that desirable.'[92]

It should be noted that in addition to the foregoing provisions, section 19 empowers a police officer to require information stored in electronic form to be converted into a format that is both visible and legible, eg hard copy, which can be taken away.[93] However, this power is subject to the restriction that he must have reasonable grounds for believing that the information relates to an offence which he is investigating, or that it has been obtained as a result of the commission of an offence. In both cases, it must be necessary to take the information away so as to prevent it being concealed, lost, tampered with or destroyed. Importantly, section 19 does not entitle a police officer to seize items which he has reasonable grounds for believing are subject to legal privilege.[94] 'Items subject to legal privilege' are defined by section 10 of PACE as being: communications between a professional legal adviser and his client or person representing his client which relate to the giving of legal advice to the client; communications between adviser and client or any representative thereof or any other person which are made in connection with or contemplation of legal proceedings and for the purposes of such proceedings; and, items which are enclosed with or referred to in such communications and which are made in connection with the giving of legal advice or the contemplation of legal proceedings for the purposes of those proceedings.

[90] Section 19(1). [91] [2000] 1 WLR 254. [92] At 264. [93] Section 19(4).
[94] A power of seizure does exist, however, under Part 2 of the Criminal Justice and Police Act 2001 which is discussed at pp. 732–733.

As with other police powers, some guidance is given in the Codes of Practice as to the manner in which the power of seizure ought to be exercised. Many of the section 19 provisions are in fact reproduced in a paraphrased version in Code B, but paragraph 7.4 is an exception to this trend. It provides that:

'An officer may decide it is not appropriate to seize property because of an explanation from the person holding it but may nevertheless have reasonable grounds for believing that it was obtained in consequence of an offence by some person. In these circumstances, the officer should identify the property to the holder, inform the holder of their suspicions and explain the holder may be liable to civil or criminal proceedings if they dispose of, alter or destroy the property.'

(i) Additional powers of seizure

Sections 50–60 and Schedules 1 and 2 to the Criminal Justice and Police Act 2001 make provision for additional powers of seizure either from premises[95] or the person.[96] By virtue of section 50, where a person who is lawfully on premises finds anything on those premises which he has reasonable grounds for believing may contain something for which he is authorised to search on those premises, an existing power of seizure to which section 50 applies,[97] or the power of seizure referred by section 50(2), entitles that person to seize the relevant item or article in order to make a determination elsewhere as to whether he is entitled to seize. The power of seizure is exercisable only where it is not reasonably practicable to make the determination or separate the seizable property from the non-seizable property at the relevant premises.[98] The following factors are relevant to the issue of 'reasonable practicability':

- how long it would take to carry out the determination or separation on those premises;
- the number of persons that would be required to carry out the determination/separation on those premises within a reasonable period;
- whether the determination/separation if carried out on the premises would involve damage to property;
- the apparatus or equipment that would be required to carry out the determination/ separation.[99]

In effect, section 50 permits the seizure of legally privileged material which would otherwise be prohibited under section 19(6) of PACE. Such a power is considered to be necessary because of the practical difficulties which may sometimes arise where the police are required to search through large volumes of material, or material which is not easily accessible, and there is a danger that a restricted search may lead to important evidence being overlooked. A corresponding power of seizure applies in relation to a search of a person.[100]

Where the section 50 or section 51 power has been exercised, there is a duty on the person exercising it to give the occupier of the premises, or the person from whom the seizure was made, written notice specifying, amongst other things, what has been seized and the grounds on which the seizure powers have been exercised.[101] Section 53 of the 2001 Act is concerned

---

[95] Section 50.   [96] Section 51.

[97] These are specified in Schedule 1, Pt 1 to the 2001 Act. For present purposes it need only be noted that the powers of seizure conferred under Parts 2 and 3 of PACE fall within the scope of section 50 of the 2001 Act.

[98] Section 50(1)(c).   [99] Section 50(3).   [100] See section 51.   [101] Section 52(1) and (4).

with the subsequent examination of the seized material. Legally privileged material which is inextricably linked to material which is evidence of the commission of an offence can be retained under the authority of this section. Generally, however, there is an obligation to return items subject to legal privilege,[102] as there is in relation to excluded and special procedure material.[103] A person with a 'relevant interest'[104] in seized property can apply to the appropriate judicial authority, ie a Crown Court judge in England and Wales, for the return of the whole or part of the seized property.[105] There are several grounds for making such an application. They include that there was no power to make the seizure or that the seized property is or contains an item subject to legal privilege whose seizure was not authorised. The Crown Court judge has the power to dismiss the application with the result that the seized property is retained either in whole or in part by the police, or order the property's return. A failure to comply with an order made by a judge under section 59 amounts to a contempt of court.[106]

(f) Arrest

In the course of his discussion of the right to personal freedom in chapter V of *An Introduction to the Study of the Law of the Constitution*,[107] Professor AV Dicey asserted that: 'The right to personal liberty as understood in England means in substance a person's right not to be subjected to imprisonment, arrest, or other physical coercion in any manner that does not admit of legal justification.'[108] Despite the antiquity of these sentiments, they nevertheless contain several important propositions about the concept of arrest. First, Professor Dicey's words clearly stress the very nature of an arrest which involves the deprivation of an individual's liberty. Thus in *Spicer v Holt*,[109] Viscount Dilhorne observed:

' "Arrest" is an ordinary English word . . . Whether or not a person has been arrested depends not on the legality of the arrest but on whether he has been deprived of his liberty to go where he pleases.'[110]

In many instances, this deprivation of liberty will be against the individual's will, and hence there will be a need for compulsion as a necessary element of the arrest. The most straightforward means by which a person making an arrest can indicate to the person being arrested that he is under arrest is for him to take the arm of that person, thus signifying detention. However, it is possible that words alone may suffice to convey the existence of compulsion, provided that they are such as to leave the arrested person in no doubt as to the fact of his arrest. In *Alderson v Booth*,[111] a police officer who gave the defendant a breathalyser test which resulted in a positive reading announced to the defendant 'I shall have to ask you to come to the police station for further tests.' The defendant complied with the request, but at his trial on the charge of driving with an excess of alcohol in his blood, he succeeded in raising the defence that he could not be convicted of the offence because he had not been lawfully arrested by the police officer. The prosecutor's appeal against the defendant's acquittal was later dismissed by the Divisional Court, despite Lord Parker CJ's stated surprise at the fact that the justices believed the defendant's claim that he was not aware that he was under compulsion when he

---

[102] Section 54.   [103] Section 55.   [104] See section 59(11).   [105] Section 59(2).
[106] Section 59(9).   [107] (10th edn, 1959).   [108] At 207–208.   [109] [1977] AC 987.
[110] At 1000. In *Lewis v Chief Constable of South Wales Constabulary* [1991] 1 All ER 206, it was held, amongst other things, that this pre-PACE definition of an arrest remained good law in the light of the subsequent enactment of PACE.   [111] [1969] 2 QB 216.

went to the police station. In order to avoid future confusion in relation to this matter, the former Lord Chief Justice offered the following advice:

'I would only say this, that if what I have said is correct in law, it is advisable that police officers should use some very clear words to bring home to a person that he is under compulsion. It certainly must not be left in the state that a defendant can go into the witness-box and merely say "I did not think I was under compulsion". If difficulties for the future are to be avoided, it seems to me that by far and away the simplest thing is for a police officer to say "I arrest you". If the defendant goes to the police station after hearing those words, it seems to me that he simply could not be believed if he thereafter said "I did not think there was any compulsion, I was only going voluntarily".'[112]

The second important proposition to emerge from Professor Dicey's words is that for an arrest to be lawful, the power to arrest in the circumstances of a given case must have been derived from legal authority. Such legal authority may take the form of a warrant which is issued by a magistrate for the arrest of a person in accordance with section 1 of the Magistrates' Courts Act 1980. The majority of the arrests which take place in this country are not, however, authorised by a warrant. Rather, the sources of authority for these more commonly used powers of arrest are statute and common law. Since the sole power of arrest at common law arises in respect of a breach of the peace, which was dealt with in chapter 11 (see pp. 647–649), it is the statutory powers of arrest which are the more significant.

Formerly it was the case that in addition to the general arrest power set out in section 24 of PACE, a great many statutes conferred specific powers of arrest in relation to particular offences. The law on arrest has recently been rationalised as a consequence of reforms made by the Serious Organised Crime and Police Act 2005. In the discussion which follows, it will be necessary to consider the legal position both before and after those reforms.

(i) Arrest for any offence

As originally enacted, the powers of arrest set out in PACE distinguished between 'arrestable' and 'non-arrestable' offences. Essentially 'arrestable' offences were the more serious offences for which the penalty was fixed by law, eg murder, treason and genocide. In addition, other serious offences, such as manslaughter, rape, robbery, burglary, theft, criminal damage and arson also fell within the definition of an arrestable offence by virtue of the fact that they carry a maximum penalty of at least five years' imprisonment. Finally, section 24(2) and Schedule 1A of PACE specified a number of other offences which were deemed to be arrestable offences even though they did not satisfy either of the criteria outlined above.[113]

Under the original section 24, a police officer had the power to arrest a person where he had reasonable grounds for suspecting that an arrestable offence had been committed and he had reasonable grounds for suspecting the arrested person to be guilty of the offence. In addition, a police officer had the power to arrest anyone who was either about to commit an arrestable offence, or whom he had reasonable grounds for suspecting was about to commit an arrestable offence. A further power of arrest existed in relation to persons who were in the act of committing an arrestable offence or whom were reasonably suspected of being in the act of

---

[112] At 221.

[113] These included, for example, the taking of a motor vehicle or other conveyance without authority and any of the offences capable of being committed under the Football (Offences) Act 1991, eg the throwing of missiles or the chanting of indecent or racial abuse.

committing an arrestable offence. This power of arrest could also be exercised by private citizens.

Section 25 of PACE authorised a police officer (but not a private citizen) to arrest a person for a non-arrestable offence where he had reasonable grounds for suspecting that an offence had been committed and that one of the general arrest conditions applied. These general arrest conditions fell into two categories: the identity or address of the person to be arrested; or their behaviour. Thus, for example, failure to furnish a name or address when requested to do so by a police officer could activate the section 25 power of arrest where the relevant person was suspected of having committed a non-arrestable offence. Thus in *Nicholas v Parsonage*,[114] it was held that a defendant who had been riding a bicycle without due care and attention contrary to section 18 of the Road Traffic Act 1972 had been lawfully arrested under section 25(1) and (3) of PACE where he had twice refused to give his name and address on request. For an arrest to be valid under section 25, it was necessary to show that the arresting officer had the relevant general arrest condition in mind at the time of the arrest (a subjective test), and that the facts were such as to prove the existence of that condition (an objective test).[115]

In August 2004, the Home Office published a consultation paper, *Policing: Modernising Police Powers to Meet Community Needs*, in which it sought views on how key police powers such as the power of arrest might be reformed. In the opinion of the Home Office, although PACE had achieved 'some success' in clarifying powers of arrest 'by establishing a systematic structure based on clear principles of necessity and seriousness', it was nevertheless felt that there was 'a complex and often bewildering array of powers and procedures' to be followed. In short, the statutory definition of an 'arrestable offence' coupled with the fact that specific statutory powers of arrest were still to be found in enactments other than PACE[116] meant that the police were not always clear as to whether or not they had a power of arrest in a given situation. The consultation paper also noted that there was a 'common perception' that police officers had a power of arrest wherever they had reasonable grounds to suspect that an offence had been committed. Accordingly, as the solution to this 'confusion', the consultation paper proposed to extend the police power of arrest to all offences, however minor.

This important proposal did not meet with universal support. For example, the Human Rights organisation *Liberty* took the view that it was a disproportionate response which amounted to a 'lowest common denominator' approach to arrest powers. Rather than extend the power of arrest to all offences, *Liberty* argued that any problem in relation to arrest powers could be resolved by greater clarity[117] and improved police training. Nevertheless, the Government went ahead with the result that the text of the new section 24 of PACE[118] largely reflects the proposals set out in the earlier consultation paper.

'24 Arrest without a warrant: constables

(1) A constable may arrest without a warrant —

    (a) anyone who is about to commit an offence;

    (b) anyone who is in the act of committing an offence;

---

[114] [1987] RTR 199.

[115] See, for example, *Edwards v DPP* (1993) 97 Cr App R 301.

[116] For example, sections 3(6), 4(3), 4A(4) and 5(4) of the Public Order Act 1986 formerly empowered the police to arrest a person who had committed an offence contrary to the relevant section.

[117] This would have entailed providing a definitive list of powers of arrest complemented by information on how they were to be exercised.

[118] As substituted by section 110(1) of the Serious Organised Crime and Police Act 2005.

(c) anyone whom he has reasonable grounds for suspecting to be about to commit an offence;

(d) anyone whom he has reasonable grounds for suspecting to be committing an offence.

(2) If a constable has reasonable grounds for suspecting that an offence has been committed, he may arrest without a warrant anyone whom he has reasonable grounds to suspect of being guilty of it.

(3) If an offence has been committed, a constable may arrest without a warrant —

(a) anyone who is guilty of the offence;

(b) anyone whom he has reasonable grounds for suspecting to be guilty of it.

(4) But the power of summary arrest conferred by subsection (1), (2) or (3) is exercisable only if the constable has reasonable grounds of believing that for any of the reasons mentioned in subsection (5) it is necessary to arrest the person in question.

(5) The reasons are—

(a) to enable the name of the person in question to be ascertained (in the case where the constable does not know, and cannot readily ascertain, the person's name, or has reasonable grounds for doubting whether a name given by the person as his name is his real name);

(b) correspondingly as regards the person's address.

(c) to prevent the person in question —

(i) causing physical injury to himself or any other person;

(ii) suffering physical injury;

(iii) causing loss of or damage to property;

(iv) committing an offence against public decency;

(v) causing an unlawful obstruction of the highway.

(d) to protect a child or other vulnerable person from the person in question.

(e) to allow the prompt and effective investigation of the offence or of the conduct of the person in question;

(f) to prevent any prosecution for the offence from being hindered by the disappearance of the person in question.

(6) Subsection (5)(c)(iv) applies only where members of the public going about their normal business cannot reasonably be expected to avoid the person in question.'

The key difference between section 24 as originally enacted and the new section 24 is that the police power of arrest now relates to *any offence* and not just an arrestable offence as was formerly the case. However, such a power only becomes exercisable where a police officer has reasonable grounds for believing that an arrest is necessary for any of the reasons specified in section 24(5)(a)–(f). These necessity criteria broadly reflect the general arrest conditions which were formerly set out in section 25 of PACE.[119] Under this provision, the police were entitled to make an arrest where a non-arrestable offence had been committed and one of the general arrest conditions applied. These conditions fell into two categories: the identity and address of the relevant person; or the behaviour of that person. Thus, as we have already seen, in *Nicholas v Parsonage*[120] it was held that a defendant who had been riding a bicycle without due care and attention contrary to section 18 of the Road Traffic Act 1972 had been lawfully arrested under section 25(1) and (3) where he had twice refused to give his name and address on request.

---

[119] Section 25 of PACE has been repealed by section 110(2) of the Serious Organised Crime and Police Act 2005.　　　　　　　　　　　　　　　　　　　　　　　[120] [1987] RTR 199. See p. 735.

Although there are many overlaps between the former general arrest conditions and the new necessity criteria, section 24(5) does not simply restate the previous position. The necessity criterion set out in section 24(5)(e), that an arrest is necessary for the prompt and effective investigation of the offence, is new. It is also potentially very wide in its application. During the committee stage of the Serious Organised Crime and Police Bill, one member of Standing Committee D argued that it was a 'catch-all provision' which would provide 'an open door to an officer to arrest on fairly trivial grounds'.[121] In response, a government minister assured the Committee that guidance on the exercise of the power would be set out in a forthcoming new Code of Practice relating to arrest powers.[122] In Code of Practice G,[123] it is stated that section 24(5)(e) may apply where an officer has reasonable grounds for believing that the person to be arrested: has made false statements; has made statements which cannot be readily verified; has presented false evidence; may steal or destroy evidence; may make contact with co-suspects or conspirators; may intimidate or threaten or make contact with witnesses; or where it is necessary to obtain evidence by questioning.[124] Where a police officer is considering arresting a person for an indictable offence (which triggers the exercise of consequential powers such as entry and search),[125] Code of Practice G informs him that an arrest may be necessary for the reasons stated in section 24(5)(e) where there is a need to: enter and search any premises occupied or controlled by the person; search the person; prevent contact with others; or take fingerprints, footwear impressions, samples or photographs of the suspect.

Under section 25, for an arrest to be valid it was necessary to show that the arresting officer had the relevant general arrest condition in mind at the time of arrest (a subjective test), and that the facts were such as to prove the existence of that condition (an objective test).[126] It would seem that the same tests will apply to the necessity criteria under the new section 24(5). Therefore, where an officer arrests a person, for the arrest to be lawful the officer will have to have in mind one of the necessity criteria set out in section 24(5)(a)–(f)[127] and the facts of the case must be such as to show that the officer's belief was reasonable in the circumstances.

(ii) Citizen's arrest

Under section 24 of PACE as originally enacted, powers of arrest were conferred on the ordinary citizen as well as on the police officer.[128] However, there were limits on the citizen's power of arrest. It was confined to a situation where either an arrestable offence was in the process of being committed or where an arrestable offence had been committed. In the case of

---

[121] Per Dominic Grieve MP, Standing Committee D, sixth sitting, 18 January 2005, at col 250.

[122] It is a moot point whether this was an entirely satisfactory response to the Committee's concerns given that there was no text of a draft Code of Practice on arrest powers before the Committee at the relevant time.

[123] The provisions of the Code apply to arrests made under the authority of the new section 24 from midnight on 31 December 2005 onwards. Code of Practice G is discussed more fully at pp. 745–746.

[124] Code of Practice G, para 2.9.

[125] These are exercisable under section 18 of PACE which was discussed at pp. 725–729.

[126] See, for example, *Edwards v DPP* (1993) 97 Cr App R 301.

[127] Code of Practice G makes it clear that the necessity criteria are 'exhaustive': see para 2.7. In other words, since only these criteria apply, the police are not entitled to form the view that an arrest is necessary for any reason other than those stated.

[128] The citizen's power of arrest does, however, predate PACE. It originally existed at common law: see *Walters v W H Smith & Son Ltd* [1914] 1 KB 595 and the discussion therein.

the former situation, a citizen could arrest any person who was in the act of committing an arrestable offence or whom they reasonably believed was so acting. In the latter situation, a citizen was empowered to arrest any person who was guilty of an arrestable offence or whom the citizen had reasonable grounds for suspecting to be guilty of the offence.[129]

Where the power of arrest was exercised in respect of an arrestable offence which was claimed to have been committed, if the arrested person was subsequently acquitted, the basis for the original arrest had never in law existed and the arrest was thereby rendered unlawful. Accordingly, a person who was detained in these circumstances would be entitled to use force to resist their unlawful detention and they may even recover damages were they to institute civil proceedings.

R v Self [1992] 1 WLR 657

The appellant was seen by a store detective to put a bar of chocolate in his pocket and then leave the shop without paying for it. The store detective and a shop assistant followed the appellant and tried to arrest him, but they only managed to do so with the help of a member of the public who declared that he was making a citizen's arrest. Prior to the appellant's final apprehension, he had assaulted both the shop assistant and the member of the public and thus, in addition to theft, he was charged with two counts of assault with intent to prevent his lawful detention contrary to section 38 of the Offences Against the Person Act 1861. At his trial, the appellant was acquitted of the theft charge but convicted of the two assault charges. On appeal, he argued that since the power of citizen's arrest for an arrestable offence under section 24(5) of PACE only arose where the person arrested was guilty of the offence, or where he was suspected on reasonable grounds to be guilty of the offence, it followed that his acquittal on the theft charge meant that he should not have been arrested by the shop assistant and the member of the public. Accordingly, it was claimed that the appellant should not have been convicted of the section 38 offences since he was merely seeking to resist an unlawful arrest. The Court of Appeal upheld the appellant's appeal on this basis and therefore quashed his convictions.

Garland LJ, at 661

'. . . in the judgment of this court, the words of section 24 do not admit of argument. Subsection (5) makes it abundantly clear that the powers of arrest without a warrant where an arrestable offence has been committed require as a condition precedent an offence committed. If subsequently there is an acquittal of the alleged offence no offence has been committed. The power to arrest is confined to the person guilty of the offence or anyone who the person making the arrest has reasonable grounds for suspecting to be guilty of it. But of course if he is not guilty there can be no valid suspicion . . .

If it is necessary to go further, one contrasts the words of subsection (5) with subsection (6), the very much wider powers given to a constable who has reasonable ground for suspecting that an arrestable offence has been committed. However, it is said on behalf of the Crown that the court should not be - assiduous to restrict the citizen's powers of arrest and that, by going back to subsection (4) and looking at the words there, "anyone who is in the act of committing an arrestable offence", perhaps those words can be used to cover the sort of situation that arose in this case where somebody is apparently making good his escape. Having committed the offence of theft, can it be said, asks Mr Sleeman [counsel for the Crown], that the thief is not in substance still committing the offence while running away?

He asks, rhetorically, should the court have to inquire into the exact moment when the ingredients of theft come together—dishonesty, appropriation, intention permanently to deprive—when to

---

[129] In practice, citizen's arrests are more likely to be made by persons who 'police' particular environments, eg store detectives or nightclub security staff, than by the man or woman who is simply walking down the street.

analyse the offence carefully may produce absurd results so that in one set of circumstances the offence may be complete and the situation fall within subsection (5) and in another be still being committed and fall within subsection (4).

The view of this court is that little profit can be had from taking examples and trying to reduce them to absurdity. The words of the statute are clear and applying those words to this case there was no arrestable offence committed. It necessarily follows that the two offences under section 38 of the Offences against the Person Act could not be committed because there was no power to apprehend or detain the appellant.'

In the earlier case of *Walters v W H Smith & Son Ltd*,[130] Sir Rufus Isaacs CJ remarked in the present context that 'the law seems to operate somewhat harshly upon the defendants'.[131] The decision in *Self* confirms this to be the case. Although the case was undoubtedly correctly decided, it does demonstrate the dilemma faced by a store detective.[132] If he were to arrest a person on the basis that he reasonably believed that they were committing an arrestable offence, if he was subsequently shown to be wrong in that belief, he would not necessarily be liable for an unlawful arrest so long as his belief was held to be reasonable in the circumstances. If, however, as in *Self*, the person was arrested for having committed an offence but was subsequently acquitted, the arrest would be unlawful because the commission of the offence was a 'condition precedent' of the power to arrest. Writing shortly after the decision in *Self*, Stannard contended that the 'moral' which emerges from the case:

'. . . would seem to be that a store detective who does not want his power of arrest to be negated by the caprices of a jury acquittal should strike while the iron is hot; that is to say, he should make sure he arrests his suspect before the theft is complete'.[133]

In its seventh report published in 1965,[134] the Criminal Law Revision Committee considered amongst other things the citizen's power of arrest. It advocated the retention of the power but not its extension. For the majority of the Committee, it was doubted:

'whether it would be desirable, or acceptable to public opinion, to increase the powers of arrest enjoyed by private persons; and they think that there is a strong argument in policy that a private person should, if it is at all doubtful whether the offence was committed, put the matter in the hands of the police or . . . take the risk of liability if he acts on his own responsibility'.[135]

When the Home Office returned to the subject some forty years later in *Policing: Modernising Police Powers to Meet Community Needs*, it too advocated the retention of a citizen's power of arrest which would continue to be more limited than the powers of arrest available to the police. Thus it envisaged a power of arrest which would be 'restricted to where the need for immediate action is such as to preclude the reasonable possibility of involving a police officer' and which would, in addition, only be capable of being exercised where an arrest appeared necessary to prevent: the person evading justice; or, interference with or harm to other persons; or the loss of or harm to property. Its proposals are largely reflected in the new section 24A of PACE.[136]

---

[130] [1914] 1 KB 595.   [131] At 606.
[132] See the comment on the case by Professor JC Smith, [1992] Crim LR 573.
[133] See Stannard, 'The Store Detective's Dilemma' (1994) 58 J Crim L 393 at 394.
[134] Cmnd 2659 (1965).   [135] Ibid., at para 15.
[136] Section 24 as originally enacted contained the arrest powers of both the police officer and the ordinary citizen. The distinction between those powers has now been underlined by their presence in different sections, the substituted section 24 and the inserted section 24A.

'24A Arrest without warrant: other persons

(1) A person other than a constable may arrest without a warrant —

    (a) anyone who is in the act of committing an indictable offence;

    (b) anyone whom he has reasonable grounds for suspecting to be committing an indictable offence.

(2) Where an indictable offence has been committed, a person other than a constable may arrest without a warrant —

    (a) anyone who is guilty of the offence;

    (b) anyone whom he has reasonable grounds for suspecting to be guilty of it.

(3) But the power of summary arrest conferred by subsection (1) or (2) is exercisable only if —

    (a) the person making the arrest has reasonable grounds for believing that for any of the reasons mentioned in subsection (4) it is necessary to arrest the person in question; and

    (b) it appears to the person making the arrest that it is not reasonably practicable for a constable to make it instead.

(4) The reasons are to prevent the person in question —

    (a) causing physical injury to himself or any other person;

    (b) suffering physical injury;

    (c) causing loss of or damage to property; or

    (d) making off before a constable can assume responsibility for him.'

It will be noted that the citizen's power of arrest is exercisable only in respect of 'indictable' offences.[137] Unlike a police officer's power of arrest, it does not apply to any offence. It will also be noted that in accordance with the previous position, the citizen's power of arrest does not extend to indictable offences which are about to be committed.[138] Further limitations on the citizen's power of arrest are set out in section 24A(3) and (4). It is evident from these that a citizen's arrest will only be the appropriate course of action to take where it is necessary for one of the reasons specified in subsection (4)(a)–(d), and where it is not reasonably practicable for a police officer rather than a citizen to make the arrest.

(iii) Reasonable suspicion

'Reasonable suspicion' is a central concept in relation to the exercise of several important police powers, including the power of arrest.[139] This was true of section 24 of PACE as originally enacted and it remains true of the new version of section 24, as set out above. The role of 'reasonable suspicion' is to safeguard the individual against the arbitrary or random use of police powers. It is surprising, therefore, that despite its undoubted importance, there is no

---

[137] An indictable offence is essentially a more serious criminal offence than a summary offence. Accordingly, it is triable in the Crown Court rather than before magistrates.

[138] In its consultation paper, the Home Office had proposed to extend the citizen's power of arrest to offences which were about to be committed. However, the proposal did not appear in the Bill which was subsequently introduced.

[139] Thus, for example, police powers of stop and search can generally only be exercised where an officer reasonably suspects that the person to be searched is in possession of a relevant article. For an exception to this general rule, see the power of stop and search in section 60 of the Criminal Justice and Public Order Act 1994.

definition of what is meant by 'reasonable suspicion' in PACE itself. Neither is the concept defined in the new Code of Practice G, on the statutory power of arrest.[140] The position in relation to the arrest power can therefore be contrasted with that which relates to the police powers of stop and search. In the relevant Code of Practice,[141] some guidance is given as to what may or may not amount to 'reasonable suspicion' in that context.[142] Thus the Code states, amongst other things, that:

'Reasonable grounds for suspicion depend on the circumstances in each case. There must be an objective basis for that suspicion based on facts, information and/or intelligence . . . Reasonable suspicion can never be supported on the basis of personal factors alone without reliable supporting intelligence or information or some specific behaviour by the person concerned . . . Reasonable suspicion cannot be based on generalisations or stereotypical images of certain groups or categories of people as more likely to be involved in criminal activity . . .'[143]

In the absence of a statutory (or Code of Practice) definition of 'reasonable suspicion' for the purposes of the arrest power it is necessary to have regard to how the courts have interpreted this concept in the present context.

O'Hara v Chief Constable of the Royal Ulster Constabulary [1997] AC 286

The claimant was arrested at his home pursuant to section 12(1) of the Prevention of Terrorism (Temporary Provisions) Act 1984. The arresting officer had no basis for suspecting the claimant to have been involved in the commission of acts of terrorism other than what he had been told in a briefing earlier that same day. At that briefing a senior colleague informed him that the claimant had been involved in a murder. The claimant was subsequently released without charge. He brought an action against the chief constable in which he sought damages for wrongful arrest. At the trial, it was held that the police officer had a reasonable suspicion of the claimant's involvement in the murder based on the information given to him at the briefing. Accordingly, the arrest had fallen within the scope of section 12(1). The Northern Ireland Court of Appeal dismissed an appeal against that decision, as did the House of Lords.

Lord Steyn, at 289–293

'The constable made the arrest in connection with a murder which was undoubtedly an act of terrorism within the meaning of section 12(1) of the Act of 1984. It was common ground that subjectively the constable had the necessary suspicion. The question was whether the constable objectively had reasonable grounds for suspecting that the [claimant] was concerned in the murder. The constable said in evidence that his reasonable grounds for suspecting the [claimant] were based on a briefing by a superior officer. He was told that the [claimant] had been involved in the murder. The constable said that the superior officer ordered him to arrest the [claimant] . . . The trial judge described the evidence as scanty. But he inferred that the briefing afforded reasonable grounds for the necessary suspicion. In other words the judge inferred that some further details must have been given in the briefing. The legal burden was on the Chief Constable to prove the existence of reasonable grounds for suspicion. Nevertheless I am persuaded that the judge was entitled on the sparse materials before him to infer the existence of reasonable grounds for suspicion . . .

Section 12(1) authorises an arrest without warrant only where the constable has "reasonable grounds for" suspicion. An arrest is therefore not lawful if the arresting officer honestly but erroneously believes that he has reasonable grounds for arrest but there are unknown to him in fact in existence reasonable grounds for the necessary suspicion, eg because another officer has information pointing to the guilt of the suspect. It would be difficult without doing violence to the wording of the statute to read it in any other way.

A strong argument can be made that in arresting a suspect without warrant a constable ought to be able to rely on information in the possession of another officer and not communicated to him . . . Arguably that ought as a matter of policy to provide him with a defence to a claim for wrongful arrest. Such considerations may possibly explain why article 5(1) of the European Convention for the Protection of Human Rights and Fundamental Freedoms . . . contains a more flexible provision. It reads as follows:

> "Everyone has the right to liberty and security of person. No one shall be deprived of his liberty save in the following cases and in accordance with a procedure prescribed by law: . . . (c) the lawful arrest or detention of a person effected for the purpose of bringing him before the competent legal author-ity on reasonable suspicion of having committed an offence or when it is reasonably considered necessary to prevent his committing an offence or fleeing after having done so; . . ."

It is clear from the drafting technique employed in article 5(1)(c), and in particular the use of the passive tense, that it contemplates a broader test of whether a reasonable suspicion exists and does not con-fine it to matters present in the mind of the arresting officer. That is also the effect of the judgment of the European Court of Human Rights in *Fox, Campbell and Hartley* . . . But section 12(1), and similar provisions, cannot be approached in this way: they categorise as reasonable grounds for suspicion only matters present in the mind of the constable . . .

Certain general propositions about the powers of constables under a section such as section 12(1) can now be summarized. (1) In order to have a reasonable suspicion the constable need not have evidence amounting to a prima facie case. Ex hypothesi one is considering a preliminary stage of the investigation and information from an informer or a tip-off from a member of the public may be enough: *Hussein v Chong Fook Kam* [1970] AC 942, 949. (2) Hearsay information may therefore afford a constable reasonable grounds to arrest. Such information may come from other officers: *Hussein's* case, ibid. (3) The information which causes the constable to be suspicious of the individual must be in existence to the knowledge of the police officer at the time he makes the arrest. (4) The executive "discretion" to arrest or not, as Lord Diplock described it in *Mohammed-Holgate v Duke* [1984] AC 437, 446, vests in the constable, who is engaged on the decision to arrest or not, and not in his superior officers.

Given the independent responsibility and accountability of a constable under a provision such as section 12(1) . . . it seems to follow that the mere fact that an arresting officer has been instructed by a superior officer to effect the arrest is not capable of amounting to reasonable grounds for the neces-sary suspicion within the meaning of section 12(1). It is accepted, and rightly accepted, that a mere request without any further information by an equal ranking officer, or a junior officer, is incapable of amounting to reasonable grounds for the necessary suspicion. How can the badge of the superior officer, and the fact that he gave an order, make a difference?'

Lord Hope, at 297–298

'It is now commonplace for Parliament to enable powers which may interfere with the liberty of the person to be exercised without warrant where the person who exercises these powers has reasonable grounds for suspecting that the person against whom they are to be exercised has committed or is committing an offence. The protection of the subject lies in the nature of the test which has to be applied in order to determine whether the requirement that there be reasonable grounds for the suspicion is satisfied.

My Lords, the test which section 12(1) . . . has laid down is a simple but practical one. It relates entirely to what is in the mind of the arresting officer when the power is exercised. In part it is a subjective test, because he must have formed a genuine suspicion in his own mind that the person has been concerned in acts of terrorism. In part also it is an objective one, because there must also be reasonable grounds for the suspicion which he has formed. But the application of the objective test does not require the court to look beyond what was in the mind of the arresting officer. It is the grounds which were in his mind at the time which must be found to be reasonable grounds for the suspicion which he has formed. All that the objective test requires is that these grounds be examined objectively and that they be judged at the time when the power was exercised.

This means that the point does not depend on whether the arresting officer himself thought at that time that they were reasonable. The question is whether a reasonable man would be of that opinion, having regard to the information which was in the mind of the arresting officer. It is the arresting officer's own account of the information which he had which matters, not what was observed by or known to anyone else. The information acted on by the arresting officer need not be based on his own observations, as he is entitled to form a suspicion based on what he has been told. His reasonable suspicion may be based on information which has been given to him anonymously or it may be based on information, perhaps in the course of an emergency, which turns out later to be wrong. As it is the information which is in his mind alone which is relevant however, it is not necessary to go on to prove what was known to his informant or that any facts on which he based his suspicion were in fact true. The question whether it provided reasonable grounds for the suspicion depends on the source of his information and its content, seen in the light of the whole surrounding circumstances.'

It is therefore apparent from these passages in the judgment in *O'Hara* that the test for 'reasonable suspicion' in the present context consists of both a subjective and an objective element. It is only if the arresting officer had a suspicion in his own mind at the time of the arrest, and that when viewed objectively that suspicion was reasonable, that an arrest will be lawful. Although this constitutes an important safeguard against the abuse of the arrest power, it should not be forgotten that, as the following words of Lord Devlin in *Hussein v Chong Fook Kam*[144] explain, 'suspicion' falls a long way short of prima facie proof:

'Suspicion in its ordinary meaning is a state of conjecture or surmise where proof is lacking; "I suspect but I cannot prove". Suspicion arises at or near the starting point of an investigation of which the obtaining of prima facie proof is the end. When such proof has been obtained, the police case is complete; it is ready for trial and passes on to its next stage. It is indeed desirable as a general rule that an arrest should not be made until a case is complete. But if an arrest before that were forbidden, it would seriously hamper the police . . .'.[145]

The approach taken by the House of Lords in *O'Hara* was subsequently held to be compatible with article 5(1)(c) of the ECHR by the European Court of Human Rights. In *O'Hara v UK*,[146] that court emphasized that 'the "reasonableness" of the suspicion on which the arrest must be based forms an essential part of the safeguard against arbitrary arrest and detention laid down in Article 5(1)(c) of the Convention'.[147] In its judgment, the safeguard required 'the existence of some facts or information which would satisfy an objective observer that the person arrested may have committed the offence'.[148] However, the European Court was at pains to stress that the standard imposed by article 5(1)(c) 'does not presuppose that the police have sufficient evidence to bring charges at the time of arrest'. In a passage redolent of the remarks of Lord Devlin in *Hussein*, the court observed:

'The object of questioning during detention under sub-paragraph (c) of Article 5(1) is to further the criminal investigation by confirming or dispelling the concrete suspicion grounding the arrest. Thus

---

[144] [1970] AC 942.
[145] At 948. See also the earlier remarks of Scott LJ in *Dumbell v Roberts* [1944] 1 All ER 326 at 329.
[146] (2002) 34 EHRR 32.   [147] At para 34.   [148] Ibid.

facts which raise a suspicion need not be of the same level as those necessary to justify a conviction, or even the bringing of a charge which comes at the next stage of the process of criminal investigation.'[149]

The House of Lords decision in *O'Hara* makes plain that a 'reasonable suspicion' in the mind of an arresting officer can be based on information received from another, eg an informant or a colleague. Thus in *Hough v Chief Constable of Staffordshire Constabulary*,[150] the claimant had been arrested on suspicion of being in possession of a firearm on the strength of an entry on the national police computer posted by a police officer in a different force which warned that he may well be armed. The claimant subsequently sued for unlawful arrest and was awarded £10,000 damages at trial. On appeal, however, the Court of Appeal took a rather different view of the matter. Given the importance of the decision in *O'Hara*, Simon Brown LJ observed that it was 'a matter of some surprise and regret that it appears not to have been brought to the judge's attention' in the present case. Had it been cited before the county court, the Court of Appeal was firmly of the opinion that the case would have been decided in favour of the chief constable since the principle which *O'Hara* establishes could be applied to the facts of *Hough*. Thus although a police officer could 'never be a "mere conduit" for someone else', since the authorities clearly showed that a reasonable suspicion justifying an arrest could be based on information received from a third party, there was no reason why that information could not come from an apparently responsible entry on the national police computer.[151] This does not mean, however, that all entries on the computer will necessarily satisfy the reasonable suspicion requirement. As Simon Brown LJ was at pains to stress in *Hough* itself, where a situation lacked urgency and the surrounding circumstances dictated that there was a need for further enquiry before a reasonable suspicion could properly crystallize, then the entry alone would not suffice. It is evident therefore that each case will turn upon its own particular facts.

The decision in *O'Hara* has subsequently been applied in *Cumming and others v Chief Constable of Northumbria Police*[152] and *Al Fayed and others v Commissioner of Police of the Metropolis*.[153] In both cases, the differently constituted Courts of Appeal also applied the approach advocated by Woolf LJ (as he then was) in *Castorina v Chief Constable of Surrey*.[154] In that case, Woolf LJ had identified three questions posed by a reasonable suspicion requirement in an arrest power[155] as follows:

'(1) Did the arresting officer suspect that the person who was arrested was guilty of the offence? The answer to this question depends entirely on the findings of fact of the officer's state of mind.

(2) Assuming the officer had the necessary suspicion, was there reasonable cause for that suspicion? This is a purely objective requirement to be determined by the judge if necessary on facts found by a jury.

(3) If the answer to the previous two questions is in the affirmative, then the officer has a discretion which entitled him to make an arrest and in relation to that discretion the question arises as to whether the discretion has been exercised in accordance with the principles laid down . . . in . . . *Wednesbury*.'[156]

---

[149] At para 36. [150] (Unreported), *The Times*, 15 February 2001.

[151] Although such an entry could justify the formation of a reasonable suspicion in the mind of an arresting officer, the Court of Appeal left open the possibility of an officer who had made an entry being sued where it could be shown that he had been negligent. [152] [2003] EWCA Civ 1844.

[153] [2004] EWCA Civ 1579. [154] [1996] LGR 241.

[155] The relevant power was the original section 24(6) of PACE.

[156] [1996] LGR 241 at 249. For a discussion of the *Wednesbury* principles, see pp. 563–565.

Questions (1) and (2) will be for the police to establish on the balance of probabilities. If they are able to show that the arresting officer did have a suspicion and that on the facts known to him, that suspicion was reasonable, the arrest will be lawful unless the claimant is able to show that in exercising his discretion to arrest, the officer acted contrary to the *Wednesbury* principles, eg by failing to take into account a relevant factor or by taking into account an irrelevant factor.

The matter to be determined in *Cumming* was whether the police had been entitled to arrest six council employees on suspicion of having perverted the course of justice by interfering with security video tape recordings made at their place of work (a CCTV room) which appeared to show the commission of a criminal offence. The police had been able as a result of their investigations to narrow the number of suspects down to an irreducible minimum of six. They knew that only one or possibly two of the suspects had interfered with the recordings, but on the basis that all of them had had the opportunity to do so, they arrested all six in order to expedite the investigation and get a confession from the guilty party.[157] The Court of Appeal held[158] that there was nothing in principle which prevented opportunity from amounting to reasonable grounds for suspicion. Moreover, there was nothing in principle wrong with arresting more than one person even where the crime in question could only have been committed by one person. Accordingly, the Court of Appeal upheld the lawfulness of the appellants' arrest.

Interestingly, in the later case of *Al Fayed*, where the Court of Appeal held that police officers had lawfully arrested a number of persons on suspicion of being jointly involved in the theft of and/or criminal damage to the contents of a deposit box stored in the safe depository at Harrod's Department Store, Auld LJ's comments on the decision in *Cumming* would seem to suggest that where the police arrest on the basis of having had the opportunity to commit the relevant offence, it need not be incumbent on them to eliminate all other suspects before they are able to arrest those whom they decide to arrest. In his opinion, it was 'all a matter of degree, in which the strength of the opportunity, whether or not unique to the person or persons arrested, has to be considered in the context of all the other information available to the arresting officer'.[159]

(iv) Code of Practice G

As originally enacted, the duty which sections 60 and 66 of PACE impose on the Secretary of State to draw up codes of practice in respect of the exercise of certain police powers did not extend to arrest. Now, however, as a consequence of an amendment made by the Serious Organised Crime and Police Act 2005, that statutory duty also encompasses arrest. Thus in accordance with that duty, the Secretary of State has drawn up Code of Practice G which deals with the 'statutory power of police to arrest persons suspected of involvement in a criminal offence'.[160] Code G makes it clear to police officers (if it was not already), that the use of the arrest power 'must be fully justified' and that officers exercising the power 'should consider if

---

[157] In *Holgate-Mohammed v Duke* [1984] AC 437 (see p. 706), the House of Lords held that it was lawful to arrest for this latter purpose. [158] In the case of Brooke LJ, he did so with stated unease: at [46].

[159] [2004] EWCA Civ 1579 at [56].

[160] At para 1.1. Code of Practice G therefore does not apply to an arrest at common law for a breach of the peace (see pp. 647–649). Neither, for that matter, will it apply to a citizen's powers of arrest under section 24A.

the necessary objectives can be met by other, less intrusive means'.[161] Thus the power of 'arrest must never be used simply because it can be used'.[162] Code G also makes it clear that 'it is essential that it is exercised in a non-discriminatory and proportionate manner'.[163]

Moving from the more general principles which apply to arrests to the specific content of the new section 24 powers, Code G makes it clear that despite the existence of the necessity criteria in section 24(5), it 'remains an operational decision at the discretion of the arresting officer' as to: what action he may take at the point of contact with an individual; which (if any) of the necessity criteria applies to the individual; and, whether to arrest, report for summons, issue a fixed penalty notice, etc.[164] It follows from this, therefore, that the existence of one or more necessity criteria does not mean that an arrest must follow. The reforms to section 24 of PACE have not transformed a power into a duty; a police officer retains a discretion as to how best to deal with a particular situation and in exercising that discretion, he may choose to arrest provided that the requirements of section 24 are satisfied.

In effecting an arrest, police officers are obliged to caution a person as follows:

'You do not have to say anything. But it may harm your defence if you do not mention when questioned something which you later rely on in Court. Anything you do say may be given in evidence.'[165]

Code G makes it clear that 'minor deviations' from this form of words do not constitute a breach of the Code provided that the sense of the caution has been preserved.[166]

The final section of Code G is concerned with the recording of certain information relating to an arrest. The relevant information comprises: the nature and circumstances of the offence leading to the arrest; the reason(s) why the arrest was necessary; the giving of the caution; and, anything said by the person at the time of the arrest.[167] Such information must be recorded either 'in his pocket book or by other methods used for recording information'.

(v) Information to be given on arrest

'28 Information to be given on arrest

(1) Subject to subsection (5) below, where a person is arrested, otherwise than by being informed that he is under arrest, the arrest is not lawful unless the person arrested is informed that he is under arrest as soon as is practicable after his arrest.

(2) Where a person is arrested by a constable, subsection (1) above applies regardless of whether the fact of the arrest is obvious.

(3) Subject to subsection (5) below, no arrest is lawful unless the person arrested is informed of the ground for the arrest at the time of, or as soon as is practicable after, the arrest.

(4) Where a person is arrested by a constable, subsection (3) above applies regardless of whether the ground for the arrest is obvious.

---

[161] Para 1.3. Presumably what the Code really means is that *prior* to exercising the statutory power of arrest, police officers ought to have given some thought to the alternative means of dealing with the situation.
[162] Ibid.
[163] Ibid. Although this should always have been the case, it is especially important now in the light of the Human Rights Act 1998. [164] Para 2.4.
[165] Para 3.5.
[166] Para 3.6. Note 5 to Code G states that 'if it appears a person does not understand the caution, the people giving it should explain it in their own words'. [167] Para 4.1.

(5) Nothing in this section is to be taken to require a person to be informed—

    (a) that he is under arrest; or

    (b) of the ground for arrest,

if it was not reasonably practicable for him to be so informed by reason of his having escaped from arrest before the information could be given.'

It is a necessary ingredient of an arrest that the person being arrested must be informed both of the fact that they are under arrest, and the grounds for the arrest in order that they may have an 'immediate opportunity of explanation or self-exculpation'.[168] Prior to the enactment of PACE the leading authority as to what the common law required following an arrest was the House of Lords decision in *Christie v Leachinsky*.[169] In that case, which concerned a claim for damages for false imprisonment and trespass to the person in respect of an arrest effected by police, Viscount Simon was of the opinion that the following five propositions could be gleaned from the text books and judicial decisions:

'1. If a policeman arrests without warrant on reasonable suspicion of felony, or of other crime of a sort which does not require a warrant, he must in ordinary circumstances inform the person arrested of the true ground of arrest. He is not entitled to keep the reason to himself or to give a reason which is not the true reason. In other words, a citizen is entitled to know on what charge or on suspicion of what crime he is seized.

2. If the citizen is not so informed, but is nevertheless seized, the policeman, apart from certain exceptions, is liable for false imprisonment.

3. The requirement that the person arrested should be informed of the reason why he is seized naturally does not exist if the circumstances are such that he must know the general nature of the alleged offence for which he is detained.

4. The requirement that he should be so informed does not mean that technical or precise language need be used. The matter is a matter of substance, and turns on the elementary proposition that in this country a person is, prima facie, entitled to his freedom and is only required to submit to restraint on his freedom if he knows in substance the reason why it is claimed that this restraint should be imposed.

5. The person arrested cannot complain that he has not been supplied with the above information as and when he should be, if he himself produces the situation which makes it practically impossible to inform him, eg by immediate counter-attack or by running away.'[170]

To quite a large extent these propositions are reflected in the words of section 28 of PACE 1984.[171] Thus it is necessary, for example, for a police officer to inform an arrested person of the reason why they have been arrested at the time of the arrest or, alternatively, as soon as it is practicable to do so.[172] However, in direct contrast to the third proposition advanced in *Christie v Leachinsky*, if it is a police officer who has effected an arrest, he or she must comply with the terms of section 28(3) even where the ground for arrest is obvious.[173] Thus if a police officer apprehended a burglar leaving a house with a bag slung over his shoulder containing articles which he had clearly stolen from the house, the police officer would need to state that the arrest was for the offence of burglary even though in the circumstances described, it would be perfectly obvious to the burglar why he was being arrested.

Viscount Simon's fourth proposition has subsequently been elaborated upon in several cases. In *Abbassy v Commissioner of the Police for the Metropolis*,[174] for example, the Court of

---

[168] Per Sedley LJ in *Taylor v Chief Constable of Thames Valley Police* [2004] 1 WLR 3115 at [58].

[169] [1947] AC 573.   [170] At 587–588.

[171] As was recommended by the Royal Commission on Criminal Procedure, Cmnd 8092, at para 3.87.

[172] Section 28(3).   [173] Section 28(4).   [174] [1990] 1 WLR 385.

Appeal stressed that the question whether a person has been properly informed of the grounds for their arrest was a question of fact to be determined by a jury rather than a matter of law for a judge. In the opinion of Purchas LJ, there was:

'. . . no mandate in the common law for a requirement that a constable exercising his powers of arrest without warrant should specify the particular crime for which the arrest is being made, provided that one or more of such alternatives present to his mind were arrestable offences. Nor does the arresting constable have to impart the information to the arrested person in the form of a technical statutory or common law definition. In my judgment, it is sufficient that commonplace words be used, the obvious meaning of which informs the person arrested of the offence or type of offences for which he is being arrested.'[175]

In assessing the sufficiency of the information given to the person being arrested, the courts therefore seek to apply an *objective* test having regard to the information which was reasonably available to the arresting officer. Whether or not the words used satisfy the test is a matter which can be determined equally as well on appeal as at first instance. There is no 'magic formula' of words to be used.[176] Although it is desirable for a police officer to utter the word 'arrest' when it is that power that he is using, it is not a prerequisite of a valid arrest.[177] Expressions such as 'You're nicked' may suffice provided that when viewed objectively, they are sufficiently clear to inform the person being arrested that they are no longer free to go. Thus in *Clarke v Chief Constable of North Wales Police*,[178] Sedley LJ remarked:

'Although no constable ever admits to saying "You're nicked for handling this gear" or "I'm having you for nicking this motor", either will do and, I have no doubt, frequently does.'[179]

Section 28 makes no stipulation as to the identity of the person imparting the relevant information. In the vast majority of cases, that person is likely to be the arresting officer. However, the requirements of section 28 may still be met where the information is given by another. Thus in *DPP v L*,[180] an initially unlawful arrest was subsequently made lawful when the reason for the respondent's arrest was recorded by the custody officer. The Divisional Court was prepared to infer from the entry in the custody record, which had been made in the respondent's presence, that she had been told of the reason for her arrest. In effect, therefore, the entry had regularised matters. Whilst there may be sound practical reasons why a court should adopt such an inference in that it marks a point in time when the requirements of section 28 are deemed to have been complied with, such an approach is not without difficulties, given that section 28 is for the benefit of the arrested person.

In addition to a custody officer, an officer present at the time of an arrest who is not in fact the arresting officer may also supply the section 28 information. Thus in *Dhesi v Chief Constable of the West Midlands Police*,[181] where the defendant was arrested by a police dog handler and told to walk towards another officer who informed him that he was 'under arrest for affray', it was held by the Court of Appeal that the arrest was lawful. In delivering the judgment of the Court, Stuart-Smith LJ observed that:

'The importance of section 28 is that the arrested person should know that he is under arrest and the reason for it. It can make no conceivable difference by whom that information is given provided it is

---

[175] At 399.
[176] See *R v Inwood* [1973] 2 All ER 645 where Stephenson LJ stated: 'There is no magic formula; only the obligation to make it plain to the suspect by what is said and done that he is no longer a free man' (at 649).
[177] See *R v Brosch* [1988] Crim LR 743.   [178] (Unreported) April 5, 2000.
[179] At para 36.   [180] [1999] Crim LR 752.   [181] *The Times*, May 9, 2000 (CA).

given at the relevant time or as soon as practicable thereafter. It is not necessary that it should be the person who actually deprives the subject of his liberty who gives that information.'

Over the years, section 28 has generated a not inconsiderable body of case law. However, in a recent case, the Court of Appeal positively discouraged recourse to past authorities when determining whether the requirements of section 28 had been complied with.

....

Taylor v Chief Constable of Thames Valley Police [2004] 1 WLR 3155

The respondent and his mother came down from Liverpool where they lived, in order to attend an anti-vivisection demonstration at a farm in Oxfordshire. The demonstration was large and violent. In order to identify those involved in the violence, a number of videos and photograph albums were produced by the police. At a subsequent demonstration at the same location, teams of police 'spotters' were deployed to see whether any of those present at the earlier demonstration were also present at the later demonstration. The intention was to arrest any persons who were suspected of having committed public order offences at the earlier demonstration. The respondent was identified by two spotters as a person seen throwing a rock or rocks from an adjacent field in the direction of the farmhouse on one of the videos. A more junior officer was instructed to arrest the respondent. She did so using the following words: 'I am arresting you on suspicion of violent disorder on April 18, 1998 at Hillgrove Farm'. The respondent, who was ten years old at the time, was then detained in a police van along with his mother. Subsequently he was presented before the custody sergeant for processing at 19.09. At 19.45 he was placed in a detention room and his interview (in his mother's presence) began. The interview was concluded at 21.53 and he was finally released at 23.00 following his acceptance of a formal caution. The respondent subsequently brought a claim in which it was alleged that his arrest had been unlawful and that he was therefore entitled to damages for false imprisonment, assault and trespass to the person.

At trial, it was held that the claimant's arrest had been unlawful on the basis that he had not been informed of the ground for his arrest in a manner sufficient to comply with section 28(3). It was also held that the claimant's detention had been unlawfully prolonged in respect of the period 20.15–21.21 and he was therefore awarded £1,500 damages. The Chief Constable appealed. The Court of Appeal held that the words used had satisfied the requirements of section 28(3) and the arrest had therefore been lawful. However, the detention for the period specified had been unlawful and the trial judge had therefore been right to make an award of damages.

Clarke LJ

'23. . . . The relevant principles remain those set out in *Christie v Leachinsky* . . . It seems to me that the best statement of those principles as articulated in more recent times is not to be found in an English case at all but in para 40 of the decision in *Fox, Campbell and Hartley v United Kingdom* (1990) 13 EHRR 157, 170. The court was there of course considering, not section 28(3) of PACE, but article 5(2) of the Convention for the Protection of Human Rights and Fundamental Freedoms which provides: "Everyone who is arrested shall be informed promptly, in a language which he understands, of the reasons for his arrest and of any charge against him".

24. The court said, at p. 170, para 40:

"Paragraph (2) of article 5 contains the elementary safeguard that any person arrested should know why he is being deprived of his liberty. This protection is an integral part of the scheme of protection afforded by article 5: by virtue of paragraph (2) any person arrested must be told in non-technical language that he can understand, the essential legal and factual grounds for his arrest, so as to be able, if he sees fit, to apply to a court to challenge its lawfulness in accordance with paragraph (4). Whilst this information must be conveyed promptly . . . it need not be related in its entirety by the arresting officer at the very moment of the arrest. Whether the content and promptness of the information conveyed were sufficient is to be assessed in each case according to its special features."

25. The wording of article 5(2) and of section 28(3) of PACE are not of course the same. Nor are the words used by the European Court of Human Rights the same as those of Viscount Simon[182] . . . or as those used in any of the other cases I have mentioned,[183] but to my mind the principles expressed are essentially the same . . .

26. In the light of all the authorities I would hold that the modern approach to the application of section 28(3) is that set out in para 40 of the judgment in *Fox, Campbell and Hartley v United Kingdom* . . . The question is thus whether, having regard to all the circumstances of the particular case, the person arrested was told in simple, non-technical language that he could understand, the essential legal and factual grounds for his arrest. In the light of the case law as it has developed I doubt whether it will in the future be necessary or desirable to consider the cases in any detail, or perhaps at all. It seems to me that in the vast majority of cases, it will be sufficient to ask the question posed by the European Court of Human Rights.'

The decision in *Taylor* is of some importance in the present context. It makes it clear that section 28 cases turn on their own particular facts and that in determining whether or not the requirements of that section have been complied with, English courts should apply the approach advocated by the ECtHR in *Fox, Campbell and Hartley v United Kingdom*.[184] In the case of persons who are deaf or who are unable to understand English, an arrest may still be lawful despite the apparent difficulties involved in communicating the section 28 information to the arrested person. Thus in *Tims v John Lewis & Co Ltd*,[185] which involved an action for false imprisonment relating to the arrest of a 'rather deaf' mother and her daughter by store detectives on suspicion of theft, Lord Goddard CJ opined:

'I do not think the decision of the House of Lords[186] means that if an officer is arresting a deaf person he has to possess himself of a speaking-trumpet or something of that sort, or shout at the top of his voice. He must do what a reasonable person would do in the circumstances . . . If a police officer who is not able to speak French has to arrest a Frenchman who does not speak English, he can only tell him in English for what he is arresting him, and take him to the police station until some officer who does speak the language or some interpreter comes to explain the charge on which he has been arrested to the person arrested.'[187]

Although the decision of the Court of Appeal was later reversed by the House of Lords on a different point,[188] no doubt was cast upon the *obiter* remarks of Lord Goddard quoted above. Indeed, his reasoning on this point was followed in *Wheatley v Lodge*,[189] where a man who was totally deaf and unable to lip-read had been arrested by a police officer for a drink-driving offence. Before the magistrates, the information against the respondent had been dismissed on the ground that he had not properly been arrested under the road traffic legislation despite the fact that the arresting officer had done all that would be required to effect an arrest under

[182] The words used in *Christie v Leachinsky* [1947] AC 573, quoted at p. 747.

[183] Clarke LJ had referred to: *Murphy v Oxford* (unreported) 15 February 1985; *Abbassy v Metropolitan Police Comr* [1990] 1 WLR 385; *Mercer v Chief Constable of the Lancashire Constabulary* [1991] 1 WLR 367; *Wilson v Chief Constable of the Lancashire Constabulary* (unreported) 23 November 2000; and *Clarke v Chief Constable of North Wales Police* (unreported) 5 April 2000.

[184] (1990) 13 EHRR 157. The decision in *Taylor* has subsequently been applied in *R v Fiak* [2005] EWCA Crim 2381 and *Faulkner (R on the application of) v Secretary of State for the Home Department* [2005] EWHC 2567 (Admin).   [185] [1951] 2 KB 459.

[186] In *Christie v Leachinsky* [1947] AC 573.   [187] [1951] 2 KB 459 at 467.

[188] See [1952] AC 676.   [189] [1971] 1 WLR 29.

normal circumstances. However, on appeal, the Court of Appeal concluded that *Tims* was an exception to the general rule stated in *Christie v Leachinsky*. Accordingly, in the words of Browne J in *Wheatley*:

'. . . if a police officer is arresting a deaf person or somebody who cannot speak English, what he has to do is to do what is reasonable, what a reasonable person would do in the circumstances'.[190]

If a police officer fails to comply with the requirement in section 28(3), the arrest will be unlawful from the time at which it became practicable to inform the arrested person of the ground for the arrest to the time when such information was conveyed. Thus in *Lewis v Chief Constable of the South Wales Constabulary*,[191] the two claimants were arrested by a police officer on suspicion of burglary and were taken to a police station. They were not told of the reason for their arrest until they arrived at the police station, which in one case was some ten minutes after the claimant had been arrested and in the other case, 23 minutes after her arrest. The claimants were detained for approximately five hours whereupon they were released without being charged. They sued the Chief Constable for false arrest and wrongful imprisonment, claiming that they were entitled to be compensated for the whole period of their detention. However, the trial judge ruled that although their arrests were initially unlawful due to the failure to comply with section 28(3) of PACE, their arrests subsequently became lawful when they were informed of the reason for the arrests at the police station, and thus they were only entitled to damages for unlawful detentions which had lasted ten and 23 minutes, respectively. Accordingly, they were each awarded £200 damages by the jury. Their appeal from this ruling was dismissed by the Court of Appeal on the basis that their initially unlawful arrests had become lawful from the moment when section 28(3) had been properly complied with. Thus they had been unlawfully detained for a matter of minutes rather than hours.[192]

Where an arrested person is properly informed of the reason for their arrest at some later point in time, this compliance with section 28(3) does not serve to retrospectively transform an unlawful arrest into a lawful arrest. Rather, as the decision in *Lewis* clearly demonstrates, the duration of the unlawful arrest will be calculated from the time at which it became practicable to inform the arrested person of the ground for arrest, to the time at which this information was actually given, at which point the arrest will then become a lawful arrest. A claimant who sues for damages in these circumstances will thus only be entitled to be compensated for the period of the unlawful detention. Conversely, what was initially a lawful arrest because it was not practicable to inform the person of the ground for arrest will become an unlawful arrest from the time at which it was practicable to give such information, where such information was not in fact given.

....

Director of Public Prosecutions v Hawkins [1988] 1 WLR 1166

The respondent was observed committing an offence for which he could be lawfully arrested by a police officer on patrol duty. The officer accordingly left his patrol car and took the respondent by the arm, announcing as he did so, 'You are under arrest.' A struggle ensued immediately involving three police officers and the respondent, and therefore it became impracticable to comply with the requirement laid down in section 28(3) of the Police and Criminal Evidence Act 1984, that an arrested person should be notified of the reason for their arrest. It remained impracticable to comply with section 28(3) until the respondent's arrival at the police station but, even then, the justices found as a matter of fact that he had either not been informed of the reason for his arrest or that he had been given a wrong reason. Accordingly, they dismissed informations against the respondent in which he had been charged with three offences of assaulting a police officer in the execution of his duty contrary to section 51(1) of the Police Act 1964, and one offence of using threatening, abusive or insulting words or behaviour contrary to section 5 of the Public Order Act 1986. On appeal by the prosecutor by way of case stated, the Divisional Court held that the failure to comply with section 28(3) did not take the police officer outside the execution of his duty and that, therefore, the justices' dismissals would be set aside and the case would be remitted back to the justices in order that they could continue the hearing.

Parker LJ, at 1170

'When a police officer makes an arrest which he is lawfully entitled to make but is unable at the time to state the ground because it is impracticable to do so, it is plain on the wording of the section that it is his duty to maintain the arrest until it is practicable to inform the arrested person of that ground. If, when it does become practicable, he fails to do so, then the arrest is unlawful, but that does not mean that acts, which were previously done and were, when done, done in the execution of duty, become, retrospectively, acts which were not done in the execution of duty. The Act certainly does not say so and contentions founded upon other consequences of an arrest being unlawful do not assist.

In my judgment the position is clear. It is impossible to contend that an officer who makes an arrest which he could lawfully make but is prevented by immediate violence from stating the ground of the arrest is not under a duty to state the ground of arrest as soon as he can. It is also impossible to contend that he is not under a duty to maintain the arrest until that moment arrives. If, when it does arrive, he then fails to carry out his duty to state the ground I am quite unable to see that such failure can have any effect on what has gone before unless specific provision is made. Here it is not.

The essential fallacy in the defendant's argument is, in my view, in the assumption that the right to resist an arrest which could not from the start have been lawfully made confers a right to resist an arrest which could be lawfully made and which was being lawfully pursued at the time when the person concerned committed assaults on the arresting officer or his colleagues.'

Simon Brown LJ, at 1171–1172

'The defendant submits not, arguing essentially as follows. (1) It is the plain effect of section 28(3) that the arrest here was unlawful. True, that fact would not be ascertainable until the end of the period in question; only then could it be known whether or not the arresting officer's earlier conduct was to be validated. But there is no reason why the lawfulness or otherwise of the arrest should not meanwhile remain in limbo. Rather the unambiguous language of section 28(3) requires that it must. (2) It is well established on the highest authority that a prisoner need not submit to an unlawful arrest but may instead use all reasonable force to free himself from the police officer's custody. (I may call this the *Christie v Leachinsky* [1947] AC 573 principle, although of course that case concerned damages for false imprisonment rather than a defence to a charge of assaulting a police officer in the execution of his duty; the principle has, however, often been applied in this latter context.) (3) The arrest in the instant case ultimately proved to be unlawful. The respondent was, therefore, entitled to resist it.

Forcefully and attractively although this argument was advanced I unhesitatingly reject it. Its central fallacy seems to me to lie in the unwarranted assumption that the *Christie v Leachinsky* principle can properly be extended to determine retrospectively the legal character of the conduct in question, ie to legalise by reference to subsequent events what at the time was apparently a criminal assault on the police officer attempting to execute his duty. I say "apparently a criminal assault" because there can be no doubt here but that the police officer was entitled to approach the respondent with a view to arresting him (it is common ground, indeed, that an assault on the officer at that stage would have been unlawful irrespective of what thereafter occurred), than to arrest him and then to restrain him. Indeed his duty required him to take such actions. I recognise of course that by virtue of section 28(3) the arrest ultimately proved to be unlawful. But that is not to say that all the earlier steps taken during the course of events leading to that ultimate position must themselves be regarded as unlawful. Still less does it follow that conduct on the part of the police officer which at the time was not only permitted but positively required of him in the execution of his duty can become retrospectively invalidated by reference to some later failure (a failure which, I may add, could well have been that of some officer other than himself).

The answer to the question posed in this appeal is, I have no doubt, this. Section 28(3) plainly dictates the circumstances in which an arrest may be found to have been unlawful and it determines decisively the consequences following the time at which that becomes apparent. In my judgment, however, it says nothing in respect of the intermediate period during which it is not practicable to inform the person arrested of the ground for his arrest. Least of all does it supply the answer to the question, hitherto unconsidered by the authorities, whether a police officer is acting in the execution of his duty during that intermediate period. That is a question which I regard as logically separate and apart from the eventual lawfulness or otherwise of the arrest on which he is engaged. Unless I were driven inexorably by the statute to accept the respondent's argument I would decline to do so: it would certainly produce the most bizarre and unwelcome results. I feel no such compulsion. In the result I concur with Parker LJ's conclusion that this appeal must be allowed.'

(vi) 'Assisting police with their enquiries'

'29 Voluntary attendance at a police station etc

(1) Where for the purpose of assisting with an investigation a person attends voluntarily at a police station or at any other place where a constable is present or accompanies a constable to a police station or any such other place without having been arrested—

    (a) he shall be entitled to leave at will unless he is placed under arrest;

    (b) he shall be informed at once that he is under arrest if a decision is taken by a constable to prevent him from leaving at will.'

The expression 'assisting police with their enquiries' which the trial judge in *R v Inwood*[193] described as a 'wonder phrase', is sometimes used by the media to denote the fact that the person in question is present at a police station in a voluntary capacity. He or she is there to answer questions put to them as part of an investigation, but since their attendance is voluntary, they are at liberty to leave whenever they wish, irrespective of whether the process of questioning has in fact been completed. If they do attempt to leave and are prevented from doing so, this detention will be unlawful unless it is done for the purpose of putting the person under arrest.[194] In addition, the phrase 'assisting' or 'helping police with their enquiries' may be used by the media to convey the meaning that while a person has in fact been arrested, they have not as yet been charged with a particular offence. However, it is important to appreciate that in whichever context the phrase is being used, it is unlawful for the police to detain a person to help them with their enquiries. In *R v Lemsatef*,[195] where the appellant had been detained under the Customs and Excise Act 1952 as part of an investigation into cannabis importation, in delivering the judgment of the Court of Appeal Lawton LJ stated:

' . . . it must be clearly understood that neither customs officers, nor police officers have any right to detain somebody for the purposes of getting them to help with their enquiries. Police officers either

---

[193] [1973] 1 WLR 647.   [194] Section 29(1)(a).   [195] [1977] 1 WLR 812.

rest for an offence or they do not arrest at all. Customs either detain for an offence or they do not
tain at all. The law is clear. Neither arrest nor detention can properly be carried out without
the accused person being told the offence for which he is being arrested. There is no such offence as
"helping police with their enquiries".'[196]

v. Assault on and Wilful Obstruction of the Police

'89 Assaults on constables

(1) Any person who assaults a constable in the execution of his duty, or a person assisting a constable
in the execution of his duty, shall be guilty of an offence and liable on summary conviction to imprisonment for a term not exceeding six months or to a fine not exceeding level 5 on the standard scale,
or to both.

(2) Any person who resists or wilfully obstructs a constable in the execution of his duty, or a person
assisting a constable in the execution of his duty, shall be guilty of an offence and liable on summary
conviction to imprisonment for a term not exceeding one month or to a fine not exceeding level 3 on
the standard scale, or to both.

(3) . . . '

Section 89 of the Police Act 1996 is the most recent in a line of statutory provisions including,
amongst others, section 51(1) and (3) of the Police Act 1964, which deal with the offences of
assaulting, resisting or wilfully obstructing a police officer in the execution of his or her duty.
The offences are designed to afford the police some degree of additional protection while
they are involved in the conduct of their duties, and since it is considered to be in the public
interest that this should be so, a conviction for a section 89 assault will result in the imposition
of a higher penalty than if the defendant were convicted of a common assault. However, while
the section 89 offences are stated with relative ease, to actually secure a conviction for the
relevant offence has sometimes proved to be a rather more difficult task. The difficulty lies not
so much in determining whether an assault has been committed for this is an offence which is
well known to the criminal law, but rather it concerns what is meant by the concept of 'wilful
obstruction' and, moreover, the requirement that the police officer was acting within the
execution of his or her duty at the time that the assault, resistance or wilful obstruction took
place.

(a) 'Wilful obstruction'

It would seem that the term 'obstruction' as originally used in the context of an offence against
the police implied that the defendant would be guilty where his conduct involved an interference with police duties which fell just short of conduct amounting to an assault. However,

---

[196] At 816.

since section 89 speaks only in terms of 'obstruction' and not 'physical obstruction', the word has accordingly been given a wide meaning by the courts.[197] Conduct which has been held by the courts to amount to an obstruction includes: shouting a warning when it was feared that the police were about to raid a pub in respect of 'after hours' drinking;[198] drinking from a bottle of whisky in order to frustrate a breathalyser test;[199] and, refusing to comply with a police officer's direction to reverse the wrong way down a one-way street where a road traffic accident had occurred.[200]

Where a police officer stops a person in the street in order to ask him or her some questions relating to a current investigation, if that person refuses to answer those questions then clearly they are obstructing the police officer. Their conduct is not such as to physically prevent the performance of a duty, but nevertheless their refusal to answer the police officer's questions does make it more difficult for that officer to carry out his investigation. In order to be guilty of a section 89 offence, however, it is necessary that the obstruction be 'wilful'; a word which has been interpreted to mean an obstruction which is either intentional or without lawful excuse.

Rice v Connolly [1966] 2 QB 414

A police constable was investigating a number of breaking offences in the early hours of one morning when he noticed that the appellant was behaving in a suspicious manner by looking into shop windows and looking round generally. He approached the appellant and asked him several questions, including what was his name and address and where was he going. The appellant refused to give his full name and address, replying instead, 'Rice, Convamore Road', which was in fact correct as far as it went. In addition, he refused to accompany the officer to a police box where it was hoped that a proper identification would be made. The appellant was accordingly arrested and charged with the offence of wilfully obstructing a police officer in the execution of his duty contrary to section 51(3) of the Police Act 1964. On appeal, the Divisional Court held that since it had not been established that the appellant's obstruction was 'wilful', his conviction should be quashed.

Lord Parker CJ, at 419–420

'What the prosecution have to prove is that there was an obstructing of a constable, that the constable was at the time acting in the execution of his duty, and that the person obstructing did so wilfully. To carry the matter a little further, it is in my view clear that to "obstruct" in section 51(3) is to do any act which makes it more difficult for the police to carry out their duty . . . It is also in my judgment clear that it is part of the obligations and duties of a police constable to take all steps which appear to him necessary for keeping the peace, for preventing crime or for protecting property from criminal injury. There is no exhaustive definition of the powers and obligations of the police, but they are at least those, and they would further include the duty to detect crime and to bring an offender to justice.

Pausing there, it seems to me quite clear that the defendant was making it more difficult for the police to carry out their duties, and that the police at the time and throughout were acting in accordance with their duties. The only remaining ingredient and the one upon which in my judgment this case revolves, is whether the obstructing of which the appellant was guilty was a wilful obstruction. 'Wilful' in this context not only in my judgment means 'intentional' but something which is done

---

[197] This is certainly the case in England and Wales. In Scotland, however, as Bailey, Harris and Ormerod note, this offence has been confined to physical obstruction: see *Civil Liberties: Cases and Materials* (5th edn, 2001), at p. 168 where the authors cite *Curlett v M'Kechnie* 1938 JC 176 in support of the point.

[198] *Hinchcliffe v Sheldon* [1955] 1 WLR 1207.   [199] *Dibble v Ingleton* [1972] 1 QB 480.

[200] *Johnson v Phillips* [1975] 3 All ER 682.

without lawful excuse, and that indeed is conceded by counsel who appears for the prosecution in this case. Accordingly, the sole question here is whether the appellant had a lawful excuse for refusing to answer the questions put to him. In my judgment he had. It seems to me quite clear that though every citizen has a moral duty or, if you like, a social duty to assist the police, there is no legal duty to that effect, and indeed the whole basis of the common law is that right of the individual to refuse to answer questions put to him by persons in authority, and to refuse to accompany those in authority to any particular place; short, of course, of arrest.

Counsel for the respondent has pointed out that it is undoubtedly an obstruction, and has been so held, for a person questioned by the police to tell a "cock-and-bull" story, to put the police off by giving them false information, and I think he would say: well, what is the real distinction, it is very little away from giving false information to giving no information at all; if that does in fact make it more difficult for the police to carry out their duties then there is a wilful obstruction.

In my judgment there is all the difference in the world between deliberately telling a false story, something which on no view a citizen has a right to do, and preserving silence or refusing to answer, something which he has every right to do. Accordingly, in my judgment, looked on in that perfectly general way, it was not shown that the refusal of the appellant to answer the questions or to accompany the police officer in the first instance to the police box was an obstruction without lawful excuse.'

Thus it would seem that in the case of the person who is stopped by the police in order to answer some questions, the giving of false answers which that person believed to be true would not amount to wilful obstruction for the purposes of section 89. However, a person who deliberately answered questions untruthfully so as to mislead the police (the 'cock-and-bull' story) would be guilty of the offence.[201] In the New Zealand case *Mathews v Dwan*,[202] where M was asked by a police officer whether a wanted man, L, had been in a particular house either that night or during the course of the day, his false assertion that L had not been there was held by the Supreme Court to be an obstruction of a police officer in the execution of his duty.[203]

The decision in *Rice v Connolly* is authority for the proposition that the citizen is not under a legal obligation to answer questions posed by the police, although it may be thought that that person has a social or moral obligation to assist the police in the absence of a good reason for not doing so. A refusal to answer police questions would not therefore amount to the offence of wilful obstruction contrary to section 89 of the Police Act 1996.[204] However, in the more recent case *Ricketts v Cox*,[205] the Divisional Court appear to have qualified this general principle by holding that a defendant can be guilty of wilful obstruction where he behaves in an abusive, uncooperative and hostile manner towards a police officer who is asking him some questions. In so finding, the Court relied upon the words of James J in *Rice v Connolly* where, following an expression of agreement with Lord Parker CJ's judgment, the former stated that:

'For my own part, I would add only this, that I would not go so far as to say that there may not be circumstances in which the manner of a person together with his silence could amount to an

[201] In addition to *Rice v Connolly*, see also the obiter remarks of Darling J in *Bastable v Little* [1907] 1 KB 59 at 63.
[202] [1949] NZLR 1037.   [203] An offence contrary to section 76 of the Police Offences Act 1927 (NZ).
[204] Running away from a police officer who is investigating the commission of an offence does, however, go beyond the right not to have to answer police questions and thus constitutes a willful obstruction: see *Sekfali, Banamira and Ouham v Department of Public Prosecutions* [2006] EWHC 894 (Admin).
[205] (1981) 74 CR App R 298.

obstruction within the section; whether they do remains to be decided in any case that happens hereafter, not in this case, in which it has not been argued.'[206]

The difficulty with the decision in *Rickets v Cox* is that the defendant was found guilty of wilful obstruction on account of his use of obscene language and his generally unhelpful manner, yet had he politely replied to the police that he did not wish to answer their questions, he would not have been guilty of the offence as *Rice v Connolly* makes clear. However, in both instances, the defendant's conduct was obstructing the police in the execution of their duties. It seems likely that if there were now a repetition of the events in *Rickets v Cox*, the more appropriate offence with which to charge the defendant would be section 4 of the Public Order Act 1986.[207]

People who obstruct the police in the execution of their duty do not necessarily do so as a consequence of an ill will or a hostile motive towards the police. On some occasions the obstruction may be the result of a feeling that there is a moral duty to act where, for example, a person wishes to make a police officer aware of his belief that the officer is in fact arresting the wrong person.

Hills v Ellis [1983] QB 680

While leaving a football match, the appellant saw two men engaged in a fight. The appellant formed an opinion as to which one of the men was the innocent party and thus when a police officer arrested that same man, the appellant intervened to point out the policeman's error. However, the noise of the crowd prevented him from making himself heard and thus he grabbed the police officer's elbow in order to make his point. The appellant was warned by another police officer that he would be arrested if he did not desist, but he ignored the warning and was accordingly arrested and charged with wilfully obstructing a police officer in the execution of his duty contrary to section 51(3) of the Police Act 1964. The appellant was convicted by magistrates, and on appeal, he contended that there had been no wilful obstruction of the police officer since he had acted with a lawful excuse throughout; he had a moral duty to draw the policeman's attention to his mistake. In addition, the appellant claimed that he had not acted with hostility towards the police officer. However, his conviction was upheld by the Divisional Court since a citizen does not have a lawful excuse to interfere with a lawful arrest. In addition, the court noted that motive is irrelevant in criminal law; what matters is what the defendant intended.

Griffiths LJ, at 684–685

'What is submitted in this case on behalf of the appellant is that his action was not wilful in the sense of being done without lawful excuse, because he had a moral duty to draw to the attention of the officer that he was arresting the wrong man. I cannot accept that submission. Here was an officer, acting in the course of his duty, arresting a man. It would be quite intolerable if citizens, who may genuinely believe the wrong man was being arrested, were entitled to lay hands on the police and obstruct them in that arrest because they thought that some other person should be arrested. One has only got to state the proposition to see the enormous abuse to which any such power on the part of the citizen might be put. A private citizen has no lawful excuse to interfere with a lawful arrest by a police officer.'

McCullough J, at 686

'Hostility suggests emotion and motive, but motive and emotion are alike irrelevant in criminal law. What matters is intention, that is what state of affairs the defendant intended to bring about. What motive he had while so intending is irrelevant.

[206] [1966] 2 QB 414 at 421.   [207] See pp. 657–663 where this offence is discussed.

What is meant by an "intention to obstruct"? I would construe "wilfully obstructs" as doing deliberate actions with the intention of bringing about a state of affairs which, objectively regarded, amount to an obstruction as that phrase was explained by Lord Parker CJ in *Rice v Connolly* . . . [1966] 2 QB 414 at 419 [p. 755] ie making it more difficult for the police to carry out their duty. The fact that the defendant might not himself have called that state of affairs an obstruction is, to my mind, immaterial. This is not to say that it is enough to do deliberate actions which, in fact, obstruct; there must be an intention that those actions should result in the further state of affairs to which I have been referring.

If I may give an example. D interferes while a police officer, P, is arresting X, and delays the arrest. It is not enough that his deliberate actions in fact delay the arrest. If D intends to prevent P from arresting X, then D is guilty because it is his intention to do that which, objectively regarded, amounts to an obstruction, that is to say, to prevent the arrest. D's motives for wanting to prevent the arrest are immaterial. He is guilty even though he believes the officer is arresting the wrong man. He is guilty even though he does not appreciate that interfering with the arrest amounts to what would be regarded objectively as an obstruction.'

As the decision in *Hills v Ellis* highlights, the criminal law is concerned with what the defendant intended where the charge is one of wilful obstruction, rather than with the defendant's motive. Motive can at best serve as a mitigating factor in the determination of sentence. Accordingly, provided that a defendant intended to do that which constitutes an obstruction, he will be guilty of a section 89(2) offence.

Lewis v Cox [1984] 3 WLR 875

The defendant was present when his friend (Marsh) was arrested by police officers and placed in the back of a police van. The defendant opened the van's rear door and asked his friend where he was being taken, at which point he was informed by the appellant policeman that he would be arrested for obstruction if he continued to open the van door. Despite this warning, however, the defendant once again opened the door when the van was in the process of pulling away. Accordingly he was arrested and charged with the wilful obstruction of a police officer in the execution of his duty contrary to section 51(3) of the Police Act 1964. The magistrates dismissed the charge but, on appeal, the Divisional Court held that the defendant's conduct did amount to a wilful obstruction. Accordingly, the case was remitted to the magistrates with a direction to convict.

Webster J, at 882

'Counsel for the defendant relies on the fact that the justices found (thereby indicating that they accepted his evidence) that the defendant opened the door in order to (that is to say with the intention of) asking Marsh where he was being taken. But in my view a court is not obliged, at any rate in the context of this subsection, to assume that a defendant has only one intention and to find what that intention was, or even to assume that, if he has two intentions, it must find the predominant intention. If, for instance, a person runs into the road and holds up the traffic in order to prevent an accident, he clearly has two intentions: one is to hold up the traffic, and the other (which is the motive of that intention) is to prevent an accident. But motive is irrelevant to intention in the criminal law, and although it may constitute a lawful excuse where absence of a lawful excuse is an element of the crime in question, as it is in the case of an offence under s 51(3) of the 1964 Act (see per Lord Parker CJ in *Rice v Connolly* . . . [1966] 2 QB 414 at 419 [p. 755]), it has not been suggested that in this case the defendant had a lawful excuse for opening the van door on the second occasion.

In my view, therefore, if the justices had also asked themselves whether the defendant had, by opening the door, intended to make it more difficult for the police to perform their duties in order to carry out his intention of asking where Marsh was to be taken they must, on the evidence, have been satisfied so as to feel sure that he had such intention.

Although the question whether a defendant's conduct is aimed at the police may not be an unhelpful question in certain circumstances, where, as here, a defendant intended to do one thing in order to carry out his intention of doing another, that test, which might be appropriate if the court had to find what was the defendant's predominant intention, can, in my view, mislead the court if it is not necessary to do that.

For my part I conclude, therefore, that if the justices had directed themselves properly in the way in which I have set out, they must, on the evidence, have decided that the defendant, when he opened the door on the second occasion, intended to make it more difficult for the police to carry out their duties, even though that was not his predominant intention, and they ought, therefore, to have convicted him of the charge against him.'

Kerr LJ, at 882–883

'The actus reus is the doing of an act which has the effect of making it impossible or more difficult for members of the police to carry out their duty. The word "wilfully" clearly imports an additional requirement of mens rea. The act must not only have been done deliberately, but with the knowledge and intention that it will have this obstructive effect. But in the absence of a lawful excuse, the defendant's purpose or reason for doing the act is irrelevant, whether this be directly hostile to, or "aimed at", the police, or whether he has some other purpose or reason. Indeed, in the majority of cases the intention to obstruct the police will not be simply "anti-police", but will stem from some underlying reason or objective of the defendant which he can only achieve by an act of intentional obstruction. This may be to assist an offender, which could be termed "hostile" to the police. Equally, the motivation could be public spirited, for instance, by intervening on behalf of someone whom the defendant believes to be innocent, as in Hills v Ellis . . . [1983] QB 680 [p. 757]. Or it may be for some neutral reason, for instance because the defendant considers that something else should have a higher priority than the duty on which the police officer is immediately engaged. In all such cases, if the defendant intentionally does an act which he realises will, in fact, have the effect of obstructing the police in the sense defined above, he will in my view be guilty of having done so "wilfully", with the necessary mens rea. In the absence of a lawful excuse, the defendant's underlying intention, reason or purpose for intentionally obstructing the police is irrelevant, because the intention to obstruct is present at the same time.'

(b) Execution of duty

In addition to the question of determining what type of conduct amounts to 'wilful obstruction' for the purposes of section 89, a further difficulty which is common to all three offences is the requirement that at the time when the police officer was assaulted, resisted or wilfully obstructed, he or she was acting in the execution of their duty. An exhaustive definition of the duties of the police is not to be found in statute, and the courts have generally expressed an unwillingness to formulate their own definition. In *R v Waterfield and another*,[208] Ashworth J observed:

'In the judgment of this court it would be difficult . . . to reduce within specific limits the general terms in which the duties of police constables have been expressed. In most cases it is probably more convenient to consider what the police constable was actually doing and in particular whether such

---

[208] [1964] 1 QB 164.

conduct was prima facie an unlawful interference with a person's liberty or property. If so, it is then relevant to consider whether (a) such conduct falls within the general scope of any duty imposed by statute or recognised at common law and (b) whether such conduct, albeit within the general scope of such a duty, involved an unjustifiable use of powers associated with the duty.'[209]

Similarly in *Chief Constable of Kent v V*,[210] Donaldson LJ remarked that:

'The Chief Constable's duties have never been exhaustively defined. It has always proved unnecessary, difficult and probably unwise to do so and I would certainly not attempt such a feat in this appeal.'[211]

However, in a report published in 1962,[212] the Royal Commission on the Police stated that the duties of the police included the following:

'First, the police have a duty to maintain law and order and to protect persons and property. Secondly, they have a duty to prevent crime. Thirdly, they are responsible for the detection of criminals and in the course of interrogating suspected persons they have a part to play in the early stages of the judicial process acting under restraint . . . Eighthly, they have by long tradition a duty to befriend anyone who needs their help and they may at any time be called upon to cope with minor or major emergencies.'

The courts have been presented with a number of cases in which it has been necessary to decide whether a police officer was acting within the execution of his or her duty at the time that he or she was assaulted etc. Frequently the conduct which it is alleged has taken the police officer outside the execution of their duty amounts to an attempt to detain a person in order to question them, as in the cases extracted below.[213]

....

Kenlin v Gardiner [1967] 2 QB 510

Two schoolboys, who were performing an errand by visiting houses to remind members of their school rugby team of a forthcoming match, aroused the suspicion of two plain clothes police officers by their actions. Accordingly, the officers approached the boys and one of them displayed his warrant card as he asked the boys what was the purpose of their calling at the houses. The boys did not believe that the two men before them were police officers and thus they made to run away. One of the boys was prevented from doing so by an officer who caught hold of his arm. A struggle ensued during which the boy punched and kicked the officer. The other boy also struck out when he was grasped by a police officer. Both boys were charged with assaulting a police officer in the execution of his duty contrary to section 51(1) of the Police Act 1964. In the opinion of the magistrates, the police officers had acted at all times within the execution of their duty, and thus the boys were convicted of the assault although each was granted an absolute discharge. On appeal, the Divisional Court held that their convictions should be quashed.

Winn LJ, at 518–519

'Now this case comes before this court with—I say this deliberately though without any intention to be insulting to either counsel—some tendency to put it forward as a cause célèbre, a state trial. In my own view it is nothing of the kind; it is quite a simple and normal case where misunderstandings led to an unfortunate consequence which need not have involved any prosecution.

---

[209] At 170–171.   [210] [1983] QB 34.
[211] At 46. See also the remarks of Lord Goddard CJ in *Rice v Connolly* [1966] 2 QB 414 at 419.
[212] Cmnd 1728.
[213] See also *Ludlow v Burgess* (1971) 25 Cr App R 227, and *Bentley v Brudzinski* (1982) 75 Cr App R 217.

The boys undoubtedly assaulted the police officers: there cannot be any doubt about that, they struck them and kicked them; but the question is whether that was a justifiable or unjustified assault; and that again . . . depends entirely on whether the answer of self-defence was available to these two boys in the particular circumstances. Of course, in the case of a charge of assault under section 51(1) of the Police Act, 1964, as in the case of any charge of assault, the defence or justification—I prefer to call it a justification, because it must always be borne in mind that it is for the prosecution to exclude justification and not for the defendant to establish it—the justification of self-defence is available just as it is in the case of any other assault. That is subject to this, that if the self-defence, in this case self-defence by the two boys against a prior assault such as had been committed, in a technical sense, by the police officers taking hold of an arm of each of these boys, was self-defence against an assault which was justified in law, as, for instance, a lawful arrest, then in law self-defence cannot afford justification for assault in resistance to justified assault by police officers. So one comes back to the question in the end, in the ultimate analysis: was this officer entitled in law to take hold of the first boy by the arm—of course the same situation arises with the other officer in regard to the second boy a little later—justified in committing that technical assault by the exercise of any power which he as a police constable in the precise circumstances prevailing at that exact moment possessed?

I regret, really, that I feel myself compelled to say that the answer to that question must be in the negative. This officer might or might not in the particular circumstances have possessed a power to arrest these boys. I leave that question open, saying no more than that I feel some doubt whether he would have had a power of arrest: but on the assumption that he had a power to arrest, it is to my mind perfectly plain that neither of these officers purported to arrest either of these boys. What was done was not done as an integral step in the process of arresting, but was done in order to secure an opportunity, by detaining the boys from escape, to put to them or to either of them the question which was regarded as the test question to satisfy the officers whether or not it would be right in the circumstances, and having regard to the answer obtained from that question, if any, to arrest them.

I regret to say that I think that there was a technical assault by the police officer. From which it follows that the justification of self-defence exerted or exercised by these two boys is not negatived by any justifiable character of the initial assault. It is plain in my own view that it was within the province of the justices to decide whether there was any excess in exercising privilege of self-defence. The court is not asked to send back this case to the justices—that would have given it a quite inflated importance—for them to decide just what was the ambit of the self-defence permissible in the circumstances, what were the reasonable or unreasonable features of the conduct of the boys in seeking to defend themselves. It suffices to say that the self-defence justification was available to these boys, and that it is not shown on the facts found by the justices that there was an excess of that liberty.'

Collins v Wilcock [1984] 1 WLR 1172

Two police officers on duty in a police car suspected that two women were soliciting for the purposes of prostitution. Accordingly, the appellant was asked to get into the police car in order that she could be questioned. However, she refused to do so and walked away. One of the two officers, a police-woman, therefore got out of the car and proceeded to follow the appellant so that she might question her as to her identity and conduct and possibly caution her if she was suspected of being a prostitute. This course of action was in accordance with the approved police procedure for administering cautions prior to charging a woman with being a prostitute contrary to section 1 of the Street Offences Act 1959. The appellant again refused to speak to the policewoman and was still in the process of walking away when the policewoman took hold of the appellant's arm in order to detain her. A struggle ensued during which the appellant swore at the policewoman and scratched the officer's arm with her finger-nails. In respect of this conduct, she was convicted by magistrates of the offence of assaulting a police officer in the execution of her duty contrary to section 51(1) of the Police Act 1964. Her appeal against conviction turned on the question whether the policewoman was acting in the execution of her duty at the time that the assault took place. In allowing her appeal and hence quashing her conviction, the Divisional Court took the view that since the policewoman had attempted to unlawfully detain the appellant, she was not acting in the execution of her duty at the relevant time.

Robert Goff LJ, at 1176–1180

'In considering this question, which is drawn in wide terms, we think it important to observe that in this case it is found as a fact that the respondent took hold of the appellant by the left arm to restrain her. Before considering the question as drawn, we think it right to consider whether, on the facts found in the case, the magistrate could properly hold that the respondent was acting in the execution of her duty. In order to consider this question, it is desirable that we should expose the underlying principles.

The law draws a distinction, in terms more easily understood by philologists than by ordinary citizens, between an assault and a battery. An assault is an act which causes another person to apprehend the infliction of immediate, unlawful, force on the person; a battery is the actual infliction of unlawful force on another person. Both assault and battery are forms of trespass to the person. Another form of trespass to the person is false imprisonment, which is the unlawful imposition of constraint on another's freedom of movement from a particular place. The requisite mental element is of no relevance in the present case.

We are here concerned primarily with battery. The fundamental principle, plain and incontestable, is that every person's body is inviolate. It has long been established that any touching of another person, however slight, may amount to a battery. So Holt CJ held in 1704 that "the least touching of another in anger is a battery": see *Cole v Turner* (1704 6 Mod Rep 149, 90 ER 958). The breadth of the principle reflects the fundamental nature of the interest so protected; as Blackstone wrote in his *Commentaries*, "the law cannot draw the line between different degrees of violence, and therefore totally prohibits the first at the lowest stage of it; every man's person being sacred, and no other having a right to meddle with it, in any the slightest manner" (see 3 Bl Com 120). The effect is that everybody is protected not only against physical injury but against any form of physical molestation.

But so widely drawn a principle must inevitably be subject to exceptions. For example, children may be subjected to reasonable punishment; people may be subjected to the lawful exercise of the power of arrest; and reasonable force may be used in self-defence or for the prevention of crime. But, apart from these special instances where the control or constraint is lawful, a broader exception has been created to allow for the exigencies of everyday life. Generally speaking, consent is a defence to battery; and most of the physical contacts of ordinary life are not actionable because they are impliedly consented to by all who move in society and so expose themselves to the risk of bodily contact. So nobody can complain of the jostling which is inevitable from his presence in, for example, a supermarket, an underground station or a busy street; nor can a person who attends a party complain if his hand is seized in friendship, or even if his back is (within reason) slapped (see *Tuberville v Savage* (1669) 1 Mod Rep 3, 86 ER 684). Although such cases are regarded as examples of implied consent, it is more common nowadays to treat them as falling within a general exception embracing all physical contact which is generally acceptable in the ordinary conduct of daily life. We observe that, although in the past it has sometimes been stated that a battery is only committed where the action is "angry, or revengeful, or rude, or insolent" (see 1 Hawk PC c 62, s 2), we think that nowadays it is more realistic, and indeed more accurate, to state the broad underlying principle, subject to the broad exception.

Among such forms of conduct, long held to be acceptable, is touching a person for the purpose of engaging his attention, though of course using no greater degree of physical contact than is reasonably necessary in the circumstances for that purpose. So, for example, it was held by the Court of Common Pleas in 1807 that a touch by a constable's staff on the shoulder of a man who had climbed on a gentleman's railing to gain a better view of a mad ox, the touch being only to engage the man's attention, did not amount to a battery (see *Wiffin v Kincard* (1807) 2 Bos & PNR 471, 127 ER 713; for another example, see *Coward v Baddeley* (1859) 4 H & N 478, 157 ER 927). But a distinction is drawn between a touch to draw a man's attention, which is generally acceptable, and a physical restraint, which is not. So we find Parke B observing in *Rawlings v Till* (1837) M & W 28 at 29, 150 ER 1042, with reference to *Wiffin v Kincard*, that "There the touch was merely to engage a man's attention, not to put a restraint on his person". Furthermore, persistent touching to gain attention in the face of obvious disregard may transcend the norms of acceptable behaviour, and so be outside the exception. We do not say that more than one touch is never permitted; for example, the lost or distressed may surely be permitted a second touch, or possibly even more, on a reluctant or impervious sleeve or shoulder, as may a person who is acting reasonably in the exercise of a duty. In each case, the test must be whether the physical contact so persisted in has in the circumstances gone beyond generally acceptable standards of conduct; and the answer to that question will depend on the facts of the particular case.

The distinction drawn by Parke B in *Rawlings v Till* is of importance in the case of police officers. Of course, a police officer may subject another to restraint when he lawfully exercises his power of arrest; and he has other statutory powers, for example, his power to stop, search and detain persons . . . with which we are not concerned. But, putting such cases aside, police officers have for present purposes no greater rights than ordinary citizens. It follows that, subject to such cases, physical contact by a police officer with another person may be unlawful as a battery, just as it might be if he was an ordinary member of the public. But a police officer has his rights as a citizen, as well as his duties as a policeman. A police officer may wish to engage a man's attention, for example if he wishes to question him. If he lays his hand on the man's sleeve or taps his shoulder for that purpose, he commits no wrong. He may even do so more than once; for he is under a duty to prevent and investigate crime, and so his seeking further, in the exercise of that duty, to engage a man's attention in order to speak to him may in circumstances be regarded as acceptable (see *Donnelly v Jackman* [1970] 1 All ER 987, [1970] 1 WLR 562). But if, taking into account the nature of his duty, his use of physical contact in the face of non co-operation persists beyond generally acceptable standards of conduct, his action will become unlawful; and if a police officer restrains a man, for example, by gripping his arm or his shoulder, then his action will also be unlawful, unless he is lawfully exercising his power of arrest. A police officer has no power to require a man to answer him, though he has the advantage of authority, enhanced as it is by the uniform which the state provides and requires him to wear, in seeking a response to his inquiry. What is not permitted, however, is the unlawful use of force or the unlawful threat (actual or implicit) to use force; and, excepting the lawful exercise of his power of arrest, the lawfulness of a police officer's conduct is judged by the same criteria as are applied to the conduct of any ordinary citizen of this country.'

[Robert Goff LJ then proceeded to consider the facts of several earlier cases in which similar issues to those raised in the present case were decided, before continuing as follows:]

'We now return to the facts of the present case. Before us, counsel for the respondent police officer sought to justify her conduct, first by submitting that, since the practice of cautioning women found loitering or soliciting in public places for the purposes of prostitution is recognised by s 2 of the 1959 Act, therefore it is implicit in the statute that police officers have a power to caution, and for that purpose they must have the power to stop and detain women in order to find out their names and addresses and, if appropriate, caution them. This submission, which accords with the opinion expressed by the magistrate, we are unable to accept. The fact that the statute recognises the practice of cautioning by providing a review procedure does not, in our judgment, carry with it an implication that police officers have the power to stop and detain women for the purpose of implementing the system of cautioning. If it had been intended to confer any such power on police officers that power could and should, in our judgment, have been expressly conferred by the statute.

Next, counsel for the respondent submitted that the purpose of the police officer was simply to carry out the cautioning procedure and that, having regard to that purpose, her action could not be regarded as unlawful. Again, we cannot accept that submission. If the physical contact went beyond what is allowed by law, the mere fact that the police officer has the laudable intention of carrying out the cautioning procedure in accordance with established practice cannot, we think, have the effect of rendering her action lawful. Finally, counsel for the respondent submitted that the question whether the respondent was or was not acting in the execution of her duty was a question of fact for the magistrate to decide; and that he was entitled, on the facts found by him, to conclude that the respondent had been acting lawfully. We cannot agree. The fact is that the respondent took hold of the appellant by the left arm to restrain her. In so acting, she was not proceeding to arrest the appellant; and since her action went beyond the generally acceptable conduct of touching a person to engage his or her attention, it must follow, in our judgment, that her action constituted battery on the appellant, and was therefore unlawful. It follows that the appellant's appeal must be allowed, and her conviction quashed.

We turn finally to the question posed by the magistrate for our consideration. As we have already observed, this question is in wide general terms. Furthermore, the word "detaining" can be used in more than one sense. For example, it is a commonplace of ordinary life that one person may request another to stop and speak to him; if the latter complies with the request, he may be said to do so willingly or unwillingly, and in either event the first person may be said to be "stopping and detaining" the latter. There is nothing unlawful in such an act. If a police officer so "stops and detains" another person, he in our opinion commits no unlawful act, despite the fact that his uniform may give his request a certain authority and so render it more likely to be complied with. But if a police officer, not exercising his power of arrest, nevertheless reinforces his request with the actual use of force, or with the threat (actual or implicit) to use force if the other person does not comply, then his act in thereby detaining the other person will be unlawful. In the former event, his action will constitute a battery; in the latter event, detention of the other person will amount to false imprisonment. Whether the action of a police officer in any particular case is to be regarded as lawful or unlawful must be a question to be decided on the facts of the case.'

The degree of physical contact involved in a touching together with the underlying purpose of the police officer weigh heavily in the court's consideration of the matter. Thus a trivial or *de minimis* touching of another by a police officer has been held not to take that officer outside the execution of his duty.

Donnelly v Jackman [1970] 1 WLR 562

The appellant was walking along the pavement when a uniformed police officer came up to him and asked him to stop and speak to him. The police officer was in the process of making enquiries into an offence which he had reason to believe the appellant might have committed. Despite his requests, however, the appellant ignored the officer and continued to walk. At one point, the police officer tapped the appellant on the shoulder, whereupon the appellant turned round and tapped the officer on the chest declaring as he did so that 'Now we are even, copper'. It was apparent that the appellant had no intention of stopping, but nevertheless the police officer tapped him on the shoulder once again, whereupon the appellant turned round and punched the officer. The appellant was convicted of assaulting the officer in the execution of his duty contrary to section 51(1) of the Police Act 1964. On appeal, the Divisional Court held that the policeman's actions had not taken him outside the execution of his duty and that therefore the appellant had been rightly convicted.

Talbot J, at 564–565

'The principal question it seems to me is whether the officer was acting in the execution of his duty, and a secondary question, whether anything he did caused him to cease to be acting in the execution of his duty. When considering what the duties of the officer were, I do not think that I can do better than cite the words of Lord Parker CJ in *Rice v Connolly*, when he said:

"It is also in my judgment clear that it is part of the obligations and duties of a police constable to take all steps which appear to him necessary for keeping the peace, for preventing crime or for protecting property from criminal injury."

Furthermore, in considering the problem whether the officer went outside the ambit of his duties so as to be ceasing to be acting therein, I would refer to the words of Ashworth J taken from *R v Waterfield* . . .'

[Talbot J then proceeded to quote the passage from that judgment which has been extracted above][214]

'Turning to the facts of this matter, it is not very clear what precisely the justices meant or found when they said that the officer touched the appellant on the shoulder, but whatever it was that they really did mean, it seems clear to me that they must have felt that it was a minimal matter by the way in which they treated this matter and the result of the case. When one considers the problem: was this officer acting in the course of his duty, in my view one ought to bear in mind that it is not every trivial interference with a citizen's liberty that amounts to a course of conduct sufficient to take the officer out of the course of his duties. In my judgment the facts that the justices found in this case do not justify the view that the officer was not acting in the execution of his duty when he went up to the appellant and wanted to speak to him. Therefore the assault was rightly found to be an assault on the officer whilst acting in the execution of his duties, and I would dismiss this appeal.'

In the light of the difficulties which are associated with the assessment of whether a touching is trivial in nature and hence within the bounds of acceptable conduct, there is a distinct possibility that differently constituted courts may arrive at different conclusions in relation to facts which are on the face of it very similar.

A case which exemplifies the nature of the considerations which need to be taken into account by a court in the context of a charge of assaulting a police officer is *Mepstead v DPP*.[215] The facts of this case were that the appellant parked his van in such a position as to cause an obstruction of the highway despite being told not to do so by a police officer. By the time that he returned to his vehicle, one of two police officers was in the process of issuing a fixed penalty notice in respect of the parking offence. At this stage the appellant became agitated and abusive, and accordingly one of the police officers took him by the arm and said 'Don't be silly, calm down, it's only a ticket'. The appellant reacted violently, kicking out at one police officer and swinging a hand containing his vehicle keys at the other. He was arrested and convicted of assaulting a police officer in the execution of his duty. The central issue for the Divisional Court in determining whether the stipendiary magistrate had been right to convict was thus whether the police officer's act of taking hold of the appellant's arm was such as to take that officer outside the execution of his duty. In holding that it was not, the Divisional Court based their decision on two factors: the purpose of the police officer when he took hold of the appellant's arm; and, the length of time for which the arm was actually held. It was found by the magistrate as a matter of fact that when the police officer took hold of the appellant's arm his intention was neither to arrest nor detain him, but rather he did so for the purpose of drawing the appellant's attention to the nature of what was being said to him and in order to try to calm the situation down. Accordingly, in the opinion of the Divisional Court, the degree of physical contact in the instant case did not exceed that which was permissible by the ordinary standards of everyday life.[216] Although there was no finding of fact as to how long the arm was actually held, the Divisional Court made the assumption that it could not have been for very long since 'otherwise the magistrate could not have reached a conclusion that it was solely an attempt to draw his attention to what was being said'. Interestingly therefore, there may be a period of time, the Divisional Court thought it to be a minute or just

---

[214] See pp. 759–760.   [215] (1995) 160 JP 475.

[216] In *R (on the application of Bucher) v DPP* [2003] EWHC 580 (Admin), the Administrative Court held that a custody officer had been acting within the execution of his duty when he was assaulted whilst physically removing a disruptive person from the custody suite. Similarly in the earlier case of *Smith v DPP* [2001] EWHC 55 (Admin), it was held that taking a person by the arm in order to move them aside so that police officers could enter a house to investigate an abandoned 999 call did not take the relevant officer outside the execution of his duty.

a little more, beyond which it might be difficult to deny that the intention was to detain that person. If the detainer is a police officer, such conduct will take that officer outside the execution of his or her duty, unless of course it was done for the purposes of effecting a lawful arrest or in order to prevent a breach of the peace.[217]

In several of the cases on section 89 (and its statutory predecessor), it is evident that the judiciary have been concerned that conduct which was clearly criminal has gone unpunished because at the time that the alleged offence was committed, the officer was acting *outside* the execution of his duty. In order to prevent this state of affairs from continuing, Donaldson LJ offered the following piece of practical advice to the prosecution when giving judgment in *Bentley v Brudzinski*:[218]

'I hope that police prosecutors will consider making an alternative charge of common assault when they have reason to think that there may be a technical challenge to the officer's authority and when the reaction of the citizen has been wholly unjustifiable. This will enable the limits of an officer's authority to be defined, whilst at the same time doing justice and giving the police officers the support which they are entitled to expect.'[219]

Charging the offence of common assault as an alternative to assault upon a police officer in the execution of his duty would thus provide the prosecution with the means of securing a conviction since 'acting within the execution of his duty' is not an ingredient of the former offence. Nevertheless, the advice proffered by Donaldson LJ does not always appear to have been heeded. Thus in *C v DPP*,[220] where it was held on appeal that a police officer had acted outside the execution of his duty when he took a minor by the elbow and was consequently assaulted by her boyfriend, Kennedy LJ observed:

'Where . . . there is any doubt as to whether at the particular moment when the violence was offered, the police officer was acting in the execution of his duty, or as the magistrates put it in the present case, performing a "socially desirable act", it seems to me to follow, as the night the day, that the charge laid should be one of common assault. The prosecution should not undertake the burden of proving unnecessarily that the officer was, indeed, acting in the execution of his duty.'[221]

FURTHER READING

Bailey SH, Harris DJ and Jones BL *Civil Liberties: Cases and Materials* (5th edn, Butterworths, London, 2001).

Bevan V and Lidstone K *The Investigation of Crime: A Guide to Police Powers* (2nd edn, Butterworths, London, 1996).

English J and Card R *Police Law* (9th edn, OUP, Oxford, 2005).

Jason-Lloyd L *An Introduction to Policing and Police Powers* (2nd edn, Routledge-Cavendish, London, 2005).

Levenson H and Fairweather F *Police Powers: A Practitioner's Guide* (3rd edn, Legal Action Group, London, 1995).

Mead D 'The Likely Effect of the Human Rights Act on Everyday Policing Decisions in England and Wales' (2000) 5(1) J Civ Lib 5.

[217] See *Albert v Lavin* [1982] AC 546, which was discussed at p. 649.
[218] (1982) 75 Cr App R 217.   [219] At 226.   [220] [2003] EWHC 2780 (Admin).
[221] At [24].

Reiner R *The Politics of the Police* (3rd edn, OUP, Oxford, 2000).

Smith G 'Reasonable Suspicion: Time for a Re-evaluation?' (2002) IJSL 1.

Stannard JE 'The Store Detective's Dilemma' (1994) 58 J Crim L 393.

Stone R *Textbook on Civil Liberties & Human Rights* (6th edn, OUP, Oxford, 2006).

Zander M *The Police and Criminal Evidence Act 1984* (5th edn, Sweet & Maxwell, London, 2005).

13 EUROPEAN CONVENTION ON HUMAN RIGHTS AND FUNDAMENTAL FREEDOMS AND THE HUMAN RIGHTS ACT 1998

1. The European Convention on Human Rights and Fundamental Freedoms

The ancestry of the European Convention on Human Rights and Fundamental Freedoms (ECHR) can be traced back to the Universal Declaration of Human Rights (UDHR) of 1948, itself a statement of a collection of human rights which are wider in scope than those rights guaranteed by the ECHR, although since it only has the status of a declaration, such rights are morally rather than legally enforceable. The desire to promote European unity and a respect for human rights was much evident in the post Second World War Europe. Prior to the war, the view among the sovereign states of Europe and indeed the world generally had been that the way in which a state treated its citizens was very much a matter to be dealt with by the state itself. Violations of human rights and freedoms were regarded as being internal political issues beyond the jurisdiction of the international community. However, the catastrophic events associated with the Second World War, particularly in Nazi Germany and the occupied territories, clearly demonstrated that a laissez-faire approach to the protection of human rights was no longer either appropriate or justified. Accordingly, on 5 May 1949, the Council of Europe was established by virtue of the signing of the statute of the same name. Its purpose was to promote unity where once there had been war,[1] and in order to achieve this objective, it drew up the ECHR which was originally signed in Rome on 4 November 1950 by

---

[1] Lord Woolf has contended that the ECHR was 'conceived as an "early warning system" to prevent states from lapsing into totalitarianism': see *Review of the Working Methods of the European Court of Human Rights*, (December 2005) at 7.

15 member states.[2] The Convention actually came into force on 3 September 1953 following its ratification by ten of its signatories. It is important to note that the Council which, at the time of writing, consists of some 46 member states, is a body completely unrelated to the European Community (EC). Admittedly each member state of the EC is also a member of the Council of Europe, but the two are distinct entities with their own institutions.

The ECHR, which is in many respects the lasting achievement of the Council of Europe, is a broad-based statement of rights and freedoms which the signatories are obliged to guarantee to their citizens.[3] It consists of a series of articles and protocols which define the substantive rights protected by the Treaty as well as detailing various procedural matters. In to this latter category falls the creation and staffing of the Convention's institutional bodies, the Committee of Ministers and the European Court of Human Rights (ECtHR). The existence of a number of protocols to the Convention is a reflection of the fact that human rights thinking has developed since the Convention was first drawn up. The protocols therefore constitute a mechanism by which the ECHR is able to take account of and adapt to these developments, thus avoiding the risk that it will come to be viewed as an anachronism by subsequent generations. Protocols are only binding upon those states that have ratified them. Thus although the United Kingdom is, for example, a party to the First Protocol[4] which entitles the state's citizens to the peaceful enjoyment of their possessions, and maintains that no one shall be denied the right to education, the United Kingdom is not a party to the Seventh Protocol to the Convention,[5] which states, inter alia, that: 'Everyone convicted of a criminal offence by a tribunal shall have the right to have his conviction or sentence reviewed by a higher tribunal.'[6] After some considerable delay, the UK signed the Sixth Protocol[7] which provides for the abolition of the death penalty. It was able to do so in May 1999 following the enactment of the Crime and Disorder Act 1998, section 36 of which abolished the death penalty for the offences of treason and piracy, the last remaining capital offences recognised in English criminal law. However, it is worth noting that at the time of writing, it appears that the UK government has no intention of signing Protocol 12[8] which seeks to impose a general prohibition on discrimination in respect of the enjoyment of any right set forth by law, ie not just those rights set out in the Convention itself.

....

Convention for the Protection of Human Rights and Fundamental Freedoms
(Rome, 4 November 1950)

'The Governments signatory hereto, being Members of the Council of Europe,

Considering the Universal Declaration of Human Rights proclaimed by the General Assembly of the United Nations on 10 December 1948;

Considering that this Declaration aims at securing the universal and effective recognition and observance of the rights therein declared;

Considering that the aim of the Council of Europe is the achievement of greater unity between its Members and that one of the methods by which that aim is to be pursued is the maintenance and further realisation of Human Rights and Fundamental Freedoms;

Reaffirming their profound belief in those Fundamental Freedoms which are the foundation of justice and peace in the world and are best maintained on the one hand by an effective political

---

[2] For a discussion of the UK's role in the process, see Marston, 'The United Kingdom's Part in the Preparation of the European Convention on Human Rights, 1950' (1993) 42 ICLQ 796.

[3] See article 1.   [4] Cmd 9221.   [5] (1984) 7 EHRR 1.   [6] See article 2.

[7] (1983) 5 EHRR 167.

[8] This was opened for signing on 4 November 2000, the 50th anniversary of the Convention.

democracy and on the other by a common understanding and observance of the Human Rights upon which they depend;

Being resolved, as the Governments of European countries which are like-minded and have a common heritage of political traditions, ideals, freedom and the rule of law, to take the first steps for the collective enforcement of certain of the rights stated in the Universal Declaration;

Have agreed as follows:

Article 1

The High Contracting parties shall secure to everyone within their jurisdiction the rights and freedoms defined in Section 1 of this Convention.

Section 1

Article 2

1. Everyone's right to life shall be protected by law. No one shall be deprived of his life intentionally save in the execution of a sentence of a court following his conviction of a crime for which the penalty is provided by law.

2. Deprivation of life shall not be regarded as inflicted in contravention of this Article when it results from the use of force which is no more than absolutely necessary:
    a. in defence of any person from unlawful violence;
    b. in order to effect a lawful arrest or to prevent the escape of a person lawfully detained;
    c. in action lawfully taken for the purpose of quelling a riot or insurrection.

Article 3

No one shall be subjected to torture or to inhuman or degrading treatment or punishment.

Article 4

1. No one shall be held in slavery or servitude.

2. No one shall be required to perform forced or compulsory labour.

3. For the purpose of this Article the term 'forced or compulsory labour' shall not include:
    a. any work required to be done in the ordinary course of detention imposed according to the provisions of Article 5 of this Convention or during conditional release from such detention;
    b. any service of a military character or, in case of conscientious objectors in countries where they are recognised, service exacted instead of compulsory military service;
    c. any service exacted in case of an emergency or calamity threatening the life or well-being of the community;
    d. any work or service which forms part of normal civic obligations.

Article 5

1. Everyone has the right to liberty and security of person. No one shall be deprived of this liberty save in the following cases and in accordance with a procedure prescribed by law:
    a. the lawful detention of a person after conviction by a competent court;
    b. the lawful arrest or detention of a person for non-compliance with the lawful order of a court or in order to secure the fulfilment of any obligation prescribed by law;
    c. the lawful arrest or detention of a person effected for the purpose of bringing him before the competent legal authority on reasonable suspicion of having committed an offence or when it is reasonably considered necessary to prevent his committing an offence or fleeing after having done so;
    d. the detention of a minor by lawful order for the purpose of educational supervision or his lawful detention for the purpose of bringing him before the competent legal authority;

   e. the lawful detention of persons for the prevention of the spreading of infectious diseases, of persons of unsound mind, alcoholics or drug addicts or vagrants;

   f. the lawful arrest or detention of a person to prevent his effecting an unauthorised entry into the country or of a person against whom action is being taken with a view to deportation or extradition.

2. Everyone who is arrested shall be informed promptly, in a language which he understands, of the reasons for his arrest and of any charge against him.

3. Everyone arrested or detained in accordance with the provisions of paragraph 1(c) of this Article shall be brought promptly before a judge or other officer authorised by law to exercise judicial power and shall be entitled to trial within a reasonable time or to release pending trial. Release may be conditioned by guarantees to appear for trial.

4. Everyone who is deprived of his liberty by arrest or detention shall be entitled to take proceedings by which the lawfulness of his detention shall be decided speedily by a court and his release ordered if the detention is not lawful.

5. Everyone who has been the victim of arrest or detention in contravention of the provisions of this Article shall have an enforceable right to compensation.

Article 6

1. In the determination of his civil rights and obligations or of any criminal charge against him, everyone is entitled to a fair and public hearing within a reasonable time by an independent and impartial tribunal established by law. Judgment shall be pronounced publicly but the press and the public may be excluded from all or part of the trial in the interest of morals, public order or national security in a democratic society, where the interests of juveniles or the protection of the private life of the parties so require, or to the extent strictly necessary in the opinion of the court in special circumstances where publicity would prejudice the interests of justice.

2. Everyone charged with a criminal offence shall be presumed innocent until proved guilty according to law.

3. Everyone charged with a criminal offence has the following minimum rights:

   a. to be informed promptly, in a language which he understands and in detail, of the nature and cause of the accusation against him;

   b. to have adequate time and facilities for the preparation of his defence;

   c. to defend himself in person or through legal assistance of his own choosing or, if he has not sufficient means to pay for legal assistance, to be given it free when the interests of justice so require;

   d. to examine or have examined witnesses against him and to obtain the attendance and examination of witnesses on his behalf under the same conditions as witnesses against him;

   e. to have the free assistance of an interpreter if he cannot understand or speak the language used in court.

Article 7

1. No one shall be held guilty of any criminal offence on account of any act or omission which did not constitute a criminal offence under national or international law at the time when it was committed. Nor shall a heavier penalty be imposed than the one that was applicable at the time the criminal offence was committed.

2. This Article shall not prejudice the trial and punishment of any person for any act or omission which, at the time when it was committed, was criminal according to the general principles of law recognised by civilised nations.

Article 8

1. Everyone has the right to respect for his private and family life, his home and his correspondence.

2. There shall be no interference by a public authority with the exercise of this right except such as in accordance with the law and is necessary in a democratic society in the interests of national security, public safety or the economic well-being of the country, for the prevention of disorder or crime, for the protection of health or morals, or for the protection of the rights and freedoms of others.

Article 9

1. Everyone has the right to freedom of thought, conscience and religion; this right includes freedom to change his religion or belief and freedom, either alone or in community with others and in public or private, to manifest his religion or belief, in worship, teaching, practice and observance.

2. Freedom to manifest one's religion or beliefs shall be subject only to such limitations as are prescribed by law and are necessary in a democratic society in the interests of public safety, for the protection of public order, health or morals, or for the protection of the rights and freedoms of others.

Article 10

1. Everyone has the right to freedom of expression. This right shall include freedom to hold opinions and to receive and impart information and ideas without interference by public authority and regardless of frontiers. This Article shall not prevent states from requiring the licensing of broadcasting, television or cinema enterprises.

2. The exercise of these freedoms, since it carries with it duties and responsibilities, may be subject to such formalities, conditions, restrictions or penalties as are prescribed by law and are necessary in a democratic society, in the interests of national security, territorial integrity or public safety, for the prevention of disorder or crime, for the protection of health or morals, for the protection of the reputation or rights of others, for preventing the disclosure of information received in confidence, or for maintaining the authority and impartiality of the judiciary.

Article 11

1. Everyone has the right to freedom of peaceful assembly and to freedom of association with others, including the right to form and to join trade unions for the protection of his interests.

2. No restrictions shall be placed on the exercise of these rights other than such as are prescribed by law and are necessary in a democratic society in the interests of national security or public safety, for the prevention of disorder or crime, for the protection of health or morals or for the protection of the rights and freedoms of others. This Article shall not prevent the imposition of lawful restrictions on the exercise of these rights by members of the armed forces, of the police or of the administration of the State.

Article 12

Men and women of marriageable age have the right to marry and to found a family, according to the national laws governing the exercise of this right.

Article 13

Everyone whose rights and freedoms as set forth in this Convention are violated shall have an effective remedy before a national authority notwithstanding that the violation has been committed by persons acting in an official capacity.

Article 14

The enjoyment of the rights and freedoms set forth in this Convention shall be secured without discrimination on any ground such as sex, colour, language, religion, political or other opinion, national or social origin, association with a national minority, property, birth or other status.

Article 15

1. In time of war or other public emergency threatening the life of the nation any High Contracting Party may take measures derogating from its obligations under this Convention to the extent strictly required by the exigencies of the situation, provided that such measures are not inconsistent with its other obligations under international law.

2. No derogation from Article 2, except in respect of deaths resulting from lawful acts of war, or from Articles 3, 4 (paragraph 1) and 7 shall be made under this provision.

3. Any High Contracting Party availing itself of this right of derogation shall keep the Secretary General of the Council of Europe fully informed of the measures which it has taken and the reasons therefor. It shall also inform the Secretary General of the Council of Europe when such measures have ceased to operate and the provisions of the Convention are again being fully executed.

Article 16

Nothing in Articles 10, 11 and 14 shall be regarded as preventing the High Contracting Parties from imposing restrictions on the political activity of aliens.

Article 17

Nothing in this Convention may be interpreted as implying for any state, group or person any right to engage in any activity or perform any act aimed at the destruction of any of the rights and freedoms set forth herein or at their limitation to a greater extent than is provided for in the Convention.

Article 18

The restrictions permitted under this Convention to the said rights and freedoms shall not be applied for any purpose other than those for which they have been prescribed.'

In terms of the subject matter of the substantive rights, the Convention ensures: protection of the right to life (article 2); freedom from torture, inhuman or degrading treatment (article 3); freedom from slavery, forced or compulsory labour (article 4); protection of the right to liberty and security of person (article 5); protection of the right to a fair and public hearing in civil and criminal proceedings (article 6); freedom from retrospective criminal laws or increased sentencing (article 7); protection of the right to privacy and respect for family life, home and correspondence (article 8); freedom of thought, conscience and religion (article 9); freedom of expression (article 10); freedom of assembly and association (article 11); protection of the right to marry and found a family (article 12); the provision of an effective domestic remedy for any violation of the Convention (article 13); and, the enjoyment of the rights and freedoms of the Convention without discrimination on any ground (article 14).

Stated in these relatively bald terms, the rights and freedoms guaranteed by the ECHR can be seen to be quite wide-ranging in their scope. If they were to be categorised, it would not be unfair to say that the Convention places greater emphasis on the protection of civil and political rights as opposed to economic and social rights.[9] Indeed, it is a moot point whether it is appropriate for economic and social rights to feature in human rights documents at all. Professor Maurice Cranston, for example, has argued that some of the rights contained in the UDHR, most notably those to be found in articles 22 onwards, are clearly distinct from what one would ordinarily consider to be fundamental human rights and freedoms. Article 24 of the UDHR, for example, states that 'Everyone has the right to rest and leisure, including reasonable limitation of working hours and periodic holidays with pay'. In Professor

---

[9] Thus in *Brown v Stott* [2003] 1 AC 681, Lord Bingham observed that the ECHR is concerned with rights and freedoms which are 'of real importance in a modern democracy governed by the rule of law': at 703.

Cranston's opinion, such inclusions in a human rights text have a detrimental effect since they 'push *all* talk of human rights out of the clear realm of the morally compelling into the twilight world of utopian aspiration'.[10]

On closer inspection, it quickly becomes apparent that few of the rights listed in the ECHR can be said to be absolute in nature. Article 3 which states that 'No one shall be subjected to torture or to inhuman or degrading treatment or punishment', is an example of an absolute right, but on the whole, the Convention rights are subject to exceptions. Thus while article 2 guarantees the protection by law of everyone's right to life, exceptions to this right are provided for by the article itself such as where a state retains capital punishment for certain offences specified by law. Article 7 prohibits retrospective or *ex post facto* criminal legislation and the imposition of higher penalties than those originally provided for at the time that the offence was committed. However, by virtue of paragraph 2 of the same article, a defendant will not avoid liability for his or her acts or omissions if at the time of their commission, such acts or omissions were 'criminal according to the general principles of law recognised by civilised nations'. Thus in *SW v UK; CR v UK*,[11] where the applicants had been found guilty by domestic courts of either raping or attempting to rape their wives,[12] and had subsequently applied to the ECtHR on the ground that their convictions breached article 7(1) of the ECHR because marital rape had not been an offence at the relevant time, both the Commission and the ECtHR were agreed that there had been no violation of the ECHR. In the judgment of the ECtHR, the development of the criminal law through judicial interpretation had reached a stage at which it was reasonably foreseeable that the courts would no longer recognise an immunity from prosecution in respect of this conduct.[13]

In the case of articles 8–11 of the ECHR, it is evident that provision is made for potentially wide-ranging exceptions to the rights and freedoms which the articles seek to protect. The need for qualification is inevitable, however, given that the exercise of a right by an individual is likely to have adverse impacts on the rights of others. Thus, for example, unrestricted freedom of expression in the form of a completely unfettered press has the potential to impact upon the private lives of those in the public eye.[14]

II. The Institutions

(a) Introduction

Prior to the institutional reforms introduced by Protocol 11 to the Convention, the European Commission on Human Rights was a central cog in the Strasbourg machine. It performed a number of important functions, such as determining whether or not an application was admissible within the meaning of the admissibility criteria laid down in the Convention.[15] This aspect of the Commission's role was vital in that it served as a means of filtering out

---

[10] See *What are Human Rights?* (Bodley Head, London, 1973) at p. 68.   [11] (1995) 21 EHRR 363.
[12] See *R v R* [1991] 2 All ER 257 (CA); [1991] 4 All ER 481 (HL).
[13] For a case where the ECtHR held that there had been a violation of article 7, see *Welch v UK* (1995) 20 EHRR 247.   [14] See *Campbell v Mirror Group Newspapers* [2004] 1 AC 457, which is extracted below.
[15] See further pp. 787–785.

applications which might otherwise have wasted the time of the Court or the Committee of Ministers. The Commission also had a central role to play in trying to broker what is known as a 'friendly settlement'.[16] However, the increase in the number of signatories to the Convention and the corresponding expansion in the numbers of actual and potential applicants meant that neither the Commission nor the Court could effectively manage their respective workloads. Institutional reform was therefore necessary. The matter was fully debated at national government level and by several committees of experts and, ultimately, a consensus started to emerge that the necessary reform was the establishment of a new single full-time court which would perform the functions of both the Commission and the ECtHR. This proposal was subsequently endorsed in the Vienna Declaration of 9 October 1993 at a meeting of the Council of Europe's heads of state and government. Protocol 11 to the Convention, which made the necessary amendments to the Convention, was opened for signing in May 1994. It entered into force on 1 November 1998 and its reforms took effect one year from that date. Accordingly, the Commission ceased to be a Convention institution in November 1999 when its functions were transferred to what has become a full-time ECtHR. The composition, powers and functions of the reformed Court will be considered in due course. First, however, it is necessary to say something about two other European institutions: the Committee of Ministers; and, the Parliamentary Assembly.

(b) Committee of Ministers

Although the Committee of Ministers is considered here as an institution of the Convention, it is in fact a creation of the Statute of the Council of Europe of 1949 which predates the Convention. Its membership consists of the various ministers of foreign affairs for each of the states which are part of the Council of Europe, though in practice, when the Committee is not sitting in one of its formal sessions held during the course of a year, ministerial deputies act as the representative of the state. The Committee of Ministers is therefore without doubt a political body. Nevertheless, by virtue of former article 32 of the Convention, it was possible for the Committee to perform what was in truth a judicial function: the determination of whether there had been a violation of the Convention in a particular case. The jurisdiction of the Committee of Ministers took effect where three months had passed since it had received a Commission report on the merits of a complaint and the matter had not been referred to the Court. Despite the fact that in practice the Committee dealt with those relatively mundane cases which either did not raise important Convention issues or which had effectively been conceded by the state since it had taken the necessary remedial action at the domestic level prior to a ruling, its jurisdiction was not without controversy since it was questionable whether a political body ought to make judicial decisions. These concerns were addressed by Protocol 11 which abolished the Committee's judicial role.

The remaining task of the Committee is, therefore, the supervision of the execution of the judgments of the ECtHR. Where the Court has delivered judgment sitting either as a Chamber or Grand Chamber, such a judgment is declared to be final in the circumstances set out in article 44 of the Convention.[17] By virtue of article 46(1), the High Contracting Parties are obliged to abide by the ruling of the Court in any case in which they were one of the parties.

[16] See further pp. 788–789. [17] See further pp. 778, 779.

The Committee's role is provided for in article 46(2) which declares that: 'The final judgment of the Court shall be transmitted to the Committee of Ministers which shall supervise its execution.'[18] The precise nature of the supervisory process is provided for in Rules for the application of article 46. Foremost among the Rules' requirements is that the state shall inform the Committee of the measures that it has taken in order to comply with the Court ruling. It is then necessary for the Committee to form an opinion as to whether these measures are in fact sufficient for the purposes of abiding by the Court's ruling. Its role in the supervisory process is completed, therefore, when it issues a resolution in which it is stated that the necessary remedial measures have in fact been taken.

It has been suggested that the implementation of the judgments of the ECHR is the 'Achilles heel of the entire Convention system'[19] in that the Committee of Ministers is effectively powerless to deal with those states which consistently fail to comply with ECtHR rulings. More specifically, the supervision process has been criticised for being 'insufficiently rigorous', inaccessible and lacking in transparency.[20] Evidently there is cause for concern since non-compliance casts a shadow over the credibility of the entire Convention system. It therefore seems that further courses of action ought to be pursued by the Committee to facilitate its supervisory task. These might include: peer pressure at its meetings and insistence that a state respects its duty to comply; increased frequency of the examination of the cases; and, adoption of an interim resolution setting out the execution measures which are planned.[21]

(c) The Parliamentary Assembly

The Parliamentary Assembly of the Council of Europe held its first session on 10 August 1949. Its membership consists of representatives (and their substitutes) from the member states of the Council of Europe who are appointed or elected from the national or federal Parliament of that state. As with the EC's European Parliament,[22] the number of members of the Parliamentary Assembly for each state is determined according to the size of the state's population. The larger states such as France, Italy, Germany, Russia and the UK each have eighteen representatives (and eighteen substitutes), whereas the smaller states such as Andorra and San Marino each have two representatives (and two substitutes). The total number of members of the Assembly (representatives and their substitutes) currently stands at 630.

Since the Parliamentary Assembly is the parliamentary organ of the Council of Europe, it follows that in common with the Committee of Ministers, it is not a Convention institution. Accordingly, for present purposes it is unnecessary to consider matters such as the political groupings within the Assembly or its committee structure. What is worth noting, however, is that under article 22 of the ECHR, the Parliamentary Assembly is responsible for electing the

---

[18] It has been observed by one commentator that although article 46(2) stipulates the power or function of the Committee, it is 'without further reference to methodology': see Leach, 'The effectiveness of the Committee of Ministers in supervising enforcement of judgments of the European Court of Human Rights' [2006] PL 443 at 444.

[19] See Greer, 'Protocol 14 and the Future of the European Court of Human Rights' [2005] PL 83 at 92.

[20] See Leach [2006] PL 443 at 451–452.

[21] For a discussion of these and other steps, see Leach [2006] PL 443 at 446–449.

[22] See p. 300.

judges to the ECtHR. Each High Contracting Party nominates a list of three individuals from which the Assembly elects a judge in respect of each state. In the case of the UK, the three nominees for election to the reformed Court in 1998 were submitted following a selection process which involved the public advertisement of the post and the interview of a short list of five candidates from the original number of thity-three.

(d) European Court of Human Rights (ECtHR)

The ECtHR came into existence on 21 January 1959. Originally its jurisdiction to deal with human rights matters had to be individually recognised by the High Contracting Parties to the Convention. Now, however, as a consequence of a reform introduced by Protocol 11, the jurisdiction of the Court is automatic. Initially referrals to the Court did not occur with any great frequency, as is evidenced by the fact that between the years 1959 and 1973, the Court heard only eleven cases. However, with the passage of time, the Court became such a vital part of the Convention machinery that institutional reform was necessary in order for it to effec-tively manage its increasing workload.

The composition, structure and jurisdiction of the reformed Court is dealt with in section II of the Convention. Thus, by virtue of article 20, the Court consists of a number of judges equal to that of the High Contracting Parties (46 at the time of writing). In terms of the credentials of the candidates themselves, article 21(1) demands that they be persons of 'high moral character and must either possess the qualifications required for appointment to high judicial office or be jurisconsults of recognised competence'. Once elected to the Court, judges sit in their individual capacity. In other words, they are at Strasbourg to perform the role of a judge, rather than to act as a representative of a High Contracting Party. It follows, therefore, that during their term of office, judges are not permitted to engage in any activity which is incompatible with 'their independence, impartiality or with the demands of a full-time office'.[23] It is worth noting at this juncture that section 18 of the Human Rights Act 1998 is concerned with the consequences flowing from the appointment of a UK judge to the ECtHR. Under this provision, the holder of a judicial office (in England and Wales, a judge of the Court of Appeal, the High Court or a Circuit Judge) may become a judge of the Court without having to relinquish his domestic office. However, while he is a judge of the Court, he is not required to perform the duties of his domestic judicial office. Currently, the UK's judge at the European Court of Human Rights is Sir Nicholas Bratza, who was appointed to the Queen's Bench Division of the High Court on 30 October 1998.

The members of the ECtHR are elected by the Parliamentary Assembly in respect of each High Contracting Party by a majority of votes cast from a list of three candidates nominated by the High Contracting Party.[24] Judges are elected for a period of six years, although they may be re-elected.[25] In order to prevent wholesale changes to the composition of the Court which may have had a detrimental effect upon its judicial activity, article 23 staggered the expiry of the terms of office of some of the members of the Court elected at the first election. Thus for half of the judges elected at the first election, their terms of office expired at the end of three years. Those to whom this applied were chosen by lot by the Secretary General of the Council of Europe. The terms of office of judges expire when they reach the age of 70.[26] They may not

---

[23] Article 21(3).   [24] Article 22.   [25] Article 23(1).   [26] Article 23(6).

be dismissed from office unless the other judges of the Court decide by a two-thirds majority that the relevant judge has ceased to fulfil the required conditions.[27]

(i) Plenary Court, Committees, Chambers and the Grand Chamber

The European Court of Human Rights exists in a number of different guises. The Plenary Court, which consists of all 46 judges, does not exercise a judicial function. Instead, it is concerned with matters such as: the election of a President of the Court and one or two Vice-Presidents for a period of three years; the setting up of Chambers of the Court; the election of Presidents of the Chambers; and, the adoption of the Rules of the Court.[28] Under the Rules, the Court is divided into four sections, each of which reflects a geographical and gender balance as well as taking account of the various different legal systems of the High Contracting Parties. When considering cases brought before it, the Court may sit in one of three guises: as a Committee (three judges); a Chamber (seven judges); or, as a Grand Chamber (seventeen judges).

Committees are set up by the Chambers for a fixed period of time. They perform an important task formerly performed by the Commission; they determine the admissibility of applications made by individuals under article 34.[29] A Committee may, acting unanimously, declare such an application to be inadmissible or strike it out of its list of cases.[30] Striking out may occur where, for example, the applicant does not intend to pursue his application or the matter has been resolved.[31] A decision of a Committee is final.

Where no decision has been reached under article 28, it will be for a Chamber to decide on the admissibility and merits of an individual application.[32] A Chamber also has the jurisdiction to decide on the admissibility and merits of inter-state applications.[33] Save in exceptional cases, article 29(3) requires that the decision on admissibility shall be taken separately from the decision on the merits of an application. When hearing a case, the judge elected in respect of the High Contracting Party concerned shall sit as an *ex officio* member of the Chamber. If there is no such judge, or if the relevant judge is unable to sit, a person of the state's choice shall sit as a judge.[34] A Chamber may relinquish its jurisdiction to determine a case where that case raises a serious question affecting the interpretation of the Convention or its protocols, or where to determine the case may produce a result which is inconsistent with a previous judgment of the Court. Relinquishment may only occur, however, if neither party to the case objects. Assuming that a case has not been relinquished to a Grand Chamber, the judgment of a Chamber will only become final when: the parties declare that they will not request that the case be referred to the Grand Chamber; or, three months have passed since the date of the decision and no referral to the Grand Chamber has been requested; or, a panel of the Grand Chamber has rejected a request from any of the parties that a case be referred to it.[35]

The Grand Chamber is the largest forum in which the Court exercises a judicial function. As with the other guises, its composition is fluid. Its membership does include, however, the President of the Court, the Vice Presidents, the Presidents of the Chambers and other judges chosen in accordance with the Rules of the Court.[36] The Grand Chamber essentially performs

---

[27] Article 24.   [28] Article 26.   [29] See further p. 786.   [30] Article 28.
[31] Article 37(1).   [32] Article 29(1).   [33] See further pp. 786–787.   [34] Article 27(2).
[35] Article 44(2).   [36] Article 27(3).

three functions. As has already been noted, it determines individual or inter-state applications which have been relinquished to it. It also determines cases which have been referred to it under article 43. For it to exercise this latter jurisdiction, however, one of the parties to a case must have requested that the case be referred to the Grand Chamber within three months of the date of the judgment of the Chamber. Moreover, a panel of five judges of the Grand Chamber will have to be satisfied that the case raises a serious question relating to the interpretation of the Convention or its protocols, or a serious issue of general importance, before the Grand Chamber will hear the case.[37] A judgment of the Grand Chamber is final.[38]

The other function of the Grand Chamber is to consider requests for advisory opinions submitted under article 47. Such requests are made by the Committee of Ministers following a majority vote in favour of seeking an advisory opinion. The Court may give advisory opinions concerning the interpretation of the Convention and its protocols. Whether or not a request for an advisory opinion is within its competence is a matter for the Court.[39] Where an advisory opinion is given, it shall be communicated to the Committee of Ministers.[40] It shall be accompanied by reasons and any dissenting judge is permitted to deliver a separate opinion.[41]

The jurisdiction of the ECtHR extends to all matters relating to the interpretation of the Convention and its protocols.[42] In the event of a dispute as to whether the Court has jurisdiction, it shall determine the matter. The hearings of the Court, which are adversarial in nature, are conducted in public unless the Court considers that exceptional circumstances require otherwise.[43] In reaching a decision in a particular case, the members of the Court are not bound by previous judgments. However, although there is no doctrine of precedent as such, the Court will tend to follow its previous decisions in the interests of legal certainty and the establishment of a coherent and logical body of human rights case law. Nevertheless, a departure from a previous decision may be justified where, for example, it is felt that the changing needs of society require a different interpretation of a right or freedom guaranteed by the Convention. Alternatively, the ECtHR may decline to follow one of its own previous decisions where it later becomes apparent that it was based on an incomplete understanding of domestic legal principle.[44]

Reasons are required to be given for the judgments of the Court and its decisions as to the admissibility of an application.[45] Where the Court takes the view that there has been a partial or complete failure to comply with a Convention obligation and that the domestic law of the High Contracting Party only provides for partial reparation, the Court's final decision may include the requirement that the state 'afford just satisfaction to the injured party'.[46] 'Just satisfaction' essentially means that the Court will make an award of compensation to the injured party for pecuniary or non-pecuniary damage suffered, and/or, for the costs and expenses that have been incurred in bringing proceedings. Such an outcome is, however, comparatively rare. Thus in 2005, although the ECtHR reached in excess of 1,100 judgments, only eight included just satisfaction.[47] In the overwhelming majority of cases, the Court takes the view that its decision in favour of the applicant is in itself a sufficient remedy for the

---

[37] Article 43(2). For an example of a case where a Panel accepted a request, see *Hirst v UK (No. 2)* (2006) 42 EHRR 41, discussed further below. [38] Article 44(1).

[39] Article 48.   [40] Article 49(3).   [41] Article 49(1) and (2).   [42] Article 37(1).

[43] Article 40.

[44] See *Z v UK* (2002) 34 EHRR 97, where the ECtHR declined to follow *Osman v UK* (2000) 29 EHRR 245 in the light of the House of Lords decision in *Barnett v London Borough of Enfield* [2001] 2 AC 550. See further below. [45] Article 45(1).

[46] Article 41.   [47] See *Survey of Activities for 2005*, at p. 31.

violation of the Convention. That decision will refrain from dictating to the High Contracting Party what sort of legislative or administrative action is necessary at a domestic level in order to comply with the terms of the judgment; that is a matter for the High Contracting Party.

(ii) The effect of the Court's rulings on domestic law and practice

The binding nature of the Court's rulings by virtue of article 46 of the ECHR does mean, however, that if the Court were to conclude that either English law or administrative practice was in breach of the Convention, the UK government would be obliged to ensure that the necessary corrective measures were taken. Such measures were necessary, for example, as a consequence of the ruling in *The Sunday Times v United Kingdom*,[48] where the ECtHR held that the granting of an injunction to restrain the publication of a newspaper article amounted to a violation of article 10 of the Convention. In purported compliance with the Court's judgment, the UK Parliament enacted the Contempt of Court Act 1981 which also gave effect to the main recommendations of the Phillimore Committee[49] which had been set up in 1971 to look into the law of contempt.

A further example of a legislative initiative being precipitated by a Strasbourg ruling is the Interception of Communications Act 1985 which followed the decision in *Malone v UK*.[50] In *Malone v Metropolitan Police Commr*,[51] it was held in the Chancery Division that although there was no specific statutory provision authorising the tapping of Malone's telephone, nevertheless the court was obliged to find against the plaintiff since there was no discernible right in relation to a person's telephone communications that merited protection. This conclusion was reached by Sir Robert Megarry V-C despite his view that telephone tapping was an area which 'cries out for legislation'. However, following the exhaustion of the domestic remedies, the matter was taken to Strasbourg and the ECtHR came to the conclusion that the UK law on the interception of communications was in breach of article 8 of the Convention on account of the fact that it was 'somewhat obscure and open to differing interpretations'. This lack of clarity meant, therefore, that there was no adequate indication as to when public authorities were likely to exercise a discretion in favour of authorising a telephone tap, and thus the citizen was deprived of even the minimum degree of legal protection required by the rule of law.

The impact made upon English law and administrative practice by rulings from Strasbourg is clearly important. In more recent times, significant judgments have continued to be handed down by the ECtHR. Often these have centred upon article 6 of the ECHR and the right to a fair hearing in the determination of an individual's civil rights and obligations, or of any criminal charge made against him, by an independent and impartial tribunal. Thus in *V v United Kingdom; T v United Kingdom*,[52] it was held, among other things, that the conduct of the trial of Jon Venables and Robert Thompson for the murder of Jamie Bulger had amounted to a violation of article 6(1) of the ECHR, as had the setting of the tariff by the Home Secretary following their conviction. Similarly in *Kingsley v United Kingdom*,[53] it was held that the applicant had not received a fair hearing contrary to article 6(1) where an allegation of bias against a supervisory board had been determined in judicial review proceedings.

---

[48] (1979) 2 EHRR 245. [49] Cmnd 5794 (1976). [50] (1984) 7 EHRR 14.
[51] [1979] 2 All ER 620. [52] (1999) 30 EHRR 121. [53] (2002) 35 EHRR 10.

(iii) Reform of the European Court of Human Rights

Although the creation of a single unified Court represents an important development in the history of the ECHR, the backlog of cases faced by the Court has continued to grow despite institutional reform. The significant increase in the number of applications between 1991 and 1999,[54] has been followed by exponential growth. Thus in 2000, the ECtHR received a little less than 8,000 more applications than it had received the previous year. By 2004, the number of new applications lodged had grown to 44,128. This figure is only approximately 10,000 less than the total number of applications received by the Court between the years 1955 and 1990. The rapid increase in the number of applications can of course be attributed to the accession of new High Contracting Parties since 1994 with the result that by 2004, the number of potential applicants under the Convention system stood at 800 million people. However, the increase can also be partly attributed to the citizens of the old High Contracting Parties making more use of the existing machinery. Thus, for example, whereas in 2003 the ECtHR received 1,396 applications from UK citizens, by 2005, that figure had increased to 1,652.[55] It has been suggested by one commentator that this latter phenomenon is 'most probably' due to 'the publicity given to important cases, coupled with better knowledge of the Convention machinery and a growing tendency to turn to the judiciary in general'.[56]

In the light of this continuing and increasing backlog of cases, it was realised that if the long-term effectiveness of the Court was to be achieved, further institutional reform was necessary. Accordingly, at the Ministerial Conference on Human Rights held in Rome on 3–4 November 2000,[57] a resolution was passed which called upon the Committee of Ministers to undertake several activities, including a thorough study of the potential options for ensuring the future effectiveness of the Court. The Committee responded by establishing an Evaluation Group to look into the matter. It submitted its Report on 27 September 2001.[58] At the same time, the Steering Committee for Human Rights set up a Reflection Group on the Reinforcement of the Human Rights Protection Mechanism. The important work undertaken by these bodies influenced the content of a number of declarations adopted by the Committee of Ministers during the period November 2001–May 2003 relating to the long-term effectiveness of the Court. The most significant step in the reform process occurred, however, when the Steering Committee was instructed to prepare a draft amending protocol to the Convention. Protocol 14 was accordingly opened for signature on 13 May 2004. In a decision made concurrently, the Committee of Ministers committed themselves to ratifying the protocol within two years, ie by 13 May 2006. At the time of writing, however, Protocol 14 has yet to enter into force.

The key features of Protocol 14 will be considered shortly. However, prior to doing so it ought to be acknowledged that other reform options were considered and ultimately rejected as part of the discussion process. Thus, for example, one idea which was mooted was the establishment of a number of regional human rights tribunals throughout Europe with the Strasbourg Court taking on the role of a tribunal of last instance. The idea was rejected,

---

[54] Part V of the *Survey of Activities for 2005* reveals that in 1991, 6,104 applications were lodged with the ECtHR. By 1999, this figure had risen to 22,617: see p. 33.

[55] See *Survey of Activities for 2005*, at p. 35.

[56] Beernaert, 'Protocol 14 and new Strasbourg procedures: Towards greater efficiency? And at what price?' [2004] EHRLR 544 at 544.   [57] The 50th anniversary of the opening for signature of the Convention.

[58] Doc. EG Court (2001) 1.

however, on both principled and practical grounds; it was felt that it would create a very real risk of diverging case law, and that the cost implications were too great. Alternatively, it was proposed that the task of filtering applications could be undertaken by a separate non-judicial body. This was also rejected, however, on the principled grounds that it would be contrary to the fundamental premises that such work needed to be carried out within the judicial framework of the Court and that, within the Court, different categories of judges should be avoided. A proposal to increase the number of full-time elected judges in the Court was also rejected.

(iv) Protocol 14

Protocol 14 seeks to address the problem of the ever-expanding caseload of the ECtHR by amending the ECHR in three crucial areas: the filtering of applications; the admissibility criteria; and, measures for dealing with repetitive cases. Under the amended Convention, the task of determining whether or not an application is admissible will be carried out by a *single judge* rather than by at least three judges as is presently the case. This new mechanism therefore remains true to the principle that the task of filtering applications ought to be carried out by judges. On the face of it, there is no reason to think that it will not prove to be effective in speeding up that process. Moreover, objections to the loss of collegiate decision-making can be countered with the observation that in practice, admissibility decisions are frequently made on the basis of an opinion expressed in a rapporteur's note with which the other two judges rarely disagree.[59]

The second key amendment which Protocol 14 will make to the ECHR, the insertion of an additional admissibility requirement into article 35,[60] is more controversial. In the future, it will also be possible to declare an application inadmissible where 'the applicant has not suffered a significant disadvantage'. This provision is, however, subject to three important safeguards. First, it will not prevent an application being declared admissible where respect for human rights as defined in the ECHR and the protocols thereto requires it. Secondly, it does not permit any case to be rejected on this ground that has not been duly considered by a domestic tribunal. Thirdly, it is an admissibility criterion which will only be able to be applied by the Chambers and the Grand Chamber in the first two years following the entry into force of Protocol 14.[61] Thereafter, however, it can be applied by a single judge or a Committee.

The key phrase in the new admissibility requirement is 'significant disadvantage'. Clearly its purpose is to weed out those applications where it can be said that the applicant has only suffered some very minor or trivial disadvantage. In the *Explanatory Report* on Protocol 14, it is stated that the new admissibility criterion will 'provide the Court with an additional tool which should assist it in its filtering work and allow it to devote more time to cases which warrant examination on the merits'.[62] However, it is questionable whether it will make for a more expeditious filtering process. As one commentator has pointed out, assessing whether or not an application falls within the scope of the admissibility requirement and whether the first two safeguards apply 'will inevitably require an in-depth study of the case file and probably make decisions on admissibility more complex and time consuming, rather than more

---

[59] See Beernaert, [2004] EHRLR 544 at 549.

[60] For a discussion of the current admissibility criteria, see further pp. 787–788.

[61] See article 20(2) of Protocol 14. [62] At para 70.

efficient'.[63] Concerns have also been expressed as to whether the new admissibility requirement amounts to an inappropriate inroad into the right of individual petition.[64] Its likely effect will be to prevent some legitimate cases involving a breach of the Convention from receiving a merits determination rather than serving as a means whereby applications which are already unmeritorious under the current admissibility criteria can be more effectively filtered out. Indeed, the point seems to have been accepted by the Council of Europe itself since it is stated in the *Explanatory Report* on Protocol 14 that: 'The new criterion may lead to certain cases being declared inadmissible which might have resulted in a judgment without it.'[65]

The incidence of repetitive applications, ie applications raising identical or very similar issues to those already determined, has undoubtedly contributed greatly to the increased workload of the Court. Protocol 14 therefore seeks to address this problem by amending the Convention so as to enable a Committee to declare an application admissible and at the same time reach a decision on its merits. This will be possible 'if the underlying question in the case, concerning the interpretation or the application of the Convention or the Protocols thereto, is already the subject of well-established case-law of the Court'. Such an amendment is therefore likely to expedite the determination of applications which raise issues which have previously been determined by the Court. It is uncontroversial in that it adheres to the principles of judicial and collegiate decision-making whilst at the same time upholding the right of individual petition.[66]

Although the focus of the present discussion has been on the key amendments which Protocol 14 will make to the ECHR, there are other miscellaneous amendments which are worthy of note. Thus under the reformed ECHR judicial tenure will be altered so that in the future, a judge will be able to serve a maximum period of nine years with no possibility of re-election rather than the present six-year period with the possibility of re-election. Protocol 14 will also enhance the role which the Committee of Ministers performs in relation to supervising the execution of ECtHR judgments. Thus under a new article 46, where the Committee considers that its role is being hindered by a problem of interpretation, it will be entitled to refer the matter to the Court for a ruling. Such a referral must, however, achieve the support of a two-thirds majority of the Committee's representatives. A further new power, the power to refer to the ECtHR the question whether a state has failed to fulfil its obligation to comply with a ruling of the Court, will also require a two-thirds majority support among the Committee's representatives. It is also subject to the restriction that it can only be exercised following the service of a formal notice on the state setting out the basis of the Committee's belief that it has refused to abide by a final judgment of the Court. This power, which mirrors the power which the European Commission has in relation to the judgments of the European Court of Justice,[67] has the potential to bring about the more effective execution of ECtHR judgments.

A further amendment to note relates to friendly settlements. Under the amended Convention, it will be possible for these to be reached at any stage of the proceedings rather than after an application has been declared admissible as is presently the case. In the event that a friendly settlement has been reached, the new article 39 will require the Court to strike the

[63] See Beernaert, [2004] EHRLR 544 at 553–554.
[64] See, for example, the views of the Parliamentary Assembly, Opinion No. 251 (2004) (28 April 2004) at para 11, and those of the Joint Committee on Human Rights—*Protocol No. 14 to the European Convention on Human Rights*, First Report of session 2004–05 (HL Paper 8, HC 106) at para 34.
[65] At para 79.   [66] See Beernaert, [2004] EHRLR 544 at 551.   [67] See p. 332.

case out of its list. This will be achieved in the form of a decision which will summarise the facts of the case and the solution reached. The Committee of Ministers will then be notified of the decision since it will be responsible for supervising the execution of the friendly settlement in accordance with the Court's decision. Finally, it should be noted that by amending article 59 of the ECHR, Protocol 14 will make it possible for the EU to accede to the Convention.

The raft of amendments which Protocol 14 seeks to make to the ECHR have as their central target the Court's burgeoning caseload. Action at the international level to deal with this problem is of course entirely appropriate. However, it should not be forgotten that one of the causes of the problem is the failure of the High Contracting Parties to properly secure for their citizens the rights and freedoms set out in the Convention. It is evident that some states are worse than others in this regard. Thus of the 1,105 judgments which the ECtHR delivered in 2005, five states accounted for more than 60 per cent of this figure.[68] Accordingly, it is self-evident that reforms to the ECHR need to be complimented by measures at the domestic level if the problem of the Court's caseload is to be solved. If they have not done so already, High Contracting Parties need to ensure that within their boundaries they have available effective mechanisms for either preventing or providing redress for violations of the ECHR, and that draft legislation and administrative practices are systematically screened in order to ensure that they are Convention compliant.[69]

(v) Further reform?

It has been argued that Protocol 14 represents a 'missed opportunity' and that it 'is likely at best, to be only a partial success'.[70] Assuming that this view proves to be correct, it is not inappropriate to speculate on how the ECtHR and the Convention machinery may be further reformed in the future. A radical reform proposed by one commentator would entail dispensing with all the current and new admissibility criteria and replacing them instead with a single inadmissibility criterion couched as follows:

'the application does not raise an allegation of a Convention violation which, in the opinion of the Court, is sufficiently serious for the applicant, the respondent state, and/or for Europe as a whole to warrant adjudication on the merits'.[71]

In deciding whether or not the alleged violation was 'sufficiently serious', it is argued that the ECtHR would be entitled to have regard to the old and new admissibility criteria, but that it would not be bound to do so. This reform would therefore seek to tackle the problem of the Court's ever-increasing workload by according that body considerable discretion as to those applications which it either will or will not hear.

Not all reforms need, however, to make amendments to the Convention. Thus in May 2005, a 'Group of Wise Persons' was set up at the Third Council of Europe Summit held in Warsaw. That Group has been given the task of 'drawing up a comprehensive strategy to secure the

[68] See *Survey of Activities for 2005*, at p. 26. The five states were: Turkey; Ukraine; Greece; Russia; and Italy. The number of Court judgments made in relation to Turkey, 290, accounted for 26.24 per cent of the total number of judgments in 2005.
[69] In the UK, this is what the Human Rights Act 1998 and the work of the Joint Committee on Human Rights seeks to achieve (see further pp. 896–897).
[70] See Greer, 'Protocol 14 and the future of the European Court of Human Rights' [2005] PL 83 at 85.
[71] Greer, [2005] PL 83 at 106.

long-term effectiveness of the European Convention on Human Rights and its control mechanism' which is likely to mean that in the future, it will suggest reforms which will require amendment of the ECHR. However, one of the members of that Group, the former Lord Chief Justice, Lord Woolf, was invited by the Secretary General of the Council of Europe and the President of the ECtHR to consider what might be done in the short term to address the problem of the Court's ever-growing workload. In December 2005, he published a *Review of the Working Methods of the European Court of Human Rights*, the purpose of which was to 'suggest administrative steps that can be taken, without amending the Convention, to allow the Court to cope with its current and projected caseload, and pending more fundamental reform'.[72] The *Review* contains a number of recommendations. These include: redefining what constitutes an application; establishing satellite offices of the Court's Registry in those countries which produce high numbers of inadmissible applications; encouraging the greater use of national Ombudsmen and Alternative Dispute Resolution; the Court making a greater use of 'pilot judgments' and then dealing summarily with repetitive cases; the establishment of a central training unit for lawyers; and, providing a formal induction programme for new judges which would include intensive language training where appropriate.

For present purposes it is appropriate to say a little more by way of explanation about some but not all of these recommendations. Thus in relation to the first recommendation, the *Review* contends that the ECtHR should be tougher on what constitutes an 'application', so that only properly completed application forms will be registered on the Court's system.[73] It argues that implementing this recommendation will prevent approximately 10,500 applications a year from appearing in the Court's statistics. It denies, however, that this represents an attack on the right of individual petition. Instead, it argues that it is a practice which has been adopted by other courts and that it ought to be the responsibility of the applicant to know the nature of their complaint and to provide the information necessary for the application to be processed.

The *Review's* recommendation that satellite offices of the Registry should be established would in effect create a satellite filtering system which could operate in those countries which generate high volumes of inadmissible applications. It is envisaged that such offices could work in a number of different ways. Thus they could assist those whose intended application either appeared to be admissible or raised an admissibility issue by providing an application form and guidance on submitting an application. Where a complaint was clearly inadmissible, the satellite office staff could provide information on the Court's admissibility criteria and on how the matter might be dealt with using domestic remedies and alternative dispute mechanisms. Where an applicant wishes to proceed with a clearly inadmissible case, that person is of course entitled to do so by virtue of the right of individual petition.[74] However, the *Review* contends that the satellite office could still involve itself in such a case by sending a note along with the application form explaining why it took the view that it was inadmissible. In the opinion of the *Review*, there are several advantages of a satellite filter system. Not least of these is that it would be 'far cheaper' to establish offices in High Contracting Parties than further increase the size of the Strasbourg staff, and that it 'should be politically attractive to national governments, as many problems could be resolved at the local level, rather than at the international level in Strasbourg'.[75]

The final recommendation to be considered here is the pilot judgment procedure. The *Review* notes that in *Broniowski v Poland*,[76] the ECtHR reached a judgment in which it found

---

[72] At 4.   [73] At 21.   [74] See further p. 786.   [75] At 30–31.
[76] Application No. 31443/96, judgment 28/09/2005.

that there had been a breach of article 1 of the First Protocol to the ECHR. However, given that there was a whole class of individuals who had suffered similarly due to an internal systemic failure, the judgment was designated a pilot judgment. This meant that in executing the judgment, the Polish government was required to take general measures which took account of the many other people who had been adversely affected. Pending the implementation of these general measures, all other applications were adjourned. Thus the pilot judgment procedure has considerable potential as a means of dealing with repetitive cases. The *Review* therefore recommends that priority ought to be given to any cases in the Court's workload which might be candidates for pilot judgments, and that all similar cases ought to be stayed pending the outcome of the relevant cases.

(vi) Right of individual petition

Article 34 of the Convention stipulates that 'any person, non-governmental organisation or group of individuals' may apply to the Court where they claim to be the 'victim' of a violation by one of the High Contracting Parties of the rights set out in the Convention or its protocols. The importance of this provision ought not to be overlooked. In essence, it is due to the existence of article 34 (and its predecessor, former article 25) that the ECtHR has been supplied with a wide-ranging and expansive diet of applications. Such applications have played a central role in the development of the Court's jurisprudence and collectively they have ensured that the Court has remained thoroughly occupied in the performance of its interpretative function. In all likelihood, this would not have been the case had its competence been confined to inter-state applications alone.[77] However, while article 34 has clearly provided the individual with the opportunity of gaining access to an independent international machinery for the settlement of human rights disputes, the individual right of petition was not originally an automatic corollary of the ratification of the Convention. Rather, it was dependent upon a declaration by the High Contracting Party that it recognised the competence of the Commission to receive such applications. Thus although the UK ratified the Convention in 1951, it did not recognise the right of individual petition until 1966.

Although the reforms introduced by Protocol 11 were primarily concerned with institutional matters, they were not exclusively so. One important non-institutional change which has taken place has been the move to a mandatory right of access to the Court. The ability of the individual to take a case to Strasbourg is therefore no longer dependent upon a declaration by the relevant High Contracting Party.

(vii) Inter-state applications

Article 33 of the Convention declares that:

'Any High Contracting Party may refer to the Court any alleged breach of the provisions of the Convention and the protocols thereto by another High Contracting Party.'

Unlike the position under article 34, the right of state referral is not dependent upon the state concerned being a 'victim' of the alleged breach of the Convention. However, while inter-state

---

[77] See below.

applications are a theoretical possibility, in practice they are not often made. The case of *Ireland v United Kingdom*,[78] where the Irish government successfully argued that interrogation techniques used on suspected terrorists in Northern Ireland amounted to torture or inhuman or degrading treatment, is, therefore, a rare example of an inter-state application that has been referred to the Court. The reason for this rather limited recourse to article 33 is not difficult to determine. To allege that a fellow signatory to the Convention is in fact breaching the terms of the ECHR is inevitably a divisive course of action which may threaten the stability of the Council of Europe and lead to the breakdown of diplomatic relations between the states concerned. Thus rather than seek confrontation in the very public nature implicit in article 33, inter-state human rights disputes are more likely to be resolved by way of a combination of discrete discussion and negotiation which results in an agreement that it is neither a threat to diplomatic relations nor the protection of human rights. In short, a friendly settlement[79] may be reached between states.

(viii) Admissibility criteria

In order for an individual or inter-state application to be both accepted and proceeded with, it is necessary that it fulfils the admissibility criteria laid down in article 35 of the Convention. In the case of either an individual or state application, the Court may only deal with the matter after all domestic remedies have been exhausted,[80] and if the application has been made within a period of six months from the date on which the final decision was taken.[81] However, with regard to individual applications, further criteria need to be satisfied before the matter can be dealt with. Accordingly, the Court is precluded from dealing with an article 35 application which is either anonymous, or which is 'substantially the same as a matter that has already been examined by the Court or has already been submitted to another procedure of international investigation or settlement and contains no relevant new information'.[82] Moreover, article 35(3) instructs the Court to treat as inadmissible any article 34 application which it considers to be 'incompatible with the provisions of the Convention or the protocols thereto, manifestly ill-founded, or an abuse of the right of application'. Thus the article 35 criteria are a mixture of procedural requirements such as the six-month time limit, and substantive requirements such as that the application is not 'manifestly ill-founded' which clearly involves a consideration of the application's merits. The important task of determining the admissibility of an application is, as we have already seen, performed by either a Committee or a Chamber of the Court.

The jurisprudence of the former Commission and the Court is extensive in relation to the various admissibility criteria referred to above. The requirement that an applicant must first have exhausted all domestic remedies before taking the matter to Strasbourg has, for example, been interpreted in such a way that both the adequacy and effectiveness of the remedy are factors to be taken into account. Where it is alleged that domestic law does not provide a remedy for the applicant's complaint, the burden of proof will be on the state to establish that

---

[78] (1978) 2 EHRR 25.   [79] See p. 788.

[80] See, for example, *D v Ireland*, Application No. 26499/02, which was declared inadmissible by a Chamber of the ECtHR in July 2006 on the ground that the applicant had not exhausted domestic remedies because she had failed to bring an action before the Irish courts.   [81] Article 35(1).

[82] Article 35(2)(b).

this is not so. However, if the state is able to claim that domestic remedies do in fact exist, it will then become the responsibility of the applicant to prove that such remedies are either inadequate or ineffective. Turning to the matter of the six-month rule, in *Kelly v United Kingdom*,[83] the Commission stressed that the purpose of the rule is to promote certainty of the law and to ensure that those cases which raise relevant issues under the Convention are dealt with within a reasonable time. Moreover, the Commission took the view that the six-month time limit ensures that the facts of the case are still relatively fresh at the time that the application is heard.

(ix) Friendly settlements

By virtue of article 38 of the ECHR, the Court is required to conduct an investigation into the merits of those complaints which have satisfied the admissibility criteria. At the same time, article 38(1)(b) confers a duty on the Court to:

'. . . place itself at the disposal of the parties concerned with a view to securing a friendly settlement of the matter on the basis of respect for human rights as defined in the Convention and the protocols thereto.'

This friendly settlement process was initially used quite sparingly as a means of resolving disputes between parties, but its popularity has increased in more recent times due to its inherent advantages.[84] With the ever expanding case load of the ECtHR and hence the increasing number of decisions which are being handed down by the Court, a body of human rights case law is now clearly established under the Convention. It follows, therefore, that novel complaints are less frequent occurrences than they once were in the early days of the Convention, and thus there is now a greater chance of being able to predict the likely outcome of a case before the Court. Friendly settlement negotiations are confidential.[85] Thus if a settlement cannot be reached and the case is heard by the Court, neither party is permitted to rely upon anything that was said during the course of those negotiations.[86] The principal advantage of the friendly settlement process for the state is that it provides a means by which the adverse impact of publicity can be avoided or at least reduced. Although article 39 provides that if a friendly settlement is reached, the Court shall strike the case out of its list by means of a decision which shall be confined to a brief statement of the facts and the solution reached, this is far less politically embarrassing for the state than being found by the Court to have acted in breach of the Convention. Indeed, if the state subscribes to the common practice of insisting that the settlement contains a clause to the effect that it is without prejudice to its submission that there has been no breach of the Convention, then depending upon the other terms of the settlement, the state's reputation for being a respecter of human rights may still remain relatively intact. For the applicant, a friendly settlement has obvious attractions in that it represents a relatively quick resolution of the matter whereas the alternative may be potentially lengthy and costly legal proceedings. In addition, the applicant may receive an undertaking from the state that he or she will be financially compensated, and there is the

---

[83] (1985) 8 EHRR 45, 42 DR 205.

[84] Thus in 2005, of the 1,150 judgments reached by the ECtHR, 37 were friendly settlements: see *Survey of Activities for 2005*, at p. 31.　　　　　　　　　　　　　　　　　　[85] Article 38(2).

[86] See rule 62(2) of the Rules of the Court.

possibility that the settlement will contain a commitment on the part of the state to change an administrative practice or to seek to introduce an amendment to legislation.

In one particular example of a friendly settlement, *Channel 4 TV v United Kingdom*,[87] Channel 4's intention to produce a daily television programme considering the day's proceedings in the trial of Clive Ponting, a former civil servant accused of having breached the Official Secrets Act, had been defeated by way of an order made at the outset by the trial judge under the Contempt of Court Act 1981. The judge refused to hear argument from the television company on this matter and accordingly, Channel 4, the production company and the National Union of Journalists made a submission to the Commission to the effect that the absence of a domestic remedy in relation to the court order amounted to a breach of article 13 of the Convention. The complaint was declared admissible by the Commission, but the matter was settled at a meeting attended by the parties together with the Secretary to the Commission and a member of the Secretariat. Included in the settlement was an undertaking that the Government would seek to introduce an amendment to the Criminal Justice Bill, which was before Parliament at the time, to afford a right of appeal to those persons who were affected by the making of an order under section 4 of the Contempt of Court Act 1981. The amendment to the Bill, which ultimately became section 159 of the Criminal Justice Act 1988, has subsequently been relied upon by journalists in a number of cases.[88]

Friendly settlements are thus an important means of resolving disputes concerning human rights issues and, as in the above example, they may be of benefit not only to the applicant but also to others where they involve a change to the law. As was noted previously, in the case of an inter-state application, a friendly settlement may act as a means of preserving and possibly even improving diplomatic relations between states. Thus in the case of *Denmark v Turkey*,[89] a judgment was delivered in which the Court expressed its satisfaction with a friendly settlement reached between the states. The application had concerned an allegation by a Danish citizen that he had been subjected to ill-treatment in violation of article 3 whilst being detained in Turkey. The friendly settlement consisted of a number of elements, including an agreement by the Turkish government to pay the Danish government compensation. More importantly, however, the settlement contained a declaration by the Turkish government in which it expressed regret at 'the occurrence of occasional and individual cases of torture and ill-treatment' and which set out the changes that had been made to the Turkish Penal Code in order to redefine and prevent torture and ill-treatment. With regard to diplomatic relations between the states, the friendly settlement noted that the governments had agreed to establish a continuous bilateral political dialogue.

(x) Doctrine of a margin of appreciation

An important feature of the jurisprudence of the ECtHR is what is known as the doctrine of a 'margin of appreciation'. This doctrine effectively allows a signatory to the Convention a degree of latitude in terms of the exceptions to the rights set out in the Convention, especially in relation to articles 8–11. These articles expressly provide for a departure from the fundamental human right in question if it is 'necessary in a democratic society' in the interests of one of a number of factors which include: national security, public safety, the protection of

[87] (1985) DR 56/156. [88] See, for example, *R v Beck, ex p Daily Telegraph plc* [1993] 2 All ER 177.
[89] Application No. 34382/97, 5 April 2000.

public order, health or morals, or, the protection of the rights and freedoms of others. In the leading case *Handyside v United Kingdom*,[90] where the applicant had been convicted under the Obscene Publications Acts of 1959 and 1964 of having in his possession obscene books for publication for gain, the ECtHR was required to consider whether the conviction was justified on the grounds of the 'protection of morals' within the meaning of article 10(2). In finding that it was so justified, the Court ventured the following explanation as to the rationale underlying the doctrine of a margin of appreciation:

'By reason of their direct and continuous contact with the vital forces of their countries, state authorities are in principle in a better position than the international judge to give an opinion on the exact content of those requirements [of morals] as well as on the "necessity" of a "restriction" or "penalty" intended to meet them.'[91]

In theory, therefore, the margin of appreciation appears to confer a wide measure of discretion upon the High Contracting Party as to the manner in which it complies with its Convention obligations. Not only may it fail to meet an obligation where a specified exception applies but also, the doctrine appears to imply that it is the state which is best placed to determine what action was required in the particular case. Where the Convention provision is article 15,[92] opinions may differ as to whether it is entirely appropriate for a state to be accorded a wide margin of appreciation as to the appropriate action to be taken in order to combat an emergency situation. At first glance, it may appear that in such circumstances there is little if any scrutiny in relation to a state's compliance with the Convention so that even if the matter does reach Strasbourg, the Court will merely rubber-stamp the state's action. However, the doctrine does not give a state a completely free hand to act in whichever manner it sees fit. Rather, a margin of appreciation suggests limits within which a state must operate. Thus in some cases a margin of appreciation may be wide, as with article 15 matters, but in all cases, what the margin of appreciation allows will depend upon the particular circumstances. Moreover, it should not be forgotten that the doctrine operates within the context of European supervision. Even in relation to national emergency matters, the European Court of Human Rights is in a position to rule on whether, for example, the state measure has gone beyond the 'extent strictly required by the exigencies' of the situation.[93]

Thus while the doctrine of a margin of appreciation may have something of the air of a concession to contracting parties in that it appears to facilitate a less rigid application of the Convention, it does reflect the fact that the onus is upon the signatory to ensure that human rights are properly protected within its boundaries. The Convention undoubtedly has an important role to play in helping to attain this objective, but an absence of genuine state commitment to these ideals is fatal to their attainment even where the state is a signatory to the ECHR.

The doctrine of a margin of appreciation is patently concerned with the relationship between the ECtHR and the national authorities. Accordingly, it has no direct application in respect of the relationship between national courts and national authorities. However, as will become apparent later in this chapter, when dealing with cases under the Human Rights Act 1998, UK courts have shown, on occasions, a willingness to *defer* to the judgment of Parliament or other domestic decision-making bodies where human rights issues are at stake.

[90] (1976) 1 EHRR 737.   [91] At para 48.   [92] See p. 791.
[93] See *Brannigan and McBride v United Kingdom* (1993) 17 EHRR 539.

(xi) Derogation

By virtue of article 15 of the ECHR, a High Contracting Party is permitted to derogate from its obligations under the Convention in 'time of war or other public emergency threatening the life of the nation'. There are, however, limitations placed upon what is an obvious concession to the High Contracting Parties. The first such limitation is that the measures taken in derogation must only be 'to the extent strictly required by the exigencies of the situation'. Moreover, any such measures must not be inconsistent with other international law obligations. A further limitation is that certain of the Convention rights are non-derogable.[94] Thus, for example, even in time of war or other public emergency threatening the life of the nation, a state would be acting contrary to the ECHR if it were to carry out torture or treat anyone within its boundaries in an inhuman or degrading manner. Where a state does wish to derogate from its Convention obligations it must keep the Secretary General of the Council of Europe fully informed of the measures which it has taken and the reasons for them.[95] The Secretary General must also be notified when the derogation is at an end.

This important provision has been invoked by the UK in the context of Northern Ireland. Indeed, the very fact that a derogation in respect of article 5(3) existed at the time that the Human Rights Act was enacted explains why its drafters were required to make provision for a 'designated derogation'.[96] Subsequently, however, that derogation was withdrawn and the Act was amended accordingly.[97]

III. Status of the Convention in UK Law

The United Kingdom is, in terms of international treaties and conventions, a dualist state. Essentially this means that for such an instrument to take effect in domestic law, it is necessary for it to be incorporated by way of an Act of Parliament. This traditional approach has determined, for example, that in order for the Treaty of Rome to take effect in the UK together with subsequent European amending provisions such as the Single European Act and the Maastricht Treaty, it was necessary to pass the European Communities Act 1972 and the subsequent amendment Acts of 1986 and 1993 respectively.[98] The legal status of treaties in English law was considered by Lord Oliver in *Maclaine Watson v Department of Trade*,[99] where his Lordship stated that:

'Treaties, as it is sometimes expressed, are not self-executing. Quite simply, a treaty is not part of English law unless and until it has been incorporated into the law by legislation. So far as individuals are concerned, it is *res inter alios acta* from which they cannot derive rights and by which they cannot be deprived of rights or subjected to obligations; and it is outside the purview of the court not only because it is made in the conduct of foreign relations, which are a prerogative of the Crown, but also because, as a source of rights and obligations, it is irrelevant.'[100]

---

[94] Article 15(2).　　[95] Article 15(3).　　[96] See section 14 and Schedule 3 to the 1998 Act.
[97] See the Human Rights Act (Amendment) Order 2001, SI 2001/1216.　　[98] See pp. 335–336.
[99] [1989] 3 All ER 523.　　[100] At 544–545.

For almost 50 years, the ECHR was an example of an international agreement which was not a 'source of rights' for UK citizens. Despite having ratified the Convention in 1951, successive UK governments of different political persuasions saw fit not to incorporate it into domestic law, even if the Lord Chancellor of the time, Lord Jowitt, was of the opinion in 1951 that incorporation was a corollary of ratification. The failure to incorporate meant, therefore, that the ECHR had no binding force in English law. Thus in *Ahmad v Inner London Education Authority*,[101] for example, Lord Denning was correct when he observed that 'the Convention is not part of our English law'. However, as a signatory to the Convention, the UK was clearly under an obligation to ensure that its citizens enjoyed the rights set out in the ECHR. Moreover, where the courts were faced with the task of interpreting domestic legislation which was capable of bearing more than one meaning, one of which conformed with the terms of the Convention and the other of which did not, a principle of construction had arisen whereby the courts would presume, in the absence of express words to the contrary, that Parliament intended to legislate in conformity with the Convention: see *R v Secretary of State for the Home Department, ex p Brind*.[102] This point was made by Lord Diplock in *Garland v British Rail Engineering Ltd*,[103] when he observed that:

' . . . it is a principle of construction of United Kingdom statutes . . . that the words of a statute passed after a treaty has been signed and dealing with the subject matter of the international obligation of the United Kingdom, are to be construed, if they are reasonably capable of bearing such a meaning, as intended to carry out the obligation, and not to be inconsistent with it'.[104]

As a principle, however, it was capable of being rebutted by the clear and unambiguous words of a statute. Thus if Parliament wished to legislate inconsistently with its obligations under the Convention, it could do so, and all that a court could do when faced with such an incompatibility would be to give effect to the will of Parliament in accordance with the doctrine of the legislative supremacy of Parliament.[105] Although it was unlikely that a British government would deliberately legislate in this manner, it was clear that the courts would be relatively powerless to resist legislation which rode roughshod over the rights and freedoms of the citizen. It was, therefore, against the general backdrop of increasing executive power and with its potential for abuse firmly in mind, that arguments for the incorporation of the ECHR into domestic law began to be advocated.

Prominent amongst the advocates for incorporation were some senior members of the judiciary. The traditional role of the courts has been to protect the individual against the unwarranted and unnecessary interference from other individuals and the state. Historically the common law has been regarded as a mechanism by which the judiciary can safeguard the rights and freedoms of the individual. Indeed, prior to the Human Rights Act 1998 (see below), it was sometimes argued that the ability of the common law to perform this important function rendered it unnecessary to incorporate the ECHR. Thus, for example, in *Attorney General v Guardian Newspapers (No. 2)*[106] (one of the 'Spycatcher' judgments), Lord Goff of Chieveley stated that:

'Finally, I wish to observe that I can see no inconsistency between English law on this subject and article 10 of the Convention for the Protection of Human Rights and Fundamental Freedoms . . . This is scarcely surprising, since we may pride ourselves on the fact that freedom of speech has existed in this country perhaps as long as, if not longer than, it has existed in any other country in the world. The only difference is that, whereas article 10 of the convention, in accordance with its avowed purpose,

---

[101] [1978] 1 All ER 574.   [102] [1991] 1 AC 696.   [103] [1982] 2 All ER 402.
[104] At 415.   [105] See chapter 2.   [106] [1988] 3 All ER 545.

proceeds to state a fundamental right and then to qualify it, we in this country (where everybody is free to do anything, subject only to the provisions of the law,) proceed rather on an assumption of freedom of speech, and turn to our law to discover the established exceptions to it.'[107]

However, in an earlier 'Spycatcher' judgment, *Attorney General v Guardian Newspapers Ltd*,[108] in which the majority of the House of Lords upheld an interim injunction to suspend the publication of extracts from the memoirs of a former member of the British security service, Lord Bridge made the following observations during the course of his dissenting judgment:

'Having no written constitution, we have no equivalent in our law of the First Amendment to the Constitution of the United States of America. Some think that puts freedom of speech on too lofty a pedestal. Perhaps they are right. We have not adopted as part of our law the European Convention for the Protection of Human Rights and Fundamental Freedoms to which this country is a signatory. Many think that we should. I have hitherto not been of that persuasion, in large part because I have had confidence in the capacity of the common law to safeguard the fundamental freedoms essential to a free society including the right to freedom of speech which is specifically safeguarded by article 10 of the Convention. My confidence is seriously undermined by your Lordships' decision.'[109]

The seeds of doubt were sown. Arguments in favour of the incorporation of the ECHR were also advanced by senior judges when speaking in an extra-judicial capacity.[110] Whereas some of their predecessors in the mid-1970s, most notably the then Lord Chancellor, Lord Elwyn Jones, and Lord Denning MR, had spoken out against a private members' Bill which had sought to incorporate the ECHR into domestic law on the basis that the Convention was 'framed in such wide and general terms' and would lead to a great deal of litigation by 'disgruntled people who will bring proceedings before the courts challenging the orderly system of our society', by the mid-1990s, a new generation of senior judges were of a different opinion. Thus, for example, Sir Thomas Bingham (as he then was) used the vehicle of the Denning Lecture of the Bar Association for Commerce, Finance and Industry to consider the arguments against incorporation since he regarded 'the positive case as clear and the burden as lying on the opponents to make good their grounds of opposition'.[111]

IV. The EU Charter of Fundamental Rights

At the Cologne Summit on June 4, 1999, the European Council decided to draw up a Charter of Fundamental Human Rights for the EU. The drafting task was entrusted to a Convention consisting of fifteen representatives of the Heads of State or Government, sixteen Members of the European Parliament, thirty Members of national Parliaments, and an EU Commissioner representing the President of the Commission. The results of that drafting process were published on September 28, 2000.

The Draft Charter is made up of a preamble and 54 articles. The articles, which are divided up into seven chapters, represent a far more broadly based statement of rights than does the ECHR. The substantive rights which form the basis of the ECHR are to be found in

[107] At 660.   [108] [1987] 3 All ER 316.   [109] At 346.
[110] See, for example, the remarks of the then Master of the Rolls, Sir Thomas Bingham, in 'The European Convention on Human Rights: Time to Incorporate' (1993) 109 LQR 390.   [111] Ibid. at 399.

chapters I and II of the Draft. However, even these chapters go beyond the statement of rights which can be categorised as civil or political in nature. Thus in Chapter II which is entitled 'Freedoms', in addition to rights such as liberty and security, respect for private and family life, freedom of thought, conscience and religion and freedom of expression, association and assembly, further rights are stated such as the right to education, the freedom to choose an occupation and the right to engage in work and, the freedom to conduct a business. These rights and freedoms are patently social and economic in nature as are the rights specified in Chapter IV ('Solidarity'). To quite a large extent, therefore, the Draft Charter is an amalgam of the rights set out in the ECHR and the European Social Chapter. The inclusion of economic and social rights in the text raises questions as to the justiciability of those rights which in turn raises questions as to the legal status of the Charter.

The House of Lords Select Committee on the European Union has looked into the matter of an EU Charter of Fundamental Rights and has noted in its Eighth report of session 2000–01, that such a Charter 'has proved from the outset to be controversial and it has produced a variety of reactions in discussion papers'.[112] With regard to the legal status of the Charter, the report notes that the Committee heard a wide variety of views on this issue. These ranged from that of the UK government, which saw the Charter as 'a showcase of existing rights' which should not be legally binding, to that of the European Parliament, which desired a Charter that was legally binding and incorporated into the Treaty. Interestingly, the report notes that there was only limited support from the witnesses heard by the Select Committee for the view that the Charter should not be a legally binding instrument. Although the Select Committee considered that a declaratory statement as advocated by the UK government had some value in that it would provide 'an over-arching and unifying framework' to draw together the human rights which are currently 'scattered throughout the Treaties', in the final analysis, it saw the EU's accession to the ECHR as the best means of providing 'a firm and consistent foundation for fundamental rights in the Union'.[113]

The Charter has been incorporated as Part II of the Treaty establishing a Constitution for Europe. At the time of writing, however, the Constitution is not in force because it was rejected in referenda held in France and the Netherlands. Accordingly, since the future of the draft Constitutional Treaty is presently unclear, it follows that a cloud also hangs over the future of the Charter.

v. The Human Rights Act 1998

(a) Background to the Act

To some extent, the background to the Human Rights Act 1998 (HRA) has been considered in head III (above), at least in terms of a growing judicial recognition of the need to incorporate the ECHR into English law. However, in order for this to be achieved, it was necessary to pass an Act of Parliament. As was suggested above, attempts were made prior to the HRA to achieve incorporation using the vehicle of the Private Member's Bill. However, all such attempts

---

[112] HL Paper 67, at para 6.

[113] At para 154. This is of course now possible given the reforms which Protocol 14 makes to the ECHR: see p. 781.

failed. It therefore became apparent that for incorporation to take place, it was necessary for it to become the policy of a political party capable of forming a government. Prior to the general election of May 1997, the Labour Party under the leadership of Tony Blair stated in its manifesto under the sub-heading 'Real rights for citizens' that:

'Citizens should have statutory rights to enforce their human rights in the UK courts. We will by statute incorporate the European Convention on Human Rights into UK law to bring these rights home and allow our people access to them in their national courts. The incorporation of the European Convention will establish a floor, not a ceiling, for human rights.'

Following its electoral success, the Labour government set about fulfilling its manifesto pledge. In October 1997 it published a White Paper, *Rights Brought Home: The Human Rights Bill*,[114] in which it argued that the case for incorporation was based on factors such as the time delay and excessive cost involved in bringing a case before the ECtHR.[115] On average, it was suggested that a case took five years to be heard by the Court after all domestic remedies had been exhausted and that it cost £30,000. Attention was also drawn to the UK's approach to the Convention, which was regarded as not having properly reflected the importance of the ECHR (as evidenced by the number of cases in which the Commission and Court had found violations of Convention rights against the UK), and the fact that incorporation would ensure that Convention rights were 'brought much more fully into the jurisprudence of the courts throughout the United Kingdom, and their interpretation will thus be far more subtly and powerfully woven into our law'.[116] Bringing rights home in the sense of allowing British citizens to directly enforce those rights against the state in the national courts would have further advantages: it would enable UK courts to 'make a distinctively British contribution to the development of the jurisprudence of human rights in Europe'; and, it would lead to the closer scrutiny of the human rights implications of new legislation and new policies introduced by the government of the day.

Following prolonged parliamentary debate, the Human Rights Bill was eventually passed by both Houses and received royal assent on 9 November 1998. However, many of its provisions did not take immediate effect.[117] Given the potentially radical change which it was likely to effect in terms of the enforcement and protection of Convention rights, it was perhaps not so very surprising that a period of delay was necessary. The courts needed to be given the opportunity to become more familiar with the rights which may now be argued before them, and public authorities needed time to consider how these rights would affect their relationships with individuals. Thus the bulk of the HRA did not enter into force until 2 October 2000. In the discussion which follows, a number of important issues arising from incorporation will be considered. However, as a preliminary, something must be said about precisely what the HRA has incorporated into UK law.

---

[114] Cm 3782 (1997).

[115] It has been suggested that the government made the case for incorporation on 'very mundane grounds': see Clayton, 'Judicial Deference and "Democratic Dialogue": the legitimacy of judicial intervention under the Human Rights Act 1998' [2004] PL 33 at 38.   [116] Cm 3782, at para 1.14.

[117] In drafting those provisions it has been contended that the government drew heavily upon the Canadian Charter of Rights and Freedoms: see Clayton, [2004] PL 33 at 45.

(b) The scope of incorporation

'1 The Convention rights

(1) In this Act "the Convention rights" means the rights and fundamental freedoms set out in—

      (a) Articles 2 to 12 and 14 of the Convention,[118]
      (b) Articles 1 to 3 of the First Protocol, and
      (c) Articles 1 and 2 of the Sixth Protocol,

  as read with Articles 16 to 18 of the Convention.

(2) Those Articles are to have effect for the purposes of this Act subject to any designated derogation or reservation (as to which see sections 14 and 15).

(3) The Articles are set out in Schedule 1.

(4) The Secretary of State may by order make such amendments to this Act as he considers appropriate to reflect the effect, in relation to the United Kingdom, of a protocol.

(5) In subsection (4) "protocol" means a protocol to the Convention—

      (a) which the United Kingdom has ratified; or
      (b) which the United Kingdom has signed with a view to ratification.

(6) No amendment may be made by an order under subsection (4) so as to come into force before the protocol concerned is in force in relation to the United Kingdom.

Schedule 1

Part II

The First Protocol

Article 1

Protection of property

Every natural or legal person is entitled to the peaceful enjoyment of his possessions. No one shall be deprived of his possessions except in the public interest and subject to the conditions provided for by law and by the general principles of international law.

  The preceding provisions shall not, however, in any way impair the right of a State to enforce such laws as it deems necessary to control the use of property in accordance with the general interest or to secure the payment of taxes or other contributions or penalties.

Article 2

Right to education

No person shall be denied the right to education. In the exercise of any functions which it assumes in relation to education and to teaching, the State shall respect the right of parents to ensure such education and teaching in conformity with their own religious and philosophical convictions.

---

[118] See pp. 770–772 above for the text of articles 2–14.

Article 3
Right to free elections
The High Contracting Parties undertake to hold free elections at reasonable intervals by secret ballot, under conditions which will ensure the free expression of the opinion of the people in the choice of the legislature.

Part III
The Sixth Protocol

Article 1
Abolition of the death penalty
The death penalty shall be abolished. No one shall be condemned to such penalty or executed.

Article 2
Death penalty in time of war
A State may make provision in its law for the death penalty in respect of acts committed in time of war or of imminent threat of war; such penalty shall be applied only in the instances laid down in the law and in accordance with its provisions. The State shall communicate to the Secretary General of the Council of Europe the relevant provisions of that law.'

Although it is sometimes stated that the HRA has incorporated the ECHR into UK law, this is not strictly true for two very good reasons. First, many of the Convention's 59 articles and a number of its protocols fall outside the scope of the HRA's definition of 'Convention rights'.[119] More important, however, is the fact that what the Act has actually done is to create domestic rights which are expressed in the same terms as those set out in the ECHR. Thus as Lord Hoffmann observed in *In re McKerr*,[120] the rights in the HRA 'are domestic rights, not international rights'.[121] Their source is therefore the HRA, not the ECHR.

With regard to the substantive rights contained in section I of the ECHR, it is worth noting that article 13 (right to an effective remedy) has been omitted from the definition of 'Convention rights' in the HRA. In resisting an amendment moved during the Committee stage of the Bill in the House of Lords which would have included article 13 as a Convention right, the then Lord Chancellor, Lord Irvine, argued that the remedial provisions contained in the Bill, particularly what is now section 8, met the requirements of article 13 and therefore made its inclusion unnecessary. Some support for this view is to be found in the recent case of *Secretary of State for the Home Department v MB*,[122] where the Lord Chief Justice, Lord Phillips, contended that partial effect is given to the obligations imposed under article 13 by sections 6–9 of the HRA. However, in his judgment, the effect was only partial because 'if legislation is incompatible with the Convention right, the only remedy available is a declaration of incompatibility'.[123] There are those, however, such as Professor Feldman[124] who take the view that it is 'clear that Article 13 rights cannot be protected adequately by the remedial regime in the Act'. If this is the case then, as he suggests, the courts may well be prevailed upon to interpret the remedial provisions in the HRA in a way which is compatible with article 13 given the view expressed by the former Lord Chancellor, the Bill's promoter.

---

[119] See section 1 of the 1998 Act, above.   [120] [2004] 1 WLR 807.   [121] At [63].
[122] [2006] EWCA Civ 1140. Discussed at p. 842.   [123] At [34].
[124] 'Remedies for Violations of Convention Rights under the Human Rights Act' [1998] EHRLR 691.

(c) Freedom of expression and freedom of thought, conscience and religion

'12 Freedom of expression

(1) This section applies if a court is considering whether to grant any relief which, if granted, might affect the exercise of the Convention right to freedom of expression.

(2) If the person against whom the application for relief is made ("the respondent") is neither present nor represented, no such relief is to be granted unless the court is satisfied—

    (a) that the applicant has taken all practicable steps to notify the respondent; or

    (b) that there are compelling reasons why the respondent should not be notified.

(3) No such relief is to be granted so as to restrain publication before trial unless the court is satisfied that the applicant is likely to establish that publication should not be allowed.

(4) The court must have particular regard to the importance of the Convention right to freedom of expression and, where the proceedings relate to material which the respondent claims, or which appears to the court, to be journalistic, literary or artistic material (or to conduct connected with such material), to—

    (a) the extent to which—

        (i) the material has, or is about to, become available to the public; or

        (ii) it is, or would be, in the public interest for the material to be published;

    (b) any relevant privacy code.

(5) In this section—

    "court" includes a tribunal; and

    "relief" includes any remedy or order (other than in criminal proceedings).'

Of all the rights and freedoms set out in the ECHR it is only freedom of expression (article 10) and freedom of thought, conscience and religion (article 9) which are expressly mentioned in the main body of the HRA. The reason for this is that during the passage of the Human Rights Bill, concerns were expressed by both the press and the churches that the legislation may provide the basis for the assertion and subsequent judicial recognition of rights which might conflict with these fundamental freedoms. It was felt, for example, that the Act may become a vehicle for gay couples to assert that they have a right to marry (article 12 of the ECHR) and that if such a right were upheld by the courts, it would run counter to religious teachings and doctrine.[125]

Section 12 of the HRA places an elaborate emphasis upon the importance of freedom of expression. This freedom is clearly vulnerable to infringement by the assertion of a right to privacy based on article 8 of the ECHR. Although English law had not prior to the HRA recognised a right to privacy as a separate cause of action, the possibility that such a right would be developed by the courts under the Act was widely commented upon prior to its enactment. Thus, for example, during the course of the second reading debate on the HR Bill in the House of Lords, Lord Irvine indicated that in his opinion, such a development was a likely consequence of incorporation. Moreover, on several occasions, the current senior Law Lord, Lord Bingham, had spoken extra-judicially about a right to privacy. On one such

---

[125] See now the Civil Partnership Act 2004 which allows same sex couples to register as civil partners (sections 1–3).

occasion in answer to the question 'should there be a law to protect rights or personal privacy?', Lord Bingham observed that:

'To a very large extent the law already does protect personal privacy; but to the extent that it does not, it should. The right must be narrowly drawn, to give full effect to the right to free speech and the public's right to know. It should strike only at significant infringements, such as would cause substantial distress to an ordinary phlegmatic person. My preference would be for legislation, which would mean that the rules which the courts applied would carry the imprimatur of democratic approval. But if, for whatever reason, legislation is not forthcoming, I think it almost inevitable that cases will arise in which the need to give relief is obvious and pressing; and when such cases do arise, I do not think the courts will.'[126]

There was an 'obvious and pressing' need for relief, at least from the point of view of the claimants, in the cases of *Douglas and others v Hello Ltd*[127] and *Thompson & Venables v News Group Newspapers Ltd & Associated Newspapers Ltd & MGM Ltd.*[128] In both cases, it was necessary for the court to consider whether or not to grant injunctive relief and if so, on what basis. Interestingly, in view of the potential for the development of a tort of privacy under the HRA, both courts regarded privacy as being capable of falling within the scope of the common law right to confidence. Later, in *Wainwright v Home Office,*[129] the House of Lords unequivocally stated that privacy rights could be protected for the purposes of article 8 of the EHCR without the development of a separate tort of privacy. Moreover, as we shall see, in *Campbell v Mirror Group Newspapers,*[130] their Lordships felt able to extend an existing cause of action, breach of confidence, to protect the claimant's privacy rights.

The provisions of section 12 are concerned with various matters relating to freedom of expression. Thus section 12(2) seeks to restrict the granting of 'gagging orders' by the courts which would have the effect of preventing publication by the media of the matter to which the order relates. In the past, it has not been uncommon for such orders to be sought *ex parte*, thus preventing the respondent from being able to make representations to the court as to why the order should not be made. By virtue of section 12(2), this can now only happen where the court is satisfied that the applicant has taken all practicable steps to notify the respondent or there are compelling reasons why the respondent should not be notified. A gagging order may still be sought *ex parte* therefore, where, for example, the court considers that notification of an application would cause an unscrupulous respondent to effectively defeat the application by publishing the matter before any order could be made.

The effect of section 12(3) was considered by the House of Lords in *Cream Holdings Ltd v Banarjee.*[131] In this case, the claimants had sought and had been granted an injunction to restrain the further publication of confidential information which a former employee had passed to a local newspaper. That information suggested that there had been financial irregularities involving a director of the complainant company and a local council official which potentially amounted to corruption. In allowing the appeal against the grant of an injunction, Lord Nicholls, who gave the leading judgment, focused on the meaning of section 12(3), in particular the significance of the word 'likely' in the provision.[132] In his opinion, it was a word which had 'several different shades of meaning' depending on the context in which it was being used.[133] He noted that section 12(3) had been enacted to allay fears that the freedom of

---

[126] 'Opinion: Should there be a law to protect rights of personal privacy?' [1996] EHRLR 450 at 461–462.
[127] [2001] QB 967.   [128] [2001] 2 WLR 1038.   [129] [2004] 2 AC 406.
[130] [2004] 2 AC 457, extracted at p. 871.   [131] [2005] 1 AC 253.
[132] In a far briefer judgment, Lord Scott commented that the issue raised by the appeal was 'one of great importance': at [29].   [133] At [12].

the press may be adversely affected by the incorporation of article 8 rights into domestic law. He also noted that Parliament sought to do this by setting a higher threshold for the grant of interlocutory injunctions against the media than that established previously by their Lordships in *Amercian Cyanamid Co v Ethicon Ltd*.[134] However, despite these considerations, Lord Nicholls was not prepared to accept the submission made on behalf of the appellant that 'likely' in section 12(3) meant 'more likely than not' or 'probably'. In his opinion:

' . . . Section 12(3) makes the likelihood of success at trial an essential element in the court's consideration of whether to make an interim order. But in order to achieve the necessary flexibility the degree of likelihood of success at the trial needed to satisfy section 12(3) must depend on the circumstances. There can be no single, rigid standard governing all applications for interim restraint orders. Rather, on its proper construction the effect of section 12(3) is that the court is not to make an interim restraint order unless satisfied the applicant's prospects of success at the trial are sufficiently favourable to justify such an order being made in the particular circumstances of the case. As to what degree of likelihood makes the prospects of success "sufficiently favourable", the general approach should be that courts will be exceedingly slow to make interim restraint orders where the applicant has not satisfied the court he will probably ("more likely than not") succeed at the trial. In general, that should be the threshold an applicant must cross before the court embarks on exercising its discretion, duly taking into account the relevant jurisprudence on article 10 and any countervailing Convention rights. But there will be cases where it is necessary for a court to depart from this general approach and a lesser degree of likelihood will suffice as a prerequisite. Circumstances where this may be so include . . . where the potential adverse consequences of disclosure are particularly grave, or where a short-lived injunction is needed to enable the court to hear and give proper consideration to an application for interim relief pending the trial or any relevant appeal.'[135]

Thus it is evident from *Cream Holdings Ltd* that section 12(3) of the HRA calls for a measure of *flexibility* as to the standard to be applied where a court is determining whether to grant an interim injunction. In their Lordships' opinion, the general approach which they advocated 'does not accord inappropriate weight to the Convention right of freedom of expression as compared with the right to respect for private life or other Convention rights'.[136] In the later case of *Greene v Associated Newspapers Ltd*,[137] where the claimant had sought to obtain an interim injunction to prevent a newspaper from publishing an allegedly defamatory statement, the Court of Appeal applied the test laid down in *Bonnard v Perryman*,[138] ie that an injunction would only be granted where the claimant was able to demonstrate that the alleged libel was plainly untrue. In its judgment, that test had survived the enactment of section 12(3) due to the well established principle that 'a rule of the common law is not extinguished by statute unless the statute makes this clear by express provision or by clear implication'.[139] Accordingly, the House of Lords' decision in *Cream Holdings Ltd* did not apply in the present context because it 'was concerned with an entirely different subject matter (the protection of confidential information)'[140] which called for a different standard to be applied since as Lord Nicholls had observed in that case, 'confidentiality, once breached, is lost for ever'.[141]

---

[134] [1975] AC 396. In that case, it was held that an applicant for an injunction needed to establish a 'real prospect' of success at a subsequent trial before an injunction would be granted.
[135] [2005] 1 AC 253 at [22].   [136] At [23].   [137] [2005] 3 WLR 281.   [138] [1891] 2 Ch 269.
[139] Per Lord Hutton in *R (Rottman) v Chief Commissioner of Police of the Metropolis* [2002] 2 AC 692 at [75]. See also the remarks of Lord Reid in *Black-Clawson International Ltd v Papierwerke Waldof-Aschaffenburg AG* [1975] AC 591 at 614.   [140] [2005] 3 WLR 281 at [60].
[141] [2005] 1 AC 253 at [18].

It is clear from the wording of section 12(4) that Parliament was in tune with the judiciary in anticipating that a likely consequence of the HRA would be the development of a tort of privacy.[142] In effect, the provision is designed to ensure that journalistic, literary or artistic material is afforded some measure of protection against the grant of injunctive relief where it is argued by the applicant that the publication of such material would violate their right to privacy. Thus where the material is already in the public domain (or is about to be so) or publication would be in the public interest, it would seem that section 12(4) encourages a court hearing an application for an injunction to allow freedom of expression to win out over the right to privacy. Thus in *Lakeside Homes Ltd v BBC*,[143] where the claimant applied for an interim injunction to restrain the BBC from broadcasting a programme relating to the standards of care at one of its nursing homes, the court was concerned with the conflict between breach of confidence and breach of contract on the one had, and freedom of expression on the other. The programme, which was claimed by the BBC to be a serious investigative broadcast which examined issues of public interest in Wales, contained some material which had been obtained by carrying out undercover filming within the home as well as interviews with members of staff and relatives of residents. In refusing to grant the injunction sought, Cresswell J noted that having 'particular regard to a right' (broadly what section 12(4) states) implied that 'the court should, where appropriate, give it greater weight than competing rights'. In his opinion, in applying section 12 of the HRA, he was not satisfied that the claimant was likely to establish at trial that publication should not be allowed. In reaching such a conclusion he had regard to a number of factors, including the importance of the Convention right to freedom of expression (article 10) and that if the BBC's contentions were correct, it was in the public interest that serious failures in the care of the elderly should be made public.

In accordance with the construction which Cresswell J placed on the words 'have particular regard to' in section 12(4) of the 1998 Act, it should be noted that having regard to a right is not, of course, the same thing as affording that right unlimited protection against encroachment from competing rights. The courts retain a discretion as to whether or not to grant an injunction in any particular case and each case will, accordingly, turn upon its own particular facts. What section 12(4) does is to tilt the balance of the scales in favour of freedom of expression when a court is hearing a claim for an injunction to prevent publication; it does not cause the scales to fail to register the weight of competing rights.

'13 Freedom of thought, conscience and religion

(1) If a court's determination of any question arising under this Act might affect the exercise by a religious organisation (itself or its members collectively) of the Convention right to freedom of thought, conscience and religion, it must have particular regard to the importance of that right.

(2) In this section "court" includes a tribunal.'

Section 13 of the HRA seeks to remind the courts of the importance of the right to freedom of thought, conscience and religion when hearing cases which may impinge upon that right. The section does not, however, act as restraint upon such a development. A court will be entitled to determine the balance between the article 9 freedom and some other right in favour of that other right when it considers it appropriate to do so. Thus in the example already mentioned,

---

[142] In *Douglas v Hello! Ltd* [2001] QB 967, Sedley LJ felt that the effect of subsection (4) was to 'put beyond question the direct applicability of at least one article of the Convention—in the jargon, its horizontal effect': at [133]. [143] (Unreported), 14 November 2000.

allowing the 'right' of gay couples to marry to trump freedom of thought, conscience and religion would not be to act in a way which was inconsistent with section 13 of the HRA, provided that a court paid particular attention to the importance of the latter right.

Lester and Pannick have argued that section 13 of the HRA 'serves no sensible purpose' for a variety of reasons. In their opinion, rather than inhibit religious freedom, the HRA will actually operate to the benefit of religious organisations in that it will provide a hitherto non-existent protection for religious freedom in English law. Moreover, they argue that since the Act is aimed at public authorities, it is only when the Churches perform a public function, eg ceremonies of marriage and the provision of education in church schools, that they will fall within the scope of the Act. Having regard to the case law of the ECtHR (and the Commission), the authors further contend that the Convention has not been used to date 'to damage the interests of religious organisations, or to force them to carry out acts contrary to religious principle, and there is no good reason for fearing that English courts will apply the Convention in any different manner in the future'.[144]

(d) Interpretation

'2 Interpretation of Convention rights

(1) A court or tribunal determining a question which has arisen in connection with a Convention right must take into account any—

  (a) judgment, decision, declaration or advisory opinion of the European Court of Human Rights,
  (b) opinion of the Commission given in a report adopted under Article 31 of the Convention,
  (c) decision of the Commission in connection with Article 26 or 27(2) of the Convention, or
  (d) decision of the Committee of Ministers taken under Article 46 of the Convention,

whenever made or given, so far as, in the opinion of the court or tribunal, it is relevant to the proceedings in which that question has arisen.

(2) Evidence of any judgment, decision, declaration or opinion of which account may have to be taken under this section is to be given in proceedings before any court or tribunal in such manner as may be provided by rules.

(3) In this section "rules" means rules of court or, in the case of proceedings before a tribunal, rules made for the purpose of this section—

  (a) by the Lord Chancellor or the Secretary of State, in relation to any proceedings outside Scotland;
  (b) by the Secretary of State, in relation to proceedings in Scotland; or
  (c) by a Northern Ireland department, in relation to proceedings before a tribunal in Northern Ireland—

    (i) which deals with transferred matters; and
    (ii) for which no rules made under paragraph (a) are in force.

3 Interpretation of legislation

(1) So far as it is possible to do so, primary legislation and subordinate legislation must be read and given effect in a way which is compatible with the Convention rights.

(2) This section—

---

[144] See *Human Rights Law and Practice* (2nd edn, 2004), at para 2.13 (pp. 66–67).

(a) applies to primary legislation and subordinate legislation whenever enacted;

(b) does not affect the validity, continuing operation or enforcement of any incompatible primary legislation; and

(c) does not affect the validity, continuing operation or enforcement of any incompatible subordinate legislation if (disregarding any possibility of revocation) primary legislation prevents removal of the incompatibility.'

Given that as from October 2, 2000, UK citizens have been able to rely upon Convention rights before their national courts and tribunals, it follows that the courts and tribunals have been required to interpret: (i) the scope of the Convention rights themselves; and (ii) the legislation (primary and secondary) which it is alleged infringes a Convention right. In performing the former task, section 2 of the HRA requires a court or tribunal to 'take into account' the jurisprudence of the Strasbourg institutions where the court or tribunal is of the opinion that it is relevant to the proceedings before it. There is clearly much common sense in such a provision. Judges who may have been largely unfamiliar with the rights contained in the ECHR (at least until they received training in anticipation of the commencement of the larger part of the Act) will obviously derive great assistance from the decisions of the Court, the Commission[145] and the Committee of Ministers. However, it is important to note that domestic courts and tribunals are not bound by the decisions of the Strasbourg institutions: they must have regard to them, but they need not follow them given that the meaning and application of the rights under the HRA is a matter for the domestic courts rather than the ECtHR.[146] Thus in *R (Alconbury Developments Ltd and others) v Secretary of State for the Environment, Transport and the Regions*,[147] Lord Slynn observed:

'Although the Human Rights Act 1998 does not provide that a national court is bound by these decisions it is obliged to take account of them so far as they are relevant. In the absence of some special circumstances it seems to me that the court should follow any clear and constant jurisprudence of the European Court of Human Rights. If it does not do so there is at least a possibility that the case will go to that court, which is likely in the ordinary case to follow its own constant jurisprudence.'[148]

Similarly in the later immigration case *R (Ullah) v Special Ajudicator*,[149] Lord Bingham opined:

'In determining the present question, the House is required by section 2(1) of the Human Rights Act 1998 to take into account any relevant Strasbourg case law. While such case law is not strictly binding, it has been held that courts should, in the absence of some special circumstances, follow any clear and constant jurisprudence of the ECtHR . . . This reflects the fact that the European Convention is an international instrument, the correct interpretation of which can be authoritatively expounded only by the ECtHR. From this it follows that a national court subject to a duty such as that imposed by section 2 should not without strong reason dilute or weaken the effect of the Strasbourg case law. It is indeed unlawful under section 6 of the 1998 Act for a public authority, including a court, to act in a way which is incompatible with a conviction right. It is of course open to member states to provide for rights more generous than those guaranteed by the convention, but such provision should not be the product of interpretation of the convention by national courts, since the meaning of the convention should be

---

[145] Although this body no longer exists (see p. 775), during its lifetime it contributed significantly to the jurisprudence of the Convention. It would seem that its decisions ought not necessarily to be regarded as carrying less weight than those of the Court, although much will depend upon the nature of the individual case: see the remarks of Collins J in *R (on the application of Boughton) v Her Majesty's Treasury* [2005] EWHC 1914 (Admin) at [18].   [146] See the remarks of Lord Hoffmann in *Re McKerr* [2004] 1 WLR 807 at [63]–[64].
[147] [2003] 2 AC 295.   [148] At [26].   [149] [2004] 3 WLR 23.

uniform throughout the states party to it. The duty of national courts is to keep pace with the Strasbourg jurisprudence as it evolves over time: no more, but certainly no less.'[150]

In practice, as the words of Lord Slynn in *Alconbury* imply, it seems unlikely that there will be much in the way of divergence between the judgments of the European Court and the domestic courts vis-à-vis the content of Convention rights. Where a divergence may occur, however, is in respect of the qualifications to which many of those rights are subject. As we have already seen in *Handyside v United Kingdom*,[151] the ECtHR accepted that a High Contracting Party might be accorded a *margin of appreciation* when it claims that a departure from a Convention right falls within the scope of a permitted exception to that right. The rationale for this doctrine was that state authorities are better placed than the international judge to determine what was required due to their proximity to events. Is a UK judge likely to regard himself as being similarly distanced from 'contact with the vital forces' of the nation? The answer to this question is to be found in the notion of judicial deference, which is discussed at pp. 805–814. In the meantime, however, it should be noted that the HRA contains another aid to interpretation: section 19.

'19 Statements of compatibility

(1) A Minister of the Crown in charge of a Bill in either House of Parliament must, before Second Reading of the Bill—

    (a) make a statement to the effect that in his view the provisions of the Bill are compatible with the Convention rights ("a statement of compatibility"); or

    (b) make a statement to the effect that although he is unable to make a statement of compatibility the government nevertheless wishes the House to proceed with the Bill.

(3) The statement must be in writing and be published in such manner as the Minister making it considers appropriate.'

This provision came into force some time before the bulk of the HRA. As was noted in chapter 1, where we speculated as to whether or not it might be regarded as having subjected Parliament to a manner and form limitation on the way in which it legislates, it requires a minister who is introducing a Bill before Parliament to make a statement prior to the Bill's Second Reading that it is in his view compatible with the Convention rights, or that if it is not, the government nevertheless wishes to proceed with the measure. The purpose behind this provision is therefore to ensure that the human rights implications of government legislation are properly thought through before a Bill is introduced in Parliament. Statements of compatibility have been routinely appended to Bills since this provision came into effect. For present purposes, the issue which needs to be considered is what effect such a statement will have upon a court which is required to determine whether the resultant Act is compatible with Convention rights. Speaking extra-judicially, Lord Hoffmann has stated that he attaches great importance to section 19 and that he:

' . . . would be very reluctant to decide that such a measure was not in fact compatible. And I think it is important that Ministers of the Crown should know that such statements will not be regarded as mere formalities but need to be made with careful thought and on responsible advice, because they will carry great weight with the courts.'[152]

Clearly the intention underlying section 19 would be frustrated if statements of compatibility were appended to Bills as a matter of course. However, a pertinent question in this context is

---

[150] At [20].   [151] (1976) 1 EHRR 737.

[152] 'Human Rights and the House of Lords' (1999) 62 MLR 159 at 162.

how likely is it that a government will introduce a Bill in respect of which it feels unable to make a statement of compatibility? In other words, what is the likelihood of a government deliberately seeking to legislate contrary to Convention rights?

(e) Judicial deference

As we have already noted, the 'margin of appreciation' is an important doctrine to emerge from the jurisprudence of the ECtHR. Essentially this doctrine allows signatories to the Convention a degree of latitude in terms of placing restrictions on Convention rights on the basis that state authorities are better placed than an international court to determine the necessity and extent of those restrictions. By its very nature, the doctrine of a margin of appreciation cannot apply domestically since a domestic court possesses a knowledge of the domestic legal system and the surrounding circumstances which the international court does not. Nevertheless, since the enactment of the HRA, the courts have recognised that in some matters, they will defer to the judgment of public authorities. The extent to which they will do so is of course a very important issue given that under the HRA, the courts' role 'is as guardian of human rights'.[153] A balance needs to be struck between too much deference on the one hand, whereby public authorities are permitted to interfere with Convention rights as and when they please, and excessive judicial activism on the other.[154] In striking this balance, it would appear that the courts will have regard to factors such as: the nature of the right which is affected, ie whether it is a qualified or unqualified right; whether matters of constitutional importance are concerned; whether the impugned act or decision is based on social, economic or political factors; and whether the courts themselves have particular expertise in respect of the matter, eg it involves an important feature of the criminal justice system. Thus in *R v DPP, ex p Kebeline*,[155] Lord Hope observed:

'Difficult choices may need to be made by the executive or the legislature between the rights of the individual and the needs of society. In some circumstances it will be appropriate for the courts to recognise that there is an area of judgment within which the judiciary will defer, on democratic grounds, to the considered opinion of the elected body or person whose act or decision is said to be incompatible with the Convention . . . It will be easier for such an area of judgment to be recognised where the issues involve questions of social or economic policy, much less so where the rights are of high constitutional importance or are of a kind where the courts are especially well placed to assess the need for protection.'[156]

In the cases which have been heard by the courts under the HRA the judges have recognised the need for deference in respect of a number of matters, including soci-economic matters,[157] moral and ethical issues,[158] and matters of national security.[159] However, given the youthfulness of the HRA and the nature of the task which the courts are required to perform under

[153] Per Simon Brown LJ (as he then was) in *International Transport Roth GmbH v Secretary of State for the Home Department* [2003] QB 728 at [27].
[154] In *International Transport*, Simon Brown LJ commented that in the context of the HRA, 'Constitutional dangers exist no less in too little judicial activism as in too much': Ibid., at [54].
[155] [2000] 2 AC 326.   [156] At 381.
[157] See, for example, *Poplar Housing and Regeneration Community Association v Donoghue* [2001] EWCA Civ 595, extracted at p. 502.
[158] See, for example, *R (on the application of Pretty) v DPP* [2002] 1 AC 800, extracted at p. 815.
[159] See, for example, *A v Secretary of State for the Home Department* [2004] UKHL 56, extracted at p. 66.

section 3 of the Act,[160] it is inevitable that the courts have trodden a cautious path in relation to deference.[161] It is also inevitable that there are differences of opinion as to the nature of the courts' role under the HRA.

R (on the application of Prolife Alliance) v British Broadcasting Corporation
[2004] 1 AC 185

The claimants were a political party which was opposed to abortion. In the 2001 general election, they fielded enough candidates in Wales (six) to entitle them to make a party election broadcast. The content of the proposed broadcast was devoted to explaining the various types of abortion. Graphic images of aborted foetuses were a central feature of the proposed broadcast. By virtue of section 6(1)(a) of the Broadcasting Act 1990, broadcasters are under an obligation to ensure, so far as they can, that their programmes do not contain material which is likely to be offensive to public feeling. The BBC was under a similar non-statutory obligation pursuant to paragraph 5.1(d) of its agreement with the Secretary of State.

In the light of these obligations, the broadcasters refused to screen the graphic images as part of the proposed broadcast. They did not, however, object to the proposed soundtrack. Prolife Alliance initially commenced judicial review proceedings against the BBC. They were refused permission to proceed. Accordingly, they submitted two further versions of the broadcast to the broadcasters. Neither revised version was deemed acceptable. Finally, a fourth version was submitted and unanimously approved. This version replaced the graphic images with a blank screen bearing the word 'censored' accompanied by a soundtrack which described the images which could not be shown. This version was broadcast in Wales five days prior to the general election of 7 June 2001.

Prolife Alliance appealed to the Court of Appeal against the refusal to grant them permission to proceed. The Court granted the permission and heard the substantive case. It concluded that the BBC's refusal to broadcast the party election broadcast had been unlawful.[162] The BBC appealed against that ruling. The House of Lords held by a majority of four to one (Lord Scott dissenting) that the BBC had been entitled to refuse to broadcast the party election broadcast on the ground that it would be contrary to the public interest to do so.

Lord Nicholls

'6. Freedom of political speech is a freedom of the very highest importance in any country which lays claim to being a democracy. Restrictions on this freedom need to be examined rigorously by all concerned, not least the courts. The courts, as independent and impartial bodies, are charged with a vital supervisory role. Under the Human Rights Act 1998 they must decide whether legislation, and the conduct of public authorities, are compatible with Convention rights and fundamental freedoms. Where there is incompatibility the courts must grant appropriate remedial relief.

. . .

---

[160] For a discussion of the interpretative obligation under section 3, see pp. 61–64.

[161] Clayton has pointed out that there was 'very little discussion of the respective roles of courts and Parliament before human rights litigation commenced': see 'Judicial Deference and "Democratic Dialogue": The Legitimacy of Judicial Intervention under the Human Rights Act 1998' [2004] PL 33 at 39.

[162] [2002] 2 All ER 756.

8. The foundation of ProLife Alliance's case is article 10 of the European Convention on Human Rights. Article 10 does not entitle ProLife Alliance or anyone else to make free television broadcasts. Article 10 confers no such right. But that by no means exhausts the application of article 10 in this context. In this context the principle underlying article 10 requires that access to an important public medium of communication should not be refused on discriminatory, arbitrary or unreasonable grounds. Nor should access be granted subject to discriminatory, arbitrary or unreasonable conditions. A restriction on the content of a programme, produced by a political party to promote its stated aims, must be justified. Otherwise it will not be acceptable. This is especially so where, as here, the restriction operates by way of prior restraint. On its face prior restraint is seriously inimical to freedom of political communication.

. . .

10 . . . For present purposes what matters is that before your Lordships' House ProLife Alliance accepted, no doubt for good reasons, that the offensive material restriction is not in itself an infringement of Pro-Life Alliance's Convention right under article 10. The appeal proceeded on this footing. The only issue before the House is the second, narrower question. The question is this: should the court, in the exercise of its supervisory role, interfere with the broadcasters' decisions that the offensive material restriction precluded them from transmitting the programme proposed by ProLife Alliance?

. . .

16. As it was, the Court of Appeal in effect carried out its own balancing exercise between the requirements of freedom of political speech and the protection of the public from being unduly distressed in their own homes. That was not a legitimate exercise for the courts in this case. Parliament has decided where the balance shall be held. The latter interest prevails over the former to the extent that the offensive material ban applies without distinction to all television programmes, including party broadcasts. In the absence of a successful claim that the offensive material restriction is not compatible with the Convention rights of ProLife Alliance, it is not for the courts to find that broadcasters acted unlawfully when they did no more than give effect to the statutory and other obligations binding on them . . .'

Lord Hoffmann

'Freedom of political speech

. . .

(a) The nature of the right under article 10

55. First, the primary right protected by article 10 is the right of every citizen not to be *prevented* from expressing his opinions. He has the right to "receive and impart information and ideas without *interference* by public authority" (emphasis supplied).

56. In the present case, that primary right was not engaged. There was nothing that the Alliance was prevented from doing. It enjoyed the same free speech as every other citizen. By virtue of its entitlement to a PEB it had more access to the homes of its fellow citizens than other single-issue groups which could not afford to register as a political party and put up six deposits.

57. There is no human right to use a television channel. Parliament has required the broadcasters to allow political parties to broadcast but has done so subject to conditions, both as to qualification for a PEB and as to its contents. No one disputes the necessity for qualifying conditions. It would obviously not be possible to give every grouping which registers as a political party a PPB or PEB. The issue in this case is about the condition as to contents, namely that it should not offend against standards of truth and decency.

58. The fact that no one has a right to broadcast on television does not mean that article 10 has no application to such broadcasts. But the nature of the right in such cases is different. Instead of being a right not to be prevented from expressing one's opinions, it becomes a right to fair consideration for being afforded the opportunity to do so; a right not to have one's access to public media denied on discriminatory, arbitrary or unreasonable grounds.

59. A recent example of the application of this principle is the decision of the Privy Council in *Benjamin v Minister of Information and Broadcasting* [2001] 1 WLR 1040. Mr Benjamin was host of a phone-in programme on government-controlled Anguilla Radio. The government suspended his programme because he had aired a politically controversial question (whether Anguilla should have a lottery) on which the government wished to stop discussion. Lord Slynn of Hadley, at p. 1048, paras 26, 27, accepted that Mr Benjamin had no primary right to broadcast. But he did have a right not to have his access to the medium denied on politically discriminatory grounds. Lord Slynn, at p. 1052, described the Government's action as "arbitrary or capricious". This is something which very much engages the freedom of political speech protected by article 10.

60. The same approach can be found in the jurisprudence of the European Court of Human Rights. In *Haider v Austria* (1995) 83-A DR 66 the Commission rejected the complaint of Mr Haider, the Austrian politician, that (among other things) his opinions had not been given enough time on television, as manifestly unfounded. It said, at p. 74:

> "The Commission recalls that article 10 of the Convention cannot be taken to include a general and unfettered right for any private citizen or organisation to have access to broadcasting time on radio or television in order to forward his opinion, save under exceptional circumstances, for instance if one political party is excluded from broadcasting facilities at election time while other parties are given broadcasting time . . ."

62. In my opinion, therefore, the Court of Appeal asked itself the wrong question. It treated the case as if it concerned the primary right not to be prevented from expressing one's political views and concluded that questions of taste and decency were not an adequate ground for censorship. The real issue in the case is whether the requirements of taste and decency are a discriminatory, arbitrary or unreasonable condition for allowing a political party free access at election time to a particular public medium, namely television.

. . .

71. . . . . And at this point it is also relevant to consider the response of the court to the complaint of the Alliance (Application No 41869/98) about the rejection of its PEB in the 1997 election. On 26 June 2000 the registrar of the court wrote to the Alliance saying that "in accordance with the general instructions received from the court" he drew their attention to "certain shortcomings" in the application. The indication given by the registrar was that the court might consider that the taste and decency requirements were not an "arbitrary or unreasonable" interference with their access to television. Subsequently the court, after noting that the Alliance had been informed of "possible obstacles" to the admissibility of the application, rejected it as not disclosing "any appearance of a violation of the rights and freedoms set out in the Convention . . ."

72. The Court of Appeal treated this decision as an aberration to which no attention should be paid. But, like Scott Baker J, I think that it is very significant. The test applied in the letter from the registrar, namely, whether the restriction on the content of the PEB was "arbitrary or unreasonable", seems to me precisely the test which ought to be applied. It is more in accordance with the jurisprudence of the European Court and a proper analysis of the nature of the right in question than the fundamentalist approach of the Court of Appeal.

73. In my opinion therefore, there is no public interest in exempting PEBs from the taste and decency requirements on the ground that their message requires them to broadcast offensive material. The Alliance had no human right to be invited to the party and it is not unreasonable for Parliament to provide that those invited should behave themselves.

(d) Deference

74. There is a good deal of discussion in the judgment of Laws LJ about whether "deference" should be paid to the decision-makers . . . Laws LJ treated the broadcasters as having decided to censor the Alliance broadcast and dismissed their argument that they were trying to apply statutory standards of taste and decency. But the question I am now addressing is whether Parliament was entitled to require PEBs to comply with standards of taste and decency and so the relevant decision-maker is Parliament.

75. My Lords, although the word "deference" is now very popular in describing the relationship between the judicial and the other branches of government, I do not think that its overtones of servility, or perhaps gracious concession, are appropriate to describe what is happening. In a society based upon the rule of law and the separation of powers, it is necessary to decide which branch of government has in any particular instance the decision-making power and what the legal limits of that power are. That is a question of law and must therefore be decided by the courts.

76. This means that the courts themselves often have to decide the limits of their own decision-making power. That is inevitable. But it does not mean that their allocation of decision-making power to the other branches of government is a matter of courtesy or deference. The principles upon which decision-making powers are allocated are principles of law. The courts are the independent branch of government and the legislature and executive are, directly and indirectly respectively, the elected branches of government. Independence makes the courts more suited to deciding some kinds of questions and being elected makes the legislature or executive more suited to deciding others. The allocation of these decision-making responsibilities is based upon recognised principles. The principle that the independence of the courts is necessary for a proper decision of disputed legal rights or claims of violation of human rights is a legal principle. It is reflected in article 6 of the Convention. On the other hand, the principle that majority approval is necessary for a proper decision on policy or allocation of resources is also a legal principle. Likewise, when a court decides that a decision is within the proper competence of the legislature or executive, it is not showing deference. It is deciding the law.

77. In this particular case, the decision to make all broadcasts subject to taste and decency requirements represents Parliament's view that, as the Annan Committee put it, in paragraph 16.3, "public opinion cannot be totally disregarded in the pursuit of liberty". That seems to me an entirely proper decision for Parliament as representative of the people to make. For the reasons I have given, it involves no arbitrary or unreasonable restriction on the right of free speech.

The decision by the broadcasters

. . .

79. In my view the only route by which one can arrive at such a conclusion is that of the Court of Appeal, which is to say that the broadcasters were not entitled to apply standards of truth and decency at all. But I have already explained why I do not think that this route is legitimate. Once one accepts that the broadcasters were entitled to apply generally accepted standards, I do not see how it is possible for a court to say that they were wrong.

80. Public opinion in these matters is often diverse, sometimes unexpected and in constant flux. Generally accepted standards on these questions are not a matter of intuition on the part of elderly male judges . . .'

Lord Scott

'94. The decision to refuse to broadcast the programme was communicated to the Alliance by a letter of 17 May 2001 from the BBC. The letter said that the BBC, and the ITV broadcasters, had concluded that "it would be wrong to broadcast these images which would be offensive to very large numbers of viewers". Was this a conclusion to which a reasonable decision maker, paying due regard to the Alliance's right to impart information about abortions to the electorate subject only to what was necessary in a democratic society to protect the rights of others, could have come?

95. In my opinion, it was not. The restrictions on the broadcasting of material offending against good taste and decency and of material offensive to public feeling were drafted so as to be capable of application to all programmes, whether light entertainment, serious drama, historical or other documentaries, news reports, party political programmes, or whatever. But material that might be required to be rejected in one type of programme might be unexceptionable in another. The judgment of the decision maker would need to take into account the type of programme of which the material formed part as well as the audience at which the programme was directed. This was a party election broadcast directed at the electorate. He, or she, would need to apply the prescribed standard having regard to these factors and to the need that the application be compatible with the guarantees of freedom of expression contained in article 10.

96. The conclusion to which the broadcasters came could not, in my opinion, have been reached without a significant and fatal undervaluing of two connected features of the case: first, that the programme was to constitute a party election broadcast; second, that the only relevant criterion for a justifiable rejection on offensiveness grounds was that the rejection be necessary for the protection of the right of homeowners not to be subjected to offensive material in their own homes.

97. The importance of the general election context of the Alliance's proposed programme cannot be overstated. We are fortunate enough to live in what is often described as, and I believe to be, a mature democracy. In a mature democracy political parties are entitled, and expected, to place their policies before the public so that the public can express its opinion on them at the polls. The constitutional importance of this entitlement and expectation is enhanced at election time.

98. If, as here, a political party's desired election broadcast is factually accurate, not sensationalised, and is relevant to a lawful policy on which its candidates are standing for election, I find it difficult to understand on what possible basis it could properly be rejected as being "offensive to public feeling". Voters in a mature democracy may strongly disagree with a policy being promoted by a televised party political broadcast but ought not to be offended by the fact that the policy is being promoted nor, if the promotion is factually accurate and not sensationalised, by the content of the programme. Indeed, in my opinion, the public in a mature democracy are not entitled to be offended by the broadcasting of such a programme. A refusal to transmit such a programme based upon the belief that the programme would be "offensive to very large numbers of viewers" (the letter of 17 May 2001) would not, in my opinion, be capable of being described as "necessary in a democratic society . . . for the protection of . . . rights of others". Such a refusal would, on the contrary, be positively inimical to the values of a democratic society, to which values it must be assumed that the public adhere.

99. One of the disturbing features of our present democracy is so-called voter-apathy. The percentage of registered voters who vote at general elections is regrettably low. A broadcasters' mind-set that rejects a party election television programme, dealing with an issue of undeniable public importance such as abortion, on the ground that large numbers of the voting public would find the programme "offensive" denigrates the voting public, treats them like children who need to be protected from the unpleasant realities of life, seriously undervalues their political maturity and can only promote the voter-apathy to which I have referred.

100. For these reasons the decision of the BBC and the other broadcasters to refuse to transmit the Alliance's desired programme was, in my opinion, a decision to which no reasonable decision maker, applying the standards prescribed by paragraph 5(1)(d) of the BBC Agreement and section 6(1)(a) of the 1990 Act, and properly directing itself in accordance with article 10, could have come. I find myself in full agreement with the Court of Appeal and would dismiss this appeal.'

Lord Walker

'124. In forming their judgments the broadcasters were required to (and, as the letter of 17 May 2001 shows, did) take account of the character of the Alliance's programme as a PEB (although one concerned with a single issue which many would regard as an issue of ethics rather than party politics). The European Court of Human Rights has recognised the special importance of freedom of expression at the time of an election: *Bowman v United Kingdom* 26 EHRR 1, 18, para 42. But even in that context the freedom is not absolute: see para 43 of the same judgment. The broadcasters also had to take into account the special power and intrusiveness of television. They are, by their training and experience, well qualified (so far as anybody, elected or unelected, could claim to be well qualified) to assess the Alliance's PEB as against other more or less shocking material which might have been included in news or current affairs programmes, and to form a view about its likely impact on viewers in Wales (the only country where the "CENSORED" version was eventually shown). In making those assessments the broadcasters were reviewing not programmes produced or commissioned by their own organisations, but programmes produced by or for political parties over which (except as regards offensive material) the broadcasters had no control. They could not themselves make editorial changes, but had to accept or reject the ready-made programme in its entirety.

. . .

132. Some of these cases speak of the national court, on judicial review, according to administrative decision-makers a margin of appreciation. But since the coming into force of the 1998 Act it has become clear that that expression is confusing and therefore inapposite. The correct principle is that the court should in appropriate cases show some deference to the national legislature or to official decision-makers: see the observations of Lord Hope of Craighead in *R v Director of Public Prosecutions, Ex p Kebilene* [2000] 2 AC 326, 380–381 and those of Lord Steyn in *Brown v Stott* [2003] 1 AC 681, 710–711. Lord Hope favoured the expression "discretionary area of judgment" put forward by Lord Lester of Herne Hill QC and David Pannick QC in *Human Rights Law and Practice* (1999), p. 74. This lead was followed by the Court of Appeal in *R (Mahmood) v Secretary of State for the Home Department* [2001] 1 WLR 840; Laws LJ referred, at p. 855, para 33, to the need for a "principled distance" between the decision-maker's decision on the merits and the court's adjudication.

. . .

136. The valuable academic work referred to by Lord Steyn in the *Daly* case has also been discussed in detail by Lord Hope in *R v Shayler* [2003] 1 AC 247, 284–287, paras 72–79. Finally (as to the authorities bearing on this part of the case) I would refer to the dissenting judgment of Laws LJ in *International Transport Roth Gmbh v Secretary of State for the Home Department* [2003] QB 728, 765–767 . . . The whole passage is of great interest but I will highlight four principles which Laws LJ put forward (with the citation of appropriate authority) for the deference which the judicial arm of government should show to the other arms of government: (1) "greater deference is to be paid to an Act of Parliament than to a decision of the executive or subordinate measure" (para 83); (2) "there is more scope for deference 'where the Convention itself requires a balance to be struck, much less so where the right is stated in terms which are unqualified' (per Lord Hope in *R v Secretary of State for the Home Department, Ex p Kebilene* [2000] 2 AC 326, 381)" (para 84); (3) "greater deference will be due to the democratic powers where the subject matter in hand is peculiarly within their constitutional responsibility, and less when it lies more particularly within the constitutional responsibility of the courts" (para 85); (4) "greater or less deference will be due according to whether the subject matter lies more readily within the actual or potential expertise of the democratic powers or the courts" (para 87).

137. The second of these principles is certainly applicable in the present case and is of the greatest importance. Striking a fair balance between individual rights and the general interest of the community is inherent in the whole of the Convention: *Sporrong and Lönnroth v Sweden* (1982) 5 EHRR 35, 52, para 69. The other three points made by Laws LJ are thought-provoking but I do not find them particularly helpful in determining this appeal, for several reasons. In this case (as in many cases raising human rights issues) responsibility for the alleged infringement of human rights cannot be laid entirely at the door of Parliament or at the door of an executive decision-maker. Responsibility for the alleged infringement is as it were spread between the two . . . Moreover the court's (or the common law's) role as the constitutional guardian of free speech is a proposition with which many newspaper publishers might quarrel (. . . although in recent years your Lordships' House has fully recognised the central

constitutional importance of free speech). A third difficulty is that the principles stated by Laws LJ do not allow, at any rate expressly, for the manner (which may be direct and central, or indirect and peripheral) in which Convention rights are engaged in the case before the court.

. . .

139. So the court's task is, not to substitute its own view for that of the broadcasters, but to review their decision with an intensity appropriate to all the circumstances of the case. Here the relevant factors include the following. (1) There is no challenge to the statutory (or in the case of the BBC quasi-statutory) requirement for exclusion of what I have (as shorthand) called "offensive material". That requirement is expressed in imprecise terms which call for a value judgment to be made. The challenge is to the value judgment made by the broadcasters. (2) Their remit was limited (for reasons not inimical to free speech) to a single decision either to accept or to reject the programme as presented to them. In making that decision the broadcasters were bound (in accordance with their respective codes) to have regard to the special power and pervasiveness of television. (3) Although your Lordships do not know the identities of all those involved in the decision, Ms Sloman is undoubtedly a broadcaster of great experience and high reputation. There is no reason to think that she and the others involved failed to approach their task responsibly and with a predisposition towards free speech. No doubt is cast on the good faith of any of them. (4) Free speech is particularly important in the political arena, especially at the time of a general election. That is why specific arrangements are made for PEBs, but the fact that PEBs are not immune from the general requirement to avoid offensive material is only a limited restriction on free speech, and it applies equally to all political parties. There was no arbitrary discrimination against the Alliance. (5) The effect of the decision was to deprive the Alliance of the opportunity of making a broadcast using disturbing images of the consequences of abortion. The Alliance still had (and used) the opportunity to broadcast its chosen text, and it was still at liberty to use a variety of other means of communicating its message. In that respect article 10, although engaged, was not engaged as fully as if there had been some total ban.'

The decision in *Prolife Alliance* has come to be regarded as important in the context of the developing domestic law on human rights and in particular the notion of 'deference' despite the fact that two of the Law Lords who heard the appeal never referred to 'deference' during the course of their speeches.[163] Indeed, it has been suggested that Lord Nicholls' speech is 'the antithesis of deference'[164] in that it envisages a robust approach by the courts with little concession to latitude when determining the lawfulness of a decision in the human rights context. Nevertheless, *Prolife Alliance* has attracted most comment in relation to what Lord Hoffmann had to say on 'deference', a term which he pointedly eschewed on the grounds of 'its overtones of servility, or perhaps gracious concession'.[165] Although it may now be more appropriate to talk in terms of a 'discretionary area of judgment'[166] rather than 'deference' to describe the relationship between the courts and the decision-makers under the HRA, terminology is of secondary importance. What matters most is the basis on which the courts will defer to or recognise that a decision falls within the discretionary area of judgment of the decision-maker, and the extent of that deference or discretion. For Lord Hoffmann, deference is based on the separation of powers and related constitutional principles, such as the independence of the judiciary and the democratic legitimacy of Parliament. Accordingly, there will be cases, and *Prolife Alliance* is one such case, where decisions on certain matters will be left to the decision-maker. In Lord Hoffmann's opinion, the courts lacked the institutional

---

[163] Lords Nicholls and Scott.

[164] See MacDonald, '*R (on the application of Prolife Alliance) v BBC*: Political Speech and the Standard of Review' [2003] EHRLR 651 at 656.   [165] At [75], extracted above.

[166] A term used by Lester and Pannick in *Human Rights Law and Practice* (2nd edn, 2004) at para 3.19 (p. 95), and approved by Lord Hope in *R v DPP, ex p Kebilene* [2000] AC 326 at 380–381.

capacity to decide on the central issue raised by the facts of *Prolife Alliance*; the offensiveness of the material which had been included in the proposed party election broadcast. Parliament had decided that that particular judgment was to be made by the broadcasters themselves.

It has been contended that Lord Hoffmann's comments in *Prolife Alliance* on the ability of the broadcasters rather than the courts to make the judgment as to what public opinion required were 'heavy with deference'.[167] Whilst this is undoubtedly true, the flexibility and developing nature of deference is demonstrated by *A v Secretary of State for the Home Department*,[168] where Lord Hoffmann himself was very non-deferential when, unlike the other eight Law Lords who heard the appeal, he declined to accept the government's view that there was a terrorist threat to the life of the nation sufficient to justify the imposition of detention without trial for non-UK citizens pursuant to section 23 of the Anti-terrorism Crime and Security Act 2001.

Lord Hoffmann's remarks in *Prolife Alliance* have been subject to criticism in both academic and judicial quarters. Thus, for example, Professor Jowell has opined:

'Lord Hoffmann is right that it is for the courts to decide the scope of rights, but there is no magic legal or other formula to identify the "discretionary area of judgment" available to the reviewed body. In deciding whether matters such as national security, or public interest, or morals should be permitted to prevail over a right, the courts must consider not only the rational exercise of discretion by the reviewed body but also the imperatives of a rights-based democracy. In the course of some of the steps in the process of this assessment the courts may properly acknowledge their own institutional limitations. In so doing, however, they should guard against a presumption that matters of public interest are outside their competence and be ever aware that they are now the ultimate arbiters (although not ultimate guarantors) of the necessary qualities of a democracy in which the popular will is no longer always expected to prevail.'[169]

The former Law Lord, Lord Steyn, has also expressed his disagreement with Lord Hoffmann's approach to the issue of deference. Writing extra-judicially, Lord Steyn has commended the 'balanced approach' advocated by Professor Jowell on the basis that although it acknowledges that on occasions there will be a need to defer to the acts or decisions of the other branches of government, it does not seek to create a legal principle which requires the courts to abstain from ruling on policy matters and other areas of discretionary judgment. Thus 'at the risk of over-simplification', Lord Steyn summarises what he believes ought to be the position as follows:

'The rule of law requires that courts do not surrender their responsibilities. So far as the courts desist from making decisions in a particular case it should not be on grounds of separation of powers, or other constitutional principle. Deference may lead courts not to make their own judgments on an issue. The degree of deference which the courts should show will, of course, depend on and vary with the context. The true justification for a court exceptionally declining to decide an issue, which is within its jurisdiction, is the relative institutional competence or capacity of the branches of government.'[170]

Clayton has argued that the relationship between decision-makers and the courts under the HRA 'would become easier if it were possible to devise a constitutional theory of adjudication'.[171] Accordingly, having regard to the experience of the Canadian courts in interpreting

---

[167] See Jowell, 'Judicial deference: servility, civility or institutional capacity' [2003] PL 592 at 600.
[168] [2005] 2 AC 68.   [169] [2003] PL 592 at 599.
[170] 'Deference: a Tangled Story' [2005] PL 346 at 352.
[171] 'Judicial Deference and "Democratic Dialogue": The Legitimacy of Judicial Intervention under the Human Rights Act 1998' [2004] PL 33 at 40.

the Charter of Rights and Freedoms, he points to the emergence of a 'democratic dialogue' between the courts and the legislature whereby an adverse judicial decision is the catalyst for a public debate as to Charter values. Applying this principle to the HRA, Clayton contends that 'the opportunity for dialogue between the courts and the legislature arises where the court is unable to construe legislation compatibly with Convention rights under section 3'.[172] He does, however, acknowledge that where section 3 is used to accord statutory words a meaning which Parliament never intended, it is difficult to claim that this amounts to a 'democratic dialogue'. Nevertheless, he opines:

'the idea of a democratic dialogue provides a helpful starting point in formulating a theory of constitutional adjudication. It articulates the fact that a judicial pronouncement routinely prompts a response from those whose decision is being reviewed. The need to defer to Parliament or the executive is less compelling once it is acknowledged that the HRA envisages the other branches of government will have a second bite of the cherry.'[173]

(f) The impact of the Human Rights Act 1998

The entry into force of the HRA has almost inevitably led to a marked increase in the number of human rights arguments which are raised before the courts. As a result, a substantial body of case law has developed. During the period October 2000–July 2006, 552 'human rights' cases were heard by the appellate committee.[174] Of the 354 cases which the House of Lords decided during this period, approximately one third involved a substantive consideration of the HRA. Nevertheless, despite this significant case load, it is evident that the courts have taken a robust approach to human rights arguments. Shortly after the HRA came into force, it was made clear that specious human rights arguments would not be tolerated. Thus, in *Daniels v Walker*,[175] the Court of Appeal rejected the argument that whether a defendant should be allowed to have the claimant examined by a consultant occupational therapist had anything to do with human rights. In the words of Lord Woolf MR (as he then was):

'Article 6 [of the ECHR] has no possible relevance to this appeal. Quite apart from the fact that the Act is not in force, if the court is not going to be taken down blind alleys it is essential that counsel, and those who instruct counsel, take a responsible attitude as to when it is right to raise a Human Rights Act point . . . When the 1998 Act becomes law, counsel will need to show self restraint if it is not to be discredited.'[176]

It is worth noting that the Family Division of the High Court has issued a practice direction on the citation of those authorities referred to in section 2 of the HRA.[177] In the direction it is stated that: (i) the authority cited to the court shall be an authoritative and complete report; (ii) the court must be provided with a list of authorities it is intended to cite and copies of the reports; and (iii) that copies of the complete original texts issued by the European Court and Commission may be used, either in paper form or from the Court's judgment database (available on the internet).

---

[172] Ibid., at 46.   [173] Ibid., at 47.
[174] See *Review of the Implementation of the Human Rights Act*, Department for Constitutional Affairs, (July 2006), at 10.   [175] (Unreported), 3 May 2000.
[176] At [23].   [177] See [2000] 4 All ER 288.

Where the HRA is argued in a case, it does not necessarily follow that it will have an effect on the final outcome. This may be due to one of several reasons. For example, it is possible that the arguments advanced do not in fact relate to a right which is protected by the ECHR. This occurred in a House of Lords case where it was unsuccessfully argued that the ECHR contained an implied right to assisted suicide.

R (Pretty) v Director of Public Prosecutions (Secretary of State for the Home Department intervening) [2002] 1 AC 800

The claimant suffered from motor neurone disease, a progressive and degenerative terminal illness. Anxious to avoid a distressing and humiliating death, she wished to take her own life. However, her condition meant that she was unable to do so. She therefore sought to enlist the help of her husband to commit suicide. Since assisting a suicide is an offence contrary to section 2(1) of the Suicide Act 1961, the claimant sought an undertaking from the Director of Public Prosecutions (DPP) that if her husband were to help her to die, the DPP would not consent to a prosecution as required by section 2(4) of the 1961 Act. The DPP refused to give such an undertaking. The claimant therefore applied for judicial review of that decision. The Divisional Court upheld the Director's decision and refused relief.[178] The claimant therefore appealed to the House of Lords. It was argued on her behalf that the refusal to allow her to commit assisted suicide constituted a breach of articles 2, 3, 8, 9 and 14 of the ECHR. The House of Lords held unanimously that the appeal should be dismissed.

Lord Bingham

'1. . . . It is on the Convention, brought into force in this country by the Human Rights Act 1998, that Mrs Pretty's claim to relief depends. It is accepted by her counsel on her behalf that under the common law of England she could not have hoped to succeed.

Article 2 of the Convention

. . .

4. On behalf of Mrs Pretty it is submitted that article 2 protects not life itself but the right to life. The purpose of the article is to protect individuals from third parties (the state and public authorities). But the article recognises that it is for the individual to choose whether or not to live and so protects the individual's right to self-determination in relation to issues of life and death. Thus a person may refuse life-saving or life-prolonging medical treatment, and may lawfully choose to commit suicide. The article acknowledges that right of the individual. While most people want to live, some want to die, and the article protects both rights. The right to die is not the antithesis of the right to life but the corollary of it, and the state has a positive obligation to protect both.

5. The Secretary of State has advanced a number of unanswerable objections to this argument which were rightly upheld by the Divisional Court. The starting point must be the language of the article. The thrust of this is to reflect the sanctity which, particularly in western eyes, attaches to life. The article protects the right to life and prevents the deliberate taking of life save in very narrowly defined circumstances. An article with that effect cannot be interpreted as conferring a right to die or to enlist the aid of another in bringing about one's own death. In his argument for Mrs Pretty, Mr Havers was at pains to limit his argument to assisted suicide, accepting that the right claimed could not extend to cover an intentional consensual killing (usually described in this context as "voluntary euthanasia", but regarded in English law as murder). The right claimed would be sufficient to cover Mrs Pretty's case and counsel's unwillingness to go further is understandable. But there is in logic no justification for drawing a line at this point. If article 2 does confer a right to self-determination in relation to life and

---

[178] [2001] EWHC 788 (Admin).

death, and if a person were so gravely disabled as to be unable to perform any act whatever to cause his or her own death, it would necessarily follow in logic that such a person would have a right to be killed at the hands of a third party without giving any help to the third party and the state would be in breach of the Convention if it were to interfere with the exercise of that right. No such right can possibly be derived from an article having the object already defined.

6. It is true that some of the guaranteed Convention rights have been interpreted as conferring rights not to do that which is the antithesis of what there is an express right to do. Article 11, for example, confers a right not to join an association (*Young, James and Webster v United Kingdom* (1981) 4 EHRR 38), article 9 embraces a right to freedom from any compulsion to express thoughts or change an opinion or divulge convictions (Clayton & Tomlinson, *The Law of Human Rights* (2000), p 974, para 14.49) and I would for my part be inclined to infer that article 12 confers a right not to marry (but see Clayton & Tomlinson, p 913, para 13.76). It cannot however be suggested (to take some obvious examples) that articles 3, 4, 5 and 6 confer an implied right to do or experience the opposite of that which the articles guarantee. Whatever the benefits which, in the view of many, attach to voluntary euthanasia, suicide, physician-assisted suicide and suicide assisted without the intervention of a physician, these are not benefits which derive protection from an article framed to protect the sanctity of life.

. . .

9. In the Convention field the authority of domestic decisions is necessarily limited and, as already noted, Mrs Pretty bases her case on the Convention. But it is worthy of note that her argument is inconsistent with two principles deeply embedded in English law. The first is a distinction between the taking of one's own life by one's own act and the taking of life through the intervention or with the help of a third party. The former has been permissible since suicide ceased to be a crime in 1961. The latter has continued to be proscribed . . . It is not enough for Mrs Pretty to show that the United Kingdom would not be acting inconsistently with the Convention if it were to permit assisted suicide; she must go further and establish that the United Kingdom is in breach of the Convention by failing to permit it or would be in breach of the Convention if it did not permit it. Such a contention is in my opinion untenable, as the Divisional Court rightly held.

. . .

Article 3 of the Convention

12. For the Secretary of State it was submitted that in the present case article 3 of the Convention is not engaged at all but that if any of the rights protected by that article are engaged they do not include a right to die . . .

13. Article 3 enshrines one of the fundamental values of democratic societies and its prohibition of the proscribed treatment is absolute: *D v United Kingdom* 24 EHRR 423, 447, para 47. Article 3 is, as I think, complementary to article 2. As article 2 requires states to respect and safeguard the lives of individuals within their jurisdiction, so article 3 obliges them to respect the physical and human integrity of such individuals. There is in my opinion nothing in article 3 which bears on an individual's right to live or to choose not to live. That is not its sphere of application; indeed, as is clear from *X v Germany* above, a state may on occasion be justified in inflicting treatment which would otherwise be in breach of article 3 in order to serve the ends of article 2. Moreover, the absolute and unqualified prohibition on a member state inflicting the proscribed treatment requires that "treatment" should not be given an unrestricted or extravagant meaning. It cannot, in my opinion, be plausibly suggested that the Director or any other agent of the United Kingdom is inflicting the proscribed treatment on Mrs Pretty, whose suffering derives from her cruel disease.

14. The authority most helpful to Mrs Pretty is *D v United Kingdom* 24 EHRR 423 which concerned the removal to St Kitts of a man in the later stages of AIDS. The Convention challenge was to implementation of the removal decision having regard to the applicant's medical condition, the absence of facilities to provide adequate treatment, care or support in St Kitts and the disruption of a regime in the United

Kingdom which had afforded him sophisticated treatment and medication in a compassionate environment. It was held that implementation of the decision to remove the applicant to St Kitts would amount in the circumstances to inhuman treatment by the United Kingdom in violation of article 3. In that case the state was proposing to take direct action against the applicant, the inevitable effect of which would be a severe increase in his suffering and a shortening of his life. The proposed deportation could fairly be regarded as "treatment". An analogy might be found in the present case if a public official had forbidden the provision to Mrs Pretty of pain-killing or palliative drugs. But here the proscribed treatment is said to be the Director's refusal of proleptic immunity from prosecution to Mr Pretty if he commits a crime. By no legitimate process of interpretation can that refusal be held to fall within the negative prohibition of article 3.

Article 8 of the Convention

. . .

26. I would for my part accept the Secretary of State's submission that Mrs Pretty's rights under article 8 are not engaged at all. If, however, that conclusion is wrong, and the prohibition of assisted suicide in section 2 of the 1961 Act infringes her Convention right under article 8, it is necessary to consider whether the infringement is shown by the Secretary of State to be justifiable under the terms of article 8(2) . . .

28. . . . It would be by no means fatal to the legal validity of section 2(1) of the 1961 Act if the response of the United Kingdom to this problem of assisted suicide were shown to be unique, but it is shown to be in accordance with a very broad international consensus. Assisted suicide and consensual killing are unlawful in all Convention countries except the Netherlands, but even if the Dutch Termination of Life on Request and Assisted Suicide (Review Procedures) Act 2001 and the Dutch Criminal Code were operative in this country it would not relieve Mr Pretty of liability under article 294 of the Dutch Criminal Code if he were to assist Mrs Pretty to take her own life as he would wish to do.

. . .

30. If section 2(1) infringes any Convention right of Mrs Pretty, and recognising the heavy burden which lies on a member state seeking to justify such an infringement, I conclude that the Secretary of State has shown ample grounds to justify the existing law and the current application of it. That is not to say that no other law or application would be consistent with the Convention; it is simply to say that the present legislative and practical regime do not offend the Convention.

Article 9 of the Convention

31. It is unnecessary to recite the terms of article 9 of the Convention, to which very little argument was addressed. It is an article which protects freedom of thought, conscience and religion and the manifestation of religion or belief in worship, teaching, practice or observance. One may accept that Mrs Pretty has a sincere belief in the virtue of assisted suicide. She is free to hold and express that belief. But her belief cannot found a requirement that her husband should be absolved from the consequences of conduct which, although it would be consistent with her belief, is proscribed by the criminal law. And if she were able to establish an infringement of her right, the justification shown by the state in relation to article 8 would still defeat it.

Article 14 of the Convention

. . .

33. The European Court of Human Rights has repeatedly held that article 14 is not autonomous but has effect only in relation to Convention rights. As it was put in *Van Raalte v The Netherlands* (1997) 24 EHRR 503, 516, para 33:

"As the court has consistently held, article 14 of the Convention complements the other substantive provisions of the Convention and the Protocols. It has no independent existence since it has effect solely in relation to 'the enjoyment of the rights and freedoms' safeguarded by those provisions. Although the application of article 14 does not presuppose a breach of those provisions—and to this extent it is autonomous—there can be no room for its application unless the facts at issue fall within the ambit of one or more of the latter."

See also *Botta v Italy* (1998) 26 EHRR 241, 259, para 39.

34. If, as I have concluded, none of the articles on which Mrs Pretty relies gives her the right which she has claimed, it follows that article 14 would not avail her even if she could establish that the operation of section 2(1) is discriminatory. A claim under this article must fail on this ground.

35. If, contrary to my opinion, Mrs Pretty's rights under one or other of the articles are engaged, it would be necessary to examine whether section 2(1) of the 1961 Act is discriminatory. She contends that the section is discriminatory because it prevents the disabled, but not the able-bodied, exercising their right to commit suicide. This argument is in my opinion based on a misconception. The law confers no right to commit suicide. Suicide was always, as a crime, anomalous, since it was the only crime with which no defendant could ever be charged. The main effect of the criminalisation of suicide was to penalise those who attempted to take their own lives and failed, and secondary parties. Suicide itself (and with it attempted suicide) was decriminalised because recognition of the common law offence was not thought to act as a deterrent, because it cast an unwarranted stigma on innocent members of the suicide's family and because it led to the distasteful result that patients recovering in hospital from a failed suicide attempt were prosecuted, in effect, for their lack of success. But while the 1961 Act abrogated the rule of law whereby it was a crime for a person to commit (or attempt to commit) suicide, it conferred no right on anyone to do so. Had that been its object there would have been no justification for penalising by a potentially very long term of imprisonment one who aided, abetted, counselled or procured the exercise or attempted exercise by another of that right. The policy of the law remained firmly adverse to suicide, as section 2(1) makes clear.

36. The criminal law cannot in any event be criticised as objectionably discriminatory because it applies to all. Although in some instances criminal statutes recognise exceptions based on youth, the broad policy of the criminal law is to apply offence-creating provisions to all and to give weight to personal circumstances either at the stage of considering whether or not to prosecute or, in the event of conviction, when penalty is to be considered. The criminal law does not ordinarily distinguish between willing victims and others: *Laskey, Jaggard and Brown v United Kingdom* 24 EHRR 39. Provisions criminalising drunkenness or misuse of drugs or theft do not exempt those addicted to alcohol or drugs, or the poor and hungry. "Mercy killing", as it is often called, is in law killing. If the criminal law sought to proscribe the conduct of those who assisted the suicide of the vulnerable, but exonerated those who assisted the suicide of the non-vulnerable, it could not be administered fairly and in a way which would command respect.'

Lord Steyn

'41. . . . . The specific question before the House is whether the appellant is entitled to a declaration that the Director of Public Prosecutions is obliged to undertake in advance that, if she is assisted by her husband in committing suicide, he will not be prosecuted under section 2(1) of the Suicide Act 1961 . . . Her case is squarely founded on the Human Rights Act 1998, which incorporated the European Convention on Human Rights into English law. For her to succeed it is not enough to show that the European Convention allows member states to legalise assisted suicide. She must establish that at least that part of section 2(1) of the 1961 Act which makes aiding or abetting suicide a crime is in conflict with her Convention rights. In other words, she must persuade the House that the European Convention compels member states of the Council of Europe to legalise assisted suicide.

. . .

The reach of human right's texts

56. . . . The aspirational text of the Universal Declaration was the point of departure and inspiration of the European Convention which opened for signature in 1950. It is to be noted, however, that the

European Convention embodied in some respects a narrower view of human rights than the Universal Declaration. The framers of the European Convention required a shorter and uncontroversial text which would secure general acceptance among European nations. Thus the European Convention contains, unlike the Universal Declaration, no guarantees of economic, social and cultural rights . . . The language of the European Convention is often open textured . . . The generality of the language permits adaptation of the European Convention to modern conditions. It is also, however, necessary to take into account that in the field of fundamental beliefs the European Court of Human Rights does not readily adopt a creative role contrary to a European consensus, or virtual consensus. The fact is that among the 41 member states[179]—North, South, East and West—there are deep cultural and religious differences in regard to euthanasia and assisted suicide. The legalisation of euthanasia and assisted suicide as adopted in the Netherlands would be unacceptable to predominantly Roman Catholic countries in Europe. The idea that the European Convention requires states to render lawful euthanasia and assisted suicide (as opposed to allowing democratically elected legislatures to adopt measures to that effect) must therefore be approached with scepticism. That does not involve support for the proposition that one must go back to the original intent of the European Convention. On the contrary, approaching the European Convention as a living instrument, the fact is that an interpretation requiring states to legalise euthanasia and assisted suicide would not only be enormously controversial but profoundly unacceptable to the peoples of many member states.

Policy grounds

57. If section 2 of the 1961 Act is held to be incompatible with the European Convention, a right to commit assisted suicide would not be doctor assisted and would not be subject to safeguards introduced in the Netherlands. In a valuable essay Professor Michael Freeman trenchantly observed "A repeal of section 2 of the Suicide Act 1961, without more, would not be rational policy-making. We would need a 'Death with Dignity Act' to fill the lacuna": "Death, Dying and the Human Rights Act 1998" (1999) 52 CLP 218, 237. That must be right. In our parliamentary democracy, and I apprehend in many member states of the Council of Europe, such a fundamental change cannot be brought about by judicial creativity. If it is to be considered at all, it requires a detailed and effective regulatory proposal. In these circumstances it is difficult to see how a process of interpretation of Convention rights can yield a result with all the necessary inbuilt protections. Essentially, it must be a matter for democratic debate and decision making by legislatures.

vi. The specific articles

58. In combination the contextual factors which I have alluded to justify an initial disbelief that any of the articles of the European Convention could possibly bear the strong meaning for which counsel for Mrs Pretty must argue. Despite his incisive arguments the position is in my opinion clear. None of the articles can bear the interpretation put forward.

Right to life

59. . . . . Counsel for Mrs Pretty argued that article 2 and in particular its first sentence acknowledges that it is for the individual to choose whether to live or die and that it protects her right of self determination in relation to issues of life and death. This interpretation is not sustainable. The purpose of article 2(1) is clear. It enunciates the principle of the sanctity of life and provides a guarantee that no individual "shall be deprived of life" by means of intentional human intervention. The interpretation now put forward is the exact opposite, viz a right of Mrs Pretty to end her life by means of intentional human intervention. Nothing in the article or the jurisprudence of the European Court of Human Rights can assist Mrs Pretty's case on this article.

---

[179] There are now 46 High Contracting Parties.

Prohibition of torture

60. . . . For my part article 3 is not engaged. The word "treatment" must take its colour from the context in which it appears. While I would not wish to give a narrow interpretation to what may constitute degrading treatment, the concept appears singularly inapt to convey the idea that the state must guarantee to individuals a right to die with the deliberate assistance of third parties. So radical a step, infringing the sanctity of life principle, would have required far more explicit wording. But counsel argues that there is support for his argument to be found in the jurisprudence of the ECHR on the "positive obligations" of a state to render effective the protection of article 3. For this proposition he cites the decision of the ECHR in *D v United Kingdom* (1997) 24 EHRR 423. The case concerned the intended deportation of an individual in the final stages of an incurable disease to St Kitts where there would not be adequate treatment for the disease. The ECHR held that in the exceptional circumstances of the case the implementation of the decision to remove the individual to St Kitts would amount to inhuman treatment by the UK. Unlike *D v United Kingdom* the present case does not involve any positive action (comparable to the intended deportation) nor is there any risk of a failure to treat her properly. Instead the complaint is that the state is guilty of a failure to repeal section 2(1) of the 1961 Act. The present case plainly does not involve "inhuman or degrading treatment".

Right to respect for private life and family

61. . . . Counsel submitted that this article explicitly recognises the principle of the personal autonomy of every individual. He argues that this principle necessarily involves a guarantee as against the state of the right to choose when and how to die. None of the decisions cited in regard to article 8 assist this argument. It must fail on the ground that the guarantee under article 8 prohibits interference with the way in which an individual leads his life and it does not relate to the manner in which he wishes to die.

62. If I had been of the view that article 8 was engaged, I would have held (in agreement with the Divisional Court) that the interference with the guarantee was justified. There was a submission to the contrary based on the argument that the scope of section 2(1) is disproportionate to its aim. This contention was founded on the supposition that Mrs Pretty and others in her position are not vulnerable. It is a sufficient answer that there is a broad class of persons presently protected by section 2 who are vulnerable. It was therefore well within the range of discretion of Parliament to strike the balance between the interests of the community and the rights of individuals in the way reflected in section 2(1).

Freedom of thought, conscience and religion

63. . . . Counsel submitted that Mrs Pretty is entitled to manifest her belief in assisted suicide by committing it. This cannot be right. This article was never intended to give individuals a right to perform any acts in pursuance of whatever beliefs they may hold, eg to attack places where experiments are conducted on animals. The article does not yield support for the specific proposition for which it is invoked. In any event, for the reasons already discussed, section 2 is a legitimate, rational and proportionate response to the wider problem of vulnerable people who would otherwise feel compelled to commit suicide.

Prohibition of discrimination

64. . . . Counsel submits that Mrs Pretty is in effect treated less favourably than those who are physically capable of ending their lives. The Divisional Court held that article 14 is not engaged. The alleged discrimination can only be established if the facts of the case fall within articles 2, 3, 8 or 9: *Botta v Italy* (1998) 26 EHRR 241, 259, para 39. They do not. This is a sufficient reason to reject this argument. But there is a more fundamental reason. The condition of terminally ill individuals, like Mrs Pretty, will vary. The majority will be vulnerable. It is the vulnerability of the class of persons which provides the rationale for making the aiding and abetting of suicide an offence under section 2(1) of the 1961 Act. A class of individuals is protected by section 2(1) because they are in need of protection.

The statutory provision does not therefore treat individuals in a discriminatory manner. There is no unequal treatment before the law . . .

. . .

viii. Conclusion

68. The logic of the European Convention does not justify the conclusion that the House must rule that a state is obliged to legalise assisted suicide. It does not require the state to repeal a provision such as section 2(1) of the 1961 Act. On the other hand, it is open to a democratic legislature to introduce such a measure. Our Parliament, if so minded, may therefore repeal section 2(1) and put in its place a regulated system for assisted suicide (presumably doctor assisted) with appropriate safeguards.'

Lord Hope

'74. . . . The argument has therefore focused on Mrs Pretty's rights under the Human Rights Act 1998 and on the powers of the Director. It proceeds in this way. Firstly, it is said that the Director has power to give the undertaking which has been sought. Second, there is the fact that section 6(1) of the Human Rights Act 1998 makes it unlawful for a public authority to act in a way which is incompatible with a Convention right. So the argument asserts that the Director is obliged to give the undertaking, because to withhold it would be incompatible with Mrs Pretty's Convention rights. Third, it is said that if the Director does not have power to give the undertaking, section 2(1) of the 1961 Act is incompatible with her Convention rights as it imposes a blanket and indiscriminate ban on all assisted suicides.

Section 6(1) of the Human Rights Act 1998

75. Had it not been for the Human Rights Act 1998, Mrs Pretty's case that the Director was obliged to give the undertaking would have been unarguable. Section 2(4) of the Suicide Act 1961 leaves no room for doubt on this point. It leaves decisions as to whether or not a contravention of section 2(1) of the Act should be prosecuted to the discretion of the Director. But the Director is a public authority for the purposes of section 6(1) of the 1998 Act. It is unlawful for him to act in a way which is incompatible with a Convention right. Section 6(6) provides that "an act" for this purpose includes a failure to act. A decision as to whether or not to prosecute has been held to be an act for the purposes of section 57(2) of the Scotland Act 1998: *Brown v Stott* [2001] 2 WLR 817. I see no reason why the words "an act" in section 6(1) of the Human Rights Act 1998, which applies throughout the United Kingdom, should be construed differently. I would hold that a decision by the Director whether or not to prosecute is an act for the purposes of that subsection.

76. Mr Havers seeks to apply section 6(1) to the refusal of the Director to give an undertaking that he would not prosecute Mr Pretty. But in my opinion the words "an act", construed with the benefit of section 6(6), do not require a public authority to do something which it has no power to do. A refusal by a public authority to do something which it has no power to do is not a failure to act. A public authority can only act within its powers. Section 6(1) is concerned with acts which are otherwise lawful but are made unlawful by the 1998 Act on Convention grounds. The Director cannot be held to have acted unlawfully within the meaning of section 6(1) of the 1998 Act when he declined to give the undertaking unless it can be demonstrated that the undertaking was one that he had power to give.

. . .

The Director's powers

79. The question whether or not a law officer (I include in that expression the Director as well as the Government Law Officers) should or should not consent to a prosecution is one which the judiciary must approach with caution and with due deference. Issues of policy may well be involved, and they should be left to the Government Law Officers to answer for in Parliament. The issues of fact will be involved, and they may not be suitable for discussion in open court before trial. In practice therefore our system of public prosecution depends to a large extent on the integrity and judgment of the public

prosecutor. He is likely to be in the best position to judge what is in the public interest. His judgment must be respected by the judiciary. It is against that background that I approach the question whether the Director has power to give the undertaking which has been sought.

80. It is important to identify precisely what it is that is being sought from the Director. He is not being asked simply for a statement about the policy which he will follow in cases of assisted suicide. If that was all that was being asked for, I would not regard it as beyond his powers to make the statement. Mr Perry has submitted that he has no such power, but I would not accept that argument. In my opinion the Director is entitled to form a policy as to the criteria which he will apply when he is exercising his discretion under section 2(4) of the 1961 Act. If he has such a policy, it seems to me to follow that he is entitled to promulgate it. I would hold that these matters lie entirely within the scope of the discretion which has been given to him by the Act.

. . .

82. But I do not see how the Director could be compelled to issue a statement of policy. In Scotland the question whether such statements should be issued are regarded as being entirely a matter for the Lord Advocate. It has never been suggested that he could be ordered to do this by the court. But in any event it is not as a statement of policy that the undertaking has been sought. What Mrs Pretty seeks is an undertaking, before the event occurs, that if her husband helps her to commit suicide he will not be prosecuted. I am not aware of any case where the Lord Advocate has given an undertaking of that kind. It is not his function to permit individuals to commit acts which the law treats as criminal.'

Lord Hobhouse

'114. . . . The undertaking which the appellant requested was not one which the Director as the holder of the statutory office had the authority or power to give and it would have been improper for him to give the undertaking whatever the merits of the appellant's solicitor's arguments. Under section 2(4) of the 1961 Act his role is confined to giving his consent to the institution of proceedings for an offence under section 2. This presupposes that an alleged offence has been committed and that he can exercise his discretion under section 2(4) in relation to all the circumstances disclosed by the evidence of what has occurred as the Code issued under section 10 of the 1985 Act makes clear. The functions of the Director do not include giving undertakings in advance of the event as to how he would exercise that discretion on hypothetical facts. Even after the event, the Director has no investigatory powers and is dependent upon evidence supplied to him by others, normally the police.

. . .

117. The request for the undertaking was a request for the grant of an immunity from prosecution equivalent to the grant of a dispensation from the operation of the criminal law or an anticipatory pardon. Even if there was a power to grant a pardon, it could not be exercised in advance. As Lord Bridge of Harwich said in *Attorney General of Trinidad and Tobago v Phillip* [1995] 1 AC 396, 411:

> "However while a pardon can expunge past offences, a power to pardon cannot be used to dispense with criminal responsibility for an offence which has not yet been committed. This is a principle of general application which is of the greatest importance. The state cannot be allowed to use a power to pardon to enable the law to be set aside by permitting it to be contravened with impunity."

Likewise any purported executive power to suspend or dispense with a law or the execution of a law, save under an express statutory authority, has been unlawful since at least 1688.'

In reaching its decision in *Pretty* it was necessary for the House of Lords to consider carefully articles 2, 3, 8, 9 and 14 of the ECHR in order to determine whether any of the rights contained therein could form the basis of a right to assisted suicide. However, as the extracts above make clear, their Lordships were unanimously of the opinion that none of the Convention rights applied. Despite the recognition by Lord Steyn that the ECHR is a 'living instrument', which calls on the courts to interpret the content of those rights which it protects with an eye to the needs and expectations of modern day society, none of their Lordships considered that any of the articles could be interpreted in such a way as to encompass the right which the claimant sought to have protected. This does not mean of course that a law on assisted suicide would be incompatible with the ECHR. The precise wording of a law on assisted suicide together with the provision of adequate safeguards to prevent its abuse would clearly be a matter for Parliament rather than the courts. Hence it is not in the least surprising that the House of Lords was not prepared to allow the HRA to be used as the vehicle for introducing such a right into English law when hitherto, Parliament has not seen fit to legislate upon the subject.

Putting to one side the Convention rights arguments which featured so prominently in the judgment in *Pretty*, the case is also of interest because it firmly establishes that for the purpose of section 6(1) and (6) of the HRA, the prohibition on a public authority acting or failing to act in a way which is incompatible with a Convention right does not require that authority to do something which it is not empowered to do. Thus although the DPP was clearly a 'public authority' for the purposes of the HRA, his power under the Suicide Act 1961 was limited to deciding whether or not a prosecution ought to be brought for an offence already committed. It did not entitle him to confer an immunity from prosecution in respect of an offence which may be committed at some point in the future. As we saw in chapter 1 (p. 12), the power to suspend and dispense with laws was made illegal under the Bill of Rights 1688.

Assuming that a Convention right is engaged in proceedings, it may be that a court will rule that any interference with that right was justified. This will require a court to carefully consider the qualifications and limits to which many of the rights protected by the ECHR are subject. Thus in an important House of Lords decision on whether a school pupil had the right to wear the jilbab, the majority of their Lordships took the view that the school uniform policy did not interfere with the pupil's article 9 rights. Alternatively, even if it did, that interference was justified by the need to protect the rights of others.

R (SB) v Governors of Denbigh High School [2006] 2 WLR 719

The claimant was a Muslim who attended a mixed-sex, multi-community school which was outside her family's catchment area. The school had devised a uniform policy after consulting with parents, students, staff and the imams of three local mosques. That policy offered female pupils three options. One of the options was the wearing of the shalwar kameeze, a combination of a sleeveless smock-like dress with a square neckline which allowed for the wearing of a school tie, together with loose trousers tapering at the ankles. Female pupils were also permitted to wear headscarves in the school's colours. The claimant wore the shalwar kameeze during her first two years at the school. However, by the beginning of her third year, she had decided that the garment did not comply with the requirements of her religious beliefs. She therefore attended school along with her brother and another male wearing the jilbab, a long coat-like garment designed to conceal the shape of the female body. She was asked to go home and return to school wearing her uniform. She refused to do so and thus remained absent from school. Attempts were subsequently made to provide the claimant with some out of school tuition. However, as a result of the dispute, she lost nearly two years' schooling. Eventually she joined another school in the area where the wearing of the jilbab was permitted.

The claimant sought judicial review of the decision not to allow her to school wearing a jilbab. She claimed that her exclusion from the school was unlawful because it limited her right to manifest her religion under article 9(1) of the ECHR, and because it violated her right to education under article 2 of the First Protocol to the ECHR. At first instance, her claim was dismissed.[180] On appeal, however, the Court of Appeal accepted her contentions. It therefore granted a declaration that she had been excluded from school without following the appropriate procedures and that her rights under article 9(1) had been violated.[181] The Governors of the school appealed with the support of the Secretary of State. The House of Lords allowed the appeal.

Lord Bingham

'2. It is important to stress at the outset that this case concerns a particular pupil and a particular school in a particular place at a particular time. It must be resolved on the facts which are now, for purposes of the appeal, agreed. The House is not, and could not be, invited to rule whether Islamic dress, or any feature of Islamic dress, should or should not be permitted in the schools of this country. That would be a most inappropriate question for the House in its judicial capacity, and it is not one which I shall seek to address . . .

Article 9 of the Convention

20. . . . . The fundamental importance of this right in a pluralistic, multi-cultural society was clearly explained by my noble and learned friend, Lord Nicholls of Birkenhead, in *R (Williamson) v Secretary of State for Education and Employment* [2005] 2 AC 246, paras 15–19, and by the South African Constitutional Court in *Christian Education South Africa v Minister of Education* [2001] 1 LRC 441, para 36. This is not in doubt. As pointed out by Lord Nicholls in para 16 of the passage cited, article 9 protects both the right to hold a belief, which is absolute, and a right to manifest belief, which is qualified.

21. It is common ground in these proceedings that at all material times the respondent sincerely held the religious belief which she professed to hold. It was not the less a religious belief because her belief may have changed, as it probably did, or because it was a belief shared by a small minority of people. Thus it is accepted, obviously rightly, that article 9(1) is engaged or applicable. That in itself makes this a significant case, since any sincere religious belief must command respect, particularly when derived from an ancient and respected religion. The main questions for consideration are, accordingly, whether the respondent's freedom to manifest her belief by her dress was subject to limitation (or, as it has more often been called, interference) within the meaning of article 9(2) and, if so, whether such limitation or interference was justified under that provision.

. . .

Interference

23. The Strasbourg institutions have not been at all ready to find an interference with the right to manifest religious belief in practice or observance where a person has voluntarily accepted an employment or role which does not accommodate that practice or observance and there are other means open to the person to practise or observe his or her religion without undue hardship or inconvenience. Thus in *X v Denmark* (1976) 5 DR 157 a clergyman was held to have accepted the discipline of his church when he took employment, and his right to leave the church guaranteed his freedom of religion. His claim under article 9 failed. In *Kjeldsen, Busk Madsen and Pedersen v Denmark* (1976) 1 EHRR 711, paras 54 and 57, parents' philosophical and religious objections to sex education in state schools was rejected on the ground that they could send their children to state schools or educate them at home. The applicant's article 9 claim in *Ahmad's* case, paras 13, 14 and 15, failed because he had accepted a contract which did not provide for him to absent himself from his teaching duties to attend prayers, he had not brought his religious requirements to the employer's notice when seeking employment and he was at all times free to seek other employment which would accommodate his religious observance. *Karaduman v Turkey* (1993) 74 DR 93 is a strong case. The applicant was denied a certificate of graduation because a photograph of her without a headscarf was required and she was unwilling for

religious reasons to be photographed without a headscarf. The commission found, at p. 109, no interference with her article 9 right because, at p. 108:

"by choosing to pursue her higher education in a secular university a student submits to those university rules, which may make the freedom of students to manifest their religion subject to restrictions as to place and manner intended to ensure harmonious coexistence between students of different beliefs."

In rejecting the applicant's claim in *Konttinen v Finland* (1996) 87-A DR 68 the commission pointed out, at p. 75, para 1, that he had not been pressured to change his religious views or prevented from manifesting his religion or belief; having found that his working hours conflicted with his religious convictions, he was free to relinquish his post. An application by a child punished for refusing to attend a National Day parade in contravention of her beliefs as a Jehovah's Witness, to which her parents were also party, was similarly unsuccessful in *Valsamis v Greece* (1996) 24 EHRR 294. It was held, para 38, that article 9 did not confer a right to exemption from disciplinary rules which applied generally and in a neutral manner and that there had been no interference with the child's right to freedom to manifest her religion or belief. In *Stedman v United Kingdom* (1997) 23 EHRR CD 168 it was fatal to the applicant's article 9 claim that she was free to resign rather than work on Sundays. The applicant in *Kalaç v Turkey* (1997) 27 EHRR 552, paras 28–29, failed because he had, in choosing a military career, accepted of his own accord a system of military discipline that by its nature implied the possibility of special limitations on certain rights and freedoms, and he had been able to fulfil the ordinary obligations of Muslim belief. In *Jewish Liturgical Association Cha'are Ve Tsedek v France* (2000) 9 BHRC 27, para 81, the applicants' challenge to the regulation of ritual slaughter in France, which did not satisfy their exacting religious standards, was rejected because they could easily obtain supplies of meat, slaughtered in accordance with those standards, from Belgium.

24. This line of authority has been criticised by the Court of Appeal as overly restrictive (*Copsey v WWB Devon Clays Ltd* [2005] ICR 1789, paras 31–39, 44–66), and in *Williamson's* case [2005] 2 AC 246, para 39, the House questioned whether alternative means of accommodating a manifestation of religious belief had, as suggested in the *Jewish Liturgical* case, para 80, to be "impossible" before a claim of interference under article 9 could succeed. But the authorities do in my opinion support the proposition with which I prefaced para 23 of this opinion. Even if it be accepted that the Strasbourg institutions have erred on the side of strictness in rejecting complaints of interference, there remains a coherent and remarkably consistent body of authority which our domestic courts must take into account and which shows that interference is not easily established.

25. . . . . I am of opinion that in this case (unlike *Williamson's* case, at para 41, where a different conclusion was reached) there was no interference with the respondent's right to manifest her belief in practice or observance. I appreciate, however, that my noble and learned friends, Lord Nicholls and Baroness Hale of Richmond, incline to a different opinion. It follows that this is a debatable question, which gives the issue of justification under article 9(2) particular significance.

Justification

26. To be justified under article 9(2) a limitation or interference must be (a) prescribed by law and (b) necessary in a democratic society for a permissible purpose, that is, it must be directed to a legitimate purpose and must be proportionate in scope and effect. It was faintly argued for the respondent that the school's uniform policy was not prescribed by law, but both the judge (para 78) and the Court of Appeal [2005] 1 WLR 3372, paras 61, 83 and 90, held otherwise, and rightly so. The school authorities had statutory authority to lay down rules on uniform, and those rules were very clearly communicated to those affected by them. It was not suggested that the rules were not made for the legitimate purpose of protecting the rights and freedoms of others. So the issue is whether the rules and the school's insistence on them were in all the circumstances proportionate. This raises an important procedural question on the court's approach to proportionality and, depending on the answer to that, a question of substance . . .

29. I am persuaded that the Court of Appeal's approach to this procedural question was mistaken, for three main reasons. First, the purpose of the Human Rights Act 1998 was not to enlarge the rights or remedies of those in the United Kingdom whose Convention rights have been violated but to enable those rights and remedies to be asserted and enforced by the domestic courts of this country and not only by recourse to Strasbourg. This is clearly established by authorities such as *Aston Cantlow and Wilmcote with Billesley Parochial Church Council v Wallbank* [2004] 1 AC 546, paras 6–7, 44 [p. 860]; *R (Greenfield) v Secretary of State for the Home Department* [2005] 1 WLR 673, paras 18–19; and *R (Quark Fishing Ltd) v Secretary of State for Foreign and Commonwealth Affairs* [2005] 3 WLR 837, paras 25, 33, 34, 88 and 92. But the focus at Strasbourg is not and has never been on whether a challenged decision or action is the product of a defective decision-making process, but on whether, in the case under consideration, the applicant's Convention rights have been violated. . . . But the House has been referred to no case in which the Strasbourg court has found a violation of Convention right on the strength of failure by a national authority to follow the sort of reasoning process laid down by the Court of Appeal. This pragmatic approach is fully reflected in the 1998 Act. The unlawfulness proscribed by section 6(1) is acting in a way which is incompatible with a Convention right, not relying on a defective process of reasoning, and action may be brought under section 7(1) only by a person who is a victim of an unlawful act.

30. Secondly, it is clear that the court's approach to an issue of proportionality under the Convention must go beyond that traditionally adopted to judicial review in a domestic setting. The inadequacy of that approach was exposed in *Smith and Grady v United Kingdom* (1999) 29 EHRR 493, para 138 [p. 582], and the new approach required under the 1998 Act was described by Lord Steyn in *R (Daly) v Secretary of State for the Home Department* [2001] 2 AC 532, paras 25–28 [p. 403], in terms which have never to my knowledge been questioned. There is no shift to a merits review, but the intensity of review is greater than was previously appropriate, and greater even than the heightened scrutiny test adopted by the Court of Appeal in *R v Ministry of Defence, Ex p Smith* [1996] QB 517, 554 [p. 579]. The domestic court must now make a value judgment, an evaluation, by reference to the circumstances prevailing at the relevant time: *Wilson v First County Trust Ltd (No 2)* [2004] 1 AC 816, paras 62–67. Proportionality must be judged objectively, by the court: *R (Williamson) v Secretary of State for Education and Employment* [2005] 2 AC 246, para 51 [p. 828] . . .

31. Thirdly, . . . I consider that the Court of Appeal's approach would introduce "a new formalism" and be "a recipe for judicialisation on an unprecedented scale". The Court of Appeal's decision-making prescription would be admirable guidance to a lower court or legal tribunal, but cannot be required of a head teacher and governors, even with a solicitor to help them. If, in such a case, it appears that such a body has conscientiously paid attention to all human rights considerations, no doubt a challenger's task will be the harder. But what matters in any case is the practical outcome, not the quality of the decision-making process that led to it.

. . .

34. On the agreed facts, the school was in my opinion fully justified in acting as it did. It had taken immense pains to devise a uniform policy which respected Muslim beliefs but did so in an inclusive, unthreatening and uncompetitive way. The rules laid down were as far from being mindless as uniform rules could ever be. The school had enjoyed a period of harmony and success to which the uniform policy was thought to contribute. On further enquiry it still appeared that the rules were acceptable to mainstream Muslim opinion. It was feared that acceding to the respondent's request would or might have significant adverse repercussions. It would in my opinion be irresponsible of any court, lacking the experience, background and detailed knowledge of the head teacher, staff and governors, to overrule their judgment on a matter as sensitive as this. The power of decision has been given to them for the compelling reason that they are best placed to exercise it, and I see no reason to disturb their decision . . .

Article 2 of the First Protocol

36. The question is whether, between 3 September 2002 and the date, some two years later, of the respondent's admission to another school, the appellants denied her access to the general level of educational provision available in this country. In my opinion they did not. A two-year interruption in the education of any child must always be a subject for profound regret. But it was the result of the respondent's unwillingness to comply with a rule to which, as I have concluded, the school were entitled to adhere, and, since her religious convictions forbade compliance, of her failure to secure prompt admission to another school where her religious convictions could be accommodated.'

Lord Nicholls

'41. . . . Your Lordships would allow this appeal. So would I. Your Lordships' reasons are twofold: (1) the school's refusal to allow Shabina Begum to wear a jilbab at school did not interfere with her article 9 right to manifest her religion and, even if it did, (2) the school's decision was objectively justified. I agree with the second reason. I am not so sure about the first. I think this may over-estimate the ease with which Shabina could move to another, more suitable school and under-estimate the disruption this would be likely to cause to her education. I would prefer that in this type of case the school is called upon to explain and justify its decision, as did the Denbigh High School in the present case.'

Lord Hoffmann

'50. I accept that wearing a jilbab to a mixed school was, for her, a manifestation of her religion. The fact that most other Muslims might not have thought it necessary is irrelevant. But her right was not in my opinion infringed because there was nothing to stop her from going to a school where her religion did not require a jilbab or where she was allowed to wear one. Article 9 does not require that one should be allowed to manifest one's religion at any time and place of one's own choosing . . .

58. Even if there had been an infringement of Shabina's rights under article 9, I would, like the judge, have been of opinion that the infringement was justified under article 9(2). The school was entitled to consider that the rules about uniform were necessary for the protection of the rights and freedoms of others . . .

63. In applying the Convention rights which have been reproduced as part of domestic law by the Human Rights Act 1998, the concept of the margin of appreciation has, as such, no application. It is for the courts of the United Kingdom to decide how the area of judgment allowed by that margin should be distributed between the legislative, executive and judicial branches of government . . .

64. In my opinion a domestic court should accept the decision of Parliament to allow individual schools to make their own decisions about uniforms . . .

68. . . . In domestic judicial review, the court is usually concerned with whether the decision-maker reached his decision in the right way rather than whether he got what the court might think to be the right answer. But article 9 is concerned with substance, not procedure. It confers no right to have a decision made in any particular way. What matters is the result: was the right to manifest a religious belief restricted in a way which is not justified under article 9(2)? The fact that the decision-maker is allowed an area of judgment in imposing requirements which may have the effect of restricting the right does not entitle a court to say that a justifiable and proportionate restriction should be struck down because the decision-maker did not approach the question in the structured way in which a judge might have done. Head teachers and governors cannot be expected to make such decisions with textbooks on human rights law at their elbows. The most that can be said is that the way in which the school approached the problem may help to persuade a judge that its answer fell within the area of judgment accorded to it by the law.'

Baroness Hale

'92. I too agree that this appeal should be allowed. Most of your Lordships take the view that Shabina Begum's right to manifest her religion was not infringed because she had chosen to attend this school knowing full well what the school uniform was. It was she who had changed her mind about what her religion required of her, rather than the school which had changed its policy. I am uneasy about this. The reality is that the choice of secondary school is usually made by parents or guardians rather than by the child herself. The child is on the brink of, but has not yet reached, adolescence. She may have views but they are unlikely to be decisive. More importantly, she has not yet reached the critical stage in her development where this particular choice may matter to her.

93. . . . I am therefore inclined to agree with my noble and learned friend, Lord Nicholls of Birkenhead, that there was an interference with Shabina Begum's right to manifest her religion.

94. However, I am in no doubt that that interference was justified. It had the legitimate aim of protecting the rights and freedoms of others. The question is whether it was proportionate to that aim. This is a more difficult and delicate question in this case than it would be in the case of many similar manifestations of religious belief. If a Sikh man wears a turban or a Jewish man a yamoulka, we can readily assume that it was his free choice to adopt the dress dictated by the teachings of his religion. I would make the same assumption about an adult Muslim woman who chooses to wear the Islamic headscarf . . .

98. . . . Social cohesion is promoted by the uniform elements of shirt, tie and jumper, and the requirement that all outer garments be in the school colour. But cultural and religious diversity is respected by allowing girls to wear either a skirt, trousers, or the shalwar kameez, and by allowing those who wished to do so to wear the hijab. This was indeed a thoughtful and proportionate response to reconciling the complexities of the situation. This is demonstrated by the fact that girls have subsequently expressed their concern that if the jilbab were to be allowed they would face pressure to adopt it even though they do not wish to do so . . .'

Since the enactment of the HRA, there have been several other important cases in the field of education law. These have been concerned with the use of corporal punishment and a challenge to a disciplinary exclusion from school.

R (Williamson and others) v Secretary of State for Education and Employment [2005] 2 AC 246

The claimants were either teachers or parents who sent their children to independent private schools which sought to provide a Christian education based on biblical observance. As part of the disciplinary regime at the schools, a mild form of corporal punishment was employed. The claimants contended that it was a fundamental part of their Christian beliefs that discipline should be administered in this way. They therefore argued that section 548 of the Education Act 1996, which sought to prohibit the use of corporal punishment by teachers in both independent and state schools, interfered with: their freedom to manifest their religion or beliefs contrary to article 9(1) of the ECHR; their right to education in conformity with their religious convictions, contrary to article 2 of the First Protocol to the ECHR; and their right to respect for family life, contrary to article 8 of the ECHR. At first instance, their claim was dismissed,[182] and a subsequent appeal to the Court of Appeal was also dismissed.[183] The claimants therefore appealed to the House of Lords. It also held that the appeal should be dismissed, but for different reasons to those of the Court of Appeal.

Lord Nicholls

'2. My Lords, corporal punishment of children is a controversial subject. It arouses strong feelings, both for and against. In this country there is now a total ban on the use of corporal punishment in all schools. The claimants in these proceedings contend this ban is incompatible with their Convention rights under the Human Rights Act 1998.

---

[182] [2001] EWHC 960 (Admin); [2002] 1 FLR 493.   [183] [2003] QB 1300.

3. The present state of the law has developed in stages over the last 20 years. In the 1970s two mothers, Mrs Campbell from Strathclyde and Mrs Cosans from Fife, objected to their children being subjected to corporal punishment in state schools. Their complaint to the European Court of Human Rights was upheld. The state had failed to respect their "philosophical convictions" on this subject, contrary to article 2 of the First Protocol to the European Convention on Human Rights: *Campbell and Cosans v United Kingdom* (1982) 4 EHRR 293. That was in 1982. Parliament then changed the law, by the Education (No 2) Act 1986, section 47. Since 1987 school teachers in maintained schools (state schools) have had no right to administer corporal punishment to school pupils. This ban applied also to children attending non-maintained schools (independent schools) who received public funding, for instance, under the assisted places scheme.

4. In 1993, in response to the decision of the European Court of Human Rights in *Costello-Roberts v United Kingdom* (1993) 19 EHRR 112, Parliament intervened again. This time the intervention was aimed at the severity with which corporal punishment could be administered at school to children outside the scope of the 1986 Act, that is, privately-funded children at independent schools. Article 3 of the European Convention imposes on states a positive obligation to take steps to ensure individuals are not subjected to inhuman or degrading punishment. The steps taken by the state should provide effective protection, in particular, for children and other vulnerable individuals: *Z v United Kingdom* (2001) 34 EHRR 97, 131, para 73. In order to comply with this obligation Parliament enacted that corporal punishment of children could not be justified if it was "inhuman or degrading": section 293 of the Education Act 1993. In deciding whether punishment is inhuman or degrading regard should be had to all the circumstances, including the reason for giving the corporal punishment, how soon after the event it was given, its nature, the manner and circumstances in which it was given, the persons involved, and its mental and physical effects.

5. The next stage in the development of the law was the extension of the ban on the use of corporal punishment to all pupils attending all types of school. That was in 1998. So now the ban applies to privately-funded children attending independent schools. It is this extension of the ban which is under challenge in these proceedings. Unlike Mrs Campbell and Mrs Cosans, the claimants in the present proceedings do not object to the use of corporal punishment. Quite the contrary: they support the use of corporal punishment and object to the statutory ban. So the present case raises the converse of the issue raised in the *Campbell and Cosans* case.

Section 548 of the Education Act 1996

11. The statutory provision under challenge is section 548(1) of the Education Act 1996, as amended by the School Standards and Framework Act 1998. The first issue in these proceedings concerns the proper interpretation of this provision. Section 548(1) provides:

> "Corporal punishment given by, or on the authority of, a member of staff to a child—(a) for whom education is provided at any school . . . cannot be justified in any proceedings on the ground that it was given in pursuance of a right exercisable by the member of staff by virtue of his position as such."

Corporal punishment means punishment which, justification apart, constitutes battery: section 548(4). Member of staff includes a teacher at the school in control or charge of the child: section 548(6). Child means a person under the age of 18: section 548(7).

12. The claimants contend this statutory provision does not apply where parents, having the common law right to discipline their child, expressly delegate this right to a teacher. Then the teacher is exercising an expressly delegated power, not acting as a teacher "as such". This interpretation of section 548 would, it is said, accord proper respect to the deliberate decision of parents in respect of the education and disciplining of their children.

13. I consider this interpretation of section 548 is not tenable. It is unnecessary to consider the origins of a teacher's disciplinary powers in relation to school pupils or the extent to which a parent's disciplinary powers are expressly delegable. Suffice to say, the plain purpose of section 548(1) was to

prohibit the use of corporal punishment by all teachers in all schools. The claimants' interpretation, if right, would defeat this purpose. The claimants' interpretation would mean the ban on the use of corporal punishment by teachers could be sidestepped by parents expressly giving their consent to the infliction of corporal punishment on their child. Thus the ban would not be mandatory in its operation. It would be optional, at the choice of the parents.

14. In my view the phrase "by virtue of his position as such" in section 548(1)(a) is apt to limit the application of section 548(1) to corporal punishment given by a teacher while acting as a teacher, that is, while discharging his functions as a teacher. It excludes cases where, for example, a teacher is himself a parent and is acting in that capacity when punishing a child. Read in context, this phrase is not apt to draw a distinction between cases where the teacher has been expressly authorised by the parents and cases where he has not. In the former case as much as the latter administration of corporal punishment by a teacher derives from a right exercisable by him by virtue of his position as a teacher within the meaning of section 548.

. . .

Freedom of belief and the Convention rights

16. . . . This freedom is not confined to freedom to hold a religious belief. It includes the right to express and practise one's beliefs. Without this, freedom of religion would be emasculated. Invariably religious faiths call for more than belief. To a greater or lesser extent adherents are required or encouraged to act in certain ways, most obviously and directly in forms of communal or personal worship, supplication and meditation. But under article 9 there is a difference between freedom to hold a belief and freedom to express or "manifest" a belief. The former right, freedom of belief, is absolute. The latter right, freedom to manifest belief, is qualified.

17. This is to be expected, because the way a belief is expressed in practice may impact on others. Familiar instances of conduct shaped by particular religious beliefs are the days or times when worship is prescribed or encouraged, the need to abstain from work on certain days, forms of dress, rituals connected with the preparation of food, the need for total abstinence from certain types of food or drink, and the need for abstinence from all or some types of food at certain times. In a more generalised and non-specific form the tenets of a religion may affect the entirety of a believer's way of life: for example, "thou shalt love thy neighbour as thyself". The manner in which children should be brought up is another subject on which religious teachings are not silent. So in a pluralist society a balance has to be held between freedom to practise one's own beliefs and the interests of others affected by those practices . . .

The claimants' beliefs

22. It is necessary first to clarify the court's role in identifying a religious belief calling for protection under article 9. When the genuineness of a claimant's professed belief is an issue in the proceedings the court will inquire into and decide this issue as a question of fact. This is a limited inquiry. The court is concerned to ensure an assertion of religious belief is made in good faith . . . But, emphatically, it is not for the court to embark on an inquiry into the asserted belief and judge its "validity" by some objective standard such as the source material upon which the claimant founds his belief or the orthodox teaching of the religion in question or the extent to which the claimant's belief conforms to or differs from the views of others professing the same religion. Freedom of religion protects the subjective belief of an individual. . . . Each individual is at liberty to hold his own religious beliefs, however irrational or inconsistent they may seem to some, however surprising.

23. Everyone, therefore, is entitled to hold whatever beliefs he wishes. But when questions of "manifestation" arise, as they usually do in this type of case, a belief must satisfy some modest, objective minimum requirements. These threshold requirements are implicit in article 9 of the European Convention and comparable guarantees in other human rights instruments. The belief must be consistent with basic standards of human dignity or integrity. Manifestation of a religious belief, for instance, which involved subjecting others to torture or inhuman punishment would not qualify for protection.

The belief must relate to matters more than merely trivial. It must possess an adequate degree of seriousness and importance. As has been said, it must be a belief on a fundamental problem. With religious belief this requisite is readily satisfied. The belief must also be coherent in the sense of being intelligible and capable of being understood.

24. This leaves on one side the difficult question of the criteria to be applied in deciding whether a belief is to be characterised as religious. This question will seldom, if ever, arise under the European Convention. It does not arise in the present case. In the present case it does not matter whether the claimants' beliefs regarding the corporal punishment of children are categorised as religious. Article 9 embraces freedom of thought, conscience and religion. The atheist, the agnostic, and the sceptic are as much entitled to freedom to hold and manifest their beliefs as the theist. These beliefs are placed on an equal footing for the purpose of this guaranteed freedom. Thus, if its manifestation is to attract protection under article 9 a non-religious belief, as much as a religious belief, must satisfy the modest threshold requirements implicit in this article. In particular, for its manifestation to be protected by article 9 a non-religious belief must relate to an aspect of human life or behaviour of comparable importance to that normally found with religious beliefs. Article 9 is apt, therefore, to include a belief such as pacifism: *Arrowsmith v United Kingdom* (1978) 3 EHRR 218. The position is much the same with regard to the respect guaranteed to a parent's "religious and philosophical convictions" under article 2 of the First Protocol: see *Campbell and Cosans v United Kingdom* (1982) 4 EHRR 293.

. . .

27. . . . Corporal punishment, even corporal punishment administered by teachers at school, can be administered in widely differing circumstances, in widely differing ways and with widely differing degrees of severity. Not surprisingly, in the *Costello-Roberts* case the European Court of Human Rights confirmed that not every act of corporal punishment of a child at school violates article 3 or article 8, even though to some extent it may adversely affect a child's physical and moral integrity. Not every act of corporal punishment will adversely affect a child's physical and moral integrity to an extent sufficient to constitute a violation of those articles. This being so, it is difficult to see how all corporal punishment of children, however mildly administered, is of its nature so contrary to a child's integrity that a belief in its infliction is necessarily excluded from the protection of article 9. It is difficult to see how corporal punishment, administered in circumstances and in a way which does not violate articles 3 or 8, can at the same time be so contrary to personal integrity that belief in its administration is ipso facto excluded from the scope of article 9.

Manifesting the claimant's beliefs in practice

. . .

35. In the present case the essence of the parents' beliefs is that, as part of their proper upbringing, when necessary children should be disciplined in a particular way at home and at school. It follows that when parents administer corporal punishment to their children in accordance with these beliefs they are manifesting these beliefs. Similarly, they are manifesting their beliefs when they authorise a child's school to administer corporal punishment. Or, put more broadly, the claimant parents manifest their beliefs on corporal punishment when they place their children in a school where corporal punishment is practised. Article 9 is therefore engaged in the present case in respect of the claimant parents.

36. Similarly, and contrary to the Secretary of State's submissions, the claimant parents' rights under article 2 of the First Protocol are also engaged in this case. "Education" in this article is wide enough to include the manner in which discipline is maintained in a school.

37. Thus far under this head I have been considering the position of the claimant parents. I turn to the position of the claimant teachers. The right protected by the second sentence of article 2 of the First Protocol is, expressly, a right of the parents, not the teachers. Thus the claimant teachers have no claim under this article. As to article 9, the teachers' beliefs in this case are ancillary to those of the parents, in that their beliefs concern the role of schools in furthering the parents' obligations in respect of the upbringing of their children. The teachers do not assert a belief in the administration of corporal

punishment irrespective of the wishes of the parents. They do not assert a belief to be obliged to administer corporal punishment separate from, or independently of, the parental obligations in this regard. So the teachers' beliefs do not call for separate consideration from those of the parents. The beliefs of the parents and the teachers stand or fall together under article 9.

Interference

38. The next step is to consider whether section 548 constitutes an interference with the claimant parents' manifestation of their beliefs. What constitutes interference depends on all the circumstances of the case, including the extent to which in the circumstances an individual can reasonably expect to be at liberty to manifest his beliefs in practice . . .

40. In the present case the Secretary of State contended that section 548 did not interfere materially with the claimant parents' manifestation of their beliefs. He submitted that section 548 left open to the parents several adequate, alternative courses of action: the parents could attend school on request and themselves administer the corporal punishment to the child; or the parents could administer the desired corporal punishment when the child comes home after school; or, if the need for immediate punishment is part of the claimants' beliefs, they could educate their children at home.

41. I cannot accept these suggested alternatives would be adequate. That a parent should make himself available on call to attend school to administer corporal punishment should his child be guilty of indiscipline deserving of such punishment strikes me as unrealistic for many parents. Parental administration of corporal punishment at home at the end of the day would be significantly different from immediate teacher administration of corporal punishment at school. As to home education, there is no reason to suppose that in general the claimant parents, or other parents with like beliefs, have the personal skills needed to educate their children at home or the financial means needed to employ home tutors. I consider section 548 does interfere materially with the claimant parents' rights under article 9 and article 2 of the First Protocol.

"Justification"

42. The final step is to consider whether this interference is justified. In the case of article 9 the issue is whether the Secretary of State can show that section 548 satisfies the requirements of article 9(2) . . .

48. . . . . The interference with the manifestation of the claimants' beliefs effected by section 548 readily meets the criterion that it must be prescribed by law. The ban has been prescribed by primary legislation in clear terms.

49. Equally I am in no doubt this interference is, within the meaning of article 9, "necessary in a democratic society . . . for the protection of the rights and freedoms of others". The statutory ban pursues a legitimate aim: children are vulnerable, and the aim of the legislation is to protect them and promote their wellbeing. Corporal punishment involves deliberately inflicting physical violence. The legislation is intended to protect children against the distress, pain and other harmful effects this infliction of physical violence may cause. That corporal punishment may have these harmful effects is self-evident.

50. Further, the means chosen to achieve this aim are appropriate and not disproportionate in their adverse impact on parents who believe that carefully-controlled administration of corporal punishment to a mild degree can be beneficial, for this reason: the legislature was entitled to take the view that, overall and balancing the conflicting considerations, all corporal punishment of children at school is undesirable and unnecessary and that other, non-violent means of discipline are available and preferable. On this Parliament was entitled, if it saw fit, to lead and guide public opinion. Parliament was further entitled to take the view that a universal ban was the appropriate way to achieve the desired end. Parliament was entitled to decide that, contrary to the claimants' submissions, a universal ban is preferable to a selective ban which exempts schools where the parents or teachers have an ideological belief in the efficacy and desirability of a mild degree of carefully controlled corporal punishment.

51. Parliament was entitled to take this course because this issue is one of broad social policy. As such it is pre-eminently well suited for decision by Parliament. The legislature is to be accorded a

considerable degree of latitude in deciding which course should be selected as the best course in the interests of school children as a whole . . .

52. For these reasons I am satisfied section 548 does not violate the rights of the claimants, either parents or teachers, under article 9. For the same reasons there has been no violation of the claimant parents' rights under article 2 of the First Protocol. . . . The present case cannot be regarded as comparable to *Campbell and Cosans v United Kingdom* . . . In the present case, unlike in the *Campbell* case, the claimants' beliefs involve inflicting physical violence on children in an institutional setting. Parliament was bound to respect the claimants' beliefs in this regard, but was entitled to decide that manifestation of these beliefs in practice was not in the best interests of children. I would dismiss this appeal.'

Lord Walker

'55. There are two reasons why it is unnecessary for the House to grapple with the definition of religion. One is that article 9 protects, not just the forum internum of religious belief, but "freedom of thought, conscience and religion". This is coupled with the individual's (qualified) freedom "to manifest his religion or belief, in worship, teaching, practice and observance". Similarly article 2 of the First Protocol refers not just to religious beliefs but to "religious and philosophical convictions". Plainly these expressions cover a wider field than even the most expansive notion of religion. Pacifism, vegetarianism and total abstinence from alcohol are uncontroversial examples of beliefs which would fall within article 9 (of course pacifism or any comparable belief may be based on religious convictions, but equally it may be based on ethical convictions which are not religious but humanist) . . . It is to be noted that section 13 of the Human Rights Act 1998 is more restricted, referring to the exercise of article 9 rights "by a religious organisation (itself or its members collectively)". But little reliance was placed, in argument, on section 13.

56. The other reason why the House need not grapple with the problem of definition is that it is not in dispute that Christianity is a religion, and that the appellants are sincere, practising Christians . . .

57. . . . Later in this opinion I shall suggest that it may be unwise to take a rigidly analytical approach to the application of article 9. But assuming for the moment that the issue is to be analysed in terms of (i) the existence of a belief, (ii) its manifestation, (iii) interference with the manifested belief and (iv) justification of the interference, I doubt whether it is right for the court . . . to impose an evaluative filter at the first stage, especially when religious beliefs are involved. For the court to adjudicate on the seriousness, cogency and coherence of theological beliefs is . . . to take the court beyond its legitimate role . . . Only in clear and extreme cases can a claim to religious belief be disregarded entirely, as in *X v United Kingdom* (1977) 11 DR 55 (no evidence of the existence of the "Wicca" religion).

58. A filter is certainly needed, because it is quite clear (as Mason ACJ and Brennan J put it crisply in the *Church of the New Faith* case (1983) 154 CLR 120, 136) that "Religious conviction is not a solvent of legal obligation". In my opinion the filters are to be found (first) in the concept of manifestation of religion or belief and (second) in article 9(2), which qualifies an individual's freedom to manifest his religion or beliefs (in the four ways mentioned in article 9(1), worship, teaching, practice and observance) . . .

62. The first necessary filter, I suggest, in order to prevent article 9 becoming unmanageably diffuse and unpredictable in its operation, is the notion of manifestation of a belief. Although freedom of thought and conscience is "also a precious asset for atheists, agnostics, sceptics and the unconcerned" (*Kokkinakis v Greece* (1993) 17 EHRR 397, 418, para 31), the notion of manifesting a belief is particularly appropriate to the area of religious belief. Most religions require or encourage communal acts of worship of various sorts, preaching, public professions of faith and practices and observances of various sorts (including habits of dress and diet). There will usually be a central core of required belief and observance and relatively peripheral matters observed by only the most devout. These can all be called manifestations of a religious belief. By contrast the manifestation or promotion of secular beliefs (or "causes") tends to be focused on articles 10 and 11, although reliance may be placed on article 9 also.

63. It is clear that not every act which is in some way motivated or inspired by religious belief is to be regarded as the manifestation of religious belief . . .

65. The second filter is article 9(2) . . .

66. . . . At the beginning of his oral submissions Mr Dingemans [counsel for the claimants] . . . - suggested that the Strasbourg jurisprudence on article 9 lacks a principled and consistent approach. I would not give much weight to that criticism. This is an area in which a rigidly analytical approach, dividing the case into watertight issues, to be decided seriatim, may not always be the best way forward. The court may conclude that a claimant has a sincere opinion which could just about be described as a religious belief, and that the claimant's conduct in accordance with that belief could just about be described as a manifestation of it. But the fact that the claimant may have only just scraped over those two thresholds should not be disregarded in determining the issue of interference or in the exercise of balancing interests and testing proportionality which is required under article 9(2) if (perhaps by giving the claimant the benefit of the doubt) the court gets that far.

. . .

69. I would give the appellants the benefit of the doubt in getting to article 9(2), but for the reasons given by Lord Nicholls and Baroness Hale they must fail at that stage. Nor does article 2 of the First Protocol assist them, since it is aimed at preventing state indoctrination, and must be applied in conformity with other articles of the Convention . . .'

Baroness Hale

'74. The practice of corporal punishment involves what would otherwise be an assault upon another person. The essential question, therefore, has always been whether the legislation achieves a fair balance between the rights and freedoms of the parents and teachers and the rights, freedoms and interests, not only of their children, but also of any other children who might be affected by the persistence of corporal punishment in some schools. The mechanism for achieving that balance lies in article 9(2) . . .

78. . . . I am prepared to accept that the practice of corporal punishment in these schools is a manifestation of the parents' and teachers' beliefs: a belief that as a last resort children may need physical correction as part of their education can only be manifested by correcting them in that way. I find it difficult to understand how a ban on that practice is anything other than a limitation of the right to manifest that belief: the belief in question is not only a belief that parents should be able to punish their children but that such punishment is an essential part of the sort of Christian education in which these parents and teachers believe. I am deeply troubled by the solution adopted in the Court of Appeal, which depended upon the parents' continued right to punish the children themselves. The real question is whether any limits set by the state can be justified under article 9(2).

79. Those limits must fulfil the three well-known criteria: (1) they must be prescribed by law, as this undoubtedly is; (2) they must pursue a legitimate aim; and (3) they must be necessary in a democratic society: the "notion of necessity implies that the interference corresponds to a pressing social need and, in particular, that it is proportionate to the legitimate aim pursued": see, for example, *Pretty v United Kingdom* (2002) 35 EHRR 1, 38, para 70.

80. There can be no doubt that the ban on corporal punishment in schools pursues the legitimate aim of protecting the rights and freedoms of children. It has long been held that these are not limited to their rights under the European Convention. The appellants were anxious to stress that the corporal punishment in which they believe would not breach the child's rights under either article 3 or article 8. But it can still be legitimate for the state to prohibit it for the sake of the child. A child has the same right as anyone else not to be assaulted; the defence of lawful chastisement is an exception to that right . . . . Even if it could be shown that a particular act of corporal punishment was in the interests of the individual child, it is clear that a universal or blanket ban may be justified to protect a vulnerable class: see *Pretty v United Kingdom*, para 74 . . .

86. With such an array of international and professional support, it is quite impossible to say that Parliament was not entitled to limit the practice of corporal punishment in all schools in order to protect the rights and freedoms of all children. Furthermore, the state has a positive obligation to protect children from inhuman or degrading punishment which violates their rights under article 3. But prohibiting only such punishment as would violate their rights under article 3 (or possibly article 8) would bring difficult problems of definition, demarcation and enforcement. . . . The appellants' solution is that they and other schools which share their views should be exempted from the ban. But this would raise exactly the same problems. How could it be justified in terms of the rights and protection of the child to allow some schools to inflict corporal punishment while prohibiting the rest from doing so? If a child has a right to be brought up without institutional violence, as he does, that right should be respected whether or not his parents and teachers believe otherwise.'

A v Head Teacher and Governors of Lord Grey School [2006] 2 WLR 690

The claimant had been excluded from school following a fire in a classroom which was under investigation by the police. He was subsequently charged with arson, although it was later decided to discontinue any criminal proceedings against him. The claimant was without schooling from March 2001 to January 2002. Up until June 2001 he was given self-assessed work to complete. On the cessation of the 45 days' temporary exclusion period as permitted by section 64(2) of the School Standards and Framework Act 1998, the claimant and his parents were invited to attend a meeting at the school to discuss his reintegration. They failed to attend and accordingly, the Head Teacher wrote to the family informing them that the claimant's name would be removed from the school roll. This occurred in October 2001. Subsequently the claimant's parents declined an offer made to them by the local authority to provide alternative education through its pupil referral unit. Eventually the claimant started at a new school in January 2002.

The claimant sought damages under sections 6 and 8 of the Human Rights Act 1998 for breach of the right to education under article 3 of the First Protocol to the ECHR. At first instance his claim failed because although his exclusion from March to July 2001 was found to be unlawful, it was nevertheless held to be sensible and reasonable and hence did not involve a breach of article 2.[184] On appeal, the Court of Appeal held that although the defendants were not liable for the period of exclusion until June 2001, they were liable for damages for the period after that, since his exclusion had by then become unlawful.[185] The defendants appealed to the House of Lords which held unanimously that the appeal be allowed (Baroness Hale for different reasons to those of the other Law Lords).

Lord Bingham

'Article 2 of the First Protocol

10. . . . The article was adopted after some years of debate, during which some states, including the United Kingdom, resisted the imposition of a positive obligation. Clayton and Tomlinson . . . attribute the relative paucity of Strasbourg authority on the right to education to its limited scope.

11. The leading Strasbourg authority on the content of the article remains the *Belgian Linguistic Case (No 2)* (1968) 1 EHRR 252. The case arose from the wish of French-speaking Belgian parents that their children should be taught in French, and the facts are in no way analogous with those here. But the court explored the meaning of the article in terms that remain highly pertinent . . .

"3 . . . To determine the scope of the 'right to education', within the meaning of the first sentence of article 2 of the Protocol, the court must bear in mind the aim of this provision. It notes in this context that all member states of the Council of Europe possessed, at the time of the opening of the Protocol

---

[184] [2003] 4 All ER 1317.   [185] [2004] QB 1231.

to their signature, and still do possess, a general and official educational system. There neither was, nor is now, therefore, any question of requiring each state to establish such a system, but merely of guaranteeing to persons subject to the jurisdiction of the contracting parties the right, in principle, to avail themselves of the means of instruction existing at a given time. The Convention lays down no specific obligations concerning the extent of these means and the manner of their organisation or subsidisation. In particular, the first sentence of article 2 does not specify the language in which education must be conducted in order that the right to education should be respected. It does not contain precise provisions similar to those which appear in articles 5(2) and 6(3)(a) and (e). However, the right to education would be meaningless if it did not imply, in favour of its beneficiaries, the right to be educated in the national language or in one of the national languages, as the case may be.

4. The first sentence of article 2 of the Protocol consequently guarantees, in the first place, a right of access to educational institutions existing at a given time, but such access constitutes only a part of the right to education. For the 'right to education' to be effective, it is further necessary that, inter alia, the individual who is the beneficiary should have the possibility of drawing profit from the education received, that is to say, the right to obtain, in conformity with the rules in force in each state, and in one form or another, official recognition of the studies which he has completed. . . .

5. The right to education guaranteed by the first sentence of article 2 of the Protocol by its very nature calls for regulation by the state, regulation which may vary in time and place according to the needs and resources of the community and of individuals. It goes without saying that such regulation must never injure the substance if the right to education nor conflict with other rights enshrined in the Convention . . ."

12. The court's judgment in the *Belgian Linguistic Case (No 2)* has been cited and relied on in a number of later decisions such as *Kjeldsen, Busk Madsen and Pedersen v Denmark* (1976) 1 EHRR 711, *Campbell and Cosans v UK* (1982) 4 EHRR 293, *Sahin v Turkey* (Application No 44774/98), (unreported) 10 November 2005, Grand Chamber, and *Timishev v Russia* (Application Nos 55762/00 and 55974/00) (unreported) 13 December 2005. In later decisions the reasoning in that case has been followed but elaborated. It has been held that article 2 is dominated by its first sentence (*Kjeldsen*, para 52; *Campbell and Cosans*, para 40) but the article must be read as a whole (*Kjelsden*, para 52), and given the indispensable and fundamental role of education in a democratic society a restrictive interpretation of the first sentence would not be consistent with the aim or purpose of that provision: *Sahin*, para 137; *Timishev*, para 64. But the right to education is not absolute (*Sahin*, para 154): it is subject to regulation by the state, but that regulation must not impair the essence of the right or deprive it of effectiveness: *Campbell and Cosans*, para 41; *Sahin*, para 154. It is not contrary to article 2 for pupils to be suspended or expelled, provided that national regulations do not prevent them enrolling in another establishment to pursue their studies (*Yanasik v Turkey* (1993) 74 DR 14), but even this qualification is not absolute: *Sulak v Turkey* (1996) 84-A DR 98. The imposition of disciplinary penalties is an integral part of the process whereby a school seeks to achieve the object for which it was established, including the development and moulding of the character and mental powers of its pupils: *Sahin*, para 156.

13. In *Coster v UK* (2001) 33 EHRR 479, para 135, Her Majesty's Government submitted that article 2 did not confer a right to be educated at a particular school. The court did not expressly accept or reject that submission. Such an interpretation was, however, adopted by the Court of Appeal in *S, T and P v Brent London Borough Council* [2002] ELR 556, para 9 . . .

21. For the purposes of this appeal I am content to accept the proposition, accepted by both courts below and agreed between counsel, that the school excluded the respondent in breach of domestic law from 8 March onwards. But I must register some unease at this conclusion.[186] The immense damage done to the vulnerable children by indefinite, unnecessary or improperly-motivated

---

[186] Lord Scott was prepared to go so far as to express the opinion that the decision of the lower courts had been wrong on this point. In his judgment, the exclusion of A was 'at no stage unlawful under domestic law': at [70]. Baroness Hale, however, could not agree that the school had behaved reasonably towards A: at [78].

exclusions from state schools is well-known, and none could doubt the need for tight control of the exercise of this important power. But the School Standards and Framework Act 1998 and the guidance issued under it seem to me singularly inapt to regulate the problem which confronted the school in this case and which must confront other schools in comparable cases . . .

24. The Strasbourg jurisprudence, summarised above . . . makes clear how article 2 should be interpreted. The underlying premise of the article was that all existing member states of the Council of Europe had, and all future member states would have, an established system of state education. It was intended to guarantee fair and non-discriminatory access to that system by those within the jurisdiction of the respective states. The fundamental importance of education in a modern democratic state was recognised to require no less. But the guarantee is, in comparison with most other Convention guarantees, a weak one, and deliberately so. There is no right to education of a particular kind or quality, other than that prevailing in the state. There is no Convention guarantee of compliance with domestic law. There is no Convention guarantee of education at or by a particular institution. There is no Convention objection to the expulsion of a pupil from an educational institution on disciplinary grounds, unless (in the ordinary way) there is no alternative source of state education open to the pupil (as in *Eren v Turkey* (Application No 60856/00) (unreported) 7 February 2006). The test, as always under the Convention, is a highly pragmatic one, to be applied to the specific facts of the case: have the authorities of the state acted so as to deny to a pupil effective access to such educational facilities as the state provides for such pupils? In this case, attention must be focused on the school, as the only public authority the respondent sued, and (for reasons already given) on the period from 7 June 2001 to 20 January 2002.

25. The question, therefore, is whether between those dates the school denied the respondent effective access to such educational facilities as this country provides. In my opinion, the facts compel the conclusion that it did not. It invited the respondent's parents to collect work, which they did not. It referred the respondent to the LEA's access panel, which referred him to the pupil referral unit, an education provider; the pupil referral unit's offer of tuition was declined. The school arranged a meeting to discuss the respondent's re-admission, which the respondent's family chose not to attend. The head teacher's reaction to this non-attendance was criticised in the courts below as over-hasty. Perhaps so. But I am not altogether surprised that she treated this unjustified non-attendance as a repudiation by the family of the pupil–school relationship. She again gave the parents contact details at the pupil referral unit. The LEA's attempts during the autumn to secure the respondent's readmission to the school or admission to another school were thwarted by the family's uncertainty what they wanted. As soon as they made up their minds, a place (although not at the school) was promptly found. The retention of the respondent's name on the roll of the school in July, and its removal in October, although much relied on in argument, were events unknown to the respondent and his family at the time, and had no causal effect or legal consequence. It is a matter for regret when any pupil, not least an able pupil like the respondent, loses months of schooling. But that is not a result which can, in this case, be laid at the door of the school.'

Lord Hoffmann

'57. Except in cases in which the applicant has been wholly excluded from some sector of the domestic educational system, the European Court's jurisprudence on article 2 of the First Protocol has never shown any interest in the procedures by which the applicant was denied entry to or expelled from a particular educational establishment. Such procedures may be relevant to rights under other articles, such as article 6 or 14, but article 2 of the First Protocol is concerned only with results: was the applicant denied the basic minimum of education available under the domestic system? For this purpose it is necessary to look at the domestic system as a whole. Thus in *Yasanik v Turkey* (1993) 74 DR 14, where the applicant had been expelled from a military academy, the commission said that there was no denial of the right to education because the Turkish education system also included civilian establishments in which he could enrol.

58. I think that by parity of reasoning, the availability of teaching at the pupil referral unit meant that the respondent had not been denied the right to education. As the necessary minimum of education was available, the Strasbourg court would not in my opinion concern itself with whether the fact that the respondent was obliged to attend the pupil referral unit rather than The Lord Grey School was in accordance with domestic law or not. I think that Stanley Burnton J summarized the European jurisprudence accurately when he said, in the passage which I have quoted in para 50 above, that if suitable and adequate alternative arrangements are available but the pupil's parents decide that the child should not use them, neither the school nor the LEA will have acted inconsistently with the child's rights under article 2 of the First Protocol, and [2003] 4 All ER 1337, para 84, that "this is the position whether or not the expulsion from the school is lawful under domestic law."

59. I do not think that *Timishev v Russia* (Application Nos 55762/00 and 55974/00) (unreported) 13 December 2005, upon which Miss Booth for the respondent relied, and *Eren v Turkey* (Application No 60856/00) (unreported) 7 February 2006, which was drawn to the attention of the House after the conclusion of the argument, support a contrary view. In the *Timishev* case the applicant's children were excluded from school because he was not registered as resident in the area. His appeal to the domestic courts was dismissed, although the Government subsequently conceded that the exclusion was unlawful by Russian law. There was no suggestion that any alternative education had been available. The court said, at para 66:

"the Convention and its Protocols do not tolerate a denial of the right to education. The Government confirmed that Russian law did not allow the exercise of that right by children to be made conditional on the registration of their parents' residence. It follows that the applicant's children were denied the right to education provided by domestic law. Their exclusion from school was therefore incompatible with the requirements of article 2 of Protocol No 1."

60. In my opinion this does not mean that the failure to provide education was a breach of the Convention because it was in breach of domestic law. It was a breach of the Convention because it was a failure to provide education. The court's reference to domestic law was to rebut an argument that such a failure could be justified, in accordance with the *Belgian Linguistic Case (No 2)* 1 EHRR 252, as being part of the Russian domestic educational system. Likewise, in the *Eren* case the applicant was wholly excluded from the Turkish university system on grounds which the European court found to be arbitrary and lacking "a legal and rational basis."

61. In the present case, where the respondent was not excluded from school education, he would in my opinion have had no claim at Strasbourg. And if no claim can be made in Strasbourg, it follows that there cannot have been an infringement of a Convention right giving rise to a claim under section 6 of the Human Rights Act 1998: see *R (Quark Fishing Ltd) v Secretary of State for Foreign and Commonwealth Affairs* [2005] 3 WLR 837. It is in my view illegitimate to promote the public law duty of the school, not giving rise to a private right of action, to a duty under section 6 of the Human Rights Act 1998 remediable by a claim for damages, by saying that in domestic law the school bore the "primary duty to educate the child". The correct approach is first to ask whether there was a denial of a Convention right. In the case of article 2 of the First Protocol, that would have required a systemic failure of the educational system which resulted in the respondent not having access to a minimum level of education. As there was no such failure, that is the end of the matter. It is only if a denial of a Convention right is established that one examines domestic law in order to discover which public authority, if any, is liable under article 6. This is an inquiry which can sometimes give rise to difficult questions of causation and which can make it necessary to ask which public authority bore the primary duty to act in accordance with the Convention. But no such question arises in this case.'

Lord Scott

'65. The paradoxical conclusion that to send the boys home and keep them away from the school until the criminal proceedings were resolved had been unlawful was attributable to the assumption that their exclusion from the school was an exclusion to which sections 64–68 of the School Standards and Framework Act 1998 applied. It was common ground that the school had not complied with the statutory requirements of a section 64 exclusion. But the assumption that the exclusion of the boys from the school was an exclusion to which section 64 applied was, in my opinion, mistaken . . .

68. I am unable to understand on what basis it was thought that the three boys had been kept away from the school "on disciplinary grounds". The head teacher had not concluded, and was not in a position in which she could have concluded, that any of them was responsible for the fire or guilty of any disciplinary offence. Their enforced absence from the school was a management decision. At the time the decision was taken there was nothing for which any of the boys could fairly have been disciplined.

69. . . . The situation that confronted Mrs Telfer on 8 March 2001 and Ms Pavlou shortly thereafter is, in my opinion, another example where sensible and responsible management of a school may require a pupil to be kept temporarily away from the school. It would, in my opinion, be lamentable if, by an application of sections 64–68 to situations to which they could never have been intended to apply, managers of schools found themselves placed in a statutory straitjacket and prevented from taking sensible decisions to deal with unusual situations.'

Baroness Hale

'72. I wish that I found this case as plain as your Lordships have done. Education plays an indispensable and fundamental role in a democratic society: see *Sahin v Turkey* (Application No 44774/98) 10 November 2005, para 137. Without it, children will not grow up to play their part in the adult world, to exercise their rights but also to meet their responsibilities. That is why children must not be denied their right to the education which the state provides for them. On the plain facts of this case, Abdul Hakim Ali was denied the education which ought to have been provided for him under our national educational system from 13 July 2001 until he started at his new school in January 2002. No-one has suggested that this was his fault . . .

79. Section 6(1) of the Human Rights Act 1998 reads simply: "It is unlawful for a public authority to act in a way which is incompatible with a Convention right." The school is undoubtedly a public authority within the meaning of the 1998 Act. The simple question for us, therefore, is whether the school acted in a way which was incompatible with one of Abdul Hakim's Convention rights. The right in question is that contained in the first sentence of article 2 of the First Protocol: "No person shall be denied the right to education." It was not the object of the Protocol to prescribe any particular educational system, syllabus or curriculum. It was premised on the existence of a developed educational system in each of the member states at the time. Its object was, as my noble and learned friend, Lord Bingham of Cornhill, has said, to guarantee fair and non-discriminatory access to the educational system established in the particular member state. But that, it seems to me, is exactly what was denied to Abdul Hakim in this case.

80. Of course, any educational system is entitled to have rules and disciplinary procedures to enforce those rules. Discipline is an integral part of the educational process. But what the school did in this case did not comply with the established system of pupil discipline. The school effectively excluded a pupil when it had no good reason to do so and without affording him any of the procedural protection afforded by the established system . . .

83. This case seems to me to be the paradigm of a case in which it would be just and appropriate to grant to Abdul Hakim a declaration that the school had acted in a way which was incompatible with his right to education, by effectively excluding him permanently from school without a good reason to do so. However, he brought an action for damages, not a declaration. In my view, it is not necessary to make an award of damages to afford him just satisfaction in this case. He is not to be blamed for the failure of his family to take up the various offers which were made, or for the delay in deciding what they wanted to do, and thus in getting him into another school. But, in view of the findings of the judge, it would not be just to make the school pay damages for the consequences. It is not necessary in any event, as Abdul Hakim returned to the school system and has obviously made good use of it.

84. I would therefore allow the appeal but for rather different reasons from those given by your Lordships.'

(i) Counter-terrorism

In chapter 2 we considered the very important decision of the House of Lords in *A v Secretary of State for the Home Department*.[187] It will be remembered that in that case, their Lordships concluded that section 23 of the Anti-terrorism, Crime and Security Act 2001 was incompatible with articles 5 and 14 of the ECHR because it provided for detention without trial for non-UK nationals who were suspected of terrorist activity, whereas UK nationals who were similarly suspected were not subject to the same detention regime. The declaration of incompatibility which their Lordships issued pursuant to section 4 of the HRA caused the government to rethink its position on the detention of such individuals.[188] Although there is nothing in the HRA which compels the amendment or repeal of a provision in primary legislation which has been declared to be incompatible with a Convention right, it would clearly be contrary to the spirit of that Act if the government were to stubbornly refuse to react. Indeed, it has been suggested by one commentator that not accepting the declaration of incompatibility 'would have enhanced the risk of adverse comment by the European Court of Human Rights to which the case would be taken in due course,[189] on the efficacy of a Declaration of Incompatibility as a remedy, thus necessitating consideration of again redrawing the constitutional balance between lawmakers and judiciary over the validity of legislation'.[190]

Ultimately it was decided to introduce a 'control order' regime under the authority of a new piece of legislation, the Prevention of Terrorism Act 2005. However, behind this sparse statement lies an altogether more involved story. Space does not permit a detailed consideration of the full background to the enactment of the 2005 Act,[191] suffice it to say that the Bill endured a troubled passage through Parliament. This was as a consequence of the proposed content of the 'control order' regime and the haste with which the measure was passed through Parliament.[192] Thus, for example, a provision in the Bill as originally drafted which provided that all forms of control order were to be made by the Secretary of State provoked strong criticism on the ground that it vested too much power in the hands of the executive. Accordingly, the government relented with the result that two types of control order may now be made under the authority of the 2005 Act: a non-derogating control order made by the

[187] [2004] UKHL 56.

[188] Their Lordships also quashed the designated derogation order, the Human Rights Act 1998 (Designated Derogation) Order 2001, SI 2001/3644, which the government had made in order to put section 23 of the 2001 Act on the statute book.

[189] At the time of writing, the applicants are pursuing an application to the ECtHR. However, it relates to their continued detention in the interim between the House of Lords' decision in *A v Secretary of State for the Home Department* and their release following the establishment of the control order regime under Prevention of Terrorism Act 2005.

[190] Bonner, 'Checking the Executive? Detention without Trial, Control Orders, Due Process and Human Rights' (2006) 12 EPL 45 at 59.

[191] For that the reader may usefully consult the *Current Law Statutes* version of the 2005 Act with annotations by Hoffman and Rowe.

[192] With regard to the issue of haste, it was contended by the Joint Committee on Human Rights that this had made it impossible for the Committee properly to scrutinise the Bill for compatibility with human rights: see Tenth Report for session 2004–05, (HL Paper 68, HC 334), at para 1.

Secretary of State;[193] and a derogating control order made by a High Court judge.[194] The latter type of control order is 'derogating' in that it imposes obligations which are incompatible with an individual's right to liberty under article 5 of the ECHR. In other words, it is a control order which authorises the detention without trial of the individual. To date, no derogating control orders have been made.

Although non-derogating control orders are made by the Secretary of State, they are subject to judicial supervision.[195] Thus the Secretary of State will either apply to the High Court for permission to make a non-derogating control order, or he will make such an order and subsequently have that decision reviewed by the High Court. In either case, the function of the court will be to determine whether the Secretary of State's decision is *obviously flawed*.[196]

Section 1 of the 2005 Act is principally concerned with the obligations which may be imposed on an individual under the terms of a control order. The Secretary of State (or a court in the case of a derogating control order) has the power to impose such obligations as are 'considered necessary for purposes connected with preventing or restricting involvement . . . in terrorism-related activity'.[197] Section 1(4) sets out a non-exhaustive list of obligations which may be imposed:

'(a) a prohibition or restriction on his possession or use of specified articles or substances;

(b) a prohibition or restriction on his use of specified services or specified facilities, or on his carrying on specified activities;

(c) a restriction in respect of his work or other occupation, or in respect of his business;

(d) a restriction on his association or communications with specified persons or with other persons generally;

(e) a restriction in respect of his place of residence or on the persons to whom he gives access to his place of residence;

(f) a prohibition on his being at specified places or within a specified area at specified times or on specified days;

(g) a prohibition or restriction on his movements to, from or within the United Kingdom, a specified part of the United Kingdom or a specified place or area within the United Kingdom;

(h) a requirement on him to comply with such other prohibitions or restrictions on his movements as may be imposed, for a period not exceeding 24 hours, by directions given to him in the specified manner, by a specified person and for the purpose of securing compliance with other obligations imposed by or under the order;

(i) a requirement on him to surrender his passport, or anything in his possession to which a prohibition or restriction imposed by the order relates, to a specified person for a period not exceeding the period for which the order remains in force;

(j) a requirement on him to give access to specified persons to his place of residence or to other premises to which he has power to grant access;

(k) a requirement on him to allow specified persons to search that place or any such premises for the purpose of ascertaining whether obligations imposed by or under the order have been, are being or are about to be contravened;

(l) a requirement on him to allow specified persons, either for that purpose or for the purpose of securing that the order is complied with, to remove anything found in that place or on any such

---

[193] See section 2.   [194] Section 4.   [195] Section 3.
[196] See section 3(2)(a), (2)(b), and (3)(b).   [197] Section 1(3).

premises and to subject it to tests or to retain it for a period not exceeding the period for which the order remains in force;

(m) a requirement on him to allow himself to be photographed;

(n) a requirement on him to co-operate with specified arrangements for enabling his movements, communications or other activities to be monitored by electronic or other means;

(o) a requirement on him to comply with a demand made in the specified manner to provide information to a specified person in accordance with the demand;

(p) a requirement on him to report to a specified person at specified times and places.'

It is evident that these obligations are very wide-ranging. They allow the government to impose restrictions on an individual which have important implications for their Convention rights and the rights of those with whom they reside.[198] Since on the face of it the requirements of a control order can amount to little short of house arrest, it is not surprising that both the procedure for making control orders and the content of such orders has been the subject of legal challenge in the courts.

In the first of these challenges it was held by the Administrative Court that the procedures in section 3 of the 2005 Act relating to the supervision by the courts of non-derogating control orders made by the Secretary of State were incompatible with the claimant's right to a fair hearing under article 6 of the ECHR. In the words of Sullivan J:

'The thin veneer of legality which is sought to be applied by section 3 of the Act cannot disguise the reality. That controlee's rights under the Convention are being determined not by an independent court in compliance with Article 6.1, but by executive decision-making, untrammeled by any prospect of effective judicial supervision.'[199]

However, in *Secretary of State for the Home Department v MB*,[200] the Court of Appeal upheld the Secretary of State's appeal against that declaration. In so doing, that court noted that there were two elements to the Secretary of State's decision to make a non-derogating control order: the need for reasonable grounds for suspecting that the controlled person either is or has been involved in terrorism-related activity (an assessment of fact); and a determination that it is necessary to make an order for the purposes of protecting the public from a risk of terrorism (a value judgment).[201] The critical issue of fact in *MB* was therefore whether there were reasonable grounds to suspect that the respondent had been engaged in terrorism related activity. Ordinarily, fairness would require that MB should have been informed of the basis of the Secretary of State's suspicions so that he could address those facts. However, the 2005 Act provides for the use of 'closed material', ie material which is not disclosed to the controlee on the grounds that to do so may compromise national security. The issue in *MB* was therefore whether article 6 required an absolute standard of fairness or, whether it was permissible to depart from that standard in the interests of national security. In the judgment of the Court of Appeal, the scheme of the 2005 Act, with its provisions for review by the courts of the making of a non-derogating control order, together with the use of a special advocate[202] in respect of closed material and the rules of the court made pursuant to paragraph 4 of the Schedule to the

---

[198] It should not be forgotten that by, for example, requiring that an individual permit his telephone conversations to be monitored, a control order will allow the telephone conversations of others resident in the house to be monitored as well.   [199] [2006] EWHC 1000 (Admin) at [96].

[200] [2006] EWCA Civ 1140.   [201] At [57].

[202] A lawyer who, by reason of having undergone security clearance, is permitted to see closed material.

Act were safeguards which were sufficient to make the process of making a control order compatible with article 6.[203]

It should be noted in passing that in relation to the second element of the Secretary of State's decision, the Court of Appeal was of the view that he should be paid a 'degree of deference' on the basis that he was 'better placed than the court to decide the measures that are necessary to protect the public against the activities of a terrorist suspect'.[204] In its judgment, such an approach was supported by both domestic and Strasbourg case law.[205] Nevertheless, the most important word here would appear to be 'degree' rather than 'deference' since the Court of Appeal did consider that there would still be 'scope for the court to give intense scrutiny to the necessity for each of the obligations imposed on an individual under a control order'.[206] Moreover, this was a task which a court *must* perform.

The effect of obligations imposed under control orders on those subject to them was the issue before the court in a further legal challenge in *Secretary of State for the Home Department v JJ, KK, GG, HH, NN and LL*.[207] The obligations in the six control orders subject to challenge were essentially the same. They included a curfew provision which required that each respondent was to remain within his residence (a one bedroom flat) for a period of eighteen hours a day. During the six hour period when they were permitted to leave their flats (10 a.m.–4.00 p.m.), the respondents were confined to restricted urban areas, the largest of which was 72 square kilometres. These areas had been carefully delineated so as not to extend to where the respondents had previously lived (with one exception) but nevertheless to allow each of them access to various facilities and amenities, including a mosque, a hospital and shops. At first instance, Sullivan J held that the obligations imposed by the control orders amounted to a deprivation of liberty contrary to article 5 of the ECHR.[208] In so doing, he had taken as his starting point the curfew provision and had paid regard to other matters, such as the ability to admit or refuse visitors to the respondents' abodes, in order to make a *value judgment* as to whether in the circumstances the control orders effected a deprivation of liberty. On appeal, the Court of Appeal agreed that the control orders were contrary to article 5. Their Lordships also agreed that Sullivan J had been right to conclude that he had the jurisdiction to quash *ultra vires* orders rather than modify their terms or direct the Secretary of State to do so. In the opinion of the Court of Appeal, devising a new package of obligations was 'an exercise that the Secretary of State is very much better placed to perform than the court'.[209]

The decisions in both cases are of some importance in that they show a willingness on the part of the courts to carefully examine the government's use of the control order regime to deal with those whom it believes represent a threat to the security of the nation. Section 23 of the Anti-terrorism, Crime and Security Act 2001 effectively authorised internment,[210] ie detention without trial, and therefore it is not so very surprising that it failed to survive the legal challenge in *A v Secretary of State for the Home Department*. However, the government's response to the House of Lords' decision, the establishment of a control order regime under the 2005 Act, is also not free from controversy. The very significant restrictions which may be imposed on the individuals' rights and freedoms under a control order made such orders an inevitable focus of legal challenge. In the two cases discussed above, we see judicial

[203] At [86].   [204] At [64].

[205] The judgments in *Home Department v Rehman* [2003] AC 153 and *Ireland v UK* (1978) 2 EHRR 25 were cited in support of the point.   [206] [2006] EWCA Civ 1140 at [65].

[207] [2006] EWHC 1623 (Admin); [2006] EWCA Civ 1141.   [208] [2006] EWHC 1623 (Admin).

[209] [2006] EWCA Civ 1141 at [27].

[210] A practice which has previously been adopted by British governments in time of war or in order to deal with suspected terrorists in Northern Ireland during the early 1970s.

recognition of the undoubted fact that the government has a very difficult task to perform when taking steps to counter a terrorist threat. However, we also see the courts ready to carry out their traditional role, that of protecting the rights of the individual against unlawful state interference. In a further recent case, the House of Lords was required to consider the lawfulness of other measures put in place to combat the threat of terrorism, the police powers of stop and search under the Terrorism Act 2000.

....

R (Gillan and another) v Commissioner of Police of the Metropolis and another [2006] 2 WLR 537

An arms fair being held in London had been the subject of protests. The policing strategy involved the use of stop and search powers under section 44 of the Terrorism Act 2000. The appellants, a student and a journalist, had been stopped and searched pursuant to those powers. Neither search had resulted in the discovery of any incriminating evidence, ie articles to be used in connection with terrorist activities. The appellants had sought to challenge the lawfulness of their being stopped and searched in claims for judicial review. They contended that: the authorisation under the Terrorism Act 2000 had been *ultra vires*; that the use of the authorisation by the police officers had been contrary to the legislative purpose of the Act and hence unlawful, and that the guidance given to the officers regarding their powers had been inadequate and misleading; and, that the decisions to authorise and use the stop and search powers under sections 44 and 45 of the 2000 Act had constituted a dispro-portionate interference with the appellants' rights under articles 5, 8, 9, 10 and 11 of the ECHR. None of these grounds of challenge succeeded before the Divisional Court.[211] Neither were the appellants successful when they appealed to the Court of Appeal on different grounds.[212] They therefore appealed to the House of Lords which unanimously dismissed their appeal.

Lord Bingham

'1. It is an old and cherished tradition of our country that everyone should be free to go about their business in the streets of the land, confident that they will not be stopped and searched by the police unless reasonably suspected of having committed a criminal offence. So jealously has this tradition been guarded that it has almost become a constitutional principle. But it is not an absolute rule. There are, and have for some years been, statutory exceptions to it. These appeals concern an exception now found in sections 44 to 47 of the Terrorism Act 2000. The appellant claimants challenge the use made of these sections and, in the last resort, the sections themselves. Since any departure from the ordinary rule calls for careful scrutiny, their challenge raises issues of general importance.

. . .

9. In dispensing with the condition of reasonable suspicion, section 45(1)(b) departs from the ordinary and salutary rule found in provisions such as section 1 of the Police and Criminal Evidence Act 1984, section 47 of the Firearms Act 1968, section 23 of the Misuse of Drugs Act 1971 and (as noted above) sections 41–43 of the 2000 Act itself. But such departure is not without precedent. A similar (although more specific and more time-limited) departure is found in section 60 of the Criminal Justice and Public Order Act 1994, where incidents involving serious violence are reasonably believed to be imminent. More pertinently, because addressed to the prevention of terrorism, a similar departure was made in section 13A of the 1989 Act, inserted by section 81 of the 1994 Act . . . It is also noteworthy that section 45(1)(b) is not the only provision of the 2000 Act which dispenses with the condition of reasonable suspicion: Schedule 7 to the Act makes detailed provision for the stopping and questioning

---

[211] [2003] EWHC 2545 (Admin).   [212] [2005] QB 388.

of those embarking and disembarking at ports and airports, without reasonable suspicion, supplemented by a power to detain for a period of up to nine hours.

III. The issues

12 . . . The claimant's case has changed somewhat as it has progressed through the courts. It was presented to the House under four main heads.

A. Construction

13. The argument centred on the expression "expedient" in section 44(3). The claimants pointed to the Divisional Court's description of these stop and search powers as "extraordinary" and as "sweeping and far beyond anything ever permitted by common law powers" (para 44 of the judgment), a description echoed by the Court of Appeal (para 8), and suggested that Parliament could not have intended to sanction police intrusion into the freedom of individuals unless it was necessary that the police have such a power. Reliance was placed on the principle of legality articulated in *R v Secretary of State for the Home Department, Ex p Simms* [2000] 2 AC 115, 130, 131. Reliance was also placed on Home Office Circular 038/2004 (1 July 2004), *Authorisations of Stop and Search Powers under Section 44 of the Terrorism Act*, addressed to chief officers of police, which emphasised that "Powers should only be authorised where they are absolutely necessary to support a force's anti-terrorism operations". The claimants submitted that section 44(3) should be interpreted as permitting an authorisation to be made only if the decision-maker has reasonable grounds for considering that the powers are necessary and suitable, in all the circumstances, for the prevention of terrorism.

14. I would for my part reject this argument for one short and simple reason. "Expedient" has a meaning quite distinct from "necessary". Parliament chose the first word, also used in section 13A of the 1989 Act, not the second. There is no warrant for treating Parliament as having meant something which it did not say. But there are other reasons also for rejecting the argument. It is true, as already recognised, that section 45(1)(b), in dispensing with the condition of reasonable suspicion, departs from the normal rule applicable where a constable exercises a power to stop and search. One would therefore incline, within the permissible limits of interpretation, to give "expedient" a meaning no wider than the context requires. But examination of the statutory context shows that the authorisation and exercise of the power are very closely regulated, leaving no room for the inference that Parliament did not mean what it said. There is indeed every indication that Parliament appreciated the significance of the power it was conferring but thought it an appropriate measure to protect the public against the grave risks posed by terrorism, provided the power was subject to effective constraints. The legislation embodies a series of such constraints. First, an authorisation under section 44(1) or (2) may be given only if the person giving it considers (and, it goes without saying, reasonably considers) it expedient "for the prevention of acts of terrorism". The authorisation must be directed to that overriding objective. Secondly, the authorisation may be given only by a very senior police officer. Thirdly, the authorisation cannot extend beyond the boundary of a police force area, and need not extend so far. Fourthly, the authorisation is limited to a period of 28 days, and need not be for so long. Fifthly, the authorisation must be reported to the Secretary of State forthwith. Sixthly, the authorisation lapses after 48 hours if not confirmed by the Secretary of State. Seventhly, the Secretary of State may abbreviate the term of an authorisation, or cancel it with effect from a specified time. Eighthly, a renewed authorisation is subject to the same confirmation procedure. Ninthly, the powers conferred on a constable by an authorisation under sections 44(1) or (2) may only be exercised to search for articles of a kind which could be used in connection with terrorism. Tenthly, Parliament made provision in section 126 for reports on the working of the Act to be made to it at least once a year, which have in the event been made with commendable thoroughness, fairness and expertise by Lord Carlile of Berriew QC. Lastly, it is clear that any misuse of the power to authorise or confirm or search will expose the authorising officer, the Secretary of State or the constable, as the case may be, to corrective legal action.

15. The principle of legality has no application in this context, since even if these sections are accepted as infringing a fundamental human right, itself a debatable proposition, they do not do so by

general words but by provisions of a detailed, specific and unambiguous character. Nor are the claimants assisted by the Home Office circular. This may well represent a cautious official response to the claimants' challenge, and to the urging of Lord Carlile that these powers be sparingly used. But it cannot, even arguably, affect the construction of section 44(3). The effect of that sub-section is that an authorisation may be given if, and only if, the person giving it considers it likely that these stop and search powers will be of significant practical value and utility in seeking to achieve the public end to which these sections are directed, the prevention of acts of terrorism.

B. Authorisation and confirmation

. . .

17. The claimants' first ground of attack on the authorisation and confirmation was based on their geographical coverage. This, they said, was excessive: even if there was justification for conferring such exceptional powers in areas of central London offering the most spectacular targets for terrorist violence, there could be no need for them in the dormitory suburbs of outer London, which offered no such targets. This is not, in my opinion, an unattractive submission, but it founders on two major obstacles. First, the Assistant Commissioner in his witness statement, having addressed the terrorist threat to the United Kingdom in general and London in particular in August–September 2003, expressly said:

"(I was particularly conscious that the number and range of particular terrorism targets in London was numerous and geographically spread throughout the entire Metropolitan Police District)."

This aspect was also addressed in the witness statement of Catherine Byrne, a senior Home Office civil servant, on behalf of the Secretary of State:

"17. In this context it is also simply impracticable to attempt to differentiate between some parts of the Metropolitan Police area and others. As I have already indicated potential targets within the London area are not limited to central London, but exist throughout the metropolitan area. Moreover, the powers under sections 44 and 45 of the 2000 Act are aimed not simply at disrupting any attempted attack 'at the last possible moment' but are intended to enable police forces, where appropriate, to ensure that any attempted attack is disrupted at an early stage, and certainly well before any serious harm could be done to members of the public or to property. It must also be remembered that the powers under sections 44 and 45 of the 2000 Act are simply one element of the strategy adopted by the Metropolitan Police (in conjunction with the City of London police) to combat the risk posed by terrorists. This is a point made in the reasons supporting both authorisa-tions made by the Commissioner [of Police of the Metropolis]. Further, the powers under sections 44 and 45 of the 2000 Act play a legitimate part in focused intelligence-gathering operations. These can be directed either for the purpose of disrupting identified risks or (equally legitimately) as a means of obtaining information that can lead to the identification of potential risks."

There is no evidence of any kind to contradict or undermine this testimony. Secondly, as both these witness statements make clear, the Assistant Commissioner and the Secretary of State independently paid attention to secret security intelligence when making the judgments which they respectively did. An offer to explore this evidence before the Divisional Court hearing, subject to procedural safeguards, was made to the claimants but not taken up. In the result, therefore, the House has before it what appear to be considered and informed evaluations of the terrorist threat on one side and effectively nothing save a measure of scepticism on the other. There is no basis on which the defendants' evidence can be rejected. This is not a question of deference but of what in *A v Secretary of State for the Home Department* [2005] 2 AC 68, 102, para 29, was called "relative institutional competence".

18. The claimants' second, and main, ground of attack was directed to the succession of authorisa-tions which had had effect throughout the Metropolitan Police District since February 2001, continuing until September 2003. It was, they suggested, one thing to authorise the exercise of an exceptional

power to counter a particular and specific threat, but quite another to authorise what was, in effect, a continuous ban throughout the London area. Again this is not an unattractive submission. One can imagine that an authorisation renewed month after month might become the product of a routine bureaucratic exercise and not of the informed consideration which sections 44 and 46 clearly require. But all the authorisations and confirmations relevant to these appeals conformed with the statutory limits on duration and area. Renewal was expressly authorised by section 46(7). The authorisations and confirmations complied with the letter of the statute. The evidence of the Assistant Commissioner and Catherine Byrne does not support, and indeed contradicts, the inference of a routine bureaucratic exercise. It may well be that Parliament, legislating before the events of September 2001, did not envisage a continuous succession of authorisations. But it clearly intended that the section 44 powers should be available to be exercised when a terrorist threat was apprehended which such exercise would help to address, and the pattern of renewals which developed up to September 2003 (it is understood the pattern has since changed) was itself a product of Parliament's principled refusal to confer these exceptional stop and search powers on a continuing, countrywide basis. Reporting on the operation of the 2000 Act during the years 2002 and 2003, Lord Carlile (*Report on the Operation in 2002 and 2003 of the Terrorism Act 2000*, para 86) found that sections 44 and 45 remained necessary and proportional to the continuing and serious risk of terrorism, and regarded London as "a special case, having vulnerable assets and relevant residential pockets in almost every borough".

. . .

C. The Human Rights Act 1998 and the European Convention

20. The appellants addressed argument on articles 5, 8, 10 and 11 of the European Convention on Human Rights. It is necessary to consider these articles separately.

Article 5

. . .

22. It is clear that the giving of an authorisation by a senior officer and its confirmation by the Secretary of State cannot, of themselves, infringe the Convention rights of anyone. Thus the threshold question is whether, if a person is stopped and searched in accordance with the procedure prescribed by sections 44 and 45 and Code A, he is "deprived of his liberty" within the autonomous meaning of that expression in article 5(1). The claimants contend that he is so deprived, even if only for a short time, since the police officer has the power to require compliance with the procedure; a member of the public will not feel that his compliance is voluntary; the officer has a power to detain, which he may or may not exercise (section 45(4)); reasonable force may be used to enforce compliance (section 114(2)); and non-compliance is criminally punishable. Thus a member of the public has no effective choice but to submit, for as long as the procedure takes. The defendants for their part do not, I think, contend that compliance with the procedure is in any meaningful sense voluntary; but they submit that viewed objectively, and in the absence of special circumstances, the procedure involves a temporary restriction of movement and not anything which can sensibly be called a deprivation of liberty.

. . .

24. The task of the House is eased by the substantial agreement of the parties on the correct approach in principle. Perhaps the clearest exposition of principle by the Strasbourg court is to be found in *Guzzardi v Italy* (1980) 3 EHRR 333, an exposition repeatedly cited in later cases. The case concerned an applicant who, pending his criminal trial, was subject for over 16 months to a form of internal exile on an island off the coast of Sardinia. He was specially supervised in an area of 2.5 square kilometres. He was held to have suffered a deprivation of his liberty. The Commission reached this conclusion (para 90) because of the small area in which the applicant had been confined, the almost permanent supervision to which he had been subject, the all but complete impossibility of his making social contacts and the length of his enforced stay. The Italian Government challenged this analysis on

a number of grounds (para 91). The court observed, at paras 92–93:

> "92. The court recalls that in proclaiming the 'right to liberty', paragraph 1 of article 5 is contemplating the physical liberty of the person; its aim is to ensure that no one should be dispossessed of this liberty in an arbitrary fashion. As was pointed out by those appearing before the court, the paragraph is not concerned with mere restrictions on liberty of movement; such restrictions are governed by article 2 of Protocol No 4 which has not been ratified by Italy. In order to determine whether someone has been 'deprived of his liberty' within the meaning of article 5, the starting point must be his concrete situation and account must be taken of a whole range of criteria such as the type, duration, effects and manner of implementation of the measure in question.
>
> 93. The difference between deprivation of and restriction upon liberty is nonetheless merely one of degree or intensity, and not one of nature or substance. Although the process of classification into one or other of these categories sometimes proves to be no easy task in that some borderline cases are a matter of pure opinion, the court cannot avoid making the selection upon which the applicability or inapplicability of article 5 depends."

The court continued, in para 95:

> "The Government's reasoning (see para 91 above) is not without weight. It demonstrates very clearly the extent of the difference between the applicant's treatment on Asinara and classic detention in prison or strict arrest imposed on a serviceman. Deprivation of liberty may, however, take numerous other forms. Their variety is being increased by developments in legal standards and in attitudes; and the Convention is to be interpreted in the light of the notions currently prevailing in democratic states."

The court went on to review the special features of the applicant's situation, and held:

> "It is admittedly not possible to speak of 'deprivation of liberty' on the strength of any one of these factors taken individually, but cumulatively and in combination they certainly raise an issue of categorisation from the viewpoint of article 5. In certain respects the treatment complained of resembles detention in an 'open prison' or committal to a disciplinary unit."

25. . . . I would accept that when a person is stopped and searched under sections 44 and 45 the procedure has the features on which the appellants rely. On the other hand, the procedure will ordinarily be relatively brief. The person stopped will not be arrested, handcuffed, confined or removed to any different place. I do not think, in the absence of special circumstances, such a person should be regarded as being detained in the sense of confined or kept in custody, but more properly of being detained in the sense of kept from proceeding or kept waiting. There is no deprivation of liberty.

Article 8

. . .

28. The claimants contended that exercise of the section 45 stop and search power necessarily involves an interference with the exercise of the article 8(1) right, and therefore had to be justified under article 8(2). The defendants did not accept that there would necessarily be such interference, but accepted that there might, as where (for instance) an officer in the course of a search perused an address book, or diary, or correspondence. I have no doubt but that the defendants' concession is rightly made. I am, however, doubtful whether an ordinary superficial search of the person can be said to show a lack of respect for private life. It is true that "private life" has been generously construed to embrace wide rights to personal autonomy. But it is clear Convention jurisprudence that intrusions must reach a certain level of seriousness to engage the operation of the Convention, which is, after all, concerned with human rights and fundamental freedoms, and I incline to the view that an ordinary superficial search of the person and an opening of bags, of the kind to which passengers uncomplainingly submit at airports, for example, can scarcely be said to reach that level.

29. If, again, the lawfulness of the search is assumed at this stage, there can be little question that it is directed to objects recognised by article 8(2). The search must still be necessary in a democratic

society, and so proportionate. But if the exercise of the power is duly authorised and confirmed, and if the power is exercised for the only purpose for which it may permissibly be exercised (ie to search for articles of a kind which could be used in connection with terrorism: section 45(1)(a)), it would in my opinion be impossible to regard a proper exercise of the power, in accordance with Code A, as other than proportionate when seeking to counter the great danger of terrorism.

Articles 10 and 11

30. The power to stop and search under sections 44–45 may, if misused, infringe the Convention rights to free expression and free assembly protected by articles 10 and 11, as would be the case, for example, if the power were used to silence a heckler at a political meeting. I find it hard to conceive of circumstances in which the power, properly exercised in accordance with the statute and Code A, could be held to restrict those rights in a way which infringed either of those articles. But if it did, and subject always to compliance with the "prescribed by law" condition discussed below, I would expect the restriction to fall within the heads of justification provided in articles 10(2) and 11(2).

D. Lawfulness

31. The expressions "prescribed by law" in article 5(1), 5(1)(b), 10(2) and 11(2) and "in accordance with the law" in article 8(2) are to be understood as bearing the same meaning. What is that meaning?

. . .

34. The lawfulness requirement in the Convention addresses supremely important features of the rule of law. The exercise of power by public officials, as it affects members of the public, must be governed by clear and publicly accessible rules of law. The public must not be vulnerable to interference by public officials acting on any personal whim, caprice, malice, predilection or purpose other than that for which the power was conferred. This is what, in this context, is meant by arbitrariness, which is the antithesis of legality. This is the test which any interference with or derogation from a Convention right must meet if a violation is to be avoided.

35. The stop and search regime under review does in my opinion meet that test. The 2000 Act informs the public that these powers are, if duly authorised and confirmed, available. It defines and limits the powers with considerable precision. Code A, a public document, describes the procedure in detail. The Act and the Code do not require the fact or the details of any authorisation to be publicised in any way, even retrospectively, but I doubt if they are to be regarded as "law" rather than as a procedure for bringing the law into potential effect. In any event, it would stultify a potentially valuable source of public protection to require notice of an authorisation or confirmation to be publicised prospectively. The efficacy of a measure such as this will be gravely weakened if potential offenders are alerted in advance. Anyone stopped and searched must be told, by the constable, all he needs to know. In exercising the power the constable is not free to act arbitrarily, and will be open to civil suit if he does. It is true that he need have no suspicion before stopping and searching a member of the public. This cannot, realistically, be interpreted as a warrant to stop and search people who are obviously not terrorist suspects, which would be futile and time-wasting. It is to ensure that a constable is not deterred from stopping and searching a person whom he does suspect as a potential terrorist by the fear that he could not show reasonable grounds for his suspicion. It is not suggested that the constables in these cases exercised their powers in a discriminatory manner (an impossible contention on the facts), and I prefer to say nothing on the subject of discrimination.'

Lord Hope

'Discrimination

41. One has only to observe the huge numbers of people moving every day through this country's transport network to appreciate the fact that it would be wholly counter-productive for the police to be compelled to exercise the section 44 power in these circumstances on a basis that was a purely random one. Those they might wish to stop for very good reasons would slip through the net as the

process of random selection was being conducted. A brief study of the selection process would be enough to guide the terrorist as to how to organise his movements so that he could remain undetected. A system that is to be effective has to be flexible. Precise rules cannot be laid down in advance. Much has to be left to the discretion of the individual police officer.

42. Common sense tells us that the nature of the terrorist threat will play a large part in the selection process. Typically terrorist acts are planned, organised and perpetrated by people acting together to promote a common cause rather than by individuals. They will have a common agenda. They are likely to be linked to sectors of the community that, because of their racial, ethnic or geographical origins, are readily identifiable . . .

43. What then if it is found that the police are using the section 44 power more frequently to stop Asians than other racial groups in the community? Does this amount to direct discrimination contrary to domestic law, as Mr Rabinder Singh suggested from time to time in the course of his argument? The issue does not arise directly in this case, of course, because neither of the claimants is of Asian origin. But it cannot be overlooked . . .

44. . . . The use of the section 44 power on racial grounds is not exempt from being treated as discriminatory simply because of the purpose for which it is being exercised. It is no answer to say that the time and place for the exercise of the section 44 power was selected in response to the threat of a terrorist outrage . . . Discrimination on racial grounds is unlawful whether or not, in any given case, the assumptions on which it was based turn out to be justified.

45. Where then does this leave the police officer when he is deciding whom to stop and search in the exercise of the section 44 power? The key must surely lie in the point which Baroness Hale made in her speech in the *Roma Rights* case,[213] at p. 59h, para 82, that the object of the legislation is to ensure that each person is treated as an individual and not assumed to be like other members of the group. That was the trap into which the immigration officers fell at Prague airport, as the evidence showed that all Roma were being treated in the same way simply because they were Roma. So a police officer who stops and searches a person who appears to be Asian in the exercise of the section 44 power must have other, further, good reasons for doing so. It cannot be stressed too strongly that the mere fact that the person appears to be of Asian origin is not a legitimate reason for its exercise.

46. Times and places will vary, of course, and the numbers and mixture of people of different races and ethnic backgrounds that one sees using buses, railways and the London Underground may not be typical of the places where authorisations are given throughout the country. But a decision to use the section 44 power will in practice always be based on more than the mere fact of a person's racial or ethnic origin if it is to be used properly and effectively, especially in places where people are present in large numbers. The selection process will be more precisely targeted, even if in the end it is based more on a hunch than on something that can be precisely articulated or identified. Age, behaviour and general appearance other than that relating to the person's racial or ethnic background will have a part to play in suggesting that a particular person might possibly have in his possession an article of a kind which could be used in connection with terrorism. An appearance which suggests that the person is of Asian origin may attract the constable's attention in the first place. But a further selection process will have to be undertaken, perhaps on the spur of the moment otherwise the opportunity will be lost, before the power is exercised. It is this further selection process that makes the difference between what is inherently discriminatory and what is not.

47. On balance, therefore, I think that it is not inevitable that stopping persons who are of Asian origin in the exercise of the section 44 power will be found to be discriminatory. But the risk that it will be employed in a discriminatory fashion cannot be discounted entirely. No more can the risk that the power will be used on occasions, as the claimants claim but has yet to be established by evidence, for a purpose that has nothing to do with the prevention of acts of terrorism. These thoughts lead to the

[213] *R (European Roma Rights Centre) v Immigration Officer at Prague Airport (United Nations High Comr for Refugees intervening)* [2005] 2 AC 1.

problem of satisfying the test of legal certainty. This must be done if the use of the section 44 power is not to be open to the objection that it is, by its very nature, arbitrary.

Legal certainty

. . .

52. The question whether the process is in accordance with the law for the purposes of the Convention is not answered merely by a finding that it is lawful under domestic law. That is only the first stage in the analysis: see *R v Governor of Brockhill Prison, Ex p Evans No 2* [2001] 2 AC 19, 38b–e. There are two further questions that must be answered. One is whether, assuming that the process is lawful under domestic law, it nevertheless fails to comply with the general requirements of the Convention as to the quality of the law in question. These requirements are based on the principle that any restrictions on the rights and freedoms of the individual must be prescribed by law in a way that is sufficiently accessible and sufficiently precise to enable the individual to foresee the consequences. The other is whether, assuming again that the two previous criteria are met, the process is nevertheless open to criticism on the ground that it is arbitrary. The claimants submit that the criterion of foreseeability is not met because the powers are widely drawn, and because the public does not have access to the authorisations which are not published. They also submit that, because it is so difficult to detect an improper or discriminatory use of it, the power that is given to the constable is arbitrary.

53. The criterion of lawfulness can be examined in four stages. First there is the legislation. Next, there is the general guidance that is given by Code A as to how the powers under section 44 are to be exercised. Then there are the authorisations themselves, whose issue is a necessary preliminary to the exercise of the section 44 power and which the Secretary of State must confirm. Finally, and crucially, there is the exercise of the power by the police officers who are authorised to make use of it.

. . .

55. . . . The use of the section 44 power has to be seen in the context of the legislation that provides for it. The need for its use at any given time and in any given place to be authorised, and for the authorisation to be confirmed within 48 hours, provides a background of law that is readily accessible to the citizen. It provides a system of regulatory control over the exercise of the power which enables the person who is stopped and searched, if he wishes, to test its legality in the courts. In that event the authorisation and the confirmation of it will of necessity, to enable the law to be tested properly, become relevant evidence. The guidance in paragraph 2.25 of Code A warns the constable that the power is to be used only for reasons connected with terrorism, and that particular care must be taken not to discriminate against members of minority ethnic groups when it is being exercised. It is no more precise than that. But it serves as a reminder that there is a structure of law within which the power must be exercised. A constable who acts within these limits is not exercising the section 44 power arbitrarily.

56. . . . the sufficiency of these measures must be balanced against the nature and degree of the interference with the citizen's Convention rights which is likely to result from the exercise of the power that has been given to the public authority. The things that a constable can do when exercising the section 44 power are limited by the provisions of section 45(3) and (4). He may not require the person to remove any clothing in public except that which is specified, and the person may be detained only for such time as is reasonably required to permit the search to be carried out at or near the place where the person or vehicle has been stopped. The extent of the intrusion is not very great given the obvious importance of the purpose for which it is being resorted to. In my opinion the structure of law within which it is to be exercised is sufficient in all the circumstances to meet the requirement of legality.

57. It should be noted, of course, that the best safeguard against the abuse of the power in practice is likely to be found in the training, supervision and discipline of the constables who are to be entrusted with its exercise. Public confidence in the police and good relations with those who belong to the ethnic minorities are of the highest importance when extraordinary powers of the kind that are under scrutiny in this case are being exercised. The law will provide remedies if the power to stop and search

is improperly exercised. But these are remedies of last resort. Prevention of any abuse of the power in the first place, and a tighter control over its use from the top, must be the first priority.'

Lord Scott

. . .

'61. The claimants, in challenging the validity of the stop and search authorisation in reliance on which the police officers stopped and searched them, contend that the authorisation, and its confirmation by the Home Secretary, constituted an excessive and disproportionate response to the threat of terrorist activity in London at that time. They say that the authorisation and confirmation went outside the boundaries of a reasonable response to that threat.

62. The problem, to my mind, with a challenge of this character is that an assessment of the reasonableness of the response requires an assessment of the degree of seriousness of the terrorist threat to which the authorisation was a response. This latter assessment will in most cases require some knowledge of the intelligence material on which the police and the Home Secretary relied when making their own assessment of that threat and of what should be done in response to it. The claimants have not contended that the giving of a section 44 authorisation could never be a proportionate response to a threat of terrorist activity. They accept, and indeed contend, that a balance must be struck between, on the one hand, the degree of interference with ordinary liberties brought about by police exercising their section 44 stop and search powers and, on the other hand, the degree of risk to the public posed by the terrorist threat as it appears from the available intelligence material.

63. The claimants say that when this balance is struck the giving of the authorisation can be judged to be a disproportionate response. I disagree for two reasons. First, the interference with the fundamental rights of individuals brought about by a police power to stop and search without the need for reasonable suspicion of wrongdoing is not, in my opinion, of overwhelming weight. It is not an interference of the same order as, for example, an indefinite detention on undisclosed grounds. A stop and search will often be very annoying to the person concerned, and may sometimes produce a feeling of humiliation or a perception of victimisation or discrimination; but any invasion of privacy will be shortlived and any deprivation of liberty will usually be no more than theoretical. These are the matters that must go into one side of the scale when the balance is struck. What goes into the other side of the scale must depend on the intelligence material that has been relied on as justifying, or requiring, the giving of the authorisation. I would not, speaking for myself, expect a challenge to the validity of a section 44 stop and search authorisation, based on the alleged disproportionate nature of that response to a perceived threat of terrorism, to be able to succeed without the court having had an opportunity to review the intelligence material that had been relied on.

64. In the present case the Divisional Court did not have that opportunity . . . . In that state of the evidence the Divisional Court could not reasonably have concluded that the authorisation was a disproportionate response to the threat of terrorist activity in London appearing from the available intelligence material. Nor could the Court of Appeal and nor, in my opinion, can your Lordships. What the position would have been had the underlying intelligence material been reviewed it is impossible to tell.

. . .

67. . . . Whether a stop and search is random depends on whether the question is asked from the point of view of the searcher or that of the searched. From the point of view of the person searched the police officer's choice of him or her to be subjected to a search may seem entirely random, or may seem absurd or discriminatory or vindictive. But from the point of view of the police officer, it is difficult to see how the choice could ever be a random one. A policy of stopping and searching every tenth person is not a random search; it is a search that follows a pattern. The pattern would allow the police officer no room for judgment as to who to stop and search. It would therefore be a pattern designed to

minimise the chances of achieving the statutory purpose of combating terrorism. In the real world a police officer will always have some reason for selecting a particular individual as a person to be stopped and searched. The reason does not have to be based on grounds for suspicion: see section 45(1)(b). It may be based . . . on no more than a professional's intuition. Or it may be because the person selected conforms to some extent in the mind of the police officer to a stereotype of a person who might possibly be in possession of articles "which could be used in connection with terrorism": section 45(1)(a).'

Lord Brown

'71. . . . The appeal does, however, raise points of real constitutional importance and on one partic- ular aspect of it I would still like to express certain thoughts of my own.

. . .

80. . . . It seems to me inevitable, however, that so long as the principal terrorist risk against which use of the section 44 power has been authorised is that from al Qaeda, a disproportionate number of those stopped and searched will be of Asian appearance (particularly if they happen to be carrying rucksacks or wearing apparently bulky clothing capable of containing terrorist-related items).

81. Is such a conclusion inimical to Convention jurisprudence or, indeed, inconsistent with domestic discrimination law? In my judgment it is not, provided only that police officers exercising this power on the ground pay proper heed to paragraph 2.25 of Code A:

"The selection of persons stopped under section 44 of the Terrorism Act 2000 should reflect an objective assessment of the threat posed by the various terrorist groups active in Great Britain. The powers must not be used to stop and search for reasons unconnected with terrorism. Officers must take particular care not to discriminate against members of minority ethnic groups in the exercise of these powers. There may be circumstances, however, where it is appropriate for officers to take account of a person's ethnic origin in selecting persons to be stopped in response to a specific terrorist threat (for example, some international terrorist groups are associated with particular eth- nic identities)."

Ethnic origin accordingly can and properly should be taken into account in deciding whether and whom to stop and search provided always that the power is used sensitively and the selection is made for reasons connected with the perceived terrorist threat and not on grounds of racial discrimination.

. . .

92. Of course it is important, indeed imperative, not to imperil good community relations, not to exacerbate a minority's feelings of alienation and victimisation, so that the use of these supposed preventative powers could tend actually to promote rather than counter the present terrorist threat. I repeat, therefore, as Lord Carlile has consistently done in his annual reports, that these stop and search powers ought to be used only sparingly. But I cannot accept that, thus used, they can be impugned either as arbitrary or as "inherently and systematically discriminatory" (Lord Steyn's charac- terisation of the Prague operation) simply because they are used selectively to target those regarded by the police as most likely to be carrying terrorist connected articles, even if this leads, as usually it will, to the deployment of this power against a higher proportion of people from one ethnic group than another. I conclude rather that not merely is such selective use of the power legitimate; it is its only legitimate use. To stop and search those regarded as presenting no conceivable threat whatever (particularly when that leaves officers unable to stop those about whom they feel an instinctive unease) would itself constitute an abuse of the power. Then indeed would the power be being exercised arbitrarily.'

The decision in *Gillan* is of interest for a number of reasons, not least of which is that it provides the answer to a question which had not previously been determined by the courts;

whether a stop and search carried out by a police officer under the authority of a statutory power amounted to a deprivation of liberty for the purposes of article 5 of the ECHR. Lord Bingham (with whom the other Law Lords agreed) was unequivocal on the point; there was no deprivation of liberty involved when a person was stopped and searched since they were 'detained' only in the sense of being kept waiting while the search was carried out, rather than 'detained' in the sense of being taken into custody.[214] It does not follow from this, however, that a stop and search might not engage the protection of article 5. Lord Bingham prefaced his remarks with the qualification 'in the absence of special circumstances'. Presumably, therefore, a stop and search may constitute a detention if it were to last for some time beyond what could be regarded as reasonable in the circumstances. It does not appear possible, however, to set an arbitrary time limit beyond which a stop and search will have become a detention; it will depend upon the facts of the case. Assuming that the duration of a stop and search was long enough to invoke the protection of article 5, it would then of course be necessary for a court to consider whether it fell within the scope of any of the exceptions set out in article 5 itself. Of these, the most likely to apply would be article 5(1)(b) which permits the lawful arrest or detention of a person on several grounds, including in order 'to secure the fulfilment of any obligation prescribed by law'.[215]

Although it was not necessary for the purposes of determining the appeal in *Gillan*, several of their Lordships expressed views on the practical exercise of the stop and search power. In particular, they dealt with the difficult issue of where to draw the line between a discriminatory and a non-discriminatory exercise of the power. The guidance which emerges from the judgments is clear. The use of the section 44 power on racial grounds is discriminatory and hence unlawful. However, in exercising his discretion as to which persons to stop and search, a police officer is entitled to take into account ethnic origin provided that he also takes into account other relevant factors as part of the selection process. Thus stopping and searching a young Asian male for no reason other than his ethnicity is discriminatory, whereas stopping and searching a young Asian male who is dressed in bulky clothing and who is carrying a rucksack is not, even though an element of stereotyping will have featured in the selection process.

(ii) Repeal or amendment?

In the DCA's *Review of the Implementation of the Human Rights Act*, it is noted that a number of myths have grown up around the HRA since its enactment. These myths have taken the following forms:

'There are three different types of myth in play. First, there are those which derive from the reporting (and often partial reporting) of the launch of cases but not their ultimate outcomes. These leave the impression in the public mind that a wide range of claims are successful when in fact they are not—and have often effectively been laughed out of court. Secondly, there are the pure urban myths: instances of situations in which someone (often it may not even be clear who) has said that human rights require some bizarre outcome or other, and this is subsequently trotted out as established fact. Finally, there are rumours and impressions which take root through a particular case or decision, and which then provide the backdrop against which all subsequent issues of the type in question are played out.'[216]

---

[214] At [25], extracted above.

[215] This was the view of the former Lord Chief Justice, Lord Woolf, when *Gillan* was heard by the Court of Appeal: see [2005] QB 388 at [44].　　　　　　　　　　　　　　　　　　　　　　[216] At 30.

Although the evidence in support of these myths is largely anecdotal, their identification in the *Review* is significant in that it serves to highlight how the effect of the HRA can so easily be misrepresented. Indeed, the extent of that misrepresentation has been such as to lead to calls for the UK to withdraw from the ECHR or repeal or amend the HRA. In relation to the former, although this is a course of action which the government could take, the *Review* makes it clear that it would leave the UK 'fatally undermined in any efforts to encourage better human rights implementation by other members of the Council of Europe and our position in lobbying for human rights implementation by states elsewhere in the world would also be affected'.[217] The repeal of the HRA is also considered in the *Review*, as its amendment. The former would result in the restoration of the legal framework which existed before the HRA was enacted.[218] However, it is a 'matter for speculation'[219] as to how the law would have changed since the Act came into force in October 2000. Amendment may therefore be a more feasible course of action. The *Review* notes that in theory, it might be possible to place particular emphasis on the importance of public safety in the HRA in order to address concerns that as things currently stand, too often the balance between the interests of the individual and those of the wider society favours the former. Overall, however, the tone of the *Review* seems to be against legislative reform. Rather, it stresses that there is 'an urgent need for the public as well as the wider public sector to be better informed about the benefits which the HRA has given to ordinary people, and to debunk many of the myths which have grown up around the Convention rights and the way in which they have been applied, both domestically and in Strasbourg'.[220] It remains to be seen how the laudable aim of 'myth-busting' will be achieved in practice.

(iii) A continuing role for Strasbourg

Incorporating Convention rights into domestic law so that those rights may now be argued before our own courts is a very important development towards the establishment of a human rights culture in the UK. The hope that incorporation would lead to significantly less adverse decisions against the UK government by the ECtHR seems to have been borne out in practice.[221] Incorporation does not mean, however, that the ECtHR has ceased to have a role to play in relation to the UK's human rights compliance. It may still be called upon to determine whether as a matter of international law, the UK has failed to comply with a Convention right. Although this may occur following a domestic court ruling that a public authority has acted incompatibly with a Convention right, it is unlikely that the government would choose not to act upon a section 4 declaration of incompatibility which has been upheld on appeal. More likely, therefore, is a scenario whereby a claim brought before the domestic courts has been held not to involve the breach of a Convention right under the HRA but the claimant is not satisfied by this outcome and, having exhausted his domestic remedies, decides to apply to Strasbourg. This is what happened in relation to the policy of preventing all convicted prisoners from having the right to vote in parliamentary and local government elections.

In *R (on the application of Pearson) v Secretary of State for the Home Department*,[222] the three claimants were all convicted prisoners who had unsuccessfully applied for their names to be

[217] At 37.   [218] At 38.   [219] Ibid.   [220] At 42.
[221] See *Review of the Implementation of the Human Rights Act*, DCA (July 2006), at 4.
[222] [2001] EWHC 239 (Admin); [2001] HRLR 39.

placed on the electoral register. Accordingly, they sought judicial review of that decision and a declaration that section 3(1) of the Representation of the People Act 1983 (which was the basis of their disenfranchisement) was incompatible with article 3 of the First Protocol to, and article 14 of the ECHR. In dismissing their applications, the Divisional Court accepted that in the light of the decision of the ECtHR in *Mathieu-Mohin and Clerfayt v Belgium*,[223] article 3 of the First Protocol was wide enough to include the right to vote as well as the right to stand in an election. It also noted, however, that the disenfranchisement of all convicted prisoners had been considered by the European Commission on three occasions and that on each occasion, the complaint had been ruled to be manifestly ill-founded and hence inadmissible.[224] Thus in the light of the domestic approach to prisoners voting which had involved successive governments taking the view that prisoners convicted of serious crimes had lost the moral authority to vote, and the fact that different states have different approaches to the issue, the Divisional Court did not accept that the UK's broad approach to disenfranchisement was contrary to the ECHR. Interestingly, despite recognizing that the right to vote was a matter of 'high constitutional importance', the Divisional Court accepted that it must 'afford some leeway to the legislator' and that if the UK's position were to change in the future, this was 'plainly a matter for Parliament not for the courts'.[225]

The applicants sought permission to appeal against the decision of the Divisional Court but the appeal permission was refused on the ground that the case had no real prospect of success. Accordingly, one of the applicants applied to Strasbourg. Before a chamber of the ECtHR, it was held that the exclusion from voting imposed on convicted prisoners was disproportionate since it fell outside the scope of an acceptable margin of appreciation and that it therefore amounted to a violation of the ECHR. The government appealed and the case was heard by the Grand Chamber of the ECtHR. It took advantage of the opportunity afforded by the appeal in *Hirst v UK (No. 2)*[226] to emphasise that the rights guaranteed by article 3 of the First Protocol are 'crucial to establishing and maintaining the foundations of an effective and meaningful democracy governed by the rule of law'.[227] The Grand Chamber noted that although in the twenty-first century universal suffrage had become the 'basic principle' in democratic states, the rights bestowed by article 3 were not absolute and that there was room for a margin of appreciation in this sphere. That margin was wide. Nevertheless, it was subject to European supervision since it was ultimately for the ECtHR to decide whether the requirements of article 3 of the First Protocol had been complied with.

Having regard to the case before it, the Grand Chamber underlined that prisoners in general continue to enjoy all the rights and freedoms guaranteed under the ECHR, save for the right to liberty. It had been submitted on behalf of the UK government that the ban on voting pursued the aims of: preventing crime by sanctioning the conduct of convicted prisoners; enhancing civic responsibility and respect for the rule of law; and, conferring an additional punishment on convicted prisoners. Although the Grand Chamber accepted that these were all legitimate aims, it nevertheless ruled that even allowing for a wide margin of appreciation, section 3 of the 1983 Act was a 'blunt instrument'[228] which provided for a general, automatic and indiscriminate restriction on a vitally important Convention right. It therefore held by twelve votes to five that since section 3 fell outside any acceptable margin of appreciation, it was incompatible with article 3 of the First Protocol to the ECHR.

[223] (1987) 10 EHRR 1.
[224] See *X v Netherlands* [1974] 1 DR 87; *H v Netherlands* [1983] 33 DR 242; and *Holland v Ireland* [1998] 93A DR 15.
[225] At [41]. This is clearly the language of judicial deference, an issue which was discussed at pp. 805–814.
[226] (2006) 42 EHRR 41.   [227] At [58].   [228] At [82].

Faced with this adverse ruling from the ECtHR it was incumbent on the UK government to ensure that the law was amended. This could have been achieved by either a remedial order made pursuant to section 10 of the HRA[229] or primary legislation. In a written statement published on 2 February 2006, the Secretary of State indicated that as a consequence of the complexity of the issues involved, a full public consultation would be embarked upon in order to give all interested parties the opportunity to participate in the debate. At the time of writing, however, the consultation document has yet to be published. It should be noted that the JCHR has expressed regret that the government did not take advantage of the opportunity afforded by the Electoral Administration Bill to make the necessary changes to the law.[230] Those changes may have included a more targeted ban on prisoners voting which related to offences of a particular gravity. They may also have included conferring a discretion on a sentencing judge to deprive a convicted person of the right to vote whilst incarcerated where it was felt appropriate to do so.

As we have already noted, in the White Paper which preceded the introduction of the HR Bill, the government considered that one of the benefits of incorporating Convention rights into domestic law would be that English judges would consequently be able to make a distinctive contribution to the evolving jurisprudence of the ECtHR. In its *Review of the Implementation of the Human Rights Act*, the Department for Constitutional Affairs is of the view that this has in fact happened since it contends that the HRA has 'established a "dialogue" between English judges and the European Court of Human Rights'[231] with the result that 'the close analytical attention paid by English courts to the European Convention on Human Rights case law is respected in Strasbourg, and has been influential on the way it approaches English cases'.[232] That close analytical attention is evident in a number of the cases extracted in this chapter. The *Review* later supports its earlier point when commenting how the House of Lords' analysis of the courts-martial system in *R v Spear and others*[233] was very influential in causing the ECtHR to effectively overrule significant parts of its earlier judgment in *Morris v UK*[234] when it came to re-examine the issues in *Cooper v UK*.[235]

It is evident, therefore, that in accordance with section 2 of the HRA, English courts have paid close attention to the decisions of the ECtHR and that for its part, that court has taken account of the decisions of the English courts. Thus in the words of Lord Steyn, it has been a 'two-way process'.[236] In addition to the example of the courts-martial system, it is worth noting that in *Z v UK*,[237] the ECtHR declined to follow its own previous decision in *Osman v UK*,[238] where it had held that an exclusion of liability in negligence in relation to the acts or omissions of police officers when conducting a criminal investigation amounted to a disproportionate restriction on the right of access to a court contrary to article 6(1) of the ECHR. That decision was the subject of criticism in some quarters.[239] Accordingly in *Z v UK*, the ECtHR acknowledged that its earlier decision had been based on an understanding of the

---

[229] Remedial orders are discussed more fully below.

[230] See Eleventh Report of the 2005–06 session, (HL Paper 115, HC 899) at para 1.42.

[231] (July 2006), at 4. [232] Ibid. [233] [2003] 1 AC 734. [234] (2002) 34 EHRR 52.

[235] (2004) 39 EHRR 8. See *Review of the Implementation of the Human Rights Act*, at 34.

[236] '2000–2005: Laying the Foundations of Human Rights Law in the United Kingdom' [2005] EHRLR 349 at 361. [237] (2002) 34 EHRR 97.

[238] (2000) 29 EHRR 245.

[239] See, for example, the remarks of Lord Hoffmann in 'Human Rights and the House of Lords' (1999) 62 MLR 159 at 164.

domestic law of negligence which now needed to be refined following the House of Lords decision in *Barrett v London Borough of Enfield*.[240]

(g) Public authorities

'6. Acts of public authorities

(1) It is unlawful for a public authority to act in a way which is incompatible with a Convention right.

(2) Subsection (1) does not apply to an act if—

    (a) as the result of one or more provisions of primary legislation, the authority could not have acted differently; or

    (b) in the case of one or more provisions of, or made under, primary legislation which cannot be read or given effect in a way which is compatible with the Convention rights, the authority was acting so as to give effect to or enforce those provisions.

(3) In this section "public authority" includes—

    (a) a court or tribunal, and

    (b) any person certain of whose functions are functions of a public nature,

but does not include either House of Parliament or a person exercising functions in connection with proceedings in Parliament.

(4) In subsection (3) "Parliament" does not include the House of Lords in its judicial capacity.

(5) In relation to a particular act, a person is not a public authority by virtue only of subsection (3)(b) if the nature of the act is private.

(6) "An act" includes a failure to act but does not include a failure to—

    (a) introduce in, or lay before, Parliament a proposal for legislation; or

    (b) make any primary legislation or remedial order.'

Section 6 is a vitally important provision in the HRA in that it makes it unlawful for a 'public authority' to act in a way which is incompatible with a Convention right. As such, it has created a new cause of action for which a remedy can be sought under section 7 of the HRA.[241] The general principle is, however, subject to exceptions. Thus it is not unlawful for a public authority to act incompatibly with a Convention right if it is compelled to do so by a provision in primary legislation.[242] Neither does it act unlawfully if it is acting in accordance with a provision of primary or secondary legislation which cannot be read or given effect in a way which is compatible with a Convention right.[243] Moreover, although section 6 is clear that an 'act' includes a failure to act, it expressly excludes certain failures from the definition. Thus, for example, if a court were to declare that a provision of an Act of Parliament was incompatible with a Convention right pursuant to section 4 of the HRA,[244] a failure by a government

---

[240] [2001] 2 AC 550. This example is cited in the *Review of the Implementation of the Human Rights Act* at 11, and by Lord Steyn in '2000–2005: Laying the Foundations of Human Rights Law in the United Kingdom' [2005] EHRLR 349 at 361.   [241] See the remarks of Lord Nicholls in *Re McKerr* [2004] 1 WLR 807 at [17].

[242] Section 6(2)(a).

[243] Section 6(2)(b). See the obiter remarks of Lord Nicholls in *Aston Cantlow and Wilmcote with Billesley Parochial Church Council v Wallbank* [2004] 1 AC 546 at [19], extracted at p. 860.

[244] See p. 64 for a discussion on the constitutional implications of a declaration of incompatibility.

minister to make a remedial order under section 10 of the Act[245] would not be contrary to section 6.[246] Finally, it is worth noting that 'it is now settled law that section 6 is not retrospective'.[247] In other words, section 6 relates to acts or a failure to act by a public authority which occurred after the HRA came into force, ie after 2 October 2000.

Given the importance of the meaning of 'public authority' in the present context, it is a little surprising that the HRA only partially defines the term. Thus we are informed that the courts[248] and tribunals *are* public authorities for the purposes of the HRA and that both Houses of Parliament, with the exception of the House of Lords sitting in its judicial capacity,[249] are *not* a public authority. The *exclusion* relating to Parliament is of course necessary in order to ensure that the doctrine of the legislative supremacy of Parliament is maintained.[250] Were it otherwise, Parliament would act unlawfully every time it made legislation which was incompatible with a Convention right. The HRA does not therefore impose a legal restriction on its ability to enact incompatible legislation. The *inclusion* of courts and tribunals and the House of Lords sitting in its judicial capacity requires that in the discharge of their functions, they must act in a way which is compatible with Convention rights. The implications of this inclusion will be examined later in this chapter when we consider whether or not it can be said that the HRA has horizontal effect.

In addition to referring to courts and tribunals, section 6(3) provides that a person is a 'public authority' for the purposes of the HRA where certain of their functions are functions of a public nature. However, it is further provided that in relation to a particular act, a person is not a public authority if the nature of the relevant act is private.[251] Thus, for example, it has been contended that 'a private security firm would be required to comply with Convention rights in its running of a prison, but not in its provision of security to a supermarket'.[252] This example demonstrates that it is the nature of the function which a body is performing at the relevant time which is crucial to the determination of whether it was acting as a public authority for the purposes of the HRA.

It follows from the above that there are two categories[253] of 'public authority' under the HRA: 'core' public authorities[254] which English law has traditionally recognised as being public authorities, eg government departments, local authorities, prisons, the armed forces and the police, which predominantly operate in the public law domain and are therefore subject to the HRA in all that they do;[255] and, 'functional' public authorities[256] which are not

---

[245] The power to make remedial orders under section 10 is discussed further at pp. 889–893.

[246] Section 6(6).   [247] Per Lord Steyn in *Re McKerr* [2004] 1 WLR 807 at [48].

[248] In *Government of the United States of America v Montgomery (No. 2)* [2003] 1 WLR 1916, the former Lord Chief Justice, Lord Woolf, made it clear that 'the court referred to in section 6 is a court in this jurisdiction': at [22].

[249] Once the Supreme Court which is provided for under the Constitutional Reform Act 2005 is operational, it will be necessary to amend this exclusion.   [250] See chapter 2 for a discussion of this doctrine.

[251] Section 6(5).

[252] See *The Meaning of Public Authority under the Human Rights Act*, Joint Committee of Human Rights, Seventh Report for the 2003–04 session, (HL Paper 39, HC 382), at para 6.

[253] Three if courts and tribunals are regarded as being a separate category: see the remarks of Lord Hope in *Aston Cantlow and Wilmcote with Billesley Parochial Church Council v Wallbank* [2004] 1 AC 546 at [35].

[254] Professor Oliver has referred to these as 'true' public authorities: see 'The Frontiers of the State: Public Authorities and Public Functions under the Human Rights Act' [2000] PL 476 at 480.

[255] Thus a 'core' public authority exercising a clearly private law function would nevertheless be subject to the terms of the HRA.

[256] On occasion this category is also referred to as 'hybrid' public authorities to denote that the body in question has characteristics of both a public and private nature. However, as the Joint Committee on Human

'core' public authorities but which nevertheless perform some functions of a public nature which hence makes it appropriate for them to be subject to the terms of the HRA in respect of the exercise of those functions. This latter category of public authority reflects the fact that in the modern day, privatisation and contracting-out has ensured that there are many private providers of public services.

Several of the leading cases on the meaning of 'public authority' for the purposes of the HRA have previously been considered. Thus for present purposes, the Court of Appeal decisions in *Poplar Housing and Regeneration Community Association v Donoghue*[257] and *R (on the application of Heather) v Leonard Cheshire Foundation*[258] need not detain us further. Instead, the focus of our attention will be on a case where the House of Lords was asked to decide whether a parochial church council was a public authority within the meaning of section 6(1) of the HRA, and on those cases which have been decided since *Aston Cantlow*.

....

Aston Cantlow and Wilmcote with Billesley Parochial Church Council v Wallbank [2004] 1 AC 546

In their capacity as freehold owners of certain rectorial land, the lay rectors were subject to a common law obligation to repair the chancel of the parish church. The chancel fell into disrepair and the Parochial Church Council (PCC) exercised its statutory power to enforce that obligation by serving notices on the rectors pursuant to section 2(1) of the Chancel Repairs Act 1932. There was a dispute as to whether the rectors were liable and the PCC subsequently brought proceedings under section 2(2) of the 1932 Act to cover the costs of the chancel repairs (approximately £95,000). On a preliminary issue, the judge at first instance held that the rectors were liable for the cost of the repairs.[259] On appeal, however, the Court of Appeal held[260] that since the PCC was a public authority for the purposes of section 6 of the HRA, it had acted unlawfully by bringing proceedings for recovery of the cost of repairs in violation of the rectors' Convention right under article 1 of the First Protocol to the ECHR. The PCC's appeal to the House of Lords was upheld on the basis that it was neither a 'core' nor a 'functional' public authority for the purposes of the HRA.

Lord Nicholls

'4. At first sight the Human Rights Act 1998 might seem to have nothing to do with the present case. The events giving rise to the litigation occurred, and the decision of Ferris J was given, before the Act came into force. But the decision of the Court of Appeal [2002] Ch 51 was based on the provisions of the Human Rights Act, and this decision has wide financial implications for the Church of England, going far beyond the outcome of this particular case . . . Accordingly, in order to obtain the decision of the House on this point, the plaintiff parochial church council conceded that the Human Rights Act 1998 applies in this case . . .

5. Assuming the Human Rights Act 1998 is applicable in this case, the overall question is whether the plaintiff's prosecution of proceedings against Mr and Mrs Wallbank is rendered unlawful by section 6 of the Act as an act by a public authority which is incompatible with a Convention right. In answering this question the initial step is to consider whether the plaintiff is "a public authority".

6. The expression "public authority" is not defined in the Act, nor is it a recognised term of art in English law, that is, an expression with a specific recognised meaning. The word "public" is a term of

Rights has pointed out, the term 'hybrid' is 'unhelpful' because it is the nature of the function which the bodies perform rather than their intrinsic nature which brings them within the ambit of the HRA: see Seventh Report for the 2003–04 session, at para 7.

[257] [2001] EWCA Civ 595, p. 502.   [258] [2001] EWHC 429 (Admin), p. 504.
[259] This decision was reached before the HRA came into force.   [260] [2002] Ch 51.

uncertain import, used with many different shades of meaning: public policy, public rights of way, public property, public authority (in the Public Authorities Protection Act 1893 (56 & 57 Vict c 61)), public nuisance, public house, public school, public company. So in the present case the statutory context is all important. As to that, the broad purpose sought to be achieved by section 6(1) is not in doubt. The purpose is that those bodies for whose acts the state is answerable before the European Court of Human Rights shall in future be subject to a domestic law obligation not to act incompatibly with Convention rights. If they act in breach of this legal obligation victims may henceforth obtain redress from the courts of this country. In future victims should not need to travel to Strasbourg.

7. Conformably with this purpose, the phrase "a public authority" in section 6(1) is essentially a reference to a body whose nature is governmental in a broad sense of that expression. It is in respect of organisations of this nature that the government is answerable under the European Convention on Human Rights. Hence, under the Human Rights Act 1998 a body of this nature is required to act compatibly with Convention rights in everything it does. The most obvious examples are government departments, local authorities, the police and the armed forces. Behind the instinctive classification of these organisations as bodies whose nature is governmental lie factors such as the possession of special powers, democratic accountability, public funding in whole or in part, an obligation to act only in the public interest, and a statutory constitution . . .

8. A further, general point should be noted. One consequence of being a "core" public authority, namely, an authority falling within section 6 without reference to section 6(3), is that the body in question does not itself enjoy Convention rights. It is difficult to see how a core public authority could ever claim to be a victim of an infringement of a Convention right. A core public authority seems inherently incapable of satisfying the Convention description of a victim: "any person, *non-governmental organisation* or group of individuals" (article 34, with emphasis added). Only victims of an unlawful act may bring proceedings under section 7 of the Human Rights Act 1998, and the Convention description of a victim has been incorporated into the Act, by section 7(7). This feature, that a core public authority is incapable of having Convention rights of its own, is a matter to be borne in mind when considering whether or not a particular body is a core public authority. In itself this feature throws some light on how the expression "public authority" should be understood and applied. It must always be relevant to consider whether Parliament can have intended that the body in question should have no Convention rights.

9. In a modern developed state governmental functions extend far beyond maintenance of law and order and defence of the realm. Further, the manner in which wide ranging governmental functions are discharged varies considerably. In the interests of efficiency and economy, and for other reasons, functions of a governmental nature are frequently discharged by non-governmental bodies. Sometimes this will be a consequence of privatisation, sometimes not. One obvious example is the running of prisons by commercial organisations. Another is the discharge of regulatory functions by organisations in the private sector, for instance, the Law Society. Section 6(3)(b) gathers this type of case into the embrace of section 6 by including within the phrase "public authority" any person whose functions include "functions of a public nature". This extension of the expression "public authority" does not apply to a person if the nature of the act in question is "private".

10. Again, the statute does not amplify what the expression "public " and its counterpart "private" mean in this context. But, here also, given the statutory context already mentioned and the repetition of the description "public", essentially the contrast being drawn is between functions of a governmental nature and functions, or acts, which are not of that nature. I stress, however, that this is no more than a useful guide. The phrase used in the Act is public function, not governmental function.

11. Unlike a core public authority, a "hybrid" public authority, exercising both public functions and non-public functions, is not absolutely disabled from having Convention rights. A hybrid public authority is not a public authority in respect of an act of a private nature. Here again, as with section 6(1), this feature throws some light on the approach to be adopted when interpreting section 6(3)(b). Giving a generously wide scope to the expression "public function" in section 6(3)(b) will

further the statutory aim of promoting the observance of human rights values without depriving the bodies in question of the ability themselves to rely on Convention rights when necessary.

12. What, then, is the touchstone to be used in deciding whether a function is public for this purpose? Clearly there is no single test of universal application. There cannot be, given the diverse nature of governmental functions and the variety of means by which these functions are discharged today. Factors to be taken into account include the extent to which in carrying out the relevant function the body is publicly funded, or is exercising statutory powers, or is taking the place of central government or local authorities, or is providing a public service.

13. Turning to the facts in the present case, I do not think parochial church councils are "core" public authorities. Historically the Church of England has discharged an important and influential role in the life of this country. As the established church it still has special links with central government. But the Church of England remains essentially a religious organisation. This is so even though some of the emanations of the church discharge functions which may qualify as governmental. Church schools and the conduct of marriage services are two instances. The legislative powers of the General Synod of the Church of England are another. This should not be regarded as infecting the Church of England as a whole, or its emanations in general, with the character of a governmental organisation.

14. As to parochial church councils, their constitution and functions lend no support to the view that they should be characterised as governmental organisations or, more precisely, in the language of the statute, public authorities. Parochial church councils are established as corporate bodies under a church measure, now the Parochial Church Councils (Powers) Measure 1956. For historical reasons this unique form of legislation, having the same force as a statute, is the way the Church of England governs its affairs. But the essential role of a parochial church council is to provide a formal means, prescribed by the Church of England, whereby ex officio and elected members of the local church promote the mission of the Church and discharge financial responsibilities in respect of their own parish church, including responsibilities regarding maintenance of the fabric of the building. This smacks of a church body engaged in self-governance and promotion of its affairs. This is far removed from the type of body whose acts engage the responsibility of the state under the European Convention.

. . .

16. I turn next to consider whether a parochial church council is a hybrid public authority. For this purpose it is not necessary to analyse each of the functions of a parochial church council and see if any of them is a public function. What matters is whether the particular act done by the plaintiff council of which complaint is made is a private act as contrasted with the discharge of a public function. The impugned act is enforcement of Mr and Mrs Wallbank's liability, as lay rectors, for the repair of the chancel of the church of St John the Baptist at Aston Cantlow. As I see it, the only respect in which there is any "public" involvement is that parishioners have certain rights to attend church services and in respect of marriage and burial services. To that extent the state of repair of the church building may be said to affect rights of the public. But I do not think this suffices to characterise actions taken by the parochial church council for the repair of the church as "public". If a parochial church council enters into a contract with a builder for the repair of the chancel arch, that could hardly be described as a public act. Likewise when a parochial church council enforces, in accordance with the provisions of the Chancel Repairs Act 1932, a burdensome incident attached to the ownership of certain pieces of land: there is nothing particularly "public" about this. This is no more a public act than is the enforcement of a restrictive covenant of which church land has the benefit.

. . .

19. I add only that even if section 6(1) is applicable in this type of case, and even if the provisions of the 1932 Act are incompatible with Mr and Mrs Wallbank's Convention rights under article 1 of the First Protocol, even so the plaintiff council would not be acting unlawfully in enforcing Mr and Mrs Wallbank's liability as lay rectors. Like sections 3(2) and 4(6), section 6(2) of the Human Rights Act 1998 is concerned to preserve the primacy, and legitimacy, of primary legislation. This is one of the basic

principles of the Human Rights Act . . . Here, section 2 of the Chancel Repairs Act 1932 provides that if the defendant would have been liable to be admonished to repair the chancel by the appropriate ecclesiastical court, the court shall give judgment for the cost of putting the chancel in repair. When a parochial church council acts pursuant to that provision it is acting within the scope of the exception set out in section 6(2)(b).'

Lord Hope

'41. . . . The words "public" and "authority" in section 6(1), "functions of a public nature" in section 6(3)(b) and "private" in section 6(5) are, of course, important. The word "public" suggests that there are some persons which may be described as authorities that are nevertheless private and not public. The word "authority" suggests that the person has regulatory or coercive powers given to it by statute or by the common law. The combination of these two words in the single unqualified phrase "public authority" suggests that it is the nature of the person itself, not the functions which it may perform, that is determinative. Section 6(1) does not distinguish between public and private functions. It assumes that everything that a "core" public authority does is a public function. It applies to everything that a person does in that capacity. This suggests that some care needs to be taken to limit this category to cases where it is clear that this over-arching treatment is appropriate. The phrase "functions of a public nature" in section 6(3), on the other hand, does not make that assumption. It requires a distinction to be drawn between functions which are public and those which are private. It has a much wider reach, and it is sensitive to the facts of each case. It is the function that the person is performing that is determinative of the question whether it is, for the purposes of that case, a "hybrid" public authority. The question whether section 6(5) applies to a particular act depends on the nature of the act which is in question in each case.

. . .

47. The test as to whether a person or body is or is not a "core" public authority for the purposes of section 6(1) is not capable of being defined precisely. But it can at least be said that a distinction should be drawn between those persons who, in Convention terms, are governmental organisations on the one hand and those who are non-governmental organisations on the other. A person who would be regarded as a non-governmental organisation within the meaning of article 34 ought not to be regarded as a "core" public authority for the purposes of section 6. That would deprive it of the rights enjoyed by the victims of acts which are incompatible with Convention rights that are made unlawful by section 6(1) . . . It would undermine the protections against state control which are the hallmarks of a liberal democracy.'

Lord Hobhouse

'85. The Human Rights Act 1998 and section 6 do not contain any complete or general definition of the term "a public authority". Section 6 does however contain a secondary definition in subsections (3)(b) and (5) as including, in respect of acts which are not of a private nature, persons (or bodies) certain of whose functions are functions of a public nature. This secondary category has been described as "hybrid" public authorities. It requires a two-fold assessment, first of the body's functions, and secondly of the particular act in question. The body must be one of which at least some, but not all, of its functions are of a public nature. This leaves what by inference from subsection (3)(b) is the primary category, ie, a person or body all of whose functions are of a public nature. This category has conveniently been called by the commentators a "core" public authority. For this category, there is no second requirement; the section potentially applies to everything that they do regardless of whether it is an act of a private or public nature.

86. Is a PCC a "core" public authority? The answer I would give to this question is that it is clearly not. Its functions, as identified above from the relevant statutory provisions, clearly include matters which are concerned only with the pastoral and organisational concerns of the diocese and the congregation

of believers in the parish. It acts in the sectional not the public interest. The most that can be said is that it is a creature of a church measure having the force of a statute—but that is not suggested to be conclusive—and that some aspects of the Church of England which is the "established church" are of wider general interest and not of importance to the congregation alone. Thus the priest ministering in the parish may have responsibilities that are certainly not public, such as the supervision of the liturgies used or advising about doctrine, but may have other responsibilities which are of a public nature, such as a responsibility for marriages and burials and the keeping of registers. But the PCC itself does not have such public responsibilities nor are its functions public; it is essentially a domestic religious body. The fact that the Church of England is the established church of England may mean that various bodies within that Church may as a result perform public functions. But it does not follow that PCCs themselves perform any such functions. . . .'

Lord Rodger

'160. The obligation under article 1 has bound the United Kingdom ever since the Convention came into force. Since 1966 individuals have been able to bring proceedings in Strasbourg to ensure that the United Kingdom complies with that obligation. Prima facie, therefore, when Parliament enacted the 1998 Act "to give further effect to rights and freedoms guaranteed under the European Convention on Human Rights", the intention was to make provision in our domestic law to ensure that the bodies carrying out the functions of government in the United Kingdom observed the rights and freedoms set out in the Convention. Parliament chose to bring this about by enacting inter alia section 6(1), which makes it unlawful for "a public authority" to act in a way that is incompatible with a Convention right. A purposive construction of that section accordingly indicates that the essential characteristic of a public authority is that it carries out a function of government which would engage the responsibility of the United Kingdom before the Strasbourg organs.

. . .

166. . . . what matters is that the PCC's general function is to carry out the religious mission of the Church in the parish, rather than to exercise any governmental power. Moreover, the PCC is not in any sense under the supervision of the state: under section 9 of the 1956 Measure it is the bishop who has certain powers in relation to the PCC's activities. In these circumstances the fact that the PCC is constituted as a body corporate under the 1956 Measure is irrelevant. For these reasons, in respectful disagreement with the Court of Appeal, I consider that the PCC is not a core public authority for the purposes of section 6 of the Act.'

The leading judgment in *Aston Cantlow* was delivered by Lord Nicholls. Its most significant feature was the call for a 'generously wide' interpretation of functions of a public nature in section 6(3)(b) of the HRA although somewhat ironically, this was not enough to allow the lay rectors to win their claim in the case itself.[261] In advocating a 'generously wide' approach which was in keeping with the aim of the HRA, ie promoting the observance of human rights values, Lord Nicholls acknowledged that there was no universal test for determining a function of a public nature. Nevertheless, he did identify certain 'touchstones' which were to be taken into account.[262] These included the extent to which the relevant body was: publicly funded; exercising statutory powers; taking the place of central government or local authorities; or providing a public service. According a function of a public nature a broad meaning has been welcomed in some quarters.[263] However, it is not a view which is immune from criticism. Despite its evident attractions in terms of securing the better protection of human rights for a larger constituency, Professor Oliver has argued that the wider implications which

[261] See Oliver, 'Functions of a public nature under the Human Rights Act' [2004] PL 329 at 342.
[262] At [12]. [263] See, for example, the views of the JCHR discussed at p. 865.

flow from a policy of generous interpretation mean that on balance, it is an undesirable approach to take. In her opinion, a broad or generous interpretation could create the risk of fruitless litigation between private parties. This would create legal uncertainty which would in turn have a negative impact upon the way in which many bodies carried out their functions. Professor Oliver is also of the view that a generous interpretation has the potential to be 'discriminatory and unacceptably anomalous' if the nature of a function performed by a private person or organisation depended upon the identity of the contractual parties, or whether there was a contract at all. Finally, Professor Oliver expresses concern that a generous interpretation would require the courts to have to strike a balance between the interests and rights of a complainant and those of private service providers. As she rightly points out, 'the Convention articles are not helpful here, not having been drafted with this 'private' balance in mind'.[264] Accordingly, in the light of these criticisms, Professor Oliver argues that:

'. . . the only sure criterion for "function of a public nature" in the absence of statutory provisions elaborating the concept is that the body is exercising physically coercive powers (such as detaining prisoners and restraining mental patients) either for the protection of the coerced person or in the public interest, or is exercising special authority (including licensing professional and other activity and exercising non-consensual disciplinary powers in the public interest) over those it deals with, which would be unlawful unless specifically authorised by statute or exercised in accordance with special common law requirements . . .'.[265]

(i) The Joint Committee on Human Rights' view

The Joint Committee on Human Rights (JCHR)[266] has been critical of the current state of the law regarding the meaning of 'public authority' for the purposes of the HRA. In its Seventh Report of session 2003–04,[267] the JCHR notes that the meaning of 'public authority' is the subject of continuing judicial development,[268] and it expresses the view that the broad approach which the House of Lords took to the interpretation of 'functional public authorities' in *Aston Cantlow* is to be preferred to the 'predominantly "institutional" rather than "functional" approach'[269] taken by the Court of Appeal in both *Poplar* and *Leonard Cheshire*. Having summarised the relevant case law up to the date of publication, the JCHR points out that a private body is likely to be a functional public authority for the purposes of the HRA if: its structures and work are closely linked with the delegating or contracting out state body; or it is exercising powers of a public nature directly assigned to it by statute; or, it is exercising coercive powers devolved from the state.[270] However, the JCHR also identifies a number of other factors as relevant to the question whether a body falls within the scope of

---

[264] [2004] PL 329 at 344.   [265] [2004] PL 329 at 345.
[266] See pp. 896–897 for the functions of the JCHR.
[267] *The Meaning of Public Authority Under the Human Rights Act*, (HL Paper 39, HC 382). Lord Steyn has described the report as being a 'balanced and impressive review': see '2000–2005: Laying the Foundations of Human Rights Law in the United Kingdom' [2005] EHRLR 349 at 356. For a full discussion of the JCHR's report, see Sunkin 'Pushing forward the frontiers of Human Rights protection: the Meaning of Public Authority under the Human Rights Act' [2004] PL 643.
[268] At para 10. The nature of this continuing development will become apparent in the discussion below.
[269] At para 39.   [270] At para 40.

section 6(3)(b). These are:

- the fact of delegation from a state body;
- the fact of supervision by a state regulatory body;
- public funding;
- the public interest in the functions being performed; or
- motivation of serving the public interest, rather than profit.[271]

In the opinion of the JCHR, the tests which have been applied by the courts have led to 'many instances where an organisation "stands in the shoes of the state" and yet does not have responsibilities under the Human Rights Act'.[272] Since the Committee takes the view that this amounts to a gap in human rights protection which is contrary to both the spirit of the legislation and the legislators' intention, it considers how the problem might be solved. A number of potential solutions are considered. These are: amending the HRA in various ways, eg redefining public functions, scheduling public authorities, designating public authorities or public functions; protecting human rights by inserting terms in contracts between state bodies and private organisations which provide services, or between a private organisation and the recipient of services; or providing authoritative guidance which clarifies when an organisation is likely to be a public authority under the HRA and the responsibilities to which it is therefore subject.[273] However, the solution which the JCHR prefers is the improved interpretation of section 6(3)(b) in accordance with certain general principles. Thus the Committee emphasizes that it is important that the test which should be applied under section 6(3)(b) is a 'functional rather than an institutional' test. In its view, 'a function is a public one when government has taken responsibility for it'[274] in the public interest. Thus although a public function will often be carried out under direct statutory authority, it does not follow that such statutory authority is a prerequisite of a public function. Indirect statutory authority may arise, as the JCHR notes, where, for example, a private body contracts with a local authority to provide the housing which the local authority is under a statutory duty to provide. In the words of the Report, 'the loss of a single step in proximity to the statutory duty does not change the nature of the function, nor the nature of its capacity to interfere with Convention rights'.[275] Neither does the JCHR consider that institutional proximity to the state ought necessarily to be the determining factor. Rather, it contends that:

'. . . as a matter of broad principle, a body is a functional public authority performing a public function under section 6(3)(b) of the Human Rights Act where it exercises a function that has its origin in governmental responsibilities . . . in such a way as to compel individuals to rely on that body for realization of their Convention human rights'.[276]

(ii) The post-Aston Cantlow authorities

The first post-*Aston Cantlow* authority to consider is the Court of Appeal decision in *R (Beer (trading as Hammer Trout Farm)) v Hampshire Farmers' Markets Ltd.*[277] In this case, the claimant had been an accepted stallholder at a farmers' market since the council had first established farmers' markets pursuant to the Local Government and Housing Act 1989.

---

[271] Ibid.   [272] At para 41.
[273] These potential solutions are considered in chapters 5–7 of the Report.   [274] At para 138.
[275] At para 142.   [276] At para 157.   [277] [2004] 1 WLR 233.

In 2001, the council handed over the running of the markets to a company whose registered address was initially at the council's offices. The council continued to provide some finance and facilities to the company, including the use of an office and a computer. The company's secretary was an employee of the council and that person later became the company's business development manager and one of its directors. In 2002, the claimant applied to participate in the market programme. However, his application was rejected. The claimant therefore brought a judicial review claim which was successful at first instance.[278] On appeal, the Court of Appeal was required to determine two issues: whether Hampshire Farmers' Markets Ltd was a body which was susceptible to judicial review; and, whether the company was a 'public authority' for the purposes of section 6 of the HRA.

In giving the leading judgment, Dyson LJ observed that the tests for a functional public authority under the HRA and for amenability to judicial review were, 'for practical purposes', the same. In other words, they would usually admit of the same answer, although this need not necessarily be so. His Lordship also rejected the suggestion that the speeches in *Aston Cantlow* cast doubt on what had been said in either *Poplar* or *Leonard Cheshire*. In his view, the two cases remained a 'useful guide to amenability to judicial review'.[279] Having regard to the facts of the case before him, Dyson LJ drew attention to a number of factors which supported the finding that the company was susceptible to judicial review and that in rejecting the claimant's application for a licence, it had been acting as a public authority for the purposes of section 6 of the HRA. These factors were that: the company owed its existence to the council which had set it up using its statutory powers; the company had stepped into the shoes of the council in that it was performing the same functions as had previously been performed by the council, to the same end and in substantially the same way; the council had supported the company in a number of respects, eg the registered office, the use of the computer etc; and that the markets had been held on publicly owned land to which the public had access.

The next case to take into account is *Cameron v Network Rail Infrastructure Ltd*.[280] Here, the claimants had sought damages under the HRA on the grounds that the death of their mother in the Potters Bar train crash on 10 May 2002 due to a points failure had involved breaches of articles 2 and 8 of the ECHR. It was therefore a necessary ingredient of the claims that if they were to succeed, the defendants had to be a public authority at the material time, ie at the date of the accident. In holding that the defendants were neither a 'core' public authority nor a 'functional' public authority, Sir Michael Turner cited extensively from the speeches of the House of Lords in *Aston Cantlow*, which he believed ought to 'be accorded the utmost respect'. Nevertheless, he was of the opinion that 'there is an element of circulatory in all the attempts which have been made to identify the key legal elements of what constitutes a core public authority'.[281] Having regard to the case before him, the judge recognised that 'a simple list of functions and duties will not suffice to determine the question which is at issue here'.[282] However, he did accept that 'descending in some detail to what will be the determining factors' was necessary. Those factors were: the business of running a railway was not intrinsically an activity of government; there was a clear commercial objective in Railtrack's performance, ie to make profits for its shareholders, and it had been stripped of any regulatory function prior to the train crash; there was no obligation on Railtrack to conduct its operations in a manner subservient to the public interest; Railtrack was not democratically accountable to central or local government; Railtrack's board of directors was appointed by the company and their

---

[278] [2002] EWHC 2559 (Admin).   [279] At [15].   [280] [2006] EWHC 1133 (QB).
[281] At [23].   [282] At [29].

appointment was not subject to government influence or control; Railtrack possessed no special powers and neither did it enjoy immunities which might have been indications of 'publicness' had they existed; and Railtrack was not publicly funded. Collectively, therefore, these factors led inexorably to the conclusion that Railtrack was not a public body for the purposes of the HRA and hence the claim failed.

The meaning of 'public authority' for the purposes of the HRA was also at issue in *R (on the application of Johnson and others) v London Borough of Havering.*[283] The claimants were representative residents of care homes owned and controlled by the local authority. They sought to challenge prospective contractual arrangements for the transfer of the care homes to a private sector provider. They argued that the transfer would deprive them of effective protection for their human rights and that this would therefore be unlawful under section 6(1) of the HRA since it would amount to a failure by the local authority to act in a way which was compatible with Convention rights. The claim for judicial review therefore raised two issues of principle: (i) whether a private body which had made arrangements with a local authority in the exercise of that authority's functions under sections 21 and 26 of the National Assistance Act 1948 could be said to itself exercise functions of a public nature within the meaning of section 6(3)(b) so that it was a public authority for the purposes of section 6(1) of the HRA; and (ii), whether the transfer of a home to the private sector would be unlawful under section 6(1).

The Secretary of State intervened in *Johnson* in order to argue for a wide interpretation of 'public authority' so as to cover the elderly and vulnerable receiving care from a private provider in the circumstances described above.[284] However, Forbes J, sitting in the Administrative Court, considered himself bound by the Court of Appeal authority in *Poplar* and *Leonard Cheshire* which, he believed, had not been overruled by the House of Lords in *Aston Cantlow* despite arguments to the contrary advanced on behalf of the Secretary of State.[285] Accordingly, during the course of his judgment, he cited the following passage from the judgment of Lord Woolf CJ in *Poplar* on two separate occasions:

'The purpose of section 6(3)(b) is to deal with hybrid bodies which have both public and private functions. It is not to make a body, which does not have responsibilities to the public, a public body merely because it performs acts on behalf of a public body which would constitute public functions were such acts to be performed by the public body itself and an act can remain of a private nature even though it is performed because another body is under a public duty to ensure that that act is performed.'[286]

Thus in the opinion of Forbes J, if the transfer of the care homes were to take place in the present case, it would not mean that the private provider would be acting as a public authority for the purposes of the HRA in subsequently running those homes. What then of the residents' Convention rights? Against whom would they be enforceable?

It was held by Forbes J that the short answer to these questions was 'the local authority'. In his judgment, the transfer of the homes to the private sector would not absolve the council from its duty under section 6(1) of the HRA to act compatibly with Convention rights. Thus if a transfer were to take place, the council 'would continue to be obliged to take appropriate

---

[283] [2006] EWHC 1714 (Admin).

[284] In *Review of the Implementation of the Human Rights Act*, the DCA made reference to this intervention: at 28.

[285] As we have seen, this had also been the view of the Court of Appeal in *R (Beer (trading as Hammer Trout Farm)) v Hampshire Farmers' Markets Ltd* [2004] 1 WLR 233.

[286] *Poplar Housing and Regeneration Community Association Ltd v Donoghue* [2001] EWCA Civ 595 at [59]. See p. 503.

steps (for example) to safeguard the lives of the claimants, to protect them from inhuman and degrading treatment and to safeguard their private and family life, home and correspondence'.[287] Accordingly, a transfer would not be contrary to section 6(1) of the HRA.

Of the three decisions referred to above, it is *Johnson* which is perhaps of greatest interest in that it suggests that where a local authority contracts out services to the private sector which it would otherwise perform itself, the local authority will remain liable under the HRA for a subsequent breach of Convention rights. In other words, although the private sector provider is not a 'public authority' for the purposes of the HRA, the local authority is and it will therefore remain under an obligation to ensure that Convention rights are not breached by the private provider. This is a potentially significant ruling which may have important consequences for human rights protection in the UK. Although the approach which Forbes J favours prevents a local authority from contracting out of its human rights responsibilities under the HRA, there is a case for arguing that the indirect form of accountability envisaged is not in keeping with the establishment of a human rights culture in the UK. The JCHR has expressed concerns about this development. In its opinion, such a culture will 'not be promoted by removing from those delivering sensitive services the responsibility for compliance with, and the liability for breaches of, those human rights standards'.[288] It thus remains to be seen what the appeal courts will make of this issue when they have the opportunity to consider it.

(h) Does the HRA have horizontal effect?

Borrowing from European Law and the doctrine of direct effects[289] at the suggestion of Professor Wade, it is necessary to consider whether Convention rights under the HRA are enforceable against private individuals (horizontal effect) as well as being enforceable against the state (vertical effect). Section 6(1) of the HRA states that it is unlawful for a 'public authority' to act in a way which is incompatible with a Convention right. Thus at first glance, it would appear that relations between private individuals do not come within the scope of the Act. Certainly this seems to have been the view of the government both before and during the passage of the HRA. In *Rights Brought Home*,[290] it was stated that:

'The definition of what constitutes a public authority is in wide terms. Examples of persons or organisations whose acts or omissions it is intended should be able to be challenged include central government (including executive agencies); local government; the police; immigration officers; prisons; courts and tribunals themselves; and, to the extent that they are exercising public functions, companies responsible for areas of activity which were previously within the pubic sector, such as the privatised utilities. The actions of Parliament, however, are excluded.'[291]

Similarly during the course of the debate on the second reading of the HR Bill in the House of Lords, the then Lord Chancellor, Lord Irvine, explained the application of the Bill to public authorities in the following terms:

'We decided, first of all, that a provision of this kind should apply only to public authorities, however defined, and not to private individuals. That reflects the arrangements for taking cases to the

---

[287] [2006] EWHC 1714 (Admin) at [44].
[288] *The Meaning of Public Authority under the Human Rights Act*, Seventh Report of session 2003–04, at para 85.
[289] See pp. 351–362.
[290] Cm 3782 (1997).   [291] At para 2.2.

convention institutions in Strasbourg. The convention had its origins in a desire to protect people from the misuse of power by the state, rather than from actions of private individuals. Someone who takes a case to Strasbourg is proceeding against the United Kingdom Government, rather than against a private individual. We also decided that we should apply the Bill to a wide rather than a narrow range of public authorities, so as to provide as much protection as possible to those who claim that their rights have been infringed.'[292]

Professor Wade has argued, however, that whatever the government's intention, the words used in section 6(1) are capable of bearing a different construction. By including courts and tribunals within the definition of 'public authority' for the purposes of the Act, it follows that they will have to act in a manner which is compatible with Convention rights when determining disputes which come before them. No problem arises where the dispute is between an individual and the state. Where, however, the dispute is between private parties, a court or tribunal will still be required to deliver a judgment which is compatible with Convention rights. Thus in Professor Wade's opinion, Convention rights will be capable of being enforced against private individuals and bodies as well as against the state.

Support for this contention (Professor Wade has described it as the 'literal argument') is to be found in *Human Rights: Law and Practice*, where the authors state that:

'Because the courts are public authorities, they have a duty to ensure that Convention rights are protected even in litigation between private parties. The obligation of the court under s.6 will apply where the Convention has effect on the legal relationship between private parties because the state (acting through its courts) is obliged, under the Convention, to protect individuals against breaches of their rights.'[293]

Given the remarks of Lord Irvine quoted above, it is perhaps a little surprising that a further statement made by the former Lord Chancellor in response to a proposed amendment to the Bill has been placed in a central position in the debate as to the horizontal effect of the Human Rights Act 1998. In what Lord Justice Buxton has described as a passage 'which is rapidly becoming the best-known paragraph in the whole of *Hansard*', the Lord Chancellor said that:

'We . . . believe that it is right as a matter of principle for the courts to have the duty of acting compatibly with the Convention not only in cases involving other public authorities but also in developing the common law in deciding cases between individuals. Why should they not? In preparing this Bill, we have taken the view that it is the other course, that of excluding Convention considerations altogether from cases between individuals, which would have to be justified. We do not think that that would be justifiable; nor, indeed, do we think that it would be practicable.'[294]

Professor Wade has argued that this latter statement, which is clearly in conflict with the former Lord Chancellor's earlier pronouncements must in effect impliedly repeal those earlier remarks. However, Lord Justice Buxton has taken rather a different view of the matter.[295] In his opinion, Professor Wade is mistaken in believing that the HRA has horizontal effect. Instead Lord Justice Buxton argues that having regard to the wording of the Convention rights themselves and the jurisprudence of the ECtHR, it follows that those rights are enforceable by the individual against the state and emanations of the state, and not against other individuals. He argues, for example, that the wording of article 8 is such that it confers a right on the individual not to be interfered with by a public authority. He also argues, as indeed he must, that

[292] HL Debates, 3 November 1997, cols 1231–1232.
[293] Lester and Pannick, *Human Rights: Law and Practice* (2nd edn, 2004), at p. 45 (fn 3).
[294] HL Debates, 24 November 1997, col 783.
[295] See 'The Human Rights Act and Private Law' (2000) 116 LQR 48.

Lord Irvine's parliamentary remarks ought to be treated with 'considerable caution'. In short, he makes the case for vertical effect alone. In response, however, Professor Wade has suggested that article 8 is capable of bearing a different construction so that its first limb can be regarded as creating an unlimited general right enforceable by the individual against both the state and another individual, whereas the second limb recognises instances where the state but not the individual may interfere with such a right.[296]

It is clear from the eminence of those who have participated in the 'horizontal effect debate'[297] and the contrasting nature of their views that there are genuine and real difficulties involved in determining the exact scope of the HRA. Although the matter raises interesting intellectual issues, its significance really lies at a practical level. Whether or not individuals are able to enforce Convention rights under the Act against other individuals as well as against public authorities is a fundamentally important question. Although there is a general absence of authoritative case law which directly addresses the point, it does seem that in certain circumstances, the courts have recognised the horizontal application of the HRA.

Campbell v Mirror Group Newspapers Ltd [2004] 2 AC 457

The claimant was a famous model who had courted publicity throughout her career. In the past she had condemned drug taking and had publicly stated that she was not and never had been a drug addict. The defendant newspaper published a series of articles in which it disclosed that she was a recovering drug addict who was seeking therapy from a self-help group for her addiction. The articles included details of the group meetings which she had attended and showed photographs of her as she was leaving a meeting. The claimant sought damages for breach of confidentiality in respect of the articles. Although she accepted that the newspaper had been entitled to publicise the fact of her addiction and that she had been receiving treatment, it was argued that the newspaper had acted in breach of confidence by obtaining and publishing additional details concerning the therapy and the photographs.

At first instance, Morland J gave judgment for the claimant.[298] On appeal, that decision was reversed by the Court of Appeal which held that the disclosure of the additional material had been peripheral and a legitimate part of a journalistic package designed to provide clear evidence that the claimant had lied to the public about her drug addiction.[299] The claimant appealed to the House of Lords. Their Lordships held by a majority of three to two that the claimant's right to privacy (as protected by the law of breach of confidence) had been breached, and that she was therefore entitled to damages.

Lord Nicholls

'17. The time has come to recognise that the values enshrined in articles 8 and 10 are now part of the cause of action for breach of confidence. As Lord Woolf CJ has said, the courts have been able to achieve this result by absorbing the rights protected by articles 8 and 10 into this cause of action: *A v B plc* [2003] QB 195, 202, para 4. Further, it should now be recognised that for this purpose these values are of general application. The values embodied in articles 8 and 10 are as much applicable in disputes between individuals or between an individual and a non-governmental body such as a newspaper as they are in disputes between individuals and a public authority.

18. In reaching this conclusion it is not necessary to pursue the controversial question whether the European Convention itself has this wider effect. Nor is it necessary to decide whether the duty imposed on courts by section 6 of the Human Rights Act 1998 extends to questions of substantive law

---

[296] See 'Horizons of Horizontality' (2000) 116 LQR 217.
[297] See also the views of Murray Hunt QC in 'The Horizontal Effect of the Human Rights Act' [1998] PL 423.
[298] [2002] EWHC 499 (QB); [2002] HRLR 28.   [299] [2003] QB 633.

as distinct from questions of practice and procedure. It is sufficient to recognise that the values under-lying articles 8 and 10 are not confined to disputes between individuals and public authorities. This approach has been adopted by the courts in several recent decisions, reported and unreported, where individuals have complained of press intrusion . . .'

Lord Hoffmann

'49. . . . Until the Human Rights Act 1998 came into force, there was no equivalent in English domes-tic law of article 8 of the European Convention or the equivalent articles in other international human rights instruments which guarantee rights of privacy. So the courts of the United Kingdom did not have to decide what such guarantees meant. Even now that the equivalent of article 8 has been enacted as part of English law, it is not directly concerned with the protection of privacy against private persons or corporations. It is, by virtue of section 6 of the 1998 Act, a guarantee of privacy only against public authorities. Although the Convention, as an international instrument, may impose upon the United Kingdom an obligation to take some steps (whether by statute or otherwise) to protect rights of privacy against invasion by private individuals, it does not follow that such an obligation would have any counterpart in domestic law.'

Lord Hope

'82. The question in this case is whether the publicity which the respondents gave to Miss Campbell's drug addiction and to the therapy which she was receiving for it in an article which was published in the "Mirror" newspaper on 1 February 2001 is actionable on the ground of breach of confidence. Miss Campbell cannot complain about the fact that publicity was given in this article to the fact that she was a drug addict. This was a matter of legitimate public comment, as she had not only lied about her addic-tion but had sought to benefit from this by comparing herself with others in the fashion business who were addicted. As the Court of Appeal observed [2003] QB 633, 658, para 43, where a public figure chooses to make untrue pronouncements abut his or her private life, the press will normally be entitled to put the record straight.

. . .

Was the information confidential?

88. The information contained in the article consisted of the following five elements: (1) the fact that Miss Campbell was a drug addict; (2) the fact that she was receiving treatment for her addiction; (3) the fact that the treatment which she was receiving was provided by Narcotics Anonymous; (4) details of the treatment—for how long, how frequently and at what times of day she had been receiving it, the nature of it and extent of her commitment to the process; and (5) a visual portrayal by means of photographs of her when she was leaving the place where treatment had been taking place.

. . .

95. I think that the judge was right to regard the details of Miss Campbell's attendance at Narcotics Anonymous as private information which imported a duty of confidence. He said that information relating to Miss Campbell's therapy for drug addiction giving details that it was by regular attendance at Narcotics Anonymous meetings was easily identifiable as private. With reference to the guidance that the Court of Appeal gave in A v B plc [2003] QB 195, 206, para 11(vii), he said that it was obvious that there existed a private interest in this fact that was worthy of protection. The Court of Appeal, on the other hand, seem to have regarded the receipt of therapy from Narcotics Anonymous as less worthy of protection in comparison with treatment for the condition administered by medical practitioners. I would not make that distinction. Views may differ as to what is the best treatment for an addiction. But it is well known that persons who are addicted to the taking of illegal drugs or to alcohol can benefit from meetings at which they discuss and face up to their addiction. The private nature of these meetings encourages addicts to attend them in the belief that they can do so anonymously.

The assurance of privacy is an essential part of the exercise. The therapy is at risk of being damaged if the duty of confidence which the participants owe to each other is breached by making details of the therapy, such as where, when and how often it is being undertaken, public. I would hold that these details are obviously private.

. . .

98. Where the person is suffering from a condition that is in need of treatment one has to try, in order to assess whether the disclosure would be objectionable, to put oneself into the shoes of a reasonable person who is in need of that treatment. Otherwise the exercise is divorced from its context. The fact that no objection could be taken to disclosure of the first two elements in the article does not mean that they must be left out of account in a consideration as to whether disclosure of the other elements was objectionable. The article must be read as a whole along with the photographs to give a proper perspective to each element. The context was that of a drug addict who was receiving treatment. It is her sensibilities that needed to be taken into account. Critical to this exercise was an assessment of whether disclosure of the details would be liable to disrupt her treatment. It does not require much imagination to appreciate the sense of unease that disclosure of these details would be liable to engender, especially when they were accompanied by a covertly taken photograph. The message that it conveyed was that somebody, somewhere, was following her, was well aware of what was going on and was prepared to disclose the facts to the media. I would expect a drug addict who was trying to benefit from meetings to discuss her problem anonymously with other addicts to find this distressing and highly offensive.

99. The approach which the Court of Appeal took to this issue seems to me, with great respect, to be quite unreal. I do not think that they had a sound basis for differing from the conclusion reached by the trial judge as to whether the information was private. They were also in error, in my opinion, when they were asking themselves whether the disclosure would have offended the reasonable man of ordinary susceptibilities. The mind that they examined was the mind of the reader: para 54. This is wrong. It greatly reduces the level of protection that is afforded to the right of privacy. The mind that has to be examined is that, not of the reader in general, but of the person who is affected by the publicity. The question is what a reasonable person of ordinary sensibilities would feel if she was placed in the same position as the claimant and faced with the same publicity.

. . .

The competing rights of free speech and privacy

. . .

105. The context for this exercise is provided by articles 8 and 10 of the Convention. The rights guaranteed by these articles are qualified rights. Article 8(1) protects the right to respect for private life, but recognition is given in article 8(2) to the protection of the rights and freedoms of others. Article 10(1) protects the right to freedom of expression, but article 10(2) recognises the need to protect the rights and freedoms of others. The effect of these provisions is that the right to privacy which lies at the heart of an action for breach of confidence has to be balanced against the right of the media to impart information to the public. And the right of the media to impart information to the public has to be balanced in its turn against the respect that must be given to private life.

. . .

111. Section 12(4) of the Human Rights Act 1998 provides . . . But, as Sedley LJ said in *Douglas v Hello! Ltd* [2001] QB 967, 1003, para 133, you cannot have particular regard to article 10 without having equally particular regard at the very least to article 8: see also *In re S (A Child) (Identification: Restrictions on Publication)* [2004] Fam 43, 72, para 52 where Hale LJ said that section 12(4) does not give either article pre-eminence over the other. These observations seem to me to be entirely consistent with the jurisprudence of the European court, as is the following passage in Sedley LJ's

opinion in *Douglas*, at p. 1005, para 137:

> "The case being one which affects the Convention right of freedom of expression, section 12 of the Human Rights Act 1998 requires the court to have regard to article 10 (as, in its absence, would section 6). This, however, cannot, consistently with section 3 and article 17, give the article 10(1) right of free expression a presumptive priority over other rights. What it does is require the court to consider article 10(2) along with article 10(1), and by doing so to bring into the frame the conflicting right to respect for privacy. This right, contained in article 8 and reflected in English law, is in turn qualified in both contexts by the right of others to free expression. The outcome, which self-evidently has to be the same under both articles, is determined principally by considerations of proportionality."

Striking the balance

112. There is no doubt that the presentation of the material that it was legitimate to convey to the public in this case without breaching the duty of confidence was a matter for the journalists. The choice of language used to convey information and ideas, and decisions as to whether or not to accompany the printed word by the use of photographs, are pre-eminently editorial matters with which the court will not interfere. The respondents are also entitled to claim that they should be accorded a reasonable margin of appreciation in taking decisions as to what details needed to be included in the article to give it credibility. This is an essential part of the journalistic exercise.

113. But decisions about the publication of material that is private to the individual raise issues that are not simply about presentation and editing. Any interference with the public interest in disclosure has to be balanced against the interference with the right of the individual to respect for their private life. The decisions that are then taken are open to review by the court. The tests which the court must apply are the familiar ones. They are whether publication of the material pursues a legitimate aim and whether the benefits that will be achieved by its publication are proportionate to the harm that may be done by the interference with the right to privacy. The jurisprudence of the European Court of Human Rights explains how these principles are to be understood and applied in the context of the facts of each case. Any restriction of the right to freedom of expression must be subjected to very close scrutiny. But so too must any restriction of the right to respect for private life. Neither article 8 nor article 10 has any pre-eminence over the other in the conduct of this exercise. As Resolution 1165 of the Parliamentary Assembly of the Council of Europe (1998), para 11, pointed out, they are neither absolute nor in any hierarchical order, since they are of equal value in a democratic society.

The article 10 right

114. In the present case it is convenient to begin by looking at the matter from the standpoint of the respondents' assertion of the article 10 right and the court's duty as a public authority under section 6(1) of the Human Rights Act 1998, which section 12(4) reinforces, not to act in a way which is incompatible with that Convention right.

The article 8 right

. . .

120. As for the other side of the balance, a person's right to privacy may be limited by the public's interest in knowing about certain traits of her personality and certain aspects of her private life . . . But it is not enough to deprive Miss Campbell of her right to privacy that she is a celebrity and that her private life is newsworthy. A margin of appreciation must, of course, be given to the journalist. Weight must be given to this. But to treat these details merely as background was to undervalue the importance that was to be attached to the need, if Miss Campbell was to be protected, to keep these details private. And it is hard to see that there was any compelling need for the public to know the name of the organisation that she was attending for the therapy, or for the other details of it to be set out. The presentation of the article indicates that this was not fully appreciated when the decision was taken to

publish these details. The decision to publish the photographs suggests that greater weight was being given to the wish to publish a story that would attract interest rather than to the wish to maintain its credibility.

121. Had it not been for the publication of the photographs, and looking to the text only, I would have been inclined to regard the balance between these rights as about even. Such is the effect of the margin of appreciation that must, in a doubtful case, be given to the journalist. In that situation the proper conclusion to draw would have been that it had not been shown that the restriction on the article 10 right for which Miss Campbell argues was justified on grounds of proportionality. But the text cannot be separated from the photographs. The words "Therapy: Naomi outside meeting" underneath the photograph on the front page and the words "Hugs: Naomi, dressed in jeans and baseball hat, arrives for a lunchtime group meeting this week" underneath the photograph on p. 13 were designed to link what might otherwise have been anonymous and uninformative pictures with the main text. The reader would undoubtedly make that link, and so too would the reasonable person of ordinary sensibilities. The reasonable person of ordinary sensibilities would also regard publication of the covertly taken photographs, and the fact that they were linked with the text in this way, as adding greatly overall to the intrusion which the article as a whole made into her private life.

. . .

123. . . . Miss Campbell could not have complained if the photographs had been taken to show the scene in the street by a passer-by and later published simply as street scenes. But these were not just pictures of a street scene where she happened to be when the photographs were taken. They were taken deliberately, in secret and with a view to their publication in conjunction with the article. The zoom lens was directed at the doorway of the place where the meeting had been taking place. The faces of others in the doorway were pixelated so as not to reveal their identity. Hers was not, the photographs were published and her privacy was invaded. The argument that the publication of the photograph added credibility to the story has little weight. The photograph was not self-explanatory. Neither the place nor the person were instantly recognisable. The reader only had the editor's word as to the truth of these details.

124. Any person in Miss Campbell's position, assuming her to be of ordinary sensibilities but assuming also that she had been photographed surreptitiously outside the place where she been receiving therapy for drug addiction, would have known what they were and would have been distressed on seeing the photographs. She would have seen their publication, in conjunction with the article which revealed what she had been doing when she was photographed and other details about her engagement in the therapy, as a gross interference with her right to respect for her private life. In my opinion this additional element in the publication is more than enough to outweigh the right to freedom of expression which the defendants are asserting in this case.

Conclusion

125. Despite the weight that must be given to the right to freedom of expression that the press needs if it is to play its role effectively, I would hold that there was here an infringement of Miss Campbell's right to privacy that cannot be justified. In my opinion publication of the third, fourth and fifth elements in the article (see para 88) was an invasion of that right for which she is entitled to damages. I would allow the appeal and restore the orders that were made by the trial judge.'

Baroness Hale

'126. My Lords, this case raises some big questions. How is the balance to be struck between everyone's right to respect for their private and family life under article 8 of the European Convention on Human Rights and everyone's right to freedom of expression, including the freedom to receive and impart information and ideas under article 10? How do those rights come into play in a dispute between two private persons? But the parties are largely agreed about the answers to these. They disagree about where that balance is to be struck in the individual case. In particular, how far is a newspaper able to go in publishing what would otherwise be confidential information about a celebrity in order to set the record straight? And does it matter that the article was illustrated by a covertly taken photograph?

. . .

The basic principles

132. Neither party to this appeal has challenged the basic principles which have emerged from the Court of Appeal in the wake of the Human Rights Act 1998. The 1998 Act does not create any new cause of action between private persons. But if there is a relevant cause of action applicable, the court as a public authority must act compatibly with both parties' Convention rights. In a case such as this, the relevant vehicle will usually be the action for breach of confidence, as Lord Woolf CJ held in *A v B plc* [2003] QB 195, 202, para 4:

> "[Articles 8 and 10] have provided new parameters within which the court will decide, in an action for breach of confidence, whether a person is entitled to have his privacy protected by the court or whether the restriction of freedom of expression which such protection involves cannot be justified. The court's approach to the issues which the applications raise has been modified because, under section 6 of the 1998 Act, the court, as a public authority, is required not to 'act in a way which is incompatible with a Convention right'. The court is able to achieve this by absorbing the rights which articles 8 and 10 protect into the long-established action for breach of confidence. This involves giving a new strength and breadth to the action so that it accommodates the requirements of these articles."

133. . . . But the courts will not invent a new cause of action to cover types of activity which were not previously covered: see *Wainwright v Home Office* [2004] 2 AC 406. Mrs Wainwright and her disabled son suffered a gross invasion of their privacy when they were strip-searched before visiting another son in prison. The common law in this country is powerless to protect them. As they suffered at the hands of a public authority, the Human Rights Act 1998 would have given them a remedy if it had been in force at the time, but it was not. That case indicates that our law cannot, even if it wanted to, develop a general tort of invasion of privacy. But where existing remedies are available, the court not only can but must balance the competing Convention rights of the parties.

Striking the balance

. . .

145. It has always been accepted that information about a person's health and treatment for ill-health is both private and confidential. This stems not only from the confidentiality of the doctor–patient relationship but from the nature of the information itself . . .

146. The Court of Appeal in this case held that the information revealed here was not in the same category as clinical medical records. That may be so, in the sense that it was not the notes made by a doctor when consulted by a patient. But the information was of exactly the same kind as that which would be recorded by a doctor on those notes: the presenting problem was addiction to illegal drugs, the diagnosis was no doubt the same, and the prescription was therapy, including the self-help group therapy offered by regular attendance at Narcotics Anonymous.

147. I start, therefore, from the fact—indeed, it is common ground—that all of the information about Miss Campbell's addiction and attendance at NA which was revealed in the "Daily Mirror" article was both private and confidential, because it related to an important aspect of Miss Campbell's physical and mental health and the treatment she was receiving for it. It had also been received from an insider in breach of confidence. That simple fact has been obscured by the concession properly made on her

behalf that the newspaper's countervailing freedom of expression did serve to justify the publication of some of this information. But the starting point must be that it was all private and its publication required specific justification.'

The decision in *Campbell* has some important things to say about the balancing exercise which a court is required to engage in where there is a conflict between the rights contained in articles 8 and 10 of the ECHR. Thus, for example, it confirms that in carrying out that exercise, a court is not to regard either right as being pre-eminent over the other. However, for present purposes, the case is of particular interest in relation to what it tells us about the horizontal application of the HRA. Of the five Law Lords who heard the appeal, three effectively held that the Act does not have direct horizontal effect as between private parties.[300] However, whilst the HRA cannot be the basis of a new cause of action between private parties,[301] Convention rights can be relied upon in established causes of action between such parties. Put another way, the common law may be developed by the courts to reflect Convention rights. The decision of the majority in *Campbell* thus indicates judicial support for *indirect* horizontal effect; the claimant's article 8 rights were allowed to shape and be reflected in the established cause of action for breach of confidence. Similarly in the earlier cases of *Douglas v Hello! Ltd*[302] and *Thompson & Venables v News Group Newspapers Ltd*,[303] Convention rights were relied upon in actions brought against parties which were patently not public authorities for the purposes of the HRA. Thus in *Thompson & Venables*, Dame Elizabeth Butler Sloss observed:

'That obligation on the court [under section 6(1) of the HRA] does not seem to me to encompass the creation of a free-standing cause of action based directly upon the articles of the convention . . . The duty on the court, in my view, is to act compatibly with convention rights in adjudicating upon existing common law causes of action, and that includes a positive as well as a negative obligation.'[304]

The lively academic debate about the horizontal effect of the HRA where private parties have sought to invoke Convention rights when bringing common law claims[305] can be contrasted with the more muted discussion on the reach of the HRA where the dispute between the parties involves the interpretation of statutory provisions. Thus, for example, in *Ghaidan v Godin-Mendoza*,[306] where the case turned on the meaning of 'spouse' in paragraph 2 of Schedule 1 to the Rent Act 1977, no argument appears to have been raised at any stage of the proceedings as to the application of the HRA despite the fact that both parties were clearly private individuals. The strength of the interpretive obligation which section 3 of the HRA imposes on the courts was such as to render irrelevant the identities of the parties. Thus as one commentator has observed, in cases such as *Ghaidan v Godin-Mendoza*,[307] the real 'defendant' becomes in effect the statutory provision which is the basis of the dispute.[308]

[300] See the remarks of Lord Hoffmann at [49] and Baroness Hale at [132], with whom Lord Carswell agreed.
[301] See the House of Lords judgment in *Wainwright v Home Office* [2004] 2 AC 406.
[302] [2001] QB 967.   [303] [2001] 2 WLR 1038.   [304] At [27].
[305] In addition to those articles mentioned above, see also Raphael, 'The Problem of Horizontal Effect' [2000] EHRLR 493, and Young, 'Remedial and Substantive Horizontality: the common law and *Douglas v Hello Ltd*' [2002] PL 232.   [306] [2004] UKHL 30. See p. 62.
[307] See also *Wilson v First County Trust Ltd (No. 2)* [2001] 3 All ER 228, where the dispute centred on the interpretation of section 127 of the Consumer Credit Act 1974.
[308] See Loveland, *Constitutional Law, Administrative Law, and Human Rights: A Critical Introduction*, (4th edn, 2006), at p. 755.

(i) Enforcing Convention rights

'7 Proceedings

(1) A person who claims that a public authority has acted (or proposes to act) in a way which is made unlawful by section 6(1) may—

    (a) bring proceedings against the authority under this Act in the appropriate court or tribunal, or

    (b) rely on the Convention right or rights concerned in any legal proceedings,

but only if he is (or would be) a victim of the unlawful act.

(2) In subsection (1)(a) "appropriate court or tribunal" means such court or tribunal as may be determined in accordance with rules; and proceedings against an authority include a counterclaim or similar proceeding.

(3) If the proceedings are brought on an application for judicial review, the applicant is to be taken to have a sufficient interest in relation to the unlawful activity only if he is, or would be, a victim of that act.

(4) If the proceedings are made by way of a petition for judicial review in Scotland, the applicant shall be taken to have title and interest to sue in relation to the unlawful act only if he is, or would be, a victim of that act.

(5) Proceedings under subsection (1)(a) must be brought before the end of—

    (a) the period of one year beginning with the date on which the act is complained of took place; or

    (b) such longer period as the court or tribunal considers equitable having regard to all the circumstances,

but that is subject to any rule imposing a stricter time limit in relation to the procedure in question.

(6) In subsection (1)(b) "legal proceedings" includes—

    (a) proceedings brought by or at the instigation of a public authority; and

    (b) an appeal against the decision of a court or tribunal.

(7) For the purposes of this section, a person is a victim of an unlawful act only if he would be a victim for the purposes of Article 34 of the Convention if the proceedings were brought in the European Court of Human Rights in respect of that act.

(8) Nothing in this Act creates a criminal offence.

(9) In this section "rules" means—

    (a) in relation to proceedings before a court or tribunal outside Scotland, rules made by the Lord Chancellor or the Secretary of State for the purposes of this section or rules of court.

    (b) In relation to proceedings before a court or tribunal in Scotland, rules made by the Secretary of State for those purposes.

    (c) In relation to proceedings before a tribunal in Northern Ireland—

        (i) which deals with transferred matters; and

        (ii) for which no rules made under paragraph (a) are in force,

rules made by a Northern Ireland department for those purposes,

and includes provision made by order under section 1 of the Courts and Legal Services Act 1990.

(10) In making rules, regard must be had to section 9.

(11) The Minister who has power to make rules in relation to a particular tribunal may, to the extent he considers it necessary to ensure that the tribunal can provide an appropriate remedy in relation to

an act (or proposed act) of a public authority which is (or would be) unlawful as a result of section 6(1), by order add to—

(a) the relief or remedies which the tribunal may grant; or

(b) the grounds on which it may grant any of them.

(12) An order made under subsection (11) may contain such incidental, supplemental, consequential or transitional provision as the Minister making it considers appropriate.

(13) "The Minister" includes the Northern Ireland department concerned.'

It is clear from the terms of section 7(1) of the HRA that a person who is the 'victim' of an unlawful act, ie an act which is incompatible with a Convention right, may bring proceedings under the HRA against the relevant public authority. Moreover, where the proceedings (civil or criminal) have been brought against the 'victim', he or she is entitled to rely on Convention rights in those proceedings. In short, human rights arguments may be used either as a sword or a shield.

Where the victim of an unlawful act instigates proceedings against a public authority, he or she is required to do so within one year of the date on which the act complained of took place.[309] This one year period may be extended by a court or tribunal if it considers that it is equitable to do so having regard to all the circumstances of the case.

In adopting the 'victim' requirement, the HRA has borrowed directly from article 34 of the ECHR. The significance of this is most apparent where an individual wishes to bring a human rights case by way of an application for judicial review. As we have already seen in chapter 9, whether or not an individual has locus standi to make such a challenge is dependent upon them being able to demonstrate that they have a 'sufficient interest' in the matter to which the application relates. The requirement of 'sufficient interest' was formerly interpreted quite restrictively by the courts. However, it is possible to argue that in more recent times, the courts have taken a more liberal approach to standing in cases such as *R v Inspectorate of Pollution, ex p Greenpeace Ltd (No. 2)*[310] and *R v Secretary of State for Foreign Affairs, ex p World Development Movement Ltd.*[311] In effect, representative applicants in the form of pressure groups, trade unions and the Equal Opportunities Commission have been deemed to have locus standi in judicial review cases. Under the HRA, however, where an applicant seeks judicial review to uphold a Convention right, the requirement of 'sufficient interest' will only be satisfied if the applicant is a 'victim' of the alleged unlawful act.[312] In short, it is the Convention's 'victim' test which applies to human rights judicial review cases. However, as Marriott and Nicol have noted, it is clear from the decisions of both the ECtHR and the Commission in cases such as *Norris and National Gay Federation v Ireland*[313] and *Purcell v Ireland*[314] that representative applicants do not satisfy the 'victim' test. It therefore follows, in the words of the authors, that:

'If domestic courts are obliged to follow the restrictive ECHR victim jurisprudence it is highly probable that the representative plaintiff will be denied direct access to judicial review on fundamental rights matters.'[315]

The parallel between the Convention and the HRA on the issue of standing was clearly intended by the government. Whether or not it is a good thing is, however, a rather different

---

[309] Section 7(5)(a).   [310] [1994] 4 All ER 329.   [311] [1995] 1 All ER 611. See pp. 509–513.
[312] Section 7(3).   [313] (1984) 44 DR 132.   [314] (1991) 70 DR 262.
[315] 'The Human Rights Act: Representative Standing and the Victim Culture' [1998] EHRLR 730 at 736–737.

matter. As Marriott and Nicol have pointed out, the rules on standing under the Convention 'represent a hard-fought international compromise' which at least calls into question why they should be applied in the domestic context. There is, however, a further more fundamental difficulty with the standing requirement under the HRA.

'11 Safeguard for existing human rights

A person's reliance on a Convention right does not restrict—

> (a) any other right or freedom conferred on him by or under any law having effect in any part of the United Kingdom; or
>
> (b) his right to make any claim or bring any proceedings which he could make or bring apart from sections 7 to 9. '

Section 11 of the HRA amounts to a safeguard of existing human rights. It provides that reliance on a Convention right does not restrict any other right or freedom conferred on the individual by or under any law. Neither does it restrict the right of that person to make a claim or bring proceedings in respect of that other right or freedom. Thus it is possible for a person to seek to enforce a human right by way of judicial review where it is argued that the right stems from the common law or European Community law rather than under the HRA. If such an application were to be made, locus standi would be determined on the basis of sufficient interest rather than the victim test. Thus, in the words of Marriott and Nicol, there is the potential that this 'duality of tests will cause needless complexity'.

(j) Judicial remedies

'4 Declaration of incompatibility

(1) Subsection (2) applies in any proceedings in which a court determines whether a provision of primary legislation is compatible with a Convention right.

(2) If the court is satisfied that the provision is incompatible with a Convention right, it may make a declaration of that incompatibility.

(3) Subsection (4) applies in any proceedings in which a court determines whether a provision of subordinate legislation, made in the exercise of a power conferred by primary legislation, is compatible with a Convention right.

(4) If the court is satisfied—

> (a) that the provision is incompatible with a Convention right, and
>
> (b) that (disregarding any possibility of revocation) the primary legislation concerned prevents removal of the incompatibility,

it may make a declaration of that incompatibility.

(5) In this section "court" means—

> (a) the House of Lords;
>
> (b) the Judicial Committee of the Privy Council;
>
> (c) the Courts-Martial Appeal Court;
>
> (d) in Scotland, the High Court of Justiciary sitting otherwise than as a trial court or the Court of Session;
>
> (e) in England and Wales or Northern Ireland, the High Court or the Court of Appeal.

(6) A declaration under this section ("a declaration of incompatibility")—

    (a) does not affect the validity, continuing operation or enforcement of the provision in respect of which it is given; and

    (b) is not binding on the parties to the proceedings in which it is made.'

A declaration of incompatibility under section 4 of the HRA is a remedy which lies within the discretion of a court to grant where it is satisfied that a provision in an Act of Parliament is contrary to a Convention right.[316] However, since this particular form of remedy has already been considered in chapter 1, it will not be discussed further in this section.

'8 Judicial Remedies

(1) In relation to any act (or proposed act) of a public authority which the court finds is (or would be) unlawful, it may grant such relief or remedy, or make such order, within its powers as it considers just and appropriate.

(2) But damages may be awarded only by a court which has power to award damages, or to order the payment of compensation, in civil proceedings.

(3) No award of damages is to be made unless, taking account of all the circumstances of the case, including—

    (a) any other relief or remedy granted, or order made, in relation to the act in question (by that or any other court), and

    (b) the consequences of any decision (of that or any other court) in respect of that act,

the court is satisfied that the award is necessary to afford just satisfaction to the person in whose favour it is made.

(4) In determining—

    (a) whether to award damages, or

    (b) the amount of an award,

the court must take into account the principles applied by the European Court of Human Rights in relation to the award of compensation under Article 41 of the Convention.

(5) A public authority against which damages are awarded is to be treated—

    (a) in Scotland, for the purposes of section 3 of the Law Reform (Miscellaneous Provisions) (Scotland) Act 1940 as if the award were made in an action of damages in which the authority has been found liable in respect of loss or damage to the person to whom the award is made;

    (b) for the purposes of the Civil Liability (Contribution) Act 1978 as liable in respect of damage suffered by the person to whom the award is made.

(6) In this section—

"court" includes a tribunal;
"damages" means damages for an unlawful act of a public authority; and
"unlawful" means unlawful under section 6(1).'

Where a court finds that the act of a public authority is or would be unlawful by reason of being incompatible with a Convention right, it may grant such relief or remedy or make such order as it considers appropriate.[317] This provision is, however, subject to an important caveat. A court may only grant such relief etc which is 'within its powers'. In other words, section 8(1)

---

[316] See, for example, *R (on the application of Alconbury) v Secretary of State for the Home Department* [2003] 1 AC 837, *Bellinger v Bellinger* [2003] 2 AC 467, and *A v Secretary of State for the Home Department* [2005] 2 AC 68. [317] Section 8(1) of the HRA.

does not empower a court to grant any form of relief which it could not have granted previously. Thus, for example, even if a court hearing a criminal prosecution was satisfied that the defendant was the victim of a breach of a Convention right, it would not have the power to award damages or compensation. Such a power remains with the civil courts. It is worth noting, however, that if a Minister considers that it is necessary to ensure that a tribunal can provide an appropriate remedy in relation to an act (or proposed act) of a public authority which is or would be unlawful, then he has the power to make rules to add to the relief or remedies that the tribunal may grant, or the grounds on which they may be granted.[318]

Injunctive relief is clearly a form of remedy which a claimant may seek in order to protect a Convention right.[319] No award of damages is to be made in an action brought under the HRA, however, unless having regard to other forms of relief granted, a court is satisfied that it is necessary to award just satisfaction to the claimant.[320] When determining whether or not to award damages or, if damages are to be awarded, their amount, a court must have regard to the principles applied by the ECtHR in relation to just satisfaction awarded under article 41 of the ECHR.[321] These principles must only be considered, however, where the action for damages is brought under the HRA. As Professor Feldman has noted, where damages are sought in a traditional action in tort, such as trespass, nuisance or false imprisonment, those damages will be assessed 'according to the traditional measure, usually designed to put the plaintiff as near as possible into the position which he or she would have been had the tort not occurred'[322] even though the action may be affected by the HRA. Nevertheless, as he subsequently points out, 'it will not always be easy to distinguish satisfactorily between ordinary actions for damages and actions against public authorities for violations of Convention rights, for two reasons'.[323] The first reason which he identifies is the potential ambiguity surrounding the definition of 'public authority'. Professor Feldman's second reason is that since rules governing tortious liability are developed by the courts, it follows that they 'will have to give way to Convention rights where they prove to be incompatible with them'.[324]

The issue of awarding damages for breach of a Convention right was recently considered by the House of Lords in the context of article 6.

....

R (Greenfield) v Secretary of State for the Home Department [2005] 1 WLR 673

The claimant was a prisoner serving a two-year sentence at a private prison when he failed a random drugs test contrary to rule 51(9) of the Prison Rules 1999. At a hearing before the deputy controller,[325] the claimant was refused legal representation. The charge against him was found proved and he was ordered to serve an additional 21 days in prison as his punishment. The deputy controller's decision was confirmed on review by an area prison manager. The claimant sought judicial review. He claimed that the deputy controller's decisions had infringed his right to a fair trial under article 6(1) of the ECHR. His application was dismissed by the Divisional Court,[326] and an appeal against that decision was

---

[318] Section 7(11).

[319] See, for example, *Thompson and Venables v News Group Newspapers Ltd & Associated Newspapers Ltd & MGN Ltd* [2001] 2 WLR 1038.   [320] Section 8(3).

[321] Section 8(4).

[322] Feldman, 'Remedies for Violations of Convention Rights under the Human Rights Act' [1998] EHRLR 691 at 703.   [323] Ibid.

[324] Ibid.

[325] The private sector equivalent of a deputy governor in a state-run prison. A deputy controller is still, however, a Crown servant for whom the Secretary of State is responsible.

[326] See [2001] 1 WLR 1731.

dismissed by the Court of Appeal.[327] However, following the decision of the ECtHR in *Ezeh and Connors v United Kingdom*,[328] the Secretary of State accepted that the prison proceedings against the claimant had constituted a criminal charge within the meaning of article 6 of the ECHR, that the deputy controller was not an independent and impartial tribunal for the purposes of article 6, and that the claimant had been wrongly denied access to legal representation. Accordingly, his subsequent appeal to the House of Lords was limited to a consideration of whether or not he was entitled to damages for a breach of his Convention rights.

Lord Bingham

'Just satisfaction and damages

5. The expectation therefore is, and has always been, that a member state found to have violated the Convention will act promptly to prevent a repetition of the violation, and in this way the primary object of the Convention is served.

6. The Convention has always, however, made provision for affording just satisfaction to the injured party. Article 41 of the Convention, repeating the substance of article 50 of the original version, now provides:

> "*Just satisfaction*: If the court finds that there has been a violation of the Convention or the protocols thereto, and if the internal law of the high contracting party concerned allows only partial reparation to be made, the court shall, if necessary, afford just satisfaction to the injured party."

Article 41 is not one of the articles scheduled to the 1998 Act, but it is reflected in section 8 of the Act . . . It is evident that under article 41 there are three preconditions to an award of just satisfaction: (1) that the court should have found a violation; (2) that the domestic law of the member state should allow only partial reparation to be made; and (3) that it should be necessary to afford just satisfaction to the injured party. There are also preconditions to an award of damages by a domestic court under section 8: (1) that a finding of unlawfulness or prospective unlawfulness should be made based on breach or prospective breach by a public authority of a Convention right; (2) that the court should have power to award damages, or order the payment of compensation, in civil proceedings; (3) that the court should be satisfied, taking account of all the circumstances of the particular case, that an award of damages is necessary to afford just satisfaction to the person in whose favour it is made; and (4) that the court should consider an award of damages to be just and appropriate. It would seem to be clear that a domestic court may not award damages unless satisfied that it is necessary to do so, but if satisfied that it is necessary to do so it is hard to see how the court could consider it other than just and appropriate to do so. In deciding whether to award damages, and if so how much, the court is not strictly bound by the principles applied by the European court in awarding compensation under article 41 of the Convention, but it must take those principles into account. It is, therefore, to Strasbourg that British courts must look for guidance on the award of damages.

Damages for breach of article 6

7. It is desirable for present purposes to concentrate on the Strasbourg approach to the award of damages on finding that article 6 has been violated. Article 6 seeks to ensure that everyone, in the determination of their civil rights and obligations or of any criminal charge against them, shall enjoy a fair and public hearing within a reasonable time by an independent and impartial tribunal established by law with judgment given in public. Criminal charges entail additional rights: the presumption of innocence, the right to be informed of the charge, the right of a person to defend the charge himself or through legal assistance of his own choosing. These are important rights, and significant violations are not to be lightly regarded. But they have one feature which distinguishes them from violations of articles such as article 3, where an applicant has been tortured, or article 4, where he has been

[327] See [2002] 1 WLR 545.   [328] (2002) 35 EHRR 691; (2003) 39 EHRR 1.

enslaved, or article 8, where a child has been unjustifiably removed from its family; that it does not follow from a finding that the trial process has involved a breach of an article 6 right that the outcome of the trial process was wrong or would have been otherwise had the breach not occurred. There is an obvious contrast with article 5, guaranteeing the right to liberty and security of the person, which provides in paragraph 5: "Everyone who has been the victim of arrest or detention in contravention of the provisions of this article shall have an enforceable right to compensation." There is a risk of error if Strasbourg decisions given in relation to one article of the Convention are read across as applicable to another.

8. In the great majority of cases in which the European court has found a violation of article 6 it has treated the finding of the violation as, in itself, just satisfaction under article 41. Very many examples could be cited, but it is enough to refer, among relatively recent cases, to *Benham v United Kingdom* (1996) 22 EHRR 293, para 68, *Findlay v United Kingdom* (1997) 24 EHRR 221, para 88, *Perks v United Kingdom* (1999) 30 EHRR 33, para 82, in relation to the seven applicants other than Mr Perks, *Kingsley v United Kingdom* (Application No 35605/97) (unreported) 7 November 2000, para 63; (2002) 35 EHRR 177, paras 42–43, *Ezeh and Connors v United Kingdom* (2002) 35 EHRR 691, para 114; (2003) 39 EHRR 1, para 143 and *GW v United Kingdom* (Application No 34155/96) (unreported) 15 June 2004, para 53. Both *Kingsley* and *Ezeh and Connors* were referred on to a Grand Chamber. In most of these cases the court declined to speculate on what the outcome of the particular proceedings would have been had the violation not occurred.

9. The routine treatment of a finding of violation as, in itself, just satisfaction for the violation found reflects the point already made that the focus of the Convention is on the protection of human rights and not the award of compensation. . . . Thus the Court of Appeal (Lord Woolf CJ, Lord Phillips of Worth Matravers MR and Auld LJ) were in my opinion right to say in *Anufrijeva v Southwark London Borough Council* [2004] QB 1124, paras 52–53:

> "52. . . . The remedy of damages generally plays a less prominent role in actions based on breaches of the articles of the Convention, than in actions based on breaches of private law obligations where, more often than not, the only remedy claimed is damages.
>
> 53. Where an infringement of an individual's human rights has occurred, the concern will usually be to bring the infringement to an end and any question of compensation will be of secondary, if any, importance."

Where article 6 is found to have been breached, the outcome will often be that a decision is quashed and a retrial ordered, which will vindicate the victim's Convention right.

10. . . . A recent statement of particular authority, since given by a Grand Chamber on a reference specifically directed to the issue of just satisfaction under article 41, is found in *Kingsley v United Kingdom* 35 EHRR 177, para 40:

> "The court recalls that it is well established that the principle underlying the provision of just satis-faction for a breach of article 6 is that the applicant should as far as possible be put in the position he would have enjoyed had the proceedings complied with the Convention's requirements. The court will award monetary compensation under article 41 only where it is satisfied that the loss or damage complained of was actually caused by the violation it has found, since the state cannot be required to pay damages in respect of losses for which it is not responsible."

11. As appears from the passage just cited, the court has ordinarily been willing to depart from its practice of finding a violation of article 6 to be, in itself, just satisfaction under article 41 only where the court finds a causal connection between the violation found and the loss for which an applicant claims to be compensated. Such claim may be for specific heads of loss, such as loss of earnings or profits, said to be attributable to the violation. The court has described this as pecuniary loss, which appears to represent what English lawyers call special damage. This head does not call for consideration here. It is enough to say that the court has looked for a causal connection, and has on the whole been slow to award such compensation.

12. More germane to the present case is a second head of claim for what English lawyers would call general damages and the court tends to call, but not always consistently, non-pecuniary damage. A claim under this head may be put on the straightforward basis that but for the Convention violation found the outcome of the proceedings would probably have been different and more favourable to the applicant, or on the more problematical basis that the violation deprived the applicant of an opportunity to achieve a different result which was not in all the circumstances of the case a valueless opportunity. While in the ordinary way the court has not been easily persuaded on this last basis, it has in some cases accepted it: see *Goddi v Italy* (1984) 6 EHRR 457, para 35 ("a loss of real opportunities"), *Colozza v Italy* (1985) 7 EHRR 516, para 38 ("a loss of real opportunities"), *Lechner and Hess v Austria* (1987) 9 EHRR 490, para 64 ("some loss of real opportunities"), *Weeks v United Kingdom* (1988) 13 EHRR 435, para 13 ("a loss of opportunities"), *O v United Kingdom* (1988) 13 EHRR 578, para 12 ("some loss of real opportunities") and *Delta v France* 16 EHRR 574, para 43 ("a loss of real opportunities").

. . .

14. . . . Thus while the court laid down in the authoritative case of *Kingsley* in the passage quoted in para 10 above, and repeated in *Edwards and Lewis v United Kingdom* 27 October 2004, paras 46 and 49, that the court will award monetary compensation under article 41 only where it is satisfied that the loss or damage complained of was actually caused by the violation it has found, and it has repeatedly stressed that it will not speculate on what the outcome of the proceedings would have been but for the violation, it has on occasion been willing in appropriate cases to make an award if of opinion that the applicant has been deprived of a real chance of a better outcome.

15. Counsel for the appellant relied on these variations of language to criticise the jurisprudence of the court as showing a lack of principle. The criticism is in my view misplaced. In the absence of a clear causal connection, the court's standard response has been to treat the finding of violation without more as just satisfaction . . . But it has softened this response where it was persuaded that justice required it to do so. The variations of language used are such as occur when a court addresses itself to the detailed facts of the case before it, rather than endlessly reproducing a form of words stored in the court's word processor. Wisely, in my opinion, the court has not sought to lay down hard and fast rules in a field which pre-eminently calls for a case by case judgment, and the court's language may be taken to reflect its assessment of the differing levels of probability held to attach to the causal connection found in individual cases.

16. A second head of general or non-pecuniary damage has been variously described . . . In considering claims under this head the court has, consistently with its general approach, only been willing to award compensation for anxiety and frustration (however described) attributable to the article 6 violation. It has recognised that for very many people involvement in legal proceedings is bound to cause anxiety irrespective of any article 6 breach, and no award is made in such cases. In some cases the court has found on the facts that the applicant had suffered attributable anxiety and frustration . . . In other cases the court has found that the applicant "must have" suffered such feelings . . . or that it is reasonable to assume he did . . . To gain an award under this head it is not necessary for the applicant to show that but for the violation the outcome of the proceedings would, or would probably, or even might, have been different, and in cases of delay the outcome may not be significant at all. But the court has been very sparing in making awards . . .

17. Where, having found a violation of article 6, the court has made an award of monetary compensation under article 41, under either of the heads of general damages considered in this opinion, whether for loss of procedural opportunity or anxiety and frustration, the sums awarded have been noteworthy for their modesty. . . . It made plain in *Osman v United Kingdom* (1998) 29 EHRR 245, para 164:

"The court notes that it conducts its assessment of what an applicant is entitled to by way of just satisfaction in accordance with the principles laid down in its case law under article 50 [now article 41] and not by reference to the principles or scales of assessment used by domestic courts."

It made the same point in an article 5 case, *Curley v United Kingdom* (2000) 31 EHRR 401, para 46:

> "It does not, however, consider that the domestic scales of compensation applicable to unlawful detention apply in the present case where there has been no equivalent finding of unlawfulness."

18. It was submitted for the appellant that courts in England and Wales, when exercising their power to award damages under section 8 of the 1998 Act, should apply domestic scales of damages. . . . Counsel also relied on the decisions of Sullivan J in *R (Bernard) v Enfield London Borough Council* [2003] HRLR 111, para 45, Stanley Burnton J in *R (KB) v South London and South West Region Mental Health Review Tribunal* [2004] QB 936, paras 47 and 53 and the Court of Appeal in *Anufrijeva v Southwark London Borough Council* [2004] QB 1124, paras 73 and 74, to suggest that awards under section 8 should not be on the low side as compared with tortious awards, that English courts should be free to depart from the scale of damages awarded by the European court and that English awards by appropriate courts or bodies should provide the appropriate comparator. In calculating awards for anxiety and frustration, counsel suggested, the scales of damages awarded by English courts and tribunals in discrimination cases provided an appropriate comparison.

19. None of the three English cases cited involved a violation of article 6, and to that extent they have only a limited bearing on the present problem. But there are in my opinion broader reasons why this approach should not be followed. First, the 1998 Act is not a tort statute. Its objects are different and broader. Even in a case where a finding of violation is not judged to afford the applicant just satisfaction, such a finding will be an important part of his remedy and an important vindication of the right he has asserted. Damages need not ordinarily be awarded to encourage high standards of compliance by member states, since they are already bound in international law to perform their duties under the Convention in good faith, although it may be different if there is felt to be a need to encourage compliance by individual officials or classes of official. Secondly, the purpose of incorporating the Convention in domestic law through the 1998 Act was not to give victims better remedies at home than they could recover in Strasbourg but to give them the same remedies without the delay and expense of resort to Strasbourg. This intention was clearly expressed in the *White Paper Rights Brought Home: The Human Rights Bill* (1997) (Cm 3782), para 2.6:

> "The Bill provides that, in considering an award of damages on Convention grounds, the courts are to take into account the principles applied by the European Court of Human Rights in awarding compensation, so that people will be able to receive compensation from a domestic court equivalent to what they would have received in Strasbourg."

Thirdly, section 8(4) requires a domestic court to take into account the principles applied by the European court under article 41 not only in determining whether to award damages but also in determining the amount of an award. There could be no clearer indication that courts in this country should look to Strasbourg and not to domestic precedents. The appellant contended that the levels of Strasbourg awards are not "principles" applied by the court, but this is a legalistic distinction which is contradicted by the White Paper and the language of section 8 and has no place in a decision on the quantum of an award, to which principle has little application. The court routinely describes its awards as equitable, which I take to mean that they are not precisely calculated but are judged by the court to be fair in the individual case. Judges in England and Wales must also make a similar judgment in the case before them. They are not inflexibly bound by Strasbourg awards in what may be different cases. But they should not aim to be significantly more or less generous than the court might be expected to be, in a case where it was willing to make an award at all.

. . .

The appeal

26. The appellant's complaints that the charge against him had involved the determination of a criminal charge, that article 6 of the Convention required that charge to be determined by an independent and impartial tribunal, that Mr Parry was not such a tribunal and that he should not have

been denied the right to be legally represented are now vindicated by a finding in his favour at the highest judicial level based on a public concession by the Secretary of State. This would seem on its face to be pre-eminently a case in which the finding in the appellant's favour affords just satisfaction and in which, applying Strasbourg principles, the award of damages is not necessary. . . .

28. . . . It is now accepted that Mr Parry lacked the structural independence and impartiality required for such adjudications. But he appears to have conducted this adjudication with exemplary conscientiousness, patience and regard for the appellant's interests. The standard of proof would have been very familiar to him if not to the appellant. The appellant struck Mr Parry as articulate and alert, and the contrary was not suggested when legal representation was sought before the substantive hearing. The issue for Mr Parry was whether he believed the appellant and his witness. Clearly he did not. A legal representative might have persuaded Mr Parry or another tribunal to take a different view or he might not. It is inappropriate to speculate.

29. A claim to damages for anxiety and frustration was also advanced, on the basis that the appellant did not think the charge against him would be fairly tried, because the prison authorities were biased against prisoners. It may readily be accepted that the appellant did think this, as many other prisoners have no doubt done. At the time, however, adjudication by a governor or deputy governor (or their private prison counterparts, also Crown servants) was the norm. The appellant had no expectation of any other procedure, and was treated no differently from anyone else. The conduct of the adjudication itself, as already noted, appears to have been exemplary. There is no special feature of this case which warrants an award of damages.'

The House of Lords' decision in *Greenfield* thus makes it clear that in determining whether or not to make an award of damages under section 8 of the HRA, the courts will pay close attention to the jurisprudence of the European Court on this matter, as they are required to do by the HRA itself.[329] In particular, the courts are likely to consider the Strasbourg jurisprudence on the award of just satisfaction for breaches of the *same article* as that which is at issue in the domestic proceedings because as Lord Bingham observed: 'There is a risk of error if Strasbourg decisions given in relation to one article of the Convention are read across as applicable to another.'[330] It is also apparent from *Greenfield* that whether or not a court should exercise its discretion in favour of an award of damages is dependent upon the existence of a causative link between the loss or damage complained of and the breach of the Convention right. In the absence of such a link, damages would not be an appropriate remedy.

The Strasbourg jurisprudence reveals that the ECtHR has generally been reluctant to award just satisfaction in relation to breaches of article 6 for the reasons articulated by Lord Bingham in *Greenfield*. Often, the judgment in itself is regarded as sufficient redress for the applicant. Since the coming into force of the HRA, it has been contended that the domestic courts have awarded damages for a breach of a Convention right on only three occasions.[331] In one of these cases,[332] *Van Colle v Chief Constable of Hertfordshire Police*,[333] an award of £50,000 was made in respect of the murder of a prosecution witness which was attributable to the culpable failure of the police to take the appropriate measures to prevent a known risk. Such failings therefore amounted to a breach of articles 2 and 8 of the ECHR. In giving judgment in

[329] See section 8(4), referred to above.

[330] At [7] of the judgment in *Greenfield*, extracted above. Note, however, that in *Van Colle v Chief Constable of Hertfordshire Police* [2006] 3 All ER 963, Cox J was satisfied that there was no risk of error where the decision of the ECtHR in *E v UK* [2002] 3 FLR 700 relating to a breach of article 3 was read across as applicable to the breach of article 2 in *Van Colle* itself.

[331] See *Review of the Implementation of the Human Rights Act*, Department for Constitutional Affairs (July 2006), at 18.

[332] The other two being: *R (Bernard) v Enfield London Borough Council* [2003] HRLR 111 and *R (KB) v Mental Health Review Tribunal* [2004] QB 936.   [333] [2006] 3 All ER 963.

Van Colle, Cox J noted the 'fact-sensitive approach' advocated by Lord Bingham in *Greenfield* which ought to guide domestic courts when exercising their discretion to make an award of damages under the HRA for the breach of a Convention right. Applying that approach to the facts of *Van Colle*, Cox J observed:

'In order for the court to be satisfied that an award of damages is necessary to afford just satisfaction to a victim of the state's breach of article 2, the victim does not have to prove causation of damage on the "but for" test.[334] In this case the proper question . . . is whether the protective measures that were reasonably open to DC Ridley in the circumstances would have had a real prospect of altering the outcome and avoiding Giles's death. The answer to that question is plainly yes. Indeed, on the evidence I consider it to be more likely than not that Giles's death would have been avoided had these steps been taken. DC Ridley fairly accepted in cross-examination that, if he had complied with the witness protection policy, there would have been a real prospect that Giles's life would have been saved.'[335]

Van Colle thus provides a useful illustration of the kind of circumstances in which damages were the most appropriate remedy for what had occurred since unlike the majority of article 6 cases, the court could be sure that the outcome would have been different had there been no violation of article 2. Such a finding is also consistent with the Strasbourg jurisprudence which indicates that the ECtHR is normally inclined to award damages for a violation of article 2.[336]

Once a domestic court has decided that there has been a violation of a Convention right and that an award of damages would be an appropriate remedy for any loss or damage incurred, it must further exercise its discretion as to the level of damages to award. In *Anufrijeva v Southwark London Borough Council*,[337] the Court of Appeal held:

' . . . the levels of damages awarded in respect of torts and reflected in the guidelines issued by the Judicial Studies Board (JSB), the levels of awards made by the Criminal Injuries Compensation Board and by the Parliamentary Ombudsman and the Local Government Ombudsman (LGO) may all provide some rough guidance where the consequences of the infringement of human rights are similar to that being considered in the comparator selected . . .'.[338]

In reaching such a conclusion in *Anufrijeva*, the Court of Appeal also approved of remarks made by Sullivan J in *R (Bernard) v Enfield London Borough Council*.[339] In that case, it was observed that awards made under section 8(3) of the HRA ought not to be minimal since this would serve to undermine the underlying policy of the Act, that public authorities should respect Convention rights. Sullivan J therefore advocated a 'restrained' or 'moderate' approach to quantum which would serve the dual purpose of encouraging public authorities to comply with their Convention obligations whilst not unduly depleting their ability to provide essential service for others.[340]

The jurisprudence to date in relation to section 8 of the HRA thus reflects a reluctance on the part of the courts to make an award of damages for a breach of a Convention right, save in exceptional circumstances. Thus, for example, in *Bernard*, Sullivan J held that the local authority's failure to provide the claimants with accommodation suitable to their assessed needs in breach of section 21 of the National Assistance Act 1948 amounted to 'an extreme example of maladministration'.[341] The jurisprudence also demonstrates an unwillingness to

---

[334] The test applied in tortious actions.   [335] At [105].
[336] At [108]. For examples where this has occurred, see: *Akkoç v Turkey* (2002) 34 EHRR 1173; *Tas v Turkey* (2001) 33 EHRR 325; *Semsi Omen v Turkey* [2002] ECHR 22876/93; and *Edwards v UK* (2002) 12 BHRC 190.
[337] [2004] QB 1124.   [338] At [74].   [339] [2003] HLR 27.   [340] At [58]–[59].
[341] At [60].

establish guidelines on the quantum of damages to be awarded. Accordingly, it follows that in determining the amount of an award in a case, the courts will be much influenced by the facts of that particular case and will derive only limited assistance from comparisons with tortious actions.[342]

(k) Remedial orders

'10. Power to take remedial action

(1) This section applies if—

    (a) a provision of legislation has been declared under section 4 to be incompatible with a Convention right and, if an appeal lies—

        (i) all persons who may appeal have stated in writing that they do not intend to do so;

        (ii) the time for bringing an appeal has expired and no appeal has been brought within that time; or

        (iii) an appeal brought within that time has been determined or abandoned; or

    (b) it appears to a Minister of the Crown or Her Majesty in Council that, having regard to a finding of the European Court of Human Rights made after the coming into force of this section in proceedings against the United Kingdom, a provision of legislation is incompatible with an obligation of the United Kingdom arising from the Convention.

(2) If a Minister of the Crown considers that there are compelling reasons for proceeding under this section, he may by order make such amendments to the legislation as he considers necessary to remove the incompatibility.

(3) If, in the case of subordinate legislation, a Minister of the Crown considers—

    (a) that it is necessary to amend the primary legislation under which the subordinate legislation in question was made, in order to enable the incompatibility to be removed, and

    (b) that there are compelling reasons for proceeding under this section,

he may by order make such amendments to the primary legislation as he considers necessary.

(4) This section also applies where the provision in question is in subordinate legislation and has been quashed, or declared invalid, by reason of incompatibility with a Convention right and the Minister proposes to proceed under paragraph 2(b) of Schedule 2.

(5) If the legislation is an Order in Council, the power conferred by subsection (2) or (3) is exercisable by Her Majesty in Council.

(6) In this section "legislation" does not include a Measure of the Church Assembly or of the General Synod of the Church of England.

(7) Schedule 2 makes further provision about remedial orders.'

Section 10 of the HRA provides for the making of remedial orders in order to remove an incompatibility between domestic law and a Convention right. In other words, a power is conferred upon Ministers to amend primary legislation by making secondary legislation. There are two catalysts for making a remedial order: a declaration of incompatibility made by a domestic court; or, where a judgment of the ECtHR appears to have identified an

---

[342] See the remarks of Lord Bingham in *Greenfield* at [19], (p. 886).

incompatibility in UK law.[343] However, before a minister is able to use the section 10 power, he must first consider that there are 'compelling reasons' for so doing. The HRA is silent as to the nature of these compelling reasons. Accordingly, useful regard may be had to the views of the Joint Committee on Human Rights (JCHR) which plays an important role in relation to the HRA and human rights issues generally.[344] In its Seventh Report for the 2001–02 session, that Committee noted that 'as a matter of general constitutional principle, it is desirable for amendments to primary legislation to be made by way of a Bill'. It also noted that an incompatibility can potentially be removed far more quickly through the use of primary legislation than the non-urgent remedial order procedure. Nevertheless, the Committee identified the following non-exhaustive list of factors as potentially compelling reasons why the remedial order procedure might be used in preference to the normal procedure for amending primary legislation:

- where the amendment relates to a body of legislation which is currently under review and which is likely to be subject to major reform, it may be felt inappropriate to introduce a Bill which relates to just a small part of the field to be dealt with by the larger Bill;
- the legislative timetable may be full with other important legislation, some of which might include emergency legislation;
- where the remedial order procedure would cause less delay than waiting for a slot in the legislative timetable;
- where the need to avoid undue delay is particularly pressing because the incompatibility either affects or potentially affects the life, liberty, safety or physical or mental wellbeing of the individual.[345]

These factors, together with any others which he may take into account, will help a minister decide whether or not to use the section 10 power since it should not be forgotten that it is a *power* which section 10 confers; it does not impose a duty on the executive to make remedial orders. Indeed, were a minister to fail to make a remedial order following a section 4 declaration of incompatibility this would not amount to an unlawful act under the HRA.[346] Ministerial discretion in respect of remedial orders also extends to the appropriate procedure to be followed when making an order.

'Schedule 2

Remedial orders

Orders

1.—(1) A remedial order may—
- (a) contain such incidental, supplemental, consequential or transitional provision as the person making it considers appropriate;
- (b) be made so as to have effect from a date earlier than that on which it is made;
- (c) make provision for the delegation of specific functions;
- (d) make different provision for different cases.

(2) The power conferred by sub-paragraph (1)(a) includes—
- (a) power to amend primary legislation (including primary legislation other than that which contains the incompatible provision); and

---

[343] Section 10(1)(a) and (b).   [344] See further p. 893.   [345] At para 33.
[346] See section 6(6)(b) of the HRA set out above.

(b) power to amend or revoke subordinate legislation (including subordinate legislation other than that which contains the incompatible provision).

(3) A remedial order may be made so as to have the same extent as the legislation which it affects.

(4) No person is to be guilty of an offence solely as a result of the retrospective effect of a remedial order.

Procedure

2. No remedial order may be made unless—

(a) a draft of the order has been approved by a resolution of each House of Parliament made after the end of the period of 60 days beginning with the day on which the draft was laid; or

(b) it is declared in the order that it appears to the person making it that, because of the urgency of the matter, it is necessary to make the order without a draft being so approved.

Orders laid in draft

3.—(1) No draft may be laid under paragraph 2(a) unless—

(a) the person proposing to make the order has laid before Parliament a document which contains a draft of the proposed order and the required information; and

(b) the period of 60 days, beginning with the day on which the document required by this sub-paragraph was laid, has ended.

(2) If representations have been made during that period, the draft laid under paragraph 2(a) must be accompanied by a statement containing—

(a) a summary of the representations; and

(b) if, as a result of the representations, the proposed order has been changed, details of the changes.

Urgent cases

4.—(1) If a remedial order ("the original order") is made without being approved in draft, the person making it must lay it before Parliament, accompanied by the required information, after it is made.

(2) If representations have been made during the period of 60 days beginning with the day on which the original order was made, the person making it must (after the end of that period) lay before Parliament a statement containing—

(a) a summary of the representations; and

(b) if, as a result of the representations, he considers it appropriate to make changes to the original order, details of the changes.

(3) If sub-paragraph (2)(b) applies, the person making the statement must—

(a) make a further remedial order replacing the original order; and

(b) lay the replacement order before Parliament.

(4) If, at the end of the period of 120 days beginning with the day on which the original order was made, a resolution has not been passed by each House approving the original or replacement order, the order ceases to have effect (but without that affecting anything previously done under either order or the power to make a fresh remedial order).

Definitions

5. In this Schedule—

"representations" means representations about a remedial order (or proposed remedial order) made to the person making (or proposing to make) it and includes any relevant Parliamentary report or resolution; and "required information" means—

    (a) an explanation of the incompatibility which the order (or proposed order) seeks to remove, including particulars of the relevant declaration, finding or order; and

    (b) a statement of the reasons for proceeding under section 10 and for making an order in those terms.

Calculating periods

6. In calculating any period for the purposes of this Schedule, no account is to be taken of any time during which—

    (a) Parliament is dissolved or prorogued; or

    (b) both Houses are adjourned for more than four days.'

Just as there are two catalysts for making a remedial order, so there are two procedures which may be followed when making the order: the non-urgent procedure; and the urgent procedure. Under the former, the minister is required to lay a draft of the proposed order before Parliament and then consult upon it before subsequently laying a draft order before Parliament which is then subject to the affirmative resolution procedure, ie it will not come into force unless it is approved by a resolution of both Houses during the specified period. In an urgent case, the minister may make a remedial order without it first being approved in draft. Such an order will cease to have effect, however, if it has not been approved by both Houses during the specified period.

The HRA gives no indication as to when it might be appropriate to follow the urgent procedure for making a remedial order in preference to the non-urgent procedure. Accordingly, it would seem permissible once again to have regard to the views of the JCHR. In its Seventh Report for the 2001–02 session, the Committee expressed the view that the 'decisive factor' in deciding which procedure is appropriate 'should be the current and foreseeable impact of the incompatibility on anyone who might be affected by it'.[347] It also drew attention to the following non-exhaustive list of factors which are likely to be relevant to the decision:

- the significance of the rights which are or might be affected by the incompatibility;
- the seriousness of the consequences for identifiable individuals or groups from allowing the continuance of an incompatibility with a Convention right;
- the adequacy of compensation arrangements as a way of militating the effects of the incompatibility;
- the number of people affected;
- alternative ways of mitigating the effect of the incompatibility pending amendment to primary legislation.[348]

In relation to the first of these factors, it should be noted that the JCHR has identified those Convention rights which it considers to be significant and hence meriting the use of the urgent procedure where there is incompatibility. These are: the right to life (article 2); the right to be free of torture or inhuman or degrading treatment (article 3); the right to be free of servitude and forced labour (article 4); and, the right to liberty (article 5). It is also worth noting in relation to the third factor that the adequacy of compensation arrangements may act as either a militating or mitigating factor. Thus, for example, if there was no right to

[347] At para 36.   [348] At para 37.

compensation or if the likely level of compensation was insufficient to mitigate the harmful effects of the incompatibility, the JCHR considers that 'it would strengthen the case for using the urgent procedure'.[349]

To date, remedial orders have been made very sparingly. Although the government has sought to remedy all those declarations of incompatibility which have been made under section 4 of the HRA,[350] in almost all of the cases this has been achieved through primary legislation.[351] Thus, for example, in the light of the House of Lords ruling in *R (on the application of Anderson) v Secretary of State for the Home Department*,[352] the Criminal Justice Act 2003 has established a new system governing the release of prisoners convicted of murder and sentenced to a mandatory life sentence which does not involve the Secretary of State.[353] The section 10 procedures have only been used once in relation to a domestic court decision, following a ruling by the Court of Appeal in *R(H) v Mental Health Review Tribunal, North and East London Region*[354] that sections 72 and 73 of the Mental Health Act 1983 were incompatible with article 5 of the ECHR on the basis that they prevented the tribunal from ordering the release of a patient who had been compulsorily detained unless the patient could satisfy the tribunal that the criteria for detention no longer applied. The incompatibility was subsequently removed by the Mental Health Act 1983 (Remedial) Order 2001.[355] Accordingly, the onus has now shifted so that under the new provisions, a tribunal is required to release a compulsorily detained patient unless it is satisfied that the criteria for detention continue to be satisfied.

A decision of the ECtHR has also acted as the catalyst for the making of a remedial order.[356] Thus following the ruling in *Grieves v UK*,[357] where it was held that certain features of the Royal Navy court martial system were contrary to article 6(1) of the ECHR, the government made the Naval Discipline Act 1957 (Remedial) Order 2004.[358] It should be noted that in both the cases referred to, the remedial orders were made using the *urgent* procedure. In the case of the Mental Health Act 1983 (Remedial) Order, this was only after a draft of the order had originally been laid before Parliament under the non-urgent procedure and the JCHR had pointed out that the continued detention of patients pending a change in the law justified the use of the urgent procedure.[359] The urgent procedure was followed at the outset for the Naval Discipline Act 1957 (Remedial) Order since it would not have been possible to conduct another court martial which was not incompatible with article 6(1) of the ECHR following the decision in *Grieves v UK*.

[349] Ibid.

[350] In the *Review of the Implementation of the Human Rights Act*, Department for Constitutional Affairs, (July 2006), the DCA states that at the date of publication, declarations of incompatibility had been made in 15 cases, two of which were subject to appeal, and that declarations had been overturned on appeal in a further five cases: at p. 17. In *Ghaidan v Godin-Mendoza* [2004] AC 557, Lord Steyn included an appendix to his opinion in which he identified all those section 4 declarations which had been made at the time of the judgment in that appeal.

[351] See *Review of the Implementation of the Human Rights Act*, DCA (July 2006), at p. 17.

[352] [2002] UKHL 46, extracted in chapter 2.   [353] See chapter 7 of the 2003 Act.

[354] [2001] 3 WLR 512.   [355] SI 2001/3712.

[356] At the time of writing a draft Marriage Act 1949 (Remedial) Order is before Parliament. This seeks to amend the 1949 Act so as to remove the incompatibility between its prohibition on in-laws marrying and article 12 of the ECHR which was identified by the ECtHR in *B v UK* (2006) 42 EHRR 11.

[357] (2004) 39 EHRR 7.   [358] SI 2004/66.

[359] See Sixth Report 2001–02 session, (HL Paper 57, HC 472), at paras 30–36.

(l) Derogations and reservations

'14 Derogations

(1) In this Act "designated derogation" means

. . . any derogation by the United Kingdom from an Article of the Convention, or of any protocol to the Convention, which is designated for the purposes of this Act in an order made by the Secretary of State.[360]

(2) . . .[361]

(3) If a designated derogation is amended or replaced it ceases to be a designated derogation.

(4) But subsection (3) does not prevent the Secretary of State from exercising his power under subsection (1) . . . to make a fresh designation order in respect of the Article concerned.[362]

(5) The Secretary of State must by order make such amendments to Schedule 3 as he considers appropriate to reflect—

    (a) any designation order; or

    (b) the effect of subsection (3).

(6) A designation order may be made in anticipation of the making by the United Kingdom of a proposed designation.'

Section 14 provides for what the HRA terms a 'designated derogation'. Essentially this amounts to a derogation by the UK government from any article of or protocol to the ECHR. Only the Secretary of State has the power to make a designated derogation order. Any order which is made ceases to be a designated derogation if it is subsequently amended or replaced.[363] However, the Secretary of State retains the power to make a fresh designation order in respect of the same article where he considers it appropriate to do so.[364]

'16 Period for which designated derogations have effect

(1) If it has not already been withdrawn by the United Kingdom, a designated derogation ceases to have effect for the purposes of this Act . . . at the end of the period of five years beginning with the date on which the order designating it was made.[365]

(2) At any time before the period—

    (a) fixed by subsection (1) . . . , or[366]

    (b) extended by an order under this subsection,

comes to an end, the Secretary of State may by order extend it by a further period of five years.

(3) An order under section 14(1) . . . ceases to have effect at the end of the period for consideration, unless a resolution has been passed by each House approving the order.[367]

---

[360] The words omitted were repealed by the Human Rights Act (Amendment) Order 2001, SI 2001/1216, article 2(a).   [361] Subsection (2) was repealed by SI 2001/1216, article 2(b).

[362] The words omitted were repealed by SI 2001/1216, article 2(c).

[363] Section 14(3).   [364] Section 14(4).

[365] The words omitted in subsection (1) were repealed by SI 2001/1216, article 3(a).

[366] The words omitted in subsection (2) were repealed by SI 2001/1216, article 2(b).

[367] The words omitted in subsection (3) were repealed by SI 2001/1216, article 3(c).

(4) Subsection (3) does not effect—

    (a) anything done in reliance on the order; or

    (b) the power to make a fresh order under section 14(1)(b).

(5) In subsection (3) "period for consideration" means the period of forty days beginning with the day on which the order was made.

(6) In calculating the period for consideration, no account is to be taken of any time during which—

    (a) Parliament is dissolved or prorogued; or

    (b) Both Houses are adjourned for more than four days.

(7) If a designated derogation is withdrawn by the United Kingdom, the Secretary of State must by order make such amendments to this Act as he considers are required to reflect that withdrawal.'

Section 16 imposes a temporal restriction on the life of a designated derogation. In effect, such an order ceases to have effect after five years from the date on which it was made.[368] However, the life of a designated derogation order may be extended by a further period of five years.[369] The UK formerly had derogations entered in respect of article 5(1)(f) and 5(3) of the ECHR. In the case of the former, the derogation was entered as a consequence of the extended power of detention contained in the Anti-terrorism, Crime and Security Act 2001, which it was felt may be inconsistent with the obligations under article 5(1)(f).[370] That derogation was subsequently quashed by the House of Lords in *A v Secretary of State for the Home Department*,[371] and the repeal of the detention provisions in the 2001 Act, which had been declared by their Lordships to be incompatible with articles 5 and 14 of the ECHR, was effected by section 16(2)(a) of the Prevention of Terrorism Act 2005.[372]

'15 Reservations

(1) In this Act "designated reservation" means—

    (a) the United Kingdom's reservation to Article 2 of the First Protocol to the Convention; and

    (b) any other reservation by the United Kingdom to an Article of the Convention, or of any protocol to the Convention, which is designated for the purposes of this Act in an order made by the Secretary of State.

(2) The text of the reservation referred to in subsection (1)(a) is set out in Part II of Schedule 3.

(3) If a designated reservation is withdrawn wholly or in part it ceases to be a designated reservation.

(4) But subsection (3) does not prevent the Secretary of State from exercising his power under subsection (1)(b) to make a fresh designation order in respect of the Article concerned.

(5) The Secretary of State must by order make such amendments to this Act as he considers appropriate to reflect—

    (a) any designation order; or

    (b) the effect of subsection (3).'

The High Contracting Parties are permitted by virtue of article 57 of the ECHR to enter reservations in respect of Convention provisions 'to the extent that any law then in force in its territory is not in conformity with the provision'. Specific reservations are thus allowed

[368] Section 16(1).   [369] Section 16(2).

[370] See the Human Rights Act 1998 (Designated Derogation) Order 2001, SI 2001/3644.

[371] [2005] 2 AC 68.

[372] Part I of Schedule 3 to the HRA 1998 was accordingly repealed: see the Human Rights Act (Amendment) Order 2005, SI 2005/1071.

whereas reservations of a general character are not. Section 15 of the HRA recognises the fact that the UK government has a reservation in place in respect of article 2 of the First Protocol to the ECHR. This provision is concerned with the right to education. The principle affirmed in the second sentence of article 2 states that in examining any functions in relation to education and teaching, the state is required to respect the rights of parents to ensure that such education and teaching conforms to their own religious and philosophical convictions. The UK's reservation in respect of article 2 has been in place since March 1952. It makes it clear that the UK accepts the principle affirmed in article 2 to the extent that is it compatible with the provision of efficient instruction and training, and the avoidance of unreasonable expenditure.[373] Any other reservation which the UK government chose to make would also be recognised under section 15. The existing reservation (and any future reservations) are subject to a periodic review as set out in section 17.

'17 Periodic review of designated reservations

(1) The appropriate Minister must review the designated reservation referred to in section 15(1)(a)—

    (a) before the end of the period of five years beginning with the date on which section 1(2) came into force; and

    (b) if that designation is still in force, before the end of the period of five years beginning with the date on which the last report relating to it was laid under subsection (3).

(2) The appropriate Minister must review each of the other designated reservations (if any)—

    (a) before the end of the period of five years beginning with the date on which the order designating the reservation first came into force; and

    (b) if the designation is still in force, before the end of the period of five years beginning with the date on which the last report relating to it was laid under subsection (3).

(3) The Minister conducting a review under this section must prepare a report on the result of the review and lay a copy of it before each House of Parliament.'

(m) The Joint Committee on Human Rights

The Joint Committee on Human Rights (JCHR) was originally established in January 2001.[374] It consists of six members of the House of Commons and six members of the House of Lords. The terms of reference of the JCHR are set out in Standing Orders of both Houses.[375] Thus the Committee is required to consider:

'(a) matters relating to human rights in the United Kingdom (but excluding consideration of individual cases);

(b) proposals for remedial orders, draft remedial orders and remedial orders made under section 10 of and laid under Schedule 2 to the Human Rights Act 1998; and

(c) in respect of draft remedial orders and remedial orders, whether the special attention of the House should be drawn to them on any of the grounds specified in Standing Order No. 151 (Statutory Instruments (Joint Committee)).'[376]

---

[373] See Schedule 3, Pt II of the HRA.
[374] See *Erskine May Parliamentary Practice* (23rd edn, 2004), at p. 844.
[375] See House of Commons Standing Order No. 152B.   [376] HC Standing Order No. 152B(2)(a)–(c).

Term of reference (a) is broad despite the limitation in parenthesis. In practice it has meant that the JCHR has set about scrutinising Bills introduced in Parliament in order to assess the human rights implications of the proposed legislation. Where the Committee is of the view that there is an incompatibility between a Bill and a Convention right, this will be drawn to the attention of both Houses in the form of a report on the Bill. The result is that Parliament is therefore able to debate the measure with a more informed awareness of its human rights implications. The JCHR's terms of reference also require it to report on remedial orders, and where necessary, to draw the attention of Parliament to draft or remedial orders on certain specified grounds. These grounds include that the order: imposes a charge on public revenues; appears to make unusual or unexpected use of the power under which it is made; gives doubt as to whether it is intra vires; or, is defective in drafting. Two of the grounds on which the Joint Committee on Statutory Instruments may draw a statutory instrument to the special attention of the House (under Standing Order No. 151) do not apply to the JCHR. These are that the order: may have been made in pursuance of an enactment excluding it from challenge in the courts; or, that it purports to have retrospective effect when the parent Act does not expressly authorize it. This latter ground is patently non-applicable because the HRA expressly authorises retrospective remedial orders.

In addition to the foregoing, from time to time the JCHR publishes reports on more general matters of importance relating to human rights. Thus, for example, it has produced reports on the meaning of 'public authority' for the purposes of section 6 of the HRA,[377] deaths in custody,[378] and the case for a Human Rights Commission.[379] In order to facilitate the conduct of its functions, the JCHR has the power to send for persons, papers and records, to sit notwithstanding an adjournment of the House, and to appoint special advisers to supply information or elucidate matters of complexity.[380]

FURTHER READING

Beernaert M-A 'Protocol 14 and New Strasbourg Procedures: Towards Greater Efficiency? And at What Price?' [2004] EHRLR 544.

Bingham Lord 'The European Convention on Human Rights: Time to Incorporate' (1993) 109 LQR 390.

Bonner D 'Checking the Executive? Detention without Trial, Control Orders, Due Process and Human Rights' (2006) 12 EPL 45.

Buxton Sir Richard 'The Human Rights Act and Private Law' (2000) 116 LQR 48.

Clayton R 'Judicial Deference and "Democratic Dialogue": The Legitimacy of Judicial Intervention Under the Human Rights Act 1998' [2004] PL 33.

Clements L, Mole N and Simmons A *European Human Rights: Taking a Case Under the Convention* (2nd edn, Sweet & Maxwell, London, 1998).

Cranston M *What are Human Rights?* (Bodley Head, London, 1973).

---

[377] Seventh Report for the 2003–04 session, (HL Paper 39, HC 382). See above where the content of this report is discussed. [378] Third Report for the 2004–05 session, (HL Paper 15-II, VC 137-II).
[379] Twenty-second Report for the 2001–02 session, (HL Paper 160, HC 1142).
[380] HC Standing Order No. 152B(7)(a) and (b).

Dickson B *Human Rights and the European Convention* (Sweet & Maxwell, London, 1997).

Duffy P and Stanley P *Human Rights Act 1998* (Current Law Annotated Statutes).

Farran S *The UK before the European Court of Human Rights: Case Law and Commentary* (Blackstone Press Ltd, London, 1996).

Fawcett JES *The Application of the European Convention on Human Rights* (2nd edn, Clarendon Press, Oxford, 1987).

Feldman D 'Remedies for Violations of Convention Rights under the Human Rights Act' [1998] EHRLR 691.

Greer S 'Protocol 14 and the Future of the European Court of Human Rights' [2005] PL 83.

Grosz S, Beatson J, Duffy P and Sedley LJ *Human Rights: The 1998 Act and the European Convention* (Sweet and Maxwell, London, 2000).

Harris DJ, O'Boyle M and Warbrick C *Law of the European Convention on Human Rights* (Butterworths, London, 1995).

Hoffmann Lord 'Human Rights and the House of Lords' (1999) 62 MLR 159.

Hunt M 'The Horizontal Effect of the Human Rights Act' [1998] PL 423.

Jacobs FG and White RCA *The European Convention on Human Rights* (4th edn, Clarendon Press, Oxford, 2006).

Janis MW, Kay RS and Bradley AW *European Human Rights Law: Text and Materials* (2nd edn, Clarendon Press, New York, 2000).

Jowell J 'Judicial Deference: Servility, Civility or Institutional Capacity' [2003] PL 592.

Leach P 'The Effectiveness of the Committee of Ministers in Supervising Enforcement of Judgments of the European Court of Human Rights' [2006] PL 443.

MacDonald A '*R (on the application of Prolife Alliance) v BBC*: Political Speech and the Standard of Review' [2003] EHRLR 651.

Lester Lord and Pannick D *Human Rights Law and Practice* (2nd edn, Butterworths, London, 2004).

Loveland I *Constitutional Law, Administrative Law and Human Rights: A Critical Introduction* (4th edn, OUP, Oxford, 2006).

Marriott J and Nicol D 'The Human Rights Act, Representative Standing and the Victim Culture' [1998] EHRLR 730.

Marston G 'The United Kingdom's Part in the Preparation of the European Convention on Human Rights, 1950' (1993) 42 ICLQ 796.

Morgan J 'Privacy, Confidence and Horizontal Effect: "Hello" Trouble' (2003) 62 CLJ 444.

Oliver D 'Functions of a Public Nature under the Human Rights Act' [2004] PL 328.

Raphael T 'The Problem of Horizontal Effect' [2000] EHRLR 493.

Sedley Sir Stephen 'The Rocks or the Open Sea: Where is the Human Rights Act Heading' (2005) 32 J Law & Soc 3.

Steyn Lord 'Deference: a Tangled Story' [2005] PL 346.

Steyn Lord '2000–2005: Laying the Foundations of Human Rights Law in the United Kingdom' [2005] EHRLR 349.

Sunkin M 'Pushing Forward the Frontiers of Human Rights Protection: The Meaning of Public Authority under the Human Rights Act' [2004] PL 643.

Wade Professor Sir William 'Horizons of Horizontality' (2000) 116 LQR 217.

Young A 'Remedial and Substantive Horizontality: The Common Law and *Douglas v Hello Ltd*' [2002] PL 232.

Yourow CH *The Margin of Appreciation Doctrine in the Dynamics of European Human Rights Jurisprudence* (Kluwer, The Hague, 1996).

INDEX